SELWYN'S
LAW OF EMPLOYMENT

Twenty-first Edition

ASTRA EMIR

MA (Oxon), LLM (Lond), Barrister-at-Law

OXFORD
UNIVERSITY PRESS

OXFORD
UNIVERSITY PRESS

Great Clarendon Street, Oxford, OX2 6DP,
United Kingdom

Oxford University Press is a department of the University of Oxford.
It furthers the University's objective of excellence in research, scholarship,
and education by publishing worldwide. Oxford is a registered trade mark of
Oxford University Press in the UK and in certain other countries

© Astra Emir 2020

The moral rights of the author have been asserted

Eighteenth Edition 2014
Nineteenth Edition 2016
Twentieth Edition 2018

Impression: 1

Public sector information reproduced under Open Government Licence v3.0
(http://www.nationalarchives.gov.uk/doc/open-government-licence/open-government-licence.htm)

Published in the United States of America by Oxford University Press
198 Madison Avenue, New York, NY 10016, United States of America

British Library Cataloguing in Publication Data
Data available

Library of Congress Control Number: 2020937790

ISBN 978–0–19–883663–6

Printed in Great Britain by
Bell & Bain Ltd., Glasgow

Preface

The aim of this book is to provide a practical, clear and easy-to-follow text setting out the main elements of Employment Law. As always, this edition includes the most important new case law as well as the new statutes and statutory instruments, and to assist readers, a new 'summary' feature has been added to the end of chapters.

The issue of Brexit looms large in the country as a whole, but has not yet affected Employment Law. The European Union (Withdrawal) Act 2018 provides that the law in the UK will remain the same until and unless it is specifically changed. While Parliament was distracted by Brexit, much of the planned legislation was put on hold, including the changes expected as a result of the publication of the Good Work Plan. Where possible, these expected changes have been highlighted in the text, but it is not yet known when or if these will come in. Any changes will, of course, appear in the online Ancillary Resource Centre, which is updated at least twice a year, in a handy chapter-by-chapter format, and has the latest cases and legislation to complement the text.

Note that the figures for statutory payments, a week's pay, etc are up to date as of April 2020 The latest figures will be found on the online Ancillary Resource Centre at www.oup.com/uk/selwyn21e/

I would like to thank all at OUP for their expert assistance in preparing this book for publication, and to Simon and Jasmine Davey for their patience.

Astra Emir

For Stephen

University Centre at
Blackburn
College

Telephone: 01254 292165

Please return this book on or before the last date shown

Notes on EU legislation and on Coronavirus Legislation

EU legislation and Brexit

The impact of the European Union on the UK employment law is set out in chapter one. The immediate effect of Brexit will not change this, as all EU legislation will continue as before unless expressly repealed by the UK.

Note that while some laws come from the EU, and some are domestic, they can often be a mixture of the two, whether they are domestic laws which have then been expanded by Europe, or European laws which are then made more generous by Parliament. There is also the impact of the European Court of Justice, which has helped to reinterpret some elements which were not in British law. Again, this legislation and interpretation of cases will not change unless a decision is made expressly to do so.

It should also be clarified that the European Convention on Human Rights, which forms the basis of the Human Rights Act, has nothing to do with the European Union. It arises instead as a result of the UK's membership of the Council of Europe, which we have been in since 1950. Brexit will have no effect on this. Even if the government eventually decides to do away with the Human Rights Act 1998, the UK will still be a member of the Council of Europe and still subject to the Convention.

The EU is considered in chapter 1 of this book, and the law is set out as it currently stands. Any changes will appear in the bi-annual update on the online updates on the OUP website.

Coronavirus Legislation

In March 2020, a raft of temporary legislation came into force to deal with the Coronavirus situation, and some of it significantly impacts employers and employees. Most of the changes affect chapter 7. The most significant for our purposes are the following:

Furlough

S75 of the Coronavirus Act 2020 lifts the on cap on the Government giving financial assistance to Industry (originally set out in the Industrial Development Act 1982) if the assistance is to address the impact of COVID-19. S76 gives the HMRC powers to do this by means of the Coronavirus Job Retention Scheme. The scheme applies from 1 March 2020, and is initially for three months. Employers can claim for 80% of furloughed employees' usual monthly wage costs, up to £2,500 a month, plus the associated Employer National Insurance contributions and minimum automatic enrolment employer pension contributions on that wage. Employers can use this scheme anytime during this period. The scheme is open to all UK employers that had created and started a PAYE payroll scheme on 28 February 2020. Guidance is provided on the ACAS website.

Sick Pay

The Statutory Sick Pay (General) (Coronavirus Amendment) Regulations 2020 (in force 13 March 2020) and the Statutory Sick Pay (Coronavirus) (Suspension of Waiting Days and General Amendment) Regulations 2020 amend the Statutory Sick Pay (General) Regulations 1982 (in force 28th March 2020). Together they provide that if an employee is incapacitated for work for a reason related to coronavirus, and the period of incapacity arose on or after 13 March 2020, then the limitation with the usual sick pay rules that sick pay is not payable for the first three days (the 'waiting days') is suspended, and so the sick pay is payable immediately.

A reason related to coronavirus covers not just if someone is ill with the coronavirus, but also if that person is ill and self-isolating for 7 days, or if the person lives with someone who is ill and is self-isolating for 14 days.

There is a requirement for the Secretary of State to keep these regulations under review.

Working Time

The Working Time (Coronavirus) (Amendment) Regulations 2020 amend the Working Time Regulations and came into force on 27th March 2020 and relate to the four weeks of annual leave deriving from European Law. Where the leave remains untaken at the end of a leave year, regulation 13.9 of the original regulations prevents that leave being carried forward into the next year. These new regulations amend that, and state that where at the end of a leave year it has not been reasonably practicable for a worker to take some or all of the leave that he was entitled to under the WTR, and that this is because of the effects of the coronavirus (whether these effects are on the worker, the employer, the wider economy or society), then the untaken leave can be carried forward and taken in the following two leave years.

Regulation 4 provides that any of this leave that is carried over and is untaken at the termination of employment can be paid in lieu.

General

The Health Protection (Coronavirus, Restrictions) (England) Regulations 2020, in force 26 March 2020 and expire after six months. They deal with the restrictions on movement (and thus employees having to work from home except where it is not reasonably possible for that person to do so) and the closure of certain businesses, with an obligation on the Secretary of State to review the restrictions every 21 days. There is a fixed penalty scheme for breach of the regulations, and offences can be prosecuted.

3rd April 2020

New to this edition

- Introductory note on employment-related Coronavirus legislation.
- 'Background' introductory sections provide an overview of each chapter, while summaries help consolidate student's learning.
- Updated case law on a range of topics including *López Ribalda v. Spain* concerning privacy, *Ali v Capita Customer Management Ltd* on discrimination in maternity and shared parental pay, and *High Court in Shelbourne v Cancer Research UK* and *Bellman v Northampton Recruitment Ltd* relating to vicarious liability at social events.
- Statutory changes to the law including the Parental Bereavement (Leave and Pay) Act 2018, the Conduct Regulations for Agency Workers, changes made by the Employment Rights (Miscellaneous Amendments) Regulations 2019, the Employment Rights Act 1996 (Itemised Pay Statement) (Amendment) (No. 2) Order 2018 and the Trade Secrets (Enforcement, etc) Regulations 2018.

Contents

Table of Statutes

Table of Statutory Instruments

Table of European Legislation

Table of International Treaties and Conventions

Table of Cases

1

The Institutions of Employment Law

Background

1.1 Throughout this book we will look at the detail of employment law, the legislation and case law, but in this chapter the sources and institutions of employment law are introduced, such as the courts and quasi-legal institutions which play a role in helping to enforce the law in some way.

1.2 Employment law derives mostly from statutes, coming from Parliament, a number of which originate in Directives from the European Union. This legislation is still part of the UK law unless it is expressly repealed, and so is included here, and the EU and its institutions are also considered in this chapter.

1.3 Statutes are interpreted by the courts, and the body of case law that arises also forms part of the law, as does the common law, which is law made by judges, such as contract law, and this chapter looks at the main courts and tribunals that consider employment law, namely the Employment Tribunal and the Employment Appeal Tribunal. Also important are the various institutions which help with conciliation and enforcement of the law. We start by considering the courts, then the institutions, and conclude with the sources of the legislation and the Human Rights Act.

Employment Tribunals

1.4 Employment tribunals hear the majority of employment cases, and the procedure for these is dealt with in Chapter 20.

1.5 The constitutional basis for employment tribunals can be found in the Employment Tribunals Act 1996. An employment tribunal is an inferior court, exercising the judicial powers of the state for the purpose of the Contempt of Court Act 1981, s 19, and contempt of court proceedings may be brought if there is an attempt to pervert the course of justice or any other breach of the Act (*Peach Grey & Co v Sommers*[1]).

1.6 An employment tribunal generally consists of an employment judge and two lay members, although employment judges now have powers to sit alone more often. The employment judge must be a lawyer, and may be full-time or part-time. The lay members, who are all part-time, are appointed from both sides of industry as representatives of employers' organisations and trade unions. The judge can sit with just one lay member if the parties agree. Each member of the employment tribunal has an equal vote (except in the case of a judge and one member, in which case the judge has a casting vote), and although decisions can be reached by a majority vote, in practice it appears that, despite the somewhat diverse backgrounds, 96% of all decisions reached

---

[1] [1995] ICR 549, [1995] IRLR 363.

are unanimous. In the remaining cases, the 'wingmembers' are just as likely to unite in outvoting the employment judge as the latter is likely to have the support of one or the other member. In cases of sex discrimination it is desirable to have one member of either sex, and in race discrimination cases a member who has special experience of race relations, but there is no absolute legal requirement that an employment tribunal should be so composed (*Habib v Elkington & Co Ltd*[2]). An employment judge or member should not have any connection with any of the parties who appear before them (see para 20.92), nor with any of the witnesses (*University of Swansea v Cornelius*[3]). However, the fact that the employment judge or members know an advocate who appears before them should not cause any problem, unless there is a close relationship between them.

1.7 An employment judge has the power to sit alone in unfair dismissal cases, and in the following circumstances (ETA, s 4):

(a) the following complaints made under TULR(C)A, ie s 68A (unauthorised or excessive deductions of trade union subscriptions), s 87 (unauthorised deduction of contribution to a political fund), ss 161, 165, 166 (application for interim relief etc), s 192 (failure by employer to pay a protective award);

(b) a complaint under the Pension Schemes Act 1993, s 126;

(c) proceedings brought under the following provisions of the Employment Rights Act 1996, ie s 11 (failure to give written statement of terms and conditions), s 23 (unauthorised deductions from wages), s 34 (failure to make a guarantee payment), s 70 (failure to pay remuneration following suspension on medical grounds), s 111 (unfair dismissal), ss 128, 131, 132 (application for interim relief etc), s 163 (right to or amount of redundancy payment), s 170 (reference following an application to the Secretary of State for a redundancy payment), s 188 (rights of employee on employer's insolvency), s 206(4) (appointment of an appropriate person where there is no personal representative of a deceased employee);

(d) complaints brought under the Transfer of Undertakings (Protection of Employment) Regulations 2006, reg 15(10) (failure to pay compensation in pursuance of an order made following a failure to consult on a transfer);

(e) complaints made under the National Minimum Wage Act 1998, s 11 (failure to allow access to records), s 19 (appeal by an employer against an enforcement notice), s 22 (appeal against a penalty notice);

(f) proceedings brought under the provisions of the Employment Tribunals Extension of Jurisdiction (England and Wales) Order 1994 and Employment Tribunals Extension of Jurisdiction (Scotland) Order 1994 (breach of contract claims);

(g) proceedings in which the parties give their written consent to be heard by an employment judge alone;

(h) proceedings in which the person against whom they are brought does not contest the case;

(i) complaints relating to the non-payment of holiday pay;

(j) stage one of equal pay cases.

---

[2] [1981] ICR 435, [1981] IRLR 344, EAT.   [3] [1988] ICR 735, EAT.

1.8 However, in any of the circumstances in para 1.6, the employment judge may at any stage decide to have the case heard by a full tribunal:

(a) where there is a likelihood of a dispute arising from the facts;

(b) where there is a likelihood of an issue of law arising;

(c) having taken into account the views of any of the parties;

(d) where there are other proceedings which might be heard concurrently and which do not come within the above categories which enable an employment judge to sit alone.

1.9 If the employment judge decides to hear the case sitting alone, he is under a continuing duty to keep that decision under review. Thus, if it becomes evident that the parties intend to call a number of witnesses, this would be a clear indication that the claim should be heard by a full tribunal (*Clarke v Arriva Kent Thameside Ltd*[4]). Indeed, an employment judge should not sit alone, even if all the parties agree to him so doing, where there is a likelihood of a dispute on the facts (*Sogbetun v Hackney London Borough*[5]).

1.10 The main jurisdiction of employment tribunals is to deal with claims made under the following statutory provisions:

(a) Employment Agencies Act 1973;

(b) Health and Safety at Work etc Act 1974;

(c) Industrial Training Act 1982;

(d) Trade Union and Labour Relations (Consolidation) Act 1992;

(e) Pension Schemes Act 1993;

(f) Employment Rights Act 1996;

(g) National Minimum Wage Act 1998;

(h) Employment Relations Act 1999;

(i) Equality Act 2006;

(j) Equality Act 2010;

(k) Work and Families Act 2014.

Employment tribunals also have jurisdiction to deal with claims made under the following statutory instruments, among others:

(a) Safety Representatives and Safety Committee Regulations 1977;

(b) Industrial Tribunals (Interest) Order 1990;

(c) Employment Tribunals Extension of Jurisdiction Order 1994;

(d) Suspension from Work (on Maternity Grounds) Order 1994;

(e) Health and Safety (Consultation with Employees) Regulations 1996;

(f) Working Time Regulations 1998;

(g) National Minimum Wage Regulations 1999;

(h) Maternity and Parental Leave etc Regulations 1999;

(i) Transnational Information and Consultation of Employees Regulations 1999;

(j) Part-time Workers (Prevention of Less Favourable Treatment) Regulations 2000;

---

[4] [2001] All ER (D) 485 (Jul), EAT.   [5] [1998] ICR 1264, [1998] IRLR 676, EAT.

(k) Employment Relations (Offshore Employment) Order 2000;

(l) Right to Time Off for Study or Training Regulations 2001;

(m) Fixed-term Employees (Prevention of Less Favourable Treatment) Regulations 2002;

(n) Paternity and Adoption Leave Regulations 2002;

(o) Flexible Working (Eligibility, Complaints and Remedies) Regulations 2002;

(p) Flexible Working (Procedural Requirements) Regulations 2002;

(q) Information and Consultation of Employees Regulations 2004;

(r) Transfer of Undertakings (Protection of Employment) Regulations 2006;

(s) Occupational and Personal Pension Schemes (Consultation with Employees) Regulations 2006;

(t) Companies (Cross Border Mergers) Regulations 2007;

(u) European Public Limited Liability Company (Employee Involvement) (Great Britain) Regulations 2009;

(v) Agency Workers Regulations 2010;

(w) Employment Relations Act 1999 (Blacklists) Regulations 2010;

(x) Time off Work for Study or Training Regulations 2010;

(y) Additional Paternity Leave Regulations 2010;

(z) Additional Paternity Leave (Adoption from Overseas) Regulations 2010.

Employment tribunals have jurisdiction to apply EU law to claims made under UK law, ie as laid down in specific UK legislation (eg Equality Act). But there is no jurisdiction to hear or determine 'free-standing' claims based on the Treaty of Rome or an EU Directive, outside the domestic statutory framework (*Biggs v Somerset County Council*[6]). Also, there is no jurisdiction to hear '*Francovich*'-style claims (*Secretary of State for Employment v Mann*[7]). An employment tribunal does have a duty to apply EU law to the extent of disapplying an offending provision in UK legislation if it is inconsistent with EU law (see *Redcar & Cleveland Borough Council v Bainbridge*,[8] paras 1.43 and 5.34).

1.11 The procedure before employment tribunals is governed by the Employment Tribunals (Constitution and Rules of Procedure) Regulations 2013. These regulations provide for the making and rejection of claims, appearance by respondents, case management, further particulars, witness attendance orders, pre-hearing review, procedure at the hearing, applications for review, award of costs, extension of time, joinder of parties, default judgments, electronic communications, and other miscellaneous matters. Generally speaking the tribunal has a wide discretion in operating its procedures, and its decision can only be challenged on appeal where the discretion was wrongly exercised because of a mistake of law, a disregard of principle, or a misapplication of the facts, or because the tribunal took into account irrelevant matters or failed to take into account relevant matters, or where the decision was outside the generous ambit within which a reasonable disagreement is possible (*Noorani v Merseyside TEC Ltd*[9]) (see Chapter 20).

---

[6] [1996] ICR 364, [1996] IRLR 203.
[7] [1996] ICR 197, [1996] IRLR 4, EAT; revsd [1997] ICR 209, CA; aff'd on other grounds sub nom *Mann v Secretary of State for Employment* [1999] ICR 898, [1999] All ER (D) 791.
[8] [2005] EWCA Civ 726, [2005] IRLR 504.   [9] [1999] IRLR 184, CA.

A. **Territorial Jurisdiction**

1.12 The jurisdiction of employment tribunals is based on particular statutory provisions. Thus, certain sections of TULR(C)A do not apply to employment where an employee works outside Great Britain, ie access to employment (ss 137–143), inducement and detriment (ss 145A–151), time off for trade union duties and activities (ss 168–173), and duty to notify Secretary of State of redundancies (ss 193–194).

1.13 The territorial jurisdiction of the Employment Rights Act was originally found in s 196, which excluded a number of claims where the employee ordinarily worked outside Great Britain, but the section was repealed in 1999 (in order to comply with the Posted Workers Directive) and not replaced. It thus fell to the courts to devise tests for determining the territorial jurisdiction in respect of various statutory claims which were brought.

1.14 The leading case on territorial jurisdiction is the House of Lords' decision in *Lawson v Serco Ltd*,[10] where it was held that claimants could be divided into three categories:

(a) *Standard cases.* The question to be asked here is, was the claimant working in Great Britain? The contract of employment will be a major factor, but attention must also be paid to what happens in practice.

(b) *Peripatetic employees.* Here, the factual 'base' test could be used, eg where the employee lived, where he was paying taxes and where his work was organised from (*Todd v British Midlands Airways Ltd*[11]), where his duty begins and where it ends (*Diggins v Condor Marine*[12]). Where the employee is working is a question of fact for the tribunal: *Ravat v Halliburton Manufacturing & Services Ltd*,[13] where the Supreme Court emphasised the need for a sufficiently close connection between the employment and Great Britain, stronger than with the country where the employee works.

(c) *Expatriate employees.* Generally, the employee must rely on the law where he is working, but there are two major exceptions, ie where an employee is posted abroad for the purpose of a business carried on in Great Britain, and an expatriate working in an extraterritorial enclave in a foreign country. Thus, in *Lawson v Serco Ltd*[14] the claimant was employed by a British company to work as a security supervisor on Ascension Island, a British Overseas Dependency with no local population. It was held that the connection with the employment relationship and the United Kingdom was overwhelmingly strong, and the claimant was entitled to pursue his claim for unfair dismissal in this country. This was also the case in *Duncombe v Secretary of State for Children, Schools and Families*,[15] where teachers were employed by the Secretary of State for Children, Schools and Families to work in European Schools abroad. Their employment was held to have an overwhelmingly closer connection with Britain and with British employment law than with any other system of law.

1.15 However, there are bound to be difficult decisions to be made regarding an employee who works abroad for a British employer for the purpose of a business carried on in the UK, eg a sales representative, or a newspaper correspondent whose dispatches are sent to different countries (*Financial Times v Bishop*[16]). The correct approach when considering the territorial scope of the right to claim is to consider the place of employment as being the major determining factor, and there is no room for using the

---

[10] [2006] UKHL 3, [2006] ICR 250, [2006] IRLR 289.   [11] [1978] IRLR 370, (1978) ICR 959.
[12] [2009] EWCA Civ 1133, [2010] ICR 213, [2010] IRLR 119.   [13] [2012] UKSC 1, [2012] IRLR 315 SC.
[14] [2006] UKHL 3, [2006] 1 All ER 823, [2006] ICR 250, [2006] IRLR 289.   [15] (No. 2) [2011] UKSC 36.
[16] [2003] UKEAT 0147_03_2511.

'substantial connection with Great Britain' approach. It is only in exceptional circumstances that the employment tribunal will have jurisdiction where the employee works wholly abroad (*Dolphin Drilling Personnel PTE Ltd v Winks*[17]). In *Hughes v Alan Dick & Co Ltd*[18] the claimant was employed by a British company to work in Nigeria. It was held that the employment tribunal had no jurisdiction to hear his claim for unfair dismissal. Although he was recruited in England, worked for a British firm for a business conducted in a foreign country, and was paid in sterling to a British bank account, all of his work was carried out in the context of a substantial business operation carried on in Nigeria, and the connection with that country was greater and stronger than that of the United Kingdom. However, in *Lodge v Dignity & Choice in Dying & Anor*[19] an employee did not lose her right to bring a claim under the Employment Rights Act 1996 (ERA) merely because, instead of working as a physical employee in a British office, she worked abroad as a virtual employee of an employer based in Britain and was subject to Australian taxes. It was found that she was in no different position to an employee who is posted abroad with his or her consent, and that the examples given in *Lawson v Serco* (para 1.14) are illustrations rather than rules. By contrast, in *Olsen v Gearbulk Services Ltd & Anor*,[20] a Danish claimant who lived in Switzerland and had rejected a contract governed by UK law, and who took care to structure his contract to ensure that he never spent the required number of days in the UK to be subject to UK tax, could not bring a claim even though he spent more time in the UK than any other office. In another example following *Lawson*, it was decided that British seafarers who were employed on ships which operated mainly outside of UK territorial waters would 'ordinarily work in Great Britain' if they did so from a base in Britain, but they would not if they did not begin and end their tours of duty from a British port (*R (Fleet Maritime Services (Bermuda) Limited) v The Pensions Regulator*[21]).

1.16 If the respondent is a company registered in Great Britain, it is resident here even though it carries on business elsewhere (*Odeco (UK) Inc v Peacham*[22]), and it may carry on a business in Great Britain even though it has no registered office here (*Knulty v Eloc Electro Optick Communicatie BV*[23]). The focus should be on whom the employee works for, rather than his role or duties (*Green v SIG Trading Ltd*[24]).

1.17 The Equality Act 2010 is also silent on the question of territorial jurisdiction (unlike many of the repealed regulations), apart from certain provisions relating to ships, hovercraft, and offshore work, and such questions must be determined by the employment tribunals in accordance with the principles outlined. In *R (on the application of Hottak) v Secretary of State for Foreign and Commonwealth Affairs*,[25] however, the Court of Appeal applied *Lawson* when considering jurisdiction under the Equality Act.

1.18 Whether the work is for the purpose of a business carried on in Great Britain is to be determined in the light of the jurisdictional rules outlined in *Lawson v Serco Ltd*,[26] because, although that case concerned the issue of unfair dismissal, it is likely that the principles outlined therein will also apply to the various anti-discrimination provisions (*Williams v University of Nottingham*[27]).

1.19 Where an employee raises a claim under UK law which is derived from EU law, it is the duty of an employment tribunal to give effect to the EU-derived entitlement, even though the work is performed by a foreign national outside Great Britain. In *Bleuse v MBT Transport*

---

[17] [2009] UKEAT 0049_08_2104.   [18] [2008] EWHC 2695, QB.   [19] UKEAT/0252/14.
[20] UKEAT/0345/14.   [21] [2015] EWHC 3744.   [22] [1979] ICR 823.   [23] [1979] ICR 827.
[24] UKEAT/0282/16/DA.   [25] [2016] EWCA Civ 438, CA.
[26] [2006] UKHL 3, [2006] 1 All ER 823, [2006] ICR 250, [2006] IRLR 289.   [27] [2007] IRLR 660.

Ltd[28] a German employee, who worked as a driver in Europe but never worked in the United Kingdom, was able to make a claim for holiday pay against his British employer because the Working Time Regulations were intended to implement an EU Directive. Since most anti-discrimination rights are so derived, it seems clear that the wider tests will apply to claims brought under the Equality Act. Thus, in *Mangold v Helm*[29] it was held that non-discrimination is a fundamental principle of EU law, which can be relied upon against private individuals as well as the state. Thus, workers in the private sector, as well as those in the public sector, will be able to claim even though their connection with Great Britain is somewhat tenuous.

1.20 Contractual entitlements are separate from statutory employment rights. The parties are free to agree the law applicable to their employment contracts, subject to international conventions, the including Rome I and II Regulations, the Posting of Workers Directive, and the Brussels I Regulation, which generally provide that the employment rights of the country with which the employment is closely connected shall apply. Breach of contract claims (eg under the Employment Tribunals Extension of Jurisdiction Order) shadow the jurisdiction of the civil courts (*Dickie v Cathay Pacific Airways Ltd*[30]).

B. **Legal Aid**

1.21 Legal aid is not generally available in England and Wales, although there is provision in the Legal Aid, Sentencing and Punishment of Offenders Act 2012 where the lack of legal aid would breach an individual's rights under the European Convention on Human Rights, or to the provision of services under EU law. In Scotland the system is more generous, but it is still only granted if (a) the applicant is unable to fund or find alternative representation elsewhere, (b) the case is an arguable one, and (c) the case is too complex to allow the applicant to present it to a minimum standard of effectiveness.

C. **Claims for Breach of Contract**

1.22 Under the Employment Tribunals Extension of Jurisdiction (England and Wales) Order 1994, and the Employment Tribunals Extension of Jurisdiction (Scotland) Order 1994, employment tribunals have jurisdiction to hear claims for damages for breach of a contract of employment, or any other contract (subject to certain exceptions, see para 1.24) connected with employment, including a claim for a sum due under such a contract, and a claim for the recovery of a sum in pursuance of any enactment relating to the terms or performance of such a contract. The claim must be outstanding on the termination of the employee's employment, which is the moment in time when the employee ceases to work for the employer (*Miller Bros & FP Butler Ltd v Johnston*[31]), and the maximum award which can be made in respect of any number of claims is £25,000. The claim must be brought within three months from the effective date of termination of the contract of employment (or within three months from the last day when the employee worked in the employment which has been terminated) with the usual extension of time if it was not reasonably practicable to bring the claim within that time (see also para 20.6). There is no requirement that the employee should have been employed for any particular period of employment before bringing a claim under the Order.

1.23 Once an employee has lodged such a claim, the employer may lodge a counterclaim in respect of breach of contract by the employee, within six weeks (or, if not reasonably practicable to do so, within such further time as the employment tribunal considers to be

---

[28] [2008] ICR 488, [2008] IRLR 264.   [29] [2006] All ER (EC) 383, [2006] IRLR 143.
[30] [2005] EWCA Civ 599, [2005] ICR 1436, [2005] IRLR 624.
[31] [2002] ICR 744, [2002] IRLR 386, [2002] All ER (D) 220, EAT.

reasonable). The counterclaim is not limited by the amount of the original claim, and may be continued irrespective of what happens to the original claim, as long as it has been presented before the employee's claim has been settled or withdrawn. Indeed, if the employee's breach of contract claim fails because it was not presented within the appropriate time limits, the employer's counterclaim, validly presented, can still proceed (*Patel v RCMS Ltd*[32]).

1.24 Neither the employee nor the employer can bring a claim or counterclaim in respect of:

    (a) damages for personal injuries;

    (b) breach of a term requiring the employer to provide living accommodation for the employee, or a term imposing an obligation on either of them in connection with the provision of living accommodation;

    (c) a term relating to intellectual property;

    (d) a term imposing an obligation of confidence;

    (e) a term which is a covenant in restraint of trade.

1.25 One effect of the Order is to give an alternative route for claims (other than the exceptions in para 1.24) which would otherwise have to be brought in the county court, although it should be noted that there are a number of differences in the respective jurisdictions and procedures (see para 8.3). Another effect of the Order is to enable employment tribunals to deal with matters which hitherto were not within the scope of the Wages Act 1986 (now Employment Rights Act 1996, ss 13–22, see para 8.5), in particular claims for payments in lieu of notice, holiday pay, advances, etc. Again, there are differences between the Order and the Act, and it will be necessary to scrutinise the nature of a claim very carefully in order to bring it under the appropriate heading.

1.26 If a claimant is successful in recovering £25,000 under the provisions of the Order, he cannot recover any excess of that amount by instituting subsequent High Court proceedings in respect of a wrongful dismissal claim (*Fraser v Hlmad Ltd*[33]).

1.27 If a claimant wishes to claim more than £25,000 under a contract, or needs a longer time limit to bring the claim, then the action should be initiated in a court rather than an employment tribunal.

D. Mediation

1.28 Judicial mediation is available as an alternative to employment tribunal proceedings. The mediator, who will be a tribunal judge trained in alternative dispute resolution, will try to assist the parties to resolve their dispute by mutual agreement. Cases which are suitable for judicial mediation will be identified at the sift stage or preliminary hearing, and if all parties agree to this course being adopted, mediation will take place in private, and the proceedings will be entirely confidential. ACAS also provides access to mediation.

Employment Appeal Tribunal (Employment Tribunals Act 1996, ss 20–37)

1.29 This tribunal consists of judges of the High Court appointed by the Judicial Appointments Commission on the recommendation of the Lord Chancellor in England, and the Lord President of the Court of Session in Scotland, plus other members (appointed on the

---

[32] [1999] IRLR 161, EAT.   [33] [2006] EWCA Civ 738.

joint recommendations of the Lord Chancellor and the Secretary of State) who have special knowledge or experience of industrial relations as representatives of employers or of workers. The Employment Appeal Tribunal (the EAT) is a superior court of record, with a central office in London, but it may sit anywhere in the country, and one or more divisions of the EAT may sit at the same time. In practice, hearings take place either in London or Edinburgh.

1.30 The jurisdiction of the EAT is as follows:

(a) to hear appeals on points of law from decisions of employment tribunals under the various statutory provisions set out in s 21 of the Employment Tribunals Act 1996, which generally cover most, but not all, of the jurisdiction enjoyed by employment tribunals (see para 1.10). In particular, it should be noted that appeals against decisions of an employment tribunal relating to the issue of improvement notices and prohibition notices go to the Divisional Court. The reason is that a breach of these notices amounts to a criminal offence, and the EAT only has specific civil jurisdiction. There have been a few cases where the relevant statutory provision has inadvertently not been included in s 21 of the Employment Tribunals Act, with the result that the EAT lacked jurisdiction to hear an appeal: see eg *Wolstenholme v Refreshment Systems Ltd (t/a Northern Vending Services)*;[34]

(b) to hear appeals from the decisions of the Certification Officer on various matters arising out of the Trade Union and Labour Relations (Consolidation) Act 1992 (TULR(C)A; see Chapter 22);

(c) to hear appeals from the decisions of the Central Arbitration Committee arising from the Transnational Information and Consultation of Employees Regulations 1999, the Information and Consultation of Employees Regulations 2004 (see Chapter 23), and the European Public Limited Liability Company (Employee Involvement) (Great Britain) Regulations 2009.

1.31 The procedure before the EAT is governed by the Employment Appeal Tribunal Rules 1993, which have been amended several times in order to align procedures with those followed by employment tribunals. Thus, the overriding objective of the Rules is to enable the EAT to deal with cases justly, including, so far as practicable, ensuring that the parties are on equal footing, dealing with cases in ways which are proportionate to the importance and complexity of the issues, ensuring that cases are dealt with expeditiously and fairly and saving expense. The Rules lay down the procedure to be followed when lodging an appeal, although if a judge or Registrar thinks that an appeal has no reasonable grounds of succeeding, or is an abuse of process, he can notify the appellant accordingly, and order that no further action be taken in the matter. Further details of the procedure before the EAT can be found in Practice Direction 2018, which supersedes all previous directions.

A party may appear before the EAT in person, or be represented by a solicitor, barrister, representative of a trade union or employers' association, or any other person whom he desires to represent him. Costs will not normally be awarded by the EAT, although there is a power to make a costs order if the proceedings brought by a party were unnecessary, improper, or vexatious, or there has been unreasonable delay or other unreasonable conduct in bringing or conducting the proceedings. The EAT may make a costs order in favour of a litigant in person, and also make a wasted costs order against a party's representative if there have been improper, unreasonable, or negligent acts on his part.

In June 2013, the ERRA 2013 amended s 28(2) and (3) of ETA so that now cases in the EAT are heard by a judge sitting alone except where he directs that they are to be heard by a judge and either two or four lay members. This reversed the previous position.

[34] [2004] All ER (D) 185 (Mar), EAT.

If a judge feels that there may be a conflict of interest because he (or a member of his family) has had some form of professional or personal connection with one of the parties, he should ensure that the full facts are placed before the parties, with an explanation. If there is a real chance of an objection, he should ascertain whether there is another judge who can hear the case (*Jones v DAS Legal Expenses Insurance Co Ltd*[35]). For example, there is an objection to an advocate appearing before the EAT if he is also a part-time judge in that tribunal, and such action is contrary to Art 6 of the Human Rights Convention as being a violation of the right to a fair hearing (*Lawal v Northern Spirit Ltd*[36]). Further guidance on judicial bias is also found in *Locabail (UK) Ltd v Bayfield Properties Ltd*.[37] A restriction on proceedings order may be made to prevent vexatious litigants wasting court time (rr 13–17), and a restricting reporting order may be made in cases where sexual misconduct is alleged (r 23) or disability discrimination (r 23A). It is an offence punishable by a fine not exceeding level 5 on the standard scale (unlimited for offences committed after 13 March 2015) to act in contravention of such an order.

1.32 An appeal can only be entertained by the EAT if there is a genuine dispute between the parties (*IMI Yorkshire Imperial Ltd v Olender*[38]) and appeals should not be pursued with other ulterior motives (*Baker v Superite Tools Ltd*[39]). The function of the EAT is only to see that the ET's decisions are lawfully made, so it is obliged to remit a case to the employment tribunal where there is an issue of fact to be decided, unless the parties agree otherwise (*Jafri v Lincoln College*[40]). A further appeal will lie on a point of law to the Court of Appeal or, in Scotland, to the Court of Session, and a final appeal will lie to the Supreme Court (formerly the House of Lords). At any time, however, a tribunal or court can refer a case to the European Court of Justice in Luxembourg if a question arises as to the application of European law (see para 1.77).

Other Courts

1.33 While the majority of employment-related cases start in the Employment Tribunal and can be appealed to the EAT, some cases (such as contractual claims) can also be brought in the County Court or, for higher value claims, the High Court. Appeals from the EAT and High Court lie to the Court of Appeal, and then to the Supreme Court. This was originally the function of the House of Lords, but the Constitutional Reform Act 2005 paved the way for the abolition of the House of Lords as the highest court of appeal, with its powers and functions being transferred to a new Supreme Court. Earlier decisions of the House of Lords will, of course, still be binding on lower courts and tribunals. The Supreme Court commenced functioning in October 2009.

The Court of Justice of the European Union is considered in the section on the European Union below.

Advisory, Conciliation and Arbitration Service (ACAS)

1.34 The Advisory, Conciliation and Arbitration Service (ACAS) was placed on a statutory basis by the Employment Protection Act 1975 and continued by virtue of the Trade Union and Labour Relations (Consolidation) Act 1992 (TULR(C)A, s 247). It has a general duty to promote the improvement of industrial relations. Its work is directed by a Council, which consists of a chairman and eleven employer, trade union and independent members

---

[35] [2003] EWCA Civ 1071, [2004] IRLR 218.   [36] [2003] UKHL 35.   [37] [2000] QB 451.
[38] [1982] ICR 69, EAT.   [39] [1986] ICR 189, EAT.   [40] [2014] EWCA Civ 449.

appointed by the Secretary of State. The appointments will be initially for a period of five years, and may be renewed for a further period (TULR(C)A, s 248).

1.35 ACAS will appoint its own staff, including a secretary, and will also provide staff for the Certification Officer and the Central Arbitration Committee. Although it will perform its functions on behalf of the Crown, it shall not be subject to any directions from any minister as to the manner in which it is to exercise any of those functions. It is this complete independence from government control which is a distinguishing feature of ACAS. It will make an annual report on its activities and those of the Central Arbitration Committee to the Secretary of State, which will be laid before Parliament and published.

Whenever it thinks it appropriate to do so, ACAS may charge a fee for its services, and also the Secretary of State may direct ACAS to charge fees, either at a full economic cost or a specified proportion or percentage of the economic cost. However, ACAS must notify the person concerned that a fee may or will be charged (TULR(C)A, s 251A).

1.36 The function of ACAS can be examined under the following headings:

A. **Advice**

1.37 ACAS may, on request or otherwise, give employers, employers' associations, workers, and trade unions such advice as it thinks appropriate on matters connected with or likely to affect industrial relations. General advice on this topic may also be published (TULR(C)A, s 213). ACAS has produced a number of Advisory Booklets and Advice Leaflets on a wide range of topics with the aim of giving advice to employers and employees about employment rights generally.

B. **Conciliation**

1.38 Where a trade dispute exists or is apprehended, ACAS may offer its assistance to the parties, either on its own volition or at the request of any party, with a view to bringing about a settlement. This may be achieved by conciliation or other means, and by the appointment, if necessary, of someone outside ACAS whose assistance may be used. Due regard will be given to the desirability of encouraging the parties to use any appropriate agreed procedures (TULR(C)A, s 210).

If there is a dispute over union recognition, ACAS may be invited to use its conciliation role. At the request of both parties, it may hold a ballot of workers involved in the dispute, and/or ascertain the strength of union membership of such workers. However, any such request may be withdrawn by either side, whereupon ACAS shall cease to take any further steps in the matter (TULR(C)A, s 210A).

1.39 It should be noted that for conciliation purposes, the definition of 'trade dispute' is the old definition (based on the Employment Protection Act 1975), now contained in TULR(C)A, s 218, not the more restricted definition (based on the Trade Union and Labour Relations Act 1974) now contained in TULR(C)A, s 244. The effect is to give ACAS a wider conciliation brief.

1.40 Conciliation officers will also be appointed for the purpose of settling by conciliation certain matters which are, or could be, the subject of proceedings before an employment tribunal under any legislation, whenever passed (TULR(C)A, s 211), provided the relevant legislation so indicates (see Employment Tribunals Act 1996, s 18).

1.41 The Enterprise and Regulatory Reform Act (ERRA) 2013, ss 7–9 introduced a further type of individual pre-trial conciliation scheme from April 2014, by inserting ss 18A and 18B to the Employment Tribunals Act 1996 (ETA). The aim of this 'Early Conciliation' scheme is to reduce the number of employment tribunal cases and extend the former pre-claim conciliation system, which was very successful.

A person who wants to make an employment tribunal claim is therefore obliged to contact ACAS first, by submitting an 'Early Conciliation' form giving basic details. ACAS will then contact the claimant to obtain further details and offer conciliation. If this is accepted, then ACAS will take steps to resolve the matter within one month. If the matter is not resolved, or the parties refuse conciliation, then ACAS will issue a certificate to the claimant. The claimant will not be permitted to make a claim to the tribunal without this.

Submission of the Early Conciliation form will 'stop the clock' on the time limit on submitting a claim (see para 20.5), and the clock will restart when the certificate is issued by ACAS.

In practice, a large number of claims made to employment tribunals are disposed of as a result of the intervention of the conciliation officer. The majority of these will be settled on the basis of the employer making some financial payment to the claimant, and the rest will be withdrawn or a private settlement reached.

1.42 Anything communicated to the conciliation officer in connection with the performance of his functions shall not be admissible in evidence in any proceedings before the tribunal without the consent of the party who communicated it. So far as dismissals are concerned, he shall try to promote the re-engagement or reinstatement of the claimant by the employer or by a successor or associated employer on terms appearing to him to be equitable or, if this is not possible, to try to promote a settlement on the sum to be paid by way of compensation. Apart from certain specific instances (see para 20.40), it is not possible for a person to contract out of his statutory rights, and any agreement to this effect is generally void, but this rule does not apply to any agreement reached through the intervention of the conciliation officer, and any such settlement agreed between the parties will be legally binding (ERA, s 203(2)(e)).

1.43 In *Clarke v Redcar and Cleveland Borough Council*,[41] the EAT restated the principles which guide the conciliation process:

(a) ACAS officers have no responsibility to see that the terms of the settlement are fair on the employee.

(b) The expression 'promote a settlement' requires a liberal construction which will enable the officer to take such action as is appropriate in the circumstances of the case.

(c) ACAS officers must never advise on the merits of the case being brought by the claimant.

The employment tribunal should only be concerned with whether the officer has purported to act under s 18 of ETA.

It is only when the officer has acted in bad faith or has adopted unfair methods when promoting a settlement that the agreement reached under s 18 of ETA can be set aside and not bar subsequent proceedings. Thus, if the parties have reached an agreement, the conciliation officer should not get involved in the merits but merely record it on the appropriate form and obtain the parties' signatures (*Moore v Dupont Furniture Products*[42]). Indeed, an agreement reached orally between the parties under the auspices of the conciliation officer is equally binding (*Gilbert v Kembridge Fibres*[43]).

---

[41] [2006] IRLR 324.   [42] [1982] ICR 84, [1982] IRLR 31.   [43] [1984] ICR 188, [1984] IRLR 52, EAT.

1.44 In *Hennessy v Craigmyle & Co Ltd*,[44] the claimant was told that he would be dismissed summarily but, provided he signed an agreement which had been prepared by the conciliation officer giving up his rights to bring a complaint before an employment tribunal, he would be treated as having been made redundant, and would be given certain monies. After taking legal advice, he signed the agreement, but subsequently brought a claim for unfair dismissal. He alleged that his consent had been obtained by economic duress, and hence was void. The argument was dismissed by the employment tribunal, the EAT, and the Court of Appeal. Economic duress was a ground for avoiding an agreement only if the claimant's will was so overborne that his consent was vitiated because he had no real alternative. In this case there was such an alternative, for he could have refused to sign the agreement and taken his chance in the employment tribunal. In any case, whether economic duress exists is a question of fact for the employment tribunal to determine.

1.45 ACAS also has a free helpline. Either employers or employees (or their representatives) may approach ACAS for assistance over a dispute that has not been resolved by the use of internal grievance or disciplinary procedures, in advance of any formal complaint. If this fails, the right to make a complaint to an employment tribunal is still available.

C. **Arbitration**

1.46 The ACAS arbitration scheme is an alternative to tribunal proceedings and can be used for unfair dismissal claims or those relating to flexible working. At the request of one or more parties to a trade dispute, but with the consent of all of them, ACAS may refer any matter to arbitration for settlement, either by a person appointed from outside ACAS, or by the Central Arbitration Committee. However, arbitration is not to be used unless the parties have exhausted agreed procedures for negotiation or the settlement of disputes, unless there is a special reason which justifies arbitration as an alternative to those procedures (TULR(C)A, s 212). With the consent of all the parties, ACAS may decide to publish the award. The Arbitration Act 1996 does not apply to any arbitration under this section, and thus the award is not capable of being legally enforced in a court of law.

In an effort to reduce the number of cases going to employment tribunals, and to avoid the intense legalism which is frequently found there, TULR(C)A s 212A enabled ACAS to introduce an arbitration alternative, whereby claims for unfair dismissal (only) may, with the agreement of both parties, be heard in private by a single arbitrator. The scheme only operates when both sides have signed a COT3 or a settlement agreement (see para 20.40). The arbitrator will be appointed from a special panel of ACAS arbitrators; the actual hearing will be as informal as possible, and held in private at a convenient location. By agreeing to submit to ACAS arbitration, both parties waive their rights to raise any jurisdictional issues, eg whether time limits have been observed, whether there was or was not a dismissal, etc. A constructive dismissal case can only be heard if both parties agree that there was in fact a dismissal.

The parties will be invited to submit a written statement of their case in advance of the hearing, and will be expected to cooperate in the production of relevant documents. The arbitrator will adopt an inquisitorial approach, ie he will generally ask the questions and seek out the relevant facts, rather than leaving it to the parties to adopt the traditional adversarial approach to the case. Legal representation is not necessary. Strict legal principles and legal precedents will not be followed, but the arbitrator will take account of the general principles of fairness and good practice set out in the ACAS Code of Practice on 'Disciplinary and Grievance Procedures' and the ACAS Handbook 'Discipline at Work'.

[44] [1986] ICR 461, [1986] IRLR 300 CA.

The arbitrator can make awards (which will be confidential to the parties and ACAS) identical to those which could be made by an employment tribunal (see Chapter 17). An award will generally be binding, and no appeal will be permitted, except where there is a point of EC law or the Human Rights Act 1998 is relevant, or where there is an allegation of serious irregularity.

The scheme will not be suitable for cases where there is a jurisdictional issue (eg was the applicant an employee, etc), where there are complex legal issues involved (eg was there a transfer of an undertaking), or where issues arising out of the implementation of EC law are concerned (eg Working Time Regulations, sex discrimination cases, etc). If issues other than unfair dismissal are revealed, these must be settled, withdrawn, or heard by an employment tribunal.

If the arbitrator recommends that the employee is re-engaged or reinstated, this order can be enforced, if necessary, by an employment tribunal. Continuity of employment will be preserved.

Full details of the scheme can be found in the ACAS Arbitration Scheme (Great Britain) Order 2004.

D. **Enquiries**

1.47 ACAS may enquire into industrial relations generally, or in a particular industry, or in a particular undertaking. After taking into account the views of the parties, such findings may be published (TULR(C)A, s 214).

E. **Codes of Practice**

1.48 ACAS may issue Codes of Practice containing such practical guidance as it thinks fit for the purpose of promoting the improvement of industrial relations (TULR(C)A, s 199). Five Codes are currently in force, namely:

(a) Disciplinary and Grievance Procedures;

(b) Disclosure of Information to Trade Unions;

(c) Time Off for Trade Union Duties and Activities;

(d) Settlement Agreements;

(e) Handling in a Reasonable Manner Requests to Work Flexibly.

1.49 The codes are first prepared and published in draft form, and then ACAS shall consider any representations made about them (and if necessary modify them) before they are finally submitted to the Secretary of State. If he approves, he shall lay them before Parliament. If he does not approve, he will give reasons for withholding his approval. After completing the Parliamentary procedure, the code will be issued in the form of a draft by ACAS and will come into effect on a day appointed by the Secretary of State. A failure on the part of any person to observe a code shall not of itself make him liable to any proceedings, but in any proceedings before an employment tribunal or the Central Arbitration Committee the code will be admissible in evidence, and any relevant provision shall be taken into account in determining the issue (TULR(C)A, s 207) (see *Lock v Cardiff Rly Co*[45]).

1.50 A Code of Practice may be revised or revoked with the approval of the Secretary of State (TULR(C)A, ss 201–202).

---

[45] [1998] IRLR 358, 599 IRLB 6, EAT.

F. **Guidance**

1.51 ACAS also publishes on its website a range of guidance leaflets on areas such as:

- National Minimum Wage and National Living Wage;
- Pay deductions;
- Holidays;
- Redundancy;
- Working hours;
- Discipline;
- Terminating employment (notice periods and pay);
- Zero-hours contracts;
- Equality and discrimination;
- Transfer of undertakings.

Certification Officer (TULR(C)A, s 254)

1.52 The post of Certification Officer was originally created to take over certain administrative functions exercised in connection with trade unions, although nowadays he has wide powers of investigation and supervision over matters such as register of members, accounting records, elections, breaches of union rules, funds for political objects, and so on (see Chapter 22). He is appointed by the Secretary of State, and will make an annual report to him and also to ACAS. Although the staff of the Certification Officer is provided by ACAS, he is completely independent of that organisation.

Since TULRA 1974 (now TULR(C)A, s 2), the Certification Officer has kept a list of organisations which are trade unions and employers' associations within the legal definition. Since the Employment Protection Act 1975 (now TULR(C)A, s 6) he has issued certificates of independence to those trade unions which have applied and meet the necessary criteria (see Chapter 22). He has issued a booklet entitled 'Guidance for trade unions wishing to apply for a certificate of independence'. He has taken custody of all documents held by his predecessors since 1871, and will keep these for public inspection, along with the list of trade unions and records of all applications for certificates of independence (TULR(C)A, ss 255–258). The Certification Officer has wide powers in respect of complaints by trade union members of alleged breaches of trade union law and trade union rules, and can make declarations and orders on a number of matters, which may be enforced in the same manner as an order of the courts (see Chapter 22). An appeal from his decisions may be made on a point of law to the Employment Appeal Tribunal.

The Certification Officer may also strike out an application or complaint on the ground that it is scandalous, vexatious, has no reasonable prospect of success, or is otherwise misconceived, or refuse to entertain an application by a vexatious litigant (TULR(C)A, ss 256A–256AA).

Central Arbitration Committee

1.53 This body has 27 members, consisting of a chairman and six deputy chairmen and other persons appointed from representatives of employers and workers who are experienced in industrial relations, appointed by the Secretary of State (after consultation with ACAS). The Central Arbitration Committee (CAC) will exercise its functions on behalf of the Crown, but will not be subject to directions of any kind from any ministers as to the manner in which those functions are to be exercised. CAC has a central role in the statutory scheme for the recognition of trade unions, created by the Employment Relations Act 1999 (see Chapter 23). In performing its functions, CAC must have regard to the object of encouraging and promoting fair and efficient practices and arrangements in the workplace, although it will remain neutral on the issue of collective bargaining. CAC will continue to exercise its former statutory functions to adjudicate on claims relating to disclosure of information for collective bargaining purposes brought under TULR(C)A, s 183 (see para 23.15) and will also adjudicate on certain disputes arising out of the provisions of the Transnational Information and Consultation of Employees Regulations 1999 (see para 23.134), and the Information and Consultation Regulations 2004 (see para 23.144).

CAC also resolves disputes concerning the provision of information, consultation, and participation arising from the European Public Limited Liability Company (Employee Involvement) (Great Britain) Regulations 2009, and can act as a voluntary arbitration body following a reference from ACAS under TULR(C)A, s 212.

Industrial Training Boards

1.54 The Industrial Training Act 1982 enables the minister to set up training boards in any industry in order to provide for industrial and commercial training of persons who are over school-leaving age. Only three such statutory boards are currently operating (construction, engineering construction, and film).

1.55 To meet its expenses a board may impose a levy on employers in the industry, which is assessed by reference to a percentage of the payroll. For this purpose a board may require employers to furnish returns and information, and keep and produce records (eg, see Industrial Training Levy (Construction Industry Training Board) Order 2012). An employer who has been assessed for a levy may appeal to an employment tribunal which may rescind or reduce or increase it as the tribunal determines (see Employment Tribunals (Constitution and Rules of Procedure) Regulations 2013).

Equality and Human Rights Commission

1.56 The Equality Act 2006 created a new institution, called the Equality and Human Rights Commission (EHRC), which took over the existing functions of the Equal Opportunities Commission, the Commission for Racial Equality, and the Disability Rights Commission, but with additional responsibilities and wider powers.

Basically, the EHRC has the fundamental duty to create a society in which:

(a) people's ability to achieve their potential is not limited by prejudice or discrimination;

(b) there is respect for and protection of each individual's human rights;

(c) there is respect for the dignity and worth of each individual;

(d) each individual has an equal opportunity to participate in society; and

(e) there is mutual respect between groups based on understanding and valuing of diversity and on shared respect for equality and human rights.

1.57 The EHRC has wider functions than its predecessors, and will draw up a strategic plan showing the activities to be undertaken in pursuance of its statutory powers. In addition to taking over the work of the existing Commissions, the EHRC will assume responsibility for promoting understanding of the importance of equality and diversity, and work towards the elimination of unlawful discrimination in the areas of race, sex, religion or belief, sexual orientation, sexual reassignment, age, disability, and the promotion of human rights. It will promote good relations between and within different groups, encourage good practice in the area of relations between different groups, and work towards the elimination of prejudice, hatred of, and hostility towards members of groups. It will monitor the effectiveness of equality and human rights enactments, give advice to the government, and make recommendations. It will issue (and revise, where necessary) Codes of Practice, which must be approved in draft by the Secretary of State, and be subject to the negative approval parliamentary procedure.

1.58 The EHRC can make enquiries into matters relating to its duties in respect of equality and diversity, human rights, disabilities, and groups. It can make grants and carry out investigations. If, following an investigation, it is satisfied that a person has committed an unlawful act, it can issue an unlawful act notice, which may be followed by requiring that person to prepare an action plan for the purpose of avoiding repetition or continuance of the unlawful act. As an alternative, the Commission may enter into a legally enforceable agreement whereby the person concerned undertakes not to commit (or prepare to commit) an unlawful act, and in return the Commission undertakes not to proceed with an investigation or issue an unlawful act notice.

Health and Safety Executive

1.59 The former Health and Safety Commission and the Health and Safety Executive were abolished by the Legislative Reform (Health and Safety Executive) Order 2008 and replaced by a new unitary organisation called the Health and Safety Executive (HSE). This consists of 11 non-executive members appointed by the Secretary of State. Three members are appointed after consultation with employers' associations, three members are appointed after consultation with employees' associations, one member is appointed after consultation with organisations representing local authorities, and up to four members are appointed after consultation with professional bodies and devolved administrations. The new HSE appoints a chief executive. All the powers and functions of the old Commission and Executive were transferred to the new organisation.

1.60 It is the duty of HSE to do such things and make such arrangements as it considers appropriate for the general purposes of the Health and Safety at Work Act 1974. In particular, HSE shall:

(a) assist and encourage persons concerned with matters relevant to those purposes to further those purposes;

(b) make arrangements as it considers appropriate for the carrying out of research and the publication of the results of research, and the provision of training and information, and encourage research and the provision of training and information by others;

(c) make arrangements to provide information and advisory services to government departments, local authorities, employers, employees and their organisations, and other purposes concerned with matters relevant to the general purposes of the Act.

1.61 HSE will submit proposals to the Secretary of State, provide particulars of what it proposes to do for the purpose of carrying out its functions, ensure that its activities are in accordance with proposals approved by, and give effect to any directions issued by, the Secretary of State. However, the Secretary of State may not give directions with regard to the enforcement of the relevant statutory provisions in any particular case.

1.62 HSE may carry out an investigation or hold an enquiry into any matter, occurrence, or situation, in accordance with the Health and Safety Inquiries (Procedure) Regulations 1975. It will issue guidance to local authorities and work with them to establish best practice and consistency in the enforcement of health and safety law. The enforcement powers of HSE and local authorities remain unchanged.

Low Pay Commission

1.63 This body, which consists of a chairman and eight other members appointed by the Secretary of State, was put on a statutory basis by the National Minimum Wage Act 1998, and is responsible for recommending to the Secretary of State the level of the national minimum wage.

The Role of the Government

1.64 The responsibility for employment law issues is shared by a number of government departments, including the Department for Business, Energy and Industrial Strategy, the Department for Transport, the Ministry of Housing, Communities and Local Government, the Department for Work and Pensions, and so forth, each headed by a Secretary of State. Within these departments, junior ministers deal with a wide range of issues, such as employment relations generally, employment tribunals, ACAS and CAC, health and safety, race, sex and disability issues, job action programmes, maternity, paternity, and adoption matters, pensions, work permits, adult and youth training, and so on.

Codes of Practice

1.65 Codes of practice may be issued by the Advisory, Conciliation and Arbitration Service, the Equality and Human Rights Commission, the Health and Safety Executive, and the Secretary of State. A failure by a person to comply with a provision in the code will not, by itself, render a person liable for criminal or civil proceedings, but in any such proceedings a relevant code shall be admissible in evidence, and be taken account of by a court or tribunal when determining any issue before it. In other words, they do not have the force of law, but can be persuasive.

1.66 The Secretary of State has power to issue Codes of Practice (TULR(C)A, s 203), and codes have been issued on Picketing, Industrial Action Ballots and Notice to Employers, and Access to Workers during Recognition and Derecognition Ballots. It is of interest to note that whereas codes of practice which have been issued by ACAS and EHRC are admissible before employment tribunals, those issued by the Secretary of State are also admissible in the courts.

The Impact of the European Union

1.67 As from 1 January 1973, the United Kingdom became a member of the European Union, and by the European Communities Act 1972 (s 2) all obligations arising out of the various treaties which set up the EU were given legal effect in this country without further enactment. In 2018 the European Union (Withdrawal) Act was published, repealing the 1972 Act. After the UK leaves the EU, all laws will continue as before, and legislation will remain unless expressly repealed. This is discussed further in the 'Note on EU legislation' at the beginning of this book. European law, which overrides domestic provisions, will for

the time being therefore remain of particular importance in the study of domestic employment law. In order to understand European Union law, we must examine the treaties, the
institutions, and the nature of the legal rules which take effect.

A. Treaty of Rome

1.68 This Treaty was signed in 1957 by the original six founding states (France, West
Germany, Italy, Belgium, the Netherlands, and Luxembourg). The UK, Ireland, and
Denmark acceded to the Treaty in 1973, Greece joined in 1981, Spain and Portugal became
full members in 1992, and Austria, Finland, and Sweden joined in 1995. The original Treaty
required unanimity between all the member states before laws could be passed, although
subsequently a system of qualified majority voting has been introduced. So far as is relevant,
Art 140 of the Treaty stated that one of the objects of the Community was to harmonise laws
relating to 'employment, labour law and working conditions, basic and advanced training,
social security, protection against occupational accidents and diseases, occupational hygiene, law of trade unions, and collective bargaining between workers and employers'. The
Treaty of Amsterdam brought about a renumbering of the Articles of the Treaty of Rome.

B. Treaty of Lisbon

1.69 The Lisbon Treaty makes the Charter on Fundamental Human Rights legally binding on EU institutions, but this only affects member states when they are implementing EU
law. Additionally, the UK Government has secured an opt-out protocol, which means that
no court or tribunal can find the laws or practices of the UK to be inconsistent with the
fundamental rights and freedoms of the Charter.

1.70 The Lisbon Treaty renamed the Treaty of Rome as the Treaty on the Functioning of
the European Union (TFEU) and the Maastricht Treaty as the Treaty on European Union
(TEU). The co-decision legislative procedure has been rebranded as the ordinary legislative
procedure, whereby the European Commission will propose legislation, which then has to
be passed by the Council of Ministers and the European Parliament before it becomes law.
Some of the Articles of the Treaty of Rome have been renumbered (eg Art 141 on equal pay
is now Art 157).

C. Expansion of the EU

1.71 At the meeting in Maastricht in 1992, the EU adopted criteria for other states to
become members of the Union. The conditions were stable institutions guaranteeing democracy, the rule of law, human rights, and respect for and protection of minorities, a
functioning market economy, and the ability to take on the obligations of political, economic, and monetary union. As a result, a further ten countries joined the European Union
in 2004, ie Cyprus, Czech Republic, Estonia, Hungary, Latvia, Lithuania, Malta, Poland,
Slovak Republic, and Slovenia. Romania and Bulgaria joined in 2007, and Croatia in 2013,
bringing the total membership of the EU to 28. Macedonia, Iceland, Montenegro, Turkey,
and Serbia are candidate countries which have applied to join.

D. EU Institutions

Council of Ministers

1.72 This is the supreme policy-making body of the EU. Each meeting of the Council is
attended by a minister from each member state. Usually, this will be the respective prime
ministers or foreign secretaries, but sometimes, when specific detailed proposals are being

discussed, the respective 'portfolio' ministers will attend. One member of the Council will hold the presidency for six months and then the position rotates. The Council is assisted by a Secretariat (comprising a staff of some 2,500) and preparatory work for the meetings is undertaken by frequent meetings of senior civil servants from the respective countries, known as the Committee of Permanent Representatives (Coreper).

The Commission

1.73 This is sometimes described as being the 'bureaucracy' of the Union, but perhaps a more accurate description would be the 'engine room'. Each member state appoints one independent commissioner, Each commissioner has certain departmental responsibilities and is assisted by a cabinet and directorate general. Decisions are taken on a collegiate basis.

1.74 The Commission has the responsibility of initiating and drafting proposals for approval by the Council. It acts as a mediator between states, and as a 'watchdog' to ensure that EU rules are being observed. Indeed, if the Commission considers that a member state is failing to comply with an EU law, it can take enforcement action by referring the alleged breach to the European Court of Justice for a ruling (see para 1.76).

European Parliament

1.75 This body sits in Strasbourg and Brussels and currently consists of 751 members of the European Parliament (MEPs) elected directly from each member state. It can express an opinion to the Council of Ministers on proposals which emanate from the Commission, can submit questions to both institutions, and can, as a final sanction, dismiss the Commission on a vote of censure passed by a two-thirds majority. The Lisbon Treaty increased the involvement of the European Parliament through an extended co-decision process with the Council of Ministers.

Court of Justice of the European Communities

1.76 This Court sits in Luxembourg and comprises 28 judges (one from each country) and nine advocates general. Appointments are made for six years. The Court gives rulings on the interpretation of European law, either on a reference from the Commission, at the request of the courts of a member state, or on a claim brought by an individual person or corporation in a member state. Once it has given its ruling the matter is then referred back to the courts of the member state for compliance.

European Union Law

1.77 For the purpose of this book, the law of the European Union consists of (a) Articles of the Treaty of Rome, (b) Directives passed by the Council of Ministers, (c) Recommendations, and (d) Decisions of the European Court of Justice. It must be borne in mind that any common law or statutory rule which is contrary to European law is void, and if there is any conflict between European law and UK law, the former is to be applied. Indeed, if, in any preliminary proceedings, it appears that the sole obstacle towards granting interim relief is a rule of national law which is in conflict with European law, that national law has to be set aside (*R v Secretary of State for Transport, ex p Factortame (No 2)*[46]). Further, the UK courts have now held that an organisation (*R v Secretary of State for Employment, ex p Equal*

---

[46] Case C-213/89 [1991] 1 AC 603, [1991] 1 All ER 70, ECJ; apld sub nom *R v Secretary of State for Transport, ex p Factortame Ltd (No 2)* [1991] 1 AC 603, sub nom *Factortame Ltd v Secretary of State for Transport (No 2)* [1991] 1 All ER 70, HL.

Opportunities Commission[47]) or a private individual (*R v Secretary of State for Employment, ex p Seymour-Smith and Perez*[48]) can bring an action for a declaration that UK law does not correctly implement EU law.

A. Articles of the Treaty

1.78 If an article of the Treaty on the Functioning of the European Union (TFEU) is clear, precise, unconditional, requires no further implementation, and does not give any discretion to member states, it is directly applicable and becomes an integral part of the law of member states (*Defrenne v Sabena*[49]). For example, Art 157 (formerly 119) of the Treaty provides: 'Each Member State shall ensure and maintain the application of the principle that men and women should receive equal pay for equal work'. This article has been invoked in a number of cases, and has been held to confer a distinct legal right on an individual, which can be enforced in national courts, in addition to any legal right conferred by national law (*Garland v British Rail Engineering Ltd*[50]). Similarly, Art 45 (formerly 48) of the Treaty on the Functioning of the European Union provides that member states shall ensure the free movement of workers within the Community without discrimination as regards employment, remuneration, and other conditions of work and employment, and this too has a direct legal effect (*Van Duyn v Home Office (No 2)*[51]). Thus if a national of a member state wishes to obtain employment in the United Kingdom, he does not need a work permit, and he must be given equal access to social security benefits, holidays, equal pay, etc.

B. Directives

1.79 A Directive passed by the Council of Ministers is binding as to the result to be achieved, but the national authorities are given a choice of form and methods. However, as Directives are binding on member states, it is the duty of those states to implement them, and if the state fails to do so, an individual may seek to enforce the terms of the Directive against a state in its capacity as an employer (*Marshall v Southampton and South West Hampshire Area Health Authority*[52]). For this purpose, 'the state' includes anybody which is an emanation of the state (eg a nationalised industry) or which provides a public service under the control of the state. In other words, a state cannot take advantage of its own failure to comply with European law (*Foster v British Gas*[53]).

---

[47] [1993] 1 All ER 1022, [1993] ICR 251, [1993] IRLR 10, CA; on appeal [1995] 1 AC 1, [1994] IRLR 176, sub nom *Equal Opportunities Commission v Secretary of State for Employment* [1994] 1 All ER 910, [1994] ICR 317, HL.

[48] [1994] IRLR 448, DC; aff'd on other grounds [1996] All ER (EC) 1, [1995] ICR 889, [1995] IRLR 464, CA; revsd [1997] 2 All ER 273, [1997] 1 WLR 473, [1997] ICR 371, [1997] IRLR 315, 56 IRLB 15, HL; refd sub nom *R v Secretary of State for Employment, ex p Seymour-Smith*: Case C-167/97 [1999] 2 AC 554, [1999] ICR 447, [1999] IRLR 253, ECJ; apld sub nom *R v Secretary of State for Employment, ex p Seymour-Smith (No 2)* [2000] 1 All ER 857, [2000] ICR 244, [2000] IRLR 263, HL.

[49] Case C-43/75 [1981] 1 All ER 122, [1976] ECR 455, [1976] ICR 547, ECJ.

[50] [1983] 2 AC 751, [1982] ICR 420, HL; refd 12/81 [1983] 2 AC 751, [1982] 2 All ER 402, [1982] ECR 359, [1982] 1 CMLR 696, [1982] ICR 420, [1982] IRLR 111, ECJ; apld [1983] 2 AC 751, [1982] 2 All ER 402, [1982] ICR 420, [1982] IRLR 257, HL.

[51] Case C-41/74 [1975] Ch 358, [1975] 3 All ER 190, [1974] ECR 1337, ECJ.

[52] [1983] 2 AC 751, [1982] ICR 420, HL; refd 12/81 [1983] 2 AC 751, [1982] 2 All ER 402, [1982] ECR 359, [1982] ICR 420, [1982] IRLR 111, ECJ; apld [1983] 2 AC 751, [1982] 2 All ER 402 [1982] ICR 420, [1982] IRLR 257, HL.

[53] Case C-188/89 [1991] 1 QB 405, [1990] 3 All ER 897, [1990] ECR I–3313, [1991] ICR 84, [1990] IRLR 353, ECJ.

In *Doughty v Rolls-Royce plc*,[54] the Court of Appeal laid down three criteria to be applied in considering whether or not any particular body is 'an emanation of the State' following principles laid down by the European Court in *Foster v British Gas*. These are:

whether the entity was made responsible, pursuant to a measure adopted by the state, for providing a public service;

whether the service it provided was under the control of the state; and

whether it possessed or claimed to exercise any special powers.

Thus, although Rolls-Royce was 100% owned by the state, it was a commercial undertaking rather than a state body for the purpose of enforcing the provisions of a Directive.

For example, in *Impact v Ministry of Agriculture & Food*[55] the European Court of Justice (ECJ) held that the non-discrimination provisions of the Fixed-Term Workers Directive (99/70/EC) were sufficiently 'clear, precise and unconditional' to have a direct effect, and can thus be enforced directly against a public authority irrespective of the provisions of national law. This would include, for example, pension entitlements that were discriminatory. However, the provisions that provide for the conversion of successive fixed-term contracts into permanent ones did not have a direct effect, although national law should be interpreted consistently with the Directive if this was possible.

1.80 In strict legal theory, a Directive is not enforceable against a non-state body or a private individual. Thus, if there are no national rules on a subject, it is not permissible to rely on the provisions of a Directive as the basis of a claim. However, the European Court of Justice has gone a great deal further in a number of cases. In *Dekker v Stichting Vormingscentrum voor Jong Volwassenen (VJV-Centrum) Plus*,[56] it was held that it is permissible to rely on the provisions of a Directive in order to interpret national law, and in particular those provisions of national law which were designed to implement a Directive. Thus the European Court will interpret national law in the light of the language and aims of the Directive. In *Marleasing SA v La Comercial Internacional de Alimentación*,[57] the Court went still further. They stated:

> It follows from the obligation on member states to take all measures appropriate to ensure the performance of their obligation to achieve the results provided for in Directives, that in applying national law, whether it was a case of provisions prior to or subsequent to the Directive, the national court called on to interpret it was required to do so as far as possible in the light of the wording and purpose of the Directive in order to achieve the result sought by the Directive.

Finally, in a historic decision, the European Court stated that if a member state fails to take the necessary steps to achieve the results required by a Directive, an individual who suffers damage thereby may sue the state for the loss suffered which results from that failure. In *Francovich v Italy*,[58] the Italian Government had failed to implement EC Directive 80/987 on the protection of employees on an employer's insolvency. In consequence, an employee was unable to recover wages owed to him following his employer's insolvency, and he sued the Italian Government for compensation. It was held that his claim could succeed as long as three conditions were satisfied. These were that: (a) the result required by the Directive includes the conferring of rights for the benefit of individuals, (b) the contents of those rights may be determined by reference

---

[54] [1992] IRLR 126, sub nom *Rolls-Royce plc v Doughty* [1992] ICR 538, CA.
[55] [2009] All ER (EC) 306, [2008] ECR I–2483, [2008] IRLR 552.
[56] Case C-177/88 [1990] ECR I–3941, [1992] ICR 325, [1991] IRLR 27, ECJ.
[57] Case C-106/89 [1990] ECR I–4135, ECJ.
[58] Case C-6/90 and 9/90 [1991] ECR I–5357, [1995] ICR 722, [1992] IRLR 84, ECJ.

to the provisions of the Directive, and (c) there is a causal link between the breach of the obligation of the state and the damage suffered by the person affected.

Since these three conditions were met, the claim succeeded. However, the European Court appeared to suggest that a claim could be made not only when a member state fails to implement the terms of a Directive, but also when it incorrectly implements a Directive. Further, national courts are the appropriate forum for such claims, without the necessity of seeking a remedy in the European Court. However it should be noted that in *R v Secretary of State for Transport, ex p Factortame*,[59] the Advocate-General expressed the view that such liability would only arise if the breach was 'manifest and serious', which suggests that inadvertent or unwitting breaches of European law may not necessarily attract such a remedy.

A *Francovich* claim must be brought within the six-year period laid down in the Limitation Act 1980 (*Spencer v Secretary of State for Work and Pensions*[60]).

Thus, although Directives are addressed to member states, and can be enforced by intended beneficiaries against the state, there also appears to be an interesting remedy against a state which fails to implement or incorrectly implements a Directive by persons who suffer damage thereby.

It should be noted that *Francovich*-style claims arising from an alleged failure by a state properly to implement a Directive must be brought in the High Court, not an employment tribunal (*Secretary of State for Employment v Mann*[61]). In *Brasserie du Pêcheur SA v Germany*,[62] the European Court of Justice gave guidance on the principles and approach to be adopted when national courts deal with *Francovich*-type claims. The three issues considered were liability, damages, and retrospection.

So far as liability was concerned, the Court stated that there was no difference in principle between those EU rights which were directly or indirectly applicable. Thus a right arising out of the Treaty (eg Art 141) or a right against a state body by a state employee (*Foster v British Gas*[63]) is to be treated in the same way as those rights which were indirectly applicable (*Marleasing SA v La Comercial Internacional de Alimentación*[64]). Further, the state was to be considered as a single entity, and thus it did not matter if the breach was attributable to the executive, the legislature, or the judiciary.

If the EU rule confers a wide discretion (as do some Directives), it must be established that it was intended to confer rights on an individual. If so, the next question to answer is whether the breach was 'sufficiently serious' in that there was a manifest and serious disregard of the discretion. This is for the national courts to decide, taking into account the clarity and precision of the rule that has been breached, the measure of the discretion given to national authorities, whether the breach was voluntary or involuntary, whether any error of law was excusable or inexcusable, whether it was caused or contributed to by any position taken by an EU institution, and the general adoption or retention of national measures which are contrary to EU law. A breach will be sufficiently serious if it has continued despite a judgment finding that there has been a breach, or where there has been a previous legal ruling from the ECJ making it clear that there has been an infringement.

So far as damages are concerned, the Court stated that national rules must not make it impossible or extremely difficult for an individual to obtain reparation, and damages awarded must be commensurate with the loss suffered. The criteria should not be less

---

[59] Case C-48/93 [1996] QB 404, [1996] ECR I–1029, [1996] All ER (EC) 301, [1996] IRLR 267, ECJ; apld [1998] 1 All ER 736n, DC; aff'd, [1998] Eu LR 456, [1999] 2 All ER 640n, CA; aff'd [2000] 1 AC 524, [1999] 4 All ER 906, [1999] 43 LS Gaz R 32, HL.

[60] [2008] EWCA Civ 750, [2009] 1 All ER 314, [2008] ICR 1359, [2008] IRLR 911.   [61] n 17.

[62] Case C-46/93 [1996] QB 404, [1996] ECR I–1029, [1996] All ER (EC) 301, [1996] IRLR 267, ECJ; apld [1998] 1 All ER 736n, DC; aff'd [1998] Eu LR 456, [1999] 2 All ER 640n, CA; aff'd [2000] 1 AC 524, [1999] 4 All ER 906, [1999], HL.

[63] n 46.   [64] Case C-106/89 [1990] ECR I–4135, ECJ.

favourable than those applicable to similar claims based on domestic law. However, a national court is entitled to enquire into the steps taken by a complainant to mitigate the loss, in particular having regard to available legal remedies.

Finally, so far as retrospection was concerned, the ECJ was of the opinion that the main issue was whether the breach was sufficiently serious. If it was, then there was no temporal limit on the effect of an ECJ judgment. However, claims could be subjected to substantive and procedural limitations imposed by national law, which could take into account principles of legal certainty by applying time limits on claims.

If a Directive is not capable of having direct effect, but is then subsequently transposed into domestic law, national courts are required to interpret the legislation in a manner which gives effect to the aims of the Directive, from the date that the period for transposition into national law has expired (*Adeneler v Ellinikos Organismos Galaktos*[65]).

1.81 There are a number of Directives which have a particular bearing on employment law, and which have been implemented by UK legislation, such as:

- Directive 75/117/EEC (Equal Pay)
- Directive 76/207/EEC (Equal Treatment)
- Directive 75/129/EEC (Collective Redundancies)
- Directive 77/187/EEC (Acquired Rights)
- Directive 79/7/EEC (Equal Treatment in Social Security Matters)
- Directive 86/378/EEC (Equal Treatment in Occupational Social Security Schemes)
- Directive 86/613/EEC (Equal Treatment for Self-employed)
- Directive 80/987/EEC (Employers' Insolvency)
- Directive 91/533/EEC (Proof of Employment Relationship)
- Directive 93/104/EEC (Working Time)
- Directive 94/45/EC (European Works Councils)
- Directive 94/33/EC (Protection of Young People at Work)
- Directive 96/34/EC (Parental Leave)
- Directive 97/81/EC (Part-time Work)
- Directive 96/71/EC (Posted Workers) (revised Directive18/957/EU)
- Directive 99/70/EC (Fixed-term Workers)
- Directive 97/80/EC (Burden of Proof)
- Directive 2000/78/EC (Equal Treatment in Employment and Occupation)
- Directive 2000/43/EC (Equal Treatment between Persons Irrespective of Racial or Ethnic Origins)
- Directive 2002/14/EC (Information and Consultation)
- Directive 2008/104/EC (Agency Workers Directive)
- Directive 2010/18/EU (Parental Leave)

C. **Other Directives**

1.82 A number of other Directives (such as those relating to health and safety at work in Chapter 11 or the General Data Protection Regulation in Chapter 10) have also been

---

[65] Case C-212/04 [2006] ECR I–6057, [2006] IRLR 716, [2007] All ER (EC) 82, ECJ.

passed by the Council of Ministers. In 2006 all seven measures dealing with the implementation of the principle of equal opportunities and equal treatment of men and women in matters of employment and occupation were consolidated into the Equal Treatment Directive 2006/54/EC with effect from August 2009. Most recently The EU Transparent and Predictable Working Conditions Directive, which applies to workers and employees, has been agreed. It is not clear yet if this will apply to the UK, depending on what the future relationship will be. Member states will have to implement it by 2022. The Directive is expected to set out, among other things, new minimum standards to ensure that all workers, including those on atypical contracts, will have more predictability and clarity in relation to their working conditions.

D. Recommendations

1.83 A Recommendation made under Community law has no binding effect, and cannot be relied upon to enforce a legal right in a national court. However, in *Grimaldi v Fonds des Maladies Professionnelles*,[66] the European Court of Justice held that national courts are bound to take Recommendations into account when determining disputes which are referred to them, in particular when they clarify the interpretation of laws passed to implement them, or when they are designed to supplement binding Community measures.

1.84 Recommendations have been made on such topics as the employment of disabled persons, hours of work and holidays generally, flexible retirement, vocational training for women, and sexual harassment.

E. Decisions of the Court of Justice of the European Union

1.85 The Court of Justice of the European Union has jurisdiction under Art 234 of the Treaty of the Functioning of the European Union to give rulings concerning the interpretation of the Treaty or Regulations or Directives made by the Council of Ministers. A member state may be taken to the Court by another state or by the European Commission (see *EC Commission v United Kingdom*,[67] para 18.69). A UK court may, but is not bound to, make a reference to the Court if it is necessary to enable a decision to be made (see *Macarthys Ltd v Smith*,[68] para 5.12). Once the Court has given its opinion, the matter is referred back to the national court for the application of the opinion to the facts of the case (see *Jenkins v Kingsgate (Clothing Productions) Ltd*[69]).

1.86 It should be noted that there are no specified time limits for bringing a claim under European law, as the provisions of the Treaty of Rome came into force upon accession (see *Stevens v Bexley Health Authority*[70]). Time will start to run against a state body from the day the state makes good its failure to comply with the objectives laid down in the Directive (*Cannon v Barnsley Metropolitan Borough Council*[71]). However, the European Court may,

---

[66] Case C-322/88 [1989] ECR 4407, [1990] IRLR 400, ECJ.

[67] Case C-382/92 [1994] ECR I–2435, [1994] ICR 664, [1994] IRLR 392, ECJ.

[68] Case C-129/79 [1978] 2 All ER 746, [1978] ICR 500, [1978] IRLR 10, on appeal [1979] 3 All ER 325, [1979] ICR 785, [1979] IRLR 316, refd [1981] QB 180, [1981] 1 All ER 111, [1980] ICR 672, [1980] IRLR 210, apld [1981] QB 180, [1981] 1 All ER 111, [1980] ICR 672, [1980] IRLR 210, CA.

[69] [1981] ICR 715, [1981] IRLR 388, EAT.

[70] [1989] ICR 224, [1989] IRLR 240, EAT.   [71] [1992] ICR 698, [1992] IRLR 474, EAT.

when giving a ruling, indicate that this shall only apply to claims lodged at the date of the ruling (*Barber v Guardian Royal Exchange*[72]).

1.87 If a person is seeking to enforce a private right which has come to light as a result of the interpretation of EC law by the European Court, national domestic procedures relating to time limits must be adhered to. Thus in *Biggs v Somerset County Council*[73] the applicant was a teacher who worked for 14 hours per week. She was dismissed in 1976 but, relying on the House of Lords' decision in *R v Secretary of State for Employment, ex p Equal Opportunities Commission*[74] (which held that the 'hours' requirement was discriminatory and contrary to the EC Equal Treatment Directive), brought a claim for unfair dismissal in 1994. It was held that her claim was out of time. She was not seeking to enforce a Community right (there is no EC right to be unfairly dismissed), and there is no separate procedure for bringing claims under EC law (see also *Setiya v East Yorkshire Health Authority*[75] and Chapter 20). (Note that in case law before 2011 the court was referred to as the ECJ; after that time it became the Court of Justice of the European Union (CJEU).)

Human Rights Act 1998

1.88 In order to prevent a re-occurrence of the horrors and atrocities which took place before and during the Second World War, the European Convention for the Protection of Human Rights and Fundamental Freedoms was signed in 1950. Note that this derives from the Council of Europe, and not the European Union, and so would be unaffected by the future relationship between the UK and the EU.

1.89 Many European countries subsequently incorporated the Convention into their domestic law, but UK citizens who wished to assert a Convention right were forced to petition the European Court of Human Rights in Strasbourg. The UK Government would always give effect to any ruling from that court, but the Convention itself was not enforceable in UK courts.

1.90 Despite the financial and practical difficulties involved in pursuing a claim under the Convention, some notable decisions were given against the UK Government in circumstances where the ordinary legal system could not or would not provide a remedy. For example, in *R v Admiralty Board of the Defence Council, ex p Lustig-Prean*,[76] the Court of Appeal refused to interfere with a decision to discharge the applicant from the Royal Navy on the grounds that he was a homosexual, and he thus brought proceedings in the European Court of Human Rights. That Court held (*Lustig-Prean v United Kingdom*[77]) that a decision to discharge homosexuals from the armed forces on grounds of their sexual orientation was a violation of their right to respect for their private lives, and thus was contrary to Art 8 of the Convention. The outcome was the lifting of the ban on homosexual men and women joining or staying in the armed forces. A similar outcome was reached in three other cases (see *Smith v United Kingdom*[78]).

---

[72] n 60.　　　　[73] n 16.　　　　[74] n 40.　　　　[75] [1995] IRLR 348, EAT.
[76] [1996] QB 517, [1996] ICR 740, sub nom *R v Ministry of Defence, ex p Smith* [1996] 1 All ER 257, [1996] IRLR 100, CA.　　　　　　　　　　　　　　　　　　[77] (1999) 29 EHRR 548, ECtHR.
[78] (Applications 33985/96 and 33986/96) 29 EHRR 493, [1999] ECHR 33985/96, ECtHR.

1.91 The Human Rights Act 1998 is designed to give effect to the rights and freedoms guaranteed under the Convention, by effectively incorporating it into UK law. It came into force in October 2000 and its basic provisions may be summarised as follows:

> A court or tribunal determining a question which has arisen in connection with a Convention right must take into account any judgment, decision, declaration or advisory opinion of the European Court of Human Rights. But although it is mandatory to take these into account, the court or tribunal is given a discretion whether to follow that decision etc (see *Kleinwort Benson Ltd v Glasgow City Council*[79]). It has long been recognised that the Convention is a 'living instrument', and a previous decision of the Court need not be followed if it is out of step with current practices and opinions, or if it is unpersuasive. Further, the Court itself developed the doctrine of 'the margin of appreciation' which recognised the relatively restrained scrutiny of national law.
>
> So far as it is possible to do so, primary and subordinate legislation must be read and given effect in a way which is compatible with Convention rights. Thus, if a court or tribunal has a choice to interpret a statute in two ways, one of which is compatible with the Convention and one not, the former interpretation must prevail (see *Marleasing*, para 1.80). This obligation arises whenever the statutory provisions were passed. But if a statute has only one possible meaning, effect must be given to it accordingly.
>
> If a court (not a tribunal) is satisfied that a provision in primary legislation is incompatible with a Convention right, it may make a declaration of incompatibility, although before doing so it must give the Crown notice of such intention, so as to enable the Crown to be joined as a party to the proceedings. Such a declaration does not affect the validity of the provision in question, nor is it binding on the parties to the proceedings, but, once made, doubtless Parliament will consider taking steps to ensure compliance with the Convention.

It is unlawful for a public authority to act in a way which is incompatible with a Convention right.

There is some uncertainty as to which bodies are 'public authorities', which will doubtless be the subject of case law, but courts and tribunals are certainly within the meaning of the term. A person aggrieved by such an act may bring proceedings in an appropriate legal venue, and certain remedies, including compensation, are available.

1.92 So far as the law of employment is concerned, there are a number of possible implications arising from the Act. An employee cannot lodge a claim in an employment tribunal based directly on a Convention right, but in any claim brought in a tribunal based on domestic law the tribunal will take those rights into account, unless prohibited from so doing by domestic law. It should be borne in mind that some of the rights are hedged with qualifications. The following Articles of the Convention may well be relevant to employment situations:

(a) *Article 4* states that 'no one shall be required to perform forced or compulsory labour'. In *R (on the application of Reilly & Anor) v Secretary of State for Work and Pensions*,[80] the Supreme Court held that making jobseeker's allowance (JSA) conditional on work or work-related activity does not constitute forced labour, as it was work forming part of 'normal civic obligations'. This is not the type of exploitative conduct at which Art 4 is aimed (although fault was found with the regulations for other reasons).

[79] Case C-346/93 [1996] QB 57, [1995] ECR I–615, [1995] All ER (EC) 514, ECJ; re-heard [1996] QB 678, [1996] 2 All ER 257, CA; revsd [1999] 1 AC 153, [1997] 4 All ER 641, HL.
[80] [2013] UKSC 68.

(b) *Article 6.* In the determination of a person's civil rights and obligations, everyone is entitled to a fair and public hearing within a reasonable time by an independent and impartial tribunal established by law. Thus in *Somjee v United Kingdom*[81] three claims before an employment tribunal and the Employment Appeal Tribunal took more than seven years to be resolved. The European Court held that this violated Art 6 of the Convention. If a person is charged with misconduct before a public body, this is a determination of his civil rights, and the protection in Art 6 applies. Thus he is entitled to have a fair hearing, ie to know in good time the nature of the charges, be given adequate time to prepare his case, to question witnesses, and to call evidence, etc (*R v Securities & Futures Authority Ltd, ex p Fleurose*[82]).

It was suggested in *Smith v Secretary of State for Trade and Industry*[83] that the independence of employment tribunals themselves was in doubt, because the Secretary of State exercised control over the appointment, tenure, and pay of lay members, but subsequently changes were made in these matters which allayed the fears of any conflict of interest or lack of impartiality, and it has now been accepted that employment tribunals are impartial and independent within the meaning of Art 6 (*Scanfuture UK Ltd v Secretary of State for Trade and Industry*[84]). It has been held that there is an objection to an advocate appearing before the Employment Appeal Tribunal if he is also a part-time judge of that Tribunal, because there was a real possibility that lay members who had sat with him in that capacity might subconsciously be biased in favour of submissions made in his capacity as an advocate (*Lawal v Northern Spirit Ltd*, see para 1.31). On the other hand, s 40 of the Health and Safety at Work Act (see para 11.74), which reverses the burden of proof which would ordinarily apply in criminal proceedings, did not violate Art 6. Balancing the fundamental rights of the individual with the general interests of the community in ensuring health and safety at work, the reversal was justified as necessary and proportionate, and therefore compatible with the Convention (*Davies v Health and Safety Executive*[85]).

It is not a violation of Art 6 for an employer to refuse an employee the right of legal representation at a disciplinary hearing, even when the ultimate sanction is likely to be the loss of a job. But a different consideration will apply if the sanction could result in being deprived of an opportunity to practice his or her chosen career, or where some other serious consequence could result, eg being placed on the sex offenders register. In *G v X School*[86] a teacher was brought before a disciplinary body charged with an allegation of sexual misconduct with a 15-year-old student. If the allegations were established this could have adversely affected his whole career. It was held that although he was not facing a criminal charge, the serious nature of the allegations and the severity of the consequences meant that he was entitled to have legal representation under Art 6 of the Convention. A similar view appears to have been taken in *Kulkarni v Milton Keynes Hospital NHS Foundation Trust*,[87] where a junior doctor was accused of inappropriately touching a female patient. It was stated obiter that if an adverse outcome of the case was so potentially damaging as to make it highly unlikely that he would be able to work in his chosen profession, then Art 6 requires that he be given the right to legal representation (see also the discussion in 12.27).

[81] (Application 42116/98) [2002] IRLR 886, [2002] All ER (D) 214 (Oct), ECtHR.
[82] [2002] IRLR 297, CA.   [83] [2000] ICR 69, [2000] IRLR 6, EAT.
[84] [2001] ICR 1096, [2001] IRLR 416, EAT.
[85] [2002] EWCA Crim 2949, [2003] IRLR 170, [2002] All ER (D) 275 (Dec).
[86] [2010] EWCA Civ 1, [2010] 2 All ER 555, [2010] IRLR 222.
[87] [2009] EWCA Civ 789, [2010] ICR 101, [2009] IRLR 829.

These decisions only affect public employers, who are required to act in a way compatible with Convention rights. Whether the principle can be extended to private employers has yet to be determined.

The Convention will not assist a claimant to pursue whims and fancies. In *Khan v Vignette Europe Ltd*[88] an employment tribunal refused to grant an adjournment mid-way through a hearing so that the claimant could experience a period of mental and spiritual purity during Ramadan. It was held that the decision did not violate his right to a fair trial under Art 6.

Where a fundamental principle of EU law is concerned, such as the right to a fair hearing, domestic courts must disapply a provision which stands in its way. In *Kücükdeveci v Swedex GmbH & Co KG*[89] and *Aklagaren v Fransson*[90] (see also para 17.4(f)) the ECJ confirmed that where a fundamental principle of EU law is concerned, such as the right to a fair hearing, domestic courts must disapply a provision which stands in its way. This was done in *Benkharbouche v Sudan*,[91] where the State Immunity Act 1978 prevented domestic workers employed by two embassies from bringing claims. The EAT held that its provisions were to be disapplied by the Charter of Fundamental Rights of the European Union in relation to discrimination and working time claims. Further claims of unfair dismissal and the minimum wage were not covered, as they did not derive from EU law. The EAT effectively held that as a result of the Lisbon Treaty, the EU charter was now directly applicable in the UK, and the tribunal was therefore bound to disapply UK law which conflicted with these principles even between private litigants. This is a significant decision, which could mean that even where the ERA does not allow a statutory provision to be disapplied, EU law will require a tribunal to do so where it concerns EU law. This was affirmed by the Court of Appeal and Supreme Court (also see *Reyes v Al-Malki & Anor*[92]).

(c) *Article 8.* Everyone has the right to respect for his private and family life, his home, and his correspondence. This right is subject to certain qualifications, ie when the interference is by a public authority in accordance with the law, and is necessary in a democratic society in the interests of national security, public safety, or the economic well-being of the country, for the prevention of disorder or crime, for the protection of health or morals, or for the protection of rights and freedoms of others. In *McGowan v Scottish Water*[93] the employer obtained evidence through covert surveillance that the employee had been falsifying his time sheets. The employee claimed that he had been unfairly dismissed, arguing that his right to respect for his private life under Art 8 of the Convention had been breached. His claim was dismissed by the EAT. The interference with his rights was justified under Art 8(2), in that the employer's actions were 'in accordance with the law and necessary for the prevention of disorder or crime'.

The right to respect for private life includes the right to privacy with respect to a person's sexual orientation. The European Court in *Smith v United Kingdom*[94] held that to discriminate against a person on grounds of his/her sexual orientation was a violation of Art 8 of the Convention, and this was transposed into UK law by the Employment Equality (Sexual Orientation) Regulations 2003 (now within the Equality Act—see para 4.1).

---

[88] Employment Appeals Tribunal, 14 January 2010.   [89] Case C-555/07.   [90] Section 1.01.

[91] *Benkharbouche v Embassy of the Republic of Sudan* UKEAT/0401/12; *Janah v Libya* UKEAT/0020/13, affirmed [2015] EWCA Civ 33 CA and [2017] UKSC 62 SC.

[92] [2017] UKSC 61.   [93] [2005] IRLR 167, EAT.   [94] (1999) 29 EHRR 493.

An employee has a reasonable expectation of privacy in respect of private telephone calls. In *Halford v United Kingdom*[95] the employee was a senior police officer who alleged that her employer had tapped a private work telephone, in order to obtain details of a claim for sex discrimination she was pursuing. The European Court of Human Rights held that as she had not been given any prior indication that her telephone calls were liable to interception, there had been a breach of Art 8.

The right to privacy in respect of correspondence clearly includes unauthorised monitoring by employers of telephone calls, email communications, and the use of the internet at the workplace. An employer must therefore seek to justify any such interference by relying on one of the qualifications mentioned earlier, or by notifying employees that such interception may take place at any time (*Barbulescu v Romania*,[96] see also *López Ribalda v Spain*, 10.45). The position was further clarified by the Telecommunications (Lawful Business Practice) (Interception of Communications) Regulations 2000, designed to ensure compliance with the Telecommunications Data Protection Directive (EC 97/66), which permits the interception and monitoring of telephone calls, email communications, etc, for certain specified purposes (see para 10.47). Further to the GDPR, these were replaced by the Investigatory Powers (Interception by Businesses etc. for Monitoring and Record-Keeping Purposes) Regulations 2018, although they are largely the same. Art 8 of the Convention does not, however, apply in respect of the commission of a criminal offence in a public place (*X v Y*[97]). There are a number of other possibilities arising out of Art 8, including the lawfulness of mandatory medical examinations, confidentiality of medical reports, etc. It is unlikely that any remedy will exist in cases where an employee has given his consent to such action, or where there is a contractual power to do so, and the qualifications to Art 8 must always be borne in mind.

This right is further discussed in Chapter 10.

(d) *Article 9*. This Article provides for the right to freedom of thought, conscience, and religion, but it is subject to the same qualifications as are found in Art 8, relating to the limitations imposed in the interests of national security, public safety, economic well-being of the country, preventing disorder or crime, protecting health and morals, and protecting the rights and freedoms of others. Thus in *Ahmad v United Kingdom*[98] the employers refused to permit a devout Muslim to take 45 minutes off work every Friday in order to pray at the local mosque. Instead, they offered to reduce his working hours from a five-day week to four and a half days. He refused this offer, arguing that he would suffer a loss of pay and benefits if he accepted, and resigned, claiming that he had been constructively dismissed. His claim was dismissed by an employment tribunal, and an appeal to the European Court of Human Rights was rejected. By offering to reduce his working hours to enable him to attend the local mosque in his own time the employers had not infringed his right to practise his religion. Similarly, in *Stedman v United Kingdom*[99] a woman's contract of employment required her to work on Sundays. She refused to do so, and was dismissed. She claimed that the dismissal was in breach of Art 9 of the Convention, but it was held that it was her refusal to comply with her contractual obligations, not her religious beliefs, which led to her dismissal. See also the religious discrimination cases of *Ewieda*, etc, in para 4.160.

[95] (Application 20605/92) (1997) 24 EHRR 523, [1997] IRLR 471, [1998] Crim LR 753, ECtHR.
[96] C 61496/08, Grand Chamber.   [97] [2004] EWCA Civ 662, [2004] ICR 1634, CA.
[98] (Application 8160/78) (1981) 4 EHRR 126, EComHR.   [99] (1997) 23 EHRR CD 168.

(e) *Article 10.* This Article provides that everyone has the right to freedom of expression, including the freedom to hold opinions and receive and impart information and ideas without interference by a public authority. Again, the exercise of such freedoms may be limited by such formalities, conditions, restrictions, or penalties as are prescribed by law, and are necessary in a democratic society, in the interests of national security, territorial integrity, or public safety, for the prevention of disorder or crime, for the protection of health or morals, for the protection of the reputation of others, for preventing the disclosure of information received in confidence, or for maintaining the authority and impartiality of the judiciary.

Thus freedom of speech is covered by the Convention, but hedged with a number of well-recognised limitations. In *Ahmed v United Kingdom*,[100] the Local Government Officers (Political Restrictions) Regulations 1990 restricted the political activities of certain categories of local government officials. The applicant, who was a solicitor employed by one local authority, wished to stand as a candidate in the local elections in another area, but was obliged to withdraw his candidature. He claimed that his rights to freedom of expression had been infringed, but the European Court of Human Rights dismissed his claim. The restrictions imposed were 'prescribed by law', and they pursued a legitimate aim of aiming to ensure effective political democracy at the local level. The Court also applied the doctrine of 'margin of appreciation', ie leaving it to the contracting state to assess whether pressing social needs existed. In this case, the regulations had been passed following a thorough enquiry, and were a valid response by the legislature.

It could be argued that a requirement to follow a particular dress code potentially violates the right to freedom of expression, although a rule which applies to both men and women—and is designed to enforce a common standard of conventionality—is not discriminatory on grounds of sex (*Smith v Safeways plc*[101]) and such rules are unlikely to come within the scope of the Convention. In *Kara v United Kingdom*[102] the Commission of Human Rights dismissed a claim by a male cross-dresser who wore female clothing at work, holding that a requirement to wear appropriate clothing was in accordance with the law and appropriate.

(f) *Article 11.* This states that everyone has the right to freedom of assembly and to freedom of association with others, including the right to form and join trade unions (see *Wilson v United Kingdom*,[103] para 21.49) for the protection of their interests. Again, there are the usual qualifications to this right, and, in addition, the Convention permits the imposition of lawful restrictions on the exercise of these rights by members of the armed forces, the police, and the administration of the state.

Freedom of assembly and freedom of association also implies a freedom not to assemble or associate. In *Young, James and Webster v United Kingdom*[104] it was held that a requirement to join a trade union which did not exist when workers were first employed (with the threat of a dismissal if there was a failure to do so) amounted to an interference with freedom guaranteed under Art 11. It was wrong to compel someone to join an association contrary to their convictions. Also, the prohibition of the right of a trade union to exclude a person from membership because he held political views which were inimical to the trade union, contained in s 174(1) of TULR(C)A, was held by the ECJ in *ASLEF v UK*[105] to violate Art 11 (see para 21.17).

---

[100] [1998] ECHR 78. [101] [1996] ICR 868, [1996] IRLR 456, CA.
[102] Unreported (Application 36528/97), ECtHR.
[103] (Applications 30668/96, 30679/96 and 30678/96) [2002] IRLR 568, [2002] All ER (D) 35 (Jul), ECtHR.
[104] (Applications 7601/76 and 7806/77) 4 EHRR 38, [1981] IRLR 408, ECtHR.
[105] (Application 11002/05) [2007] IRLR 361, (2007) 45 EHRR 34, ECtHR.

Article 11 contains no express right to strike (*Ministry of Justice v Prison Officers Association*[106]), but in *Demir v Turkey*[107] the European Court of Human Rights ruled that the right to strike is a human right recognised and protected in international law, and may only be limited in strictly defined circumstances. In this case, the Turkish Government issued a general ban on strike action by civil servants when a Turkish trade union organised a national action day for the recognition of the right to collective bargaining in the public sector. It was held that there was breach of Art 11 of the Convention on Human Rights, because the action taken was in violation of the rights of employees to form trade unions and bargain collectively.

It has been held that the provisions of the Trade Union and Labour Relations (Consolidation) Act 1992, with its stringent provisions and limitations on strike and other industrial action offend against the Convention, because balloting, industrial action notices, etc are prescribed by law, and it could be argued that these rules are necessary in a democratic society (*Metrobus v UNITE*[108]). It has also been suggested that the restriction on the number of pickets contained in the Code of Practice on Picketing (see para 1.66) is capable of being challenged, on the ground that there is no such restriction on any other form of public demonstration. However, Codes of Practice are not law, and a violation does not automatically lead to a breach of the law.

(g) *Article 14.* This states that the enjoyment of the rights and freedoms in the Convention shall be secured without discrimination on any ground such as sex, race, colour, language, religion, political or other opinion, national or social origin, association with a national minority, property, birth or other status. It is effectively therefore a catch-all in protecting the other rights in the Convention. It was considered in the case of *Gilham v Ministry of Justice*,[109] where the question was whether a judge could be a worker and so able to claim whistleblowing protection under the Employment Rights Act. The Supreme Court found that article 14 was engaged as she had been prevented from using her article 10 rights, and so interpreted the relevant sections of the ERA to read that she was a worker under the second limb of ERA 230 (see 2.70).

Summary

- Employment law comes from statutes and common law.
- Some employment law comes from the EU. This will remain unless the UK specifically legislates otherwise.
- The Human Rights Act 1998 enshrines the European Convention of Human Rights, which derives from the Council of Europe. The UK/EU relationship therefore has no effect on the HRA.
- Most employment law cases are heard in the Employment Tribunal, with appeals to the EAT.
- Some cases are heard in the County Court and High Court, with appeals to the Court of Appeal and Supreme Court.
- There are a number of institutions to assist in conciliation and the enforcement of the law.
- ACAS provides advice, conciliation and arbitration, among other things.

[106] [2008] ICR 702.   [107] [2009] IRLR 766, (2009) 48 EHRR 54.
[108] [2009] EWCA Civ 829, [2010] ICR 173, [2009] IRLR 851.   [109] [2019] UKSC 44.

2

The Nature of a Contract
of Employment

Background

2.1 The complex form of modern industrial and commercial organisation enables people to work under a variety of legal arrangements which may be entirely satisfactory to all concerned, but which are difficult to rationalise into well-defined categories necessary for the purpose of legal analysis. Legal rights and responsibilities are frequently at the mercy of verbal distinctions, for modern terminology does not assist in the process of drawing precise lines between different economic relationships. The nineteenth-century concept of 'master and servant', though somewhat servile by today's standards, at least had the merit of elegant simplicity.

2.2 It is the task of the employment tribunal to establish the true relationship between the parties. If there is a contractual document, the answer will normally be found therein. However, if it is asserted that the document does not represent or describe the true relationship, the tribunal is entitled to consider not only the words of the written contract at its inception and, where appropriate, the subsequent conduct of the parties, but also whether the true relationship is in fact something different. If the document can be shown to be a sham it can be wholly disregarded. If the evidence establishes that the true relationship was, and intended to be, something different from what is described in the document, then it is the true relationship, with its essential terms of mutuality of obligation and the obligation of personal service, which defines the contract (*Protectacoat Firthglow Ltd v Szilagyi;*[1] *Autoclenz v Belcher*[2]). It has to be asked what was the true agreement between the parties in all the circumstances of the case (of which the written agreement is only a part), and to examine all the relevant evidence, including how the parties conducted themselves in practice. The relative bargaining power of the parties must also be taken into account in deciding whether the terms of any written agreement in truth represent what was agreed—*Autoclenz v Belcher*.[3] This was followed by the Employment Appeal Tribunal (EAT) in *Uber v Aslam* (para 2.65), which pointed out that the contract had been drafted by 'armies of lawyers' and did not reflect the reality of the situation.

2.3 It is undoubtedly true that the courts have generally taken policy considerations into account when trying to devise 'tests' for determining into which category a particular person will fall. The fact that there is an inadequate statutory definition, coupled with inconsistent legal decisions based on different criteria which are adopted in order to achieve a particular end result, means that there is confusion and uncertainty in what is, after all, a fundamental feature of employment law. The modern trend is to widen the scope of the law by extending legal rights to 'workers', but the 'economic man' refuses to be placed in neat legal pigeonholes.

---

[1] [2009] EWCA Civ 98, [2009] ICR 835, [2009] IRLR 365.   [2] [2011] UKSC 41.   [3] *Ibid.*

2.4 This issue of employment status has come to the fore in recent years because of the rise of new business models and the so-called 'gig economy', where a person is paid for each 'gig' that they do, such as a delivery or car journey. Organisations say this helps flexibility but means individuals do not get the rights that 'workers' are entitled to, and it has led to a number of cases where they have been found to be workers (paras 2.20 and 2.29). This was the subject of the Taylor Review of Employment Practices in the Modern Economy and led to the governmental Good Work Plan 2018. The government has stated that it intends to align the current framework or employment and taxation, and provide greater clarity. It is not yet known what form this will take (although there is legislation expected which will extend the operation of the off-payroll working rules (IR35) to private companies). There are also plans to allow workers to request a more stable contract after 26 weeks, but again it is not known when these will happen.

Parties to a Contract of Employment

A. **Employers**

2.5 In this book we will deal mainly with the legal relationship which exists between the employer and his employees, and, to a limited extent, between the employer and his workers (see para 2.20 for the definition of 'worker'). These terms are bland enough to state, but give rise to considerable problems in practice. The employer is usually a readily identifiable entity, and may be defined as any person, partnership, corporate body, or unincorporated association who (or which) employs one or more persons under a contract of employment, although this definition is not particularly helpful. In the building industry, for example, an 'employer' is the term used for someone who 'engages' a main contractor, whereas he ought properly to be described as 'the client' (eg, see Construction (Design and Management) Regulations 2007). Frequently, the 'acts' of the employer are in reality done by various levels of management, who are themselves employees, yet it is 'the employer' who will be called to account (eg *Courtaulds Northern Textiles v Andrew*[4]). If the employer is an unincorporated association, a person employed by it will be employed by the members of the management committee for the time being (*Affleck v Newcastle Mind*[5]). A co-operative, on the other hand, might be an association of self-employed persons (*Addison v London Philharmonic Orchestra Ltd*[6]).

Associated Employer

2.6 Certain legal consequences may flow from the fact that an employer is part of a group of employers, provided the respective employers are 'associated employers' in the legal sense. ERA, s 231 states that two employers shall be treated as being associated if:

(a) one is a company, of which the other (directly or indirectly) has control, or

(b) both are companies of which a third person (directly or indirectly) has control (*Spanlite Structures Ltd v Jarrett*[7]).

2.7 Companies in this connection means limited companies, not other forms of statutory bodies corporate (*Hasley v Fair Employment Agency*[8]). But the definition covers companies which are incorporated under foreign law (*Hancill v Marcon Engineering Ltd*[9]) and partnerships of companies (*Pinkney v Sandpiper Drilling Ltd*[10]). The hardship which would

---

[4] [1979] IRLR 84, EAT.   [5] [1999] ICR 852, [1999] IRLR 405, EAT.   [6] [1981] ICR 261.
[7] [1973] ICR 465, [1973] IRLR 280, NIRC.   [8] [1989] IRLR 106, NICA.
[9] [1990] ICR 103, [1990] IRLR 51, EAT.   [10] [1989] ICR 389, [1989] IRLR 425, EAT.

otherwise be caused to employees in the public sector who are not employed by companies as defined has been somewhat mitigated by special legislation covering local government employees (Redundancy Payments (Local Government) (Modification) Order 1983), and continuity has been preserved for teachers in schools run by local government authorities and health service employees (ERA, s 218(7)–(10) (see para 13.40)).

2.8 'Control' is a legal, not factual, concept, and is determined by the number of votes attached to shares which can exercise control of a company in general meeting (*Secretary of State for Employment v Newbold*[11]). De facto control, ie, how the company is run in practice, is not sufficient (*Washington Arts Association Ltd v Forster*[12]). A negative control, ie a 50% shareholding, is not sufficient (*Hair Colour Consultants v Mena*[13]). It has been suggested that control by a person may be exercised by a group of persons, provided that in fact they act as one (*Zarb and Samuels v British and Brazilian Produce Co (Sales) Ltd*[14]), but this point has been seriously doubted (*South West Launderettes Ltd v Laidler*[15]), and there are a number of conflicting decisions on this point (compare *Russell v Elmdon Freight Terminal Ltd*[16] with *Tice v Cartwright*[17]).

2.9 There are a number of legislative provisions where the fact that two employers are associated employers in the legal sense is important (see, in particular, para 13.40):

(a) An employee who is taken into the employment of another employer, who, at the time of the change, is an associated employer, will find that his period of employment is continuous, and the change does not break continuity (ERA, s 218(6)). If there is a gap between the two employments, continuity may be preserved by the provision of ERA, s 212 (*Bentley Engineering Ltd v Crown and Miller*,[18] see para 13.20).

(b) The definition of redundancy contained in ERA, s 139(1) (see para 18.12) is extended so that the business of associated employers shall be treated as one business.

(c) An offer of re-engagement in redundancy situations, made under ERA, s 138 or 141, can be made by an employer or an associated employer (ERA, s 146).

(d) Independent advice given by a lawyer on a compromise agreement must not be given by a lawyer who is employed by or acting for the employer or an associated employer (ERA, s 203(3B)).

(e) The reference in TULR(C)A, s 182(1) to the disclosure of information for collective bargaining purposes (see para 23.15) exempts information communicated in confidence by an associated employer.

(f) An equal pay claim may be made if a comparator is employed by an associated employer (Equal Pay Act 1970, s 1(6), see *Scullard v Knowles*, para 5.6).[19]

(g) An employee may be able to count employment with an associated employer for the purpose of obtaining the higher rate national minimum wage (National Minimum Wage Regulations, reg 13(2)).

2.10 But if the statute does not refer to an associated employer, then clearly no duty is imposed. Thus, there is a requirement for an employer to consult on redundancies if 20 or more employees are to be made redundant at the same establishment; several associated employers can therefore each make 19 employees redundant without involving the duty to consult (*E Green & Son (Castings) Ltd v Association of Scientific, Technical and Management Staffs*[20]).

---

[11] [1981] IRLR 305, EAT.　　[12] [1983] ICR 346, EAT.　　[13] [1984] ICR 671, [1984] IRLR 386, EAT
[14] [1978] IRLR 78, EAT.　　[15] [1986] IRLR 68, EAT; on appeal [1986] ICR 455, [1986] IRLR 305, CA
[16] [1989] ICR 629, EAT.　　[17] [1999] ICR 769, EAT.　　[18] [1976] ICR 225, [1976] IRLR 146, D(
[19] [1996] ICR 399, [1996] IRLR 344, EAT.　　[20] [1984] ICR 352, [1984] IRLR 135, EAT.

Employees of associated employers cannot be aggregated to pass the threshold of 20 employees in order to create a bargaining unit for the purpose of statutory recognition procedures (*GPMU v Derry Print Ltd*[21]).

B. **Directors**

2.11 A person who is a director of a limited company is not an employee of that company by virtue of his directorship, but he will be an employee if he has a service contract with the company, which can be express or implied. Every company must keep a copy of every written service agreement, or a written memorandum of a service agreement which is not in writing (Companies Act 2006, s 228). As a director, he can be voted out of office at any time by a simple majority of shareholders' votes at a general meeting of the company, but as an employee he will have all the protections afforded either by his service agreement or the rules of modern employment law. However, a company may not give a director security of employment for more than two years, unless the arrangement has been approved by a resolution of the company in general meeting (Companies Act 2006, s 188).

2.12 A service contract between a company and a director can be either express or implied. In the absence of a written agreement or memorandum, it must be ascertained if the person concerned worked as a director and only occasionally worked in the capacity of an employee, or if he kept regular working hours, or worked full-time and spent only short or insignificant periods on his duties as a director (*Folami v Nigerline (UK) Ltd*[22]). Thus, if remuneration is by way of directors' fees rather than by a salary, if tax and national insurance contributions are not paid on the remuneration, and if there is an absence of a service agreement as required by s 228 of the Companies Act, it is unlikely that a director will be regarded as an employee of the company (*Parsons v Albert J Parsons & Sons Ltd*[23]). However, in *Stack v Ajar-Tec Ltd*,[24] a director who was an investor and shareholder was removed from his position. In order to bring a claim of unfair dismissal he would have to show he was an employee, and to bring a claim for unlawful deductions from wages he would have to show he was a worker. He had no written contract and had never been remunerated. He was found to be both a worker and an employee. The Court of Appeal also found that a contract can be formed partly expressly and partly by implication. It is also possible for the law to change a person's legal status in accordance with the circumstances. In *Road Transport Industry Training Board v Readers Garage Ltd*,[25] the question was whether an industrial training levy could be assessed on the earnings of a controlling director who also worked as an employee, and the court held that if there was a contract of service implied between him and the company, the employment tribunal must assess how much of his drawings from the company were in respect of that service, and assess the levy on that amount. Any sum he received in his capacity as a director would not be assessed for levy purposes.

2.13 In the past the courts had difficulty in deciding whether a controlling director of a company could also be regarded as an employee of the company. The 1961 decision of the Privy Council in *Lee v Lee's Air Farming Ltd*[26] was authority for the proposition that a limited company is a separate legal entity, distinct from the persons who control it, and thus, in theory, there is no reason why a sole shareholder could not be regarded as an employee of the company. But this theory sat uncomfortably with modern employment law concepts of unfair dismissal and other employment rights, and the issue was complicated by a number of factors, including whether tax and national insurance was paid, the hours worked,

---

[21] [2002] IRLR 380.   [22] [1978] ICR 277, EAT.   [23] [1979] ICR 271, [1979] IRLR 117, CA.
[24] [2015] EWCA Civ 46.   [25] (1969) 6 KIR 137, 113 Sol Jo 125, DC.   [26] [1961] AC 12.

whether holidays were taken, whether a written contract was in existence, whether guarantees/personal loans were given, and so on. Thus, if a person was a sole shareholder of a company, how could he dismiss himself? In particular, in recent years the courts had been faced with a number of conflicting decisions dealing with claims made by company directors for redundancy payments following the liquidation of their company.

2.14 Clarification on this issue was given by the Court of Appeal in *Secretary of State for the Department of Business Enterprise and Regulatory Reform v Neufeld*.[27] Here, the claimant owned 90% of the shares in a company, and was also the managing director. When the company went into liquidation, he sought a redundancy payment from the Secretary of State under s 188 of ERA (see para 18.67). He argued that he was also an employee of the company, having worked as part of the sales team. The employment judge found against him, partly because the claimant had given personal guarantees in respect of the company's liabilities, had lent money to it, and had not taken his full holiday entitlement. The decision was reversed by the EAT, and the Court of Appeal dismissed an appeal by the Secretary of State. The court held that there is no reason why someone who is a shareholder and director of a company cannot also be an employee of the company. Similarly, there is no reason in principle why someone whose shareholding gives him total control of the company cannot be an employee. To determine what is ultimately a question of fact, the employment tribunal must start by asking two questions, namely (a) whether the putative contract is in fact a sham, and (b) assuming it is genuine, whether it amounts to a contract of employment or is a contract for services.

2.15 It is likely that the putative contract will be a sham if it is a formal written contract of employment, or a board minute or memorandum purporting to create a contract of employment (presumably because it is unlikely that the director/majority shareholder will sign a contract with himself). Thus the enquiry will investigate the circumstances in which the document was created. The same principle will apply if the alleged contract is an oral one (see *Snook v London and West Riding Investments*[28]).

2.16 If the contract is not a sham, then a number of considerations must be taken into account. Thus, the fact that the claimant is a majority shareholder, or indeed the sole shareholder is not normally relevant to the enquiry whether or not the claimed contract amounts to a contract of employment. Nor is the fact that he will have share capital invested in the company, or that he made loans to it, or personally guaranteed its obligations. The Court of Appeal broadly accepted the guidance set out in *Clark v Clark Construction Initiatives Ltd*[29] by Elias J. If the contract does not appear to be a sham, the burden of seeking to deny its effect lies upon the party making that assertion (in most cases this will be the Secretary of State). Thus, if the individual pays tax and insurance as an employee, works the hours, and takes the stipulated holidays, it is likely that a genuine employment relationship exists.

C. **Business Consultants**

2.17 A person who works in a consultancy or advisory capacity is capable of being an employee, depending on the legal and factual arrangements which are made. In *Bromsgrove Casting and Machining Ltd v Martin*,[30] the applicant was a managing director of a company. He ceased to hold office, but continued to work as a director and consultant. There was no provision as to the number of hours to be worked, and his salary was unchanged. He

---

[27] [2009] EWCA Civ 280, [2009] 3 All ER 790, [2009] ICR 1183, [2009] IRLR 475.
[28] [1967] 2 QB 786, [1967] 1 All ER 518.   [29] [2008] EWCA Civ 1446, [2009] ICR 718.
[30] [1977] 3 All ER 487, [1977] ICR 417, EAT.

was then dismissed, and he brought a complaint of unfair dismissal. It was held that in his capacity as a consultant, he was retained, not employed. His employment only came into being when he was actually called upon to give advice. Therefore, the employment tribunal should have enquired into the number of hours he was normally required to give advice, to see whether or not his contract was for the requisite number of hours per week in order to qualify for protection from unfair dismissal (NB: this is no longer a prerequisite for such a claim, as there is no longer an hour's threshold for claiming unfair dismissal).

D. **Partners**

2.18 'A partnership is the relation which subsists between persons carrying on a business in common with a view of profit' (Partnership Act 1890, s 1). There is no reference to the sharing of that profit. Thus a person may be a partner even though he does not share in the profit of the firm (*M Young Legal Associates Ltd v Zahid Solicitors*[31]). Even if he does share in some profit, there is no minimum threshold that has to be reached in relation to his rights either to profits or to his involvement in management before he can be regarded as a partner rather than an employee (*Tiffin v Lester Aldridge LLP*[32]).

A salaried partner may be (or may not, depending on the facts of the case) a partner, although it has been suggested that the term should be avoided because it creates confusion (*Stekel v Ellice*[33]). A partner in a limited partnership is not an employee (*Kovats v TFO Management LLP*[34]) but a salaried partner can be an employee (Limited Liability Partnerships Act 2000, s 4(4)), and an equity partner can be a worker (*Winkelhof*, para 2.20).

Architects and dentists frequently engage 'associates', and may make contractual arrangements which suit all concerned, but in law such persons, however designated, are probably employees. However, the contract of engagement may specify to the contrary. A junior partner, however, is a partner with (usually) a lesser share of the profits/smaller say in the conduct of the partnership business. The modern vogue for co-partnership and profit-sharing schemes may well throw up further problems in the future, for although the mere fact of sharing profits is not evidence that a partnership exists (Partnership Act 1890, s 3), it could, together with other relevant circumstances, lead to that conclusion (see *Glasgow v Independent Printing Co*[35]).

2.19 If an employee is employed by a partnership, which ceases to trade, he may be able to recover a redundancy payment from the National Insurance Fund if he can show that he has taken all reasonable steps to recover the payment (ERA, s 166). But in order to obtain arrears of pay, notice money, holiday pay, and compensation for unfair dismissal under s 182 of ERA, he would have to show that the employer is insolvent, which means that each and every one of the partners must be adjudged bankrupt. As long as there is a partner who is solvent, it is from such a person that the employee must first seek payment (*Secretary of State for Trade and Industry v Forde*[36]).

E. **Workers**

2.20 Consider the term 'worker'. This can mean 'anyone who works for a living', and would thus include all from a managing director of a large public company to a machine operator in an engineering factory; a bookmaker's clerk on a race track to a surgeon in a hospital; or even a partner in an LLP(*Clyde & Co LLP v Winkelhof*[37]). Nowadays it is surely a mistake

---

[31] [2006] EWCA Civ 613.   [32] [2012] EWCA Civ 35.   [33] [1973] 1 WLR 191, [1973] 1 All ER 465.
[34] [2009] ICR 1140.   [35] [1901] 2 IR 278, 34 ILTR 66.   [36] [1997] ICR 231, [1997] IRLR 387, EAT.
[37] [2014] UKSC 32.

to use the term with a socio-economic undertone. On the other hand, the term 'workman' has, in the past, been given a more precise legal meaning, though it appears to be falling into legislative disuse as legal rights are given a wider scope.

2.21 Whatever the currently acceptable meanings of these terms may be, it is clear that the law can place within its ambit anyone it wishes. Thus there are two main definitions of the term 'worker' currently in use, with some minor variations in particular circumstances.

2.22 Section 296 of TULR(C)A provides that a worker is an individual who works or seeks to work:

(a) under a contract of employment, or

(b) under any other contract whereby he undertakes to do or perform personally any work or services for another party to the contract who is not a professional client of his, or

(c) in employment under or for the purposes of a government department (otherwise than as a member of the armed forces) in so far as such employment does not come within (a) or (b) above.

2.23 At the same time, ss 224(6) and 235 of the Act define a contract of employment, for the purpose of the secondary action provisions (see para 23.74) and the balloting provisions (see para 23.47), as including a contract under which one person personally does work or performs services for another.

2.24 Section 230 of ERA defines the term worker in similar, but not identical terms, ie an individual who has entered into or works under (or worked under):

(a) a contract of employment, or

(b) any other contract whereby the individual undertakes to do or perform personally any work or services for another party to the contract whose status is not by virtue of the contract that of client or customer of any profession or business undertaking carried on by the individual.

(The reason the definition does not deal with Crown employment is because there are other specific provisions which take effect, ie ss 191–192.)

But when the terms 'shop worker' or 'betting worker' are used in this Act (see Chapter 8), they refer to employees, not workers!

2.25 The Trade Union and Labour Relations (Consolidation) Act deals with the rights of workers and employees. Part II of the Employment Rights Act, which deals with deductions from wages etc (see Chapter 8), applies to workers, as do the protected disclosure provisions contained in Pt IVA of the Act (see Chapter 10), albeit with a somewhat extended definition of the term (see s 43K). The National Minimum Wage Act 1998, the Working Time Regulations 1998, and the Part-time Workers (Prevention of Less Favourable Treatment) Regulations 2000 all apply to workers. The result is that when the term 'worker' is used, certain employment rights are extended to cover a wider group of persons, in line with the trend in modern employment law.

2.26 A 'worker', for some purposes, may have rights which are identical to those enjoyed by an employee, even though he is clearly not an employee and is self-employed. Thus in *Flynn v Torith Ltd*,[38] the applicant worked as a self-employed joiner on a building site. He claimed he was entitled to holiday pay under the Working Time Regulations. The EAT

---

[38] [2003] All ER (D) 45 (Jan).

noted that the regulations applied to 'a worker', which is defined as being an individual who works under 'any other contract, whereby the individual undertakes to do or perform personally any work or services for another party to the contract'. The phrase 'any other contract' in reg 2(1) in those regulations was wide ranging, and included persons who worked under a contract to provide services or perform work for another, other than under a contract of employment. The only exception to reg 2(1) is an individual carrying on a profession or business undertaking of which the other party was a client. Thus the claimant was entitled to holiday pay.

2.27 The Equality Act 2010 applies to anyone who is employed under a contract of service or of apprenticeship, or a contract personally to execute any work or labour. Thus the Act applies to employees and self-employed persons.

2.28 Various groups of workers are excluded from some (but not all) legal rights for reasons of policy, eg mariners and share fishermen, and there are a few groups who are outside the protection of employment law altogether, eg office holders (see para 2.65). For clergymen, see para 2.69. A number of cases with implications for the 'gig' economy have highlighted the definition of 'worker' (see para 2.65).

F. Employees

2.29 The term 'employee' is defined in ERA, s 230 as an individual who enters into or works under (or, where the employment has ceased, worked under) a contract of employment, which is a contract of service or apprenticeship, whether express or implied, and (if it is express) whether oral or in writing. The definition in TULR(C)A, s 295 is similar. Since the term 'employee' is narrower than the term 'worker' it follows that most of the rights contained in ERA are limited to employees, apart from certain specific provisions, eg, ss 13–27 (see para 8.5) and ss 43A–43K (see para 10.75). Thus all employees are workers, but not all workers are employees (*Broadbent v Crisp*[39]).

2.30 An employee, though easy to define, is not so easy to describe, for the relationship between A (the employer) and B (the employee) is complicated by the fact that there is also a relationship between B and the state. It is possible that a person can be an employee for one purpose, but not an employee for another. Thus in *Challinor v Taylor*,[40] a taxi driver was the night driver of a cab which was used during the day by the owner. The latter paid for the fuel, insurance, and maintenance of the car, and took 65% of the gross takings. He also paid the cost of the employer's contribution towards the driver's national insurance. The driver, however, was assessed for income tax purposes as a self-employed person under Schedule D. The owner sold the taxi and the driver was thus redundant. It was held that he was not an employee, and therefore not entitled to a redundancy payment.

2.31 There is no reason in principle why an employee cannot have more than two employers, and, provided he is within the appropriate protection of the law, pursue his legal remedies against either of them (*Prison Officers Association v Gough*[41]). Indeed, it is possible for an employee to have two contracts of employment with the same employer, so that if he is dismissed from his employment under one contract, he may pursue his remedy whilst still leaving the other contract subsisting (*Throsby v Imperial College of Science and Technology*[42]).

---

[39] [1974] 1 All ER 1052, [1974] ICR 248, NIRC.   [40] [1972] ICR 129, NIRC.   [41] EAT/0405/09.
[42] [1978] QB 438, [1978] 2 All ER 465, [1978] ICR 357, EAT; aff'd sub nom *Dixon v BBC* [1979] QB 546, [1979] 2 All ER 112, [1979] ICR 281, [1979] IRLR 114, CA.

G. **Employee Shareholders**

2.32 The Growth and Infrastructure Act, s 31 introduced the new status of employee shareholder in September 2013, by inserting a new s 205A of the ERA 1996. There has to be an agreement between the employee and the employer (who has to be a company) that the former will become an employee shareholder, and the employee will issue shares worth at least £2,000 to the employee. (The first £2,000 of shares will be free of tax and national insurance.) The company has to give the individual a written statement setting out his status as an employee shareholder, and the rights which attach to the shares. The rights relating to his status are set out in sub-s (5).

2.33 If an employee enters into this agreement, he will lose various employment rights. Section 205A(2) provides that an employee shareholder will not have:

(a) the right to make an application under s 63D (request to undertake study or training),

(b) the right to make an application under s 80F (request for flexible working),

(c) the right under s 94 not to be unfairly dismissed (except note that this does not apply in a s 108 Health and Safety case, as set out in sub-s (10), a dismissal which is automatically unfair, or one which would be a contravention of the Equality Act), or

(d) the right under s 135 to a redundancy payment.

2.34 An employee shareholder also has to give longer notice (16 weeks) to notify the employer of the intention to return to work during a maternity/paternity/adoption leave period.

2.35 Before such an agreement can be valid, the employee shareholder has to have received advice from an independent adviser, and the employer has to pay the reasonable costs of that advice (sub-ss (6) and (7)). The employee also has seven days in which to change his mind (sub-s (6)).

2.36 An employee will be protected from being subjected to a detriment for refusing to accept an employee-shareholder contract.

Employee, Worker, or Self-employed?

A. **Contract of Service**

2.37 The basic division for our purposes is between those who are employed persons and those who are self-employed, and the distinction between these categories is that the employed person works under a contract *of* service, whereas the self-employed person works under a contract *for* services, although in recent years cases on the distinction between workers and the self-employed have also come to the fore (para 2.65). It is easy to state this distinction, but in practice it has proved difficult to draw it, and over the years the courts have developed a number of tests designed to produce a given result. Fundamentally, for the relationship of employer/employee to exist, there must be a contract of employment, either express or implied. It follows that if there is no contract of any sort between the parties, there cannot be a contract of employment, and the fact that a worker is taxed as an employee under IR35 or pays Class 1 national insurance contributions is irrelevant (*O'Murphy v Hewlett Packard Ltd*[43]).

---

[43] [2002] IRLR 4, [2001] All ER (D) 91 (Sep), EAT.

Control test

2.38 An important criterion for determining whether or not the relationship of employer/ employee exists is the extent to which a person is under the direction and control of the other party with regard to the manner in which the work is done (*Narich Pty Ltd v Payroll Tax Comr*[44]). Indeed, in the nineteenth century, control was regarded as the sole determining factor. Thus if the employer could tell the employee not only what to do, but how to do it, then a contract of service existed (*Yewens v Noakes*[45]). In modern conditions the application of such a test is clearly unreal. An employee may be highly skilled and qualified, and employed specifically because he has professional training and competence, so that the employer is frequently unable (as well as being unwilling) to instruct the employee as to how the work is to be done. Despite this difficulty, some modern decisions have added to the control test a refinement which looks for *the right to control* as being the determinant factor (*Gibb v United Steel Companies Ltd*[46]) or even the existence of the right to control, even though this is seldom if ever exercised in practice. It is clear that the greater the degree of control which is exercisable by the employer, the more likely it will be that the contract is one of service (*Whittaker v Minister of Pensions and National Insurance*),[47] but 'the greater the skill required for an employee's work the less significant is control in determining whether the employee is under a contract of service' (*Beloff v Pressdram*[48]). Ultimately, though, it is the contractual right to control which is important, not necessarily day-to-day control. In *Troutbeck SA v White & Anor*,[49] a couple were employed to look after a farm, and were left to decide for themselves how to go about running the farm. While there was a low level of control, it was not completely absent, and so there was an employment relationship.

2.39 But the exercise of a degree of control is not conclusive. In *Hitchcock v Post Office*,[50] the applicant ran a sub-post office as part of a shop he owned. Although the Post Office exercised control over many of its activities, it was held that this was because of the need to ensure financial control and security, rather than being a control over managerial functions. Consequently, the sub-postmaster was not an employee of the Post Office.

Organisational *Test*

2.40 In *Stevenson, Jordan and Harrison Ltd v MacDonald and Evans*,[51] Denning LJ suggested a more up-to-date test. 'Under a contract of service', he said, 'a man is employed as part of the business and his work is done as an integral part of the business'. This 'organisational' test has certain advantages, particularly in relation to skilled employees who are 'integrated' into an enterprise, eg doctors, nurses, etc, in respect of whom the control test is inappropriate. In *Whittaker v Minister of Pensions and National Insurance* a trapeze artiste broke her wrist as a result of a fall in her act. It was held that she was an integral part of the circus business and thus an employee for the purpose of claiming industrial injuries benefit.

Mutuality of Obligations

2.41 Mutuality of obligations and the elements of control are usually seen as essential prerequisites for a contract of employment to exist, whether the claimant is a worker or an employee (*Montgomery v Johnson Underwood Ltd*[52]). There must also be an irreducible level of personal service (*MacFarlane v Glasgow City Council*[53]). The question to be decided

---

[44] [1984] ICR 286, PC.   [45] (1880) 6 QBD 530, CA.   [46] [1957] 2 All ER 110.
[47] [1967] 1 QB 156, [1966] 3 All ER 631.   [48] [1973] 1 All ER 241.
[49] [2013] EWCA Civ 1171, [2013] IRLR 286.   [50] [1980] ICR 100, EAT.
[51] (1952) 69 RPC 10, [1952] 1 TLR 101, CA.
[52] [2001] EWCA Civ 318, [2001] ICR 819, [2001] IRLR 269.   [53] [2001] IRLR 7.

is whether the claimant is a worker, or an employee, or a self-employed businessman. To answer this, there must be a finding on (a) whether there is one contract or a succession of short-term contracts, (b) if there is one contract did the employer undertake to provide a minimum amount of work, (c) was there such control as to turn the arrangement into a contract of employment, and (d) was the claimant obliged to do a minimum amount of work (*Cotswold Developments Construction Ltd v Williams*[54])?

2.42 There must be an obligation on the part of the employer to provide work, and an equal obligation upon the worker to do the work when offered. If these features are not present, it is likely that no contract of employment exists. Thus in *Bebbington v Palmer (t/a Sturry News)*[55] a 14-year-old schoolboy was engaged to work on a paper round. When he did not turn up for work, other arrangements were made. There was no written contract, he was only paid on the days he worked, and he received no sick pay or holiday pay. Following an argument with his mother about the time when he was required to work, the employer stopped his paper round. His claim for unfair dismissal was dismissed. The EAT held that there was a lack of mutuality of obligations which were the irreducible minimum of the existence of a contract of employment.

2.43 Thus if the employer can decline to offer work, or the worker can refuse to do the work when offered, it is likely that no contract of employment exists. However, mutuality can be inferred from how the contract operated in practice over a period of time. In *Prater v Cornwall County Council*[56] the claimant was employed as a home tutor to teach children who were unable to attend school. The council was under no obligation to offer to send pupils to the claimant, and equally she was under no obligation to accept pupils sent to her. In practice, she never refused offers over a period of ten years, during which time she had a succession of individual teaching contracts. It was held that mutuality of obligations existed, and although there were gaps between the individual contracts, she could rely on the provisions of s 212 of ERA (see Chapter 13), and her claim based on continuity of employment succeeded.

2.44 Mutuality of obligations also requires the essential element of personal service. Thus if a worker is permitted to provide a substitute to do the work, no contract of employment can exist. In *Ready Mixed Concrete (South East) Ltd v Ministry of Pensions and National Insurance*,[57] a firm dismissed all its drivers, sold all the lorries to them, and re-employed them under a contract which contained obligations capable of leading to the conclusion that they were either employees or self-employed workers. Thus, the drivers had to wear the company's uniform, place the lorries at the disposal of the firm for a certain number of hours, only use them for the company's business, obey the orders of the foreman, and sell the lorries back to the company at an agreed valuation. On the other hand, the drivers had to maintain the lorries at their own expense and pay all the running costs. A driver could own more than one lorry, and could engage a substitute driver. They paid their own national insurance contributions, had no set hours or meal breaks, and made their own decisions on how to drive the lorries and which routes to take. McKenna J held that there were three conditions necessary to establish whether a contract of employment existed. The first was that the employee agreed to provide his own labour and skill in the performance of a service for the employer, the second was that there must be some element of control exercisable by the employer, and the third was that the other terms of the contract must not be inconsistent with the existence of a contract of employment. The fact that the

---

[54] [2006] IRLR 181.   [55] EAT/0371/09.
[56] [2006] EWCA Civ 102, [2006] 2 All ER 1013, [2006] ICR 731, [2006] IRLR 362.
[57] [1968] 1 All ER 433, (1968) 2 QB 497.

drivers could (and did) employ a substitute was clearly a crucial factor in determining that they were self-employed haulage contractors.

2.45 But the fact that a contract permits a person to have the limited ability to delegate performance to another person is not conclusive. In *MacFarlane v Glasgow City Council*[58] the claimant was a part-time lecturer. If he was unable to take a class he could arrange for someone else to do it for him, but that person had to be selected from a register held by the local authority, and sometimes it was the local authority which organised the replacement. It was held that the claimant was an employee. There is a distinction between obtaining a substitute because one is unable to do the work and a general power to delegate performance at will (*Staffordshire Sentinel Newspapers Ltd v Potter*[59]). If the right to substitute is fettered, there may well be an employment contract (*Weight Watchers (UK) Ltd & Ors v HMRC*[60]—although this was not an employment law case).

2.46 The element of control is also a factor in determining whether mutuality of obligations exist. Thus if a claimant is genuinely running his own business, then again he cannot be an employee. In *Bacica v Muir*[61] the claimant had his own business accounts, was in receipt of an allowance for business overheads, and worked for others whenever he wished. On the facts, he was clearly a self-employed person.

2.47 The fact that there is no entitlement to sick pay is merely one of the indications that there is a lack of mutuality of obligations (*Clark v Oxfordshire Health Authority*[62]), and a similar conclusion was reached in a case concerning the payment of income tax and national insurance contributions. In *Parade Park Hotel v Commrs of HM Revenue & Customs*[63] a worker carried out maintenance at a hotel. The hotel did not have to offer him work, and he was under no obligation to accept work. He provided his own tools and equipment, and paid his own national insurance stamps and income tax. It was held that he was self-employed.

2.48 If the contract is so drafted as to exclude a finding of employment relationship, it will normally be upheld. In *Cochrane v A D Bly Construction Ltd*[64] the claimant was given a written contract which contained a clause stating that the employer was not obliged to offer work, the claimant was not obliged to accept an offer of work. It was further stated that the parties did not wish to create or imply any mutuality of obligations whatsoever. It was held that the claimant was neither a worker nor an employee for the purpose of the Working Time Regulations. But in a similar situation that arose in *ABC News International v Gizbert*,[65] it was held that there was an implied obligation on the claimant to decide in good faith whether or not to accept or reject assignments, and mutuality could be implied into the arrangements.

2.49 If a clause in a contract is so unrealistic when compared with what happens in practice, the employment tribunals will ignore it altogether. Thus, the fact that the contract states that there is no obligation on the worker to do the work personally, or that he can provide a substitute, or can refuse to accept the work offered, or is described as a self-employed sub-contractor, etc, these clauses will be disregarded if they do not reflect the reality of the relationship between the parties (*Consistent Group Ltd v Kalwak*,[66] see para 2.157).

Entrepreneurial Test

2.50 Sometimes the entrepreneurial test seems to be the dominating feature. The problem is looked at from a self-employed person's point of view, and the question asked, 'Is he in business on his own?' Again, no exhaustive list of considerations can be formulated.

---

[58] [2001] IRLR 7.   [59] [2004] IRLR 752.   [60] (2011) FTC/57–59/2010 [2011] BTC 1895.
[61] [2006] IRLR 35.   [62] [1998] IRLR 125.   [63] [2007] STC (SCD) 430, [2007] STI 1183.
[64] EAT/0243/05.   [65] EAT/0160/06.   [66] [2007] IRLR 560, EAT.

Does he provide his own equipment? Does he hire his own helpers? Is there any degree of financial responsibility for investment or degree of risk? Does he undertake any other sort of commission, business, or employment? Is there any opportunity to profit from sound management? These questions were raised in *Market Investigations Ltd v Minister of Social Security*,[67] where a company employed women on a part-time basis to do market research. They could work as they chose, but according to a set pattern. It was held that the women were employees, and not employed in business 'on their own'. The more unskilled and untrained a person is, the less likely it will be that the employment tribunal will hold that he is running his own business. In *Airfix Footwear Ltd v Cope*,[68] the applicant was a home-worker making heels for shoes manufactured by the respondent company. She was provided with the necessary equipment and material, and worked in accordance with instructions given to her. The EAT upheld a finding that she was an employee. On the other hand, in *Argent v Minister of Social Security*,[69] an actor taught drama on a part-time basis at a school. It was held that he was a self-employed lecturer.

2.51 In *Withers v Flackwell Health Football Supporters' Club*,[70] the EAT stated that difficult cases could be resolved by using industrial, rather than legal, terminology. Hence, the person could be asked a simple question: 'Are you your own boss?'

2.52 This pragmatic approach was taken even further in *Davis v New England College of Arundel*,[71] where the claimant was engaged as a lecturer on a yearly renewable contract. He specifically asked to be treated as being self-employed as he wished to retain that status for income tax and national insurance purposes. He was not re-engaged, and claimed that he had been unfairly dismissed. It was held that to determine whether or not he was an employee, the matter had to be looked at objectively. His request to be treated as being self-employed, and the fact that the college so regarded him, did not alter the nature of the contractual relationship between him and his employer. In reality, he was an employee of the college, and hence he was entitled to bring a claim. It is the essence of the arrangement, rather than the form, which is the determinant factor (*Tyne and Clyde Warehouses Ltd v Hamerton*[72]).

2.53 The difficulties inherent in such cases can be seen in *Massey v Crown Life Insurance Co*,[73] where the claimant was an employee of the respondents. It was then agreed that he should be treated as being self-employed, and a new agreement to this effect was signed. Although his actual duties were identical, the claimant was taxed under Schedule D, and paid self-employed insurance. He was then dismissed, and claimed unfair dismissal. It was held that he was working under a contract for services. While the parties cannot alter the nature of their relationship by putting a different label on it, where the situation was in doubt, or was ambiguous, an agreement which stipulated the nature of the relationship affords strong evidence of what it is. In this case, there was a genuine attempt to change the legal situation to that of an independent contractor. There was no attempt to deceive the Revenue. It was a genuine agreement to enable the applicant to be treated as being self-employed. Consequently, he could not claim that his dismissal was unfair.

Multifactorial Approach

2.54 The rule that no single factor can, by itself, be conclusive is illustrated by the decision of the EAT in *City and East London FHS Authority v Durcan*.[74] The claimant ran his own dental practice on a self-employed basis. Once each week, he worked on a rota at a

---

[67] [1969] 2 QB 173, [1968] 3 All ER 732, EAT. [68] [1978] ICR 1210, [1978] IRLR 396, EAT.
[69] [1968] 3 All ER 208. [70] [1981] IRLR 307, EAT. [71] [1977] ICR 6, EAT.
[72] [1978] ICR 661, EAT. [73] [1978] 2 All ER 576, [1978] ICR 590, [1978] IRLR 31, CA.
[74] EAT 721/96.

local hospital, providing emergency services. He was paid a fixed fee, made his own arrangements for tax and national insurance, and, if he was unable to attend, had to make arrangements for a replacement. When the hospital trust sought to reduce the number of hours worked, he claimed that he had been constructively and unfairly dismissed. The respondents resisted the claim, arguing that he was self-employed. The EAT noted that the claimant used the hospital's premises, equipment, and medicines, but, on the other hand, he was not subject to any form of control as to how the work was to be done. The fact that he had to provide a replacement if he was unable to attend was not fatal to the existence of an employment contract, because the replacement had to be on an approved list, and this was not inconsistent with the modern trend towards job-sharing. It was true that the claimant did not enjoy the usual benefits of employment status, including sick pay, holiday pay, and notice rights, nor did he have the right to pursue any grievance procedure or take advantage of any disciplinary procedure. He had to treat any patient who attended for treatment, but his remuneration was not dependent on the number of patients who attended, and thus there was no risk of profit or loss from his working activities. The label attached to the relationship was not determinative of the worker's legal status, although it could tip the balance if all the relevant factors were evenly balanced. Mutuality of obligation is an important factor, but again not conclusive. Nor was it relevant that he worked only for a limited number of hours each week, because since the removal of the eight hour per week qualification, employment tribunals will increasingly be called upon to determine the legal status of workers who only work for a few hours each week. Taking into account all the considerations, the EAT refused to disturb the decision of the employment tribunal that the claimant was an employee, and was therefore entitled to pursue his claim.

2.55 Following *Quashie v Stringfellows Restaurant Ltd*,[75] in *Secretary of State for Justice v Windle and Arada*,[76] freelance interpreters who accepted work on a case-by-case basis were found not to be employees for the purposes of the Equality Act 2010. There was no obligation on the claimants to accept any assignment, and so there was no mutuality of obligation. The court said that the fact that a person supplying services is only doing so on an assignment-by-assignment basis may tend to indicate a degree of independence, or lack of subordination, in the relationship while at work which is incompatible with employee status even in the extended sense.

2.56 Whether someone is a worker rather than self-employed is also an issue because workers are entitled to certain statutory rights (para 2.66), and can be seen in the 'gig economy' cases. Uber drivers were found to be workers rather than self-employed (as described in their contracts) in *Uber BV v Aslam and others*.[77] This is one of a pattern of cases, such as *Dewhurst v CitySprint UK Ltd*,[78] in which a cycle courier was found to be a worker, and *Pimlico Plumbers & Mullins v Smith*,[79] where the Court of Appeal ruled that a plumber described as self-employed was in fact a worker. These cases obviously are decided on their own facts, but all have in common a certain level of control, and the fact that the claimants were described by the employer as self-employed but depended on personal service, as described in s 230(b). It does, however, depends on the facts of each case—for example, in *IWGB Union & Roofoods Limited t/a Deliveroo*,[80] a claim for union recognition, the CAC found that Deliveroo drivers were self-employed, particularly as there was an unpoliced right of substitution (and the High Court rejected an application for judicial review[81]). There has however been a reference to the CJEU by an Employment Tribunal as to whether Yodel couriers were workers. The reference includes the question of whether the right to

[75] [2012] EWCA Civ 1735.   [76] [2016] EWCA Civ 459.   [77] [2018] EWCA Civ 2748.
[78] ET/2202512/2016.   [79] [2017] EWCA Civ 51.   [80] TUR1/985(2016).
[81] [2018] EWHC 3342 (Admin).

use a substitute means they cannot be found to be a worker. (Note that foster parents, however, are not workers (*Sindicatul Familia Constanța and Others*[82]).)

2.57 An employment tribunal should therefore take the following factors into account, and make its determination accordingly:

(a) the contractual provisions (*BSM (1257) Ltd v Secretary of State for Social Services*);[83] and whether or not those provisions do represent the true relationship between the parties (see *Secretary of State for the Department of Business Enterprise and Regulatory Reform v Neufeld*,[84] para 2.14);

(b) the degree of control exercised by the employer (*Global Plant Ltd v Secretary of State for Health and Social Security*);[85]

(c) the obligation on the employer to provide work (*Nethermere (St Neots) Ltd v Gardiner*);[86]

(d) the obligation on the employee to do the work (*Ahmet v Trusthouse Forte Catering Ltd*);[87]

(e) the duty of personal service (*Ready Mixed Concrete Ltd (South East) v Minister of Pensions and National Insurance*);[88]

(f) the provision of tools, equipment, instruments, etc (*Willy Scheidegger Swiss Typewriting School (London) Ltd v Minister of Social Security*);[89]

(g) the arrangements made for tax, national insurance, VAT, statutory sick pay (*Davis v New England College of Arundel*);[90]

(h) the opportunity to work for other employers (*WHPT Housing Association Ltd v Secretary of State for Social Services*);[91]

(i) other contractual provisions, including holiday pay, sick pay, notice, fees, expenses, etc (*Tyne and Clyde Warehouses Ltd v Hamerton*);[92]

(j) the degree of financial risk and the responsibility for investment and management (*Market Investigations Ltd v Minister of Social Security*);[93]

(k) whether the relationship of being self-employed is a genuine one, or whether there is an attempt to avoid modern protective legislation (*Young & Woods Ltd v West*);[94]

(l) the number of assignments, the duration of the engagement, and the risk of running bad debts (*Hall v Lorimer*);[95]

(m) the presence or absence of mutuality of the obligation to provide or do the work (*Carmichael v National Power plc*[96]).

2.58 No single factor, by itself, is conclusive, and all the relevant circumstances must be considered. As long as the employment tribunals take these into account, their decision is a question of fact, not law, and their findings (either way) cannot normally be challenged (*O'Kelly v Trusthouse Forte plc*,[97] and see *Hall v Lorimer*) unless they took a view on the facts which would not reasonably be sustained (*Lee Ting Sang v Chung Chi-Keung*[98]). However, if

---

[82] [2018] EUECJ C-147/17.   [83] [1978] ICR 894.
[84] [2009] EWCA Civ 280, [2009] 3 All ER 790, [2009] ICR 1183, [2009] IRLR 475.
[85] [1972] 1 QB 139, [1971] 3 All ER 385.
[86] [1984] ICR 612, sub nom *Nethermere (St Neots) Ltd v Taverna and Gardiner* [1984] IRLR 240, CA.
[87] Unreported.   [88] n 55.   [89] (1968) 5 KIR 65.   [90] n 69.   [91] [1981] ICR 737.
[92] n 70.   [93] n 65.   [94] [1980] IRLR 201, CA.
[95] [1992] ICR 739; aff'd [1994] 1 All ER 250, [1994] ICR 218, [1994] IRLR 171, CA.
[96] [1998] ICR 1167, [1998] IRLR 301, CA; revsd [1999] 4 All ER 897, [1999] ICR 1226, [2000] IRLR 43, HL.
[97] [1984] QB 90, [1983] 3 All ER 456, [1983] ICR 728, [1983] IRLR 369, CA.
[98] [1990] 2 AC 374, [1990] ICR 409, [1990] IRLR 236.

there is a written contract which determines the relationship between the parties, the interpretation of that contract is a question of law, which can be considered on appeal (*Davies v Presbyterian Church of Wales*[99]).

B. Why the Distinction is Important

2.59 Before a clear and satisfactory answer can be given to the question 'who is an employee?' or 'who is a worker?' we may well need to pose a second one, namely, 'for what purpose is the question being asked?' A part-time lecturer may well be a self-employed person for income tax purposes but an employee in relation to national insurance contributions, and he may well be an employed person (using the 'organisational test') if the issue is raised as to the vicarious liability of his employer for wrongful acts committed by him during the course of his work. The pragmatic approach adopted by the courts is to say that the matter is a question of fact, to be determined by the evidence in each case. For example, in *Maurice Graham Ltd v Brunswick*,[100] a company engaged self-employed bricklayers, who paid their own income tax and were responsible for their own national insurance contributions. The company was convicted of breaches of the Construction (Health and Welfare) Regulations 1966, and argued on appeal that those regulations only applied to 'employees', not independent contractors. It was held that though the outward arrangement gave the appearance of a worker being an independent contractor, this was not conclusive. The company controlled and supervised the men and supplied them with the necessary equipment and materials, and the court refused to disturb the convictions.

2.60 There are a number of reasons for stressing the importance of this distinction between a contract of service and a contract for services, although recent decisions are tending to minimise this importance.

Tax Reasons

2.61 Under the Social Security Contributions and Benefits Act 1992 an employer must pay secondary Class 1 contributions in respect of employed earners (the primary contribution being made on an earnings-related basis by the employed earner—which term includes an office holder). Self-employed earners pay a flat-rate Class 2 contribution, and in addition a Class 4 contribution based on the gains or profits derived which are chargeable to income tax (see *Lane v Shire Roofing Co Ltd*[101]). They must also complete their own self-assessment tax form. The employer does not need to deduct PAYE income tax in respect of his self-employed independent contractors, and he need not pay a levy for industrial training purposes. An independent sub-contractor may have to charge VAT on services supplied, which would not be so if he were an employee. But it must be stressed that it is the substance of the relationship which will count, not the form. Thus if a person is an employee in the legal sense, the employer's obligations will arise despite any artificial attempt or arrangements made to avoid such duties (*Pennington v Minister of Social Security*[102]). Nor does the fact that a person pays his own national insurance and is responsible for his own income tax payments necessarily mean that he is a self-employed person. In *Jennings v Westwood Engineering Ltd*[103] the applicant was offered employment. He was told that he could work at a lower rate of remuneration on PAYE, or at a higher rate paying his own tax and insurance, and he chose the latter option. It was held that he was employed under a contract of employment nonetheless. Conversely, in *President of the Methodist Conference v Parfitt*[104]

---

[99] [1986] 1 All ER 705, [1986] ICR 280, [1986] IRLR 194, HL.
[100] (1974) 16 KIR 158, 118 Sol Jo 294, DC.   [101] [1995] IRLR 493, CA.   [102] Unreported.
[103] [1975] IRLR 245.   [104] [1984] ICR 176.

the fact that the applicant paid Class 1 national insurance and was taxed under Schedule E did not in itself make him an employee.

Liability Issues

2.62 An employer will not normally be vicariously liable for the tortious acts (civil wrongs) committed by independent contractors (though there are certain exceptions to this rule), whereas he would be so liable for torts committed by his employees in the course of their employment which cause injury or damage to third parties (see Chapter 10). Two contrasting cases will illustrate this point. In *Hillyer v St Bartholomew's Hospital*,[105] the plaintiff selected a consultant who negligently performed an operation. It was held that the hospital was not liable, because the consultant was an independent contractor who was merely using the facilities of the hospital. On the other hand, in *Cassidy v Ministry of Health*,[106] a resident surgeon operated negligently on the plaintiff, and it was held that the hospital board, as the employer, was liable.

Health and Safety Issues

2.63 An employer owes a duty at common law to his employees to take reasonable care for their safety, whereas these duties do not normally apply with respect to his independent contractors, although again there are exceptions. Thus in *McArdle v Andmac Roofing Co*,[107] the claimant worked for one of several sub-contractors who were employed on converting a building at a holiday camp, who were all under the direction of Pontins (Contractors) Ltd. The latter had made no arrangements for safety precautions with the sub-contractors, and as a result the claimant suffered severe injuries when he fell off a roof. It was held that the main contractors (Pontins) assumed the responsibility of co-ordinating the work, and were therefore under a duty to ensure that reasonable safety precautions were taken for all those who were working on the job, even though they were not the employers of those who were working. The duties owed by the employer to his employees under the Health and Safety at Work etc Act 1974 and regulations made under the Act are more extensive than those owed to independent contractors (see Chapter 11). In practice this may mean that a self-employed person who is injured whilst at work may be unable to claim any compensation from the employer, and additionally will be unable to claim industrial injuries benefit and/or sick pay.

Statutory Rights

2.64 Many statutory rights apply only to employees, not to workers. For example, an employee is entitled to all the rights contained in the Employment Rights Act, including a written statement of terms of employment, itemised pay statement, maternity, paternity, parental and adoption rights, guarantee pay, medical suspension pay, time off work, unfair dismissal, redundancy rights, etc. Despite the appellation, shop workers and betting workers are employees. The Flexible Working Regulations, Fixed-term Employees Regulations, Transfer of Undertaking Regulations, etc apply to employees, as does the Health and Safety at Work Act and many regulations issued thereunder. A court may be able to make an attachment of earnings order whereby an employer is obliged to make certain deductions from the earnings of an employee, which would not be possible if the person concerned was a (self-employed) worker. On the other hand, the protection of wages and the public interest disclosure provisions of ERA apply to workers (which includes employees), as do the Part-time Workers Regulations, Working Time Regulations, the various pieces of discrimination legislation, the National Minimum Wage Act and parts of the Trade Union and Labour Relations (Consolidation) Act.

---

[105] [1909] 2 KB 820, CA. [106] [1951] 2 KB 343, [1951] 1 All ER 574, CA.
[107] [1967] 1 All ER 583, CA.

2.65 The difference between workers and the self-employed can also be an issue. This is important because workers have some statutory rights that the self-employed do not, such as national minimum wage, holiday pay, working time, etc (although these rights are fewer than those of employees). This is aptly illustrated by several gig economy cases (para 2.65).

Other Categories of Parties to a Contract of Employment

A. Office Holders

2.66 A special category of persons exists who are technically known as office holders. They are not employed by virtue of a contract of employment, and therefore have certain privileges attached to their position. A judge, for example, holds office during good behaviour and may only be dismissed on a resolution passed by both Houses of Parliament. A magistrate is also an office holder (*Knight v A-G*[108]). However, some office holders may also have a contract of employment, eg a stipendiary reader in the Church of England (*Barthorpe v Exeter Diocesan Board of Finance Ltd*[109]). In *102 Social Club and Institute v Bickerton*,[110] a club secretary was paid an honorarium of £225 per year. The EAT held that the employment tribunal should consider whether the money was paid by way of a salary for services rendered, or whether it was an honorarium for work done as a member of the club in his capacity as an office holder. In the former case only would he be regarded as being an employee. An elected officer of a trade union is not an employee (*Unite the Union v Nailard*[111]).

2.67 In *Lincolnshire County Council v Hopper*,[112] the council appointed the claimant as a registrar. The council also paid her remuneration, determined her hours of work, and made provision for her pension. However, the Registration Services Act 1953 stated that a registrar holds office during the pleasure of the Registrar General. It was held that the claimant was an office holder, not an employee. The council did not have the power to dismiss the claimant, which is an essential element of an employment relationship.

2.68 Regular earnings received by an office holder are more akin to remuneration for work done than by way of honorarium for tenure of office. Thus his claim for the money is closely analogous to a claim for a salary due under a contract of employment. It follows that the office holder must be willing and able to render the services required of him, and that if he refuses to perform his duties (as a form of industrial action) his paymaster is entitled to withhold the relevant part of his remuneration (*Miles v Wakefield Metropolitan District Council*[113]).

2.69 In *Johnson v Ryan*,[114] the EAT held that there were three categories of office holders, namely:

  (a) an office holder whose rights and duties are defined by the office they hold, and not by any contract (such as a police officer);

  (b) persons who have the title of office holder, but who are in reality employees with a contract of service; and

  (c) workers who are both office holders and employees, such as company directors.

2.70 Indeed, there is a fourth category of office holder, namely a worker who is not necessarily an employee. In *Perceval-Price v Department of Economic Development*,[115]

---

[108] [1979] ICR 194, EAT.   [109] [1979] ICR 900, EAT.   [110] [1977] ICR 911, EAT.
[111] UKEAT/0300/15.   [112] [2002] All ER (D) 401 (May), EAT.
[113] [1984] ICR 332; on appeal [1985] 1 All ER 905, [1985] ICR 363, [1985] IRLR 108, CA; revsd [1987] AC 539, [1987] 1 All ER 1089, [1987] ICR 368, [1987] IRLR 193, HL.   [114] [2000] ICR 236, EAT.
[115] [2000] IRLR 380, NICA.

the Northern Ireland Court of Appeal held that full-time holders of judicial posts in tribunals were 'workers' for the purpose of Art 141 of the Treaty of Rome, and hence provisions in domestic law which provided that statutory officers were not to be regarded as employed under a contract of service had to be disapplied. Part-time judges (known as daily fee-paid judges) are also regarded as workers (*O'Brien v Ministry of Justice*[116]) and as such are entitled to pro-rata pensions given to full-time judges under regulation 17 of the Part-time Workers (Prevention of Less Favourable Treatment) Regulations 2000. So far as EU law is concerned, the criterion was the existence of an employment relationship, regardless of the legal nature of that relationship and its purpose. In *Gilham v Ministry of Justice*[117] it was found that s230(3) ERA 1996 (which was domestic law rather than derived from the EU, as in *O'Brien*) can also be interpreted so as to find that a judge can be a worker with domestic law rights (also see 1.107). As in *Preston v President of the Methodist Conference* (para 2.70) therefore, office-holder status and employment/worker status are not mutually exclusive.

There is little doubt that the categories of people who nowadays could properly be described as 'office holders' is declining, because formerly the offices in question were attached to incorporeal hereditaments, and many such titles are nowadays largely obsolete. In *R v BBC, ex p Lavelle*,[118] Woolf J commented: 'The distinctions which previously existed between pure cases of master and servant and cases where a person holds an office are no longer clear.'

A useful summary of the legal position of office holders can be found in *Percy v Church of Scotland Board of National Mission* (para 2.71).

B. Ministers of Religion

2.71 It had long been thought that ministers of religion had few (if any) employment rights, as they were not employed under a contract of employment, having regard to the spiritual nature of their work (*President of the Methodist Conference v Parfitt*[119]), or were office holders (*Diocese of Southwark v Coker*).[120] This type of simplistic reasoning was rejected by the House of Lords in *Percy v Church of Scotland Board of National Mission*,[121] where the claimant was appointed as an ordained minister. It was alleged that she had an affair with a married elder of the parish. She was suspended from her duties pending preparation for a disciplinary hearing, and eventually resigned. She brought proceedings in an employment tribunal alleging unfair dismissal sex discrimination, arguing that in similar circumstances the church would not have taken such action against a male minister. Her claim was dismissed by an employment tribunal, on the ground that, having regard to the essentially religious nature of her duties, she was not employed under a contract of employment as defined in the Employment Rights Act and the Sex Discrimination Act. The decision was upheld by the EAT and Court of Session, but the House of Lords found in her favour on the sex discrimination point.

It was held that there was an offer and acceptance of a church post for a specific period, with detailed provision for the claimant's duties, remuneration, travel expenses, holidays, and accommodation. As such, there was clearly an intention to create legal relations. Further, the claimant was employed under a contract 'personally to execute any work or labour' as defined in s 82(1) of the Sex Discrimination Act, and hence her claim for sex discrimination could proceed.

It is important to note that although the claimant originally claimed unfair dismissal, this matter was not pursued on appeal to the House of Lords, and the decision only applies to those legislative provisions which define 'employment' in a manner similar to the then Sex Discrimination Act, s 82(1).

---

[116] [2013] UKSC 6.   [117] [2019] UKSC 44.   [118] [1983] 1 All ER 241, [1983] ICR 99, [1982] IRLR 404.
[119] n 94.   [120] [1996] ICR 896, EAT; aff'd [1998] ICR 140, CA.   [121] [2006] IRLR 195, HL.

There is no presumption that a minister and a church do not intend to enter into legal relations, and an individual can be an employee as well as an office holder. The test of whether or not a minister of religion is an employee must be resolved by ascertaining whether the normal tests for employment are satisfied in relation to that particular church and that particular minister. The decision was upheld by the Court of Appeal, who made it clear, however, that the case is not authority for a general finding that ministers of religion are employees. In *President of the Methodist Conference v Preston*[122] the Supreme Court emphasised that one had to look at the manner in which a minister is engaged, and the rules governing his service. These both depend on the intentions of the parties, and the factual background, which includes the fundamentally spiritual purpose of a minister of religion. The question is whether the parties intended these benefits and burdens of the ministry to be the subject of a legally binding agreement between them. The correct approach is to examine the rules and practices of the particular church, and any special arrangements made with the particular minister. Therefore in *Sharpe v The Bishop of Worcester*[123] a rector, who was the holder of a statutory office, was found to be neither an employee who could claim unfair dismissal, nor a worker who could bring a whistleblowing detriment claim, as there was no contract.

Tribunals will therefore need to analyse the facts carefully, and the answer will probably vary from church to church and religion to religion before reaching a conclusion. The existence of a religious dogma that was opposed to the existence of a contract of employment would be an important factor. An employment tribunal is entitled to have regard to the historic background and ethos of the religion concerned, in particular its independence from the state, and the fact that employment status would be inconsistent with the beliefs of the religion in question (*MacDonald v Free Presbyterian Church of Scotland*[124]).

Further, to impose a contract of employment on a religion that was doctrinally opposed to it would be a breach of Art 9 of the European Convention on Human Rights (freedom of religion).

2.72 Church of England clergy now enjoy a parallel regime of employment-type rights, which cover such matters as stipend, accommodation, education, training, time off, capability, and grievance procedures, etc. They also have the right to claim unfair dismissal before an employment tribunal (Ecclesiastical Offices (Terms of Service) Regulations 2009). However, existing case law will continue to apply to ministers of other religions.

C. **Crown Employees**

2.73 The precise legal nature of the relationship between the Crown and civil servants has long been a moot point, but it now appears that since such arrangements have an intention to create legal relations, a contract of employment exists, enforceable by private law remedies (*R v Lord Chancellor's Department, ex p Nangle*[125]). The provisions of the Equality Act 2010 do apply to the Crown. Most of the provisions of the Employment Rights Act 1996 apply to Crown employees, except those relating to rights to minimum periods of notice, redundancy payments, Sunday working for shop and betting office workers, and rights on insolvency. There are restrictions on the disclosure of information based on grounds of national security, but a minister can no longer exclude the rights of certain employments on that ground (Employment Relations Act 1999, Sch 8). The provisions of TULR(C)A similarly apply, except the power of the court to make an order against an employer in respect of a failure to ensure that a check-off arrangement excludes a payment to the political fund of a

---

[122] [2013] UKSC 29.   [123] [2015] EWCA Civ 399.   [124] [2010] CSOH 55, 2010 GWD 16–303.
[125] [1992] 1 All ER 897, [1991] ICR 743, [1991] IRLR 343.

trade union (s 87), failure to comply with a declaration of the Central Arbitration Committee requiring an employer to disclose information for collective bargaining purposes (s 184), and the procedure for consulting with trade unions on redundancies (ss 188–194).

2.74 Members of the staff of the House of Commons have been accorded the same statutory protection in most fields as that enjoyed by Crown employees by virtue of ERA, s 195, with the House of Commons Commission (or the Speaker) being the employer. Staff employed by the House of Lords also have a similar full range of protections, except in relation to time off work for public duties connected with political activities and other minor exceptions (see ERA, s 194 and TULR(C)A, s 277).

2.75 However, where a person holds any office or employment under the Crown which does not constitute a contract of employment, those terms shall be deemed to be such a contract for the purpose of the law relating to the liability in tort of any person who commits an act which induces another to break a contract, or interferes with the performance of any contract (or induces the interference), or consists of a threat that a contract will be broken or its performance interfered with. In other words, Crown servants will be deemed to have contracts of employment for the purpose of tort liability arising out of industrial action, unless the protections of TULR(C)A, s 219 apply.

D. **Armed Forces**

2.76 Various provisions in the Employment Rights Act apply to members of the naval, military, or air forces of the Crown. These include written particulars, antenatal care, suspension on medical and maternity grounds, rights to maternity leave of absence, written reasons for dismissal, and unfair dismissal. The Equality Act 2010 also applies, but nothing is to be rendered unlawful if it was done for the purpose of ensuring combat effectiveness. Although there is a general rule that a member of the Armed Forces should go through service redress procedures before complaining to an employment tribunal, this is no longer always the case (see Race Relations (Complaints to Employment Tribunals) (Armed Forces) Regulations 1997, Equal Pay (Complaints to Employment Tribunals) (Armed Forces) Regulations 1997, and Sex Discrimination (Complaints to Employment Tribunals) (Armed Forces) Regulations 1997).

E. **Health Service Employees**

2.77 Employees of the National Health Service or Health Trusts have the full range of employment protection rights (now including the right to redundancy payments, see National Health Service and Community Care Act 1990, s 60).

F. **Police**

2.78 A person is employed in the police service if he serves as a member of any constabulary maintained by virtue of an enactment, or in any capacity by virtue of which he has the powers or privileges of a constable. This includes special constables, but not police cadets (*Wiltshire Police Authority v Wynn*[126]), nor prison officers, who are now 'workers' for the purpose of ERA and TULR(C)A (see Criminal Justice and Public Order Act 1994, s 126(1)). Otherwise, policemen, even though they may be engaged under a contract of employment in the police service, have few employment law rights. Thus, they are not entitled

---

[126] [1981] QB 95, [1980] ICR 649, CA.

to an itemised pay statement, guarantee pay, rights under the Working Time Regulations, protection for employee representatives, rights in protected disclosure cases, leave for domestic reasons, time off work for public duties, time off work as an employee representative, suspension from work on medical or maternity grounds, right to return to work after childbirth, written reasons for dismissal, and unfair dismissal (except in health and safety cases), even in respect of conduct which occurs when they are not exercising the privileges or powers of a constable (*Home Office v Robinson*[127]). Nor can they claim in respect of unlawful deductions from wages (*Metropolitan Police Comr v Lowrey-Nesbitt*[128]). A policeman does have the right to have written particulars of his terms and conditions of employment, minimum periods of notice, and redundancy pay.

2.79 A policeman is deemed to be employed by the chief constable or the police authority for the purpose of the Equality Act 2010 in respect of any act done by him, or the authority in relation to discrimination in employment, but not acts committed outside the course of employment (*Waters v Metropolitan Police Comr*[129]). The Police (Health and Safety) Act 1997 applies the provisions of the Health and Safety at Work etc Act 1974 (see Police (Health and Safety) Regulations 1999) to holders of the office of constable (ie police, including police cadets), even though they are not employed under a contract of employment. For this purpose, the Chief Officer shall be treated as a corporation sole or distinct juristica (Serious Organised Crime and Police Act 2005, s 158). The Police Federation is to be treated as a recognised trade union for the purpose of appointing and consultation with safety representatives.

2.80 A policeman cannot be dismissed without a proper hearing in accordance with the rules of natural justice (*Ridge v Baldwin*[130]) (see Police Act 1996, ss 84–85), and, in the event of wrongful dismissal, he has the right to be reinstated. Police cadets are persons training to become police officers, and are not employees (*Wiltshire Police Authority v Wynn*).

G. **Those Employees with Special Legal Status**

2.81 Over the years a number of different groups of employees had additionally acquired a special legal status which overrode the existence of their contracts of employment (see, eg, *McClelland v Northern Ireland General Health Services Board*[131]), but 'status' relating to a person's occupation is now in decline, and in this sense it may be truly said that in employment law, 'there is a movement from status to contract'. Thus registered dock workers no longer enjoy the special protection which they had under the dock labour scheme (see Dock Work Act 1989), and tenure for all university staff appointed or promoted after 20 November 1987 has been abolished (Education Reform Act 1988, s 203). In respect of university academic staff appointed prior to that date, regard must be had to the terms of their appointment. If these state that dismissal is only possible for 'good cause' then it is not possible to dismiss for any other reason, eg redundancy (*Pearce v University of Aston in Birmingham*[132]).

2.82 On the other hand, there are many groups of workers who have special protections and advantages by virtue of their situation, including pregnant women, trade unionists, safety representatives, etc, and in this respect, therefore, 'status' still retains a certain significance.

[127] [1982] ICR 31, [1981] IRLR 524, EAT.   [128] [1999] ICR 401, EAT.
[129] [1995] ICR 510, [1995] IRLR 531, EAT; aff'd [1997] ICR 1073, [1997] IRLR 589, CA; revsd [2004] 4 All ER 934, [2000] 1 WLR 1607, [2000] ICR 1064, HL.
[130] [1963] 1 QB 539, [1961] 2 All ER 523; aff'd [1963] 1 QB 539, [1962] 1 All ER 834, CA; revsd [1964] AC 40, [1963] 2 All ER 66, [1963] 2 WLR 935, HL.
[131] [1957] 2 All ER 129, HL.   [132] [1991] 2 All ER 461, CA.

H. **Temporary Employees**

2.83 A temporary employee has all the rights of any other employee as long as he has the appropriate length of service. An exception here is to be found in ERA, s 106, which states that if an employee is employed on a temporary basis in order to replace a woman who has been given maternity leave or adoption leave or to replace someone suspended on medical grounds, and the latter returns to work, the dismissal of the temporary employee will amount to some other substantial reason for the dismissal, but without prejudice to the rule that the employer must still show that he acted reasonably in dismissing the employee. It is essential that the employee has been informed in writing that the employment will be terminated when the absent employee returns to work. However, since it is unlikely that the temporary employee will have obtained the two-year qualifying period of employment, s 106 has little value.

2.84 If a temporary worker is taken on with the expectation that, assuming all goes well, s/he will be made a permanent employee, it is probable that a contract of employment will retrospectively be implied, so as to enable the employee to obtain continuity from the date when the engagement first began. This is so even though the original engagement was made on the clear understanding that no contract of employment came into existence (*Royal National Lifeboat Institution v Bushaway*[133]).

I. **Part-time Workers**

2.85 The Part-time Workers (Prevention of Less Favourable Treatment) Regulations 2000 (as amended) are designed to implement EC Directive 97/81/EEC, and to ensure that part-time workers are to be treated no less favourably, in relation to terms and conditions of employment, than a comparable full-time worker whether or not the latter is on a permanent or fixed-term contract. However, less favourable treatment will not be unlawful if it is objectively justified.

2.86 Before these regulations, any rights enjoyed by part-time workers were inextricably bound up with claims of sex discrimination, on the basis that since the majority of part-time workers were women, any less favourable treatment which occurred was because of their sex (eg *R v Secretary of State for Employment, ex p Equal Opportunities Commission*, see para 1.77). The Part-time Workers (Prevention of Less Favourable Treatment) Regulations 2000 undoubtedly go some way towards the elimination of such claims. But the regulations only apply to direct discrimination, which is capable of being justified, whereas the Equality Act 2010 applies to direct and indirect discrimination, and only the latter is capable of being justified. The part-time worker will always have to find a full-time comparator of either sex for the purpose of showing less favourable treatment, whereas under the Equality Act 2010 the search is for a person of the opposite sex.

2.87 The regulations apply to 'workers', not just employees. A worker is an individual who has entered into or works/worked under:

(a) a contract of employment;

(b) any other contract, whether express or implied, whereby the individual undertakes to do or perform personally any work or services for another party to the contract whose status is not by virtue of the contract that of a client or customer of any profession or business undertaking carried on by the individual.

---

[133] [2005] IRLR 674, EAT.

2.88 In other words, a worker is anyone who works for another person (not necessarily under a contract of employment) other than in a professional or business relationship. Only genuinely self-employed persons are excluded from the regulations.

2.89 A part-time worker is defined as one who is paid wholly or in part by reference to the time he works and, having regard to the custom and practice of the employer in relation to workers employed by the worker's employer under the same type of contract, is not identifiable as a full-time worker. Conversely, a full-time worker is a worker who is paid wholly or in part by reference to the time he works and, having regard to the custom and practice of the employer in relation to workers employed by the worker's employer under the same type of contract, is identifiable as a full-time worker.

2.90 In order to avoid being subjected to less favourable treatment, the part-time worker must be able to compare his treatment with that given to a full-time worker. This involves finding the comparator—not a hypothetical one (*Carl v University of Sheffield*[134]). A full-time worker will be comparable if:

(a) both workers are employed by the same employer under the same type of contract, and engaged in the same or broadly similar work, having regard, where relevant, to whether they have a similar level of qualifications, skills, and experience, and

(b) the full-time worker works or is based at the same establishment as the part-time worker or, where there is no full-time worker working or based at that establishment, works or is based at a different establishment and satisfies the above requirements. A part-time worker, whether permanent or on a fixed-term contract, can compare himself with a full-time permanent worker or worker on a fixed-term contract.

2.91 In *Matthews v Kent & Medway Towns Fire Authority*,[135] the House of Lords held that part-time firefighters could compare themselves with whole-time firefighters. The term 'the same type of contract' should not be read in an over precise way, thus allowing employers to take part-timers outside the scope of the regulations by setting different terms for them. The fact that not all part-time workers are treated adversely does not mean that a claim for discrimination cannot be made by those who are treated less favourably, if being part-time was the reason for their adverse treatment (*Sharma v Manchester City Council*[136]).

2.92 A full-time worker who becomes a part-time worker can compare his treatment with the way he was treated when he was full-time. A worker who has had a period of absence (which cannot exceed more than 12 months) and then returns to work at the same job or to a job at the same level but with fewer hours can compare his treatment with the way he was treated prior to his absence.

2.93 A part-time worker has the right not to be treated by his employer less favourably than a full-time worker is treated, as regards the terms of his contract, or be subjected to any detriment by any act, or deliberate failure to act, of his employer (reg 5). However, this right only applies if the treatment is on the ground that the worker is a part-time worker, and cannot be justified on objective grounds. A pro rata principle must be applied unless it is inappropriate to do so. Thus, where a comparable full-time worker is entitled to receive pay or any other benefit, a part-time worker is entitled to receive not less than the proportion of that pay or benefit that the number of his weekly working hours bears to the number of weekly working hours of the comparable full-time worker.

---

[134] [2009] ICR 1286, [2009] IRLR 616.
[135] [2004] ICR 257, [2003] IRLR 732, [2003] All ER (D) 90 (Aug), EAT.   [136] [2008] ICR 623.

2.94 If a part-time worker considers that he is receiving less favourable treatment than a full-time worker (bearing in mind the pro rata principle) he may request from his employer a written statement giving particulars of the reasons for the treatment. The employer shall provide the statement within 21 days, but if, in subsequent tribunal proceedings, the tribunal finds that the employer deliberately and without reasonable excuse omitted to provide the statement or finds that the written statement is evasive or equivocal, the tribunal may draw any inference which it considers to be just and equitable to draw, including an inference that the employer has infringed the right in question (reg 6).

2.95 An interesting point dealing with part-time workers arose in *McMenemy v Capita Services*,[137] where an employee claimed holiday pay in lieu of bank holidays that fell on a Monday, a day on which he did not work. It was held that he had not been discriminated against when compared with a full-time employee. He received no pay for bank holidays which fell on a Monday because he did not work on Mondays. A full-time worker who worked from (say) Tuesday to Saturday would have been treated in the same way.

2.96 It is thus clear that as a matter of principle, part-time workers must be paid the same rate of pay as comparable full-time workers. Contractual sick pay, maternity pay, access to pension schemes, access to training, holiday entitlement, etc must all be no less favourable, on a pro rata basis. Statutory rights, such as time off work (see Chapter 7), apply. Any different treatment, eg on redundancy selection or severance payments, must be capable of being justified (*Barry v Midland Bank plc*[138]). Thus to select an employee for redundancy because of his part-time status is to treat the employee less favourably, and is likely to be an unfair dismissal (*Hendrickson Europe Ltd v Pipe*[139]). But if a part-time worker works overtime, he will not be entitled to any overtime premium which a full-time worker receives until he works the normal standard working hours of the full-time worker. Also, since a part-time worker is not required to pay national insurance contributions if his or her wages are below the lower earning limit, this may result in the exclusion from the right to receive statutory maternity pay, statutory adoption pay, and statutory sick pay.

2.97 A worker has the right not to suffer a detriment because he brought proceedings under the regulations, or requested a written statement, or gave evidence or information in connection with such proceedings brought by any worker, or otherwise did anything under the regulations, or alleged that the employer had infringed the regulations, or refused to forgo a right conferred by the regulations, or because the employer believed that the worker has done or intends to do any of these things. It will also be an automatic unfair dismissal to dismiss an employee (but not a worker) on any of those grounds (reg 7).

2.98 A worker may lodge a complaint to an employment tribunal that his rights under the regulations have been violated (within the usual time limits: see Chapter 20). The burden will be on the employer to identify the grounds for any less favourable treatment or detriment. The tribunal can make the usual awards (declaration, compensation, and recommendation) but not compensation for injury to feelings. The claimant is under a duty to mitigate the loss, and the rules on contributory conduct apply.

2.99 The regulations provide that so far as the police are concerned, the holding of an office of constable or police cadet (otherwise than under a contract of employment) shall be treated as being employment under a contract of employment. The regulations also

---

[137] [2006] IRLR 761, EAT(SC); aff'd [2007] IRLR 400, IH (Ex Div).
[138] [1997] ICR 192, EAT; aff'd [1998] 1 All ER 805, [1999] ICR 319, [1998] IRLR 138, CA; aff'd [1999] 3 All ER 974, [1999] ICR 859, [1999] IRLR 581, HL. [139] [2003] All ER (D) 280 (Apr), EAT.

apply to Crown employment, members of the armed forces, staff of the House of Lords and House of Commons, but not, apparently, to an individual in his capacity as the holder of a judicial office if he is remunerated on a daily fee-paid basis (*Christie v Department for Constitutional Affairs*[140]).

2.100 A set of guidance notes has been issued to assist in compliance with the regulations. Basically, these suggest that, unless there is some objective justification, part-time workers should receive the same treatment as full-time comparable workers when considering hourly rates of pay, contractual sick pay and maternity pay (applied pro rata), access to pensions schemes, training, holiday entitlement, contractual maternity and parental leave, career breaks, selection for redundancy, etc. Less favourable treatment may be objectively justified if it is intended to achieve a legitimate objective, it is necessary to achieve that objective, and it is an appropriate way of doing so.

J. Probationary Employees

2.101 The essence of a probationary appointment is that the employer retains the right not to confirm the appointment after a specified period, particularly on the grounds of capability. The majority of the tribunal in *Donn v Greater London Council*[141] thought that the tests which are applied to a probationary employee are not necessarily the same as those which apply to a confirmed appointment, and a decision not to retain a probationer may be justified even though a similar decision made with respect to a fully established employee may not be. This view has been followed on a number of occasions (eg *Hamblin v London Borough of Ealing*[142]), for a probationary employee must know that he is on trial, and must therefore establish his suitability for the post. The employer, however, must give the employee a proper opportunity to prove himself, and give a warning if the required standards are not being met (*Post Office v Mughal*[143]). A probationary employee is still an employee, and is therefore entitled to have appropriate guidance and advice (*Inner London Education Authority v Lloyd*[144]).

2.102 Certainly, if the probationary period is less than two years, few problems will arise, but a longer probationary period could create difficulties. In *Weston v University College, Swansea*,[145] the applicant was appointed as a lecturer for the probationary period of three years. At the end of this time he was not placed on the permanent staff. It was held that he was entitled to pursue his complaint in respect of his alleged unfair dismissal, for his contract was not for a fixed term. The employer must still show that he acted reasonably in dismissing a probationer and that the reason was within the statutory requirements, and it is submitted that if a different test is to be applied, the employer must show a valid reason why a probationary period of such a length of time is required in order to establish the suitability of the employee for the post in question.

2.103 If an employee is told that his appointment is subject to a probationary period of a certain length of time, this does not give him a legal right to be employed for that length of time, and the employer may lawfully dismiss him before that period has expired (*Dalgleish v Kew House Farm Ltd*[146]) as long as he is given his correct contractual notice (*Fosca Services (UK) Ltd v Birkett*[147]).

---

[140] [2007] ICR 1553, EAT.   [141] IDS Brief 65.   [142] [1975] IRLR 354.
[143] [1977] ICR 763, [1977] IRLR 178, EAT.   [144] [1981] IRLR 394, CA.   [145] [1975] IRLR 102.
[146] [1982] IRLR 251, CA.   [147] [1996] IRLR 325, EAT.

K. **Trainees**

2.104 Section 230 of ERA defines a contract of employment as 'a contract of service or apprenticeship, whether express or implied, and (if it is express) whether it is oral or in writing'. It is clear, therefore, that a trainee can be employed under a contract of employment, and this includes, for example, a trainee employed by a solicitor (*Oliver v JP Malnick & Co*[148]). However, not all such trainees are so employed. In *Wiltshire Police Authority v Wynn* (see para 2.78), it was held that police cadets are not employees, but persons who are training to become policemen. During their training, even though they are being paid, they are not employed under a contract of employment. Similarly, in *Daley v Allied Suppliers Ltd*,[149] a young black girl was working on a Youth Opportunities scheme operated by the respondents. She alleged that she had been discriminated against on the ground of race, but it was held that the Race Relations Act was not applicable, as she was not a person employed within the meaning of s 4 and s 78 of the Act.

2.105 Indeed, the fact that young people on work experience courses are not employees has caused some concern, particularly in relation to their health and safety, for many of the duties owed by an employer are only owed to employees. Consequently the Health and Safety (Training for Employment) Regulations 1990 apply the provisions of the Health and Safety at Work etc Act 1974 to youth trainees as if they were employees.

2.106 A youth training scheme is a tripartite relationship between the individual, the employer, and the training provider. Generally, the employer agrees to employ the trainee for the term of the training, and although the training is provided by a third party, the employer has somewhat wider responsibilities to the trainee than to an ordinary employee. Such arrangements, generally referred to as 'Modern Apprenticeship Agreements', are capable of amounting to a traditional contract of apprenticeship, because they secure wages for the apprentice during the period of apprenticeship, they provide training to enable the apprentice to obtain skills and give status in the labour market on successful completion of the training (*Flett v Matheson*[150]).

L. **Apprentices**

2.107 A contract of apprenticeship is an agreement whereby the apprentice binds himself to his employer in order to learn a trade, and the employer on his part agrees to teach and instruct him. The contract must be in writing and signed by the parties, and cannot be terminated by the employer except for grave misconduct (such as theft) or a refusal to attend to his duties. However, it appears that there is no longer any need for a formal apprenticeship agreement to be entered into; to give a statement of terms and conditions which described a person as an 'apprentice sheet metal worker' was sufficient to create a contract of apprenticeship in *Wallace v C A Roofing Services Ltd*,[151] and it was not possible to terminate that contract on grounds of redundancy. An apprentice who is wrongfully dismissed may claim by way of damages not only his immediate loss, but a sum representing the value of his loss of future prospects as a qualified person (*Dunk v George Waller & Son Ltd*[152]). Also, since an employer is, in one sense, *in loco parentis* to an apprentice, a certain latitude must be shown in respect of minor lapses in conduct. For example, in *Shortland v Chantrill*,[153] an apprentice was criticised by a managing director about his work, and he retorted 'You couldn't have done any fucking better'. For this, he was dismissed. It was held that the

---

[148] [1983] 3 All ER 795, [1983] ICR 708, [1983] IRLR 456, 127 Sol Jo 646, EAT.
[149] [1983] ICR 90, [1983] IRLR 14, EAT.   [150] [2006] EWCA 53, [2005] ICR 1134, [2005] IRLR 412.
[151] [1996] IRLR 435.   [152] [1970] 2 QB 163, [1970] 2 All ER 630, CA.   [153] [1975] IRLR 208.

dismissal was unfair; one isolated step of impudence did not warrant the termination of an apprenticeship which had only ten months to run.

2.108 An apprentice is employed for the duration of the apprenticeship, and may not be dismissed until it expires (other than for good cause). An apprenticeship differs from a contract of employment in that it is not terminable on notice, and, if there are provisions in the agreement which are inconsistent with the employer's normal terms and conditions of employment, it is the apprenticeship agreement which must prevail. In particular, an employer cannot dismiss an apprentice for reason of redundancy (*Whitely v Marton Electrical Ltd*[154]).

2.109 The Apprenticeship, Skills, Children and Learning Act 2009 (which mainly applies to England and Wales) provides that a person completes an apprenticeship if the standard completion conditions are met, ie a recognised apprenticeship agreement in connection with an apprenticeship framework. The certifying authority will issue apprenticeship certificates on completion. The Act also requires apprenticeship agreements to be treated as a contract of employment, which will give an apprentice all the usual employment rights. In addition, The Institute for Apprenticeships, an independent body to regulate the quality of apprenticeships, was established by the 2009 Act (as amended by the Enterprise Act 2016).

2.110 Section 6 of the Deregulation Act 2015 replaced apprenticeships in England with English Apprentices, which simplifies the scheme and allows employers to design apprenticeship standards for their own sectors. Such apprenticeships continue to be contracts of service, as with non-English Apprentices.

From April 2017, all employers with a pay bill over £3 million a year have to pay an apprenticeship levy of 0.5% of the wage bill (including wages, bonuses, commissions, and pension contributions, but not benefits in kind), minus £15,000.

M. **Those Under the Age of 18**

Minors

2.111 A contract of employment entered into by a minor (ie a person under the age of 18) is a valid agreement provided that on the whole it is substantially for his benefit. Otherwise, it will be void. Even though the contract contains terms which are onerous or detrimental to his interests, one must look at the effect of the whole agreement. In *De Francesco v Barnum*,[155] a 14-year-old girl bound herself by an apprenticeship deed to the claimant in order to become a professional dancer. She agreed not to marry during this time, and to perform engagements only with the plaintiff's permission. The claimant was under no obligation to provide engagements, but when he did, the pay was somewhat ungenerous. It was held that the deed was void, for it was totally unreasonable, and was not in the interests of the girl. By contrast, in *Clements v London and North-Western Rly Co*,[156] where a boy entered into the defendants' employment on terms which excluded his right to sue under the Employers' Liability Act 1880, in respect of injuries suffered during his employment. Instead, he was covered by the company's own insurance scheme, which had a wider range of protection, though the benefits were somewhat lower than the State scheme. It was held that on the whole the contract was to his advantage and was therefore binding. In *Denmark Productions Ltd v Boscobel Productions Ltd*,[157] a contract by four infant members of a pop group to employ a manager was held to be binding, and in *Chaplin v Leslie Frewin (Publishers) Ltd*,[158] the son of a famous film star contracted to assign to a firm of publishers

---

[154] [2003] ICR 495, [2003] IRLR 492, [1999] All ER (D) 370 (Nov), EAT.
[155] 45 Ch D 430, [1886–90] All ER Rep 414.   [156] [1894] 2 QB 482, [1891–4] All ER Rep Ext 1461, CA.
[157] [1969] 1 QB 699, [1968] 3 All ER 513, CA.   [158] [1966] Ch 71, [1965] 3 All ER 764, CA.

a book containing his life story. This too, was held to be binding, as it conferred a financial benefit on him.

Young Persons

2.112 A young person is any person who has not attained the age of 18, and therefore includes children of any age. This is not to be confused with a young worker (a term used, for example, in the Working Time Regulations 1998), which refers to a person who has attained the age of 15 but not the age of 18 and who is over compulsory school age.

2.113 Special protection is given to young persons by the Management of Health and Safety at Work Regulations 1999. Before employing a young person, the employer must make a risk assessment, taking into account his inexperience, lack of awareness of risks and immaturity, the fitting and layout of the workplace, exposure to physical, biological, and chemical agents, the way work equipment is handled, the organisation of the processes, the extent to which health and safety training is provided, and the risks from certain dangerous processes. Employers must ensure that young persons are protected at work from any risks to their health and safety which are a consequence of their lack of experience, absence of awareness of risks and lack of maturity. Special provision has been made for young workers in the Working Time Regulations 1998 (see para 7.62).

Children

2.114 The Children (Protection at Work) Regulations 1998–2000 deal with the employment of children below the minimum school leaving age, and amend the provisions of the Children and Young Persons Acts 1933 and 1963 and the Children and Young Persons (Scotland) Act 1937 in order to implement the requirements of Directive 94/33/EC on the Protection of Young Persons at Work.

The general principle is that a child under the age of 14 may not be employed in any work, other than as an employee of his parent or guardian in light agricultural work or horticultural work on an occasional basis. However, children over the age of 13 may be employed in categories of light work specified in local authorities' byelaws. Light work is defined as being work which does not jeopardise a child's safety, health, development, attendance at school, or participation in work experience. Children have the right to have a two-week break from any employment in school holidays. Local authorities have the power to prohibit the employment of children who are employed in a manner which may be prejudicial to their health or render them unfit to obtain the benefit of full-time education, and they may impose restrictions on such employment (Education Act 1996, s 559).

This legislation, together with the Children (Performances) Regulations 1968 (see also Children (Performance) (Amendment) (Wales) Regulations 2007), extends controls on the employment of children in performances, including sport, advertising and modelling. A licence may be obtained from any justice of the peace if it is proposed to take a child abroad for these purposes.

Further information about these rules can be obtained from the education welfare office of a local education authority. Local authorities have the power to prohibit the employment of children who are employed in a manner which may be prejudicial to their health or render them unfit to obtain the benefit of full-time education, and they may also impose restrictions on such employment (Education Act 1996, s 559). A child may not be employed in an industrial undertaking or on a sea-going boat, unless the undertaking or boat is one in which only members of the child's family are employed (Employment of Women, Young Persons, and Children Act 1920, ss 1–3). A child may not be employed in a factory (Education Act 1918, s 14) nor employed underground in a mine, except for the purpose of receiving prescribed instruction (Mines and Quarries Act 1954, s 124). A child may not be required to lift, carry, or move anything so heavy as to be likely to cause injury.

2.115 Schoolchildren may be employed for work experience from the beginning of the school term preceding the start of the school year in which they become entitled to leave school (Education (Work Experience) Act 1973, s 1, as amended).

N. **Domestic Servants**

2.116 A domestic servant is an employee, and, provided she has the requisite periods of continuous employment, may claim appropriate statutory rights. She may claim redundancy payment, for employment in a private household is deemed to be a business like any other. However, this does not apply if she is a close relative of the employer (see para 18.64). Nor do the special rules relating to the transfer of a business apply, except where the head of the household dies, for here there may be a transfer to the new head of the household for redundancy purposes (see ERA, s 175 and *Ranger v Brown*[159]).

O. **Foreign Employees**

2.117 A person who is not a national of a member state of the European Economic Area (ie European Union, Iceland, Liechtenstein and Norway), or who is not a Commonwealth citizen with the right of abode, must obtain the necessary permission to take up employment in the United Kingdom, otherwise the employment will be illegal. The Immigration Rules currently in force detail a number of different categories of workers who may be granted entry clearance to enter this country for specified periods of time, with or without work permits, and the conditions which will be attached thereto if they wish to take up employment. A points-based system of immigration control is in place, which replaced the previous categories of persons entitled to come from non-EU countries. There are five tiers: Tier 1 high value migrants, entrepreneurs and innovators; Tier 2 skilled workers with job offers to fill shortages in the labour market; Tier 3 unskilled temporary seasonal labour (this category has been suspended indefinitely, as the United Kingdom expects to fill such jobs from EU workers); Tier 4 students; and Tier 5 temporary workers (eg working holiday-makers). A consideration of these matters is outside the scope of this book, but information can be obtained from UK Visas and Immigration.

2.118 The illegality of the employment has three potential consequences. In the first place, a person who is employed under an illegal contract cannot acquire any legal rights under that contract. Thus he will have few employment rights (*Sharma v Hindu Temple*,[160] but see para 3.7 and 4.198). Additionally, if the contract was legal at one time, periods when the contract became illegal will not count towards continuity of employment, and will also break continuity (*Bamgbose v Royal Star and Garter Home*[161]).

2.119 Second, the Immigration, Asylum and Nationality Act 2006, s 15 provides that the Secretary of State may apply for a penalty notice against a person who employs an adult who is subject to immigration control, and:

(a) who has not been granted leave to enter or remain in the United Kingdom, or

(b) whose leave to enter or remain has expired, or is invalid, or

(c) who is subject to a condition prohibiting employment.

The amount of the penalty notice will be prescribed by regulations, currently up to £20,000 if the employment was due to negligence. The employer may object to the penalty notice,

---

[159] [1978] 2 All ER 726, [1978] ICR 603, EAT.   [160] Unreported.   [161] UKEAT/841/95.

and the Secretary of State may cancel, reduce, increase, or confirm it. In the alternative, an appeal against the penalty notice may be made to a county court (or sheriff's court).

The Secretary of State will issue a Code of Practice, specifying the factors to be considered in determining the amount of the penalty notice. The Code will also give advice on how to avoid a penalty under s 15, or an offence under s 21, without contravening the Equality Act 2010.

Third, it is also a criminal offence to employ a person who is subject to the immigration controls referred to earlier, when the employer (or a person how has responsibility within the body for an aspect of employment) knows or has reasonable cause to believe that the person is not entitled to work. The offence is punishable on indictment with a maximum of two years' imprisonment, or a fine, or both, and on summary conviction to 12 months' imprisonment (six months in Scotland) or a fine, or both (s 21). Where an offence is committed by a body corporate, any director, manager, secretary, or similar officer (or person purporting to act as such) will be jointly liable, if the offence was committed with his consent, or connivance, or attributable to any neglect on his part. The above offence does not apply if the employee was an asylum seeker who has been given written permission to work, or an asylum seeker who had permission to work before appealing against a refusal to grant asylum. It will be a defence for the employer to show that before the employment began, he was shown a document which related to the employee, and which was of a description specified in an order made by the Secretary of State. The documents which are acceptable are set out in the Immigration (Restrictions on Employment) Order 2007, as amended, and basically consist of secure documents, which are either a UK or EEA passport, national identity card or UK residence permit, or the originals of certain other documents which will confirm that the holder is entitled to take the employment in question. A copy of the document must be kept for the duration of the employment and for a further six months after it ends.

2.120 The purpose behind the legislation was to try to limit the number of foreign nationals working here illegally. However, the requirement that before permitting a person to commence employment, the employer must ask certain questions and seek confirmation of nationality or status raises issues of race discrimination (*Dhatt v McDonalds Hamburgers Ltd*[162]). The EHRC has issued guidelines for employers which contain a number of 'good practice recommendations'.

2.121 If the employment of a foreign worker is perfectly legal, then he will have all the employment protection rights which are applicable to his case, in the same manner as a UK or EU national, apart from being able to obtain employment in certain official posts.

2.122 The Immigration Act 2016 also establishes a new Director of Labour Market Enforcement to oversee the relevant enforcement agencies (Gangmasters and Labour Abuse Authority, Employment Agency Standards Inspectorate, and the National Minimum Wage enforcement team), and requires public authorities to ensure that each person who works for them in a customer-facing role speaks fluent English.

P. Posted Workers

2.123 A posted worker is a worker who is sent from one EU member state to another state on a temporary basis in order to carry out some work in that other state. EC Directive 96/71/EC is designed to ensure a level playing field between member states, so that employers do not acquire a competitive edge by paying workers less favourable terms and conditions than

---

[162] [1988] ICR 591, EAT; aff'd [1991] 3 All ER 692, [1991] ICR 238, [1991] IRLR 130, CA.

the worker would otherwise earn according to the laws and practices in that other member state. They could, however, retain any terms and conditions which were more favourable under their existing contracts. This was updated by The Posted Workers Enforcement Directive (2014/67/EU), implemented in the UK by the Posted Workers (Enforcement of Employment Rights) Regulations 2016 (SI 2016/539), which came into force in June 2016.

Q. **Working Abroad**

2.124 An employee may be required to work outside the United Kingdom either permanently or on a temporary basis. The requirement will stem from an express term of the contract of employment, or by virtue of an implied term, when it is 'obvious' from the nature of the job and/or the employer's business.

2.125 If the employee is required to work outside the United Kingdom for more than one month, then, in addition to the matters which need to be contained in the written statement of terms and conditions given under ERA, s 1, the statement must:

(a) state the period for which the employee is to work outside the United Kingdom;

(b) state the currency in which remuneration is to be paid;

(c) give details of any additional remuneration paid and/or any extra benefits provided by reason of the requirement to work outside the United Kingdom; and

(d) specify any terms and conditions relating to the employee's return to the United Kingdom (s 1(4)(k)).

These details must be provided before the employee leaves the United Kingdom.

2.126 The parties can decide for themselves whether the contract will be governed by UK law or by the law of another country, although this cannot deprive the employee of the right to claim under the laws of the country in which he works. Otherwise the Contract (Applicable Law) Act 1990 provides that the contract will be governed by the law of the country in which the employee habitually carries out his duties. If this cannot be ascertained with certainty, the law to be applied will be the law of the country in which the employer's business is situated. Further, the Civil Jurisdiction and Judgments Act 1982 provides that if the employer is domiciled in a member state of the European Union, he can be sued in the courts of that state or in the courts of the state where the employee habitually carries out his work.

2.127 Any period spent working abroad will count for the purpose of computing the period of continuous employment (ERA, s 215(1)), but will only count for redundancy purposes if national insurance contributions are made in respect of such periods (ERA, s 215(4)). However, weeks of overseas employment do not break continuity for redundancy purposes, but the start of any such period will be postponed by seven days for each week that does not thus count.

2.128 There is no implied term that an employer will provide personal accident insurance for the benefit of a person who is required to work abroad. Nor is the employer obliged to give specific advice on special risks, or to advise the employee to take out his own personal accident insurance (*Reid v Rush & Tompkins Group plc*,[163] and see para 10.34). Nor can a duty in tort be imposed to expand contractual duties.

---

[163] [1989] 3 All ER 228, [1990] ICR 61, [1989] IRLR 265, CA.

R. **Offshore Employment**

2.129 Offshore employment is defined as employment for the purposes of activities: (a) in the territorial waters of the United Kingdom; or (b) connected with the exploration of the seabed or subsoil, or the exploration of their natural resources, in the United Kingdom sector of the continental shelf; or (c) connected with the exploration or exploitation, in a foreign sector of the continental shelf, of a cross-boundary petroleum field and renewable energy zones (eg wind farms) (ERA, s 201; TULR(C)A, s 287).

2.130 Orders have been made extending the provisions of various employment legislation to offshore employment, including the Employment Rights Act 1996 (except time off work for public duties), Equality Act 2010, National Minimum Wage Act 1998, and Trade Union and Labour Relations (Consolidation) Act 1992. Employment in the Frigg Gas Field comes within the scope of the various Acts if the employer is a British company, or has a place of business in Great Britain from which the activities are directed.

S. **Retainers**

2.131 A person who is retained for employment is not an employee merely because he is 'on call' even though he is paid during that time. Employment involves work or other activity carried out for the employer. In *Suffolk County Council v Secretary of State for the Environment*,[164] it was held that a retained fireman, who was permanently on call, was not an employee, for a contractual obligation to remain on call within a prescribed area did not constitute employment. His hours of work only began when he was on duty following a call.

However, a different result was reached in *British Nursing Association v Inland Revenue (National Minimum Wage Compliance Team)*,[165] where the employers provided a 'bank' of nurses for emergency duties. A booking system operated a 24-hour service. During the day, nurses could be contacted at the employer's premises, but at night they had to be contacted at their homes. The National Minimum Wage Compliance Team took the view that those nurses engaged on the night shift were entitled to a minimum hourly rate for all hours they were on duty, but the employers argued that the nurses were not actually working during their shift. Although they were required to be available to take telephone calls, they could spend their shift doing other activities, such as watching television or reading, etc. It was held that the nurses were entitled to the national minimum wage for all the hours they were on duty. They had to hold themselves ready to answer the telephone, they could not pick and choose the times at which they had to answer the telephone, and there was a continuing obligation throughout the night to be available (see para 7.59 for further discussion).

T. **Fixed-term Contracts**

2.132 A fixed-term contract is a contract of employment for a specified period of time, ie, with a defined beginning and a defined end (*Wiltshire County Council v National Association of Teachers in Further and Higher Education and Guy*[166]). As a general rule, such a contract cannot be terminated before its expiry date except for gross misconduct or by mutual agreement (*Lyritzis v Inmarsat*[167]). However, a contract can still be for a fixed

---

[164] (1983) 82 LGR 557; revsd 83 LGR 130, [1984] ICR 882, [1985] IRLR 24, HL.
[165] [2001] IRLR 659, [2001] All ER (D) 59 (Aug), EAT; aff'd [2002] EWCA Civ 494, [2003] ICR 19, [2002] IRLR 480, [2002] All ER (D) 419 (Mar).
[166] [1978] ICR 968, [1978] IRLR 301, EAT; aff'd [1980] ICR 455, [1980] IRLR 198, CA.
[167] Unreported.

term if it contains within it a provision enabling either side to terminate it on giving notice before the term expires (*Allen v National Australia Group Europe Ltd*[168]). A contract of apprenticeship is a classic example of a fixed-term contract (*Wallace v CA Roofing Services Ltd*, para 2.107).

The Fixed-term Employees (Prevention of Less Favourable) Treatment Regulations 2002

2.133 These regulations implement the Fixed-term Workers Directive (1999/70/EC). The regulations apply to employees (not workers) and are designed to introduce the principle of non-discrimination between those working on fixed-term contracts and comparators who are permanent employees. The main beneficiaries of the regulations will be employees who are employed in order to cover for employees who are on statutory periods of absence (maternity leave, adoption leave, parental leave, etc), those employed in periods of peak demand, those who are employed on contracts to carry out specific tasks, eg setting up a database, teachers in higher education, senior staff employed in the health service, etc.

2.134 A fixed-term contract is defined as being a contract of employment that, under its provisions determining how it will terminate in the normal course, will terminate (a) on the expiry of a specific term, or (b) on the completion of a particular task, or (c) on the occurrence or non-occurrence of any specific event other than the attainment by the employee of any normal and bona fide retiring age.

2.135 The regulations do not apply to agency workers, or to those working under a contract of apprenticeship, or on government training schemes, or doing work experience not exceeding one year as part of a higher education course.

2.136 The regulations do not provide for permanent employees to have the right to compare themselves with fixed-term employees, and so it is possible to treat the latter more favourably than the former, provided, of course, that no other aspect of employment law is infringed, such as sex discrimination etc.

Terms Not Less Favourable

2.137 A fixed-term employee has the right not to be treated by his employer less favourably than a comparable permanent employee with regard to the terms of the contract, including any period of service qualification relating to a particular condition of service, the opportunity to receive training, or the opportunity to secure permanent employment in the establishment. He will also have the right not to suffer any other detriment by any act (or deliberate failure to act) of his employer. However, this right only applies if the treatment in question is on the ground that the employee is a fixed-term employee, and the treatment is not justified on objective grounds. The comparable permanent employee must be employed by the same employer at the same establishment (other locations can be considered if there is no one appropriate at the same establishment) and be an employee who is engaged on the same or broadly similar work, having regard to whether they have a similar level of qualifications and skills. A hypothetical comparator will not suffice. An employee is not a comparable permanent employee if his employment has ceased.

2.138 Terms which must be no less favourable include pay and pensions. Where appropriate, a 'pro rata' principle is to be applied, which means that the fixed-term employee is entitled to such proportions of pay or other benefits as is reasonable bearing in mind the length of his contract of employment and the basis on which pay, or other benefits,

---

[168] [2004] IRLR 847, EAT.

is offered. An employee on a fixed-term contract of three months or less has the right to receive statutory sick pay, and, after one month's continuous employment, is entitled to a week's notice if the contract is terminated, and also has the right to receive guarantee payment and payment on medical suspension. But the non-renewal of a fixed term contract does not, by itself, amount to less favourable treatment (*Department for Work and Pensions v Webby*[169]).

2.139 It is, however, possible to justify the unequal treatment on objective grounds. In order to be objectively justified, the unequal treatment should be aimed at achieving a legitimate business objective, be necessary to achieve that objective, and be an appropriate way of achieving it. If the treatment by an employer of a fixed-term employee is less favourable than the treatment meted out to a comparable permanent employee, it will amount to objective justification if, taken as a whole, the terms and conditions of a fixed-term employee are at least as favourable as those which apply to a comparable permanent employee. Thus it is permissible to take a 'package' approach, as opposed to a term-by-term approach (as in equal pay cases). Higher salaries, or more holidays, etc can compensate for the lack of other benefits such as pensions, provided that the package as a whole is equivalent to or better than that of a permanent employee.

2.140 A fixed-term employee has the right to be informed of any permanent suitable vacancies, and may bring a claim in respect of the employer's failure to do so within three months from the date on which other individuals, whether employees or not, were informed of the vacancy.

The Four-year Rule and Other Rights

2.141 Where there is a fixed-term contract or a succession of such contracts which result in the employee being employed for four years or more, the contract will be deemed to be a contract of indefinite duration (unless there is objective justification when the contract was made or renewed), and the minimum period of notice provisions of ERA, ss 86–91 will apply (see para 15.4). The employee also has the right to request a written statement from his employer either giving reasons why his contract remains fixed-term beyond the four-year limitation period, or confirming that it has become open-ended. It should be noted that a fixed-term contract does not become a permanent contract until it is renewed. If it is renewed before the four-year point, it will become permanent as soon as the four-year point is reached. If it is renewed after the four-year point, it became permanent on renewal.

2.142 To benefit from the four-year rule, the employee would need to show that he has been continuously employed within the meaning of ERA, ss 210–219 (see Chapter 13). In particular, if a week's absence from work is not covered by s 212(3) (see para 13.24), continuity of employment will be broken. Thus if there is a gap of more than one week between successive fixed-term contracts, such contracts cannot be turned into a permanent contract under the four-year rule. The situation revealed in *Booth v United States of America* (see para 13.2) remains unaffected.[170]

2.143 The requirement which permits an employee to opt out of his right to receive a redundancy payment is repealed, although contracts which were in force prior to the commencement of the regulations are able to retain this waiver during their term (see para 18.64).

2.144 A fixed-term employee will have the right to request in writing from his employer a written statement giving particulars of the reasons for any less favourable treatment, and the employer must reply within 21 days of the request. An identical right exists for

---

[169] [2004] EWCA Civ 1745, CA.   [170] [1999] IRLR 16, 611 IRLB 9, EAT.

an employee who considers that his contract is one of indefinite duration under the four-year rule to make a similar request for confirmation that the contract is to be so regarded. There is no remedy if the employer fails to comply with either of these requests, but if, in proceedings before an employment tribunal to enforce the fixed-term employee's rights under the regulations, it is shown that the employer deliberately and without reasonable excuse omitted to provide the written statement, or that it was evasive or equivocal, the tribunal may draw an inference that the employer has infringed the right in question. If an employee considers that he is a permanent employee under the four-year rule, he may present an application to an employment tribunal for a declaration to that effect, but he cannot do so unless he has previously requested a statement from his employer and the employer has failed to provide one. He must also still be employed by the employer.

2.145 An employee has the right not to suffer a detriment, or be dismissed, because he did an act under the regulations, and may also bring a claim alleging unequal treatment contrary to the regulations. The claim must be brought within three months of the alleged infringement, although the tribunal can consider a complaint which is out of time if it considers that it is just and equitable to do so. If the employment tribunal finds in his favour, it may make a declaration as to the rights of the complainant and the employer, award compensation, and make a recommendation that the employer takes steps to obviate or reduce the adverse effects complained of. The compensation award shall be that which the tribunal considers to be just and equitable, and may include the loss of benefits and reasonable expenses. However, if the claim is based on less favourable treatment, there can be no award in respect of injured feelings.

Continuity Rules

2.146 In respect of a fixed-term contract of short duration, the normal continuity rules apply on renewal (see Chapter 13), including the statutory presumption in favour of continuity (ERA, s 210(5)). This may enable an employee whose employment was intended to be temporary to obtain various employment protection rights in appropriate circumstances. The normal rules about giving statutory notice do not apply when the contract period expires, except where an employee has been employed under a fixed-term contract of one month or less, and has actually been employed for three months or more (ERA, s 86(4)).

Expiry of the Fixed Term

2.147 If a fixed-term contract is not renewed on expiry, that will not amount to a dismissal at common law, because the contract has been terminated automatically by effluxion of time. However, non-renewal under the same contract will be a dismissal for the purpose of ERA. Whether the dismissal was fair or unfair will be determined by whether or not the employer can show that he acted reasonably in not renewing the contract. If the contract is terminated prior to the expiry of the fixed term, the employee will have the normal rights in respect of breach of contract (see Chapter 15), and the employer will be liable to pay the employee for the rest of the term, subject to the employee's duty to mitigate against his loss. He will also have the right to claim unfair dismissal, provided he has been employed for the requisite period of continuous employment. However, if the contract is terminated by mutual agreement, no dismissal has taken place (*Lyritzis v Inmarsat*), although a mutual acknowledgement that the contract will terminate on the fixed date will be a dismissal nonetheless (*Thames Television v Wallis*[171]). Nor will there be a dismissal for redundancy payment purposes if the employee is employed under a new contract which takes effect within four weeks of the expiry of the old (ERA, s 138(1)). A dismissal will take place if

---

[171] [1979] IRLR 136, EAT.

the new contract is substantially different from the old (ERA, s 138(2–6)), but the right to obtain a redundancy payment will be lost if the employee unreasonably refuses an offer on the same or different terms (ERA, s 141).

U. Secondment of Employees

2.148 Occasionally, an employer will second an employee to another employer, either for a specific task or for a specific period of time. This arrangement can give rise to a number of legal problems, eg (a) the status of the seconded employee during the period of second-ment and after it has concluded; (b) which employer is to accept liability if the seconded employee injures a third party; (c) which employer will be liable if the employee suffers an injury. Only the first of these comes under employment law and is covered by this book.

2.149 In *Fitton v City of Edinburgh Council*[172] the claimant was employed in the council's education department. She was then seconded to ELLP, another corporate body that pro-vided educational services. It was intended that the secondment would last for 12 months, but it was later agreed to be open-ended. The council agreed that if the secondment came to an end she would be guaranteed a comparable post. The council continued to pay her salary, but this was done on the basis of a financial arrangement with ELLP. The claim-ant did no work for the council, and the council could no longer require her to work for them. After working for ELLP for two years, she resigned her employment with them, and brought claims for constructive dismissal, sex discrimination, and sexual harassment against the council. The EAT upheld the finding of an employment tribunal that she was not employed by the council during her open-ended secondment. The irreducible mini-mum requirements of mutuality of agreement and control were absent. The fact that the arrangement used the term 'secondment' was not, by itself, determinative of the matter, if the facts established that the 'seconded employee' had, in practice, been transferred from one employer to another.

Status of the Seconded Worker During, and After, the Period of Employment

2.150 The status of the employee who has been seconded can be a problem. Is he an employee of the original employer, or of the employer to whom he has been seconded? What are his continuity rights if either employer terminates the contract? Is there an im-pact on the employment contract by virtue of the Transfer of Undertakings (Protection of Employment) Regulations? What is his pension position during the period of secondment? Some of these questions were raised in *Astley v Celtec Ltd*,[173] but the answers given were somewhat inconclusive.

2.151 What is the position of an employee who has been seconded to work abroad? It is now established that an employee working in another country may, in some circumstances, be able to bring a claim under UK employment legislation (see *Serco Ltd v Lawson*, para 1.14), but the position of seconded employees is not clear. Two problems are apparent, namely (a) who will be the employer against whom a claim is to be made, and (b) will the UK employment tribunals have jurisdiction to deal with a claim made by an employee who once worked in the United Kingdom, but who is then seconded to work abroad? It is a tru-ism to state that each case will have to be determined on its own facts, but the trend is toward permitting such actions wherever possible (eg, see *Crofts v Cathay Pacific Airways Ltd*[174]).

2.152 An allied problem arises if an employee takes a 'career break'. If the employee is expected to resign, continuity of employment is likely to be broken (*Curr v Marks &*

---

[172] EATS/0010/07.   [173] (C-478/03) (2005) *Times*, 9 June.   [174] [2005] IRLR 423.

Spencer plc[175]), but if he is on some form of leave of absence, continuity will be preserved by virtue of ERA, s 212(3)(c) (see para 13.24).

V. **Agency Workers**

Employment Agency or Employment Business?

2.153 An employer may turn to an agency to provide him with staff for a specific purpose or definite or indefinite period of time. The Conduct of Employment Agencies and Employment Businesses Regulations 2003–2010 set out the minimum standards which govern the conduct of the private recruitment industry. Generally, such agencies must comply with the legislation on equal opportunities, equal pay, health and safety, national minimum wage, working time, etc, and there is a gov.uk Guidance Note clarifying various issues.

An employment agency undertakes to find work for a work seeker, and once the worker is suitably placed, the agency will drop out of the picture, having obtained a fee from the worker's employer for its services.

On the other hand, an employment business is an organisation which supplies workers to hirers, often on a temporary basis (the term 'worker' is used in a neutral sense). The worker will do work for the hirer, but as a general rule the employment relationship is with the employment business, and it is the business which pays the worker his wages. The terms of the contract between the employment business and the worker shall specify in writing whether the worker is employed by the employment business under a contract of service or apprenticeship or a contract for services, and, in any case, other terms and conditions relating to remuneration, notice, annual leave, etc.

Status of Agency Workers

2.154 In practice, there are three different scenarios to consider when dealing with the status of agency workers. The first arises out of employment legislation, when it has to be determined whether or not the worker is legally an employee, for such issues as unfair dismissal, redundancy payments, and other rights that exist for employees. The second issue arises when prosecutions are considered under the Health and Safety at Work Act and associated regulations, which generally speaking only apply to employees, although under the Management of Health and Safety at Work Regulations 1999 an employer also owes duties to visiting workers and temporary workers. Thirdly, claims for injuries based on common law negligence or vicarious liability are sometimes treated by the courts in a more relaxed manner, as the real defendant is the insurance company, not the employer!

2.155 In view of some difficult and frequently irreconcilable decisions it is trite to observe that it all depends on the facts of each case. The courts and tribunals have to decide whether the worker is an employee of the employment business (*McMeecham v Secretary of State for Employment*[176]), an employee of the client end-user (*Dacas v Brook Street Bureau*[177]), or an employee of neither (*Bunce v Postworth Ltd*[178]).

2.156 One has to start with the terms of the contract between the worker and the employment business, although the label put on the contract is only determinative of the relationship between the parties if, having considered all the relevant factors, there is still some

---

[175] [2002] All ER (D) 76 (Mar), EAT; revsd [2002] EWCA Civ 1852, [2003] ICR 443, [2003] IRLR 74, [2002] All ER (D) 205 (Dec).

[176] [1995] ICR 444, [1995] IRLR 461, EAT; aff'd [1997] ICR 549, [1997] IRLR 353, CA.

[177] [2003] IRLR 190, [2003] All ER (D) 241 (Jan), EAT; revsd [2004] EWCA Civ 217, [2004] All ER (D) 125 (Mar).   [178] [2005] EWCA Civ 490, [2005] IRLR 557.

doubt about the worker's true status. In *McMeecham v Secretary of State for Employment* the claimant worked for an employment business under a series of temporary contracts. The terms of his engagement specifically stated that he was self-employed, but he was paid on a weekly basis when he worked, and tax and national insurance contributions were deducted. The business became insolvent and the claimant sought to recover wages owed to him from the National Insurance Fund (under ERA, s 182). In allowing his claim, the Court of Appeal drew a distinction between the general terms of engagement which existed with the employment business and the specific engagements a worker undertakes. In respect of the latter a single engagement was capable of giving rise to a contract of employment, even though the worker might not be entitled to employee status under his general terms of engagement.

2.157 In *Consistent Group Ltd v Kalwak*[179] the EAT expressed the view that the fact that the contract provides for unrealistic possibilities will not alter the true nature of the relationship if this is different from what happens in reality, and this view was expressly endorsed in *Protectacoat Firthglow Ltd v Szilagyi*[180] and by the Supreme Court in *Autoclenz v Belcher* (para 2.2). The employment tribunal should adopt a robust and sensible view in order to prevent the substance of the relationship from being undermined by form. Clauses that are designed to prevent the relationship from being that of employer/employee (with the consequent dilution of employment rights) will only be upheld if the documentation realistically reflects what might be expected to occur (*Redrow Homes (Yorkshire) Ltd v Buckborough*[181]). The decision in *Protectacoat* was strengthened in *Autoclenz Ltd v Belcher*, where it was stressed that the proper approach is to consider whether the written terms reflect the true intentions of the parties. It is not enough to argue that a clause has never been activated, if it is genuine. Thus, provisions that state that the employer has no obligation to provide work, or that the worker is under no obligation to do the work, or that the worker could provide a substitute if necessary, are not conclusive of anything, if they do not represent the true intent of the parties.

2.158 In the absence of a formal contract between the parties, it is necessary to draw conclusions about the legal nature of their relationship from all the surrounding circumstances, including how they act in practice. Thus in *Hewlett Packard Ltd v O'Murphy*,[182] a computer specialist set up his own limited company which then contracted with an employment business, which in turn provided his services to the respondent company. Even though the arrangement lasted for some years, and the worker was under the respondent's control so far as performance and discipline were concerned, the strict legal position was that there was no contractual nexus between the worker and the respondents, and his claim for unfair dismissal failed. The existence of 'one too many contracts' (ie between the individual service company—agency—end-user) was fatal to the claim.

2.159 In a number of cases, the existence of a contract of employment between the worker and client has been implied (eg see *Dacas v Brook Street Bureau*) but this can only be done if there is strong evidence that the agency worker has been integrated into the end-user's organisation, and treated on a day-to-day basis in the same way as it treats its own employees (*Franks v Reuters Ltd*[183]). Thus if the agency worker has a contract of employment with

---

[179] [2008] EWCA Civ 430; [2008] IRLR 505 (note that the EAT view in this case was specifically approved by the SC in *Autoclenz v Belcher*, as opposed to the judgment of the CA in *Kalwak*).

[180] [2009] EWCA Civ 98, [2009] ICR 835, [2009] IRLR 365.   [181] [2009] IRLR 34.

[182] [2002] IRLR 4, [2001] All ER (D) 91 (Sep), EAT.

[183] [2002] All ER (D) 239 (Jun), EAT; revsd [2003] EWCA Civ 417, [2003] ICR 1166, [2003] IRLR 423 [2003] All ER (D) 160 (Apr).

the agency, this would negate the existence of a contract of employment with the end-user client, and there is thus no necessity to imply a contract of employment between them (*Cairns v Visteon Ltd*[184]).

2.160 Sometimes a more cautious approach to the status of agency workers appears to be taken. In *Craigie v Haringey*[185] the EAT held that there was no necessity to imply a contract of employment between an agency worker and an end-user, and *Dacas v Brook Street Bureau* was not followed on this point. Further, the mere fact that an employee looked like an employee of the end-user, acted like an employee, and was treated like an employee does not mean that tribunals should therefore imply a contract of employment (*Heatherwood & Wexham Park Hospitals NHS Trust v Kulubowila;*[186] see also *Astbury v Gist*[187]). In *James v Greenwich Council,*[188] the claimant provided her services to the council for five years. Her contract with the agency stated that she was employed under a contract for services, and that no employment relationship existed with either the agency or the client. The council did not pay her wages, but made a payment to the agency. She was not subject to the council's disciplinary or grievance procedure, was not entitled to sick pay or holiday pay, and, when absent from work, was replaced by another agency worker. When she was not allowed to return to work after a period of sickness absence, she claimed unfair dismissal against the council, arguing that in view of the length of time she had worked for them, an implied contract of employment had come into existence. Her claim was dismissed by the employment tribunal, the EAT, and the Court of Appeal. The fact that the arrangement had existed for a considerable length of time did not, per se, give rise to an implied contract of employment, for it is only in cases of necessity that such a contract can be implied.

2.161 It would appear that employment tribunals nowadays are more likely to give preference to contractually expressed intentions over the manner in which the relationship with the agency worker has worked in practice (*Astbury v Gist*) unless the documentation is totally unrealistic (*Consistent Group Ltd v Kalwak*, para 2.157).

2.162 The presence or absence of mutuality is a significant factor to be considered. In *Bunce v Postworth Ltd (t/a Skyblue),*[189] the claimant registered for work with Postworth, an employment business. The written agreement described the claimant as 'an associate', and stated that it was a contract for services and not intended to give rise to a contract of employment. Postworth were not obliged to obtain work for the claimant, and in turn the claimant was not obliged to accept work offered. When he accepted work, he was obliged to accept the directions, supervision, and instructions of any person in the client organisation to whom he was responsible, and to conform to the client's normal hours of work, and rules and regulations. Postworth paid the claimant's wages and holiday pay, but not sick pay. Over a period of one year, the claimant accepted 142 assignments, most of which were with the same client. However, after complaints were received about the quality of his work, Postworth informed him that the arrangement was terminated. His claim for unfair dismissal was rejected by the employment tribunal, the EAT, and the Court of Appeal. So far as Postworth were concerned, there was an absence of control. So far as the client was concerned, there was an absence of mutuality. For the claimant, it had been argued that he had an 'umbrella' contract, which covered all the separate arrangements made with Postworth, but the argument was dismissed by the Court of Appeal, who pointed out that the very detailed provisions in the contract left no room for implying an overall contract.

---

[184] [2007] ICR 616, [2007] IRLR 175.   [185] EAT/0556/06.   [186] EAT/0633/06.
[187] EAT/0619/06/DA, EAT/0446/04/LA.
[188] [2007] ICR 577, [2007] IRLR 168, EAT; aff'd [2008] EWCA Civ 35, [2008] ICR 545, [2008] IRLR 302.
[189] n 170.

Further, the fact that the claimant worked for more than one end user was fatal to the 'umbrella contract' argument.

2.163 An employee who is supplied by an agency on a temporary appointment and who is then taken on as a full-time employee has continuity of employment from the date his temporary appointment commenced (*RNLI v Bushaway*[190]).

Agency Workers Regulations 2010

2.164 The Agency Workers Regulations 2010 apply to workers supplied by temporary work agencies, ie agencies that introduce workers to hirers for temporary work only. They do not apply to employment agencies, as these look for permanent employment for workers. An agency worker is defined as an individual who is supplied by a temporary work agency to work for and under the direction of a hirer. The agency worker can be employed by the agency or treated as a worker by the hirer, but genuinely self-employed persons are excluded. Workers who work through an 'umbrella company' (which is usually used to exploit tax loopholes) or who are engaged by an intermediary are within the scope of the regulations.

2.165 An agency worker is entitled to the same basic working conditions and employment conditions as he would have if he had been recruited by the hirer directly, with the same terms and conditions of employment that are ordinarily included in contracts of employees of the hirer, whether by collective agreement or otherwise (reg 5). The relevant terms and conditions are those enjoyed by comparable employees of the hirer. A comparable employee is one who is, together with the agency worker, working for and under the supervision and direction of the hirer, and engaged on broadly similar work, having regard to whether they have a similar level of qualifications and skills, and based at the same establishment.

2.166 The relevant terms and conditions that must be applied to the agency worker are terms and conditions relating to pay, duration of working time, night work, rest periods, rest breaks, and annual leave. 'Pay' means any sum payable, including fees, bonus, commission, holiday pay, or other emoluments referable to the employment, but excluding the monetary value of benefits in kind, occupational sick pay, maternity, paternity and adoption pay, redundancy payments, profit-sharing schemes, etc. Bonuses that relate to personal and individual performances are included, but not those linked to long-term organisational performance.

2.167 The agency worker is entitled to be treated no less favourably than a comparable worker in relation to collective facilities provided by the hirer (reg 12). These include canteen or other similar facilities, childcare facilities, and transport services, although less favourable treatment can be justified on objective grounds. During the assignment, the agency worker is entitled to be informed by the hirer of any relevant vacant posts with the hirer, and must be given the same opportunity as a comparable worker to find permanent employment with the hirer (reg 13). These are known as 'day one' rights. While agency workers have the right to be told about vacant posts, however, they do not have the right to be considered on an equal footing with permanent staff (*Coles v Ministry of Defence*[191]). Nor is there a right to the same number of contractual hours of work as those of a permanent employee comparator (*Kocur v Angard Staffing Solutions Limited*[192]). The Directive only seeks to provide equal treatment in relation to basic working conditions. There is no general right for a temporary agency worker to be treated no less favourably than a direct

---

[190] [2005] IRLR 674, EAT.   [191] EAT/0403/14.   [192] [2019] EWCA Civ 1185.

employee: instead, the principle of equal treatment is confined to working time and pay. This is so that the flexibility of hiring agency workers is retained.

2.168 To qualify for equal treatment, however, an agency worker must be employed in the same role for 12 continuous calendar weeks (part of a week counts as a full week). If there is a break between assignments, there are a number of circumstances when the break can be ignored for the purpose of computing continuity, ie for any reason up to six weeks, for sickness or injury up to 26 weeks, and periods of absence due to maternity leave, paternity leave, jury service, and so on (see reg 7(8)). The 12-week period must be continuous, with the agency worker doing the same job with the same hirer. If there is a break during an assignment, continuity is only broken if the break is for six calendar weeks or more.

2.169 Continuity will also be broken if the worker is given a new role with substantially different duties (reg 7(3)). But the work or duties must be substantially different from those that made up the previous assignment, and the employment agency must inform the agency worker in writing of the type of work he will be required to do in the new role. Further, the agency worker will be deemed to have satisfied the 12-week qualifying period if he is otherwise prevented from doing so by the structure of assignments. This will arise when the agency worker has completed two or more assignments with a particular hirer, or has worked in two or more substantially different roles with the same hirer, and the most likely explanation for it is that the hirer (or the agency) intended to prevent the agency worker from being entitled to equal treatment (reg 9). If an employment tribunal decides that the hirer's motive for moving the agency worker to a different job, or otherwise breaking the 12-week period, is to prevent the agency worker from obtaining equal treatment, it may make an award that the agency worker is entitled to equal treatment from the date from which he would otherwise be entitled, and a further award of up to £5,000 in respect of the breach of the equal treatment rule.

2.170 Liability for a breach of reg 5 (para 2.167) lies with the temporary work agency to the extent that it is responsible for the breach, although not if the agency has taken reasonable steps to obtain relevant information from the hirer about basic working and employment conditions in force with the hirer and, having received such information, acted reasonably in determining what the agency worker's basic working and employment conditions should be at the end of the qualifying period until the agency worker ceases to be entitled to the rights in reg 5 (see reg 14). To the extent that the temporary work agency is not liable under reg 14, the hirer will be liable for a breach of reg 5 to the extent that it is responsible for the breach.

2.171 If an agency worker considers that the hirer or temporary work agency have infringed his reg 5 rights, he may make a written request to the temporary work agency for a written statement containing information relating to the treatment in question. The temporary work agency shall respond within 28 days, setting out the relevant information relating to basic working and employment conditions of the workers of the hirer, the factors the temporary work agency considered when determining the basic working conditions that applied to the agency worker. If no response has been received within 30 days, the agency worker may request the hirer to provide a written statement containing information relating to the relevant basic working and employment conditions of workers of the hirer. Also, if the agency worker considers that he has not been given access to collective facilities or amenities (reg 12), or information regarding vacant posts with the hirer (reg 13), he may request the hirer to provide a written statement containing information relating to the treatment in question. The hirer shall respond to such a request with relevant information within 28 days.

2.172 An agency worker who is an employee has the right not to be unfairly dismissed because he has brought proceedings under the regulations, or done a number of acts in connection with his rights. He also has the right not to suffer a detriment as a result of any act, or deliberate failure to act, by the temporary work agency or the hirer (reg 17). An application may be made to an employment tribunal that the temporary work agency or the hirer has infringed a right conferred on the agency worker by regs 5, 9, 12, 13, or 17(2). If the employment tribunal finds the complaint well founded, it may make a declaration as to the rights of the complainant, order the respondent to pay compensation to him, and make a recommendation that the respondent takes action for the purpose of obviating or reducing the adverse effect on the complainant of any matter to which the complaint relates.

2.173 Consequential amendments have been made to a number of existing legislative provisions, including the Trade Union and Labour Relations (Consolidation) Act, Employment Rights Act, Safety Representative and Safety Committees Regulations, Management of Health and Safety at Work Regulations, Transfer of Undertakings (Protection of Employment) Regulations, and so on.

2.174 It is not possible to contract out of the provisions of these regulations (reg 15).

Information document for agency workers

2.175 The Conduct of Employment Agencies and Employment Businesses (Amendment) Regulations 2019 (known as the Conduct Regulations) will come into force on 6 April 2020. These will require employment agencies to provide a key information document setting out their terms and benefits to those looking for agency work to those who are looking for work. These key facts include the type of contract, the rate of renumeration and holiday entitlement, who is responsible for their employment, any pay from an intermediary, any fee and any benefits. This requirement will be overseen by the Employment Agency Standards Inspectorate.

W. Casual Workers and Global Contracts

2.176 There are some workers who are employed on short-term periodic contracts, with various breaks in between, whose status has been the subject of a number of judicial decisions. If the employer is under no obligation to provide work, and if the worker is under no obligation to accept an offer of work, a contract of employment cannot exist. This is so even though during actual periods of working, income tax and national insurance contributions are deducted, for administrative reasons (*Stevedoring & Haulage Services Ltd v Fuller*[193]). Attempts have been made to treat such workers as being employed under one 'global contract' but with very limited success. A global contract cannot exist unless there is an irreducible minimum of obligations to offer and accept work existing between the parties (*Clark v Oxfordshire Health Authority*[194]), and it cannot be brought into existence merely by counting together a number of individual contracts which may have subsisted over a period of time (*Hellyer Bros Ltd v McLeod*[195]). In particular, where the terms upon which casual work is offered and accepted expressly negate mutuality of obligations, eg if the employment is specifically stated to be for an 'ad hoc or casual basis' or 'as and when required', there can be no global or overarching contract. The courts will not invent an implied term which specifically overrides the express term (*Stevedoring & Haulage Services Ltd v Fuller*).

---

[193] [2001] EWCA Civ 651, [2001] IRLR 627, [2001] All ER (D) 106 (May).
[194] [1998] IRLR 125, CA.
[195] [1987] ICR 526, 131 Sol Jo 805, sub nom *McLeod v Hellyer Bros Ltd* [1987] IRLR 232, CA.

In *Carmichael v National Power plc*,[196] the appellant was engaged as a guide at a power station. She was paid for the number of hours worked, and had tax and national insurance deducted. Her contract stated that she was employed 'on a casual and as required basis'. The Court of Appeal held that, on the facts of the case, there was an implied term that the employer would offer her a reasonable amount of work, and that if so offered, she would carry out a reasonable amount of work. Thus it was held that a contract of employment existed. However, the House of Lords disagreed, and held that she was not an employee. The absence of mutuality of obligation will frequently be determinative of the matter, for if a person is not obliged to offer work, and the other party is not obliged to accept the work when offered, there is an absence of the irreducible minimum of mutual obligation necessary to create a contract of employment (see para 2.41). It would therefore appear that the fact that a contract is repeated does not create a global contract of employment.

Zero Hours Contracts

2.177 There has been a growth in the use of casual contracts in recent years, becoming known as 'zero hours' contracts. For the protection of such workers, s 153 of the Small Business, Enterprise and Employment Act 2015 inserted s 27A into the ERA, prohibiting the use of exclusivity clauses in such contracts. The Exclusivity Terms in Zero Hour Contracts (Redress) Regulations 2015 came into force on 11 January 2016. S27A(3) providing that any zero hours contract which prohibits the worker from doing work or performing services under another contract or under any other arrangement is unenforceable.

The regulations go further, and regulation 2 states that an employee who works under a zero hours contract is to be regarded as automatically unfairly dismissed if the main reason for the dismissal is that he or she breached the provision in s27A(3), and that such a worker should not be subject to a detriment.

Regulation 3 provides for a complaint to the employment tribunal and regulation 4 for a remedy.

X. **Modern Slavery**

2.178 Section 1 of the Modern Slavery Act 2015 (MSA) makes it an offence knowingly to hold another person in slavery or servitude, or to require him to perform forced or compulsory labour, the maximum penalty on indictment being life, and on summary conviction 12 months or a fine or both.

The part of the MSA that is likely to have most impact on employers is set out in s 54 relating to transparency in supply chains. This requires commercial organisations which supply goods and services, and which have a turnover not less than £36 million to prepare a slavery and human trafficking statement for each financial year of the organisation, showing that slavery and human trafficking are not taking place in their business or supply chains. Information which can be provided is set out in s 54(5). If the organisation has a website, it must publish the statement on it, and if it does not have one, it must provide a copy within 30 days of any request.

Summary

- Associated employers can also be employers.
- People who work may be employees, workers, or self-employed.

---

[196] n 86.

- The distinction is important because employees have the full panoply of employment rights.
- Workers also have some rights, such as working time, whistleblowing, etc.
- There are a number of different tests to determine whether someone is an employee.
- These are tests such as the control test, organisational test, mutuality of obligation, and entrepreneurial approach. These lead to a multifactorial approach, which includes one or more of these.
- All the facts of the case must be considered when deciding if someone is an employee.
- There are also categories such as office-holders, partners, directors, etc.
- There are special rules for fixed-term workers, who are generally deemed to be on indefinite contracts after four years.
- There are also special rules for agency workers, who are entitled to equal treatment after 12 weeks.

3

The Formation of a Contract of Employment

Background

3.1 A contract of employment can be entered into formally or informally. It can emerge as a result of interviews, negotiations, exchange of letters, or a casual conversation at the factory door. It can be made orally or in writing, although apprenticeship deeds and articles for merchant seamen by definition must be written. But essentially it is a contract like any other contract, and in principle subject to the general contractual rules of the common law.

3.2 However, traditional legal reasoning based on the law of contract does not always sit comfortably with the expansion of workers' rights which has occurred over the past few decades, partly because of the acknowledged inequality of bargaining power between the parties, but also because a contract of employment involves a continuing relationship, unlike most other forms of contracts which are generally single transactions. In the world of employment, the parties have to live together and work together over a period of time. There has to be an element of trust and confidence. Consequently, the courts have thus developed and expanded the doctrine of the implied term of trust and respect which is sometimes used to override strict contractual obligations, on the basis that the exercise of contractual powers by management is subject to that power being exercised reasonably and not in an unconscionable manner. Thus issues such as discretionary bonuses (*Clark v BET plc*[1]), non-contractual share options (*Mallone v BPB Industries Ltd*[2]), implementation of mobility clauses (*United Bank Ltd v Akhtar*[3]), payment of non-contractual national pay rates (*Glendale Managed Services v Graham*[4]), capricious or inequitable favouritism in non-contractual pay awards (*FC Gardner v Beresford*[5]), etc, are well outside traditional contractual doctrines. Equally, the exercise of strict contractual rights which have the effect of depriving an employee of valuable benefits may also be frustrated by the use of the implied term doctrine (*Aspden v Webbs Poultry*[6]), although more recently adherence to strict contractual principles can be noted. The law of contract, when applied to employment situations, is not static.

The Contract of Employment

3.3 There must be an offer of employment, and an acceptance of that offer. In *Wishart v National Association of Citizens Advice Bureaux Ltd*,[7] the claimant was offered a job 'subject to the receipt of satisfactory references'. The defendants received references from the claimant's existing employer which indicated that he had been absent from work through illness

---

[1] [1997] IRLR 348.
[2] [2001] All ER (D) 28 (Mar); aff'd [2002] EWCA Civ 126, [2002] ICR 1045, [2002] All ER (D) 242 (Feb).
[3] [1989] IRLR 503, EAT.   [4] [2003] EWCA Civ 773, [2003] IRLR 465, [2003] All ER (D) 225 (May).
[5] [1978] IRLR 63.   [6] [1996] IRLR 521.   [7] [1990] ICR 794, [1990] IRLR 393, CA.

for a considerable number of days, and consequently the offer was withdrawn. The claimant sought an interlocutory injunction to restrain the defendants from appointing anyone else to the post and requiring them to provide him with the job in question. The injunction was granted by a deputy High Court Judge, but on appeal the decision was reversed by the Court of Appeal. On the facts, there was a conditional offer of employment, and the only obligation on the defendants was to consider the references in good faith. Whether or not the references were satisfactory was a subjective matter. The Court of Appeal suggested that it was possible to make a conditional offer of employment subject to something which could be objectively determined, eg the passing of a medical examination, but that did not apply in this case.

3.4 If an employer makes an offer of employment, which is accepted, and before the date of performance the employer withdraws the offer, the disappointed employee is entitled to damages for breach of contract. These will usually be assessed according to the loss suffered, ie the lawful notice the putative employee would have been entitled to receive had he commenced the employment less any mitigation of the loss, unless there is a collateral contract (see para 16.8). Further, such a claim for lawful notice may be brought in the employment tribunal under the provisions of the Employment Tribunals Extension of Jurisdiction Order (see para 1.40), which permits employment tribunals to hear claims arising or outstanding 'on the termination of the employee's employment', even though, as in this case, the employment had not commenced. The phrase has to be construed as meaning 'on the termination of the employee's contract of employment' (*Sarker v South Tees Acute Hospitals NHS Trust*[8]).

3.5 Conversely, if the employer makes a job offer which contains a 'no show' clause (ie a clause which provides that the employee would pay a specified amount if he fails to take up the employment) the amount can be liquidated damages, and not a penalty. In *Tullett Prebon Group Ltd v Ghaleb El-Hajjali*[9] the defendant was a successful broker with recognised skills. He was invited to join the plaintiffs' firm, and was advised by solicitors throughout the negotiations. His attention was specifically drawn to the 'no show' clause, and he was informed that if he breached it he would be liable for a sum equal to 50% of his net basic salary plus 50% of the signing payment that the plaintiffs had agreed to pay him. He then changed his mind about taking up the employment, and he was sued for the sum of £293,000. It was held that the clause was not a penalty clause, but liquidated damages. The defendant had received expert legal advice throughout the negotiations, and was well aware that the plaintiffs would sue if he breached the 'no show' clause. The amount claimed was not extravagant or unconscionable when compared with the loss the plaintiffs had suffered.

3.6 In addition, there must be an intention to create legal relations (see *R v Lord Chancellor's Department, ex p Nangle*,[10] para 2.73). Although there may be an element of personal service, if the object of the relationship is not employment but something else (eg training), there is an absence of an intention to create legal relationship (*M & P Steelcraft Ltd v Ellis*). There must be consideration (but this doctrine does not apply in Scotland) and the absence of vitiating elements (mistake, misrepresentation, illegality, etc). The consideration for the contract is that the employee agrees to work for the employer in return for remuneration. Thus a person who does voluntary work cannot benefit from legal employment rights because he is not employed under a contract of employment (*Melhuish v Redbridge Citizens Advice Bureau*[11]), there being no consideration for his services (*South East Sheffield Citizens Advice Bureau v Grayson*[12]).

---

[8] [1997] ICR 673, [1997] IRLR 328, EAT.   [9] [2008] EWHC 1924 (QB), [2008] IRLR 760.
[10] [1992] 1 All ER 897, [1991] ICR 743, [1991] IRLR 343.   [11] [2005] IRLR 419, EAT.
[12] Unreported.

3.7 If an employee is seeking to rely on, or enforce, or found a claim on a contract of employment, that contract must not be tainted with illegality, for it is contrary to public policy to claim statutory protection in respect of an illegal contract, eg when seeking compensation for unfair dismissal or a redundancy payment. But if the protection or remedy sought does not involve relying on or enforcing the contract of employment, the illegality of that contract is not a bar to a claim. Thus, a person may claim for discrimination even though the contract is illegal (*Leighton v Michael*[13] and see *Hall v Woolston Hall Leisure Ltd*, and *Hounga v Allen*,[14] para 4.199), but if the contract is central to the claim, eg in unfair dismissal complaints, and is tainted with illegality, it will be unenforceable (*Zarkasi v Anindita & Anor*[15]). In *Cole v Fred Stacey Ltd*,[16] the employee was given an additional payment which was not taxed as income. He was subsequently made redundant, but it was held that he was not entitled to a redundancy payment, as the contract was illegal and unenforceable, being a contract to defraud the Revenue (see also *Tomlinson v Dick Evans U Drive Ltd*[17]), but see *Enfield Technical Services v Payne* para 3.10. In *Rastegarnia v Richmond Design*,[18] the applicant, who came from Iran, had been granted a work permit for a specific job. Without obtaining permission from the Department of Employment he changed his job and went to work for the respondents. He was subsequently dismissed, but his claim for unfair dismissal was rejected. His employment was unlawful, and he could not obtain any legal rights thereunder.

3.8 If a contract is lawful when entered into, and is intended by the parties to be performed legally, the fact that some of the work carried out is tainted with illegality will not render the whole contract unenforceable (*Colen v Cebrian (UK) Ltd*[19]). Thus in *Blue Chip Trading Ltd v Helbawi*[20] a foreign student was subject to an immigration condition that prohibited him from working more than 20 hours a week during term time. He subsequently claimed that he had not been paid the national minimum wage. His employer contended that the contract was tainted with illegality, because in some weeks he had worked over 20 hours a week. It was held that the legal and illegal parts of his contract could be severed, and whilst he could not claim the national minimum wage for work done when he was in breach of the immigration condition, he could succeed in a claim for those hours worked when he was not in fact in breach.

3.9 The fact that a contract of employment is ultra vires the employer's power to enter into it does not render that contract void for all purposes, and an employee employed under an ultra vires contract can still bring a claim for unfair dismissal, because his rights are determined by statute (*Shrewsbury & Telford Hospital NHS Trust v Lairikyengban*[21]).

3.10 In *Salvesen v Simons*,[22] it was held that if the terms of the contract are designed to avoid or postpone the payment of income tax then the contract is illegal, and it matters not that the parties are unaware of the illegality, but this decision has been doubted. The test for illegality is some form of misrepresentation or some deliberate attempt to conceal the true nature of the employment situation. A contract will not be rendered unlawful merely because the parties have wrongly labelled the relationship or entered into an agreement which deprives the Inland Revenue (now HMRC) of tax (*Enfield Technical Services v Payne*[23]).

3.11 The fact that the employer makes an occasional tax-free payment to the employee does not render the contract illegal, for this is not part of the remuneration as defined in

---

[13] [1995] ICR 1091, [1996] IRLR 67, EAT.   [14] [2014] UKSC 47.   [15] [2011] UKEAT/0400.
[16] [1974] IRLR 73, 9 ITR 11.   [17] [1978] ICR 639, [1978] IRLR 77, EAT.   [18] Unreported.
[19] [2003] EWCA Civ 1676, [2004] ICR 568, [2004] IRLR 210.   [20] [2009] IRLR 128.
[21] [2010] ICR 66.   [22] [1994] ICR 409, [1994] IRLR 52, EAT.
[23] [2008] EWCA Civ 393, [2008] ICR 1423, [2008] IRLR 500, (2008) *Times*, 2 June.

the contract of employment (*Annandale Engineering v Samson*[24]). Nor is a legitimate tax avoidance scheme unlawful, provided it is a proper method of reducing liability for tax and national insurance contributions, and has been (or would be) disclosed to the Inland Revenue (*Lightfoot v D & J Sporting Ltd*[25]).

3.12 A fraud or dishonesty against an employer by an employee, whilst it may be grounds for dismissal, does not make the contract inherently illegal so as to make it void ab initio (*Broaders v Kalkare Property Maintenance Ltd*[26]).

3.13 Nor will the contract be unenforceable for illegality if the employee does not receive any benefit from the illegality. In *Hewcastle Catering Ltd v Ahmed*,[27] the employers devised a scheme to avoid paying VAT, and gave certain instructions to the employees to facilitate the scheme. The employees did not receive any direct benefit. Following investigations by Customs and Excise, the employers were prosecuted and the employees were called as prosecution witnesses. They were subsequently dismissed, and claimed that the dismissals were unfair. The employers argued that the contracts of employment, being tainted with illegality, were unenforceable, but this claim was rejected. The employers had involved the employees in the fraud, but the employees did not benefit from it and were not essential parties to it. It would be contrary to public policy to deny the employees compensation when the employers had involved them in the fraud and dismissed them because they gave evidence in criminal proceedings taken against the employers.

3.14 If the alleged illegality lies in the performance of the contract, then a distinction must be drawn between the cases where the contractual obligation is to do an act which is unlawful and those where the obligations are capable of being performed lawfully, but which were in fact performed by unlawful means. In *Coral Leisure Group Ltd v Barnett*,[28] the claimant was dismissed from his post as a public relations executive. It was alleged that part of his duties was to keep rich punters happy by obtaining for them, among other things, the services of prostitutes. It was held that the fact that an immoral or unlawful act was committed during the course of the employment did not render the contract void, unless it was entered into with the object of doing that unlawful or immoral act, or the contract itself (as opposed to the mode of performance) was prohibited by law.

3.15 But the contract will only be void if the party seeking to enforce it was aware of the illegality. If it can be shown that the employee was not a party to the illegality, or did not know about it, he can still rely on the contract as an innocent party (*Davidson v Pillay*[29]). The test is not whether the employee ought to have known of the illegality, but whether he actually did know (*Corby v Morrison (t/a The Card Shop)*[30]). Thus if an employee is paid part of his wages in cash as a tax-free payment, the essential question to ask is, has the employee knowingly been a party to a deception on the Revenue (*Newland v Simons & Willer (Hairdressers) Ltd*[31])?

3.16 Although the basic rule is that the law does not uphold illegal agreements, the Court of Appeal in *Okedina v Chikale*[32] found that where an exploited Malawian national (who had been paid less than £5 per day) outstayed her visa and was therefore employed illegally, could still bring a claim for unfair dismissal and unlawful deduction from wages. The Immigration, Asylum and Nationality Act 2006 imposed penalties on those who employed people illegally, and did not deny a remedy to the employees themselves.

---

24 [1994] IRLR 59, EAT.   25 [1996] IRLR 64, EAT.   26 [1990] IRLR 421, EAT.
27 [1992] ICR 626, [1991] IRLR 473, CA.   28 [1981] ICR 503, [1981] IRLR 204, EAT.
29 [1979] IRLR 275.   30 [1980] ICR 564, [1980] IRLR 218, EAT.
31 [1981] ICR 521, [1981] IRLR 359, EAT.   32 [2019] EWCA Civ 1393.

Terms and Conditions

3.17 It is usual to speak of the 'terms and conditions of employment' which are part of every contract of employment, although no attempt ever appears to have been made to define or delineate this expression (but see *Cory Lighterage v Transport and General Workers' Union*[33] and *Universe Tankships v ITWF*[34]). It is submitted that the terms of the employment are bilateral, ie they are part of the agreement made between the employer and employee, whereas the conditions of employment are unilateral instructions which are laid down by the employer. The result is that a change in the terms can only be made by an express or implied agreement to that effect, whereas a condition can be changed by the employer unilaterally at any time (see *Cadoux v Central Regional Council*[35]) on giving reasonable notice.

3.18 For the terms of a contract of employment to apply, there must be certainty as to the commitment entered into. In *Judge v Crown Leisure Ltd*,[36] an employer made a promise to the claimant at a staff Christmas party that the employee would be put on roughly the same level of remuneration as other managers. This was held not to be legally enforceable. The words used were too vague to amount to a contractual commitment.

3.19 If an employer has a code of practice, or issues a policy statement, such documents do not necessarily constitute employment terms. In *Wandsworth London Borough Council v D'silva*,[37] the local authority issued a code of practice on staff sickness, to which they proposed to make changes unilaterally. The Court of Appeal found that the code merely set out good practice which management intended to follow, but did not constitute contractual requirements. Similarly, an equal opportunities policy was a mere statement of policy in generalised terms, and did not give rise to contractual obligations (*Grant v South-West Trains Ltd*[38]). In *Pendragon plc v Jackson*,[39] the employer inserted a clause into a share option scheme which stated that the scheme was non-contractual. It was held that the employee had no legal entitlement to any benefits under the scheme. The employers had discharged the burden of proof to show that the scheme was not intended to create a legally binding contract.

3.20 But although a policy or practice set out in a staff manual may not be contractual, if it is relied upon by an employee, it cannot be changed unilaterally to his detriment, because that would be a breach of the implied term of trust and confidence (*French v Barclays Bank plc*[40]).

3.21 Terms of employment can be found in express or implied agreements, collective agreements, and various statutory provisions; conditions of employment are usually contained in works rules, disciplinary and grievance procedures, and job descriptions. Care should be taken not to place a term or condition in the wrong category. For example, it may be a term of a contract that an employee shall be entitled to six weeks' holiday per year; it will be a condition that he shall take those holidays at particular times of the year. A term will specify the number of hours he shall work; a condition will instruct him as to when he shall work those hours. A term will specify his employment duties; a condition will lay down how he shall perform those duties. The fact of payment is a term; the mode of payment is a condition.

---

[33] [1973] 2 All ER 558, [1973] ICR 339, [1973] IRLR 152, CA.

[34] [1981] ICR 129, [1980] IRLR 239; varied [1981] ICR 129, [1980] IRLR 363, CA; on appeal [1983] 1 AC 366, [1982] 2 All ER 67, [1982] ICR 262, [1982] IRLR 200, HL.   [35] [1986] IRLR 131, Ct of Sess.

[36] [2005] EWCA Civ 571, [2005] IRLR 823.   [37] [1998] IRLR 193, CA.

[38] (C-249/96) [1998] ECR I-621, [1998] All ER (EC) 193, [1998] ICR 449, [1998] IRLR 206 [1998] 1 FLR 839, ECJ.   [39] [1998] ICR 215, [1998] IRLR 17, EAT.

[40] [1998] IRLR 646, CA.

A. **Interpretation of Terms**

3.22 Under the modern law of employment, contractual terms are subject to an over-riding obligation of trust and respect. In *United Bank Ltd v Akhtar*,[41] the claimant was subject to a clause in his contract which required him to work anywhere in Great Britain. On 5 June he was informed that as from 8 June he would be required to transfer from Leeds to a branch in Birmingham. He requested that the transfer be delayed for three months, because of his wife's illness, and also the impending sale of his house. This request was refused. He then asked if he could take 24 days' leave due to him to enable him to sort out his affairs, and he offered to commence work in Birmingham on 10 July, but he received no reply to this request. His pay was then stopped as from 5 June, so he resigned and claimed he had been constructively dismissed. His claim succeeded. There was an implied term in his contract that the employers would give reasonable notice if they wished to exercise their rights under the mobility clause (see *White v Reflecting Roadstuds Ltd*,[42] para 17.34).

3.23 Similarly, an employer may still be acting fairly even though he dismisses an employee in circumstances which amount to a breach of contract by the employer, for statutory rights and obligations exist concurrent with, but are sometimes different from, those which exist at common law (see *Hooper v British Railways Board*[43]).

3.24 In *Farrant v Woodroffe School*,[44] the claimant was employed as a laboratory technician at a school. Following a reorganisation of technical support services he was required to transfer from the science department where he worked and divide his time between other departments. He refused to accept the new job description and was dismissed. The dismissal was held to be fair. The employers had given him ample warning of the proposed change, had fully consulted with him, and thus had acted reasonably in the circumstances in dismissing him. The lawfulness of the instruction is not by itself determinative of the fairness of a dismissal.

3.25 Where the terms of a contract of employment are ambiguous, it is open to the courts to look at the practice adopted by the parties, and to attach considerable importance to it as indicating the proper interpretation of contractual terms (*Dunlop Tyres Ltd v Blows*[45]).

B. **Express Terms**

3.26 At the conclusion of the negotiations the parties may have expressly stated the terms which form the basis of the contract. These terms may deal with wages, salaries, commissions, bonuses, hours of work, the nature of the duties, holidays, overtime, sick pay, pension schemes, and so on. The task of the courts and tribunals is to interpret the meaning of such express terms in a manner consistent with industrial realism. Thus in *Cole v Midland Display Ltd*,[46] the employee was a manager employed on a 'staff' basis. He refused to do overtime without pay, and his subsequent dismissal was held to be fair. The essence of being employed as 'staff' meant that he was guaranteed his wages whether there was work or not, and during sickness. In return, 'staff' are apparently required to work reasonable overtime without pay if required to do so.

---

[41] n 4.   [42] [1991] ICR 733, [1991] IRLR 331, EAT.   [43] n 1.
[44] [1998] ICR 184, [1998] IRLR 176, EAT.
[45] [2001] EWCA Civ 1032, [2001] IRLR 629, [2001] All ER (D) 179 (Jun).
[46] [1973] IRLR 62, NIRC.

3.27 On the other hand, in *Redbridge London Borough Council v Fishman*,[47] the employee was appointed as a teacher in charge of a resource centre. Gradually, she was asked to teach more and more, and was eventually dismissed when she refused. Her dismissal was held to be unfair. A headteacher could require teachers to do work other than that for which they were engaged, provided that such requests were reasonable. In this case, the teaching was ancillary to her main job, which was as a director of the resource centre. Consequently, the headmaster's instructions went beyond the strict contractual obligations of the employee, and were therefore unreasonable.

3.28 Although it may be permissible to refer to statements made in a job advertisement to ascertain the terms of a contract (*Tayside Regional Council v McIntosh*[48]), such statement cannot override the express terms. In *Deeley v British Rail Engineering Ltd*,[49] the employers advertised for a 'Sales Engineer (Export)'. The claimant applied for the job and was appointed, but his contract was for a 'Sales Engineer'. It was held that there were no grounds for implying the word 'Export' into his contract.

3.29 If there is an express term in the contract which permits an employee to have short-term or long-term sickness benefits, or there is in force a permanent health insurance scheme, the employer cannot bring these to an end by dismissing the employee (*Adin v Sedco Forex International Resources Ltd*[50]), and it is probable that there is also an implied term that the employer will not dismiss an employee who is off work sick while covered by such a scheme (*Aspden v Webbs Poultry and Meat Group (Holdings) Ltd*). If the employer has the right to terminate the scheme without prior notice, benefits under the scheme will continue until the employee is notified of the change (*Bainbridge v Circuit Foil UK Ltd*[51]).

3.30 An express term may be used to negate a liability. In *Petrie v MacFisheries Ltd*,[52] the employers posted a notice stating that half pay for sickness would be paid as an act of grace by the company to all employees with over six months' service. All the employees knew of the position and the company acted on it consistently. It was held that the company was not bound to make payments when employees were off sick.

3.31 If an employer provides facilities for his employee's property (eg car parks, cloak-rooms, etc) he cannot restrict his liability for death or personal injury resulting from negligence, and he may only be able to restrict or exclude his liability for damage to the employee's property by a term in the contract which is reasonable in the circumstances (Unfair Contract Terms Act 1977, s 2).

3.32 If the employee is in breach of a contractual term this will be ground for dismissal. Equally, if the employer is in breach, the employee may accept the breach and bring a claim for constructive dismissal (see Chapter 17). In either event, the fairness or unfairness of the dismissal has to be determined in accordance with established legal principles, though clearly the breach of a contractual term must be regarded with greater seriousness than the breach of a non-contractual term. In *Martin v Solus Schall*,[53] the claimant signed a contract which included a clause stating 'you will be expected to work such overtime as is necessary to ensure continuity of service'. This was held to be a contractual obligation, and on the facts his dismissal for refusing to do overtime was fair.

3.33 Whether a breach by the employer of a term in a contract is so fundamental as to amount to a repudiatory breach will depend on the nature of the breach and the circumstances which gave rise to it. Thus, if there is a non-payment of agreed wages, or an

---

[47] [1978] ICR 569, [1978] IRLR 69, EAT.   [48] [1982] IRLR 272, EAT.   [49] [1980] IRLR 147, CA.
[50] [1997] IRLR 280, Ct of Sess.   [51] [1997] ICR 541, [1997] IRLR 305, CA.
[52] [1940] 1 KB 258, [1939] 4 All ER 281, CA.   [53] [1979] IRLR 1, EAT.

interference by the employer with a salary package, a distinction must be drawn between the employer's failure to pay, or his delay in paying, and his deliberate refusal to do so. A unilateral reduction in pay diminishes the value of the employee's remuneration, and undermines the whole foundation of the contract of employment. But if the failure to pay is a result of temporary fault in the employer's technology, or a simple accounting error or mistake, or due to accident or illness etc, it would be open to the court to hold that the breach did not go to the root of the contract although this may amount to a 'deduction' under ERA, s 13 (see *Elizabeth Claire Care Management v Francis*,[54] para 8.22). A repeated or persistent failure or delay, or one which was unexplained, might lead the court to hold that the breach was indeed repudiatory (*Cantor Fitzgerald International v Callaghan*[55]).

3.34 At one time it was thought that a breach of contract by an employee amounted to a 'constructive resignation', but this view is now regarded as being incorrect (see *London Transport Executive v Clarke*,[56] para 17.52). The legal position is that the employer may 'accept' the breach or not, as he wishes. If he does accept the breach, he dismisses the employee, and the fairness of the dismissal must be justified in accordance with the usual principles (see Chapter 17).

A strike by an employee is a breach of contract, as is a refusal to perform contractual duties. Either of these events gives rise to legal consequences, including the right of the employer to deduct a sum of money from the wages or salary of the employee, calculated on a proportional basis (*Sim v Rotherham Metropolitan Borough Council*[57]).

C. Implied Terms

3.35 Occasionally the courts and tribunals are prepared to imply a term into the contract in circumstances where the parties did not expressly insert a term to meet a particular contingency. The theory adopted was that the term in question was so obvious that the parties did not see the need to state it expressly. Clearly, a certain amount of judicial hindsight is required in order to imply a term after a dispute has arisen, and there is frequent room for disagreement on whether or not the court was correct in making its assumptions. However, in *Mears v Safecar Security Ltd*,[58] the Court of Appeal held that the correct approach was to consider all the facts and circumstances before implying a term into the contract, including the way the parties had carried out the contract since it was formed (further guidance was also given by the Supreme Court in *Marks & Spencer plc v BNP Paribas*,[59] a non-employment case). There is no presumption either way about an implied term. For example, in *O'Grady v M Saper Ltd*,[60] the employee claimed his wages for a period in which he had been off work through sickness. He had been away sick before, and had not received any wages. Indeed, he never asked for them nor expected them, until he saw an item in a newspaper which led him to believe that he might be able to claim. It was held that there was an implied term that he would not be paid.

3.36 The original justification for the implied term theory was the need to give business efficacy to the contract, but there is now a much wider approach, implying terms which are a necessary incident of a definable category of contractual relationship. In *Scally v Southern Health and Social Services Board*,[61] the claimant was a doctor, whose terms and conditions

---

[54] [2005] IRLR 858.   [55] [1999] 2 All ER 411, [1999] ICR 639, [1999] IRLR 234, CA.
[56] [1980] ICR 532, EAT; revsd [1981] ICR 355, [1981] IRLR 166, CA.
[57] [1986] 3 All ER 387, [1986] ICR 897, [1986] IRLR 391.
[58] [1983] QB 54, [1982] 2 All ER 865, [1982] ICR 626, [1982] IRLR 183, CA.
[59] [2015] UKSC 72.   [60] [1940] 2 KB 469, [1940] 3 All ER 527, CA.
[61] [1992] 1 AC 294, [1991] 4 All ER 563, [1991] ICR 771, [1991] IRLR 522, HL.

of employment were to be found in a statutory scheme. This scheme gave doctors the right to purchase added years of pension entitlement, but this valuable right had to be exercised within certain time limits. The claimant was never informed about the scheme, and so he failed to exercise his option to purchase the added years' pension. When he did discover the existence of the scheme, he was outside the time limits. He claimed that his employers had broken an implied term of the contract by failing to take reasonable steps to bring to his notice his right to enhance his pension entitlement by the purchase of added years. The House of Lords unanimously upheld his claim. It was noted that the terms of the contract had not been negotiated with the individual employee, but were negotiated with a representative body or otherwise incorporated by reference. The contract thus contained a valuable right for the employee, but this was contingent on him taking action to avail himself of the benefit. He could not be expected to do this unless the term was drawn to his attention. There was an implied term, therefore, that the employer could take reasonable steps to bring the provisions of the pension scheme to the employee's attention, so that he could enjoy its benefits if he so wished.

3.37 But there is no implied term in a contract of employment that an employer will take reasonable care for the economic well-being of an employee. In *Crossley v Faithful and Gould Holdings Ltd*,[62] a senior employee wished to resign his employment due to ill health. His employer did not advise him that if he did so he would lose entitlements under a permanent health insurance scheme, and he claimed that there was an implied term that his employer should have warned him about the effect of his retirement on his entitlement to that benefit. The Court of Appeal dismissed his claim. The claimant was a senior employee who should have been familiar with the terms of the insurance scheme, and he also had access to expert advice. It would impose an unfair and unreasonable burden on employers to imply a term that they should assume responsibility for financial advice in relation to benefits accruing from employment. The Court of Appeal noted that in *Scally's* case the House of Lords set out three strict criteria which had to be satisfied before placing a duty on an employer to inform employees of contractual benefits, one of which was that the employee cannot reasonably be expected to be aware of the particular term. This criterion was not satisfied in the instant case. But the EAT has held that there is an implied term that an employer will take reasonable steps to ascertain whether an employee is entitled to the benefit of an ill health retirement scheme, and it could be an unfair dismissal if the employee is thereby deprived of the benefits under the scheme (*First Leeds v Haigh*[63]).

3.38 It is not possible to imply terms which are too vague or unpredictable to be given efficacy, or to which the parties would not have agreed had the matter been drawn to their attention (*Lake v Essex County Council*[64]). Thus, in *Cresswell v Board of Inland Revenue*,[65] staff employed by the Inland Revenue habitually carried out their tasks by dealing manually with files and records. The Inland Revenue introduced a programme of computerisation, and the claimant alleged that in so doing there was a breach of contract, arguing that there was an implied term that he could not be required to perform tasks or carry out functions in a manner other than that which they had habitually used by custom and practice. He sought a declaration that he could not be required to operate computerised systems. It was held that the employers were not in breach of the contract by requiring employees to use computer systems. An employee is expected to adapt himself to new methods and techniques introduced in the course of his employment. It is a question of fact whether the retraining involved the acquisition of such esoteric skills that it would not be reasonable

---

[62] [2004] EWCA Civ 293, [2004] All ER (D) 295 (Mar).   [63] [2008] IRLR 182, EAT.
[64] [1979] ICR 577, [1979] IRLR 241, CA.   [65] [1984] 2 All ER 713, [1984] ICR 508, [1984] IRLR 190.

to expect the employee to acquire them. Nowadays, it is not unusual to ask an employee to acquire basic skills such as retrieving information from a computer or feeding information into one. However, the employer must be expected to provide any necessary training for the acquisition of these skills.

3.39 If exceptional circumstances arise, there is an implied term that an employee can be asked to perform duties which are outside his strict contractual obligations. Thus in *Luke v Stoke-on-Trent CC*,[66] an employee claimed she had been bullied. After the matter was investigated, she was offered temporary redeployment, which involved her doing work which was outside her contractual obligations. When she refused to accept the temporary change, her employers stopped paying her wages. Her subsequent claim against her employer was dismissed. The work was suitable for her to perform, she would have suffered no disadvantage in terms of contractual benefits or status, and the change in her duties was a temporary matter, designed to meet an exceptional circumstance.

3.40 Legal decisions have established that there is an implied term that an employer will treat the employee with respect and trust, and will not treat an employee in an arbitrary or vindictive manner. Thus, falsely to accuse an employee of theft (*Robinson v Crompton Parkinson Ltd*[67]), unreasonably to deny an employee an increase in remuneration which had been granted to other employees (*FC Gardner Ltd v Beresford*[68]), and, in the case of a large firm, to refuse to give an employee time off work to deal with a domestic emergency (*Warner v Barbers Stores*[69]), have all been held to amount to conduct by the employer which could constitute a breach of the implied term that the employer should treat an employee fairly and reasonably.

3.41 It may be possible to imply a term by reference to the practices of the industry and/or the national agreements which are in force. For example, in *Stevenson v Teesside Bridge and Engineering Ltd*,[70] a steel erector's employment was governed by the national agreement for the time being in force in the industry. Although there was no express term in his contract stating that he was expected to work away from home, this was clearly envisaged, for the national agreement made provision for lodging allowances, travelling expenses, etc. The court held that there was an implied term in his contract that he could be sent anywhere to work, for it was recognised that in the construction steel industry, where sites are, by their very nature, scattered around the country, employees know that mobility is a feature of their employment.

3.42 There is an implied term that the employer will not prevent the employee from performing his contract of employment, or delay or hinder him so as to prevent him from earning his full remuneration, but the employer is entitled to take steps which may improve that performance, and to see that the work is done in a proper manner, for example, by engaging time and motion experts (*Davies v Richard Johnson & Nephew Ltd*[71]). If an employee is contractually obliged to do overtime without pay, there is an implied term that the requirements of overtime will always be reasonable and would not be excessive (*Gilbert v Goldstone Ltd*[72]). On the other hand, if a contract of employment is silent on the actual place of work, it may be necessary to imply a term to give that contract business efficacy. In *Jones v Associated Tunnelling Co Ltd*,[73] it was held that there was an implied term that the employers were entitled to require the employee to work anywhere within a reasonable daily commuting distance from his home.

---

[66] [2007] IRLR 305, EAT; aff'd [2007] EWCA Civ 761, [2007] IRLR 777, [2007] ICR 1678.
[67] [1978] ICR 401, [1978] IRLR 61, EAT.   [68] n 6.   [69] [1978] IRLR 109, EAT.
[70] [1971] 1 All ER 296, DC.   [71] (1934) 78 Sol Jo 877, 51 TLR 115.
[72] [1977] 1 All ER 423, [1977] ICR 36, [1976] IRLR 257, EAT.   [73] [1981] IRLR 477, EAT.

3.43 An implied term is sometimes used to give the contract business efficacy (or business common sense: see *Marshall v Alexander Sloan & Co Ltd*[74]). Thus if a contract provides for the payment of sick pay, but is silent on the period for which it is payable, there is an implied term that the obligation is for a reasonable period only (*Howman & Son v Blyth*[75]).

3.44 There is also an implied term that the employer will not conduct his business in a fraudulent and dishonest manner so as to cause damage to the employees' reputation and consequently place him at a disadvantage in the labour market (*Malik v BCCI SA*[76]). However, a claimant must be able to show that the failure to obtain fresh employment was because of the stigma (*BCCI SA v Ali (No 3)*[77]).

3.45 The original basis for the implied term theory was that it is the court's (or tribunal's) view about a provision that was 'obvious' where the contract was silent. In *Shell UK Ltd v Lostock Garage Ltd*,[78] Lord Denning suggested that if a contract of employment did not define the obligations of the parties, the courts (or tribunals) should ask what would be reasonable in the general run of such cases, and then say what the obligation shall be. This view was followed in *Pepper and Hope v Daish*[79] and appears to have general acceptance, even though there is a fundamental difference between importing into a contract an implied term which is 'obvious' and one which is 'reasonable'. The courts have gone on to express the view that there is an implied term that the employer will not conduct himself in a manner likely to destroy or seriously damage the relationship of confidence and trust between the employer and employee, and if the conduct has that effect, then the question of whether there has been a reasonable and proper cause for the behaviour must be considered. If such reasonable and proper cause could not be shown, the employer would be acting in a manner which no reasonable employer would adopt. Thus to offer a particular benefit to the entirety of one class of employees bar one is capable of being an act calculated to seriously damage or destroy the trust and confidence between the employer and that employee (*BG plc v O'Brien*[80]). If it is done without reasonable and proper cause, it would be a breach of the employer's obligation of fair dealing (*Johnson v Unisys Ltd*[81]). But if the employer had reasonable and proper cause to act in the manner he did, then even though there are adverse consequences to the employee, there is no breach of the implied duty of trust and confidence (*Hilton v Shiner Ltd*[82]).

3.46 The implied term of trust and respect is both positive and negative, in the sense that it may require the employer to do something, as opposed to refrain from doing something. Thus there can be a breach of the term if an employer decides not to offer an employee a new contract, or a variation of the old one. There is an obligation to treat employees in a fair and even-handed manner (*Transco plc v O'Brien*[83]).

3.47 The contracts of employment of professional employees do not always detail the contractual obligations, and these may be defined by reference to the nature of the profession and the obligations incumbent on those who follow that profession (*Sim v Rotherham Metropolitan District Council*, see para 3.38).

---

[74] [1981] IRLR 264.   [75] [1983] ICR 416, [1983] IRLR 139.
[76] [1995] 3 All ER 545, [1996] ICR 406, [1995] IRLR 375, CA; revsd [1998] AC 20, [1997] 3 All ER 1, [1997] ICR 606, [1997] IRLR 462, HL.
[77] [2001] UKHL 8, [2002] 1 AC 251, [2001] 1 All ER 961, [2001] ICR 337, [2001] IRLR 292, [2001] All ER (D) 06 (Mar).
[78] [1977] 1 All ER 481, CA.   [79] [1980] IRLR 13, EAT.   [80] [2002] ICR 721, (2002) IRLR 444.
[81] [1999] 1 All ER 854, [1999] ICR 809, [1999] IRLR 90, CA; aff'd [2001] UKHL 13, [2003] 1 AC 518, [2001] 2 All ER 801, [2001] ICR 480, [2001] IRLR 279, [2001] All ER (D) 274 (Mar).
[82] [2001] IRLR 727, [2001] All ER (D) 316 (May), EAT.
[83] [2001] IRLR, [2001] All ER (D) 169 (May), EAT; aff'd sub nom *O'Brien v Transco plc (formerly BG plc)* [2002] EWCA Civ 379, [2002] ICR 721, [2002] IRLR 444, [2002] All ER (D) 80 (Mar).

3.48 There is no implied term that an employer will look after the employee's property (clothes, car, etc) which are left on the employer's premises (*Edwards v West Herts Group Hospital Management Committee*),[84] though there is an obligation under the Workplace (Health, Safety and Welfare) Regulations 1992 for employers to provide suitable and sufficient accommodation for clothing which is not worn during working hours, and if there is a statutory obligation to do something, a failure to comply with that requirement will amount to a breach of an implied term (*W A Goold (Pearmak) Ltd v McConnell*[85]). Nor is there an implied term that an employee will be entitled to work overtime if the employer is not contractually obliged to provide overtime (*McClory v Post Office*[86]).

3.49 There is no implied term that the employer will provide personal accident insurance for the benefit of an employee who is required to work abroad, or that the employer should give specific advice on special risks, and advise the employee to take out personal accident insurance (see *Reid v Rush & Tompkins Group plc*, para 10.34). Nor can a duty in tort be imposed to enlarge on contractual duties.

If there is no agreement on the matters which should be included in the written statement which has to be given to employees under the provisions of s 1 of the Employment Rights Act 1996, it is not be possible to rely on an implied term concerning matters which ought to be, but are not, set out in the statement (eg whether an employee is entitled to accrued holiday pay on a pro rata basis, see *Morley v Heritage plc*[87], but see now Working Time Regulations, para 7.53).

3.50 It is clear that if an employer breaks an express term of the contract, the employee may 'accept' the breach, resign from his employment, and claim that he has been 'constructively' dismissed (see para 17.21). This is equally true in the case of a breach of an implied term, and in particular when the conduct of the employer amounts to a breach of the implied term of mutual trust and confidence which must exist between the parties (*Post Office v Roberts*[88]). These developments will be considered in detail in Chapter 17.

3.51 A term can only be implied into a contract of employment if it would have existed at the time the contract was made. Thus, generally speaking, it is not possible to imply a term when there is a changed situation (*Casson Beckman & Partners v Papi*[89]). Nor can an implied term be used to override an express term, although it may be used as a means of qualifying or explaining an express term (*Stevedoring & Haulage Services Ltd v Fuller*, see para 2.177).

3.52 It is not for the judiciary to speculate on what might have been agreed. Thus in *Ali v Christian Salvesen Food Services Ltd*,[90] individual contracts of employment were varied by a collective agreement. Certain topics had been omitted, and the Court refused to fill in the gaps.

D. **Statutory Terms**

3.53 Superimposed on all contracts of employment are a number of statutory terms. These are in addition to a considerable number of statutory 'rights' which have been created by various legislative provisions. Thus the Equality Act 2010 imports an equality clause into contracts of employment, minimum wages for appropriately qualified persons are guaranteed by the National Minimum Wage Act 1998, and various employment rights are

---

[84] [1957] 1 All ER 541, CA.   [85] [1995] IRLR 516, EAT.
[86] [1993] 1 All ER 457, [1992] ICR 758, [1993] IRLR 159.   [87] [1993] IRLR 400, CA.
[88] [1980] IRLR 347, EAT.   [89] [1991] BCLC 299, [1991] BCC 68, CA.
[90] [1996] ICR 1, [1995] IRLR 624, EAT; revsd [1997] 1 All ER 721, [1997] ICR 25, [1997] IRLR 17, CA.

contained in the Employment Rights Act 1996 and various regulations, etc. These statutory terms may be improved upon by agreement between the parties, but any attempt to oust them will be of no effect.

E. **Collective Agreements**

Express Incorporation of the Terms of a Collective Agreement

3.54 A collective agreement is an agreement made between an employers' association, or a single employer, on the one hand, and a trade union, on the other, which, as well as laying down the procedure which will govern the relationship between the signatories, will also provide for the terms and conditions of employment of those covered by the agreement. There are currently about 6.3 million employees who are members of trade unions, and many of these, but not all, will doubtless be covered by such agreements; there is also an unknown number of non-trade unionists in respect of whom their employer will apply the terms of a relevant collective agreement. There are, however, a number of different situations to consider. There can be a national or federation agreement, made between an employers' association and a trade union, on the conclusion of which the individual employers who are members of the association will start to apply its provisions to their employees. There is no rule of law which requires this, only the practice of industrial relations. The terms of the agreement will be binding in law on the individual employer and the employee if, and only if, they are expressly or impliedly incorporated into the individual contract of employment. The same rule applies to a local or plant agreement, which is usually made between a single employer and a trade union. Also, there are some employers who, though not members of the employers' association, voluntarily undertake to observe the terms of a negotiated agreement.

3.55 In *Framptons Ltd v Badger*[91] the EAT gave a useful summary of the effect of a collective agreement on the contract of employment, as follows:

(a) employees do not derive rights directly from the collective agreement. The parties to the agreement are the employer and the union, and the union does not act as agent for its members;

(b) there is a presumption that the collective agreement is not intended to be legally enforceable as between the parties. Nonetheless, the rights and obligations found in the collective agreement can bind the employer and employee by being incorporated into the individual's contract of employment;

(c) incorporation can operate expressly or by implication. In order to determine whether this has occurred, it is necessary to focus on the relationship between the employer and the employee, not the employer and the trade union;

(d) not all terms typically found in a collective agreement will be incorporated. The terms must be suitable to take effect as contractual terms. Some terms will not be suitable, because they are too vague or aspirational;

(e) the terms of a collective agreement may continue to operate and bind the parties to the individual contract even when the collective agreement is brought to an end, and even possibly when the employer has withdrawn recognition from the union;

(f) there is a strong presumption that the parties to the individual contract of employment will have intended that the terms shall continue to be derived from the collective agreement, even after that agreement has ceased to have effect, if the consequence of not doing so is that there would be no binding contractual terms at all.

---

[91] EAT/0138/06.

3.56 Certain terms contained in a collective agreement govern the relationship between the trade union and the employer. Other terms are designed to benefit individual employees, and this becomes part of the contract of employment (*National Coal Board v National Union of Mineworkers*[92]). These latter terms are said to have a 'normative' effect. In *Alexander v Standard Telephones and Cables plc*,[93] the claimant was employed on the basis of the terms contained in a collective agreement. The agreement contained a redundancy procedure, which stated that LIFO ('last in first out') would be the basis of selection in the event of compulsory redundancies. The company wished to select on the basis of skills and flexibility, and the claimant sought an injunction to prevent this. The application failed, but it was suggested that there was an arguable case that the terms of the collective agreement formed part of his contract of employment. Any remedy for breach of that contract would lie in an action for damages and the case was sent for trial on that basis (see para 3.60).

3.57 The authority of a trade union to enter into agreements which will be binding on its members vis-à-vis their employers stems from express authority, from implied authority, or by virtue of the law of agency. Express authority will normally arise when a trade union (or an authorised official) is asked or is invited to negotiate on a specific issue which affects its members. Implied authority arises when a union negotiates nationally or locally on matters which affect all members (eg wage increases), and usually is inferred from the conduct of the parties and the circumstances of the case. Under the law of agency, a union would need ostensible or apparent authority to negotiate with an employer or employers. The mere fact that an employee is also a member of a trade union does not necessarily mean that the union has that authority (*Burton Group Ltd v Smith*[94]), although nowadays the courts appear to be more willing to accept that a trade union official (or shop steward, in appropriate circumstances) has apparent or ostensible authority to negotiate a revision of terms and conditions of employment (*Harris v Richard Lawson Autologistics Ltd*[95]).

3.58 The 'normative' terms of a collective agreement may be incorporated into the individual contract of employment by an express provision to this effect. For example, employment may be undertaken on the basis of 'union rates of pay', or 'union conditions'. It is at least arguable that the former term refers solely to the wages rates clauses in the collective agreement, whilst the latter term may be somewhat wider, and may include other provisions. In *Jewell v Neptune Concrete Ltd*[96] the employee's written particulars stated that his rate of wages was to be based on the national agreement. It was held that this did not, by itself, incorporate the working rule agreement's lay-off provisions into his contract of employment. Employees who work for public bodies are normally engaged on the basis of the appropriate scale laid down by the negotiating bodies and the only scope for individual bargaining may be on the precise point of entry into the scale for salary purposes. Thus, in *Knox v Down District Council*[97] the Northern Ireland Court of Appeal were prepared to incorporate into the employee's contract of employment an assisted car purchase scheme which had been negotiated by the National Joint Council, the terms of which were expressly incorporated into his contract. In *National Coal Board v Galley*,[98] the defendant was employed on the basis of 'the national agreements for the time being in force'. These agreements required him to do a certain amount of overtime, and when he refused to do a Saturday morning shift it was held that he was in breach of his contract.

[92] [1986] ICR 736, [1986] IRLR 439.   [93] [1990] ICR 291, [1990] IRLR 55.
[94] [1977] IRLR 351, EAT.
[95] [2002] EWCA Civ 442, [2002] ICR 765, [2002] IRLR 476, [2002] All ER (D) 214 (Mar).
[96] [1975] IRLR 147.   [97] [1981] IRLR 452, NICA.   [98] [1958] 1 All ER 91, CA.

3.59 Frequently the terms of a collective agreement will be expressly incorporated into the individual contract by means of the statement given to the employee under ERA, s 1. In *Camden Exhibition and Display Ltd v Lynott*,[99] notices issued to the employees stated that their hours of work, wages, etc, would be in accordance with the working rule laid down by the National Joint Council for the industry. Rule 6 of this agreement stated that 'Overtime required to ensure the due and proper performance of contracts shall not be subject to restriction, but may be worked by mutual agreement and direct arrangement between the employer and operatives concerned.' Workmen who were dissatisfied with a wage award decided to cease overtime working. It was held that r 6 was a term of the contracts of employment of each employee. However, its effect was obscure. Lord Denning thought that it meant that the workmen would not collectively impose an overtime ban, but Russell LJ thought that the rule did not import into the contract of any individual an agreement not to limit overtime save for a reason special to himself.

3.60 To determine whether or not the terms of a collective agreement can be incorporated into an individual's contract of employment, regard must be had to the contractual intentions of the parties. In *Alexander v Standard Telephones and Cables plc*,[100] the claimant was given a statement of written particulars, issued under ERA, s 1. This stated that the basic terms and conditions of employment were in accordance with and subject to the provisions of a plant agreement negotiated by his employers and a trade union. One of the terms of the collective agreement provided that in the event of redundancy, selection will be on the basis of service with the employers. When the company wished to make a number of employees redundant, it was decided to retain employees whose skills and flexibility were best suited to the circumstances. The trade union insisted that selection should be on the basis of length of service. After negotiations broke down, the employers went ahead with their proposals, and the claimant was one of those dismissed. He sought an interlocutory injunction to restrain the employers from terminating his employment without applying the principles of collective agreement, but this was refused. He also claimed damages for breach of contract, arguing that he would have continued in his employment until retiring age.

His claim for damages was dismissed. The only relevant document applicable to the claimant's employment was the written statement issued under ERA, s 1. This had to be construed in accordance with the relevant contractual principles. The statutory statement did not deal with redundancy matters, and therefore it did not incorporate the terms of the collective agreement into his contract of employment. The collective agreement itself, not being a contract, could be incorporated into the individual contract of employment if there was a cogent indication that this was intended. However, the clauses in question had to be considered in the context of a joint consultation scheme of a procedure agreement, and it was not sufficiently cogently worded to support the inference of incorporation into the individual contract of employment. In *Malone v British Airways plc*[101] it was held that the terms of a collective agreement which set out minimum cabin crew numbers for aircraft on long-haul flights did not form part of the cabin staff's employment contracts, and an application for an injunction to prevent the airline from reducing cabin crew numbers was refused. It had not been intended that the statement in the collective agreement would be incorporated and thus enforceable by individual employees.

A contrary view was taken by the Court of Session in *Anderson v Pringle of Scotland Ltd*,[102] where the claimant's terms and conditions of employment were in accordance with the agreement made between the employer and a trade union. This agreement contained, inter alia, a redundancy procedure which provided that selection for redundancy was on

---

[99] [1966] 1 QB 555.   [100] n 94.   [101] [2011] IRLR 32, [2010] EWCA Civ 1225, [2011] ICR 125.
[102] [1998] IRLR 64, OH.

the basis of last in first out (LIFO). When the employers decided to make a large number of employees redundant, they decided not to follow that procedure, but instead to use a selective scheme. The claimant would not have been selected under LIFO because of his long service, but he was to be chosen for redundancy under the selective scheme. He sought an injunction to prevent the employers from selecting for redundancy on any basis other than LIFO. The court granted the injunction. It was decided that the relevant terms of the collective agreement made between the employers and the trade union had been incorporated into the contracts of employment of the individual employees. Further, although the injunction would appear to have the effect of enforcing the performance of a contract of employment—which is not normally permissible (see Chapter 10)—in this case there was no loss of trust or confidence in the employee, for the issues were the mechanics of dismissal rather than the principles of dismissal. Whilst it might be difficult for the employer to abide by the LIFO selection system, it was not unfair to hold them to the agreement they had made (see also *Edinburgh Council v Brown*[103]).

The terms of the collective agreement must be suitable for incorporation into the individual contract of employment. In *Griffiths v Buckinghamshire County Council*[104] a redundancy procedure agreement negotiated between the employers and a trade union recommended that 12 months' notice of impending redundancies should be given. It was held that this was advisory in nature, and was a procedural, not a contractual obligation. Equally, a statement made in a collective agreement that the employer will not institute a compulsory redundancy programme is aspirational, and not intended to be incorporated into any individual's contract of employment (*MG Rover Group Ltd v Kaur*[105]).

3.61 Once the terms of a collective agreement are incorporated into the individual contract of employment, they are part of that contract, and cannot be unilaterally altered.

In *Robertson v British Gas Corpn*[106] the employee was appointed as a gas meter reader/collector, his letter of appointment stating that an incentive bonus scheme would apply. The terms of this scheme were negotiated between the employers and a trade union. Subsequently the employers gave notice to the trade union to terminate the scheme, and no new scheme was negotiated. The employee brought an action for arrears of pay. It was held that the letter of appointment was a binding contract, which gave the right to an incentive bonus scheme. Although the collective agreement had no legal force as between the signatories, it was incorporated into the employee's contract, and the employers could not terminate the scheme unilaterally.

3.62 A different result was reached in *Airlie v Edinburgh District Council*,[107] where the employers entered into a collective agreement with trade unions representing workers in the direct labour organisation which contained, inter alia, a bonus scheme. The scheme was incorporated into the individual contract of employment, but a clause permitted the employers to alter it after consultation with the unions. When the department was making a loss, the employers wanted to alter the scheme. The unions agreed that alterations had to be made, but there was a failure to reach agreement. Nonetheless, the employers modified the scheme, which resulted in a reduction in the wages of the employees concerned. It was claimed that an unlawful deduction had been made from wages, but the claim was dismissed by an employment tribunal and the EAT. The employers had properly consulted the unions about the changes, but there was nothing in the scheme which required the agreement of either the employees or the trade unions concerned.

3.63 Indeed, the fact that the collective agreement contains a clause to the effect that its terms are binding in honour only does not affect the legal enforceability of those terms

[103] [1999] IRLR 208, EAT.   [104] [1994] ICR 265.   [105] [2005] IRLR 40, CA.
[106] [1983] ICR 351.   [107] [1996] IRLR 516, EAT.

which are expressly or impliedly incorporated into the individual contract (*Marley v Forward Trust Group Ltd*[108]). However, a distinction must always be made between contractual terms, which are bilateral in effect, and rules, which are unilateral. The latter do not have a legally binding effect (*Cadoux v Central Regional Council*, see para 3.17).

Implied Incorporation of the Terms of a Collective Agreement

3.64 It is equally possible to incorporate the terms of a collective agreement into an individual contract of employment by implication. In certain types of employment it will be 'assumed' that employees are employed on the basis of union/management agreements. Thus, in *MacLea v Essex Line Ltd*,[109] the plaintiff took a job as a seaman, and the court implied into his contract the contents of an agreement made by the National Maritime Board, which was the negotiating forum for the industry. In *Wilton Ltd v Peebles*[110] employers had paid to their employees for 20 years the annual pay increases negotiated by a national agreement made between the trade unions and the employers' trade association, and the EAT confirmed that, despite the absence of any written terms of employment or oral agreement as to pay, there was an implied term that the wages of employees were to be those stipulated in the national agreement.

3.65 If a contract of employment (or the written particulars which evidence that contract) states that pay will 'normally be in accordance with' nationally negotiated rates, 'as adopted from time to time', or if there is collective agreement which has not been specifically incorporated into the individual contract, then there is an implied term that the employer will inform the employee if and when there is a departure from the normal situation. An employee is entitled to assume that such national rates will be applied unless he is informed to the contrary (*Glendale Managed Services v Graham*, see para 3.2).

3.66 The terms of a collective agreement can also be incorporated into an individual's contract of employment by virtue of custom and practice, provided the custom and practice is reasonable, certain, and notorious. In *Henry v London General Transport Services Ltd*,[111] the employers, in preparation for a management buy-out, entered into negotiations with a trade union over changes to the employees' terms and conditions of employment. These negotiations resulted in a framework agreement which set out new and less advantageous terms and conditions, including reduced rates of pay. After holding workplace meetings, the union informed the employer that the majority of the staff affected had consented to the new terms, and these were subsequently put into effect. A number of dissident employees brought claims in an employment tribunal alleging unlawful deductions from wages (see Chapter 8). It was held that the tradition of collective bargaining between the employer and the trade union was sufficient to enable fundamental changes to be made in the employees' contract of employment, by virtue of custom and practice.

3.67 If the employers are not members of the employers' association, there is little scope for the implied incorporation of the terms of an industry-wide collective agreement into the individual contract of employment. There would have to be strong evidence to indicate that the agreement had been so incorporated by way of custom and practice (*Hamilton v Futura Floors Ltd*[112]).

Changing the Terms of a Collective Agreement

3.68 Terms which are incorporated into the contract of employment as a result of a collective agreement remain part of that contract until or unless they are changed either by

---

[108] [1986] ICR 115, [1986] IRLR 43, EAT; revsd [1986] ICR 891, [1986] IRLR 369, CA.
[109] (1933) Ll L Rep 254.   [110] Unreported.
[111] [2000] All ER (D) 2049, EAT; aff'd [2002] EWCA Civ 488, [2002] IRLR 472, [2002] All ER (D) 322 (Mar).
[112] [1990] IRLR 478, OH.

agreement with the employees concerned or under a specific right contained in the contract. The trade union is not, per se, an agent of its members with authority unilaterally to negotiate a variation. Thus, in *Lee v GEC Plessey Telecommunications*,[113] the employers had reached an agreement with trade unions in 1985 which gave enhanced redundancy terms to its employees. In 1990 they purported to withdraw those terms, but, following objections from the unions, negotiations took place on revised terms. An agreement appeared to have been reached which enabled the employers to withdraw the enhanced redundancy payments and substitute less favourable terms, but this was on the basis that there would be no further redundancies in the future. However, redundancies were announced, and individual employees brought an action for a declaration that the attempt to vary the enhanced redundancy terms was ineffective. Their claim succeeded in the High Court. It was not necessary to give fresh consideration every time a new collective agreement was reached, for a continuation by the workforce in their employment was a value attributed to the employer. Although the employers could unilaterally determine the collective agreement, this would not be effective to change the terms contained in the individual contracts of employment. Nor were the trade unions acting as agents for their members when they attempted to negotiate the change. They were acting in a collective manner, not on behalf of each individual.

3.69 Another example is *Burke v Royal Liverpool University Hospital NHS Trust*,[114] where the claimant was employed as a domestic worker. Her terms and conditions of employment were regulated by a Whitley Council agreement. In order to assist the trust in submitting a competitive tender, the two recognised trade unions agreed to less favourable terms and conditions than those previously enjoyed. The tender was successful, the lower wage rates were put into effect, but the claimant made a complaint under the protection of wages provisions of the ERA, claiming that an unlawful deduction had been made to her wages. An employment tribunal held that the agreement made between the unions and the trust constituted a collective agreement which has the effect of incorporating the new terms and conditions into the claimant's contract of employment. An appeal against this decision was dismissed. The claimant had signed the new contract, the consideration for her agreement to accept a reduction in her wages was the greater sense of security of employment, and the agreement was capable of being incorporated into her contract of employment.

3.70 If an agreement states that its terms can be changed after consultation, that does not require the agreement of the parties, and, provided the consultation is carried out in good faith, changes can be made unilaterally (*Airlie v Edinburgh District Council*, para 3.62).

Collective Agreements and Non-unionists

3.71 Just as the terms of a collective agreement may be binding on a non-federated employer who assents to it, so also will those terms apply to a non-unionist if his contract of employment states so expressly. In the absence of such express incorporation, the collective agreement will not apply. In *Singh v British Steel Corpn*,[115] the employee's contract stated that he was to work a 15-shift system over a five-day week. He resigned from his trade union, and instructed his employers to cease paying the union subscription under a check-off agreement. The union then negotiated a new agreement with the employers which provided for a 21-shift system over a seven-day week, but the employee refused to agree to this, and was dismissed. It was held that there was nothing in his contract which permitted a change in the system of working, either by the employers unilaterally or by means of a collective agreement. The tribunal thought that while he was a member of the union he was bound by such agreements because it was his negotiating body, but when he

[113] [1993] IRLR 383.   [114] [1997] ICR 730, EAT.   [115] [1974] IRLR 131.

left he ceased to be bound. The union and the employers had no power to vary the terms of his agreement without his consent.

3.72 There is clearly less scope for the implied incorporation of the terms of a collective agreement into the contracts of employment of non-unionists. In *London Passenger Transport Board v Moscrop*,[116] a collective agreement provided that an employee on a disciplinary charge could be accompanied by a trade union official. The claimant was a member of another union which had not been a party to the agreement, and he wished to be accompanied by an official of his own union. It was held that the terms of the agreement were not necessarily applicable to employees who were not members of the signatory union. In *Singh v British Steel Corpn* (para 3.71) it was equally held that there was no implied term of his contract that as a non-union member he would be bound by union agreements.

Backdating Agreements

3.73 A further problem can arise when the terms of a collective agreement are backdated. As a general rule, it would seem that there is no implied term in a contract of employment that a wage award can be backdated, although this may come about by an express agreement to that effect. However, an express agreement cannot override the statutory position. In *Leyland Vehicles Ltd v Reston*[117] the claimant was made redundant in February, and received his redundancy payment calculated on the basis of the wages he was then receiving. In April a new wage agreement was negotiated with the union, and this was backdated to January. The claimant contended that his redundancy pay should be calculated so as to take account of the increase in his wage rate, but his claim was dismissed by the EAT. Section 225 of ERA refers to the amount of pay actually payable at the calculation date. It does not include increases made by agreement concluded after the employment has ended, even though the agreement provided for the backdating of the increase. The payment of a backdated wage increase to employees who have left the firm is usually a matter to be considered on an *ex gratia* basis.

Conflicting Collective Agreements

3.74 A difficulty sometimes arises when there is an overlap between the national agreement and a local agreement which covers the same or similar ground. In *Clift v West Riding County Council*[118] the claimant was paid less by virtue of a local agreement than he would have received on the basis of a national agreement. It was held that since the local agreement was later in time, its terms prevailed. But the 'latest agreement prevails' doctrine is not a rule of law, as *Gascol Conversions Ltd v Mercer*[119] demonstrates. Here, a national agreement provided that the working week should be 40 hours, and overtime worked as necessary. It also stated that if the national agreement was at variance with any local agreement, the national agreement was to prevail. A subsequent local agreement provided that the working week should be 54 hours. The employee was made redundant, and the question arose as to whether his redundancy payment was to be calculated on the basis of a normal working week of 40 hours or one of 54 hours. The Court of Appeal held that the employee was employed on the basis of the national agreement, and though it was at variance with the local agreement, its terms took precedence.

Which Terms are Employment Terms?

3.75 Another difficulty is to determine which terms of a collective agreement are to be incorporated into the individual contract of employment. Clearly, there are many terms which are capable of such incorporation, such as wage rates, hours, overtime payments,

---

[116] [1942] AC 332, [1942] 1 All ER 97, HL.   [117] [1981] ICR 403, [1981] IRLR 19, EAT.
[118] (1964) *Times*, 16 July.   [119] [1974] ICR 420, [1974] IRLR 155, CA.

travel allowances, and so on. Equally, there are other terms which govern the relationship which is to exist between the signatories, and have no relevance to the individual contract of employment. For example, in *Gallagher v Post Office*,[120] the defendants recognised two trade unions for negotiating purposes, and informed their employees that they were entitled to join either union. Recognition was then withdrawn from one union, and the claimant alleged that this constituted a breach of contract. It was held that there was no term, express or implied, that the Post Office should continue to recognise the union to which the claimant belonged. Any statement about recognition was purely informative, and not part of the contract of employment of any individual employee.

3.76 Some difficulty has been experienced in the past with the 'no strike' clause, or the procedural aspects of settling disputes. In *Rookes v Barnard*,[121] this clause was held to have been incorporated into the contracts of employment of the employees, but as the point was conceded rather than argued, the case adds little to our knowledge of the subject. A great deal may well turn on the precise wording of the agreement. Supposing this wording states 'the union will not call a strike until the procedure for settling the dispute is exhausted'. This is an obligation on the union, and is not part of the contracts of employment of the employees. Supposing the agreement states 'the employees will not go on strike until the procedure for settling the dispute is exhausted'. This term is clearly capable of being so incorporated. However, by TULR(C)A, s 180, the incorporation of such a clause will not be binding unless:

(a) the collective agreement is in writing;

(b) it expressly states that the terms are to be incorporated into the individual contract;

(c) a copy of the collective agreement is reasonably accessible to the employees concerned;

(d) the agreement is made by an independent trade union; and

(e) the individual contract of employment expressly or impliedly incorporates the terms of the collective agreement.

However, it must be borne in mind that a strike, whether in breach of a collective agreement or not, is always a breach of contract at common law, so that the effect of s 180 must be minimal.

F. Custom as a Source of Employment Terms

3.77 It is sometimes argued that terms of employment can be found in those practices which are customary in a particular industry or local area, or even within a single firm (as in *Park Cakes Ltd v Shumba & Ors*,[122] where the Court of Appeal held that enhanced redundancy payments paid over a period of time can become contractually binding through custom and practice). Support for this view can also be gleaned from the case of *Sagar v Ridehalgh*,[123] where a deduction from the wages of a cotton weaver for bad workmanship was upheld by virtue of the existence of a long-standing custom of the trade which, apparently, was well known. The general rule is that a custom must be reasonable, notorious, and certain (*Devonald v Rosser & Sons*[124]). It must also not be contrary to law, and strictly proved. Custom can even override a policy statement where an employee benefit

---

[120] [1970] 3 All ER 712.

[121] [1963] 1 QB 623, [1961] 2 All ER 825; revsd [1963] 1 QB 623, [1962] 2 All ER 579, CA; revsd in part [1964] AC 1129, [1964] 1 All ER 367, HL.

[122] [2013] EWCA Civ 974.   [123] [1930] 2 Ch 117; revsd [1931] 1 Ch 310, [1930] All ER Rep 288, CA.

[124] [1906] 2 KB 728.

is described as being 'ex gratia' (*Albion Automotive Ltd v Walker*[125]), but an alleged custom cannot be in conflict with an express term of the contract (*Dunlop Tyres Ltd v Blow*[126]).

3.78 In *Hardwick v Leeds Area Health Authority*,[127] the claimant was dismissed after exhausting her period of sick pay, which was an entitlement of two months on full pay and two months on half pay. This was in accordance with the normal practice of the Health Service. It was held that such an automatic rule, whereby an employee could be dismissed irrespective of the circumstances, was totally outmoded and unreasonable, and the dismissal was held to be unfair. In *Singh v British Steel Corpn* (para 3.71) the fact that the claimant had considered himself in the past to be bound by trade union agreements was not sufficient evidence to establish a custom to that effect. Moreover, in *Gascol Conversions v Mercer* (para 3.74) the court stated that if the parties had reduced the contract to writing, it is not permissible to say that they intended something else, and thus it would appear that a custom cannot override a written statement of the terms of employment.

3.79 This point has considerable implications when, as sometimes happens, an appeal is made to 'custom and practice' as a basis of employment terms. It is true that in *Heaton's Transport Ltd v Transport and General Workers' Union*[128] the House of Lords upheld custom and practice as being the basis of the authority of a shop steward to initiate action on behalf of a trade union, but this was a case where the union rule book was silent on the point. However, it might be easier to argue that 'custom and practice' can override the terms of a collective agreement which has been incorporated into an employment contract (see *Parry v Holst & Co*,[129] para 3.107). It is also arguable that a 'custom' is different from a 'practice'. The former has a legal significance which the latter does not possess. In *Spencer Jones v Timmens Freeman*,[130] it was a 'common practice' in the hairdressing trade for shops to be open on Saturday afternoons, but this did not make it a custom.

3.80 Clear and compelling evidence is required to establish that a custom and practice exists (*Henry v London General Transport Services Ltd*[131]). In *Samways v Swan Hunter Shipbuilders Ltd*[132] the claimant, who was originally employed as a labourer, was appointed as a chargeman over a gang, and was given an additional £4 per week allowance. The company then informed him that owing to a reduction in production, it was necessary to withdraw the allowance, and he was offered employment as a labourer. It was held that this constituted a dismissal for reason of redundancy, as there was a reduction in the requirements of the company for chargemen. An argument by the company that, by virtue of custom and practice, chargemen's allowances were temporary payments for additional responsibility so long as this lasted was rejected by the tribunal, who thought that the 'allowance' was in fact remuneration. That other men had, in the past, reverted from the job of chargeman to their former positions was not sufficient to establish a custom, for their conduct could be explained on the ground that they wanted to keep their job with the firm, and it did not follow that they were contractually bound to do so.

3.81 It is submitted that with the increasing formalisation of contracts of employment, the scope for custom and practice as a source of employment terms has decreased, and indeed there is very little by way of modern legal authorities which could indicate that 'custom and practice' have any relevance in modern employment law. For example, in *Quinn v Calder Industrial Materials Ltd*,[133] a policy document was issued to all member companies of a

[125] [2002] EWCA Civ 946.   [126] [2001] EWCA Civ 1032, [2001] IRLR 629.
[127] [1975] IRLR 319.
[128] [1997] AC 15, [1972] 2 All ER 1214, CA; revsd [1973] AC 15, [1972] 3 All ER 101, [1972] ICR 308, [1972] IRLR 25, HL.   [129] (1968) 3 ITR 317, DC.
[130] [1974] IRLR 325.   [131] n 112.   [132] [1975] IRLR 190.   [133] [1996] IRLR 126, EAT.

group holding company, which contained guidelines on additional redundancy payments. The document had not been formally communicated to the employees or their trade unions, although its terms were generally known. Indeed, enhanced redundancy payments based on the document had been made on four occasions, although a decision to do so had to be made by higher management on each such occasion. When the claimant was made redundant, he was not given any enhanced redundancy payment, and he contended that the employers were in breach of their contractual obligation. He argued that his entitlement to enhanced payments had been incorporated into his contract through custom and practice. His claim failed. Factors to be taken into account include whether management had drawn the attention of employees to the policy, whether it had been followed without exception for a substantial period, and whether employees had a genuine expectation that the terms of the policy would be applied to them. In the circumstances, it was not possible to infer that the policy document had achieved the status of a contractual obligation. But a different conclusion on somewhat similar facts was reached in *Harlow v Artemis International Corporation Ltd*,[134] where an additional ground for holding that an enhanced redundancy payment policy was contractual was that it was also part of the individual's contract of employment through 'custom and practice' (see *Keeley v Fosroc International Ltd*,[135] para 3.84).

G. **Works/Staff Rules**

3.82 These are generally set out in staff handbooks, although some employers issue booklets or post notices containing the rules of the workplace. Such rules can either be part of the contractual terms or unilaterally imposed instructions, a distinction which is important because in the former case they can only be changed by mutual assent and agreement, whereas in the latter case the employer may, at any time and on reasonable notice, change them (see *Cadoux v Central Regional Council*[136]) and substitute new instructions or impose new obligations, and a failure by the employee to obey would be a breach of his duty to follow all lawful and reasonable orders.

3.83 Thus in *Bateman v Asda Stores Ltd*[137] the firm's staff handbook contained details of pay and other conditions of employment, which were incorporated into the contracts of employment of all staff. One clause read: 'The Company reserve the right to review, revise, amend or replace the contents of this handbook, and introduce new policies from time to time reflecting the changing needs of the business.' It was proposed to bring in a new pay structure, which was implemented after due consultation. A number of staff brought claims alleging unlawful deduction of wages, breach of contract, and unfair dismissal, but these were dismissed by an employment tribunal and the decision was upheld on appeal by the EAT. The changes were within the terms of the handbook, and were made in a manner that did not breach the implied term of trust and confidence.

3.84 The courts appear to be more willing to incorporate the terms of a company's handbook as part of the contract of employment by looking at the importance of the provision to the overall bargain, including the employee's remuneration package. For example, even though an enhanced redundancy package is expressed to be discretionary, it may be contractual if there is evidence that it has been consistently applied in the past, and it is proper for the court to enforce a discretionary power (see *Keeley v Fosroc International Ltd*, para 3.81). In *Small v Boots Co plc*[138] a bonus scheme, which was stated in the staff handbook to be discretionary and not intended to be contractual, was nonetheless held to have a contractual

---

[134] [2008] EWHC 1126 (QB), [2008] IRLR 629.   [135] [2006] EWCA Civ 1277, [2006] IRLR 961.
[136] n 37.   [137] [2010] IRLR 370.   [138] [2009] IRLR 328.

effect. The term 'discretionary' may be attached to the decision whether or not to pay a bonus at all, or it may refer to the method of calculating the bonus, or it may refer to the amount of the bonus. All the relevant circumstances must be taken into account, including the invariable practice of making payments over many years.

3.85 But a code of practice to be invoked in cases of long-term sickness (*Wandsworth London Borough Council v D'silva*, see para 3.19) and an equal opportunities policy (*Grant v South-West Trains Ltd*, para 3.19) were statements of policies in general terms, and not contractual documents (but see *French v Barclays Bank plc*, para 3.20).

3.86 The fact that a change in the company's rules bears hard on a particular individual does not justify an inference that the employer has acted in such a way as to repudiate the contract of employment. In *Secretary of State for Employment v Associated Society of Locomotive Engineers and Firemen*,[139] railwaymen proposed to engage in a work-to-rule campaign. If the rule book, by which they were working, was a part of their contracts of employment, then by adhering to it, albeit strictly, they could hardly be said to be breaking their contracts. However, one of the rules stated that employees should 'make every ef-fort to facilitate the working of trains and prevent unavoidable delay', which would clearly prohibit any deliberate attempt to interpret the rules in such a way as to achieve disruption of services, and to that extent there was clearly a breach of contract on either view of their legal significance. But Lord Denning held that the rules were 'in no way terms of his (ie the individual railwayman's) contract of employment. They were only instructions to a man on how he was to do his work.' It will clearly be an implied term of his contract of employment that he will interpret those rules reasonably.

3.87 In *Peake v Automotive Products*[140] it was held that the contents of a rule book were non-contractual administrative arrangements for running the factory. If this view is cor-rect, then works rules are non-negotiable instructions laid down by the employer. They may deal with all manner of subjects, including the method of performing the work, safety policy, disciplinary matters, concessions and privileges, and so on. A breach of the rules may lead to appropriate penalties. In *Blake v Berkel Auto Scales Co Ltd*[141] an employee was summarily dismissed for a serious breach of the company's rules, and the dismissal was held to be fair. Indeed, a rule may be enforced even though the employee is in no way blame-worthy. In *Jeffries v BP Tanker Co Ltd*[142] the company had a rule that an employee with a history of cardiac disease should not be employed at sea as a radio officer, and an employee who had had two heart attacks was held to have been fairly dismissed, even though he had made an excellent recovery. The rule in this case was more in the nature of company policy.

3.88 But this does not mean that an employer can lay down rules and act on them in an au-tocratic manner, for the courts and tribunals will use the test of reasonableness to circum-scribe management prerogatives. The rules must be clear and unambiguous; their contents must be made known to the employees, and be reasonable in the circumstances. Thus in *Talbot v Hugh H Fulton Ltd*[143] an employee was dismissed for having long hair, contrary to the works rules. It was held that this would only be reasonable if there was a safety hazard, and if the exact length which was acceptable was made known. Presumably the rule should have applied to female employees as well, otherwise it would have been discriminatory. (For a further discussion of dress codes, see para 4.21.)

---

[139] [1972] 2 QB 443, [1972] 2 All ER 853, [1972] ICR 7; aff'd sub nom *Secretary of State for Employment v Associated Society of Locomotive Engineers and Firemen (No 2)* [1972] 2 QB 455, [1972] 2 All ER 949, [1972] ICR 19, CA.

[140] [1977] QB 780, [1977] ICR 480, [1977] IRLR 105; revsd [1978] 1 All ER 106, [1977] ICR 968 sub nom *Automotive Products Ltd v Peake* [1977] IRLR 365, CA.

[141] [1974] IRLR 272.   [142] [1974] IRLR 260.   [143] [1975] IRLR 52.

3.89 There may be circumstances when some aspects of the works rules can be regarded as contractual terms, despite their unilateral nature. In *Briggs v Imperial Chemical Industries Ltd*[144] the claimant was employed as a process worker at a cyanide plant. The employers decided to pull the plant down and build another one, and consequently he was asked to work elsewhere in the firm as a process worker. He refused and claimed that he was entitled to a redundancy payment. The Divisional Court dismissed his appeal from an employment tribunal finding that he was not entitled. His terms of employment were governed by the statement given under ERA, s 1 (see para 3.109), which stated that his pay would vary with the job he was performing, and clearly this contemplated that he could be transferred from one job to another. Also, he had been issued with a booklet containing the works rules of the factory, r 17 of which stated 'You must accept the right of management to transfer you to another job with a higher or lower rate of pay, whether day work, night work or shift work.' The court held that r 17 was a term of his employment, but this is probably because there was some implied (if obscure) reference to the works rules in his contract of employment. It would seem to follow that if the contract makes express reference to the works rules as being part of the contract of employment, they will more readily be regarded as part of the contractual terms. In *Singh v Lyons Maid Ltd*[145] it was a requirement of the company that employees should not wear beards; this was in order to maintain the company's high standards of hygiene. The applicant knew of this rule, but nonetheless grew a beard in accordance with his religious beliefs. The dismissal was held to be fair (before the introduction of religious discrimination legislation). He had refused to obey a contractual term which the employers felt to be fundamental and which did not appear to be unreasonable.

3.90 At this stage it can only be said that the legal significance of the rules is a question of fact, to be determined by the circumstances of each case. For example, if the company's rule permits security guards to search employees before they leave the premises, will a refusal to be searched amount to a breach of an express term of the contract, or will it amount to a breach of the duty to obey a lawful (and reasonable) order? If a company does not have such a 'search' policy, but wishes to introduce one, can it be done unilaterally, or must the consent of each individual employee be obtained? Would a refusal to agree to be searched amount to 'some other substantial reason' for dismissal, by analogy with *R S Components Ltd v Irwin* (see Chapter 19[146])? In *Trotter v Grattan plc*,[147] the employer, with the support of trade unions, introduced a random body search policy, in order to minimise thefts from the premises. The claimant objected to the policy and resigned, claiming constructive dismissal. An employment tribunal held that this was a unilateral variation of the claimant's contract and amounted to a breach of the implied term of trust and confidence, entitling the claimant to resign. However, it went on to hold that the dismissal was for 'some other substantial reason', and in the circumstances, fair.

Other Aspects of the Contract of Employment

A. Disciplinary and Grievance Procedures

3.91 It is generally a condition of the contract that the employment is subject to the disciplinary and grievance procedures which are in force from time to time. These procedures are unilateral in the sense that it is the employer's responsibility to draw them up, with the co-operation of the employees and/or any relevant trade union if possible, without such assistance if necessary. Some form of incorporation into the individual contract of

---

[144] (1968) 5 KIR 492, 3 ITR 276, 112 Sol Jo 541, DC.   [145] [1975] IRLR 328.
[146] [1974] 1 All ER 41, [1973] ICR 535, [1973] IRLR 239, NIRC.   [147] IDS Brief 757 18.

such conditions is also desirable, especially if these procedures are contained in a collective agreement, for this will then avoid the problems of incorporation so far as non-unionists are concerned.

3.92 But if a disciplinary procedure is incorporated into the contract, it must be adhered to, and a failure may attract the usual legal remedies. In *Jones v Lee and Guilding*,[148] the claimant was dismissed from his post as headmaster of a Roman Catholic school after he had divorced his wife and remarried. His conditions of tenure stated that before any decision to dismiss a teacher was taken, the teacher had a right to be heard and to be represented before the local education authority. This procedure had not been followed, and the Court of Appeal granted an injunction restraining the school managers from purporting to dismiss the claimant without a hearing being held by the local education authority. In *Gunton v London Borough of Richmond*,[149] the claimant was given one month's notice of dismissal, though the disciplinary procedure, which was conceded to be part of his contract of employment, had not been fully implemented. The Court of Appeal held that his damages for wrongful dismissal should be limited to the loss he had suffered, which was assessed by reference to a reasonable period it would have taken the employer to implement the disciplinary procedure. (The decision was followed, albeit with some reluctance, by another division of the Court of Appeal: see *Boyo v Lambeth London Borough Council*.)[150]

3.93 Disciplinary procedures, discussed in Chapter 12, are designed to ensure that the employee is given every possible opportunity to put right any conduct which is likely to be the subject of critical appraisal; to this extent, the object of the procedure is corrective rather than punitive. Grievance procedures are designed to ensure that the individual employee has a proper outlet for such complaints that he may have, so as to prevent an employee from nursing a grievance.

B. Job Description

3.94 It is common to draw up and give to an employee a job description document, detailing the nature of his duties. Again, this should be a unilateral document, and should be specific enough to identify the employee's tasks, yet general enough to enable variations to take place within the context of the contract. The ambit of contractual obligations is not the same as the ambit of the duties which an employee in fact performs. This is especially true in small firms, where greater flexibility is needed, and thus the former may be wider than the latter (*Glitz v Watford Electric Co Ltd*[151]). An employer may be able to change the job description provided the proposed work is still within the contractual obligations.

3.95 The fact that a job description contains a flexibility clause does not give the employer carte blanche to change the fundamental nature of the employee's work. Any job change without the employee's assent must be qualified by the requirement that the change must be reasonable, and within the scope of the employee's contract (*Land Securities Trillium Ltd v Thornley*[152]).

C. Variation of Contractual Terms

3.96 Any variation does, like any other express term, have to be certain. Thus an announcement made by an employer to all the workforce can amount to a variation if it is in sufficiently certain terms and there is an intention to create legal relations (*Dresdner*

---

[148] [1980] ICR 310, [1980] IRLR 67, CA.   [149] [1980] 3 All ER 577, [1980] ICR 755, [1980] IRLR 321, CA.
[150] [1994] ICR 727, [1995] IRLR 50, CA.   [151] [1979] IRLR 89, EAT.   [152] [2005] IRLR 765.

Kleinwort Ltd v Commerzbank AG v Attrill).[153] The terms of the contract of employment may only be varied with the consent of both parties, and there is no power which enables one side to act unilaterally, unless the contract unambiguously provides for a unilateral variation (*Security Facilities Division v Hayes*[154] and see para 3.104). It follows that a unilateral variation which is not accepted amounts to the repudiation of the contract. Thus if an employee is demoted, this will be repudiatory conduct by the employer, and a consequent resignation by the employee will be an acceptance of the repudiation and hence is, in law, a dismissal by the employer (see *Marriott v Oxford and District Co-operative Society (No 2)*[155]). But if, subsequent to the variation, the employee stays on with the firm for a considerable length of time, it is likely that he may be regarded as having accepted the change, and the modified contract will be in existence. This may be regarded as implied acceptance (see *Wess v Science Museum Group*[156]). Where an employee protests about the change, but continues with the employment, it is a question of fact in each case as to whether or not he has accepted it (albeit under protest). If an employee continues to work under revised terms and conditions, albeit under protest, for a considerable length of time, it will be extremely difficult to conclude other than that he has accepted the revised terms (*Henry v London General Transport Services Ltd*, para 3.66). In *Khatri v Cooperative Centrale Raiffeisen-Boerenleenbank BA*,[157] however, a trader did not sign a variation letter presented by the employer, and was not pressed to do so. He continued to work for the bank. It was held that nothing in his conduct implied his acceptance of the change. The employer had purported unilaterally to change the terms of the contract, but the fact that the employee continued to work did not automatically mean acceptance of changes which were disadvantageous to him.

3.97 The employer unilaterally varies the contract if he insists that the employee performs duties other than those contained in the contract, as in *Dwyer v Superguard Ltd*,[158] where the applicant was engaged as a telephonist/typist. Typing work declined, and she was under-employed. She was asked to take on other work, splitting invoices, but she refused and was dismissed. This was held to be unfair, for her contract could only be varied with her consent. However, such a situation could be dealt with in future cases either by stating in the contract an obligation 'to perform such other duties as may be assigned from time to time', or by declaring a redundancy situation and making an offer of alternative employment.

3.98 An employer has no right unilaterally to vary the terms of a contract of employment, eg by reducing wages or salaries (*Miller v Hamworthy Engineering Ltd*),[159] and if he does so, the employee is entitled to a common law remedy for the whole of the time the employer is in breach, and not merely for the period of notice which the employer could lawfully give to terminate the contract. In *Rigby v Ferodo Ltd*[160] the claimant's wages were £192 per week, and his contract of employment terminable by 12 weeks' notice. As a result of a financial crisis, the employers tried to get the trade unions to agree to wage reductions, but the unions refused to agree. The employers then unilaterally reduced the plaintiff's wages by £30 per week. The claimant continued to work at the lower rate, but issued a writ claiming damages for breach of contract. The House of Lords upheld his claim. The employers had unilaterally repudiated the contract, but the employee had not accepted that repudiation, and thus the contract had not been terminated by the reduction in wages. Thus the employee was entitled to damages for the breach of contract for the whole of the period of the breach, and

---

[153] [2013] EWCA Civ 394. [154] [2001] IRLR 81, CA.
[155] [1969] 1 All ER 471; revsd [1970] 1 QB 186, [1969] 3 All ER 1126, CA. [156] UKEAT/0120/14/DM.
[157] [2010] EWCA 397. [158] Unreported. [159] [1986] ICR 846, [1986] IRLR 461, CA.
[160] [1987] ICR 457, [1987] IRLR 61, CA; aff'd [1988] ICR 29, [1987] IRLR 516, HL.

not for the period after 12 weeks when the employers could have lawfully terminated the contract. Whether a shop steward has apparent or ostensible authority to negotiate changes in terms and conditions of employment is a question of mixed fact and law, to be resolved according to the facts of each case (*Harris v Richard Lawson Autologistics Ltd*, para 3.57).

3.99 An employee has been 'dismissed' for the purpose of ERA, s 95(1) even though he remained in employment. Thus in *Alcan Extrusions v Yates*[161] the employers wished to impose a new working pattern system, which had the effect of reducing the employees' earnings. After negotiations with trade unions had failed, the new pattern was unilaterally imposed. Employees sent a pro forma reply to the employers, stating that they would work the new system under protest, reserving their rights to claim unfair dismissal and/or redundancy payments. It was held they had been dismissed. Where an employer unilaterally imposes radically different terms of employment, that could amount to a dismissal if the changes constitute a very substantial departure from the old contract. In this case, the old contract had been removed, and a new, substantially inferior, contract had been substituted.

3.100 But a contract of employment cannot remain static over the years, and some element of change is inevitable. In strict law, a variation must be mutually agreed by both sides, but if an employee refuses to accept such a change this does not mean that he can exercise a power of veto over any new proposal. Ultimately, the employer retains an equal right lawfully to terminate the contract. In *Grix v Munford Ltd*[162] the employee was dismissed when she refused to work a new shift system at a service station, which the employers had claimed was necessary on the grounds of efficiency and financial expediency. The employment tribunal, in holding that the dismissal was fair, gave some guidelines on the approach which employers should adopt in these circumstances. They should consult fully and properly with the employee, and they must give reasonable and due consideration to any objections or alternative suggestions. It is also necessary to prove that the change is necessary, and thus amounts to 'some other substantial reason' should a dismissal prove to be necessary. It is not necessarily unfair to dismiss an employee who refuses to obey an order which is outside the terms of his contract, for the test is focused on the reasonableness of the employer's actions, not whether the employer was in breach of the contract (*Farrant v Woodroffe School*, para 3.24; see also *Luke v Stoke-on-Trent CC*, para 3.39). In *Bowater Containers Ltd v McCormack*,[163] the claimant was a supervisor. After a reorganisation, it was decided that another small section should come under his supervision. He refused to take on these additional duties, as he maintained that he was not contractually obliged to do so. His dismissal was held to be unfair by the employment tribunal, but the decision was reversed by the EAT. The reason for the dismissal, ie consequent on the reorganisation, was some other substantial reason and, in the circumstances, the employers had acted reasonably.

3.101 It is possible to dismiss an employee (with proper notice) and then offer to rehire him on new terms and conditions. There are a number of variations with such a policy, all of which give rise to legal complications. The simplest situation arises if the reason for the dismissal was redundancy, for then the provisions of ss 138–141 of ERA will come into effect (see chapter 18). If there is a TUPE situation the variation must be unconnected with the transfer, or an economic, technical, or organisational reason entailing a change in the workforce, or a reason connected with a business rescue provision (see Chapter 9). A change in terms and conditions can be permitted by an express term in the contract (eg a flexibility or mobility clause), or when the change has been made by a collective agreement which has been incorporated expressly or impliedly into the employee's contract of employment.

---

[161] [1996] IRLR 327, EAT.   [162] Unreported.   [163] [1980] IRLR 50, EAT.

3.102 If an employer wishes unilaterally to change the terms or nature of the contractual obligations, and the employee objects to the change, he has two choices; (a) he could refuse to work under the new terms, and, if the employer still insists on imposing them, he can resign and claim constructive dismissal, or (b) he can work under the new terms under protest, and sue for breach of contract. But if he agrees to work under the new terms until matters are resolved, a subsequent refusal to comply with them can constitute a refusal to obey a lawful order, for which he may be dismissed (*Robinson v Tescom Corporation*[164]).

3.103 Thus if the employer wishes to vary the contract, and the employee refuses to accept the variation, the employer must give notice to terminate the contract (*Rigby v Ferodo Ltd*[165]). This will, of course, amount to a dismissal, and would normally give the employee a right to bring a claim for unfair dismissal. In such proceedings, the employment tribunal may make a finding as to the advantages to the employers of the proposed changes, and whether it was reasonable for them to implement them by terminating the contract and offering a new one. The question then becomes one of whether the employers acted reasonably in dismissing the employee for his refusal to enter into the new contract (*Chubb Fire Security Ltd v Harper*[166]). To answer this question, the nature of the new offer, the advantages to the employer, and the method of handling the situation, the incentives offered, etc all become relevant considerations (*Hollister v National Farmers' Union*[167]). The dismissal will be fair if the offer is one which a reasonable employer would make in the circumstances (*Richmond Precision Engineering Ltd v Pearce*[168]). The employment tribunal should not look solely at the advantages and disadvantages of the new contract from the employee's point of view, but should also consider and take into account the benefits to the employer in seeking to impose the change (*Catamaran Cruisers v Williams*[169]).

3.104 However, the express terms of the contract may permit substantial variations, and if this is so the other party is bound to accept, whether he agrees in principle or not. The terms may expressly permit a change in the location of employment, or the duties of the employee, or any other relevant matter. In *Bex v Securicor Transport Ltd*[170] it was a condition of the employee's contract that the nature of his work could be changed by the company. When they appointed him to another position, which he regarded as a demotion, he resigned. It was held that as the employers were expressly entitled to require the employee to serve the company in any capacity, there had been no breach of contract by the employer, and consequently his resignation did not amount to a dismissal. He had the choice of carrying out his contract, or resigning.

3.105 Although an oral variation to the contract can be made where both parties agree, where there is an express term stating 'No Oral Modification', then a subsequent oral variation is not valid (*Rock Advertising Ltd v MWB Business Exchange Centres Ltd*[171]).

3.106 An implied variation, accepted by both sides, may be inferred from the parties' conduct. In *Armstrong Whitworth Rolls v Mustard*,[172] when the employee was engaged, his hours were fixed by a national agreement, and he worked an eight-hour shift for five days per week. One of his workmates left, and he was asked to work 12-hour shifts for five days per week. This arrangement continued for seven years, and when he was eventually made redundant, it was held that his redundancy payment was to be based on a normal working week of 60 hours. Although there was no express mutual agreement to vary his hours, such agreement could clearly be inferred from the conduct of the parties.

---

[164] [2008] IRLR 408.   [165] [1988] ICR 29, [1987] IRLR 516.   [166] [1983] IRLR 311, EAT.

[167] [1978] ICR 712, [1978] IRLR 161, EAT; revsd [1979] ICR 542, [1979] IRLR 238, CA.

[168] [1985] IRLR 179, EAT.   [169] [1994] IRLR 386, EAT.   [170] [1972] IRLR 68.

[171] [2018] UKSC 24.   [172] [1971] 1 All ER 598, DC.

3.107 A contract may also be varied by virtue of the terms of a collective agreement. In *Parry v Holst* (see para 3.79) the claimant's employment was expressly governed by the terms of the Working Rule Agreement of the Civil Engineering Construction Conciliation Board, Clause XD (f) of which provided that '[a]t the discretion of the employer, an operative may be transferred at any time during the period of his employment from one job to another'. The employee's work in South Wales came to an end, and his employers asked him to work in Somerset. He refused, and claimed a redundancy payment. It was held that he was not entitled. His employment was subject to the Working Rule Agreement, which provided for travelling and shift allowances, and there was nothing unusual about the employers' request. However, if the proposed transfer had been so unreasonable that it could be said to be outside the contemplation of the parties to the contract, then the literal application of Clause XD (f) would be precluded. Also, it was suggested that the Clause would not apply if there was a custom and practice of a particular company which would have the effect of varying the way the rule operated. None of these considerations applied in this case, and the application for a redundancy payment was rejected.

3.108 Where a variation of an existing contract is based on a change brought about by a revised collective agreement, the change will only be binding on individual employees if it is accepted by them, or if they were collectively represented at the time the change was agreed (*Land and Wilson v West Yorkshire Metropolitan County Council*[173]). Thus employees who are not union members, or who are members of another union, are not necessarily bound by the change. But if the collective agreement is expressly incorporated into the individual's contract, or if the union has authority to negotiate a change, the variation will bind (*Nelson and Woollett v Post Office*[174]).

D. Written Particulars of the Contract of Employment

3.109 Section 1 of the Employment Rights Act 1996 provides that no later than the commencement of employment (before 6 April 2020 this was 'no later than two months'), the employer shall give to the employee a written statement containing the following information:

(1) (a) the names of the employer and employee;

(b) the date when the employment began;

(c) the date on which the employee's period of continuous employment began, taking into account any employment with a previous employer which counts towards continuity;

(2) as at a specified date, not more than seven days before the statement is given (or the instalment of a statement given under section 2(4) ERA):

(a) the scale or rate of remuneration, or the method of calculating remuneration;

(b) the intervals at which remuneration is paid;

(c) any terms and conditions relating to
(i)   normal working hours,
(ii) the days of the week the worker is required to work, and
(iii) whether or not such hours or days may be variable, and if they may be how they vary or how that variation is to be determined.;

[173] [1981] ICR 334, [1981] IRLR 87, CA.   [174] [1978] IRLR 548, EAT.

(d) any terms and conditions relating to:

(i) entitlement to holidays, including public holidays, and holiday pay (being sufficient to calculate the entitlement, including accrued holiday pay on the termination of employment);

(ii) incapacity for work due to sickness or injury, including any provision for sick pay and any other paid leave;

(iii) pensions and pension schemes;

(iv) any other benefits provided by the employer;

(e) the length of notice the employee is obliged to give, and entitled to receive to determine the employment;

(f) the title of the employee's job;

(g) if the employment is not intended to be permanent, the period for which it is expected to continue; if it is for a fixed term, the date when it is to end;

(ga) any probationary period, including any conditions and its duration;

(h) either the place of work or, where the employee is required or permitted to work at various places, an indication of that, and of the address of the employer;

(j) any collective agreement which directly affects the terms and conditions of employment; where the employer is not a party to the agreement, the persons by whom they are made;

(k) where the employee is required to work outside the United Kingdom for more than one month:

(i) the period for which he is to work outside the United Kingdom;

(ii) the currency in which remuneration is to be paid while so working;

(iii) any additional remuneration payable to him, and any benefits to be provided by reason of his working abroad; and

(iv) any terms and conditions relating to his return to the United Kingdom;

(l) any training entitlement provided by the employer,

(m) any part of that training entitlement which the employer requires the worker to complete, and

(n) any other training which the employer requires the worker to complete and which the employer will not bear the cost of.

3.110 So far as the matters in para 3.109 are concerned, it should be noted that:

(a) if there are no particulars to be entered under any of these headings, that fact should be stated;

(b) the written statement may refer the employee to the provisions of some other document which he has a reasonable opportunity of reading in the course of his employment, or which is made reasonably accessible to him in some other way, in respect of sick pay and pension schemes;

(c) all the above particulars may be given in instalments except terms and conditions relating to pensions, collective agreements, and details given to employees who are to work outside the United Kingdom. These terms may be contained in a separate document or documents.

A statement, insofar as it relates to the particulars required by section1(4)(d)(iii), (j) and (l) and the note required by section 3—

(a); and

(b) must be given not later than two months after the beginning of the employment, even where the employment ends before that date;

3.111 In addition to the matters required to be given by s 1, s 3(1) requires that the statement shall include a note:

(a) specifying any disciplinary rules applicable to the employee or referring him to the provisions of a document which is reasonably accessible to him specifying such rules;

(b) specifying any procedure applicable to the taking of disciplinary decisions relating to the employee, or a decision to dismiss him, or referring to the provisions of a document which is reasonably accessible to him and which specifies such procedure;

(c) specifying (by description or otherwise) a person to whom the employee can apply if dissatisfied with any disciplinary decision relating to him, or any decision to dismiss him.

3.112 However, the s 3 requirements do not apply to rules, disciplinary decisions, decisions to dismiss, grievances, or procedures relating to health and safety at work.

3.113 Sections 7A and 7B of ERA (inserted by the Employment Act 2002) provide that the employer meets his obligation under s 1 and s 3 if he provides a written contract of employment or letter of engagement at the beginning of employment which provides the s 1 and s 3 information.

3.114 If there is any change in the matters specified in the written particulars, the employer shall give, within one month of the change, the relevant particulars (s 4(1)).

3.115 It must be borne in mind that the statement given by virtue of s 1 is not necessarily a contract, and is not conclusive evidence of that contract (*System Floors (UK) Ltd v Daniel*[175]). But it certainly helps to establish what those contractual terms were, and a failure by an employer to provide such a statement may well lead an employment tribunal to draw adverse presumptions against that employer in subsequent litigation, should the terms of the contract be in dispute.

3.116 If an employer does not provide the written statement under s 1, or if it is incomplete, the employee can require a reference to be made to an employment tribunal to determine what particulars ought to be included in such a statement. But this power only extends to matters which should be in the statement in accordance with the above statutory requirements. The tribunal has no power to amend or rewrite a contract of employment merely because there is some misunderstanding about its meaning (*Construction Industry Training Board v Leighton*[176]).

3.117 An employment tribunal may only state those terms which have been agreed. They cannot remake the contract and insert terms which should have been agreed. 'Mandatory' terms can be determined by looking at all the evidence, including the express, implied, and statutory terms. If there has been no agreement on the 'non-mandatory' terms, the employment tribunal should record this (*Eagland v British Telecommunications plc*[177]). There is no power to insert terms which have not been agreed. For example, in *Cuthbertson v AML Distributors*[178] a tribunal declined to state whether three months' notice was reasonable for a senior executive, because this was a common law concept that would have to be determined in the ordinary courts.

---

[175] [1982] ICR 54, [1981] IRLR 475, EAT.
[176] [1978] 2 All ER 723, [1978] IRLR 60, sub nom *Leighton v Construction Industry Training Board* [1978] ICR 577, EAT.
[177] [1990] ICR 248, [1990] IRLR 328, EAT; aff'd [1993] ICR 644, [1992] IRLR 323, CA.
[178] [1975] IRLR 228.

3.118 The Employment Act 2002, s 38 provides for various sanctions to be applied when an employer fails to give the written statement under ERA, s 1 or the statement of changes under s 4(1) in respect of proceedings brought relating to a claim by an employee under any jurisdiction listed in Sch 5 (see Chapter 12). If, in respect of such proceedings, the employment tribunal finds in favour of the employee but makes no award in respect of the claim, and, at the time proceedings were begun, the employer was in breach of his duty to give a written statement of employment particulars or particulars of change, the tribunal must make an award of the minimum amount of two weeks' pay, and may, if it considers it just and equitable in all the circumstances, award the maximum amount of four weeks' pay. Equally, if the employment tribunal does make an award in respect of the claim, it must increase the award by two or four weeks' pay. In either case, these awards need not be made if there are exceptional circumstances which would make the award or increase unjust or inequitable. It must be borne in mind that the Employment Act 2002, s 38, does not give employees a free-standing claim to compensation for incomplete or inaccurate written particulars. It only applies when a claim is being brought under one of the jurisdictions set out in Sch 5 to the Act (see Chapter 12). A reference under ERA, s 11 is not specified in Sch 5, and therefore does not, by itself, give rise to any claim for compensation.

The week's pay is calculated in accordance with ERA, ss 220–224 (see Chapter 14), with the statutory maximum to be applied.

E. Itemised Pay Statement (Employment Rights Act 1996, ss 8–10)

3.119 Every worker (this was extended from 'every employee' by the Employment Rights Act 1996 (Itemised Pay Statement) (Amendment) (No. 2) Order 2018 from 6 April 2019) has the right to be given by his employer an itemised pay statement, giving particulars of the gross amount of wages or salary, the amount of any variable or fixed deductions, and the purposes for which they are made, the net wages or salary payable and, where the net amount is paid in different ways, the amount and method of each part-payment. A pay statement need not contain separate particulars or fixed deductions as long as the aggregate amount of all deductions is stated and the employer had given to the employee a standing statement of fixed deductions which contains all the relevant details. Such standing statement must be reissued every 12 months.

3.120 The right to have an itemised statement is not conditional upon an employee making a request for one (*Coales v John Wood (Solicitors) & Co*[179]). If an employer fails to give an itemised pay statement, the employee may require a reference to be made to an employment tribunal, to determine what particulars ought to be included in such a statement. But where the tribunal finds that the employer has failed to give an employee any itemised pay statement, or that it does not give the required particulars concerning deductions, the tribunal shall make a declaration to that effect (*Coales v John Wood & Co*) and, if there have been any unnotified deductions from the employee's pay within 13 weeks preceding the date of the application for the reference to the tribunal, then the tribunal may award that the employer shall pay to the employee the aggregate of the deductions made. However, no application for a tribunal reference can be made more than three months after the employment has ceased. The requirement to give an itemised pay statement does not apply to employees who work outside Great Britain, share fishermen, or merchant seamen.

F. Holidays

3.121 It will be recalled (see para 3.108) that the written statement to be given to employees under ERA, s 1 shall include any terms and conditions relating to entitlement to holidays, including public holidays and holiday pay, the particulars being sufficient to enable

---

[179] [1986] ICR 71, [1986] IRLR 129, EAT.

the employee's entitlement to be precisely calculated, including any entitlement to accrued holiday pay on the termination of the employment. Under the provisions of the Working Time Regulations 1998 (as amended) workers are entitled to 28 days' holiday from April 2009 (see para 7.73). Other than the provisions contained in the contract (or the written statement if used as evidence of the contract), there is no legal entitlement to bank or public holidays, and these may be used to discharge the employer's liability under the Working Time Regulations. Under the regulations, accrued holiday pay is payable on termination of the employment, but if the worker's entitlement is in excess of the statutory entitlement, then on termination of employment there may be problems in calculating the contractual entitlement (*Taylor v East Midlands Offender Employment*[180]).

G. **Occupational Pension Schemes**

3.122 The Occupational Pension Schemes (Disclosure of Information) Regulations 1986 require an employer who runs an occupational pension scheme to disclose automatically certain information to members and beneficiaries, including details of the scheme, rights of leavers, amount of pension payable to a new pensioner, and options available to persons on the death of a member or beneficiary. Other information is to be disclosed on request, including trust deeds and rules, benefit statements, the trustees' annual report, and the actuarial valuation report.

3.123 The persons entitled to this information include current members and deferred pensioners, prospective members and their spouses, and recognised independent trade unions (except that the latter are not entitled to benefit statements).

3.124 In October 2012, the auto-enrolment into a pension scheme for employees aged 22 or over and earning more than the tax threshold came into force. The scheme applies to all employers, including new businesses and small employers with fewer than 50 employees. Employers without a pension scheme can use the National Employment Savings Trust (NEST), which is a government-sponsored scheme. Employees who do not wish to take part have to opt out.

Summary

- A contract of employment is an agreement between the employer and employee.
- All contracts have to have an offer, acceptance, consideration and intention to create legal relations.
- Express terms are those which are specifically set out in the contract and agreed upon (eg salaries, hours of work, etc).
- Implied terms are implied by the courts where the term is so obvious the parties did not see the need to state it expressly.
- Statutory terms (eg the Equality Act) are implied into all contracts of employment.
- Collective agreements can be incorporated.
- Terms cannot be changed unilaterally by one party.
- The ERA 1996 sets out written particulars that have to be given to employees at the start of employment.
- Workers as well as employees are entitled to an itemised pay slip.

---

[180] [2000] IRLR 760, EAT.

4

Equality in Employment

Background

4.1 The Equality Act 2010 is a major piece of legislation. It purports to harmonise all the law dealing with the prevention of discrimination and the promotion of equality in society. It consists of 218 sections and 28 schedules, and applies across all sectors of public life, including employment, services, public functions, premises, education, associations, public sector equality duty, transport, and so on.

4.2 The Act repeals or revokes most of the previous law on the subject, makes some amendments to case law, and purports to strengthen the law in certain areas. Somewhat unusually, each page of the Act is accompanied by explanatory notes, which are for guidance only, and not to be regarded as being an authoritative interpretation. Also unusually, much of the Act is written in plain English, in an attempt to simplify many of the complex concepts.

4.3 In this chapter, only those provisions of the Act that impact on employment law will be considered. These are generally to be found in Parts 5, 8, 9, 10, and 11 of the Act, together with provisions found in various schedules. Other than those instances where specific legal decisions have been replaced by the Act (eg the decision in *Malcolm v London Borough of Lewisham*[1]) most of the old case law will presumably still apply, until modified or interpreted in accordance with the new provisions. Thus, pre-2010 legal decisions are included in the following text, with the reservation that they must be used with care, more by way of example and illustration, and are not to be taken as being authoritative unless and until confirmed by subsequent legal decisions. It is expected that the higher courts will adopt a pro-active approach to the legislation, consistent with the policy objectives.

4.4 Because of the way in which anti-discrimination legislation has been enacted over the years, a number of variations have occurred in the legislative provisions, which, though minor, have tended to produce significant differences in the approach taken by the courts and tribunals in specific instances. One of the aims of the Equality Act is to ensure uniformity of approach across the board where possible.

4.5 The Act commences with the key concepts of equality, which are the protected characteristics, and which are the main object of the Act's provisions. This is then followed by the prohibited conduct in respect of those characteristics, which are the anti-discrimination provisions. However, each of the protected characteristics must be examined separately, because not all the prohibited conduct will necessarily be applicable in each case.

---

[1] [2008] UKHL 43, [2008] 1 AC 1399, [2008] 4 All ER 525, [2008] IRLR 700.

4.6 The next section deals with the application of the prohibited conduct to the various protected characteristics in the field of employment, which is the major concern of this book. The Act then deals with equality of terms (formerly found in the Equal Pay Act 1970), followed by the relevant enforcement provisions. Finally, there are some miscellaneous provisions that are common to a number of the protected characteristics.

4.7 Provisions contained in the Act which deal with public sector duties, services, occupational pension schemes, local authorities, education, transport, taxis, railways, etc are outside the scope of this book.

A. **Repeals and Revocations**

4.8 The following important legislative provisions have been repealed or revoked:

(a) Equal Pay Act 1970;

(b) Sex Discrimination Act 1975;

(c) Race Relations Act 1976;

(d) Sex Discrimination Act 1986;

(e) Employment Act 1989 ss 1–7, 9;

(f) Disability Discrimination Act 1995;

(g) Equality Act 2006 (ss 25, 26, 33, 43, 81, Part 2 and Part 4, and part of Sch 3);

(h) Employment Equality (Religion or Belief) Regulations 2003;

(i) Employment Equality (Sexual Orientation) Regulations 2003;

(j) Employment Equality (Age) Regulations 2006.

Key Concepts

4.9 The key concepts of the Act are the protected characteristics and the prohibited conduct in relation to those characteristics.

A. **Protected Characteristics (ss 4–12, 18)**

4.10 The protected characteristics are given in alphabetical order, as follows:

(1) age;

(2) disability;

(3) gender reassignment;

(4) marriage and civil partnership;

(5) pregnancy and maternity;

(6) race;

(7) religion or belief;

(8) sex;

(9) sexual orientation.

4.11 While these characteristics are based largely on definitions contained in the repealed legislation, certain modifications have been made to some of them.

B. **Prohibited Conduct (ss 13–27)**

4.12 Subject to certain exceptions, the prohibited conduct in relation to the protected characteristics that has general applicability is as follows:

(a) direct discrimination;

(b) discrimination arising from disability;

(c) gender reassignment discrimination;

(d) pregnancy and maternity discrimination (work);

(e) indirect discrimination;

(f) duty to make adjustments;

(g) harassment;

(h) victimisation.

(There was originally proposed a further type of prohibited conduct known as combined (or dual) discrimination, but the government has indicated that this is unlikely to be brought into force.)

4.13 Again, while largely based on the repealed discrimination law, a number of modifications have been made, mainly with a view to harmonising and simplifying the application of the prohibited conduct to the protected characteristics.

Prohibited Conduct

4.14 We can now examine the various types of prohibited conduct, noting, in particular, some of the changes made to the legislation by the Act.

A. **Direct Discrimination (s 13)**

4.15 A person discriminates against another if, because of a protected characteristic, he treats that other less favourably than he treats or would treat others.

4.16 As well as the obvious type of direct discrimination, there are several subtle implications arising from the wording of s 13.

(a) *Associative discrimination.* The definition in s 13 does not refer to the protected characteristic of any particular person, and hence associative discrimination is clearly covered. This arises when a person is discriminated against because of his/her association with a person who has the protected characteristic. In *Coleman v Attridge Law*[2] the claimant claimed that she was subjected to unfair treatment because she had a disabled son who required care. Although there was nothing in the Disability Discrimination Act that dealt with this point, the European Court held that associative discrimination was within the scope of the Employment Equality Directive 2000/78. This finding is now confirmed by this wording. It has also been found that a company can be discriminated against because of the protected characteristic of an associated person (*EAD Solicitors v Abrams*[3]). Associative discrimination does not, however, extend to an employer's duty to make reasonable adjustments (*Hainsworth v Ministry of Defence*[4]).

---

[2] [2010] ICR 242, [2010] IRLR 10.   [3] UKEAT/0054/15.   [4] [2014] EWCA Civ 763.

(b) *Perceptive discrimination.* The Explanatory Notes suggest that discrimination can occur if a person treats another less favourably because it is believed that that other has a protected characteristic. For example, it would be perceptive discrimination if a person with a foreign sounding name applies for a job but is not appointed because the employer thinks that the applicant is from an African country. Perceptive discrimination does not apply to the protected characteristics of marriage and civil partnerships.

(c) *Deterred discrimination.* If an employer gives an indication that persons who have a particular protected characteristic would not be considered for the post, this can amount to an act of deterred direct discrimination. This is because of the inclusion of the words '*or would treat*'. It must be shown that the person with the characteristic genuinely intended to apply for the post, and was suitably qualified for it. Otherwise it cannot be said that the person suffered less favourable treatment. If the indication is contained in an advertisement, this could result in a case being brought by the Equality and Human Rights Commission, even though no identifiable person with the protected characteristic could be found (see *Centrum voor gelijkheid van kansen v Firma Feryn*[5] and para 4.209).

4.17 Less favourable treatment must be distinguished from unfavourable treatment. Less favourable treatment requires a comparator, unfavourable treatment does not.

4.18 Section 13 is subject to the following qualifications:

(a) If the protected characteristic is age, there is no discrimination if it can be shown that the treatment is a proportionate way of achieving a legitimate aim (see para 4.69).

(b) If the protected characteristic is disability, there is no discrimination if the person with the disability is treated or would be treated in a way that is permitted by the Act, and another person who does not have the disability is not treated in that way. Thus more favourable treatment of a disabled person is permitted.

(c) If the protected characteristic is marriage or civil partnership, there is discrimination only if the treatment is because a person is married or a civil partner. In other words, associative discrimination does not apply to this protected characteristic.

(d) If the protected characteristic is race, less favourable treatment includes segregation but not congregation, if this is the wish of those concerned (see *Pel Ltd v Modgill*[6]).

(e) If the person discriminated against is a man, no account is to be taken of special treatment afforded to a woman in connection with pregnancy or childbirth. Provisions in a contract relating to pay and contractual terms are excluded from s 13, because they are otherwise dealt with in ss 64–79, which replicate the equal pay provisions (see Chapter 5). (Note that under the Workplace (Health and Safety) Regulations 1992 suitable facilities must be provided for pregnant women and nursing mothers.)

(f) For work-related pregnancy and maternity discrimination, the test is whether a woman has been treated unfavourably, not less favourably, reflecting the fact that there is no need for a woman in such circumstances to compare the treatment with that offered to a comparator (see s 18, paras 4.133 and 4.136).

---

[5] [2008] All ER (EC) 1127, [2008] ECR I–5187, [2008] ICR 1390, [2008] IRLR 732.
[6] [1980] IRLR 142, EAT.

B. **Motive for Direct Discrimination**

4.19 The test for determining whether or not an act was an act of direct discrimination is objective, not subjective. In other words, regard must be had to what was done, not the reasons or motives behind what was done. The question to be asked is 'was the person so treated because of the protected characteristic?' A benign motive, however laudable, can still be discriminatory. Thus in *James v Eastleigh Borough Council*,[7] Mr and Mrs James were both aged 61. The local authority adopted a policy whereby children under the age of three, and members of the public over pensionable age, were permitted free entry into the local swimming pool, whereas everyone else had to pay the 75p entrance fee. Mr James complained that he had been discriminated against because of his sex, as he was required to pay an entrance fee whereas his wife was not. The House of Lords upheld his contention. The purity of the discriminator's subjective motive, intention, or reason for discriminating cannot save the criterion applied from the objective taint of discrimination on grounds of sex. The reason why the local authority adopted this particular policy, ie to benefit state pensioners, cannot affect the fact that men were treated less favourably than women.

4.20 A person can discriminate directly even though he is unaware that he is doing so. It may happen as a result of an inbuilt social prejudice or as a result of making a stereotype assumption. In *Skyrail Oceanic Ltd v Coleman*[8] the claimant worked as a booking clerk in a travel agency. She then became engaged to a man who worked for a rival firm. The two employers discussed the matter amicably, as it appeared there could be the possibility of the leakage of confidential information. It was agreed that as the husband-to-be would be the breadwinner of the family, the wife would be dismissed. The Court of Appeal upheld her claim for unfair dismissal. An assumption that men are more likely to be the breadwinner of a family was an assumption based on sex, and a dismissal based on that assumption amounted to an act of sex discrimination. However, following *CLIFIS (UK) Limited v Reynolds* (para 4.226), knowledge of a disability cannot be imputed to a decision-maker, even where it is already known to others in the organisation. A tribunal should therefore be concerned only with the actual motivation, intention, and knowledge of that decision maker (*Gallop v Newport City Council*[9]).

4.21 But the treatment afforded must be less favourable, and the fact that it is different does not mean that it is less favourable. The test is an objective one, not subjective, so it makes no difference if the claimant thinks that the treatment is less favourable. In *Smith v Safeways Stores*[10] a male assistant who worked in the delicatessen department of a supermarket was dismissed because his ponytail hairstyle breached the company's rule that hairstyles should not be unconventional, and should not be permitted to grow below collar length. The Court of Appeal held that a code governing the appearance of male and female employees, which laid down conventional standards, and was even-handed in its approach, was not discriminatory on grounds of sex. There is a distinction between discrimination between the sexes (which may be permissible) and discrimination against one or another of the sexes, which is forbidden by the Act. In other words, there is a difference between treating differently and treating less favourably. There is no discrimination where dress code compliance requirements apply equally between the sexes (*Dansie v Commissioner of Police for Metropolis*[11]). In *Burrett v West Birmingham Health Authority*[12] male and female nurses were required to wear a uniform. Female nurses wore a starched cap, which had no practical or hygienic purpose. The claimant thought that the wearing of this cap was

---

[7] [1990] 2 AC 751, [1990] 2 All ER 607, [1990] ICR 554, [1990] IRLR 288.
[8] [1981] ICR 864, [1981] IRLR 398.   [9] UKEAT/0118/15.   [10] [1996] ICR 868, (1996) IRLR 456.
[11] EAT/0234/09.   [12] [1994] IRLR 7, EAT.

demeaning and undignified, and when she refused to wear one she was transferred to another department where she had less opportunity to work overtime. She claimed that she had been unlawfully discriminated against, but her claim was dismissed. The fact that there was a different uniform for men and women did not constitute less favourable treatment. Nor was the fact that she felt that she was being treated less favourably relevant, for the test of direct discrimination is an objective one, for the employment tribunal to determine (see also *Stewart v Cleveland Guest (Engineering) Ltd*[13]).

4.22 Unreasonable behaviour, by itself, does not equate with unlawful discrimination. In *Bahl v Law Society*[14] it was stated that all discriminatory behaviour is unreasonable, but not all unreasonable behaviour is discriminatory. Similarly, all racial language is offensive, but not all offensive language is racist. The fact that the victim of such treatment is of a particular sex or racial group etc is not conclusive of the perpetrator's actions. True, the burden of proof may be on the perpetrator, and adverse conclusions may be drawn in the absence of a satisfactory explanation, but if the alleged hostile action has nothing to do with the relevant protected characteristic, no discrimination has occurred.

C. Indirect Discrimination (s 19)

4.23 A person indirectly discriminates against another if:

    (a) he applies a provision, criterion or practice (PCP) which is discriminatory in relation to that other's protected characteristic;

    (b) the provision, criterion or practice is applied to persons who do not share that characteristic and puts or would put persons who do share that characteristic at a particular disadvantage compared with persons who do not share it;

    (c) it puts or would put an individual with that characteristic at a disadvantage; and

    (d) it cannot be shown that it is a proportionate means of achieving a legitimate aim.

4.24 Thus the provision, criterion or practice can apply generally to persons with a protected characteristic, or to an individual who has that characteristic. The claimant does not have to show why a particular action places the group of which they are part at a disadvantage, simply that it does, and all the workers affected by the PCP in question should be considered in the pool (*Essop v Home Office and Naeem v Secretary of State for Justice*[15]).

Further, perceived discrimination is covered. For example, if there is a criterion that a job applicant should be able to work a night shift, a woman who is otherwise qualified but is unable to comply with the criterion because she has young children to care for would be able to claim that she has been indirectly discriminated against on grounds of sex. The employer would have to show that the criterion is a proportionate means of achieving a legitimate aim. However, the woman must be able to show that she was genuinely deterred from applying for the job because of the criterion (see *Keane v Investigo*, para 4.212).

4.25 There is no specific provision in the Equality Act for associative indirect discrimination. In the case of *CHEZ Razpredelenie Bulgaria AD v Komisia za ot diskriminatsia*,[16] however, the ECJ found that a person can claim indirect discrimination even if he is not a member of the racial group, if he nevertheless suffers as a result of the treatment complained of, as the wording of the Race Directive does not state that he has to share the characteristic. This contrasts with the Equality Act, where a claimant has to have the same

---

[13] [1994] ICR 535, [1994] IRLR 440 EAT.   [14] [2004] EWCA Civ 1070, [2004] IRLR 799.
[15] [2017] UKSC 27.   [16] C-83/14.

characteristic as the protected group, and indeed has recently been reinforced in *UK Border Agency v Essop*,[17] where the court found that the employee has to show that the PCP affects both the group with the protected characteristic and himself. This makes the Equality Act incompatible with the Directive and it may therefore lead to amendment.

4.26 An important distinction between direct and indirect discrimination is that so far as the former is concerned, there is no defence of justification, whereas indirect discrimination can be justified if it is a proportionate means of achieving a legitimate end.

4.27 When determining whether a provision, criterion or practice was indirectly discriminatory, the employment tribunal must strike an objective balance between the discriminatory effect of the provision and the reasonable needs of the business. There must be a real need for the provision, and it must be appropriate and reasonably necessary (*Network Rail Infrastructures Ltd v Gammie*[18]).

4.28 Indirect discrimination applies to all the protected characteristics except pregnancy and maternity.

D. **Comparators (s 23)**

4.29 For the purpose of s 13 (direct discrimination), s 19 (indirect discrimination), and s 20 (duty to make adjustments), on a comparison of cases there must be no material difference between the circumstances relating to each case. In other words, the treatment of the claimant must be compared with that of an actual or hypothetical person who does not share the same protected characteristics as the claimant, but whose circumstances are otherwise not materially different. Thus, for example, if the claimant is blind and applying for a job as a computer operator, he is to be compared with a person who is not blind but who is applying for a job as a computer operator. In *Bullock v Alice Ottley School*[19] the employers decided to establish a common retiring age for all members of their staff, irrespective of sex. Teaching, administrative, and domestic staff had to retire at the age of 60, whereas gardeners and maintenance staff had to retire at 65. The claimant was required to retire at the age of 60, and she claimed that she had been discriminated against on grounds of sex because all the gardening and maintenance staff who stayed on until 65 were men. The Court of Appeal dismissed her claim. The comparison between the two groups could not be made, because there were special difficulties in recruiting gardening and maintenance staff that justified them having a later retiring age. The relevant circumstances had to be those circumstances that were relevant to the comparison.

4.30 Similarly, a comparison between persons of different racial groups must be such that the relevant circumstances are the same or not materially different. In *Wakeman v Quick Corpn*,[20] Japanese managers who worked for a financial institution were paid more than locally recruited managers. It was held that the higher rate of pay was attributed to their status as secondees. As such, their circumstances were materially different from those of the claimant, who was English, so no proper comparison could be made. Choosing a comparator is a question of fact and degree, and it is open to a tribunal to hold that the people chosen were appropriate comparators, despite the fact the situations being compared were not the same, if there is sufficient evidence they were comparable: *Hewage v Grampian Health Board*.[21]

---

[17] [2015] EWCA Civ 609.   [18] EATS/0044/08.   [19] [1993] ICR 138, [1992] IRLR 564.
[20] [1999] IRLR 424.   [21] [2012] UKSC 37.

4.31 If there is no actual comparator, the employment tribunal must create a hypothetical one, drawing a careful inference from all the available evidence (*Shamoon v Chief Constable of the Royal Ulster Constabulary*[22]), but again the circumstances must not be materially different.

E. Discriminator's Characteristics (s 24)

4.32 So far as direct discrimination is concerned (s 13), it is irrelevant that the alleged discriminator has the same protected characteristics as the person discriminated against.

F. Harassment (s 26)

4.33 The Act defines three types of harassment that are of general application, and a further definition of harassment which relates specifically to employment situations (see s 40, para 4.56).

(a) A person harasses another if he engages in unwanted conduct which has the purpose or effect of violating that other person's dignity, or creating an intimidating, hostile, degrading, humiliating, or offensive environment for that person. Motivation is irrelevant. This type of harassment applies to all the protected characteristics apart from pregnancy and maternity, and marriage and civil partnership.

(b) A person harasses another if he engages in any form of unwanted verbal or non-verbal or physical conduct of a sexual nature that has the effect of violating a person's dignity, or creating an intimidating, hostile, degrading, humiliating, or offensive environment for that other. This type of harassment applies to all the protected characteristics.

(c) The third type of harassment is where one or more persons engage in conduct of a sexual nature, or that is related to gender reassignment or sex, and has the purpose or effect of violating another person's dignity, or creating a hostile, degrading, humiliating, or offensive environment, and because the person offended rejects or refuses to submit to the conduct he is treated less favourably than he would have been had he not rejected or submitted to the conduct. Again, this type of harassment applies to all the protected characteristics.

4.34 In deciding whether the conduct has that effect, the perception of the person allegedly harassed must be taken into account, as well as the other circumstances of the case and whether it was reasonable for the conduct to have that effect.

4.35 Conduct is 'unwanted' in the sense of being 'unwelcome' or 'uninvited' (*Insitu Cleaning Co Ltd v Heads*[23]). A single incident can give rise to harassment under this section (*Bracebridge Engineering Ltd v Darby*[24]). If the conduct is of a sexual nature, the fact that similar treatment is meted out to men as well as to women is irrelevant (*Driskel v Peninsula Business Services*[25]).

4.36 If an employer has reason to believe that sexual harassment is taking place, it is incumbent on him to investigate the matter, and to take some action, if necessary, without waiting for a formal complaint to be made. A failure to do so could well amount to a breach of the implied term of trust and confidence (*Reed & Bull Information Systems Ltd v Stedman*[26]).

---

[22] [2003] UKHL 11, [2003] 2 All ER 26, [2003] ICR 337, [2003] IRLR 285.
[23] [1995] IRLR 4, EAT.   [24] [1990] IRLR 3, EAT.   [25] [2000] IRLR 151, EAT.
[26] [1991] IRLR 299, EAT.

4.37 In *Richmond Pharmacology v Dhaliwal*[27] the EAT warned against encouraging a climate of hypersensitivity in harassment cases, stating that not every case of racially slanted adverse comment or conduct may constitute a violation of a person's dignity, and presumably the same approach would apply to allegations of sexual harassment. For example, if a woman's actions are themselves provocative, it can hardly be said that she has suffered an injury to her feelings (*Wileman v Minilec Engineering Ltd*[28]).

G. **Victimisation (s 27)**

4.38 A person victimises another on grounds of any of the protected characteristics if he subjects that person to a detriment because he:

(a) brings proceedings under the Act;

(b) gives evidence or information in connection with proceedings;

(c) does any other thing for the purpose of or in connection with the Act;

(d) makes an allegation that another person has contravened the Act.

4.39 All that is necessary is for the claimant to show that the alleged victimiser was motivated because of one of the protected acts. The acts do not even have to have been made by the claimant himself, so long as he was subjected by the employer to a detriment because of the protected acts of others (*Thompson v London Central Bus Company Ltd*[29]). Subconscious motivation will suffice (*Nagarajan v London Regional Transport*[30]). Whether the actions of the employer constitute victimisation would depend on the perception of the employee who alleges victimisation, but the perception must be reasonable. In *Chief Constable of West Yorkshire v Khan*[31] a police officer made a complaint to an employment tribunal alleging that he had been the victim of race discrimination, in that his application for promotion had not been supported. Before the claim was heard he applied for promotion to another police force, who wrote to his present employers for a reference. The latter's chief constable refused to provide the reference because he feared that it would prejudice his own case before the impending tribunal hearing. The claimant brought a claim alleging he had been victimised, but the claim was dismissed. The refusal to provide a reference was not because the claimant had brought proceedings in the employment tribunal, but because the chief constable wished to preserve his legal position in relation to those proceedings.

4.40 However, the giving of false evidence or information or making a false allegation is not protected if the information or allegation is given or made in bad faith (*Cornelius v University College of Swansea*[32]).

4.41 A claim alleging victimisation may be brought against a former employer who refuses to pay an employment tribunal award if the reason for non-compliance was related to the fact that the ex-employee has brought tribunal proceedings (*Rank Nemo (DMS) Ltd v Coutinho*[33]). However, a victimisation claim cannot be brought in respect of a failure by the employer to comply with an order made by the employment tribunal for reinstatement

---

[27] [2009] ICR 724, [2009] IRLR 336.   [28] [1988] ICR 318, [1988] IRLR 144, EAT.

[29] UKEAT/0108/15.

[30] [1995] ICR 520, [1994] IRLR 61, EAT; aff'd sub nom [1998] IRLR 73, CA; revsd [2000] 1 AC 501, [1999] 4 ALL ER 65, [1999] 3 WLR 425, [1999] ICR 877, [1999] IRLR 572.

[31] [2000] ICR 1169, [2000] All ER (D) 237, CA; revsd [2001] UKHL 48, [2001] ICR 1065, [2001] IRLR 830, [2001] All ER (D) 158 (Oct); sub nom *Khan v Chief Constable of West Yorkshire Police* [2001] 4 All ER 834.

[32] [1987] IRLR 141, CA.

[33] [2009] EWCA Civ 454, [2009] ICR 1296, [2009] IRLR 672, (2009) *Times*, 8 June.

or re-engagement, because the Employment Rights Act, s 132 provides its own remedy for that failure.

4.42 In order to establish that a person was victimised, it must be shown that s/he did one of the protected acts (but see *Thompson v London Central Bus Company Ltd* para 4.39), and that s/he suffered a detriment for doing so (*Aziz v Trinity Street Taxis Ltd*[34]). If an employer makes an honest and reasonable attempt to compromise proceedings in a dispute with employees by trying to persuade them to settle those proceedings, this does not amount to victimisation, but great care needs to be taken in such circumstances. In *St Helen's Borough Council v Derbyshire*[35] the employer sent letters to a number of women employees warning them that if they continued to pursue an equal pay claim, and succeeded, a number of members of staff would have to be made redundant. It was held that this amounted to an attempt to bring undue pressure to settle or abandon the claim, and constituted victimisation. Had the letter been sent to legal advisers there would have been no problem. But the letters were sent not only to the claimants, but also to other workers who had in fact settled their own claims, and who would no doubt have expressed their anger or disapproval with the claimants' action. Thus the letter constituted a detriment by reason that the women in question had brought an equal pay claim.

4.43 A person may be victimised even though the employment relationship has ended, if the conduct in question would have contravened the Act had it occurred during that relationship (see para 4.200). The Equal Treatment Directive would be undermined if the employer was permitted to take discriminatory action after the employment had ceased (*Coote v Granada Hospitality Ltd*[36]). While it is not specifically mentioned in the Act, the Court of Appeal in *Jessemey v Rowstock*[37] confirmed that a claim can be brought. It seems to be an involuntary omission as it appears in the Explanatory Notes.

4.44 There is no requirement for a comparator in cases of victimisation (*Woodhouse v West North West Homes Leeds Ltd* UKEAT/0007/12).

Discrimination in Employment

4.45 Sections 39–40 draw into the employment field the various forms of prohibited conduct relating to discrimination that are contained in ss 13–25, harassment in s 26, and victimisation in s 27. Section 39 deals with discrimination and victimisation by the employer, and s 40 deals with harassment by the employer.

A. Discrimination and Victimisation in Employment: s 39(1)–(4)

4.46 An employer must not discriminate against or victimise a person with any of the protected characteristics (subject to the exceptions noted at para 4.54):

(a) in the arrangements he makes for deciding to whom to offer employment;

(b) as to the terms on which he offers employment. This does not apply with respect to the protected characteristics of sex or pregnancy or maternity, unless, were the employee to accept the offer, an equality clause or rule would apply, or unless the term was directly discriminatory, or a breach of s 13 (see para 4.15);

(c) by not offering employment (s 39(1)).

---

[34] [1986] IRLR 435, EAT; aff'd [1989] QB 463, [1988] 2 All ER 860, [1988] 3 WLR 79, [1988] ICR 534, [1988] IRLR 204, CA.   [35] [2007] UKHL 16, [2007] 3 All ER 81, [2007] ICR 841, [2007] IRLR 540.   [36] [1998] IRLR 656 ECJ.   [37] [2014] EWCA Civ 185.

4.47 Discrimination against job applicants with a particular protected characteristic can take many forms. There can be associative discrimination, perceived discrimination, and deterred discrimination (see para 4.16). Job advertisements can be discriminatory, even though no potential victim is identified (*Centrum voor gelijkheld van kansen v NV Firma Feryn*[38]), as they are part of 'the arrangements for deciding to whom to offer employment', as are questions asked at job interviews (*Saunders v Richmond-upon-Thames London Borough Council*[39]) or statements made at the actual interview (*Brennan v J H Dewhurst Ltd*[40]). Note that there is no right for an unsuccessful job applicant to have disclosure about the successful one; however, the refusal to disclose such information may be a factor to be taken into account when making a decision about discrimination: *Meister v Speech Design Carrier Systems GmbH*.[41]

4.48 To refuse to offer employment to a woman because 'it is a man's job' (*Batisha v Say*[42]) or to refuse to offer a man a job because women would not work with him (*Munro v Allied Suppliers*[43]) is also discriminatory.

4.49 An employer must not discriminate against an employee of his who has the protected characteristic or victimise him/her:

    (a) as to the terms of that employee's employment. As noted in para 4.18 this does not apply to terms which may be subject to an equality clause (see para 5.16). However, if there are minor differences in the terms of employment offered to men and women, these may be ignored under the de minimis rule (*Jeremiah v Ministry of Defence*[44]);

    (b) in the way the employer affords (or does not afford) the employee access to opportunities for promotion, transfer, or training, or for receiving any other benefit, facility, or service. However, positive action may be encouraged (see para 4.208);

    (c) by dismissing the employee;

    (d) by subjecting the employee to any other detriment (s 39(2)).

4.50 A dismissal includes the non-renewal of a fixed-term contract, including a period expiring by reference to an event or circumstances (see para 17.19) (although it will not be a dismissal if immediately after the termination the employment is renewed on the same terms), and a constructive dismissal (see para 17.21).

4.51 A detriment can take many forms. Thus to dismiss a woman following a disciplinary hearing which she was unable to attend because of a pregnancy-related illness amounted to a detriment in *Abbey National plc v Formoso*.[45] A failure to carry out a risk assessment when employing women of child-bearing age, as required by reg 16 of the Management of Health and Safety at Work Regulations (see para 11.64), was to subject the claimant to a detriment in *Day v T Pickles Farms Ltd*,[46] as was a failure to investigate an allegation of sexual harassment in *Coyne v Home Office*.[47] To put women on short-time working in preference to men was held to subject women to a detriment in *Morris v Scott*.[48]

4.52 A detriment may exist even though the employee is compensated for it. In *Jeremiah v Ministry of Defence*[49] it was the practice of the employer not to require women to do certain dirty work as they did not wish to take showers afterwards. When men did the work, they

---

[38] [2008] ICR 1390, (2008) IRLR 732.   [39] [1978] ICR 75, [1977] IRLR 362.
[40] [1984] ICR 52, [1983] IRLR 357.   [41] C-415/10, ECJ.
[42] [1977] IRLIB, [1977] IRLR 6.   [43] [1977] IRLIB.
[44] [1980] QB 87, [1979] 3 WLR 857, [1979] 3 All ER 833, [1980] ICR 13, [1979] IRLR 436.
[45] [1999] IRLR 222.   [46] [1999] IRLR 217.   [47] [2000] ICR 1443, [2000] IRLR 838.
[48] [1976] IRLR 238.   [49] n 39.

received extra pay. It was held that the fact that the men received an additional payment for the work in question did not mean that a detriment had not been suffered. An employer cannot buy the right to discriminate.

4.53 But there is no detriment if the job application is not genuine, or if the applicant has no intention of accepting the job (see *Keane v Investigo*, para 4.212). This is also the case with the Equal Treatment Directive (*Kratzer v R+V Allgemeine Versicherung*[50]).

B. Occupational Requirements (Sch 9)

4.54 Schedule 9 (para 1) sets out exceptions to s 39(1)(a) (arrangements for offering employment), s 39(1)(c) (failure to offer employment), s 39(2)(b) (opportunities for promotion etc), and s 39(2)(c) (dismissal), when applying a requirement to have a particular protected characteristic is, having regard to the nature or context of the work, an occupational requirement. The application of the requirement must be a proportionate means of achieving a legitimate aim, and the person to whom it is applied must not meet it (or the employer must have reasonable grounds for not being satisfied that the person concerned does meet it). Particular occupational requirements for the protected characteristics are dealt with under their respective headings. Occupational requirements apply to direct and indirect discrimination, not to cases of harassment or victimisation.

4.55 There are also particular occupational requirements exceptions relating to the protected characteristics or sex, transsexual people, civil partners, and marriage, and when the employment is for the purpose of an organised religion.

C. Employer Harassment (s 40)

4.56 An employer must not harass an employee of his, or an applicant for employment.

4.57 Anything done by a person in the course of his employment shall be treated as done by his employer as well as by him, whether or not the act was done with the employer's knowledge or approval. This is the effect of the doctrine of vicarious liability. Thus in *Jones v Tower Boot Co Ltd*[51] an employee was racially harassed at work, by having to suffer physical and verbal abuse from his fellow employees. It was argued for the employer that the acts were not committed in the course of employment because it was no part of their work to do such things, which were unauthorised and unconnected with anything they were employed to do. The Court of Appeal rejected the argument, and held the employer liable for race discrimination. The words 'in the course of his employment' were to be given a purposive construction.

4.58 The Enterprise and Regulatory Reform Act 2013 removed liability for third party harassment from 1 October 2013, and the law on this reverted to the position before the Equality Act. This was set out in *Pearce v Governing Body of Mayfield School; Macdonald v Advocate General for Scotland* [2003] ICR 937,[52] where the House of Lords stated that while an employer's failure to prevent third parties committing acts of harassment could amount to discrimination, this could only be the case if the steps were not taken because of the employee's protected characteristic. A claimant can also bring an action under the general harassment provisions of the Act (s 26, para 4.33) or claim that the employer's failure to take steps could amount to a fundamental breach, entitling the employee to resign and claim constructive dismissal (para 17.21).

---

[50] C 423/15.   [51] [1997] 2 All ER 406, [1997] ICR 254, [1997] IRLR 168.   [52] [2003] UKHL 34.

4.59 If an act of harassment takes place at a social gathering of work colleagues, it is for the employment tribunal to consider whether the circumstances can be treated as an extension of the employment. Factors to consider include (a) whether the conduct took place on the employer's premises, (b) whether the persons were still on duty, (c) whether the gathering was organised by or on behalf of the employer, and (d) whether the incidents took place immediately after work. These matters are to be questions of fact to be determined by the employment tribunal (*Chief Constable of Lincolnshire v Stubbs*;[53] see also 10.110).

4.60 It is the objective nature of the alleged harassment itself that is determinative, not the circumstances of the victim. Thus to subject a person to homophobic abuse, even though it is known to the harassers that the victim is not homosexual, can still amount to harassment. Such abuse is on grounds of sexual orientation, amounts to unwanted conduct, has the effect of violating the victim's dignity or creating a degrading, humiliating, or offensive environment, and should reasonably be considered to have that effect (*English v Thomas Sanderson Blinds Ltd*[54]).

4.61 A common law action for the tort of harassment may be brought under the provisions of the Protection from Harassment Act 1997 (see para 10.115), although it is expected that most cases will be brought under the provisions mentioned earlier.

Protected Characteristics/Prohibited Conduct

4.62 The protected characteristics and the prohibited conduct can now be drawn together, with the emphasis on discrimination in employment generally.

A. Age

Direct Discrimination; Age (Equality Act, s 13(2))

4.63 A person discriminates against another if because of a person's age he treats that other less favourably than he treats others ('age' in this connection refers not only to a person's age but also to persons in a particular age group, eg 41–50-year-old persons). Associative, perceived, and deterred discrimination also apply. For example, it would amount to discrimination if an employer treats an employee less favourably because the employee is caring for an elderly relative. However, there is no discrimination on grounds of age if it can be shown that the treatment so accorded is a proportionate means of achieving a legitimate aim. In *Incorporated Trustees of the National Council on Aging v Secretary of State for Business, Enterprise and Regulatory Reform*[55] (the *Heyday* case) the European Court of Justice held that it was permissible for a state to derogate from the principle in EC Directive 2000/78/EC (Equal Treatment in Employment) that prohibits discrimination on grounds of age only in respect of measures that are justified by legitimate social objectives, including matters of employment policy, the labour market, or vocational training. It is for national courts to decide whether legislation is consistent with such legitimate aims, and whether the means chosen are appropriate and necessary to achieve those aims.

4.64 A Spanish law that permitted compulsory retirement on the ground of age was held by the ECJ not to be in breach of the EC Equal Treatment Directive. The legislation was

---

[53] [1999] ICR 547, [1999] IRLR 81.
[54] [2008] EWCA Civ 1421, [2009] 2 All ER 468, [2009] ICR 543, [2009] IRLR 206.
[55] [2009] All ER (EC) 619, [2009] ICR 1080, [2009] IRLR 373.

held to be an appropriate and necessary means of checking unemployment and encouraging recruitment. The discriminatory effect was objectively justified (*Palacios de la Villa v Cortefiel el Servicios SA*[56]). Similarly, in *Wolf v Stadt Frankfurt am Main*[57] the ECJ held that a requirement that applicants for jobs in the fire service should be under the age of 30 was justifiable as a genuine and determining occupational requirement. It was noted that firefighting and rescue duties were only carried out by younger officers, and that recruitment at an older age would have the consequences that too large a number of firemen could not be assigned to the most physically demanding duties. However, a maximum recruitment age of 30 for police officers was held to be discriminatory in *Mario Vital Pérez v Ayuntamiento de Oviedo*.[58] Although the ECJ accepted that the concern to ensure the operational capacity and proper functioning of the police service is a legitimate objective, and that possessing certain physical capabilities may be regarded as a genuine and determining occupational requirement, the article must be interpreted strictly. It distinguished this case from *Wolf v Stadt Frankfurt* as the level of fitness required here was not as high as for firefighters and there was insufficient evidence to show that imposing the age requirement was appropriate or necessary. An age requirement based on the physical demands of a job will not always be justifiable, as it depends on the circumstances of the case. It was however justified in *Gorka Salaberria Sorondo v Academia Vasca de Policia y Emergencias*,[59] which was distinguished from *Pérez*, where the duties were less physical with fewer frontline operational activities, and older officers were entitled to work fewer hours, so younger recruits were needed to ensure a full service.

4.65 Also, as already noted, discrimination on grounds of age is permitted for benefits which relate to childcare of children. Thus, the provision of childcare facilities for children under a certain age is permissible, even though this could amount to associative discrimination in respect of an employee who has a child above that age.

Indirect Discrimination (s 19)

4.66 The statutory definition of indirect discrimination has been noted in para 4.23. So far as its application to age is concerned, indirect discrimination is aimed at disguised age barriers. In *Homer v Chief Constable of West Yorkshire Police*,[60] it was a requirement for promotion that a post-holder should have a law degree. The claimant, who was 61 years of age, could not comply with that requirement before he retired, and he claimed the requirement was indirectly discriminatory. His claim succeeded. The particular disadvantage suffered by the claimant stemmed from the fact that his working life would have come to an end before he could qualify, and thus was an inevitable result of age, and the requirement to obtain a law degree was therefore one which indirectly discriminated against him on grounds of age. The case was returned to the tribunal to consider justification.

4.67 The other anti-discrimination provisions of the Act apply to the protected characteristic of age, ie s 19 (indirect discrimination), s 26 (harassment), s 27 (victimisation), s 39 (discrimination in employment), and s 40 (harassment by employers of employees and job applicants). Thus in *London Borough of Tower Hamlets v Wooster*[61] a 49-year-old man was dismissed for reasons of redundancy. There was evidence that the employer's failure to deploy him was a desire to avoid his becoming entitled to an early retirement pension, and it was held that the claimant had suffered unlawful age discrimination.

---

[56] [2008] All ER (EC) 249, [2009] ICR 1111, [2007] IRLR 989.   [57] [2010] IRLR 244.
[58] C-416/13.   [59] [2016] EUECJ C-258/15.   [60] [2012] UKSC 15.   [61] [2009] IRLR 980.

Repeal of Default Retirement Age

4.68 The Employment Equality (Repeal of Retirement Age Provisions) Regulations 2011[62] repealed the default retirement age that was previously set out in Sch 9 of the Equality Act 2010 and Sch 6 of the Employment Equality (Age) Regulations 2006. The regulations also removed retirement as a fair reason for dismissal from the Employment Rights Act 1996. Dismissal for retirement reasons therefore, if justified, will be deemed to be some other substantial reason (SOSR) (see Chapter 17).

The employer is not precluded from setting a retirement age, but he will have to have an objective justification in each case, by showing that the compulsory retirement is a proportionate means of achieving a legitimate aim. The Supreme Court in *Seldon v Clarkson, Wright & Jakes*[63] gave guidance on what might constitute objective justification, saying that aims must be related to a general public interest, and not just specific to the business in question. The employer in *Woodcock v Cumbria Primary Care Trust*[64] had dismissed the claimant prematurely on grounds of redundancy so as to avoid his eligibility for early retirement, thereby saving between £500,000 and £1 million. The court said the cost saving cannot of itself justify discrimination on the grounds of age. The question is whether the cost saving is a proportionate means of achieving the legitimate aim. Here, it was acceptable as the legitimate aim was the need to reorganise and make redundancies.

Long-service Benefits (Equality Act, Sch 9, para 10)

4.69 The general principle is that it is lawful to use length of service as a criterion for the provision of an additional benefit, facility, or service. However, if an employee feels that he is at a disadvantage because the employer has used this criterion in relation to another employee, the employer would have an absolute defence where the benefit in question was awarded in relation to service of five years or less. If the length of service exceeds five years, then the exception applies if the employer could show that the reason the criterion was used was to fulfil a business need of the undertaking, eg by encouraging loyalty or motivation, or rewarding the experience of some or all of his workers. In other words, if an employee has been employed for less than five years, he is entitled to complain if he is not given a benefit based on long service whereas another employee has been given such a benefit. To resist such a complaint, the employer must show the 'business need' of encouraging loyalty, etc.

Enhanced Redundancy Payments (Equality Act, Sch 9, para 13)

4.70 It is permissible for an employer to make an enhanced redundancy payment in which there is an in-built age factor, provided certain conditions are met. These are:

(a) the employee must be redundant (within the meaning of ERA, s 135). Employees who have less than two years' service may also be given an enhanced redundancy payment, as well as employees who volunteer to take redundancy;

(b) the method of calculation must be the same for all employees who are made redundant;

(c) the calculation is based on the statutory multiplier, ie one and a half weeks' pay for each year of employment in which the employee was not below the age of 41, one week's pay for a year of employment in which he was not below the age of 22, and half a week's pay for each year of employment below the age of 22;

(d) no more than 20 years' service is to count.

---

[62] SI 2011/1069.   [63] [2010] IRLR 865, [2010] EWCA Civ 899, CA, [2012] UKSC 16, SC.
[64] [2012] EWCA Civ 330.

4.71 The employer may make an enhanced redundancy payment that is in excess of the statutory cap used for a week's pay purpose, and may increase the multiplier used to calculate the payment for each year's employment by more than one.

4.72 Length of service as a criterion for redundancy selection is prima facie discriminatory against younger workers, although there is an exception in respect of service-related benefits where the service to be taken into account is five years or less.

4.73 However, the use by an employer of a length of service criterion within a selection matrix for redundancy is a proportionate means of achieving a legitimate aim of advancing an employment policy that achieved a peaceable process of redundancy selection agreed with the recognised trade unions. Giving credit for length of service in a redundancy selection policy was considered to be a benefit under reg 32 of the Employment Equality (Age) Regulations, (now Sch 9 of the Equality Act; see *Rolls-Royce plc v Unite*[65]). In *Lockwood Department of Work and Pensions*[66] it was held that a voluntary redundancy scheme which provided enhanced benefits for older employees to reflect the comparative difficulty of loss of employment suffered by them was justified. It was a proportionate means to achieve the legitimate aim of producing a proportionate financial cushion for the older workers until alternative employment was found.

4.74 There will be a consequential knock-on effect on contractual redundancy schemes, which are generally more beneficial than the state scheme. These will have to be reconsidered in the light of the new law and suitably amended to remove any semblance of age discrimination other than that permitted. The employer would need to show that long service 'fulfils a business need', etc. Thus in *MacCulloch v ICI plc*[67] the employer operated an enhanced contractual redundancy payment scheme whereby payments were increased in accordance with age and length of service. However, because of its complexity, it did not come under the exception to the anti-discrimination provisions contained in reg 33 of the Employment Equality (Age) Regulations. The claimant, who was made redundant, complained that the scheme was discriminatory under reg 33 of the regulations. The employer sought to rely on the defence of justification, arguing that there were three legitimate aims, namely (a) encouraging loyalty, (b) helping older workers who are more vulnerable in the job market if they are made redundant, and (c) encouraging older workers to take redundancy, thus freeing up senior posts for younger workers, avoiding compulsory redundancies, and making it easier to manage change. However, while the EAT accepted that the scheme had identified certain legitimate aims, the claim was remitted back to the employment tribunal for further evidence on whether the means adopted were proportionate to those aims, having regard to the significant detriment suffered by the claimant. It was pointed out that legitimate aims and proportionality are two separate issues, and both need to be addressed.

Exceptions

4.75 There are exceptions in respect of an act done in order to comply with a statutory requirement (*Renfrewshire Council v Martin*[68]), on grounds of national security, national minimum wage, and positive action (but not positive discrimination).

B. **Disability**

4.76 The provisions relating to disability can be found in the Equality Act 2010, ss 15, 20–21, 39–40, 60, and Schs 1, 8, and 9, together with regulations to be made. The appropriate Minister may issue guidance about matters to be taken into account.

---

[65] [2009] EWCA Civ 387, [2010] ICR 1, [2009] IRLR 576.   [66] [2013] EWCA Civ 1195.
[67] [2008] ICR 1334, (2008) IRLR 846.   [68] [2010] All ER (D) 44 (Nov).

Regulations

4.77 The Minister will make regulations that will make provision for:

(a) conditions of a prescribed description to be an impairment;

(b) prescribed circumstances in which an effect is to be treated as being, or as not being, long term;

(c) prescribed circumstances when a severe disfigurement is not to be treated as having a substantial adverse effect on a person's ability to carry out normal day-to-day activities;

(d) the effect of a prescribed description on the ability of a person to carry out normal day-to-day activities to be treated as being, or as not being, a substantial adverse effect.

4.78 Regulations will also be made making provision for:

(a) persons of prescribed descriptions to be treated as having disabilities (deemed disabilities);

(b) circumstances in which a person who has a disability is to be treated as no longer having the disability;

(c) a condition of a prescribed description to be treated as being, or not being, progressive.

Guidance

4.79 The Minister may issue guidance (subject to Parliamentary approval), which may give examples of:

(a) the effects that it would, or would not, be reasonable, in relation to particular activities, to regard as substantial adverse effects;

(b) substantial adverse effects that it would, or would not, be reasonable to regard as long-term.

4.80 In determining whether a person is a disabled person, an adjudicating body (ie an employment tribunal) must take account of such guidance as it thinks is relevant. Current guidance is provided by the Equality Act 2010 (Disability) Regulations 2010.[69]

Definition of Disability (s 6, Sch 1)

4.81 A person has a disability if he has a physical or mental impairment, which has a substantial and long-term adverse effect on his ability to carry out normal day-to-day activities. The fact that a person is disabled within the meaning of other legislation (eg for the purpose of disability living allowance) does not mean that he comes within the definition of disability within the meaning of the Act.

4.82 There are thus three elements to consider, namely (a) impairment (physical or mental), (b) substantial and long-term adverse effect, and (c) normal day-to-day activities. The text that follows includes the pre-2010 case law and various regulations on disability discrimination, which are likely to be replicated.

Physical or Mental Impairment

4.83 The physical impairment must be real, and not the result of functional overlay (ie where the symptoms are imaginary manifestations of an individual's psychological state: see *Rugamer v Sony Music Entertainments UK Ltd*[70]). But if there are physical symptoms,

---

[69] SI 2010/2128.   [70] [2002] EWCA Civ 1074, [2002] ICR 1498, [2002] IRLR 711.

the existence or non-existence of a physical cause is irrelevant (*College of Ripon and York St John v Hobbs*[71]), because an impairment may exist without any physical or mental causation. In other words, a claimant needs to show an impairment, but not why the impairment exists, ie by reference to a particular physical or mental illness. But if there is a dispute as to the nature of the impairment it is for the claimant to prove that it is physical or mental in character (*Millar v Inland Revenue Commissioners*[72]). A medical adviser can express an opinion about diagnosis, prognosis, and observation of day-to-day activities, but it is for the employment tribunal to determine whether or not a person is disabled, and not for them merely to adopt the opinion of the medical adviser (*Abadeh v British Telecommunications plc*[73]). Direct discrimination claims must be decided in accordance with the evidence, not 'stereotyping' on the basis of assumed characteristics, such as assumptions that a tribunal made about the claimant's particular mental illness rather than on the basis of up-to-date medical evidence about the effect of his illness on his ability to continue in the employment (*Aylott v Stockton-on-Tees Borough Council*).[74]

4.84 Addictions to alcohol, nicotine, or other substances do not amount to an impairment for the purpose of the Act, although if there is a physical or mental impairment, the fact that it was caused by such addiction is not relevant (*Power v Panasonic UK Ltd*[75]). What matters is the impairment, not how it is caused. A tendency to pyromania, kleptomania, physical or sexual abuse, exhibitionism, or voyeurism are not impairments. Seasonal allergic rhinitis (hay fever) is excluded, but not if it aggravates another condition. Also excluded are tattoos or the piercing of the body by objects for decorative or non-medical purposes (Equality Act 2010 (Disability) Regulations 2010).

4.85 Persons who suffer from certain progressive illnesses, eg, HIV infection, cancer, or multiple sclerosis, will be deemed to be disabled from the point in time of diagnosis, although certain types of minor cancers which respond to quick and effective treatment may be excluded by regulations. The Disability Discrimination (Blind and Partially Sighted Persons) Regulations 2003 provided that anyone certified or registered blind or partially sighted is deemed to be disabled for the purpose of the Act, and will no longer be required to establish that being blind or partially sighted has a substantial adverse effect on day-to-day activities.

4.86 The perception that there is a disability is also discriminatory. In *Chief Constable of Norfolk v Coffey*[76] the Court of Appeal found that it was discriminatory to refuse the claimant a transfer because of a perception that her hearing loss, which had never caused any problems and which was not a disability within the meaning of the Act, would affect her ability to work in the future.

4.87 However, any impairment, whether physical or mental, which ceases to have a substantial effect on a person's ability to carry out normal day-to-day activities is to be treated as continuing to have that effect if it is likely to recur. The likelihood of recurrence is to be judged at the date of the actual discrimination, and the fact that a recurrence takes place subsequently cannot be taken into account by the employment tribunal (*Richmond Adult Community College v McDougall*[77]).

Substantial and Long-term Effects

4.88 The effect of an impairment is long term if it has lasted for 12 months, or is likely to last for at least 12 months, or is likely to last for the rest of a person's life. The ECJ has found

---

[71] [2002] IRLR 185.   [72] 2006 SC 155.   [73] [2001] ICR 156, [2001] IRLR 23.
[74] [2010] IRLR 994, CA.   [75] [2003] IRLR 151.
[76] [2019] EWCA Civ 1061.   [77] [2008] EWCA Civ 4, [2008] ICR 431, [2008] IRLR 227.

that, depending on the fact of the case, a temporary capacity can be a disability (*Daoudi v Bootes Plus SL*[78]).

4.89 An impairment that ceases to have a substantial adverse effect on day-to-day activities is to be treated as still having that effect 'if that effect is likely to recur'. The word 'likely' means 'could well happen', not the stricter test of 'more probable than not'. Thus if a person is not actually suffering from an underlying condition at a particular moment in time, but remains susceptible to it, s/he is disabled for the purpose of the legislation (*SCA Packaging Ltd v Boyle*[79]). In assessing the likelihood of an impairment recurring, an employment tribunal should only take into account the evidence that was available at the time of the alleged act complained of, and not events that occur after the alleged act but before the tribunal hearing (*Richmond Adult Community College v McDougall*[80]).

4.90 The effect of a condition or illness that is likely to develop from another illness or condition is to be taken into account when forming an assessment of whether the original illness or condition was likely to have lasted for at least 12 months (*Patel v Oldham Metropolitan Borough Council*[81]).

4.91 A severe disfigurement is to be treated as having a substantial adverse effect on a person's ability to carry out normal day-to-day activities, although regulations may exclude certain severe disfigurements, including those that were deliberately acquired.

4.92 An impairment is to be treated as having a substantial adverse effect on the ability of the person concerned to carry out normal day-to-day activities if:

(a) measures are being taken to treat or correct it, and

(b) but for those measures, the impairment would be likely to have such effect.

4.93 Measures include medical treatment and the use of a prosthesis or other aid, but not, in relation to a person's sight, the extent to which the impairment is correctable by spectacles or contact lenses, or other prescribed measures.

4.94 When determining whether a disability had a substantial adverse effect, account must be taken of the 'deduced effect', ie the likely effect upon the person's capability if aid or treatment is withdrawn. Thus, if a person is suffering from anxiety, he can be assessed as if he was not receiving counselling sessions from a psychologist (*Kapidia v London Borough of Lambeth*[82]). Account cannot be taken of events that occur after the alleged discriminatory act in order to determine the likelihood of a recurrence of a disability, but the statute does not require a prophesy to be made (*McDougall v Richmond Adult Community Centre*[83]).

4.95 To assess whether or not an impairment has a substantial adverse effect, a tribunal should concentrate on what a claimant cannot do, or can only do with difficulty, and not on what he can do (*Aderemi v London & South East Railway*[84]). A tribunal should not adopt a narrow approach and should look at the effects of the impairments rather than just the question of diagnosis (*Nissa v Waverly Education Foundation Ltd*[85]).When considering what is a 'substantial' effect, unless a matter can be classified as 'trivial' or 'insubstantial', then it must be substantial (*Aderemi v London & South East Railway*).

4.96 It is no longer necessary for a mental impairment to arise from 'a clinically well-recognised illness', and thus physical and mental illnesses are to be treated alike from a

---

[78] [2016] EUECJ C-395/15.
[79] [2009] UKHL 37, [2009] 4 All ER 1181, [2009] ICR 1056, [2009] IRLR 746.   [80] n 68.
[81] [2010] ICR 603, [2010] IRLR 280.   [82] [2000] IRLR 699, (2000) All ER (D) 785.
[83] n 68.   [84] EAT/0316/12.   [85] UKEAT/0135/18.

diagnostic point of view. But vague expressions, such as 'depression', 'anxiety', 'stress', or 'nervous debility', will not, by themselves, lead to a conclusion that the person is disabled. Many instances of such illnesses do not last for a long period, and thus would fail to meet the requirement that the impairment must have a substantial and long-term adverse effect. If they do, however, it would count as a disability. In *Walker v Sita Information Networking Computing Ltd*[86] a tribunal was wrong to say that an obese claimant was not disabled because there was no recognisable pathological or mental cause for his symptoms, but should rather have looked at what effect the impairments had on everyday life. The focus should therefore be on the effect of the person's symptoms rather than their cause. The EAT said that the obesity was not a disability itself, but could make it more likely that a claimant would be disabled. Similarly, in *FOA, acting on behalf of Karsten Kaltoft v Kommunernes Landsforening, acting on behalf of the Municipality of Billund*[87] the ECJ found that while obesity does not in itself constitute a 'disability', if it entails a limitation which results in an impairment, such as reduced mobility or medical conditions which cause discomfort while carrying out duties, and the limitation is a long-term one, then it can amount to a disability.

Normal day-to-day activities

4.97 The Act has dropped the list requirement in earlier legislation, which stated that an impairment is to be taken as affecting normal day-to-day activities only if it affected a person with regard to mobility, manual dexterity, physical coordination, continence, ability to lift, carry, or move everyday objects, speech, hearing, eyesight, memory, or ability to concentrate, learn, or understand, or perception of risks of physical danger. The view was taken that such limitations were no longer necessary.

4.98 Whether an impairment has a substantial effect on a person's ability to carry out normal day-to-day activities should not be judged by reference to whether he is able to carry out his job (*Goodwin v Patent Office*[88]), but evidence as to how he carries out his duties at work can be relevant in assessing the employee's credibility, provided that the duties carried out can be regarded as being normal day-to-day activities (*Law Hospital NHS Trust v Rush*[89]). If the effect of the impairment fluctuates, and is exacerbated by conditions at work, then an employee's ability to perform normal day-to-day activities both while at work and while not at work is to be taken into account when assessing whether the impairment has a substantial and long-term adverse effect (*Cruickshank v VAW Motorcast Ltd*[90]).

4.99 The playing of games or sports does not constitute 'normal day-to-day activities', because such activities are only normal for a particular group of persons (*Coca-Cola Enterprises Ltd v Shergill*[91]). But it is normal for a woman to put rollers in her hair and apply make-up to her face (*Ekpe v Metropolitan Police Comr*[92]).

4.100 'Normal day-to-day activities' does not apply to specialist skills that are required for some employment situations, but can include activities that are to be found across a range of employment situations. Warehouse work, for example, such as lifting up to 25kg, can count as normal day-to-day activities (*Banaszczyk v Booker Ltd*[93]), as there are a number of workers in the UK whose job may include the same lifting tasks. In *Chief Constable of Dumfries & Galloway v Adams*[94] a police officer, who suffered from ME, had mobility problems when working on a night shift. As the work activity was 'normal' in the sense it applied to a range of different work situations (because there are a number of employees who work on night shifts), it was held that the employee was disabled within the meaning of the Act.

---

[86] UKEAT/0097/12.   [87] Case C 354/13.   [88] [1999] ICR 302, [1999] IRLR 4.
[89] 2002 SC 24, [2001] IRLR 611.   [90] [2002] ICR 729, [2002] ICR 24.
[91] [2002] All ER (D) 02 (Sep).   [92] [2001] ICR 1084, [2001] IRLR 605.   [93] UKEAT/0132/15.
[94] [2009] ICR 1034, [2009] IRLR 612.

Discrimination Arising from Disability (s 15)

4.101 A person discriminates against a disabled person if:

(a) he treats him unfavourably because of something arising in consequence of the disabled person's disability; and

(b) it cannot be shown that the treatment is a proportionate means of achieving a legitimate aim.

4.102 The first part of this section reverses the decision in *London Borough of Lewisham v Malcolm*,[95] which required the treatment of a disabled person to be 'less favourable' when compared with the treatment afforded to a non-disabled person. Section 15 is dealing with unfavourable treatment, and thus a comparator is not required. If the treatment results in the disabled person suffering a detriment, this will amount to discrimination. Associative, perceived, and deterred discrimination also apply. But there will be no discrimination if the alleged discriminator does not know, and could not reasonably be expected to know, that the person discriminated against has the disability.

4.103 The provisions of s 19 (indirect discrimination), s 26 (harassment), s 27 (victimisation), s 39 (discrimination in employment), and s 40 (harassment) apply in disability cases.

4.104 However, the treatment will not be unfavourable under s 39 if it is a proportionate way of achieving a legitimate aim. For example, the provisions designed to prevent discrimination on grounds of disability are subordinate to health and safety law. In *Farmiloe v Lane Group plc*[96] the claimant worked in a warehouse. He could not wear safety boots because he suffered with psoriasis. A local authority health and safety officer required him to wear safety boots, and threatened enforcement action if he failed to do so. The employers approached various footwear manufacturers, but none could provide suitable safety footwear. As there was no other employment available for him, he was dismissed. It was held that even though he had been discriminated against because of his disability, the principles of health and safety law overrode the principles behind the Disability Discrimination Act. The employers had made an effort to provide a reasonable adjustment and, as there was none available, and no other suitable employment for him, the claimant was fairly dismissed.

4.105 So too in *McCall v Post Office*,[97] where the claimant, unknown to his employers, suffered from epilepsy. He was employed as a cleaner, but had several fits of short duration. The personnel department took medical advice, and were told that he should be employed in a 'no risk' area. Unfortunately, there was no suitable vacancy, and he was dismissed. It was held that the dismissal was fair. On medical advice the employee had to be moved to a safe area, but as there was none available, it was in his interests (and in the interests of other employees) that he be dismissed.

4.106 There only needs to be a loose causal link between the disability and the unfavourable treatment; the test does not have to be a stringent one (*Hall v Chief Constable of West Yorkshire*[98]).

4.107 There is no discrimination if the person with the disability is treated in a way permitted by the Act and another person who does not have the disability is not treated in that way. Thus more favourable treatment of a disabled person is permitted. On the other hand, discriminatory treatment will be justified if it arises from performance-related pay, eligibility for and contributions to occupational pension schemes, and permits for incapacitated persons under the agricultural wages legislation (see Disability Discrimination (Employment) Regulations 1996).

---

[95] [2008] UKHL 43, [2008] 1 AC 1399, [2008] 4 All ER 525, [2008] IRLR 700.   [96] [2004] PIQR P22.
[97] IRLR LIB.   [98] EAT/0057/15.

4.108 Further, there is nothing in the Act that prohibits an employer from requiring a job claimant to undergo a pre-recruitment medical examination and, if a person refuses such a request, there is no obligation to offer him employment (*X v EC Commission*,[99] but see s 60, para 4.110). If a disabled person is dismissed, it must be shown that the disability-related reason was present in the employer's mind when the decision to dismiss was taken (*Taylor v OCS Group Ltd*[100]).

4.109 Thus once a disability is revealed, it will be necessary to obtain a proper assessment of the disabling condition, the prognosis, the effect of the disability on the employee's (or job applicant's) ability to undertake duties, the effect of the physical features of the workplace, and the steps that might be taken to reduce or remove the disadvantages to which the disabled person would otherwise be subjected (*Mid-Staffordshire General Hospitals NHS Trust v Cambridge*[101]).

Enquiries about Disability and Health (s 60)

4.110 A person to whom an application for work is made must not ask the job applicant about his health before offering him work or before including the job applicant in a pool of candidates from which selection for employment is to be made. A contravention of s 60 is enforceable as an unlawful act by the Commission under Part I of the Equality Act 2006 (see s 120(8)).

4.111 Asking about the health of a job applicant does not, by itself, mean that there is a contravention of a relevant disability provision (s 60(3)), but conduct in reliance on information given in response may be a contravention. If this does occur and the job applicant is not progressed to the next stage or is not appointed to the post, and he brings a claim alleging discrimination to an employment tribunal, the burden of proof (in s 136(2)) will be on the employer to show that the reason did not contravene s 39(1)(a) (arrangements for employment) or s 39(1)(c) (failure to offer employment). In the absence of a satisfactory explanation, the employment tribunal can conclude that a contravention of the Act has occurred (s 60(5)).

4.112 However, s 60 does not prohibit an employer from asking questions for the purpose of:

(a) establishing whether the job applicant is able to comply with a requirement to undergo an assessment designed to give an indication of the applicant's suitability for the work concerned, or whether there would be a duty on the employer to make reasonable adjustments in connection with the requirement to undergo an assessment;

(b) establishing whether the job applicant will be able to carry out a function that is intrinsic to the work;

(c) monitoring diversity in the range of persons applying to the employer for work;

(d) establishing whether the employer can take lawful positive action under s 159;

(e) if there is a work requirement to have a particular disability, ascertaining if the job applicant has that particular disability. The requirement must be an occupational requirement and its application must be a proportionate means of achieving a legitimate aim.

4.113 Section 60 does not apply to anything done for the purpose of vetting applicants for work for reasons of national security.

---

[99] [1995] IRLR 320.   [100] [2006] EWCA Civ 702, [2006] ICR 1602, [2006] IRLR 613.
[101] [2003] IRLR 566.

Occupational Requirement

4.114 There is no contravention of the employment provisions relating to disability if, having regard to the nature or context of the work, a requirement to have or not to have a particular disability is an occupational requirement, the requirement is a proportionate means of achieving a legitimate aim, and the person concerned does not meet it.

Duty to Make Adjustments (s 20, Sch 8)

4.115 The duty to make reasonable adjustments comprises three requirements:

(a) Where a provision, criterion or practice puts a disabled person at a substantial disadvantage in relation to a non-disabled person, the employer must take such steps as are reasonable to avoid the disadvantage.

(b) Reasonable steps must be taken to ensure that a disabled person is not disadvantaged because of a physical feature, which may be because of the design or construction of a building, the approach, exit from, or access to a building, a fixture or fitting, or furniture, furnishings, materials, equipment, or other chattel in or on the premises, or any other physical element or quality. The steps to be taken include removing the physical feature in question, or altering it, or providing a reasonable means of avoiding it.

(c) Reasonable steps must also be taken to provide auxiliary aids or an auxiliary service where necessary to avoid a disadvantage.

4.116 A person discriminates against a disabled person if he fails to comply with any of these three requirements. So far as the first or third requirements are concerned, if they relate to the provision of information, steps must be taken to ensure that the information is provided in an accessible format. Further, the person on whom the burden to make the adjustments is placed cannot require the disabled person to pay for the costs of the adjustments unless there is an express provision to the contrary (s 20(7)).

4.117 If the employer is under a binding obligation to obtain the consent of another person to make alteration to the premises he occupies, or to vary the terms of the tenancy, or to obtain the consent of another person to an alteration to common parts, it is always reasonable for him to have to take steps to obtain consent, but it is never reasonable for him to have to make the alteration before the consent is obtained.

4.118 The duty applies in respect of job applicants as well as employees. The employer is not subject to this duty if he does not know and could not reasonably be expected to know that the job applicant has a disability or that an employee is likely to be placed at the disadvantage mentioned in the three requirements listed at para 4.115. An employer cannot rely solely on an occupational health report when considering disability, but should ask specific practical questions (*Gallop v Newport City Council*[102]). An employment tribunal may substitute its own view for that of the employer when considering whether or not an adjustment is reasonable in the circumstances.

4.119 The Minister may make regulations dealing with, inter alia, whether a particular step could amount to a reasonable adjustment, what is or what is not a provision, criterion, or practice or a physical feature, and things that are or are not to be treated as auxiliary aids. It is likely that the regulations will deal with making adjustments to the premises, allocating the disabled person's duties to another person, transferring him to fill an existing vacancy, altering working hours, assigning to him a different place of work, permitting him to be absent during working hours for rehabilitation, assessment, and/or treatment, providing training, acquiring or modifying equipment, modifying instructions or reference manuals or procedures for assessment or testing, providing a reader or interpreter, supplying auxiliary aids, and so on. But these suggestions will be illustrative, not exhaustive (*Chief Constable of South Yorkshire Police v Jelic*[103]).

4.120 In considering whether an employer has made reasonable adjustments, the operational needs of the employer and the interests of other employees may be taken into account (*Chief Constable of Lincolnshire Police v Weaver*[104]), as well as the extent to which the adjustment would prevent the discriminatory effect. The nature of the activities, the size of the employer's undertaking, and the financial implications of the adjustment may also be a relevant consideration (*O'Hanlon v Commissioners for HM Revenue & Customs*[105]). Reasonable adjustments must be job related. The employer is not bound to provide personal carers or special facilities (eg a disabled toilet must be provided, but not assistance in going to the toilet (*Kenny v Hampshire Constabulary*[106])). It is not a reasonable adjustment to continue to pay full pay or enhanced sick pay (*O'Hanlon v HM Revenue & Customs*[107]) to an employee who is off work for a disability-related reason when other employees do not receive such treatment, because this would not help the employee to return to work (*Fowler v Waltham Forest*[108]). But it can be a reasonable adjustment to move a disabled employee to a different place of work within the organisation if this would best achieve the necessary aim (*Garrett v Lidl Ltd*[109]), or swap the role of a disabled person with that of another employee (*Chief Constable of South Yorkshire Police v Jelic*[110]) if such steps would best achieve the necessary aim.

4.121 An employer's failure to make a reasonable adjustment that is inadvertent, eg through lack of diligence or competence, is to be regarded as a decision to make a deliberate omission, and thus a failure for the purpose of the time limits that apply to a claimant. It is up to the employer to assert an intervening date that could be taken as being the date when the 'decision to make an omission' from which date time will run (*Matuszowicz v Kingston upon Hull City Council*[111]).

C. **Gender Reassignment**

4.122 A person has the protected characteristic of gender reassignment if s/he is proposing to undergo, is undergoing, or has undergone a process for the purpose of reassigning that person's sex by changing physiological or other attributes of sex. This definition includes transsexual (the term used in the legislation) people, and it is no longer necessary for a person to be under medical supervision for reassignment purposes. It should be noted that once a person has undergone gender reassignment and obtained formal recognition under the Gender Recognition Act 2004, that person is entitled to be treated in all respects as a person of the acquired gender (see *Chief Constable of Yorkshire v A*[112]).

Discrimination on Grounds of Gender Reassignment (s 16)

4.123 If a person is undergoing treatment for gender reassignment (as defined in s 7), it will be discrimination if he is treated less favourably than he would be treated if he was absent from work because of sickness or injury, or for some other reason, and it would not be reasonable for him to be treated less favourably.

---

[103] [2010] IRLR 744, EAT.   [104] EAT/0622/07.   [105] [2007] ICR 1359, (2007) IRLR 404.
[106] [1999] ICR 27, [1999] IRLR 76.   [107] n 90.   [108] [2007] All ER (D) 126.
[109] EAT/0541/08.   [110] n 89.
[111] [2009] EWCA Civ 22, [2009] 3 All ER 685, [2009] ICR 1170, [2009] IRLR 288.
[112] [2004] ICR 806, (2004) IRLR 573, [2005] AC 51.

4.124 The anti-discrimination provisions of the Act apply, ie direct discrimination (s 13), indirect discrimination (s 19), harassment (s 26), victimisation (s 27), discrimination or victimisation in employment (s 39), and harassment by employers of employees and job applicants (s 40).

Occupational Requirements (Sch 9)

4.125 There is no contravention of the employment provisions if, having regard to the nature or context of the work, a requirement not to be a transsexual person is an occupational requirement, the requirement is a proportionate means of achieving a legitimate aim, and the person concerned does not meet it.

D. **Marriage and Civil Partnership**

4.126 A civil partnership is a relationship that has been entered into by two persons of the same sex that has been registered under the Civil Partnership Act 2004, and for all intents and purposes is to be treated to the same extent as a legal marriage (Civil Partnership Act 2004 (Amendment to Subordinate Legislation) Order 2005).

Direct Discrimination (s 13)

4.127 A person discriminates against another person if because of the protected characteristic of marriage or civil partnership he treats that person less favourably than he would treat another person. It is permissible to discriminate against a single person of either sex, but not in favour of such a person, because that would amount to discrimination against a married person. Thus if a firm were to offer special preferential mortgage facilities to its staff, then if these were made available to married men, they must be made available to married women (*Sun Alliance & London Insurance Co v Dudman*[113]), but it would be permissible to exclude a single person of either sex from the scheme. Associative discrimination only applies when the victim is married or a civil partner. Note that it has been held that if an employer treats a woman less favourably not because she is married per se, but because she is married to a particular man, then this does not amount to discrimination (*Hawkins v Atex Group Limited*[114]).

4.128 The other anti-discrimination provisions of the Act apply, ie s 19 (indirect discrimination), s 27 (victimisation), s 39 (discrimination or victimisation in employment), and s 40 (harassment).

4.129 Note that harassment under sub-s (1) of s 26 (unwanted conduct) (para 4.33) does not apply to the relevant protected characteristic of marriage and civil partnership, but sub-ss (2) and (3) of s 26 (ie harassment of a sexual nature) do apply, because s 26(1) refers to a 'relevant protected characteristic' whereas sub-ss (2) and (3) do not appear to be so limited.

4.130 There are no occupational requirements exemptions for the employment aspects of this protected characteristic other than for the purpose of organised religion (see para 4.168).

E. **Pregnancy and Maternity**

4.131 A woman becomes pregnant from the date when she carries a fertilised egg inside her body. If she has had in vitro fertilisation, the earliest point at which pregnancy begins is the date the fertilised ova are implanted into the woman's uterus (*Mayr v Backerei und Konditorei Gerhard Flocker OHG*[115]), at least until the end of the protected period (*Sahota v Home Office*[116]). It has also been suggested that a woman who is in an advanced stage

---

[113] [1978] ICR 551, [1978] IRLR 169.   [114] EAT/0302/11.
[115] [2008] All ER (EC) 613, [2008] IRLR 387, [2008] 1 FLR 1242.   [116] EAT/0342/09.

of her IVF treatment prior to implantation is also protected from dismissal and/or detriment for that reason by virtue of the Equal Treatment Directive. The pregnancy ceases if she has a miscarriage or abortion, the baby is born prematurely, or she gives birth in the normal manner.

4.132 However, so far as the discrimination provisions are concerned, she will not have the protection from the prohibited conduct of pregnancy unless the employer knows she is pregnant, or unless there are symptoms from which the employer can reasonably suspect she is pregnant (*Ramdoolar v Bycity Ltd*[117]).

4.133 There are a number of other protective legislative provisions that apply to pregnant women and women who have given birth. These include time off work for antenatal care, risk assessments, suspension on maternity grounds, facilities for breastfeeding, maternity leave, maternity pay, the right to return to work, and written reason for dismissal.

Direct Discrimination (s 13)

4.134 A person discriminates against a woman if because of the protected characteristic of pregnancy or maternity he treats her less favourably than he would treat others. More favourable special treatment is, of course, permitted. As already noted, there is no prohibited conduct of indirect discrimination in relation to pregnancy and maternity, as s 18 (para 4.137) provides sufficient protection.

4.135 So if a rule applies equally to men and women, but adversely affects pregnant women, it will be discriminatory. Thus in *Brown v Rentokil Ltd*[118] the employer had a rule which stated that any employee who was absent from work because of sickness for more than 26 weeks would be dismissed. The claimant had a series of pregnancy-related illnesses, and was dismissed after 26 weeks' absence. The European Court held that it was contrary to the Equal Treatment Directive to dismiss a woman at any time for absence due to pregnancy or pregnancy-related illnesses, even though a man absent for that period would have been dismissed.

4.136 However, if the person discriminated against is a man, no account is to be taken of special treatment afforded to a woman in connection with pregnancy or childbirth.

Discrimination at Work (s 18)

4.137 A person discriminates against a woman if, in the protected period in relation to a pregnancy of hers, he treats her unfavourably because of her pregnancy or because of an illness suffered by her because of her pregnancy. The protected period begins when the pregnancy begins, and ends:

  (a) if she has the right to ordinary and additional maternity leave, at the end of the additional maternity leave period or when she returns to work after the pregnancy if earlier;

  (b) if she does not have that right, at the end of two weeks beginning with the end of the pregnancy.

(As already noted, 'unfavourable treatment' in s 18 does not require a comparator).

4.138 A person discriminates against a woman if he treats her unfavourably because she is on compulsory maternity leave or she is exercising or seeking to exercise the right to ordinary or additional maternity leave.

---

[117] [2005] ICR 368.
[118] [1998] All ER (EC) 791, [1998] ICR 790, [1998] IRLR 445, [1998] 2 FLR 649.

4.139 There are three circumstances to consider:

(a) If a woman is pregnant and applies for or remains in employment, any unfavourable treatment because of her pregnancy would be discrimination. In *Dekker v Stichting Vormingcentrum*[119] a refusal to employ a pregnant woman because of adverse financial consequences that would be suffered by the employer was held by the ECJ to be an act of discrimination. An extreme situation arose in *O'Neill v Governors of St Thomas More School*,[120] where the claimant, who was unmarried, was employed to teach religion at a Roman Catholic school. She was expected to teach the ideologies and ethos of the Catholic faith to her pupils. She then announced that she was pregnant as a result of having an affair with a Roman Catholic priest who used to visit the school, and who was well known locally. She took maternity leave and then announced her intention to return to work. When the school governors refused to permit this she claimed she had been discriminated on grounds of pregnancy. Her claim was upheld by the EAT. The treatment complained of was because of pregnancy and maternity, and the factors that motivated the discriminator were irrelevant.

(b) During the appropriate maternity leave period, the fact that a woman receives different treatment does not necessarily become unlawful if the treatment is lawful by national legislation. Thus in *Gillespie v Northern Ireland Health and Social Services Board*[121] a woman argued that she was entitled to receive full pay during her maternity leave, arguing that it was because of her pregnancy that she was receiving the lower statutory maternity pay. It was held by the ECJ that it was for national legislatures to set the rates of maternity pay, provided this was not so low as to defeat the purpose of maternity leave.

(c) When her leave period ends her special protection ends, and unfavourable treatment will only be unlawful if a man would have been treated more favourably. Thus in *Handelsog (acting on behalf of Larsson) v Dansk Handel & Service*[122] a woman remained absent from work after the conclusion of her maternity leave because of an illness that was caused by her pregnancy. She was dismissed because of her absences, and claimed that she had been discriminated against. It was held by the European Court that, outside the period of maternity leave laid down by national law, a woman has no more protection than a man would have had in respect of absences caused through illness.

4.140 Where a woman is treated unfavourably because of her pregnancy or a pregnancy-related illness, and the decision to treat her in that way was taken during the protected period but not implemented until after the end of that period, the treatment is still regarded as occurring during the protected period (s 18(5)).

4.141 The anti-discrimination provisions of the Act apply, ie s 27 (victimisation), discrimination or victimisation in employment (s 39), and harassment by employers of employees and job applicants (s 40). Note that the indirect discrimination provisions of s 19 and harassment under s 26(1) do not apply to the pregnancy and maternity characteristic.

Occupational Requirement

4.142 There is no occupational requirement exclusion in respect of pregnancy and maternity, because of the operation of s 18 (see para 4.137). There is no indirect discrimination

---

[119] [1990] ECR I–3941, [1992] ICR 325, [1991] IRLR 27.   [120] [1997] ICR 33, (1996) IRLR 372.
[121] [1996] All ER (EC) 284, [1996] ICR 498, [1996] IRLR 214.   [122] [1997] IRLR 643.

provision for this protected characteristic, and hence it is not possible to apply a provision, requirement, or practice relating to pregnancy or maternity that could be an occupational requirement.

F. **Race**

4.143 Race includes colour, nationality, and ethnic or national origins. A racial group can be made up of two or more different racial groups, eg 'black/British'. Nationality and national origins are separate concepts: the former refers to citizenship, whereas the latter term refers to historical and/geographical features that would at some point in time reveal the existence of a nation. Thus England and Scotland were once separate nations and it was unlawful to discriminate against a person because of his national origins from either country (*BBC Scotland v Souster*[123]). In *Gwynedd County Council v Jones*[124] it was accepted that Welshmen were a distinct ethnic group. The term 'ethnic' is wider than 'race'. In *Mandla v Dowell Lee*[125] it was held that an ethnic group must regard itself as a distinct community by virtue of certain characteristics, including a long shared history, a cultural tradition, and other factors that set them apart from others in the community. Thus Sikhs who are born in the United Kingdom still retain their ethnicity (*Mandla v Dowell Lee*[126]), as do gypsies (*Dawkins v Department of the Environment*[127]). Jews share the characteristics of being an ethnic group (*Seide v Gillette Industries*[128]) and a racial and religious group (*R (E) v Jewish Free School*[129]).

4.144 The Act confers on a minister a power to specify that 'caste' shall be an aspect of race, which would bring certain groups from the Indian subcontinent etc within the scope of the Act. In *Chandhok & Anor v Tirkey*,[130] the EAT found that, although 'caste' is not specifically outlawed under s 9(1) of the Equality Act, it could be capable of coming within 'ethnic origins'. 'Ethnic origins' has a wide and flexible ambit, including characteristics which are determinable by 'descent', and it could therefore be covered depending on the facts of the case.

Direct Discrimination (s 13)

4.145 A person discriminates against another if, because of the protected characteristic of race, he treats that person less favourably than he treats others. Less favourable treatment includes segregation (*Pel Ltd v Modgill*[131]), but not congregation (if that is the wish of all concerned). It is irrelevant that the alleged discriminator has the same religion or belief as the person discriminated against.

4.146 Associative discrimination (see para 4.16) has always been applied in race cases. In *Zarczynska v Levy*[132] a barmaid alleged she was dismissed for refusing to obey an order not to serve black persons in a pub, and the EAT held that even though she was personally not discriminated against on grounds of her race, she was entitled to pursue her claim. In *Wilson v TB Steelworks*[133] a white woman was on the point of being offered employment, but when she disclosed that her husband was black, the offer was withdrawn. It was held that this amounted to unlawful discrimination.

---

[123] 2001 SC 458, [2001] IRLR 150.   [124] [1986] ICR 833.
[125] [1983] 2 AC 548, [1983] 1 All ER 1062, [1983] ICR 385, [1983] IRLR 209.
[126] n 111.   [127] [1993] ICR 517, [1993] IRLR 284.   [128] [1980] IRLR 427.
[129] [2010] IRLR 136, (2010) 1 All ER 319.
[130] EAT/0190/14, [2015] IRLR 195.   [131] [1980] IRLR 142.
[132] [1979] 1 All ER 814, [1979] ICR 184, [1978] IRLR 532.   [133] IDS Brief 150, 23662/77/ET.

4.147 The motive for the discrimination is irrelevant. In *R v Commission for Racial Equality, ex p Westminster City Council*[134] a black man applied for a job as a refuse collector. He was given a temporary appointment, but this was later withdrawn, as it was feared that other workers would take industrial action if his employment was continued. It was held that the Commission for Racial Equality was entitled to issue a non-discrimination notice. For an employer to give in to such threats would frustrate the purpose of the legislation. In *Amnesty International v Ahmed*[135] the claimant was not offered promotion because it was feared that her ethnicity would compromise the employer's impartiality. It was held that the employer's motive, however benign, was irrelevant to establishing direct discrimination on grounds of race.

4.148 The fact that an employee suffers a sense of grievance does not by itself mean that he has been treated less favourably than others, and an employee who, for sound reasons, is treated differently but no less generously than others in a different racial group does not necessarily mean that he has suffered a detriment (*Barclays Bank Ltd v Kapur*[136]).

4.149 To adopt a screening policy, whereby members of a particular racial group are eliminated from consideration for employment is discrimination, even though the discriminator is unaware of whether a particular job applicant is a member of that group (*Simon v Brimham Associates*[137]). However, it is permissible to request, as part of the employment arrangements, that the job applicant produces evidence of his right to work in the United Kingdom (*Dhatt v McDonald's Hamburgers Ltd*[138]).

4.150 Discrimination on grounds of birth, nationality, descent, or residence is permitted for employment with certain civil service posts and other public bodies (the Race Relations (Prescribed Public Bodies) Regulations 1994 are likely to be replicated).

Indirect Discrimination (s 19)

4.151 A person discriminates against a person who has the protected characteristic of race if he applies a provision, criterion or practice which is discriminatory of that person, puts him at a disadvantage, and cannot be shown to be a proportionate means of achieving a legitimate aim.

4.152 To determine whether or not the provision, criterion or practice is proportionate, the employment tribunal should decide (a) whether the objective was legitimate, (b) whether the means used to achieve that objective were reasonable, and (c) whether those means were justified when balanced between the discriminatory effect upon the claimant's racial group and the needs of those applying the provision, criterion or practice (*St Matthias Church of England School v Crizzle*[139]). In *Panesar v Nestle & Co Ltd*[140] a chocolate factory had a rule that prohibited employees wearing beards and long hair. This was indirectly discriminatory against the claimant, who was a Sikh, but the Court of Appeal held that the condition was justified in the interests of hygiene and safety.

4.153 Section 23 of the Act provides that on a comparison of cases for the purpose of ss 14 and 19 there must be no material difference between the circumstances relating to each case. In *Wakeman v Quick Corpn*,[141] Japanese managers, who were seconded from Japan to work in England, were paid more than locally recruited managers. It was held that the higher rate of pay was attributed to their status as secondees. As such their circumstances

---

[134] [1985] ICR 827, [1985] IRLR 426.   [135] [2009] ICR 1450, [2009] IRLR 884.
[136] [1991] 2 AC 355, [1991] 1 All ER 646, [1991] ICR 208, [1991] IRLR 136.
[137] [1987] ICR 596, [1987] IRLR 307.   [138] [1991] 3 All ER 692, [1991] ICR 238, [1991] IRLR 130.
[139] [1993] ICR 401, [1993] IRLR 472.   [140] [1980] ICR 144, [1980] IRLR 64.
[141] [1999] IRLR 424.

were materially different from those of the claimant, who was English, so no proper comparison could be made between them.

4.154 The other anti-discrimination provisions of the Act apply to the protected characteristic of race, ie s 26 (harassment), s 27 (victimisation), s 39 (discrimination and victimisation in employment), and s 40 (harassment by employers of employees and job applicants).

Occupational Requirement (Sch 9)

4.155 There is no contravention of the employment provisions if, having regard to the nature or context of the work, a requirement to be or not to be of a particular race is an occupational requirement, the requirement is a proportionate means of achieving a legitimate aim, and the person concerned does not meet it.

4.156 It is possible that the provision of personal service promoting the welfare of a racial group may, in particular cases, amount to an occupational requirement on racial grounds (*Tottenham Green Under Fives' Centre v Marshall*[142]), but in *Lambeth London Borough Council v Commission for Racial Equality*[143] the Court of Appeal refused to uphold the decision of a local authority to confine applications for the vacant posts in their housing benefits department to applicants from the Afro-Caribbean or Asian communities, because the jobs were basically managerial in nature, and did not involve the provision of personal services promoting the welfare of a particular racial group.

G. **Religion or Belief**

4.157 Religion means any religion, and belief means any religious or philosophical belief. A lack of belief (eg atheism, humanism, etc) is also covered. As well as the more obvious religions that are within the definition (Christianity, Judaism, Islamism, Hinduism, etc), it is thought that the provisions apply to other religions, such as Baha'i, Buddhism, Rastafarianism, Scientology, Zoroastrianism, etc.

4.158 Philosophical beliefs are more difficult to define. In *Grainger Ltd v Nicholson*[144] the EAT stated that a philosophical belief (a) must be genuinely held, (b) must be a belief and not an opinion or viewpoint based on the present state of information available, (c) must be a belief as to a weighty and substantial aspect of human life and behaviour, (d) must attain a certain level of cogency, seriousness, cohesion, and importance, and (e) must be worthy of respect in a democratic society, not incompatible with human dignity, not in conflict with the fundamental rights of others. Thus the belief must be more than an opinion based on perceived logic or information. It is thought that political beliefs, such as communism, socialism, etc, are not within the protection of the Act (see *Baggs v Fudge*[145]), but it will be for the employment tribunal to draw parameters on what do or do not constitute philosophical beliefs. The Guidance to the Act states that Darwinism is not within the provisions, but this must be considered to be doubtful. In *Grainger plc v Nicholson*[146] it was held that a belief that climate change was man-made was, if genuinely held, a philosophical belief for the purpose of the Religion and Belief Regulations. It was further suggested that while support for a political party would not come within the regulations, belief based on a political philosophy, such as Marxism, communism, etc, could be. The EAT has also held that a belief in spirituality could be regarded as a religious belief (*Power v Greater Manchester Police Authority*[147]). The regulations would not protect a racist or homophobic political

---

[142] [1991] ICR 320, (1991) IRLR 162.   [143] [1990] ICR 768, [1990] IRLR 231.
[144] [2010] 2 All ER 253, [2010] ICR 360, [2010] IRLR 4.   [145] 1400114/05/ET.   [146] n 130.
[147] EAT/0087/10.

philosophy, because such beliefs would not be worthy of respect in a democratic society, and would therefore offend against Art 9 of the European Convention on Human Rights.

4.159 A person still has the protection of the Act where they have a sincere belief about something, even if it is not a core component of the particular faith—*Mba v The Mayor & Burgesses of the London Borough of Merton*.[148] On the facts of that case, however, it was proportionate for Ms Mba to be required to work on a Sunday, as she was required to do so by virtue of her contract and there was no other viable or practicable way of running the care home effectively.

4.160 In some cases, there is a conflict between the religion of the employee and the requirements of the employer. The European Court of Human Rights jointly heard the four cases of *Eweida, Ladele, Chaplin and Macfarlane v UK*,[149] all of whom were committed Christians. The court found in favour of Ms Eweida but not the other applicants. In *Eweida*, an employee of BA was not permitted to wear a visible cross with her uniform. The domestic courts were found to have accorded too much weight to the employer's wish to project a certain image, and there was no evidence of any real encroachment on the interests of others. Ms Eweida's cross was discreet and cannot have detracted from her personal appearance. In the case of *Chaplin*, however, the court emphasised that the reason for asking her to remove the cross, namely the protection of health and safety on a hospital ward, was inherently of a greater magnitude than that which applied in respect of Ms Eweida. Moreover, this is a field where the domestic authorities must be allowed a wide margin of appreciation. The hospital managers were better placed to make decisions about clinical safety than a court. For *Ladele* (a registrar who refused to perform civil partnerships for homosexual couples) and *Macfarlane* (a counsellor who did not want to treat gay couples) the aim pursued by the local authority, which was to secure the rights of others and provide a service without discrimination, was legitimate. The court generally allows the national authorities a wide margin of appreciation when it comes to striking a balance between competing Convention rights and here they did not exceed that margin (see also the non-employment case of *Bull & Bull v Hall & Preddy*,[150] where the Supreme Court decided a similar point). Following this judgment, the Equality and Human Rights Commission provided further guidance on religion and equality in the workplace.

4.161 In *Achbita and another v G4S Secure Solutions NV*,[151] however, a rule prohibiting the wearing of any visible signs of political, philosophical, or religious belief which applied to all employees was found by the ECJ not to be direct discrimination against a Muslim who wore a headscarf, as it was not treating one religion less favourably than another. Neither was it indirect discrimination, as an employer's desire to project an image of neutrality in relation to customer-facing employees was a legitimate aim. In *Bougnaoui v Micropole SA*,[152] by contrast, dismissing a Muslim employee for refusing to remove a headscarf when meeting a particular customer was direct discrimination, as 'religion' includes the manifestations of that religion. She was treated less favourably compared to someone who had not manifested their religion. It was also indirect discrimination, and could not be justified. Discrimination is only lawful if it is based on a genuine occupation requirement and limited to matters which are absolutely necessary.

4.162 On a slightly different point, in *Apelogun-Gabriels v London Borough of Lambeth*[153] the claimant was a committed Christian who distributed to his colleagues quotations from

---

[148] [2013] EWCA Civ 1562.
[149] (Applications 48420/10, 59842/10, 51671/10, and 36516/10), [2013] ECHR 37.
[150] [2013] UKSC 73.
[151] (C 157/15), [2017] EUECJ C-157/15.   [152] (C-188/15).
[153] [2001] EWCA Civ 1853, [2002] ICR 713, [2002] IRLR 116.

the Bible that condemned homosexuality. He was dismissed, and he claimed religious discrimination. It was held that his dismissal was because he distributed homophobic materials, and was not because of his religious beliefs. If an employee is seeking to promote a
religion or belief contrary to instructions, his dismissal is due not to his religion or belief,
but his actions in disobeying a lawful order from his employer (*Chondol v Liverpool City
Council*;[154] also see *Kuteh v Dartford and Gravesham NHS Trust*[155] re improper proselytising
resulting in a fair dismissal).

4.163 The employer must know or be aware of the religious or philosophical belief of the
claimant, otherwise it cannot be claimed that there has been an act of discrimination. In
McClintock v Department of Constitutional Affairs[156] it was held that it would be absurd if
an employer was to be held liable for religious discrimination when the employee had not
made known his religious beliefs.

Direct Discrimination (s 13)

4.164 A person discriminates against another if, because of the protected characteristic of
religion or belief, he treats that person less favourably than he treats others. It is irrelevant
that the discriminator has the same religion or belief as the person discriminated against.
It did not constitute direct discrimination on grounds of religion for a local authority to require a female Muslim teacher to remove her full face veil while teaching her class. Another
woman teacher, whether Muslim or not, who wore a veil for a reason other than her religious belief would have received the same treatment from her employer and hence there
was no direct discrimination (*Azmi v Kirklees Metropolitan Borough Council*[157]).

Indirect Discrimination (s 19)

4.165 A person discriminates against a person who has the protected characteristic of
religion or belief if he applies a provision, criterion or practice that is discriminatory of that
person, puts him at a disadvantage, and cannot be shown to be a proportionate means of
achieving a legitimate aim. In *Azmi v Kirklees Metropolitan Borough Council*[158] it was held
that there was no indirect discrimination, as the requirement was a proportionate means of
achieving a legitimate aim. It is possible that the application of a dress code that adversely
affected persons of certain religions may amount to indirect discrimination that would
have to be justified, depending on the circumstances.

4.166 The other anti-discrimination provisions of the Act apply, ie s 26 (harassment), s 27
(victimisation), s 39 (discrimination and victimisation in employment), and s 40 (harassment by third parties).

Exception for Occupational Requirement (Equality Act, Sch 9)

4.167 Certain provisions of the Act do not apply if it can be shown that the employment
is for the purposes of organised religion, the post is an occupational requirement, and the
application of the requirement is a proportionate means of complying with the doctrines of
that religion. The requirement must arise because of the nature or context of the work, and
must engage the compliance principle, ie it is applied so as to comply with the doctrines
of the religion, or the non-conflict principle, ie to avoid conflicting with the strongly held
religious convictions of a significant number of the religion's followers, and if the person to
whom the requirement is applied does not meet it. The exceptions are s 39(1)(a) (arrangements for determining employment), s 39(1)(c) (refusing to offer employment), s 39(2)(b)
(access to promotion etc), and s 39(2)(c) (dismissal). The requirement can be to be of a

---

[154] EAT/0298/08.   [155] [2019] EWCA Civ 818.   [156] [2008] IRLR 29.
[157] [2007] ICR 1154, [2007] IRLR 484.   [158] n 140.

particular sex, or not to be a transsexual person, or not to be married or a civil partner, or not to be married to, or a civil partner of, a person who has a living former spouse, or relating to the circumstances in which a marriage or civil partnership came to an end, or a requirement related to sexual orientation.

4.168 The exceptions apply for purposes of organised religion. There is also a general exception from the employment provisions where a person with an ethos based on religion does not contravene the provisions in s 39 by applying in relation to work a requirement to be of a particular religion or belief, and it can be shown that, having regard to that ethos and to the nature of the work, it is an occupational requirement the application of which is a proportionate means of achieving a legitimate aim, and the person to whom it is applied does not meet it. Thus the nature of the work may involve leading or assisting in the observance of liturgical or ritualistic practices of the religion, or promoting the doctrine of the religion. However, the application of the requirement to be of a particular religion must be a proportionate means of achieving a legitimate aim. In *Glasgow City Council v McNab*[159] an atheist teacher was not interviewed for the post of acting principal teacher of pastoral care at a local authority-maintained school. The EAT upheld a decision that he had been discriminated against on grounds of his beliefs. The job of pastoral care did not require that the holder be a Roman Catholic, and it was not proportionate to apply such a requirement. Consequently the defence of occupational requirement failed.

4.169 However, under s 124A of the Schools Standard Framework Act 1998, designated independent schools are permitted to give preference in the appointment, promotion, and remuneration of persons whose religious opinions are in accordance with the tenets of the school.

H. **Sex**

4.170 This refers to the biological state of being a man or a woman.

Direct Discrimination (s 13)

4.171 A person discriminates against another if, because of the protected characteristic of sex, he treats that person less favourably than he treats others.

4.172 The motive for the discriminator's action is irrelevant. In *Grieg v Community Industry*[160] the claimant and another woman were appointed to two jobs, which involved working with men. The other woman failed to turn up for work, and so the claimant was not allowed to start work, as in the past there had been problems with one woman working alone with men. It was held that this constituted direct discrimination; the motive of the employers was irrelevant. This is so even though the action taken was well-intentioned, and for the protection of an employee (see *Amnesty International v Ahmed*,[161] para 4.147).

4.173 To establish direct discrimination, an employment tribunal should first identify an actual comparator, and then compare the treatment of the claimant with that afforded to a person of the other sex. The actual comparator's situation should be, in all material respects, identical to the claimant's. Where there is no actual comparator, the employment tribunal must create a hypothetical comparator, which can be done by carefully drawing inferences from all the available evidence (*Shamoon v Chief Constable of the Royal Ulster Constabulary*[162]).

---

[159] [2007] IRLR 476.   [160] [1979] ICR 356, [1979] IRLR 158.   [161] n 121.
[162] [2003] ICR 337, [2003] IRLR 285.

4.174 It will amount to discrimination if persons from one sex are given preferential treatment in terms of recruitment or promotion etc, in order to redress an imbalance of the sexes, but this does not prevent positive action in appropriate circumstances (see para 4.208). An employer does not unlawfully discriminate against a woman if he fails to treat her more favourably than a man (*Kenny v Ministry of Defence*[163]).

Indirect Discrimination (s 19)

4.175 An employer discriminates against a person who has the protected characteristic of sex if he applies a provision, criterion or practice that is discriminatory of that person, puts him/her at a disadvantage, and cannot be shown to be a proportionate means of achieving a legitimate aim.

4.176 An important distinction between direct and indirect discrimination is that so far as direct discrimination is concerned, there is no defence of justification, whereas in indirect discrimination, justification may be raised as a defence if it is a proportionate means of achieving a legitimate end. It is for the employment tribunal to determine where the provision, criterion or practice at issue is reasonably necessary (*Hardys & Hanson plc v Lax*[164]). There must be a real need for the provision etc, and it must be appropriate and reasonably necessary (*Network Rail Infrastructures Ltd v Gammie*[165]). Thus in *Ypourgos Esoterikon v Kalliri*[166] the ECJ held that a height requirement for Greek police was indirectly discriminatory against women, and could not be justified as it was not necessary or appropriate for its objective of ensuring the necessary physical capability for the job. A specific test of physical ability could be used instead.

4.177 Thus a provision that requires a woman to work overtime, or a refusal to permit her to return to work on a part-time basis (*Home Office v Holmes*[167]), or a refusal to permit her to work from home where this is feasible (*Lockwood v Crawley Warren Group Ltd*[168]) could all amount to a provision that puts her at a disadvantage (eg because of childminding difficulties) that would amount to indirect discrimination unless the provision etc is a proportionate means of achieving a legitimate aim. In *London Underground Ltd v Edwards*[169] the claimant was employed as a train driver, generally working from 8.00am until 4.00pm. As part of a cost-saving plan, the employer introduced a new system, which required her to commence work at 4.45am. As a single mother with a young child, she was not prepared to work the new system, and she resigned, claiming indirect discrimination. The EAT held that the employment tribunal was entitled to take into account their common knowledge that a proportionately larger number of women had childcare responsibilities than men, and, having regard to her length of service (ten years) and the fact that the demands of her family would be less in the future, the employer should have made arrangements to accommodate her personal requirements.

4.178 But it is possible to show that the application of the provision is proportionate and that the aim is legitimate. In *Briggs v North Eastern Education and Library Board*[170] the Northern Ireland Court of Appeal took the view that a contractual provision that was imposed on a school teacher that she should assist in the taking of games outside school hours was a requirement which was justified irrespective of sex or age or marital status, etc. A balance must be drawn between the discriminatory effect of the provision and the

---

[163] Unreported.   [164] [2005] EWCA Civ 846, [2005] ICR 1565, [2005] IRLR 726.
[165] EATS/0044/08.   [166] [2017] EUECJ C-409/16.
[167] [1984] 3 All ER 549, [1984] ICR 678, [1984] IRLR 299.
[168] EAT/1176/99, [2001] Emp LR 322.   [169] [1999] ICR 494, [1998] IRLR 364.
[170] [1990] IRLR 181.

reasonable needs of the employer, objectively determined (see also *Bilka-Kaufhaus v Weber von Hartz*[171]). Further economic factors, such as cost, can be weighed in the balance in assessing proportionality (*Cross v British Airways*[172]).

4.179 A person may discriminate (directly or indirectly) even though he is unaware that he is doing so. This may happen because of an inbuilt prejudice or the making of a stereotype assumption that a man is the 'breadwinner' of the family (*Skyrail Oceanic v Coleman*[173]). In *Gubala v Crompton Parkinson*[174] the choice of dismissal in a redundancy situation lay between a man and a woman. The woman had longer overall service, but the employers took into account the fact that the man was 58 years old, and had a family to support and a mortgage to keep up. The woman was young and married, with a husband who was working, and she was therefore dismissed for reason of redundancy. It was held that this amounted to unlawful discrimination; the tribunal refused to accept the 'breadwinner' criteria as a basis for redundancy selection.

4.180 On the other hand, it does not depend on whether the recipient thinks that the treatment is less favourable, for the test is an objective one for the employment tribunal to determine (*Burrett v West Birmingham Health Authority*[175]). Thus it has been held that a code governing the appearance of male and female employees, which was even-handed in its approach, was not discriminatory on grounds of sex. There is a distinction between discrimination between the sexes (which may be permissible) and discrimination against one or another of the sexes, which is not permitted (*Smith v Safeway plc*[176]).

Discrimination in Employment (s 39)

4.181 We have already noted (para 4.46) the general provisions dealing with the employment or non-employment of persons with a protected characteristic. Thus to refuse to employ a woman because 'it is a man's job' is an example of direct discrimination (*Batisha v Say*[177]), but if the unfavourable treatment has nothing to do with the sex of the person concerned, there is no direct discrimination (*Moberly v Commonwealth Hall (University of London)*[178]).

4.182 A comparison of the cases of persons of different sex must be such that the relevant circumstances in the one case are the same, or not materially different, in the other. Thus in *Thorn v Meggitt Engineering Ltd*[179] a woman was refused employment as a radial driller because she was neither tall enough nor strong enough, and it was held that no direct discrimination had occurred. The reason for the treatment meted out had nothing to do with that characteristic. In *Steere v Morris Bros*[180] a woman applied for a job as a heavy goods vehicle driver. When she was refused employment she claimed that she had been discriminated against. However, the employers were able to show that the reason she was not offered the job was because she lived too far away from the place of employment. The reason for her non-appointment had nothing to do with her sex, and no comparative person was involved.

4.183 Direct discrimination, however well intentioned, is not capable of being justified. In *Moyhing v Barts & London NHS Trust*[181] the claimant was a male student nurse who was required to be chaperoned when carrying out an electrocardiogram procedure on female patients. This was because it was inevitable that he would be touching the

---

[171] [1986] ECR 1607, [1987] ICR 110, [1986] IRLR 317.

[172] [2006] EWCA Civ 549, [2006] ICR 1239, [2006] IRLR 804.

[173] [1981] ICR 864, [1981] IRLR 398, (1981) *Times*, 28 July. [174] [1977] IRLR 10.

[175] [1994] IRLR 7. [176] n 7. [177] [1977] IRLR 6. [178] [1977] ICR 791, [1977] IRLR 176.

[179] [1976] IRLR 241. [180] IDS Handbook. [181] [2006] IRLR 860.

patient's breasts, and the policy was felt to be necessary in order to avoid the risks of claims of assault upon female patients and/or false accusations of assault against male nurses. The claimant claimed that this policy treated him as a second-class person, and demonstrated a widespread assumption that female nurses were automatically suited to provide personal care and that it was inappropriate for male nurses to provide intimate care for female patients. The EAT agreed that the claimant had suffered a detriment. That there were good and objective reasons for the policy was no defence, because there was no legal basis for treating male and female nurses differently so as to cause a detriment.

4.184 Provisions in an offer of employment or in the terms of employment which relate to pay are excluded from ss 13 and 39, because these are otherwise dealt with in ss 64–79, which replicate the equal pay provisions.

4.185 There is clearly an overlap with the characteristic of sex and marriage and pregnancy. Thus to refuse to promote a woman because she is married to a work colleague would be indirect discrimination on grounds of sex as well as being direct and indirect discrimination on grounds of marital status (*Chief Constable of Bedfordshire Constabulary v Graham*[182]). On the other hand, a dress code that differentiates between requirements for men and for women is not discriminatory on grounds of sex provided it is applied in an even-handed manner (*Smith v Safeways plc*[183]).

4.186 The provisions of s 27 (victimisation) and s 40 (harassment) apply to the protected characteristic of sex.

Occupational Requirement (Sch 9)

4.187 There is no contravention of the employment provisions in s 37 if, having regard to the nature or context of the work, a requirement to be or not to be of a particular sex is an occupational requirement, the requirement is a proportionate means of achieving a legitimate aim, and the person concerned does not meet it.

4.188 The Guidance Notes state that the occupational requirement must be crucial to the post, and not merely one of several important factors. There is a heavy burden of proof on those who seek to rely on an occupational requirement. Examples of occupational requirements that may still apply are:

(a) the job calls for authentic male or female characteristics (eg in a play or film);

(b) there are considerations of decency or privacy (eg public changing rooms, see eg *Etam plc v Rowan*;[184] *Sisley v Britannia Security Systems Ltd*[185]);

(c) the job involves living in a private home where a person of one sex might object to the presence of a person of the other sex;

(d) the job involves living in accommodation where there are no separate sleeping facilities (see Sch 23);

(e) the job needs to be held by a man because it is likely to be performed in a country whose laws or customs are such that the duties could not be performed by a woman;

(f) there may be religious or strongly held cultural objections to the job being done by a person of one sex.

---

[182] [2002] IRLR 239.   [183] n 7.   [184] [1989] IRLR 150.   [185] [1983] ICR 628, [1983] IRLR 404.

I. **Sexual Orientation**

4.189 This means a person's sexual orientation to persons of the same sex (ie a homosexual man or lesbian), persons of the opposite sex (ie a heterosexual person), or persons of either sex (ie a bisexual person). It does not cover particular sexual practices or fetishes, eg sadomasochism, or paedophile activities etc.

4.190 The provisions on direct discrimination (s 13), indirect discrimination (s 19), harassment (s 26), victimisation (s 27), discrimination or victimisation in employment (s 39), and harassment by employer (s 40) apply.

4.191 Indirect discrimination may occur when a provision, criterion or practice is applied that puts a person of a particular sexual orientation at a disadvantage when compared with others.

4.192 So far as harassment is concerned it is the objective nature of the alleged harassment itself that is determinative, not the circumstances of the victim. Thus to subject a person to homophobic abuse, even though it is known to the harassers that the victim was not homosexual, can still amount to harassment. Such abuse is on grounds of sexual orientation, amounts to unwanted conduct, has the effect of violating the victim's dignity or creating a degrading, humiliating, or offensive environment, and should reasonably be considered to have that effect (*English v Thomas Sanderson Blinds Ltd*[186]). To harass a person because of his/her association with another who has the protected characteristic is also covered. On the other hand, a gay employee who had disclosed his sexual orientation in a previous job could not complain of discrimination when the manager in his new job, without any discriminatory purpose, revealed his sexual orientation to colleagues against his wishes. He may have been upset that he could not release the information in his own way, but that did not constitute harassment (*Grant v HM Land Registry*).[187]

Occupational Requirements (Sch 9)

4.193 So far as s 39 (discrimination in employment) is concerned, there may be two occupational requirements. The first is where the nature of the employment is such that a particular sexual orientation is a proportionate means of achieving a legitimate aim, and the person concerned does not meet that requirement. The second applies to employment for the purposes of an organised religion, where there is a requirement as to sexual orientation in order to comply with the doctrines of the religion, or to avoid conflicting with the religious convictions of a significant number of the religions followers. Again, there is a heavy burden of proof on those who seek to rely on this exception.

Common Provisions

4.194 A number of provisions in the Equality Act are common to all of the protected characteristics.

A. **Application of the Act**

4.195 The employment provisions of the Equality Act apply in respect of persons who are employed. 'Employment' for the purpose of the Act means employment under a contract of service or apprenticeship or a contract personally to do work (s 83). Thus self-employed persons are included in the definition (see *Allonby v Accrington and Rossendale College*[188]),

---

[186] [2008] EWCA Civ 1421, [2009] 2 All ER 468, [2009] ICR 543, [2009] IRLR 206.
[187] [2011] IRLR 748, CA, [2011] EWCA Civ 769.
[188] [2005] All ER (EC) 289, [2004] ICR 1328, [2004] IRLR 224.

but not volunteer workers (*X v Mid-Sussex CAB*[189]). The dominant purpose of the contract must be to carry out the work personally. Personal responsibility is not, by itself, sufficient (*Mirror Group Newspapers Ltd v Gunning*[190]). Nor is an option to carry out the work personally (*Inland Revenue Commissioners v Post Office Ltd*[191]). There must be a personal obligation to perform the work or labour, and that performance must be the dominant purpose of the contract (*Mingeley v Pennock and Ivory*[192]). But the fact that a contract permits the provision of a substitute worker does not take that contract outside the provisions as long as the right to provide a replacement is limited in some way (*Byrne Brothers (Formwork) Ltd v Baird*[193]). A blanket right to provide a substitute is unlikely to meet the requirement of personal service (*Hawkins v Darken*[194]).

4.196 The Act is silent on territorial jurisdiction (unlike such provisions formerly found in the various anti-discrimination regulations) and it is left to the employment tribunals to determine whether the law applies in any particular case, which will depend on how close is the connection between the employment relationship and Great Britain. Certain principles can be gleaned from the decision in *Lawson v Serco Ltd*,[195] and other such cases (see para 1.14). In *British Airways plc v Mak*, a case decided on previous discrimination legislation, the Court of Appeal ruled that cabin crew based in Hong Kong and who worked on flights between there and London were to be regarded as doing their work 'partly in Great Britain', which meant that their employment was to be treated as being at an 'establishment' in Great Britain, even though they did not actually work at an 'establishment' at all.[196]

4.197 The Act also applies to Crown employment, employment as a relevant member of the staff of the House of Commons and House of Lords, and service in the armed forces. Offshore workers (who work on oil and gas rigs, and renewable energy installations) will be covered by an order in council.

B. Lawful Discrimination (Sch 22)

4.198 There is no discrimination of a person with the protected characteristics if action is taken to comply with an enactment. Thus, it is permissible to refuse to sell alcohol or cigarettes to a person under the age of 18, a disabled person may be fairly dismissed if it is necessary to comply with health or safety requirements (see *Farmiloe v Lane Group plc*,[197] para 4.104), special treatment may be given on grounds of pregnancy or maternity, health and safety legislation may be passed for the special protection of women, certain educational appointments may be restricted to persons of a particular religion, there are lawful restrictions on the appointment of foreign nationals to certain posts in the security and intelligence services, and so on.

C. Illegal Contracts

4.199 The fact that a person is employed under a contract of employment that is tainted with illegality will not necessarily exclude the operation of the anti-discrimination provisions of the Act (*Hall v Woolston Hall Leisure Centre*[198]). If a claimant is seeking to enforce a contract of employment that is tainted with illegality, it will probably be unenforceable, but if the remedy sought does not involve relying on the illegal contract, eg a claim of race or

---

[189] [2012] UKSC 59.   [190] [1986] 1 All ER 385, [1986] ICR 145, [1986] IRLR 27.
[191] [2003] ICR 546, (2003) IRLR 199.   [192] [2004] EWCA Civ 328, [2004] ICR 727, [2004] IRLR 373.
[193] [2002] ICR 667, [2002] IRLR 96.   [194] [2004] EWCA Civ 1755.
[195] [2006] UKHL 3, [2006] 1 All ER 823, [2006] ICR 250, [2006] IRLR 289.
[196] [2011] EWCA Civ 184.   [197] [2004] PIQR P22.
[198] [2000] 4 All ER 787, [2001] ICR 99, [2000] IRLR 578.

sex discrimination, the illegality is no bar to the claim (see para 3.7). An illegal immigrant can therefore still bring a claim for discrimination, where there is an insufficiently close connection between that and the immigration offence (*Hounga v Allen*[199]).

D. Relationships that Have Ended (s 108)

4.200 A person must not discriminate against another if the discrimination arises out of or is closely connected to the relationship that used to exist between them, and the conduct is of a description that would have contravened the Act if it had occurred during the relationship. This provision may have implications, for example, in respect of a refusal to give a reference (see *Rhys-Harper v Relaxation Group plc*[200]). Similarly, a person must not harass another if the harassment arises out of and is closely connected to a relationship that used to exist between them and the conduct would have contravened the Act had it occurred during the relationship.

4.201 Discrimination and harassment that takes place during an appeal against a dismissal (when technically the employee is no longer employed, see *J Sainsbury Ltd v Savage*[201]) or in the giving of a reference (*D'Souza v London Borough of Lambeth*[202]) is thus actionable in respect of all of the protected characteristics.

E. Liability of Employers (s 109)

4.202 Anything done by an employee in the course of his employment must be treated as also done by the employer, and it does not matter whether the thing is done with the employer's knowledge or approval. The phrase 'in the course of employment' has to be construed by an employment tribunal in a layman's sense, as a question of fact (*Jones v Tower Boot Co Ltd*[203]). However, it will be a defence for the employer to show that he took all reasonable steps to prevent that person from doing the thing or from doing anything of that description. Thus if the employer can show, for example, that he had given proper training to his employees to prevent discrimination and harassment, published an equal opportunities policy and was unaware that unlawful acts were being done, he may be able to successfully raise the defence. For example, in *Tower Hamlets v Balgobin*[204] the EAT commented that it was difficult to see what steps could have been taken by an employer to prevent harassment from occurring. The employment tribunal must consider whether the employer took any steps at all to prevent an employee from committing an act of discrimination, and then consider what further steps could have been taken which were reasonably practicable (*Canniffe v East Ridings of Yorkshire Council*[205]). In *Martins v Marks & Spencer plc*,[206] the Court of Appeal considered the firm's equal opportunity policy, their compliance with the Code of Practice on selection procedures, criteria, and interviewing, and the inclusion on the interviewing panel of a person with an interest in recruiting from ethnic minorities, and held that in the circumstances the employers had made out a defence.

4.203 But s 109 does not exonerate the individual employee from liability and proceedings may be taken against the latter for a contravention of the Act by virtue of s 110, although there would be no contravention if the employee relied on a statement by his employer that what he did was not a contravention of the Act and it was reasonable for him to rely on that statement.

[199] [2014] UKSC 47.
[200] [2003] UKHL 33, [2003] 4 All ER 1113, [2003] ICR 867, [2003] IRLR 484.
[201] [1981] ICR 1, [1980] IRLR 109.   [202] [2003] ICR 867, (2003) IRLR 484.
[203] [1997] IRLR 168, (1997) ICR 254.   [204] [1987] ICR 829, [1987] IRLR 401.
[205] [2000] IRLR 555.   [206] [1998] ICR 1005, [1998] IRLR 326.

4.204 A discrimination claim can therefore be made against the individual discriminator as well as the employer, and compensation can be awarded on the basis of joint and several liability (*London Borough of Hackney v Sivanandan*).[207]

F. Instructing, Causing or Inducing Discrimination (s 111)

4.205 A person must not instruct, cause or induce (directly or indirectly) another person to do anything with respect to a third person that would contravene s 39 (discrimination in employment, see eg, para 4.46) or s 108 (relationships that have ended, see para 4.200) or s 112 (aiding a contravention, see para 4.207). A refusal to follow an instruction to discriminate on a prohibited ground was held to be unlawful discrimination in *Weathersfield Ltd v Sargent*.[208]

4.206 Proceeding for a contravention of s 111 may be brought by:

(a) the person to whom the instruction or inducement was given, if he is subjected to a detriment as a result of the instruction or inducement;

(b) the person against whom the instruction or inducement was directed if he suffers a detriment as a result of the instruction or inducement (even though the instruction is not carried out);

(c) the Equality and Human Rights Commission (see eg *Commission for Racial Equality v Imperial Society for Teachers of Dancing*[209]).

G. Aiding Contraventions (s 112)

4.207 A person must not knowingly help another person to do anything that contravenes s 39 (discrimination in employment, see eg para 4.48) or s 108 (relationships that have ended, see para 4.200) or s 111 (instructing, causing or inducing discrimination, see earlier). The help must be substantial or productive, but not so insignificant as to be negligible (*Anyanwu v South Bank Student Union*[210]). A general attitude of helpfulness by the alleged aider is not enough to establish liability (*Hallam v Avery*[211]). There is no contravention of s 112 if the person who is asked to help relies on a statement that the act for which the help is asked does not contravene the Act, and it is reasonable for him to do so.

H. Positive Action; Recruitment and Promotion (s 159)

4.208 An employer is permitted to take the protected characteristics into consideration when deciding whether to recruit or promote persons with that characteristic because they are under-represented in the workforce. But such positive action will only apply when the candidates for recruitment or promotion are equally qualified (*Abrahamsson and Anderson v Fogelqvist*[212]). 'Qualification' does not refer to academic achievements, but work experience, skills, and other competences can be taken into consideration. The action in question must be a proportionate means of achieving the aims of overcoming any disadvantage associated with the characteristic or enabling such disadvantaged persons to participate in an activity. A target scheme for recruitment, selection, and promotion is not precluded by EC law if the scheme does not ensure that persons with the protected characteristic were automatically and unconditionally offered preferential treatment over those who do

---

[207] [2011] IRLR 740.   [208] [1999] ICR 425, [1999] IRLR 94.   [209] [1983] ICR 473, [1983] IRLR 315.
[210] (2003) *Times*, 5 December, [2003] All ER (D) 285 (Nov).
[211] [2001] UKHL 15, [2001] ICR 408, [2001] IRLR.   [212] [2002] ICR 932, [2000] IRLR 732.

not share that characteristic (*Badeck v Hessischer*[213]). Thus positive discrimination is unlawful but positive action may be encouraged (*EFTA Surveillance Authority v Kingdom of Norway*[214]). More favourable treatment of those with the protected characteristic is not permitted, other than as permitted by the Act (eg on grounds of pregnancy and maternity).

I. Discriminatory Advertisements

4.209 The European Court has ruled that a discriminatory advertisement was direct discrimination even though there is no identifiable complainant. In *Centrum voor gelijkheid van kansen v Firma Feryn*[215] the employer was a company that specialised in installing security gates. A director of the company publicly stated that he would not employ immigrants because of the reluctance of customers to give such persons access to their homes during installation work. It was held that this constituted race discrimination and gave rise to a presumption of the existence of a recruitment policy that is directly discriminatory. The burden of proof would then shift to the employer to show that the actual recruitment practice did not correspond with the statement made. However, it was open to member states to decide whether to pass legislation to enable an appropriate body to bring proceedings in such cases where there is no identifiable victim.

4.210 Proceedings in respect of discriminatory job advertisements may be brought by the Equality and Human Rights Commission (see para 4.239).

J. Job Advertisements

4.211 Job advertisements must not fall foul of anti-discrimination legislation. It is also clear that the wording of s 39 means that the publishing of an advertisement is part of the arrangements a person makes 'for deciding to whom to offer employment'.

4.212 Thus to advertise for a 'young person', 'attractive female', or 'Afro-Asian ethnicity', etc would be contrary to the age, sex, and race anti-discriminatory provisions respectively, and would fall within the scope of s 39. But a person would only be able to make a claim of such discrimination if s/he had a genuine intention of applying for the post, but was deterred from doing so by the nature of the advertisement. In *Keane v Investigo*[216] the claimant was an accountant in her early 50s. She applied for more than 20 jobs which were advertised as being suitable for a recently qualified accountant, and when she was not offered interviews she brought claims of age discrimination. Several such claims were settled out of court, but the present employer decided to resist the claim. It was held that her job applications were not bona fide, and by being turned down for a job which she had no genuine intention of accepting she had not suffered a detriment, or been treated unfavourably, or put at a disadvantage. (It is unclear the effect that *CHEZ Razpredelenie Bulgaria AD v Komisia za ot diskriminatsia* (para 4.25) will have on this.)

K. Conduct Giving Rise to Separate Proceedings (s 140)

4.213 If two or more separate proceedings are brought under the Act, with at least one being for a contravention of s 111 (instructing, causing or inducing contraventions), a court may transfer proceedings to an employment tribunal, and an employment tribunal may transfer the proceedings to a court, and the jurisdiction of the court or tribunal is transferred accordingly.

[213] [2000] All ER (EC) 289.   [214] [2008] 1 CMLR 44.   [215] n 3.   [216] EAT/0389/09.

L. Unenforceable Terms (s 142)

4.214 A term of a contract is unenforceable against a person in so far as it constitutes, promotes, or provides for treatment that is of a description prohibited by the Act. On an application by a person who has an interest in a contract, a county court (or sheriff's court) may make an order for an unenforceable term to be removed or modified.

M. Restriction on Contracting Out (s 144)

4.215 A term of a contract is unenforceable by a person in whose favour it would operate in so far as it purports to exclude or limit a provision of the Act. However, this does not apply to a contract that settles a claim in respect of which the employment tribunal has jurisdiction (see s 120) if the contract:

  (a) is made with the assistance of a conciliation officer (see para 1.40); or

  (b) is a qualifying compromise contract. A qualified compromise contract is one drawn up by an independent adviser, provided the conditions set out in s 141 of the Employment Rights Act are complied with (see para 20.40);

  (c) is a contract settled as a result of an arbitration award made in accordance with the scheme set out in s 212A of the Trade Union and Labour Relations Act 1992 (see para 1.46).

N. Void and Unenforceable Terms (s 145)

4.216 A term of a collective agreement is void in so far as it constitutes, promotes, or provides for treatment of a description prohibited by the Act. A rule of an undertaking is unenforceable against a person in so far as it constitutes, promotes, or provides for treatment of the person that is of a description prohibited by the Act. This includes a rule made by an employer for application to employees, persons who apply for employment, and persons the employer considers for employment. An application to an employment tribunal may also be made for a declaration that a term in a collective agreement that may be discriminatory in the future be declared unenforceable (s 146). It is also not possible to contract out of provisions made under the Act (eg by regulations).

O. National Security (s 192)

4.217 A person does not contravene the Act by doing, for the purpose of safeguarding national security, anything it is proportionate to do for that purpose. Section 60 (enquiries about disability and health) does not apply to anything done for the purpose of vetting applicants for work for reasons of national security. So far as remedies are concerned, any recommendation made in national security cases can only be made in respect of the complainant, not other persons (s 125).

4.218 Proceedings in cases that involve national security come within the provisions of the Employment Rights Act 1996 (see para 17.167).

P. Death of a Claimant

4.219 A cause of action under the Equality Act can be continued after the death of the claimant by his personal representatives, under the provisions of the Law Reform (Miscellaneous Provisions) Act 1934 (*Lewisham and Guys Mental Health NHS Trust v Andrews*[217]).

---

[217] [1999] ICR 774, [1999] IRLR 407.

Q. **Other Provisions**

4.220 There are further provisions in the Act that relate specifically to contract workers (s 41), police (s 42), partnerships (s 44), barristers (s 47), advocates (s 48), personal office holders (s 49), appointments to public offices (s 50), qualification bodies (s 53), employment service providers (s 55), trade organisations (s 57), official business of local authorities (s 58), and occupational pension schemes (s 61: but see Sch 9 Part 2 for exceptions).

Submitting a Complaint

A. **Jurisdiction (s 120)**

4.221 An employment tribunal has jurisdiction to determine a complaint arising from Part V of the Act, which includes the work provisions contained in s 39 (discrimination in employment), s 40 (harassment), s 108 (relationships that have ended), s 111 (instructing and causing discrimination), s 112 (aiding a contravention), and ss 64–79 (equality of terms). A civil court may strike out a claim relating to a non-discrimination rule if it appears that this could more conveniently be determined by an employment tribunal, and may also refer a matter to the employment tribunal for determination. The territorial jurisdiction must be determined by employment tribunals in accordance with the principles set out in *Lawson v Serco Ltd*[218] and, since most of the anti-discrimination provisions have their origins in EU law, the decisions in *Bleuse v MBT Transport*[219] (see para 1.19).

B. **Time Limits (s 123)**

4.222 Proceedings on a complaint within s 120 may not be brought after the end of a period of three months starting with the date of the act to which the complaint relates, or such other period as the employment tribunal thinks just and equitable.

4.223 Conduct that extended over a period of time is to be treated as done at the end of that period, and a failure to do a thing is to be treated as occurring when the person in question decided on it. Thus a claim based on continuing discrimination may be brought up to three months after the discrimination has ceased (*Calder v James Finlay Corpn Ltd*[220]). But a distinction must be made between an act of continuing discrimination and an act of discrimination that has continuing consequences. In the latter case, the time limit of three months will normally apply. In *Clarke v Hampshire Electro-Plating Co Ltd*[221] the claimant, who is black, saw an advertisement for a supervisory job with his present employers. On 25 April he saw his employer about the vacancy, but was told he would not be considered. On 4 September a white man was appointed to the job, and the claimant then submitted a claim, alleging he had been discriminated against on grounds of race. An employment tribunal held that his complaint was out of time, but if there was discrimination it dated from 25 April. On appeal the decision was reversed by the EAT. Time will start to run from the date the cause of action crystallised, not from when the claimant felt he had been discriminated against. The cause of action had not crystallised when his application for promotion was rejected but from the date when the white man was appointed, and this provided the comparison that enabled him to believe that he had been discriminated against.

---

[218] [2006] UKHL 3, [2006] 1 All ER 823, [2006] ICR 250, [2006] IRLR 289.
[219] [2008] ICR 488, [2008] IRLR 264.
[220] [1989] ICR 157.   [221] [1992] ICR 312, [1991] IRLR 490.

4.224 A somewhat different result was reached in *Sougrin v Haringey Health Authority*,[222] where the claimant, a black nurse, appealed internally against her employer's decision to place her in a certain salary grade. Her appeal was unsuccessful, although an appeal by a white colleague succeeded. Six months later she submitted her application to an employment tribunal, arguing that she had been discriminated, on grounds of race, and that the discrimination was a continuing act. It was held by the Court of Appeal that she had not submitted her application within the statutory time limit. The decision to reject her appeal was a one-off act with continuing consequences that resulted in her being paid less than the white colleague. There was no suggestion that the employers had a policy to pay black nurses less than white nurses. Had there been evidence of such a policy, it would have been possible to argue that there was an act of continuing discrimination but, since there was no such evidence, her claim was out of time.

4.225 But if there is a deliberate omission to do something, time will run from the date when the discriminator was in a position to do that thing (*Swithland Motors plc v Clarke*[223]).

C. **Burden of Proof (s 136)**

4.226 If there are facts from which an employment tribunal could decide, in the absence of any other explanation, that a person has contravened a provision in the Act, the tribunal must hold that the contravention has occurred, unless the person shows that he did not contravene the provision. This reversal of proof now applies to all the protected characteristics. The reversal of the burden of proof also applies when making enquiries about disability and health (see s 60, para 4.110). However, where the burden shifts to the employer to show a non-discriminatory explanation for the decision, it does not impose a blanket obligation to prove the absence of discrimination in every act of every employee that formed part of the chain of causation leading to the act complained of (*CLFIS v Reynolds*[224]).

4.227 It will be recalled that unreasonable behaviour, by itself, does not equate with unlawful discriminatory behaviour. In *Law Society v Bahl*[225] it was stated that all unlawful discriminatory behaviour is always unreasonable, but not all unreasonable behaviour is necessarily unlawfully discriminatory. Similarly, all racist language is offensive, but not all offensive language is racist, and the fact that members of a racial group are treated differently does not, by itself, constitute unlawful discrimination. It must be shown that the treatment was less favourable on grounds of race (*Barclays Bank plc v Kapur*[226]). Equally, the fact that the recipient of the offensive treatment is a woman, or disabled, etc, says nothing about the perpetrator's actions. Thus if A is dismissed, and A is a woman, it does not necessarily follow that A was dismissed because she is a woman. If B is black, and B suffers a detriment, it does not necessarily follow that B has suffered the detriment because he is black. If hostile action has nothing to do with the relevant protected characteristic, no unlawful discrimination has occurred.

4.228 The fact that the employer already employs persons of different protected characteristics is not conclusive (*Johnson v Timber Tailors (Midlands) Ltd*[227]) but it is a relevant consideration of evidential value (*Piperdy v UEM Parker Glass*[228]). If an employer's replies to a questionnaire sent by the EHRC are evasive, it could lead to an inference that discrimination took place (*Virdee v EEC Quarries Ltd*[229]). Evidence of events that took place

[222] [1992] ICR 650, [1992] IRLR 416.   [223] [1994] ICR 231, [1994] IRLR 275.
[224] [2015] EWCA Civ 439.   [225] n 11.
[226] [1991] 2 AC 355, [1991] 1 All ER 646, [1991] ICR 208, [1991] IRLR 136.
[227] [1978] IRLR 146.   [228] IDS Supplement.   [229] [1978] IRLR 295.

subsequent to the alleged act of discrimination is admissible where it is logically probative of a relevant fact (*Chattopadhyay v Headmaster of Holloway School*[230]).

4.229 A claimant may be able to obtain the discovery of existing statistics showing the number of persons from groups with different protected characteristics who have applied for posts, been engaged, or been promoted, for such evidence may have some probative value from which inferences of discriminatory practices may be drawn (*West Midlands Passenger Transport Executive v Singh*[231]). But an employment tribunal cannot order a respondent to produce details of the composition of the workforce where such evidence does not exist, for this is not 'discovery' of documents, nor 'particulars' of the grounds on which the claimants seek to rely.

D. **Transfer of Proceedings (s 140)**

4.230 If there are two or more separate proceedings being brought under the Act, with at least one of them dealing with a contravention of s 111 (instructing, causing or inducing discrimination, see para 4.205), proceedings may be transferred to or from a county court (or sheriff's court) or an employment tribunal, and the court or tribunal shall have jurisdiction to deal with the proceedings so transferred.

E. **Remedies (s 124)**

4.231 If there has been a contravention of a provision mentioned in s 120 (see para 4.221) the employment tribunal may make the following remedies:

(a) a declaration as to the rights of the complainant and respondent in relation to the matters to which the proceedings relate;

(b) order the respondent to pay compensation to the complainant. The amount of the award should correspond to the amount that would be awarded by a county court or sheriff under s 119, and generally speaking is equivalent to the amounts that would flow from claims in tort, including an award in respect of injured feelings;

(c) make an appropriate recommendation. This will be that within a specified period the respondent takes specified steps for the purpose of obviating or reducing the adverse effect of any matter to which the proceedings relate on the complainant. Although the Explanatory Notes suggest that this power could be used for the benefit of persons other than the claimant, eg other employees, or to make improvements in the employer's policies and/or procedures, the Deregulation Act 2015 removes the power to make a wider recommendation—the recommendation has to relate to the claimant. If the respondent fails, without reasonable excuse, to comply with the appropriate recommendation so far as it relates to the claimant, the tribunal can make or increase the compensation award. However, the Act is silent on how, if at all, other persons who are not parties to the proceedings can enforce any such recommendation. The power to make a recommendation does not apply to equal pay claims (s 113(6)).

4.232 If there has been a contravention of s 19 (indirect discrimination), and the employment tribunal is satisfied that the provision, criterion or practice was not applied with the intention of discriminating against the complainant, it must not make an award of compensation unless it first considers whether to make a declaration or a recommendation.

---

[230] [1982] ICR 132, [1981] IRLR 487.
[231] [1988] 2 All ER 873, [1988] ICR 614, [1988] IRLR 186.

4.233 Damages may include an award for injury to feelings, which is fundamental to a claim based on discrimination (*Murray v Powertech (Scotland) Ltd*[232]). There can be an award for injury to feelings even where the claimant did not know about the motivation of the discriminator, as in *Taylor v XLN Telecom Ltd*[233] where a black employee who brought a grievance complaining of race discrimination was dismissed, ostensibly for poor performance. He suffered distress and psychiatric injury as a result of the dismissal, but did not know then that the dismissal was in part prompted by his grievance relating to discrimination. The EAT held that it was nonetheless an injury attributable to the discriminatory conduct.

4.234 The award will usually fall within three 'Vento' bands, depending on the frequency and nature of the wrongful act (*Vento v Chief Constable of West Yorkshire Police (No 2)*.[234] Since *De Souza v Vinci Construction (UK) Ltd*[235]), these have been updated annually. From April 2020 the lower band is between £900 and £9,000; the middle band between £9,000 and £27,000; and the top band between £27,000 and £45,000; with exceptional cases exceeding this.

4.235 An award may also be made for psychiatric illness suffered as a result of sex discrimination and/or harassment (*HM Prison Service v Salmon*[236]).

There is currently no limit on the amount that can be awarded, which can include aggravated damages if the injury was inflicted by conduct that was high-handed, malicious, insulting, or oppressive (*HM Prison Service v Johnson*[237]), and such damages should not be aggregated with or treated as part of the damages awarded for injury to feelings (*Scott v Commissioners of Inland Revenue*[238]), but see para 20.98.

4.236 It must be borne in mind that ss 123–124 (see paras 4.221 and 4.230) apply only to complaints brought under the Equality Act, and there are some differences from the provisions that apply to complaints made under the Employment Rights Act, for which see Chapter 17.

F. Interest on Awards (s 139)

4.237 Interest on the compensation element (but not on the award to injured feelings) may be awarded, both in respect of the period up to the date when the compensation was assessed and the period following the promulgation of the award (but not if the full amount is paid within 14 days): see Employment Tribunals (Interest on Awards in Discrimination Cases) Regulations 1996, as amended.

4.238 The minister may make regulations for enabling an employment tribunal to include interest on an amount awarded by it in proceedings under the Act. It is likely that the pattern laid down in the Employment Tribunals (Interest on Awards in Discrimination Cases) Regulations 1996 (no longer in force) will be followed.

Enforcement by the Commission: Equality Act 2006

4.239 The enforcement powers of the Equality and Human Rights Commission can be found in the Equality Act 2006 (as amended). The Commission may bring proceedings

---

[232] [1992] IRLR 257.   [233] [2010] IRLR 499, EAT.   [234] [2002] EWCA Civ 1871.
[235] Ltd [2017] EWCA Civ 879.   [236] [2001] IRLR 425.   [237] [2007] IRLR 951.
[238] [2004] EWCA Civ 400, [2004] ICR 1410, [2004] IRLR 713.

under that Act in respect of alleged violation of provisions in the Equality Act 2010 dealing with direct discrimination (s 13), discrimination arising from disability (s 15), gender reassignment disability (s 16), pregnancy and maternity discrimination (s 18), the application of a provision, criterion or practice that by virtue of s 19 of the 2010 Act amounts to indirect discrimination, enquiries about disability and health, and relationships that have ended (s 108(1)) in so far as these provisions relate to the prohibited conduct of the protected characteristics in the employment field. It is immaterial whether the Commission knows or suspects that a person has been affected by the unlawful act (Equality Act 2006, s 24A). The proceedings must commence within six months of the act complained of, and an injunction may be obtained from a county court or sheriff court to restrain a person from repeating the unlawful act at any time within five years of a non-discrimination notice (Equality Act 2006, ss 71–72). The Commission may also bring a preliminary action in an employment tribunal on behalf of a person, even though that person has not made a complaint, and the employment tribunal can make an order of rights or a recommendation that appropriate action be taken to obviate or reduce the adverse effect of the discrimination (Equality Act 2006, s 73).

4.240 The Commission has power to investigate whether an unlawful act has been committed (Equality Act 2006, s 20) and, if so, may issue a notice requiring the person to whom it is given to prepare an action plan for the purpose of avoiding repetition or continuation of the unlawful act. An appeal against the notice may be made to the employment tribunal or county court as appropriate (Equality Act 2006, ss 21–22). The Commission may also enter into an agreement with a person under which he undertakes not to commit unlawful acts of a specific kind, and to take (or refrain from taking) other specified action.

4.241 The Commission may also apply to the court for an injunction (or interdict in Scotland) to restrain a person from committing an unlawful act or requiring him to comply with his undertaking, for example regarding unlawful advertising or instructions or pressure to discriminate. The Commission may give assistance in legal proceedings, and costs and legal representation may also be given to individuals in appropriate cases. It may intervene in legal proceedings, and in order to assist a person in obtaining the necessary information, the Commission may issue a questionnaire that can be sent to the alleged discriminator.

4.242 The Commission may carry out formal investigations, either on its own initiative or at the request of the Secretary of State, with specific terms of reference, and notice will be given to the persons affected. If the investigation is confined to the activities of a named person, an opportunity must be given for them to make oral or written representations (*Re Prestige Group plc*[239]). A person may be required to furnish information, or to attend a hearing and give oral evidence on specified matters, and to produce relevant documents. If a person fails or refuses to comply, the Commission may apply to a county court (or sheriff's court) for an order requiring him to comply, and a failure to do so is punishable in as like manner as neglecting a witness summons. Wilfully to alter, suppress, conceal, or destroy a document, or knowingly or recklessly to make a statement that is false in a material particular, is an offence, punishable on summary conviction by a fine not exceeding level 5 on the standard scale.

4.243 If, in the course of its investigations, the Commission is satisfied that a person is committing an unlawful discriminatory act, or contravening an equality clause (s 66 of the 2010 Act), the Commission may issue a non-discriminatory notice. It must first inform the person of its intentions, specifying the ground, and give him an opportunity to make oral

---

[239] [1984] ICR 473, [1984] IRLR 166.

or written representations (*Re Prestige Group plc*[240]). An appeal may be lodged to an employment tribunal within six weeks against any requirement, and the tribunal may quash the requirement it thinks to be unreasonable, or substitute its own directions. On such appeal, it is open to the person against whom the order has been made to challenge any finding of fact relating to the order (*Commission for Racial Equality v Amari Plastics*[241]). A public register of non-discrimination notices shall be kept, and if at any time within five years of the notice becoming final it appears to the Commission that the discriminatory act has been or is likely to be repeated, the Commission may apply to the county court for an injunction to restrain the person from doing so.

4.244 New codes of practice specific to the Equality Act have also been issued by the Commission and replace those that were issued by the previous commissions.

Other Protected Groups

A. **Rehabilitated Persons**

4.245 The Rehabilitation of Offenders Act 1974 seeks to ensure that if a person has made a genuine effort to rehabilitate into society after conviction for a serious criminal offence, he may be spared the indignity and embarrassment of subsequently having to disclose his unsavoury past. Provided he does not commit a serious offence within the rehabilitation period, he may, at the end of that time, be regarded as a rehabilitated person, and his conviction will be treated as having been 'wiped off the slate'. The Act is somewhat complex, but the general rule is that the length of the rehabilitation period will depend on the age of the offender at the time of conviction and the sentence given for the offence, and so the period will vary. The Legal Aid, Sentencing and Punishment of Offenders Act 2012 (LASPO) made changes to the Rehabilitation of Offenders Act 1974 and came into force in March 2014. This reduces the length of time before a conviction becomes 'spent', and is retrospective, so it applies to pre-existing convictions. For custodial and community sentences, the rehabilitation period will start from the end of the total sentence imposed by the court (including the licence period), not from the day of release. The rehabilitation period includes an additional 'buffer period' that runs from the end of the sentence. This buffer period is determined by the length of total sentence imposed. Therefore a conviction is deemed to be spent once a certain amount of time has elapsed (the 'buffer period') after the sentence, rather than conviction, as it had been before the amendment (this is except for fines, when it is from the date of conviction). The rehabilitation period depends on the sentence that was given, not the offence committed, and the periods operate on a sliding scale (see para 4.249). A sentence of imprisonment of more than four years (previously 30 months) will never become 'spent'. Once a person has become 'rehabilitated' evidence of his previous conviction is not generally admissible, and he may not be asked about it or, if he is asked, he need not tell the truth, and may deny his previous conviction.

4.246 So far as the law of employment is concerned, s 4(3)(b) of the Act provides that (subject to certain exceptions) a 'spent' conviction, or failure to disclose such, shall not be grounds for dismissing or excluding a person from any office, profession, occupation, or employment, or for prejudicing him in any way in any occupation or employment. However, the limits of the section need to be noted. At common law, an employer has the right to please himself whether or not to employ someone and although to refuse to employ a rehabilitated person may be to 'exclude' him, the section provides no remedy for a

[240] n 220.   [241] [1982] QB 1194, [1982] 2 All ER 499, [1982] ICR 304.

person who may feel that he has been discriminated against. Equally, a refusal to promote a rehabilitated person may amount to prejudicing him in that employment, but again no remedy is provided. On the other hand, if an employee who was a rehabilitated person was dismissed, and the sole ground was the discovery of his past convictions, this would undoubtedly amount to an unfair dismissal if he was otherwise within the protection of the Employment Rights Act (see Chapter 17). In *Hendry v Scottish Liberal Club*,[242] one of the reasons why the claimant was dismissed was connected with the discovery that he had been convicted many years ago of possessing cannabis. This conviction was 'spent' within the meaning of the Act, and hence it was not a statutory reason for dismissal.

4.247 In *Property Guards Ltd v Taylor and Kershaw*[243] the two claimants were employed as security guards. On commencing their employment they signed a statement to the effect that they had never been guilty of a criminal offence. When the employers discovered that they had both been convicted of minor offences of dishonesty, they were dismissed. The EAT upheld the finding of the employment tribunal that the dismissals were unfair. In both cases the convictions were 'spent' within the meaning of the Act. They were entitled not to disclose their previous convictions.

4.248 If an employer subsequently discovers that the employee has had a previous conviction, he must make all necessary enquiries to ascertain whether or not the conviction is spent before he starts taking action. In *Brooks v Ladbroke Lucky Seven Entertainment*,[244] the claimant was dismissed when it was discovered that he had had a prior conviction. It was argued on behalf of the employer that the dismissal was necessary in view of the nature of their business (as a gambling club), and as they did not know that the conviction was spent, they were not acting unreasonably. It was held that the employer should have sought further information about the nature of the offence and the penalty imposed, and a failure to do so rendered the dismissal unfair.

4.249 The main rehabilitation periods are as follows:

Sentence	Rehabilitation period
Imprisonment over 4 years	never spent
Imprisonment over 30 months	sentence plus 7 years
Imprisonment 6–30 months	sentence plus 4 years
Imprisonment less than 6 months	sentence plus 2 years
Fine	1 year
community order	sentence plus 1 year
Conditional discharge/supervision order	varies between 1 year and length of order
Absolute discharge	6 months
Caution	immediately
Conditional caution	3 months

These limits apply from the end date of the sentence (including the licence period). Note that for offenders under 18 at the time of conviction, these periods are halved, except for custodial sentences up to six months, where the buffer period will be 18 months. Further protection for those with minor convictions came from the Supreme Court in *R v Secretary of State for the Home Department*,[245] where it found that the requirement to disclose these cautions was a breach of the individual's right to a private life and could jeopardise their

---

[242] [1977] IRLR 5.   [243] [1982] IRLR 175, EAT.   [244] [1977] IRLIB.   [245] [2014] UKSC 35.

future careers. The court said the disclosures 'were not necessary in a democratic society' and were not based on any rational assessment of risk. Since then the Home Office has introduced a system to filter out single minor convictions or cautions. Cautions given to adults are removed from records checks after six years, while cautions given to children are filtered out after two years.

4.250 The rules relating to enhanced certificates for work with children and disabled adults (which are stricter than for other certificates) were considered in the *Lorraine Gallagher*[246] case, where the Supreme Court found that the rules were disproportionate in that they required disclosure for old multiple convictions even where they were minor ones, and did not distinguish between cautions/reprimands and convictions for juveniles, and so issued a declaration of incompatibility. This may lead to the rules being amended.

4.251 The Act does not apply to questions which are asked of a person in order to assess the suitability of a person for admission to the professions of medical practitioner, barrister, accountant, solicitor, dentist, dental hygienist or auxiliary, veterinary surgeon, nurse, midwife, ophthalmic or dispensing optician, or pharmaceutical chemist, or a Scottish registered teacher. Such people must still tell the truth about their previous convictions. Nor can a person tell a lie if the questions are asked for the purpose of assessing his suitability for the following employments, namely, certain legal appointments and offices, certain employment connected with the punishment of offenders, constables, traffic wardens, probation officers, carers, and employment with children, further education teachers, proprietors of independent schools, certain local government social workers, hospital workers, persons who work for building societies or who provide financial services, youth club leaders, and employment with cadet forces. Certain other occupations are also excluded from the provisions of the Act (see the Rehabilitation of Offenders Act 1974 (Exceptions) Orders 1975 (as amended), and see *Wood v Coverage Care Ltd*).[247]

B. Access to Criminal Records

4.252 Employers who wish to know whether an applicant for employment has or has not got a criminal record may be able to use the procedures set out in the Police Act 1997, which makes arrangements for access to criminal records for employment-related purposes. This Act enables a criminal record check to be made available by the Disclosure and Barring Service (formerly the Criminal Records Bureau) from computerised national criminal records, in response to an application by a person who is the subject of the check or by a registered organisation.

4.253 It is a criminal offence to require employees or applicants to provide criminal record information themselves through a subject access request. Employers should instead use the Disclosure and Barring Service.

Criminal Conviction Certificate (s 112)

4.254 This certificate gives prescribed details of every conviction which is recorded in central police records. A 'conviction' for this purpose means a conviction within the meaning of the Rehabilitation of Offenders Act, other than a conviction which is spent. Alternatively, the certificate will record that there is no conviction. An employer cannot apply direct to the Criminal Records Agency for this certificate, but can request that the job applicant provides one as a prerequisite for employment.

---

[246] *In the matter of an application by Lorraine Gallagher for Judicial Review (Northern Ireland), etc* [2019] UKSC 3.   [247] [1996] IRLR 264, EAT.

Criminal Record Certificate (s 113)

4.255 This is a more detailed certificate, which will record every matter recorded in central police records, including a conviction which is spent under the Rehabilitation of Offenders Act. This certificate can be asked for by a person seeking employment in one of the occupations where a conviction under the Rehabilitation of Offenders Act must be disclosed, even though it would otherwise be spent. An application for this type of certificate will be made by the subject of the check, countersigned by a person who is listed in a register to be kept by the Secretary of State as being likely to employ persons in occupations which are excluded from that Act. It is likely that this certificate will be sought by persons who wish to be employed in a large number of occupations which are exempt from the 1974 Act, including the judiciary, police, Crown employment, probation officers, prison staff, professional groups generally, banking and financial services, carers/social workers, etc.

Enhanced Criminal Record Certificate (s 115)

4.256 This certificate, as well as containing the information found in the criminal record certificate, may contain additional information provided by local police forces, including cautions and relevant non-conviction information. This certificate will be used when seeking employment caring for or being in sole charge of persons under the age of 18 or vulnerable adults, or being involved in training or supervising them. Again, the application will be made by the job applicant, and countersigned by the registered person.

4.257 It is an offence for members and staff of any registered body to make an unauthorised disclosure of any information provided in a criminal records check or enhanced criminal records check.

4.258 A code of practice on the operation of the provisions of the Police Act has been issued.

C. Unfair Recruitment (TULR(C)A, s 137)

4.259 There are provisions in the Trade Union and Labour Relations (Consolidation) Act 1992 which protect a person from being refused employment on grounds of trade union membership or non-membership. These matters will be considered in Chapter 21.

D. Employment of Women

4.260 Most of the statutory provisions passed for the protection of female employees have been repealed in so far as they enabled different treatment to be accorded to women. Thus women may clean parts of machinery while in motion, work underground in mines, and perform a number of other tasks which were previously not open to them (see Employment Act 1989, s 9). This is in accordance with the Equal Treatment Directive (see para 1.82) and the desire of the government to reduce the legislative and administrative burdens on industry.

4.261 However, a number of statutory provisions relating to the health and safety of women have been retained, particularly dealing with those risks associated with pregnancy, childbirth, and other risks specifically affecting women (see para 6.12). Thus a woman may not work in a factory within four weeks of childbirth (Factories Act 1961, Sch 5, Public Health Act 1936, s 205), or in any employment within two weeks of childbirth (Maternity (Compulsory Leave) Regulations 1994). Women are prohibited from working in certain processes and activities involving lead products (including lead paint); there are limits on exposure to ionising radiations, and there is a prohibition on working at sea while pregnant

(Employment Act 1989, Sch 1). Indeed, it is lawful to discriminate against a woman in so far as it is necessary to comply with the restrictions mentioned in para 4.198.

4.262 Restrictions on hours of work (including overtime and night work) for women were abolished in the Sex Discrimination Act 1986 (s 7) but the position is now governed by the Employment Act 1989 (s 1), which effectively nullifies any statutory provision which produces discrimination as regards access to employment and working conditions.

E. Employment of Young Persons

4.263 Legislative provisions dealing with the health and safety of young persons (defined as persons over compulsory school leaving age) can be found in the Management of Health and Safety at Work Regulations 1999 (see para 11.64), and restrictions on the hours of work of young workers can be found in the Working Time Regulations 1998 (see para 7.6).

F. Adult Workers

4.264 The sole remaining legislation imposing restrictions on the hours of work of adult workers are (1) Mines and Quarries Act 1954 (underground miners), (2) Hours of Employment (Conventions) Act 1936 (sheet glass workers), (3) Shops (Early Closing Days) Act 1965 (shop assistants), and (4) Transport Act 1968 (vehicle drivers) and the Working Time Regulations (see para 7.57).

Summary

- Equality law was consolidated by the Equality Act 2010.
- There are nine protected characteristics, and subject to certain exceptions, the list of prohibited conduct is applicable to each characteristic.
- Most types of prohibited conduct require a comparator, whether real or hypothetical. Again there are certain exceptions.
- There are special provisions for the protected characteristic of disability.
- Direct discrimination is when someone treats another less favourably than another because of a protected characteristic. There are also rules relating to perceptive and deterred discrimination.
- Direct discrimination cannot be justified (apart from for age), but there are provisions for occupational requirements.
- Indirect discrimination can be justified.
- There are three types of harassment.
- Victimisation is prohibited.
- Rehabilitated persons are also protected under the Rehabilitation of Offenders Act 1974.

5

Equal Pay

Background

5.1 Article 157 of the Treaty on the Functioning of the European Union (formerly Art 141 of the Treaty of Rome) provides that member states shall maintain the application of the principle that men and women shall receive equal pay for equal work. Directive 75/117/EEC (Equal Pay Directive) states that the principle of equal pay means for the same work or work to which equal value has been attributed. Article 157 has direct effect (*Defrenne v Sabena*[1]), and thus it is clear that the overriding views of the European Court, when interpreting Art 157 and the Directive, must be applied.

5.2 'Pay' is a very wide concept, and means 'the ordinary basic or minimum wage or salary, and any other consideration, whether in cash or in kind, which a worker receives, directly or indirectly, in respect of his employment from his employer' (*Barber v Guardian Royal Exchange*[2]). All sorts of benefits must be equalised, including Christmas bonuses (*Lewen v Denda*[3]), travel facilities (*Garland v British Rail Engineering Ltd*[4]), and remuneration provisions (*Worringham v Lloyds Bank*[5]).

5.3 The equal pay provisions apply to employment under a contract of employment, contract of apprenticeship, or contract to do work personally (s 80). Thus workers are within the scope of the provisions, as well as employees. In *Quinnen v Hovells*[6] the claimant was a self-employed salesman engaged by the respondents to demonstrate goods for sale in a department store. He complained that two female demonstrators who were employees of the respondents were receiving a higher rate of pay, and the EAT held that he was entitled to have his claim considered on its merits, for the definition of employment clearly covered self-employed persons.

5.4 In principle, the burden of proof lies upon a claimant to show that, on the balance of probabilities, s/he is not receiving equal pay, but in *Handels-og v Dansk Arbejdsgiverforening*[7] (the 'Danfoss' case) the ECJ held that if a pay system manifestly produces inequalities of pay between the sexes, the burden of proof lies upon the employer to show that the criteria used that produces those inequalities are not discriminatory. Thus once there is a suspicion of discrimination in pay scales, the burden of proof shifts to the employer to justify pay differentials (*Enderby v Frenchay Health Authority*[8]).

Equality of Terms (Equality Act, ss 64–79)

5.5 The Equal Pay Act 1970 has been repealed, and its provisions re-enacted in ss 64–79 of the Equality Act 2010. Many of the interpretive decisions from the 1970 Act are repeated in the following text, with the usual caveat that the interpretation of reforming legislation is never static.

---

[1] [2000] ECR I–6155.   [2] [1991] 1 QB 344, [1990] 2 All ER 660, [1990] ICR 616, [1990] IRLR 240.
[3] (2000) IRLR 67, (2000) ICR 648.   [4] [1983] 2 AC 751, [1982] ICR 420, [1982] IRLR 257.
[5] [1982] 3 All ER 373, [1982] ICR 299, [1982] IRLR 74.   [6] [1984] ICR 525, [1984] IRLR 227.
[7] [1992] ICR 332, [1991] IRLR 31.   [8] [2000] ICR 612, [2000] IRLR 257.

5.6 The provisions of ss 64–70 apply when a person is employed on work that is equal to the work that is done by a comparator of the opposite sex. A person is a comparator if s/he is employed by the same employer or an associated employer (see para 2.6) and they both work at the same establishment (s 79). But this only applies if the employers concerned are 'companies'. Statutory agencies, whether or not they are under the control of the government, are not associate employers (*Hasley v Fair Employment Agency*[9]), because there is a distinction between 'bodies corporate' and 'companies' (*Gardiner v London Borough of Merton*[10]), but it is possible that this limitation is incompatible with the requirements of EC law (*Scullard v Knowles and Southern Regional Council*[11]). If they are employed by the same employer or associated employer, but work at different establishments, they are comparators if common terms of employment apply at those establishments. If work is not done at the same establishment it is to be treated as being done at the establishment with which it has the closest connection (s 80).

5.7 A major problem is to determine whether terms and conditions are 'common' as between two establishments (*British Coal Corpn v Smith*[12]). Thus if terms and conditions are governed by the same collective agreement, they will be common (*Barclays Bank plc v James*[13]). Having a common employer is not the same thing as being 'in the same employment', or having pay and conditions attributed to a 'single source' (*Lawrence v Regent Office Care Ltd*[14]), because there must be a single source responsible for the difference in pay (*Allonby v Accrington and Rossendale College*[15]). Thus in *Robertson v Department for Environment, Food and Rural Affairs*[16] male civil servants sought equal pay with senior secretaries employed in a different government department. The claim failed. Although they were in common employment, responsibilities for terms and conditions of employment had been transferred to the individual government departments, and thus there was no single source of the pay structure.

5.8 If a claimant seeks to rely on a comparator who is employed at a different establishment, there must be a real possibility of the comparator doing the same or a broadly similar job. The claimant must then show that the terms and conditions on which s/he would be employed are broadly similar to those on which s/he is currently employed. In the case of *North v Dumfries and Galloway Council*,[17] female school workers, such as classroom assistants, learning assistants, and nursery nurses, sought to compare themselves with male manual workers employed as groundsmen, road workers, refuse drivers, refuse collectors, and a leisure attendant. The comparators were employed by the same local authority, but at depots rather than schools. The Supreme Court said that the question was: if the comparators were employed at the same establishment, would they be employed on the same or broadly similar terms and conditions to those applicable in their current place of work? The comparators sometimes did occasionally do work at schools, and when they did there was no change in their terms and conditions, and so the female workers succeeded.

5.9 If there is a single source of pay for both, such as a parent company, comparison can be made independently of whether the unequal treatment arises from legislation or collective agreements, or whether the employment is in the same establishment (*ASDA Stores Ltd v Brierley & Ors*[18]). Here, female employees in retail stores were able to compare themselves with higher paid men working in distribution centres, as their work was of equal value.

---

[9] [1989] IRLR 106.   [10] [1981] QB 269, [1981] ICR 186, [1980] IRLR 472.
[11] [1996] ICR 399, [1996] IRLR 344.   [12] [1996] 3 All ER 97, [1996] ICR 515, [1996] IRLR 399.
[13] [1990] ICR 333, [1990] IRLR 90.   [14] [2003] ICR 1092, [2002] IRLR 822.
[15] [2005] All ER (EC) 289, [2004] ICR 1328, [2004] IRLR 224.
[16] [2005] EWCA Civ 138, [2005] ICR 750, [2005] IRLR 363.
[17] [2013] UKSC 45.   [18] UKEAT/0011/17/DM; see also on appeal [2016] EWCA Civ 566.

5.10 If a claim for equal pay is brought under Art 157 of the Treaty, the pay of the comparator must be attributable to a single source, but in cases where the claim was brought under the Equality Act the single source was not required, provided the comparator was in the same employment (*North Cumbria Acute Hospitals NHS Trust v Potter*[19]).

5.11 An equality clause is only applicable when there is an actual comparator of the opposite sex. Thus a woman who believes that she is poorly paid has no remedy in the absence of a male comparator (see observations of Elias J in *Walton Centre for Neurology NHS Trust v Bewley*[20]). But it has been held that if there is sufficient statistical evidence to support the assertion that women, as a class, are paid less than men, an equal value claim may lie under the provisions of Art 157 of the Treaty, even in the absence of a male comparator (*Grundy v British Airways plc*[21]), and a claim for sex discrimination could also be made (s 71).

5.12 It is possible to use a former employee as a comparator. In *Macarthys Ltd v Smith*[22] a man was employed as a stock room manager, and was paid £60 per week. He left the job, and four months later the woman claimant was appointed as stockroom manageress and was paid £50 per week. The European Court upheld her claim, holding that the principle of equal pay for equal work applied to the situation where a woman received less pay than a male predecessor, provided they were both doing the same or broadly similar work.

5.13 A part-timer can use a full-time employee as a comparator. In *British Airways Plc v Pinaud*[23] a cabin crew worker who worked 53.5 percent of the number of days of her full time comparator was entitled to the same ratio of pay, and not 50 percent. It had been held that a woman cannot claim equal pay with a man who succeeds her in her job, because to hold otherwise would have been an exercise in speculation as to what would have happened if they had been employed contemporaneously (*Walton Centre for Neurology NHS Trust v Bewley*[24]). However, s 64(2) of the Equality Act now provides that the relevant type of work is not restricted to work that is done contemporaneously, thus opening the possibility that a claim may be made citing a successor as well as a predecessor or a comparator (see *Diocese of Hallam Trustees v Connaughton*[25]).

5.14 A woman can choose the man with whom she wishes to be compared. Thus, if she is getting equal pay with some men, she can still seek equal pay with a man who is paid at a higher rate, if their work is the same or broadly similar or has an equal value (*Ainsworth v Glass Tubes and Components*[26]).

5.15 A 'piggyback' claim may be brought by a man by comparing himself with a woman who has succeeded in an equal pay claim against a more highly paid male comparator. The claim may be brought contingently, ie even before the woman's right to equal pay has been established (*Hartlepool Borough Council v Llewellyn*[27]). If the woman's claim is successful and a tribunal award is made, the man is entitled to arrears of pay for the same period as the female comparator.

Sex Equality Clause (s 66)

5.16 A sex equality clause is to be treated as being included in the terms under which persons are employed. Thus, any term in a contract that is less favourable than that of a

---

[19] [2009] IRLR 900.   [20] [2008] ICR 1047, [2008] IRLR 588.
[21] [2007] EWCA Civ 1020, [2008] IRLR 74.
[22] [1981] QB 180, [1981] 1 All ER 111, [1980] ICR 672, [1980] IRLR 210.
[23] [2018] EWCA Civ 2427.   [24] [2008] ICR 1047, [2008] IRLR 588.
[25] [1996] ICR 860, [1996] IRLR 505.   [26] [1977] ICR 347, [1977] IRLR 74.
[27] [2009] ICR 1426, [2009] IRLR 796.

comparator of the opposite sex is to be modified so as to ensure that it is not less favourable, and similarly a term that contains a benefit in the contract of a comparator of the opposite sex is to be included. If the contract of employment does not contain any term equivalent to that enjoyed by the comparator, the equality clause operates to insert such a term.

5.17 When considering an equality clause, the correct approach is to look at the situation term by term, so that a claimant can succeed in relation to any one particular element of the employment terms. The package approach, whereby more favourable terms can be set off against less favourable terms, is wrong (*Jorgensen v Foreningen AF Speciallaeger Sygesikringens Forhandlingsudvalg*[28]).

5.18 The equality clause applies not only in respect of remuneration, but also other benefits and facilities that are part of the contract of employment. This includes holiday entitlement, cars, privileged access to sports facilities, fringe benefits that continue after the employment has ended, eg travel facilities granted to retired rail workers (*Garland v British Rail Engineering Ltd*[29]), contributions to a pension scheme (*Worringham v Lloyds Bank*[30]), allowances to compensate for loss of earnings whilst on a training course (*Davies v Neath Port Talbot County Borough Council*[31]), severance payments (*Barber v Guardian Royal Exchange Assurance Group*[32]), and so on. But men cannot complain because women have certain advantages because of pregnancy or maternity, and similarly, women cannot claim full pay whilst on maternity leave (*Gillespie v Northern Health and Service Board*[33]).

5.19 The equality clause is not designed to produce absolute parity in contractual terms. Thus, if there is a non-discriminatory reason for an additional element in a man's pay (eg a special allowance for working unsocial hours: see *Electrolux Ltd v Hutchinson*[34]), the equality clause will not operate. In *Stadt Lengerich v Helmig*[35] employees who worked beyond 'normal working time' were entitled to overtime payments. Normal working time was defined as full-time working. The claimants, who worked part-time, argued that this was discriminatory, because even though they worked beyond their normal working hours, they would not receive the overtime payment until their working hours exceeded the equivalent of the full-time employees' hours. The European Court held that there was no unequal pay as between full-time and part-time employees, because their overall pay was the same for the number of hours worked. A part-time employee who worked for 19 hours would have received the same pay as a full-time employee who worked the same number of hours.

5.20 If the same rule applies equally to men and women, and to both full-time and part-time employees, the fact that some women are less well off in consequence is irrelevant. In *Barry v Midland Bank*[36] a contractual redundancy scheme, which provided for severance pay to be based on final salary at the date of termination, did not breach the Equal Pay Act, even though part-time women received less under the scheme than full-time employees. Their final salary was less because they were working fewer hours, and the calculation of the severance scheme was made on the same basis as part-time male employees.

5.21 Neither the sex equality clause nor a maternity equality clause (see para 5.54) apply in relation to terms of work affected by compliance with laws regulating the employment of women or the special treatment afforded to women in connection with pregnancy or childbirth (Sch 7). Thus if there is a pay differential resulting from the restrictions on employing women in certain processes, eg Control of Lead at Work Regulations 2002, Ionising Radiations Regulations 1999, etc, unequal pay is possible. Nor does it have any effect in

---

[28] [2000] IRLR 726.   [29] [1983] 2 AC 751, [1982] ICR 420, [1982] IRLR 257.
[30] [1982] 3 All ER 373, [1982] ICR 299, [1982] IRLR 74.   [31] [1999] ICR 1132, [1999] IRLR 769.
[32] [1991] 1 QB 344, [1990] 2 All ER 660, [1990] ICR 616, [1990] IRLR 240.
[33] [1997] IRLR 410.   [34] [1977] ICR 252.   [35] [1996] ICR 35, [1995] IRLR 216.
[36] [1999] 3 All ER 974, [1999] ICR 859, [1999] IRLR 581.

relation to terms of work affording special treatment to women in connection with pregnancy or childbirth.

Equal Work (s 65)

5.22 The work of an employee is equal to the work of another colleague if:

(a) it is like work;

(b) it is rated as equivalent;

(c) it is of equal value.

A. **Like Work (s 65)**

5.23 Work is like work if it is the same or broadly similar, and such differences as there are between the work are not of practical importance in relation to the terms of their work. It is thus necessary to have regard to the frequency with which the differences between the work occur in practice, and the nature and extent of the differences. In *Capper Pass Ltd v Lawton*[37] a woman worked as a cook in a company directors' dining room, providing lunches for between 10 and 20 persons. She sought equal pay with two assistant chefs who worked in the factory canteen, and who prepared 350 meals each day. Other differences were that she worked 40 hours per week and had no supervisor, whereas the men worked 45 hours per week and were under the supervision of a head chef. The EAT upheld a decision that she was entitled to equal pay with the male chefs. The work did not have to be the same; it was sufficient if it was broadly similar and the differences were not of practical importance. It would have been wrong to take a too pedantic approach, or to find they were not on like work because of insubstantial differences.

5.24 If there are differences in the work done, the employment tribunal must assess if it was reasonable to expect those differences to be reflected in wage settlements. Three such differences may be noted.

5.25 *(i) Different duties.* In *Noble v David Gold & Son (Holdings) Ltd*[38] men worked in a warehouse loading and unloading, whereas women did lighter work such as sorting, packing, and labelling. The Court of Appeal agreed with the finding of the employment tribunal that women were not on like work. Nor was the work broadly similar, for the differences were of practical importance in relation to terms and conditions of employment.

5.26 If there is a difference in the contractual obligations, this may negate equal pay, but it must be ascertained what happens in practice, and whether some other form of payment could be made for the different contractual obligations. In *Electrolux Ltd v Hutchinson*[39] men and women were performing broadly similar work, but the men were graded at a higher rate. The employers argued that the men had different contractual obligations, such as accepting transfer to different work, working compulsory overtime, and working nights. The EAT upheld a decision that the women were entitled to equal pay. The question had to be asked: what happened in practice? If and when the men performed these additional obligations, the situation could be dealt with by paying additional premiums.

5.27 But if male employees received different training, and thus could be called upon to perform different duties, they are not employed on the same work as women

---

[37] [1977] QB 852, [1977] 2 All ER 11, [1977] ICR 83, [1976] IRLR 366.
[38] [1980] ICR 543, [1980] IRLR 253.   [39] [1977] ICR 252.

(*Angestelltenbetriebsrat der Wiener v Wiener*[40]). As discussed in 5.25, in *Noble v David Gold & Son (Holdings) Ltd*[41] men worked in a warehouse loading and unloading, whereas women did lighter work such as sorting, packing, and labelling. The Court of Appeal upheld a decision of the employment tribunal that the women were not on like work. Nor was the work broadly similar, for the differences were of practical importance in relation to terms and conditions of employment. Also, the mere fact that a woman carried out the duties of a man for a short period of time or as a deputy as a temporary measure does not entitle the woman to equal pay with that man, for basically their responsibilities are different (*Ford v Weston (Chemists) Ltd*[42]).

5.28 *(ii) Different hours.* In *Dugdale v Kraft Foods Ltd*[43] men and women worked on broadly similar work, but the men had to do a compulsory night shift and there was a voluntary shift on Sunday mornings. It was held that the time at which the work is performed is by itself no bar to equal pay at the basic rate. The men could be compensated for these extra burdens by receiving a night shift payment or premium.

5.29 But this reasoning only applies when the difference in pay for hours worked applies only to men. If men and women work different hours to other employees, then the difference between the former and the latter has nothing to do with the sex of the employees, and thus basic rates can vary between the employees concerned (*Kerr v Lister & Co Ltd*[44]). Nor is there a breach of the equality clause if the employer makes a priority payment to employees who work on a rotating 24/7 shift pattern, even though women with child-caring responsibilities are unable to work those hours (*Blackburn v Chief Constable of West Midlands Police*[45]).

5.30 *(iii) Different responsibilities.* In *Eaton Ltd v Nuttall*,[46] a man and a woman worked on like work, but the man received higher pay because his responsibilities were greater. He handled more expensive products, and consequently a mistake by him would have had more serious financial consequences. The EAT held that it was proper to take into account the additional responsibilities which the job entailed.

B. **Work Rated as Equivalent (s 65(4))**

5.31 Work is rated as equivalent if a job evaluation study gives equal value to the jobs in terms of the demands made, or would give equal value if the job evaluation was not made on a sex-specific system, ie a system that sets different values for men and women. A system is sex-specific if it sets values for men different from those it sets for women.

5.32 A woman's work will be considered to have been rated equivalent to that of a man if it has been given equal value under a properly conducted job evaluation scheme, in terms of the different demands made upon an employee, eg, effort, skill, decision-making, etc. Such a scheme must be gender neutral and capable of satisfying the test of being thorough in analysis and impartial in application (*Eaton Ltd v Nuttall*[47]). Once it is established that it is a genuine scheme it must be accepted by the parties and employment tribunal, for the latter cannot be an appeal court from a valid scheme.

5.33 It is irrelevant if there emerges a difference between men and women in the actual points scored under the scheme, if there is no difference in the allocation to a particular

---

[40] [2000] ICR 1134, [1999] IRLR 804.   [41] n 37.   [42] (1977) 12 ITR 369.
[43] [1977] 1 All ER 454, [1977] ICR 48, [1976] IRLR 368.   [44] [1977] IRLR 259.
[45] [2008] EWCA Civ 1208, [2009] IRLR 135.
[46] [1977] 3 All ER 1131, [1977] ICR 272, [1977] IRLR 71.   [47] n 46.

salary grade. In *Springboard Sunderland Trust v Robson*[48] the claimant was awarded 400 following a job evaluation, which was increased to 410 following an appeal. She claimed equal pay with a man who had been awarded 428 points. The relevant salary scale for the grade in question was 410–449 points. Thus, although the jobs were not rated as equivalent to her comparator, her claim succeeded, because what mattered was the grade that was allocated to her following the evaluation, rather than the values assigned to her under the evaluation.

5.34 An unusual case was *Redcar and Cleveland Borough Council v Bainbridge*,[49] where a job evaluation scheme graded men lower than women, but nonetheless the men received higher pay. Clearly the jobs were not, strictly speaking, rated as equivalent, but the Court of Appeal had no difficulty in finding that the principle of equal pay had been breached. Relying on European law, the court gave a purposive interpretation of the Equal Pay Act by adding words to it, so that it read 'A woman is to be regarded as employed on work rated as equivalent with that of any men if, but only if, her job and their job have been given an equal value *or her job has been given a higher* value.' Under the Equality Act, there is little doubt that such a finding would be a breach of the equality clause and amount to sex discrimination under s 39.

5.35 However, if a job evaluation scheme produced a small, albeit significant, difference between the claimant and her comparator, it cannot be said that the two jobs are rated as equivalent (*Home Office v Bailey*[50]).

C. **Work of Equal Value (s 65(6))**

5.36 Work is of equal value if it is not like work nor work rated as equivalent, but is equal in terms of the demands made by reference to such factors as effort, skill, and decision-making.

5.37 Where a question arises as to whether one person's work is of equal value to another's, the tribunal may, before determining the question, require a member of the panel of independent experts (who is designated by ACAS for the purpose) to prepare a report on the question (s 131). If the requirement has not been withdrawn, the tribunal must not determine the question unless it has received the report. If no report is commissioned by the employment tribunal, the tribunal shall not determine the matter without giving the parties an opportunity to adduce their own evidence (*Wood v William Ball Ltd*[51]). If there has been a job evaluation study that results in different values being given, that conclusion must be accepted unless there are reasonable grounds for suspecting that the evaluation was based on a system that discriminated because of sex, or that it is otherwise unreliable, for example if it was out of date (Equality Act, s 131).

5.38 Work that is rated under a job evaluation scheme and work rated under an equal value assessment are two different exercises. The fact that jobs have been rated as equivalent in the job evaluation scheme does not set up a presumption that they were of equal value. Moreover, an equal value claim may not be brought if the claim could be brought under the provisions for like work or work rated as equivalent (*Hovell v Ashford & St Peter's Hospital NHS Trust*[52]).

5.39 The Employment Tribunals (Equal Value) Rules of Procedure, contained in the Employment Tribunals (Constitution and Rules of Procedure) Regulations 2013, Sch 3, set out the procedure for dealing with equal value claims. Such cases form a small proportion of cases that come before employment tribunals, but because of their complexity,

---

[48] [1992] ICR 554, [1992] IRLR 261.   [49] [2008] EWCA Civ 885, [2009] ICR 133, [2008] IRLR 776.
[50] [2005] IRLR 757.   [51] [2000] ICR 277, [1999] IRLR 773.
[52] [2009] EWCA Civ 670, [2009] ICR 1545, [2009] IRLR 734.

sometimes involving large numbers of claimants, they take up a disproportionate amount of time. Employment tribunals have wide powers of case management, with timetables set out depending on whether or not evidence is being given by an independent expert appointed by the tribunal. Standard directions require an early exchange of information, with particular reference to identifying the areas of disagreement. There are also special rules that apply if the parties appoint their own experts, including a requirement that those experts prepare a joint report on matters on which they agree and disagree. Annexed to the Rules of Procedure is a timetable, in the form of a flowchart which indicates that an equal value claim that does not involve an independent expert should be heard within 25 weeks, and a claim that does involve an independent expert should be heard within 37 weeks.

5.40 In *Hayward v Cammell Laird Shipbuilders Ltd*[53] the claimant, a canteen worker, was paid at a lower rate than certain skilled workers, but she enjoyed superior sickness benefits, paid meal breaks, and extra holidays. An independent expert concluded that her work was of equal value to the male comparators, but an employment tribunal dismissed her claim, holding that the terms and conditions *as a whole* must be not less favourable. Thus although her cash pay was less than the comparators, her other terms and conditions, which were more favourable, had to be taken into consideration. However, the House of Lords upheld her claim, holding that the employment tribunal should have considered each individual term which was not less favourable, and did not require a holding that terms as a whole should be not less favourable.

5.41 But the 'term-by-term' approach, if taken literally, could result in an equal pay claim ending up with unequal pay, which would defeat the purpose of the legislation. In *Degnan v Redcar Borough Council*[54] the Court of Appeal avoided such result by stating that the 'term' in question must be the same subject matter. Thus basic rates, bonuses, and attendance allowance were all part of one 'term' on remuneration, thus preventing a female claimant from cherry-picking the most advantageous part of a remuneration package of a number of male employees. However, in *Knowsley Hospitals NHS Trust v Brownbill*,[55] the Court of Appeal made clear that *Degnan* turned on its own special facts and did not give rise to an exception to the principle in *Hayward*. Equal pay claimants were entitled to compare the distinct contractual terms in their contracts governing the rate of pay for working unsocial hours to a similar term in the contracts of their male comparators, even though the women, overall, received higher pay than the men. Basing equal pay claims on a term-by-term comparison follows *Barber v Guardian Royal Exchange Assurance Group*,[56] which emphasised the importance of transparency.

5.42 An equal value claim may be brought by a woman even though she works with men doing the same work and who are paid the same as she, as long as there is another man earning a higher wage with whom she wishes to be compared. In *Pickstone v Freemans plc*[57] the claimant was a warehouse operative, who worked alongside other male warehouse operatives, all of whom received the same pay. She brought an equal value claim, naming as her comparator a male checker warehouse operative who was earning a higher rate. It was held that her claim succeeded. To hold otherwise would enable an unscrupulous employer to defeat equal value claims by ensuring that one man who worked alongside women was paid the same.

---

[53] [1988] AC 894, [1988] 2 All ER 257, [1988] ICR 464, [1988] IRLR 257.
[54] [2005] EWCA Civ 726, [2005] IRLR 615.   [55] [2011] EWCA Civ 903.   [56] nn 2, 31.
[57] [1989] AC 66, [1988] 2 All ER 803, [1988] ICR 697, [1988] IRLR 357.

Defence of Material Factor (s 69)

5.43 The sex equality clause will not take effect if the employer shows that the difference between the terms of persons of the opposite sex is because of a material factor, reliance on which:

(a) does not involve treating an employee less favourably because of the employee's sex than the employer would treat another employee of the opposite sex, and

(b) is a proportionate means of achieving a legitimate aim.

5.44 Pre-2010 cases held that length of service is an appropriate method of achieving the legitimate aim of rewarding experience required, which enables a worker to perform his duties better (*Cadman v Health and Safety Executive*[58]), but since length of service tends to disadvantage women—because they generally work for shorter periods of time than men—an employer would have to produce good and convincing reasons if the pay scale is arguably too long. Long-service-based increments must be shown to reward greater skill or experience, or achieve other aims such as the retention of labour (*Wilson v Health and Safety Executive*[59]). True, it was stated in *Handels-og-Kontorfuntionaerernes Forbund I Danmark v Dansk (acting for Danfloss)*[60] that '[l]ength of service goes hand in hand with experience, and since experience generally enables the employee to perform his duties better, the employer is free to reward him without having to establish the importance it has in the performance of specific tasks entrusted to the employee', but in *Cadman* it was stated that if the employee provides evidence that raises 'serious doubts' as to whether the general rule applies in a particular case, the employer will still have to prove objective justification. Thus it is not sufficient merely to state the fact of long-service increments without some attempt to justify them (*Honeywell Ltd v Scott*[61]).

5.45 Other non-sex material factors could be additional responsibility allowances (*Waddington v Leicester Council for Voluntary Services*[62]), extra pay for academic qualifications (*Murray v East Lothian Regional Council*[63]), long-service increments, a genuine mistake in putting an employee in the wrong grade (*Yorkshire Blood Transfusions Service v Plaskitt*[64]), productivity bonuses (*Redcar and Cleveland Borough Council v Bainbridge*[65]), antisocial working hours (*Chief Constable of West Midlands Police v Blackburn*[66]), differences in the place where the work was being done (*NAAFI v Varley*[67]), and differences between day work and night work (*Kerr v Lister & Co Ltd*[68]). Economic factors, such as a change in the volume of work that reflects the profitability of the firm (*Albion Shipping Agency v Arnold*[69]) or the need to attract qualified staff of either sex may also amount to a material factor (*Rainey v Greater Glasgow Health Board*[70]). Incentive bonus schemes may amount to a material factor, but if they maintain a pay differential between male dominated groups they should be monitored to ensure that they do what they are supposed to do, otherwise they will not amount to a material factor (*Hartlepool Borough Council v Dolphin*[71]). In an indirect sex discrimination equal pay case where the claimant has established that the factor relied on has an adverse disparate impact on women, if the employer can establish

[58] [2007] All ER (EC) 1, [2006] ICR 1623, [2006] IRLR 969.
[59] [2009] EWCA Civ 1074, [2010] ICR 302, [2010] IRLR 59.
[60] [1997] 2 CMLR 915, [1997] IRLR 643.   [61] IDS Handbook.
[62] [1977] ICR 266, [1977] IRLR 32.   [63] [1977] CLY 972.   [64] [1994] ICR 74.
[65] [2008] EWCA Civ 885, [2009] ICR 133, [2008] IRLR 776.   [66] n 45.
[67] (1976) *Times*, 25 October.   [68] [1977] IRLR 259.   [69] [1982] ICR 22, [1981] IRLR 525.
[70] [1987] AC 224, [1987] 1 All ER 65, [1987] UKHL 16, [1987] ICR 129, [1987] IRLR 26.
[71] [2009] IRLR 168, (2008) 152(38) SJLB 30.

that the reason for the difference in pay is not sex-tainted, then there is no need to objectively justify the difference (*Armstrong v Newcastle NHS Foundation Trust*[72]); however, the decision in *Essop* and *Naeem* (para 4.24) that there is no need for a 'reason why' in indirect discrimination may cast doubt on this.

5.46 The fact that benefits were paid to men under productivity schemes that were not discriminatory when they were introduced was not a sufficient justification where there was no longer a link between actual productivity and the bonus (*Council of the City of Sunderland v Brennan*[73]). The fact that rates of pay were agreed by collective bargaining is a factor that can be taken into account, but cannot be the only basis of justification (*Kenny v Minister for Justice*[74]).

5.47 A grading scheme which operates according to skill, experience, and ability, and which is genuine, and which is applied irrespective of the sex of the workers, is not rendered inoperative by the Act (*National Vulcan Engineering Insurance Group v Wade*[75]).

5.48 Pay protection schemes that are only offered to employees who would suffer as a result of the implementation of a job evaluation study are unlawful if they perpetuate historical indirect sex discrimination. Phasing out pay discrimination by cushioning the blow of pay cuts can be a legitimate objective, but may not be objectively justified if no thought is given to mitigating the continuing discriminatory effect (*Redcar and Cleveland Borough Council v Bainbridge*[76]). The long-term objective of reducing inequality between a man's and woman's terms of work is always to be regarded as a legitimate aim (s 69(3)).

5.49 The fact that a pay protection scheme has been negotiated with a trade union is not a justification for discrimination. Negotiators should pay attention to the possibility that differentials may have an adverse disparate impact on employees of a particular gender (*British Airways plc v Grundy*[77]).

5.50 'Red circle' treatment, ie the protection of a person's wages because of a demotion, transfer, or downgrade, etc, is permissible (*Forex Neptune (Overseas) Ltd v Miller*[78]) but the employment tribunal must be satisfied that the reason for the red circling has nothing to do with the sex of the person concerned (*Methven v Cow Industrial Polymers Ltd*[79]). Thus if there is direct discrimination, the material factor defence can never apply, because objective justification is not possible. It is possible that indirect discrimination can be objectively justified as long as the employer can disprove the influence of sex as a factor (*Middlesbrough Borough Council v Surtees*[80]).

5.51 Red circling of a comparator for a good reason is still a material factor defence, but there is an obligation to try to diminish its effects over time (usually by not increasing the red-circled pay to allow others to catch up (*Fearnon v Smurfit Corrugated Cases Ltd*[81])).

5.52 The mere attaching of a label of 'red circling' will not, by itself, constitute a material factor (*Honeywell Ltd v Scott*), particularly if past discrimination has contributed to the unequal pay (*Snoxell v Vauxhall Motors Ltd*[82]).

---

[72] [2006] IRLR 124.   [73] [2012] EWCA Civ 413.   [74] Case C-427/11; [2013] WLR (D) 87.
[75] [1979] QB 132, [1978] 3 All ER 121, [1978] ICR 800, [1978] IRLR 225.   [76] nn 46, 65.
[77] n 21.   [78] [1987] ICR 170.   [79] [1980] ICR 463, [1980] IRLR 289.
[80] [2008] EWCA Civ 885, [2009] ICR 133, [2008] IRLR 776.   [81] [2009] IRLR 132.
[82] [1977] ICR 700.

Sex Discrimination in Relation to Contractual Pay (s 71)

5.53 There may be circumstances where the absence of a comparator makes it impossible for the equality clause to operate (eg because a woman has no male colleague doing equal work with whom to compare), but nonetheless there is evidence of direct discrimination on grounds of sex (eg where the employer states that he would pay the employee more if she was a man). In these circumstances a claim for direct discrimination may be made under s 13 of the Act in respect of contractual pay even in the absence of a comparator.

Maternity Equality Clause (s 73)

5.54 The terms of employment of a woman must include a maternity equality clause. This means that any pay increase she receives (or would have received were she not on maternity leave) is to be taken into account in the calculation of her maternity pay. Pay (including any bonus) must be paid to her at the time she would otherwise have received it had she not been on maternity leave. On her return to work following maternity leave she is entitled to any pay increase she would have received had she not been on maternity leave.

Pay Structures etc

5.55 Any discrimination that is sex-based must be eliminated from an employer's pay structure, employment conditions, and collective agreements. An individual who considers that the terms of a collective agreement could have effect as being contrary to the principle of equal treatment may present a claim to an employment tribunal. This applies to actual and potential employees. If the complaint is well founded, the employment tribunal will declare the term to be void.

Discussions about Pay (s 77)

5.56 A term of a person's work that purports to prevent or restrict that person from disclosing or seeking to disclose information about the terms of his/her work is unenforceable against that person, as is a term that is designed to prevent a person from seeking such information from a colleague or a former colleague. A relevant pay discussion is a discussion with a colleague about pay, and which relates to whether there is a connection between pay and having (or not having) a particular protected characteristic, and where a colleague includes a former colleague in relation to the work in question. The discussion must be about pay, because s 77 does not cover discussions about other terms and conditions of employment. Thus a confidentiality clause, which purports to restrict a person from disclosing or seeking to disclose pay (including bonuses) with either colleagues or others (including, for example, a trade union official), would be unenforceable if it is made for the purpose of establishing a connection between pay and a protected characteristic. The taking of disciplinary action against a person for entering into such discussions amounts to victimisation under s 27 (para 4.38).

Gender Pay Gap Reporting (s 78)

5.57 The Equality Act 2010 (Gender Pay Gap Information) Regulations 2017 apply to any organisation which has 250 or more employees, which should publish and report specific figures about their gender pay gap. This is the difference between the average earnings of men and women, expressed relative to men's earnings. The example given in gov.uk is eg 'women earn 15% less than men per hour'. The Equality Act 2010 (Specific Duties and Public Authorities) Regulations 2017 similarly apply to the public sector. This data must be published on the employer's website and reported to the government online. If an employer has fewer than 250 employees, then it can publish and report voluntarily.

The figures must be calculated using a snapshot date, which is 31 March for public sector organisations and 5 April for businesses and charities, and the information must be published within a year of that date.

Equal Pay Audit

5.58 Section 98 of the Enterprise and Regulatory Reform Act 2013 amends the Equality Act by introducing a new s 139A, which allows for regulations to be made to extend the powers of employment tribunals to require employers to conduct an equal pay audit, if the tribunal finds that they have discriminated on pay.

Jurisdiction (s 127)

5.59 An employment tribunal has jurisdiction to determine a complaint that relates to a breach of an equality clause. As well as complaints brought by a worker, an employer can seek a declaration as to the rights of the parties in the event of a dispute as to the effect of an equality clause, and a court may refer a claim or counterclaim that could more conveniently be dealt with in the employment tribunal.

5.60 Note that a claim can also be brought in the High Court (*Birmingham City Council v Abdulla* (n.85) and *ASDA Stores Ltd v Brierley & Ors* (n.18)). There is no power for a tribunal to transfer a case to the High Court, or to order a stay for the purpose of a claim being brought in that venue (*Asda Stores*).

Burden of Proof (s 136)

5.61 If there are facts from which the employment tribunal could decide, in the absence of any other explanation, that the employer has contravened the provision concerned, the complaint must be upheld, but not if the employer satisfies the employment tribunal that there was no such contravention. The burden is therefore on the employer (*Kenny v Minister for Justice*, see para 5.46).

Time Limits (s 129)

5.62 A claim for the breach of an equality clause must normally be brought either during the employment or within six months of the end of the employment. Time will run from when the claimant left the employment, not from the time when s/he left the actual job on which the claim was based (*National Power plc v Young*[83]). However, if there has been a deliberate concealment by the employer of relevant information, without knowledge of which

---

[83] [2004] EWHC 2972 (QB).

the worker could not reasonably be expected to bring the proceedings, or if the worker has been under an incapacity, the time limit will be extended to the end of the period of six months from the date when the concealment was first discovered or the incapacity ceased, as the case may be.

5.63 If an employee is transferred from one employer to another, in circumstances where the transfer is governed by TUPE (see Chapter 9) employment with the transferor and transferee does not constitute a single period of employment. Thus, retrospective claims in respect of the pre-transfer period against the old employer must be brought within six months of the transfer date (*Gutridge v Sodexo Ltd*[84]).

5.64 In *Birmingham City Council (Appellant) v Abdulla & Ors (Respondents)*,[85] an equal pay claim which was brought outside the six months permitted by the employment tribunal was brought as a breach of contract claim in the ordinary courts (as equal pay relates to an implied equality clause in every contract), which have a time limit of six years (five in Scotland). This was because the six-month time limit in the tribunal cannot be extended on the grounds that it is just and equitable, unlike other types of discrimination claims. The defendants applied to have the claim struck out as an abuse of process. This was rejected by the Supreme Court on the basis that the six-month limitation period set for employment tribunal claims had never been made extendable, which suggested that Parliament recognised the availability of an alternative claim process in the High Court. The claim could therefore be brought in the High Court under the longer limitation period.

Remedies (s 132)

5.65 If the tribunal finds that there has been a breach of the equality clause, it may:

(a) make a declaration as to the rights of the parties;

(b) order an award by way of arrears of pay to the complainant.

5.66 The claim can only be in respect of the salary the comparator was receiving, ignoring any potential increments which could have been earned. In *Enderby v Frenchay Health Authority*[86] the claimant worked for a health authority for six years. She successfully made an equal value claim, using as her comparator a man who had only been employed for one year. She argued that she was entitled to the pay her comparator would have received had he been employed as long as she, ie to include the potential increments he would have had. The Court of Appeal held that she was entitled to receive the same pay as her comparator was currently receiving (see also *Evesham v North Hertfordshire Health Authority*[87]).

Backdating Awards

5.67 In England and Wales, the award in respect of equal pay and equal value claims cannot be backdated more than six years from the time when proceedings were instituted, and in Scotland the award cannot be backdated more than five years from when proceedings were commenced. An award in respect of a job evaluation scheme can only be backdated to the date when the scheme came into force (*Bainbridge v Redcar and Cleveland*

---

[84] [2009] EWCA Civ 729, [2009] ICR 1486, [2009] IRLR 721.   [85] [2012] UKSC 47.
[86] [2000] ICR 612, [2000] IRLR 257.   [87] [2000] ICR 612, [2000] IRLR 257.

Borough Council[88]). An award of interest may be made, calculated in accordance with the provisions of the Sex Discrimination and Equal Pay (Remedies) Regulations 1993. No compensation for injured feelings may be awarded (*City of Newcastle upon Tyne v Allen*[89]).

Summary

- The law relating to Equal Pay is set out in the Equality Act ss 64–69.

- It applies when someone does equal work to someone of the opposite sex, then they should be paid the same, unless there is a reason not related to sex that explains the difference.

- Equal work means like work (same or broadly similar), work rated as equivalent (in a job evaluation study) or work of equal value (in terms of the demands made by reference to eg effort, skill and decision-making).

- An equality clause should be looked at term by term, and applies not only to renumeration, but also other benefits.

- There is a defence of material factor, ie that it did not involve treating less favourably because of sex, and that it was a proportionate means of achieving a legitimate aim.

- A claim can be brought within six months in an employment tribunal or six years as a breach of contract claim in the courts.

---

[88] nn 49, 65, 76.   [89] [1995] CLY 3664.

6

Family Friendly Rights

Background

6.1 In this chapter we shall consider various family friendly rights designed to assist employees with parental and childcare responsibilities. These are maternity rights generally, ordinary and additional maternity leave, ordinary and additional adoption leave, parental leave, paternity leave, caring for dependants, and applications for flexible working. The relevant statutory provisions are based on the implementation of a number of EU Directives, and to that extent EU jurisprudence must be considered where appropriate.

6.2 For the purposes of the Employment Rights Act 1996, childbirth is defined as the birth of a living child or the birth of a child whether living or dead after 24 weeks of pregnancy. Certain rights to be considered also apply on the adoption of a child.

Maternity Rights

A. **Time Off Work for Antenatal Care (ERA, ss 55–57)**

6.3 An employee who is pregnant, and who, on the advice of a registered medical practitioner, registered midwife, or registered health visitor, has made an appointment to attend any place for the purpose of receiving antenatal care, shall have the right not to be unreasonably refused time off work during her working hours to enable her to keep that appointment. This right arises from the moment the woman commences her employment, and is irrespective of the number of hours or days worked (but see para 6.6) or whether or not she is a permanent or temporary employee. The size of the employer's undertaking is also irrelevant. The only women who do not enjoy this right are those who are not employed under a contract of employment, or who are share fisherwomen, or women employed as members of any constabulary.

6.4 If requested to do so, she must produce a certificate stating that she is pregnant. (A woman who has had in vitro fertilisation is pregnant from the time when the fertilised ovary is implanted in her uterus (*Mayr v Backerei und Konditorei Gerhard Flockner OHG*[1]).) She must produce some documentary evidence of the antenatal appointment (but not the first appointment).

6.5 She is entitled to be paid for the period of her absence at the appropriate hourly rate (calculated in accordance with the provisions of s 56). If she is refused time off work, or if she is not paid for the time off taken, she may make a complaint to an employment tribunal (within three months of the date of the appointment in question, or within such further time as the employment tribunal considers to be reasonable) that her employer has

---

[1] [2008] All ER (EC) 613, [2008] IRLR 387, [2008] 1 FLR 1242.

unreasonably refused to permit her to have time off work, or has failed to pay her the whole or part of the amount to which she claims she was entitled. If the employment tribunal upholds her complaint, it will make a declaration to that effect, and also award her the amount of remuneration to which she is entitled (s 57).

6.6 It should be noted that the right is not to be unreasonably refused time off work. Thus it may be possible to argue that in particular circumstances it would be reasonable for the woman to make arrangements for antenatal care outside working hours (eg in the case of a woman who works part-time, or less than five days each week). Antenatal care is not defined in the Act, but undoubtedly includes antenatal relaxation classes and (possibly) classes in parentcraft, provided she attends on the advice of a medical practitioner etc (see *Gregory v Tudsbury Ltd*[2]).

6.7 An employer cannot defeat a woman's statutory rights by rearranging her working hours or requiring her to work additional hours to make up for time lost (*Edgar v Giorgine Inns Ltd*[3]). On the other hand, if a woman abuses the time off provisions, and takes additional time off work for activities which are not antenatal care, she will have no rights under the Act, and will be subject to the usual consequences which flow from disciplinary proceedings (*Gough v County Sports (Wales) Ltd*[4]).

6.8 If an employer refuses to pay a pregnant woman when she takes time off work for antenatal care, then as well as bringing a claim under s 57(5) of ERA for the amount due, she may also claim that she has suffered a detriment under reg 19 of the Maternity and Parental Leave etc Regulations, for which compensation may be awarded, including an award in respect of injury to feelings.

Right for Partners to Accompany to Antenatal Appointments

6.9 The right for partners to unpaid time off to accompany the mother to up to two antenatal appointments was brought in by s 127 of the Children and Families Act 2014 (adding s 57ZE to the ERA) and came into force on 1 October 2014. This right is unpaid and capped at six and a half hours per appointment.

6.10 The employer is not entitled to ask for evidence of the appointment, as this is the property of the mother. He is, however, entitled to ask the employee for a declaration stating the date and time of the appointment, that the employee qualifies for the unpaid time off through his or her relationship with the mother or child, and that the time off is for the purpose of attending an antenatal appointment with the expectant mother that has been made on the advice of a registered medical practitioner, nurse, or midwife.

6.11 There is no qualifying period, and the right applies to the father, the mother's partner (even if these are different people—they both get the right), and intended parents of surrogate babies. Agency workers will, of course, have to have been working for the same employer for 12 weeks. If the time off is refused, or the employee or agency worker is subjected to a detriment, he can bring a claim to the employment tribunal within three months.

B. **Risk Assessment and Suspension on Maternity Grounds**

6.12 Under the Management of Health and Safety at Work Regulations 1999 (see Chapter 11) every employer is required to carry out a risk assessment designed to ensure the health and safety at work of new or expectant mothers, defined as employees who are pregnant, who have given birth within the preceding six months, or who are breastfeeding.

---

[2] [1982] IRLR 267.   [3] Unreported.   [4] Unreported.

6.13 The first requirement is that where the workforce includes women of childbearing age, *and* the work is of a kind which could involve risk to the health or safety (because of pregnancy or maternity) to a new or expectant mother, or to that of her baby, from any processes or working conditions, or from physical, biological, or chemical agents (including those set out in Annexes I and II of Directive 92/85/EEC), the employer shall carry out a risk assessment; see reg 16. It should be noted that the provisions of the Management of Health and Safety at Work Regulations now confer a right of action in civil proceedings (see para 11.59). Thus in *Day v T Pickles Farm Ltd* the EAT thought that the failure to carry out a risk assessment on a woman of childbearing age could amount to sex discrimination and may also amount to a repudiatory breach of contract by the employer entitling the employee to resign and claim she has been constructively dismissed (*Bunning v GT Bunning & Sons Ltd*[5]). Similarly, the ECJ, in *Otero Ramos v Servicio Galego de Saude*,[6] found a failure to conduct a proper risk assessment for a breastfeeding mother could amount to sex discrimination.

6.14 The physical agents referred to are those which are likely to cause foetal lesions or disrupt placental attachment, eg shocks, movement, ionising or non-ionising radiation, extremes of heat or cold, travel, mental or physical fatigue, etc. The biological agents include those set out in Directive 90/679/EEC (the Biological Agents Directive) in so far as it is known that these agents can endanger the health of a woman or her unborn child. The chemical agents include dangerous substances set out in Directive 90/393/EEC (Carcinogens at Work Directive), Annex I. Also included are certain industrial processes, underground mining work, pressurised enclosures (eg underwater diving), work with certain viruses (unless immunised), and lead and lead derivatives. After the risk assessment has been carried out, the employer must provide all female workers of childbearing age with comprehensible and relevant information of the risks to their health identified by the assessment, and also with details of the preventative and protective measures which need to be taken to comply with the relevant statutory provisions (see Chapter 11).

6.15 Once the employer is aware that a woman employee is pregnant, or is breastfeeding, a second risk assessment needs to be made in respect of that woman, to ascertain what measures need to be taken to avoid the risk to her health. These risks could be heavy lifting, prolonged standing, night work, early shift work, work-related stress, threats from customers, exposure to nauseating smells, working excessive hours, lack of rest breaks, and so on. If measures cannot be taken to avoid the risk, the employer must alter her working hours or, if this is not feasible or would not avoid the risk, she should be offered alternative employment or put on paid leave of absence (ERA s 67, and reg 16(3) of the Maternity etc Regulations). The risk assessment does not need to be in writing when relating to a particular individual, because it is the employer's 'thought process' which is relevant (*Stevenson v J M Skinner & Co*[7]). Avoiding the risk does not mean eliminating it altogether. It means reducing the risk to the lowest acceptable level (*New Southern Railways Ltd v Quinn*[8]). It should be noted that an employer is not obliged to alter her working conditions or working hours, or to suspend her from work, unless she has informed him in writing that she is pregnant, or has given birth within the previous six months, or is breastfeeding.

6.16 Next, if a new or expectant mother works at night, and a certificate from a registered medical practitioner or registered midwife shows that it is necessary for her health or safety that she should not be at work for any period identified in the certificate, then the employer shall suspend her from work (subject to ERA, s 66 below). There is also a requirement

---

[5] EAT/0136/03.   [6] Case C-2017/789.
[7] UKEAT/0584/07.   [8] [2006] ICR 761, [2006] IRLR 266.

under health and safety legislation for an employer to provide suitable rest facilities for a pregnant woman, or a woman who has given birth within the previous six months or who is breastfeeding (Workplace (Health, Safety and Welfare) Regulations 1992, reg 25 (4)).

6.17 The maternity provisions stem from ERA, s 66 because the Management of Health and Safety at Work Regulations are specified as being the 'relevant statutory provision' for the purpose of that section (see Suspension from Work (on Maternity Grounds) Order 1994). Additionally, a woman is entitled to be suspended from work on maternity grounds due to any recommendation contained in an approved code of practice issued by the Health and Safety Executive under the Health and Safety at Work etc Act 1974, s 16 (see Chapter 11).

Following on from her right to be suspended on maternity grounds, a woman will have two further rights.

Alternative Work (ERA, s 67)

6.18 Before suspending a woman on maternity grounds, the employer, if he has available suitable alternative work, shall offer it to her. The alternative work must be of a kind which is suitable for her, and appropriate in the circumstances (see *Iske v P & O European Ferries (Dover) Ltd*[9]). If the terms and conditions differ from her normal contract of employment, they must not be substantially less favourable (see *British Airways (European Operations at Gatwick) Ltd v Moore and Botterill*[10]). A failure to make such an offer entitles the woman to bring a complaint to an employment tribunal, within the usual time limits, which may make an award of compensation as the employment tribunal considers to be just and equitable in all the circumstances.

She is not entitled to be paid, however, if the employer offers her suitable alternative work which she unreasonably refuses to do.

6.19 The Pregnant Workers Directive (92/85/EEC) contains an absolute and express prohibition on exposure to the listed risks. However, the Management Regulations, reg 16 requires that risks to the health of a pregnant woman shall be avoided, which means that if the risk cannot be eliminated in its entirety, it must be reduced to its lowest acceptable level. Thus, if it is decided to remove a pregnant woman from her present job because of a perceived health or safety risk, this can be a pointless exercise if the new job offer contains equally perceived risks. To use a hypothetical risk as an excuse to demote a woman from her job (with a consequential reduction in salary) can amount to a detriment contrary to ERA, s 47C, and a failure to offer alternative employment on terms not substantially less favourable is contrary to ERA, s 67. It may be discrimination on grounds of sex, and could give rise to a potential constructive dismissal claim (*New Southern Railway Ltd v Quinn*[11]).

Maternity Suspension Pay (ERA, s 68)

6.20 A woman who is suspended from work on maternity grounds is entitled to be paid a week's pay in respect of each week of suspension, reduced proportionately if the suspension is for less than a week. She is entitled to be paid her normal hourly rate of pay (ie the week's pay will be divided by the number of normal working hours). If her working hours vary from week to week they are to be averaged over the previous 12 working weeks. If she has not completed 12 weeks' service, an average shall be estimated from the agreed terms and conditions and from the work pattern of others in comparable jobs. A failure by the employer to pay the whole or any part of the remuneration due entitles the woman to bring a complaint to an employment tribunal, which, if it finds the complaint well founded, shall order the employer to pay the amount of remuneration due to her.

---

[9] [1997] IRLR 401, EAT.   [10] [2000] ICR 678, [2000] IRLR 296, EAT.   [11] [2006] ICR 761, EAT.

6.21 Finally, it should be noted that no period of continuous employment is required for a woman to have these rights (in contrast to the general right to be suspended on medical grounds—see para 7.10—where continuous employment of one month is required).

C. Maternity Leave (ERA, ss 71–74, Maternity and Parental Leave etc Regulations 1999 as amended)

6.22 There are three periods of maternity leave:

(a) Compulsory maternity leave. This prevents a woman from working for the period of two weeks immediately following the date of childbirth.

(b) Ordinary maternity leave (OML). All pregnant women are entitled to take 26 weeks OML irrespective of their length of service, provided they satisfy the relevant conditions.

(c) Additional maternity leave (AML). All women are entitled to a further 26 weeks AML at the end of their OML, irrespective of their length of service.

(NB Entitlement to ordinary and additional maternity leave must not be confused with entitlement to Statutory Maternity Pay (SMP) or Maternity Allowance (MA), for which see paras 6.59 and 6.68.)

Compulsory Maternity Leave (ERA, s 72(1))

6.23 The taking of ordinary maternity leave or additional maternity leave is optional for women who are pregnant, not compulsory. Some women may want to return to work as soon as possible after the birth, but ERA, s 72 provides that an employer shall not permit a woman to work within two weeks of childbirth. A contravention of this provision can lead to a fine of not exceeding Level 2 on the standard scale. Any prohibition arising under the Health and Safety at Work Act will also apply. Also, it is an offence (punishable by a fine of up to Level 1 on the standard scale) to permit a woman to work in a factory within four weeks of childbirth (Public Health Act 1936, s 205; Factories Act 1961, Sch 5).

Ordinary Maternity Leave and Additional Maternity Leave

6.24 The Maternity and Parental Leave etc Regulations 1999 were amended in 2008 so as to remove the distinction between ordinary and additional maternity leave and the distinction between ordinary and additional adoption leave. This means in effect that certain benefits, such as company cars, gym membership, health insurance, etc, which used to apply only during ordinary maternity and ordinary adoption leave, will now apply throughout additional maternity and additional adoption leave. Seniority and personal length of service rights (eg pay increments) will continue throughout both periods. The only practical difference nowadays between ordinary and additional maternity leave and ordinary and additional adoption leave concerns the right to return to work and the non-accrual of pension rights during the unpaid part of additional leave. Terms and conditions relating to remuneration remain unaffected.

6.25 An employee (not a worker) who is appropriately qualified is entitled to 26 weeks' ordinary maternity leave and a further 26 weeks' additional maternity leave. This is irrespective of her length of service or whether or not she is a temporary or permanent employee. The only exclusions are in respect of members of the armed forces, share fisherwomen, members of the constabulary, and agency workers who are not employed under a contract of employment by the agency or hirer. In order to qualify for maternity leave, the employee must notify her employer (in writing if he so requests) no later than the end of the 15th week before the expected week of confinement of:

(a) her pregnancy;

(b) the expected week of childbirth; and

(c) the date on which she intends her ordinary maternity leave period to start. This may start any time from the beginning of the 11th week before the expected week of confinement.

6.26 If it is not reasonably practicable for her to give 15 weeks' notice of her intention to take maternity leave, she must do so as soon as is reasonably practicable. If the employer so requests, she must produce for inspection a certificate from a registered medical practitioner or a registered midwife stating the expected week of childbirth. If she wishes to vary the date of the commencement of her ordinary maternity leave, she must give at least 28 days' notice, or, if that is not reasonably practicable, as much as is reasonably practicable.

6.27 On receipt of the notice, the employer must notify the employee, within 28 days, of the date on which her additional maternity leave will end. If he fails to do so, he will not be able to complain if she returns to work too early or too late, and the employee may have a remedy under regs 19–20 in respect of detriment or dismissal.

6.28 Maternity leave will start on either (a) the date she has notified to her employer as the date she intends it to start, or (b) the day which follows the first day after the beginning of the fourth week before the EWC on which she is absent from work wholly or partly because of her pregnancy, or (c) the day that follows the day on which childbirth occurs. She can vary the date on which she intends to start her maternity leave by giving her employer notice of the new date 28 days before the date originally specified, or 28 days before the date on which she intends her maternity leave to start, or, if that is not reasonably practicable, then as soon as is reasonably practicable. However, the revised date cannot be earlier than the beginning of the 11th week before the EWC, and the notification must be in writing if the employer so requests.

6.29 However, there are two exceptions to the notification requirements. These are:

(a) if the maternity leave commences with the day which follows the first day after the beginning of the fourth week before the EWC on which she is absent from work wholly or partly because of pregnancy; or

(b) if her maternity leave commences with the day which follows the day on which childbirth occurs.

6.30 In both cases she must notify the employer as soon as is reasonably practicable (in writing if he so requests) that she will be absent from work because of pregnancy or because she has given birth, and the date on which either event took place.

Terms and Conditions During Ordinary Maternity Leave

6.31 An employee who takes maternity leave is entitled to the benefit of all the terms and conditions of employment which would have applied had she not been absent, whether or not they arise under her contract of employment. In other words, she is to be treated as if her contract of employment continues during her maternity leave. The only exception is that she is not entitled to terms and conditions relating to remuneration. Thus contractual and non-contractual benefits, other than sums which would have been payable by way of wages or salary, must be continued, eg life and medical insurance, private use of a company car, mortgage subsidies, etc. Whether profit-related pay, bonuses, and commissions which arise after the commencement of maternity leave are payable will depend on the purpose for which and the terms under which these payments are to be made. The test is whether or not these can be defined as being 'wages or salary'.

6.32 A woman who takes maternity leave during a year when a bonus is payable must be paid the bonus for the periods when she is at work and for the fortnight of compulsory maternity leave. The general principle was laid down by the European Court in *Lewen v Denda*[12] that an employer is entitled to make a pro rata deduction for work done during the employee's absence on maternity leave (except when on compulsory maternity leave). Any such deduction does not amount to sex discrimination because of the exclusion that relates to the payment of money during such leave (*Hoyland v Asda Stores Ltd*[13]). The employee cannot take contractual annual leave during her maternity leave, as this would come under the remuneration exclusion. She will be entitled to take statutory paid annual leave during a period other than the period of her maternity leave, because maternity leave is not a holiday, and the time spent by a woman on maternity leave cannot count against her holiday entitlement. This means that her annual holiday entitlement must be taken either before the start of maternity leave or after its expiry (*Merino Gomez v Continental Industrias del Caucho*[14]), although it is not certain if this rule applies if the current holiday year has expired.

6.33 Similarly, a woman who gives in her notice during her absence on maternity leave (or who is given notice by her employer) is entitled to be paid for the statutory notice period (ERA, s 88(1)(cc)), although this will not apply to notice given by either party if the period of notice to be given by the employer under the contract is at least one week longer than the statutory notice period (*Scotts Company (UK) Ltd v Budd*[15]). However, she would not be entitled to contractual notice pay, as this would fall to be excluded under the definition of remuneration (ERA, s 71).

6.34 For her part, during the period of maternity leave, the employee is bound by any obligations which arise under her terms and conditions of employment. Thus, she is still an employee, and must abide by relevant contractual obligations, such as confidentiality, etc (see Chapter 10). Obviously, she is not required to turn up for work, as this would be inconsistent with her statutory right, but she can agree to 'keeping in touch' days (see para 6.38).

Additional Maternity Leave

6.35 An employee who is entitled to ordinary maternity leave is entitled to a further period of six months additional maternity leave, which must commence immediately following the end of the period of ordinary maternity leave. The only distinction between the two types of leave is that during additional maternity leave, she will not be entitled to accrued pension rights during the latter part of additional maternity leave (ie for the last 13 weeks), and her right to return to work is slightly more restricted.

Terms and Conditions During Additional Maternity Leave (reg 17)

6.36 During the period of additional maternity leave, the employee is entitled to the benefit of the employer's implied obligation of trust and confidence. She is also entitled to any terms and conditions relating to notice on termination by her employer,

---

[12] [2000] IRLR 67, (2000) ICR 648.   [13] [2006] IRLR 468.
[14] Case C-342/01, [2004] 2 CMLR 38, [2004] All ER (D) 350 (Mar), ECJ.
[15] [2004] ICR 299, [2003] IRLR 145, [2002] All ER (D) 58 (Nov), EAT.

compensation in the event of redundancy, and the benefit of any disciplinary or griev-ance procedures. For her part, she is bound by any terms and conditions relating to the giving of notice by her, non-disclosure of confidential information, the acceptance of gifts or other benefits from third parties, and her participation in any other business. However, statutory annual leave entitlement under the Working Time Regulations will continue to accrue, as will her right to statutory notice on dismissal (see s 88(1)(c), at para 6.33).

6.37 The period of additional maternity leave will count towards the period of continuous employment for the purpose of statutory employment rights, but not for the purpose of assessing contractual rights which depend on length of service, eg contractual leave provi-sions, annual increments, seniority rights, etc.

Reasonable Contact (reg 12A)

6.38 The employer and employee may agree to make reasonable contact with each other from time to time during the maternity leave period, and this will not bring that period to an end. It is suggested that this can be for the purpose of discussing details of the return to work, communicating information, informing the employee of promotion opportunities, etc. Contact may be by any suitable means, eg telephone, email, personal visits, etc.

Work During Maternity Leave Period (reg 12A)

6.39 An employee may carry out up to ten days' work for her employer during the statu-tory leave period without bringing that period to an end. These are known as 'Keeping in Touch' or KIT days. Work, which includes training, will count as a full day if it is done for part of a day. The type of work that the employee may carry out will be a matter for agree-ment between the parties, but it would normally be any activity which would ordinarily be classed as work under the woman's contract of employment. She is entitled to be paid on an agreed basis, and her entitlement to statutory maternity pay will not be affected. Any such work will not extend the total duration of the maternity leave period. However, no such work can be done within the two weeks following childbirth.

6.40 A woman who refuses to keep in touch or to work during her maternity leave period is protected from suffering a detriment or dismissal in consequence of that refusal.

Returning to Work after Ordinary Maternity Leave (regs 18(1), 18A(1), 10)

6.41 After taking ordinary maternity leave, an employee is entitled to return to the job in which she was employed before her absence, with seniority, pension, and similar as they would have been had she not been absent, and on terms and conditions not less favourable than those that would have applied if she had not been absent. Her period of absence dur-ing ordinary maternity leave will count as continuous employment for the purpose of any rights or benefits that depend on an employee's length of service, eg service-related pay in-crements. A refusal to permit her to return to her old job may amount to a dismissal, which could be unfair, and may also amount to direct discrimination.

6.42 However, there are certain exceptions to this rule. The first arises where she has taken two or more consecutive periods of statutory leave, which include the ordinary leave period, and any period of additional maternity leave, or additional adoption leave, or any period of parental leave lasting more than four weeks. If it is not reasonably prac-ticable for a reason other than redundancy for her to return to the same job, then she is entitled to be offered another job that is suitable and appropriate for her to do in the circumstances.

6.43 The second exception arises where a redundancy situation arises during the maternity leave, and it is not practicable to continue to employ her under the existing contract. In this situation she is entitled to be offered any suitable alternative employment, on terms and conditions that are not substantially less favourable (reg 18(4), reg 10). The work must be suitable and appropriate, and its provisions as to the capacity and place in which she is to be employed, and other terms and conditions, not substantially less favourable to her than if she had continued to be employed under the previous contract. The new contract must take effect immediately on the ending of the previous contract. If a suitable vacancy exists, and the employer fails to offer it to her, the dismissal will be automatically unfair under s 99 of ERA if the principle reason was redundancy (reg 20(l)(b)). However, if there is no such vacancy, her dismissal for reason of redundancy will be fair. If she unreasonably refuses the offer, her dismissal will be fair, and she may lose her entitlement to a redundancy payment (ERA, s 141). If she is made redundant, then in addition to her redundancy payment (if she qualifies), she will be entitled to her notice period, and a written statement of the reasons for her dismissal.

6.44 Where the respondent had to choose between a man and a woman on maternity leave when deciding whom to make redundant, it was not reasonably necessary to give the female comparator a maximum notional score. There were more proportionate means available to ensure she did not lose out in the redundancy exercise because of her maternity absence, otherwise there was a risk of sex discrimination against the male claimant (*Eversheds Legal Services Ltd v De Belin*[16]).

6.45 Finally, she will not be entitled to return to her old job if she has indicated that she does not wish to do so (eg because she wishes to change her location of work, or to work different hours, etc). However, a failure by an employer to accommodate the changed situation may amount to sex discrimination.

6.46 The 'job' to which she is entitled to return means the nature of the work she was employed to do in accordance with her contract, ie the same job she was doing before she went on maternity leave, and the capacity and place where she was employed. If there have been changes during her absence, these will be irrelevant as long as the contractual obligations are the same (*Edgell v Lloyd's Register of Shipping*[17]). In *Blundell v St Andrew's Catholic Primary School*[18] the claimant was a primary school teacher. It was the policy of the school to rotate teachers every two years. The claimant taught the reception class when she went on maternity leave, but when she returned to work she was allocated year 2. She claimed she had not been allowed to return to work at the job at which she was employed before her absence. Her claim was dismissed. Taking into account the nature, capacity, and location of the respective jobs, the statutory requirements were satisfied. She had been offered her old job as a primary school teacher.

Returning to Work after Additional Maternity Leave (regs 18(2), 18A(2))

6.47 The position is similar, but not identical, in the case of a return to work after additional maternity leave. She is entitled to return to her old job, with her seniority, pension, and similar rights as they would have been had she not been absent from work, on terms and conditions not less favourable than those that would have applied had she not been absent. Her period of absence during additional maternity leave will count towards continuity of employment for the purpose of the various statutory rights. However, there are two exceptions to this rule. First, her pension rights under an employment-related benefits

---

[16] [2011] IRLR 448.   [17] [1977] IRLR 463.   [18] [2007] ICR 1451, [2007] IRLR 652.

scheme will have been suspended during the period of unpaid maternity leave, so that such rights are preserved as if the two periods on either side of the unpaid maternity leave were continuous. Second, where it is not reasonably practicable, for a reason other than redundancy, for an employer to permit her to return to her old job after taking additional maternity leave, she is entitled to be offered another job that is both suitable and appropriate for her to do in the circumstances.

Redundancy During Maternity Leave (reg 10)

6.48 If it is not practicable for reason of redundancy for her employer to continue to employ her under her existing contract, the employee is entitled to be offered a suitable alternative vacancy, with the employer, his successor, or an associated employer (reg 10). The new contract must take effect immediately on the ending of the old one. The work must be suitable and appropriate for her to do in the circumstances, and the capacity and place of employment and other terms and conditions must be not substantially less favourable that if she had continued to work under the old contract. If such a suitable vacancy exists, and the employer fails to offer it to her, the dismissal will be automatically unfair under ERA, s 99. However, if there is genuinely no such vacancy, she will be entitled to a redundancy payment, although if she unreasonably refuses the offer, she may lose her right to a redundancy payment (ERA, s 141). If the employer fails to observe the appropriate procedure for selecting employees for redundancy (consultation, proper notice, search for alternatives, etc) she may claim unfair dismissal in the ordinary way, and possibly claim sex discrimination. When selecting for redundancy an employer cannot assess those who have been off work on parental leave on different criteria to those who have not been on leave—*Riezniece v Zemkopības Ministrija*.[19] Obviously, if her selection was due to her pregnancy or the fact that she took maternity leave, this will again be automatically unfair (reg 20(2)).

6.49 It should be remembered that the employer's duty to offer alternative employment to a woman who has been on maternity leave is an absolute one, ie the offer must be in preference to any other employee who is similarly affected by the redundancy situation but who has not been absent on maternity leave. This applies even though the woman is actually on maternity leave at the time the redundancy situation arises. The work, however, only needs to be offered if it is suitable for her in the circumstances (*Simpson v Endsleigh Insurance Services*[20]). A failure to notify a woman who is on maternity leave that there is a suitable vacancy for which she could have applied is a fundamental breach of the implied term of trust and confidence, entitling her to resign and claim constructive dismissal (*Visa International Services Association v Paul*[21]).

6.50 There is no need for her to give notice to her employer of the date when she will be returning to work after maternity leave or additional maternity leave. It will be recalled (see para 6.27) that once the employer has received notice that she intends to take maternity leave or additional maternity leave, he must write to her within 28 days confirming the date on which she is due to return to work. However, if she wishes to return earlier, she must give at least eight weeks' notice of her intention to do so. If she returns to work without giving this notice, the employer is entitled to postpone her return to a date which will secure eight weeks' notice (but not beyond the 26-week period of maternity leave or the 52-week period of additional maternity leave). If she actually returns to work without giving the notice, she is not entitled to be paid her contractual remuneration.

6.51 The general rule is that once maternity leave or additional maternity leave comes to an end, the employee has no right to postpone her return to work any longer. There are,

---

[19] Case C-7/12, [2013] WLR (D) 247.   [20] UKEAT/544/09, [2011] ICR 75.   [21] [2004] IRLR 42.

however, three circumstances when she may do so. First, if the employer has failed to notify the employee of the date when her leave would end, and she reasonably believes that the period has not ended (regs 19(2)–20(3)). Second, if she is sick at the end of her maternity leave, she is entitled to be treated in the same way as any other employee who is off work sick. Thus she will have an entitlement to sick pay, and, if the absence is likely to last a length of time, the usual procedure for dealing with the long-term sick employee should be adopted (see para 17.89). Third, she may postpone her return to work by adding on another leave period, eg annual holidays, parental leave etc.

6.52 If the employee fails to return to work after her leave entitlement has come to an end, she should be treated as an unauthorised absentee, and dealt with under the appropriate disciplinary procedure. If she wishes to return to work, but the employer refuses to permit her to do so, this will amount to an automatically unfair dismissal if the reason was because she had given birth or exercised her rights to take maternity leave or additional maternity leave.

6.53. There are proposals to extend reg 10 to offer protection for six months after the mother's return to work. It is not yet known when this will happen.

D. **Remedies**

6.54 An employee is entitled not to be subjected to any detriment because she is pregnant, gave birth to a child, was suspended from work on maternity grounds, or took ordinary or additional maternity leave (ERA, s 47C). She will be deemed to have been automatically unfairly dismissed if the reason for her dismissal was that she was pregnant, gave birth to a child, or took ordinary or additional maternity leave. It will also be unfair to select her for redundancy for any of these reasons (ERA, s 99, reg 20). According to the European Court of Justice it is not contrary to the Equal Treatment Directive to dismiss a woman after her maternity leave has come to an end because of absences due to a pregnancy-related illness, even though that illness first appeared during her pregnancy (*Handels-og v Dansk Handel*, see para 4.139).

6.55 The dismissal of a pregnant woman who is unable to complete a fixed-term contract is sex discrimination under the Equal Treatment Directive and Pregnant Workers Directive, even if the woman knew she was pregnant when she was recruited, did not tell her employer, and her presence at work is essential for the proper functioning of the employer's business (*Tele-Danmark A/S v Handels (HK) per Brandt-Nielsen*[22]). Equally, the non-renewal of a fixed-term contract on grounds of pregnancy is discrimination, although not if the reason for the non-renewal had nothing to do with the fact of pregnancy (*Jiminez Melgar v Ayuntamiento de los Barrios*[23]).

6.56 Of course, if the employer did not know that she was pregnant, and dismisses her for a reason unconnected with her pregnancy, she will not be able to claim that her dismissal was contrary to s 99 of ERA. An employer must know or believe in the existence of an employee's pregnancy in order to be liable for automatically unfair dismissal (*Del Monte Foods v Mundon*[24] approved in *Ramdoolar v Bycity Ltd*[25]). Equally, if she is selected for redundancy, and the pregnancy or childbirth had nothing to do with her selection, then her right to a redundancy payment falls to be considered under s 135.

---

[22] Case C-109/00, [2001] All ER (EC) 941, [2001] IRLR 853, [2001] All ER (D) 37 (Oct), ECJ.
[23] Case C-438/99, [2001] IRLR 848, [2001] All ER (D) 42 (Oct), ECJ.
[24] [1980] ICR 694, [1980] IRLR 224.   [25] [2005] ICR 368, EAT.

6.57 If an employer has engaged a temporary replacement to do the work of a woman who is absent because of pregnancy or childbirth, then, if he has informed him/her in writing that the employment will be terminated on the return to work of the latter, and the employer does in fact dismiss the temporary replacement in order to make room for the woman returning from maternity leave, the dismissal shall be regarded as being for some other substantial reason of a kind to justify the dismissal, but the employer must still show that he acted reasonably in treating that reason as a sufficient ground for dismissal (see Chapter 17). The same rule applies when a replacement is taken on when a woman is suspended on medical or maternity grounds (ERA, s 106).

6.58 An employee may exercise her contractual or statutory rights, whichever is the more favourable. Her remedy for a breach of her contractual rights (other than in respect of remuneration) is by way of a claim for breach of contract in the county court, or a breach of contract claim under the provisions of the Employment Tribunals Extension of Jurisdiction Order (see para 1.40) where the claim is outstanding on the termination of her employment. She may also claim that she has suffered a detriment contrary to reg 19, or claim unfair dismissal under reg 10 or reg 20.

6.59 Finally, a woman who is dismissed at any time while she is pregnant or after childbirth when the maternity leave period ends by reason of the dismissal is entitled to be given written reasons for her dismissal, without any request being made (see para 17.176). This rule will also apply if an employee is dismissed while absent from work during an ordinary or additional adoption leave period (see para 6.71). In both cases, no period of continuous employment is required (ERA, s 92(4), (4A)).

E. **Statutory Maternity Pay (SMP)**

6.60 The Statutory Maternity Pay (General) Regulations 1986 (as amended) make provision for SMP to be paid by employers, and recouped by them from the national insurance contributions they pay to the Revenue. SMP is payable for a period of 39 weeks to employees who satisfy the conditions of eligibility.

6.61 The first qualification for SMP is that the woman must be an 'employed earner', ie one whose earnings attract a liability for employers' Class 1 national insurance contributions. This concept is slightly wider than the definition of 'employee' generally used in employment law, and refers to a woman who is gainfully employed under a contract of service or an office holder whose earnings are chargeable to income tax under Schedule E. The result could well be that a woman may be regarded as self-employed for SMP purposes and thus not entitled to this benefit (eg because no Class 1 contributions are being made) but an employee for the purpose of employment protection rights, and thus be able to benefit from the provisions relating to maternity leave and the right to return to work. A woman who is employed by a foreign organisation with no place of business in the United Kingdom will also not qualify for SMP, although women who work within the European Community are so entitled.

6.62 Second, she must have been continuously employed (not necessarily working) for a period of 26 weeks immediately before the 15th week before the expected week of confinement. There is no minimum number of hours' qualification, she does not need to be actually working as long as the contract of employment is in existence, and there are a number of provisions which help her to retain continuity where it would otherwise be broken.

6.63 Third, she must satisfy the earnings rule, ie her average earnings (including overtime and bonuses) must be at or above the lower earnings limit at which national insurance contributions are payable (£120per week from April 2020. Note that all figures are updated annually). Average earnings are to be calculated over a period of eight weeks ending with the last pay day before the end of the qualifying week.

6.64 Fourth, she must produce a medical certificate stating the expected week of confinement, and give 28 days' notice to her employer of the date when she expects the liability for SMP to begin.

6.65 Finally, SMP is not payable for weeks when she is actually working, and there are additional exclusions in respect of women who are taken into legal custody or who go outside the European Economic Area, and on the death of the employer, and if she changes her employer after her baby is born.

6.66 SMP is payable at two rates. For the first six weeks, SMP is earnings-related, ie 90% of the employee's average weekly earnings. The remaining 33 weeks are paid at the prescribed rate, or 90% of average earnings if this is less than the prescribed rate (currently £151.20. SMP is subject to tax and NI contributions, and any other lawful deductions (eg pension contributions, trade union subscriptions etc). Any contractual remuneration (eg contractual sick pay or maternity pay) can be offset. (As with other pay under these regulations, an employer can enhance it above the statutory limit (and see *Ali v Capita Customer Management Ltd*, 6.108)).

6.67 If a woman is entitled to a pay increase before the start of her maternity leave, or would have been awarded such an increase had she not been absent on statutory maternity leave, this must be taken into account when calculating her entitlement to SMP. If, during the period of maternity leave, she becomes entitled to a pay increase, the employer must re-calculate her SMP entitlement accordingly (Statutory Maternity Pay (General) Regulations, reg 21(7)). If an existing employee feels that she has been denied such entitlement in the past, she has six years from the date of the ruling in *Alabaster v Woolwich Bank*[26] to request a recalculation of her payment.

6.68 There are a number of provisions dealing with special situations which may arise, and which may affect entitlement to SMP. These include the dismissal of a woman because she is pregnant, when the employer becomes insolvent, or if she is detained in legal custody, or working during the maternity pay period, etc.

F. Maternity Allowance (Social Security Contributions and Benefits Act 1992)

6.69 A woman who does not qualify for statutory maternity pay may be entitled to maternity allowance (MA) paid to her direct by the Department for Work and Pensions. She must show that:

(a) she is pregnant, and has reached the start of the 11th week prior to the expected week of confinement;

(b) she has been employed as an employed earner or self-employed earner for at least 26 weeks in the 66 weeks preceding the EWC. These weeks do not have to be continuous, nor do they have to be with the same employer;

(c) her average weekly earnings are not less than the maternity allowance threshold in any of the 13 weeks in the test period (currently £30 per week). Earnings from more than one job will count if necessary.

---

[26] [2005] EWCA Civ 508, [2005] ICR 1246, [2005] IRLR 576.

6.70 Maternity allowance is paid for a period of 39 weeks, at a weekly rate of 90% of average weekly earnings, or the prescribed rate (currently £151.20 whichever is the smaller sum). It is not payable to women who travel outside the European Economic Area, or who are in legal custody.

Adoption Leave (Paternity and Adoption Leave Regulations 2002)

6.71 To qualify for ordinary adoption leave, the employee must:

(a) have been matched with a child by an adoption agency, and must have agreed that the child should be placed with him or her for adoption;

(b) provide evidence of his/her entitlement; and

(c) inform the employer of the date when the child is expected to be placed for adoption and the date on which the employee has chosen for the leave period to begin.

6.72 The employer, for his part, must inform the employee of the date when the leave period entitlement will end, taking into account any additional adoption leave period to which the employee will be entitled. There are special provisions dealing with the situation arising from the interruption or termination of the child's placement. The ordinary adoption leave period is 26 weeks.

6.73 An employee who takes ordinary adoption leave is also entitled to additional adoption leave, which will last for a period of 26 weeks beginning on the day after the last day of ordinary adoption leave.

6.74 Adoption leave is available only where a child is newly placed with adoptive parents, and only one parent, the 'primary adopter', is entitled to it. It is a matter for the couple to decide which of them this shall be. The other parent may be entitled to take time off equivalent to paternity leave and shared parental leave if he or she meets the relevant statutory criteria.

6.75 An employee who takes ordinary and additional adoption leave has the same rights as those enjoyed by a woman taking ordinary and additional maternity leave. During the leave period, the employee is entitled to the benefit of the terms and conditions of employment that would have applied if s/he had not been absent, excluding terms relating to remuneration (but statutory adoption pay is payable if the employee qualifies for this). This could include contractual benefits, such as membership of a health club, use of mobile telephones, company car, etc. S/he is entitled to the benefit of the employer's implied obligation of trust and confidence, and any terms relating to termination, redundancy payments, and disciplinary and grievance procedures, etc. For her/his part, the employee is bound by the obligations of good faith, the giving of notice, disclosure of confidential information, the taking of other employment, etc.

6.76 The whole period of adoption leave does not break continuity of employment and will count for continuity purposes and for the purpose of assessing entitlement to contractual rights, such as assessing seniority, pay increments, etc, except that the additional adoption leave period does not count for accrued pension rights purposes.

A. Reasonable Contact

6.77 The employer and employee may agree to make reasonable contact with each other from time to time during the adoption leave period, which will not affect the rights of either party. It is suggested that this could be for the purpose of discussing details of return to work, communicating information, informing the employee of promotion opportunities, etc. Contact may be by any suitable means, eg telephone, emails, personal visits, etc.

B. Work During the Adoption Leave Period

6.78 An employee may carry out up to ten days' work for the employer during the adoption leave period without bringing that period to an end. Work, which includes training, will count as a full day if it is done for part of a day. The type of work that the employee may carry out will be a matter for agreement between the parties, but it would normally be any activity that would ordinarily be classed as work under the employee's contract of employment. He/she will be entitled to be paid on an agreed basis, and entitlement to statutory maternity pay will not be affected. Any period of work will not extend the total duration of the adoption leave period.

C. Returning to Work after Adoption Leave

6.79 An employee who returns to work after ordinary adoption leave is entitled to return to the same job, with seniority, pension rights, and other terms and conditions that are not less favourable than if s/he had not been absent. No notice of return to work need be given (it will be recalled that the employer will have already specified the date for return to work). However, if the employee wishes to return to work on a date before the end of the adoption leave period, eight weeks' notice of the intention to return early must be given (16 weeks for employee shareholders).

6.80 An employee who returns to work after the additional adoption leave period is entitled to return to the same job, on the same terms and conditions as if they had not been absent. However, if it is not reasonably practical for the employer to continue to employ the employee under the existing contract of employment, then, where there is a suitable and appropriate vacancy, the employee is entitled to be offered alternative employment with the employer (or the employer's successor or an associated employer).

6.81 If the employee unreasonably refuses that offer, the reasonableness of the employee's dismissal (or resignation) will be tested in the usual way under the provisions of ERA, s 94(4).

D. Remedies

6.82 An employee has the right not to be subjected to any detriment because s/he took adoption leave, and it will generally be an unfair dismissal to dismiss the employee because adoption leave was taken.

E. Statutory Adoption Pay (SAP)

6.83 To qualify for statutory adoption pay, the adopter must:

(a) have been in employed earner's employment for a continuous period of at least 26 weeks;

(b) have normal weekly earnings in the eight weeks ending with the week in which the adopter is notified of the match which are not less than the lower earnings limit for the payment of national insurance contributions;

(c) have elected to receive SAP (and not SPP).

6.84 The employee must give evidence of his/her entitlement to SAP, and there are provisions relating to disentitlement if the employee works for the employer or another employer during the SAP period, if the adopter is entitled to statutory sick pay, in legal custody, etc. SAP is payable for a continuous period of 26 weeks during ordinary adoption leave and for a further 13 weeks if additional adoption leave is taken, at a rate which is the lesser of 90% of the employee's normal weekly earnings or the prescribed rate (currently £151.20). Contractual remuneration can be offset.

Recoupment by employer

6.85 An employer who pays SMP, SPP, or SAP is entitled to recover from HMRC 92% of the amount paid out. A 'small employer', ie one whose gross NI contributions payments (including employers' and employees' contributions) is £45,000 or less in the qualifying tax year, is entitled to recover 103% (including secondary national insurance) of the payments made.

Paternity Leave (Paternity and Adoption Leave Regulations 2002, as Amended)

6.86 In addition to taking 18 weeks' unpaid parental leave (see para 6.109), and the opportunity to take shared parental leave (see para 6.96), a father (or male or female partner of the mother) is entitled to take one or two weeks' paternity leave on the birth or adoption of a child, with pay at the statutory rate. Although 'paternity' is a peculiarly male concept, there are several circumstances when a woman may take paternity leave. Thus, if the partner of the birth mother or adoptive mother is a woman, then she will be entitled to paternity leave if she is a woman who has, or who expects to have, the main responsibility for raising the child. Also, if, when a couple adopt a child, the adoptive father takes adoption leave, the adoptive mother is entitled to take paternity leave. And if two people of the same sex living together adopt a child, one may take adoption leave and the other may take paternity leave.

6.87 The rules relating to paternity leave cater for paternity on the birth of a child and paternity arising from adoption. So far as the former is concerned, the right to paternity leave applies to employees (not workers) who have been continuously employed for at least 26 weeks ending with the week immediately preceding the 14th week before the expected week of birth. The employee must be the father of the child, or the mother's husband or partner. Whether he is or is not the father of the child, he must have or expect to have responsibility for the upbringing of the child. A 'partner' is a person who lives with the mother in an enduring family relationship, whether of the same or different sex, but must not be a relative of the mother.

6.88 So far as adoption is concerned, paternity leave may be taken in respect of a child who is under the age of 18 (there are special provisions relating to children who are adopted from overseas). Again, the employee must have been employed for at least 26 weeks ending with the week in which the child's adopter is notified of having been matched with the child. The employee must be married to or the partner of the adopter, and have the main responsibility for the upbringing of the child. Again, a partner is a person (whether of the same or different sex) who lives with the adopter in an enduring family relationship.

6.89 An employee who wishes to take paternity leave can choose to take either one week's or two weeks' leave. He cannot take odd days or non-consecutive weeks (a week, in this connection, is a period of seven days). The leave cannot be taken before the child is born (or the child is placed with the adopter) and must be taken within 56 days of the birth or placement. The employee must give his employer notice of the date from when he will take his leave, and the length of absence. If the employer so requests, the employee must provide a signed declaration stating (a) that the purpose of the absence from work is to take care of the child or support the child's mother (or adopter), (b) that he is the father of the child (or the mother's husband or partner) and that he expects to have responsibility for the upbringing of the child.

6.90 There are further provisions dealing with the effect of premature birth, stillbirth or the death of the child's mother, and multiple births, when only one period of paternity leave may be taken.

6.91 An employee who is absent from work on paternity leave is entitled to the benefit of all of the terms and conditions of employment that would have applied if he had not been absent (excluding terms and conditions concerning remuneration), and is bound by any obligation under those terms except in so far as they are inconsistent with his right to take paternity leave. S/he is entitled to return from his leave to the job in which he was employed before his absence, on terms and conditions not less favourable than those which would have applied had he not been absent. If, however, s/he has taken paternity leave as well as additional maternity leave or additional adoption leave, the right to return is limited to the considerations which apply in respect of those latter leave periods (see paras 6.47 and 6.78).

6.92 Otherwise, an employee is entitled not to be subjected to a detriment because s/he took paternity leave, and it will also be automatically unfair to dismiss a person because s/he took such leave.

6.93 In *Atkins v Coyle Personnel plc*,[27] an employee was dismissed while on paternity leave because he had engaged in an angry exchange of emails and telephone conversations with his manager. It was held that his dismissal was not connected with the fact that he took paternity leave, but because of the heated argument with his manager. It may have been associated with paternity leave, but was not connected with it.

Statutory Paternity Pay (SPP)

6.94 Statutory paternity pay (SPP) is payable to an employee who satisfies the conditions of eligibility. These are:

(a) he must have been employed for a continuous period of 26 weeks ending with the week immediately preceding the 14th week before the expected week of the child's birth, or the week in which the adopter was notified of the match being made;

(b) his normal weekly earnings in the eight weeks ending with the relevant week are not less than the lower earnings limit for the payment of NI contributions;

(c) he gives at least 28 days' notice before the date from which he expects SPP or SAP to be paid (or, if that is not reasonably practicable, as soon as is reasonably practicable);

(d) he provides evidence of the child's birth, and provides a written declaration that he meets the conditions as to the relationship with the child's mother.

6.95 Currently, statutory paternity pay is payable for two weeks at a weekly rate of either 90% of average weekly earnings or the prescribed rate (currently £ 151.20, whichever is the lesser sum).

---

[27] [2008] IRLR 420.

Shared Parental Leave

6.96 The Shared Parental Leave Regulations 2014 came into force on 5 April 2015 and give the mother the choice of converting part of her maternity leave (but not the compulsory maternity leave element) to shared parental leave (SPL), which she can share with her partner. If she chooses not to do so, her maternity leave entitlement will be unchanged.

6.97 The partner must have a specific relationship to the mother and baby, and can be the child's father, the mother's husband or civil partner at the time of the birth, or a partner who lives with her and the child in an 'enduring family relationship' (reg 3).

6.98 It is for the mother or primary adopter to decide whether to end her maternity or adoption leave early and opt into SPL. If the parents both meet the qualifying requirements, they will need to decide how they divide their total SPL and pay entitlement between them. The scheme is designed to be flexible, so that parents, their partners, or adoptive parents can share the remaining 'pot' of leave. They can be off work at the same time, or they can take it in turns. The leave is taken in up to three blocks of time, and a parent can return to work and then take another block later.

6.99 SPL may be taken at any time within the period which begins on the date the child is born or date of the placement and ends 52 weeks after that date. Leave must be taken in complete weeks and can either be taken in a continuous period, which an employer cannot refuse, or in discontinuous periods (that is, separate periods which are not continuous), which the employer can refuse.

A. **Eligibility**

6.100 To be eligible for SPL:

(a) the mother (or adopter) must be entitled to maternity or adoption leave, or statutory maternity or adoption pay or maternity allowance, and must share the main responsibility for caring for the child with the child's father or her partner;

(b) she must have worked for the same employer for at least 26 weeks at the end of the 15th week before the due date and still be employed in the first week that SPL is to be taken;

(c) her partner must have worked for 26 weeks (not necessarily in a row) in the 66 weeks leading up to the due date and have earned above the maternity allowance threshold of £30 a week in 13 of those 66 weeks;

(d) her partner can be employed, self-employed, or an agency worker.

6.101 Sometimes only one parent in a couple is eligible to get SPL, which means that they are unable to share the leave between them. In such a case, that parent can still use SPL to book the leave in separate blocks even if her partner is unable to share it, as it is more flexible than maternity leave.

B. **Notifying the Employer**

6.102 An employee who opts for SPL must notify his or her employer and book the leave with at least eight weeks' notice, stating:

(a) how much leave is available;

(b) how much leave s/he is entitled to take;

(c) how much leave s/he is intending to take; and

(d) how s/he expects to take it.

6.103 Each eligible employee can give his or her employer up to three separate notices. Each notice can be for a block of leave, or the notice may be for a pattern of 'discontinuous' leave involving different periods of leave. If a parent asks for discontinuous blocks of leave in a notification, the employer can refuse and require that the total weeks of leave in the notice be taken in a single continuous block.

C. **Rights During SPL**

6.104 Parents have certain rights during SPL, which mirror those of AML:

(a) Contractual terms will remain in place. Employees will remain entitled to all contractual terms and benefits (apart from pay) and will continue to accrue holidays.

(b) In addition to the ten keeping in touch (KIT) days that a mother on maternity leave has, each parent taking SPL would be entitled to 20 days as SPL in touch days (SPLIT). Like KIT days, an employer cannot require an employee to attend work during shared parental leave, nor can an employee insist on attending work during a period of SPL. Employees are protected against suffering a detriment as a result of their decision whether or not to use SPLIT days.

(c) Employees are protected from detriment if they apply for or take SPL, or the employer thinks that they may do so.

Shared Parental Pay

6.105 Shared parental pay (ShPP) has the same qualifying requirements as statutory maternity and paternity pay. In other words, as well as passing the continuity test above, the parent should also have earned an average salary of the lower earnings limit or more for the eight weeks prior to the 15th week before the EWC.

6.106 Before taking up the entitlement to ShPP, the mother or adopter has to serve a written curtailment notice under the Pay Curtailment Regulations 2014 (or, if she is receiving MA, the Maternity Allowance Regulations 2014). At least eight weeks' notice of the date of curtailment must be given.

6.107 Note that an employer can enhance statutory maternity pay above the SMP limit. It has been held that it would not be discriminatory to do this just for women on maternity leave, and not for men on shared parental leave (*Ali v Capita Customer Management Ltd*[28]), as maternity leave is there for the health of the mother to deal with the trauma of having a child, and cannot be compared with shared parental leave. This appears to be a practical decision, avoiding the effect of companies withdrawing such enhanced pay from women. The case was not brought as one of indirect discrimination, for example because more men than women take shared parental leave/pay, even though women are entitled to it. If it had, there may have been a different result.

---

[28] [2019] EWCA Civ 900.

Parental Leave (Maternity and Parental Leave Regulations 1999–2001, regs 13–21)

6.108 An employee (man or woman) who has been continuously employed for one year, and has (or expects to have) parental responsibility for a child, is entitled to have parental leave for a period of up to 18 weeks. This changed from a 13-week entitlement in March 2013. Note that this should not be confused with shared parental leave (para 6.96), which is a replacement for some of a mother's maternity leave. Parental leave is an additional right for each parent.

6.109 The qualifying period of one year's employment will be measured backwards from the date when the leave is to start. There are more favourable rules in respect of parents of disabled children, who will be entitled, in certain circumstances, to count service with a previous employer (see reg 13(1A)).

6.110 A person has responsibility for a child if s/he has parental responsibility within the meaning of s 3 of the Children Act 1989 (as amended by the Adoption and Children Act 2002) or s 1(3) of the Children (Scotland) Act 1995. A mother automatically acquires parental responsibility; a father will do so if he is married to the child's mother or, in the case of an unmarried father, if he registers the birth jointly with the mother. Parental responsibility may also be acquired by a court order or by a formal agreement with the child's mother. Thus guardians and adoptive parents qualify for parental leave, but not step-parents or foster parents. However, the right does not apply to members of the armed forces, share fishermen, or members of the constabulary.

6.111 Parental leave may be taken as soon as the child is born or adopted, and the right will last until the child reaches the age of 18 (this was previously the age of five until 5 April 2015, except in the case of disabled children).

6.112 Unlike paternity leave, maternity leave, and adoption leave, there is no requirement that parental leave shall be with pay, although other social security benefits may be available (income support, housing and council tax benefit, etc) as appropriate.

6.113 An employee may only take up to four weeks' parental leave in any one year (Sch 2, para 8) in respect of any individual child. Leave may only be taken in weekly blocks; thus if an employee takes less than a week's leave it will count as one week out of his total 18-week entitlement (*South Central Trains Ltd v Rodway*[29]). However, if the child is in receipt of disability living allowance, greater flexibility is allowed, and leave may be taken on a daily basis, so that up to 20 individual days' leave may be taken in any one year.

6.114 During parental leave, the employee's terms and conditions of employment are the same as those which are applicable during additional maternity leave. The employee is entitled to the benefit of the employer's obligation of trust and confidence, and any terms and conditions relating to notice of termination, compensation in the event of redundancy, and disciplinary and grievance procedures. For his or her part, the employee is bound by the obligation of good faith, and any terms and conditions relating to the giving of notice of termination, the disclosure of confidential information, the acceptance of gifts or other benefits, and participation in any other business. A period of leave will count as continuous service for the purpose of statutory employment protection rights.

6.115 If the employee has taken up to four weeks' parental leave (whether or not this was added on to paternity leave, ordinary maternity leave, or ordinary adoption leave), s/he is entitled to return to the job s/he was doing before the absence. If parental leave followed a

---

[29] [2004] IRLR 777, EAT.

period of additional maternity leave or additional adoption leave or lasted more than four weeks, s/he is entitled to return to the job s/he was doing before the absence unless it is not reasonably practicable for the employer to permit the employee to return to the job, in which case the employer must offer a job which is suitable and appropriate for him/her to do in the circumstances. The terms and conditions must be no less favourable than those which would have applied if the employee had not been absent.

6.116 The regulations give power to employers and employees to enter into agreements which provide for a certain flexibility, by means of a collective agreement or a workforce agreement which must be incorporated into the individual contract of employment (see Sch 1 to the regulations). In the absence of any such agreement, the default provisions of Sch 2 will apply. This states that the employee gives at least 21 days' notice of the dates when leave is being taken, and the employer is entitled to request proof of entitlement. A father who wishes to take leave in respect of a child not yet born can give 21 days' notice of the expected week of confinement, and he may start his leave as soon as the baby is actually born, even if this is earlier or later than the anticipated date of birth. Adoptive parents must also give 21 days' notice, although if this is not reasonably practicable, notice must be given as soon as is reasonably practicable. Except in relation to new fathers and adoptive parents, the employer may postpone the leave where he considers that the operation of the business would be unduly disrupted if the employee took the leave during the period in question, but the postponement cannot be for more than six months.

6.117 An employee may present a complaint to an employment tribunal that his employer has unreasonably postponed a period of parental leave, or has prevented him from taking such leave. If the employment tribunal find the complaint well founded, it shall make a declaration to that effect, and may award compensation to the employee, the amount being such as is considered to be just and equitable, having regard to the employer's behaviour and any loss suffered by the employee (ERA, s 80).

6.118 An employee has the right not to suffer a detriment because s/he took parental leave (ERA, s 47C) and it will be an automatically unfair dismissal to dismiss an employee because s/he took or sought to take parental leave (ERA, s 99).

Parental Bereavement Leave

6.119 The Parental Bereavement (Leave and Pay) Act 2018 came into force in April 2020. It provides a right to primary carers to time off work following the death of a child. Parents or carers will be entitled to at least two weeks' leave following the loss of a child under the age of 18 or a stillbirth after 24 weeks of pregnancy. Employees with 26 weeks' continuous service will be entitled to paid leave at the statutory rate or 90% of average earnings, whichever is the lower. The leave will be unpaid for those without such service.

To Care for Dependants (ERA, s 57A)

6.120 An employee is entitled to be permitted by his employer to take a reasonable amount of time off work during the employee's working hours in order to take action which is necessary:

(a) to provide assistance on an occasion when a dependant falls ill, gives birth, or is injured or assaulted;

(b) to make arrangements for the provision of care for a dependant who is ill or injured;

(c) in consequence of the death of a dependant;

(d) because of an unexpected disruption or termination of arrangements for the care of a dependant; or

(e) to deal with an incident which involves the child of the employee and which occurs unexpectedly in a period during which an educational establishment which the child attends is responsible for him.

6.121 In *Royal Bank of Scotland v Harrison* the unavailability of a childminder was 'unexpected' and therefore it was 'necessary' for the employee to take a day off work, even though she had two weeks' notice of the unavailability of the childminder. However, the longer the time available to make alternative arrangements, the less likely it will be that the employee can establish the necessity.

6.122 Time off work under s 57A(1)(c) in order to take action which is necessary in consequence of the death of a dependant does not include the right to have time off work to deal with the emotional effect of a bereavement (*Forster v Cartwright Black*).[30]

6.123 The employee must tell his employer the reason for the absence as soon as is reasonably practicable, and also inform him how long he expects to be absent.

6.124 A dependant is a spouse, child, parent, or person living in the same household as the employee, otherwise than by reason of his being an employee, tenant, lodger, or boarder. Additionally, for the purpose of para 6.121(a) and (b), a dependant can also be any person who reasonably relies on the employee for assistance on an occasion when he falls ill or is injured or assaulted, or to make arrangements for the provision of care in the event of illness or injury. For the purpose of (d), a dependant can also include any person who reasonably relies on the employee to make arrangements for the provision of care.

6.125 There is no service qualification for the enjoyment of these rights, but equally there is no requirement on the employer to pay an employee who takes such time off work. Any such entitlement must depend on the terms of the contract of employment.

6.126 An employee may complain to an employment tribunal (within the usual time limits) that his employer has unreasonably refused to permit him to take time off work for any of the purposes referred to earlier, and, if the complaint is well founded, the tribunal will make a declaration, and may award compensation as it considers to be just and equitable. Also, an employee has the right not to suffer a detriment because he took such time off work, and it will be automatically unfair to dismiss an employee for taking time off work for the purposes referred to. In *Qua v John Ford Morrison (Solicitors)*[31] the EAT gave guidance on how time off work for dependants' leave should be properly exercised, and the tests to be applied in determining whether there has been an automatically unfair dismissal under s 57A where the principal reason for the dismissal was that the employee had taken time off work to look after a dependant.

Flexible Working Arrangements (ERA, ss 80F–80I)

6.127 In recent years there appears to have developed a greater interest in finding alternatives to conventional full-time and part-time employment, partly with a view to trying to avoid legal responsibilities (which has had very limited success) but mainly due to

---

[30] [2004] ICR 1728, EAT.   [31] [2003] ICR 482, [2003] IRLR 184, [2003] All ER (D) 29 (Jan), EAT.

the genuine need of employers and employees for new-style flexible working arrangements, which can, in certain circumstances, be commercially advantageous to both sides. Flexitime itself has had a long history, but arrangements such as job-sharing, performance contracts, zero hours contracts, annualised hours contracts, home-working, etc, are now being used with greater frequency. However, because statutory rules were not designed to deal with these arrangements, legal disputes arising out of them had to be dealt with by the use of a certain amount of judicial creativity (see *Chief Constable of Avon and Somerset v Chew*[32]).

6.128 The Employment Act 2002 gave a right for an employee to request flexible working arrangements, by inserting new ss 80F–80I into the Employment Rights Act 1996. This was originally for those who cared for an adult or child only, but was amended by s 131 of the Children and Families Act 2014 (CFA) to remove the requirement to be a carer and so extend to all qualifying employees. The right does not apply to those in to the armed forces, police officers, share fishermen, and employee shareholders. The CFA also removed the statutory procedure that had been in place. Instead, there is an ACAS code of practice.

6.129 There is no actual right to work flexibly; the right is only one to make a request. The Act only requires an employer to 'consider the request in a reasonable manner'. A remedy may only arise on an application to an employment tribunal if it can be shown that the employer has failed to do so, or has based his decision on incorrect facts. The relevant rules were originally laid down in the Flexible Working (Procedural Requirements) Regulations 2002, and the Flexible Working (Eligibility, Complaints and Remedies) Regulations 2002 (as amended). From 8 March 2013 the Parental Leave (EU Directive) Regulations extended the right to request flexible working to employed agency workers returning from maternity/paternity leave. These provisions have since been updated by Part 9 of the CFA 2014, amending the ERA.

A. **Application for Flexible Working**

6.130 An application for flexible working may be made by a qualifying employee, ie s/he must have been continuously employed for a period of 26 weeks at the date the application is made.

6.131 Only one application may be made in any 12-month period, and if the application is accepted, the resultant change to terms and conditions will be permanent.
The application may relate to a change of:

(a) the hours the employee is required to work;

(b) the times the employee is required to work;

(c) the place where the employee is required to work;

(d) such other aspects of the employee's terms and conditions of employment as may be specified in regulations.

6.132 The application, which must be in writing, must specify the change applied for, and the date from which the proposed change will be effective, and must explain what effect, if any, the change will have on the employer's business and how such effect may be dealt with.

6.133 The employer has to consider the request in a reasonable manner and notify the employee of his decision within three months, or such longer period as may be agreed

---

[32] [2001] All ER (D) 101 (Sep), EAT.

between the parties. This period does not have to be agreed in writing, and the agreement to extend the time can be made retrospectively, as long as it is made within three months of the expiry of the original time limit. If the application is accepted, it will operate as a variation of the terms and conditions of employment of the employee's contract, which will be binding until and unless there is a further agreed variation (unless agreed on a time-limited basis). If the application is refused, the employer has to hear an appeal within three months, unless an extension has been agreed.

6.134 The employer will be under no duty to consider the application where the employee notifies him that it has been withdrawn, or if the employee fails without reasonable cause to attend a meeting more than once, or refuses without reasonable cause to provide the employer with further information needed in order to assess whether the contract should be varied.

6.135 The employer may refuse the request only for one of the following reasons:

(a) the burden of additional costs;

(b) the detrimental effect on ability to meet customer demand;

(c) the inability to reorganise work among existing staff;

(d) the inability to recruit additional staff;

(e) the detrimental impact on quality;

(f) the detrimental impact on performance;

(g) the lack of work during the periods when the employee proposes to work;

(h) the planned structural changes;

(i) other grounds which the Secretary of State may specify from time to time.

6.136 If the employer and employee are unable to reach an amicable agreement on the application for flexible working, then, if both parties agree, resort may be had to the ACAS Arbitration Scheme (see para 1.13). By so doing, the employee waives the right to present a claim to an employment tribunal. The decision of the arbitrator will be final. Otherwise, the employee may make a claim to an employment tribunal, on the ground that the employer has failed to comply with the procedural requirements as set out in the regulations, or has based his decision to reject the application on incorrect facts. It should be noted that the tribunal's role is merely to verify whether the employer has followed the correct procedure and to examine any disputed facts. The tribunal does not have the power to question the commercial validity of the employer's decision, nor can it substitute its own judgment on the business reasons for those of the employer. But the tribunal is entitled to look at the ground asserted by the employer as the reason why he did not grant the application, and to ascertain if it was factually correct. This may involve an examination of the evidence as to the circumstances surrounding the application, the effect of granting it, whether there would be any potential disruption, and the attitude of customers and other members of staff (*Commotion Ltd v Rutty*[33]). If it finds the complaint to be well founded, the tribunal must make a declaration, and may make an order requiring the employer to reconsider the application. An award of compensation may be made, of such amount as the tribunal thinks just and equitable, up to a maximum of eight weeks' pay.

6.137 There is the usual protection against an employee suffering a detriment because an application for flexible working was made, and it will be automatically unfair to dismiss an employee for a reason relating to any such application.

---

[33] [2006] ICR 290, EAT.

Summary

- A pregnant employee can have paid time off for antenatal care from the start of her employment. Partners have a right to accompany her for two of these appointments.

- Employers must carry out risk assessments for new or expectant mothers, and find alternative work or otherwise suspend a woman on maternity grounds if there is a risk to health.

- There are three periods of maternity leave—CML, OML, and AML. CML is two weeks (four in a factory), OML and AML both 26 weeks. Rights of return are slightly different. Adoption leave mirrors these.

- There is also a right to unpaid parental leave for up to 18 weeks until the age of 18.

- Partners of the mother of a child have a right to two weeks paternity leave, or shared parental leave.

- The right to request flexible working is a right to have that request considered reasonably, not a right to have it granted.

7

Employment Protection

Background

7.1 In this chapter we will consider a number of miscellaneous legal rights given to employees in the Employment Rights Act 1996 and other legislation. These are minimum standards which can be exceeded by agreement or negotiation, but they cannot be denied to an employee.

Guarantee Payments (ERA, ss 28–35)

7.2 Provided an employee has been continuously employed for at least one month, the employer is bound to pay him a guarantee payment in respect of any whole day in which the employee is not provided with work because:

(a) there is a diminution in the requirements of the employer's business for work of the kind which the employee is employed to do, or

(b) any other occurrence affecting the normal working of the employer's business in relation to work of that kind.

In *North v Pavleigh Ltd*[1] the owner of a company closed his factory for Jewish holidays. The employment tribunal held that no guarantee payment could be claimed. Section 28 only applies to a diminution of work, or an 'occurrence', such as a power failure or national disaster. It was not intended to cover the religious habits of the proprietor.

7.3 A guarantee payment is not payable if the workless day occurs in consequence of a trade dispute involving any employee of the employer or of any associated employer. In *Garvey v J & J Maybank (Oldham) Ltd*[2] there was a national lorry drivers' strike, and pickets at the employer's entrance refused to let the firm's own lorries in or out. The employer ordered the firm's drivers (who were not involved in the strike) to cross picket lines, but they refused. As a result, there were insufficient supplies coming into the firm, and the claimant was laid off. It was held that he was not entitled to guarantee pay. The refusal of the drivers to cross the picket lines meant that the lay-off occurred in consequence of a trade dispute. Nor is the employee entitled to the payment if the employer offers to provide alternative work which is suitable in all the circumstances (whether or not it is within the employee's contract) and he unreasonably refuses that offer (*Purdy v Willowbrook International Ltd*[3]). Employees who had agreed to a temporary reduction in their work were entitled to a guarantee payment under s 28 (*Abercrombie & Ors v AGA Rangemaster Ltd*[4]). The claimants agreed to work four days a week rather than five when market conditions deteriorated. The respondent refused to pay them guarantee payments for the fifth day. It was held that during the currency of the agreement, Fridays were days on which they were normally contracted to work, and as no work was provided, they were entitled to guarantee payments.

---

[1] [1977] IRLR 461.   [2] [1979] IRLR 408.   [3] [1977] IRLR 388.   [4] [2013] EWCA Civ 1148.

The employee must also comply with reasonable requirements imposed by the employer with a view to ensuring that his services are available (*Meadows v Faithful Overalls Ltd*[5]). Guarantee pay is only payable in respect of days on which the employee would otherwise be required to be at work (*Mailway (Southern) Ltd v Willsher*[6]).

7.4 The employee is entitled to be paid at the guaranteed hourly rate (which is one week's pay divided by the number of normal working hours) for the number of normal working hours in respect of any whole day he is laid off. He is entitled to be paid for five working days in any period of three months, at a maximum prescribed daily rate (currently £30 (ERA, s 31)). In other words, the present position is that an employee will be entitled to the prescribed daily rate for a maximum of 20 days in each year. If the employee already has a contractual right to remuneration in respect of a workless day (eg by means of a collective agreement, etc), then any payment made under that agreement will go towards discharging the employer's liability to make the statutory guarantee payment, and equally, the latter will go towards discharging the contractual liability. If there is a guaranteed week agreement in existence, then the contractual remuneration shall be apportioned rateably between the workless days, and the statutory minimum will be used to 'top up' as appropriate. However, workless days when a contractual payment is made are taken into account when calculating the number of days guarantee pay is payable in any period of three months (*Cartwright v G Clancey Ltd*[7]). It should be noted that if a contractual or statutory guarantee payment is being made, the employee is not entitled to apply for jobseeker's allowance.

7.5 If an employer fails or refuses to pay the whole or part of the guarantee payment, the employee may complain within three months to an employment tribunal. If they find the complaint well founded, they will order the employer to pay to the claimant the amount due to him.

7.6 If there is a collective agreement in force which already relates to guarantee payments, then all the parties thereto may apply to the appropriate minister for an exemption order. This will be granted if he is satisfied that the statutory provisions should not apply to those employees, but the collective agreement must contain provisions for an aggrieved employee to take a dispute about non-payment of the guarantee payment either to arbitration (or other procedure) or to an employment tribunal. A number of such exemption orders have been granted.

Suspension on Medical Grounds (ERA, ss 64–65)

7.7 Provided an employee has been employed for not less than one month, he will be entitled to be paid remuneration if he is suspended from work in consequence of a requirement imposed by certain statutory provisions or a recommendation made in a code of practice issued or approved under s 16 of the Health and Safety at Work etc Act 1974 (see Chapter 11). The statutory provisions in question are (a) Control of Lead at Work Regulations 2002, (b) Ionising Radiations Regulations 1999, and (c) Control of Substances Hazardous to Health Regulations 2002. If a health risk occurs within the scope of these provisions, certain processes must be suspended, and the result now is that in these circumstances the affected employees will be entitled to be paid for a period of up to six months from the day when the suspension period begins. An employee is not entitled to be paid during the suspension period if he is incapable of work because of illness or injury, or if he unreasonably refuses alternative work offered to him by the employer (whether within the terms of his contract or not), or if he does not make himself available for work.

[5] [1977] IRLR 330.   [6] [1978] ICR 511, [1978] IRLR 322.
[7] [1983] ICR 552, [1983] IRLR 355, EAT.

7.8 An employee who is thus suspended on medical grounds is entitled to a week's pay in respect of each week the suspension lasts, and though the contractual right to remuneration is unaffected, the contractual and statutory remuneration can be set off against each other as appropriate. If the employer fails to pay the whole or any part of the employee's remuneration, the latter may present a complaint to the employment tribunal within three months, and if it finds the complaint well founded, it shall order the employer to pay to the employee the amount due to him.

7.9 It must be stressed that a medical suspension payment can only be claimed if the employee is fit for work. In *Stallite Batteries Co Ltd v Appleton*,[8] the claimant became ill after falling into a skip containing lead paste. In consequence, his blood lead level exceeded the limit laid down in the Control of Lead at Work Regulations 1998, but no medical suspension certificate was issued by the employment medical adviser. Nonetheless, the applicant's own doctor considered that he was not fit for work. The EAT held that he was not entitled to a medical suspension payment. He was not available for work due to sickness, and his claim was excluded by s 65(3) of the Act.

7.10 If an employee is dismissed for a reason which would otherwise amount to a medical suspension, he is only required to have been employed for one month (instead of two years) in order to present a claim for unfair dismissal (s 65(1)).

7.11 If the employer wishes to engage a temporary employee to take the place of the suspended employee, then, as long as he has informed the temporary employee in writing that the employment will be terminated when the suspension has ended, a dismissal of the temporary employee in order to allow the suspended employee to return to work will amount to 'some other substantial reason' for the dismissal (see Chapter 17), although the employer will still have to show that he acted reasonably.

7.12 For medical suspension from work on maternity grounds, see Chapter 6.

Time Off Work

A. **For Public Duties (ERA, s 50)**

7.13 An employer shall permit an employee of his who is a justice of the peace to take time off during his working hours for the purpose of performing any of the duties of his office (see *Riley-Williams v Argos Ltd*[9]).

7.14 An employer shall also permit an employee who is a member of certain specified bodies to take time off work during his working hours for the purpose of attending at a meeting of the body or its committees or sub-committees, and to do any other thing approved by the body for the purpose of discharging its functions. The specified bodies are:

(a) a local authority (including the Common Council of the City of London, a National Parks Authority and the Broads Authority);

(b) a statutory tribunal;

(c) a police authority or police member of the National Criminal Intelligence Service;

(d) a board of prison visitors or prison visiting committee;

(e) a relevant health body (including a National Health Service trust, a health authority or health board);

---

[8] HSLB 147, EAT.   [9] [2003] All ER (D) 58 (Jul), EAT.

(f) a relevant education body (managing or governing body of an educational establishment maintained by a local authority or (in Scotland) a school or college council
or governing body of further education);

(g) the Environment Agency or the Scottish Environment Protection Agency;

(h) Service Authority for the National Criminal Intelligence Service or the National
Crime Squad;

(i) Scottish Water or Water Customer Consultation Panel;

(j) General Teaching Council for England and for Wales.

7.15 There is no requirement that the employee be paid for taking time off work under s
50. The amount of time off permitted for these purposes, the occasions on which, and the
conditions subject to which time off may be taken are those that are reasonable in all the
circumstances, having regard in particular to:

(a) how much time off is required for the performance of the duties;

(b) how much time off the employee has had already in respect of trade union duties
and activities; and

(c) the circumstances of the employer's business and the effect of the employee's absence on the running of that business.

7.16 In *Walters v British Steel Corpn*[10] the claimant was transferred to an essential job, and
it was difficult to release him for certain public duties. When he took the job, he had agreed
that his public duties would take second place. Consideration of safety required certain
minimum manning levels, and his colleagues refused to cover for him. It was held that he
was not entitled to time off work for public duties, as the circumstances of the employer's
business had to be taken into account.

7.17 In considering the amount of time off to be given under s 50, the needs of the
employee to perform his public duties adequately must be balanced carefully with the requirements of the employer to have the work done. In *Emmerson v IRC*[11] the claimant was
the leader of the opposition party on Portsmouth Council. He had been given 18 days' leave
(paid) each year to perform his duties, but this was insufficient. His application for further
unpaid leave of absence was refused by his employers, as it was argued that he could not be
spared from his job. The employment tribunal thought that the problem could be overcome
by appointing a deputy to give him some assistance, for in other areas there was more than
one person doing the same job as the claimant, who should not be put at a disadvantage
because he was extra-efficient. Since the claimant was prepared to use some of his own
holidays for public duties, the tribunal thought that he should be given a further 12 days'
leave of absence without pay. However, in *Corner v Buckinghamshire County Council*,[12] the
EAT held that the employment tribunal has no power to make any recommendations of
this nature, or to impose conditions.

7.18 Section 50 requires the employer to give time off work to the employee. Rearranging
hours of work or swapping duties so that the same number of hours are worked is not giving time off (*Ratcliffe v Dorset County Council*[13]).

7.19 It has been noted that there is no legal requirement that the employee be paid for
time off work under s 50. But if he is refused time off, he may present a complaint to an

---

[10] IDS Brief 150.   [11] [1977] IRLR 458.   [12] [1978] ICR 836, [1978] IRLR 320, EAT.
[13] [1978] IRLR 191.

employment tribunal within the usual period of three months from the date of refusal. The employment tribunal must take account of all the relevant considerations (*Borders Regional Council v Maule*[14]), including the employee's efforts to reorganise his commitments so as to produce a reasonable pattern of work, and if the complaint is upheld, the tribunal shall make a declaration and may award compensation of such amount as it considers just and equitable, having regard to the employer's default and any loss sustained by the employee.

B. **For Occupational Pension Scheme Trustees (ERA, s 58)**

7.20 An employee who is a trustee of an occupational pension scheme is entitled to be given time off work, with pay during working hours, for the purpose of:

(a) performing any of his duties as such a trustee; or

(b) undergoing training relevant to the performance of those duties.

7.21 The amount of time off which the employee is to be permitted to take, the purpose for which, the occasions on which, and any conditions subject to which time off may be taken are those that are reasonable in all the circumstances, having regard to:

(a) how much time off is required for the performance of the duties as a trustee of the scheme and to undergo the relevant training; and

(b) the circumstances of the employer's business and the effect of the employee's absence on the running of that business.

7.22 The employee must be paid his normal remuneration, or his average hourly earnings, or a fair estimate of those earnings, for the time off work under these provisions. If the employer refuses to permit him to take time off work, or refuses to pay for time off work taken, a complaint may be made to an employment tribunal. If the complaint is upheld, the employment tribunal shall make a declaration to that effect, and make an award of compensation to the employee as it thinks just and equitable.

C. **For Employee Representatives (ERA, s 61)**

7.23 An employee who is a representative of an independent trade union, or an elected employee representative (or candidate for election), has the right to be allowed reasonable time off work, with pay, for the purpose of performing his functions as such when the employer is required to consult on redundancies (see para 18.69) or on transfers of undertakings (see para 9.76). He is entitled to have access to the affected employees, and such accommodation and facilities as may be appropriate.

7.24 Time off work may also be claimed under the following statutory provisions:

(a) Transnational Information and Consultation of Employees Regulations 1999;

(b) European Public Limited Liability Company (Employer Involvement) (Great Britain) Regulations 2009;

(c) Information and Consultation of Employees Regulations 2004;

(d) Occupational and Personal Pension Schemes Regulations 2006;

(e) European Cooperative Society (Involvement of Employees) Regulations 2006;

(f) Companies (Cross-Border Mergers) Regulations 2007.

---

[14] [1993] IRLR 199, EAT.

7.25 An employee representative has the right not to suffer a detriment because he performed any function or activity as such, and it will be an automatic unfair dismissal to dismiss him for the same reason.

D. **For Young Person for Study or Training (ERA, s 63A)**

7.26 An employee who:

(a) is aged 16 or 17;

(b) is not in full time secondary or further education; and

(c) has not attained certain minimum standards of education as set out in the Right to Time Off Work for Study or Training Regulations 2001 (and/or the Right to Time Off Work for Study or Training (Scotland) Regulations 1999),

is entitled to be permitted by his employer to take time off during the employee's working hours in order to undertake study or training leading to the relevant qualification, which is an external qualification, the attainment of which would contribute to the attainment of one of the prescribed standards set out in the regulations and would be likely to enhance the employee's employment prospects (whether with his employer or otherwise). If an employee is aged 18 but began such studies before attaining that age, he is entitled to continue until he ceases to be 18.

7.27 The amount of time off, the occasions on which, and any conditions subject to which time off may be taken are those that are reasonable in all the circumstances, having regard to:

(a) the requirements of the employee's study or training, and

(b) the circumstances of the employer's business and the effect of the employee's time off on the running of that business.

7.28 The employee is entitled to be paid whilst taking time off work for study or training purposes, at the appropriate hourly rate, calculated in accordance with the normal rules which define 'week's pay' and 'normal working hours' (see ERA, ss 220–229, 234, para 14.1). A complaint may be made to an employment tribunal, within the usual time limits, that the employer has unreasonably refused to permit the employee to have time off work as required by s 63A, or has failed to pay the whole or part of the remuneration due to him. If the complaint is upheld, the tribunal will make a declaration and award the remuneration due.

E. **Time Off for Study or Training (ERA, s 63D)**

7.29 Section 63D of the Employment Rights Act (inserted by the Apprenticeships, Skills, Children and Learning Act 2009) creates a right for a qualifying employee to make a request for time off work in order to pursue a course of study or training, the purpose of which is to improve the employee's effectiveness in the employer's business and the performance of the employer's business.

7.30 The right to apply for time off for study or training applies to employees who work for firms that employ more than 250 employees. There is no requirement that the employer shall pay the employee while he is taking time off; nor is the employer required to pay for the training or study.

7.31 A qualifying employee must have been employed for a period of at least 26 weeks, and not be an agency worker or a person in respect of whom learning needs are already catered for (eg young persons).

7.32 The study or training may be undertaken on the employer's premises, or in the employee's home, or elsewhere, and could be during or outside the employee's working hours, supervised by the employer or someone else, undertaken with or without supervision, within or outside the United Kingdom, and need not be intended to lead to an award of a qualification to the employee. More than one course of study or training may be included in one request, but the employee must not have made a request within the previous 12 months (although in certain circumstances a previous request made within that period may be ignored). There is no limit to the amount of time off an employee may request, or whether the course of study or training shall be full-time or part-time. These matters will fall to be taken into account when the employer considers the request.

7.33 The Employee Study and Training (Procedural Requirements) Regulations generally follow the Flexible Working Regulations, and lay down the procedures to be followed for the making and consideration of a request. The employee's application (known as a s 63D application) must:

    (a) give the following details of the proposed course of study or training:

        (i)   its subject matter;

        (ii)   where it would take place;

        (iii) who would provide or supervise it;

        (iv) what qualification (if any) it would lead to; and

    (b) explain how the employee thinks the proposed study or training would improve:

        (i)   the employee's effectiveness in the employer's business; and

        (ii)   the performance of the employer's business.

Dealing with the Request

7.34 When the employer receives the s 63D application from the employee, then, provided the employee has not submitted an earlier application within the previous 12 months (other than a request which has to be ignored: see reg 3), the employer must consider the application and, within 28 days, hold a meeting with the employee to discuss the request, at a time and place convenient to both parties. The employee will have the right to be accompanied at the meeting by a companion, and the meeting may be delayed if the companion is not available.

7.35 The employer is entitled to seek further information about the proposed course of study or training, and if the employee refuses to supply this, the request may be taken as having been withdrawn. Otherwise, within 14 days of the meeting, the employer must give the employee a written notice of the decision, stating the grounds for the refusal with an explanation as to why those grounds apply. The application may be refused (in whole or in part) on a number of permissible grounds, which are:

    (a) the proposed study or training would not improve:

        (i)   the employee's effectiveness in the employer's business; or

        (ii)   the performance of the employer's business;

    (b) the burden of additional costs;

    (c) the detrimental effect of ability to meet customer demand;

    (d) the inability to reorganise work among existing staff;

    (e) the inability to recruit additional staff;

(f) the detrimental impact on quality;

(g) the detrimental impact on performance;

(h) the insufficiency of work during the periods the employee proposes to work;

(i) planned structural changes;

(j) any other grounds specified by the Secretary of State in regulations.

7.36 The employee will have a right to appeal within 14 days against the refusal, and a meeting to consider the appeal must be held within 14 days, and the decision must be notified to the employee within 14 days. If the appeal is dismissed, the grounds on which the appeal was dismissed must be stated.

7.37 If the s 63D application is granted, the employer must give the employee notice of the decision, in writing, and dated. The notice must give details of the subject of the study or training, where and when it will take place, who will provide or supervise it, and what qualifications (if any) it will lead to. The notice must also make clear whether any remuneration will be paid for the time spent on study or training, whether there will be any changes in the employee's working hours in order to accommodate the study or training, and how tuition fees or other direct costs are to be met.

7.38 If the application is granted in part, or varied, the employer's notice must make clear the variation agreed to, and be supported by written evidence of the employee's agreement to the variation.

7.39 For his part, the employee must inform the employer:

(a) if he fails to start the agreed study or training;

(b) if he fails to complete the agreed study or training;

(c) if he undertakes or proposes to undertake study or training that differs from the agreed study or training.

Complaints to Employment Tribunal (s 63(I))

7.40 An employee may present a complaint to an employment tribunal that the employer has failed to deal with the application in accordance with the regulations or refused on a ground other than the permissible ones, or that the employer's decision to refuse the application is based on incorrect facts. The complaint must be brought within three months of the date when the employee was notified of the decision on the appeal or the employer was in breach of the statutory provisions, or such further period as the employment tribunal considers reasonable. On such a complaint the employment tribunal may make an order requiring the employer to reconsider the application, or make an award of compensation to the employee as is thought to be just and equitable, not exceeding eight weeks' pay (capped).

7.41 An employee has the right not to be subjected to a detriment because he made or proposed to make a s 63D application, and it would be an automatically unfair dismissal if the making of such an application was the reason for the dismissal.

F. Other Time Off Work

7.42 Time off work may also be claimed in order to care for dependants (see para 6.121), for trade union duties and activities (see para 21.66) and for redundant employees to look for work (see para 18.38).

Statutory Sick Pay (SSP)

A. How the Scheme Works

7.43 Under the provisions of the Social Security Contributions and Benefits Act 1992, ss 151–163 and the Statutory Sick Pay (General) Regulations 1982 employers will be responsible for paying to their employees' statutory sick pay in respect of the first 28 weeks of absence through sickness (£95.85 per week in 2020) (see addendum for Coronavirus changes).

7.44 Originally, the whole amount of SSP paid out by employers could be recovered by means of deductions from national insurance contributions sent to the Revenue, and there was also in existence a small employer's relief. However, these regimes have now been abolished and replaced by a percentage threshold scheme (PTS) designed to help all employers if they have a large number of employees off sick at the same time.

7.45 To understand the scheme, certain expressions must be defined:

(a) *A day of incapacity for work*
This is any day when an employee is incapable, by reasons of some specific disease or mental or bodily disablement, of doing work of a kind he might reasonably be expected to do.

(b) *A period of incapacity for work*
This means any period of four or more consecutive days, each of which is a day of incapacity for work in relation to the employee's contract of employment.

(c) *A period of entitlement*
This period starts with the first day of incapacity for work, and ends when either:

    i.   the period of incapacity has ended, or

    ii.   the entitlement to SSP has been used up, or

    iii.   the contract of employment is terminated, or

    iv.   a woman who is pregnant becomes disqualified under the provisions of the Act.

(d) *Qualifying days*
These are days on which the employee is required by his contract of employment to be available for work.

B. Qualifying Conditions

7.46 To qualify for SSP, three conditions must be satisfied, namely:

(a) the employee's day of incapacity for work must form part of the period of incapacity for work (ie four or more consecutive days);

(b) the day must be within the period of entitlement;

(c) the day must be a qualifying day.

If there are two periods of incapacity (for the same or different reasons) separated by not more than eight weeks, they will be treated as a single period of incapacity. This means that an employee will not have to requalify with another three 'waiting days'. Moreover, if an employee leaves his job and starts another one, his period of incapacity with his previous employer counts with his new one.

7.47 The entitlement to SSP is a flat-rate payment for a maximum period of 28 weeks in any one period of entitlement of three years or in any one tax year. Thereafter, the employee will be able to claim employment and support allowance. SSP is payable to all employees who meet the qualifying conditions and whose average weekly earnings are above the level at which national insurance contributions are payable.

7.48 The above provisions apply to part-time employees (provided they earn the requisite amounts) and there is no minimum service qualification. SSP will be deemed remuneration, and therefore subject to deductions in respect of tax and national insurance contributions. Married women and widows who pay reduced national insurance contributions will qualify for SSP even though they do not qualify for employment and support allowance. Note that agency workers are also entitled to SSP.

C. Exclusions from Entitlement

7.49 The following employees are excluded from entitlement:

(a) employees who are incapacitated from work for less than four days;

(b) employees who earn less than the current lower earnings limit (£120 per week from April 2020 averaged over an eight-week period;

(c) pregnant women whose first day of sickness is within the disqualifying period (ie 18 weeks beginning with the eleventh week prior to the expected week of confinement), or who are receiving SMP or MA;

(d) employees who would be workless on the day when the period of entitlement would begin because of a trade dispute, unless they can prove that they did not take part in the strike or did not have a direct interest in it;

(e) employees who are sick on the day they are due to start new employment (employment and support allowance may be payable);

(f) employees whose first day of sickness is within eight weeks of a claim in respect of one of the following state benefits—employment and support allowance, invalidity pension, maternity allowance, or a previous entitlement to incapacity benefit or severe disablement allowance;

(g) employees who are in legal custody or who are outside the European Economic Area.

D. Enforcement

7.50 If an employee has not been paid SSP, he may refer the matter to HM Revenue & Customs. A decision made in the employee's favour can be enforced in the county court, should this be necessary. Certain questions may be referred directly to the Secretary of State for Work and Pensions for a decision, namely:

(a) whether a person is, or was, the employee or employer of another person;

(b) whether an employer is entitled to deduct SSP from his contribution payments;

(c) whether two or more contracts of employment, or two or more employers, shall be treated as one for SSP purposes.

7.51 Any agreement which purports to exclude, limit, or modify an employee's entitlement to SSP shall be void, but this does not prevent an employer from operating a sick pay scheme which is more favourable than the statutory scheme. Contractual sick pay may discharge the employer's liability for SSP, and any SSP payment will discharge contractual liability for the relevant days.

E. **Self-certification of Illness and Fit Notes**

7.52 Doctors are required to issue fit notes after seven days of absence from work. Employees who need to self-certify four or more days' absence should fill in form SC2, which helps to determine if they are entitled to SSP. The form must be completed and signed by the employee, which amounts to a self-certification of absence through illness. If the illness lasts for a period longer than seven days, a Statement of Fitness for Work can be obtained from the doctor. The traditional sick note, issued by general practitioners, has been replaced by these 'fit notes' in which the GP will spell out the tasks the worker can perform. The fit note allows the doctor to advise one of two options:

(a) not fit for work, where the assessment of the employee is that he should refrain from work for a stated period of time;

(b) may be fit for work, where the assessment of the employee's condition does not necessarily mean he cannot return to work; however, he may not be able to complete all of his normal duties or hours, or may need some support to help him undertake his normal duties.

The guidance in relation to fit notes emphasises the importance of assessing an individual's health in relation to work in general, and not just in relation to one specific role. The doctor may be able to advise on what 'reasonable adjustments' could be made, eg altered hours, changed duties, workplace adaptations, etc, although the fit note is qualified by the addition of 'if available, and with your employer's agreement'. Moreover, a doctor may not necessarily be familiar with the resources available to the employer, and there is likely to be considerable disagreement over what amounts to a reasonable adjustment in the circumstances and whether a doctor is sufficiently well informed to make certain suggestions.

The fit note also has implications for employees who have been dismissed after a long-term absence caused by injury or illness. If the absence is due to a disability within the meaning of the Equality Act 2010, the employer must take appropriate steps or risk a finding of unfair dismissal. A GP's view, while not being conclusive, will contain more information about an individual's condition and functional ability, and the reasonableness of the dismissal may be open to challenge if there has been a failure to consider the suggested reasonable adjustments.

Working Time Regulations 1998 (as amended)

A. **The Regulations**

7.53 These regulations came into force in October 1998 and are designed to implement the provisions of the Working Time Directive (93/104/EC) and the Young Workers Directive (94/33/EC). They were amended in 1999 and in 2003 to extend coverage to non-mobile transport workers in the sea, inland waterways and fishing sectors, all workers in the railway and offshore sectors, and all workers in the aviation industry who are not covered by the separate Aviation Directive (2000/79/EC), and to mobile workers in the road transport industry in 2005.

7.54 Generally, the regulations give a series of rights to 'workers', a term which is wider than 'employees', and which also applies to a person working under a contract 'to do or perform personally any work or services for another party to the contract whose status is not by virtue of the contract that of a client or customer of any profession or business undertaking carried on by the individual' (reg 2(1)). This clearly covers casual, freelance, and some self-employed workers, other than self-employed persons who are pursuing a professional or business activity on their own account. Thus in *Byrne Bros (Formwork) Ltd v Baird*[15] the claimant was a self-employed worker employed under a sub-contractor's agreement. He was taxed under Schedule D. The employer was not obliged to provide work, and the claimant was not obliged to do the work personally, although he was paid on a time basis. He claimed holiday pay for the Christmas and New Year closure under the Working Time Regulations. An employment tribunal upheld his claim, and the EAT confirmed the decision. As a 'labour-only sub-contractor' he undertook personally to provide work or services, and he did not work as part of 'any profession or business undertaking'. Thus he was a worker within the meaning of the regulations (see also *Cavil v Barratt Homes Ltd*[16]). So too are bricklayers who work in gangs and who are paid by the employer directly to each gang member (*JNJ Bricklaying Ltd v Stacey*[17]).

7.55 The regulations do not apply to certain seafarers, sea fishermen, and workers who work on inland waterways, each of whom have their own special sector provisions. Non-mobile workers in the transport industry are included, but mobile workers in that industry are covered by the Road Transport (Working Time) Regulations 2005. There is partial exclusion for mobile staff who work in civil aviation (again covered by sector-specific provisions), and for activities of the armed forces and police or specific activities in connection with civil protection services which inevitably conflict with the regulations.

7.56 The main provisions of the Working Time Regulations 1998, as amended, are as follows.

B. The Main Provisions

Regulation 4 (maximum weekly working time)

7.57 A worker's average working time for each seven-day period, including overtime, must not exceed 48 hours in any period of 17 weeks, although in certain circumstances (reg 21, special cases) the reference period can be 26 weeks, or 52 weeks if permitted by a collective agreement or workforce agreement (reg 23(b)). The regulation will not apply if the worker agrees in writing to working more than 48 hours each week (reg 5). The agreement may be for a specified or an indefinite period, but may be terminated by either side giving the appropriate notice of not less than seven days and not more than three months. For a worker to opt out of the 48-hour week, the consent must be expressly and freely given (*Pfeiffer v Deutsches Rotes Kreuz*[18]).

To calculate the average hours in any reference period, the formula to be applied is:

$$\frac{A + B}{C}$$

7.58 This requires some explanation. In any reference period, there will be days when the employee will not work, because of annual holidays, sick leave, maternity leave, etc. Clearly, to exclude those days from the calculation would distort the average hours worked. Therefore, those 'excluded days' must be added back in to the calculation. 'A' is the total number of hours worked during the reference period; 'B' is the total number of hours worked immediately after the reference period during the number of days equivalent to the number of excluded days. 'C' will be the number of weeks in the reference period. Thus

---

[15] [2002] ICR 667, [2001] All ER (D) 321 (Nov), EAT, [2002] IRLR 96.
[16] [2003] All ER (D) 06 (Jul), EAT.   [17] [2003] All ER (D) 96 (Jul), EAT.   [18] [2005] IRLR 137.

the formula (A+B÷C) will give the average number of hours in the reference period, which will, in effect, be extended by the equivalent number of 'excluded' days.

7.59 If a relevant agreement is provided for successive 17-week reference periods, then each reference period will be self-contained, for the purpose of calculating average working hours. In the absence of any such agreement, the reference period will be a 'rolling' 17-week period, ie each week will be the start of a new 17-week reference period. If a worker is required to remain at his place of work, even though he is not actually working, this is working time for the purpose of the regulations (*Sindicato de Médicos de Asistencia Pública (SIMAP) v Conselleria de Sanidad y Consumo de la Generalidad Valenciana*[19]). However, if the worker is permitted to be away from his place of work when on call, and accordingly free to pursue other activities, the on-call time does not amount to working time until he is called upon by the employer to work. If a person is permitted to sleep while on call, the period of inactivity is still on-call time (*Landeshaupstadt Kiel v Jaeger*[20]); Where a paramedic had to stay within a three-mile radius of the ambulance station, and respond to calls within three minutes, this was working time, following *Landeshauptstadt Kiel*, as the employer restricted where a worker can be during on-call hours, and their time was not their own (*Truslove v Scottish Ambulance Service*[21])., Also in *Ville de Nivelles v. Matzak*,[22] a firefighter was required to be on stand-by withineight minutes of the workplace. This was found by the ECJ to be working time, even though it was spent at home, because there was an obligation to be physically present at a location decided by the employer.

7.60 Time spent by mobile workers travelling from home to customers' premises counts as working time (*Federacion de Servicios Privados del sindicato Comisiones obreras v Tyco Integrated Security SL*[23]).

7.61 An employer cannot insist that a worker works hours of work in excess of the restrictions imposed by the Working Time Regulations, and a dismissal for refusing to do so is automatically unfair under s 101A of ERA. The one year's qualifying period of employment for unfair dismissal does not apply in these circumstances (*McLean v Rainbow Homeloans Ltd*[24]).

Regulations 5A, 6A, 7 (Young Worker)

7.62 The working time of a young worker (ie who has attained the age of 15 but not the age of 18 and who is over compulsory school leaving age) shall not exceed eight hours per day or 40 hours per week. A young worker shall not work during the restricted period, which is between 10pm and 6am or 11pm and 7am. An employer shall not assign a young worker to work during the restricted period unless the employer has ensured that the young worker will have the opportunity of a free assessment of his health and capacities before he takes up the assignment, and thereafter at such regular intervals as may be appropriate in his case.

Regulation 6 (Length of Night Work)

7.63 The normal hours of work for a night worker (defined in reg 2) shall not exceed eight in any 24-hour period, again with the average being assessed over a 17-week period (which can be fixed successive 17-week periods, as set out in a relevant agreement, or, failing such agreement, a 'rolling' 17-week period). In *R v A-G for Northern Ireland, ex p Burns*[25] the claimant worked a cycle of 15 shifts of eight hours' duration. During five of these, at least three hours of her working time fell between 11pm and 6am. It was held that she was a

---

[19] [2001] All ER (EC) 609, [2001] ICR 1116, [2000] IRLR 845.
[20] [2004] ICR 1528, (2004) All ER (EC) 604.   [21] UKEATS/0053/13/JW.   [22] Case C 518/15.
[23] Case C-266/14.   [24] [2007] IRLR 14.   [25] [1999] IRLR 315.

night worker within the meaning of reg 6. It was noted that the Directive defined a night worker as a person who works at night 'as a normal course', and this phrase was to be construed as meaning 'as a regular feature'.

7.64 An employer shall ensure that no night worker whose work involves special hazards or heavy physical or mental strain works for more than eight hours in any 24-hour period. The work shall be regarded as involving special hazards or physical or mental strain if it is identified as such in a collective agreement or a workforce agreement, or in a risk assessment carried out under the Management of Health and Safety at Work Regulations 1999. Further, a night worker will be entitled to a free health assessment before he takes up the assignment, with further such assessments at regular intervals. If a registered medical practitioner advises the employer that a worker employed by him is suffering from health problems connected with night work, then, if possible, the employer should transfer the worker to other work for which he is suited, undertaken at times so that he ceases to be a night worker.

7.65 To calculate the average working hours of a night worker, the normal working hours during the reference period must be divided by the number of working days in that period. The formula is:

$$A \div (B - C)$$

Again, an explanation is required.

7.66 From the number of 24-hour periods during the reference period ('B') must be deducted the number of hours (divided by 24 to equate days) which comprise or are included in the weekly rest periods, as provided for in reg 11 ('C'). The amount of the normal working hours during the reference period ('A') can thus be ascertained by dividing the normal working hours during the reference period by the number of working days in that period.

7.67 If a worker has worked for less than 17 weeks, the average will be calculated by reference to the period since the worker started to work for the employer.

Regulation 8 (Pattern of Work)

7.68 Where the pattern according to which the employer organises work is such as to put the health and safety of a worker employed by him at risk, in particular because the work is monotonous or the work-rate is predetermined, the employer shall ensure that the worker is given adequate rest breaks.

Regulation 9 (Records)

7.69 An employer shall keep records of the maximum weekly working time, length of night working, health assessments, etc, of night workers, in respect of each worker in relation to whom they apply, and keep such records for two years.

Regulation 10 (Daily Rest)

7.70 An adult worker is entitled to a rest period of not less than 11 consecutive hours in each 24-hour period during which he works for an employer, although a young worker is entitled to a rest period of 12 consecutive hours.

Regulation 11 (Weekly Rest Periods)

7.71 A worker is entitled to an uninterrupted rest period of not less than 24 hours in each seven-day period during which he works for his employer, although this can be changed to two uninterrupted periods of 24 hours in each 14-day period, or one uninterrupted period of 48 hours in each 14-day period. A young worker is entitled to a rest period of not less than 48 hours in any seven-day period, although this can be altered in certain circumstances.

Regulation 12 (Rest Breaks)

7.72 Where a worker's daily working time is more than six hours, he is entitled to a rest break, which shall be for an uninterrupted period of 20 minutes (unless a collective agreement or workforce agreement specifies otherwise), to be spent away from the workstation. A young worker who works for more than four and a half hours shall be entitled to a rest break of at least 30 minutes, spent away from the workstation.

A rest break must have an ascertainable beginning and end. If a worker is 'on call' the fact that he can take a rest break is not sufficient if he is subject to instant recall whilst having a break (*McCartney v Oversley House Management*[26]). Rest breaks are not to be regarded as time spent on call if the worker is not to be interrupted save in exceptional circumstances, even if the break is taken on site (*Martin v Southern Health and Social Care Trust*[27]).

Regulation 13 (Annual Leave Entitlement)

7.73 Under the Working Time (Amendment) Regulations 2007, statutory minimum annual leave was increased to 5.6 weeks from April 2009 (ie 28 days) for a worker who works five days a week, pro rata for workers who work part time. Public holidays may be included in this entitlement, but there is no legal entitlement to take time off work on the actual public holidays. Further, employers who at present grant time off for public holidays do not have to provide workers with any additional leave. A worker is entitled to receive his normal weekly pay during these holidays, calculated in accordance with ss 221–224 of ERA. Normal weekly pay includes any usual supplements (such as flight supplements for airline pilots, *Williams v British Airways plc*),[28] and see *Bear Scotland* (7.86).

7.74 Entitlement to statutory holidays applies to all workers, not just those who are employees in the legal sense. Thus self-employed workers, casual employees, part-time employees, etc are all entitled to holidays with pay, the only exception being a person who is a client or customer of any profession or business undertaking. Agency workers are also entitled to holiday pay.

7.75 A holiday year may be fixed by a relevant agreement, which can be a workforce agreement that meets the requirements of Sch 1 of the Working Time Regulations, or a collective agreement with a recognised trade union, or a written contract of employment. In the absence of any such agreement, the holiday year will run from October each year or, in respect of workers who commenced work after 1 October 1998, from their start date and each subsequent anniversary.

7.76 The European Court has held that if a full-time worker becomes a part-time worker during the course of a year, and has not taken his full entitlement to annual leave before he changes, the employer cannot reduce the right to annual leave that the worker has already accumulated during the period of full-time employment but has not been able to take while working full-time (*Zentralbetriebsrat der Landeskrankenhaüser Tirols*[29]).

7.77 If a worker leaves his employment having taken less holiday than his entitlement at the time of leaving, he is entitled to be paid in respect of the untaken holiday period. If he leaves his employment having taken more holiday than his legal entitlement the relevant agreement may provide for a deduction in pay in respect of the excess holiday period.

---

[26] [2006] IRLR 514.   [27] [2010] IRLR 1048.   [28] Case C-155/10.
[29] Case C-486/08, [2010] IRLR 631.

7.78 To ascertain how much leave is owed on termination, the formula to use is $(A \times B)-C$, where 'A' is the period of leave the worker is entitled to under the regulations, 'B' is the portion of the leave year which has expired prior to the effective date of termination, and 'C' is the period of leave already taken by the worker. If a relevant agreement so permits, a worker who has already taken holiday entitlement in excess of his statutory entitlement can be required to compensate the employer, either by way of a payment or by doing additional work.

Where the contract of employment is terminated during the course of a leave year, and the employee has not taken his leave entitlement, reg 14(3) provides that he shall receive a payment in lieu, which shall be such sum as is provided for in a relevant agreement, or, if there are no such provisions, the formula $(A \times B)-C$ (para 7.77) will apply. In *Witley and District Men's Club v MacKay*[30] the employee was dismissed for gross misconduct. A relevant collective agreement provided that in such circumstances accrued holiday pay would not be payable. When the employers refused to make any such payment, the employee claimed that there was a breach of the Working Time Regulations. His claim was upheld. The words 'such sum' in reg 14(3) did not mean 'no sum'. Thus an agreement which provided for no sum to be paid in respect of outstanding leave entitlement is void by virtue of reg 35(1), as an attempt to exclude or limit the operation of the regulations. This clearly leaves open the possibility of an agreement being upheld if it provides for a minimal or token sum to be paid.

7.79 It goes without saying that clauses sometimes found in existing employment contracts which specify that an employee dismissed for reason of gross misconduct shall not be entitled to accrued statutory holiday pay are no longer valid although this rule would not apply in respect of additional contractual entitlement.

7.80 An employer can insist that offshore employees who work two weeks on and two weeks off take their annual leave during the 26 weeks of onshore time (*Russell v Transocean International Resources Ltd*).[31]

7.81 The worker may give notice to the employer of the dates when he wishes to take his holidays, subject to the employer requiring the worker to take his holidays on particular dates. The worker must give twice the number of days' notice as days' leave he wishes to take. The employer can prevent the employee taking leave on a particular day by giving notice equivalent to the same number of days as the length of leave the employee wishes to take. However, the notice provisions are capable of being overridden by a relevant agreement, which may provide for longer (or shorter) periods of notice.

7.82 If an employee fails to comply with the notice requirements as set out in his contract of employment he will lose his entitlement to statutory leave. In *Lyons v Mitie*[32] the contract stated that applications for holidays must be made on a request form and submitted at least four weeks before the holiday was to begin. The employee failed to give the requisite notice, and it was held that he was no longer entitled. However, the EAT cautioned that if an employer applied their rules in such a way as to effectively defeat a worker's entitlement to annual leave, or if the employee was forced to apply for holiday late in the year because of illness, EU law may well require the employer to permit him to take leave despite the failure to give proper notice.

7.83 There are conflicting decisions on whether holiday pay must be paid at the time when the worker is taking the holiday, or whether it can properly be paid along with basic pay

---

[30] [2001] IRLR 595, [2001] All ER (D) 31 (Jun), EAT.   [31] [2011] UKSC 57.
[32] [2010] ICR 628, [2010] IRLR 288.

but in *Robinson-Steele v RD Retail Services Ltd*,[33] the ECJ held that in principle, rolled-up holiday pay is not permitted by the EC Directive. Workers who take statutory leave must be placed in the same financial position as they would be in if they were carrying on work. An arrangement whereby annual leave payments are staggered over the corresponding annual period of work is precluded by the Directive. In other words, the point in time when payment is made for annual leave must be so fixed as to ensure that the worker can take his holiday entitlement. However, if there are genuine rolled-up holiday payments, made transparently and comprehensibly, these may be offset against a worker's entitlement to payment when leave is finally taken. In other words, if the percentage of holiday pay allocated is clearly identified in the contract and/or on the payslip, and it is made clear that it is a true addition to the contractual rate of pay, credit for such payments may be given (*Lyddon v Englefield Brickworks Ltd*[34]).

7.84 Accrued holiday pay is to be calculated on the basis of the number of working days in the year (ie 233 days per year), not on the basis of a calendar year of 365 days (*Leisure Leagues UK Ltd v Maconnachie*[35]). When calculating holiday pay for the minimum four weeks' statutory annual leave required by the Working Time Directive, the court in *Bear Scotland Ltd & Ors v Fulton & Ors*[36] found that non-guaranteed (but compulsory) overtime must be taken into account, but did purport to limit this, ruling that claims for arrears of holiday pay will be out of time if there has been a break of more than three months between successive underpayments, although there was still the risk that there would be claims stretching back 16 years. The Deduction from Wages (Limitation) Regulations 2014 were therefore brought in so that claims for unlawful deductions/backdated holiday pay stemming from this decision will be limited to two years (see 8.22). The limitation applies to cases brought from 1 July 2015. The Regulations also state that the right to paid holiday is not incorporated as a contractual term. In *Lock v British Gas Trading Ltd*[37] it was similarly found that commission is payable as part of holiday pay. Also, in *Flowers v East of England Ambulance Trust*[38] it was found that voluntary overtime should be taken into account for holiday pay, as it was part of normal remuneration if it was paid over a sufficient period of time.

7.85 The holiday pay of a worker on a zero hours contract placed on short-time working can be calculated on a pro rata basis. The situation is analogous to that of the part-time worker, not of someone on long-term sick leave (*Heimann & Anor v Kaiser GmbH*[39]). If the employee leaves his employment, having taken more than his annual leave entitlement, the employer can only recover the overpayment if there is a contractual provision to this effect, ie in the contract of employment, a workforce agreement, or a collective agreement which has been incorporated into the individual contract (*Hill v Chapell*[40]).

7.86 A period of illness whilst on holiday does not count towards the minimum period of four weeks' annual paid leave. In *Pereda v Madrid Movilidad* SA[41] the claimant suffered an accident at work 14 days before the commencement of his allocated period of four weeks' annual leave. The injury lasted for six weeks, and he was thus unable to take his planned holiday. His request for an additional period of annual leave was refused. The ECJ held that there can be no derogation from the entitlement to paid annual leave. Thus if a worker decides not to take his annual leave during a period of illness, he must be granted a replacement holiday period to ensure that he is not deprived of his entitlement to rest, relaxation

---

[33] Case C-131/04, [2006] IRLR 386, ECJ.   [34] [2007] All ER (D) 198, [2008] IRLR 198.
[35] [2002] IRLR 600, [2002] All ER (D) 223 (Mar), EAT.
[36] [2015] ICR 221, [2015] IRLR 15 EAT, also EATS/0010/16.
[37] Case C-539/12, [2016] EWCA Civ 983 CA, also see EAT/0189/15.   [38] UKEAT/0235/17.
[39] Cases C-229/11 and C-230/11; [2013] IRLR 48.
[40] [2003] IRLR 19, [2002] All ER (D) 461 (May), EAT.   [41] [2009] IRLR 959.

and leisure. This principle applies if the employee falls sick before or during the annual leave period: *Asociación Nacional de Grandes Empresas de Distribución (ANGED).*[42] In *Stringer v HMRC*[43] (and *Sobczyszyn v Szkola Podstawowa w Rzeplinie*[44]) the ECJ held that a worker who is on long-term sick leave is entitled to any holiday that accrues during his sickness absence, which he can presumably take on his return to work. An employee on long-term sick leave who did not have an opportunity to take her annual leave because of her illness was entitled to have the holiday carried forward to the next leave year automatically without having to request it (*NHS Leeds v Larner*[45]). This, however, only applies to the four weeks' leave set out in the European Directive, and not the additional 1.6 weeks granted by UK law, unless the parties have agreed otherwise (*Sood Enterprises v Healy*,[46] see also *TSN v Hyvinvointialan*[47] making the same point from an EU perspective).

If the employee is dismissed while on sick leave he is entitled to pay in lieu on any un-taken leave that accumulated during his sickness absence. Where a worker has been pre-vented from taking his annual leave due to sickness, he must be allowed to take that leave when he returns in the new leave year, or receive a payment on termination (*Schulz-Hoff v Deutsche Rentenversicherung Bund*[48]).

7.87 The death of a worker does not extinguish the right to paid annual leave which he had accrued (*Bollacke v Klaas & Kock B.V. & Co*[49]).

7.88 Annual leave accrued on sick leave cannot be carried over indefinitely. In *KHS AG v Schulte*[50] the Court of Justice of the European Union allowed it to be carried over up to 15 months. In domestic law, the EAT in *Plumb v Duncan Print Group Ltd*[51] found that it can be carried forward for up to 18 months.

7.89 Note that the paid annual leave provisions in the Working Time Directive have direct effect. This means that cases such as *Stringer & Ors v HMRC* referred to earlier can be enforced directly by public sector workers (*Dominguez v Centre informatique du Centre Ouest Atlantique*[52]) without waiting for UK case law or legislation.

7.90 In *Ainsworth v Inland Revenue Commissioners*[53] the House of Lords ruled that a claim for non-payment of holiday pay may be brought under the unlawful deductions provisions of ss 13–23 of the Employment Rights Act. The significance of this ruling is that the time for bringing a complaint will run from the last date of a series of unlawful deductions, and not from the more restrictive three-month time limit as laid down in reg 30 of the Working Time Regulations.

C. Exclusions

7.91 There are a number of excluded sectors of employment and specified activities to which specific regulations do not apply, as follows.

Regulation 18

7.92 The regulations do not apply to certain seafarers, workers on sea-going fishing vessels, and workers on board certain ships and hovercrafts. These workers have their own sector-specific provisions. Non-mobile workers in road, sea, and inland waterways

---

[42] Case C-78/11.   [43] [2009] All ER (EC) 906, [2009] ICR 932, [2009] IRLR 214.
[44] Case C-178/15.   [45] [2012] EWCA Civ 1034, CA.   [46] UKEATS/0015/12.   [47] C-609/17.
[48] [2009] ICR 932, (2009) IRLR 214.   [49] Cases C-118/13 EU, C-2014, C-1755, [2014] IRLR 732.
[50] Case C-214/10, [2012] IRLR 156.   [51] UKEAT/2015/0071.
[52] Case C-282/10, [2012] IRLR 321.
[53] [2009] UKHL 31, [2009] 4 All ER 1205, [2009] ICR 985, [2009] IRLR 677.

transport (eg clerical and administrative workers) are covered by the regulations, but mobile workers have limited exclusions. If a doctor is on call, but required to remain at a hospital, then periods of inactivity—even sleeping—can constitute working time. The fact that the doctor is required to be present at the place of work determined by the employer, and be available to provide services immediately in cases of need, means that such hours must be regarded as being within the ambit of the performance of his duties (*Landeshauptstadt Kiel v Jaeger*,[54] and see 7.60).

Regulation 19

7.93 Domestic servants in a private household are excluded from reg 4 (maximum weekly working time), reg 5A (young worker), reg 6 (length of night work), reg 6A (night work by young worker), reg 7 (health assessment for night workers), and reg 8 (safe pattern of work).

Regulation 20

7.94 Workers who, on account of the specific characteristics of the activities engaged in, or where the duration of the working time cannot be measured or predetermined, or which can be determined by the worker himself. In particular:

   (a) managing executives or other persons with autonomous decision-making powers;

   (b) family workers;

   (c) workers officiating at religious ceremonies in churches and religious communities.

7.95 The above workers are excluded from reg 4 (maximum weekly working time), reg 6 (length of night work), reg 10 (daily rest), reg 11 (weekly rest period), and reg 12 (rest breaks).

Regulation 21

7.96 There is a limited exclusion for the following group of workers:

   (a) workers whose activities are such that their place of work and place of residence are distant from one another, or whose different places of work are distant from one another;

   (b) where a worker is engaged in security and surveillance activities requiring a permanent presence in order to protect property and persons, particularly security guards and caretakers or security firms;

   (c) workers whose activities involve the need for continuity or service or production, particularly:

      (i) services relating to the reception, treatment or care provided by hospitals or similar establishments (including the activities of doctors in training), residential institutions and prisons,

      (ii) work at docks or airports,

      (iii) press, radio, television, cinematographic production, postal and telecommunications services, and civil protection services,

      (iv) gas, water, and electricity production, transmission and distribution, household refuse collection and incineration,

      (v) industries in which work cannot be interrupted on technical grounds,

---

[54] Case C-151/02, [2003] IRLR 804, [2003] All ER (D) 72 (Sep), ECJ.

    (vi)   research and development activities,

    (vii) agriculture,

    (viii) the carriage of passengers on regular urban transport services;

  (d) where there is a foreseeable surge of activity, particularly in:

    (i)   agriculture,

    (ii)   tourism, and

    (iii) postal services;

  (e) where the worker's activities are affected by:

    (i)   an occurrence due to unusual and unforeseeable circumstances, beyond the control of the worker's employer, or

    (ii)   exceptional events, the consequences of which could not have been avoided despite the exercise of all due care, or

    (iii) an accident or the imminent risk of an accident;

  (f) workers in railway transport whose activities are intermittent, who work on trains and whose activities are to ensure continuity and regularity of traffic.

7.97 In respect of the above group of workers, the following regulations do not apply, namely, reg 6 (length of night work), reg 10 (daily rest periods), reg 11 (weekly rest periods), and reg 12 (rest breaks). However, if a worker is required to work during what would normally be a rest period, the employer shall allow him to have a compensatory period of rest, or, if this is not possible, afford him appropriate protection (reg 24).

Regulation 23

7.98 This regulation provides that a collective agreement or a workforce agreement may modify or exclude the following regulations in relation to particular workers, namely reg 6 (length of night work), reg 10 (daily rest), reg 11 (weekly rest period), and reg 12 (rest breaks, see *Prison Service v Bewley*[55]). So far as reg 4 (maximum weekly working time) is concerned, such agreement can substitute a different period over which the average can be worked out, not exceeding 52 weeks (in place of 17 weeks).

7.99 There are also a number of other limited exclusions in respect of shift workers, offshore workers, workers in the armed forces, and young workers affected by *force majeure* or when no adult worker is available (regs 25–27A). There are also special rules for agricultural workers (Sch 2).

D. **Enforcement**

7.100 The regulations can be enforced in three ways. First, inspectors from the Health and Safety Executive (or, in appropriate circumstances, enforcement officers of local authorities) are responsible for the enforcement of the following relevant requirements (see reg 28), namely:

  (a) the duty of an employer to take all reasonable steps to ensure that the provisions relating to the 48-hour week have been complied with, and also to keep up-to-date records of workers who are subject to an opt-out agreement;

  (b) the duty of an employer to take all reasonable steps to ensure that a young worker's working time does not exceed 8 hours per day and 40 hours in any week;

---

[55] [2004] ICR 422, [2004] All ER (D) 22 (Mar), EAT.

(c) the duty of an employer to take all reasonable steps to ensure that a night worker's normal hours of work do not exceed an average of eight hours in each 24 hours;

(d) the duty of an employer to ensure that no night worker whose work involves special hazards or heavy physical or mental strain works for more than eight hours in any 24-hour period;

(e) the duty of an employer to ensure that a young worker does not work between 10pm and 6am (or 11pm and 7am);

(f) the duty of an employer to provide a free health assessment for a night worker and for a young worker who works at night, and for the health assessment to be repeated at regular intervals;

(g) the duty of the employer to provide adequate rest breaks when the work is monotonous;

(h) the duty of the employer to keep adequate records, and to retain them for two years;

(i) where a young worker is permitted under the regulations to work at night, the duty of the employer to ensure that he is supervised by an adult worker, and be allowed a compensatory period of rest;

(j) where the application of the regulations to special cases or shift workers is excluded, the duty of the employer to ensure an equivalent compensatory period of rest;

(k) where certain mobile workers are excluded from the regulations, the duty of the employer to ensure adequate rest.

7.101 It may be noted that although the above provisions are generally enforced by health and safety inspectors, it is the duty of the Civil Aviation Authority to enforce the provisions in respect of relevant civil aviation workers, of the Maritime and Coastguard Agency in respect of mobile workers in inland waterways and lake transport, and of the Vehicle and Operator Services Agency in respect of relevant road transport workers.

7.102 The powers of inspectors to enforce the regulations are identical to those possessed by inspectors under the Health and Safety at Work Act (see para 11.10), as are the offences which may be committed by a person who obstructs, inhibits, gives false information, etc, while the inspector is exercising his powers (see reg 29 and Sch 3).

7.103 In respect of the matters just referred to, an employer may be prosecuted in the magistrates' courts, or in the Crown Court, and an unlimited fine may be imposed. Enforcement officers may also issue an Improvement Notice, requiring the employer to rectify matters specified therein, in order to ensure compliance with the statutory requirements; failure to comply with such notice can lead to a fine of up to £20,000 and/or six months' imprisonment in the magistrates' court, or an unlimited fine and/or up to two years' imprisonment in the Crown Court. Enforcement of Working Time Regulations by HSE is on a reactive basis, ie a worker must first make a complaint to the authority.

7.104 The second way in which the regulations can be enforced is by way of a complaint by a worker to an employment tribunal, alleging that the employer has failed to comply with any of the following provisions:

(a) the daily rest periods for adult or young workers (reg 10);

(b) the weekly rest periods for adult or young workers (reg 11);

(c) rest break periods for adult or young workers (reg 12);

(d) entitlement to annual leave (reg 13);

(e) entitlement to equivalent compensatory rest, where the provisions of regs 10, 11, and 12 have been excluded or modified;

(f) entitlement to compensatory rest where the provisions of regs 10 and 11 have been excluded in respect of young workers serving in the armed forces, or where the *force majeure* exemption applies;

(g) the duty of the employer to pay a worker's statutory annual leave pay, or pay for leave outstanding on the termination of employment (regs 14, 16);

(h) mobile workers, where regs 10, 11, or 12 have been excluded;

(i) young workers who are not permitted to take compensatory rest periods.

7.105 A complaint to an employment tribunal must be brought within three months from the date on which it is alleged that the exercise of the right should have been permitted, or, in the case of holiday pay, from the date when the payment should have been made, although the employment tribunal may extend the period if it was not reasonably practicable to bring the complaint earlier. If the complaint is well founded, the employment tribunal may make a declaration, and may award compensation of such amount as the tribunal considers to be just and equitable, having regard to the employer's default in refusing to permit the worker to exercise the right in question, and any loss sustained by the worker attributable to that default. In the case of holiday pay, the amount due will be awarded.

7.106 A worker will also have the right (ERA, s 45A) not to be subjected to any detriment because:

(a) he refused to comply with a requirement that the employer imposed which would be in contravention of the regulations;

(b) he refused to forgo a right conferred by the regulations;

(c) he failed to sign a workforce agreement or an individual agreement opting out of the regulations;

(d) he performed any functions or activities as a workforce representative, or as a candidate in an election for workforce representatives;

(e) he brought proceedings against the employer to enforce a right conferred by the regulations;

(f) he alleged that the employer had infringed a right conferred by the regulations.

The European Court of Justice has held that a detriment was suffered in the case of *Fuß v Stadt Halle*.[56] Here, a fire officer was timetabled to work an average of 54 hours per week. He asked his employers not to exceed the 48-hour limit in the Working Time Directive. The response of the employer was to transfer him to an office post with fewer hours, but also with lower pay, as his hours were no longer unsocial. The Court regarded the treatment as victimisation which deprived of all substance his right to a maximum 48-hour week and the fact that the Directive was intended to protect his safety and health.

7.107 An employee (not a worker) also has the right not to be unfairly dismissed for any of the above reasons (ERA, s 101A), and also the right not to be unfairly selected for redundancy (ERA, s 105(4A)). Again, the complaint must be brought within three months from the date of the act complained of, with the usual extension of time if it was not reasonably practicable to bring the complaint earlier. If the complaint is upheld, the employment tribunal will make a declaration, and may make an award of compensation, on just and equitable principles. If the employee was unfairly dismissed, no qualifying period of employment is required, interim relief may be available (see para 17.177), and the minimum basic award, as well as an additional award (of between 26 and 52 weeks' pay), may be made as appropriate.

---

[56] Case C-243/09, [2010] IRLR 1080.

7.108 The third way of enforcing the regulations is to seek an appropriate remedy for breach of contract of employment. In *Barber v RJB Mining (UK) Ltd*[57] pit deputies, although contractually obliged to work for 42 hours a week, regularly worked a considerable amount of overtime, in excess of 48 hours. They were asked to sign an agreement opting out of their rights under the regulations, but refused, and they sought from the court a declaration to the effect that they need not work at all until such time as their average working hours fell below the limit specified in reg 4(1). The High Court granted the declaration. It was held that it was clearly the intention of Parliament that their contract of employment should be read so as to provide that an employee should work no more than 48 hours a week during the relevant reference period. Thus reg 4(1) created a free-standing right which took effect as a contractual term in the contracts of employment of the pit deputies.

7.109 The mere fact that an employee works in excess of the 48-hour limit imposed by reg 4(2) does not, by itself, give rise to a claim for breach of statutory duty (see Chapter 11). The regulations themselves provide for specific methods of enforcement, ie by way of a criminal offence under reg 29 and a complaint to an employment tribunal under reg 30 (*Sayers v Cambridgeshire County Council*[58]). Whether a claim at common law in respect of work-related stress caused by working long hours would succeed will depend on whether the illness suffered was reasonably foreseeable (*Pakenham-Walsh v Connell Residential*[59]).

E. **Sunday Trading**

7.110 The Sunday Trading Act 1994 was passed to reform the law relating to the circumstances when shops may be open on Sundays, and, at the same time, gave certain protections to employees who did not wish to work on Sundays. Identical provisions apply to betting workers who work at a track for a bookmaker, or who work in a licensed betting shop. The relevant law is now set out in ERA, ss 36–43 (see also Sunday Working (Scotland) Act 2003).

7.111 If an employee is a 'protected shop worker' or an 'opted-out shop worker' he may refuse to work on Sundays. Any agreement or provision in the contract of employment will be unenforceable in so far as it requires him to work on Sundays. Further, a dismissal because an employee refuses to do Sunday work will be automatically unfair.

7.112 An employee will be a protected shop worker if:

- he was in employment as a shop worker on the day the Act came into force (26 August 1994);
- he was not employed to work only on Sunday;
- he has been continuously employed since the Act came into force and the date on which he complains of dismissal, detrimental treatment, or attempts by the employer to require him to work on Sundays under his contract of employment; and
- he has been a shop worker throughout that period of continuous employment.

A person is also a protected shop worker if he cannot be required to work on Sundays under his contract of employment, whether this was entered into before or after the Act came into force.

---

[57] [1999] ICR 679, [1999] IRLR 308, [1999] All ER (D) 244.
[58] [2006] EWHC 2029 (QB), [2007] IRLR 29.   [59] [2006] EWCA Civ 90.

7.113 An employee will be an opted-out shop worker if:

- under his contract he may be required to work on Sundays; but
- he is not employed to work only on Sundays; and
- he has given his employer an opting-out notice stating that he objects to working on Sundays.

In these circumstances, the opted-out shop worker will obtain the statutory protections after three months from when the opting-out notice was served. However, an employer has a duty to provide any employee who could potentially be an opted-out shop worker with a statement in the prescribed form explaining his rights to become an opted-out shop worker (within two months from the commencement of the employment) and if the employer fails to do this, the three-month period referred to is reduced to one month.

7.114 A protected shop worker or an opted-out shop worker may decide to give his employer an 'opting-in notice' indicating that he wishes to work on Sundays or does not object to working on Sundays, in which case he will lose his status, provided he expressly agrees to work on Sundays or a particular Sunday. It would seem that any such agreement can be verbal or in writing.

7.115 It will be an automatic unfair dismissal:

(a) to dismiss an employee who is a protected or opted-out shop worker for refusing or threatening to refuse to work on Sundays;

(b) to dismiss an employee for giving or proposing to give an opting-out notice;

(c) to select a person for redundancy because he refused to work on Sundays, or because he is a protected or opted-out shop worker;

(d) to dismiss an employee because he has asserted his rights under the Act (ERA, s 101).

However, it should be noted that an opted-out shop worker has no protection until the expiry of the three-month notice period (see para 7.113).

7.116 An employer cannot subject a person to a detriment because he is a protected or opted-out shop worker on the ground that he refuses to work on Sundays or because he has given an opting-out notice. However, an employer can offer financial or other inducements to such workers if they are prepared to work on Sundays, and those who are not so prepared are not thereby deemed to be suffering from a detriment (ERA, s 45).

7.117 An employee who has protected status will not lose that status by agreeing to work on a Sunday, provided he has not given an opting-in notice. However, an opted-out employee will lose his status once he gives an opting-in notice, although presumably he can regain that status by giving a further notice.

7.118 Finally, it should be noted that there is no requirement of a period of continuous employment, or a minimum number of hours worked, for a worker to obtain rights under the Act.

F. **Christmas Shopping**

7.119 The Christmas Day (Trading) Act 2004 prohibits a large shop from opening on Christmas Day for the serving of retail customers, but this does not apply to shops of a kind mentioned in the Sunday Trading Act 1994, Sch 1, para 3 (shops selling intoxicating liquor, motor or cycle supplies, pharmacies, petrol stations, etc). Also prohibited is the loading or unloading of goods except with the consent of local authorities. A large shop is one which has a relevant floor area exceeding 280 square metres (see also Christmas Day and New Year's Day Trading (Scotland) Act 2007).

G. **Jury Service (Juries Act 1974)**

7.120 An employee who is summoned to attend for jury service must be given time off work for that purpose, unless he is within one of the excused categories, or unless he has been excused service on application to the appropriate authority or the court. Failure to attend without reasonable cause may result in a fine being imposed of up to £1,000. A juror is entitled to claim travel and subsistence allowances, and payment for financial loss at prescribed rates. An employee has the right not to be subjected to any detriment because he has been summoned for jury service (including a coroner's jury), but a failure to pay remuneration during such absence is not a detriment unless he is entitled to be paid under his contract of employment (ERA, s 43M). It will also be automatically unfair to dismiss an employee if the reason was his attendance at jury service, but this will not apply if the employer can show that the employee's absence was likely to cause substantial injury to the employer's undertaking, the employee knew of this, and the employee unreasonably refused to apply for an excusal form or deferral of the obligation to attend (ERA, s 98B).

H. **Armed Forces Reserves**

7.121 Reservists who are called up to serve in the armed forces (including those who volunteer for such service) have their civil employment rights protected by the Reserve Forces (Safeguard of Employment) Act 1985 and the Defence Reform Act 2014. When the military service comes to an end, an employer must re-employ the employee:

(a) in the occupation in which he was last employed before the full-time service, on terms and conditions not less favourable than those which would have been applicable had he not undertaken full-time service, or

(b) if reinstatement is not reasonable and practicable, the employee must be offered the most favourable occupation, and on the most favourable terms and conditions which are reasonable and practicable in his case.

7.122 The employee must apply for reinstatement in writing, before the end of the third Monday after the full-time service has ceased, unless he was prevented from making it within that time by illness or other reasonable cause. The employer must be notified of a date (not more than three weeks) when the employee will be available for employment.

7.123 If the employer has already filled the vacancy, he cannot claim that it was not reasonably practicable to reinstate the reservist because he would have to dismiss that other person, and in practice it should be made clear to the replacement that the appointment may be for a temporary period.

7.124 A person who claims that his rights under the Act have been infringed may make an application to a reinstatement committee (see *Slaven v Thermo Engineers Ltd*[60]). They may order the employer to reinstate the employee, or make an award of compensation of between 13 and 52 weeks' pay, depending on his length of service prior to being called up. A further appeal will lie to an umpire. It is a criminal offence to fail to comply with an order of the reinstatement committee or the umpire.

7.125 If an employee is dismissed before the commencement of military service, and the reason is the call-up, then, in addition to a claim being made for unfair dismissal (for which there is no qualifying period for dismissals made after 1 October 2014), the employer again faces the prospect of being prosecuted for a criminal offence.

[60] [1992] ICR 295.

7.126 Once the employee returns to his employment, his employment will be deemed to be continuous. The period of absence will not count towards continuity, but will not break it. However, if the employee received permission from the employer to go, he will be absent from work by arrangement or agreement, and the period of absence will count under the provisions of ERA, s 212(3) (see para 13.24).

7.127 The Reserve Forces Act 1996 makes provisions which would enable a reservist to be called out for a period of up to nine months, with the consent of his employer, and for employees to enter into employee agreements with registered employers specifying the maximum liability to service of the employee as a special member, events which will terminate that liability, and other terms relating to the obligations of a special member.

I. Access to Medical Reports

7.128 The Access to Medical Reports Act 1988 gives an employee the right to refuse permission to his employer who is seeking a medical report on the employee, the right to see any such report before it is supplied to the employer, and the right to correct any errors contained in the report.

7.129 A medical report is defined as being a report relating to the physical or mental health of an individual which has been prepared by the medical practitioner who is responsible for the clinical care of the individual. This would normally be the employee's own doctor or specialist consultant. Thus the Act does not apply to examinations and reports made by a company's own medical advisers, or a specialist report made on an ad hoc basis.

7.130 If an employer wishes to obtain a medical report from the employee's own doctor (or specialist), he must inform the employee in writing that he intends to make such an application, inform the employee of his rights under the Act, and obtain the employee's consent. If the employee refuses to give his consent, that is the end of the matter, and the employer may take any other steps he deems necessary, having regard to the refusal. Alternatively, the employee may agree to the application being made, but may insist on seeing the report before it is sent to the employer. He may then refuse consent to it being sent to the employer, or request the doctor to make amendments to the report which the employee considers to be incorrect or misleading. If the doctor refuses to do this, the employee may request the doctor to attach to the report a written statement from the employee, setting out his views in respect of any part of the report which the doctor declines to amend.

7.131 A doctor is not obliged to show to an employee any part of a medical report if he is of the opinion that the disclosure would cause serious harm to the employee's physical or mental health, or would indicate the doctor's intentions with regard to another person. Also, the doctor would not give access to any part of a medical report if this would reveal information about another person (unless that person consents).

7.132 An employee is entitled to access to a medical report which has been supplied for employment purposes any time within the preceding six months.

J. Rights in Insolvency (Insolvency Act 1986, s 386, Sch 6)

7.133 If an employer becomes insolvent (through bankruptcy or liquidation) certain preferential debts are paid in priority to others. These include:

(a) up to four months' wages, up to £800 (Insolvency Act 1986, Sch 6);

(b) accrued holiday pay;

(c) any guarantee pay due under ERA, s 28;

(d) remuneration payable on medical suspension under ERA, s 64, or suspension on maternity grounds under ERA, s 66;

(e) any payment due for time off work for trade union duties (TULR(C)A, s 168), or time off to look for work (ERA, s 52) or time off for antenatal care (ERA, s 55);

(f) remuneration due under a protective award (TULR(C)A, s 189);

(g) holiday pay, contractual sick pay and statutory sick pay, and statutory maternity pay;

(h) employer contributions to occupational pensions schemes and state scheme premiums.

The maximum sum which can be treated as a preferential debt is £800.

K. Payments from the National Insurance Fund (ERA, ss 182–189)

7.134 Certain monies due to an employee as a result of the employer's insolvency may be paid by the Secretary of State out of the National Insurance Fund (see *Secretary of State for Employment v Forde*, para 2.19). He must be satisfied that the employer is insolvent (ie bankrupt, or, if a company, being wound up or in receivership, ERA, s 183), that the employee was entitled to be paid the whole or part of the monies due, that the employee has not received payment as a preferred creditor, and that the debt was incurred prior to the employer becoming insolvent. The debts are (see s 184):

(a) any arrears of pay for a period not exceeding eight weeks. This also includes any guarantee pay, remuneration or suspension on medical grounds or maternity grounds, payment for time off work for trade union duties, and the protective award (TULR(C)A, s 189);

(b) any minimum period of notice as computed by ERA, ss 86–90 (see Chapter 15). The rights of the employee to claim against the Secretary of State are no greater than those he has against the employer. In *Secretary of State for Employment v Wilson*[61] the employee was dismissed without notice, but he obtained employment immediately. His former employers went into liquidation, and he claimed four weeks' notice from the Secretary of State. It was held that he was not entitled. He was under a duty as against his former employers to mitigate against his loss, and having done so, he would have had no claim against them. Consequently, he had no claim against the Minister. But the employee is not obliged to bring into account any social security benefits received (*Westwood v Secretary of State for Employment*[62]);

(c) any holiday pay due in the preceding 12 months (but not exceeding six weeks' pay);

(d) any basic award compensation for unfair dismissal (but not a compensatory or higher award);

(e) any reasonable sum by way of reimbursement of the whole or part of a premium paid by an apprentice or articled clerk;

(f) any of the priority debts mentioned earlier (para 7.133) which have not been satisfied as preferential debts in bankruptcy or liquidation, for a period not exceeding in the aggregate eight weeks;

(g) statutory maternity pay (Statutory Maternity Pay (General) Regulations 1986).

[61] [1978] 3 All ER 137, [1978] ICR 200, [1977] IRLR 483, EAT.
[62] [1982] ICR 534, [1982] IRLR EAT; aff'd [1985] AC 20, [1983] ICR 820, [1983] IRLR 419 CA; revsd [1985] AC 20, [1984] 1 All ER 874, [1985] ICR 209, [1984] IRLR 209, HL.

It is important to note that not all debts owed by an employer to his employees are covered by the insolvency provisions of s 184, but only those which fall within the ambit of the statutory provision (*Benson v Secretary of State for Trade and Industry*[63]).

Section 183 of ERA specifies the circumstances when a company can be regarded as being insolvent, namely if (a) a winding-up or administration order, (b) the appointment of a receiver or manager, or (c) a voluntary arrangement has been approved under the Insolvency Act. The burden is on the applicant to show that one of these events has taken place. The fact that a company has ceased trading, or that it is unable to pay its debts when due or has been dissolved, does not necessarily mean that it is insolvent within the meaning of s 183 (*Secretary of State for Trade and Industry v Walden*[64]).

There is a maximum liability on the Insolvency Service of (currently) £538 per week in respect of any debt which is referable to a period of time (with a proportionate reduction for periods of less than a week). The Secretary of State is entitled to deduct tax and national insurance contributions (*Morris v Secretary of State for Employment*[65]). The person who is in charge of the winding up must provide the Secretary of State with a statement of the amount of the debt which is owed to the employee, although this is not essential if more than six months have elapsed since an application by the employee was made, and there appears to be a further delay, in which case the Secretary of State has a discretion to make the payment. The Act also provides that the Secretary of State may make payment out of the Fund in respect of any unpaid contributions which an insolvent employer has failed to make to an occupational pension scheme.

7.135 By the Insolvency of Employer (Excluded Classes) Regulations 1983, the right to claim payments on insolvency is extended to employees who, under their contracts of employment, ordinarily work in a member state of the European Community.

7.136 If the Secretary of State fails to make any of these payments, a complaint may be made to an employment tribunal within three months from his refusal (or within such further time as is reasonable). If the tribunal thinks that the payment ought to be made, it shall make a declaration to that effect, and state the amounts which the Secretary of State ought to pay.

7.137 On making the payment, the Secretary of State becomes subrogated to the rights of the employee (or pension fund) as a preferential creditor in the insolvency.

7.138 For claiming unpaid redundancy payments from the Insolvency Service, see para 18.67.

L. Post-employment Detriment

7.139 We have seen that discrimination law applies to post-employment situations (see paras 4.198–4.200). The same rule applies to a detriment which is suffered after the termination of employment in respect of all the rights contained in Part V of ERA (ie jury service, health and safety cases, Sunday working, working time, occupational pension trustees, employee representatives, time off for study leave for family reasons, tax credits, flexible working). Even though those sections deal with the rights of an employee, they also apply to an ex-employee who can allege a breach of his rights. In *Woodward v Abbey National*[66] the claimant claimed that her former employer had refused to provide her with a

---

[63] [2003] ICR 1082, [2003] All ER (D) 113, EAT.   [64] [2000] IRLR 168, EAT.
[65] [1985] ICR 522, [1985] IRLR 297, EAT.
[66] [2005] ICR 1750, EAT; revsd [2006] EWCA Civ 822, [2006] 4 All ER 1209, [2006] ICR 1436, [2006] IRLR 677.

suitable reference because she had made a protected disclosure under the whistle-blowing provisions of ERA. It was held that her claim could proceed. Thus if an employer provides an unfavourable reference or takes other steps to prevent an ex-employee from obtaining suitable employment, a claim by the ex-employee may well succeed if the reason for that action was because the employee sought to exercise a right under the various provisions of Pt V of ERA, as well as the various discrimination statutes (*Rhys-Harper v Relaxation Group plc*, para 4.200).

Summary

- The ERA 1996 sets out a number of rights to establish various minimum standards.
- Some of these rights are paid and some require a qualifying period, but not all.
- Guarantee payments are paid for days where there is a diminution of work for various reasons.
- An employee is generally entitled to be paid if suspended on medical grounds if he is fit for work.
- Time off work is available for matters such as public duties or as employee representatives, eg of a trade union.
- Time off in some situations is also available for study or training, and obligations such as jury service, armed forces, etc.
- Special rules apply for Sunday trading.
- Maximum working time is an average of 48 hours in any period of 17 weeks, unless the worker agrees otherwise in writing.
- There are other provisions for young workers, breaks, rest periods and annual leave.

8

Protection of Wages

Background

8.1 Under the provisions of the Truck Act 1831 the wages of manual workers had to be paid in current coin of the realm. That Act (together with a number of similar legislative provisions) was repealed by the Wages Act 1986, and cashless pay was made lawful for all employees. The actual mode of payment of wages is a matter for agreement between employer and employee.

8.2 A further object of the Wages Act was to prevent an employer from making a deduction from a worker's wages, or requiring the worker to make a payment to the employer (except in specifically defined circumstances), and to give added protection to workers employed in the retail trade. In consequence, the provisions of the Truck Act 1896 relating to fines and deductions were also repealed.

8.3 The Wages Act itself was repealed and re-enacted in ss 13–27 of the Employment Rights Act 1996 (ERA) and it is to this Act that reference will be made.

ERA or ETEJO?

8.4 Some confusion sometimes arises between the wages provisions of the ERA and the Employment Tribunals Extension of Jurisdiction Order (ETEJO, see para 1.22). This was made under what is now s 3 of the Employment Tribunals Act 1996 and gives jurisdiction to employment tribunals also to deal with breach of contract claims. However, there are several important differences which need to be noted, as follows:

(a) Claims under ETEJO can only be brought in respect of matters outstanding on the termination of employment, whereas ERA claims are made in respect of unlawful deductions and payments made during the existence of the contract of employment (*Capek v Lincolnshire County Council*[1]).

(b) Claims under ETEJO can only be made by employees, whereas under Pt 2 of ERA claims can be made by 'workers', a category which is somewhat wider (see s 230 and para 2.20).

(c) Under ETEJO an employer can bring a counterclaim, but this is not possible under ERA, and if an employer wishes to make some sort of 'set-off' claim, he must pursue it through the normal court machinery.

(d) A claim under ETEJO is essentially a common law claim for breach of contract, and is thus subject to the usual rules relating to mitigation of loss, whereas an ERA claim is a claim for a specific sum protected by statute, and the full sum must be awarded.

---

[1] [2000] IRLR 590, [2000] All ER (D) 749, CA.

General Restrictions on Unauthorised Deductions and Payments (ERA, ss 13, 15)

8.5 An employer must not make any deductions from the wages of any worker employed by him, nor receive any payment from him, unless:

(a) the deduction or payment is required to be made or is authorised by a statutory provision; or

(b) the deduction or payment is authorised by a relevant provision in a worker's contract of employment. This can be a written term in the contract of which the employer has given a copy prior to the making of the deduction, or a term of the contract (express or implied, and if express, orally or in writing), the existence and effect of which the employer has notified to the worker in writing. Thus in *Kerr v Sweater Shop (Scotland) Ltd*[2] it was held that the display of a notice by the employer, changing the company's rules so that a person dismissed for gross misconduct would not be paid accrued holiday pay, did not comply with the Act. The Act requires that the term must be 'notified to the worker'; this means that there must be a written notification given individually to each worker, eg by a statement inserted in the wage packet. The display of a notice was not sufficient to discharge the employer's obligation;

(c) the worker has signified in advance in writing his agreement to the deduction or payment.

These three categories need to be explored further.

A. Statutory Deduction

8.6 The most usual types of deduction to be made under this heading will be income tax and national insurance contributions. Other examples include a deduction from earnings order made under the Child Support Act 1991 (whether or not the worker was correctly liable under that order: see *Reynolds v Cornwall County Council*[3]), and an attachment of earnings order made by an appropriate court to secure payments of a maintenance order, judgment debts, fines, costs, compensation, forfeiture of recognisances, and legal aid contribution order, under the Attachment of Earnings Act 1971. The statutory provision in question must however specifically authorise the deduction or require it to be made (see *McCree v Tower Hamlets London Borough Council*[4]); an employer cannot seek to rely on a statute which does not confer a power on an employer to do an act in consequence of which the alleged deduction is made (see *Morgan v West Glamorgan County Council*[5]).

B. Contractual Authorisation

8.7 The relevant provision in a worker's contract of employment must be contained in a written document, a copy of which has been given to the worker before the employer makes the deduction, or be a contractual term (whether express or implied, and, if express, whether oral or in writing) whose effect and existence has been notified to the employee in writing before the deduction is made.

---

[2] [1996] IRLR 424, EAT.   [3] EAT1189/95.   [4] [1992] ICR 99, [1992] IRLR 56, EAT.
[5] [1995] IRLR 68, EAT.

8.8 It will be noted that the power to make the deduction need not be in the actual contract. It is sufficient if the employer has notified the worker in writing of the term. Thus an implied term, or an oral term, will suffice, provided that the notification is given to the worker individually. The mere display of a notice on a notice board will not suffice (see *Kerr v Sweater Shop (Scotland) Ltd*; para 8.5).

C. **Written Consent**

8.9 A deduction is permissible if the worker gives his written consent in advance. This provision is designed to cover those circumstances where there is no contractual term as such, but which are collateral to that contract. For example, an agreement to repay a loan made to purchase a season travel ticket, or the forfeiture of a week's pay from an employee who leaves without giving proper notice (see *Pename Ltd v Paterson*[6]), will be valid, provided the appropriate prior written notification is given, and the worker consents to it, either expressly or impliedly, ie by continuing to work once the term has been validly brought to his attention (see *Kerr v Sweater Shop (Scotland) Ltd*, para 8.5). But the agreement must indicate with sufficient clarity the source from which the deductions are to be made, ie the worker's wages, and that the worker authorises the deduction from that source. Otherwise, all that may exist is an agreement to repay a loan, not an agreement which authorises a deduction from wages. Thus in *Potter v Hunt Contracts Ltd* (paras 8.10 and 8.32)[7] the employer agreed to pay for the cost of an HGV driving course, on the understanding that the employee would repay some or all of the cost on leaving his employment. An agreement was drawn up requiring the employee to repay the fee incurred on a diminishing basis if he left the employment within two years. In fact, he left after one month, when most of the loan was still outstanding, and as this amount was more than the wages due to him on departure, he was not given any final wages. It was held that the deduction was unlawful. The loan agreement did not indicate that the repayment of the loan was to be made by way of deduction from wages.

8.10 It must further be noted that the worker's authority for the making of the deduction must not relate to anything that has happened before that authority was given. In other words, deductions must not have a retrospective effect, even if they are made with the worker's agreement. Thus a variation of a contract, or a worker's written consent, can only relate to future happenings (s 13(5), (6)). This is to prevent pressure being placed on a worker to agree or consent to deduction (*Discount Tobacco and Confectionery Ltd v Williamson*[8]).

8.11 The contractual provisions or written agreement which authorise the deductions must be clear and unambiguous, for the mere fact that the worker owes the employer money does not entitle the latter to make a deduction. Employment tribunals can be very astute in striking down terms and agreements which contain ambiguities, the benefit of the doubt being given to the worker (see *Potter v Hunt Contracts Ltd*, para 8.9). An employee's claim for part-payment of wages outstanding at the date of dismissal is not defeated by the fact that the dismissal was for reason of gross misconduct. The Apportionment Act 1870 applies when a contract of employment is terminated during the payment period, unless there is something in the contract of employment to the contrary (*Item Software (UK) Ltd v Fassihi*[9]). *Delaney v Staples* (15.12), is authority for the premise that a tribunal has

[6] [1989] IRLR 195, EAT.   [7] [1992] ICR 337, [1992] IRLR 108, EAT.
[8] [1993] ICR 371, [1993] IRLR 327, EAT.
[9] [2002] EWHC 3116 (Ch), [2003] IRLR 769, [2002] All ER (D) 62 (Dec).

jurisdiction to resolve any issue necessary to determine whether a sum claimed properly payable, including an issue as to the meaning of the contract of employment. It was followed by *Agarwal v Cardiff University & Ors*,[10] where the Court of Appeal emphasised that an employment tribunal has power to construe a contract of employment in a claim for unauthorised deduction of wages.

8.12 Even if the employer does have the right to make a deduction, he must still show that the deduction is in fact justified. Thus in *Fairfield Ltd v Skinner*[11] a van driver was given a document indicating that the employer would charge the employee for private calls made from the van telephone and for private mileage, and that the employee would be liable for any excess insurance arising from damage caused to the vehicle. When the employee was dismissed, a sum of £305 was withheld from his final pay packet. The employee brought a claim under the Act, arguing that the deduction was unlawful. The employer responded by claiming that half of the amount deducted represented damage caused to the van whilst being used privately, and the remainder was a provisional deduction for private mileage and telephone calls made. The tribunal found that the employee had carried out repairs to the van at his own expense, and there was no evidence as to how the deduction for private mileage and telephone calls had been calculated. The deduction was therefore unlawful. The fact that an employer had the right to make a deduction did not mean that he can do so if in fact the deduction is not justified on the facts of the case, and, if there was a dispute on those facts, it is for the employment tribunal to resolve the matter.

8.13 An employer is permitted to make deductions where a worker is ready and willing to perform his contract, but is remanded in custody as a result of his own actions. Such a remand is avoidable, and so the employee is not entitled to his contractual pay (*Burns v Santander UK plc*[12]).

What are 'Wages'? (ERA, s 27(1))

8.14 The term 'wages' is defined as any sum payable to the worker by his employer in connection with his employment. These include:

(a) any fee, bonus, commission, holiday pay, or other emolument referable to the employment, whether payable under his contract or otherwise;

(b) statutory sick pay, statutory maternity, paternity and adoption pay, guarantee pay, medical and maternity suspension pay, and payments for statutory time off work;

(c) payment made pursuant to a reinstatement or re-engagement order, interim relief order, or protective award.

8.15 It will be noted that the definition is very wide. It includes overtime pay (*Bruce v Wiggins Teape (Stationery) Ltd*[13]), shift payments (*Yemm v British Steel plc*[14]), guaranteed monthly payments paid as a retainer (*Thompson v Tech Communications Ltd*),[15] long-service awards (*Clarke v Hays Distribution Services Ltd*[16]), holiday pay (*Thames Water Utilities v Reynolds*[17]), accrued holiday pay (*Kerr v Sweater Shop (Scotland) Ltd*, para 8.5), commission not payable until after the employment has been terminated (*Robertson v Blackstone Franks Investment Management Ltd*[18]), and so on. A service charge added to a customer's

---

[10] [2018] EWCA Civ 2084.   [11] [1992] ICR 836, [1993] IRLR 4, EAT.   [12] [2011] IRLR 639.
[13] [1994] IRLR 536, EAT.   [14] [1994] IRLR 117, EAT.   [15] Unreported.   [16] Unreported.
[17] [1996] IRLR 186, EAT.   [18] [1998] IRLR 376, CA.

bill in a restaurant (see *Saavedra v Aceground Ltd*)[19] or a tip added to that bill when it is paid by cheque or credit card (see *Nerva v United Kingdom*[20]) is part of an employee's wages, although it is not part of the minimum wage (see para 8.45), and while the actual distribution of these monies among different employees may be allocated by the employer on a specified or discretionary basis (in accordance with the contracts of employment of his staff) he cannot appropriate part of the charge to himself, for, in doing so, he is making an unlawful deduction within the meaning of the Act. In *Kent Management Services Ltd v Butterfield*,[21] a discretionary bonus, expressed to be ex gratia, was held to be part of the employee's wages, although it was suggested obiter that if such payment was intended to be non-contractual and discretionary, and payable only on the employee achieving a satisfactory performance, words to that effect in the contract could well take the payment outside the Act.

8.16 Accrued holiday pay is 'wages' which an employee is entitled to receive unless there is an express term in the contract negating this right. For example, in *Greg May (Carpet Fitters and Contractors) Ltd v Dring*,[22] the employee's contract stated that on the termination of his employment he would be entitled to accrued holiday pay. However, this would not be paid if he was dismissed through gross misconduct. The employers dismissed the employee for what they claimed to be misconduct, and refused to pay him the accrued holiday pay. The employee complained to an employment tribunal that the employers had made an unlawful deduction. It was held that whether or not the sum 'was properly payable' was for the employment tribunal to investigate. On the facts, the employee had not been guilty of 'gross misconduct', and hence the accrued holiday pay was properly payable.

8.17 A payment in lieu of notice is not 'wages' under the Act, however, because it constitutes 'damages' for breach of contract, and is paid not in connection with the employment but in connection with its termination. In *Delaney v Staples*[23] the House of Lords held that payments made under a 'garden leave' dismissal (see paras 15.12 and 15.21) constituted wages, but other situations where a payment in lieu of wages is made or promised were not within the Act, because the essential characteristic of wages was consideration for work done under a subsisting contract of employment. Thus a payment made in respect of a period after the contract has terminated cannot be wages. The matter now is perhaps academic, since the passing of the Employment Tribunals Extension of Jurisdiction Order (see para 1.22), except perhaps for a highly paid employee whose notice rights exceed the limits laid down in that Order.

What are Not 'Wages'? (ERA, s 27(2))

8.18 The following payments are excluded from the provisions of the Act:

(a) a payment made by way of an advance under an agreement for a loan or by way of an advance of wages, although s 13 (see para 8.5) will still apply to any deduction an employer may make from a worker's wages in order to recover that advance;

(b) any payment in respect of expenses incurred by the worker in carrying out his employment. It does not matter if there is an element of profit in those expenses, it is still excluded from the Act, for any such payment does not cease to be expenses merely because the employer is generous (*Southwark London Borough v O'Brien*[24]);

[19] [1995] IRLR 198.   [20] [2002] IRLR 815, [2002] All ER (D) 137 (Sep), ECtHR.
[21] [1992] ICR 272, [1992] IRLR 394, EAT.   [22] [1990] ICR 188, [1990] IRLR 19, EAT.
[23] [1990] ICR 364, [1990] IRLR 86, EAT; on appeal [1991] 2 QB 47, [1991] 1 All ER 609, [1991] ICR 331, [1991] IRLR 112, CA; aff'd [1992] 1 AC 687, [1992] 1 All ER 944, [1992] ICR 483, [1992] IRLR 191, HL.
[24] [1996] IRLR 420, EAT.

(c) any payment by way of a pension (including pension contributions—*Somerset County Council v Chambers*[25]), allowance, or gratuity in connection with the worker's retirement or as compensation for loss of office. As noted at para 8.17, a payment in lieu of notice is not within the Act (*Foster Wheeler (London) Ltd v Jackson*[26]);

(d) any payment referable to a worker's redundancy, whether statutory or not;

(e) any payment made to a worker otherwise than in capacity as a worker;

(f) any benefits in kind are not wages, except a voucher, stamp, or similar document which is capable of being exchanged for money, goods, or services (whether on its own or together with any other such document). Thus luncheon vouchers are wages within the Act, but other benefits, such as free meals, accommodation, discounts, etc, are not. In *Leisure Employment Services v HMRC*[27] it was held that a deduction from wages of £3 per week in respect of a payment for gas and electricity was part of the provision of living accommodation, and that since the deduction was for the employer's benefit, it could not be counted towards the employees' wages.

What is a Deduction? (ERA, s 13(3))

8.19 Where the total amount of wages paid on any occasion by an employer to a worker employed by him is less than the total amount of the wages properly payable (after lawful deductions), the amount of the deficiency shall be treated as a deduction made by the employer from the worker's wages on that occasion. Thus a reduction in wages amounts to a deduction. In *Bruce v Wiggins Teape* the employers agreed to pay enhanced overtime rates to employees who worked on a rolling night shift. It was subsequently decided (without the agreement of the employees or their trade union) to withdraw the enhanced payment. An employment tribunal held that the Act dealt with deductions from pay, not with reductions, but this was reversed by the EAT. The wages properly payable included the enhanced overtime rate, which the employers could not terminate unilaterally. Thus the deductions were unauthorised and therefore unlawful. If an employer reduces the hours of work of his employees without their consent, and pays them for the reduced working hours only, this can amount to an unlawful deduction from wages (*International Packaging Corpn (UK) Ltd v Balfour*[28]). But if the employer has lawful contractual authority to transfer an employee from one shift to another, with a resultant loss of a shift premium allowance, there is no unauthorised deduction from wages within the meaning of s 13 (*Hussman Manufacturing Ltd v Weir*[29]).

8.20 If a collective agreement, the terms of which are incorporated into the individual contracts of employment of employees, expressly provides for a reduction in rates of pay (eg when there is short-time working) such a deduction would not constitute a breach of the Act, although there would be a breach if the deduction could only be made with the approval of the employees and the trade union, and such approval was not obtained. It follows that if rates of pay are contained in a collective agreement which has been incorporated into the individual contracts of employment, these can only be changed in accordance with the terms of that agreement, not unilaterally by the employer (*Davies v Hotpoint Ltd*[30]).

---

[25] UKEAT/0417/12/KN.   [26] [1990] ICR 757, [1990] IRLR 412, EAT.
[27] [2007] EWCA Civ 92, [2007] IRLR 450, [2007] ICR 1056.
[28] [2003] IRLR 11, [2002] All ER (D) 146 (Nov).   [29] [1998] IRLR 288, EAT.
[30] [1994] IRLR 538, EAT.

8.21 If there is no power in the contract of employment to demote an employee, then to do so and consequently reduce his salary would be an unlawful deduction under the Act (*Morgan v West Glamorgan County Council*, see para 8.6). It will be recalled (see para 8.15) that in *Kent Management Services Ltd v Butterfield* the EAT held that even discretionary bonuses could constitute wages properly payable, if it was in the contemplation of the parties that outstanding commissions would be paid on termination of employment.

8.22 A failure to pay wages on time can amount to a deduction from wages (*Elizabeth Claire Care Management Ltd v Francis*, see para 3.32). However, s 13(4) provides that a deficiency in wages, attributable to an error affecting the computation by an employer of the gross wages due to the employee, is not an unlawful deduction for the purpose of s 13(3). In other words, an arithmetical mistake is not an unlawful deduction, although a mistaken belief that certain monies ought not to be paid is a deduction (*Morgan v West Glamorgan County Council*, para 8.21).

8.23 Applications for holiday pay must be brought as a claim for unlawful deductions of wages under ERA, see *Ainsworth v Inland Revenue Commissioners*, para 7.90. See also *Bear Scotland*, para 7.84, and the Deduction from Wages (Limitation) Regulations 2014, which state that claims for unlawful deductions/backdated holiday pay stemming from the *Bear Scotland* decision will be limited to two years (with the exception of certain claims for unlawful deductions, such as SMP, SSP, and guarantee payments). The limitation applies to cases brought from 1 July 2015. The Regulations also state that the right to paid holiday is not incorporated as a contractual term.

Excepted Deductions and Excepted Payments (ERA, ss 14, 16)

8.24 The following deductions and payments, whether lawfully or unlawfully made, are not within the scope of the protection of wages provisions. The employee's remedy, if any, would be to sue for breach of contract in the county court (unless the employment tribunal has jurisdiction to deal with the case under the provisions of the Extension of Jurisdiction Order, see para 1.22).

(a) A deduction or payment for the purpose of reimbursing the employer in respect of an overpayment of wages (s 14(1)(a)), or an overpayment of expenses incurred by the worker in carrying out his employment (s 14(1)(b)), made to the employee for any reason. In *SIP Industrial Products Ltd v Swinn*[31] an employer withheld part of an employee's wages as a reimbursement in respect of expenses which had been fraudulently claimed. An employment tribunal took the view that this deduction was not permitted by s 14(1)(b), because what the employee had done amounted to theft, and therefore had nothing to do with expenses incurred in the course of his employment. However, the EAT held that overpaid expenses made 'for any reason' were recoverable by the employer without being in breach of the Act.

If the worker disputes that there has been an overpayment, or claims that he is not required to repay the overpayment, this matter must be resolved in the ordinary courts, under the general law relating to mistake. It is now settled that there is no difference between a mistake of law and a mistake of fact (*Kleinwort Benson Ltd v Lincoln City Council*[32]). All such overpayments are recoverable by the employer, except that he may not be able so to recover if:

[31] [1994] ICR 473, [1994] IRLR 323, EAT.   [32] [1999] 2 AC 349, [1998] 4 All ER 513, HL.

(i)   he made a representation of fact which led the employee to believe that he was entitled to treat the money overpaid as his own, and

(ii) the employee, bone fide and without notice of the mistake, consequently changed his position (eg by spending the money), and

(iii) the overpayment was not caused by the fault of the employee.

(b) A deduction made in consequence of any disciplinary proceedings held by virtue of a statutory provision (s 14(2)). This provision probably refers to disciplinary proceedings held by the police or fire service (see *Chiltern House Ltd v Chambers*[33]). Such proceedings, however, may be the subject of judicial review (*R v Leicestershire Fire Authority, ex p Thompson*[34]).

(c) A deduction made in consequence of a requirement imposed on an employer by a statutory provision to pay the money over to a public body, if the deduction is made in accordance with the relevant determination of that body (s 14(3)). This is not quite the same as the lawful deductions which can be made under s 13 (see para 8.5), and would cover a case where a public body (eg local authority) has power to require an employer to deduct a sum from the worker's wages and pay that sum to the authority in question.

(d) A deduction which is paid to a third party at the employee's request (s 14(4)). There must be a relevant provision in the contract, to which the employee has signified his consent in writing, or otherwise with the prior agreement or consent of the worker in writing. This exclusion would cover, for example, the check-off system, whereby an employer deducts trade union subscriptions from the worker's wages and pays the money to the trade union (see Chapter 21).

(e) A deduction which is made by the employer because the worker has taken part in a strike or other industrial action (s 14(5), and see *Sim v Rotherham Metropolitan Borough Council*, paras 3.33 and 3.46). Thus, if the employee is not performing any of his duties the employer may deduct an amount which represents a fair proportion of his salary (*Miles v Wakefield Metropolitan District Council*, para 2.68). If the employee alleges that the employer has deducted more than a fair proportion, his remedy is to bring an action in the county court, not in the employment tribunal. In *Sunderland Polytechnic v Evans*[35] an employee took part in a half-day strike. The employer deducted a full day's salary from the employee's monthly pay, and she complained that an unlawful deduction had been made from her wages. On her behalf, it was argued that s 14(5) only applied to a 'lawful' deduction, ie in respect of the half day she was on strike, and therefore the deduction of a full day's pay was not protected by s 14(5). The employment tribunal held that they had jurisdiction to determine if the deduction was indeed lawful, but this decision was reversed by the EAT. The EAT decided to look at *Hansard*, and it was noted that in both the House of Commons and the House of Lords, government ministers were quite clear in their views that if a worker believed that a deduction was not contractually authorised, the remedy would have to be an action in the county court, not in the employment tribunal. Thus, if the amount of the deduction is in dispute, the matter must be settled in the county court. A decision of the EAT to the contrary (*Home Office v Ayres*[36]) was disapproved.

More difficult, perhaps, is the situation where the employee is taking part in 'other industrial action', eg by working his full contractual hours but only performing part

---

[33] [1990] IRLR 88, EAT.   [34] [1979] IRLR 166, DC.   [35] [1993] ICR 392, [1993] IRLR 196, EAT.
[36] [1992] ICR 175, [1992] IRLR 59, EAT.

of his contractual duties during those hours (eg by way of protest). In such circumstances, the employer will be entitled to deduct part of the employee's wages, based on his assessment of the amount of time when the employee is not working properly (*Wiluszynski v London Borough of Tower Hamlets*[37]).

(f) A deduction made with the prior agreement of the worker to satisfy an order made by a court or tribunal requiring the payment of any amount to the employer (s 14(6)).

Deductions and Payments in Retail Employment (ERA, ss 17–18)

8.25 Special rules apply for the protection of persons who are engaged in retail employment, which is defined as:

(a) the carrying out of retail transactions, ie the sale or supply of goods or services (including financial services); or

(b) the collection by the worker of amounts payable in connection with retail transactions carried out by other persons, or other individuals in their personal capacities.

8.26 The definition covers a wide range of activities, including shop assistants, bus drivers, bank cashiers, insurance agents, petrol pump attendants, credit collectors, etc.

8.27 The Act permits an employer to make deductions or require payments from the wages of such retail workers in respect of cash shortages and/or stock deficiencies which arise in the course of retail employment. These include shortages or deficiencies arising from dishonest, negligent or other conduct by the employee, or any other event in respect of which he has a contractual liability. Nor is it relevant that the amount of the deduction or payment does not reflect the actual amount of the shortage or deficiency (s 17(4)). But an employer cannot evade the provisions of the Act by defining wages by reference to cash shortages or deficiencies, for in such circumstances the gross wages are to be treated as being the amount they would have been but for the shortage or deficiency (s 19).

8.28 Under ss 17–18 of the Act, it is permissible to make a deduction (or require a payment) in respect of cash shortages or stock deficiencies subject to two conditions. First, the requirements of s 13 (see para 8.5) must be met, ie an appropriate contractual agreement enabling the deductions (or payments) to be made. This contractual arrangement must have been agreed to before the happening of the event which was the cause of the purported deduction, because, as we have seen (see para 8.10), the Act is designed to prevent pressure being put on the employee to agree to the deduction (*Discount Tobacco and Confectionery v Williamson*, see para 8.10). Second, the deduction (or demand for payment) must not exceed 10% of the gross wages payable on the day in question (see s 18). If the shortage or deficiency is greater than the sum to be deducted or demanded the employer may continue to deduct or demand the balance on subsequent pay days, provided that on each occasion the deduction or demand does not exceed 10% of the gross wages payable.

8.29 If the employer wishes to make a demand for payment, he must do so in writing (on one of the worker's pay days) and notify him (again in writing) of the total liability, prior to receiving any payment (s 20).

---

[37] [1988] IRLR 154; on appeal [1989] ICR 493, [1989] IRLR 259, CA.

8.30 Generally, the deduction or demand must be made within 12 months from the date when the employer discovers the cash shortage or stock deficiency, except:

(a) if the deduction is one of a series of deductions in respect of the same shortage or deficiency, in which case the 12-month period applied from the first deduction or demand of the series, or

(b) if the employer ought reasonably to have discovered the cash shortage or stock deficiency earlier, in which case the 12-month period will run from the date when he ought to have discovered it, not from when he actually did so.

8.31 However, once the employment comes to an end, there is no limit on the amount which the employer may deduct or demand.

Complaints to an Employment Tribunal (ERA, s 23)

8.32 A worker may complain to an employment tribunal that his employer has:

(a) made a deduction or received a payment in contravention of ss 13–17;

(b) made a deduction which is outside the limit of 12 months as required by s 20(3);

(c) received a payment in respect of a cash shortage or stock deficiency without notifying the worker in writing of his total liability, or without making the demand in the prescribed manner as required by s 20(1);

(d) made a deduction or received a payment in excess of the limit of 10% of the gross pay on a particular day as permitted by s 21(1).

8.33 The complaint must be made within three months from the time when the deduction was made or the payment received by the employer, with the usual extension of time if the employment tribunal is satisfied that it was not reasonably practicable to present a claim earlier. The three-month period runs from the date when contractually the wages were due to be paid, not when they were actually paid (*Group 4 Nightspeed Ltd v Gilbert*[38]). If the complaint is well founded, the employment tribunal shall make a declaration to that effect, and order the employer to reimburse the worker the amount of any unauthorised deductions made or payments received plus any additional financial loss sustained by the worker.

In response to the decision in *Bear Scotland Ltd & Ors v Fulton* (para 7.84) the Deduction from Wages (Limitation) Regulations 2014, reg 2 amends s 23 of ERA so that, for complaints presented from 1 July 2015, a tribunal can only consider deductions from which the wages were paid within two years of the complaint. This does not apply to certain deductions which are set out in s 27(1)(b)–(j) of the Act, such as SMP, SSP, and guarantee payments. However a break of more than three months between non-payment or underpayment of wages breaks the series of deductions (*Fulton v Bear Scotland*[39]).

If there is an unlawful deduction or payment, which the employment tribunal orders to be repaid, the employer will lose all rights to it, and may not seek to recover that which could lawfully be claimed from the employee by bringing an action at common law (*Potter v Hunt Contracts*, see paras 8.8 and 8.10).

8.34 A claim under the provisions of Pt 2 of ERA in respect of an unlawful deduction from wages must be in respect of a specific and identifiable sum. In *Coors Brewers Ltd v Adcock*[40] the claimants claimed an amount which they alleged was due to them under a

---

[38] [1997] IRLR 398, EAT.   [39] EAT/0010/16.
[40] [2007] EWCA Civ 19, [2007] ICR 983, [2007] IRLR 440.

bonus scheme. It was held that the employment tribunal was not the correct forum for such proceedings. A claim for unliquidated damages must be brought in the county court.

8.35 Finally, an ex-employee may bring a claim under the Extension of Jurisdiction Order, provided the amount does not exceed £25,000, and the money is outstanding on the termination of employment.

National Minimum Wage

8.36 Under the provisions of the National Minimum Wage Act 1998 workers are entitled to be remunerated in any pay reference period at a rate which is not less than the national minimum wage (s 1). The actual hourly rate will be determined in regulations made by the Secretary of State (currently the National Minimum Wage (Amendment) Regulations 2018) after receiving a recommendation from the Low Pay Commission, but he may not differentiate between different areas of the country, different sectors of employment, undertakings of different sizes, persons of different ages (except, in certain circumstances, those under the age of 26), or persons of different occupations (s 2). There is no qualifying period of employment required, and no exclusion for small businesses. In 2016, a national living wage for those 25 and over was added.

8.37 The Department for Business, Innovation and Skills has produced a lengthy 'Guidance' booklet which, although not legally binding, gives guidance to employers and workers, and is a powerful aid to understanding and implementing the regulations.

8.38 The rates for the national minimum wage and national living wage from April 2020 are as follows:

(a) national living wage (workers aged 25 and over) £8.72 per hour;

(b) national minimum wage (workers aged 21 to 24) £8.20 per hour;

(c) national minimum wage (18–20-year-olds) £6.45 per hour;

(d) national minimum wage (16–17-year-olds) £4.55per hour.

8.39 Apprentices under the age of 19, or between the ages of 19–26 in the first year of their apprenticeship, are entitled to a minimum wage of £4.15per hour.

8.40 The rate for accommodation offset will increase to £57.40 per week (£8.20 per day). These figures are reviewed annually.

A. Who Qualifies for the National Minimum Wage

8.41 The Act applies to a worker who works:

(a) under a contract of employment; or

(b) any other contract whereby the individual undertakes to do work personally, other than as a client or customer of any profession or business undertaking (s 54).

In other words, only the genuinely self-employed are excluded. Thus employees, agency workers, homeworkers, etc are within the Act's provisions. In tribunal or court proceedings, the presumption is that an individual is qualified for the national minimum wage unless the employer can rebut that presumption by proving to the contrary. A review of 'worker status' was given by the EAT in *James v Redcats (Brands) Ltd*.[41]

---

[41] [2007] ICR 1006, [2007] IRLR 296.

8.42 The Act does not apply to share fishermen, voluntary workers, certain resident workers in religious communities, prisoners, and serving members of the Armed Forces. Also excluded by the National Minimum Wages Regulations 1999 are:

(a) certain workers in schemes funded by the European Social Fund, on government-funded training schemes, work experience, or temporary work schemes or schemes to help the unemployed to find work (who are not employed by the employer for whom they work under the scheme);

(b) undergraduates on sandwich course placements, trainee teachers on placement;

(c) homeless persons taking part in certain schemes under which they are provided with shelter and other benefits in return for work;

(d) au pairs, nannies, and companions who are treated as a member of the employer's family;

(e) members of the employer's family who live at home and participate in running the family business.

8.43 It has been held that pupil barristers are not engaged under a contract of apprenticeship, and therefore do not qualify for the national minimum wage (*Edmunds v Lawson*[42]). Agricultural workers covered by agriculture wages councils are entitled at least to the amount of the national minimum wage (Agricultural Wages Act 1948, Agricultural Wages (Scotland) Act 1949). Offshore workers are covered by the regulations.

B. **Calculating the Hourly Rate (reg 14)**

8.44 In order to determine whether or not a worker is being paid the national minimum wage it is necessary to determine his hourly rate. This is done by dividing the total remuneration received for the relevant pay period by the number of hours worked in that period. The pay reference period is a month, unless a worker is paid by a reference period shorter than that. Certain deductions from wages can be ignored, ie repayment of loans, contractual repayments, advance of wages, accidental overpayments, and share purchases. Lump sums paid upon retirement, suggestion schemes awards, loans, redundancy payments, and benefits in kind (other than accommodation) are not taken into account for the purpose of calculating total remuneration. Nor are premium payments for overtime or shift work.

8.45 In *Commissioners for Revenue & Customs v Annabel's (Berkeley Square) Ltd*[43] the Court of Appeal confirmed that tips distributed through a 'tronc' system do not count towards the national minimum wage.

8.46 If an employer provides a worker with free accommodation, he is credited with making an additional payment to the worker of (currently) £8.20 per day in the pay reference period for which the accommodation is provided (see *Leisure Employment Services Ltd v HM Revenue & Customs*[44]).

8.47 The hours that count for the purpose of calculating the rate of the national minimum wage depend on the type of work the worker is doing. There are four types of worker, namely:

(a) *a time worker*, who is paid according to a set or varying number of hours, or periods of time worked. In *British Nursing Association v Inland Revenue*[45] a worker was required to answer the telephone from home during a shift period. It was held that the worker was

---

[42] [2000] IRLR 18.   [43] [2009] EWCA Civ 361.
[44] [2007] EWCA Civ 92, [2007] ICR 1056, [2007] IRLR 450.
[45] [2002] EWCA Civ 494, [2003] ICR 19, [2002] IRLR 480.

on time work throughout the whole of the shift period, and not just during the periods when she was actually answering the telephone. So too a night watchman was engaged in time work throughout the whole of his shift, even during periods when he was asleep, He was 'on call throughout the entire period' (*Scottbridge Construction Ltd v Wright*[46]);

(b) *a salaried-hours worker*, who is paid for a predetermined number of minimum hours a year, and is contractually entitled to an annual salary for those hours worked in equal instalments. The fact that additional payments may be made for any over-time working, or that a bonus may be payable, does not prevent the contract being one for salaried hours (see eg *MacCartney v Oversley House Management*[47]);

(c) *an output worker*, who is paid in accordance with each piece of work produced, or task performed (sometimes referred to as piecework); and

(d) *unmeasured work*, where the worker is paid a set amount for a task or for working a certain length of time, and which is not time work, salaried hours work, or output work. This is work where the worker has no specific hours, and/or is required to work when needed or when work is available.

8.48 The hourly rate is payable for any period during which the worker is at the employer's disposal and carrying out his duties and activities (*British Nursing Association v Inland Revenue*; see para 8.47). It is payable for all times when a worker is required to be at the place of work and available for work, even though there may not be work available. But if a worker is permitted to use sleeping facilities at or near his place of work, only time when he is awake for the purpose of working will count (reg 15(1A)). In *Walton v Independent Living Organisation*[48] a carer lived on her client's premises for 24 hours each day. She was responsible for the client's washing, ironing, shopping, preparation of meals, and medication but, when not performing services for the client, she could do what she wanted. Her daily rate of pay was £31.40, and she claimed that this did not equate with the national minimum wage of (then) £3.60 per hour. Her claim failed. She was carrying out unmeasured work, not time work. The exclusion from the minimum wage legislation set out in reg 15(1A) relating to employees who are required to sleep in does not apply to those who can be required to work during the time they would otherwise be asleep. The exclusion only applies to those who are available for work, not to those who are actually working—*Burrow Down Support Services Ltd v Rossiter*.[49] This was followed in *Whittlestone v BJP Home Support Limited*,[50] where it was held that travelling time is time work, except where incidental to the duties being carried out. Where specific hours at a particular place are required, upon the pain of discipline if they are not spent at that place, and the worker is at the disposal of the employer during that period, it will normally constitute time work, even if the worker is sleeping. Terms such as 'on call' and 'core hours' can be misleading. However in *Royal Mencap Society v Tomlinson-Blake/ Shannon v Rampersad (t/a Clifton House Residential Home*[51]) the Court of Appeal decided that carers who were on call and slept at a client's home were not entitled to the minimum wage while they are asleep, meaning that only the time which is spent awake and working counts for the NMW. This has been appealed to the Supreme Court. Note that in *Esparon (t/a Middle West Residential Care Home) v Slavikovska*,[52] a care worker was required to work a number of 'sleep-in' night shifts and be available for emergency purposes. If the employer requires the employee to be on the premises pursuant to a statutory requirement to have a suitable person on the premises 'just in case', that would be a powerful indicator that he is

---

[46] [2003] IRLR 21.   [47] [2006] ICR 510, [2006] IRLR 514.
[48] [2002] ICR 1406, [2002] All ER (D) 241 (Apr), EAT; aff'd [2003] EWCA Civ 199, [2003] ICR 688, [2003] IRLR 469, [2003] All ER (D) 373 (Feb).   [49] [2008] ICR 1172.
[50] UKEAT/0128/13.   [51] [2018] EWCA Civ 1641.   [52] [2014] ICR 1037, [2014] IRLR 598, EAT.

being paid simply to be there and is thus deemed to be working regardless of whether work is actually carried out. Here the reason was to fulfil the employer's legal obligations to have staff available on the premises at all times, even if they did nothing, under regulations relating to care homes. This was therefore 'time work' under the NMW regulations.

8.49 In *Focus Care Agency Ltd v Roberts*,[53] the EAT found that there needed to be a multi-factorial approach looking at the individual facts of each case when deciding if an employee who is on call, or sleeping in, is working. It disapproved of cases where a worker is found to be working simply by being at the premises, or is provided with accommodation and is simply on call. No single factor is determinative, and potentially relevant factors are:

(a) the employer's particular purpose in engaging the worker, for example, if the employer is subject to a regulatory or contractual requirement to have someone present during the particular time that might indicate whether and the extent to which the worker is working by simply being present;

(b) The extent to which the worker's activities are restricted by the requirement to be present and at the disposal of the employer;

(c) The degree of responsibility undertaken by the worker during the period, whether for example just to call out the emergency services if needed, or if they are a night sleeper in a home for the disabled where there is a heavier responsibility;

(d) The immediacy of the requirement to provide services if something untoward occurs or an emergency arises, for example if the worker is the person who has the responsibility to take action.

8.50 Every employer will be obliged to keep records (s 9), and if a worker believes that he is being remunerated at a rate which is less than the national minimum wage, he may require his employer to produce those records, and the worker may inspect and examine them, accompanied by any other person he thinks fit. The worker must first give notice to his employer (a 'production notice'), and the employer must produce the records at the worker's place of work or any other place at which it is reasonable for the worker to attend and inspect the relevant records (s 10). If an employer fails to produce the relevant records, or fails to allow the worker to inspect them, or fails to allow the worker to be accompanied by someone, the worker may make a complaint to an employment tribunal, who, if they find the complaint to be well founded, will make a declaration to that effect, and make an award to the worker of a sum equal to 80 times the hourly amount of the national minimum wage (s 11).

C. **Enforcement by the Worker**

8.51 A worker who believes that he is being paid less than the national minimum wage may bring a claim in an employment tribunal or a county court, seeking the additional remuneration, either as a claim for unlawful deduction from wages under the Employment Rights Act (see para 8.5), or as a claim for breach of contract. On such a claim, the burden of proof is reversed, ie it will be presumed that the worker was not getting the national minimum wage until the contrary is proved by the employer (s 28).

8.52 The formula for calculating arrears of the national minimum wage takes account of the length of time since the underpayment occurred and the current rates. This is $(A/R1) \times R2$ where:

A is the amount of underpayment for the pay reference period

R1 is the worker's national minimum rate which applied at the time of the underpayment

R2 is the worker's current national minimum wage.

---

[53] [2017] UKEAT/0143/16.

In essence, this means that the worker is entitled to be paid as additional remuneration, the greater of:

(a) the shortfall between the amount paid and the amount which should have been paid under the national minimum wage applicable at the time of the underpayment, and

(b) the sum payable if the rate of the national minimum wage applying at the time of the arrears being determined had been applicable throughout the relevant period.

8.53 Further, employees have the right not to suffer a detriment or be dismissed or victimised because they brought or became involved in proceedings relating to the enforcement of the national minimum wage (ss 23 and 25). No qualifying period of employment is required.

D. **Enforcement by the State**

8.54 The responsibility for ensuring compliance with the national minimum wage lies with HM Revenue & Customs (HMRC). Officers from this department can visit employers to check if the employer is paying the national minimum wage to workers. The officers can question workers and remove copies of records.

8.55 If the officer believes that an employer has failed to pay the national minimum wage to a worker, he may serve a notice of underpayment. This will require the employer to repay arrears to each named worker and pay a financial penalty to HMRC. The penalty is 100% of the arrears owed to each worker to whom the notice relates, subject to a maximum of £20,000 per worker.

8.56 In *IRC v Bebb Travel plc*[54] it was held that the Revenue had no power to serve enforcement notices in respect of workers who, although they were paid less than the prescribed amount in the past, had left the employment in question before the enforcement notices had been issued. However, this ruling was altered by the National Minimum Wage (Enforcement Notices) Act 2003 so as to enable enforcement officers to issue notices requiring employers to make good arrears of the national minimum wage to former workers who at any time within six years prior to the issue of the notice qualified for the minimum wage. The failure to comply with an enforcement notice is a criminal offence with daily financial penalties for failing to comply. The employer may appeal against the notice, within four weeks, to an employment tribunal. The employment tribunal will dismiss the appeal unless it is established that the facts were such that the officer had no reason to serve the notice, or that no sum was due to the worker, or that the amount specified as being due is incorrect.

8.57 If the amount specified in the notice is found to be incorrect, the employment tribunal has a duty to insert the correct figure. If the evidence is unsatisfactory, the tribunal must do the best it can on the material available (*IRC v St Hermans Estate Co Ltd*[55]).

8.58 An officer may withdraw an underpayment notice, and/or replace it with another. He may also withdraw and/or replace a penalty notice if the facts are such that the officer concerned had no reason to serve the notice, or the calculation of the penalty was incorrect.

8.59 If an employer does not comply with the notice of underpayment, the enforcement officer can present a claim to an employment tribunal or the county court (or sheriff's court) on behalf of the worker.

---

[54] [2002] 4 All ER 534, [2003] ICR 201, [2002] IRLR 783, EAT; aff'd [2003] EWCA Civ 563, [2003] 3 All ER 546, [2003] ICR 1271.   [55] [2002] IRLR 788, [2002] All ER (D) 58 (Jul), EAT.

8.60 The employer can appeal to an employment tribunal against the notice of underpayment on the ground that:

   (a) at the date set out in the notice no arrears were owing;

   (b) the amount specified in the notice is incorrect; or

   (c) the amount specified in the penalty is incorrect.

8.61 A successful appeal will result in the notice being rescinded or rectified.

E. Offences (NMWA, ss 31–33)

8.62 It is an offence to:

   (a) refuse or wilfully neglect to remunerate a worker for any pay period at a rate which is at least equal to the national minimum wage;

   (b) fail to keep or preserve records;

   (c) make false entries in records;

   (d) produce or furnish any record or information which he knows to be false;

   (e) intentionally delay or obstruct an inspector, or refuse or neglect to answer any question or produce any document when required to do so.

8.63 If the offence committed by a body corporate is proved to have been committed with the consent or connivance of an officer of that body, or attributable to any neglect on his behalf, then he, as well as the body corporate, shall be guilty of an offence and liable to be proceeded against and punished accordingly.

8.64 A person guilty of an offence shall be liable on conviction to an unlimited fine (previously limited to £5,000 until March 2015).

F. Labour Market Enforcement

8.65 A further power was added by the Immigration Act 2016, and came into force in March 2016. This is a Labour Market Enforcement Order, aimed at employers who persistently commit breaches of employment law. If an employer has failed to give an undertaking that it will comply with the law, or breaches such an undertaking, HMRC can apply to a magistrates court for the order. Non-compliance with the order is an offence, with a sanction of two years' custody.

Summary

- Workers are protected from unauthorised deductions from wages.
- Claims can be brought under the ERA, or ETEJO in certain circumstances.
- There has to be contractual authorisation before a deduction can be made.
- Wages include a number of things set out in s27 ERA, such as bonus pay, commission, holiday pay, etc.
- A worker can complain to an employment tribunal in relation to an unauthorised deduction.
- The national living wage and national living wage rates are set every year.
- Employers must keep records, and payment can be enforced by the aggrieved worker or by the state.

9

Transfer of Undertakings

Background

9.1 At common law, a contract of employment was a personal contract between the employer and employee; when that relationship ceased, the contract of employment came to an end. Thus if a business was sold, the purchaser had the right to choose who he wished to employ, and the employee had the right to choose for whom he worked. Indeed, 'the right to choose for himself whom he would serve . . . constituted the main difference between a servant and a serf' (*Nokes v Doncaster Amalgamated Collieries*[1]). Thus the sale or transfer of any business resulted in the termination of any existing contract of employment because at common law an employee's contract of employment cannot be transferred to another employer without his consent (*Bolwell v Redcliffe Homes Ltd*[2]).

9.2 This position was altered by the Transfer of Undertaking (Protection of Employment) Regulations 1981 (familiarly referred to as 'TUPE'), designed to give effect to the Acquired Rights Directive (77/187/EEC). These regulations generally tried to put the transferee employer in the same position as the transferor, so that the rights and obligations contained in the contract of employment made between the transferor are passed to the transferee. Various changes to these regulations were made by the Collective Redundancies and Transfer of Undertakings (Protection of Employment) (Amendment) Regulations 1995–1999, the Pensions Act 2004, and the Transfer of Employment (Pensions Protection) Regulations 2005.

9.3 However, the application of the regulations gave rise to a number of legal and practical problems, and was not helped by a series of irreconcilable decisions from the European Court of Justice and UK courts. Difficult factual questions arose on such issues as what a transfer is, what an undertaking is, whether statutory as well as contractual rights were transferred, pension rights, and so on. The House of Lords gave its approval to the adoption of a 'purposive approach' to the regulations, which went far beyond the traditional strict and literal application of recognised canons of construction, in order that, as far as possible, the rights of employees could be safeguarded (see *Litster v Forth Dry Dock and Engineering Co Ltd*[3]). Despite this novel approach, and the fact that the regulations were amended on several occasions, a number of outstanding issues remained unresolved.

9.4 After a lengthy consultation period, the government introduced the Transfer of Undertakings (Protection of Employment) Regulations 2006. As well as seeking to clarify a number of small matters, the regulations were designed to deal with the thorny issues raised by 'service provision changes', deal with certain matters arising from transfer-related dismissals and changes to terms and conditions of employment, require the transferor to notify the transferee of the identities of the employees to be transferred, as well as all rights and liabilities that will pass with the transfer, and provide for a certain amount of flexibility in cases where the transferor is insolvent and a 'rescue bid' is mounted. But these

---

[1] [1940] AC 1014, [1940] 3 All ER 549, HL.   [2] [1999] IRLR 485, [1999] All ER (D) 33, CA.
[3] [1990] 1 AC 546, [1989] 1 All ER 1134, [1989] ICR 341, [1989] IRLR 161, HL 96.

regulations still retained the same convoluted jargon as their predecessor, and there was also concern by employers that the regulations 'gold-plated' the European Directive by being more generous. Since then, the regulations have been amended by the Collective Redundancies and Transfer of Undertakings (Protection of Employment) (Amendment) Regulations 2014, in relation to transfers taking place from 31 January 2014.

Who is Covered by the Regulations?

9.5 The regulations apply to an 'employee', defined as 'any individual who works for another person, whether under a contract of service or apprenticeship or otherwise' (reg 2(1)). This definition is somewhat wider than the one used in the Employment Rights Act, and may, for example, include agency supplied employees, casual employees, and so on. In *Mikkelson v Danmols Inventar A/S*[4] the European Court of Justice held that the meaning of the term was for the national courts to decide. However, the definition does not include persons who work under a contract for services. In *Cowell v Quilter Goodison Co Ltd*[5] the claimant was an equity partner in a firm of stockbrokers. The firm was then taken over by a limited company, which continued to employ the claimant as an employee. It was held that the claimant's service as an equity partner could not be counted for the purpose of establishing continuous employment, because he was not an 'employee' at the time of the transfer.

9.6 The regulations apply to a transfer of an undertaking, business, or part of an undertaking or business situated immediately before the transfer in the United Kingdom to another employer, where there is a transfer of an economic entity which retains its identity (reg 3(1)(a)). An 'economic entity' is an organised grouping of resources which has the objective of pursuing an economic activity, whether or not that activity is central or ancillary (reg 3(2)). The transferee will not necessarily take over the contracts of employment of those employees who are only temporarily assigned to the organised grouping, and it will be a question of fact and degree whether an employee is or is not so assigned, depending on such factors as the length of time he has been in the group, the work he does in the group, whether or not he is reassigned to other work, and so on.

9.7 However, 'an organised grouping of employees' can, in some circumstances, constitute one person, eg, if the cleaning of business premises is carried out by a single person. Thus in *Schmidt v Spar- und Leihkasse der Früheren*[6] the claimant was the sole cleaner at a branch of a bank. The bank transferred cleaning duties to a contracting firm, who dismissed the claimant when she refused to accept new terms which she considered to be inferior to those previously enjoyed. The ECJ held that (1) the fact that there was no transfer of tangible assets was not decisive in determining whether there was a transfer for the purpose of EC Directive 77/187/EEC; (2) the decisive factor was whether the business retained its identity; (3) the fact that the activity was ancillary to the main activity carried on did not exclude the operation of the Directive; and (4) the fact that the activity was carried on by a single person also did not exclude the operation of the Directive.

A. **Transfer of an Undertaking or Business**

9.8 The European Court has held that it is for the national court to consider all the factual circumstances and assess whether they are characteristic of a transfer of an undertaking within the meaning of the Directive. Thus the undertaking or business transferred must be

---

[4] Case C-105/84, [1985] ECR 2639, ECJ.   [5] [1989] IRLR 392, CA.
[6] Case C-392/92, [1995] ICR 237, [1994] IRLR 302, ECJ.

a stable economic entity, which retains identity after the transfer, but it need not be a profit-making entity (*Dr Sophie Redmond Stichting v Bartol*[7]). The business or undertaking must be transferred 'as a going concern' (*Spijkers v Gebroeders Benedik Abattoir*[8]), and thus the mere transfer of assets does not come under the regulations (*Premier Motors (Medway) Ltd v Total Oil Great Britain Ltd*[9]). The sale of equipment is not within the scope of the regulations, unless some other part of a business is transferred (*ECM (Vehicle Delivery Service) Ltd v Cox*[10]). A building contract for a single project was not treated as an undertaking, because there has to be 'a stable economic entity' (*Rygaard v Stro Molle Akustik*[11]), but this decision appears to rely heavily on the fact that it was an activity under a one-off short-term contract (see *BSG Property Services v Tuck*[12]). There is no transfer in a situation in which a municipal authority had contracted out the cleaning of its premises to a private company but then decided to terminate its contract with that company and to undertake those cleaning services itself, by hiring new staff for that purpose (*CLECE SA v Valor*[13]). If an undertaking is transferred, the Directive cannot be used to preserve the lease of commercial premises entered into by the transferor with a third party, even though the termination of that lease is likely to entail the termination of the contracts of employment of the employees transferred. The European Court has found that there can still be a transfer of undertakings under the Acquired Rights Directive even where there was a five month break between outsourcing the contracts (*Colino Sigüenza v Ayuntamiento de Valladolid*[14]). The Directive only applies to the transfer of employment relationship rights (*Kirtruna SL v Red Elite Electrodomesticos SA*[15]).

9.9 There must be the transfer of an identifiable business (*Banking Insurance and Finance Union v Barclays Bank plc*[16]) and the mere fact that staff are transferred from one status to another, eg by altering employees from direct staff to agency workers doing the same work, is not a relevant transfer (*Wynnwith Engineering Co Ltd v Bennett*[17]). The decisive factor appears to be whether the business retains an identity, but it is also necessary to take into account the nature of the undertaking concerned, whether tangible assets were transferred, the value of intangible assets at the time of the transfer, whether or not the majority of employees were taken on by the new owner, whether customers or goodwill were transferred, the degree of similarity between the activities carried on before and after the transfer, and the period, if any, during which those activities were suspended (*Rask and Christiensen v ISS Kantineservice A/S*[18]). A useful test is whether the essential business activity is carried on by the new owner (*Kenny v South Manchester College*[19]); conversely, if there is no transfer of goodwill a transfer may be outside the scope of the regulations (*Robert Seligman Corpn v Baker*[20]).

9.10 Some confusion appears to stem from the decisions of the European Court in *Suzen v Zehnacker Gebaudereinigung GmbH*[21] and *Oy Lukkene Ab v Liskojarvi*.[22] In *Suzen* it was held that in the absence of a transfer of the workforce in a labour-intensive sector the EU Directive did not apply, and in *Oy Lukenne Ab* the same conclusion was reached in a case where there was an absence of an asset transfer in an asset-reliant sector. These decisions were discussed and distinguished in a series of cases (eg, *Betts v Brintel Helicopters*,[23] *ECM*

---

[7] Case C-29/91, [1992] IRLR 366, ECJ.   [8] Case C-24/85, [1986] ECR 1119, ECJ.

[9] [1984] ICR 58, [1983] IRLR 471, EAT.

[10] [1998] ICR 631, [1998] IRLR 416, EAT; aff'd [1999] 4 All ER 669, [1999] ICR 1162, [1999] IRLR 559, CA.

[11] [1996] IRLR 51, ECJ.   [12] [1996] IRLR 134, EAT.   [13] Case C-463/09, [2011] IRLR 251.

[14] [2018] EUECJ C-472/16.   [15] [2008] ECR I–79077.   [16] [1987] ICR 495.

[17] [2002] IRLR 170, EAT.   [18] Case C-209/91, [1992] ECR I–5755, [1993] IRLR 133, ECJ.

[19] [1993] ICR 934, [1993] IRLR 265.   [20] [1983] ICR 770, EAT.

[21] Case C-13/95, [1997] ECR I–1259, [1997] All ER (EC) 289, [1997] ICR 662, [1997] IRLR 255, ECJ.

[22] Case C-172/99, [2001] All ER (EC) 544, [2001] ECR I–745, [2002] ICR 155, [2001] IRLR 171, ECJ.

[23] [1997] 2 All ER 840, [1997] ICR 792, [1997] IRLR 361, sub nom *Betts v Brintel Helicopters Ltd and KLM ERA Helicopters (UK) Ltd* [1998] 2 CMLR 22, CA.

(Vehicles Delivery Services) Ltd v Cox,[24] *OCS Cleaning Scotland Ltd v Rudden*,[25] etc), decisions which generated more heat than light. The issue was then considered in *Scottish Coal Co Ltd v McCormack*,[26] where a company took over mining operations without acquiring the outgoing company's plant or equipment. The Court of Session held that the two categories of 'labour intensive' and 'asset-reliant' were neither mutually exclusive nor exhaustively definitive. There is a range of intermediate possibilities, and the whole of the transaction, including the type of undertaking and the sector of activity in which it operates, must be looked at to see whether any particular factor is decisive. It appears that no single factor should be isolated, but a multi-factorial approach should be taken (*P & O Trans European Ltd v Initial Transport Services Ltd*[27]).

B. Transfer of Part of a Business

9.11 If part of a business is transferred, it is not necessary to show that it was a separate and self-contained business prior to the transfer. The part transferred has to be a recognisable and identifiable part of the business as a whole (*Green v Wavertree Heating and Plumbing Co Ltd*[28]), which means that ancillary activities, such as cleaning, catering, etc, are within the scope of the regulations (*Rask v ISS*, see para 9.9). Problems sometimes arise when an employee works for two or more companies in the same group, and one or more of those companies are transferred. In *Michael Peters Ltd v Farnfield*,[29] the claimant was the chief executive of Michael Peters Group Ltd, a holding company for 25 subsidiary companies. The group experienced financial difficulties, and receivers were appointed. Four of the subsidiary companies were then sold to another company, but the parent company was not a party to the sale. An employment tribunal held that all the companies formed a single economic unit, that part of the parent company had therefore been transferred, and the claimant was unfairly dismissed when he was taken on by the transferee. However, the EAT reversed the decision. It was inappropriate to apply the concept of 'single economic unit' and impermissible to pierce the veil of corporate personality. The business of the subsidiaries was not the business of the parent company. By contrast, in *Sunley Turriff Holdings Ltd v Thomson*,[30] the claimant was the company secretary and chief accountant of Lilley Construction Ltd and of Lilley Construction (Scotland) Ltd. The contract of employment was with the former company, although part of his work involved the latter. Both firms went into receivership, and the Scottish company was sold by the receiver to Sunley Turriff Holdings Ltd. It was held that the claimant's contract of employment was automatically transferred to the transferee, because he was part of the undertaking transferred. In *Albron Catering BV v FNV Bondgenoten*[31] an employee was employed by a service company within a corporate group and was then permanently assigned to another company within that group. The second company was later transferred. The European Court held that the latter company was the transferor, even though his contract was with the former, as the Directive is intended to protect employees in the event of a change of 'employer'.

9.12 Whether an employee is 'assigned' to an organised group is a question of fact in each case (*Botzen v Rotterdamsche Droogdok Maatschappij*[32]). Factors to be taken into account include the amount of time spent on a particular part of the business, the amount of value given to each part by the employee, the terms of the contract which detail the employee's duties, and how, if at all,

---

[24] [1998] ICR 631, [1998] IRLR 416, EAT; aff'd [1999] 4 All ER 669, [1999] ICR 1162, [1999] IRLR 559, [1999] All ER (D) 838, CA.   [25] EAT/290/99, IDS Brief 644.
[26] EAT/3/0034/03, (2005 CSIH 68 CS), IDS Brief 791.
[27] [2003] IRLR 128, [2002] All ER (D) 116 (Nov), EAT.   [28] [1978] ICR 928.
[29] [1995] IRLR 190, EAT.   [30] [1995] IRLR 184, EAT.
[31] Case C-242/09, [2011] IRLR 76, [2011] ICR 373.
[32] Case C-186/83, [1985] ECR 519, [1986] 2 CMLR 50, ECJ.

the cost to the employer of the employee's services was allocated between the different parts of the employer's business (see *Duncan Web Offset (Maidstone) Ltd v Cooper*[33]). Further, if an employee works at a particular job on a temporary basis, he has not been 'assigned' to the organised group in question, and thus will be outside the scope of the regulations (*Securiplan v Bademosi*[34]).

9.13 What is his position if the employee performs services in part of the undertaking transferred, and also in part of the undertaking retained? The European Court of Justice in *Botzen v RDM* stated that the Directive protects those who are assigned to the transferred part, but this is not very helpful. Two theories are suggested by UK commentators. The first is to ascertain if the employee spends most of his activities in the department transferred, or for its benefit (the so-called 'location' theory). The second is to ascertain if the employee's post is part of the staffing structure of the department transferred (the so-called 'belonging' theory). The 'location' theory appears to have some support from the decision of the ECJ in *Botzen v RDM*, but the EAT in *Duncan Webb Offset (Maidstone) Ltd v Cooper* appears to have adopted the 'belonging' approach. The question as to whether or not the employee has been 'assigned' to the part transferred and the proportion of work he did for that part was to be determined on the facts by the employment tribunal. An employee does not have to work exclusively in the part of the undertaking transferred, and all the circumstances have to be taken into account (*Buchanan-Smith v Scheicher & Co International Ltd*[35]). It would appear that TUPE 2006 adopts the *Botzen* approach, ie assigned to an organised grouping.

C. **Service Provision Change (reg 3(1)(b))**

9.14 There has always been considerable uncertainty arising from 'outsourcing' or 'contracting out' of services, and the bringing back of services 'in house'. Typically, these will be labour-intensive activities, such as cleaning services, catering, maintenance contracts, and so on. These situations are now covered by reg 3(1)(b). In *Metropolitan Resources Ltd v Churchill Dulwich Ltd*[36] it was held that the definition of 'service provision change', introduced in the 2006 version of TUPE, is to be viewed afresh, without reference to pre-2006 decisions on whether the old definition of relevant transfer (the economic entity approach) should be used. The modern test is to apply a pragmatic and common-sense approach by going through the wording of reg 3(1)(b) carefully (*Cheeseman v Brewer Contracts Ltd*[37] not followed). Thus in *Ottimo Property Services v Duncan & Anor*[38] it was found that there can be more than one client, provided they have a common purpose.

9.15 A service provision change can arise in one of three ways:

(a) activities which cease to be carried out by a person (a client) on his own behalf, and are carried out instead by another person on the client's behalf (a contractor). Normally, this would be a group of employees being transferred, but a single employee employed by the employer can be so transferred to the contractor if that employee's activities are transferred (see *Schmidt v Spar*, etc, para 9.7);

(b) activities cease to be carried out by a contractor on a client's behalf, and are carried out instead by another person (a subsequent contractor). This would occur, for example, as a result of competitive tendering;

(c) activities cease to be carried out by a contractor or a subsequent contractor on a client's behalf, and are carried out instead by the client on his own behalf. In other words, they are brought back 'in house'.

---

[33] [1995] IRLR 633, EAT.   [34] EAT/1128/02, [2003] All ER (D) 435 (Oct).
[35] [1996] ICR 613, [1996] IRLR 547, EAT.   [36] [2009] ICR 1380, [2009] IRLR 700.
[37] [2001] IRLR 144.   [38] UKEAT/0321/14.

9.16 Generally, in any of these circumstances, there will have been a transfer within the meaning of the regulations.

Organised Grouping

9.17 For a transfer to occur, there must be an organised grouping of employees which has as its principal purpose the carrying out of the activities concerned on behalf of the client. Thus if different employees are employed by a contractor to carry out an activity on behalf of a client, no transfer within the meaning of the regulations will take place if the client decides to use another contractor, because it would be unclear which employees should transfer. The group of employees is not an 'organised grouping'. A single employee can be an organised grouping where she has been deliberately assigned by the employer to a particular client. This has to be a positive decision of an employer rather than mere fortuity. When deciding whether there is a service provision change when company A takes over the provision of services from company B there is a four-stage test to carry out. First, identify the service which B provided to the client; second, list the activities which B's staff performed in order to provide that service; third, identify the employee(s) of B who normally carried out those activities; fourth, consider whether B organised the employee(s) into a grouping for the principal purpose of carrying out the listed activities (*Rynda (UK) Limited v Rhijnsburger*[39]). A tribunal can therefore look at the actual activities that are being carried out and the intention behind the grouping when considering what is the principal purpose of an organised grouping (*Tees Esk & Wear Valleys NHS v Harland*[40]).

9.18 The 2014 regulations added that activities carried on after the change must be fundamentally the same as the activities carried out previously, to reflect the position taken in the case law. It is unlikely, however, that minor differences between the nature of the tasks would matter, so long as the activities are fundamentally the same.

One-off Business Tasks

9.19 If the client intends that the activities will, following the service provision change, be carried out by the transferee in connection with a single specific event or task, or a task of short-term duration, then no transfer will occur. Thus if a client engages a contractor to perform a 'one-off' business task, or a task which will only last for a short time, the regulations will not apply if the client subsequently engages another contractor to perform the task. There may be an organised grouping of staff on the project, but the one-off buying in of services, or services of short-term duration, will not bring the regulations into operation.

Procurement/Supply of Goods for Client's Use

9.20 No transfer will occur if the activities consist wholly or mainly of the procurement or supply of goods for the client's use. Thus if a client engages a contractor to supply food to the client's canteen, a reallocation of that contract will not come within the regulations, because the main activity will be the procurement or supply of goods (it will of course, be a different matter if the client engages a contractor to operate the canteen).

Outsourcing

9.21 There is no requirement in reg 3(1)(b) that the organised grouping of employees situated in Great Britain retain its identity after the purported transfer, and it would therefore appear that the closing down of a business (eg an in-house call centre) and its transfer to another country could well come within the regulations. As well as having implications for the transferred employees, the transfer would also give rise to the operation of the consultation provisions (*Holis Metal Industries Ltd v GMB*,[41] see para 9.80).

---

[39] [2015] EWCA Civ 75.   [40] [2017] ICR 760 EAT.   [41] [2008] ICR 464, [2008] IRLR 187, EAT.

9.22 A service provision change may also occur if the activities are transferred to more than one transferee. In such circumstances liability for the transferred employees will pass to the company that took up the activities to which the employees had been assigned before the transfer (*Kimberley Group Housing Ltd v Hambley*[42]). In *OCS Group UK Ltd v Jones*[43] a catering contract was changed from a full canteen service, which supplied hot and cold food etc, to a reduced service selling pre-prepared sandwiches and salads. It was held that the new service was materially different from the old one, and it was held that no service provision change had taken place. Similarly, in *Clearsprings Management Ltd v Ankers*[44] the transferor's responsibilities were randomly distributed among three incoming contractors, and thus no single transferee could be identified as having taken over the activities formerly carried on by the transferor.

D. Transfers within Public Administration (reg 3(5))

9.23 A reorganisation of public administration, or the transfer of administrative functions between public administration (eg from central to local government, etc), will not be a relevant transfer for the purpose of the regulations. However, such transfers will come within a Governmental Statement of Practice, 'Staff Transfers in the Public Sector', which guarantees TUPE-equivalent protection for employees who are transferred from one public sector body to another. But transfers from the public sector to the private sector are within the scope of the regulations in the same way as transfers between private sector employers.

E. Employees who Work Outside the United Kingdom (reg 3(4))

9.24 In principle, the regulations apply to an undertaking situated in the United Kingdom immediately before the transfer, or, if there is a change in a service provision, where the organised grouping of employees is situated in the United Kingdom immediately before the transfer. But if the transfer of the business or service provision is governed by the law of an overseas country, and the employment of persons so employed in the business or service provision is governed by the laws of that country, the regulations will still apply if the employees concerned are an organised group of employees and the undertaking itself is situated in the United Kingdom.

The Mechanics of the Transfer

9.25 A relevant transfer may take place in a number of ways. It can be by the sale of a business (but not the sale solely of assets), a merger of two or more companies, a change of a licensee or franchisee, changing contractors or the contracting out of services, the sale of a sole trader's business or of a partnership, and so on. As long as there is a change in the identity of the employer it does not matter if a formal legal transfer has not taken place (*Landsorganisationen I Danmark v Ny Molle Kro*[45]). Thus a transfer can take place on a grant, or the surrender and regranting of a lease (*Premier Motors (Medway) Ltd v Total Oil GB Ltd*, see para 9.8), because what matters is that there has been a change in the identity of the employer, not necessarily a change in the ownership of the business. In *Young v Daniel Thwaites & Co Ltd*[46] it was held that there was a relevant transfer when a change took place

---

[42] [2008] ICR 1030, [2008] IRLR 682.   [43] UKEAT/0038/09.   [44] UKEAT/0054/08/LA.
[45] Case C-287/86, [1987] ECR 5465, [1989] ICR 330, [1989] IRLR 37, ECJ.   [46] [1977] ICR 877, EAT.

in the tenancy of a public house. However, where an employee changes from being employed by a single employer to a group, and this includes the original employer, there is no transfer of employment (*Hyde Housing Association Ltd v Layton UK*[47]).

9.26 A transfer may be effected by two or more transactions, and the absence of a contractual link between the transferor and the transferee does not preclude the existence of a transfer. In other words, the business does not need to be transferred from the transferor to the transferee. In *Dines v Initial Healthcare Services Ltd*[48] the claimant was employed by a firm of cleaners to clean at a hospital. The hospital then went to competitive tendering, and awarded the cleaning contract to another firm. The claimant was dismissed by her original employers and offered new but less favourable terms by the transferee. It was held that the transfer had taken place in two stages, ie the handing back of the cleaning contract to the hospital and the subsequent transfer of the cleaning contract to the new contractors. Hence there had been a transfer of the cleaning services, and the regulations operated.

9.27 It is also irrelevant whether or not property passes from the transferor to the transferee. Thus a concession, or a permit to operate a licence, comes within the regulations. The absence of a contractual link between the transferor and the transferee does not preclude the existence of a transfer, because this can result in two or more successive contracts which are part of the web of contractual relations, albeit that the end result (ie the transfer of assets and activities) is somewhat indirectly achieved (*Temco Service Industries SA v Imzilyen*[49]).

9.28 There is no transfer if there is a take-over of shares, because the corporate personality of the company does not change (*Brookes v Borough Care Services*[50]). Nor is there a transfer within the scope of the regulations if there is a transfer of administrative functions between public authorities (reg 3(5), *Henke v Gemeinde Schierke*,[51] but see para 9.23).

9.29 The date when a transfer takes place is the date on which responsibility as the employer for carrying on the business of the unit moves from the transferor to the transferee, and cannot be postponed to another date at the will of either party. Employment relationships existing at that date are deemed to be transferred on that date, subject only to the employee's objection to being transferred (*Celtec Ltd v Astley*[52]).

The Effect of the Transfer

A. Contracts of Employment (reg 4)

9.30 A relevant transfer shall not operate so as to terminate the contract of employment of any person employed by the transferor and assigned to the organised grouping of resources or employees that is subject to the relevant transfer, but any such contract shall have effect after the transfer as if originally made between the person so employed and the transferee. On completion of the relevant transfer, all the transferor's rights, powers, duties, and liabilities under or in connection with any such contract shall be transferred to the transferee, and any act or omission before the transfer is completed or in relation to the transferor in respect of that contract or person assigned to that organised grouping of resources or employees shall be deemed to have been an act or omission of or in relation to the transferee. Thus actual or potential claims which could be made against the transferor may be brought

---

[47] EAT/0124/15.   [48] [1995] ICR 11, [1994] IRLR 336, CA.
[49] Case C-51/00, [2002] ECR I-969, [2002] IRLR 214, [2002] All ER (D) 199 (Jan), ECJ.
[50] [1998] ICR 1198, [1998] IRLR 636, EAT.   [51] Case C-298/94, [1996] ECR I-4989, [1996] IRLR 710.
[52] Case C-478/03, *Times*, 9 June 2005.

against the transferee, eg claims for discrimination (*DJM International Ltd v Nicholas*[53]), breach of contract, unfair dismissal, redundancy payments, etc, even though these occurred before the transfer took place. Liability for an industrial accident which occurred before the transfer is also transferred, although the transferee could claim the benefit of any insurance policy belonging to the transferor which covered the accident (*Bernadone v Pall Mall Services Group Ltd*[54]). Clearly, it would make sense for the transferee to obtain an indemnity from the transferor against any such potential liabilities.

However, reg 4 does not transfer or otherwise affect the liability of any person to be prosecuted for, convicted of, or sentenced for any offence (reg 4(6)).

9.31 This is the nub of the regulations, and constitutes a form of statutory novation of the contract of employment. The transferee 'steps into the shoes' of the transferor, and the contract of employment is continuous as from the date of the original contract of employment with the transferor. Rights and liabilities which existed under the original contract continue in favour of or against the transferee. For example, in *Morris Angel & Son Ltd v Hollande*[55] the defendant was the managing director of a company. His service agreement provided that he would not seek business from any person with whom the company had done business within one year of the end of his employment. The company was then sold to the claimants, who sought to enforce the restrictive covenant. It was held that the effect of TUPE was to put the claimants in the place of the transferor company, and the covenant operated in favour of the claimants, who were the transferees.

9.32 Regulation 4 operates to include matters which were done by the transferor before the transfer, in respect of the employee transferred, even though the transferee is unaware of those matters. In *DJM International Ltd v Nicholas*[56] the claimant worked for a company for many years, but she was forced to retire when she reached the age of 60. Ten days later, she was re-engaged on a part-time basis, and two months after that, following a transfer of the undertaking, she commenced her employment with the respondent company. Five months later she was made redundant, and she brought a claim alleging that her previous employer (the transferor) had discriminated against her on grounds of sex when they terminated her employment at the age of 60 (although her claim was outside the normal three-month time limit, the employment tribunal exercised its discretion to extend the time limit). For the respondent it was argued that the contract of employment, in respect of which she was alleging sex discrimination, had been terminated before the transfer took place, and was not therefore transferred to the transferee. The EAT dismissed the argument, and upheld the claimant's right to pursue her claim. Regulation 5(2)(b) (now reg 4(2)(b)) is very wide, and applies not only to things done before the transfer in respect of the contract of employment, but also to anything done before the transfer in respect of a person's employment in that undertaking.

9.33 However, rights and liabilities are only transferred in respect of those employees who were 'employed immediately before the transfer'. In *Tsangacos v Amalgamated Chemicals Ltd*[57] the claimant lodged a claim for unfair dismissal and race discrimination in March 1995. In July 1995 the employer ceased trading, and all the staff, etc were transferred to another company. The claimant sought to join the latter employers as respondents to his claim, but this was refused by an employment tribunal chairman, and the decision was upheld on appeal. The rights and obligations of the transferor are only transferred in respect of those employees who were employed immediately before the transfer, and this clearly did not include the claimant.

[53] [1996] ICR 214, [1996] IRLR 76, EAT.
[54] [1999] IRLR 617; aff'd [2000] 3 All ER 544, [2000] IRLR 487, CA.
[55] [1993] 3 All ER 569, [1993] ICR 71, [1993] IRLR 400, CA.
[56] [1996] ICR 214, [1996] IRLR 76, EAT.   [57] [1997] ICR 154, [1997] IRLR 4, CA.

9.34 The meaning of the phrase 'employed immediately before the transfer' gave rise to a number of difficulties in the past, although the matter was resolved by the House of Lords in *Litster v Forth Dry Dock & Engineering Co Ltd* (see para 9.3). The phrase includes not only those employees who were employed immediately before the transfer, but also those who would have been so employed had they not been unfairly dismissed because of the transfer or a reason connected with the transfer that is not an economic, technical, or organisational reason entailing a change in the workforce (reg 4(3)). In other words, dismissals unconnected with the transfer are to be ignored so far as the transferee is concerned, but obligations arising from dismissals which are connected with the transfer are transferred.

Thus in *G4S Justice Services (UK) Ltd v Anstey*[58] two employees were dismissed for gross misconduct. They lodged an internal appeal, but before the hearing the business was transferred to another company. The transferor then allowed the appeals against the dismissals, and ordered their reinstatement. The transferee, however, refused to reinstate them on the basis that they were not employed 'immediately before the transfer'. It was held that the successful appeal had expunged the dismissals, and the employees should be treated as being employed by the transferor right up to the date of the transfer, and thus the transferee was obliged to reinstate them.

9.35 As a general principle, if there has been a liquidation of assets on an insolvency, reg 4 can be disapplied, and no transfer of employees takes place. However, this may not be the end of the matter, because it is possible that s 218(2) of the Employment Rights Act comes into play (*Oakland v Wellswood (Yorkshire) Ltd*, see para 13.40).

B. **Statutory Rights**

9.36 It is clear that contractual rights are thus transferred. Also transferred are statutory rights, such as claims for equal pay, maternity rights, etc, as well as liability for a protective award (*Alomo Group (Europe) Ltd v Tucker*[59]). Restrictive covenants made by the employee with the transferor are also transferred, although these may need to be re-assessed in the light of the changed situation (*Morris Angel & Son Ltd v Hollande*, para 9.31). But a non-competition clause agreed by the transferred employee will not be enforced if it occurred by reason of the transfer (*Credit Suisse v Padiachy*[60]) because an employee cannot waive rights under the contract which he had with the transferor (*Credit Suisse First Boston (Europe) Ltd v Lister*[61]).

C. **Other Benefits**

9.37 Where a contract incorporates provisions of a collective agreement, rights relating to such an agreement which come into force after the date of the transfer will not transfer under regulation 4 unless the transferee is a party to the collective bargaining (reg 4A). Terms which came into force before the transfer are still binding. This was inserted into s 4 by the 2013 regulations, and puts in statutory terms the CJEU decision in the case of *Alemo-Herron & Ors v Parkwood Leisure Ltd*,[62] where the claimant was employed by Lewisham Borough Council, with terms and conditions set out in a collective agreement made in the National Joint Council. He was subsequently transferred to the defendant employer. After the transfer, the National Joint Council awarded pay increases, but the employer refused to implement the award, as it had not been a party to the agreement and it was reached after the transfer had taken place. The European Court held that employees transferred under

---

[58] [2006] IRLR 588, EAT.   [59] [2003] IRLR 266, EAT.   [60] [1999] ICR 569, [1998] IRLR 504.
[61] [1999] ICR 794, [1998] IRLR 700, CA.   [62] Case C-426/11.

TUPE cannot after their transfer rely on collectively agreed terms and conditions where the transferee did not have the opportunity of participating in the negotiating process by which the agreement was made.

9.38 Transferees can renegotiate collectively agreed terms that do carry through one year after transfer, provided that overall the changes are no less favourable to the employee.

9.39 The question thus arises as to what other benefits are capable of being transferred, eg if the transferor employer has a permanent health insurance scheme or a profit-sharing scheme which the transferee does not have. In *Mitie Managed Services Ltd v French*[63] it was impossible for the transferee to offer the transferred employees a contractual benefit, but the EAT held that they were entitled to participate in a scheme of substantial equivalence. In *Bernadone v Pall Mall Services Group* (para 9.30) the claimant suffered an accident at work in 1996. The following year the undertaking in which she was employed was transferred to a new employer. The claimant brought proceedings for damages against the transferor and the transferee. The transferor claimed that the liability had been transferred to the transferee, a claim which was upheld by the Court of Appeal. However, the court went further and held that the transferor's right to an indemnity under their employer's liability insurance policy was also transferred by reason of TUPE on the grounds that this was a right arising from or in connection with the employee's contract of employment (see reg 17). But this does not confer additional rights on the employee to improve his situation. In other words, reg 4(1) cannot be relied upon to give a transferred employee access to benefits other than those he was entitled to before the transfer (*Jackson v Computershare Investor Services Ltd*[64]).

9.40 Obligations under a share-option or profit-sharing scheme are also transferred to the transferee (*Thompson v ASDA-MFI Group plc*[65]), which can bring about the odd result that the transferee will have to pay profit-related pay based on the employee's performance with the transferor (*Unicorn Consultancy Services Ltd v Westbrook*[66]).

9.41 Occupational pension schemes are not transferred under the regulations, either because they arise under legislation as opposed to contractual obligations, or because they were originally excluded from the Directive. That position remains basically unchanged (reg 10) and an employee whose contract of employment is so transferred is not entitled to bring a claim against the transferor for breach of contract or constructive dismissal arising out of a loss or reduction of his rights under such a scheme (reg 10(3)). However, under the Pensions Act 2004, s 257 if an employee is a member of an occupational pension scheme before the transfer, the transferee must ensure that the employee is eligible to become a member of a scheme operated by the transferee or a stakeholder arrangement. The specific requirements concerning the transferee's scheme are set out in the Transfer of Undertakings (Pension Protection) Regulations 2005. The minimum requirement is for the transferee to match the employee's contribution, up to 6% of salary, into a stakeholder pension, or offer an equivalent alternative. In the public sector, the Government will ensure the continuation of the policy set out in HM Treasury Note 'A Fair Deal for Staff Pensions', which guarantees broadly comparable occupational entitlement when there is a transfer from the public to the private sector.

9.42 Early retirement benefits do not fall within the scope of the exclusion to be found in the Directive of terms relating to old age, invalidity, or survivor's benefits, and therefore the

---

[63] [2002] IRLR 512, [2002] All ER (D) 150 (Sep), EAT.
[64] [2007] EWCA Civ 1065, [2008] IRLR 70, [2008] ICR 341.
[65] [1988] 2 All ER 722, [1988] IRLR 340, 132 Sol Jo 497.   [66] [2000] IRLR 80, EAT.

transferee is obliged to offer early retirement benefits (including, where relevant, enhanced redundancy payments) which mirror those provided to the employees by the transferor (*Martin v South Bank University*[67]).

9.43 If there is a transfer following the insolvency of the transferor, any relevant debts owed to the relevant employees (ie those transferred to the transferee and those who were unfairly dismissed by reason of the transfer or for a non-ETO reason (see para 9.57) connected with the transfer) are not transferred to the transferee, but will be met by the Secretary of State. This is in line with the existing provisions which are found in ERA, ss 166–170 and ss 182–190 (see para 7.134).

D. Variation of the Contract of Employment (reg 4(4))

9.44 Any purported variation of the contract of employment shall be void if the reason for the variation is the transfer itself but it will not be void if it is for an economic, technical or organisational reason (ETO, see para 9.57) entailing changes in the workforce (reg 4(4)). Changes in the workforce include a change to the place of work. If there is a valid ETO reason, however, this provision enables an employer and employee to agree to a change in the terms of the contract (reg 4(5)), where the terms of the contract allow the employer to make the variation. In other words, an employer cannot unilaterally change the terms and conditions of employment of the employees transferred, but there are circumstances when the employer and employee can mutually agree to a variation of those terms, provided there is a genuine ETO reason.

9.45 Equally, a variation will be valid if it was for a reason unconnected with the transfer (reg 4(5)). In *Norris v Brown & Root Ealing Technical Services*[68] employees were offered new terms of employment some two years after a transfer took place. The reason was because the employer was having cash flow difficulties. It was held that the contractual variations were not transfer-connected reasons, but because the employer was having cash flow difficulties. The unexpected loss of a major order could also be an example of circumstances which would permit a variation, as it would be unconnected with the transfer.

9.46 Although reg 4(4) provides that any change in the terms of the contract made as a result of a transfer is void (see, for example, *Wilson v St Helens BC*[69]), this does not apply to changes which are for the benefit of the employee (*Regent Security Services Ltd v Power*[70]).

9.47 The above regulation does not apply to a variation to a term or condition in a collective agreement, provided the variation takes place more than one year after the date of the transfer, and the terms and conditions of the contract are not less favourable to the employee than they were before (reg 4(5B)). This is for transfers that took place from 31 January 2014.

E. Insolvency Rights (reg 8)

9.48 If a company is put into liquidation or administration, which results in a transfer to which TUPE applies, employees who are dismissed can no longer claim against the transferor or transferee. Instead, they must seek payments from the national insurance

---

[67] Case C-4/01, [2004] IRLR 74, [2003] All ER (D) 85 (Nov), ECJ.

[68] [2002] All ER (D) 413 (Oct), EAT.

[69] [1996] ICR 711, [1996] IRLR 320, [1996] IRLR 541, EAT; revsd [1998] ICR 387, [1997] IRLR 505, CA; revsd [1999] 2 AC 52, [1998] 4 All ER 609, [1998] ICR 1141, [1998] IRLR 706, [1998] All ER (D) 516, HL.

[70] [2007] 4 All ER 354, [2007] ICR 970, [2007] IRLR 226, EAT; aff'd [2007] EWCA Civ 1188, [2008] IRLR 66, [2008] ICR 442.

fund. Further, when the transferor is in administration, its liability to pay certain debts to its employees (arrears of wages and holiday pay) does not transfer to the transferee, although the transferee will still be liable for any excess that the employees are owed above the statutory limits. Arrears that are above the statutory maximum will still transfer. Employees who are dismissed by the administrator for a reason connected with the transfer can claim arrears of wages and holiday pay up to the statutory limits from the national insurance fund. If there is an ETO reason for the dismissal, arrears of redundancy pay, wages, holiday pay, and notice pay may also be claimed from the fund. (Where, however, an employee is unfairly and wrongfully dismissed by a transferee immediately following a TUPE transfer of an administration 'pre-pack', it is the transferee, rather than the Secretary of State, who is liable for the employee's basic award and notice pay (*Pressure Coolers Ltd v Molloy*[71]).)

9.49 Regulation 8 is part of the government's pursuit of 'rescue culture' by providing that the transferee takes on an insolvent company free of those liabilities, which can now be met by the Secretary of State. However, the transfer of these liabilities to the Secretary of State does not apply if the insolvency proceedings have not been commenced at the time of the transfer (*Secretary of State for Trade and Industry v Slater*,[72] *Key2Law (Surrey) LLP v De'Antiquis*[73]).

9.50 In *Key2Law (Surrey) LLP v De'Antiquis*, the Court of Appeal (with whom the Supreme Court agreed) said that the primary objective of an administration appointment is the rescuing of the company as a going concern, and so companies in administration are not exempted from TUPE; therefore when a business is sold by an administrator, employees will transfer to the new employer and will be protected against transfer connected dismissals. Regulation 8(7) therefore does not apply in such cases.

9.51 However, a company administrator can make dismissals for an ETO reason and then sell the business without the purchaser being liable for TUPE if the reason for the dismissals was to enable the company to continue to trade. The case of *Crystal Palace FC Ltd v Kavanagh & Ors*[74] was distinguished from *Spaceright Europe Ltd v Baillavoine & Anor*.[75] In *Spaceright*, the court said for an ETO reason to be available there must be an intention to change the workforce and to continue to conduct the business, as distinct from the purpose of selling it. It is not available in the case of dismissing an employee in order to enable the administrators to make the business of the company a more attractive proposition to prospective transferees of a going concern. Here, the administrator dismissed the claimants in order to reduce the wage bill and keep the football club alive as a going concern, in the hope that there would be a sale in the future. (This is distinguished from *Spaceright*, where the reason was to make the business more attractive to the purchaser.)

9.52 A transfer occurs when there is the sale of a company subject to a 'pre-pack' administration (*Federatie Nederlanse Vakvereniging and others v Smallsteps BV*[76]).

F. Permitted Variations in Insolvency Proceedings (reg 9)

9.53 It is permissible to vary the contracts of employment of the transferee's employees when the transferor is subject to insolvency proceedings, if the objective is to safeguard employment opportunities by ensuring the survival of the undertaking which is the subject of the relevant transfer (this is to promote the 'rescue culture' in an attempt to facilitate

[71] [2011] IRLR 630.   [72] [2008] ICR 54, [2007] IRLR 928.   [73] [2011] EWCA Civ 1567, CA.
[74] [2013] EWCA Civ 1410.   [75] [2012] IRLR 212.   [76] Case C-126/16 [2017] WLR(D) 417.

employment prospects when an employer becomes insolvent). Two conditions must be present:

(a) The variation must be agreed between the transferee (or insolvency practitioner) and the appropriate representatives of the assigned employees. These will be either representatives of an independent trade union recognised by the employer, or, if there are no such representatives, employee representatives who have previously been appointed or elected who have authority to agree to the permitted variations on behalf of the employees, or employee representatives elected by assigned employees for the particular purpose.

(b) If the representation is by non-union representatives, the agreement recording the permitted variation must be in writing, and the employer must give the affected employees copies of the text of the agreement and such guidance as they might reasonably require in order to fully understand it. The agreement must then be signed by each of the representatives.

The permitted variation shall then take effect as a term or condition of the assigned employee's contract of employment in place of any term of condition it varies.

9.54 A problem may arise when a company is put into administration, because the administrator is generally appointed to carry on the business with a view to rescuing it. However, in *Oakland v Wellswood (Yorkshire) Ltd*[77] the employment tribunal found as a fact that the administrator was instituted with a view to the liquidation of the assets of the company. Thus the transfer was under the supervision of an insolvency practitioner, and reg 9 of TUPE applied.

Dismissal on Transfers (reg 7)

9.55 Where, either before or after a relevant transfer, an employee of the transferor is dismissed, this will amount to an automatically unfair dismissal if the reason for the dismissal was the transfer, unless it is for an ETO reason. (Until the 2014 regulations, it was also automatically unfair if it was for a reason connected with the transfer, but that is no longer the case.) Regulation 7(2) provides that if the employee was dismissed for an economic, technical or organisational reason which entailed a change in the workforce of either the transferor or transferee, the reason for the dismissal will be treated as either being for redundancy (if that applies) or otherwise for a substantial reason of a kind such as to justify the dismissal of an employee holding that position (*Collins v John Ansell & Partners Ltd*[78]). Thus slimming down an overstaffed workforce so as to enable the transferee to continue to operate successfully would be an ETO reason, and it is then for the employer to show that he acted reasonably in treating that reason as a sufficient reason for the dismissal. If the reason shown is redundancy (and redundancy is the commonest of the ETO reasons), the employee will be able to claim a redundancy payment.

9.56 For the defence of reg 7(2) to apply, a transferor cannot plead that the transferee had an ETO reason, and the fact that the transferee had no need for the employee transferred is irrelevant. If in fact the employee is redundant in consequence of the transfer, a fair procedure for handling the situation must be followed (*Hynd v Armstrong*).

A. **ETO Reason (regs 4, 7)**

9.57 We have seen that it is permissible to vary the contracts of employment of transferred employees (with their agreement) and to dismiss transferred employees, if there is an economic, technical or organisational (ETO) reason which entails a change in the workforce

---

[77] [2009] EWCA Civ 1094, [2010] IRLR 82.   [78] IDS Brief 659, EAT/124/99.

(however this does not necessarily mean the entirety of the workforce (*Nationwide Building Society v Benn*[79])). An ETO reason includes a change in the place of work (reg 8, 2014 regulations). The phrase 'ETO' is not defined in the regulations, and is therefore the subject of interpretation by the courts and tribunals. In a Guide to the Regulations published by the DBIS, it is suggested that an economic reason would relate to the profitability or market performance of the transferee's business, a technical reason would relate to the nature of the equipment or production processes which the transferee operates, and an organisational reason would relate to the management or organisational structure of the transferee's business.

9.58 Potentially, 'economic, technical or organisational reasons' is a wide concept, but it is generally given a restricted meaning. In *Wheeler v Patel*,[80] the EAT held that an economic reason entailing a change in the workforce must relate to the conduct of the business concerned, so that the transferor's attempt to obtain a higher price for a sale by acceding to the demands of the transferee to dismiss the workforce did not constitute an economic reason. An earlier decision to the contrary (*Anderson v Dalkeith Engineering Ltd*[81]) has been disapproved (see *Gateway Hotels Ltd v Stewart*[82]). But a redundancy dismissal brought about solely to obtain a contract is an ETO reason, and is not analogous to a dismissal brought about solely to obtain a best price for the business *(Whitehouse v Charles Blatchford & Sons Ltd*[83]). If the transferee does not need the transferor's workforce, so that a redundancy situation is produced, this is within reg 7(2) (*Meikle v McPhail*[84]). If, on the transfer of the business, employees are dismissed for reason of redundancy without the transferor being contractually required to do so, this will be evidence of the unfairness of the dismissals (*Litster v Forth Dry Dock and Engineering Co Ltd*, see paras 9.3 and 9.34). Even when there is an ETO reason which results in redundancies, the employer concerned must still act fairly in treating that reason as a sufficient reason for the dismissal (*Gibson v Ciro Cittero*[85]). The standard way of dealing with redundancies must be followed, that is, fair selection procedures, search for alternatives, full consultation with the workforce and their representatives, etc.

9.59 The decision must be one made on the need to entail changes in the workforce. Generally, this could be a change in the number of employees employed, or a change in the functions of those employed. Thus if whole job contents have to be changed because of the transfer, this may constitute a change in the workforce (*Crawford v Swinton Insurance Brokers Ltd*[86]). If something else is sought to be changed (eg the pay of the employees who are transferred) the resultant dismissal does not come within reg 7(2), and the dismissal will be unfair (*Berriman v Delabole Slate Ltd*[87]). However, this does not prevent a mutually agreed variation for an ETO reason (see reg 4(5)).

9.60 In order to ascertain whether a dismissal was for economic reasons or a reason relating to the transfer, regard has to be paid to the thought processes of the person who took the decision, which generally speaking will be the employer. In *Dynamex Friction Ltd v Amicus*[88] the managing director of a company realised that if he had to pay £2m by way of compensation to employees who had been unfairly dismissed, the company would be insolvent. He therefore placed the company in administration. The administrator decided

---

[79] UKEAT/0273/09/JOJ.   [80] [1987] ICR 631, [1987] IRLR 211, EAT.
[81] [1985] ICR 66, [1984] IRLR 429, EAT.   [82] [1988] IRLR 287, EAT.
[83] [1999] IRLR 492, [1999] All ER (D) 414, CA.   [84] [1983] IRLR 351, EAT.   [85] Unreported.
[86] [1990] ICR 95, [1990] IRLR 42, EAT.
[87] [1984] ICR 636, [1984] IRLR 394, EAT; aff'd [1985] ICR 546, sub nom *Delabole Slate Ltd v Berriman* [1985] IRLR 305, CA.   [88] [2008] EWCA Civ 381, [2009] ICR 511, [2008] IRLR 515.

to dismiss the employees because he had no money with which to pay them. There was no evidence to suggest that he dismissed the employees in order to have a better prospect of selling the business. Subsequently the administrator sold the business back to the managing director. It was held that the decision to dismiss was taken by the administrator, which was therefore an economic reason. There was no collusion between the administrator and the managing director, nor were the dismissals effected in order to escape the legitimate claims of the workforce.

9.61 If the employee is unfairly dismissed in connection with the transfer, his rights lie against the transferee, not the transferor. This is so even if the dismissal took place before the transfer, if the reason was connected with the transfer. Thus in *Allen v Stirling District Council*[89] the claimant was employed by the council's direct services department. Following competitive tendering, the work was awarded to an outside contractor. The claimant was dismissed by the council on 31 December, and the following day that outside contractor assumed responsibility for the service. The claimant brought a claim for unfair dismissal against the council, which failed. The Inner House of the Court of Session held that reg 4(2) was clear and unambiguous. All the transferor's duties and liabilities in connection with the contract of employment were transferred to the transferee. But a dismissed employee cannot compel the transferee to employ him, because the dismissal is not a legal nullity (*Wilson v St Helen's Borough Council*, see para 9.46).

9.62 If a dismissal takes place at the time of the transfer, but is for a reason unconnected with the transfer, none of the TUPE provisions apply, and the dismissal is to be tested under the usual provisions of ERA. For example, a dismissal which takes place following a disciplinary hearing would be unconnected with the transfer. So too would be the unexpected loss of a major order. A desire to harmonise terms and conditions of employment of the incoming employees with those of existing employees does not come within the ETO exception.

9.63 If an employee wishes to bring a complaint of unfair dismissal for a reason connected with the transfer under the provisions of TUPE, or wishes to claim a redundancy payment, he is still required to meet the normal qualifying period of continuous employment of two years.

Refusing a Transfer (reg 4(7))

9.64 An employee is not bound to accept the transfer. He is free to choose for whom he will work, and cannot be compelled to work for an employer against his will. He can, at any time before the transfer, object to becoming an employee of the transferee. However, if he does so object, he will not be treated, for any purpose, as having been dismissed by the transferor (losing, for example, his right to a redundancy payment, see *Katsikas v Konstantinidis*[90]). There is no particular form of refusal, but it must be clear and unequivocal, and can be made to either the transferor or transferee. A protest in advance of the transfer will not by itself amount to an objection unless it is followed by an actual refusal to consent to the transfer. Thus, it has been held that to express a preference for a redundancy payment as opposed to a transfer was not enough to constitute an objection to the transfer (*Senior Heat Treatment Ltd v Bell*[91]). The employee has to inform the transferor or transferee specifically that he objects to the transfer.

---

[89] [1994] ICR 434, [1994] IRLR 208, EAT; revsd [1995] ICR 1082, sub nom *Stirling District Council v Allen* [1995] IRLR 301.   [90] Cases C-132, 138, and 139/91, [1992] ECR I-6577, [1993] IRLR 179, ECJ.
[91] [1997] IRLR 614.

9.65 There is no requirement that prior to the transfer the transferor must inform his employees of the identity of the transferee (*Secretary of State for Trade and Industry v Cook*),[92] although the requirements on consultation (see para 9.76) in practice will mean that the identity of the transferee will be known. But if the employee does not know the identity of the transferee, and objects to being transferred as soon as he finds out, the objection will take effect retrospectively (*New ISG Ltd v Vernon*[93]).

9.66 An employee will be able to refuse to accept the transfer if it involves a substantial change in working conditions to his detriment. In these circumstances, reg 4(9) preserves the right of the employee to treat the contract of employment as having been terminated by the employer with notice (see *University of Oxford v Humphreys*[94]). What amounts to a substantial change is a matter to be determined in each individual case. Thus the loss of status, a requirement to relocate which is unacceptable, or a sound medical objection to working in new premises, etc, could amount to a substantial change in working conditions. Further, the employee may resign his employment and claim that he was constructively dismissed, although for a successful claim he would have to show that the change in working conditions amounted to a repudiatory breach of contract by the employer. In *Rossiter v Pendragon plc*[95] the claimant was a car salesman. His employer operated a commission scheme which could be withdrawn or amended without notice. The business was then transferred to the respondent employer, who changed the commission scheme so that it was less beneficial to the claimant. Because of this, the claimant resigned and claimed he had been constructively dismissed. The Court of Appeal held that since there was no repudiation of the employment contract by the respondent employer, there was no liability for constructive dismissal. A depot relocation of three and a half miles for bus drivers was not a substantial change (*Cetinsoy & Ors v London United Busways Ltd*).[96]

9.67 The test for determining whether a substantial change to working conditions is to the detriment of the transferred employee is to look at the impact of the change from the employee's reasonable viewpoint, not by balancing the views of the employer and employee (*Tapere v South London & Maudsley NHS Trust*[97]).

9.68 Damages cannot be awarded against an employer in respect of his failure to pay wages to an employee in respect of a notice period which the employee has failed to work (reg 4(10)).

Employee Liability Information (regs 11–12)

9.69 The transferor shall notify the transferee of any employee liability information, ie information known to the transferor as to his rights, powers, duties, and liabilities under or in connection with the contract of employment of any employee who is assigned to the organised grouping of resources that is the subject of the transfer. This will include:

(a) the identity and ages of employees to be transferred;

(b) the information contained in their statutory statement of particulars of employment;

---

[92] [1997] ICR 288, [1997] IRLR 150, EAT.   [93] [2007] EWHC 2665 (Ch), [2008] IRLR 115, [2008] ICR 319.
[94] [2000] 1 All ER 996, [2000] IRLR 183, CA.
[95] [2001] ICR 1265, [2001] IRLR 256, [2001] All ER (D) 412 (Feb), EAT; revsd in part [2002] EWCA Civ 745, [2002] ICR 1063, [2002] IRLR 483, [2002] All ER (D) 143 (May).
[96] UKEAT/0042/14.   [97] [2009] ICR 1563, [2009] IRLR 972.

(c) details or any formal disciplinary action or grievances raised in the previous two years;

(d) details of actual or potential legal action brought by the employees concerned in the previous two years or that the transferor has reasonable grounds to believe an employee may bring against the transferee arising out of the employee's employment with the transferor (ie, actual or potential claims); and

(e) information of any collective agreement which will have effect after the transfer in accordance with reg 5(a) (see para 9.74).

9.70 It must also include information about any employee who had been unfairly dismissed (in accordance with reg 7(1), see para 9.55) because of the transfer. Employee liability information shall contain information as at a specified date not more than 14 days before the date on which the information is notified to the transferee. The notification shall be in writing (or made available in a readily accessible form) and given not less than 28 days before the relevant transfer (or 14 days if the transfer was before 1 May 2014) or, if special circumstances make this not reasonably practicable, then as soon as is reasonably practicable thereafter. The notification may be given in instalments, and may come indirectly from a third party. If the specified information changes between the time when it has been provided and the time the transfer is completed, written notification must be given of those changes.

Remedy for Failure to Notify Employee Liability Information (reg 12)

9.71 A transferee may present a claim to an employment tribunal that the transferor has failed to comply with the above provisions relating to employee liability information. The complaint must be made within three months of the relevant transfer (with an extension of time if it was not reasonably practicable to present the complaint within that period). If the employment tribunal finds the complaint to be well founded, it shall make a declaration to that effect, and may award compensation to the transferee to be paid by the transferor. The amount of compensation shall be such as the tribunal considers to be just and equitable, having regard to the loss suffered by the transferee, and the terms of the contract between the transferee and transferor under which the transferor may be liable to pay to the transferee in respect of any failure to notify the transferee of employee liability information.

9.72 The amount of compensation shall be not less than £500 per employee in respect of whom the transferor failed to comply with the provisions in reg 11, unless the tribunal considers it just and equitable to award a lesser sum. The transferee will be expected to take steps to mitigate against the loss suffered.

9.73 The purpose of regs 11–12 is to ensure that the transferee obtains full and accurate information about the rights and obligations which will be taken on, so that these can be honoured. At the same time, both the transferor and the transferee owe a duty of care to each other and to the affected employees not to negligently misrepresent the nature of various benefits which may or may not result from the transfer (*Hagen v ICI Chemicals plc*[98]).

---

[98] [2002] IRLR 31, [2001] All ER (D) 273 (Oct).

Other Matters

A. Collective Agreements (reg 5)

9.74 Where, at the time of the transfer, there exists a collective agreement made between the transferor and a recognised trade union in respect of employees to be transferred, then, in its application in relation to them, that agreement shall have effect as if made by or on behalf of the transferee with the trade union. Thus the rights of the transferred employees under existing collective agreements are protected, but the transfer does not bestow rights under any future collective agreement (*Werhof v Freeway Traffic Systems GmbH*[99]).

B. Trade Union Recognition (reg 6)

9.75 Where, before the transfer, an independent trade union is recognised by the transferor in respect of employees who are transferred, then, after the transfer, the union shall be deemed to have been recognised by the transferee to the same extent. However, this will only apply if, after the transfer, the transferred organised grouping of resources or employees maintains an identity distinct from the remainder of the transferee's undertaking. Any agreement for recognition may subsequently be varied or rescinded.

C. Consultation on Transfers (reg 13)

9.76 On the transfer of an undertaking, it is clear that employees of the transferor and the transferee may be affected in some way. Regulation 13 provides that long enough before the relevant transfer to enable the employer of any affected employees to consult all persons who are appropriate representatives of any of the affected employees, the employer shall inform those representatives of the fact that the relevant transfer is to take place, the date of the transfer, and the reasons for it, together with:

(a) the legal, economic, and social implications of the transfer for the affected employees;

(b) the measures (if any) which he envisages he will take in relation to those employees; and

(c) the measures (if any) which the transferor envisages the transferee will take in relation to the affected employees.

For this purpose, the transferee shall give to the transferor such information as will enable the transferor to perform his duty.

9.77 The information must be delivered to the appropriate representatives (reg 13(5)) and, if either employer envisages that he will take measures in respect of any employees affected by the transfer, he shall consult with the appropriate representatives with a view to seeking their agreement to the measures to be taken. The employer will consider any representations made by the appropriate representatives, reply to them, and, if he rejects them, state his reasons. If there are special circumstances which render it not reasonably practicable for the employer to consult as required, he will take such steps towards performing that duty as are reasonably practicable in the circumstances. The language of reg 13(2)(b) obliges the employer to describe what he genuinely believes to be the legal, social, and economic implications of the transfer, but he does not have to warrant that his belief is correct (*Royal Mail Group v CWU*[100]).

---

[99] Case C-499/04, [2006] ECR I–2397, [2006] IRLR 400, ECJ.
[100] [2009] EWCA Civ 1045, [2010] ICR 83, [2009] IRLR 1046.

9.78 The appropriate representatives are the representatives of a recognised independent trade union, or, in any other case, representatives appointed or elected by them for some other purpose (who have authority to receive such information and be consulted about the transfer) or employees' representatives elected for this specific purpose. The employer shall allow the appropriate representatives access to the affected employees and shall afford them such accommodation and other facilities as may be appropriate.

9.79 If the employer has invited the affected employees to elect representatives, and the invitation was issued long enough before the time when the employer is required to give the information as required under reg 13 to allow them to elect representatives by that time, the employer will have complied with the consultation provisions if he does consult as soon as is reasonably practicable after the election of the representatives. If the employees fail to elect representatives within a reasonable time after being invited to do so, the employer shall give the information to each of the affected employees. It should be noted that, unlike the provisions on consultation on redundancies (see TULR(C)A, s 188), there is no minimum number of employees who are affected before the duty to consult arises.

9.80 The obligation to consult applies even though the business concerned is transferred out of the United Kingdom and the European Community (*Holis Metal Industries Ltd v GMB*, see para 9.21). However, there is no obligation on a transferee employer to consult with a recognised trade union after a transfer has taken place regarding changes that it proposes to make in respect of employees who have been transferred to the new employer (*UCATT v Glasgow City Council*[101]).

9.81 The 2014 regulations insert reg 13A, allowing a micro-business (which is an employer with fewer than ten employees) to inform and consult directly with all affected employees in cases where there are no existing appropriate representatives.

D. Election of Employee Representatives (reg 14)

9.82 If there is no independent trade union recognised by the employer, the affected employees are entitled to elect their representatives, and reg 14 lays down detailed requirements for such elections. These must be fair, the number of representatives must be sufficient to represent the interests of all the affected employees, the candidates for employee representatives must be affected employees, voting must be secret, no affected employee shall be unreasonably excluded from standing in the election, and so on. Employees' representatives have the right not to suffer a detriment because they performed any function or activity (including standing for election) and have the right to reasonable time off work with pay, access to the affected employees, and to be provided with appropriate accommodation and facilities. It will be an unfair dismissal to dismiss an employee because he was an employee representative or candidate, or proposed to perform any functions or activities as such.

E. Failure to Inform or Consult (reg 15)

9.83 A complaint may be made to an employment tribunal in respect of a number of potential failures by the employer, as follows:

(a) if there is a failure to arrange for the election of employee representatives, by any employees who are affected employees;

(b) if there is any other failure relating to employee representatives, by the relevant employee representative;

[101] [2009] IRLR 253.

(c) if there is a failure relating to representatives of a trade union, by the trade union;

(d) in any other case, by any of the affected employees.

9.84 In respect of any such complaint, the employer may show that there were special circumstances which rendered it not reasonably practicable to perform the duty, and that he took all such steps towards its performance as were reasonably practicable in the circumstances.

9.85 If the complaint against the transferee is well founded, the employment tribunal shall make a declaration, and order appropriate compensation to be paid. If the complaint against the transferor is well founded, the employment tribunal shall make a declaration, and order the transferor to pay appropriate compensation. If the complaint is that the transferor failed to provide information about the measures which the transferee will take in connection with the transfer (and the transferor has given notice to the transferee that the latter will be a party to the proceedings), the transferee may be ordered to pay appropriate compensation to the affected employees. The transferor and transferee shall be jointly and severally liable in respect of compensation payable. 'Appropriate compensation' means such sum not exceeding 13 weeks' pay, as the tribunal considers just and equitable having regard to the seriousness of the failure of the employer to comply with his duty. The maximum award of 13 weeks' pay should be made unless there are mitigating circumstances which would justify a reduction in the award (*Sweetin v Coral Racing*[102]).

9.86 The complaint must be presented to the employment tribunal within three months of the date when the relevant transfer is completed, or three months from the tribunal's order that a payment shall be made. There is a discretion to extend the presentation date for such further period as the tribunal thinks reasonable. An appeal against all tribunal decisions made under the regulations will lie to the EAT on a point of law.

Summary

- The 'TUPE' regulations apply to employees, which has a wider definition than in the ERA.
- The undertaking transferred must be an identifiable business, an organised grouping, a stable economic entity which retains identity after the transfer.
- If part of a business is transferred, it has to be a recognisable and identifiable part of the business as a whole to come within TUPE.
- A service provision change, eg contracting out or bringing things back in house, is covered by TUPE.
- On transfer, all the transferor's (old employer's) rights, powers, duties, and liabilities in connection with the contract of employment are transferred to the transferee (new employer). The transferee 'steps into the shoes' of the transferor.
- Statutory rights, eg maternity, etc, are also transferred.
- Any variation of the contract of employment will be void if the reason is the transfer, but will not be void if it is for an economic, technical or organisational (ETO) reason.
- The transferor shall notify the employee of any employee liability information, and failure to comply can result in a tribunal action.

---

[102] [2006] IRLR 252, EAT.

10

Performance of the Contract of Employment

Background

10.1 We have seen (in Chapter 3) that there are a number of different ways by which the terms of a contract of employment may come into existence. We must now consider a number of duties and obligations which are imposed by law on both parties during the continuance of the performance of the contract. Some of these arise by virtue of the common law, but others arise out of the implications of legislative policy.

10.2 The distinction between those duties which are imposed by law and those which operate as an implied term of the contract is not at all clear. Prior to the massive explosion in employment law, which began in the 1960s, there were few legal authorities on the contractual nature of the employment relationship, and hence the courts were readier to invent obligations as a necessary part of that relationship. Now there is no dearth of legal authority arising from the contractual aspect, and rights have developed accordingly, whether as an express or implied term of the contract. But the more terms are expressly laid down, the less scope there is for implied terms to operate. Indeed, since an implied term cannot override an express term, and since express terms can exclude an implied term, the duties imposed by law begin to assume greater importance.

Personal Nature of the Contract

10.3 A contract of employment is essentially one of personal service, which gives rise to duties and obligations on both sides, but the courts will not compel either side to carry out that contract by means of an order for specific performance or an injunction. In *Warner Bros Pictures Inc v Nelson*[1] a film actress agreed to work for the claimants, and not to work for any other film company. It was held that an injunction would be granted restraining her from breaking the negative stipulation, for while she could not work for a rival film company, there were presumably other ways in which she could earn her living. However, the injunction would not be granted if its effect would be to compel the performance of the contract. In *Whitwood Chemical Co v Hardman*[2] a manager agreed to devote the whole of his time to the company's business. He intended to work part-time for a rival company, and his employers sued for specific performance. It was held that the agreement was not enforceable, for while they could have obtained an injunction to restrain him from working for a competitor, the court would not compel him to work for the claimants.

[1] [1937] 1 KB 209, [1936] 3 All ER 160. [2] [1891] 2 Ch 416, CA.

10.4 By the same rule, the courts will not normally order an employer to continue to employ an employee (*Measham v AEEU*[3]), though there are cases where this had been done (see para 10.8) and in recent years the courts have been more willing to do so than hitherto (see the cases cited in *Wadcock v London Borough of Brent*[4]). There are also pressures on employers to offer reinstatement or re-engagement following employment tribunal proceedings (see Chapter 17) and a contract of employment may transfer from one employer to another when the Transfer of Undertakings (Protection of Employment) Regulations apply (see Chapter 9). But the rule generally remains. In *Chappell v Times Newspapers Ltd*,[5] members of a trade union were carrying on a disruptive campaign in support of a wage demand. The employers' association sent a telegram to the union stating that unless the campaign was called off, the members would be regarded as having broken their contracts of employment and thereby terminated their engagements. Several employees brought an action for an injunction to restrain their employers from terminating their contracts. It was held that, even on the assumption that the employers were acting in breach of contract, an injunction would not be granted, for to do so would be to compel specific performance by the employers. In particular, an injunction will not be granted if damages would be an adequate remedy for the alleged breach of contract (*Alexander v Standard Telephones and Cables plc*[6]).

10.5 An exceptional case was *Hill v CA Parsons & Co Ltd*,[7] where, following the making of a closed shop agreement with a trade union, the employers wrote to the claimant giving him one month's notice of dismissal because of his failure to join the union. The court thought that the claimant, who was a senior engineer, was entitled to at least six months' notice, and granted an injunction restraining the employers from treating the notice as having terminated the contract. (The effect of this was to delay the dismissal until after the coming into effect of the Industrial Relations Act 1971, which would have protected the claimant from dismissal for non-membership of the union.) But the court conceded that there were special circumstances in the case which enabled them to grant the injunction. There was no loss of confidence between the employers and the claimant, for the employers were acting under union pressure, and therefore there was no difficulty in enforcing the continuance of the contract.

10.6 *Hill v CA Parsons & Co Ltd* was followed in *Irani v Southampton and South West Hampshire Health Authority*,[8] where the claimant was employed by the defendants as a part-time ophthalmologist. The claimant quarrelled with the consultant in charge of the clinic, and he was thus dismissed, although the defendants failed to operate the disputes procedure laid down in the Whitley Council Conditions of Service. The claimant was granted an injunction preventing the defendants from implementing the decision without invoking the disputes procedure. The court advanced three reasons. First, there was no lack of confidence in the claimant, for his professional competence was not in issue. Second, the claimant was seeking the protection of the disputes procedure which was incorporated into his contract. Third, damages would not be an adequate remedy. The balance of convenience lay in the granting of the injunction.

10.7 Whether the employee retains the confidence of the employer must be judged on the circumstances of the case, including the nature of the work, the people with whom the work is to be done, and the effect on the employer's operations if the injunction is granted.

---

[3] [1994] IRLR 218.   [4] [1990] IRLR 223.
[5] [1975] 2 All ER 233, [1975] ICR 145, [1975] IRLR 90, CA.
[6] [1990] ICR 464, [1990] IRLR 723, CA.   [7] [1972] Ch 305, [1971] 3 All ER 1345, CA.
[8] [1985] ICR 590, [1985] IRLR 203.

In *Powell v London Borough of Brent*,[9] the claimant was told that she had been selected for promotion. It was then thought that the selection may have been in breach of the council's equal opportunity code, and her promotion was rescinded and the post re-advertised. The claimant brought an action for an injunction to restrain the council from treating her other than as being promoted. By the time the case came to court, she was able to show that she had worked in the senior post without any complaints about her work and there were no problems in her working relationships. It was held that the injunction would be granted. A bare assertion by her employers that there was a lack of confidence was not sufficient.

10.8 The normal remedy in such cases is for the employee who is being threatened with dismissal to seek an interlocutory injunction restraining the proposed dismissal until the trial of action. The court must then consider whether the balance of convenience requires such a course of action (see *American Cyanamid Co v Ethicon Ltd*[10]), leaving the substantial merits of the case to be argued subsequently at a full hearing. However, in *Jones v Gwent County Council*,[11] the court held that a judge can give a final ruling on any question of law or construction of document without a full trial of action, and such ruling can finally determine the matter, subject to an appeal. In this case, the claimant had been subjected to two disciplinary hearings which ended in her favour. Nonetheless the council brought further disciplinary proceedings on the ground that her return to work would cause an irrevocable breakdown in relationships between management and staff. It was decided that she should be dismissed. It was held that a declaration could be made that her dismissal was not valid, and a permanent injunction was granted, restraining the council from dismissing her other than in accordance with the proper procedure as laid down in her terms of appointment, and unless proper grounds existed.

10.9 TULR(C)A, s 236 provides that no court shall compel an employee to work or attend at a place of work through the making of an order for specific performance, or an injunction. Thus an order cannot be granted, for example, to call off a strike.

Implied Duties of the Employer

A. Implied Duty of Trust and Confidence

10.10 Now that the age when management could 'hire and fire' at will has gone, it is possible to assert that the employer has a legal duty to treat his employees with due respect and consideration, mindful of their needs and problems, sympathetic to their difficulties. It is no longer possible to treat an employee as an expendable chattel, or as an object without feelings and emotions. This duty is implicit in a number of cases which will be considered in due course when dismissal or disciplinary policies are discussed, but it is particularly evident where the employer is alleged to have been carrying out provocative conduct. In *Donovan v Invicta Airways Ltd*[12] the employee resigned after what he considered to be a number of incidents where he thought the employer was being unfair, and claimed damages for breach of contract. In the circumstances it was held that such conduct, though irritating, was not substantial enough to amount to a breach, but it was stated that there was an implied duty that each of the parties to a contract of employment should treat the other with such a degree of consideration and courtesy as would enable the contract to be carried on. Thus it is a breach of the implied term of trust and confidence to single out an employee

---

[9] [1988] ICR 176, [1987] IRLR 466, CA.
[10] [1974] FSR 312, CA; revsd [1975] AC 396, [1975] 1 All ER 504, [1975] FSR 101, HL.
[11] [1992] IRLR 521.   [12] [1969] 2 Lloyd's Rep 413, [1970] 1 Lloyd's Rep 486, CA.

on capricious grounds and to refuse to offer him the same terms as are offered to the rest of the workforce (*Transco plc v O'Brien*, see para 3.46).

10.11 It will be recalled (see para 3.44) that in *Malik v BCCI SA* the House of Lords held that there was a duty on an employer to conduct his business so as not to damage an employee's future prospects in the labour market. While the *Malik* decision was probably decided on its own facts, it does raise a number of interesting possibilities, including, for example, the case of an employee who has been dismissed for misconduct alleging that his reputation has been damaged by a false accusation, and suing accordingly. In the words of Lord Nicholls: 'Employers must take care not to damage their employees' future employment prospects by harsh and oppressive behaviour or by any other form of conduct which is unacceptable today as falling below the standards set by the implied trust and confidence term.' But if the employer had reasonable and proper cause to act in the manner he did, then even though there are adverse consequences to the employee, there is no breach of the implied duty of trust and confidence (*Hilton v Shiner Ltd*, see paras 3.45 and 17.44).

10.12 Although to carry on a business in a corrupt and dishonest manner is an example of a breach of the implied term of trust and confidence, if a former employee wishes to claim damages as a result, he must produce credible evidence that prospective employers rejected his applications for employment on such grounds (*Bank of Credit and Commerce International SA v Ali*, see para 3.44).

10.13 This duty arises at the outset of the employment, and continues during its performance right up to its termination. Employers will have to examine very closely their personnel and recruitment policies, for a mistake in selection or a failure to handle a problem in a proper manner could lead to an expensive action being brought in the future. For if an employer selects someone for a particular job, and that person does not have the necessary experience or capability for doing it, it is likely that the employer must accept some of the blame (*Bradley v Opperman Gears Ltd*[13]). As a result, many employers employ people on the basis of a probationary period in order to assess their capabilities properly. The employer also has an obligation to ensure that the employee is provided with an adequate job description, with objectives clearly mapped out, is provided with adequate facilities and support staff, and is properly trained and supervised where necessary. A failure by the employer to attend to these and similar matters may well mean that any shortcomings on the employee's part may not be entirely his own fault, and it could well be unfair to dismiss him in these circumstances (*Burrows v Ace Caravan Co (Hull) Ltd*[14]).

10.14 The frequent use of foul and abusive language by an employer can breach the implied duty of trust and confidence, entitling the employee to resign and claim constructive dismissal (*Horkulak v Cantor Fitzgerald International*[15]).

10.15 However, there are limits to the duty of trust and confidence. For example, in *University of Nottingham v Eyett*[16] it was held that the duty did not create a positive obligation on an employer to advise an employee that if he delayed taking retirement for another month, when he would have received a salary increase, his pension would have been correspondingly higher (see *Crossley v Faithful and Gould Holdings Ltd*, para 3.37). The implied duty is subject to the qualification that the employer must not act in such a way as to destroy or damage the trust and confidence which must otherwise exist between the parties without reasonable and proper cause. Thus if an employer, after a fair and full investigation,

---

[13] [1975] IRLR 13.   [14] [1972] IRLR 4.
[15] [2003] EWHC 1918 (QB), [2003] IRLR 756, [2003] All ER (D) 542 (Jul).
[16] [1999] 2 All ER 437, [1999] ICR 721, [1999] IRLR 87.

rejects a grievance raised by an employee, this will not give rise to a claim for constructive dismissal based on a breach of the implied term of trust and confidence. Equally, if the employee is himself in breach of the implied term, he cannot complain of his employer's breach (*RDF Media Group v Clements*[17]).

B. Duty to Provide Work

10.16 As a general rule, the employer is not under an obligation to provide work for his employee. As Asquith J said in *Collier v Sunday Referee Publishing Co*: 'Provided I pay my cook her wages regularly, she cannot complain if I choose to take any or all of my meals out'.[18] Indeed, there are many circumstances when the employer may find himself unable to provide work for his employees, for example, as a result of reorganisation, shortage of materials, lack of orders, etc, where the employer may prefer to keep his workforce together and pay them for doing nothing. However, there are certain special circumstances where the failure to provide work may result in the breach of a legal duty:

(a) If the failure to provide work can lead to a loss of reputation or publicity. In *Herbert Clayton and Jack Waller Ltd v Oliver*,[19] an actor was given a leading role in a musical comedy. He was subsequently offered a lesser role, but at the same salary. It was held that the employer was in breach of contract, because the nature of the work was as important as the salary to be paid.

(b) If the failure to provide work leads to a reduction in the employee's actual or potential earnings. Thus an employee is entitled to be given an opportunity to earn his commission (*Turner v Goldsmith*[20]) or to earn a reasonable sum if he is on piecework (*Devonald v Rosser & Sons*[21]). In *Bauman v Hulton Press Ltd*[22] it was held that the employers 'were bound to give the claimant a reasonable amount of work to enable him to earn that which the parties must be taken to have contemplated'. It was the lack of opportunity to earn premium payments for hours worked on nightshift and overtime which constituted the breach of contract by the employers in *Langston's* case.

(c) There are dicta in *Langston's* case which suggest that if an employee needs practice in order to maintain or develop his skills in employment, the employer is under a duty to provide a reasonable amount of work for this purpose. This view has received further support from the 'garden leave' cases (see *Provident Financial Group plc v Hayward*,[23] para 19.9).

(d) A failure to provide work may constitute a repudiation of the contract by the employer if it is possible to imply a term into the contract that the employer shall provide suitable work. This appears to be particularly true when the employee is appointed to a specific office. In *Breach v Epsylon Industries Ltd*,[24] the EAT thought that some of the earlier decisions on this subject were somewhat out of date and perhaps old-fashioned in their approach. Consequently, in modern cases there may be facts which more readily lead to the conclusion that there is an implied term to the effect that there is an obligation to provide work. In *William Hill Organisation Ltd v Tucker*[25] it was stated in the Court of Appeal that times had moved on from the

---

[17] [2007] EWHC 2892 (QB), [2008] IRLR 207.   [18] [1940] 2 KB 647, [1940] 4 All ER 234.
[19] [1930] AC 209, [1930] All ER Rep 414, HL.   [20] [1891] 1 QB 544, [1891–4] All ER Rep 384, CA.
[21] [1906] 2 KB 728, [1904–7] All ER Rep 988, CA.   [22] [1952] 2 All ER 1121.
[23] [1989] 3 All ER 298, [1989] ICR 160, [1989] IRLR 84, CA.
[24] [1976] ICR 316, [1976] IRLR 180, EAT.   [25] [1999] ICR 291, [1998] IRLR 313, CA.

days when only musicians, actors, etc were perceived as requiring regular exercise of their skills and public performances in order to keep up their reputation. All employees with specific skills are entitled to exercise those skills, even during notice periods, provided that there is work to be done (see para 19.10).

(e) If the contract of employment provides for suspension with pay pending the outcome of disciplinary enquiries, or criminal proceedings, there is no obligation on the employer to provide the employee with an opportunity to work overtime (*McClory v Post Office* (para 3.48)).

C. Duty to Pay Wages or Other Remuneration When There is No Work

10.17 The express terms of the contract will normally determine the amount of remuneration to be paid to the employee, but we must consider the situation where, because there is no work to do, the employee cannot earn his money. The question is to what extent, if at all, does the employer undertake to pay the employee wages if the employer cannot provide work for the employee to do? To seek the answer, we must state the general rule, and then seek any modification which may exist by virtue of any express or implied terms of the contract of employment.

10.18 At common law an employee who is ready and willing to work is entitled to be paid wages, even though no work is available for him, unless there is a provision in the contract which enables the employer to withhold them (*Beveridge v KLM UK Ltd*[26]). Clearly, this is the position in respect of salaried staff (who are paid weekly or monthly: see *Miller v Hamworthy Engineering Ltd*, para 3.99), and there is no legal distinction between them and hourly paid workers or pieceworkers. An hourly paid worker is entitled to be paid for the number of hours he makes himself available for work, not the number of hours the employers permit him to work, and a pieceworker, though paid for the work actually done, is entitled to expect that the employer will give him an opportunity to earn his wages. Because of this general common law rule, it was a comparatively simple matter to imply into the contract of an employee a term that he would be paid if there was no work. In *Devonald v Rosser & Sons* (see para 15.14) the plaintiff was a pieceworker. His employers closed down the factory, and gave him one month's notice. It was held that there was an implied term in his contract that the employer would find him work to do, and he recovered damages based on his prior average earnings. An argument by the employers that there was a trade custom to the contrary was rejected by the court, because a custom has to be reasonable, certain, and notorious. But if the failure to provide work was due to circumstances outside the control of the employer, different considerations could apply. In *Browning v Crumlin Valley Collieries*[27] a colliery had to close down because it was in a dangerous condition, through no fault of the employers. It was held that there was an implied term that the employers were not obliged to pay wages in these circumstances.

10.19 The common law rule, however, can be varied by an express or implied term to the contrary and, of course, a statutory provision will always override the rule. Thus if the contract states that there shall be no payment during a lay-off or in respect of short-time working, the employers will incur no obligation to pay at common law. In *Hulme v Ferranti Ltd*[28] the claimant was employed on terms that if there was no work, he would not be paid. He was laid off as a result of a strike involving other workers in the plant, and it was held that he was not entitled to be paid during that time. But the modern practice of concluding

---

[26] [2000] IRLR 765, EAT.   [27] [1926] 1 KB 522, [1926] All ER 132.   [28] [1918] 2 KB 426, DC.

guarantee payment agreements lends greater credence to the view that the present law is that in respect of hourly or pieceworkers, there is an implied term that they will not be paid during a lay-off or short-time working. For example, if an employer agrees to pay a minimum guarantee week to employees who have been employed by him for a certain period, those who do not qualify can scarcely be in a better position. The very existence of the guarantee payments rights in the Employment Rights Act 1996 (see Chapter 7) supports this view, for such rights would virtually be unnecessary if the common law rule was of general application. Nonetheless, a lay-off without pay is either a temporary suspension or a dismissal with the prospect of re-engagement, and the employer may only treat it as a suspension if there is an expressed or implied term in the contract giving him that right (*Jewell v Neptune Concrete Ltd*, para 3.58). In the absence of such a term the employee is entitled to treat the suspension as repudiatory conduct by the employer, and hence a dismissal. In appropriate circumstances (see Chapter 18) he may claim redundancy pay. Indeed, since there must be few contracts of employment which made provision for such eventuality, the Redundancy Payments Act 1965 was apparently based on the assumption that there was a general existence of an implied term that employees who are laid off or who are on short time are not entitled to be paid (see now ERA, s 147).

D. **Payment of Bonuses, etc**

10.20 If a contract of employment contains an express term which provides for the payment of a bonus (or incentive scheme), problems may arise over interpretation, but not over entitlement. In the absence of any agreement, the courts will calculate or estimate what monies the employee would have received, and include that amount in the quantum of damages (*Addis v Gramophone Co Ltd*[29]). However, difficulties frequently arise when the bonus scheme purports to be discretionary, because, in the absence of clear and precise wording (see eg *Kent Management Services Ltd v Butterfield*, paras 8.14 and 8.20), a legal obligation may nonetheless arise, as part of the implied duties of the employer. In *Mallone v BPB Industries plc* (see para 3.2) it was held that the directors of a company acted irrationally in cancelling mature share options following the employee's dismissal for poor performance, even though the contract gave them an absolute discretion to reduce these by an appropriate fraction. Thus, despite the fact that discretion is expressed to be absolute or unfettered, the courts are willing to impose limits on such management prerogatives, by implying a term that a discretion cannot be exercised in a manner which no reasonable employer would have done. But in *Ridgeway v JP Morgan Chase National Bank*[30] it was held that the employer did not act irrationally or perversely when it awarded an employee a 'nil bonus', even though a full performance review had not been carried out. The employee had lost a large sum of money in trading during the relevant period, and had done nothing in non-trading work to justify a bonus.

10.21 As a general principle, a dismissed employee cannot claim compensation for the loss of a benefit to which he is not contractually entitled (*Lavarack v Woods of Colchester Ltd*[31]), and if a bonus or other incentive scheme states that it is non-contractual the employer generally does not incur a legally binding obligation to make payments under the scheme (*Pendragon plc v Jackson (No 2)*, see para 3.19). But if there is a discretionary bonus scheme the terms of which have been notified to the employee, he will become entitled to it until he has been notified that the scheme has been changed or withdrawn (*Chequepoint UK Ltd v Radwan*[32]). There is no implied term in an employee's contract that a bonus would

---

[29] [1909] AC 488, [1908–10] All ER Rep 1, HL.   [30] 2007 IDS Brief 835.
[31] [1967] 1 QB 278, [1966] 3 All ER 683, CA.   [32] Unreported.

only be paid if the employee remained in employment or was not serving out a notice period at the date of the bonus payment (*Rutherford v Seymour Pierce Ltd*[33]). Even after a dismissal, anticipated discretionary bonus payments can be claimed on the basis that, although there was no obligation on the employer to pay, the court will assume that the discretion would have been exercised in good faith (*Clark v BET plc*, see para 3.2). Thus a refusal to make a non-contractual bonus payment will amount to a breach of contract if no reasonable employer would have exercised his discretion that way (*Clark v Nomura International*[34]). There is an implied duty on the employer to exercise his discretion in good faith, and not capriciously (*Manor House Healthcare v Hayes*[35]).

10.22 In an industry where there are high earnings and competitive activity, a discretionary bonus scheme can be regarded as being part of the remuneration structure of the employers, and a contractual benefit to the employee, as opposed to a mere declaration of the employer's right to pay a bonus if he so wishes. In such circumstances, the employee is entitled to a bona fide and rational exercise of the discretion by the employer in relation to the bonus scheme, and if the employer fails to do so, the employee is entitled to be compensated in respect of that failure (*Cantor Fitzgerald International v Horkulak*[36]).

10.23 A problem sometimes arises as to whether or not a bonus (contractual or discretionary) should be paid to a woman who is on maternity leave. The general principle was laid down by the European Court in *Lewen v Denda*[37] that where a bonus is payable in respect of work done, an employer is entitled to make a pro rata reduction in respect of the period of absence during maternity leave. She is entitled to a contractual bonus for the periods when she is at work, and also in respect of the compulsory maternity leave period, but a pro rata deduction for periods when she is not at work did not amount to unlawful sex discrimination, because s 39(6) of the Equality Act excluded benefits that consisted of payments of money when the provision of those benefits was regulated by the woman's contract of employment (*Hoyland v Asda Stores Ltd*[38]).

E. Duty of Confidentiality

10.24 Just as there is a duty on employees not to disclose confidential information about the employer's business (see para 10.69) so there is a similar duty on an employer not to disclose to third persons confidential information about the employee. This duty does not depend on any express or implied term of the contract (*Lord Advocate v Scotsman Publications Ltd*[39] per Lord Couldsfield). In *Dalgleish v Lothian and Borders Police Board*,[40] the employers held the names and addresses of all their employees. They were asked to provide this information to a local authority, for the purpose of discovering the identity of persons who had not paid the poll tax. The claimants sought an interim injunction restraining the employers from disclosing this information, which was granted. The information was not in the public domain, and was given by the employees to the employers for the purpose of the employment relationship, and for no other purpose. Hence it retained a characteristic of being confidential information, which could not be disclosed without the consent of the employees.

10.25 As well as the common law duty of confidentiality, there are statutory provisions on data protection. Originally, the EC Data Protection Directive (95/46/EC) required member

---

[33] [2010] IRLR 606, [2010] EWHC 375 (QB).   [34] [2000] IRLR 766.   [35] EAT/1196/99.
[36] [2004] IRLR 942, CA.   [37] *Lewen v Dender* [2000] IRLR 67.
[38] [2006] CSIH 21, 2006 SC 550, [2006] IRLR 468.
[39] 1988 SLT 490, Ct of Sess; aff'd sub nom *Lord Advocate v Scotsman Publications Ltd* [1990] 1 AC 812, [1989] 2 All ER 852.   [40] [1991] IRLR 422.

states to enact laws designed to protect the rights to privacy with respect to the processing of personal data, and the UK law was covered by the Data Protection Act 1998. Since then the General Data Protection Regulation (EU) 2016/679 (GDPR) was passed, which had effect in May 2018. This was supplemented by the Data Protection Act 2018, which replaced the 1998 Act.

10.26 Under the Data Protection Act 1998 and its 2018 successor workers have a right to have a copy of any information that an organisation has on them, and may apply to the court to obtain an order requiring a data controller to correct inaccurate information thereon, and seek compensation where damage or distress has been caused. The 1998 Act created the post of Information Commissioner, who produced an Employment Practices Code which gives guidance on how employment matters can be dealt with under the provisions of the Data Protection Act. After the coming into force of the 2018 Act, the Information Commissioner's Office (ICO) decreed that the replacement legislation did not affect the Code and so it is still valid.

The Code is in four parts, ie (a) Recruitment and Selection, (b) Employment Records, (c) Monitoring at Work, and (d) Information about Workers' Health. The Code itself is not legally binding, and any enforcement action has to be based on a breach of the Act. However, the relevant benchmarks would be cited by the Commissioner in such proceedings, and a disregard of those requirements is likely to mean that an employer does not comply with the Act.

10.27 Part 1 of the Code deals with advertising, applications, and verifications, shortlisting and interviews of applications, pre-employment vetting, and retention of recruitment records.

10.28 Part 2 of the Code deals with procedures and penalties for storing personal data about employees and job applicants, as well as the processes for subject access requests.

10.29 Part 3 of the Code deals with monitoring at work. It covers the use of CCTV cameras, automatic checking software to monitor the use or misuse of emails, recording telephone calls, and videoing workers who are on sickness absence to ensure that they are not, in fact, malingering. Since a balance must be drawn between the worker's right to privacy and the employer's monitoring requirements, workers must be clearly informed of the purpose of those arrangements, and the employer must be satisfied that the particular arrangement is justified by the benefits which will ensue. The decision whether to monitor or not should be made by a senior member of staff, and it should be done with a minimum of intrusiveness, with spot checks and annual audits being preferred to continuous monitoring. All employees should, as far as possible, be treated equally.

10.30 Part 4 is entitled 'Information about workers' health' and covers such topics as occupational health schemes, medical examinations and testing, drug and alcohol testing, and genetic testing. Collecting and holding information about a worker's health may be intrusive, but may be done with a clear purpose and justified by real benefits.

10.31 The 2018 Act retains many aspects of the 1998 Act, but the main changes as far as employers are concerned relate first to special personal data (s 9), such as health data, union membership, political opinion, etc, which employers can process if they meet the strict conditions under the GDPR. They can do this by obtaining explicit consent, or by having a specific policy on the matter. The policy should explain how the data controller complies with the legislation, its retention and erasure procedures, and an indication of how long the data is retained. Second, the Act allows the processing of criminal data if the same conditions are met (s 10).

The offence under s 55 DPA 1998 of unlawful obtaining of personal data is extended to include unlawful 'retention' of data without the data controller's consent, even if the data was originally obtained with consent. There are also two new offences created by the 2018 Act: (1) altering, destroying, or concealing information to be provided though a subject access request; (2) intentionally or recklessly re-identifying individuals from anonymised data.

The Information Commissioner will continue much as before, and will be required to co-operate with other supervisory bodies across the EU. The ICO will also be required to continue to keep under review a data-sharing code of practice and direct marketing code of practice.

The 2018 Act also provides for an enforcement regime in part 6, and a maximum fine of up to 20 million euros or 4% of the undertaking's total annual worldwide turnover.

F. Duty to Indemnify

10.32 Any expenses reasonably incurred by the employee in the performance of his contract ought properly to be met by the employer. Normally, one would expect express agreement to this effect, for example, for travelling or lodging allowances, but circumstances do arise when an employee spends his own money in pursuance of his employer's business, and it is submitted that he is entitled to be reimbursed. More difficult is the situation which arises when the employee commits a wrongful act. If this was done for the employer's business, and was authorised, or if the employee was acting under his employer's orders, then the employee is entitled to be indemnified for any personal loss he suffers.

10.33 For example, if an employer requires an employee to take out the firm's van, which has a defective tyre, and the employee is consequently fined, then it is reasonable to expect the employer to reimburse the amount, even though he may be prosecuted in addition. But if the work can be done in a lawful or unlawful manner, and the employee chose the latter option, the employer would not be required to reimburse such expenditure. For example, if the employee, in order to deliver some goods, parks illegally, then unless he was told to perform his work in this manner, he must bear any subsequent fine himself. In *Gregory v Ford*,[41] the claimant was injured due to the negligent driving of the defendant, whose employer did not have a valid third-party insurance policy as required by the Road Traffic Act 1988. It was held that there was an implied term of the contract that the employer would not require the employee to do an unlawful act, and therefore the employer should indemnify the employee in respect of the damages which were awarded to the claimant. In *Re Famatina Development Corpn Ltd*,[42] a consulting engineer employed by the company was asked to prepare a report on the conduct of the managing director. The latter brought an action for an alleged libel, which the engineer defended. It was held that he was entitled to be indemnified by the company for his costs in defending the action, for he had been requested by his directors to make the report, which was therefore in the course of his duties as an employee.

G. Duty to Insure

10.34 In respect of work activities taking place within the United Kingdom, an employer is obliged to take out compulsory employers' liability insurance, for the benefit of his employees, of at least £5m (Employers' Liability (Compulsory Insurance) Regulations 1998). However, an employer owes no duty in tort to any employee who is working abroad to take

---

[41] [1951] 1 All ER 121.
[42] [1914] 2 Ch 271, 83 LJ Ch 712; on appeal [1914] 2 Ch 271, 64 LJ Ch 48, 30 TLR 696, CA.

out appropriate insurance cover against special risks, or to advise the employee to take out his own cover. In *Reid v Rush & Tompkins Group plc* (see paras 2.128 and 3.39), the claimant worked for the defendants in Ethiopia. He received severe injuries in a road accident, which was the fault of the other driver, for whom the defendants were not responsible. The claimant was unable to obtain compensation from the other driver, as there is no third-party insurance in Ethiopia, and so he claimed damages from his employers. His statement of claim was struck out. An employer does not owe a duty to inform or advise on the potential danger of suffering economic loss in the form of uncompensated injuries.

H. References

10.35 In the absence of any express contractual obligation, the general rule is that an employer is under no legal duty to provide an employee or an ex-employee with a reference (*Gallear v JF Watson & Son Ltd*[43]), although in *Spring v Guardian Assurance plc* (see para 10.38) Lord Woolf suggested that there may be circumstances in which it is necessary to imply a term into a contract of employment that the employer would provide the employee with a reference, particularly in those areas of employment where it is normal practice to require a reference from a previous employer before employment is offered, eg in the financial services industry. An employer who does provide a reference about an existing employee who is seeking employment with another employer is under an obligation to ensure that it is fair and reasonable, and a failure to do so may amount to a breach of the implied duty of trust and confidence entitling the employee to resign and claim constructive dismissal. In *TSB Bank plc v Harris*[44] the employers sent a reference to a prospective employer about the employee which was factually true, but potentially misleading. Thus it stated that there were a number of complaints against her which were outstanding, but these complaints had never been drawn to her attention, and she had never had an opportunity to comment on them or to give her explanation. Her claim for constructive dismissal was upheld, even though she was considering leaving in any case. There is a difference between leaving without a job to go to and leaving in order to go to another job.

10.36 But although the duty is to provide a reference which is in substance fair, true, and accurate, it does not have to be full and comprehensive in every case. In *Bartholomew v London Borough of Hackney*[45] the local authority commenced disciplinary proceedings against the claimant, in connection with alleged irregularities. Eventually, a settlement was reached whereby the claimant took voluntary severance, and the disciplinary action was terminated. Subsequently, in response to a request for a reference, the employers stated that at the time of leaving their employment, the claimant was under suspension, disciplinary action had been commenced, but this lapsed on the claimant's departure from the employment. The claimant claimed that the employers were in breach of their legal duty of care, because the reference, although factually correct, was unfair. The Court of Appeal dismissed his claim. Although the form of the reference might have been improved upon in some respects it was not unfair, inaccurate or false. The employers also owed a duty to the recipients of the reference not to be unfair or to mislead. The only duty on the employer is to take reasonable care not to give misleading information, not to make a selective provision of information, or not to make comments which could give rise to a false or misleading inference in the mind of the recipient (*Kidd v AXA Equity and Law Life Assurance Society plc*[46]). The employer should not, in a reference, deal with matters which have not been put to the ex-employee, and which

---

[43] [1979] IRLR 306, EAT.   [44] [2000] IRLR 157, EAT.   [45] [1999] IRLR 246, CA.
[46] [2000] IRLR 301.

he has not had a fair opportunity of rebutting following a proper investigation (*Cox v Sun Alliance Life Ltd*[47]). The High Court in *Hincks v Sense Network*[48] gave guidance that where an employer gives a reference relying on the findings of an earlier investigation, it does not have to review the procedural fairness of that investigation, so long as it had a proper and legitimate basis. The Court set out guidelines, stating that while each case will depend on the surrounding facts, there are certain common features of the duty, which are:

(a) to conduct an objective and rigorous appraisal of facts and opinion, particularly negative opinion, whether those facts and opinions emerge from earlier investigations or otherwise;

(b) to take reasonable care to be satisfied that the facts set out in the reference are accurate and true and that, where an opinion is expressed, there is a proper and legitimate basis for the opinion;

(c) where an opinion is derived from an earlier investigation, to take reasonable care in considering and reviewing the underlying material so that the reference writer is able to understand the basis for the opinion and be satisfied that there is a proper and legitimate basis for the opinion;

(d) to take reasonable care to ensure that the reference is fair, in the *Bartholomew* sense, of not being misleading either by reason of what is not included or by implication, nuance or innuendo.

10.37 While, as a general rule, there is no obligation on an employer to provide a reference for an ex-employee, the situation is different if the reason for the failure or refusal was an act of unlawful discrimination under the Equality Act 2010 or the whistle-blowing provisions of ERA (see para 10.75). The Equality Act now provides that it is unlawful to discriminate against a person by subjecting him/her to a detriment, where the discrimination arises out of or is closely connected with the relevant relationship. Thus, if the reason for a failure to provide a reference was because a woman had brought a claim alleging unfair maternity dismissal, this would be an act of unlawful discrimination (*Coote v Granada Hospitality Ltd*, see para 4.43). On the other hand if the refusal was based on other considerations, no victimisation has occurred (*Chief Constable of West Yorkshire v Khan*, see para 4.39). Where an employer has victimised a former employee by giving her an adverse reference because she had previously brought discrimination proceedings against it, the employer can be liable for loss of earnings if a prospective job offer is withdrawn as a result of the reference. In *Bullimore v Pothecary Witham Weld Solicitors (No. 2)*,[49] in answer to a question about how the employment had ended, her manager referred not simply to the fact that she had resigned but also gratuitously to the fact that she had brought discrimination proceedings against the firm.

10.38 Several pitfalls can occur when providing a reference about an ex-employee to a prospective employer. First, a derogatory reference may expose the giver of the reference to an action for defamation. This may be defended on the ground that the statements made were true, or, if untrue, were made on an occasion when the law confers qualified privilege, and the statements were made without malice, in the sense of an improper motive. Next, the employer owes a duty of care to the ex-employee to ensure that the reference is not prepared carelessly or negligently, and will be consequently liable for damages in respect of any economic loss which flows from the negligent misstatement (*Spring v Guardian Assurance plc*, para 10.35). In this case, Lord Slynn suggested that the employers could avoid any

---

[47] [2001] EWCA Civ 1010, [2001] IRLR 448, [2001] All ER (D) 108 (May).
[48] [2018] EWHC 533.   [49] [2011] IRLR 18.

liability by making it clear to the ex-employee that they will only provide a reference if he accepts that there will be a disclaimer of liability to him and to the recipient.

10.39 On the other hand, to give a commendatory reference about a prospective employee which is untrue, and which is relied upon by a subsequent employer to his detriment, may well lead to an action based on deceit or negligent misstatement, unless the reference is qualified by a disclaimer of responsibility (*Hedley Byrne & Co Ltd v Heller & Partners Ltd*[50]).

10.40 A further problem associated with the provision of a reference can arise in dismissal cases. In *Castledine v Rothwell Engineering Ltd*,[51] one of the reasons given by the employer for dismissing the firm's buyer was that he was incapable of performing his job adequately. The tribunal found this difficult to reconcile with the reference given by the employer, which stated that the employee 'had carried out his duties satisfactorily, often under difficult conditions'. Not surprisingly, the tribunal found that the employee had been unfairly dismissed. And in *Haspell v Restron and Johnson Ltd*[52] the respondents gave a reference which was laudatory of the claimant. It was held that they were estopped from relying on criticisms of her performance as a reason for her dismissal.

I. **The Right to Privacy**

10.41 There are many occasions during the performance of the contract of employment when an employer will be monitoring the employee's performance, as a matter of routine. The problem arises when such actions become intrusive into an employee's private life. For example, an employer may wish to monitor the employee's telephone calls, in order to assess performance, ensure that quality standards are met and customer satisfaction is achieved, and provide a valuable record in the event of a subsequent dispute with customers or suppliers, etc. But what happens when the employee's telephone call is of a personal nature? Does this amount to an unwarranted infringement of his right to privacy?

10.42 The routine use of email and the internet by employees during working hours will exacerbate the problem. The temptation for employees to use these facilities for their own purposes is ever-increasing, whether it be for booking holidays, purchasing goods for private use, or playing games. The questions must be thus posed: can the employer (a) implement surveillance, (b) listen in and/or record such activities, and (c) take disciplinary action in the event of suspected misuse? Clearly, a balance must be drawn between the employee's right to privacy and the legitimate interests of the employer in ensuring that the employee is doing his work properly, and not abusing facilities provided.

10.43 So far as the law is concerned, Art 8 of the European Convention on Human Rights provides:

(a) Everyone has the right to respect for his private and family life, his home and his correspondence.

(b) There shall be no interference by a public authority with the exercise of this right except such as is in accordance with the law and is necessary in a democratic society in the interests of national security, public safety or the economic well-being of the country, for the prevention of disorder or crime, for the protection of health or morals, or for the protection of the rights and freedoms of others.

---

[50] [1962] 1 QB 396, [1961] 3 All ER 891, CA; aff'd [1964] AC 465, [1963] 2 All ER 575 HL.
[51] [1973] IRLR 99.   [52] [1976] IRLR 50.

10.44 It will be recalled (see para 1.88) that the Human Rights Act 1998 is designed to give effect to the provisions of the European Convention, and although this only applies to public authorities, the courts and tribunals use it as an aid in the decision-making process when dealing with the private employer.

10.45 The right to privacy was an issue in *Halford v United Kingdom* (see para 1.91), where the claimant, who was a senior police officer, alleged that she had been turned down for promotion because of her sex, and brought a claim of sex discrimination. She also alleged that her telephone calls at work and at home were being intercepted for the purpose of obtaining information to be used against her in the tribunal proceedings. The sex discrimination case was settled, but she brought further proceedings in the European Court of Human Rights, claiming that the interception of her telephone calls was an infringement of her right to privacy. Her claim succeeded. The Court held that telephone calls made from business premises may be covered by the notion of private life and correspondence within the meaning of Art 8 of the Convention. The Court refused to accept the notion that an employer could, without prior knowledge of the employee, monitor calls made by the employee on telephones provided by the employer. In *Bărbulescu v Romania* (para 1.91) an employee made extensive personal use of a work computer, knowing that this was not permitted, and was put under surveillance by his employer. He claimed that this was against his right of privacy under Article 8 ECHR. The Grand Chamber agreed, finding that an employee should be notified in advance of any monitoring. Note however *López Ribalda and Others v Spain*.[53] After finding discrepancies in stock levels, the employer supermarket installed covert video surveillance, catching cashiers stealing items and helping customers to do so. The Spanish court found the surveillance to be justified and necessary to achieve a legitimate aim. The case eventually also reached the 17-judge Grand Chamber of the ECHR, which equally found no breach of Article 8. Although the staff were not told of the surveillance, there was a reasonable suspicion of serious misconduct, the monitoring was carried out in an area open to the public, was for a limited time of ten days, and so was proportionate. There may be a different expectation in private areas, and some where heightened protection or a complete ban on video surveillance is justified, such as lavatories and cloakrooms, but that was not the case here.

10.46 The Regulation of Investigatory Powers Act 2000 makes it a criminal offence without lawful authority to intercept a communication in the course of its transmission by post or by a public or private telecommunication system. However, interceptions may be lawful if the sender or intended recipient has consented to the interception or the interceptor has a warrant (or, in certain circumstances, without a warrant, eg to comply with an EU Convention on Mutual Assistance in Criminal Matters). Interception is also permitted when done by the postal or telecommunications service provider for purposes connected with the operations of the service.

10.47 There is no problem if the person making or receiving the communication consents to its interception, but the Regulation of Investigatory Powers Act 2000 enables employees to take legal action in tort against an employer whom they believe has unlawfully intercepted a telecommunication made to a third party on the employer's network. However, such an interception is permissible under the Telecommunications (Lawful Business Practice) (Interception of Communications) Regulations 2000, which were passed to give effect to the EU Telecoms Data Protection Directive (97/66/EC) (and have now been replaced by the Investigatory Powers (Interception by Businesses etc. for Monitoring and

---

[53] Applications nos 1874/13 and 8567/13.

Record-Keeping Purposes) Regulations 2018, further to the GDPR, although they are largely the same). By virtue of these regulations, employers may legitimately monitor or record all telecommunications transmitted over their systems, without the consent of the persons making those communications, for the following purposes, namely, to establish the existence of facts, to ensure compliance with regulatory or self-regulatory practices or procedures, for quality control purposes, for the purpose of detection or prevention of crime, to ensure the effectiveness of their telecommunications systems, or to check on whether the communications in question were relevant to the employer's business.

J. Duty to Ensure the Employee's Safety

10.48 The law on compensation for injuries at work will be considered in Chapter 11. Undoubtedly the most important aspect of the employer's duty which is implied by law is the duty to take reasonable care to ensure the safety of his employees.

Implied Obligations of the Employee

A. Duty of Faithful Service

10.49 Since the relationship between the employer and employee is one of trust and confidence, the law implies into the contract of employment the term that every employee shall serve his employer faithfully. This is a fundamental obligation, and any serious or persistent course of conduct which is inconsistent with that obligation may well amount to a breach of contract. Examples which readily spring to mind include persistent lateness, incompetence, wilful neglect, and theft of the employer's property. A strike, a go-slow, a work-to-rule, a sit-in, being contrary to the fundamental nature of the contract—which is to work in return for a reward—are also within this category, and an employee may be dismissed for them (see Chapter 21). The employee undertakes to perform his duties carefully and competently, with due regard for the interests of the employer. In *Secretary of State for Employment v Associated Society of Locomotive Engineers and Firemen* (see para 3.86) Roskill LJ thought that it was an implied term that each employee would not, in obeying lawful instructions, seek to carry them out in a manner which had the effect of disrupting the employer's business. Whether the 'implied term' theory can stand up to analysis is another matter; all members of the Court of Appeal were prepared to import some form of obligation of fidelity arising from the very nature of the contract of employment.

10.50 In *Sim v Rotherham Metropolitan Borough Council* (para 3.34) it was held that the contractual obligations of a person employed in a professional capacity were those defined by the nature of his profession and the obligations incumbent on those who follow that profession.

10.51 If an employee fails to perform part of his duties, but indicates that he is prepared to perform the remainder, the employer may make it clear that he is not prepared to accept such partial performance, and may lawfully refuse to pay the employee the whole of the remuneration due (*Wiluszynski v London Borough of Tower Hamlets*, see para 8.24).

10.52 If the employee is in breach of contract, the employer may seek to recover expenditure incurred or wasted as a result of the breach. Thus in *Anglia Television Ltd v Reed* an actor agreed to play a leading role in a film. He subsequently repudiated the agreement and refused to perform. The company abandoned production of the film, and sued for the expenditure that had been wasted. It was held that both pre- and post-contractual expenditure was within the contemplation of the parties that would be wasted, and the company was entitled to recover their loss (see also *Tullett Prebon Group Ltd v Ghaleb El-Hajjali*, para 3.5).

10.53 A wrongful act which does not necessarily benefit the employee may still be a breach of fidelity if it is harmful to the employer's business. In *Dalton v Burton's Gold Medal Biscuits Ltd*[54] the employee was dismissed for falsifying the clock-card of a fellow employee, and this was held to be a fair dismissal. A more difficult situation arises if there is a conflict between the duty of fidelity on the one hand, and an obligation the employee owes by virtue of his membership of a professional organisation on the other. It is submitted that there is an implied term that the employer will not require an employee to act in a manner contrary to professional ethics, and that this would override the duty to the employer.

10.54 It is a breach of the employee's duty of faithful service to compete with the employer while he is still employed but it is not a breach if an employee indicates that he intends to take steps at some future date which will enable him to compete after the employment has ceased, in the absence of any restrictive covenant to that effect (see para 19.30). In other words, there is a distinction between an intention to set up in competition with the em-ployer in the future, and competing with the employer while still employed. In *Adamson v B & L Cleaning Services Ltd*,[55] the employee was a foreman employed by a firm of cleaning contractors. The firm had a cleaning contract worth £60,000 per year. Tenders were invited for renewal, and the employee indicated that he had requested that his name be placed on the tender list. When the employers were informed of this, they asked him to sign an undertaking not to seek to obtain any contract for industrial cleaning while still in the firm's employment, but he refused to do so, and was dismissed. The dismissal was held to be fair. He was in breach of his duty of faithful service, which justified the termination of his employment. In *Ward Evans Financial Services Ltd v Fox*[56] the employee's contract of employment provided that he would act at all times in the best interests of his employer. He purchased an 'off the shelf' company, which did not commence trading until after his employment had ended, and he also informed existing clients about the new company. It was held that he had acted in breach of his duty of fidelity. It is a breach of the duty of fidelity for an employee to email confidential company information to her personal email account, even where it is done to protect her position in forthcoming litigation against the employer, and because of concerns about compliance in order to make a report to the regulator (*Brandeaux (Advisers) UK Ltd v Chadwick*).[57]

10.55 An employee who learns of confidential matters relating to competition from a prospective employer is not bound to pass the information to his existing employer, as he would then be in breach of confidence to the new employer. In *Customer Systems Plc v Ranson*,[58] the High Court followed *Tullett Prebon v BGC Brokers*[59] and said that a duty of fidelity to a current employer does not necessarily defeat the duty of confidence to a new employer.

10.56 As a general principle, an employee's duty of fidelity does not prevent him from competing with a former employer once he has left his employment, and the freedom to do so carries with it the freedom to prepare for future activities that the employee intends to pursue once he has left his employment (*Helmet Integrated Systems Ltd v Tunnard*[60]).

---

[54] [1974] IRLR 45, NIRC.   [55] [1995] IRLR 193, EAT.
[56] [2001] EWCA Civ 1243, [2002] IRLR 120, [2001] All ER (D) 415 (Jul).
[57] [2011] IRLR 224, [2010] EWHC 3241 (QB).   [58] [2011] EWHC 3304.   [59] [2011] EWCA 131.
[60] [2006] FSR 41, PCC; aff'd [2006] EWCA Civ 1735, [2007] IRLR 126, [2007] FSR 16.

But preparatory activities undertaken by directors or senior employees are more likely to constitute breaches of fidelity and fiduciary duties (*Shepherds Investment Ltd v Walters*[61]). In any particular case, it will be necessary to identify the particular duties undertaken by the employee and to ask whether, in all the circumstances, he has placed himself in a position where he must act solely in the interests of his employer (*Nottingham University v Fishel*[62]).

10.57 An employee must not make a secret profit out of his position of trust for his own benefit, without the knowledge or informed consent of the employer, and to do so will amount to a breach of contract which will justify summary dismissal (*Neary v Dean of Westminster*[63]). If the employee is in breach of a fiduciary obligation, then, if the normal remedies of damages or injunction are not sufficient, an action for an account of profits may be brought (*A-G v Blake*[64]). It is probable that this rule also applies to overpayments of wages or expenses received by the employee (see para 8.24). Indeed, it is possible to argue that if an employee knows that he has been overpaid, and deliberately keeps the money, or spends it after he realises that he has been overpaid, then he has committed a criminal offence (*A-G's Reference (No 1 of 1983)*[65]).

B. Duty to Obey Lawful and Reasonable Orders

10.58 The employee undertakes to obey all lawful and reasonable orders. In *United Kingdom Atomic Energy Authority v Claydon*,[66] the employee's contract required him to work anywhere in the United Kingdom. He refused to transfer to another base, and was dismissed. The order was clearly lawful and reasonable, for it was within the express terms of the contract. In *Pepper v Webb*,[67] a gardener used some choice expletives accompanied by words which indicated that he had no intention of obeying his employer's instructions, and it was this refusal, rather than the language which accompanied it, which was held to be the breach of contract.

10.59 But if the employee can show that the order was unlawful, he need not obey it. In *Morrish v Henlys (Folkestone) Ltd*[68] the employee refused to falsify some records, and was dismissed. It was held that he was entitled to refuse to obey an unlawful order, and the dismissal was unfair. Whether an order is unreasonable may well be a question of fact in each case. In *Walmsley v UDEC Refrigeration Ltd*[69] the claimant was dismissed after refusing to work in Wexford in Eire on the grounds that it was a hotbed of IRA activity. He could not substantiate these allegations, and it was held that he had refused to obey a reasonable order. Had he been told to go to Belfast, a refusal may well have been justified, for this might involve a serious risk which was not contemplated at the time of the formation of the contract (*Wicks v Charles A Smethurst Ltd*[70]). An employee need not obey an order which would expose him to the risk of danger to life or liberty (*Ottoman Bank v Chakarian*[71]).

10.60 To determine whether or not an order is reasonable, principles of good industrial relations may be taken into account. Thus in *Payne v Spook Erection Ltd*,[72] a foreman was instructed to compile a merit table each week, listing the performance of 25 employees, and

---

[61] [2006] EWHC 836 (Ch), [2007] IRLR 110, [2007] FSR 15.
[62] [2000] ICR 1462, [2000] IRLR 471, [2000] All ER (D) 269.   [63] [1999] IRLR 288.
[64] [1997] Ch 84, [1996] 3 All ER 903; revsd [1998] Ch 439, [1998] 1 All ER 833, CA; aff'd on other grounds [2001] 1 AC 268, [2000] 2 All ER (Comm) 487, [2000] All ER (D) 1074, HL.
[65] [1985] QB 182, [1984] 3 All ER 369, [1984] Crim LR 570, CA.
[66] [1974] ICR 128, [1974] IRLR 6, NIRC.   [67] [1969] 2 All ER 216, CA.
[68] [1973] 2 All ER 137, [1973] ICR 482, [1973] IRLR 61, NIRC.   [69] [1972] IRLR 80.
[70] [1973] IRLR 327.   [71] [1930] AC 277, PC.   [72] [1984] IRLR 219, EAT.

to send warning letters to those whose name appeared at the bottom of the list. As he did not see all the employees each week, he refused to operate the system, as he thought that it would be based largely on guesswork. He was told that unless he operated the system he would be dismissed, but he refused to comply. An employment tribunal, although they had little sympathy with the system, held the dismissal to be fair, but the decision was reversed by the EAT. In considering whether or not a decision of an employment tribunal was perverse, matters of good industrial relations could be considered. The weekly merit rating system was clearly unfair, and to dismiss the foreman for refusing to operate an unreasonable order was also unfair.

10.61 Difficulty is frequently caused by loose contractual expressions relating to overtime. If this is stated to be voluntary, then the employee is entitled to refuse. If it is stated to be worked by arrangement, then again, it becomes a matter for negotiation. But if it is clear that some overtime is to be worked, and the negotiations are merely about the details, the refusal may well be unreasonable, particularly if this is designed to bring improper pressure to bear on the employer (*Pengilly v North Devon Farmers Ltd*[73]). As we have seen (in Chapter 3) a refusal to accept a demotion or a change in contractual terms is not necessarily unreasonable, but refusal to obey instructions which are within the contract may be unreasonable. In *Connor v Halfords Ltd*[74] the employee was obliged to 'obey all orders and instructions received from the directors'. He was dismissed because he refused to go on a training course, and the dismissal was held to be fair.

10.62 An employee who refuses to obey a lawful and reasonable order, which was given in good faith and without any ulterior motive, is in repudiatory breach of contract, which the employer may accept by dismissing him without notice or pay in lieu of notice (*Macari v Celtic Football and Athletic Co Ltd*[75]).

10.63 However, it does not follow that an employee who refuses to obey a lawful order may automatically be dismissed, any more than it can be said that an employee cannot be dismissed if he refuses to obey an order which is outside his contractual obligations, for the strict legal rights are only relevant in considering the 'lawfulness' of the dismissal, but not its fairness. Two employment tribunal decisions will illustrate this point. In *Wilson v IDR Construction Ltd*[76] the claimant was contractually bound to move from site to site in accordance with management instructions. He was asked to move to a new site, but refused, as his wife was ill, and he was having difficulty with his car. Although his refusal to obey a lawful and reasonable order would have entitled the employers to dismiss him at common law, the tribunal held that this was not an invariable rule so far as unfair dismissal law was concerned. The employers should have given him a chance to explain his refusal, taken into account the genuineness of the reason, the fact that he had never refused to change sites before, and that his refusal related only to that one day. In the circumstances, the dismissal was held to be unfair. On the other hand, in *Robinson v Flitwick Frames Ltd*[77] the claimant was dismissed following his refusal to work overtime, although he was not contractually bound to do so. All the other employees in his section worked the necessary overtime, and the claimant gave no satisfactory explanation for his refusal. The tribunal held that his dismissal was for 'some other substantial reason' and that the employers had acted reasonably in the circumstances, for it would have caused considerable problems if the claimant had to be employed on terms different from the other employees (see also *Farrant v Woodroffe School*, paras 3.24 and 17.153).

---

[73] [1973] IRLR 41, EAT.   [74] [1972] IRLR 109.   [75] [1999] IRLR 787.
[76] [1975] IRLR 260.   [77] [1975] IRLR 261.

10.64 If the employees are not prepared to give an undertaking that they will desist from future disruptive conduct, an employer may suspend them from work until they do so, and the employees, though willing to work, will not be entitled to remuneration for the period of suspension (*British Telecommunications plc v Ticehurst*[78]).

C. **Duty to Use Skill and Care**

10.65 The employee undertakes to perform his work competently, using reasonable skill and care. This, of course, must be combined with the employer's duty to provide all necessary assistance, etc (see para 10.13), but if the employer has done all he can, then a dismissal for incompetence will usually be fair. Also, the employee undertakes to take proper care of the employer's property. In *Superlux v Plaisted*[79] the employee negligently allowed some of his employer's property to be stolen from a van, for which he was held responsible. For a dismissal to be warranted, the act of negligence must be a serious one (*Comerford v Swel Foods Ltd*[80]) or a series of minor acts of neglect (*Lowndes v Specialist Heavy Engineering Ltd*,[81] para 17.82). It is an implied term of the contract of employment that an employee will exercise skill and care in the performance of his duties, and a breach of that term entitles the employer to claim damages in respect of the negligent performance of the contract. In *Janata Bank v Ahmed*,[82] the employee worked as a bank manager. It was alleged that he had been negligent in the way he carried out his duties, and after his dismissal, the bank issued a writ claiming £34,640 damages. The Court of Appeal upheld the claim. He had failed to exercise proper skill and care, as implied by his contract. It is irrelevant that the cause of action arises in contract or in tort (see *Lister v Romford Ice and Cold Storage Co Ltd*[83]).

D. **Secret Bribes and Commissions**

10.66 The employee undertakes not to accept any secret bribes or commissions or gifts, or any reward in respect of his work other than from his employer. This rule applies even though the employee is in no way influenced by the favours he has received, for there is always the possibility that there will be a suspicion that his conduct has been influenced, or that it might be affected in the future. Tips, however, are a recognised method of being paid, and do not constitute a bribe which must be disclosed. An employee can only serve one employer, and it will be inconsistent with his obligation of faithful service to accept anything from another person in respect of things done within the performance of his work. In *Boston Deep Sea Fishing and Ice Co v Ansell*[84] the defendant was a managing director of the claimant company. He placed orders for supplies with other companies, from whom he received a commission. It was held that his dismissal was justified. It is a violation of the duty of honest and faithful service for an employee to have an interest in a firm which is transacting business with his employer without disclosing that interest, and on discovering the facts, the employer is entitled to dismiss the employee summarily (*Horcal Ltd v Gatland*[85]).

10.67 The employer may also take steps to recover the amount of the bribe from the employee, and refuse to pay certain benefits which may be due (see *Tesco Stores Ltd v Pook*,[86] para 10.100).

---

[78] [1992] ICR 383, sub nom *Ticehurst and Thompson v British Telecommunications plc* [1992] IRLR 219, CA.
[79] [1958] CLY 195, *Times*, 12 December, CA.   [80] [1972] IRLR 17.
[81] [1977] ICR 1, [1976] IRLR 246, 8 BLR 76, EAT.   [82] [1981] ICR 791, [1981] IRLR 457, CA.
[83] [1957] AC 555, [1957] 1 All ER 125, HL.
[84] (1888) 39 Ch D 339, [1886–90] All ER Rep 65, 59 LT 345, CA.
[85] [1983] IRLR 459; on appeal [1984] IRLR 288, CA.   [86] [2004] IRLR 618, EAT.

10.68 The rule is easy to state, but in practice it may be hard to apply, for there is no simple line between acts which are part of social or business intercourse and bribery. No one is going to quibble if a salesman pays for a working lunch at a modest cafe for the firm's buyer. A a slap-up lunch at an expensive restaurant may fall into a different category. Some firms may anticipate this problem by laying down the standards of conduct expected from those in a position of authority who may be affected by the rule. Employees may be warned not to accept gifts from suppliers, not to accept hospitality which might have a significant value, or to allow others to pay travel or hotel bills on their behalf.

The issue of bribery has now been supplemented by legislation in the form of the Bribery Act 2010. While the details of the statute are outside the scope of this book, suffice it to say that it makes it a criminal offence for a person to bribe (s 1 active bribery) or receive a bribe (s 2 passive bribery). The Act has extraterritorial application, so that a bribe to a foreign public official can be prosecuted in the UK (s 6). It also makes it an offence for a commercial organisation to fail to prevent a bribe (s 7), but there is a defence if it can show that adequate procedures have been put in place to prevent bribery if these are necessary. Guidance on the Act can be found on the Justice website.

E. Confidential Information

10.69 There is a general rule that during the subsistence of the employment relationship, the employee must not disclose any confidential information about the employer's business to an unauthorised person. To do so will amount to a breach of contract, and a third party who induces an employee to break his contract of employment in this way may also be sued (see *Bents Brewery Co Ltd v Hogan*,[87] para 23.37). To determine whether or not the information is indeed confidential, three requirements must be satisfied, namely:

(a) the information must have the necessary quality of confidence;

(b) the information must have been imparted to the employee in circumstances which import an obligation of confidence; and

(c) there must have been an unauthorised use of the information to the detriment of the employer (*A-G v Guardian Newspapers (No 2)*[88]).

10.70 The disclosure of information such as the profitability of the business, new models or designs, modes of operation, etc, could seriously harm the employer's business. Thus in *Foster v Scaffolding (GB) Ltd*[89] the employee gave confidential information to a rival company which was to the disadvantage of his employer, and he was held to have been fairly dismissed. The unauthorised disclosure of trade secrets would also fall within this rule (*Lancashire Fires Ltd v s A Lyons & Co Ltd*[90]), and indeed information may well be so highly confidential as to amount to a trade secret (*PSM International plc v Whitehouse*[91]). But an employee's skill and knowledge are his own possessions, and are not subject to any such restrictions (*Printers and Finishers Ltd v Holloway*[92]).

10.71 It has been held that the employee is not released from this obligation even when the information has been obtained or published by a third party (*Cranleigh Precision Engineering Ltd v Bryant*[93]), although it seems likely that in such circumstances the quality

---

[87] [1945] 2 All ER 570.
[88] [1990] 1 AC 109, [1988] 3 All ER 545; aff'd [1990] 1 AC 109, [1988] 3 All ER 545, CA; aff'd [1990] 1 AC 109, [1988] 3 All ER 545, HL.   [89] (1973) (342/73) IDS Brief 13.
[90] [1999] 30 LS Gaz R 28, CA.   [91] [1992] FSR 489, [1992] IRLR 279, CA.
[92] [1964] 3 All ER 731.   [93] [1964] 3 All ER 289.

of confidence has been lost (*A-G v Guardian Newspapers (No 2)*, para 10.69). If, however an employee starts a new business with other employees who misuse confidential information without the first employee's knowledge, then she is not liable for that breach of confidence as she did not breach it (*Vestergaard Frandsen v Bestnet Europe Ltd*[94]).

10.72 If an employer discovers that an unidentifiable employee is leaking information to the press, he may be able to obtain a court order which will lead him to identify the person concerned (generally known as a 'whistle-blower'). Clearly, there is a conflict between the public interest which requires that the press shall protect the identity of its sources and the right of an employer to identify a disloyal employee, particularly when it is likely that that employee may disclose other sensitive information. In *Camelot Group plc v Centaur Communications Ltd*[95] the Court of Appeal set out certain principles which should be applied in such cases, but stressed that the resolution of such conflicts will very much depend on the facts of each case, ie the nature of the information disclosed, whether there is an allegation of wrongdoing, whether the information would eventually be in the public domain, etc. The law does not enable the press to protect the identity of a whistleblower in all circumstances.

10.73 However, there are some important exceptions to the rule against the non-disclosure of confidential information. Thus the rule will not apply if the employee is obliged by law to disclose the information. For example, an employee is under a legal duty to give any necessary information to an inspector carrying out an examination or investigation under the Health and Safety at Work etc Act 1974 (see Chapter 11) and to produce any necessary books or documents.

10.74 In recent years there has been a rise in the use of Non-Disclosure Agreements (NDAs)/confidentiality clauses, including those being used to cover up sexual harassment, racial discrimination and assault. Legislation is planned to prevent NDAs being used to prevent disclosure to certain professionals, such as the police and legal or health professionals, and to establish safeguards for such agreements.

The legislation is expected to:

a) Ensure employers make clear the limitations of a confidentiality clause, so those signing them understand what they are signing and their rights.

b) Extend current legislation so that individuals signing NDAs will get independent legal advice on the limitations of an agreement.

c) Introduce new enforcement measures to deal with illegal NDAs.

F. Public Interest Disclosures (ERA, ss 43A–43K)

10.75 Under the provisions of the Public Interest Disclosure Act 1998 (as amended by ss 17–20 of the Enterprise and Regulatory Reform Act 2013), generally known as the 'Whistle-blowers Act', or 'PIDA', which inserted ss 43A–43L into the Employment Rights Act, protection is given to a worker (a definition which is wider than that of 'employee', and indeed is wider than the definition of 'worker' contained in s 230(3), see ERA, s 43K), and includes claims by agency workers against end users—*McTigue v University Hospital Bristol NHS Foundation Trust*,[96] and even judges—*Gilham v Ministry of Justice* (paras 1.90 and 2.70)

---

[94] [2013] UKSC 31.   [95] [1999] QB 124, [1998] 1 All ER 251, [1998] IRLR 80, CA.
[96] UKEAT/0354/15.

who makes a protected disclosure to a specified individual in prescribed circumstances. The primary aim of the Act is to encourage the resolution of concerns through proper workplace procedures, and has a more limited application to a worker who decides to go outside those procedures. The Act is not limited to cases where the disclosure relates to a wrongdoing or failure by the whistleblower's employer, but includes the disclosure made about the wrongdoing of any person or organisation (*Hibbins v Hester Way Neighbourhood Project*[97]) including a detriment suffered as a result of a disclosure made about the activities of a previous employer (*BP plc v Elstone;*[98] *Onyango v Berkeley Solicitors*[99]).

10.76 There are three conditions to be satisfied for the Act to apply, namely (i) there must be a qualifying disclosure, (ii) the qualifying disclosure must be a protected disclosure, and (iii) the worker must have been dismissed or suffered a detriment in consequence of the disclosure.

10.77 (i) A qualifying disclosure must be one of the six categories of subject matter specified in ERA, s 43B, namely, any disclosure of information which, in the reasonable belief of the worker making it, tends to show one or more of the following:

(a) that a criminal offence has been committed, is being committed or is likely to be committed;

(b) that a person has failed, is failing or is likely to fail to comply with any legal obligation to which he is subject;

(c) that a miscarriage of justice has occurred, is occurring or is likely to occur;

(d) that the health or safety of any individual has been, is being or is likely to be endangered;

(e) that the environment has been, is being or is likely to be damaged; or

(f) that information tending to show any matter falling within any one of the preceding paragraphs has been, is being or is likely to be deliberately concealed.

10.78 The standard to be used when considering the above categories is the subjective one, ie the worker does not have to prove the existence of any of the above state of affairs; he merely has to show that he had a reasonable belief that this was so. He does not have to prove that some offence has actually been committed (*Baluba v Waltham Forest College*[100]). Clearly, if he fails to show that he had grounds for his belief, it may well be that a tribunal would find that his belief was not reasonable.

10.79 However the question under ERA s 103A is an objective one to be determined by the employment tribunal, so the decision-maker's belief about whether the disclosure is a protected one is therefore irrelevant (*Beatt v Croydon Health Services NHS Trust*[101]).

10.80 A disclosure will not be a qualifying disclosure if the worker commits an offence by making it (eg in breach of the Official Secrets Act), or if the information is covered by legal professional privilege. However, the substance of the disclosure can relate to matters which take place anywhere in the world.

10.81 (ii) A qualifying disclosure will be a protected disclosure if it is made in the reasonable belief of the worker making the disclosure, in the public interest, and in one of the six ways set out in the Act. In other words, the disclosure must be made through the

[97] [2009] 1 All ER 949, [2009] ICR 319, [2009] IRLR 198.   [98] [2010] IRLR 558.
[99] UKEAT/0407/12.   [100] (2007) ICR 1026, (2007) IRLR 346.   [101] [2017] EWCA Civ 401.

appropriate channels, set out in ss 43C–43H. Four of these categories are to named persons, while the further two categories are subject to more stringent conditions. The disclosure does not actually have to be in the public interest—it is sufficient if the worker reasonably believes that it is so. It does not have to be of interest to the whole public, but a relatively small group may be sufficient to satisfy the test, and the mere fact that something is in the worker's private interests does not mean it is not also in the public interest, but this depends on the facts of the case—*Chesterton Global Ltd v Nurmohamed*,[102] which laid out useful factors in deciding if it is in the public interest, by looking at:

(a) the numbers in the group whose interests the disclosure served;

(b) the nature of the interests affected and the extent to which they are affected by the wrongdoing disclosed—a disclosure of wrongdoing directly affecting a very important interest is more likely to be in the public interest than a disclosure of trivial wrongdoing affecting the same number of people;

(c) the nature of the wrongdoing disclosed—disclosure of deliberate wrongdoing is more likely to be in the public interest than the disclosure of inadvertent wrongdoing affecting the same number of people;

(d) the identity of the alleged wrongdoer, because the larger or more prominent the wrongdoer (in terms of the size of its relevant community, i.e. staff, suppliers, and clients), the more obviously should a disclosure about its activities engage the public interest, although this should not be taken too far.

10.82 The disclosure must be made to one of the following persons:

(a) to his employer, or, where the worker reasonably believes that the relevant failure relates solely or mainly to the conduct of a person other than his employer, or any other matter for which a person other than the employer has legal responsibility, to that other person;

(b) in the course of obtaining legal advice (eg to a solicitor);

(c) where the worker's employer is an individual appointed under any enactment by a minister of the Crown, or a body any of whose members are so appointed, a disclosure made to a minister of the Crown;

(d) a disclosure to a prescribed person, and the worker reasonably believes that the relevant failure falls within the prescribed category, and the information disclosed, and any allegation made, is substantially true. The persons (and bodies) to which disclosure may be made for this purpose include various regulatory bodies, local authorities, etc;

(e) in other cases, the worker must reasonably believe that the information disclosed, and any allegation contained in it, are substantially true, the disclosure is not made for personal gain, in the circumstances it was reasonable for him to make the disclosure, and it meets one of the following conditions, namely:

(i) that at the time he makes the disclosure, the worker reasonably believed that he would be subject to a detriment if he made the disclosure to his employer or to the prescribed person, or

(ii) where there is no person prescribed, the worker reasonably believes that evidence relating to the relevant failure will be concealed or destroyed if he makes the disclosure to his employer, or

---

[102] [2017] EWCA Civ 314.

(iii) the worker has previously made a disclosure to his employer or to a prescribed person of substantially the same information.

10.83 To decide whether or not it was reasonable for the worker to make the disclosure, the Act states that regard should be had to the identity of the person to whom the disclosure is made, the seriousness of the relevant failure, whether the failure is continuing or likely to occur in the future, whether the disclosure is made in breach of any duty of confidentiality owed by the employer to any other person, any action which the employer has taken which might reasonably be expected to have been taken as a result of a previous disclosure, and whether in making the disclosure to the employer the worker has complied with any procedure whose use by him was authorised by the employer.

(f) A disclosure will be protected if:

(i) the worker reasonably believes that the information disclosed, and any allegation made in it, are substantially true,

(ii) the disclosure is not made for personal gain,

(iii) the matter disclosed is of an exceptional serious nature, and

(iv) in all the circumstances, it was reasonable for the worker to make the disclosure.

10.84 A previous requirement for the disclosure to be made in good faith was removed by the ERRA 2013, although a tribunal has the power to reduce any compensation by up to 25% if it finds that a disclosure was made in bad faith. Thus when assessing compensation the whistleblower's motives for making the disclosure will be relevant. So, if he makes a disclosure because of some personal antagonism, or other improper motive, this will be evidence of a lack of good faith (*Street v Derbyshire Unemployed Workers' Centre*[103]). An employee is not protected by the whistleblowing provisions if he discloses information which he obtains by an illegal or wrongful act. In *Bolton School v Evans*[104] a teacher hacked into the school's computer system in order to demonstrate its poor security. When he was disciplined for doing so, he resigned and claimed constructive dismissal. His claim was rejected. The reason he was disciplined was not because he made a disclosure, but because he had committed an act of misconduct. There is also a distinction between giving information, which means conveying facts, and making allegations. The former comes within the whistleblowing provisions and the latter does not (*Cavendish Munro Professional Risks Management v Geduld*[105]), although it counts if the information given is also an allegation (*Kilraine v London Borough of Wandsworth*[106]).

10.85 (iii) A worker who makes a protected disclosure has the right not to suffer a detriment as a result of the disclosure. If he is an employee (but not a worker), he has the right not to be dismissed (or be made redundant) in consequence of the disclosure. Dismissal for whistleblowing can be a breach of the Article 10 right to freedom of expression (*Heinisch v Germany*[107]). It will also be automatically unfair to dismiss an employee because he made a protected disclosure covered by the Public Interest Disclosure Act (however the protected disclosure must be the sole or principal reason for the dismissal before it is deemed to be automatically unfair (*NHS Manchester v Fecitt*[108])). The two-year qualifying period of employment does not apply, and there is no ceiling on any compensation award. Interim relief is also available (ERA, s 128(1)(b)). If the worker is not an employee, he will have no

---

[103] (2007) ICR 1026, (2007) IRLR 346.
[104] [2006] IRLR 500; aff'd [2006] EWCA Civ 1653, [2007] ICR 641, [2007] IRLR 140, CA.
[105] [2010] ICR 325, [2010] IRLR 38.   [106] UKEAT/0260/15.   [107] [2011] IRLR 922.
[108] [2011] EWCA Civ 1190.

right to complain of unfair dismissal, but if he is in fact dismissed, he can claim that this amounts to a detriment.

10.86 In searching for the reason for a dismissal, courts need generally look only at the reason given by the decision-maker. But where the real reason is hidden from the decision-maker behind an invented reason, the court must penetrate through the invention (*Royal Mail Ltd v Jhuti*[109]).

10.87 The ERRA introduced a vicarious liability on an employer for a detriment committed by co-workers, or an agent of the employer, on the worker who has made a protected disclosure. It is immaterial whether the detriment was done with the knowledge or approval of the employer. There is a defence for an employer who is able to show that it took all reasonable steps to prevent the detrimental treatment.

10.88 Any agreement between the worker and his employer (including one which purports to settle legal proceedings) is void in so far as it precludes the worker from making a protected disclosure (s 43J).

10.89 The EAT gave a useful overview of the law relating to whistleblowing in *Dray Simpson v Cantor Fitzgerald Europe*.[110]

10.90 A new European Whistleblowing directive has been approved, but, because the future is currently uncertain because of Brexit, it is not yet known whether it will need to be implemented.

G. Patents, Inventions, and Copyright

10.91 The law relating to inventions made and patents taken out by employees was altered by the Patents Act 1977. According to s 39, an invention made by an employee shall belong to the employer if (a) it was made during the employee's normal duties, or if such duties were specifically assigned to him and in either case the circumstances were such that an invention might reasonably be expected to result from those duties, or (b) because of the employee's particular responsibilities, he has a special obligation to further the interests of the employer's undertaking (see *LIFFE Administration and Management v Pinkava*[111]). Any other invention made by an employee shall belong to him, notwithstanding any term to the contrary in the contract of employment (see *Reiss Engineering Co Ltd v Harris*[112]). Even if the invention belongs to the employer, the employee may apply to the Comptroller General of Patents (or Patents Court) for an award of compensation, which may be awarded if the patent is of outstanding benefit to the employer (having regard to the size and nature of the employer's undertaking) and it is just that compensation should be awarded. The amount of compensation should be a fair share of the benefit which the employer has derived, taking into account a number of factors, including (a) the nature of the employee's duties, his remuneration, etc, (b) the effort and skill provided by others, including any advice and assistance received from other employees, (c) the contribution made by the employer, whether by way of assisting in the manufacture, marketing, or other contribution, and (d) whether the invention has resulted in an outstanding benefit to the employer (s 40).

10.92 In *Kelly & Chui v GE Healthcare Ltd*[113] (believed to be the first reported successful claim under s 40 of the Patents Act 1977) two research scientists were involved in the

---

[109] [2019] UKSC 55.   [110] [2019] UKEAT 0016/18.
[111] [2006] EWHC 595 (Pat); aff'd [2007] EWCA Civ 217, [2007] 4 All ER 981, [2007] ICR 1489, CA.
[112] [1985] IRLR 232, EAT.   [113] [2009] EWHC 457 (Pat).

discovery of a compound, the patent of which was claimed by their employer, and which subsequently resulted in sales amounting to over £1bn. In a claim for 'just' compensation, the learned judge analysed the requirements of s 40, holding that 'outstanding benefit' meant something special, more than substantial or significant, and something more than one would normally expect to arise from the duties for which the employee is paid. The judge considered what the position of the company would have been had the patent not been granted, and compared this with the company's position with the benefit of the patent. In the circumstances of the case, the judge held that the patent had conferred an outstanding benefit, and made a 'just and fair' reward to the employees of £1m and £500,000 respectively.

10.93 If the invention belongs to the employee, he is free to dispose of it as he wishes. If he assigns his interest to his employer (whether by way of an assignment in the right to a patent, or a licensing arrangement, etc), then he is still entitled to apply for an award of statutory compensation, if he can show that the financial return he has received is inadequate in relation to the benefit derived from the patent by the employer and it is just that compensation should be paid in addition to the benefit received from the relevant contractual arrangement between the parties. Such compensation will amount to a fair share of the benefit which the employer has derived from the assignment or licence, taking into account, inter alia: (a) any condition granted in respect of the licence or the patent, (b) the extent to which the invention was made jointly by the employee and any other person, and (c) the contribution made by the employer in the making, developing, manufacturing, and marketing of the invention.

10.94 However, an award of compensation cannot be made if there is in force a relevant collective agreement which provides for payment of compensation for inventions made by employees. The collective agreement is only relevant if it is made by a trade union to which the employee belongs and by the employer, or an employers' association to which the employer belongs, and is in force at the time of the making of the invention. Non-unionists, therefore, may apply for compensation under the Act.

10.95 By the Copyright, Designs and Patents Act 1988, if the maker of a written work is employed under a contract of employment, the employer becomes the first owner of the copyright (s 11). This rule extends to literary, dramatic, musical, or artistic works, but it is subject to any agreement to the contrary. There are no provisions in this Act for employee compensation on the lines of the Patents Act 1977.

H. 'Moonlighting'

10.96 The employee is obliged not to act in any manner which is inconsistent with his duty of fidelity. In *Gibson v National Union of Dyers, Bleachers and Textile Workers*[114] a full-time trade union official worked in a mill during his holidays. There was clearly a conflict of interests between his union position and his spare-time employment, and his dismissal was only held to be unfair because of the manner in which it was done. Indeed, the practice of 'moonlighting' whereby an employee undertakes spare-time work outside his employment hours can raise problems, particularly if the work is in competition with the employer's business. In *Gray v C & P Pembroke Ltd*[115] the employee agreed not to be engaged in any other business without the written consent of his employer. Contrary to this agreement, he took a part-time job with a rival employer. As well as being in breach of an express term

[114] (1972) 13 KIR 143, [1972] ITR 324.   [115] (1972) (1350/72) IDS Brief 10.

of his contract, it was also a breach of fidelity, and his dismissal was held to be fair. On the other hand in *Frame v McKean & Graham Ltd*[116] the National Working Agreement for the Building Industry provided that no operative should undertake any jobbing work on his own account. This had never been enforced or referred to by the employer, and there was no mention of it in his contract of employment. The tribunal held that his dismissal for doing some work for a former customer of the firm was unfair, but the decision seems to rely heavily on the fact that the employer had, in the past, condoned his employees doing spare-time work, and even allowed them to purchase materials for this purpose.

10.97 In the absence of any contractual term, it appears that the employee may not work for a competitor in his spare time. In *Hivac Ltd v Park Royal Scientific Instruments Ltd*[117] an injunction was granted against the competitor restraining him from employing the claimant's employees who were making valves for him in their spare time. On the other hand, an employee cannot be restrained from working in a different business in his spare time which does not compete with his employer's business, provided, of course, that this does not interfere with his normal work.

10.98 An employee cannot undertake work for himself or for other persons during his working hours (*Wessex Dairies v Smith*[118]), nor can he use his employer's materials or equipment for his own purposes (ignoring matters which come within the *de minimis* rule). Thus if he uses the employer's facilities or equipment, or profits from work done by other employees under his supervision, this would amount to a breach of the duty of fidelity, and the employer would be entitled to an account of those profits (*University of Nottingham v Fishel*[119]).

I. Duty of Disclosure

10.99 An employee is under no duty to disclose to his employer facts which are inimical to the employer (except in response to a direct question), nor to disclose his own misconduct (*Bell v Lever Bros Ltd*[120]) or that of another employee (*High Court Lonmar Global Risks Ltd v West*[121]). However, if the employee acts fraudulently or dishonestly, particularly when acting on the employer's behalf in circumstances when trust and confidence are being reposed in him, then he is under a duty to disclose his own misconduct, and may be sued by the employer for any loss suffered as a direct result of that misconduct (*Item Software (UK) Ltd v Fassihi*, see para 8.11). Also, he is under a duty to disclose the misconduct of his subordinates even if, by doing so, he incriminates himself. In *Sybron Corpn v Rochem Ltd*,[122] a man called Roques was the European manager for Gamblem Chemical Co (UK) Ltd. During his employment, payments were made on his behalf by the company into a pension scheme, and on his retirement he received a lump sum payment. It was then discovered that Roques, together with several subordinates, had been conspiring to set up in direct competition with Gamblem, and the company sought restitution of the pension payments, claiming that under the rules of the pension scheme, Roques could have been dismissed for gross misconduct, and the payments would not have been made. The Court of Appeal held that the company was entitled to have the money repaid. As a senior executive, Roques was under a duty to report the continuing misconduct of his subordinates, and for this breach

---

[116] [1974] IRLR 179.   [117] [1946] Ch 169, [1946] 1 All ER 350, CA.
[118] [1935] 2 KB 80, [1935] All ER Rep 75, CA.
[119] [2000] ICR 1462, [2000] IRLR 471, [2000] All ER (D) 269.
[120] [1932] AC 161, [1931] All ER Rep 1, HL.   [121] [2011] IRLR 138.
[122] [1984] Ch 112, [1983] 2 All ER 707, [1983] ICR 801, [1983] IRLR 253, CA.

of duty he could have been dismissed summarily. The money was therefore paid under a mistake of fact, since, had Gamblem known about the breach, they could have invoked the rules of the pension fund.

10.100 An employee who takes a bribe or receives a secret commission is in breach of his duty of fidelity. The employer can recover the amount from the employee. Further, the employer would be entitled to refuse to pay certain benefits to the employee who is consequently dismissed because of taking a bribe, because there is an implied term in the contract of employment that such a breach would disentitle the employee to receive such benefits (eg share options) (*Tesco Stores Ltd v Pook*, para 10.67). The effect of this case and *Rochem* is to weaken the principle established in *Bell v Lever*.

10.101 A major problem will arise if an employee discovered a fraud or criminal offence being perpetrated within his employer's organisation. Should he report it and, if so, to whom? The police? The employer's lawyers? Senior management? Is there a duty of confidentiality which prevents reporting the fraud to persons outside the organisation, and is reporting a breach of confidence? Would the fear of job prospects being damaged be sufficient to amount to a defence in civil and/or criminal proceedings? Some answers to these questions were given in *RGB Resources plc v Rastogi*,[123] where a certified accountant was employed as a financial controller. The chief executive officer of the company and two other senior employees were implicated in the misappropriation of hundreds of millions of pounds of loan capital, and the company's liquidator took action against the directors and the financial controller for recovery of the money. For the liquidator, it was argued that as a senior executive, the defendant was under a duty to make enquiries about suspicious conduct of the other directors, and should have taken steps to prevent dishonest activities. Further, he should have disclosed these irregularities both internally and externally, but had failed to do so. It was held that the liquidator was entitled to recovery from the defendant. A senior employee is under a duty to investigate wrongdoings and, where appropriate, to make a full disclosure to internal auditors, the board of directors, or, if necessary, the police or financial watchdog. The precise course of action will have to vary in each case, but the more senior the employee the more serious the conduct in question, and the more serious the adverse effect on the employer's business is likely to be, the greater will be the duty to report and make a full disclosure to the proper person or authority.

10.102 The obligations of an employee who leaves their employment, or who is about to leave, will be considered in Chapter 19.

J. Absence Related to Unforeseen Events

10.103 Problems may arise when an employee is absent because of an unforeseen event, such as the disruption caused to international air travel in 2010 by the eruption of the Eyjafjallajökull volcano, that caused by snow or blankets of fog, or possibly those arising from a human cause, eg a terrorist attack or a spate of train strikes. More recently, of course there is the question of people having to self-isolate because of the coronavirus Covid-19). These events give rise to questions as to the rights and obligations of the employee and employer.

10.104 The starting point will always be the express provisions found in the contract of employment. For example, if an employee is to be paid by the hour, then he will only be entitled to be paid for those hours when he attends work, and his inability to get to work, however caused, will generally be irrelevant. If he is paid weekly or monthly, then he will

---

[123] [2004] All ER (D) 258 (Apr).

be entitled to be paid accordingly, as long as he is available for work. As well as contractual provisions, an employee could invoke custom and practice as a basis for his rights to be paid when absent from work (and in the Covid-19 case there is also the governmental advice that employers should voluntarily pay employees while they are obliged to self-isolate for the protection of others, although there is currently no obligation at the time of writing to do so unless someone is actually sick—para 10.1045).

10.105 Many employers will have terms that cover absences from work through illness, etc, and if there are problems arising, it is usually through the abuse of the system. For example, if the employee engages in hazardous activities outside working hours, eg rock climbing or violent sports, it is possible to reduce entitlement to sick pay in specified circumstances. But the general rule is that there is no implied term that an employee is entitled to pay whilst off work sick, even though the absence from work is not the fault of the employee. The employee must be able and willing to work, and if he is unable to attend work for a reason that is not covered by his contract, he loses his right to be paid for such absences. This will usually be done on a pro rata basis, based on the number of days lost in the calendar year (see Apportionment Act 1870, s 2, and *Miles v Wakefield Metropolitan District Council*[124]). In *Burns v Santander UK plc*[125] an employer was permitted to make deductions where a worker was ready and willing to perform his contract, but was remanded in custody as a result of his own actions. The EAT held that such a remand was avoidable, and so the employee was not entitled to his contractual pay. (It is submitted that the question remains open what the situation would be if he was acquitted of the offence—would a court still find that he had disabled himself from work?)

10.106 This is also true of the 'volcano' effect, which arises when the employee is unable to get to work through no fault of his own, eg, because flights from foreign destinations are cancelled, or strikes prevent trains from running, or violent demonstrations affect departures from tourist resorts, and so on. If an employee fails to turn up for work in such circumstances, then, whilst an employer might take a sympathetic view of the reasons for the absence, the employee is not entitled to be paid, unless, of course, he has been able to do some work remotely. The problem for the employer will be that any deduction from wages must be in accordance with the provisions of ss 13–15 of the Employment Rights Act 1996 (see para 8.5); otherwise the employee may have a claim for unlawful deduction from wages.

Employer's Vicarious Liability

10.107 If an employee commits a wrongful (ie tortious) act in the course of his employment which causes injury or damage to a third party, the employee will, of course, be personally liable. In addition, however, the employer may be vicariously liable to compensate that third party. Two reasons are usually adduced for this principle. The first is that the employer, having initiated or created the situation where the employee has been in a position to cause the harm, should properly bear the loss; the second is the more practical reason that the employee will usually be unable to meet any substantial claim for damages, whereas the employer will normally have the financial resources to do so, or, at least, will be insured against such contingencies.

10.108 There are also a number of exceptional circumstances where an employer will be liable for the tortious acts of his independent contractors; for example, if he authorises the

---

[124] [1987] AC 539, [1987] 1 All ER 1089, [1987] ICR 368, [1987] IRLR 193.
[125] [2011] IRLR 639 (see also para 8.13).

wrongful act, or where he has a responsibility to take care which cannot be delegated by employing someone else to do the work, eg if there is a hazardous task to be undertaken (see *Holliday v National Telephone Co*[126]). It is also true that in recent years the courts appear to be gradually extending this principle of legal liability, and to that extent the distinction between an independent contractor and an employee (discussed in Chapter 2) is becoming possibly less important than before. But the general rule remains as stated. It may be that a different principle applies if the activity of the sub-contractor damages property. In *Biffa Waste Services Ltd v Maschinenfabric GmbH*[127] it was held that the principle that an employer is liable for the negligence of a sub-contractor should be applied as narrowly as possible, and only where the operations concerned would be hazardous whatever precautions were taken. Note also that a union may also be liable for actions done by its lay officials in the course of performing their role (*Unite the Union v Nailard*[128]).

10.109 The major problem is to determine which acts are committed by the employee 'in the course of his employment', and there are a number of marginal situations which cause difficulty. It is clear that if the employer expressly authorises the wrongful act, he will be liable. Equally the employer will be liable if he authorises the act and the employee performs it in a wrongful manner, for this is the very essence of the legal principle under discussion. If the employer expressly forbids the act, he may still be vicariously liable if it can be shown that nonetheless the act was done in the scope of the employment, or for the purposes of the employer's business. In *Conway v George Wimpey & Co Ltd*[129] the employers issued instructions to their drivers that no person other than a fellow employee was permitted to ride as a passenger in their lorries. In breach of these instructions, a driver gave a lift to a non-employee, and the passenger was injured as a result of an accident. It was held that the employers were not liable, for the express prohibition had taken the act (of giving lifts) outside the scope of the employment. But in *Rose v Plenty*[130] the employers had made it clear that children were not allowed to travel on milk floats. In breach of this instruction, a milkman engaged a young boy to help him deliver and collect milk bottles, and as a result of negligent driving the boy was injured. The Court of Appeal held that the employers were nonetheless liable vicariously. The court distinguished cases like *Conway v George Wimpey & Co Ltd* on the ground that in the latter case, employees who disregarded instructions by giving lifts to unauthorised persons were acting outside the scope of their employment, because what they did was not for the purpose of the employers' business. In *Rose v Plenty*, the act (of giving a lift to an unauthorised person), although prohibited, was done for the purpose of the employers' business and hence was within the scope of the employment. Theft by an employee from the very container which he was instructed to fumigate was a risk reasonably incidental to the purpose for which he was employed, making it a sufficiently close connection between the employee's theft and the purpose of his employment (*Brink's Global Services Inc v Igrox Ltd*[131]).

10.110 The modern test is to concentrate on the closeness of the connection between the nature of the employment and the employee's wrongdoing (*Lister v Hesley Hall Ltd*). The idea of defining 'in the course of employment' by reference to an unauthorised or wrongful mode of doing an act authorised by the employer does not cope ideally with vicarious liability for intentional wrongdoing. Thus in *Fennelly v Connex South Eastern Ltd*[132] a ticket inspector assaulted a railway passenger following an argument. It was held that the act was committed

[126] [1899] 2 QB 392, [1895–99] All ER Rep 359, 15 TLR 483, CA.
[127] [2009] QB 725, [2008] EWCA 6.   [128] [2018] EWCA Civ 1203.
[129] [1951] 1 All ER 56, [1951] TLR 215, CA.
[130] [1976] 1 All ER 97, [1975] ICR 430, [1976] IRLR 483.
[131] [2011] IRLR 343, [2010] EWCA Civ 1207.   [132] [2001] IRLR 390, [2000] All ER (D) 2233, CA.

in the course of employment. The courts should look at the job in general terms, and not divide each step and task performed into categories and ask whether each was authorised. The test for vicarious liability is whether the tort is so closely connected with the employment, ie within what was authorised or expected of the employee, that it would be fair and just to hold the employer vicariously liable (*Gravil v Carroll*[133]). A finding of vicarious liability will only be made where there is a sufficiently close connection between the wrongdoing and the employment so that it would be fair and just to hold the employer vicariously liable. This can be distinguished from a situation where the employee's duties include an element of exercising authority and keeping order, such as a nightclub doorman. In *Mohamud v WM Morrison Supermarkets*,[134] however, vicarious liability was found where an employee of a supermarket petrol station was abusive to a customer, then followed him out of the service kiosk and violently attacked him. The Supreme Court said the 'close connection' test required a court to do two things: (1) the court had to look broadly at the nature of the job, in deciding whether the conduct was carried out in the course of employment; (2) it had to ask whether there was sufficient connection between the field of activities carried out by the employee for it to be just for the employer to be held responsible. On the facts of this case, the employee was going about his employer's business in trying to eject the customer, and the violence was a reinforcement of his doing so, and so it was fair to hold the employer vicariously liable as it was sufficiently closely connected to his job. In another case involving the same employer, the Supreme Court in *WM Morrison Supermarkets Plc v Various Claimants*,[135] overturning the decision of the Court of Appeal, found that it was not vicariously liable for the criminal actions of an employee, which in fact harmed the employer, who had taken steps to prevent such actions. The employee who had a grudge against the employer, had disclosed on the web the personal information of other employees, in breach of his duty of confidentiality and the DPA 1998.

10.111 If the employers permit the act, they cannot escape liability by prohibiting it from being done in a wrongful manner. In *Canadian Pacific Rly Co v Lockhart*,[136] the employers issued instructions that staff should not drive uninsured cars while on company business. One of their employees disregarded this prohibition, and, through negligent driving, injured the claimant. The employers were held to be vicariously liable. It was not the driving which was prohibited, and the prohibition merely limited the way in which the employee was to do his work. The same principle applies if the employee negligently performs his duties. In *Century Insurance Co Ltd v Northern Ireland Road Transport Board*,[137] a driver of a petrol lorry, whilst transferring petrol from his lorry to an underground storage tank at a garage, struck a match in order to light a cigarette. He then threw the match on the floor, and an explosion ensued. It was held that the employers were liable. He was doing that which he was employed to do, namely, deliver petrol, although he was negligent in the manner in which he was performing his work.

10.112 The fact that the employee is seeking to obtain a personal gain will not necessarily take his acts outside the course of his employment. In *Lloyd v Grace, Smith & Co*[138] a managing clerk of a firm of solicitors induced the claimant, a client of the firm, to sign some documents, which transferred the claimant's properties to him. The firm was held liable, even though they stood to obtain no personal gain from the wrongful act. The clerk was merely performing the class of duties for which he was employed. This principle was taken

---

[133] [2008] EWCA Civ 689, [2008] ICR 1222, [2008] IRLR 829.   [134] [2016] UKSC 1.
[135] [2020] UKSC 12.   [136] [1942] AC 591, [1942] 2 All ER 464, PC.
[137] [1942] AC 509, [1942] 1 All ER 491, HL.
[138] [1911] 2 KB 489, 104 LT 789, 27 TLR 409, CA; revsd [1912] AC 716, [1911–13] All ER Rep 51, 107 LT 531, 28 TLR 547, HL.

further in *Morris v CW Martin & Sons Ltd*[139] where the claimant took a fur to a furrier for cleaning. This was stolen by an employee whose duty it was to do the work, and the employers were held liable.

10.113 For the purpose of vicarious liability, an employer may be a 'deemed temporary employer'. In *Hawley v Luminar Leisure Ltd*[140] the claimant was visiting a nightclub when he was seriously injured by a doorman. The doorman was not employed by the nightclub, but by a security company to whom the nightclub had sub-contracted its security. It was held that the nightclub exercised sufficient practical control over the doorman to make it the deemed temporary employer for the purpose of vicarious liability. The doorman was subject to the nightclub's code of conduct, was generally supervised by the nightclub manager, and was given detailed instructions on where he should be stationed, who should be admitted, and what to do with troublesome customers.

10.114 One issue that arises is the situation where things happen, for example, at a work social event. The *High Court in Shelbourne v Cancer Research UK*[141] considered the extent of the duty of care at a Christmas party. The employer had undertaken a risk assessment which took account of the fact that alcohol would be consumed, and took action to restrict access to laboratories during and after the party. It was found that the employer was not vicariously liable, the court stating that 'the ascertainment of what social justice requires, which lies at the heart of the law on vicarious liability, is not a journey down a one-way street. The desirability of enabling those who have suffered injury at the hands of others to recover adequate financial compensation needs to be balanced against the wider social consequences which may ensue from achieving this result through the imposition of vicarious liability'. There were two questions which had to be answered: first, what field of activities had been entrusted to the employee; and second, whether the connection between that employment and the wrongful conduct sufficient to make the employer liable having regard to social justice. This can be contrasted with the Court of Appeal decision of *Bellman v Northampton Recruitment Ltd*,[142] where a managing director arranged an after-party at a different venue to the main Christmas party, and punched the claimant while drunk, causing serious injury. He was the directing mind and will of the company, with a wide remit, was responsible for the party himself and was in a supervisory role at the party. There was therefore sufficient connection and level of control which made it just that the company should be vicariously liable.

Harassment and Bullying

10.115 Statutory provisions relating to harassment are contained in the provisions of the Protection from Harassment Act 1997 and the Equality Act 2010. There is no statutory definition of bullying, but frequently such conduct will be associated with harassment, and there is a distinct overlap between the two concepts. Harassment, however, mainly occurs in relation to the protected characteristics, especially, but not limited to, sexual harassment, whereas bullying is indiscriminate, and can occur irrespective of a protected characteristic.

10.116 Civil liability for the tort of harassment is contained in s 1 of the Protection from Harassment Act 1997. The test is whether a reasonable person in possession of the same information would think that the course of conduct in question amounts to the harassment of another person. To amount to the statutory tort (a) the harassment must be intentional,

---

[139] [1966] 1 QB 716, [1965] 2 All ER 725, CA.   [140] [2005] EWCA Civ 18.
[141] [2019] EWHC 842.   [142] [2018] EWCA Civ 2214.

(b) the alleged offender must have known or ought to have known that he was harassing another person if a reasonable person in possession of such information at the time of the alleged conduct would so regard it, (c) the harassment includes alarming a person or causing distress, (d) there must be a course of conduct that involves harassment on at least two occasions, and (e) the same person must be the victim on each occasion.

10.117 It has been suggested that to determine whether harassment has occurred for the purpose of civil proceedings, the test is whether the gravity of the alleged misconduct would sustain criminal liability under s 2 of the Act (*Majrowski v St Thomas's NHS Trust*[143]), but this is not essential, for the courts are well able to recognise the boundaries between conduct that was unattractive, even unreasonable, and conduct that was oppressive and unacceptable (*Conn v Sunderland City Council*[144]).

10.118 In *Veakins v Kier Islington Ltd*[145] a claim for damages for harassment succeeded, albeit the employer did not seek to challenge the employee's evidence, and did not dispute vicarious liability. The victimisation and demoralisation recounted by the claimant, which reduced her to a state of clinical depression, crossed the line into conduct that was oppressive and unacceptable. The fact that a prosecutor would be reluctant to prosecute was not a conclusive factor, given the unchallenged evidence of the claimant. However, it was suggested that in the great majority of cases the remedy for high-handed or discriminatory conduct by or on behalf of an employer would be more fittingly dealt with in the employment tribunal.

10.119 As we have seen (see para 4.33) s 26 of the Equality Act provides that harassment is a prohibited conduct in a general sense, and in particular when it is harassment of a sexual nature. There is the further provision in s 40 of the Act, which is designed to prevent harassment by an employer towards his employees and towards job applicants.

10.120 There are some differences between liability for harassment under the Equality Act and a claim under the Protection from Harassment Act when an employer is faced with a claim based on vicarious liability. Under the latter Act, the statutory defence that the employer took all reasonable steps to prevent an employee from doing the act in question does not apply, and the only defence is whether it would be just and equitable to hold an employer vicariously liable. The limitation periods are not the same.

10.121 There is no statutory definition or judicial guidance on what bullying consists of. In its advisory leaflet 'Bullying and harassment at work', ACAS defines bullying as 'offensive, intimidating, malicious or insulting behaviour, an abuse or misuse of power through means intended to undermine, humiliate, denigrate or injure the recipient'. Signs of bullying may be overt or subtle. Examples include exclusion from meetings, being overloaded with work, persistent criticisms, the spreading of false or malicious rumours, being insulted, being humiliated, the threat of or infliction of physical force, and so on. For example, in *Green v DB Group Services (UK) Ltd*[146] the bullying levelled against the claimant consisted of withdrawing her name from circulation lists, withholding her post, laughing at her, and making crude comments in her direction, thus interfering with her work with the purpose of undermining her. It was held that the bullying took place in the course of employment, and the employer was vicariously liable.

10.122 Whereas liability for harassment would normally be dealt with under the various statutory provisions outlined earlier, with claims being made to an employment tribunal,

---

[143] [2006] UKHL 34, [2007] 1 AC 224, [2006] 4 All ER 395, [2006] ICR 1199, [2006] IRLR 695.
[144] [2007] EWCA Civ 1492, [2008] IRLR 324.   [145] [2009] EWCA Civ 1288, [2010] IRLR 132.
[146] [2006] EWHC 1898 (QB), [2006] IRLR 764.

liability for bullying would be determined by the general principles which govern the duty of the employer to ensure the health, safety, and welfare of his employees. Bullying can cause a number of illnesses associated with mental health and psychological problems, including stress, depression, panic attacks, anxiety, loss of confidence, and so on. The test is whether the employer knew, or ought to have known, of the existence of the state of affairs that gave rise to the illness, and whether the illness was itself reasonably foreseeable (*Banks v Ablex Ltd*[147]).

10.123 There is ample legal protection available. Under the Health and Safety at Work etc Act the employer has a duty to ensure, so far as is reasonably practicable, the health, safety, and welfare of his employees, and, in particular, to maintain a working environment that is safe. Under the Management of Health and Safety at Work Regulations 1999, an employer must carry out an assessment of the risks to which employees are exposed whilst they are at work. The employer is also under a duty to maintain the relationship of trust and confidence, and to permit bullying to take place without taking steps to investigate or prevent it will undoubtedly seriously damage the relationship of trust and confidence that must exist between the parties. There is an implied term in the contract of employment that the employer would take such steps as were reasonable to support an employee without the latter being subjected to bullying or disruption from colleagues (*Wigan Borough Council v Davies*[148]). A failure to provide such support could give rise to a claim based on constructive dismissal.

Summary

- There are contractual duties and obligations on both employers and employees.
- On employers there is a duty of implied trust and confidence, to provide work, to pay when there is not work, confidentiality, to ensure safety, etc.
- On employees there is a duty of faithful service, to obey lawful and reasonable orders, to use skill and care and not to disclose confidential information.
- The Public Interest Disclosure Act 1998 protects workers who 'blow the whistle', ie make protected disclosures.
- An employer is vicariously liable if an employee commits a wrongful act in the course of his employment.

---

[147] [2005] EWCA Civ 173, [2005] ICR 819, [2005] IRLR 357.   [148] [1979] ICR 411, [1979] IRLR 127.

11

Health and Safety at Work

Background

11.1 This chapter considers the rules and obligations on employers to keep staff safe. Health and safety law spans both criminal liability, predominantly enforced under the Health and Safety at Work Act 1974 (HASAWA), and the civil liability and duty of care of the employer. The latter can be under the tort of negligence, or various statutory instruments. Under criminal liability, an employer can be prosecuted and punished, whereas successful civil proceedings can lead to payment of damages/compensation to the aggrieved person.

Health and Safety at Work etc Act 1974

A. **Background to the Legislation**

11.2 As a result of the recommendations of the Robens Committee, the Health and Safety at Work etc Act 1974 (HAWASA) was passed. In considering the then existing laws and practices relating to health and safety, the Committee came to a number of interesting conclusions. It found that in fact there was too much law, that much of it was unsatisfactory and unintelligible, and there was overlapping jurisdiction between those bodies whose task it was to enforce the law. The result of this was that there was a general feeling of apathy in the day-to-day implementation of safety rules, and little interest was shown in the subject. The Health and Safety at Work Act thus lays down the general legal obligations of all concerned in a single enactment, with the enforcement under the control of a unified administration. The old laws (Factories Act 1961, Offices, Shops and Railway Premises Act 1963, etc) were progressively repealed and replaced by regulations and approved codes of practice which are designed to maintain and improve the standards of health, safety, and welfare. Two further reviews of the subject, by Lord Young in 2010 and Professor Löfstedt in 2011, called for changes to the system, many of which were accepted by the government. It is expected that the amount of legislation related to health and safety will be reduced or consolidated in the coming years.

11.3 The 1974 Act applies to people, not to premises. It covers all employed persons (with the exception of domestic workers), wherever they work, and brought within the orbit of safety legislation an additional 7,000,000 employees who were hitherto outside the protection of statutory rules. In addition, the Health and Safety (Training for Employment) Regulations 1990 apply the provisions of the Act to trainees on government sponsored training schemes as if they were employees. The Act also applies to people who are not employees, in so far as they may be affected by activities which are being carried on in places of work. The Deregulation Act 2015 has since taken away the liability of self-employed persons from health and safety legislation unless they conduct an 'undertaking of a prescribed description'. Regulations clarify the types of undertakings.

11.4 HASAWA applies to all employment situations, including (with appropriate modifications) to offshore installations and pipelines within UK territorial waters and areas designated under the Continental Shelf Act 1964, including construction work and diving activities. The Police (Health and Safety) Act 1997 applies the provisions of the Act to holders of the office of constable, even though they are not technically employees (Police (Health and Safety) Regulations 1999).

11.5 Next, it will be noted that obligations are placed on employers in their different capacities as manufacturers, suppliers, and importers of articles and substances to be used at work, to ensure that these can be used in safety and without risk to health. Health and safety has to be built into the design and manufacturing stages.

11.6 The emphasis of the Act is on criminal sanctions and enforcement of the law, for the Act itself (unlike some of the regulations made under the Act) does not give rise to questions of civil liability. The number of prosecutions is small compared with the number of offences revealed by inspections, for the emphasis is on co-operation rather than compulsion. In addition, however, the issuing of improvement and prohibition notices has been widely exercised, and these often have very positive effects.

11.7 Finally, there are a number of provisions designed to bring about a greater awareness by all concerned of the need to promote safety and health at work, and thus provide the impetus to the greater self-regulatory system which the Robens Committee thought to be desirable.

11.8 We can examine the provisions of the Act under five headings.

B. **Enforcement of the Act**

11.9 The overall responsibility for supervising and administering the law on health and safety lies with the Health and Safety Executive (see para 1.59), together with enforcement officers (usually designated Environmental Health Officers) of local authorities. Neither the Secretary of State nor the HSE can instruct an enforcement officer to enforce any particular provision or institute proceedings in any particular case.

Powers of Inspectors

11.10 All enforcing authorities will appoint inspectors, who will have the following powers:

(a) at any reasonable time, or, if there is a dangerous situation, at any time, to enter premises;

(b) to take with him a constable if he has reasonable cause to apprehend any serious obstruction in the execution of his duty;

(c) to take with him any other authorised person and any equipment or materials required for any purpose for which the power of entry is being exercised;

(d) to make such examination and investigation as may be necessary;

(e) to direct that any premises shall be left undisturbed so long as is reasonably necessary for the purpose of examination or investigation;

(f) to take such measures and photographs and make such recordings as he considers necessary;

(g) to take samples of any articles or substances found in any premises and of the atmosphere in, or in the vicinity of, such premises. The Secretary of State may make regulations concerning the procedure to be adopted in such cases;

(h) in the case of any article or substance likely to cause danger to health or safety, to cause it to be dismantled or subjected to any process or test, but not to damage or destroy it unless it is for the purpose of exercising his powers. If the person who has responsibilities in relation to those premises is present, and so requests, the inspector shall exercise this power in that person's presence, unless he considers that it would be prejudicial to the safety of the state to do so. In any case, before exercising these powers, he must consult with appropriate persons for the purpose of ascertaining what dangers, if any, there may be in doing what he proposes to do;

(i) in the case of any article or substance likely to cause danger to health or safety, to take possession of it, and detain it for so long as is necessary in order to examine it, to ensure it is not tampered with before he has completed his examination, and to ensure that it is available for use as evidence in any proceedings for an offence, or in respect of matters arising out of the issuing of an improvement notice or a prohibition notice. He must leave a notice giving particulars of the article or substance, stating that he has taken possession of it, and, if practicable to do so, leave a sample with a responsible person;

(j) if conducting an examination or investigation under (d) above, to require any person whom he has reasonable cause to believe to be able to give any information to answer such questions as the inspector thinks fit to ask, and to sign a declaration of the truth of his answers;

(k) to require the production of, inspect, and take copies of any entry in any books or documents which are required to be kept, and any other book or document which it is necessary for him to see for the purpose of any examination or investigation under (d), above;

(l) to require any person to afford him such facilities and assistance within that person's control or responsibilities as are necessary for him to exercise his powers;

(m) any other power which is necessary for the purpose of exercising any of the above powers.

Improvement Notices (s 21)

11.11 If an inspector is of the opinion that a person is contravening one or more relevant statutory provisions, or has done so, and the contravention is likely to be continued or repeated, he may serve on him an improvement notice, stating that opinion, specifying the relevant statutory provision, giving reasons why he is of that opinion, and requiring that person to remedy the contravention within such period as may be specified in the notice, but not less than 21 days (ie the period in which an appeal may be made—see later in the section).

Prohibition Notices (s 22)

11.12 In respect of any activity covered by a relevant statutory provision, if the inspector thinks that those activities are carried on or are likely to be carried on so as to involve a risk of serious personal injury, the inspector may serve a prohibition notice. This will state his opinion, specify the provisions which give rise to that opinion, and direct that the activities to which the notice relates shall not be carried on by or under the control of that person on whom the notice was served unless the matters specified and any associated contravention are remedied. This direction takes effect at the end of the period specified in the notice or, if the notice so declares, immediately. Prohibition notices can be issued on persons, eg for a failure to wear protective eye shields. Activities are being carried on for the purpose of s 22 even though they are temporarily suspended (eg because of an accident). If there is a possibility that the activities may be resumed, the inspector is entitled to issue a prohibition notice requiring remedial action prior to the recommencement of those activities (*RailTrack plc v Smallwood*[1]).

11.13 In the case of an improvement notice or a prohibition notice, the notice may include directions as to the measure to be taken to remedy the contravention, which may be by reference to any approved code of practice or afford a choice between different ways of remedying the contravention. However, in respect of an improvement notice relating to a building, this cannot impose more onerous requirements than those imposed by the building regulations unless there is a statutory provision to the contrary. Also, if the notice relates to the means of escape in the event of fire, the inspector must engage in prior consultations with the fire authorities. Any improvement notice or a deferred prohibition notice may be withdrawn by the inspector before the expiry of 21 days, and may also be extended by the inspector at any time when an appeal is not pending.

Appeals Against Improvement or Prohibition Notices (s 24)

11.14 An appeal from the imposition of an improvement notice or a prohibition notice may be made to the employment tribunal, which can cancel or affirm it, or affirm it with such modifications as the tribunal thinks fit. For the purpose of hearing such appeals, the tribunal may include assessors specially appointed to sit with the regular members. Once an appeal has been lodged, this will suspend the operation of the improvement notice until such time as the appeal is disposed of or withdrawn; in the case of a prohibition notice, however, the lodging of an appeal will only suspend it if the tribunal so directs, and then only from the time it does so direct.

11.15 An appeal against an improvement notice or a prohibition notice can be made on a number of grounds.

11.16 First, it could be argued that there is no breach of a statutory duty. To determine this, a tribunal may refer to any relevant code of practice and guidance note. In *Sutton & Co Ltd v Davies*[2] the employers were in breach of s 13 of the Factories Act 1961 in not guarding transmission machinery. They appealed against an improvement notice, arguing that they had operated for 27 years without an accident. The appeal was dismissed, for the requirements of the Act are absolute. But in *Brewer & Sons v Dunston*[3] the inspector issued a prohibition notice on a machine. No accident had occurred in 18 years of use, and the tribunal held that there was no evidence to support the contention that there was risk of imminent danger. The distinction is that for an improvement notice, the sole issue is whether or not there has been a breach of a statutory provision, whereas a prohibition notice is concerned with whether there is a risk of serious personal injury.

11.17 Second, an appeal may be against the time limit imposed for remedying the defect, and there the tribunal may consider any serious embarrassment which may be caused to the company, and may take into account any history of recorded accidents at the firm. A company with a good record may well be given an extension of time so as to maintain production, so long as there is no immediate risk of danger or injury, and there is a willingness to make the appropriate modifications.

11.18 A third ground for appeal may be based on the absence of any risk or danger. In *South Surbiton Co-operative Society v Wilcox*,[4] a cracked washbasin was made the subject of an improvement notice. It was argued that the breach was trivial, there was little risk to

---

[1] [2001] EWHC Admin 78, [2001] ICR 714, [2001] 09 LS Gaz R 40, 145 Sol Jo LB 52, [2001] All ER (D) 103 (Jan).   [2] Unreported.   [3] Unreported.   [4] [1975] IRLR 292.

health, and there must be many employers who are similarly in breach and who have not been served with improvement notices. Nonetheless, the notice was confirmed by the tribunal. The requirements of the Act were absolute.

11.19 But in *Associated Dairies Ltd v Hartley*,[5] an improvement notice required the company to issue safety shoes free of charge to employees. In the previous year, one employee had been injured when the wheel of a truck ran over his foot. The company employed 1,000 employees, with a high turnover. Free footwear would have cost £20,000 in the first year. The tribunal held that the expense of providing protective footwear was disproportionate to the risk, and the notice was cancelled. In this case, the Act only required the employer to do that which was reasonably practicable.

11.20 A final ground for appeal may be based on the financial inability of the employer to comply with the order. Such an appeal is doomed from the start. In *TC Harrison (Newcastle-under-Lyme) Ltd v Ramsey*,[6] the company appealed against an improvement notice which required them to paint and clean the walls of a factory, in accordance with s 1 of the Factories Act 1961. It was stated that their financial position was precarious due to difficult trading conditions, but the employment tribunal had no hesitation in confirming the notice. To do otherwise would be to allow a firm to keep its charges low so as to undercut competitors, thus obtaining an unfair advantage over those who complied with the legal requirements. An employer cannot be relieved of his statutory duties because of financial difficulties.

11.21 Unlike other proceedings before employment tribunals, appeals against improvement and prohibition notices may result in an order for costs being made against the unsuccessful party. Such an order is entirely at the discretion of the tribunal, who may take into account the conduct of the party in failing to remedy the breach, and the hopelessness or otherwise of the appeal (see Employment Tribunals (Constitution and Rules of Procedure) Regulations 2004, Sch 4). In *South Surbiton Co-operative Society v Wilcox* (see para 11.18) no order for costs was made, as the tribunal considered that the breach was trivial.

11.22 A failure to observe the requirements of a prohibition or improvement notice is a criminal offence, and it is no defence in criminal proceedings to argue that the employer has done all that is reasonably practicable to comply. The proper forum in which to argue questions of practicability is the employment tribunal (*Deary v Mansion Hide Upholstery Ltd*[7]).

11.23 An appeal against a decision of an employment tribunal relating to a prohibition or improvement notice must be made to the Divisional Court. The reason is that the failure to comply with such notices is a criminal offence and the EAT, which would normally hear appeals from employment tribunals, is only concerned with civil matters.

Crown Notices

11.24 Because there is a rule of law that the Queen cannot be prosecuted in her own courts, it is not possible to enforce prohibition and improvement notices against Crown organisations, even though they employ large numbers of employees in various government departments. Consequently, the HSE devised the Crown Notice, which will be issued when a prohibition or improvement notice would be appropriate. Such notices have only a moral sanction, but are designed to draw attention to potential hazards, and, as copies are to be given to employees' representatives, will naturally attract publicity. A number of such notices are issued annually, requiring the same action from Crown employers as

---

[5] [1979] IRLR 171.   [6] [1976] IRLR 135.   [7] [1983] ICR 610, [1983] IRLR 195.

do prohibition and improvement notices issued to other employers. If there is a failure to comply, HSE can issue a censure notice, which is a formal recording that, but for Crown immunity, the evidence would have been sufficient to provide a realistic prospect of a conviction in the courts, and prosecution would have been in the public interest.

Power to Deal with Imminent Danger (s 25)

11.25 If the inspector finds on any premises any article or substance which he has reasonable cause to believe is a cause of imminent danger of serious personal injury, he may seize it and cause it to be rendered harmless whether by destruction or otherwise. Before doing so, if it is practicable for him to do so, he will give a sample with an identifiable mark to a responsible person. Thereafter, he will prepare and sign a report giving particulars of the circumstances, and give a copy to a responsible person at those premises, and also to the owner.

Enforcement Powers of the Court (s 42)

11.26 Where a person is convicted of an offence under any relevant statutory provision, the court may, in addition to, or instead of, imposing any punishment, order him to take such steps as may be specified in the order to remedy the matters specified, within such time as may be fixed. Failure to do so may amount to contempt of court, but an application may be made for an extension of the time limit. During the period given to remedy matters, the person cannot be liable for a failure to observe the provisions. After that time, if he continues with the contravention, he can be sentenced to six months' imprisonment and/or fined up to £20,000 in the magistrates' courts (this fine is unlimited for offences committed after 12 March 2015), or up to two years' imprisonment and/or an unlimited fine in the Crown Court.

11.27 If a person is charged with an offence in connection with the acquisition of explosives, the court may order the article or substance in question to be forfeited and either destroyed or dealt with as the court so orders. However, such order cannot be made unless the court gives the owner or any other interested party an opportunity to be heard.

C. Statutory Duties on Health, Safety, and Welfare

11.28 In general, there are three sets of guiding rules which will govern the operation of the law. The first of these is the general duties laid down in ss 2–9, and which must be observed by the specified persons. The second will be the regulations, which will supplement the law. The third will be the Codes of Practice issued and approved from time to time. It must be borne in mind that a breach of the general duties laid down in ss 2–9 of the Act is a criminal offence, and does not give rise to civil proceedings (s 47), whereas a breach of the regulations will be actionable civilly if the regulations themselves provide for this. However, by the Civil Evidence Act 1968, s 11 any conviction for a criminal offence is admissible in civil proceedings as evidence that the person so convicted committed the offence, and therefore, a claimant may point to the conviction as being relevant to the issue of civil liability.

11.29 Some of the duties are absolute ones, which means that the person on whom the duty is placed must carry it out. Others are preceded by the words 'so far as is reasonably practicable'. This is a somewhat lesser standard. The employer must weigh, on the one hand, the time, trouble, expense, etc of meeting that duty against the risks involved and the nature of the obligation on the other hand. Also, the duty can only be performed against the background of current knowledge which the employer knows, or ought to know. However, in *Marshall v Gotham Co Ltd*[8] it was suggested that a precaution which

---

[8] [1954] AC 360, [1954] 1 All ER 937, HL.

was practicable would not lightly be held to be unreasonable. In other words, a duty or obligation must be performed or carried out unless it would be unreasonable to do so. Further, s 40 of the Act states that in any proceedings for a failure to comply with a duty or requirement, it will be for the accused to prove that it was not reasonably practicable to do more than was in fact done.

11.30 The fact that the duty on UK employers to ensure the health, safety, and welfare at work of all employees was imposed 'so far as is reasonably practicable' did not infringe the European Directive 89/391/EEC (*Commission of the European Communities v United Kingdom*[9]). The ECJ pointed out that Art 5(1) of the Directive does not impose no-fault liability for all accidents in the workplace. Article 5(4) provides that member states can exclude or limit the employer's responsibility where occurrences are due to unusual or unforeseeable circumstances beyond the employer's control, or to exceptional events the consequences of which could not be avoided despite the exercise of all due care.

Duties of the Employer

Duties Owed to His Employees (s 2)

11.31 It shall be the duty of every employer to ensure, so far as is reasonably practicable, the health, safety, and welfare at work of all his employees. In particular, the employer must:

(a) provide and maintain plant and systems of work that are, so far as is reasonably practicable, safe and without risks to health;

(b) make arrangements for ensuring, so far as is reasonably practicable, safety and absence of risks to health in connection with the use, handling, storage, and transport of articles and substances (see *Page v Freight Hire (Tank Haulage) Ltd*[10]);

(c) ensure the provision of such information, instruction, training, and supervision as is necessary to ensure, so far as is reasonably practicable, the health, safety, and welfare at work of his employees. If an employee has a limited command of the English language, there is need for a greater degree of training, instruction, and supervision (*Tasci v Pekalp of London Ltd*[11]). The employer must also give such information etc to his employees and to persons who are not his employees (eg to sub-contractors and their employees) if this is necessary to ensure the health and safety of the employees of the employer (*R v Swan Hunter Shipbuilders Ltd*[12]);

(d) so far as is reasonably practicable as regards any place of work under his control, ensure the maintenance of it in a condition that is safe and without risks to health, and the maintenance of means of access and egress from it that are safe and without such risks;

(e) ensure the provision and maintenance of a working environment for his employees that is, so far as is reasonably practicable, safe, without risks to health, and adequate as regards facilities and arrangements for their welfare at work.

11.32 So far as these duties are concerned, it will be noted that they bear a strong resemblance to the common law duties of care (see para 11.80), spelt out, perhaps, in greater detail. An employer is only responsible for premises over which he has actual control, but that does not absolve him from the duty of ensuring a safe system of work on the premises

---

[9] [2007] IRLR 720.   [10] [1981] 1 All ER 394, [1981] ICR 299, [1981] IRLR 13.
[11] [2001] ICR 633, [2000] All ER (D) 2157, CA.
[12] [1982] 1 All ER 264, [1981] ICR 831, [1981] IRLR 403, CA.

of another (*General Cleaning Contractors Ltd v Christmas*[13]). The duty to provide a safe working environment would cover noise, fumes, heat, etc; welfare at work is not defined, but would presumably cover washing and toilet facilities, drinking water, and possibly eating arrangements.

Written Safety Policy (s 2(3))

11.33 Except for employers who employ fewer than five employees (see *Osborne v Bill Taylor of Huyton Ltd*[14] and Employers' Health and Safety Policy Statements (Exception) Regulations 1975) it shall be the duty of every employer to prepare and revise as often as is appropriate a written statement of his general policy with respect to the health and safety at work of all his employees, and the organisation and arrangements for the time being in force for carrying out that policy, and to bring this statement to the notice of all his employees. The Act does not give any guidance on the contents of this written statement, for the object of the exercise is for each employer to sit down and think about his own safety problems and work out the necessary solutions. Clearly, this would prove to be without value if the employer merely copied out a draft scheme drawn up by someone else.

11.34 It is suggested, however, that the safety policy should at least deal with the responsibility of all employees, including the board of directors, all levels of management, supervisors and operatives, inspection procedures, arrangements for dealing with special hazards, emergency arrangements including fire drill, the provision and use of safety precautions generally, supervision, training, research, and consultative arrangements. In drawing up the safety policy, it may be sound procedure to seek advice from the Commission, the Executive, and employers' associations, and to consult with trade union representatives, but it must be stressed that the statement is not a joint consultative document, but one for which the employer has ultimate responsibility. The Act requires the statement to be brought to the notice of all employees, but no guidance is given on how this is to be done. It would clearly not be sufficient to place the statement on the notice board and hope that work people will read it as they go past, and so the more formal channels of written communication should be used. If it is known that a particular employee does not read English, presumably some other way must be found of bringing it to his notice. The employer is obliged to revise the written statement as often as may be appropriate, and it should be looked at once a year at least in the light of practical experience of operating the safety policy, and taking into account any suggestions which might be received.

Safety Representatives and Safety Committee (s 2(4), (6), (7))

11.35 A trade union which is recognised by an employer may appoint safety representatives from among the employees in respect of whom the union is recognised (*Cleveland County Council v Springett*[15]). The persons appointed need not themselves be members of the union.

11.36 The legal requirements are contained in the Safety Representatives and Safety Committees Regulations 1977 (as amended) and a Code of Practice issued and approved by the former Health and Safety Commission. An independent trade union shall notify the employer in writing of the name of the safety representative, who shall hold the appointment until the union terminates it, or he ceases to be employed at the workplace, or resigns. So far as is reasonably practicable, he shall have been employed by that employer for the preceding two years, or have had at least two years' experience in similar employment.

---

[13] [1953] AC 180, [1952] 2 All ER 1110, HL.   [14] [1982] ICR 168, [1982] IRLR 17, DC.
[15] [1985] IRLR 131, EAT.

11.37 An employer has a duty to consult with safety representatives over a wide range of issues, with a view to making and maintaining arrangements which will enable him and his employees to co-operate effectively in promoting and developing measures to ensure the health and safety at work of employees, and checking the effectiveness of those measures (s 2(6)). In particular, there shall be consultation about the introduction of measures which may substantially affect the health and safety of employees, the arrangements for appointing or nominating the safety assistant, the provision of health and safety information, the planning and organisation of health and safety training, and the health and safety consequences of the introduction of new technologies (Management of Health and Safety at Work Regulations 1999).

Additionally, the safety representative has the following functions:

(a) to investigate the potential hazards and dangerous occurrences at the workplace, and to examine the causes of accidents;

(b) to investigate complaints by any employee he represents relating to that employee's health, safety, or welfare at work;

(c) to make representations to the employer about these matters;

(d) to make representations to the employer on general matters affecting the health, safety, and welfare at work of the employees at the workplace;

(e) to carry out inspections (see para 11.39);

(f) to represent employees in consultations with inspectors of the Health and Safety Executive;

(g) to receive information from the inspectors; and

(h) to attend meetings of safety committees in his capacity as safety representative.

11.38 In order to perform these functions adequately, the employer shall permit the safety representative to have time off work with pay during his working hours, and also for the purpose of undergoing training in aspects of those functions as may be reasonable in the circumstances (see *White v Pressed Steel Fisher*[16]). To determine what is reasonable in the circumstances, regard must be had to HSE's Code of Practice. Factors to be taken into account include the contents of the course and how it relates to the particular health and safety function of the employee, and whether the training would assist him in performing those functions. The test is whether the training is reasonable in all the circumstances, not whether it was necessary (*Duthie v Bath & North East Somerset Council*[17]). The safety representative is entitled to be paid his normal earnings or average hourly earnings.

11.39 Safety representatives are entitled to carry out an inspection of the workplace at least every three months (or more frequently with the employer's consent), and also further inspections if there has been some substantial change in the conditions of work (eg by the introduction of new working processes, or the coming to light of new information disclosing a potential hazard). Inspections may also be carried out after a notifiable accident has occurred or a notifiable disease contracted, for the purpose of determining the cause. The employer shall provide reasonable facilities and assistance, but he, or his representative, may be present during the inspection.

11.40 The employer shall establish a safety committee when at least two safety representatives make such a request. For this purpose, he shall consult with these representatives, and also those of any recognised trade unions. A notice must be posted stating the composition of the committee, which must be established within three months of the request being made.

---

¹⁶ [1980] IRLR 176, EAT.   ¹⁷ [2003] ICR 1405, [2003] All ER (D) 358 (Apr), EAT.

11.41 A complaint may be made to an employment tribunal that the employer has failed to permit a safety representative to have time off work for these purposes, or has failed to pay for such time off. If the complaint is well founded, the tribunal shall make a declaration, and may make an award of compensation.

11.42 There was some doubt as to whether the Safety Representative and Safety Committee Regulations met the requirements of the 'Framework Directive' (89/391/EEC) because there was no means whereby employees in non-unionised firms could have a legal right to play their role in health and safety matters. Consequently, the Health and Safety (Consultation with Employees) Regulations 1996 were introduced. Under these regulations, an employer has two choices with respect to those employees who have no safety representative by virtue of the 1977 regulations. He can either consult with employees directly, or he can consult with one or more persons of any group of employees who were elected for the purposes of consultation, and who are referred to as 'representatives of employee safety'. There is no provision in the regulations as to how an employer shall organise any such elections, but apparently it is not necessary to have a statutory framework for this purpose (*R v Secretary of State for Trade and Industry, ex p UNISON*[18]).

11.43 Under the 1996 regulations, employers must consult with their employees, or their elected representatives of employee safety, in good time, on matters concerning their health and safety at work, and, in particular, with regard to:

(a) the introduction of any measures at the workplace which will substantially affect the health and safety of those employees;

(b) the employer's arrangements for appointing or nominating a competent person to assist him, as required by regs 6(1) and 7(1)(b) of the Management Regulations;

(c) any health and safety information he is required to provide to the employees under any relevant statutory provision;

(d) the planning and organisation of any health and safety training he is required to provide by virtue of any statutory provision; and

(e) the health and safety consequences for the employees of the introduction of new technologies into the workplace (including the planning thereof).

11.44 In such consultations, representatives of employee safety have the following functions:

(a) to make representations to the employer on potential hazards and dangerous occurrences at the workplace, which affect the employees represented;

(b) make representations to the employer on general matters affecting the health and safety of employees, in particular, on matters referred to in paras (a)–(e) (see para 11.43);

(c) represent the group of workers he represents in consultations at the workplace with health and safety inspectors.

11.45 If the employer consults with employees directly, he must make available to them such information as is necessary to enable the employees to participate fully and effectively in the consultation process. If the employer consults with representatives of employee safety, he must make available such information as is necessary to enable them to carry out their functions. But the rights and functions of employee representatives under the 1996 regulations are more limited than those which apply under the 1977 regulations.

---

[18] [1996] ICR 1003, [1996] IRLR 438.

In particular, they have no right to carry out workplace inspections, attend meetings of a safety committee, inspect statutory health and safety documents, or investigate employees' complaints and notifiable accidents or dangerous occurrences. However, such matters are provided for in the guidance notes which have been issued. An employee safety representative has the right to be paid when carrying out his functions as such, or when being trained.

Further Duties

11.46 There are further duties owed to non-employees who are lawfully on the employer's premises (s 3) to ensure, so far as is reasonably practicable, that they are not exposed to risks to their health or safety. This duty applies not only to persons who are lawfully on the employer's premises, for example, students in an educational establishment, but also persons who are outside those premises but who may be affected by the activities in question. Thus if there is a potential hazard on the employer's premises, he must provide information not only to his own employees, but also to visitors and the employees of a sub-contractor who may be working there (*R v Swan Hunter Shipbuilders Ltd*, para 11.31). Other duties relate to controllers of premises (s 4) and of manufacturers (s 6 as amended).

Duties of Employees

Duties at Work (s 7)

11.47 Every employee is under a duty while at work:

(a) to take reasonable care for the health and safety of himself and of others who may be affected by his acts or omissions at work; this could mean that an employee who failed or refused to wear or use safety precautions which are provided would be in breach of his legal duty;

(b) as regards any duty imposed on his employer or any other person, to co-operate with him so far as is necessary to enable that duty to be performed or complied with.

Duty Not to Interfere with Safety Provisions (s 8)

11.48 No persons shall intentionally or recklessly interfere with or misuse anything provided in the interest of health, safety, or welfare in pursuance of any relevant statutory provisions. This duty is wider than the old law, which was directed against 'wilful' conduct, defined as perverse or deliberate action. Intentional or reckless conduct does not need to be wilful.

Duty Not to Charge (s 9)

11.49 An employer shall not charge any employee in respect of anything done or provided in pursuance of any relevant statutory provision (see Personal Protective Equipment at Work Regulations 1992, para 11.62).

Rights of Employees

Right Not to Suffer a Detriment in Health and Safety Cases (ERA, s 44)

11.50 An employee is entitled not to be subjected to any detriment by an act or a failure to act by his employer on any of the following grounds:

(a) having been designated by the employer to carry out activities in connection with preventing or reducing risks to health and safety at work, he carried out (or proposed to carry out) those activities;

(b) being a safety representative or member of a safety committee, he performed (or proposed to perform) any functions as such or took part in consultations or in an election as an employee safety representative;

(c) if there is no safety representative or safety committee where he is, or, if there are, it is not reasonably practicable to raise such matters, he brought the employer's attention (by reasonable means) to circumstances connected with his work which he reasonably believed were harmful or potentially harmful to health or safety;

(d) in circumstances of danger which he reasonably believed to be serious and imminent and which he could not reasonably be expected to avert, he left, or proposed to leave, or, while the danger persisted, he refused to return to, his place of work or any dangerous part of his place of work;

(e) in circumstances of danger which he reasonably believed to be serious and imminent, he took, or proposed to take, appropriate steps to protect himself or other persons from the danger. This is to be judged by reference to all the circumstances, including his knowledge, and the facilities and advice available to him at the time. However, he will not have been subjected to a detriment if he was so negligent in the steps he took that the employer treated him as a reasonable employer would have done in those circumstances.

11.51 An employee who believes that he has suffered a detriment contrary to s 44 may bring a complaint before an employment tribunal within the usual time limits. If the complaint is upheld, the tribunal shall make a declaration to that effect and also award compensation to the complainant, the amount being such as the tribunal considers to be just and equitable in all the circumstances. This will include any expenses incurred and take account of any benefits lost. The employee is expected to mitigate against his loss, and the compensation award can be reduced on the ground of contributory conduct (see para 17.222).

11.52 But if a safety representative acts in respect of matters which are not within the area of the workplace for which he is a representative, or acts outside the laid-down procedure, or acts in bad faith, then it may be that he is not pursuing a genuine health and safety matter, but is pursuing a personal agenda in order to embarrass the employer. In such circumstances, he may be disciplined as appropriate (*Shillito v Van Leer (UK) Ltd*[19]).

Right Not to be Dismissed Unfairly in Certain Circumstances Involving Health and Safety Cases (ERA, s 100)

11.53 It will be unfair to dismiss an employee because of any of the following circumstances arising out of health and safety matters:

(a) having been designated by the employer to carry out activities in connection with preventing or reducing risks to health and safety at work, he carried out (or proposed to carry out) those activities. In *Healey v Excel Logistics Ltd*[20] a safety representative went to the site of another company in order to inspect an entry in that company's accident book concerning an accident which involved one of the employees he represented. His subsequent dismissal for doing so was held to be unfair, because his duties as a safety representative were not confined to incidents which took place on his employer's premises;

(b) being a safety representative or member of a safety committee, he performed (or proposed to perform) any functions as such, or took part in consultations as an employee safety representative, or in an election of representatives of employee safety;

---

[19] [1997] IRLR 495, EAT.   [20] Unreported.

(c) if there is no safety representative or safety committee where he is, or, if there are,
     it is not reasonably practicable to raise such matters, he brought the employer's at-
     tention (by reasonable means) to circumstances connected with his work which
     he reasonably believed were harmful or potentially harmful to health or safety. In
     Balfour Kilpatrick Ltd v Acheson[21] it was held that the taking of industrial action was
     not, in the circumstances, reasonable means whereby employees may bring health
     and safety concerns to the employer's attention;

(d) in circumstances of danger which he reasonably believed to be serious and immi-
     nent and which he could not reasonably be expected to avert, he left, or proposed
     to leave, or, while the danger persisted, refused to return to, his place of work or any
     dangerous part of his place of work. In *Harvest Press Ltd v McCaffrey*[22] an employee
     left work because he felt he was in danger of being injured due to the behaviour of
     another employee towards him, who had been abusive and aggressive. His dismissal
     for leaving work was held to be unfair, for s 100(1)(d) was not confined to circum-
     stances of danger which arose from working methods or equipment;

(e) in circumstances of danger which he reasonably believed to be serious and imminent,
     he took, or proposed to take, appropriate steps to protect himself or other persons
     from the danger. This is to be judged by reference to all the circumstances, including
     his knowledge, and the facilities and advice available to him at the time. Where an
     employee has a reasonable belief in danger and takes appropriate action, the employer
     must take that belief seriously and cannot dismiss him or subject him to detriment
     simply because he disagrees whether there was in fact danger (*Oudahar v Esporta
     Group Ltd*[23]). The term 'other persons' includes members of the public as well as fellow
     employees, so that a chef who was dismissed because he refused to cook food which he
     believed to be unfit for human consumption succeeded in a claim for unfair dismissal
     under s 100 (*Masiak v City Restaurants (UK) Ltd*[24]). However, his dismissal shall not be
     regarded as being unfair if he was so negligent in the steps he took that the employer
     treated him as a reasonable employer would have treated him in those circumstances.

11.54 It should be noted that if a dismissal is unfair by virtue of (a) or (b) in para 11.53, and
the employer refuses to reinstate or re-engage the employee following a tribunal order, an
additional award (see para 17.233) can be made. The test to be applied is not only whether
the employee genuinely feared for his safety, but whether that fear was based on reasonable
grounds. This is a question of fact, to be determined not only by the nature of the potential
danger, but also by the steps which the employee could have taken to follow any procedures laid down by the employer which would militate against the danger (*Kerr v Nathan's
Wastesavers Ltd*[25]). Otherwise, there is no limit on the amount of the compensation award
if the dismissal (or selection for redundancy) was contrary to s 100.

11.55 However, when it comes to a dismissal on other grounds, the protection afforded to
a safety representative is neutral. Like a shop steward, he has no specially privileged position, and thus may be selected for redundancy in accordance with the appropriate selection
criteria (*Smiths Industries Aerospace and Defence Systems v Rawlings*[26]).

Interim Relief in Health and Safety Cases (ERA, ss 128–130)

11.56 If an employee is dismissed for an inadmissible reason because he has been designated to carry out health and safety activities, or he is a safety representative or member

---

[21] [2003] IRLR 683, [2003] All ER (D) 15 (Apr), EAT.   [22] [1999] IRLR 778, EAT.
[23] [2011] IRLR 730, EAT.   [24] [1999] IRLR 780, EAT.   [25] Unreported.
[26] [1996] IRLR 656, EAT.

of a safety committee (see para 11.35) and he proposed to carry out activities as such, he may apply for interim relief within seven days following the effective date of termination of his employment. The procedure and remedies are similar to the interim relief provisions contained in TULR(C)A, ss 161–166 (see para 21.122).

D. **Health and Safety Regulations (s 15 and Sch 3)**

11.57 As has already been indicated, one of the main purposes of the Act was to replace the existing statutory provisions by regulations, and over a period of time, the 'old' law contained in the Factories Act 1961, Offices, Shops and Railway Premises Act 1963, and so forth (for a complete list, see column 3 in Sch 1 to the Act) was phased out and replaced with a system of regulations and Codes of Practice which, in combination with the other provisions of the Act, were designed to maintain and improve the standards of health, safety, and welfare. Regulations are of three general types: first, there are those which lay down standards to be applied in most or all employment situations, second, there are those which are designed to control a particular hazard which may exist in a particular industry, and third, there are those which refer to particular hazards or risks but which may be found in a number of different industries. The view appears to be held that the use of regulations as a device for laying down legal standards is a superior method to legislation, for regulations are simpler and more flexible; they can be altered more readily in accordance with experience and technological progress, and will be more manageable to those who have to implement them.

11.58 Regulations are to be made by the Secretary of State either as a result of proposals made to him by the HSE or on his own initiative, but in the latter case he must consult with the HSE and any other appropriate bodies. If the HSE makes the proposals, it, too, must consult with the appropriate government departments and other bodies (s 50).

11.59 A breach of duty imposed by regulations is, of course, punishable as a criminal offence. Additionally, a breach may give rise to civil liability, if the regulations specifically provide for this.

11.60 A number of regulations have been passed since 1974 dealing with all aspects of health and safety law. Reference should be made to an established textbook on this topic.

E. **The Impact of European Law**

11.61 Article 137 of the Treaty of Rome provides that member states shall pay particular attention to encouraging improvements, especially to the working environment, as regards the health and safety of workers. Under this article, Directives may be adopted by the qualified majority voting system, and a considerable number of such Directives have been adopted. In particular, the 'Framework Directive' (98/391/EEC) and five 'Daughter Directives' were given effect by the so-called 'six-pack' regulations (see para 11.62). The general view taken by the HSC is that the European Directives did not involve any significant change in UK law, although they do require UK law to make explicit that which is generally regarded as being implicit. Legal standards on health and safety in the UK are very high, and following EU Directives does not impose any further particularly onerous burdens on UK employers.

11.62 The so-called 'six pack' regulations came into force on 1 January 1993. These are:

(a) Management of Health and Safety at Work Regulations, which require employers to make risk assessments provide employees with appropriate health surveillance, appoint safety advisers, establish emergency procedures, provide training and information to employees etc;

(b) Personal Protective Equipment at Work Regulations—personal protective equipment (PPE) must conform to applicable EC standards;

(c) Provision and Use of Work Equipment Regulations, whereby there must be suitable and well maintained work equipment, and proper training where appropriate. Effective measures must be taken to prevent access to danger and hazards;

(d) Workplace (Health, Safety and Welfare) Regulations, which deal with the state of the workplace, its construction, temperature, lighting, seats etc;

(e) Manual Handling Operations Regulations, which set out the need for employers to avoid the need for employees to undertake manual handling operations which involve the risk of injury, and carry out assessments and take steps if such operations cannot be avoided; and

(f) Health and Safety (Display Screen Equipment) Regulations, whereby employers are required to make an analysis of workstations for the purpose of assessing health and safety risks so as to reduce these to the lowest extent reasonably practicable.

Many previous regulations were revoked, and most of the existing protective legislation found in the Factories Act 1961, Offices, Shops and Railway Premises Act 1963 etc, was repealed.

11.63 Fundamental to the law is the need to take proactive steps to ensure the health and safety at work of employees and others. These will include risk assessment in certain specified situations, provision of information to all those who may be at risk, health surveillance, the use of safety advisers, co-operation between employers, the provision of approved equipment and personal protection equipment, and so on. Employees have a duty to use the equipment etc provided in a proper manner, and to report shortcomings in the employer's protection arrangements or which represent a serious and immediate danger to health and safety.

No Smoking

11.64 The Smoke-Free (Penalties and Enforcement) Regulations 2006 came into force in England in July 2007. Similar provisions came into force in Wales and Northern Ireland in April 2007. These regulations provide that:

(a) all work premises shall be smoke free if enclosed or substantially enclosed. This is defined as meaning premises with a ceiling, unless more than 50% of the wall area is open to the outside;

(b) all occupiers of premises must display a prominent 'No Smoking' sign. The sign must be of at least A5 size, and contain the words 'No Smoking. It is against the law to smoke in these premises except in a designated room';

(c) company cars are deemed to be entirely non-smoking if they might be used by more than one person, except if it is a convertible car and the roof is open;

(d) an employer who fails to display a prominent 'No Smoking' sign may be fined a fixed penalty of £1,000. If he fails to take reasonable steps to prevent smoking he is liable to a fine of up to £2,500;

(e) an employee or a visitor who is caught smoking on work premises is liable to a fixed penalty of £200 (or £50 in Scotland).

The Smoking (Health and Social Care) (Scotland) Act 2005 came into force in March 2006 in Scotland, and regulations made thereunder provide that all workplaces, as well as clubs, pubs, etc, shall be free from tobacco smoke.

The regulations do not cover vaping, so employers should have separate policies for that.

Other Regulations

11.65 There are a considerable number of other regulations on health and safety matters which have been passed since 1974. The most important of these deal with the following topics: first aid (1981), electricity (1989), safety signs and signals (1996), confined spaces (1997), lifting operations (1998), major accident hazards (1999), ionising radiations (1999), protection of children (2000), lead (2002), hazardous substances (2002), fire precautions (2005), noise at work (2005), work at height (2005), vibrations (2005), construction (2007), employers' liability (compulsory insurance) (2008), artificial optical radiation (2012), asbestos (2012), reporting of injuries, diseases, and dangerous occurrences (2013) and so on. In addition, a number of regulations deal with specific industries and processes (railways, gas, transport, adventure activities, carriage of goods, offshore installations, compressed air, etc).

F. **Codes of Practice (s 16)**

11.66 For the purpose of providing practical guidance with respect to the general duties imposed by ss 2–7 (paras 11.33–11.49), or by any regulation or any existing statutory provisions, the HSE may approve and issue codes of practice which are suitable for that purpose. The HSE may also approve other such suitable codes which are drawn up by other persons or organisations, and thus there is no reason why a private firm or employers' organisation should not draw up its own code and submit it for approval, should this be thought desirable. One might also expect approval to be given to the existing British Standards Institution's own codes. The HSE cannot approve a code without the consent of the Secretary of State, and prior to obtaining this, must consult with government departments and other appropriate bodies. The codes may be revised from time to time, and the HSE may, if necessary, withdraw its approval from a particular code.

11.67 A failure on the part of any person to observe the provisions contained in an approved code of practice shall not of itself render that person liable to any civil or criminal proceedings, but in any such criminal proceedings, if a person is alleged to have committed an offence concerning a matter in respect of which an approved code is in force, the provisions of that code shall be admissible in evidence, and a failure to observe it shall constitute proof of the breach of duty, or contravention of the regulation or statutory provision, unless the accused can satisfy the court that he complied with the requirements of the law in some other equally efficacious manner. The codes, therefore, will be the guides to good safety practice, and if a person follows the provisions of the codes, he cannot be successfully prosecuted for an offence. If he fails to follow the relevant code, he may be guilty of an offence unless he can show that he observed the specific legal requirement some other way.

11.68 The Act contains no guidance on the use of the codes in civil proceedings, but it is likely that a failure to observe any such provision as is contained therein may well constitute prima facie evidence of negligence, which can be rebutted by evidence to the contrary.

G. **Penalties (s 33)**

11.69 Any person or body corporate (eg a company) may be charged with and convicted of an offence under the Act, and punished accordingly. In addition, if an offence committed by a body corporate is proved to have been committed with the consent or connivance of, or be attributable to any neglect on the part of, any director, manager, secretary, or other similar officer, then he, as well as the body corporate, may be guilty of an offence, and liable to be proceeded against and punished accordingly (s 37) (see *Huckerby v Elliott*[27]).

11.70 In *Armour v Skeen*,[28] a senior local government official was prosecuted for failing to prepare and carry out a safety policy, for this neglect of duty ultimately led to breaches of safety provisions which resulted in the death of an employee. It was held that the official was guilty of an offence under s 37. He was in a senior position in his organisation, and was therefore responsible for the general safety policy in his department. But in *R v Boal*[29] the accused was an assistant manager in a bookshop. Following a visit by inspectors, he was prosecuted and convicted in respect of a number of offences. On appeal, it was held that criminal liability was to be imposed on persons in authority in the company who were the 'decision makers', with the power and responsibility to decide corporate policy. As the accused was an 'underling', his conviction was quashed.

11.71 Where the commission of an offence by a person is due to the default of another person, that other person may be proceeded against, whether or not proceedings are taken against the first mentioned person (s 36). No proceedings under the Act may be brought except by an inspector, or with the consent of the Director of Public Prosecutions (in Scotland, the Procurator Fiscal).

11.72 There is an anomaly, however, in that although Crown bodies (excluding health authorities) have the same obligations under the Act as other employers, they cannot be prosecuted, and it is not possible to issue improvement or prohibition notices against the Crown (see para 11.24). However, this rule does not prevent the prosecution of individual Crown employees.

11.73 The Health and Safety (Offences) Act 2008 applies to all offences committed on or after 17 January 2009. The Act increased the penalties for most health and safety offences to £20,000, and makes imprisonment, up to 12 months in the magistrates' courts, an option for an increased number of offences. Certain offences hitherto triable in the magistrates' courts may now be tried either summarily in the magistrates' courts or on indictment in the Crown Court before a jury. If proceedings are brought on indictment, there is the possibility of an unlimited fine, and in certain specified cases, up to two years' imprisonment. In *R v Howe & Son (Engineers) Ltd*[30] the Court of Appeal gave guidance on how sentencing policies should be applied to convictions for health and safety offences.

H. Burden of Proof

11.74 As a general rule, in criminal proceedings it is for the prosecution to prove its case 'beyond reasonable doubt'. However, by the Health and Safety at Work Act, s 40, if the offence consists of a failure to comply with a duty or requirement to do something 'so far as is reasonably practicable', or to use 'the best practicable means', it shall be for the accused to prove that it was not reasonably practicable to do more than was in fact done, or that there were no better practicable means than were in fact used to satisfy the duty or requirement. When the burden of proof is thus placed on the accused, he may discharge that burden of proof on the balance of probabilities (*R v Carr-Briant*[31]). In *Davies v Health and Safety Executive* it was held that this reversal of the burden of proof did not violate Art 6 of the Convention on Human Rights (see para 1.91).

---

[27] [1970] 1 All ER 189.   [28] [1977] IRLR 310.
[29] [1992] QB 591, [1992] 3 All ER 177, [1992] ICR 495, [1992] IRLR 420, CA.
[30] [1999] 2 All ER 249, [1999] IRLR 434, (1999) 163 JP 359, [1999] Crim LR 238, [1998] All ER (D) 552, CA.
[31] [1943] KB 607, [1943] 2 All ER 156, CCA.

11.75 It is not necessary for the prosecution to identify a specific breach of duty by the defendant. It is sufficient to prove that there was a risk of injury arising from a state of affairs at work. The burden of proof then passes to the defendant under s 40 of the Act to prove that they had done all that was reasonably practicable to avoid the risk. Thus, if there has been no risk assessment, no training given, or no adequate safety precautions provided, it will be difficult for the accused to discharge that burden (*R v Chargot Ltd*[32]). But if the worker is injured because he has acted in a manner that a reasonable employer could not have foreseen, the employer cannot be successfully prosecuted, because the employee's action constitutes going 'on a frolic of his own' (*R v N Ltd*[33]).

I. Corporate Manslaughter

11.76 The Corporate Manslaughter and Corporate Homicide Act 2007 created a new offence of corporate manslaughter in England, Wales, and Northern Ireland, and corporate homicide in Scotland, which replaced the previous common law offence of manslaughter as it applied to organisations. The offence is committed when an organisation manages or organises its activities in such a way as to cause a person's death in a manner that amounts to a gross breach of duty of care. The way in which the senior managers, who play a significant role in the making of decisions about the whole or a substantial part of the organisation's activities, manage or organise its activities must be a substantial element in the breach. The breach will be gross if it falls far below what can reasonably be expected of the organisation in the circumstances.

11.77 A jury must consider such factors as (a) whether the organisation failed to comply with health and safety legislation, (b) the seriousness of the breach, (c) how much of a risk of death the breach posed. In addition, the jury may also take into account (a) the extent to which the evidence shows that there were attitudes, policies, systems, or accepted practices within the organisation which were likely to have encouraged the failure, or to have produced tolerance of it, (b) any health and safety guidance that relates to the breach issued by an authority responsible for enforcing health and safety legislation, and (c) any other relevant matter.

11.78 A prosecution under the Act can only be undertaken by the Director of Public Prosecutions (in Scotland the Procurator Fiscal). If convicted, the court will impose a fine, and may also issue a remedial order requiring the organisation to take specified steps to remedy any relevant breach or any matter resulting from the breach that caused the death, or any health and safety deficiency in the organisation's policies or practices of which the relevant breach appears to be an indication. The court may also impose a publicity order, requiring the convicted organisation to publicise specific information about its failures.

11.79 The duty of care is owed (a) by an employer to his employees or other persons working for the organisation, (b) by an occupier of premises, (c) in connection with the supply of goods or services, construction or maintenance activities, using or keeping of plant, etc, and (d) from a future date, to persons in custody.

Compensation for Injuries at Work

A. The Extent of the Duty Owed

11.80 One of the prime duties of an employer is to ensure that his employees do not suffer an accident or injury while at work. There are a number of common law rules which determine the extent of that duty, and in addition there are certain statutory provisions designed

---

[32] [2008] UKHL 73, [2009] 1 WLR 1, [2009] 2 All ER 645, [2009] ICR 263.
[33] [2008] EWCA Crim 1223.

to ensure the employee's safety which, if broken or not observed by the employer, may lead to an action for damages by an injured employee based on a breach of statutory duties, if a statutory instrument specifically provides for this.

Where the legislation sets out that a breach of statutory duty claim can be brought (see para 11.109), the two actions are run together, so that an employee may succeed for breach of the common law duty and/or a breach of the statutory duty, though, of course, only one set of damages will be awarded. The purpose of the common law rules is to compensate for injuries incurred as a result of the employer's negligence; the object of the statute will be accident prevention enforced by criminal penalties, but with a potential liability for compensation as well. But as Goddard LJ said in *Hutchinson v London and North Eastern Rly Co*, 'The real incentive for the observance by employers of their statutory duties . . . is not their liability to substantial fines, but the possibility of heavy claims for damages.'[34]

11.81 The duty owed by the employer is in respect of the employee's physical and mental health, including ill health caused by overwork (*Johnstone v Bloomsbury Health Authority*[35]), psychiatric illness (*Frost v Chief Constable of South Yorkshire Police*[36]), and stress and anxiety caused thereby (*Walker v Northumberland County Council*[37]). But if the employers do not know of the risk, or if, having knowledge, they take such steps as are reasonable in the circumstances to minimise the risk or provide appropriate healthcare, no liability arises (*Petch v Customs and Excise Comrs*[38]). A difficult case was *White v Chief Constable of South Yorkshire Police*,[39] where it was held that a policeman was not entitled to recover damages for psychiatric illness suffered as a result of assisting in the aftermath of the Hillsborough disaster, either as an employee or a rescuer. Note that the independent Stevenson/Farmer review on mental health at work, 'Thriving at Work', reports on what employers can do to improve support for employees. It makes a number of recommendations, in particular that all employers should adopt six 'mental health core standards' that lay basic foundations for an approach to workplace mental health.

11.82 Liability for psychiatric injury caused by stress at work is no different in principle from liability for physical injury. The test is whether the injury is a foreseeable breach of the employer's duty of care. It does not follow that because a claimant suffers from stress at work, and that the employer was in some way in breach of a duty to allow that to occur, that the claimant is able to establish a claim in negligence (*Hartman v South Essex Mental Health and Community Care NHS Trust*[40]). Since *Sutherland v Hatton*[41] the courts have adopted a more cautious approach to claims for damages in respect of psychiatric injury caused by stress. There, the Court of Appeal heard appeals by employers in four unconnected cases against awards of damages to employees who had stopped work because of stress-induced psychiatric illness. Three of the appeals were allowed, while the fourth was dismissed 'not without some hesitation'. The court laid down a number of practical propositions designed to help other courts deal with future claims. While conceding that it was the employer's duty to take reasonable steps to ensure the physical and mental health of his employees, it was held that in order for an employer to be liable, the stress-induced injury must be sufficiently foreseeable to be plain enough for any reasonable employer to realise that he

---

[34] [1942] 1 KB 481, [1942] 1 All ER 330, 111 LJKB 369, CA.

[35] [1992] QB 333, [1991] 2 All ER 293, [1991] ICR 269, [1991] IRLR 118, CA.

[36] [1998] QB 254, [1997] 1 All ER 540, [1997] IRLR 173, CA; revsd sub nom *White v Chief Constable of South Yorkshire Police* [1999] 2 AC 455, [1999] 1 All ER 1, [1999] ICR 216, sub nom *Frost v Chief Constable of South Yorkshire Police* 143 Sol Jo LB 51, HL.   [37] [1995] 1 All ER 737, [1995] ICR 702, [1995] IRLR 35.

[38] [1993] ICR 789, CA.   [39] [1999] IRLR 110.   [40] [2005] EWCA Civ 6.

[41] [2002] EWCA Civ 76, [2002] 2 All ER 1, [2002] ICR 613, [2002] IRLR 263; revsd [2004] UKHL 13, [2004] 2 All ER 385.

should do something about it. The Court of Appeal stated that there were no occupations which are intrinsically dangerous to mental health, that employers are entitled to assume that employees can withstand the normal pressures of the job (unless they know of some particular problem or vulnerability), and that an employee who returns to work after being absent through sickness is implying that he is fit for work, and the employer is entitled to take that at its face value. To trigger a duty to take steps, the indications of impending harm to health arising from stress at work had to be plain enough for any reasonable employer to realise that he ought to do something about it, and the employer will only be liable if he fails to take reasonable steps bearing in mind the magnitude of the risk, the gravity of the harm, the costs and practicability of preventing it, and the justification for running the risk. Thus it might be possible for the employer to suggest that the employee takes a sabbatical period of leave, or a transfer to other work, or a redistribution of the work, etc. Extra help may be provided, or a mentoring scheme introduced. But such assistance will depend very much on the employer's resources and the interests of other employees at the workplace. The fact that an employer provides a counselling service for the benefit of employees who are suffering from stress-related illnesses does not, by itself, relieve the employer of the duty of care owed. Counselling services are not a panacea by which the duty of care can be discharged (*Intel Corporation (UK) Ltd v Daw*[42]).

11.83 The court went on to point out that it is not enough that the occupational stress has caused the harm. It must be shown that it was the employer's breach of duty to take reasonable care for the health of his employees that has caused or materially contributed to the harm. An employer can only reasonably be expected to take steps which are likely to do some good, and if the only reasonable steps an employer could take in order to remove the employee from a job which is causing stress is to demote the employee or dismiss him, and the employer will not be in breach of his duty for allowing a willing employee to continue in his job. If there is no alternative solution, it is for the employee to decide whether or not to continue in the job and risk a breakdown in his health, or whether to leave the employment and look for work elsewhere. Finally, the consequence of the breach of duty may be only one of many stressful events which affected an employee's state of health, and the employer should only pay for that proportion of the harm which is attributable to his wrongdoing.

11.84 A somewhat different approach to stress at work claims was taken by the Court of Appeal in *Dickens v O2 plc*[43] where, although purporting to apply the guidelines in *Hatton*, it would seem that the requirements of reasonable foreseeability, breach of duty, and causation are not as difficult for claimants to satisfy as the reading of *Hatton* may suggest. In this case it was held that a prior claim about stress should have alerted management to the existence of a potential problem, and steps should have been taken to have the affected employee examined by occupational health personnel. It was pointed out that the guidelines in *Hatton* must be taken in the context of the case, and not applied out of context to contort a case out of recognition.

11.85 Thus an employer should always be alert to the problems likely to be suffered by a stressed employee. In *Barber v Somerset County Council*[44] the employee was the head of a department at a school. He had a very heavy workload, working between 60 and 70 hours per week. He was off work for three weeks suffering from 'overstressed/depression'. When he returned to work the school authorities were not very sympathetic towards him, and no steps were taken to improve the situation. The following term he found himself with

[42] [2007] EWCA Civ 70, [2007] 2 All ER 126, [2007] ICR 1318, [2007] IRLR 355.
[43] [2008] EWCA Civ 1144.
[44] [2002] EWCA Civ 76, [2002] 2 All ER 1, [2002] IRLR 263; revsd [2004] UKHL 13, [2004] 2 All ER 385.

the same or slightly heavier workload, and eventually left work altogether, suffering from 'moderate or severe' depression. His claim for damages was upheld by the House of Lords. A prudent employer who knew that an employee had taken some time off work because of stress caused by work overload would have investigated the situation to see how the difficulties might be improved. If an employee works hours which are in excess of the 48-hour week, or in breach of the rest provisions, with the consequence that he suffers psychiatric injury caused by overwork, this can be taken into account when consideration is given to the foreseeability of the injury (*Hone v Six Continents Retail*[45]). While every case will turn on its own facts, the principles laid down in *Stokes v Guest, Keen and Nettlefold*[46] (see para 11.109) were approved, ie 'the overall test is still the conduct of a reasonable and prudent employer, taking positive thought for the safety of his workers in the light of what he knows or ought to know'.

11.86 An employer is entitled to assume that an employee is of 'reasonable fortitude' in the absence of knowledge, actual or constructive, indicating the contrary. There will, however, be cases where such psychiatric illness will not be too remote, and will depend on the facts of the case (*Yapp v Foreign and Commonwealth Office*[47]). An employer, however, has no general obligation to make searching or intrusive enquiries and is entitled to take what he is told by his employee at face value (*Easton v B&Q plc*[48]).

11.87 The duty of the employer to take care is one aspect of the law of negligence which requires everyone to ensure that his activities do not cause injury or damage to another through an act of negligence. The standard of care which an employer must observe is, as Lord Oaksey pointed out in *Paris v Stepney Borough Council*, '[t]he care which an ordinary prudent employer would take in all the circumstances'.[49] The employer does *not* guarantee that an employee will not be injured; he only undertakes to take reasonable care, and he will only be liable if there is some lack of care on his part in failing to prevent something which was reasonably foreseeable. The employee, on his part, must be prepared to look after himself, and not expect to be able to blame the employer for every incident which takes place. In *Vinnyey v Star Paper Mills*,[50] the claimant was instructed by the foreman to clear and clean a floor area which had been made slippery by a viscous fluid. The foreman provided proper equipment and gave clear instructions. The claimant was injured when he slipped on the floor, and it was held that the employer was not liable, for there was no reasonably foreseeable risk in the performance of such a simple task.

11.88 Equally, if an employer does not know of the danger and could not be expected to know in the light of current knowledge, or did not foresee the danger and could not be expected to foresee it, he will not be liable. In *Down v Dudley Coles Long Ltd*[51] an employee was partially deafened by the noise from a cartridge-assisted hammer gun. At the then state of medical knowledge (ie in 1964), a reasonable employer would not have known of the potential danger of using this particular piece of equipment without providing safety precautions, and hence the employer was not liable for the injury. But once the danger is discovered, he must take all reasonable steps to protect his employees from the consequences of risks which have hitherto been unforeseeable. In *Wright v Dunlop Rubber Co*,[52] the employers used an anti-oxidant known as Nonox S from 1940 onwards. The manufacturers then discovered that the substance was capable of causing bladder cancer, and informed the defendants that all employees who had been exposed to it should be screened and tested. This was not done for some time, and thus the employers, as well as the manufacturers, were held liable to the claimants.

---

[45] [2005] EWCA Civ 922, CA.   [46] [1968] 1 WLR 1776, 112 Sol Jo 821.
[47] [2014] EWCA Civ 1512.   [48] [2015] EWHC 880 (QB).
[49] [1950] 1 KB 320, [1949] 2 All ER 843, CA; revsd [1951] AC 367, [1951] 1 All ER 42, HL.
[50] [1965] 1 All ER 175.   [51] Unreported, 1969.   [52] (1971) 11 KIR 311, 115 Sol Jo 366.

11.89 The matter was summarised by Swanwick J in *Stokes v Guest, Keen and Nettlefold (Bolts and Nuts) Ltd* (see para 11.85):

(a) The employer must take positive steps to ensure the safety of his employees in the light of the knowledge which he has or ought to have.

(b) The employer is entitled to follow current recognised practice unless in the light of common sense or new knowledge this is clearly unsound.

(c) Where there is developing knowledge, he must keep reasonably abreast with it, and not be too slow in applying it.

(d) If he has greater than average knowledge of the risk, he must take more than average precautions.

(e) He must weigh up the risk (in terms of the likelihood of injury and possible consequences) against the effectiveness of the precautions needed to meet the risk, and the cost and inconvenience.

11.90 Applying these tests, if the employer falls below the standards of a reasonable and prudent employer, he will be negligent. On the other hand, if the employer takes all such steps as are reasonably practicable, he will not be liable at common law (*Darby v GKN Screws and Fasteners Ltd*[53]).

11.91 If, before his dismissal, an employee acquires a cause of action at common law (whether for breach of contract or breach of the duty to take reasonable care for the employee's health and safety) that cause of action remains unimpaired by the fact that the employee has brought a statutory unfair dismissal claim. Thus a claim for damages for psychiatric injury caused, for example, by a wrongful application of the contractual disciplinary procedure may succeed (*Eastwood v Magnox Electric plc*[54]), even though there can be no award for psychiatric illness (or injury to feelings) caused by the manner of actual dismissal (*Dunnachie v Kingston upon Hull City Council*[55]).

B. Duty to Unborn Children

11.92 Under the Congenital Disabilities (Civil Liability) Act 1976, an employer may be liable to a child of an employee who is born disabled as a result of any breach of legal duty, whether imposed by statute or by common law, to the child's parent. The child may thus sue in respect of a pre-natal injury suffered, whether or not the parent suffered any injury, and whether or not the employer knew of the existence of the foetus. The right of the child to sue is contingent on the existence of a right for the parent to sue; in other words, the claim is as good as, but no better than, the claim of the parent. Any contributory negligence on the part of the parent may reduce the child's damages.

C. Personal Nature of the Duty

11.93 The duty of the employer is a personal one, in the sense that he cannot absolve himself by delegating the duty to someone else. In *Wilsons & Clyde Coal Co Ltd v English*,[56] the employer was compelled by law to employ a colliery agent who was responsible for mine safety; nonetheless, it was held that the employer was liable for an unsafe system of work in the mine. Thus it can never be a defence to argue that the employer has assigned the task of securing and maintaining safety precautions to a safety officer or other person.

---

[53] [1986] ICR 1.   [54] [2002] EWCA Civ 463, [2003] ICR 520n, [2002] IRLR 447.
[55] [2004] UKHL 36.   [56] [1938] AC 57, [1937] 3 All ER 628, HL.

11.94 Equally, the duty is owed to each employee as an individual, not to them all collectively. This means that one must take greater precautions when dealing, for example, with inexperienced employees, or with new and untrained employees or with young persons, etc, than one might do with more responsible staff. In *Paris v Stepney Borough Council* (see para 11.87) the claimant worked chipping away at rust and other superfluous rubbish which had accumulated underneath buses. Goggles were not provided for this work, for it was not customary to do so. The claimant only had one eye, and he was totally blinded when a splinter entered his good eye. It was held that the employers were liable. They should have foreseen that there was a risk of greater injury to the employee, and provided goggles for him, even though they may not have been under such a duty with respect to other employees.

11.95 Clearly, a higher standard of care must be shown to employees who lack a sufficient or adequate command of the English language, to ensure that they are properly trained and clearly instructed so as not to cause injuries to themselves and to others. In *James v Hepworth and Grandage Ltd*[57] the employers put up large notices informing employees that they should wear spats for their personal protection. Unknown to them, the claimant could not read, and when he was injured he claimed damages from his employers. His claim failed. He had observed other workmen wearing spats, and the court concluded that his failure to make enquiries meant that even if he had been informed about the notice, he would not have worn them. But with the growth of foreign labour in UK factories, the problem is likely to cause growing concern, particularly as such labour tends to concentrate in the initial stages in those industries which have serious safety hazards. The responsibility of the safety officer, as the 'agent' of the employer, to ensure that the work can be done in safety is likely to be very onerous in practice (see *Hawkins v Ian Ross (Castings) Ltd*[58]).

11.96 An employer has a duty to warn an employee of risks to his health and safety where those risks are not common knowledge and cannot be guarded against by the taking of sensible precautions, and where that knowledge would affect the employee's decision to accept the work. But the employer does not guarantee absolutely the safety of the employee. In *White v Holbrook Precision Castings Ltd*[59] the claimant was employed as a grinder. He developed Reynaud's Disease (vibration white finger) and sued for damages. His claim was dismissed. The claimant knew of the risk when he accepted the employment, and the employers were merely aware that the disease could cause minor discomfort. No precautions had ever been suggested or were viable. The claimant would still have taken the employment had he been specifically told of the risk. However, given the current state of medical and scientific knowledge, a different conclusion may well be reached nowadays (see *Shepherd v Firth Brown Ltd*[60]).

11.97 It has long been held that, as a general rule, there is no onus on an employer to remove an employee from unsafe work, the onus being on the employee to decide for himself whether to continue to take on the work (*Withers v Perry Chain Co Ltd* (see para 11.87) and *Henderson v Wakefield Shirt Co Ltd*[61]). Still less is there an obligation on the employer to dismiss the employee, if that was the only alternative. Indeed, in *Sutherland v Hatton* (see para 11.82) it was stated that if the only reasonable and effective step would have been to dismiss or demote the employee, the employer would not be in breach of his duty in allowing a willing employee to continue in the job. It is for the employee to decide whether or not to carry on in the employment and take the risk of a breakdown in his health. But there may well be cases where, despite the employee's desire to remain at work notwithstanding the risk he ran, the employer would be under a duty in law to dismiss him for his own

---

[57] [1968] 1 QB 94, [1967] 2 All ER 829, CA.   [58] [1970] 1 All ER 180.
[59] [1985] IRLR 215, CA.   [60] Unreported, 17 April 1985.   [61] [1997] PIQR P413, CA.

good so as to protect him from physical danger (see *Coxall v Goodyear GB Ltd*[62]). In unfair dismissal proceedings, the employer would have to plead some other substantial reason, ie the common law duty. If disability discrimination proceedings were brought, the defence of reasonable adjustments would have to be raised.

11.98 Modern technologies and modern working methods inevitably bring about new and special problems, and legal decisions must be adapted from existing principles to meet the factual situations which arise.

D. **The Threefold Nature of the Duty**

11.99 Although there is only one single duty on an employer to take care, it is convenient to examine the nature of that duty under three sub-headings.

Safe Plant and Appliances

11.100 This means that all the equipment, tools, machinery, plant, etc, where the employee works shall be reasonably safe for work. In *Bradford v Robinson Rentals Ltd*,[63] a driver was required to drive an unheated van on a 400-mile journey during a bitterly cold spell of weather. It was held that the employer was liable when the driver suffered frostbite as a consequence. In *Close v Steel Co of Wales Ltd*,[64] it was suggested by Lord Goddard that if an employer knows that a machine has a tendency to throw out flying parts so as to constitute a danger to the operative, this could well amount to common law negligence on the part of the employer if he fails to take reasonable precautions.

11.101 However, if an employer purchased tools or equipment from a reputable supplier, and has no knowledge of any defect in them, he will have performed his duty to take care, and will not be liable for negligence (see *Davie v New Merton Board Mills*[65]). This would not be so if the equipment was bought second-hand from, say, a scrapyard. If a remedy existed in *Davie's* case, it would be for the injured employee to sue the person responsible for the defect under the general law of negligence as propounded in the leading case of *Donoghue v Stevenson*,[66] but frequently this might prove to be difficult or impossible in practice. The employee might not be in a position to prove just who was negligent. It might be a firm of stevedores at the docks, a foreign manufacturer, and so on. In view of these problems, the law was changed with the passing of the Employers' Liability (Defective Equipment) Act 1969. This provides that if an employee suffers a personal injury in the course of his employment in consequence of a defect in equipment provided by his employers for the purpose of the employers' business, and the defect is attributable to the fault of a third party, the injury shall be deemed to be attributable to the negligence of the employer. Thus, should facts similar to *Davie's* case arise again, the employee would be able to sue his employer for the 'deemed' negligence, and the employer, for his part, would be able to recover the amount of damages paid from the third party whose fault it really was. At the same time, the Employers' Liability (Compulsory Insurance) Act 1969 was passed, to ensure that all employers had valid insurance cover to meet personal injuries claims from their employees.

11.102 If an employer is aware that there are defects in tools or equipment he has bought then he should withdraw them from circulation if he wishes to avoid liability. In *Taylor v Rover Co Ltd*[67] a batch of chisels had been badly hardened by the manufacturers. One had,

---

[62] [2002] EWCA Civ 1010, [2003] ICR 152, [2002] IRLR 742.   [63] [1967] 1 All ER 267.
[64] [1960] 2 QB 299, [1960] 2 All ER 657, CA; aff'd [1962] AC 367, [1961] 2 All ER 953, HL.
[65] [1959] AC 604, [1959] 1 All ER 346, HL.   [66] [1932] AC 562, 1932 SC, HL 31.
[67] [1966] 2 All ER 181.

in fact, shattered, without causing any injury, but the batch was still in use when another chisel shattered, injuring the claimant in his eye. The employers were held liable.

Safe System of Work

11.103 Here we must consider all the factors which concern the manner in which the work is to be done. The layout, the systems laid down, the training and supervision, the provision of warnings, protective clothing, special instructions, and so forth, are all relevant. In *Barcock v Brighton Corpn*,[68] the claimant was employed at an electricity sub-station. A certain method of testing was in operation, which was unsafe, and in consequence the claimant was injured. The employers were held liable. But if the employer gives proper instructions which the employee fails to observe, the employer will not be liable for a subsequent injury. In *Charlton v Forrest Printing Ink Co Ltd*[69] a senior employee was required to collect the firm's wages of £1,500 each Friday from the bank. Because, several years earlier, there had been a wage snatch of the firm's payroll, the managing director had given instructions that the collection arrangements should be varied each week, for example, by using taxis instead of private cars, and by going at different times and by different routes. Contrary to these instructions, in the course of time, a collecting pattern set in, and the employee suffered severe injuries when he was robbed in an attack. In the High Court, the judge found for the claimant arguing that the employers had been negligent in not employing a professional security firm, but this decision was reversed on appeal. The vast majority of firms of that size in that area made their own payroll collection, and hence the employers could not be said to be negligent in carrying on with that practice. Although there was a risk, they had taken reasonable steps to minimise or eliminate it. The Court of Appeal thought that the claimant's remedy would be through an application to the Criminal Injuries Compensation Board, which has funds for such contingencies.

11.104 If there are safety precautions laid down, the employee must be told what they are; if safety equipment is provided, it must be available for use. In *Finch v Telegraph Construction and Maintenance Co Ltd*[70] the claimant was employed as a grinder. Goggles had been provided, but he was not told where they were. The employers were held to be liable when he was injured by a flying piece of metal whilst doing his work.

11.105 But if the employer, though not providing the safety precautions, can show that even if he had provided them the employee would not have used them, he may escape liability. In *Cummings (or McWilliam) v Sir William Arrol Ltd*,[71] a steel erector fell from scaffolding and was killed. The employer had provided safety belts in the past, but these had not been used, and they had been taken away to be used on another site. It was held that even though the employer was negligent in not providing the safety belts, it was unlikely that the employee would have used them had they been available. Accordingly, the employer's negligence was not the cause of the death, since this would have occurred anyway.

11.106 The more dangerous the process, the greater the need for safety precautions. On the other hand, the employer cannot be expected to be held liable in respect of accidents which occur in simple situations, as *Vinnyey's* case (para 11.87) illustrates. A situation which gives rise to some legal difficulties is where the employer provides the safety precautions, but the employees fail or refuse to use them. Is the duty of the employer a merely passive one, to provide and do no more? Or is it an active one, to exhort, propagandise, instruct, or even compel their use? It is submitted that the answer to these questions can be given in four propositions.

---

[68] [1949] 1 KB 339, [1949] 1 All ER 251.   [69] [1978] IRLR 559; revsd [1980] IRLR 331, CA.
[70] [1949] 1 All ER 452.
[71] 1961 SC 134, Ct of Sess; aff'd sub nom *Cummings (or McWilliams) v Sir William Arrol & Co Ltd* [1962] 1 All ER 623, 1962 SC 70, HL.

(a) If the risk is an obvious one, and the injury resulting from the failure to use the precautions is not likely to be serious, then the employer's duty is a passive one of merely providing the precautions, informing the employees, and leaving it to them to decide for themselves whether or not to use them. In *Qualcast (Wolverhampton) Ltd v Haynes*,[72] an experienced workman was splashed by molten metal on his legs. Spats were available, but the employers did nothing to ensure that they were worn. The injury, though doubtless painful, was not of a serious nature, and the employers were held not liable.

(b) If the risk is that of a serious injury, then the duty of the employer is a higher one of doing all he can to ensure that the workmen will use the safety precautions which are provided. In *Nolan v Dental Manufacturing Co Ltd*[73] a toolsetter was injured when a chip flew off a grinding wheel. Because of the seriousness of the injury should such occur, it was held that the employer should have insisted that protective goggles were worn.

(c) If the risk is an insidious one, or one the seriousness of which the employee would not readily appreciate, then again, it is the duty of the employer to do all he can by way of propaganda, constant reminders, exhortations, etc, to try to get the employees to use the precautions. In *Berry v Stone Manganese and Marine Ltd*,[74] the claimant was working in an environment where the noise levels were dangerously high. Ear muffs had been provided, but no effort was made to ensure their use. It was held that as the workmen would not readily appreciate the dangers of injury to their hearing if they did not use the ear muffs, the employers were liable, as they had failed to take steps to impress on them the need to use the protective equipment.

(d) When the employer has done all he can do, when he has not only provided the protection but instructed on its use, advised on how to use it properly, pointed out the risks involved in a failure to use, and given constant reminders about its use, then he can do no more, and from that time he will be absolved from liability. Admittedly, this does not solve the problem, which is how to ensure that employees do their work safely. It is possible to make the use of safety equipment part of the contract of employment, or a provision in the works rules, and, it is submitted, a failure to observe these terms or instructions may, after due warning, enable the employer fairly to dismiss the employee. There appears to be no legal duty to do so in order to protect the employee from the physical consequences of his own folly.

11.107 The question then arises how far an employer is required to protect employees against everyday hazards and risks, as in *Kennedy v Cordia (Services) LLP* [2016] UKSC 6, where a home carer who had not been provided with protective footwear slipped on an icy path. The court found that if it had carried out a proper risk assessment, the employer, who was aware of incidents in previous years, would have learnt that attachments were available at a modest cost to reduce the risk, and had been used by other employers in a similar position. This highlights the importance of risk assessments being carried out, both in relation to the common law and to the regulatory regime set out below.

Reasonably Competent Fellow Employees

11.108 If an employer engages an incompetent person, whose actions injure another employee, the employer will be liable for failing to take reasonable care. In *Hudson v Ridge Manufacturing Co Ltd*[75] an employee who was known to be prone to committing

---

[72] [1959] AC 743, [1959] 2 All ER 38, HL.   [73] [1958] 2 All ER 449.
[74] [1972] 1 Lloyd's Rep 182, 115 Sol Jo 966.   [75] [1957] 2 QB 348, [1957] 2 All ER 229.

practical jokes carried one of his pranks too far, and injured a fellow employee. The employer was liable. The answer in these circumstances is, after due warning, to dispense firmly with the services of such a person, for he is a menace to himself and to others. On the other hand, in *Coddington v International Harvester Co of Great Britain Ltd*,[76] for a joke, an employee, M, kicked a tin of burning thinners close to X; another employee, Y, was scorched by the flames, and in the agony of the moment kicked the tin away so that it enveloped the claimant in flames, causing him severe injuries. It was held that the defendants were not liable. There was nothing in M's previous conduct which suggested that he might endanger others, and his act was completely outside the scope of his employment. If a person is injured during horseplay, he would not be able to recover damages unless he could show that the injury was caused by a failure to take care which amounted to recklessness or a very high degree of carelessness, or that it was caused with intent to do harm (*Blake v Galloway*[77]).

E. **Breach of Statutory Duty**

11.109 The Health and Safety at Work Act 1974 specifically excludes the right to bring a civil action in respect of a breach of ss 2–8. In the past, however, an action could be brought for breach of statutory duty unless the particular regulations said otherwise. On 1 October 2013, s 69 of the Enterprise and Regulatory Reform Act came into force and amended s 47 of the Health and Safety at Work Act (HSA). The aim of the amendment was to 'remove the right of civil action against employers for breach of statutory duty in relation to certain health and safety legislation, other than where such a right is specifically provided for'. This reverses the previous position, and means that no civil claim can be brought for breach of statutory duty unless a regulation expressly provides for it. It effectively removes strict liability in most cases. The position therefore reverts in the majority of cases to that of the common law, where claimants will be required to prove the employer's negligence and the courts will need to look at the employer's common law duties, such as the provision of safe plant and equipment, a safe place of work, properly qualified colleagues, and a safe system of work.

The cases in this section were mainly decided before the ERRA came into force, and so should be read with that in mind—not all of the regulations mentioned would be actionable now, but they are referred to as illustrations of the point that they make.

Four Elements

11.110 There are four elements of the tort of breach of statutory duty, namely, (a) that the defendant owed a duty to the claimant (*Hartley v Mayoh & Co*[78]), (b) that there was a failure to carry out that duty (*Chipchase v British Titan Products Co Ltd*[79]), (c) that the breach caused the damage (*McWilliams v Sir William Arrol & Co Ltd*, para 11.105), and (d) that the damage was the kind which the statute was designed to prevent (*Fytche v Wincanton Logistics plc*[80]). Claimants will generally bring such an action together with an action based on the tort of negligence, thus increasing the prospects of success, although, of course, only one amount of damages will be awarded. The main advantage in doing so is that, generally speaking, most statutory duties are absolute, ie a failure to perform the duty will inevitably mean that there has been a breach of that duty, whereas an action based on negligence is subject to various defences, eg reasonable foreseeability etc (see para 11.82).

---

[76] (1969) 6 KIR 146, 113 Sol Jo 265.   [77] [2004] EWCA Civ 814.
[78] [1953] 2 All ER 525; aff'd [1954] 1 QB 383, [1954] 1 All ER 375, CA.
[79] [1956] 1 QB 545, [1956] 1 All ER 613, CA.   [80] [2003] EWCA Civ 874.

(a) The Defendant Must Have Owed a Duty to the Claimant

11.111 Whether a duty is owed to a particular claimant is a question of construction. Thus, if a statutory provision is made for the benefit of a particular class of persons, only those in that class can take advantage of the statutory protection (*Canadian Pacific Steamships Ltd v Bryers*[81]). For example, the Management of Health and Safety at Work Regulations 1999 specify certain duties in relation generally to employees, and thus contract workers, agency workers, members of the public, etc are not so protected, and cannot sue for a breach of statutory duty by the employer. In *Ricketts v Torbay Council*[82] the claimant tripped on an uneven surface in a council car park. She sued for damages, arguing that the car park was a workplace, and under reg 12 of the Workplace (Health, Safety and Welfare) Regulations there was a requirement that every floor in a workplace and the surface of every traffic route shall be suitable for the purpose and that floors and surfaces must be free from anything that may cause any person to slip, trip, or fall. She argued that 'any person' meant any person who was lawfully there. Her claim was dismissed by the Court of Appeal. The regulations were designed to protect persons at work in the workplace. Similarly, in *Reid v Galbraith's Stores*[83] it was held that the provisions of the Offices, Shops and Railway Premises Act 1963 did not apply to a customer who was visiting the shop, as the Act was concerned with the protection of persons who worked there.

(b) There was a Failure to Carry Out that Duty

11.112 An employer will be in breach of the duty if he fails to observe the relevant statutory provision. Thus, when s 14 of the Factories Act 1961 (now repealed) stated that '[e]very part of dangerous machinery shall be securely fenced' it imposed an absolute obligation to fence, and it was no defence for an employer to argue that it was impossible to fence the dangerous part and use the machine in question. The Act thus implicitly prohibited its use, and the factory occupier used the machine at his peril (*John Summers & Sons Ltd v Frost*[84]). Similarly, reg 6 of the Provision and Use of Work Equipment Regulations 1998 provides that every employer shall ensure that work equipment is maintained in an efficient state, in efficient working order, and in good repair, and an employer was held liable when an employee was injured because the front brake on his delivery bicycle broke, even though the employer had no knowledge of the defect (*Stark v Post Office*[85]). The obligation imposed by the regulation at the time was absolute (but note that if the cause of action had occurred after 1 October 2013, there would have been no strict liability—see para 11.109).

11.113 On the other hand, if a statute or regulation imposed a duty to do something 'so far as is practicable' or 'to use the best practicable means', this is a high standard, but not an absolute one. Thus in *Richards v Highway Ironfounders (West Bromwich) Ltd*[86] it was not known at the time that an invisible dust could cause silicosis, and thus the employer could not be held liable for failing to insist that employees should wear masks. A defendant cannot be held liable for failing to use a precaution which was not then invented, or failing to protect against a danger which medical science had not yet identified (*Adsett v K & L Steelfounders and Engineers Ltd*[87]).

11.114 If a statutory provision requires that something should be done 'so far as is reasonably practicable' then again, different considerations apply. It is permissible to take into account on the one hand the danger or hazard or risk of injury which may occur, and balance it against the cost, inconvenience, time, and trouble it would take to counter it. If the risk is insignificant in relation to the cost etc likely to be incurred, then it may not

[81] [1958] AC 485, [1957] 3 All ER 572, HL.   [82] HSB No 326.   [83] 1970 SLT (Notes) 83.
[84] [1955] AC 740, [1955] 1 All ER 870, HL.   [85] [2000] All ER (D) 276, CA.
[86] [1955] 3 All ER 205, CA.   [87] [1953] 1 All ER 97n; aff'd [1953] 2 All ER 320, CA.

be reasonably practicable to take those steps (*Edwards v National Coal Board*[88]). Thus in *Marshall v Gotham & Co* (see para 11.29) the roof of a mine collapsed due to a rare geological fault, injuring a workman. The court held that the danger was a very rare one. The roof had been tested in the usual way, and any further precautions taken would not have afforded complete protection against the danger. In the circumstances, the employers had done all that was reasonable. Similarly, a failure on the part of an employer to note a trivial risk would not give rise to liability (*Furness v Midland Bank plc*[89]).

(c) The Breach Caused the Damage

11.115 The breach of the duty must have been a cause of the damage. This is the causation rule. Clearly if the damage caused is physical, there are generally few problems. When the damage caused is psychological, it is a matter of construction and evidence as to whether the damage was foreseeable. Thus in order to succeed in a claim for damages for psychiatric illness caused by stress at work, it must be established not only that it was reasonably foreseeable that overwork would lead to stress, but also that the failure to carry out a risk assessment or health surveillance would lead to a breakdown in the stressed employees' health (*Bonser v RJB Mining (UK) Ltd*[90]). If there is a failure to carry out a risk assessment as required by the Management of Health at Work Regulations (or other regulations which impose this requirement) it is a likely conclusion that that breach was in some way responsible for the accident or injury (*Griffiths v Vauxhall Motors Ltd*[91]).

11.116 But if the damage caused would have occurred even if the employer had complied with the statutory duty, there is no liability. In *McWilliams v Sir William Arrol & Co Ltd* (see paras 11.107 and 11.112), the employers provided safety belts on a site for the use of steel erectors, but as these were not being used by the employees, they were taken away to another site. A steel erector on the first site fell from scaffolding, and was killed. Although the employers were clearly in breach of their statutory duty to provide the safety belts, there was nothing to suggest that this employee, who had never used the belts before, would have worn them on the day he was killed. Thus the employers were held not liable for damages. The breach of the legal duty did not cause the damage; it would have occurred anyway.

(d) The Damage was the Kind the Statute was Designed to Prevent

11.117 The harm done must be of a type which the legislation is designed to prevent (*Gorris v Scott*[92]). Thus in *Fytche v Wincanton Logistics plc* (see para 11.12) a driver was employed to collect milk from farms. He was provided with steel-capped safety boots, which were changed every six months. Water seeped through a tiny hole in one of his boots, and, because the weather was extremely cold, he contracted frostbite. He brought a claim under reg 7 of the Personal Protective Equipment Regulations, arguing that the boots were not in an efficient state or in good repair, as required by that regulation. His claim was dismissed by the House of Lords. The purpose of the safety boots was to protect against his feet being crushed by some heavy object while he was on the farms; it was not to prevent his feet from getting wet or cold. His only remedy would be an action for common law negligence, but as the judge found that there had been no breach of the duty of care (because the defect was not known to the employers, and could not have been discovered by reasonable care) his claim under this heading failed.

Similarly, it was not the intention of Parliament to enable an action for damages to be brought in respect of a breach of the Working Time Regulations, as these provide for their own remedies (*Sayers v Cambridgeshire County Council*, para 7.109).

---

[88] [1949] 1 KB 704, [1949] 1 All ER 743, CA.   [89] Unreported, 10 November 2002.
[90] [2004] IRLR 164, CA.   [91] [2003] EWCA Civ 412, [2003] All ER (D) 167 (Mar).
[92] (1874) LR 9 Exch 125, 43 LJ Ex 92, 2 Asp MLC 282, 22 WR 575, 30 LT 431.

11.118 So far as the Management of Health and Safety at Work Regulations are concerned, there are some specific provisions which are likely to be relevant in civil litigation, including reg 3 (risk assessment), reg 6 (health surveillance), reg 8 (provisions for serious and imminent danger), reg 10 (information for employees), reg 14 (duties of employees), and reg 16 (risk assessment for new or expectant mothers). All other regulations have specific requirements, a breach of which may, in appropriate circumstances, give rise to civil liability.

F. Defences to an Action for Personal Injuries

11.119 An employer (or in reality his insurance company) may be able to raise a number of defences to an action based on negligence or breach of statutory duties, as appropriate.

Denial of Negligence

11.120 The employer may deny that he failed to take reasonable care, or claim that he did all that a reasonable employer would have done in the circumstances. In *Latimer v AEC Ltd*[93] a factory floor was made slippery owing to the interaction of water from an unprecedented rainfall with the oily surface of the floor. The management ordered sand and sawdust to be spread around, but there was not enough to cover the whole factory. The employee slipped on an untreated part and was injured. It was held that the employer had done all that a reasonable employer could have done, having regard to the nature of the risk. The only other alternative would have been to close down the factory, which would have been unreasonable in the circumstances. In *Brown v Rolls-Royce (1971) Ltd*[94] the claimant contracted dermatitis owing to the use of an industrial oil. The employers did not provide a barrier cream on the advice of their chief medical officer, who doubted its efficacy. It was again held that the employers were not liable, for they were entitled to rely on the skilled judgment of a competent adviser, and no more could be expected. Indeed, the medical officer had instituted his own preventative methods, as a result of which the incidence of dermatitis in the factory had decreased.

11.121 The duty of the non-specialist employer in these circumstances is somewhat different. After all, not every firm can be expected to employ their own medical officer. Nonetheless, they must pay attention to the current literature which is available to them, either through their employers' associations or other sources. In *Graham v Co-operative Wholesale Society Ltd*[95] the claimant worked in a furniture workshop where an electric sanding machine gave off a quantity of fine wood dust. This settled on his skin and caused dermatitis. No general precautions were taken against this, although the manager had received all the information which was commonly circulated in the trade. It was held that the employers had not been negligent. They did not know of the danger, nor ought they to have known. They had fulfilled their duty to take reasonable steps to keep their knowledge up to date.

11.122 Recent years have seen such an increase in negligence claims that many worthwhile activities (such as school outings etc) have been abandoned or restricted because of fears of potential litigation. To counter these fears, the Compensation Act 2006 provides that a court considering a claim in negligence or breach of statutory duty may, in determining whether the defendant should have taken particular steps to meet a standard of care (whether by taking precautions against a risk or otherwise), have regard to whether the requirement to take those steps might prevent a desirable activity from being undertaken at all, or to a particular extent or in a particular way, or discourage persons from undertaking functions in connection with a desirable activity. Further, an apology or an offer

---

[93] [1952] 2 QB 701, [1952] 1 All ER 1302, CA; aff'd [1953] AC 643, [1953] 2 All ER 449, HL.
[94] (1977) 12 ITR 382, EAT.   [95] [1957] 1 All ER 654.

of treatment or other redress shall not by itself amount to an admission of negligence or breach of statutory duty. The Act only applies to England and Wales.

The Injury was the Sole Fault of the Employee

11.123 If it can be shown that the accident or injury was solely due to the fault of the employee, the employer will not be liable. In *Jones v Lionite Specialities Ltd*[96] a foreman was addicted to a chemical vapour from a tank. One weekend he was found dead, having fallen into the tank. The employers were not liable. In *Brophy v Bradfield & Co Ltd*[97] a lorry driver was found dead inside a boiler house, having been overcome by the fumes. He had no reason to be there, and his employers had no reason to suspect his presence. Again, the employers were not liable. And in *Horne v Lec Refrigeration Ltd*,[98] a tool-setter had been trained to operate a machine, but was killed because of his failure to operate a safety drill. The employers were not liable, even though they were in breach of their statutory duty to ensure secure fencing.

11.124 It used to be inferred that this defence was one of *volenti non fit injuria*, ie that a person consents to the risk of being injured. But the doctrine of consent rarely succeeds in employment cases. The fact that an employee knows that he runs the risk of being injured does not mean that he consents to that risk because of the employer's negligence (*Smith v Baker & Sons*[99]). The payment of 'danger money' to specialised employees (eg stunt artistes) may indicate that there is a special risk which cannot be guarded against, and to that extent consent may be raised; but even so, the real question to be asked is: was the employer negligent in the circumstances?

11.125 Moreover, the Unfair Contract Terms Act 1977 applies to those employment situations where the employer seeks to exclude his liability for injury to the employee by means of a prominently displayed notice or even a contract term. Section 2 of the Act states that a person cannot, by reference to a contract term or to a notice, exclude or restrict his liability for death or personal injury resulting from negligence. Thus an employer cannot escape his legal responsibility if he has been negligent.

Contributory Negligence

11.126 This defence is based on the Law Reform (Contributory Negligence) Act 1945, which provides that if a person is injured, partly because of his own fault and partly due to the fault of another, damages shall be reduced to the extent the court thinks fit, having regard to the claimant's share in the responsibility for the damage. The defence is successfully raised in a number of cases. The employer will argue that even though he was negligent, so too was the injured employee, and a reduction in the amount of damages awarded will be the result. The actual percentage reduction made is scarcely based on scientific principles, and appeal courts may take a different view of the share of the blame to be apportioned.

11.127 Although in *Jayes v IMI (Kynoch) Ltd*[100] the Court of Appeal had held that there was no principle in law that rules out a finding of 100% contributory negligence, the case was disapproved by a more recent decision of the court in *Anderson v Newham College of Further Education*.[101] There is a distinction between arguing that a claimant is 100% contributorily negligent and arguing that an accident was entirely due to the fault of the claimant. Thus, if there has been a breach of a statutory duty by an employer it must be shown not only that the worker's breach of the same statutory duty was as great as that of the employer,

---

[96] (1961) 105 Sol Jo 468; revsd 105 Sol Jo 1082, CA.   [97] [1955] 3 All ER 286, CA.
[98] [1965] 2 All ER 898.   [99] [1891] AC 325.   [100] [1985] ICR 155, CA.
[101] [2002] EWCA Civ 505, [2003] ICR 212, [2002] All ER (D) 381 (Mar).

but also that the employer did all he could to ensure compliance by the worker. If there is no breach of statutory duty by the employer, no question of contributory negligence arises (*Anderson v Newham College of Further Education*).

New Intervening Act

11.128 An employer will not be liable if the injury is caused by a new intervening act, ie by a person or event over which or whom the employer has no control. In *Horton v Taplin Contracts Ltd*[102] the claimant was standing on the platform of a scaffolding tower. A fellow worker, with whom he had previously had an altercation, deliberately pushed the tower over, and the claimant suffered serious injuries. He claimed damages from his employer, alleging a breach of the Provision and Use of Work Equipment Regulations, regs 5 and 20 (work equipment must be suitable for the purpose, and work equipment must be stabilised) as well as reg 5 of the Construction (Health Safety and Welfare) Regulations (employers must keep the workplace safe for any person at work there). The claim failed. Under reg 5 of PUWER the suitability of work equipment was to be measured by taking into account those hazards which were reasonably foreseeable. The obligation to stabilise the equipment under reg 20 only arose when this was necessary for the purpose of health and safety, which introduced considerations of foreseeability. Finally, the scaffolding tower was a safe place of work; it only became unsafe as the result of the deliberate, violent, and unpredictable act of a third party.

11.129 Similarly, in *Yorkshire Traction Co Ltd v Searby*,[103] a bus driver, while sitting in his driver's seat, was assaulted by a passenger. A county court judge held that the employers had been negligent in not inserting a screen to separate the driver from passengers, and thus there was a failure to provide work equipment which was 'suitable'. The decision was reversed by the Court of Appeal. In the first place, his trade union had strongly objected to the insertion of such screens, as these were considered to be a safety hazard. Indeed, some drivers had taken action to have the screens removed from their buses. It was further found that the risk of injury to bus drivers was very low. Thus the measure of the risk, the perceived disadvantages, and the attitude of the workforce was such that the failure by the employers to fit screens did not amount to negligence at common law. So far as a breach of statutory duty is concerned, the regulations do not require complete and absolute protection. In assessing the suitability of work equipment the test for liability involved a consideration of the degree of risk. Since the incidence of injury to drivers from passengers had been very low, it could not be said that the work equipment (ie the bus) was unsuitable.

G. Limitation of Actions (Limitation Act 1980)

11.130 Any action in respect of negligence, nuisance, or breach of statutory duty which has resulted in personal injury must be brought within three years from the date when the cause of action accrued, or from the date when the claimant had knowledge of the injury. 'Knowledge' in this connection means when the injured person had knowledge:

(a) that the injury was significant;

(b) that the injury was attributable wholly or partly to the act or omission which gave rise to the legal liability;

(c) that the defendant was responsible;

(d) of any other fact supporting the bringing of an action against the defendant.

---

[102] [2002] EWCA Civ 1604, [2003] ICR 179, [2002] All ER (D) 122 (Nov).
[103] [2003] EWCA Civ 1856, [2003] All ER (D) 409 (Dec).

A person's knowledge includes knowledge which he might reasonably be expected to acquire from facts which are observable by him, or from facts ascertainable by him with the help of medical or other expert advice which it is reasonable for him to seek. The Act does not apply in Scotland, where the Prescription and Limitations (Scotland) Act applies.

Summary

- The Health and Safety at Work Act 1974 is intended to protect people, not premises.
- Liability of employers can be criminal or civil.
- The HASAWA is enforced by the HSE or local authorities.
- They can issue improvement or prohibition notices.
- Employers also have some duties to non-employees who are lawfully on their premises.
- Employees also have some duties, such as to take reasonable care.
- There are a number of regulations to protect employees, in particular the 'six-pack'.
- Claims can be made in tort for compensation for injuries at work.
- A claim for personal injury has to be brought within 3 years.

12

Disciplinary, Dismissal, and Grievance Procedures

Background

12.1 During the performance of the employment contract the employer may find it necessary, through the appropriate manager, foreman, or supervisor who is charged with the necessary responsibility, to exercise some form of disciplinary authority over the employee. This may take one of a number of forms, ranging from counselling, informal warnings, etc, through to final warning or dismissal. The prime objective must be corrective, not punishment. Disciplinary procedures and powers must be exercised in a manner that will enable the employee to retain his position as a valued member of the staff, and not used purely as a matter of form of mechanical exercise. Thus adherence to a well-drafted disciplinary procedure is an essential part of any decision-making process. Equally, there will be occasions when the employee will wish to pursue a grievance over the way he is treated, and a suitable grievance procedure is the obvious channel to be used.

Disciplinary Procedures

A. **Procedures in Operation**

12.2 From the employer's point of view, there are likely to be three categories of 'hearing', and it is important to establish from the outset the distinctions. First, there is an informal interview, at which matters can be discussed. So long as this session does not result in any form of disciplinary sanction, the worker does not have the right to be accompanied (see para 12.25) and matters are best resolved by the parties concerned. Second, there is the investigatory type of hearing, which is designed to ascertain facts and collate evidence. Again, the employee has no right to be accompanied even though the meeting could lead to disciplinary proceedings (*Skiggs v South West Trains Ltd*[1]). Finally there is the disciplinary hearing itself where certain fundamental principles will apply. The important thing is that employers should not allow the informal interview or investigatory hearing to turn into a disciplinary hearing and, if there is a possibility that this is going to happen, those hearings should be terminated and a formal disciplinary hearing convened. If an allegation is so minor that it is dealt with under the informal misconduct procedure, it would clearly be wrong to dismiss an employee for gross misconduct on the same facts (*Sakar v West London Mental Health Trust*[2]).

---

[1] [2005] IRLR 459.   [2] [2010] IRLR 508, [2010] EWCA Civ 289, CA.

Investigations by the Employer

12.3 Clearly, no disciplinary action should be taken in advance of proper investigation by the employer. But there are certain limits on the extent to which an employer may properly make enquiries into an incident, particularly if the charge is a serious one, such as theft, for there may well be an improper interference with the processes of justice (*Tesco (Holdings) Ltd v Hill*[3]). On the other hand, when a disputed allegation is made against an employee, a careful and conscientious investigation must be carried out, and the investigator must focus no less on evidence which may exculpate the employee, or at least point to his innocence. This is particularly so when the employee is suspended, and has thus been denied an opportunity of being able to contact potentially relevant witnesses (*A v B*[4]).

12.4 Whether an employer should carry out his own investigations after being informed that criminal charges are to be brought against an employee in respect of matters arising out of his employment is a question of circumstances, and the employer has a wide discretion whether to continue or postpone the hearing (*Secretary of State for Justice v Mansfield*[5]).

On the one hand, it is incumbent on an employer to embark on some form of investigation involving at least an interview with the employee, to give him an opportunity to state his position. On the other hand, if the circumstances are so blatant and sufficient to warrant a belief as to the employee's guilt, no further investigation is necessary. Within this spectrum there are many situations where a further consideration of the position should be considered before disciplinary action is taken (*Lovie Ltd v Anderson*[6]). Although an employer cannot be expected to carry out its own independent investigation in order to test the reliability of the information provided by a responsible public authority, it should not take an uncritical view of the allegations. Rather, it should insist on a sufficient degree of formality and specificity about the disclosure before contemplating taking any action against the employee on the basis of it (*A v B*).[7]

12.5 The employer is not obliged to hold a full-scale trial, but there must be a careful examination of all the relevant matters. An investigation should not be conducted with such haste that important evidence is overlooked (*Johnson Matthey Metals v Harding*[8]), nor should it be delayed so long that issues become stale and hazy in the minds of witnesses (*Marley Homecare v Dutton*[9]). An employer does not have to investigate every line of defence put forward by an employee in order for the investigation to be reasonable (*Shrestha v Genesis Housing*[10]). It is particularly important to conduct a fair investigation and test the evidence of an accuser where there could be serious consequences to the employee—in *Salford Royal NHS Foundation Trust v Roldan*[11] dismissal could have meant deportation. An employer should also investigate allegations of dishonesty involving breach of trust with care. In *Stuart v London City Airport*[12] it was unreasonable that the employer did not look into evidence which might have shown that the employee was not dishonest. There is no particular form of procedure to be adopted, as long as the employee is given a fair hearing (*Bentley Engineering Co v Mistry*[13]). If it is necessary to consider an investigation in advance of criminal proceedings, it is still possible to discuss the matter without prejudicing a fair trial (*Harris (Ipswich) Ltd v Harrison*[14]), and a decision may be made on the basis of known facts, even though the employee has been advised to remain silent. If the evidence produced is sufficiently indicative of guilt (in the absence of any explanation) the employer

---

[3] [1977] IRLR 63, EAT.   [4] [2003] IRLR 405, [2003] All ER (D) 184 (May), EAT.
[5] EAT/0539/09/RN.   [6] [1999] IRLR 164, EAT.   [7] [2010] IRLR 844.
[8] [1978] IRLR 248, EAT.   [9] [1981] IRLR 380, EAT.   [10] [2015] EWCA Civ 94.
[11] [2010] IRLR 721, CA, [2010] EWCA Civ 522.   [12] [2013] EWCA Civ 973.
[13] [1979] ICR 47, [1978] IRLR 437, EAT.   [14] [1978] ICR 1256, [1978] IRLR 382, EAT.

is entitled to take some action. If, however, there are doubts, fairness may require the employer to wait until the criminal proceedings have been concluded (*Harris and Shepherd v Courage (Eastern) Ltd*[15]). The employer has a wide discretion on whether to continue with or postpone disciplinary hearings if the employee's conduct is also being investigated by the police (*Secretary of State for Justice v Mansfield*[16]). The object in holding a full investigation is to confirm suspicions or clear up doubts as to whether or not a particular act of misconduct has occurred (see *British Home Stores v Burchell*[17]). If an employee admits the offence, there is no need for a full investigation, unless some useful information could come to light (*Royal Society for the Protection of Birds v Croucher*[18]).

12.6 When an allegation of an employee's misconduct has been made by an informant, a balance must be maintained between the need to protect the informant and respect his anonymity, and providing a fair hearing to the accused employee. In *Linfood Cash and Carry Ltd v Thomson*,[19] the EAT laid down the following guidelines which could usefully be followed:

(a) the information should be reduced into writing, although it may be necessary to 'doctor' the statement in order to prevent identification;

(b) the statement should contain all the relevant facts, including dates, times, places, etc, the opportunity of the informant to observe clearly and with accuracy circumstantial evidence, and whether the informant had any reason to fabricate the evidence, whether from a personal grudge or any other reason;

(c) further investigation should then take place to confirm, corroborate, or challenge the information;

(d) tactful enquiries should be made about the background of the informant, and to find any other information which would add to or detract from the value of the information given;

(e) if the informant is not prepared to attend the disciplinary hearing, a decision will have to be taken on whether to continue or not;

(f) if it is decided to continue, the person responsible for conducting the hearing should interview the informant, and assess the weight to be given to the information;

(g) the written statement of the informant should be made available to the employee and his representatives;

(h) if there are matters to be put to the informant, the person conducting the hearing should adjourn to make further enquiries;

(i) full and careful notes of the disciplinary hearing should be taken;

(j) evidence from the investigation officer should be prepared in a written form.

12.7 An employee who has been dismissed in consequence of information provided in this manner may however be able to obtain from the High Court an order compelling his former employer to disclose the identity of the informant, so as to pursue an appropriate remedy, eg defamation and/or malicious falsehood (*P v T Ltd*[20]).

12.8 A distinction must be drawn between the investigatory function and the disciplinary function. If the same person undertakes both, there is usually no problem, but when they are separate and distinct, there is an obligation to give an employee a hearing at both stages.

[15] [1982] ICR 530, [1982] IRLR 509, CA.   [16] [2010] UKEAT/593/09.
[17] [1980] ICR 303n, [1978] IRLR 379.   [18] [1984] ICR 604, [1984] IRLR 425, EAT.
[19] [1989] ICR 518, [1989] IRLR 235, EAT.   [20] [1997] 4 All ER 200, [1977] ICR 887.

In *Budgen & Co v Thomas*,[21] an employee was dismissed after she had signed a written confession that she had stolen a small sum of money. The matter had been investigated by the security officer, and on the basis of his report, which was sent to the company's head office, the decision to dismiss was taken. This was held to be unfair. She was an 18-year-old girl, diabetic, and subsequently claimed that she was confused at the time she signed the confession and that it was not true. It could not be said that in view of her personal circumstances the management would have dismissed her had she been given the opportunity to present her case; the person who took the decision to dismiss should at least have given her a hearing.

12.9 A person who is a witness in investigatory proceedings should not act as a judge in disciplinary proceedings, otherwise this could be regarded as a breach of the principles of natural justice. However, there may be occasions when the person who has to take the decision to dismiss is also the person who witnessed the incident, and while this can be acceptable (and indeed inevitable) it is preferable for this dual role to be avoided (*Moyes v Hylton Castle Working Men's Social Club*[22]). Also, a person who is involved in the investigatory stage should not, if possible, be involved in the appeal stage, as this would put him in a situation of being a judge in his own cause, and justice would not be done, as well as not appear to be done (*Byrne v BOC Ltd*[23]). However, in the case of small employers, this counsel of perfection may not be possible.

12.10 In those cases where witnesses are not part of the employer's organization, it is not necessary for the employer to carry out a quasi-judicial hearing, with a confrontation and cross-examination of those witnesses (*Ulsterbus Ltd v Henderson*[24]). In *Sainsbury's Supermarkets Ltd v Hitt*,[25] the Court of Appeal confirmed that the band of reasonableness approach applies to the conduct of investigations as much as to other procedural and substantive decisions to dismiss a person from his employment for conduct. Thus, provided an employer carries out an appropriate investigation, gives the employee a fair opportunity to explain his conduct, etc, it would be wrong for an employment tribunal to suggest that further investigations should have been carried out for, by doing so, they are substituting their own standards of what was an adequate investigation for the standard that could be objectively expected from a reasonable employer.

12.11 The principle of *res judicata*, namely that a person should not have to face the same allegation twice, applies only to courts and tribunals, not internal procedures: *Christou and Ward v London Borough of Haringey*[26] (although this case was on very specific facts).

B. Types of Disciplinary and Grievance Procedures

12.12 Basically, disciplinary and grievance procedures should conform to the ACAS Code of Practice Disciplinary and Grievance Procedures in Employment, which should be studied in detail by all levels of management, but note that the Code is limited to disciplinary situations relating to culpable conduct which may lead to correction or punishment. This means that employers who dismiss employees for reasons which do not give rise to a disciplinary situation do not have to follow the ACAS Code of Practice on disciplinary procedures, such as ill health dismissals (*Holmes v Qinetiq Ltd*[27]), or

---

[21] [1976] ICR 344, [1976] IRLR 174, EAT.   [22] [1986] IRLR 482, EAT.
[23] [1992] IRLR 505, EAT.   [24] [1989] IRLR 251, NICA.
[25] [2001] All ER (D) 344 (Dec), EAT; revsd [2002] EWCA Civ 1588, [2003] ICR 111, [2003] IRLR 23, [2002] All ER (D) 259 (Oct).
[26] [2013] EWCA Civ 178.   [27] UKEAT/0206/15.

dismissals for some other substantial reason where there is an irretrievable breakdown in the working relationship (*Phoenix House Limited v (1) Stockman (2) Lambis*[28]). A failure to follow the Code of Practice will not mean automatically that any action taken will inevitably be unfair (*Lewis Shops Group v Wiggins*[29]) but both sides ignore it at their peril. Employment tribunals should always consider the Code of Practice as a guide when assessing the reasonableness of any action taken, and any relevant provisions should be taken into account when determining the issues before them (*Lock v Cardiff Railway*, see para 17.71).

The ACAS Code of Practice makes the following recommendations:

(1) In relation to grievances

   (a) the employee should tell the employer of the grievance

   (b) the employer should hold a meeting with the employee to discuss the grievance

   (c) the employee should be told of the right to be accompanied

   (d) after the meeting, the employer should decide on the appropriate action

   (e) the employer should permit the employee to have a right of appeal.

(2) In relation to discipline and dismissal proceedings

   (a) the employer should first establish the facts of the case

   (b) the employer should then inform the employee of the nature of the problem

   (c) the employer should hold a meeting with the employee to discuss the matter

   (d) the employee should be told of his right to be accompanied

   (e) after the meeting, the employer should decide on the appropriate action to be taken

   (f) the employee should be given the right of appeal.

12.13 If either party unreasonably fails or refuses to follow the provisions of the Code, the employment tribunal may increase or reduce any award made by up to 25 percent, as appropriate.

12.14 There will also be the normal contractual or non-contractual disciplinary and grievance procedures (many of which will have already been in existence for some time), which are still valid and should still function, provided they meet at least the standards set down by the ACAS Code. They can, however, be more expansive. A failure to follow contractual procedures may constitute a breach of contract by the employer. This may result in (a) the employee seeking an injunction to restrain the employer from taking disciplinary action in breach of the procedure (*Peace v City of Edinburgh Council*[30]), (b) the employee resigning and claiming that he was constructively dismissed (see Chapter 17), or (c) the employee seeking damages at common law, based on the length of time he would have been employed had the appropriate procedure been followed (*Gunton v London Borough of Richmond upon Thames*, see para 3.91). A failure to follow a contractual procedure in relation to a dismissal will render that dismissal unfair (*Polkey v AE Dayton Services Ltd*[31]). If, however, the employer can show that the dismissal would have taken place even if the proper procedure had been followed, then a tribunal can make a '*Polkey*' reduction (para 17.212).

[28] UKEAT/0264/15.   [29] [1973] ICR 335, [1973] IRLR 205, NIRC.
[30] [1999] IRLR 417.   [31] [1987] UKHL 8.

C. **Drawing up Procedures**

12.15 The responsibility for drawing up disciplinary and grievance procedures is on the employer. Clearly, if he can obtain the co-operation and assistance of any relevant trade union, or of his employees, so much the better, but in the absence of any such co-operation, the employer must act unilaterally. There are practical advantages in having trade union involvement in drawing up procedures, and challenges alleging unfairness are less likely to succeed if agreed procedures are followed.

12.16 The important thing is that the employer does not have to prove that an offence took place, or even satisfy himself beyond all reasonable doubt that the employee committed the act in question. The function of the employer is to act reasonably in coming to a decision. Thus in *Ferodo Ltd v Barnes*,[32] an employee was dismissed for vandalism. The employment tribunal was not satisfied that the employee was guilty, and therefore held that the dismissal was unfair. This finding was reversed by the EAT. The question was not whether or not the employment tribunal was satisfied that the employee was guilty, but whether they were satisfied that the employer had reasonable grounds for believing that the employee had committed the offence, and had acted reasonably in dismissing for that offence. The employer is not concerned to apply standards of proof which may be relevant in a criminal court. In *Docherty v Reddy*,[33] the employee was dismissed for stealing 50p from the till. The employers took into account that they had suspected him of stealing similar sums on previous occasions, and it was held that they were entitled to have regard to their past suspicions. Clearly, a suspicion of previous theft is hardly evidence which would be admitted in a criminal court, but the issues are different. The employer is having to decide whether or not he wishes to retain the employee, not whether or not he was guilty of a particular offence. Thus the test is, what would a reasonable employer have done on the facts which he knew, taking into account the Code of Practice and current industrial relations practice (*Parkers Bakeries Ltd v Palmer*[34])? The employment tribunal must not act as a court of appeal, nor retry a case, and the fact that in subsequent criminal proceedings an employee is acquitted of a charge against him is irrelevant to the issue of whether or not the employer has acted reasonably (*Davies v GKN Birwelco (Ukside) Ltd*[35]).

12.17 Evidence which is not admissible in criminal proceedings may fairly be considered by an employer in disciplinary proceedings (*Dhaliwal v British Airways Board*[36]) and a confession which would be inadmissible in a criminal court is also properly admissible before a disciplinary board (*Morley's of Brixton Ltd v Minott*[37]).

12.18 If an employee pleaded guilty to a criminal offence in a court of law, or has been found guilty by the court, it is reasonable for an employer to believe that the offence has been committed by the employee. Any other conclusion 'would be ridiculous' (*P v Nottinghamshire County Council*[38]). The fact of conviction might well form an adequate basis for dismissal, although the nature of the offence would be a relevant factor. Thus, to dismiss for a trivial offence would not be reasonable (*Secretary of State for Scotland v Campbell*[39]). Note that an employer does not generally need to wait for the outcome of a police investigation before starting a disciplinary hearing (*North West Anglia NHS Foundation Trust v Gregg*[40]).

---

[32] [1976] ICR 439, [1976] IRLR 302, EAT.   [33] [1977] ICR 365, EAT.
[34] [1977] IRLR 215, EAT.   [35] [1976] IRLR 82.
[36] [1985] ICR 513, EAT.   [37] [1982] ICR 444, [1982] IRLR 270, EAT.
[38] [1992] ICR 706, [1992] IRLR 362, CA.   [39] [1992] IRLR 263, EAT.
[40] [2019] EWCA Civ 387.

D. **Composition of Procedural Bodies**

12.19 The composition of any disciplinary body will doubtless be determined by each employer in accordance with the size of the firm and the circumstances of each case. The procedure will lay down who can exercise authority, the extent of the authority, and the circumstances when it is exercised. For example, informal warnings may be given at a certain level by supervisors, formal warnings should be given in writing and signed by someone who has power to issue and act on them, and so on. If an appeal may be made to a disciplinary board, its composition should be specified, with due regard to providing substitutes as appropriate. Otherwise a failure to do this may result in a dismissal being rendered unfair when it may have been fair. Thus in *Westminster City Council v Cabaj*,[41] the employee was dismissed. He was entitled to appeal to an appeal tribunal consisting of three council members. At the actual hearing, only two council members turned up, and they proceeded to hear the appeal and dismissed it. The employee was not asked if he agreed to the appeal being heard by two members. The Court of Appeal held that where there is a failure to comply with a contractually enforceable disciplinary procedure, it was for the employment tribunal to determine whether a consequent dismissal is fair or unfair, and there is no automatic assumption of unfairness. The employment tribunal must decide the issue in accordance with the matters set out in ERA, s 98. But where public institutions are concerned, the persons sitting on the appeal body must have been validly appointed, and there is no power to ratify an invalid appointment (*R v Secretary of State for Education, ex p Prior*[42]). In a case concerning a public institution, when deciding who should sit on the panel regard should be had to the principle that justice must not only be done, but must also be seen to be done, and so care should be taken not only to avoid bias but also the appearance of bias (*Watson v University of Strathclyde*).[43] A disciplinary panel does not have to be composed entirely of members from outside the employer NHS Trust for it to be independent and impartial. It is sufficient that one of the three members is impartial (*R (Puri) v Bradford Teaching Hospitals NHS Foundation Trust*).[44]

12.20 In *Clark v Civil Aviation Authority*,[45] the EAT gave some broad guidance on how disciplinary proceedings should be conducted. The purpose of the meeting should be explained, those present should be identified, representation should be arranged, the employee should be informed of the allegations being made, the evidence should be presented in statement form or through witnesses, the employee or his representative should be permitted to ask questions, the employee should be permitted to call witnesses, he or his representative will then explain or argue his case, both sides can then argue on the allegations and any possible consequences, including mitigation, and the employee will finally be asked if there is any further evidence or enquiry which will help his case. The decision will then be reduced to writing (whether or not an earlier oral decision has been given).

12.21 Particular care should be taken when it is proposed to take disciplinary action against shop stewards, and the Code of Practice recommends that it is advisable to discuss the circumstances of the case with a full-time official of the union concerned. However, being a shop steward is not a passport to disciplinary immunity (*Fowler v Cammell Laird (Shipbuilders) Ltd*[46]).

---

[41] [1996] ICR 960, [1996] IRLR 399, CA. [42] [1994] ICR 877. [43] [2011] IRLR 458.
[44] [2011] IRLR 582, [2011] EWHC 970 (Admin). [45] [1991] IRLR 412, EAT. [46] [1973] IRLR 72.

E. **Conduct of Hearing**

12.22 A disciplinary hearing must be conducted fairly. To achieve this, a number of rules should be observed.

(a) The employee is entitled to know the nature of the charge against him, in sufficient detail to enable him to prepare his case (*Hutchins v British Railways Board*[47]). It is best to put this in writing, particularly if the employee's command of English is weak, so that he can get someone else to explain it to him (*Sharma v West Yorkshire Passenger Transport Executive*[48]).

In particular, he must not ultimately be disciplined or dismissed because other matters come to light which were not previously notified to him. In *Boyd v Renfrewshire Council*[49] disciplinary proceedings were taken against an employee for disrupting work by taking part in a work-to-rule. At no stage either in the letter calling him to the disciplinary hearing or during the hearing itself was he told that he was liable to dismissal. His subsequent dismissal was held to be unfair. He had not been given an opportunity to put forward matters that were relevant because of fears of harassment by fellow employees, and it was unfair to dismiss him on grounds that were significantly more serious than the complaint he expected to face at the disciplinary hearing. Had he realized that he was facing dismissal he would have given a fuller explanation for his conduct in mitigation.

Witness statements should be shown to the person accused (*Louies v Coventry Hood and Seating Co Ltd*[50]), although it is acknowledged that there may be occasions when it is necessary to preserve anonymity (*Linfood Cash and Carry Ltd v Thomson*, see para 12.6). But in *Fuller v Lloyds Bank plc*[51] an employee of the respondents was in a public house on Christmas Eve, and received severe facial injuries from a glass which the claimant held in his hand. The employers took statements from a number of witnesses, but these were not disclosed to the claimant. Following a disciplinary hearing, he was dismissed, and claimed his dismissal was unfair. An employment tribunal dismissed his claim, arguing that the claimant knew the nature of the allegations. An appeal to the EAT failed. The procedure adopted was not so defective as to make the overall result unfair. Thus there is no universal requirement of natural justice or general principles of law that in all cases a witness statement must be shown to an employee who has been accused of misconduct. It is only a failure of natural justice if the essence of the case against the employee is contained in the statements, and he has not been otherwise informed of the nature of the case against him (*Hussain v Elonex plc*[52]). There is no rule of law which requires an employer to permit an employee to cross-examine, during a disciplinary hearing, colleagues who have made allegations of misconduct by the employee. The employer must carry out a reasonable investigation into the alleged wrongdoing, not carry out a forensic or quasi-judicial investigation (*Santemera v Express Cargo Forwarding*[53]).

(b) An employee should always be given an opportunity to state his case (*Tesco (Holdings) Ltd v Hill*, see para 12.3) no matter what the circumstances are (as should an office holder: *R (Shoesmith) v OFSTED & Ors*[54]). He is entitled to plead that he did not do the alleged act, or that he did not intend the construction which has been

[47] [1974] IRLR 303.   [48] [1977] IRLIB.   [49] 2008 SCLR 578, 2008 GWD 20–333.
[50] [1990] ICR 54, [1990] IRLR 324, EAT.   [51] [1991] IRLR 336, EAT.   [52] [1999] IRLR 420, CA.
[53] [2003] IRLR 273, [2002] All ER (D) 379 (Nov), EAT.
[54] [2011] IRLR 679, [2011] EWCA Civ 642.

put on it, or that mitigating circumstances relating to his case should be taken into consideration (*Boyd v Renfrewshire Council*[55]). To dismiss a woman who, because of a pregnancy-related illness, is unable to attend a disciplinary hearing is to cause her to suffer a detriment on grounds of pregnancy, and is therefore direct discrimination (*Abbey National plc v Formoso*, see para 4.51). However, it is not essential that the employee should be present in person throughout the hearing, when all the evidence is being given, if his representative is there (*Pirelli General Cable Works v Murray*[56]). The opportunity given to an employee to 'state his case' cannot be underestimated or undervalued.

However, in rare cases, where there is no possibility of any explanation of the conduct alleged, or where misconduct is admitted by the employee, it is legally permissible (although possibly in practice undesirable) to dispense with disciplinary formalities (*Clarke v Trimoco Motor Group Ltd*[57]). Thus in *Sutherland v Sonat Offshore (UK) Inc*[58] the employers had a strict rule forbidding alcohol or drugs while employees were on a drilling unit. The appellant was given a routine drug test, which showed the presence of cannabis in his urine, and the result was confirmed in further tests. He was dismissed without being given a proper chance to state his case, but the EAT upheld a finding of an employment tribunal that his dismissal was nonetheless fair. The requirement for investigation was met by the testing procedures, there was no possibility of an error, and there was no way the substance could have been ingested by some other means, eg 'passive smoking'. Thus the employers were entitled to act on the evidence before them without involving the full disciplinary procedure.

(c) He should be permitted the right to be represented or accompanied in accordance with the procedure (*Rank Xerox (UK) Ltd v Goodchild*[59]). There is now a statutory right to be accompanied (see para 12.25).

(d) He should be informed of his right to appeal to a higher level of management, who have not previously been involved in the decision (*S C Brown Communications Ltd v Walker*[60]), or to an independent arbitrator. If he fails or refuses to exercise that right, then he does not contribute to the unfair dismissal, nor does he fail to mitigate his loss (*William Muir (Bond 9) Ltd v Lamb*[61]). As a matter of principle, a person who takes the decision to dismiss should not take any part in the appeal process (*R v Chief Constable of Merseyside Police*[62]), although it has to be conceded that this counsel of perfection cannot be applied to small firms.

12.23 As a general rule it is not appropriate for the courts to intervene to remedy minor irregularities in the course of disciplinary proceedings between employer and employee—its role is not the 'micro-management' of such proceedings: *Kulkarni v Milton Keynes Hospital NHS Foundation Trust* (paras 12.27 and 12.29). Such intervention would produce unnecessary delay and expense, but in the case of *Chhabra v West London Mental Health NHS Trust*[63] the irregularities were of a more serious nature. An HR manager altered the conclusions of a disciplinary investigation that had been carried out by another manager from a finding of ordinary misconduct to one of gross misconduct, meaning that Dr Chhabra could be summarily dismissed without notice. The Trust was found to have breached the contract by allowing the case investigator's conclusions to be amended by someone else, and so an injunction was granted. The Supreme Court held that it can intervene to restrain

[55] See n 46.   [56] [1979] IRLR 190, EAT.
[57] [1993] ICR 237, [1993] IRLR 148, EAT.   [58] EAT/186/93.   [59] [1979] IRLR 185, EAT.
[60] Unreported.   [61] [1985] IRLR 95, EAT.   [62] [2001] IRLR 442.   [63] [2013] UKSC 80.

an employer from requiring an employee to face a charge of potential gross misconduct at a disciplinary hearing if the conduct complained of is not sufficiently serious to support such a finding.

12.24 There may be a desire to record a hearing. It is not always misconduct for an employee to make a covert recording (*Phoenix House v Stockman*[64]) as such a recording is not necessarily always undertaken to entrap or gain a dishonest advantage, so an ET is not bound to conclude that the covert recording of a meeting necessarily undermines the trust and confidence between employer and employee to the extent that an employer should no longer be required to keep the employee. The EAT found that an ET is entitled to make an assessment of the circumstances, looking at the purpose for which it is made, what is recorded, and the extent of the employee's blameworthiness. That said, it considered that it is good employment practice for an employee or an employer to say if there is any intention to record a meeting save in the most pressing of circumstances; and it will generally amount to misconduct not to do so.

F. **Right to be Accompanied: Employment Relations Act 1999, ss 10–15**

12.25 Section 10 of the Employment Relations Act 1999 creates a right for a worker, when invited by his employer to attend a disciplinary or grievance hearing, to make a reasonable request to be accompanied by a single companion, who can be:

(a) an official of an independent trade union (not necessarily one recognised by the employer); or

(b) a trade union official who has been certified by the trade union as having had experience or having received training in acting as a worker's companion in such hearings (eg a shop steward); or

(c) another of the employer's workers.

The choice of companion does not have to be reasonable, so long as it is someone within the specified categories and the request to be accompanied is itself reasonable (*Toal & Anor v GB Oils Ltd*[65]).

12.26 The right to be accompanied is triggered by any hearing which has the characteristic of a disciplinary sanction, however it is described. An investigatory meeting, or one which could only result in a genuine informal warning, will not attract the statutory right to be accompanied. But a requirement to undergo retraining, coaching, or counselling is not a disciplinary sanction since it does not contain an element of penalty or punishment (*London Underground Ltd v Ferenc-Batchelor*[66]).

12.27 The companion is entitled to address the hearing in order to put the worker's case, sum up that case, respond to any views expressed at the hearing, and confer with the worker during the hearing. He is not entitled to answer questions on behalf of the worker, or address the hearing if the worker does not wish him to do so. Nor can he prevent the worker from explaining his case or prevent any other person from making a contribution to the hearing. However, there is no obligation on any person, whether or not he is a trade union official, to take on the role of companion.

12.28 As a general principle, ERA, s 10 does not confer the right to legal representation at a disciplinary or grievance hearing unless there is a provision in the contract of

---

[64] UKEAT/0284/17.   [65] UKEAT/0569/12/LA.

[66] [2003] ICR 656, [2003] IRLR 252, [2003] All ER (D) 252 (Mar), EAT.

employment or disciplinary procedure that provides for this, or the employer permits this on an 'ad hoc' basis. The right to be accompanied is confined to being accompanied by an official of a trade union or a fellow worker. However, if the consequences of the disciplinary hearing would have a serious impact upon an employee's working life, or possibly expose him to criminal charges, the courts lean to the view that he is entitled to have legal representation if he so wishes. This right is based on the European Convention on Human Rights, Art 6(1), which states that every person is entitled to a fair and public hearing, and Art 6(3), which provides that when being faced with a criminal charge, every person has the right to defend himself through legal assistance of his own choosing. In *Kulkarni v Milton Keynes Hospitals NHS Trust*[67] a doctor was charged with professional misconduct in conducting an improper examination of a female patient. As a matter of construction of the trust's procedure it was held that the doctor was entitled to be represented by a lawyer of his professional association, but the view was expressed that if disciplinary proceedings could deprive an employee of the right to practice his profession there could be an implied right to legal representation based on Art 6 of the Convention on Human Rights. Contrast this with the case of *R (Puri) v Bradford Teaching Hospitals NHS Foundation Trust* (see para 12.19), where it was held that Art 6 was not engaged. The difference is that whilst it would be difficult for Mr Puri to find employment within the NHS, it was not impossible. For Dr Kulkarni, however, it was practically impossible, as he had been found guilty of what amounted to a criminal offence, and still had to complete his training, which could only be done in the NHS. Accordingly there was insufficient link between the dismissal and a denial of the right to practise his profession to engage Art 6.

12.29 Article 6 does not therefore apply where the hearing does not deprive the claimant of the right to practise his profession. It only applies where there is a 'determination of . . . civil rights and obligations'. In *R v Governors of X School*,[68] a schoolteacher was subjected to disciplinary action following an allegation of inappropriate behaviour with a young person engaged at the school on a work-experience programme. The school's disciplinary procedure was followed by a hearing before the Independent Safeguarding Authority, which maintains a list of those to be barred from working with children, and which could place the claimant on the 'barred list'. The ISA would exercise its own judgment, and come to its own conclusion. As the school's determination dealt only with his employment, and would not have a 'substantial influence' on the ISA's decision, there was not a sufficient connection between the internal disciplinary proceedings and the ISA proceedings. The Supreme Court found that the former dealt only with his current employment, and was therefore not 'directly decisive' of the issue, and so there was no right to legal representation before the school, although there would be for the ISA hearing.

12.30 Several problems arise from these decisions. The fact that the outcome of disciplinary proceedings could result in the loss of employment does not, per se, warrant legal representation (see *Kulkarni*, para 12.28). But there are many cases when even a lesser sanction could have an equally disastrous effect on an employee's livelihood or reputation (eg an allegation of sexual misconduct), and when the need for legal representation may be just as important. We may also ask if there is a distinction between the dismissal of an employee and the dismissal of a professional person. Are we to grade employees by their ranking in the food chain in order to see if their status warrants higher standards in disciplinary proceedings, and thus give a professional person the right to legal representation which is denied to others? Finally, cases such as *Kulkarni* and *R v Governors of X School* can only apply to public sector employees who are required to act in a manner which is compatible

[67] [2009] EWCA Civ 789, [2010] ICR 101, [2009] IRLR 829. [68] [2011] IRLR 756, [2011] UKSC 30.

with the Convention. Would the courts be willing to extend the right to legal representation to the private sector? It is clear that this topic raises a number of outstanding issues, which no doubt will be the subject of judicial exploration in the coming years.

12.31 If the worker makes a request to be accompanied, but the chosen companion is not available at the time proposed for the hearing, the employer must postpone the hearing to a time proposed by the worker. The alternative time must be reasonable, and within five working days after the date proposed by the employer.

12.32 The employer shall permit a worker to have time off work for the purpose of accompanying another worker; when acting in the capacity of a trade union official, this will count as trade union duties for the purpose of TULR(C)A, ss 168–173 and thus the time off work will be with pay.

12.33 The right to be accompanied applies to workers as defined, including agency workers, homeworkers, persons in Crown employment and members of the staff of the House of Lords and House of Commons (s 13). However, persons employed by the Security Services, Secret Intelligence Service, and Government Communications Headquarters are excluded from these provisions (s 15).

12.34 A complaint may be made to an employment tribunal (within the usual time limits) that the employer has failed to permit the worker to exercise his rights under s 10; if it finds the complaint to be well founded, the tribunal shall make a compensation award of up to two weeks' pay (s 11).

12.35 A worker has the right not to suffer a detriment because he sought to be accompanied or to accompany another, and any dismissal because of the exercise of the above rights will be automatically unfair. The qualifying period of employment does not apply, and interim relief will be available, as appropriate (s 12).

G. Appeal Procedures

12.36 If the initial procedure is flawed in some way a refusal by the employer to permit an employee to exercise the right of appeal to which he is contractually entitled will render a dismissal unfair (*West Midland Co-operative Society v Tipton*[69]). If an employer's decision to dismiss would be fair at the time when the appeal machinery is exhausted, that decision does not become unfair because further information comes to light after the appeal has been dismissed (*Greenall Whitley plc v Carr*[70]).

12.37 Whether an appeal hearing should be a rehearing of all the evidence *de novo*, or a review of all the evidence with an opportunity to make further representations, is a matter of style. At one time it was thought that when an initial decision to dismiss was procedurally flawed, the defect could be cured at the appeal stage, which could be a rehearing or review, as the case may be (see *Whitbread plc v Mills*[71]). However, that approach was disapproved of in *Taylor v OCS Group Ltd* (see para 4.108), where the Court of Appeal stated that the employment tribunal should consider the fairness of the whole of the disciplinary process. If the early stage of the procedure was defective or unfair in some way, the tribunal should examine any subsequent proceedings with particular care. It must then determine whether, due to the fairness or unfairness of the procedures adopted,

---

[69] [1986] AC 536, [1986] 1 All ER 513, [1986] ICR 192, [1986] IRLR 112, HL.
[70] [1985] ICR 451, [1985] IRLR 289, EAT.
[71] [1988] ICR 776, [1988] IRLR 501, EAT.

the thoroughness (or lack of it) of the process, and the open-mindedness (or not) of the decision-maker, the overall procedure was fair, notwithstanding any deficiencies at the early stage. However, in *Adeshina v St George's University Hospitals NHS Foundation Trust & Ors*[72] it was found that where an appeal hearing is a rehearing rather than a review, this can correct a procedural flaw in the disciplinary process. It is the fairness overall which counts, and depends on the facts of the case. Procedural defects where the decision has a serious effect on the employee, however, can affect the fairness of a dismissal, even if these defects are rectified at the appeal stage (*Tykocki v Royal Bournemouth and Christchurch Hospitals NHS Foundation Trust*[73]).

12.38 However, it is very important that internal appeals procedures operated by commercial concerns should not be cramped by legal requirements which impose impossible burdens on the way they conduct their affairs. In *Rowe v Radio Rentals*[74] the claimant was alleged to have been guilty of gross misconduct, and was dismissed by the area manager. An appeal was made to the regional manager and at the hearing the area manager outlined the facts of the case and remained present throughout the hearing. It was held that the appeals procedure was perfectly fair, even though it may appear to have offended against the rules of natural justice. It was inevitable that those who take the original decision to dismiss must be in daily contact with their superiors who would be hearing the appeal. Rules about lack of contact cannot be applied in the majority of cases. The EAT quoted with approval Lord Denning in *Ward v Bradford Corpn*: 'We must not force these disciplinary bodies to become entrammelled in the nets of legal procedure. So long as they act fairly and justly, their decision should be supported.'[75]

12.39 If an employee is dismissed, but is given a right to make an appeal in accordance with the company's disciplinary procedure, what is his legal position up to the time the appeal is heard? There are two possibilities.

12.40 First, if he is dismissed (with or without notice) the dismissal takes effect from the effective date of termination, and the fact that an appeal is pending does not alter that date. In *J Sainsbury Ltd v Savage* (see para 20.27) the applicant was dismissed for gross misconduct. On the effective date of termination he did not have the requisite period of continuous employment (26 weeks, as the law then was), but by the time the appeal was heard, more than 28 weeks had elapsed since the commencement of his employment. It was held that he could not pursue a claim for unfair dismissal. Thus using domestic appeal machinery merely suspends the dismissal; if the appeal is rejected, the original decision is confirmed (*Natt v Hillingdon Area Health Authority*[76]).

12.41 Second, if he is dismissed and placed on full pay pending an internal appeal, there is a suspension which does not terminate the contract, and hence he is still an employee up to the time of the appeal hearing (*Duffy v Northampton Area Health Authority*[77]).

12.42 On the other hand, if a person is dismissed, and then his appeal against dismissal is allowed, his period of employment is to be regarded as being continuous, for it is implicit in the contract that the period between the dismissal and appeal is one of suspension, and the result of the ultimate decision of the appeal process relates back to the date of the purported dismissal (*Howgate v Fane Acoustics*[78]).

---

[72] UKEAT/0293/14; on appeal [2017] EWCA Civ 257.   [73] UKEAT/0081/16.
[74] [1982] IRLR 177.   [75] (1971) 70 LGR 27, 115 Sol Jo 606, CA.
[76] Unreported.   [77] Unreported.   [78] [1981] IRLR 161, EAT.

Disciplinary Rules

12.43 The actual rules which an employee is expected to observe can be found either in the disciplinary procedure itself, or in the works or staff rules (see Chapter 3), or even in a combination of both. At one time it was customary to write them on a prominently displayed notice posted somewhere in the works, but this is not particularly satisfactory nowadays. The important thing is that they must be brought to the employee's attention, whether on an induction course or in a specially prepared handbook or other suitable method. In *Pitts v Revertex*[79] the employer posted a notice near the canteen on a notice board stating that any employee who absented himself without authority would be guilty of gross misconduct. The applicant was found to be absent, and was dismissed. It was held that if a rule was so important, posting a notice was not sufficient. It should have been communicated individually to each employee. The need to communicate the relevant rules to the employees concerned was stressed once again in *Brooks (W) & Son v Skinner*,[80] where the employers agreed with a trade union that employees who over-indulged themselves at a Christmas party so that they were unable to attend work would be instantly dismissed. This agreement was not communicated to the employees. The applicant was dismissed for failing to turn up for work on the night shift after a Christmas party, and his dismissal was held to be unfair. He would not have realized that this conduct would attract instant dismissal, and his lack of knowledge of the rule meant that the employers had acted unreasonably.

12.44 The rules should be clear and readily understandable by all affected employers, and should not be confused with extraneous matters. In *Rigden-Murphy v Securicor Ltd*,[81] the claimant was dismissed after being seen to be breaking a company rule concerning the transfer of money from a bank to his vehicle. The rule in question was contained in a manual, which had 'Ten golden rules'. At the end, there was a statement that a failure to comply may lead to instant dismissal. Some of the 'rules' were in fact mere exhortations, such as 'Beware of complacency. Build up the habit of self-discipline'. Other rules had in the past been dealt with by a warning. It was held that the dismissal was unfair. The rules were somewhat ambiguous, in that they contained matters which were unconnected with discipline, and there was no clear line between those rules which attracted dismissal as a punishment and those which were dealt with, if at all, with lesser severity.

12.45 Employment tribunals have, in the past, been most inconsistent in dealing with rules which contain automatic as opposed to discretionary sanctions. For example, in *Jones v London Co-operative Society*[82] the staff code in a departmental store stated that an incorrect recording of a customer's purchase was a serious offence, 'and the employee *will be* summarily dismissed'. It was held that such a rule was too rigid, for it failed to distinguish between a genuine error and a calculated act. On the other hand, in *Lindsay v Fife Forge*,[83] the works rules stated that employees who left the premises without permission '*may be* subject to instant dismissal' and the employment tribunal held that this did not amount to a clear and specific warning.

12.46 The problems caused by such sophistry can be illustrated by comparing *Dalton v Burton's Gold Medal Biscuits Ltd* (see para 10.53) and *Meridian Ltd v Gomersall.*[84] In the former case, a man of 22 years' service was dismissed for a clocking offence, the works rules stating that such action 'will result in instant dismissal'. The National Industrial Relations Court held the dismissal to be fair. In the latter case, it was stated in the works rules that

---

[79] Unreported.   [80] [1984] IRLR 379.   [81] [1976] IRLR 106.
[82] [1975] IRLR 110.   [83] [1976] IRLR 47.   [84] [1977] ICR 597, [1977] IRLR 425, EAT.

anyone guilty of a clocking offence 'will render themselves liable to instant dismissal'. The EAT upheld a tribunal decision that a dismissal was unfair, because the employee might take the view that to be caught once, even suspected of doing it previously, would not necessarily lead to an instant dismissal.

12.47 The question, in reality, is not the mandatory nature of the sanction, but whether the employer acts reasonably in imposing that sanction, or whether some other equally efficacious sanction could be imposed. It must be wrong to dismiss an employee for minor misconduct no matter how strongly worded is the rule, for the mandatory nature of a disciplinary rule does not exclude the jurisdiction of the employment tribunal to decide whether or not the employer has acted reasonably (*Ladbroke Racing Ltd v Arnott*[85]). On the other hand, automatic penalties fail to permit an employer to take account of mitigating circumstances, the employee's record, general conduct, and so forth. The employer should be able to tailor the punishment to the offence, and then to the offender. He should be consistent in his procedures, but can be flexible in his punishments. In *Elliott Bros Ltd v Colverd*[86] the EAT resolved doubts by stating that there is no legal requirement that a rule must indicate that a breach would inevitably lead to a dismissal, and a rule book did not need to indicate a distinction between the possibility and inevitability of dismissal. However the rule is worded, the employer is entitled to look at all the circumstances.

12.48 An employer must be prepared to justify any alleged disparity of treatment between different employees. In *Hadjioannou v Coral Casinos Ltd*[87] the claimant was dismissed for breaking a rule which forbade socializing with members or guests at a gambling club. He argued that in the past other employees had broken the rule and had not been dismissed. In upholding a decision of the employment tribunal that the dismissal was fair, the EAT commented that action taken by the employers in previous cases was only relevant in three circumstances: (a) to show that there may be certain categories of misconduct which may be overlooked (or at least not dealt with by the sanction of dismissal), (b) if it leads to the conclusion that the purported reason for the dismissal was not the real or genuine reason, and (c) to show that some lesser penalty would have been more appropriate. The EAT went on to comment that it was of the highest importance that flexibility should be retained, and employers should not be encouraged to think that there was a 'tariff' approach to industrial misconduct (see *Paul v East Surrey District Health Authority*,[88] para 17.127).

12.49 Disparity of treatment is acceptable if culpability is not the same. In *Securicor Ltd v Smith*,[89] the claimant and another employee were security guards, collecting and delivering cash. The employers had strict rules about the way they did their work. Following an incident when the rules were breached, the employers held a disciplinary hearing, and both employees were dismissed. An appeal was made to the area manager, who affirmed the dismissals. Both employees then lodged a further appeal to a special panel set up by the company, and at this level it was decided that as one employee was less blameworthy he would not be dismissed, but the dismissal of the claimant was confirmed. An employment tribunal held that his dismissal was unfair. They held that the original decision to dismiss both men was reasonable, but the final appeal body acted unreasonably in dismissing one employee but not the other on the ground that the other employee was less blameworthy. The decision was confirmed by the EAT. However, the Court of Appeal reversed the decision. The real question was whether the final appeal panel's decision was so unreasonable that no reasonable employer would have accepted it. Indeed, had the employers refused to accept the decision of the appeal panel not to dismiss the other employee, he would

[85] [1979] IRLR 192, EAT; on appeal [1983] IRLR 154, Ct of Sess.   [86] [1979] IRLR 92, EAT.
[87] [1981] IRLR 352, EAT.   [88] [1995] IRLR 305, CA.   [89] [1989] IRLR 356, CA.

have had an unanswerable case for unfair dismissal in an employment tribunal. The appeal panel, having thoroughly investigated the matter, had distinguished the culpability of the two employees, and their decision was not unreasonable.

12.50 Similarly, disparity of treatment is permitted if disciplinary records are not the same. In *Harrow London Borough v Cunningham*,[90] the claimant and a fellow worker were found to be doing unauthorized work in circumstances which amounted to gross misconduct. The claimant was dismissed, but his fellow worker was given a final warning. The reason for this was that the claimant had already been in receipt of a final warning, whereas his fellow worker had a clean disciplinary record. The EAT said this was not unfair, as an employer is entitled to take into account aggravating factors, including an employee's previously poor disciplinary record as compared with the other employee concerned, as well as mitigating circumstances which affect one employee when compared with the other.

12.51 Once an employer lays down a particular rule, a failure to enforce it consistently may weaken any subsequent attempt to do so. In *Frame v McKean & Graham Ltd* (see para 10.96), the claimant was dismissed for doing work on his own account contrary to the working rules for the industry. His dismissal was held to be unfair. The rule had never been enforced in the past, and indeed, such conduct had been condoned. Moreover, he had not taken any work away from the employer, for the customer for whom he worked had severed the relationship with the employer.

12.52 Rules may be of a general nature, eg defining conduct which, by the generality of the law of employment, cannot be tolerated; they may be specific, defining the sort of conduct which *this* employer will not tolerate, and they may be special, dealing with instant circumstances which have not arisen hitherto.

A. General Rules

12.53 These are rules which govern conduct which is such that by common consent, disciplinary sanctions will be imposed. Examples which readily spring to mind include theft of the employer's property, theft from fellow employees, serious neglect, wilful damage, dangerous practices, and so on. It is not generally advisable to list all the matters which come under the heading of gross misconduct, for this could mean that an employee would be saved from dismissal who committed an act which was so outrageous that no one thought it would ever happen (*Gardiner v Newport County Borough Council*[91]). In *Clarkson v Brown, Muff & Co Ltd*,[92] 'gross misconduct' was defined as being 'dishonesty, arson, violence, obscenity, neglect and insubordination'. It was held that this definition did not cover an employee who had been telling lies. Some firms make it clear that the definitions of gross misconduct contained in their rules are examples only, and any list of misdeeds is not intended to be exhaustive.

B. Specific Rules

12.54 These rules cover the sort of misconduct which *this employer* will not tolerate under any circumstances. Thus each employer must judge for himself the standards which are to apply, based on his own circumstances. Thus fighting, swearing, lateness, absenteeism, drunkenness, trading, betting, and so forth may all amount to industrial misconduct which, in the individual case, attracts disciplinary sanctions. Such rules must be fair and reasonable. In *Turner v Pleasurama Casinos Ltd*,[93] the claimant was an inspector who was employed to observe gaming tables, to ensure that there was no dishonesty by croupiers. He was dismissed for 'neglect of duty' after a complaint that a croupier and a member of the public had been cheating under his nose. The allegation was denied by him, but after a full and proper investigation, the employer found against him. It was held that the dismissal was fair; the gaming world is a hard world, and even the smallest of mistakes could not be tolerated.

12.55 Provided such rules meet the standards of reasonableness (and reasonableness is for the tribunal to interpret), they can generally be enforced. In *Higham v International Stores*,[94] the claimant was given to wearing sandals and clogs, and other casual clothes. He was told that he must comply with the company's requirement to wear proper shoes and socks, and to wear a tie and overall when serving customers. After failing to heed due warnings, he was dismissed for not complying with the rules. It was held that an employer is entitled to insist on a reasonable standard of dress. What was reasonable is always a question of fact, to be determined in each case by all the circumstances. Different standards apply in different places. In this case, the shop had a smart clientele in a conventional town, and the dismissal was thus fair.

C. Special Rules

12.56 Since the rules cannot conceivably cover every possible situation, an employer must be free to lay down a rule specifically to deal with a matter which has not hitherto arisen. In *Spiller v Wallis Ltd*[95] a company rule stated that employees should not have deep emotional relationships with other members of the staff which might impair their marital status. This rule had been promulgated after an incident where the spouse of an employee had come on to the premises and created an unpleasant scene. The claimant was in fact having a love affair with a senior employee, and she refused to discontinue the relationship. Her dismissal was held to be fair. She was told of the rule, but chose not to comply. NB: Whether such a rule contravenes Art 8 of the European Convention on Human Rights (see para 1.88) is a matter upon which no doubt the tribunals will shortly adjudicate!

12.57 Finally, the interpretation of the rules, and their reasonableness, is a matter for the employment tribunal to determine. In *Palmer v Vauxhall Motors Ltd*,[96] the claimant was dismissed for spending 15 minutes in the club bar after her lunch break. It was alleged that this constituted gross misconduct in accordance with the works rules. It was held that even though the rules were somewhat ambiguous, the employment tribunal was entitled to find that the dismissal was fair. The EAT would only reverse that finding if it could be said that no person instructed in the relevant law could have come to that decision.

Disciplinary Powers

12.58 The exercise of disciplinary powers is a corrective function, not punitive. The object is to improve an employee's performance so that he can remain a valued and useful employee, not to give vent to management frustrations. The choice of the disciplinary sanction must therefore reflect this objective, and should, so far as is possible, be tailored to the individual case, bearing in mind the need to show some form of consistency in like cases. The Code of Practice should be borne in mind at all times.

---

[93] [1976] IRLR 151.   [94] Unreported.   [95] [1973] IRLR 362.   [96] [1977] ICR 24, EAT.

A. **Fines and Deductions**

12.59 It is possible to impose a fine or make a deduction for bad or negligent work, but the principles laid down to prevent unlawful deductions (see para 8.5) must be observed. There must be a specific contractual power, and in respect of persons employed in retail employment the restrictions in ERA, s 18 must be observed. Deductions or payments made in consequence of disciplinary proceedings held under a statutory provision are excluded from the Act (eg police and fire service).

12.60 The Act specifically states that the only remedy for a breach is by way of a complaint to an employment tribunal under s 23, but it is submitted that an unauthorized deduction or payment may still give rise to a complaint of constructive dismissal. Thus, in *Lethaby v Horsman Andrew and Knill Ltd*[97] the employer made a deduction from the employee's wages to cover the loss of the firm's property. This was done in the absence of any contractual authority to make such a deduction, and the employee, who refused to agree to it, resigned. It was held that this constituted repudiatory conduct by the employer of the contract, and as such constituted a dismissal (see Chapter 17).

12.61 The employer's power to fine or make deductions must be contained in the express terms of the contract, and it is no longer possible to rely on an implied term, or (more likely) a customary term to this effect. This makes a number of current employment practices of dubious validity. For example, some firms make a practice of deducting 15 minutes from the pay of an hourly worker when he is a few minutes late (known as quartering); it is doubtful if the unilateral imposition of such a practice would be upheld in law.

B. **Suspension Without Pay for Misconduct**

12.62 If there is an express term in the contract which permits the employer to suspend an employee for a specific reason, such as misconduct, the courts will uphold such a term provided the suspension is carried out in strict conformity with the laid-down procedure. Sometimes the grounds for suspension, and the procedure to be adopted, will be laid down in the works rules, and the extent to which those rules will form part of the individual contract of employment will be a question of fact in each case. Even so, if an employee is, or ought to be, aware of the practice of a firm, or if there is a custom in the trade or industry or locality, then he will be bound by it. In *Bird v British Celanese Ltd*[98] an employee was suspended for two days in accordance with the firm's practice, and this was held to be a valid exercise of disciplinary power by the employer.

12.63 Alternatively, the grounds for suspension and procedure to be adopted may be contained in a collective agreement, in which case there may be an express or implied incorporation of those terms into the individual contract of employment. In *Tomlinson v London, Midland and Scottish Rly Co*[99] a trade union negotiated with the defendant company an agreement which, inter alia, laid down the procedure for dealing with breaches of discipline, and this was held to have been incorporated into an employee's contract of employment.

12.64 It is clear that the right of suspensory lay-off must be based on a contractual power, which will be either expressed, or implied, or based on custom and practice. The courts and tribunals are quite willing to discover such a power when minor disciplinary matters are concerned, though they appear to require strict proof if there is a major disciplinary

---

[97] [1975] IRLR 119.   [98] [1945] KB 336, [1945] 1 All ER 488, CA.   [99] [1944] 1 All ER 537, CA.

matter which can lead to a dismissal. The EAT held that it may not be difficult to draw an inference that a contract contains an implied power to suspend as a disciplinary matter, or to enable an investigation to take place (*Pirie and Hunter v Crawford*[100]). But in the total absence of such a power, it is clear that the employer may not purport to exercise it, for this would virtually enable him to assess unilaterally the damages for an employee's misconduct. It further follows that if an employee is wrongfully suspended without pay, he may recover any lost pay by way of damages. In *Hanley v Pease & Partners*,[101] an employee was suspended for one day without pay, and it was held that he was entitled to the money which had been withheld.

12.65 If an employer lawfully suspends an employee, the legal position at common law appears to be that the employment has been temporarily put in abeyance, with a right for the employee to apply for reinstatement at the end of the suspension period (*Marshall v English Electric Co Ltd*[102]). Presumably there is no break in continuity of employment in these circumstances. If the suspension is wrongful, the employee will be entitled to treat this breach as repudiatory conduct by the employer, and he will be entitled to resign and sue for wrongful or unfair dismissal. In *Davies v Anglo Great Lakes Corpn*[103] an employee was suspended without pay after allowing his trade union membership to lapse, and this was held to be repudiatory conduct by the employer.

12.66 But if an employee decides to resign as a result of wrongful suspension he may find the tribunal somewhat unsympathetic, for he would have to argue that he was entitled to resign by reason of the employer's (wrongful) conduct, which the tribunal may not accept as a valid reason, particularly if the employer had reasonable cause to suspend and the employee's conduct would otherwise have to be dealt with by a dismissal which would have been fair. It can hardly be right for an employer to be saddled with the burden of compensation if he exercises a lesser disciplinary power than he might have done. Another view which may be taken is that the employee's conduct was such that it 'contributed' to the repudiation by the employer, and hence reduced compensation may be awarded. Thus if the employee's conduct is such as to warrant a dismissal, but the employer suspends him without having the contractual power to do so, an action for unfair dismissal would probably fail because the constructive dismissal would be justified because of the misconduct, while an action for wrongful dismissal is unlikely to meet with any greater success. There have been a number of cases where the tribunals have held that an employee should not have been dismissed for misconduct, but the offence warranted some lesser disciplinary measure, such as suspension, even though the employer had no contractual right to do so. Thus in *Unkles v Milanda Bread Co Ltd*[104] an employee was dismissed for smoking in breach of the company's rules. The tribunal thought that an appropriate penalty might have been a suspension for one month without pay, but there is no evidence in the report to suggest that the employer had the power to do this by virtue of the contract of employment. In seeking to encourage employers to exercise this lesser power, it would be inconsistent for the tribunals to penalize them for doing so.

C. **Precautionary Suspension**

12.67 If an employee is suspended as a precautionary measure, and not for disciplinary purposes, the position is somewhat different. In *Jones v British Rail Hovercraft Ltd*[105] the employee was suspended from duty without pay pending the outcome of investigations

---

[100] Unreported.   [101] [1915] 1 KB 698, 79 JP 230, 84 LJKB 532, [1914–15] All ER Rep 984, 112 LT 823.
[102] [1945] 1 All ER 653, 43 LGR 275, 109 JP 145, 89 Sol Jo 315, 173 LT 134, 61 TLR 379, CA.
[103] [1973] IRLR 133.   [104] [1973] IRLR 76.   [105] [1974] IRLR 279.

and proceedings against him which were brought by the police. He claimed that this amounted to a dismissal, but this argument was rejected. The rule book, which was part of his employment conditions, mentioned the distinction between precautionary and punitive suspension, and it was reasonable for the employer to take precautionary steps to protect his interest and his property. That the suspension was without pay could be dealt with by making up his back pay if the proceedings ended in his favour. In *Crawford v Suffolk Mental Health Partnership NHS Trust*[106] the Court of Appeal raised concerns that even where there is a contractual power to suspend an employee, the employer should not do so as an automatic knee-jerk reaction to an allegation of misconduct, as this can be very damaging to the employee.

12.68 The Code of Practice indicates that precautionary suspension pending investigation should be with full pay, and this is probably correct in the absence of any contrary term in the contract. This could give rise to difficulties if the investigation is outside the control of management, for this could possibly go on for weeks or months. It is submitted therefore that precautionary suspension should be with pay if there is to be an internal investigation, but this may not be the rule in the case of external investigations. If this were not so, then the only alternatives available to the employer would be to retain an employee on full pay or to dismiss him, and it is submitted that suspension without pay may turn out to be a better practice in some cases. In *Conway v Matthew, Wright & Nephew*,[107] the claimant was a night watchman, and he was charged by the police with maliciously causing damage to the company's property. The company investigated the matter, and dismissed him. Subsequently, all criminal charges against him were dropped. It was argued that the company should have suspended him pending the outcome of criminal proceedings, but it was held that there was no legal obligation to do so, as it could have been many months before such charges were disposed of. The employers were under no obligation to refrain from dismissing him until the guilty conduct was established beyond reasonable doubt in a criminal court.

12.69 However, an employer should beware of using suspension as a knee-jerk reaction to a problem, for there may well be circumstances where such action is in fact not warranted. In *Gogay v Hertfordshire County Council*[108] the claimant was a residential care worker at a children's home. A child made some vague allegations of sexual abuse, which caused the employers to suspend the claimant while investigations were carried out. These concluded that there was no truth whatsoever in the allegations and the claimant was offered reinstatement. However, she was unable to return to work because she was suffering from clinical depression brought on by the suspension, and she subsequently brought a claim for loss of earnings and damages for personal injury. It was held that her claim would succeed. The employers should have undertaken further enquiries before deciding to suspend the claimant pending an investigation into an allegation of sexual abuse. Further, the claimant could have been transferred for a short time while the enquiries proceeded, or given a short period of leave. In the circumstances, the employers were in breach of the implied term of trust and confidence, but each case must turn on its own facts (*London Borough of Lambeth v Agoreyo*[109]).

12.70 There is no reason in principle to prevent a court from granting an injunction to restrain an employer from suspending an employee whilst carrying out an investigation into an alleged wrongdoing. In *Mezey v South West London & St George's Mental NHS*

[106] [2012] EWCA Civ 138.   [107] [1977] IRLR 89, EAT.

[108] [2000] IRLR 703, [2000] Fam Law 883, [2000] All ER (D) 1057, CA.   [109] [2019] EWCA Civ 322.

Trust (No 1)[110] (see para 10.16) a consultant psychiatrist was suspended pending disciplinary proceedings. It was held that an injunction against this would be granted. In this case suspension was not a neutral act preserving the employment relationship, especially in the case of a qualified professional. It changes the status from work to no work, and inevitably casts a shadow over the employee's competence. The crucial question is whether there has been a breach of the implied term of trust and confidence (*London Borough of Lambeth v Agoreyo*[111]).

12.71 If there is an express contractual right to suspend with or without pay pending an investigation, this is subject to an implied term that the imposition of the suspension and its continuance would be on reasonable grounds. In *McClory v Post Office* (see paras 3.48 and 10.16) three postmen were involved in a fight with employees from another office, and they were arrested and charged by the police with various offences. The Post Office suspended them on full pay, but without any payment for overtime which they would otherwise have worked. After making various enquiries, they were permitted to return to work some seven months later, and subsequently were acquitted of all the criminal charges. They brought an action for a declaration that their suspension had been in breach of their contracts of employment and they also sought damages for loss of overtime pay which they would have earned but for the suspension.

It was held that there was no breach of the employment contract. There was no duty on an employer to give reasons for the suspension or to give the employee an opportunity to be heard before it was imposed. The court refused to import the rules of natural justice into what is essentially a contractual arrangement between employer and employee. There was an implied term that the employer would exercise the express contractual right to suspend and to continue to suspend, only on reasonable grounds. To hold otherwise would enable an employer to suspend indefinitely. On the facts of the case, the employer had acted reasonably, and that aspect of the claim was dismissed.

The court also dismissed the claim for loss of overtime pay. The employees could not show that they had a right to overtime pay, only an obligation to work overtime when required. There was no duty on the employer to provide overtime on a regular basis, and thus the loss of a chance to work extra hours could not constitute the basis of a legal claim.

12.72 There is no legal requirement to suspend an employee prior to the undertaking of a full investigation, and a failure to do so does not weaken an allegation of gross misconduct. As a general rule, it is unwise to draw any conclusion from the act of or absence of suspension (*East Berkshire Health Authority v Matadeen*[112]). If an employee is absent from work because he is suspended, there is no obligation for him to return to work until the suspension is lifted (*Hassan v Odeon Cinemas*[113]).

D. **Warnings**

12.73 An employer does not need contractual power to issue warnings, but frequently this will be the subject of a disciplinary code or part of the works rules. These may state the procedural steps (for example, first oral warning, first written warning, final written warning), before further disciplinary action is taken. Strict adherence to these steps is necessary and a failure by the employer to observe them may lead to difficulties in unfair dismissal proceedings. Thus, a failure to give a warning in writing as required by the agreed procedure resulted in a dismissal being held to be unfair in *Raymond v Sir Lindsay Parkinson Ltd.*[114]

---

[110] [2007] EWCA Civ 106. See also *Mezey v South West London & St George's Mental Health NHS Trust (No. 2)* [2010] IRLR 512, [2010] EWCA Civ 293, CA.   [111] See n.109.

[112] [1992] ICR 723, [1992] IRLR 336, EAT.   [113] [1998] ICR 127, EAT.   [114] [1974] IRLR 298.

12.74 Nonetheless, the warning system must be operated sensibly, not merely as a form of mechanical procedure. It is possible to give an employee a final warning for a serious misdemeanour without having first to go through the processes of informal warning, first written warning, etc; equally, the fact that an employee has received a final warning does not mean that the next occasion on which he commits an 'offence' will be visited with an automatic sanction. Either course could lead to ludicrous results. There is no substitute for a full and fair investigation of all the facts. In *Newalls Insulation Co Ltd v Blakeman*,[115] the claimant was dismissed for being absent on two occasions within 14 days, following a final warning for absenteeism. Prior to this, he had had two verbal warnings. The EAT held that the employment tribunal should look at all the circumstances of the case, and not simply whether it was reasonable to dismiss for two days' absence after the final warning. The issues were: what happened before the final warning was given, how many absences were there, why was he absent, and how did the absences fit in as part of the general picture?

12.75 A warning can deal with specific conduct which is the subject of complaint, and it should also deal with general matters, so that the totality of the employee's conduct can eventually be taken into account. This solves the problem sometimes raised by management as to whether or not, having given three warnings for one type of misconduct, it is necessary to give a further three warnings in respect of a different series of offences! Thus in *Donald Cook v Carter*,[116] the claimant received a number of warnings: one for using bad language, and a year later, another one for the same offence. Two months later he was given a final warning for inefficiency, with a threat to demote or dismiss. Three months later he was given another final warning for leaving work before the normal finishing time and he was suspended for five days. He was then guilty of inefficiency, and was dismissed. The employment tribunal held that the dismissal was unfair, in that he should have been given a further final warning, but this was reversed by the EAT. As long as the matter leading to the dismissal was properly investigated and the proper procedure followed, it was not open to the employment tribunal to find that fairness required a further warning being given, or that the employers should have suspended the employee, as they had done so previously.

12.76 This approach was confirmed by the EAT in *Auguste Noel Ltd v Curtis*,[117] where an employee was dismissed for mishandling company property. He had previously received two final written warnings for different offences. An employment tribunal held that the previous warnings were not relevant, but the decision was reversed on appeal. The existence of previous warnings, and the dates, numbers, and substance of the complaints, were all relevant matters which an employer was entitled to take into account.

12.77 It is for the employer to determine the nature of the disciplinary sanction, and, generally speaking, an employment tribunal should not attempt to assess whether or not a final warning should or should not have been given. However, if there is something to suggest that a final warning was 'manifestly inappropriate' or given without prima facie grounds, then the employment tribunal will carefully scrutinize the employer's decision.

In *Davies v Sandwell Metropolitan Borough Council*[118] the Court of Appeal emphasised that a warning in an unfair dismissal claim can only be challenged if it was issued in bad faith or was manifestly inappropriate (see also *Simmonds v Milford Club*[119]).

12.78 A final warning is a severe penalty which just stops short of a dismissal. It is frequently imposed when a dismissal is a permissible and obvious sanction but, for reasons relating to the particular employee, is not imposed. To issue a final warning in respect of

---

[115] [1976] ICR 543, [1976] IRLR 303, EAT.   [116] [1977] IRLR 88, EAT.
[117] [1990] ICR 604, [1990] IRLR 326, EAT.
[118] [2013] EWCA Civ 135.   [119] 2013 All ER (D) 182 (Mar).

a relatively minor incident of misconduct can be a disproportionate response to the employee's conduct, and may enable the employee to resign and claim constructive dismissal (*Stanley Cole (Wainfleet) Ltd v Sheridan*[120]).

12.79 If a warning is stated to last for a certain length of time, then clearly it will lapse at the end of that time. In *Bevan Ashford v Malin*[121] a letter was handed to the employee on 29 January 1992, stating that a final written warning would remain on his personal file for a period of 12 months from the date of the letter. He was dismissed following his involvement in an incident at work on 29 January 1993. The employment tribunal held that the final written warning had expired at midnight on 28 January 1993, and ought not to have been taken into account when considering the disciplinary action to be taken following the incident which occurred the following day, and the decision was confirmed by the EAT. The general rule is that penal documents should be construed strictly, and also any ambiguity has to be construed against the maker. Thus the final warning had expired the day before the conduct which led to the dismissal occurred, and could not be relied upon as a ground for dismissal. However in *Stratford v Auto Trail VR Ltd*[122] it was found that an expired warning (or, as in this case, 17 previous warnings) could be taken into account as part of the overall circumstances when considering whether a dismissal is unfair. Note that in *NHS24 v Pillar*[123] the EAT held that an employer who had taken into account previous incidents of misconduct which had not been treated at the time as misconduct was entitled to do so, as they were relevant to the disciplinary matters that were being considered. There would have been a significant risk to patients' safety if they had been ignored. The dismissal was therefore fair. If these incidents had, however, been the subject of a warning which had expired, then this would have been unfair.

12.80 The warning should refer to the past conduct which is the subject of complaint, and to future conduct. It should, where possible, state the remedial action to be taken, and should specify the period of time in which such action should be taken. Frequently, a disciplinary procedure will specify the length of time the warning will last, but perhaps a better approach is for the warning itself to state the operative period, for mechanical and automatic approaches to disciplinary problems are not sound policy. A warning can also be suspensive, when it will stay on the employee's record until such time as it is removed or can be ignored, or resolutive, which will lapse on compliance. The latter can therefore be ignored when its objective has been achieved. In *Duncan v GEC Telecommunications Ltd*[124] an employee failed to send in a medical certificate as required by the company's rules. After being warned, she sent in an appropriate certificate. A few months later she again failed to send in a medical certificate. It was held that the earlier warning had lapsed on her compliance, and therefore her dismissal was unfair.

12.81 A warning may lapse after a certain period of time, but an employer is not to be criticized because he is over-generous and extends the warning period instead of acting on it. Being over-generous is not the same as being unreasonable (*Kraft Foods Ltd v Fox*[125]). Further, a warning which is itself the subject of a pending appeal may be taken into account by an employer when considering dismissal for subsequent misconduct (*Tower Hamlets Health Authority v Anthony*[126]), and a final written warning which has expired may be taken into account in exceptional circumstances. In *Airbus UK v Webb*[127] the claimant was given

---

[120] [2003] ICR 297, [2003] IRLR 52, [2002] All ER (D) 11 (Nov), EAT; aff'd [2003] EWCA Civ 1046, [2003] 4 All ER 1181, [2003] ICR 1449, [2003] IRLR 885.

[121] [1995] ICR 453, [1995] IRLR 360, EAT.   [122] [2016] UKEAT 0116.   [123] UKEATS/0005/16.

[124] [1976] IRLR 3.   [125] [1978] ICR 311, [1977] IRLR 431, EAT.

[126] [1989] ICR 656, [1989] IRLR 394, CA.   [127] EAT/0453/06; [2008] EWCA Civ 49, CA.

a final written warning for misuse of company time, which was to stay on his record for 12 months. One month after the warning expired he, and several colleagues, were caught watching television during company time. The claimant was dismissed, although his colleagues, who had not previously had a final warning, were not. The employment tribunal and the EAT held that an expired warning could never be taken into account for dismissal purposes, but the decision was reversed by the Court of Appeal. Reliance on a final warning was a relevant factor in deciding whether the employer had acted reasonably and, though in most circumstances taking it into account would mean that a dismissal was unfair, this was not inevitably so. Reliance on an expired final warning would be the exception, rather than the rule.

12.82 Tribunals have frequently stressed the need to issue warnings before the power of dismissal is exercised. The warnings should be given by a person in authority and should be clear, incisive, and firm. They should make clear the nature of the conduct which will not be tolerated, and spell out in no uncertain terms that the consequence of a failure to heed the warning will be a dismissal. Formal warnings should be given in writing and this is of particular importance when there are language or communication problems.

12.83 Failure to follow these rules may lead to the tribunal making a finding adverse to the employer. In *Wells v West Ltd*[128] the employers gave a warning to an employee that his 'employment might be in jeopardy'. In holding that this was not a sufficient warning, the tribunal held that those who use circumlocutions will have to bear the burden which they subsequently impose. In *Bendall v Paine and Betteridge*[129] the employee was given a verbal warning that smoking would not be tolerated on the premises. It was held that a failure to give a written final warning meant that the dismissal was unfair. And in *Rosenthal v Louis Butler Ltd*[130] the employee used some offensive language to her manager. It was held that she ought to have been warned about future conduct and been given an opportunity to apologize before dismissal was warranted.

12.84 It must be stressed that there is no rule of law which requires warnings to be given in all cases; it is merely a rule of good industrial relations practice. Warnings are matters of substance, not procedure (*James v Waltham Holy Cross UDC*[131]). Whether a warning should have been given will depend on all the circumstances of the case, including its effectiveness, and the alternative course which may have been available or adopted. If a tribunal considers that, had a clear warning been given, a dismissal would not have been necessary, then it will conclude that a dismissal without such a warning will be unfair (*Jones v GEC Elliott Automation Ltd*[132]). Conversely, if a warning would have had no effect, then a failure to give one will not by itself render a dismissal unfair (*AJ Dunning & Sons (Shopfitters) Ltd v Jacomb*[133]). There should be no need to give a warning to a highly paid and qualified employee that he will be dismissed if there is dissatisfaction with his work, for he should know this. Nor is there a need to give an educated person in a responsible position a warning that he must co-operate with his head of department (*Farnborough v Governors of Edinburgh College of Art*[134]). Each case must be determined on its own merits. The circumstances surrounding the warning should be considered. In *Way v Spectrum Property Care Ltd*[135] an employer who took into account a warning given in bad faith was found not to be acting reasonably when deciding whether the employee's conduct was sufficient reason for dismissing him.

[128] [1979] IRLR 269.   [129] [1973] IRLR 44.   [130] [1972] IRLR 39.
[131] [1973] ICR 398, [1978] IRLR 202, 14 KIR 576, NIRC.   [132] [1972] IRLR 111.
[133] [1973] ICR 448, [1973] IRLR 206, NIRC.   [134] [1974] IRLR 245, NIRC.
[135] [2015] EWCA Civ 381.

12.85 If an employee is given a final warning against which he has appealed, there is no rule of law which requires the employer to await the outcome of the appeal before dismissing for another disciplinary offence (*Stein v Associated Dairies*[136]).

E. Reprimand

12.86 The same is probably true about a reprimand, which is a mark of displeasure about past conduct and a warning about the future. Tribunals have held that misconduct which is not 'gross' should in some circumstances be punished by a reprimand rather than a dismissal, though to what extent a reprimand constitutes a punishment is somewhat difficult to see. Further, employers could be forgiven for thinking that this area of tribunal law is full of hazardous speculation, for when 'misconduct' becomes 'gross' is a somewhat subjective concept. In *King v Motorway Tyres and Accessories Ltd*[137] a manager told his superior to 'fuck off' in the course of an argument. It was held that this did not amount to gross misconduct sufficient to warrant dismissal, and that in view of his long service and satisfactory record, he should have been 'severely' reprimanded. The precise distinction between a reprimand and a severe reprimand, and whether the latter is equivalent to a final warning, has yet to be decided. It is submitted that a reprimand is an appropriate sanction to be used when taking disciplinary action against management, or staff employees.

F. Demotion

12.87 An employee whose conduct is such that the employer has lost all confidence in his ability to do the job in question may be demoted, with or without review, and at a lower earning rate if this is appropriate. If there is an express power to do this in the contract or rules, then provided the sanction has been fairly exercised, there should not be any legal problem. In the absence of such a power, a demotion imposed following a disciplinary hearing is not a breach of contract when it is a lesser penalty than the dismissal which could otherwise have been imposed (*MacKay Decorators (Perth) Ltd v Millar*[138]). If the employee refuses to accept the demotion, he can either resign and claim constructive dismissal, or leave it to the employer to dismiss him. If the employer has acted fairly, and with the interests of the employee at heart, such dismissal will be fair. In *Hall v Lodge*,[139] the claimant was promoted from a supervisory post to manage a shop. Following serious stock deficiencies, her appointment was terminated and she was offered re-engagement as a supervisor at another branch, at a lower salary. This offer was refused, so she was dismissed. It was held that her dismissal was fair. The company had made a mistake in promoting her too soon to a job which was too big for her. Having realized this, they then acted fairly by considering the alternatives which were available, by offering her a post which was within her competence. However, there is no legal requirement that an employer should demote a person who is incompetent (*Bevan Harris Ltd v Gair*[140]).

12.88 But if a demotion on disciplinary grounds is out of all proportion to the offence, the employee may regard the employer as having repudiated the contract, and claim constructive dismissal. In *BBC v Beckett*,[141] the claimant was employed for 14 years as a scenic carpenter. He was negligent in his work on one occasion, and was demoted to the position of building maintenance carpenter, at a lower salary. He resigned and claimed constructive dismissal, a claim which was upheld by the employment tribunal and by the

---

[136] [1982] IRLR 447.   [137] [1975] IRLR 51.
[138] EAT/782/98.   [139] Unreported.   [140] [1981] IRLR 520, EAT.   [141] [1983] IRLR 43, EAT.

EAT. The punishment was out of all proportion to the offence, given his long period of satisfactory service.

G. Transfer

12.89 Similar considerations apply to the transfer of an employee from one department to another, or one job to another. This power, however, would be used in different circumstances. Merely to transfer an incompetent employee from one department to another is to export one's problems from one manager to another. Transfer is best used as a means of overcoming personality clashes, so as to minimize the likelihood of future problems arising, or to place an employee in a job which he can do, rather than leaving him doing work which is beyond his competence. In *High v British Railways Board*,[142] it was held that a disciplinary transfer which resulted in the employee suffering a drop in his earnings did not give rise to a claim for constructive dismissal.

H. Alternative Employment

12.90 In appropriate cases, it may be unfair to dismiss an employee without considering whether there is any alternative work he can do, notwithstanding that he cannot be permitted to continue in his old job. However, there is no requirement that this should be investigated before the decision to dismiss is taken, as opposed to after the decision has been taken but before the expiry of any period of notice which may be given. To hold otherwise would mean that an employee would be unfairly dismissed notwithstanding that during his notice period alternative employment was found for him and the notice never took effect (*P v Nottinghamshire County Council*, see para 12.18).

I. Other Sanctions

12.91 There are a number of other disciplinary powers which may be used on appropriate occasions, and provided these are exercised in accordance with the relevant rules and procedures, these should cause few problems. For example, it may be possible to withdraw privileges for a certain period of time so as to deny to an employee certain non-contractual benefits, or to provide for the loss of so many years' seniority for certain purposes (but this does not affect the operation of the legal rules relating to continuity of employment). An employee who is persistently late in starting work may have flexi-time withdrawn, as an alternative to, or a precondition of, the implementation of other disciplinary action.

J. Non-employment Situations

12.92 The disciplinary powers described in paras 12.59 to 12.90 can only apply to acts of employees committed in the course of employment. An employer has no inherent power to discipline for acts which have occurred outside the employment, though if such acts adversely affect the employer's business, he may be justified in dismissing the employee (see Chapter 17). But if an employee is convicted of an offence outside his employment which may have an effect on his job, the employer should consider the employee's long and blameless record, and consider, for example, if some other means of dealing with the situation can be found. In *Jones v R M Douglas Construction Ltd*[143] the employee, who was a plant engineer, was dismissed after being convicted of handling a stolen engine. The tribunal thought that the employer should have given some consideration to demoting him to his original

---

[142] [1979] IRLR 52, EAT.   [143] [1975] IRLR 175.

trade of mechanic/fitter. Clearly, such a power cannot be found in the contract of employment, and amounts to a unilateral assessment by the employer of the necessary steps to be taken to protect his interests. A demotion is, as we have seen, equivalent to a dismissal, and one can only assume that if such steps are taken in serious disciplinary cases, the exercise of a lesser disciplinary power short of dismissal will, in cases of grave misconduct outside the employment, also be looked upon more favourably by the tribunals.

12.93 If the employee is convicted of an offence in connection with matters outside his employment, he is still entitled to present his side of the story to his employers, and the latter should not treat the fact of conviction per se as being conclusive without at least giving a chance to the employee to state his version (*Parsons v LCC*[144]).

Summary

- The exercise of disciplinary powers is a corrective function, not punitive. The object is to improve an employee's performance.
- A grievance procedure should be available for employees.
- Employers should not allow an informal interview or investigatory hearing to turn into a disciplinary hearing.
- Provided an employer carries out an appropriate investigation and gives the employee a fair opportunity to explain his conduct, the standard is what can objectively be expected from reasonable employer.
- Disciplinary (in cases which may lead to a punishment) and grievance procedures should conform to the ACAS code on this subject.
- Failure to follow a procedure which has been set out is likely to result in any dismissal being unfair.
- This does not apply in non-punishment cases, eg ill health or SOSR.
- The employer only has to act reasonably in coming to a decision. It does not have to prove that the employee committed any specific act, or apply criminal standard of proof, or conduct a quasi-judicial investigation.
- A worker can be accompanied by a trade union official or another worker in any hearing which has the characteristic of a disciplinary sanction. There is no right to be accompanied at an investigatory hearing.
- The companion can address the hearing, but is not entitled to answer questions.
- There is no right to legal representation unless the contract provides for it.
- If the consequences for an employee are severe, such as deprivation of a profession, Article 6 ECHR may be engaged and legal representation permitted.
- Disciplinary rules the employee has to observe must be brought to their attention.

[144] (1893) 9 TLR 619.

13

Continuous Employment

Background

13.1 In order to obtain certain statutory rights, an employee has to show they have been continuously employed for a certain length of time, depending on the right in question. The statutory provisions which provide for continuity of employment are contained in ss 210–219 of the Employment Rights Act 1996, which define what is meant by 'continuously employed', and the Employment Protection (Continuity of Employment) Regulations 1996. Continuity of employment is a statutory concept, generally used for two purposes, namely (a) to determine whether an employee has been employed for a particular length of time so as to qualify for a specific statutory right, and (b) to ascertain the employee's length of employment for the purpose of obtaining certain financial benefits (ie a basic award (see para 17.189) and a redundancy payment (see para 18.65). However, for some statutory rights, known as 'day one' rights, no period of continuous employment is required.

Continuity of Employment

13.2 Continuity of employment is a concept which is only of importance in a statutory context. Thus, if an employer and employee make a private agreement to treat a particular period of employment as being continuous, this may create a private right, but cannot be used to enforce any statutory right, unless the statutory rules are also met. In *Secretary of State for Employment v Globe Elastic Thread Co Ltd*,[1] an employee worked for a company for 22 years. He was then transferred to another company, after receiving assurances that his employment would be treated as being continuous. Five years later, he was made redundant, and he sought a redundancy payment based on the combined service. The House of Lords held that he was only entitled to a statutory redundancy pay in respect of the latter five years' employment. The private agreement may have given him a contractual right against the employers, but could not be used for the purpose of enforcing a statutory right.

Similarly, in *Hanson v Fashion Industries (Hartlepool) Ltd*,[2] an employee went on strike. Nine weeks later, she was re-engaged under a contract which stated that her continuous employment was to start afresh. In subsequent litigation claiming for maternity pay, it was held that her continuous employment had not been broken by the strike, as the statutory provisions preserved her continuity, and a private agreement cannot override those provisions.

13.3 There is nothing to prevent an employer drafting contracts so as to prevent continuity, and so avoiding liability for unfair dismissal and redundancy payments. If there are legitimate breaks in employment, and re-employment does not become an arrangement by virtue of s 212(3)(c) (see para 13.24), continuity can be defeated (*Booth v USA*, see para 2.142).

---

[1] [1978] QB 86, [1978] 1 All ER 987, [1978] ICR 473, [1977] IRLR 233, EAT; aff'd [1979] QB 183, [1978] 3 All ER 954, [1978] ICR 1041, [1978] IRLR 417, CA; revsd [1980] AC 506, [1979] 2 All ER 1077, [1979] ICR 706, [1979] IRLR 327, HL.   [2] [1981] ICR 35, [1980] IRLR 393, EAT.

Counting and Computing Continuity (ERA, ss 210–219)

13.4 The counting of a period of continuous employment is done in weeks, but the computation is done in months and years (s 210(3)). This requires some explanation. The rule is that to determine if an employee's employment, whether continuous or successive or broken, can be counted as being continuous is done on a week-by-week basis, because there is a general rule that continuity is broken by a complete week which does not count towards continuity (s 210(4)), unless continuity is preserved by one of the special rules (see below). (Note that there are plans to extend the time required to break a period of continuous service to four weeks, but it is not yet known when this will happen.) A week will count, for the purpose of establishing continuity, if it is governed by a contract of employment, irrespective of the number of hours or days worked during the week. But a 'week', for the purpose of determining whether there has been a break in employment, means a complete week from Sunday ending with a Saturday (*Jennings v Salford Community Service Agency*[3]).

13.5 Continuity is not broken unless there is a complete week in which there is no contract of employment. If there is one day in any week which is governed by a contract of employment, it matters not how or why a gap occurred, or what the employee did during that gap. Thus if an employee leaves one employer to work for another employer, but returns within a week of so leaving, continuity is preserved (*Sweeney v J S Henderson (Concessionaires) Ltd*[4]).

13.6 However, the computation of the length of continuous employment is done in months and years. Thus, if an employee commences work on (say) 21 January 2016, he will have completed two years' employment on 20 January 2018, assuming there is no break of a whole week in his employment. Similarly, if he commences employment on (say) 19 August 2017, he will have been continuously employed for three months on 18 November 2017. The terms 'years' and 'months' mean calendar years and months respectively.

13.7 Thus, in order to establish a period of continuous employment, it is necessary to ascertain the day when the employment commenced, the day when it ceased, whether there were any weeks which break continuity, and whether there were any weeks which do not break continuity but which do not count towards continuity. Since 1995, this has been the same for part-time workers as for full-time workers, irrespective of the number of hours worked each week, and service before the change in 1995 is to be counted (ERA, Sch 2, para 14(1)).

13.8 The first rule to note is that there is a presumption that continuity of employment exists. Thus, once an employee can show the date on which he started work, his employment will be presumed to be continuous until the effective date of termination (s 210(5), and see *Nicoll v Nocorrode Ltd*[5]). So an employee can change his place of work, his terms of employment, or even his contract of employment, without his continuity being affected, provided he remains employed by the same employer (*Wood v York City Council*[6]) or an associated employer. An agency worker who is supplied to an employer on a temporary basis, and who is then taken on as a full-time employee, has continuity of employment from the date he started his temporary work (*RNLI v Bushaway*, see para 2.163). Continuity exists following a period of absence on maternity, paternity, adoption, parental leave, etc.

13.9 Continuity begins on the day the employee starts work under the contract of employment, although if the starting day is a non-working day (eg a holiday or a Sunday) the employment is continuous from that date, even though he does not actually commence

---

[3] [1981] ICR 399, [1981] IRLR 76, EAT.   [4] [1999] IRLR 306, EAT.
[5] [1981] ICR 348, [1981] IRLR 163.   [6] [1978] ICR 840, [1978] IRLR 228, CA.

working until a day or two later (*Salvation Army v Dewsbury*). If there are periods which do not count towards continuity but do not break continuity (see para 13.13) the commencement of the period of employment is advanced by the period in question (s 211(3)). If a written statement of terms and conditions of employment given under ERA, s 1 contains a starting date, that will not be conclusive if in fact the true starting date was different (*System Floors (UK) Ltd v Daniel*, see para 3.115).

13.10 When a period of continuous employment ends will depend on the statutory right which is being claimed by the employee. For employment rights generally, and unfair dismissal claims in particular, it will be 'the effective date of termination' (see para 20.28). If the claim is for a statutory redundancy payment, the period will end on 'the relevant date', which will normally be the effective date of termination, although there are some variations on this (ERA, ss 136(3), 145(3)(b), 145(5), 145(7), 153). There are also provisions dealing with the termination of employment on the death of the employer and employee (ERA, ss 133(1), 174, and 176(1)).

13.11 The employment must be legal for it to be continuous. Thus, any period when the employment is illegal cannot count towards continuity, and will break continuity. Therefore, if a person has no legal right to work in the UK (see para 2.119), any time spent so working cannot count towards continuity. If a legal contract becomes tainted with illegality (see para 3.7), continuity will be broken, and will have to start again from when it becomes legal. In *Hyland v J H Barker (North West) Ltd*[7] the employee was employed from 1967. For four weeks in 1982 he arranged with his employer that he would receive a tax-free lodging allowance, whereas in fact he returned home every night. Clearly, this arrangement was illegal, being an attempt to defraud the Revenue. Thus, when he was dismissed a year later, it was held that the four-week period had broken the continuity, and that therefore he lacked the necessary qualifying period of employment to bring a claim for unfair dismissal.

13.12 Continuity of employment exists if an employee commences work for a subsidiary or associated employer of the original employer, or if there is a takeover of the business (not just its assets) or on the transfer of an undertaking. Nor is it relevant that the employee's job changed. In *Lord Advocate v De Rosa*[8] the employee had been employed by Isaac Barrie (Transport) Ltd for 17 years when the business was transferred to Isaac Barrie (Contractors) Ltd. There was no interruption in his employment, but he changed his job from transport manager to docks manager. It was held that his redundancy payment was to be calculated by reference to both periods of employment, and the fact that there had been a change in his employer and in his terms and conditions of employment was irrelevant.

Preserving Continuity (s 212)

13.13 There is a general principle that if an employee is dismissed, or resigns, or his contract of employment comes to an end in some other lawful manner (frustration, project termination, etc), then, if he is subsequently re-engaged, continuity will have been broken if there is a gap of more than one week between the two employments, and he will have to start again so far as computation is concerned. However, there are a number of rules which enable an employee to preserve continuity despite the existence of a break between the two periods. Sometimes the weeks in question may be added into the counting of continuity, although sometimes they are not to be counted, even though they do not break continuity.

---

[7] [1985] ICR 861, [1985] IRLR 403 EAT.   [8] [1974] 2 All ER 849, [1974] ICR 480, [1974] IRLR 215, HL.

13.14 Any week during the whole or part of which an employee's relations with his employer are governed by a contract of employment will count when computing the employee's period of employment (s 212(1)). Thus, if an employee is off work sick, away on a holiday (see *Vernon v Event Management Catering Ltd*[9]), or otherwise absent with permission, the weeks in question will still count, as long as the contract of employment is still in existence. The whole of the period when a person is on ordinary maternity, paternity, or adoption leave will count towards continuity so far as statutory rights are concerned.

13.15 Continuity will also be preserved in the following three circumstances (see paras 13.16–13.28) (s 212(2)), provided two conditions are met. First, there must be no contract of employment subsisting (because otherwise there would be no need to rely on these provisions to preserve continuity). Second, the employee must be re-employed during the relevant period. In other words, s 212(2) does not guarantee continuity; it merely preserves it in circumstances when it would otherwise be lost.

A. Incapable of Work because of Sickness or Injury (s 212(3)(a))

13.16 For this rule to apply, the contract of employment must have been terminated (whether by dismissal or frustration or resignation, etc). If so, then if the employee is re-employed within 26 weeks, his employment will be deemed to be continuous. In other words, he is entitled to be absent from work for up to 26 weeks after his contract of employment has ended without suffering a break in continuity should he be re-employed. He must, however, have been incapable of work, not merely absent from work (*Scarlett v Godfrey Abbott Group Ltd*[10]). In *Donnelly v Kelvin International Services*[11] the employee resigned from his employment with the respondent because his doctor advised him to obtain lighter work. He obtained employment with another employer, but five weeks later resumed his employment with the respondent. He was subsequently dismissed, and his claim for unfair dismissal could only proceed if he could link the two periods of employment in order to establish the necessary continuity. An employment tribunal dismissed his claim, holding that although he had resigned his employment because of sickness, he was not incapable of work because of that sickness, because he had demonstrated his fitness for work by obtaining other employment. The EAT allowed the employee's appeal, and remitted the claim for reconsideration by another tribunal. The phrase 'incapable of work' did not mean incapable of work of any kind. It referred to the work which the employee was doing before the period which interrupted the continuity of employment, and the fact that the employee had taken up other work during the period of interruption did not mean that he had ceased to be capable of the work he was doing by reason of sickness, within the meaning of s 212(3)(a). The proper approach was to look at what happened in the intervening period between the two employments in question. If, for example, the employee took employment of light work, in the hope that he may be able to return to his previous employment in time, this may not interrupt the period of continuity. But if the intervening employment was undertaken as full-time permanent employment, then it was possible to conclude that his absence from the first employment was not because of incapacity for work.

13.17 A different result was reached in *Pearson v Kent County Council*,[12] where the employee decided to resign his employment on 31 May on health grounds. He was offered, and accepted, a less demanding job with his employers, and commenced his new position on 11 June. Four years later he was made redundant, and sought to link the two periods

---

[9]　[2007] All ER (D) 129 (Jul).　　[10]　[1978] ICR 1106, [1978] IRLR 456, EAT.
[11]　[1992] IRLR 496, EAT.　　[12]　[1992] ICR 20, [1992] IRLR 110, EAT; aff'd [1993] IRLR 165, CA.

of employment for the purpose of enhancing his claim for statutory redundancy pay. His claim failed. There was no medical reason why he could not have commenced his new job immediately after he left his former position. Thus, he was not incapable of work because of sickness or injury, and because there was a break of more than one week, the two periods of employment could not be linked to form one period of continuous employment.

B. **Absent from Work on Account of a Temporary Cessation of Work (s 212(3)(b))**

13.18 Weeks will count when an employee is absent from work (again, without a contract of employment) on account of a temporary cessation of work. This provision was probably designed to deal with those industries where there may be lay-offs, eg the construction industry, but the practical effect has been much wider (see *Fitzgerald v Hall, Russell & Co Ltd*[13]). In particular, it should be noted that a lay-off and a temporary cessation of work are the same thing (*Murray v Murray (t/a Newholme Decorators)*[14]).

13.19 The term 'cessation of work' means that the work which the employee was employed to do must have ceased (*Fitzgerald v Hall Russell & Co Ltd*) or the amount of work no longer exists. If an employee is 'laid off' because existing work has been redistributed, there has been no cessation of work (*Byrne v Birmingham City Council*[15]). Further, the work which has ceased must be paid work, not voluntary work (*University of Aston in Birmingham v Malik*[16]). Nor is the reason for the cessation relevant; it may be due to shortage of orders, shortage of supplies, cash flow problems, etc (*Hunter v Smith's Dock Co Ltd*[17]). There must be an interruption in the availability of work which, but for that interruption, would have been performed by the employee.

13.20 The absence from work must be 'temporary'. This is a question of fact, to be looked at with hindsight, not foresight. Although there is dicta in *Ford v Warwickshire County Council*[18] (see para 13.28) to suggest that 'temporary' means 'lasting only for a relatively short time', this guidance has not always been followed (eg see *Bentley Engineering Co Ltd v Crown*,[19] where a period of absence of two years was held to be temporary!). The whole of the employment history must be examined, and evidence may be adduced as to the expectations of the parties.

13.21 There have been a number of cases where employees have been employed on 'intermittent' contracts, each of varying lengths, and being separated by varying periods of non-employment. The correct approach in such cases is to consider all the relevant circumstances, and in particular to consider the lengths of the periods of absence from work in the context of the employment as a whole (*Sillars v Charrington Fuels Ltd*[20]). Sometimes employment tribunals try to circumvent this enquiry by finding that 'a global contract' exists (see para 2.175), but with mixed success. For seasonal workers, if a greater time is spent out of employment than in, the period of non-employment cannot be regarded as being an absence because of a temporary cessation of work (*Berwick Salmon Fisheries Co Ltd v Rutherford*[21]).

13.22 It will be clear that if an employee resigns, or is dismissed, and is subsequently re-employed by the employer (or an associated employer, see para 2.6) he cannot be

---

[13] [1970] AC 984, [1969] 3 All ER 1140, HL.   [14] EAT/750/93.
[15] [1987] ICR 519, [1987] IRLR 191, CA.   [16] [1984] ICR 492, EAT.   [17] [1968] 2 All ER 81, DC.
[18] [1982] ICR 520, [1982] IRLR 246, CA; revsd [1983] 2 AC 71, [1983] 1 All ER 753, [1983] ICR 273, [1983] IRLR 126, HL.   [19] [1976] ICR 225, [1976] IRLR 146, DC.
[20] [1988] ICR 505, [1988] IRLR 180, EAT; aff'd [1989] ICR 475, [1989] IRLR 152, CA.
[21] [1991] IRLR 203, EAT.

regarded as being absent from work because of a temporary cessation (*Wessex National Ltd v Long*[22]). If, during the period of absence, the employee takes what he regards as being other permanent employment, then the absence ceases to be because of the temporary cessation of work. But if he takes temporary employment, making it clear that he was seeking to be re-employed by his former employers, continuity will be preserved (*Thompson v Bristol Channel Ship Repairer and Engineers Ltd*[23]).

13.23 If a company goes into liquidation, and an employee who is thus dismissed is then employed by another company in circumstances such that both companies are owned and controlled by the same owner, continuity of employment may be preserved, and any period between the dismissal and re-employment may be treated as a temporary cessation of work (*Da Silva v Composite Mouldings & Design Ltd*[24]). This was illustrated in *Welton v Deluxe Retail (t/a Madhouse)*.[25] The claimant worked at a shop in Sheffield that closed down, and his employment was terminated. During what would have been the next working week, he agreed to accept employment with the same employer in Blackpool. His first working day was the following week. His employment was terminated a few months later and he claimed unfair dismissal. On considering whether his continuity had been broken, the EAT held that the absence was on account of a temporary cessation of work and there was a contract of employment from when he accepted the offer, notwithstanding that work had yet to be performed under it. It also confirmed that an arrangement could not be entered retrospectively so as to confer continuity.

C. Absent by Arrangement or Custom (s 212(3)(c))

13.24 Continuity is preserved if the employee's absence from work is such that, by arrangement or custom, he is regarded as continuing in the employment of his employer for any purpose. Clearly, if an employee's contract enables such absence, eg sabbatical leave, s 212(3)(c) is not relevant. The section only applies if the contract does not exist, and would cover, for example, an employee who has been seconded from one employer to another, or someone who has been given leave of absence for personal reasons. Indeed, the 'arrangement' need not have been made between the employer and the employee, but can arise from an agreement between the employer and a trade union (*Taylor v Triumph Motors Ltd*[26]). Keeping an employee 'on the books' can be an arrangement for the purpose of continuity within s 212(3)(c), especially if the contract of employment has previously been frustrated (*G F Sharp & Co Ltd v McMillan*[27]).

13.25 The arrangement must have been to preserve continuity for any purpose. In *Lloyds Bank Ltd v Secretary of State for Employment*[28] an employee worked one week on and one week off for five years. She became pregnant; the employers paid her statutory maternity pay, and sought to recover the amount from the Maternity Fund. It was held that her employment was continuous for five years, her absence was by arrangement, and, having rightfully paid her the money, they were entitled to a rebate from the Fund. But in *Letheby & Christopher Ltd v Bond*[29] a casual barmaid took leave over a Christmas period. Although this was by arrangement, there was no arrangement that the absence would preserve continuity, for she worked under a number of separate contracts, and it was not possible to say

---

[22] (1978) 13 ITR 413, EAT.

[23] [1969] 1 Lloyd's Rep 407, 6 KIR 510, 4 ITR 262, 113 Sol Jo 382, DC; aff'd [1971] 1 Lloyd's Rep 105, 8 KIR 687, 5 ITR 85, 114 Sol Jo 167, CA.   [24] [2009] ICR 416.

[25] UKEAT/0266/12.   [26] [1975] IRLR 369.   [27] [1998] IRLR 632, EAT.

[28] [1979] 2 All ER 573, [1979] ICR 258, [1979] IRLR 41, EAT.   [29] [1988] ICR 480, EAT.

that any contract of employment would have continued after the cessation of the previous contract. The absence therefore broke her continuity.

13.26 However, the arrangement must have been made before the period of absence ceases (*Murphy v A Birrell & Sons Ltd*[30]). One made after the absence has ceased may give rise to private contractual rights, but cannot affect the statutory position. Thus, in *Morris v Walsh Western Electric UK Ltd*[31] the appellant was summarily dismissed. Two months later he was re-employed, and was told by the company's general manager that the intervening period would be treated as being a period of unpaid leave. He then terminated his own employment, and claimed that the two combined periods of employment gave him sufficient continuity to bring a case of constructive dismissal. His claim was dismissed. The statutory provisions envisage that the arrangement exists when the employee is absent from work, not when he returns to work. A contrary view expressed in *Ingram v Foxon*,[32] that a retrospective arrangement could preserve continuity, was disapproved.

13.27 The 'arrangement' for the purpose of s 212(3)(c) must be such that there was a mutual recognition by the parties that the employee, although absent from work, nevertheless continues in the employment of the employer. Whether such mutual recognition in fact exists will depend on the circumstances and, in particular, any correspondence between the parties, and what the employee was told before taking the period of absence (*Curr v Marks & Spencer plc*, see para 2.152).

13.28 There are few cases dealing with 'custom' in modern employment law generally, let alone with reference to s 212(3)(c). Industry-wide customs (of the kind which would be upheld at law) rarely exist now, as the greater formalisation of contracts of employment and collective agreements takes place. Older cases (eg *Sagar v Ridehalgh*, see para 3.77) are no longer particularly relevant. But in *Gray v Burntisland Shipbuilding Co*[33] a recognised custom in the shipbuilding industry whereby workers laid off when work ran out were recalled when more work became available, was used to establish continuity under the statutory provision. In *Ford v Warwickshire County Council* (see para 13.20) the EAT commented that detailed evidence about customs in certain industries could be usefully given, and, if there was an appropriate custom in the teaching profession, it should be brought to the attention of the employment tribunal for consideration.

Re-employment after Unfair Dismissal (s 219)

13.29 The Employment Protection (Continuity of Employment) Regulations 1996 (as amended) (made under ERA, s 219) deal with the situation where a person is reinstated or re-engaged in consequence of any of the following events, namely:

(a) a claim made under an approved dismissal agreement (s 110: see para 17.4 (there are no such agreements in force at the present time));

(b) the presentation by the employee of a complaint of dismissal, ie under ERA, or in respect of sex, race, disability, or other anti-discrimination provisions;

(c) action taken by a conciliation officer of ACAS under the Employment Tribunals Act 1996, s 18 (see para 20.40);

(d) the making of a compromise agreement authorised by ERA, s 203(3);

---

[30] [1978] IRLR 458, EAT.   [31] [1997] IRLR 562, EAT.   [32] [1984] ICR 685, [1985] IRLR 5, EAT.
[33] (1967) 2 ITR 255.

(e) as a result of an arbitration award made under an approved ACAS arbitration scheme (see para 1.14);

(f) if the employment has been extended of an employee who would otherwise have retired.

13.30 In any of these circumstances, the employee's continuity of employment is deemed to be preserved, and the period beginning with the date on which the dismissal took effect, and the date when the re-engagement or reinstatement took place, will count in the computation of the employee's period of continuous employment.

13.31 The re-engagement or reinstatement must be 'in consequence of' any of these actions. The mere fact of re-engagement or reinstatement, by itself, for some other reason, will not ensure continuity (*Gardener v National Coal Board*[34]), unless the provisions of ERA, s 212(3)(c) apply, it being recalled that this cannot apply to an arrangement which purports to be retrospective (*Morris v Walsh Western UK Ltd*, para 13.26).

13.32 If an employer gives notice of dismissal and withdraws it following an appeal during the currency of the notice period, there is no break in continuity (*Brock v Minerva Dental Ltd*[35]). If an employee is dismissed and then reinstated, re-engaged, or otherwise re-employed by the employer or a successor or associated employer, the effect of reinstatement etc is to annul the dismissal (Continuity of Employment Regulations 1996 (as amended), and *Roberts v West Coast Trains Ltd*[36]) and the period of prior employment as well as the period between the dismissal and reinstatement etc will count towards continuity.

Weeks Which do not Count towards Continuity (ss 215–217)

13.33 There are certain circumstances when weeks of absence do not count towards continuity, but do not break continuity. The non-counting weeks are used to advance the starting date of the employment, by seven days for each non-counting week (s 215(2)) (except weeks spent abroad in redundancy cases: see para 13.34). The non-counting weeks arise in the following circumstances.

A. Periods Spent Working Abroad (s 215(1))

13.34 A person who works outside Great Britain is generally excluded from employment rights and weeks of employment abroad will not normally count. However, there are circumstances when a period of employment spent outside Great Britain will count in computing continuous employment as if it were employment in Great Britain. Thus, if an employee works outside Great Britain, and his contract is then varied so that he works inside Great Britain, the whole of his period of employment will be continuous for the purpose of establishing a qualifying period of employment rights generally. However, for the purpose of calculating statutory redundancy pay, a week of employment abroad will not count towards continuity (but will not break continuity) if the employee spent the whole or part of the week working abroad, and he was not an employed earner for the purpose of national insurance contributions.

B. Strikes and Lock-outs (s 216)

13.35 Any week during which, or during part of which, an employee takes part in a strike will not count towards continuity, but will not break continuity. This rule applies

---

[34] EAT/375/82.   [35] [2007] ICR 917.   [36] [2004] EWCA Civ 900, [2005] ICR 254, [2004] IRLR 788.

whether the strike is official or unofficial. However, the strike must be connected with terms and conditions of employment, and not, for example, a 'political' strike. If an employee is dismissed while on strike, and subsequently re-engaged, the weeks on strike will be deducted from his continuous employment, but continuity is preserved (*Hanson v Fashion Industries (Hartlepool) Ltd*, see para 13.3). The total number of days deducted will be the actual number of days (not the number of working days) falling in the period between the last day when the employee worked and the day when he resumed work (s 216(2)). Thus, non-working days, eg Saturday and Sunday, can be deducted. If, during a strike, an employee takes another job and is subsequently re-engaged then, if that job was a temporary one, his continuity will be preserved; but if it was a permanent job (eg there is evidence that he so regarded it) he will be treated as if he left his original employment, and continuity will be broken (*Bloomfield v Springfield Hosiery Finishing Co Ltd*[37]).

13.36 Issues sometimes arise as to whether or not the employee is 'taking part' in a strike, or is absent from work during an industrial dispute for some other reason (see *Coates v Modern Methods and Material Ltd*[38]). It is not relevant that the employer 'knows' that the employee took part in the strike, for the test is an objective one (see *Manifold Industries Ltd v Sims*[39]). Indeed, off-duty employees and employees who are away from work sick may be regarded as taking part in strike action in appropriate circumstances (see *Bolton Roadways Ltd v Edwards*[40]).

13.37 Similarly, continuity of employment is not lost if the employee is absent from work because of a lock-out (s 216(3)), but there does appear to be a difference, in that if the contract of employment still subsists, s 212(1) (see para 13.14) applies, and days when an employee is locked out will still count towards continuity. This is because s 216(1) only refers to strikes, not to lock-outs. It is only when there is no contract of employment in existence that s 216(3) provides that the number of days falling within the period between the employee's last working day and the day he resumes work are to be deducted from the start of the employee's period of continuous employment.

C. **Military Service (s 217)**

13.38 An employee who is obliged to serve as an armed forces reservist may apply under the Reserve Forces (Safeguard of Employment) Act 1985 to be reinstated in his former employment within six months of the termination of the period for which he was called up. Weeks when the employee was called up will not count towards continuity, but continuity will not be broken.

Change of Employer (s 218)

13.39 As has been noted, if there has been a transfer of an undertaking within the meaning of the TUPE regulations (see Chapter 9) there is an automatic transfer of the contract of employment from the transferor to the transferee. Curiously enough, the regulations make no mention of continuity of employment being preserved in such circumstances, although there can be little doubt that this will happen, for otherwise the UK would be in

---

[37] [1972] 1 All ER 609, [1972] ICR 91, NIRC.
[38] [1983] QB 192, [1982] 3 All ER 946, [1982] ICR 763, [1982] IRLR 318, CA.
[39] [1991] ICR 504, [1991] IRLR 242, EAT.   [40] [1987] IRLR 392, EAT.

serious breach of its obligations to transpose the Acquired Rights Directive into domestic law. It would seem that the provisions of ERA, s 218 are sufficient for this purpose, even though many of the legal decisions on this section were decided prior to the introduction of TUPE.

13.40 There are a number of circumstances to consider.

(a) There is a transfer to which TUPE applies. Regulation 5(1) states that the contract shall have effect as if originally made between the person so employed and the transferee. This clearly preserves the continuity of the employee so transferred (*Royal Ordnance plc v Pilkington*[41]).

(b) There is a transfer to which ERA, s 218(2) applies. This section provides for continuity to be preserved when there is a transfer of a trade, business, or undertaking from one employer to another. There must be a recognised and identifiable part of the business transferred, not merely a collection of assets (*Melon v Hector Powe Ltd*[42]). But s 218(2) does not depend on there being a transfer of employment under the TUPE regulations (*Oakland v Wellswood (Yorkshire) Ltd*[43]).

(c) Statutory change of employer: here ERA, s 218(3) applies when an Act of Parliament substitutes one employer for another (see *Gale v Northern General Hospital NHS Trust*,[44] where the rule was held not to apply).

(d) Although at common law the death of an employer would normally terminate the contract, ERA, s 218(4) provides that if the employee is kept on by the personal representative or trustee of the deceased employer, continuity will not be broken.

(e) If an employee is employed by two partners and one of them leaves the partnership (for whatever reason) there is no break in the continuity of employment. Section 218(5) ensures continuity when two partners are succeeded by one of them as sole principal (*Stevens v Bower*[45]).

(f) If an employee is transferred from an employer to an associated employer, the transfer does not break continuity (s 218(6)). However, the two employers must be 'associated' in the legal sense, in accordance with the definition contained in ERA, s 231 (see para 2.6).

(g) If an employee transfers from employment by the governors of a school maintained by a local education authority to employment by that authority, continuity is preserved (ERA, s 218(7)). Employees who transfer from one hospital to another, or from an NHS hospital to one with trust status, will generally have continuity preserved by ERA, s 218(8) (see also National Health Service and Community Care Act 1990, s 6), and certain senior hospital appointees whilst undergoing training, which involves being successively employed by different health authorities, have continuity for a number of employment protection rights specified in ERA (Employment Protection (Continuity of Employment of National Health Service Employees) (Modification) Order 1996). For redundancy payment purposes, if an employee transfers from one local authority to another, or to or from certain

---

[41] [1988] ICR 606, [1988] IRLR 466, EAT; revsd [1989] ICR 737, [1989] IRLR 489, CA.

[42] [1980] IRLR 80, Ct of Sess; aff'd [1981] 1 All ER 313, [1981] ICR 43, [1980] IRLR 477, HL.

[43] [2009] EWCA Civ 1094, [2010] IRLR 82.

[44] [1994] IRLR 292, CA.

[45] [2004] ICR 1582, [2004] IRLR 957, CA.

specified bodies, continuity is preserved (Redundancy Payments (Continuity of Employment in Local Government etc) (Modification) Order 1999). But a transfer to or from a body not included in Sch 1 to the Order will not give rise to continuity (*Liversidge v London Residuary Body*[46]). Similarly, continuity is preserved on a transfer from one NHS body to another (Redundancy Payments (National Health Service) (Modification) Order 1993).

13.41 In particular, it should be noted that artificial breaks in employment consequent on a transfer are not generally favoured, and s 218, combined with TUPE, are to be given a broad interpretation so as to preserve continuity where possible (*Macer v Abafast Ltd*[47]).

The Effect of the Continuity Rules

13.42 The purpose of establishing continuity of employment is to enable an employee to qualify, by virtue of the length of his employment, for certain statutory rights. In particular, however, additional years of employment which can be saved by the continuity rules are of great value to an employee whose employment ultimately comes to an end for reason of redundancy, for he can then obtain a larger redundancy payment (or an increased basic award if he was unfairly dismissed). Thus, when there is a transfer of a business from one employer to another, if there is no continuity, he can apply for his redundancy payment and then start again with his new employer; on the other hand, if there is continuity, the new employer takes over the obligations to make a redundancy payment should this prove necessary in the future. In principle, if the employer makes a redundancy payment to the employee, whose contract is then renewed by the same or another employer (eg by virtue of the TUPE Regulations, see Chapter 9), continuity of employment is broken for redundancy payment purposes (ERA, s 214). There must be a full payment of redundancy money due, and the payment must be in pursuance of a statutory obligation to pay (*Rowan v Machinery Installations (South Wales) Ltd*[48]), not a voluntary payment (*Ross v Delrosa Caterers Ltd*[49]), and must not have been paid by virtue of an employment tribunal decision (*Richards v s and H E Fielding Ltd*[50]). Continuity will also be broken if a redundancy payment has been made by the Secretary of State under the provisions of ERA, ss 166–167 (see para 18.67), provided he is satisfied that the requisite conditions for the payment have been met (*Secretary of State for Trade and Industry v Lassman*[51]).

13.43 Continuity is broken if, having been paid a redundancy payment, the employee is re-employed in circumstances in which the Continuity of Employment Regulations apply, but only for the purpose of calculating service for any future entitlement to a redundancy payment. The regulations provide however that if the employee repays the redundancy payment, continuity is restored (Employment Protection (Continuity of Employment) Regulations 1996, reg 4). See Table 13.1 below.

---

[46] [1989] ICR 228, EAT.   [47] [1990] ICR 234, [1990] IRLR 137, EAT.
[48] [1981] ICR 386, [1981] IRLR 122, EAT.   [49] [1981] ICR 393, EAT.
[50] (1966) 1 KIR 365, 1 ITR 376.   [51] [2000] ICR 1109, [2000] IRLR 411, 4 May.

Continuity Table

Table 13.1 Continuity of Employment

Statutory right	Continuous employment required
Written particulars (ERA, s 1)	Two months
Guarantee pay (ERA, s 29)	One month
Time off work to look for work or arrange training (ERA, s 52)	Two years
Medical suspension pay (ERA, s 65)	One month
Parental leave (Maternity and Parental Leave etc Regulations, reg 13)	One year
Paternity leave (Paternity and Adoption Leave Regulations 2002, reg 4)	26 weeks
Flexible working (Flexible Working (Eligibility, Complaints and Remedies) Regulations 2002, reg 3)	26 weeks
Minimum notice (ERA, s 86)	One month
Written reason for dismissal (ERA, s 92) (with exceptions)	Two years (see note 53)
Unfair dismissal (ERA, s 108) (with exceptions)	Two years
Redundancy payment (ERA, s 155)	Two years
Statutory paternity pay (Social Security Contributions and Benefits Act 1992, s 171ZA(1))	26 weeks prior to the 15th week before the EWC or the week when the child's adopter was matched with the child
Fixed term contract becoming permanent employee (Fixed term Employees (Prevention of Less Favourable Treatment) Regulations 2002 reg 8)	Four years
Agency Workers Regulations 2010	12 weeks
Time off for study or training	26 weeks

Summary

- Continuity of employment is important in order to obtain certain statutory rights.
- An employer can draft contracts to prevent continuity, although private contracts to preserve continuity cannot affect the statutory position.
- The rules of continuity are set out in ss210-219 ERA 1996.
- Continuity is not broken unless there is a complete week in which there is no contract of employment.
- Time off sick or on holiday do not break continuity if the person is still employed.
- There is no break in continuity for a temporary cessation of work or layoff.
- A reinstatement or re-engagement order by a tribunal preserves previous continuity.
- Some absences do not break continuity but do not count towards it, such as official strikes, military service, and periods spent working abroad.
- An unlawful strike (one not protected by TULRCA) breaks continuity.

14

Normal Working Hours and a Week's Pay

Normal Working Hours

A. **Employment Rights Act, ss 221–229**

14.1 In order to calculate the amount payable to an employee for the breach of certain specific statutory rights, it is necessary to ascertain the employee's weekly pay. This is done by reference to the employee's 'normal working hours'. The Employment Rights Act sets out precise formulae for working out a week's pay and, in certain specific cases, puts a cap on that amount.

B. **Contractual Provisions**

14.2 The Act envisages that there are a number of different possibilities when trying to assess an employee's 'normal working hours', and it is therefore necessary to choose the one which is most appropriate in the circumstances, so as to calculate the week's pay. To do this, one must start with a consideration of the contract of employment. So if the contract specifies normal working hours that will generally be conclusive, and it is immaterial that the employee works more or less than those hours unless it can be shown that there has been a variation (express or implied) of the contract (*ITT Components (Europe) v Kolah*[1]). If the contract is silent on this matter, the employment tribunal must infer the relevant term from what happens in practice (*Larkin v Cambos Enterprises (Stretford) Ltd*[2]). Thus, in *Armstrong Whitworth Rolls Ltd v Mustard* (see para 3.105) the contract of employment required the employee to work 40 hours per week. He was then asked to work for 60 hours per week, in order to ensure 24-hour coverage of the plant. He did this for seven years and, when made redundant, it was held that his contract of employment had been varied, so that he was entitled to a redundancy payment on the basis of a 60-hour week.

14.3 Overtime is generally excluded from normal working hours, unless it is included in the minimum number of hours fixed by the contract. In other words, it must be guaranteed by the employer and obligatory for the employee (*Tarmac Roadstone Holdings Ltd v Peacock*[3]). If the employer is entitled, but not obliged, to call for overtime working, such hours as are worked will not count towards normal working hours, even though the employee is bound to work overtime under the terms of his contract (*Lotus Cars Ltd v Sutcliffe*[4]). In *Bamsey v Albion Engineering and Manufacturing plc*[5] the employee worked under a contract that entitled him to a basic working week of 39 hours. In fact, he regularly worked a shift pattern which averaged 60 hours per week. He was paid for his period of annual leave on the

---

[1] [1977] ICR 740, [1977] IRLR 53, EAT.   [2] [1978] ICR 1247, EAT.
[3] [1973] 2 All ER 485, [1973] ICR 273, [1973] IRLR 157, CA.
[4] [1982] IRLR 381, CA.   [5] [2004] ICR 1083, CA.

basis of a 39-hour week, and he claimed that he should have been paid at the same rate as averaged, with overtime, while at work. His claim failed. The Working Time Regulations incorporated the definition of working hours contained in ERA, s 234 and overtime could only be included in a week's pay if it was obligatory on both sides as contractual obligations.

A Week's Pay

14.4 It is then necessary to establish how much the employee was paid for those hours. Remuneration, for this purpose, can be quite wide. Clearly, wages or salaries will be included, but so will contractual bonuses paid on a regular basis, eg per shift, or per site, or for undertaking additional duties (*A & B Marcusfield v Melhuish*[6]). Commission payments are also included, although a commission paid annually has to be apportioned over the period when the employee actually worked (*J & s Bickley Ltd v Washer*[7]), and consequently averaged over a period of 12 weeks (see para 14.8). Expenses do not count as remuneration if they are a reimbursement of an employee's expenditure, but do if they represent a profit in the employee's hands (*S & U Stores Ltd v Wilkes*[8]). However, expenses representing a profit must have been declared to the Revenue, otherwise the contract may be illegal (*Tomlinson v Dick Evans U Drive Ltd*, see para 3.7). Payments in kind (car, accommodation, food, etc) will not count (*Skillen v Eastwoods Froy Ltd*[9]), although it should be noted that such benefits may be taken into account when determining any relevant compensation award. Tips and gratuities do not count if they are paid by the customer, not the employer (*Palmanor Ltd v Cedron*[10]), but a service charge which is distributed among employees in a fixed proportion will count as part of a week's pay (*Tsoukka v Potomac Restaurants Ltd*[11]) (but not for the purpose of the national minimum wage, see para 8.5). A lodging allowance is not part of a week's pay, although a deduction from pay in respect of lodging clearly would be. Overtime premiums also do not count (*British Coal Corpn v Cheesbrough*[12]).

14.5 When calculating 'a week's pay' for statutory purposes, it is the gross pay which counts, not net pay (*Secretary of State for Employment v John Woodrow & Sons (Builders) Ltd*[13]). Moreover, the amount must be calculated on the basis that the employer is complying with his legal obligations. Thus, in *Cooner v P S Doal & Sons*,[14] an employee was paid less than that to which he was entitled under a Wages Council order, and it was held that it was pay under the order which counted, not the lower wage actually paid. Although the Wages Councils orders have now ceased to exist, the principle still applies to the minimum wage legislation (*Paggetti v Cobb*[15]).

A. Quantifying a Week's Pay

14.6 Having ascertained an employee's normal weekly hours, and how much he is paid for those hours, we can now work out his week's pay for statutory purposes. The following four circumstances should cover all situations.

---

[6] [1977] IRLR 484, EAT.   [7] [1977] ICR 425, EAT.
[8] [1974] 3 All ER 401, [1974] ICR 645, [1974] IRLR 283, NIRC.
[9] (1966) 2 ITR.   [10] [1978] ICR 1008, [1978] IRLR 303, EAT.   [11] (1968) 3 ITR 259.
[12] [1988] ICR 60, sub nom *National Coal Board v Cheesbrough and Secretary of State for Employment* [1988] IRLR 351, CA; revsd sub nom *British Coal Corpn v Cheesbrough* [1988] ICR 769, [1988] IRLR 351, CA; aff'd [1990] 2 AC 256, [1990] 1 All ER 641, [1990] ICR 317, [1990] IRLR 148, HL.
[13] [1983] ICR 582, [1983] IRLR 11, EAT.   [14] [1988] ICR 495, [1988] IRLR 338, EAT.
[15] [2002] IRLR 861, [2002] All ER (D) 394 (Mar), EAT.

Remuneration does not Vary (ERA, s 221(2))

14.7 If an employee's remuneration does not vary in normal working hours (whether he is an hourly or weekly paid employee, or is paid for any other period) then the amount of a week's pay is the amount which is payable under the contract of employment. If the employee is paid by the hour, then the week's pay is to be determined as if he worked his full contractual hours in that week.

Remuneration Varies with the Amount of Work (ERA, s 221(3))

14.8 If the amount of remuneration does vary with the amount of work done in the period (eg pieceworkers) the week's pay is ascertained by finding the average hourly remuneration payable in the 12 weeks ending with the calculation date. If an employee is paid on a commission basis, and so the pay varies with the work done, then remuneration should be calculated over 12 weeks, and not at a specific, frozen single week, when the commission is earned or paid (*May Gurney Ltd v Adshead*[16]). If, in any of those 12 weeks, no remuneration was payable for hours when the employee was actually at work, earlier weeks can be taken into account, so as to bring the number up to 12 (s 223). Only weeks when the employee actually works will count (*Adams v John Wright & Sons (Blackwall) Ltd*[17]). Thus, if an employee is paid for work actually done in a week, even if those earnings were abnormally low, the week will count. If an employee is a recent recruit, so that he does not have 12 weeks' employment to take into account, an employment tribunal can determine an amount which fairly represents a week's pay, taking into account the amount already received, the remuneration offered in the contract, the remuneration of comparable employees of the same employer, and remuneration received by comparable employees of other employers (ERA, s 228). Weeks with a previous employer which count towards continuity (see Chapter 13) may be taken into account (ERA, s 229).

Remuneration Varies According to the Time of Work (ERA, s 222)

14.9 If an employee is a shift worker, or works on a rota, so that the hours when he is required to work differ according to the time of the day or the day of the week, with the consequence that his remuneration will correspondingly be different, the week's pay will be the average hourly rate multiplied by the average weekly hours in the period of 12 weeks prior to the calculation date. Again, earlier weeks can be counted, if necessary (see para 14.8).

No Normal Working Hours (ERA, s 224)

14.10 If the employee had no normal working hours, the week's pay is determined by taking the employee's average weekly earnings for the period of 12 weeks prior to the calculation date. If the employee was not paid during any of those weeks, earlier weeks can be included, if necessary, to make up the 12-week period, even if the employee agreed to waive an entitlement to be paid, which otherwise was legally required to be paid (*Secretary of State for Employment v Crane*[18]).

B. **Capping a Week's Pay (ERA, s 227)**

14.11 In respect of the following claims, there is a limit to the amount of a week's pay which can be calculated (currently £538 per week). These claims are:

(a) basic award for unfair dismissal;

(b) additional award of compensation for unfair dismissal;

(c) statutory redundancy pay;

---

[16] EAT/0150/06.   [17] [1972] ICR 463, 7 ITR 191, NIRC.   [18] [1988] IRLR 238, EAT.

(d) arrears of pay (up to eight weeks), statutory notice, and holiday pay (up to six weeks) and a basic award, payable on an employer's insolvency (ERA, s 186);

(e) right not to be unjustifiably disciplined by a trade union (TULR(C)A, s 67);

(f) unreasonable exclusion from a trade union (TULR(C)A, s 176);

(g) failure to give employment particulars (Employment Act 2002: see para 3.118);

(h) failure to comply with the Flexible Working (Procedural Requirements) Regulations (see para 6.128);

(i) failure to consult under the Transfer of Undertakings (Protection of Employment) Regulations 2006;

(j) breach of right to be accompanied (Employment Relations Act 1999);

(k) duty to notify employee of retirement date and right to make a request (Employment Equality (Age) Regulations 2006);

(l) breach of time off for study or training provisions.

14.12 It will be noted that guarantee pay (see para 7.2) is limited to £30 per day (ERA, s 31) with a maximum of £150 in any period of three months (five days' pay). Pay for time off work to look for another job (see para 18.38) is limited to two-fifths of a week's pay, not capped (ERA, s 54). In all other instances where a week's pay is used for calculation purposes, it is the actual gross pay which has to be taken into account.

C. **The Calculation Date (ERA, ss 225–226)**

14.13 The date on which the calculations are to be made will differ, depending on the nature of the employee's claim. Each statutory right has its own formula. For guarantee pay (s 30), it will generally be the day on which the guarantee payment is payable (unless a new contract or variation has been entered into, in which case it will be the last day when the old contract was in force). The calculation date in respect of a claim for remuneration for time off with pay to look for work (s 52) is the day the employer gave notice of termination for reason of redundancy. For time off work for antenatal care (s 55) the calculation date is the date of the appointment, and for time off work for employee representatives (s 62) and time off work for study or training (s 63A) the calculation date is the date on which time off was taken or should have been permitted. For suspension on medical grounds (s 64) or maternity suspension (s 66), the calculation date is generally the day before the suspension begins. If a request is made for contract variation (s 80F) the calculation date is the date on which the application was made.

14.14 For redundancy payment claims, if contractual notice was given which was greater than the statutory notice which could have been given, the calculation date will be the day on which, counting backwards from the effective date of termination, the statutory notice could have been given. If less than statutory notice was given, the calculation date will be the date that notice expires, and if no notice is given, the date the contract terminated. For payments due to an employee on the employer's insolvency, the calculation date becomes the 'appropriate date', ie the date on which the employer became insolvent (for holiday pay and arrears of pay). For the basic award, it will be the later of the dates when the employer became insolvent, or the employment was terminated, or the basic award was made, as the case may be. For other payments (ie statutory notice, statutory redundancy pay), the calculation date will be the later of the dates when the employer became insolvent or the employment was terminated (ERA, s 186).

Summary

- To calculate compensation for certain rights, it is necessary to work out the weekly pay.
- This is done by reference to 'normal working hours'.
- The process is described in the ERA ss 221–229.
- It is gross pay that counts.
- A week's pay is capped for certain types of compensation in the legislation. See appendix A for further details.

15

Rights in Notice

Background

15.1 One of the features which distinguishes a contract of employment from other contractual situations is that a contract of employment is one of continuous obligation, with, generally speaking, no specified time for its ending. Thus, apart from certain exceptions (eg fixed-term contracts, summary dismissal, retirement age, project termination), if either the employer or employee wishes to terminate the contract, notice of such termination must be given. Whether or not there is a termination is a factual and legal question (see para 17.7), but to be operative, the notice must give a clear indication of the actual date of termination (*Morton Sundour Fabrics Ltd v Shaw*,[1] para 18.8). This chapter will explore the rights and duties of the parties to give and receive lawful notice in the event of a termination, ie if there is a dismissal or resignation.

Notice to be Given by the Employer

15.2 The period of notice to be given by the employer will first be determined by looking at the contract of employment, as required by ERA, s 1(4)(e).

15.3 If the contract of employment is silent on this matter, at common law, reasonable notice must be given. Again, what is reasonable will depend on the employee's position, the industry, nature of the work, etc. For example, in *Hill v C A Parsons & Co Ltd* (see paras 10.5 and 10.6), the Court of Appeal expressed the view that a senior engineer would have been entitled to between six months' and one year's notice, and there are a number of decisions (dating from the nineteenth century and the earlier part of the twentieth century) which deal with what would be reasonable notice for employees such as head gardeners, domestic servants, journalists, commercial travellers, chorus girls, hairdressers' assistants, and so on. The more senior the status, the more notice an employee is entitled to receive. Thus, in *Clark v Fahrenheit 451 (Communications) Ltd*[2] three months' notice was held to be appropriate for a director, bearing in mind his seniority and salary.

15.4 However, irrespective of the contractual terms, by statute, certain minimum periods of notice must be given (see ERA, s 86(1)). These periods are to be determined by the length of the employee's period of employment. Thus, after one month's employment, the employee is entitled to one week's notice, and this will apply until he has been employed for two years. Thereafter, he will be entitled to a week's notice in respect of each year's continual employment, ie two weeks' notice after two year's employment, up to a statutory maximum of 12 weeks' notice in respect of employment which has lasted for 12 years or more. But if contractual notice is for a period which is longer than that to be given by statute, the contractual notice will prevail.

---

[1] (1966) 2 KIR 1, 2 ITR 84, DC.   [2] [2000] All ER (D) 849.

15.5 If a contract of employment comes to an end because of the operation of the doctrine of frustration (see para 17.55), no statutory or contractual notice can be or need be given (*G F Sharp & Co Ltd v McMillan*³).

15.6 Notice to terminate a contract of employment may be given at any time, even before the employment has commenced. Thus, in *Sarker v South Tees Acute Hospitals NHS Trust* (see para 3.4), the claimant was offered a post in July, and was due to start work in October. However, the offer was withdrawn in September. The claimant brought a claim for her contractual notice, under the provisions of the Employment Tribunals Extension of Jurisdiction Order (see para 1.22). The EAT held that her contract had been terminated, and she was entitled to her contractual notice.

A. Giving Notice

15.7 Notice may be given by either side either orally or in writing. In either case, apart from summary dismissal, it will run from the day after it is given (*West v Kneels Ltd*⁴), unless a later date is specified, but it cannot operate unless the recipient has had an opportunity to know of it. Thus, if a letter giving notice to an employee is not received on a particular day (because the employee is not at home, or because of a postal strike etc), it will only operate when the employee has had a reasonable opportunity to read it (see *Brown v Southall and Knight*,⁵ para 17.5). If there is a collateral contract (see para 16.8) to the main contract, notice must be given in respect of both of them.

15.8 It is advisable for employers to include express terms relating to when notice takes effect in their employment contracts. In *Newcastle upon Tyne Hospitals NHS Foundation Trust v Haywood*,⁶ the Supreme Court extended the principles of the *Gisda Cyf v Barratt* case (see Chapter 17) which was limited to unfair dismissal claims under the ERA 1996, to the situation under common law. It found that, in the absence of an express term in the contract as to when notice takes effect, then there is an implied term when giving written notice of dismissal that notice must have been communicated or come to the mind of the addressee. In other words, it would be the date on which the dismissal notice letter came to the claimant's attention and she had a reasonable opportunity of reading it. Here, the employer was aware the employee was been on holiday and would not open the letter until her return.

15.9 The general common law rule is that once notice has been given, it cannot be unilaterally withdrawn either by the employer (*Riordan v War Office*⁷) or the employee (*Brennan v C Lindley & Co Ltd*⁸), although it can be withdrawn by mutual agreement between the parties (*Harris and Russell Ltd v Slingsby*⁹). The notice period may also be extended by mutual agreement (*Mowlem Northern Ltd v Watson*¹⁰). However, modern cases draw a distinction between the deliberate giving of notice (by either party) and a resignation or dismissal given 'in the heat of the moment'. In such circumstances (usually following some form of argument) it is incumbent on the recipient to ascertain whether the other party really meant what he said (*Kwik-Fit (GB) Ltd v Lineham*,¹¹ and see para 17.47). The validity of an unambiguous notice of dismissal which is given by mistake depended not just on what the employer intended, but also on whether it was reasonable for the employee to take it at face

---

³ [1998] IRLR 632, EAT.   ⁴ [1987] ICR 146, [1986] IRLR 430, EAT.
⁵ [1980] ICR 617, [1980] IRLR 130, EAT.   ⁶ [2018] UKSC 22.
⁷ [1959] 3 All ER 552; aff'd [1960] 3 All ER 774n, CA.   ⁸ [1974] IRLR 153, NIRC.
⁹ [1973] 3 All ER 31, [1973] ICR 454, [1973] IRLR 221, NIRC.
¹⁰ [1990] ICR 751, [1990] IRLR 500, EAT.   ¹¹ [1992] ICR 183, [1992] IRLR 156, EAT.

value and treat herself as dismissed in *C F Capital plc v Willoughby*.[12] This applies particularly to notice which is given in the heat of the moment.

15.10 If the employer gives notice to terminate the contract of employment, and during the period of that notice the employee gives a counter-notice that he intends to leave at an earlier date, the employee has still been dismissed for the reason for which the employer's notice was given (ERA, s 95(2); see *Lees v Arthur Greaves Ltd*[13]). However, if the employee resigns during the notice period, rather than giving a counter-notice, he will be regarded as not having been dismissed but as having resigned (*Walker v Cotswold Chine Home School*[14]), unless the employer agrees to him leaving, before the expiry of their notice, in which case it is treated as being a variation of the employer's notice of dismissal (*McAlwane v Boughton Estates*[15]). A resignation does not have to be accepted by the employer, nor can it be withdrawn unilaterally. If an employee gives notice to terminate his employment, and during the notice period the employer releases the employee from serving the full notice period, there is no dismissal by the employer. All that has happened is that the employee is no longer required to attend work (*Tom Findlay & Co Ltd v Devlin*[16]).

15.11 There are special provisions dealing with the counter-notice to be given by an employee because he has been laid off or put on short-time working (see para 18.33). Further, it should be noted that during the notice period, an employee retains those statutory rights relating to time off work (see ERA, ss 50–63 and TULR(C)A, ss 186–190, and see para 15.17).

B. **Taxation of Payments**

15.12 The taxation of payments on the termination of employment is covered by the Income Tax (Earnings and Pensions) Act 2003. The position is somewhat complicated because some such payments are taxable in full, some only partly so, and some not at all. The general principle is that if the payment constitutes 'earnings', such as salary to the date of termination, accrued holiday pay, benefits in kind, etc, full income tax and national insurance contributions must be deducted. Money paid as an inducement to enter into a restrictive covenant is taxable (even if it becomes unenforceable), but not the affirmation of an existing covenant. On the other hand, money paid by way of compensation for breach of contract is generally free of tax up to £30,000.

C. **Pay in Lieu of Notice**

15.13 In *Delaney v Staples* (see para 8.17), Lord Browne-Wilkinson listed four circumstances when a payment in lieu of notice may be made, with different consequences in each case. These are:

(a) the employer gives the appropriate notice of termination to the employee, but does not require him to work during the notice period. In effect, the employee is on 'garden leave'. Generally, there is no breach of contract in not requiring the employee to work until the termination date (but see para 19.8). Tax and national insurance contributions must be deducted, and restrictive covenants will normally be enforceable;

(b) the contract provides that the employer may terminate the contract, either with notice or summarily on the payment of a sum of money in lieu of notice. Here, two alternative ways are set out whereby the contract may be lawfully terminated. If the

---

[12] [2011] IRLR 985, [2011] EWCA Civ 1115.
[13] [1974] 2 All ER 393, [1974] ICR 501, [1974] IRLR 93 91.   [14] (1977) 12 ITR 342, EAT.
[15] [1973] 2 All ER 299, [1973] ICR 470, NIRC.   [16] UKEATS/0071/06/MT.

employer fails to make the payment, the employee can sue for the money as a debt. If the employer makes the payment, income tax should be deducted;

(c) the employer and employee mutually agree to bring the contract of employment to an end, for an agreed payment. Technically, there is no breach of contract, but even though the payment is not strictly 'earnings', it is taxable in full;

(d) the employer summarily dismisses the employee and makes a payment of money in lieu of notice. This is the most common category of payment in lieu of notice. Since the employer is seeking to extinguish a claim for damages (for breach of contract) the payment is free from tax up to £30,000.

15.14 It follows that if there is no payment at all made in lieu of notice (or if the payment made is in respect of a lesser period than the full notice period), any subsequent payment must be regarded as damages for breach of contract, the first £30,000 of which will not be liable to income tax.

15.15 Either party may waive his right to receive contractual or statutory notice (ERA, s 86(3)) and, in particular, an employer may decide to pay the employee in lieu of him working his notice. Indeed, if the contract of employment gives the employer an option to make a payment in lieu of notice, the employee has no right to work out his notice, or to be compensated for non-contractual benefits he would have obtained had he worked his notice (*Marshall (Cambridge) Ltd v Hamblin*[17]). But an employer cannot use the device of making a payment in lieu of notice to prevent an employee from achieving his contractual earnings, eg commissions, etc. An employee who is on piecework must be given enough work to enable him to earn his usual earnings, and this rule applies equally during the notice period (*Devonald v Rosser & Sons*, see paras 10.16 and 10.18).

15.16 The employee is also entitled to be compensated for the loss of other contractual benefits (car, health insurance, accrued holiday pay, etc) for the period had the notice been worked out. Further, it was held by the Court of Appeal in *Abrahams v Performing Rights Society*[18] that if a contract states that there is a contractual entitlement to pay in lieu of notice, the full amount due is payable and there is no duty to mitigate against any loss. The duty only arises if the employer is not contractually bound to make the payment in lieu. Thus in *Cerberus Software Ltd v Rowley*[19] the contract of employment provided that the employer could either give six months' notice of termination or make a payment on termination in lieu of notice. The claimant was dismissed without notice and without a payment in lieu. He claimed damages for wrongful dismissal. The Court of Appeal held that a provision in a contract which enabled the employer to make a payment in lieu of notice gives the employer a choice, and is inconsistent with the employee having a right to insist on such payment being made. Consequently, the employee's remedy was for damages for breach of contract, and the measure of such damages was the amount the employee would have received had the employment continued, subject to the ordinary rules relating to mitigation of damages. *Abraham v Performing Rights Society* was distinguished because in that case there was a contractual entitlement to pay in lieu, which was not subject to the duty to mitigate, whereas in *Cerberus* the employer had a choice whether or not to make a payment in lieu. In other words, there is a difference between a claim for contractual entitlement and a claim for liquidated damages. For the latter, where the claim is for damages for breach of contract, the mitigation rules apply.

---

[17] [1994] ICR 362, [1994] IRLR 260, EAT.   [18] [1995] ICR 1028, [1995] IRLR 486, CA.
[19] [2000] ICR 35, [1999] IRLR 690, EAT; revsd sub nom *Rowley v Cerberus Software Ltd* [2001] EWCA Civ 78, [2001] ICR 376, [2001] IRLR 160, [2001] All ER (D) 80 (Jan).

D. **Rights During the Notice Period (ERA, ss 88–91)**

15.17 During the period of notice, the employee will still have certain statutory rights, contained in ERA, ss 88–91. If the employer gives notice, the employee must have been employed for one month or more to obtain the statutory rights, but he will not have any of these rights if the notice to be given by the employer must be at least one week more than the statutory notice laid down in ERA, s 86(1). Thus, in *Scotts Co (UK) Ltd v Budd* (see para 6.33) the claimant was employed for 17 years, and thus entitled to statutory notice of 12 weeks. He was off work sick for two years, and the employers terminated his employment, giving him the 13 weeks' notice to which he was entitled under his contract. He claimed that he was entitled to be paid for the weeks of his notice period. His claim was dismissed by the EAT. Section 87(4) of ERA makes it quite clear that the entitlement to be paid during the notice period does not apply if the notice to terminate must be at least one week longer than the statutory period of notice. If an employee has been employed for five years, and is given four weeks' contractual notice, or five weeks' statutory notice, the provisions of ss 88–91 apply. However, if the employee gives notice (after being employed for one month or more) he will be able to enjoy these statutory rights only for the statutory notice period required of an employee, ie one week (s 86(1)), even though he gives a longer period of notice.

15.18 The statutory rights in question are as follows:

(a) Where the employee has normal working hours, he is entitled to be paid for those hours when he is ready and willing to work, but

   (i) the employer does not provide work (s 88(1)(a)), or

   (ii) the employee is incapable of work because of sickness or injury (s 88(1)(b)), or

   (iii) the employee is absent from work because of pregnancy or childbirth or parental leave, adoption leave or paternity leave (s 88(1)(c)), or

   (iv) he is absent from work in accordance with the terms of the contract relating to holidays (s 88(1)(d)).

He is entitled to be paid at the average hourly rate, produced by dividing a week's pay by the number of normal working hours. It should be noted that, for the purpose of ss 88–91, a 'week's pay' is not subject to the statutory limit which is applied in unfair dismissal and redundancy claims. Any payment made by the employer by way of sick pay, statutory sick pay, statutory maternity pay, paternity pay, statutory paternity pay, adoption pay, statutory adoption pay, holiday pay, etc, can be offset.

(b) If the employee does not have normal working hours, the employer shall pay a week's pay (or average weekly remuneration—calculated over a period of 12 weeks), for each week of the notice period, provided the employee is ready and willing to do work of a reasonable nature and amount in order to earn a week's pay (s 89(1), (2)). The employee is also entitled to be paid for periods when s/he is off work because of sickness or injury, absent through pregnancy or childbirth or parental leave, adoption leave, or paternity leave, or absent because of contractual holidays (s 89(3)). Any payments made by the employer can be offset (see (a)).

(c) ERA, s 91 provides that an employer is not required to make payments under ss 88–89 in respect of any period during which the employee is absent from work with leave from the employer granted at the request of the employee, including any period of time off work taken for the purpose of public duties, looking for work or making arrangements for retraining, antenatal care, acting as an occupational pension scheme trustee, or taking part in trade union duties and activities. At first sight this would appear to be strange, but in fact there is no problem. ERA, ss 50–63 and

TULR(C)A, ss 168–170 contain their own remedies for such absences from work, and thus the employee must pursue them under the appropriate section, without reference to ERA, ss 89–90.

15.19 Section 91 further provides that no payment is due to an employee under ss 88–89 in the following circumstances:

(a) if the employee gives notice, and then takes part in a strike;

(b) if the employer gives notice, and the employee then takes part in a strike (because he cannot be said to be ready and willing to perform some work);

(c) if, during the notice period, the employee commits an act which amounts to a breach of contract, eg something which amounts to gross misconduct, and the employer dismisses the employee forthwith (s 91).

15.20 The rights contained in ss 88–90 apply when either the employer or the employee give notice of termination of the contract. If the employer terminates the contract without notice, then the rights conferred by ss 88–90 shall be taken into account when assessing his liability for breach of contract.

Time Off to Look for Work (ERA, s 52)

15.21 An employee whose employment has been terminated because of redundancy has the right to have time off work (with pay) to look for work or make arrangements for re-training during his notice period. This topic has been dealt with in Chapter 7.

E. **Contractual Rights During Notice**

15.22 It is always open to an employer to give lawful notice to terminate the contract, and to require the employee to work during the notice period. If the employee fails or refuses to do so, he will not be entitled to his pay under s 88 (see para 15.18), because he is not able or willing to work. As an alternative, the employer may give lawful notice, but not require the employee to work during the notice period. During this period, the employee will be entitled to all the contractual benefits. For his part, the employee may be restrained from working for a competitor during the notice period, if by doing so the employer would suffer serious harm (*Evening Standard Co Ltd v Henderson*[20]). An employer may require an employee to stay at home during a notice period, even though there is no garden leave clause in the contract, if the employee's conduct exhibits a behaviour that indicates that he does not wish to be bound by the contract of employment. In such circumstances he has forfeited the right to be provided with work (*SG & R Valuation Service v Boudrais*[21]). Any right to work expressed in the contract does not trump a garden leave clause (*Christie v Johnston Carmichael*).[22]

15.23 Otherwise the fact that the employee takes another job during the notice period is not repudiatory conduct by him, in the absence of a garden leave clause (see para 19.8). Further, since the notice money is contractually due to the employee, there is no require-ment to mitigate against his loss (*Hutchings v Coinseed Ltd*[23]).

15.24 If, during the notice period, there is a wage increase (eg as a result of negotiations with a trade union) the employee is entitled to be paid that increase. However, if, subse-quent to leaving the employment, a wage increase is negotiated which is backdated to a period when the employee was working, it would appear that he has no legal entitlement to

[20] [1987] ICR 588, [1987] IRLR 64, CA.   [21] [2008] EWHC 1340 (QB); [2008] IRLR 770.
[22] [2010] IRLR 1016.   [23] [1998] IRLR 190, CA.

that increase (*Leyland Vehicles Ltd v Reston*, see para 3.72). In legal reasoning, the employee has not given 'consideration' for the increase, because he has already worked under his contract, and 'past consideration is no consideration'.

F. Dispensing with Notice

15.25 If a contract provides that an employee may be dismissed with immediate effect, he is still entitled to contractual notice or to a payment in lieu of notice (*T & K Home Improvements Ltd v Skilton*[24]). If the employee has a contractual right to pay in lieu of notice, there is no duty to mitigate (*Abrahams v Performing Rights Society*[25]).

15.26 If an employee commits a 'fundamental breach of contract' which warrants summary dismissal (see para 16.9), the employer need not give notice of termination. If the employer commits a fundamental breach of contract entitling the employee to resign and claim constructive dismissal (see para 17.21) the employee need not give notice of termination. Nor need an employer give notice if the contract had already been frustrated, and the fact that the employer keeps an employee 'on the books' when he is unlikely to return to work may be the sort of arrangement contemplated by ERA, s 212(3)(c) (see para 13.24), but no contract of employment will be in existence (*GF Sharp & Co Ltd v McMillan*[26]). If an employee is on a fixed-term contract (ie one with a fixed date of expiry) no notice of termination need be given, and a letter sent to the employee confirming that the contract will expire on a certain date is not a letter of dismissal (*London Underground Ltd v Fitzgerald*[27]). However, notice will be required if the employer wishes to terminate the contract prior to the expiry of the fixed term (*Dixon & Constanti v BBC*[28]), or if the employee wishes to resign before the end of that term, particularly if there is a restrictive covenant in force (*Thomas Marshall (Exports) Ltd v Guinle*[29]).

15.27 If an employee is on a probationary period, the successful completion of which will result in him being confirmed in his position, this is not a fixed-term contract, and he may be given lawful notice prior to the expiry of the probationary period. The employer is not obliged to employ the employee for the whole of the probationary period (*Dalgleish v Kew House Farm Ltd*, see para 2.103). A training contract may or may not be a fixed-term contract, depending on how it is worded. If it is, it cannot be brought to an end until the period of training has expired, except for gross misconduct.

15.28 A project contract expires when the project is completed, and so no notice need be given (*Ironmonger v Movefield Ltd*[30]).

G. Notice and Time Limits

15.29 Once notice (by either side) is given, the effective date of termination, for unfair dismissal and redundancy pay purposes, is the date the notice expires, and the time for bringing a complaint before an employment tribunal will run from that date. However, an employer cannot give less notice than the statute requires so as to prevent the employee from satisfying the qualifying period of employment. So, if an employee has been employed for one week less than two years, and is dismissed without notice, his effective date of termination is the day he leaves, and, not having a requisite period of two years'

[24] [2000] ICR 1162, [2000] IRLR 595, CA.   [25] [1995] ICR 1028, [1995] IRLR 486.
[26] [1998] IRLR 632, EAT.   [27] [1997] ICR 271, EAT.
[28] [1978] QB 438, [1978] 2 All ER 465, [1978] ICR 357, [1977] IRLR 337, EAT; aff'd [1979] QB 546, [1979] 2 All ER 112, [1979] ICR 281, [1979] IRLR 114, CA.
[29] [1979] Ch 227, [1978] 3 All ER 193, [1978] ICR 905, [1978] IRLR 174.   [30] [1988] IRLR 461.

continuous employment, he would appear to be unable to lodge a claim for unfair dismissal. However, ERA, s 97(2) provides that the effective date of termination is the date on which his statutory notice would have expired. In other words, he is entitled to add to the period of employment the week's notice to which he is entitled by statute. On the other hand, the dismissal will only operate for computation purposes from the date when the statutory notice expires, not from the date when his contractual notice (had it have been given) would have expired. Thus, if the employee has been employed for two weeks less than two years, and is entitled to four weeks' notice but is dismissed immediately with pay in lieu of notice, his period of continuous employment is two weeks short of the qualifying period. He is only entitled to add on the period of statutory notice, not his potential contractual notice (see *Fox Maintenance Ltd v Jackson*,[31] para 17.4). This provision also applies to constructive dismissal claims (ERA, s 97(4)). However, s 97(2)–(4) only applies for the purpose of determining the qualifying period of employment (s 108(1)), the calculation of the basic award (s 19(1)), and the calculation of a week's pay where this has been increased by the Secretary of State during the statutory notice period (s 227(3)). A similar extension of the period of continuous employment is contained in s 92(7), with respect to written reasons for dismissal. It should be noted that in general the law takes no account of fractions of a day (*Wang v University of Keele*[32]).

15.30 The continuous period of employment is not extended for the purpose of extending the time limit within which a claim for unfair dismissal may be brought. This means an unfair dismissal claim must be brought within three months of the effective date of termination (or other period permitted by law), not from when the statutory notice period would have expired. The effective date of termination is the date on which the employment relationship ends, and that date cannot be varied by any subsequent agreement between the parties. However, the notice that determines the effective date of termination can be varied, so that there can be a subsequent agreement that the effective date of termination can be brought forward or pushed backward, and time will start to run from the new date (*Palfrey v Transco plc*[33]). Finally, it may be noted that an employee who has been given notice may commence proceedings for unfair dismissal without waiting for the notice period to expire, or within three months from the effective date of termination (ERA, s 111(3)).

H. Notice Pay on Insolvency (ERA, ss 182–186)

15.31 If an employer becomes insolvent (eg bankrupt or wound up; see s 183), so that the contract of employment is no longer capable of being performed, then clearly that contract has terminated. In such circumstances, the employee may make an application for his statutory notice to be paid from the National Insurance Fund. If the Secretary of State is satisfied that the employee is so entitled, he will pay out of that Fund the amount of statutory notice set out in s 86 (as well as certain other payments, see para 7.133), although the 'week's pay' for the purpose of this provision is limited to the statutory maximum as laid down (currently £508 per week). Other contractual benefits cannot be recovered from the Fund. The employee will be under a duty to mitigate against his loss (*Westwood v Secretary of State for Employment*, see para 7.134), and an employee who obtains fresh employment immediately or during what would have been his notice period can only recover in respect of the period of loss, if any (*Secretary of State for Employment v Wilson*, see para 7.134). Any award made by the Secretary of State from the Fund will be based on pay net of income tax.

[31] [1978] ICR 110, [1977] IRLR 306, EAT.   [32] [2011] IRLR 542, EAT.   [33] [2004] IRLR 916, EAT.

Notice to be Given by the Employee

15.32 An employee is required to give due notice of termination, as laid down in his contract of employment. If there is no such term, then, in theory, he should give reasonable notice, depending on his position, the industry, etc. The statutory notice period set out in ERA, s 86(2) provides that an employee who has been continuously employed for one month or more has to give at least one week's notice.

Employer's Remedies

15.33 If the employee fails to give the required notice of termination of his contract, technically the employer has two remedies. The first arises where there is a restrictive covenant prohibiting the employee from working for a competitor etc (see Chapter 19). The employer may be able to obtain an injunction to prevent a breach of this term. However, he will not be able to obtain an order for specific performance of the contract (TULR(C)A, s 236).

15.34 Second, in theory, the employer may sue for damages for breach of contract, although such actions are virtually unknown and the most an employee stands to lose if he fails to give the requisite notice is his reputation, if any, as a responsible employee. But if, for example, in anticipation of an employee commencing work, the employer incurs considerable expenses (eg purchases equipment or machinery, or hires premises, or enters into an abortive advertising campaign), an action for damages against an employee who fails to meet his contractual obligations could well succeed (*Batty v Melillo*; and see *Tullett Prebon Group Ltd v Ghaleb El-Hajjali*,[34] para 3.5).

15.35 An employer may attempt to pre-empt this problem by providing, in the contract of employment, that he may withhold arrears of wages and/or accrued holiday pay if an employee fails to give proper notice or work out that notice in accordance with the contract.

When an employee leaves his employment without giving proper notice, the employer can elect whether to keep the contract of employment alive, so as to be able to enforce the employee's obligation not to work for anyone else. He can refuse to pay the employee any wages as the employee is no longer ready and willing to work for the employer, and this will not terminate the contract, because the employee must be ready and willing to do the work in exchange for the wages (*Sunrise Brokers LLP v Rodgers*[35]).

15.36 So far as the withholding of wages is concerned, this would appear to be perfectly legal, but only in so far as the amount withheld is a genuine pre-estimate of the loss, and not a penalty clause (*Dunlop Pneumatic Tyre Co Ltd v New Garage & Motor Co*[36]). Such deduction would not contravene ERA, s 13(1) (see para 8.5) because the deduction would have been authorised by the employee's contract of employment. For example, in *Giraud UK Ltd v Smith*[37] the employee's contract of employment required him to give four weeks' notice of termination. If he failed to give such notice, the employer would be entitled to deduct from his final payment an amount equivalent to the number of days short. When he left his employment without notice, the employers refused to pay him payments due to him, claiming that under the contract they were entitled to deduct a payment equivalent of four weeks' pay. It was held that the clause was not a lawful liquidated damage clause, because it

---

[34] [2008] EWHC 1924 (QB), [2008] IRLR 760.   [35] [2014] EWHC 2633 (QB).
[36] [1915] AC 79, [1914–15] All ER Rep 739, 111 LT 862, 30 TLR 625, HL.
[37] [2000] IRLR 763, 668 IDS Brief 7, EAT.

did not represent a genuine pre-estimate of the loss or damage suffered. Essentially, it was a penalty clause, and was unenforceable.

15.37 So far as accrued holiday pay is concerned, the provisions of reg 13 of the Working Time Regulations must be borne in mind (see para 7.73), and any such deduction would not be lawful.

Employee's Remedies

15.38 If an employer fails to give notice to the employee, or gives notice which is less than the contractual or statutory notice (whichever is the longer), the employee's remedy is to bring an action either in the ordinary courts or in the employment tribunal, under the Employment Tribunals Extension of Jurisdiction Order (see para 1.40). A court action would be appropriate if the amount claimed by way of damages is in excess of £25,000, because that is the maximum sum which could be awarded by an employment tribunal. Further, an action for breach of contract may be brought in the ordinary courts any time within six years from the breach, whereas a claim in an employment tribunal must be brought within three months beginning with the effective date of termination, or, if there was no such date, within three months from when the employee last worked, or, if it was not reasonably practicable to present the claim in either of those periods, within such further period as the employment tribunal thinks reasonable.

15.39 The claim by the employee is one for breach of contract, the measure of damages being the amount he would have earned had he been given proper notice. If there was an element of discretion in certain payments (eg annual salary increases, bonuses) it must be assumed that the employer would have exercised that discretion in good faith, and thus they form part of the loss suffered (*Clark v BET plc*, see para 3.2). The claim is subject to the common law rule that the innocent party to a breach of contract must take reasonable steps to mitigate against his loss. Thus, if the employee is dismissed without notice, and the following day he obtained fresh employment on equivalent or improved terms and conditions, then, since he has lost nothing, he is not entitled to anything (*Secretary of State for Employment v Wilson*, para 15.31). In *Hardy v Polk (Leeds) Ltd*[38] the claimant was entitled to eight weeks' contractual notice. She was unfairly dismissed without notice, but started a new job after four weeks. Her employer was not contractually obliged to make a payment in lieu of notice. It was held that as she had partially mitigated against her loss she was only entitled to compensation for four weeks. Further, credit must be given by the employee for any payment received by way of jobseeker's allowance (*Westwood v Secretary of State for Employment*, para 15.31). In other words, the object of the exercise is to place the employee in the same position financially as she would have been in had lawful notice been given.

15.40 In certain special circumstances, an employee may be able to obtain an injunction to restrain an employer from terminating the contract of employment without proper notice. Generally speaking, it has to be shown that the trust and confidence which should exist between employer and employee remains (*Hill v C A Parsons Ltd*, see para 15.3), but an injunction may also be obtained where it can be shown that the employer has failed to operate a contractual disciplinary procedure, particularly where damages would not be an adequate remedy for the manner in which a dismissal without notice was carried out. The modern test to be applied is 'the workability' of the situation (*Robb v London Borough of Hammersmith and Fulham*[39]).

---

[38] [2005] ICR 557, EAT.   [39] [1991] ICR 514, [1991] IRLR 72.

15.41 It should be noted that there is no implied term that an employee will not be unfairly dismissed and so the only damages which can be awarded at common law are those which relate to contractual notice (*Fosca Services (UK) Ltd v Birkett*, see para 16.21).

Summary

- There are certain statutory periods of notice set out in the ERA s 1 and s 86. After one month's employment, an employee is entitled to one week's notice. After two years, he will be entitled to a week's notice for each week of employment.

- The maximum statutory notice required is twelve weeks after 12 years.

- If the contract provides for more notice than statute, the contractual notice prevails.

- If the contract is frustrated, no notice need be given.

- Apart from summary dismissal, notice runs from the day after it is given.

- If given by letter, notice only operates when an employee has had a reasonable opportunity to read it.

- Notice, once given, cannot be unilaterally changed, but can be changed by agreement.

- Sections 88–91 set out certain rights of the employee during the notice period.

- If the employee commits a fundamental breach of contract, the employer does not need to give notice and can summarily dismiss.

- If sufficient notice is not given, a claim can be brought in court or employment tribunal. Court action is more appropriate if the amount claimed is more than £25,000. The time limit for a court action is also 6 years rather than three months in a tribunal.

16

Wrongful Dismissal

Background

16.1 Under the law which existed prior to 1971 an employer was entitled to dismiss an employee for any reason or no reason at all; generally, the only issues which arose related to whether or not the employee was entitled to a certain period of notice, or whether his conduct was such as to warrant summary dismissal without notice, although there were some exceptions. These matters are now largely of historical interest.

16.2 In 1971 the Industrial Relations Act created the right for many employees not to be unfairly dismissed, and though that Act was repealed, the relevant provisions were substantially re-enacted (with some minor amendments) in the Trade Union and Labour Relations Act 1974, and further changes were made by the Employment Protection Act 1975. All the relevant law was brought together in the Employment Protection (Consolidation) Act 1978, and further amendments were made in subsequent legislation. The Employment Rights Act 1996 (as amended) now contains most of the relevant statutory provisions currently in force (see Chapter 17).

16.3 But although the new legal right has largely subsumed the old common law learning, it is still necessary to examine the old law relating to wrongful and summary dismissal, because there may be situations when the common law remedy is more advantageous, or indeed, the only remedy available. In particular, we may note the following circumstances:

(a) the maximum compensatory award for unfair dismissal is £88,519 from April 2020 plus an appropriate basic award. A highly paid employee who is entitled to a long period of notice may be able to obtain substantially higher damages at common law (see *O'Laoire v Jackel International Ltd*,[1] para 16.28);

(b) an employee who lacks the relevant period of continuous employment to qualify for unfair dismissal rights may still sue for wrongful dismissal either at common law or in the employment tribunal under the provisions of ETEJO (see para 1.22). However, if the employee is summarily dismissed, or given less than the contractual notice, with the result that he lacks the necessary qualifying period of continuous employment to pursue a claim for unfair dismissal, he cannot claim damages for the loss of the opportunity to claim unfair dismissal (*Johnson v Unisys Ltd*, para 16.25);

(c) a fair dismissal may nonetheless be a wrongful dismissal if proper notice has not been given (*Treganowan v Robert Knee & Co Ltd*[2]);

(d) an application for unfair dismissal is likely to be time barred if it is not brought within three months from the effective date of termination, whereas a common law action for wrongful dismissal may be brought within six years of the breach;

---

[1] [1990] ICR 197, [1990] IRLR 70, CA.   [2] [1975] IRLR 112; aff'd [1975] ICR 405, [1975] IRLR 247.

(e) the rules relating to damages are different. In particular, a common law action does not permit a reduction for contributory conduct, and the mitigation rules are not the same;

(f) the dispute may contain a public law element, and not be concerned with strict contractual rights (*R v Secretary of State for the Home Department, ex p Benwell*[3]);

(g) a dismissal which is in breach of a contractual dismissal procedure may enable an employee to bring a common law action for breach of contract (*Shook v London Borough of Ealing*[4]) or to seek an injunction to restrain the breach (*Irani v Southampton and South West Hampshire Health Authority*, see para 10.4), or seek a declaration as to his legal rights. But the employee's remedies in such circumstances may be limited to damages for the period up to which he would have been employed had the correct procedure been followed (*Gunton v London Borough of Richmond*, see paras 3.92 and 12.14, and see *Edwards v Chesterfield Royal Hospital NHS Foundation Trust*,[5] where the Supreme Court held that employees may not recover damages in civil courts for loss suffered as a result of a breach of their contract of employment in relation to the manner of their dismissal unless the loss can be said to precede and be independent of the dismissal).

16.4 Since the jurisdiction of the employment tribunals is concurrent in many respects with that possessed by the ordinary courts, an employee will thus opt for whichever cause of action will produce the most advantageous results (see para 1.22).

16.5 If, before his dismissal, an employee has a case at common law (whether for breach of contract or breach of the duty to take reasonable care for the employee's health and safety), that cause of action is unaffected by the fact that the employee has brought a statutory unfair dismissal claim. Thus, a claim for damages for psychiatric injury caused, for example, by a wrongful application for the contractual disciplinary procedure may succeed (*Eastwood v Magnox Electric plc*, see para 11.91), even though there can be no award for psychiatric illness (or injury to feelings) caused by the manner of actual dismissal (*Dunnachie v Kingston upon Hull City Council*, see para 11.91). Damages for injury to feelings and aggravated and exemplary damages may be awarded in detriment cases, as well as race, sex, and disability cases, but not in unfair dismissal cases.

Wrongful Dismissal

16.6 There are a number of ways in which wrongful dismissal may occur:

(a) the employer terminates the employment without notice, or with less notice than the employee is entitled to receive under the terms of his contract or the statutory provisions (see Chapter 15);

(b) a fixed-term contract is terminated by the employer before the date it was due to expire;

(c) a contract for the completion of a specific task is terminated by the employer before the task has ended;

(d) the employer terminates the employment without carrying out the disciplinary procedure which has been incorporated into the employee's contract (*Gunton v London Borough of Richmond* (see para 16.3));

---

[3] [1985] QB 554, [1984] 3 All ER 854, [1984] ICR 723, [1985] IRLR 6.
[4] [1986] ICR 314, [1986] IRLR 46, EAT.   [5] [2011] UKSC 58.

(e) the employee is selected for redundancy in breach of a selection procedure which has been incorporated into his contract (*Alexander v Standard Telephones and Cables plc*, see paras 3.55, 3.59, and 10.4);

(f) the employer wrongfully repudiates the contract, his actions indicating that he no longer intends to be bound by the contract (*General Billposting Co Ltd v Atkinson*[6]). Where an employment contract is wrongfully repudiated, the contract is terminated only if and when the other party has accepted that repudiation: *Geys v Société Générale*.[7] (The Supreme Court affirmed the principle in *Gunton v LB Richmond*, see paras 3.92, 12.14, 16.3, and 16.30.) The employee 'accepts' the repudiation by resigning, or, if appropriate, keeps the contract alive and sues for whatever remedy is available (*Rigby v Ferodo*, see para 3.97). For example, if the employer has unilaterally reduced the employee's wages, a claim may be made under the appropriate provisions of the Employment Rights Act (see Chapter 8). On the other hand, if the employee delays action, he may be taken to have affirmed the contract, unless the employer has given him time to make a decision (*Bliss v South East Thames Regional Health Authority*[8]). Whether the employer has in fact repudiated the contract depends on the particular circumstances of the case (*General Billposting Co Ltd v Atkinson*). Therefore, if the employer fails or refuses to provide work for the employee (see para 10.16) or makes it impossible for the employee to do his work (*Collier v Sunday Referee Publishing Co Ltd*, see para 10.16), or unilaterally attempts to vary the contract of employment, such actions can amount to a breach of contract by the employer which the employee can accept by resigning and claiming wrongful dismissal. This is the common law counterpart of the statutory concept of 'constructive' dismissal, which will be dealt with in Chapter 17;

(g) the contract specifies that a dismissal may only take place in certain specified circumstances, or on specified grounds, and the employer dismisses for some other reason not stated in the contract (*McClelland v Northern Ireland General Health Services Board*, see para 2.80).

16.7 However, if the contract expressly permits the employer to terminate the employment without notice on the payment of a sum of money in lieu of notice, and the employer summarily dismisses the employee, the dismissal is not wrongful, whether or not the employer pays the money in lieu of notice, because he is acting within the strict terms of the contract. In such circumstances, the employee may sue for any outstanding due under the contract, as liquidated damages, and the employee is under no duty to mitigate against his loss (*Abrahams v Performing Right Society*, see para 15.16).

Collateral Contracts

16.8 At common law, when an employer terminates the contract of employment, the only remedy for the employee is to claim money for the period of notice to which he is entitled (see para 15.2). However, if the employer promises that the contract will subsist for a certain period of time, this may be a collateral contract to the main contract, and the employee may be able to claim damages for a breach of that collateral contract. In *Gill v Cape Contracts Ltd*[9] the claimant gave up his job in Belfast to go to work for the defendants in the Shetlands. He was told that the work would last for at least six months, but the

---

[6] [1908] 1 Ch 537, [1908–10] All ER Rep 619, 52 Sol Jo 240, 98 LT 482, 24 TLR 285, CA; aff'd [1909] AC 118, 78 LJ Ch 77, [1908–10] All ER Rep 619, 99 LT 943, 25 TLR 178, HL.   [7] [2012] UKSC 63.
[8] [1987] ICR 700, [1985] IRLR 308, CA.   [9] [1985] IRLR 499.

defendants repudiated the contract before he could start work. It was held that the plaintiff was entitled to damages for a breach of contract by the defendants, who had made representations which had been acted on by the claimant to his detriment. These representations formed a collateral contract to the main contract of employment.

Summary Dismissal

16.9 In *Jupiter General Insurance Co v Shroff*[10] the Privy Council stated that summary dismissal was a strong measure, to be justified only in the most exceptional circumstances. Nonetheless, there are a number of well-recognised grounds on which an employer may dismiss an employee summarily; these include gross misconduct, wilful refusal to obey a lawful and reasonable order, gross neglect, dishonesty, etc (see eg *Blyth v Scottish Liberal Club*[11]). Whether such conduct is serious enough to warrant dismissal is always a question of fact in each case, and the standards to be applied are those of the current *mores*, not those which may have become somewhat outdated. In *Wilson v Racher*, Edmund-Davies LJ said: 'Many of the decisions which are customarily cited in these cases . . . may be wholly out of accord with current social conditions.'[12] Many of the older decisions on this subject lack authority today, and must be therefore treated cautiously.

16.10 Certain principles remain constant, however. In *Sinclair v Neighbour*[13] a manager took £15 from a till and left an IOU in its place. He intended to replace the money a few days later. His conduct was regarded as being dishonest and his summary dismissal was upheld. In *Ross v Aquascutum Ltd*[14] the employee was a night-watchman. He was observed to be absent from the building he was guarding for two hours of each night, and it was held that his conduct constituted a breach of contract so serious as to justify summary dismissal. When considering conduct which results from the interaction of human personalities, it is necessary to apply the standards of ordinary people, not those of the angels. In *Pepper v Webb* (see para 10.58) a gardener was asked to do certain work, but he refused to do so in language which was somewhat vulgar. His summary dismissal was held to be justified, for by refusing to obey a lawful and reasonable order he had broken his contract. Indeed, his conduct had been such as to give rise to a history of complaints for insolence, and the incident which gave rise to his dismissal was merely the last straw. On the other hand, in *Wilson v Racher* (see para 16.9) a gardener swore at his employer using some even choicer obscenities. Although this could have amounted to gross misconduct, the court held that 'it requires very special circumstances to entitle a servant who expresses his feelings in such a grossly improper way to succeed in an action for wrongful dismissal'. On the facts of the case, the special circumstance existed, and these lay in the employer's own conduct which had provoked the outburst.

16.11 The breach of an express term of the contract or of a provision in the works rules may justify summary dismissal, provided it has been brought expressly to the attention of the employee that there is certain conduct which the employer will on no account tolerate. Certain airlines, for example, have a rule that any pilot who takes drugs (other than on medical prescription) or is discovered drunk whether on or off duty will be instantly dismissed. Other employers may specify other conduct which is detrimental to the business and which may warrant summary dismissal. For example, smoking in prohibited areas, unhygienic practices in food premises, and breach of safety rules which may lead to hazards or

---

[10] [1937] 3 All ER 67, PC.   [11] [1983] IRLR 245, Ct of Sess.
[12] [1974] ICR 428, [1974] IRLR 114, CA.   [13] [1967] 2 QB 279, [1966] 3 All ER 988, CA.
[14] [1973] IRLR 107.

risk of injury to others all constitute conduct which may, in special circumstances, warrant dismissal. In *Dunn v AAH Ltd*[15] a director's contract stated that the employee could be summarily dismissed for 'wilful neglect'. The director was also specifically told to report any potential business risk to the parent company, so that the risk could be assessed. The claimant director failed to report that a supplier company was supplying substituted products worth many millions of pounds, which potentially exposed the parent company to legal action. The Court of Appeal upheld the director's summary dismissal. Gross misconduct is a form of repudiatory conduct, for which instant dismissal was not inappropriate.

16.12 An employee is not in breach of his contract of employment merely because he indicates his intention to open a business in competition with his employer. In *Laughton and Hawley v Bapp Industrial Supplies Ltd*[16] the two claimants, who were employed by the respondents, wrote to the company's suppliers stating that they intended to commence trading in the near future, and asked for product lists, prices, and terms. When the employers discovered this, the employees were dismissed instantly without notice. The dismissals were held to be wrongful. There was no abuse of their positions as employees, no breach of any covenant in restraint of trade, and no disclosures of trade secrets or confidential information. The employees had not failed to devote their efforts to their employer's business during working hours, so their activities did not constitute gross misconduct. But where a managing director formed a new business entity, sought to persuade his employer's major client to transfer business to it, and induced two senior employees to join him in the new venture which was in direct competition with the employer, it was held that this amounted to gross misconduct warranting summary dismissal (*Marshall v Industrial Systems and Control Ltd*[17]). An employee has a duty to his employer to act in good faith and in the employer's best interests. Thus, if he seeks to divert to himself a contract which his employer is seeking to obtain with a third party, this will amount to dishonest conduct which would warrant summary dismissal (*Item Software (UK) Ltd v Fassihi*, see paras 10.97 and 16.24).

16.13 A more difficult problem arises if conduct of the employee is in the nature of neglect, which causes damage to the employer. Should one consider the act itself, which may be of a minor or major nature, or should one consider the consequences, which may be insignificant or serious? In *Savage v British India Steam Navigation Co*[18] it was stated that it was the nature of the act, not the consequences, which was relevant. A failure to observe instructions which resulted in damage was held to be of sufficient seriousness to warrant summary dismissal in *Howe v Gloucester and Severnside Co-operative Society*,[19] but excessive zeal which caused damage did not warrant such drastic measures in *Newlands v Howard & Co Ltd*[20] Neglect by senior employees who hold responsible positions appears to amount to a greater dereliction of duty than junior staff, and hence is more likely to attract instant dismissal. As a general rule, for an employee to be summarily dismissed on the grounds of neglect, the neglect should be something approaching habitual conduct, but a single act of neglect could justify instant dismissal if its consequences are likely to be serious enough (*Taylor v Alidair Ltd*[21]).

16.14 A strike is a breach of contract by the employee, and is thus an act of such a nature as to justify summary dismissal. So too is any other conduct designed to disrupt the employer's business, such as go-slow tactics, work-to-rule, etc. Persistent lateness, drunkenness, fighting, swearing, immorality, skylarking, are all examples of conduct which could attract summary dismissal in particular circumstances. But it must be stressed that although

---

[15] [2009] EWHC 692 (QB), [2010] IRLR 709, CA.   [16] [1986] ICR 634, [1986] IRLR 245, EAT.
[17] [1992] IRLR 294, EAT.   [18] (1930) 46 TLR 294.   [19] [1975] IRLR 17.
[20] [1973] IRLR 9.   [21] [1978] ICR 445, [1978] IRLR 82.

dismissal would not be wrongful at common law, in most cases the test of 'fairness' will have to be considered for the purpose of unfair dismissal claims, and this will be explored later in Chapter 17.

16.15 A summary dismissal takes effect immediately. Any rights an employee may have, eg for pay in lieu of notice, expenses, etc may be claimed by an action for damages for breach of contract in the ordinary courts (*Octavius Atkinson & Sons Ltd v Morris*[22]) or the employment tribunal (see para 1.22).

Employment Law Remedies

A. **Common Law Remedies**

16.16 Although most of the cases involving employment law are brought in employment tribunals, there are cases which for various reasons seek the old common law remedies. Actions may be brought for wrongful dismissal (see para 16.6), and also for damages based on a failure by the employer to follow contractual disciplinary procedures, the measure of damages being the loss suffered by the employee as a result of that failure (*Boyo v Lambeth London Borough Council*, see para 3.92). Also, an application may be made for an injunction to restrain an employer from purporting to act in breach of a contractual disciplinary procedure (*Jones v Lee and Guilding*, see para 3.92) and, somewhat rarely, an action seeking specific performance of the contract (*Powell v London Borough of Brent*, see para 10.7). These matters were explored in Chapter 10 (and see *Jones v Gwent County Council*, para 10.8).

16.17 If an employer acts unfairly towards an employee in such a way that the employee has acquired a cause of action at common law prior to, and independent of, a subsequent dismissal (whether fair or unfair, or whether constructive or not), the common law action is not barred by the fact that the employee has brought a statutory unfair dismissal claim (*Eastwood v Magnox Electric plc*, para 16.5).

16.18 It must be stressed that an action for wrongful dismissal is different from a claim for unfair dismissal, although there may well be some overlap in certain instances. But, in particular, it should be noted that the sole issue in a wrongful dismissal action is whether or not the employer has broken the contract of employment. The 'reasonableness' of the employer's conduct is not in issue, nor does 'contributory conduct' by the employee come into the equation. Also, care must be taken to distinguish between payments made by the employer, and awards against an employer made by a court or tribunal. It is with the latter that this chapter is concerned.

16.19 The normal remedy for wrongful dismissal is for the innocent party to bring an action for damages, although sometimes an application for an injunction or a declaration will be made. Also, if the breach of contract consists not in a dismissal, but an alteration in the terms of the contract which is not permitted by the contract, the employee can, at his option, either accept the breach and resign (claiming wrongful constructive dismissal) or refuse to accept the breach and sue on the contract as it stands, thus seeking to insist that the employer performs the contract (see *Dietman v London Borough of Brent*[23]). The majority of wrongful dismissal claims are brought in the county court or the High Court, although, with the concurrent jurisdiction conferred on employment tribunals by the Extension of

---

[22] [1988] ICR 880, EAT; revsd [1989] ICR 431, [1989] IRLR 158, CA.   [23] [1987] IRLR 146, CA.

Jurisdiction Order, more claims are now being brought under a procedure which is cheaper and comparatively expeditious.

16.20 In rare cases, an employee may seek a public law remedy, by way of judicial review, generally when a private law remedy either does not exist or would be inadequate in the circumstances (*R v Chief Constable of Merseyside Police, ex p Calveley*[24]).

Damages

16.21 The general principle in contract law (and it must be remembered that employment law is basically concerned with a contract of employment) is that the purpose of damages is to put the innocent party in the position in which he would have been had the contractual obligations been performed, in so far as it is possible to do this by a monetary award. Thus, since an employer may always give notice to terminate the contract, then this will become the starting point for any claim. If the employer terminates the contract without notice, or gives less notice than the contract or the statutory provisions require, then damages will be initially limited to the period of notice that should have been given (*Fosca Services (UK) Ltd v Birkett*, paras 2.102 and 15.40, and see Chapter 15). Similarly, if the contract was for a fixed term, and is prematurely terminated, damages will be the loss suffered by the employee as the result of the employer's action. However, if a fixed-term contract gives the employer the right to terminate before the end of that term, then damages will be limited to the notice period (*British Guiana Credit Corpn v Da Silva*[25]). If the employer is in breach because he has failed to follow a disciplinary procedure which has been incorporated into the contract, damages will be limited to the period of time it would have taken the employer to put the contractual procedure into effect (*Dietman v Brent London Borough Council*, para 16.19). An apprentice who has been wrongfully dismissed may recover damages for the loss of training and work experience he would have gained had the contract not been broken, or the diminution of his future prospects (*Dunk v George Waller & Son Ltd*, see para 2.107). Artistes may be able to recover for loss of publicity (*Withers v General Theatre Corpn*[26]), or the loss of enhancing their reputation (*Herbert Clayton & Jack Waller Ltd v Oliver*, see para 10.16).

16.22 Because there may be certain complications arising out of income tax liability and national insurance contributions, the actual computation of the financial loss may present problems. In principle, an employee is entitled to the net loss suffered (ie after the deduction of tax and national insurance), and whether one should start with the gross salary less deductions, or the net figure grossed up, will frequently depend on the amounts at stake. It would appear that the latter course is more advantageous if the amount is comparatively large, whereas the former method appears to be appropriate when the length of the notice period is relatively short (*Shove v Downs Surgical plc*[27]).

16.23 Also to be taken into account are commissions, bonuses, gratuities, etc, which were contractually due to the employee (*Addis v Gramophone Co Ltd*, see para 10.20), including an enhanced contractual redundancy payment (*Basnett v J & A Jackson Ltd*[28]) but not discretionary payments (*Lavarack v Woods of Colchester Ltd*, see para 10.21). Damages for breach of contract can also include accrued pension rights, because there is no difference between a lost pension and lost pay (*Silvey v Pendragon plc*[29]). Fringe benefits, eg company car (in so far as it was permitted for private use), subsidised mortgages, free lunches, the loss of the right to obtain share options (if there was a contractual right) or options already

---

[24] [1986] QB 424, [1986] 1 All ER 257CA.   [25] [1965] 1 WLR 248, 109 Sol Jo 30, PC.
[26] [1933] 2 KB 536, [1933] All ER Rep 385, 149 LT 487, CA.
[27] [1984] 1 All ER 7, [1984] ICR 532, [1984] IRLR 17.
[28] [1976] ICR 63, [1976] IRLR 154.   [29] [2001] EWCA Civ 784, [2001] IRLR 685.

granted (*Chapman v Aberdeen Construction Group Ltd*[30]), private medical insurance, rent-free accommodation etc, can be quantified and their value claimed. Expenses are not normally allowable, as they represent a reimbursement for expenditure incurred by the employee on behalf of the employer. Indeed, if it can be shown that the expenses were in fact a device to boost the employee's income, and were not genuinely incurred, it may be argued that this was an attempt to avoid paying income tax on the employee's salary, and, as such, the contract was illegal, and did not give rise at all to any cause of action (see para 3.7).

16.24 Also included in the compensation which may be awarded will be the loss of other actual or potential benefits, such as pension rights and/or the employer's potential pension contributions, profit sharing schemes, the lost value of share options (*Micklefield v SAC Technology*[31]), outstanding holiday pay, loss of statutory protection rights (*Stapp v Shaftesbury Society*[32]), loss of the opportunity to claim a redundancy payment (*Basnett v J & A Jackson Ltd*, para 16.23), and so on. An employee's claim for part-payment of wages outstanding at the date of dismissal is not defeated by the fact that the dismissal was for reason of gross misconduct. The Apportionment Act 1870 applies when a contract of employment is terminated during the payment period, unless there is something in the contract of employment to the contrary (*Item Software (UK) Ltd v Fassihi*, see paras 8.10 and 10.98).

16.25 At common law, no damages may be awarded for the manner of dismissal (*Addis v Gramophone Co Ltd*, para 16.23), whether by way of injured feelings, psychiatric illness, loss of reputation, or difficulty in finding fresh employment (*Boardman v Copeland Borough Council*[33]). The decision of the House of Lords in *Malik v BCCI* (see para 3.44) is concerned with a complaint relating to a breach of trust and confidence owed by the employer to his employees during the period they were employed, and is not concerned with the actual manner of dismissal (*Johnson v Unisys Ltd*, para 16.3). There can be no claim at common law for damages for psychiatric illness if an employer conducts a campaign designed to deprive an employee of his job by fabricating evidence for the purpose of conducting disciplinary proceedings. *Johnson v Unisys* established that unfairness in the manner of dismissal does not give rise to a common law action, whether it is founded on contract or tort. Such matters must be the subject of employment tribunal proceedings (*Eastwood v Magnox Electrical plc*, paras 16.5 and 16.17). But in *McCabe v Cornwall County Council*,[34] the Court of Appeal appear to have taken a somewhat different view, and permitted a claim to proceed on the basis that there is no automatic bar to such an action just because a dismissal results from the alleged breach of trust and respect.

16.26 Damages for breach of contract at common law are always subject to the rule that the innocent party must take reasonable steps to mitigate against his loss, which, in this context, involves looking for other suitable employment. Any earnings from such employment (or from self-employment) can be deducted from the loss suffered (*Shove v Downs Surgical plc*, para 16.22). The problem here, however, is that the burden of proof is on the employer to show that the employee has failed to take reasonable steps to mitigate his loss (*London and South of England Building Society v Stone*[35]). This he may be able to do either by reference to matters known to him, or by obtaining some form of discovery from the employee concerning his attempts to seek alternative employment. Whether an employee has taken reasonable steps to mitigate against his loss is a question of fact to be determined by the court, bearing in mind all the circumstances, including the employee's age,

[30] [1991] IRLR 505, 1993 SLT 1205, Ct of Sess.
[31] [1991] 1 All ER 275, [1990] 1 WLR 1002, [1990] IRLR 218.   [32] [1982] IRLR 326, CA.
[33] [2001] EWCA Civ 888, [2001] All ER (D) 99 (Jun).
[34] [2002] EWCA Civ 1887, [2003] ICR 501, [2003] IRLR 87, [2002] All ER (D) 294 (Dec).
[35] (1981) 261 Estates Gazette 463; revsd [1983] 3 All ER 105, [1983] LS Gaz R 3048, 267 Estates Gazette 69, CA.

mobility, personal commitments, qualifications, experience, and so on. For example, in *Brace v Calder*, the claimant was dismissed from a partnership as a result of a change in the partners, but offered his old job back by the new partners. He refused this offer, and it was held that he had failed to mitigate his loss, and was therefore only entitled to nominal damages. On the other hand, in *Yetton v Eastwoods Froy Ltd*,[36] a managing director was dismissed from his post, but was offered the job of assistant managing director. It was held that his refusal of this job, which was a significant step down, was not unreasonable.

16.27 It is not unusual for a contract of employment of a senior executive to contain a provision that in the event of a wrongful dismissal the employer will make a lump sum payment by way of liquidated damages, which may in fact be in excess of any amount which would be recoverable at common law (sometimes referred to as 'golden parachutes'). In principle, such damages may be unenforceable, since they may amount to being a penalty clause as they fail to take into account the duty of the employee to mitigate against his loss by seeking alternative employment. In *Murray v Leisureplay plc*[37] the contract provided that in the event of a dismissal, a chief executive would be entitled to one year's gross salary plus certain benefits. The High Court held that this provision was a penalty clause, rather than liquidated damages, and that consequently it was unenforceable. However, the decision was reversed by the Court of Appeal. The clause would only be a penalty if the party seeking to avoid the terms could show that it was 'extravagant and unconscionable' in amount. The clause may have been generous, but it was not unconscionable. A payment may be so extravagant as to be unenforceable because it is 'ultra vires': see *Gibb v Maidstone and Tunbridge Wells NHS Trust*,[38] para 20.45.

16.28 It is unusual, but not impossible, to bring a claim for unfair dismissal as well as an action for wrongful dismissal, although either the court or tribunal can stay one action, pending the outcome of the other (*Carter v Credit Change Ltd*[39]). If one claim does not fully resolve the whole matter, the second action may then be resorted to. One would expect there to be a general rule that any award made in one jurisdiction would be deducted from an award stemming from the second claim. Thus, an award made by an employment tribunal will normally identify the various headings of loss in respect of which compensation is to be awarded, and double recovery of any particular loss would not be permitted in subsequent High Court proceedings. However, where the loss is in excess of the statutory compensation award, it may not always be possible to identify the particular heading awarded by the employment tribunal, and therefore there may not be an element of double recovery. Thus, in *O'Laoire v Jackel International* (see para 16.3), an employment tribunal held that the claimant had been unfairly dismissed, and assessed his loss at £100,000. However, they could only award compensation of £8,000, which was the maximum compensation award at that time. The claimant then brought an action in the High Court, and the judge held that the sum of £8,000 had to be deducted from the damages of £100,000. However, the Court of Appeal held that this was wrong. It was clearly not possible for the employment tribunal to assess the maximum compensation award with reference to any particular head of loss, and thus the rule against double recovery did not apply.

16.29 The general principle relating to any award of damages by a court is that they should be paid net of tax (*British Transport Commission v Gourley*[40]). However, the Income Tax (Earnings and Pensions) Act 2003, ss 401–404 provide that damages for wrongful dismissal are not taxable in the hands of the recipient unless they exceed £30,000. Thereafter, tax

---

[36] [1966] 3 All ER 353.   [37] [2005] EWCA Civ 963, [2005] IRLR 946, CA.
[38] [2010] IRLR 786, [2010] EWCA Civ 678.
[39] [1979] ICR 908, [1979] IRLR 309, EAT; revsd [1980] 1 All ER 252, [1979] ICR 908, [1979] IRLR 361, CA.
[40] [1956] AC 185, [1955] 3 All ER 796, HL.

must be deducted at the employee's highest marginal rate. Thus a court must award a gross sum which, after tax, would leave the employee with a net sum which represents his loss.

Injunction/Declaration

16.30 An employee who feels that he has been wrongfully dismissed may be able to bring an action for an injunction to restrain a breach of contract, or seek a declaration as to what are his rights under the contract. These are equitable remedies, and therefore will only be granted at the court's discretion. If an application is made for an interlocutory injunction pending the trial of the action, the principles laid down in *American Cyanamid Co v Ethicon* (see para 10.8) will apply, ie (a) has the claimant shown that there is a triable issue, and (b) does the balance of convenience favour the granting of the injunction? In particular, as we have seen (para 10.3), the courts will rarely grant an injunction if the effect is to compel specific performance of the contract. Exceptionally the court will do so in perhaps two circumstances, ie (a) if there is no loss of trust and confidence in the employee (*Powell v London Borough of Brent*, para 16.16) or (b) where the dismissal was in breach of natural justice or of a contractual disciplinary procedure (*Gunton v London Borough of Richmond*, paras 16.3 and 16.6). It must be shown that damages would not be an adequate remedy (*Wadcock v London Borough of Brent*, see para 10.4). A person seeking an injunction must first of all have pursued all internal remedies in so far as they are available (*R v BBC, ex p Lavelle*, see para 2.70).

16.31 Similarly, an employee may seek a declaration as to his contractual rights. This remedy will usually be sought when an employee refuses to accept a decision by an employer which is outside the terms of the contract. For example, in *Stevenson v United Road Transport Union*[41] an employee was dismissed without being given reasons (in breach of the contractual procedure), and a declaration was granted that the dismissal, in breach of natural justice, was void. A declaration may be sought if an employer unilaterally reduces an employee's wages, or otherwise purports to act in breach of the contract (*Rigby v Ferodo Ltd*, see para 16.6). As with all equitable remedies, the employee must act expeditiously (*Dietman v London Borough of Brent*, paras 16.19 and 16.21).

Suing for Breach of Contract

16.32 An employee is not bound to accept a breach of contract which falls short of a wrongful constructive dismissal, and may, instead of suffering the breach in silence, sue for the loss suffered, while not accepting the alleged employer repudiation. Thus, in *Rigby v Ferodo Ltd* (see para 16.6), the employee recovered damages for loss of wages when the employer unilaterally reduced his earnings; in *Miller v Hamworthy Engineering Ltd* (see paras 3.97 and 10.18) an employee recovered lost pay when put on short-time working without contractual authority; and in *Keir and Williams v Hereford and Worcester County Council*,[42] damages were awarded to employees when an employer withdrew their car allowance. The correct procedure in such cases is for the employer to give lawful termination of the contract (ie by giving the requisite period of notice) and then to offer the employees new contracts with new terms before the notice period expires. A unilateral variation of the contract, by itself, is not a termination and offer of re-engagement under a new contract (*Burdett-Coutts v Hertfordshire County Council*[43]). Thus by lawfully terminating the contract, the employer avoids any liability for wrongful dismissal, although it must be borne in mind that an employee's rights to claim unfair dismissal will be unaffected. Whether the dismissal is in fact fair or unfair will depend on all the circumstances of the case (see Chapter 17).

---

[41] [1976] 3 All ER 29; aff'd [1977] 2 All ER 941, [1977] ICR 893, CA.   [42] [1985] IRLR 505.
[43] [1984] IRLR 91.

B. **Public Law Remedies**

16.33 An application may be made for judicial review, seeking to ensure that a public body carries out its public duties in a manner consistent with the legal requirements. Generally speaking, there are three grounds on which judicial review may be granted: (1) where the public body has acted illegally, ie contrary to the legal rights and duties of the parties; (2) where the public body has acted irrationally, ie where the decision arrived at was so outrageous that no sensible body or person acting responsibly could have reached that decision; and (3) where there has been a procedural impropriety, ie a failure to act with procedural fairness (*Council of Civil Service Unions v Minister for the Civil Service*,[44] per Lord Diplock). Generally speaking, judicial review is a challenge to the way in which a decision is made, rather than the correctness of the conclusion reached.

16.34 Attempts have been made by employees in the public sector to establish legal rights based on such principles, but with mixed success. The claim must be brought within the procedure laid down in the Civil Procedure Rules (judicial review) and the remedy is not generally available if a remedy based on contractual principles would suffice. There must be a further element of a public right or the enforcement of a public duty (*R v East Berkshire Health Authority, ex p Walsh*[45]).

16.35 In *McLaren v Home Office*,[46] Woolf LJ suggested that there are four general principles which apply when an employee of a public body is proposing to proceed by way of judicial review: (1) in relation to personal claims against an employer, an employee of a public body is in the same situation as other employees; (2) however, if there exists some disciplinary or other body established under the Royal prerogative or a statute to which disputes can be referred, judicial review may be the appropriate remedy; (3) if an employee of a public body is adversely affected by a decision of general application, judicial review of that decision may be sought (see *R v Secretary of State, ex p Council of Civil Service Unions*, para 16.33); (4) if disciplinary procedures are of a domestic nature, judicial review will not be sought.

16.36 However, if a person is seeking to enforce a private right which has a public law element, he can pursue his claim through the normal procedure of issuing a writ, and is not required to seek redress by means of judicial review (*Roy v Kensington and Chelsea and Westminster Family Practitioner Committee*[47]). This is of particular importance if the public law issue is raised after the time for applying for judicial review has lapsed (*Doyle v Northumbria Probation Committee*[48]).

16.37 In Scotland, however, for historical reasons, the situation is slightly different. Scots law does not depend on a distinction between public and private law, but the court will accept jurisdiction by way of judicial review to regulate the process by which decisions are taken by a person or body to whom a power has been delegated by statute, agreement, or other instrument, in order to ensure that the person or body does not exceed or abuse that power. But there must always be a tripartite relationship between the person or body to whom the power has been delegated, the person or body by whom it has been delegated, and the person for whose benefit the power is to be exercised. Strict contractual rights,

[44] [1984] IRLR 309; revsd [1984] IRLR 353, CA; aff'd sub nom *Council of Civil Service Unions v Minister for the Civil Service* [1985] AC 374, [1984] 3 All ER 935, [1985] ICR 14, sub nom *R v Secretary of State for Foreign and Commonwealth Affairs, ex p Council of Civil Service Unions* [1985] IRLR 28, HL.
[45] [1985] QB 152, [1984] 3 All ER 425, [1984] ICR 743, [1984] IRLR 278, 128 Sol Jo 664, CA.
[46] [1990] ICR 824, [1990] IRLR 338, CA.
[47] [1989] 1 Med LR 10; on appeal [1990] 1 Med LR 328, CA; aff'd [1992] 1 AC 624, [1992] 1 All ER 705, [1992] IRLR 233, HL.   [48] [1991] 4 All ER 294, [1992] ICR 121.

such as those which exist between employer and employee, are not amenable to judicial review (*West v Secretary of State for Scotland*[49]), whether they occur in the public or the private sector. Thus, where a local authority suspended a senior employee, it was exercising a power derived from the contract of employment, rather than from a statutory grant (*Blair v Lochaber District Council*[50]).

Summary

- Wrongful dismissal is a common law remedy that can be brought by an employee.
- It is a breach of contract claim and can be brought even if there is no right to claim unfair dismissal (there are occasions when it may be more advantageous to bring a claim of wrongful dismissal, as the compensatory limit may be greater, depending on which court the claim is brought in).
- It can be brought by itself or in addition to another claim, such as unfair dismissal.
- A summary dismissal is a strong measure, to be justified only in the most exceptional circumstances.
- A summary dismissal takes effect immediately, without notice.
- There are a number of grounds on which an employer may dismiss an employee summarily, including gross misconduct, wilful refusal to obey a lawful and reasonable order, gross neglect, dishonesty, etc. Whether such conduct is serious enough to warrant dismissal is always a question of fact in each case.

[49] [1992] IRLR 399, Ct of Sess.   [50] [1995] IRLR 135, Ct of Sess.

17

Unfair Dismissal

Background

17.1 The statutory provisions relating to unfair dismissal are to be found in ss 94–107 of the Employment Rights Act 1996. The interpretation of those provisions by the courts and tribunals has led to thousands of reported decisions which have laid down guidelines varying from legal ingenuity, through sound common sense, and ending up, on occasion, in cabalistic mystery! But many decisions can only be explained on their own special facts and on a consideration of the actual evidence presented to the tribunal, and it must be borne in mind that employment tribunal decisions are not, in themselves, binding precedents. Sometimes the successful claimant will be awarded reduced compensation because of his own contributory conduct, and there have been cases where a dismissal, though unfair, has resulted in a nil award.

17.2 Nonetheless, the decisions of the reported cases repay detailed study. In the first place, they give guidance to a generalised stream of thought which shows the dominant thinking in employment law; guidance on how an employer should act so as to be re-garded as being reasonable and fair, on how disciplinary procedures should be operated, and on when an employer may adopt standards which are less than those expected by a perfectionist. Second, the decided cases point out the pitfalls into which other employers have fallen, and thus enable a conscientious personnel manager so to direct his policies as to avoid those very traps. Finally, they provide interpretation of the legislative provisions which have a persuasive effect until a higher court has had an opportunity to pronounce on their validity.

17.3 Every employee to whom the Act applies has the right not to be unfairly dismissed, and the remedy for the infringement of that right is by way of a complaint to the employ-ment tribunal, and not otherwise (ERA, s 94). This means that unfair dismissal cases must go to the employment tribunals, whereas a person who wishes to sue in respect of *wrongful dismissal* must bring the action in the ordinary courts in the normal way, or in the employ-ment tribunal as appropriate (see para 16.4).

Exclusions From Unfair Dismissal

17.4 The following categories of employees are not protected by the unfair dismissal pro-visions of ERA:

(a) any employment as a master or member of the crew of a fishing vessel where the employee is remunerated by a share of the profits;

(b) merchant seamen may pursue claims for unfair dismissal provided they are em-ployed to work on ships registered in Great Britain (ie excluding Northern Ireland, the Isle of Man and the Channel Islands) unless their employment is wholly outside Great Britain, or they are not ordinarily resident in Great Britain (ERA, s 199(7), (8)).

In *Wood v Cunard Line Ltd*,[1] the claimant was engaged in Southampton, and then joined a ship which cruised around the Caribbean. It was held that his employment was wholly outside Great Britain.

Under the Employment Protection (Offshore Employment) Order 1976, employees who work in oil rigs and offshore installations in UK territorial waters or areas designated under the Continental Shelf Act 1964 are not excluded from the provisions of the Employment Rights Act 1996;

(c) apart from specific statutory provisions (see para 17.77) any employment where the employee has been continuously employed for less than two years (but see Table 13.1). The period of continuous employment begins with the day on which he is due to start work under the contract, not from the date on which he actually commences work (*Salvation Army v Dewsbury*, see para 13.9). If notice of termination is given, the day on which the notice is given must be disregarded (*West v Kneels Ltd*, see para 15.7). As has been noted (see para 15.29), an employee who had been employed for one week less than the then qualifying period of one year, and is dismissed, is entitled to add to his computation the week's statutory notice to which he is entitled (s 97(2)), but not his contractual notice (see *Fox Maintenance Ltd v Jackson*, para 15.29). But if he is dismissed without notice for gross misconduct, he cannot rely on s 97(2) 'to pull him past the post' (*Ahmed v National Car Parks Ltd*[2]).

The fact that the reason for the dismissal is designated as 'gross misconduct' does not preclude the operation of s 97(2), for the employment tribunal can enquire into the facts on their merits, and decide whether in the circumstances the employer was entitled to terminate the contract without notice. If they decide that the employer was not so entitled, s 97(2) comes into operation (*Lanton Leisure Ltd v White and Gibson*[3]).

If a person is dismissed as a result of being suspended from work on medical grounds, s/he is only required to have one month's continuous employment (see ERA, s 64(2), para 7.7).

No qualifying period of employment is required in those cases where the dismissal is automatically unfair (see para 17.77);

(d) any employment covered by a dismissals procedure agreement which has been designated and approved by the Secretary of State. This enables an employer and an independent trade union to create their own dismissals procedure which, provided it conforms with the laid-down criteria, may be approved by the Minister, and those employees covered by it are excluded from the provisions of the Act. There are no such agreements currently in force;

(e) an agreement to submit the dispute to arbitration under a scheme prepared by ACAS (see TULR(C)A, s 212A inserted by s 7 of the Employment Rights (Dispute Resolution) Act 1998) (see para 1.46);

(f) employees who work for foreign governments and other international organisations which enjoy diplomatic immunity (eg see *Gadhok v Commonwealth Secretariat*[4]) can only bring appropriate claims if that diplomatic immunity is waived; otherwise the employment tribunals have no jurisdiction (*Mukoro v European Bank for Reconstruction and Development*[5]). However, by the State Immunity Act 1978, a state is not immune in respect of proceedings relating to a contract of employment if (a) the contract was made in the United Kingdom, or (b) the work is to be wholly or

---

[1] [1989] ICR 398, [1989] IRLR 431, EAT; aff'd [1991] ICR 13, [1990] IRLR 281, CA.
[2] IDS Brief 149.   [3] [1987] IRLR 119, EAT.   [4] (1977) 12 ITR 440, CA.
[5] [1994] ICR 897, EAT.

partly performed in the United Kingdom. The Act does not apply if at the time of the claim the applicant was a national of the state concerned, or at the time when the contract was made he was neither a national of the United Kingdom nor habitually resident here, or if the parties have agreed to exclude the provisions of the Act. In *Kücükdeveci v Swedex GmbH & Co KG*[6] and *Aklagaren v Fransson*,[7] however, the ECJ confirmed that where a fundamental principle of EU law is concerned, such as the right to a fair hearing, the UK courts must disapply a provision which stands in its way. This was done in *Benkharbouche v Sudan*,[8] where the State Immunity Act 1978 (SIA) prevented domestic workers employed by two embassies from bringing claims. The Court of Appeal (affirmed by the Supreme Court) found that the blanket immunity from claims provided by s 16(1)(a) of the SIA went beyond the UK's obligations in public international law and was incompatible with Art 6 of the European Convention. The same applied to s 4(2)(b), which prevents claims where the claimant does not habitually reside in the UK. The immunity also violated Art 47 of the EU charter, and so the appellants could proceed with their claims under the WTR 1998, race discrimination and harassment;

(g) persons who serve as a member of a constabulary maintained by virtue of an enactment, or who have the powers or privileges of a constable (ERA, s 200). This includes members of the British Transport Police (*Spence v British Railways Board*[9]) but not prison officers (Criminal Justice and Public Order Act 1994, s 126);

(h) employees who work abroad (see Territorial Jurisdiction, para 1.12).

What is a Dismissal? (ERA, s 95)

17.5 As a general rule, a dismissal is not effective until it has been communicated to the employee (*Gisda Cyf v Barratt*).[10] Thus if it is sent by post, it will be effective from the time when the employee has actually read the letter, or had a reasonable opportunity to do so. In *Brown v Southall and Knight* (see para 15.7) the employers sent a letter of dismissal to the claimant who, at that date, did not have the requisite period of continuous employment. He was away on holiday when the letter arrived, and thus did not read it until he returned a week later, by which time he had the necessary qualifying period. It was held that he was entitled to pursue his claim for unfair dismissal. Of course, if he deliberately did not open the letter, or went away in order to avoid reading it, he would have been debarred from saying that the notification of the dismissal was not given to him (see also *McMaster v Manchester Airport plc*[11]).

17.6 There are four ways in which a dismissal may take place.

A. **Employer Termination**

17.7 This occurs when the contract of employment is terminated by the employer, with or without notice. It follows that (subject to the doctrine of constructive dismissal, discussed at para 17.21) if an employee resigns of his own volition, there is no dismissal. In *Elliott v Waldair (Construction) Ltd*[12] the claimant was engaged as a driver, and mainly drove a heavy lorry. It was decided that this work was too hard for him, and he was instructed to drive a smaller van. This he refused to do because it would reduce his opportunity of

---

[6] Case C-555/07.   [7] Case C-617/10.   [8] [2015] EWCA Civ 33, aff'd [2017] UKSC 62.
[9] [2001] ICR 232, [2000] All ER (D) 1956, EAT.
[10] [2010] UKSC 41, SC.   [11] [1998] IRLR 112, 593 IRLB 17, EAT.   [12] [1975] IRLR 104.

overtime earnings, and he resigned. It was held that the order to drive a different vehicle at the same hourly rate but with less opportunity to earn overtime could not be said to constitute a dismissal by the employer.

17.8 Equally, a mutually agreed termination does not amount to a dismissal. In *Harvey v Yankee Traveller Restaurant*,[13] the claimant became pregnant, and although her employer made various arrangements to accommodate her, these were not satisfactory. After a discussion with her employer, she agreed to resign. It was held that this could not amount to a dismissal.

17.9 The fact that the employer invited the employee to resign may, however, constitute a dismissal, for the alternative may be expressed or implicit in the request. In *Robertson v Securicor Transport Ltd*[14] the claimant had broken a company rule by signing for a container which had not been received. When this was discovered, he was given the alternative of resigning or being dismissed, and he chose the respectable course. It was held that he had been dismissed nonetheless. Although a resignation under duress may be a dismissal (*East Sussex County Council v Walker*[15]), an invitation to resign as an alternative to facing a disciplinary hearing which may result in a dismissal is not, by itself, a dismissal (*Martin v Glynwed Distribution Ltd*[16]). If the choice is put to the employee 'perform your contract or resign' this is not a dismissal, for the employee is making a decision not to carry out the terms of the contract which the employer is legally entitled to expect.

17.10 To falsely inveigle an employee to resign may also amount to a dismissal (*Caledonian Mining Co Ltd v Bassett and Steel*[17]), and informing an employee that he has been taken off the payroll is a dismissal (*Kirklees Metropolitan Council v Radecki*[18]).

17.11 A dismissal can take place even though the employee invites this course of action. In *Thomas v General Industrial Cleaners Ltd*[19] the claimant was in poor health, but did not wish to resign because of fears that he might lose certain benefits. He left the decision to the employers, who accepted the initiative and terminated his employment. The tribunal held that there was a dismissal by the employers.

17.12 A dismissal takes place if an employer unilaterally imposes radically different terms of employment, which are so substantially different as to have the effect of destroying the basis of the old contract. In *Alcan Extrusions v Yates* (see para 3.99) the employers unilaterally made changes in working hours, shift systems, weekend and bank holiday workings, shift premiums, etc. The employees agreed to work the new system under protest, reserving their rights to claim unfair dismissal and/or redundancy payments, which they subsequently did. An employment tribunal chairman held that they had been dismissed, and the decision was upheld by the EAT. It was not correct to argue that the imposition of contractual changes can only be characterised as a potentially repudiatory breach, giving the employee an option to resign and claim constructive dismissal. Substantial departure from the original contract constitutes a dismissal in its own right (but see *Bateman v Asda Stores Ltd*, para 3.83).

17.13 A warning that a dismissal is being contemplated in the future (eg for reason of impending redundancy etc) is not a dismissal (*Doble v Firestone Tyre and Rubber Co Ltd*[20]). A warning of a possible dismissal in the future is not a dismissal. In *Rai v Somerfield Stores Ltd*,[21] the claimant was away from work. He was informed that if he did not return to work

---

[13] [1976] IRLR 35.   [14] [1972] IRLR 70.   [15] (1972) 7 ITR 280, NIRC.

[16] [1983] ICR 511, sub nom *Martin v MBS Fastenings (Glynwed) Distribution Ltd* [1983] IRLR 198, CA.

[17] [1987] ICR 425, [1987] IRLR 165, EAT.

[18] [2009] EWCA Civ 298, [2009] ICR 1244, [2009] IRLR 555.   [19] (3964/72) IDS Supp 21.

[20] [1981] IRLR 300, EAT.   [21] [2004] IRLR 124, EAT.

by 9 April he would be dismissed. He did not turn up at work on that date, but three days earlier, on 6 April, he presented a claim of unfair dismissal to an employment tribunal. It was held that the tribunal had no jurisdiction to hear the complaint. It had been presented three days before the termination of his employment, and was therefore premature. An employee may bring a complaint once notice has been given, even though it has not expired (ERA, s 111(3)), but in this case, he had not been dismissed with or without notice. He had merely been informed of the consequences which may follow if he failed to turn up for work, but dismissal was not inevitable, for the employer could still have unilaterally withdrawn the threat.

17.14 Traditionally, the words used by the employer to denote that a dismissal has taken place are usually quite clear and explicit, but the niceties of social intercourse are not always observed in real life. In *Kendrick v Aerduct Productions*,[22] the employer told an employee to 'fuck off'. Could this be construed as being equivalent to 'you're fired'? Or was it an expression of abuse with no other ulterior implication? If the words used are ambiguous, the employment tribunal must ask themselves: what would a reasonable man understand by the expression in the context of the industry and the surrounding circumstances? In *Futty v D and D Brekkes Ltd*[23] the employee was a fish filleter. During an altercation with the foreman he was told 'if you do not like the job, you can fuck off'. He took this as a dismissal, found another job, and claimed compensation. It was held that in the context of the particular trade, the words meant no more than 'if you do not like the work you are doing, you can clock off'. Indeed, had the applicant not received a promise of another job, he would have gone back to work the following day, and hence he had resigned, and had not been dismissed. But there is little doubt that there can be circumstances where telling an employee to 'fuck off' will amount to a dismissal (*a fortiori*, telling him to 'fuck off and piss off', see *King v Webb's Poultry Products (Bradford) Ltd*[24]).

17.15 Equally, if the words used are unambiguous, the employment tribunal must give them their natural and ordinary meaning (*Sothern v Franks Charlesly & Co*[25]).

17.16 A further refinement on this theme was pursued in *Davy v Collins (Builders) Ltd*[26] During an argument, the employer said to the employee 'if you are not satisfied, you can fuck off'. The employee left and brought a claim for unfair dismissal, which failed. With dialectic ingenuity the tribunal drew a distinction between an employer saying, 'I am not satisfied, so you can fuck off', and 'If you are not satisfied, you can fuck off'. In the former case there is likely to be a dismissal; in the latter case, the employer is saying to the employee, 'If you don't like it, you can lump it', and the claimant, not liking it, lumped it!

17.17 It is thus not the actual words which are used which are significant, but the intention behind them, and this must be ascertained from all the surrounding circumstances and the accompanying words as well as the industry, the relationships between the parties, and so on (*J & J Stern v Simpson*[27]). If an employer or his manager, speaking in anger, behaves in a way which he might not do ordinarily, and utters abusive words, the employment tribunal should consider very carefully whether the words amount to a dismissal, or whether they were little more than abuse (*Chesham Shipping Ltd v Rowe*[28]). Events which followed the utterance of the offensive words and preceding the departure of the employee may be taken into account in so far as they throw light on the employer's intentions (*Tanner v DT Kean Ltd*[29]).

---

[22] [1974] IRLR 322.   [23] [1974] IRLR 130.   [24] [1975] IRLR 135.
[25] [1981] IRLR 278, CA.   [26] [1974] IRLR 324.   [27] [1983] IRLR 52, EAT.
[28] [1977] IRLR 391, EAT.   [29] [1978] IRLR 110, EAT.

17.18 Once a dismissal (or resignation) has taken place, it cannot be withdrawn unilaterally (*Harris and Russell Ltd v Slingsby*, see para 15.9), but words used in the heat of the moment and withdrawn almost immediately may be ignored, for it is vital to good industrial relations that either the employer or the employee should be given the opportunity to recant (*Martin v Yeoman Aggregates Ltd*[30]).

B. Fixed-term Contract Expires

17.19 Where the employee is employed under a limited-term contract, a dismissal takes place if that term expires without being renewed under the same contract. But a dismissal which takes place in this manner must still be tested for fairness in terms of the reasonableness of the employer's action in not renewing the contract. Thus if there is a genuine need for an employee to have a fixed-term contract (eg of a temporary nature, or for a specific purpose, etc) then it may be reasonable not to renew this after expiry. It is important that employees should not be deprived of their statutory rights by dressing up an ordinary job as a fixed-term contract (*Terry v East Sussex County Council*[31]). Further, when a fixed-term contract expires, an employer may be acting unreasonably if he fails genuinely to consider the employee for employment in some other suitable post (*Labour Party v Oakley*[32]) (see the Fixed-term Employees (Prevention of Less Favourable Treatment) Regulations 2002, para 2.135).

C. Completion of a Limited-term Contract

17.20 A limited-term contract is a contract which is not intended to be permanent and which will end either on the expiry of a fixed term, or on the performance of a specific task, or the occurrence of a specific event (or on the failure of an event to occur). If an employee is employed under such a contract which terminates by virtue of the limiting event without being renewed, this will amount to a dismissal under ERA. The effective date of termination is the date on which the termination takes effect.

D. Constructive Dismissal

What Amounts to Constructive Dismissal?

17.21 Where the employee himself terminates the contract, with or without notice, in circumstances where he is entitled to terminate it without notice by reason of the employer's conduct: this is known as 'constructive dismissal', for although the employee resigns, it is the employer's conduct which constitutes a repudiation of the contract, and the employee accepts that repudiation by resigning. The employee must clearly indicate that he is treating the contract as having been repudiated by the employer (*Logabax Ltd v Titherley*[33]), and if he fails to do so, by word or by conduct, he is not entitled to claim that he has been constructively dismissed (*Holland v Glendale Industries Ltd*[34]).

17.22 The doctrine of constructive dismissal has had a somewhat chequered history. The real problem was to determine the nature of the conduct of the employer which entitles the employee to resign. Did such conduct have to amount to an actual breach of contract by the employer, or could any unreasonable conduct by the employer be sufficient to entitle

---

[30] [1983] ICR 314, [1983] IRLR 49, EAT.

[31] [1977] 1 All ER 567, [1976] ICR 536, [1976] IRLR 332, EAT.

[32] [1987] ICR 178, [1987] IRLR 79, EAT; revsd [1988] ICR 403, sub nom *Oakley v Labour Party* [1988] IRLR 34, CA.   [33] [1977] ICR 369, [1977] IRLR 97, EAT.

[34] [1998] ICR 493, EAT.

an employee to resign? For a long time the latter theory held sway, leading to some of the most bizarre and eccentric decisions in the whole of employment law. This view was firmly disposed of by the Court of Appeal in *Western Excavating (ECC) Ltd v Sharp*,[35] and earlier decisions must be read subject to this case. The facts were that the employee was dismissed for taking unauthorised time off work. He appealed to the internal disciplinary board, which substituted a penalty of five days' suspension without pay. This he accepted, but being short of money, he asked his employers if he could have an advance on his accrued holiday pay. This was refused. He then asked if he could have a loan of £40, but this too was refused. Consequently he resigned (in order to get his holiday pay) and brought a claim for unfair dismissal, alleging that he was forced to resign by virtue of the employer's conduct. His claim was upheld by the employment tribunal; the conduct of the employers was so unreasonable that the employee could not fairly be expected to put up with it, and it justified him leaving. On appeal, the EAT was not sure that they would have come to the same decision had they heard the case, but held that the employment tribunal was entitled to come to that decision. This was reversed by the Court of Appeal. The test for constructive dismissal was to be determined by the contract test, ie did the employer's conduct amount to a breach of contract which entitled the employee to resign? The 'unreasonable conduct' theory was dismissed as leading to a finding of constructive dismissal on the most whimsical grounds. Since there had been no breach of contract by the employers in *Sharp's* case (for the employers were under no contractual obligation to make the payments which were requested) there was no dismissal, constructive or otherwise.

17.23 It follows, therefore, that only those cases where the employer's conduct amounts to a significant breach, going to the root of the contract, can be regarded as being authoritative. There must be a fundamental breach of contract by the employer, not merely a failure to act reasonably (*Wadham Stringer Commercials (London) Ltd v Brown*[36]). Thus, if the employer tries to impose a unilateral change in employment terms, such as a change in the job, a significant change in hours (*Simmonds v Dowty Seals Ltd*[37]), a lowering in earnings (*RF Hill Ltd v Mooney*[38]), a significant change in the location of employment (*Courtaulds Northern Spinning Ltd v Sibson*[39]), or a demotion, then provided there is no contractual right to do so, such conduct will entitle an employee to resign. But a failure to pay salary on the due date was held not to have been so serious a breach in *Adams v Charles Zub Associates Ltd*[40] The employer's action did not show an intention not to be bound by the contract.

17.24 It must be borne in mind that although a constructive dismissal may amount to a dismissal in law, whether the dismissal is fair or unfair has still to be determined by the facts of the case, and whether or not the employer has acted reasonably (*Industrial Rubber Products v Gillon*[41]).

Genuine Dispute over Contract

17.25 If there is a genuine dispute concerning the nature of the parties' contractual obligations, this does not indicate an intention on the part of the employer to break the contract, and hence this will not be grounds for claiming constructive dismissal. In *Frank Wright & Co Ltd v Punch*[42] the claimant claimed that he was entitled to receive cost of living increases in his salary. The employers disputed that they were contractually obliged to pay, and so he resigned, claiming constructive dismissal. The EAT held that where there was a genuine dispute as to the construction of a contract, or a genuine mistake as to fact or law, the courts

[35] [1978] QB 761, [1978] 1 All ER 713, [1978] ICR 221, [1978] IRLR 27, CA.
[36] [1983] IRLR 46, EAT.   [37] [1978] IRLR 211, EAT.   [38] [1981] IRLR 258, EAT.
[39] [1984] ICR 218, [1984] IRLR 43, EAT.   [40] [1978] IRLR 551, EAT.
[41] [1977] IRLR 389, 13 ITR 100, EAT.   [42] [1980] IRLR 217, EAT.

would be unwilling to hold that an expression of intent by a party to carry out the contract in accordance with his (possibly erroneous) interpretation amounts to a repudiation of that contract. However, more recently it has been held that what is significant in constructive dismissal cases is the impact of the employer's conduct on the employee, rather than on what the employer intended. The impact has to be assessed objectively (*Parsons v Bristol Street Motors*[43]). It has to be shown that the employer did not intend to be bound by the contract, as properly construed (*Bridgen v Lancashire County Council*[44]).

Employer's Breach of an Implied Term

17.26 More difficult are those cases where the employee claims he is entitled to resign because the employer has broken an implied term of the contract (see para 3.32) because the nature of these terms may sometimes be a matter for speculation and conjecture. In *British Aircraft Corpn v Austin*[45] a failure to investigate a complaint about the inadequacy of protective spectacles was held to be a breach of the employer's implied duty to take reasonable care for the employee's safety, and in *Graham Oxley Tool Steels Ltd v Firth*[46] it was held that there was an implied term that the employer will provide a proper working environment. If no reasonable employer would have expected the employee to work in those conditions, then there is a fundamental breach of the contract of employment (*Dutton & Clark Ltd v Daly*[47]). It will be recalled that there is an implied duty of mutual respect, and therefore any action by or on behalf of the employer which runs contrary to that duty may amount to constructive dismissal. This could be the use of foul and abusive language (*Palmanor Ltd v Cedron*, see para 14.4), making unjustifiable complaints or giving unjustified warnings (*Walker v Josiah Wedgwood*[48]), making statements which destroy or seriously damage the relationship of trust and confidence which must exist between the parties (*Courtaulds Northern Textiles Ltd v Andrew*, see para 2.5), such as ill-founded allegations of theft (*Robinson v Crompton Parkinson Ltd*, see para 3.40), offensive and insensitive conduct by a supervisor (*Hilton International Hotels (UK) Ltd v Protopapa*[49]), and so on.

17.27 Even if there is an express term in the contract enabling an employer to transfer the employee to another location, there is an implied term that the employer will give reasonable notice of the transfer and, where appropriate, relocation and other allowances will be made, so as to make it feasible for the employee to comply with the contractual obligation to transfer (*United Bank Ltd v Akhtar*, see para 3.22).

17.28 A further problem arises when the employer makes life as difficult or as uncomfortable as possible, in the hope (or expectation) that the hint will be taken, and the employee will resign. No doubt a great deal will depend on the extent of the evidence which shows whether or not the employer is in breach of an express or implied term of the contract. Situations do occur when the parties wish to part company, but the employer is scared to take the initiative for fear of having a claim brought against him, and the employee is reluctant to resign without at least having an opportunity to collect some financial reward which is available under modern legislative provisions. It is here that the vagaries of the doctrine of constructive dismissal present the greatest menace, for the uncertainties are enormous.

17.29 In *Haseltine Lake & Co v Dowler*[50] the claimant was told that there was no future with the firm for him and that he should seek another job elsewhere. Eventually he found another job, resigned his employment, and claimed he had been constructively dismissed.

---

[43] UKEAT/0581/07/2802.   [44] [1987] IRLR 58, CA.
[45] [1978] IRLR 332, EAT.   [46] [1980] IRLR 135, EAT.   [47] [1985] ICR 780, [1985] IRLR 363, EAT.
[48] [1978] ICR 744, [1978] IRLR 105, EAT.   [49] [1990] IRLR 316, EAT.
[50] [1981] ICR 222, [1981] IRLR 25, EAT.

The EAT rejected his claim. No date had been fixed by the employers for his resignation, and before a contract of employment can terminate, there must be an ascertainable date on which it came to an end. This was not a case of 'resign or you will be dismissed', and therefore there was no repudiation of the contract by the employers.

17.30 Although the 'implied term' theory has effectively replaced the unreasonable conduct test, it can be just as capricious and whimsical in its results. In *FC Gardner Ltd v Beresford* (see paras 3.2 and 3.39) an employee resigned because she had not had a pay increase for two years, whereas other employees had. It was held that although there was no express term of the contract relating to pay increases, in most cases it was possible to imply a term that an employer would not treat an employee capriciously, arbitrarily, or inequitably in matters of remuneration. This does not mean, however, that a failure to give an annual pay rise to an employee is a breach of contract, for it is impossible to say that there is an implied term to that effect. The test is whether such failure is arbitrary and capricious. Thus, if the employer can show a good reason, such as inadequate performance by the employee, there is no breach of the duty of mutual trust and confidence (*Murco Petroleum Ltd v Forge*[51]).

17.31 A constructive dismissal situation arises when the employer, without reasonable and proper cause, conducts himself in a manner calculated or likely to destroy or seriously damage the relationship of trust and confidence which must exist between the parties (*Malik v BCCI SA*[52]). A repudiatory breach of contract, once it has happened, cannot be cured by the contract breaker. Thus even though the employer attempts to 'cure' the breach before the employee resigns, there is no room for the argument that what the employer did was within the range of reasonable responses, for to do so would take away the innocent party's option of accepting the breach and resigning in response to it (*Buckland v Bournemouth University*[53]). An employer may however cure a breach of contract before it becomes repudiatory. In *Assamoi v Spirit Pub Company*,[54] an employer accepted a worker's grievance, and so the worker no longer had a breach on which to resign. There is a distinction between preventing matters escalating into a breach of the implied term of mutual trust and confidence and trying to cure a breach which has already taken place.

17.32 Occasionally, the 'unreasonable conduct' test makes a reappearance in a new guise. It will be recalled that in constructive dismissal cases, one must look for the breach of contract. There is generally no difficulty in ascertaining the express terms, but legal authorities are clear that the implied terms are discovered by looking at what was 'obvious', so obvious in fact that the parties omitted to insert them (para 3.35).

17.33 Unreasonable conduct by an employer does not, by itself, constitute constructive dismissal. The conduct must be such as to amount to a breach of contract, ie conduct which fundamentally undermines the employment relationship (*Claridge v Daler Rowney Ltd*[55]).

17.34 The EAT returned to orthodoxy in *White v Reflecting Roadstuds Ltd* (see para 3.22). Here, the employee was working in the employer's despatch department but, at his own request, he was transferred to the mixing department, which involved higher pay, but also harder work. After about a year, he requested a move to lighter work, which was not then possible. From then on, his attendance deteriorated, and, after being given a formal warning, he was transferred to the pressing department, which involved a considerable drop in

[51] [1987] ICR 282, [1987] IRLR 50, EAT.
[52] [1998] AC 20, [1997] 3 All ER 1, [1997] ICR 606, [1997] IRLR 462.
[53] [2010] EWCA Civ 121, [2010] IRLR 445.   [54] UKEAT/0050/11.
[55] [2008] ICR 1267, [2008] IRLR 672.

his pay. He then resigned, claiming that the decision to move him to another department constituted a fundamental breach of his contract of employment. In their defence, the company pointed to a flexibility clause in the contract which gave them the right to transfer employees to alternative work if the requirements of operational efficiency so dictate, and also that a willingness of employees to do so was a condition of the contract. An employment tribunal held that the express right to transfer from one department to another was subject to two implied terms, namely (a) that it would be exercised in a reasonable manner, and (b) that the transfer would not result in a unilateral reduction in the employee's pay. On appeal, the EAT reversed the decision on both grounds. On the first point, the EAT stated that to imply a term that a flexibility or mobility clause should be handled reasonably would be to introduce the 'reasonableness' test into constructive dismissal cases by the back door and would fly in the face of the authority of *Western Excavating (ECC) Ltd v Sharp* (paras 17.22 and 17.37). Although a 'capricious' decision would not create any difficulty (*United Bank Ltd v Akhtar*, para 17.27), if there are sufficient grounds for operating the clause, the employers are entitled to reach such decisions. On the second point, it was held that if an employer acts within the contract, the fact that the change results in a unilateral reduction in the employee's pay does not constitute a fundamental breach of the contract (see *Spafax Ltd v Harrison*,[56] para 17.37).

17.35 Also, if the employer is in breach, but the employee does not resign, and subsequently alleges a further breach, the employment tribunal should take into account the whole of the employer's conduct, and not merely the latest incident which led to the resignation (*Lewis v Motorworld Garages Ltd*[57]). If the employee does resign, it has to be in response, at least in part, to the fundamental breach of contract by the employer (*Meikle v Nottinghamshire County Council*[58]). The tribunal does not have to find a *principal* reason otherwise (*Logan v Celyn House Ltd*[59]).

17.36 If an employee resigns, claiming that the employer has broken the implied term of trust and confidence, can the employer counter this by arguing that in fact the employee was in breach of the same term? In *Aberdeen City Council v McNeill*[60] the employee was accused of bullying, sexual harassment, and intoxication at work. The disciplinary procedure was invoked, but the employee resigned, claiming that it was being conducted oppressively, and thus in breach of the implied term of trust and confidence. The employers countered this by arguing that in fact it was the employee who was in breach of the term, and thus he had lost the right to claim constructive dismissal, because there was no trust and confidence left for the employer to breach! The EAT held that the claimant's prior breach meant that he was not entitled to terminate his contract on the basis that his employer had breached the same term.

17.37 If an employer gives lawful notice, this is not a breach of trust and confidence so as to enable an employee to claim constructive dismissal. In *Kerry Foods Ltd v Lynch*[61] the employer wanted an employee to change from five days a week to six days, but the employee refused to do so. His employer then stated that he would be given lawful notice to terminate the contract, and then be re-engaged immediately on the new terms. Before the notice expired, the employee resigned and claimed constructive dismissal. His claim failed. There was no breach of contract by the employer.

17.38 Since the employee is claiming that the employer has broken the contract, he must resign as a result of that breach (*Holland v Glendale Industries*, para 17.21). If he continues to report to work, he may be deemed to have waived the breach, and can hardly bring a

---

[56] [1980] IRLR 442, CA.   [57] [1986] ICR 157, [1985] IRLR 465, CA.   [58] [2005] ICR 1.
[59] UKEAT/0069/12, [2012] All ER (D) 04 (Sep).   [60] [2010] IRLR 374.   [61] [2005] IRLR 680.

claim subsequently based on the employer's repudiation, for 'the law does not allow him to have his cake and eat it' (*Hunt v British Railways Board*[62]). But if he protests about the breach but stays on until he finds himself another job, he may not necessarily be deemed to have accepted the employer's breach (*Miller v Shanks & McEwan*[63]) provided that he acts reasonably expeditiously (*WE Cox Toner (International) Ltd v Crook*[64]). An employee does not necessarily affirm the contract by claiming sick pay (*Colomar Mari v Reuters*[65]). All the circumstances should be looked at, and the passage of time in itself does not amount to an affirmation, and is not to be taken in isolation (*Chindove v William Morrisons Supermarket plc*,[66] following *Buckland v Bournemouth*, para 17.31). A distinction must be drawn between the waiver of a breach and the non-waiver of a continuing breach.

17.39 If there is a series of breaches which lead the employee to look for another job before handing in his notice, the employment tribunal must consider whether those breaches were the effective cause of a resignation. They do not have to be the sole cause. If the taking of other employment was the consequence of the breaches, then the employee can claim he has been constructively dismissed (*Jones v Sirl & Son (Furnishers) Ltd*[67]). Harassment can also result in a claim for constructive dismissal, on the basis that the mutual trust and confidence that should exist between employer and employee has broken down (*Blackburn with Darwen Borough Council v Stanley*).

17.40 Constructive dismissal may occur in a 'last straw' situation. In *Lewis v Motorworld Garages Ltd* (see para 17.35) it was stated that the breach of the implied obligation of trust and confidence may consist of a series of actions on the part of the employer which cumulatively amount to a breach of the term, even though each individual incident may not do so. The 'last straw' need not itself be a breach of contract by the employer, but it must contribute, however slightly, to the sustained breach of the implied term of trust and respect. An entirely innocent act by the employer cannot be the 'last straw', even if the employee mistakenly interprets it in that light (*Omilaju v Waltham Forest London Borough Council*[68]).

17.41 When considering the 'last straw' argument in a constructive dismissal case, it is important for the employment tribunal to identify the 'last straw' act, and then consider, objectively, whether cumulatively with the earlier acts a breach of the implied term of trust and confidence has occurred (*Wishaw & District Housing Association v Moncrieff*[69]).

17.42 If the employer announces an intention to break the contract at a future date, and the employee does not accept the breach, it is open to the employer to inform the employee that the contract will be performed. The employee will thus lose the right to claim constructive dismissal (*Norwest Holst Group Administration Ltd v Harrison*[70]). On the other hand, if the employee accepts the constructive dismissal, and gives notice to terminate the contract, conduct between the resignation and termination can be taken into account when assessing compensation (*Peterborough Regional College v Gidney*[71]).

Constructive Dismissal can be Fair Dismissal

17.43 It must be stressed that the fact that there is constructive dismissal does not necessarily mean that the dismissal is unfair (*Ford v Milthorn Toleman Ltd*[72]), and there have been a number of cases where a constructive dismissal has been held to be a fair dismissal

---

[62] [1979] IRLR 379, EAT.   [63] IDS Handbook 12.   [64] [1981] ICR 823, [1981] IRLR 443, EAT.
[65] UKEAT/0539/13.   [66] UKEAT/0201/13.   [67] [1997] IRLR 493, EAT.
[68] [2004] EWCA Civ 1493, [2005] IRLR 35, CA.   [69] UKEATS/0066/08.
[70] [1984] IRLR 419, EAT; aff'd [1985] ICR 668, sub nom *Harrison v Norwest Holst Group Administration Ltd* [1985] IRLR 240, CA.   [71] EAT/1270/97, 1270A/97.
[72] [1980] IRLR 30, CA.

(eg *Savoia v Chiltern Herb Farms Ltd*[73]). Thus if an employer demotes an employee without contractual authority, this will amount to a constructive dismissal, but if the demotion was brought about by a well-founded suspicion of dishonesty, the dismissal may be fair (*Hilton v Shiner Ltd*, see paras 3.44 and 10.11). Even if it is unfair, compensation may still be reduced for contributory conduct. An employer faced with a constructive dismissal claim should be prepared to fight it on two fronts: (a) he may argue that there was no dismissal, or (b) in the alternative, if there was a dismissal, it was fair because … etc. A failure to adopt this course may result in a finding that there was a (constructive) dismissal, and, if no reason for the dismissal is advanced, it must therefore be unfair (*Derby City Council v Marshall*[74]). Whether an employer's conduct amounts to a constructive dismissal is a question of fact for the employment tribunal to determine (*Woods v W M Car Services (Peterborough) Ltd*[75]).

17.44 A failure to follow a grievance procedure is not, by itself, relevant in a constructive dismissal claim, because it is the conduct of the employer which is in issue (*Tolson v Mixenden Community School*[76]). In *Amnesty International v Ahmed*[77] (see para 4.147) it was held that although an employer's actions constituted unlawful race discrimination, this did not mean that there was a breach of the implied term of trust and respect. The employer had not acted without reasonable or proper cause, and the conduct in question was not calculated to destroy the relationship of trust and confidence that must exist between the parties.

Termination of the Contract

17.45 There are a number of ways in which a contract may come to an end, but which do not amount to a dismissal in law.

A. Resignation

17.46 If an employee resigns, then (unless it is a constructive dismissal) he has not been dismissed. If the words used by the employee are clear and unambiguous (eg 'I am leaving, I want my P45') then there are no grounds for the employment tribunal to find that the words have a significance other than their plain meaning (*BG Gale Ltd v Gilbert*[78]). If the words are ambiguous, then the test is, what would a reasonable employer have understood by those words in that context (*Tanner v Kean Ltd*, para 17.17)? If an employee is threatened that if he does not resign he will be dismissed, a consequent resignation will amount to a dismissal, but if his resignation is brought about by other factors, such as an offer of a financial inducement, this is not a dismissal (*Sheffield v Oxford Controls Co Ltd*[79] but see *Sandhu v Jan de Rijk Transport Ltd*,[80] para 17.68).

17.47 Words spoken or action taken by an employee in the heat of the moment or under extreme pressure should not necessarily be taken at face value. The employer should allow a reasonable time to elapse before accepting such an apparent resignation to see whether this was what was really intended. If the employer fails to make a proper investigation, he runs the risk that an employment tribunal may hold that there are special circumstances where the apparent resignation was not really intended by the employee (*Kwik-Fit (GB) Ltd v Lineham*, para 15.9).

---

[73] [1981] IRLR 65, EAT; aff'd [1982] IRLR 166, CA.   [74] [1979] ICR 731, [1979] IRLR 261, EAT.
[75] [1981] ICR 666, [1981] IRLR 347, EAT; aff'd [1982] ICR 693, [1982] IRLR 413, CA.
[76] [2003] IRLR 842, [2003] All ER (D) 312 (Oct), EAT.   [77] [2009] ICR 1450, [2009] IRLR 884.
[78] [1978] ICR 1149, [1978] IRLR 453, EAT.   [79] [1979] ICR 396, [1979] IRLR 133, EAT.
[80] [2007] EWCA Civ 430, [2007] IRLR 519, [2007] ICR 1137.

17.48 For a resignation to be effective to terminate the contract there must be an ascertainable date (express or implied) on which it will take effect. To say, 'I am resigning at some future point in time' is a statement of intention, not a resignation; but to say, 'I am resigning' is not ambiguous, for it indicates a present intention (*Sothern v Franks Charlesly & Co*, para 17.15). An employment tribunal is entitled to conclude on the evidence that the words of apparent resignation used by the employee 'in the heat of the moment' should not be accepted at their face value (*Sovereign House Security Services Ltd v Savage*[81]).

17.49 If the employee indicates an intention to resign, but in terms which are somewhat equivocal, so that the position is mistakenly construed by the employer as a resignation although the employee has not in fact resigned, this can be relied upon by the employer for the purpose of supplying an employment tribunal a potentially fair reason for the dismissal (for some other substantial reason, see para 17.144) even though, in error, the employer is seeking to hold the employee to the alleged resignation. What matters are the facts which led to the dismissal/resignation, not the precise label put on it by the employer (*Ely v YKK Fasteners (UK) Ltd*[82]).

17.50 A resignation does not have to be accepted by the employer, nor can it be withdrawn unilaterally. If an employee gives notice to terminate his employment and, during the notice period, the employer releases the employee from serving the full notice period, there is no dismissal by the employer. All that has happened is that the employee is no longer required to attend work (*Tom Findlay & Co Ltd v Devlin*[83]).

17.51 Whether an employee has resigned or was dismissed is a question of fact for the employment tribunal to determine, and their findings cannot be challenged unless their conclusions were such that no reasonable employment tribunal could have reached them (*Martin v Glynwed Distribution Ltd*, para 17.9).

B. **Constructive Resignation**

17.52 If a breach of contract by the employer entitles the employee to resign and claim constructive dismissal, then why should not a breach of contract by the employee entitle the employer to claim that the contract has been terminated by 'constructive resignation'? This view was supported by a number of decisions by the EAT and employment tribunals, but must be discounted in the light of the decision of the Court of Appeal in *London Transport Executive v Clarke* (see para 3.34), and all earlier decisions must be read in the light of this case. The facts were that Clarke wanted to go to Jamaica on extended unpaid leave, but permission was refused by the employers as he had already exhausted his entitlement under the rules. When he asked what would happen if he went without permission he was told that his name would be removed from the books. Nonetheless he went to Jamaica, stayed for seven weeks, and on his return he submitted a medical note, which the employment tribunal viewed 'with some surprise'. While he was away, the employers wrote to his home address, stating that if no reply was received within 14 days it would be assumed that he did not wish to continue his employment, and eventually his name was removed from the books. When he returned from Jamaica, he applied for his job back, and when this was refused, he claimed he had been unfairly dismissed. For the employers, it was argued that the applicant had 'resigned' but this view was rejected. It is trite law that if a person breaks a contract, the other party has two options; he can either accept the breach, and treat the contract as being at an end, or refuse to do so, and treat the contract as still subsisting. If he accepts the breach, he terminates the contract. Thus Clarke had been dismissed, and had

---

[81] [1989] IRLR 115, CA.   [82] [1993] IRLR 500, CA.   [83] UKEATS/0071/06/MT.

not resigned. However, the Court of Appeal then went on to find that the dismissal, in the circumstances, was fair.

17.53 There is no doubt that this analysis is correct. The reason for the doctrine of constructive dismissal is because there is a statutory provision for it (ERA, s 95(1)(c)). There is no statutory doctrine of constructive resignation. Thus if an employee walks out of his job, or commits any other breach of contract, but nonetheless claims that he is entitled to resume his work, the employer must expressly or impliedly accept the repudiation, and this will constitute a dismissal. He must then satisfy the employment tribunal that in the circumstances, having regard to the equity and substantial merits of the case, he acted reasonably in treating the repudiatory conduct as sufficient reason for dismissing the employee.

C. Implied Resignation

17.54 However, it is submitted that there may be circumstances of implied resignation or resignation by conduct. Thus, if an employee disappears and does not respond to the employer's communications, or if it is discovered that the employee is working for another employer, it may not be difficult to infer that he has resigned his employment. The point was made by Sir John Donaldson in *Harrison v George Wimpey & Co Ltd*: 'Where an employee so conducts himself as to lead a reasonable employer to believe that the employee has terminated the contract, the contract is then terminated.'[84]

D. Frustration of the Contract

17.55 If the performance of the contract of employment is rendered impossible by some intervening event, then it will be terminated by frustration, not by dismissal. In *Anyanwu v South Bank Student Union* (see para 4.207) the claimant was a salaried officer of the student union. He was expelled from the university and excluded from its premises, whereupon the student union treated his contract of employment as being at an end. A claim for unlawful discrimination was dismissed by an employment tribunal, and the decision was upheld on appeal. Impossibility of performance meant that the contract ended by frustration. Frustration can only arise where there is no fault by either party, eg where accident or illness prevents the employee (or employer) from performing the contract. Where there is fault by one party, this is repudiatory conduct, not frustration, although there is a view that this could be self-induced frustration. It is thus up to the other party to accept the repudiation and terminate the contract, or keep the contract open, as he chooses (*London Transport Executive v Clarke*, para 17.33). Clearly, if the repudiatory conduct was serious (eg being sent to prison) it would be rare for the dismissal to be categorised as being unfair (*Norris v Southampton City Council*[85]).

17.56 There are two situations which commonly occur, and which may give rise to the doctrine of frustration. The first is long-term absence through accident or illness (*Notcutt v Universal Equipment Co (London) Ltd*[86]), the second is imprisonment (*FC Shepherd & Co Ltd v Jerrom*[87]).

17.57 To decide whether or not a contract will terminate by frustration, regard must be had to the length of time the employee is likely to be away from his work and thus be unable to perform his contract, the need for the employer to obtain a replacement, the length

---

[84] (1972) 7 ITR 188, NIRC.   [85] [1982] ICR 177, [1982] IRLR 141, EAT.
[86] [1986] 3 All ER 582, [1986] ICR 414, [1986] IRLR 218, CA.
[87] [1985] ICR 552, [1985] IRLR 275, EAT; revsd [1987] QB 301, [1986] 3 All ER 589, [1986] ICR 802, [1986] IRLR 358, CA.

of time he has been employed, his position, and so forth. In cases where the employee is absent for a long time through sickness, all these factors are relevant, and in addition the employer must consider the nature of the illness (or injury), how long it has continued, and the prospects for recovery, as well as the terms of the contract, including the provision of sick pay (see *Marshall v Harland and Wolff Ltd*[88]). The mere absence from work, even for a long time, will not automatically constitute frustration. Thus in *Maxwell v Walter Howard Designs Ltd*[89] the claimant was away sick for nearly two years, during which time he sent in regular sick notes. His job, as a cabinet maker, was one which did not need to be filled by a permanent replacement, and so, despite the passage of time, it was held that the contract had not been frustrated.

17.58 But if it is clear that on the medical evidence, the employee is unlikely to return to work for a considerable time, then there must come a point at which the employer is entitled to decide that the employee will not be returning to work, and consequently treat the contract as being frustrated. The problem is establishing when, exactly, that point in time comes about, and to this question there is no easy answer (see *Scarr v FW Goodyear & Sons Ltd*[90]). In employment cases, the courts and tribunals must guard against too easy an application of the doctrine of frustration, especially when redundancy occurs, or where the true reason for the dismissal is disability (*Williams v Watsons Luxury Coaches Ltd*[91]).

17.59 In *Egg Stores (Stamford Hill) Ltd v Leibovici*,[92] the EAT stated that there may be a long process before it can be said that illness has brought about a frustration of the contract. But if the time arrives when one can say that matters have gone on for so long, and the prospects for future employment are so poor, that it is no longer practical to consider the contract as still subsisting, then frustration will occur. Among the matters to be taken into account to reach this conclusion are (1) the length of the employment, (2) how long it would have been expected to continue, (3) the nature of the job, (4) the nature, length, and effect of the illness, (5) the need to appoint a permanent replacement, (6) the risk to the employer of acquiring further obligations in respect of redundancy payments or unfair dismissals, (7) whether wages are still being paid, (8) the acts and statements of the employer in relation to the employee, including his failure to dismiss, and (9) whether in all the circumstances a reasonable employer could be expected to wait for the employee any longer. To this we may add (a) the terms of the contract as to sick pay, and (b) a consideration of the prospects of recovery (*Williams v Watsons Luxury Coaches Ltd*).

17.60 That none of these tests, by themselves, can be conclusive can be seen from the decision in *Hart v AR Marshall & Sons (Bulwell) Ltd*[93] where the claimant became sick in April 1974. In August of that year, the employers engaged a permanent replacement but the claimant continued to send in sick notes. In January 1976 he presented himself for work, but was told there was no job for him, and he was given his cards. He claimed that this constituted unfair dismissal, but the EAT upheld a tribunal finding that the contract had been frustrated. The failure by the employers to act on the absence by dismissing the claimant was not, by itself, evidence that they will continue to regard him as an employee. Otherwise an employer would be in a difficult situation with regard to a sick employee; if he dismissed him prematurely this might be unfair; if he engaged a temporary replacement, he might have to pay compensation at the end of that contract in order to permit the sick employee to return to work. Nor was the fact that the employee continued to send in sick notes indicative of anything other than that the employee was keeping in touch in case there was a

---

[88] [1972] 2 All ER 715, [1972] ICR 101, [1972] IRLR 90, NIRC.   [89] [1975] IRLR 77.
[90] [1975] IRLR 166.   [91] [1990] ICR 536, [1990] IRLR 164, EAT.
[92] [1977] ICR 260, [1976] IRLR 376, EAT.
[93] [1978] 2 All ER 413, [1977] ICR 539, [1977] IRLR 51, EAT.

prospect of future employment. The crucial factor appears to be the finding that the claimant occupied a key position, which had to be filled, and thus the contract was frustrated.

17.61 If it is clear that the employee is permanently unfit to do his job, the contract will be frustrated. The fact that the employer keeps the employee 'on the books' may be an arrangement which falls short of a contract of employment, of the sort expressly recognised in ERA, s 212(3)(c) (see para 13.24) as being relevant to the question of continuity of employment when no contract is actually in existence. But if the contract is frustrated the statutory or contractual rights to notice on termination do not apply (*G F Sharp & Co Ltd v McMillan*, see para 15.26).

17.62 Imprisonment, though self-induced, is not strictly speaking repudiatory conduct, for it does not amount to a breach of the contract of employment. But there is an inherent contradiction, because the doctrine of frustration arises when an event occurs without the fault of either party, and a person who had been given a custodial sentence will invariably be at fault. The answer appears to be that the person asserting the frustration (ie the employer) must show that there was no fault on his part, and the person against whom frustration is being asserted (ie the employee) cannot rely on his own misconduct by way of an answer (*FC Shepherd & Co Ltd v Jerrom*, para 17.56).

17.63 Frustration arises by operation of law, not a conscious decision by the parties, and whilst it is not necessary to be able to point to the exact moment in time when the relationship between the parties is dissolved, the burden of proving that the contract has been frustrated lies on the employer. Thus, if an employee is sent to prison, this can be an instantaneously frustrating event or a potentially frustrating event. Accordingly, regard has to be paid to:

(a) when it was commercially necessary for the employer to make a decision about the employee's future;

(b) what a reasonable employer would consider to be the likely length of the employee's absence; and

(c) whether it was reasonable to engage a permanent rather than a temporary replacement (*Chakki v United Yeast Co Ltd*[94]).

E. **Consensual Termination**

17.64 A consensual termination arises when the employment is terminated by mutual agreement, and the reason for that agreement is generally irrelevant (*Birch and Humber v Liverpool University*[95]). Since there is no dismissal, no statutory rights ensue. If a person is given the option of working part-time or being made redundant, and chooses the latter option, there is a dismissal for reason of redundancy, and it is not a consensual termination (*Lassman v De Vere University Arms Hotel*[96]). Also, a person who volunteers for redundancy has volunteered to be dismissed, and is entitled to a redundancy payment (*Burton Allton and Johnson Ltd v Peck*[97]).

17.65 A mutual agreement whereby the employment will come to an end on the happening of a future event is not a consensual termination. In *Igbo v Johnson Matthey Chemicals Ltd* [98] the claimant wished to take extended leave. She signed a document which stated that

[94] [1982] 2 All ER 446, [1982] ICR 140, EAT.
[95] [1985] ICR 470, [1985] IRLR 165, CA.   [96] [2003] ICR 44, [2002] All ER (D) 83 (Oct), EAT.
[97] [1975] ICR 193, [1975] IRLR 87, DC.
[98] [1986] ICR 82, [1985] IRLR 189, EAT; revsd [1986] ICR 505, [1986] IRLR 215, CA.

she agreed to return to work by a certain date, and that if she failed to do so the contract of employment would automatically terminate. She failed to return to work on the due date, and her employers treated the contract as being at an end. She claimed that she had been unfairly dismissed. The Court of Appeal applied ERA, s 203, which stipulates that any provision in an agreement shall be void in so far as it purports to limit the operation of any provision in the Act. The document she signed purported to take away her right to claim that she was unfairly dismissed, and it was therefore void. The Court of Appeal overruled earlier authorities on this topic and remitted the case to the employment tribunal to determine whether her dismissal was fair or unfair.

17.66 However, a mutual agreement to bring a contract of employment to an end, made for good consideration, after the employee had received proper advice, and made without duress, is effective. In *Logan Salton v Durham County Council*,[99] the claimant was due to attend a disciplinary hearing which was to consider a recommendation that he be dismissed. An agreement was then reached whereby, on terms, his employment would come to an end by mutual agreement. He subsequently claimed he had been unfairly dismissed, but his claim failed. The agreement was not void by virtue of ERA, s 203 because it was not a contract of employment, or the variation of a contract of employment. The EAT distinguished this type of situation from that which occurred in *Igbo v Johnson Matthey Chemicals* (see para 17.65).

17.67 The distinction between a resignation and a termination by mutual agreement is that the former is a unilateral act by the employee, whereas the latter requires the consent of both parties, because otherwise there may be a breach of contract by one party. Thus if an employee gives notice, he resigns. If the employer and employee agree that the employee may leave without giving notice, it is a mutual termination (*L Lipton Ltd v Marlborough*[100]).

17.68 However, the question 'did he jump or was he pushed?' must be determined by reference to all the surrounding circumstances. In *Sandhu v Jan de Rijk Transport Ltd* (para 17.46) the employee was called to a meeting with no indication as to its substance. He was told that his contract was to be terminated. The meeting continued, and the employee negotiated agreed terms for his departure. He subsequently claimed he had been unfairly dismissed. Relying on *Sheffield v Oxford Controls Co Ltd* (see para 17.46), the employment tribunal held that the agreement had converted the dismissal into a resignation, but the Court of Appeal reversed that decision. Earlier cases were distinguished because in them the employee had had time to consider the inevitability of the termination, and subsequently negotiate for himself a financial package, whereas in the instant case the employee had not had a full opportunity to consider his position and, in particular, take independent advice as to his rights.

Fair and Unfair Dismissal (ERA, s 98)

A. Is it Fair?

17.69 Once it has been established that a dismissal has taken place, it must then be determined whether or not the dismissal was unfair. Section 98 of the Employment Rights Act 1996 lays down five grounds on which a dismissal is capable of being fair, as follows:

   (a) a reason relating to the capability or qualifications of the employee for performing the work of the kind which he was employed by the employer to do. 'Capability'

[99] [1989] IRLR 99, EAT.   [100] [1979] IRLR 179, EAT.

includes any assessment by reference to skill, aptitude, health, or other physical or mental quality, and 'qualifications' means any degree, diploma, or other academic, technical, or professional qualification relevant to the position which the employee holds;

(b) a reason which relates to the conduct of the employee;

(c) the redundancy of the employee;

(d) because the employee could not continue to work in the position which he held without contravention (either on his part or on the part of the employer) of a restriction or a duty imposed by or under a statute;

(e) some other substantial reason such as to justify the dismissal of an employee holding the position which he held.

17.70 Whether a particular dismissal based on one or more of these reasons will be fair or unfair will depend on whether in the circumstances of the case (including the size and administrative resources of the employer's undertaking) the employer acted reasonably or unreasonably in treating the reason as a sufficient reason for dismissing the employee, and the question will be determined in accordance with equity and the substantial merits of the case (ERA, s 98(4)). Further, whereas it is for the employee to prove that he was dismissed, it is for the employer to show the reason for the dismissal, and that it was one of the potentially fair reasons. It will then be for the employment tribunal to find, on the basis of the evidence presented, whether or not the employer had acted reasonably in treating that reason as a sufficient ground for dismissal. Thus if he fails to show the reason, or fails to show a reason which is one of those listed in para 17.69, the dismissal is automatically unfair. In *Raynor v Remploy Ltd*[101] a group general manager was dismissed for alleged lack of business judgment and general inefficiency. He had been employed for five years, and the tribunal rejected the company's allegations as spurious. Since there was no evidence of incapability, the dismissal was unfair. In *Castledine v Rothwell Engineering Ltd* (see para 10.40) the tribunal refused to accept the general allegations of incompetence, pointing to the favourable reference given to an employee subsequent to his dismissal. The employer cannot expect to win his case if he fails to give or call evidence on which the tribunal can reach its conclusion on the reason for the dismissal or its reasonableness, and general allegations without such evidence will normally be insufficient. In *Whitaker v Milk Marketing Board*,[102] an artificial inseminator was dismissed for incompetence and misconduct. Although the Board mentioned various farmers who were supposed to be dissatisfied with the service they had received, none was called to give evidence, and the dismissal was held unfair.

Two-stage Procedure

17.71 Broadly speaking, there are two stages in the process of determining whether or not a dismissal was fair. The first is the means whereby the decision is reached. This involves going through proper procedures (see Chapter 12) bearing in mind especially the provisions of the Code of Practice (*Lock v Cardiff Railway Co Ltd*, paras 1.16 and 12.12), so that there is a full investigation, a proper hearing, a right to appeal, etc. The second stage is the actual decision taken, bearing in mind the reason for the dismissal, the need to consider mitigating circumstances, consistency and/or flexibility as appropriate, the terms of the contract, the size and nature of the employer's undertaking, and so on. No single factor, by itself, can be conclusive, and each case will turn on its own peculiar facts.

---

[101] [1973] IRLR 3.   [102] [1973] IRLR 100.

Has the Employer Acted Reasonably?

17.72 Further, the test is 'did the employer act reasonably?' and not 'did the employment tribunal agree with what the employer did?' (*Grundy (Teddington) Ltd v Willis*[103]). An employment tribunal is not entitled to substitute its own views for those of the employer (*Foley v Post Office*[104]). A decision on whether the employer acted reasonably is a question of fact for the employment tribunal to decide (*Iceland Frozen Foods Ltd v Jones*[105]), which can only be challenged if the decision was perverse or based on an incorrect perception of the law.

17.73 In *Anandarajah v Lord Chancellor's Department*,[106] the President of the EAT, Waite J, made a major policy statement about the use of precedents in employment tribunal hearings. Although these are of great practical assistance, they must not be relied upon as being of binding authority, but rather treated as guidelines. He continued:

> Sometimes the judgment in a particular case will be found to express, in helpful and concise language, some concept which is regularly found in this field of enquiry and it becomes of great illustrative value. But reference to such a case can never be a substitute for taking the explicit directions of the statute as a guiding principle.

17.74 To determine whether or not the employer has acted reasonably in dismissing the employee, the current test is: 'What would a reasonable employer have done?' There is a band of reasonableness within which one employer might decide to dismiss, whilst another might decide not to do so. If the circumstances of the case are such that a reasonable employer might dismiss, the dismissal will be fair even though not all the employers would take that view (*British Leyland (UK) Ltd v Swift*[107]). The 'band of reasonableness' test was challenged (somewhat belatedly) by the EAT in *Haddon v Van Den Bergh Foods Ltd*,[108] but in *HSBC v Madden*[109] the Court of Appeal disagreed, and reaffirmed the correctness of the 'range of reasonable responses' test as laid down in *Iceland Frozen Foods Ltd v Jones*. Further, the *Burchell* test (para 17.123) applied to the assessment of the fairness of the dismissal under s 98(4), not to establishing the reason for the dismissal under s 98(1)–(3).

17.75 In *Kent County Council v Gilham*[110] the Court of Appeal stressed once again that whether or not an employer acts reasonably is a question of fact for the employment tribunal. That two employment tribunals, considering the same broad issues, had reached opposite conclusions did not indicate that either had misdirected themselves in law. It is endemic in the system that different answers will be given to broadly similar situations, and the decision cannot be challenged just for that reason. But on rare occasions higher courts will interfere if the decision of the employment tribunal is thought to be perverse (*British Railways Board v Jackson*[111]). The 'range of reasonable responses' relates to facts reasonably known by the employer, not to facts found by the employment tribunal, particularly if the facts are in dispute at the tribunal hearing (*London Ambulance Service NHS Trust v Small*[112]).

17.76 The point in time at which the reasonableness of the employer's decision to dismiss is to be tested is when the employment comes to an end, not when the decision is taken, nor when the notice to terminate is given (*Stacey v Babcock Power Ltd*[113]). Thus if an initial

---

[103] [1976] ICR 323, [1976] IRLR 118.   [104] [2001] 1 All ER 550, [2000] ICR 1283, [2000] IRLR 827, CA.
[105] [1983] ICR 17, [1982] IRLR 439, EAT.   [106] [1984] IRLR 131, EAT.
[107] [1981] IRLR 91, CA.   [108] [1999] ICR 1150, [1999] IRLR 672, EAT.
[109] [2001] 1 All ER 550, [2000] ICR 1283, [2000] IRLR 827, CA.
[110] [1985] ICR 227, sub nom *Gilham v Kent County Council* [1985] IRLR 16, CA.
[111] [1994] IRLR 235, CA.   [112] [2009] EWCA Civ 220, [2009] IRLR 563.
[113] [1986] QB 308, [1986] ICR 221, [1986] IRLR 3, EAT.

decision to dismiss was unfair because of a defect in the disciplinary proceedings, it may be cured if an appeal hearing is properly conducted (see *Clark v Civil Aviation Authority*, para 12.20). The reason for the dismissal is to be assessed at the time notice of termination was given right through to the actual date of the termination of the contract (*West Kent College v Richardson*[114]). Matters which come to light after the employment has ended are generally irrelevant (*Greenall Whitley plc v Carr*, para 12.36).

Automatically Unfair Dismissals

17.77 Certain dismissals are automatically unfair, and no question arises as to whether or not the employer has acted reasonably. Nor is the length of continuous employment relevant, as a claim for automatically unfair dismissal can be brought from day one of employment. These are dismissals connected with:

(a) pregnancy or childbirth, the taking of ordinary or additional or compulsory maternity leave, ordinary or additional adoption leave, parental leave or paternity leave, or time off to look after dependants, declining to sign a workforce agreement for maternity or parental leave purposes, the performance of functions as a workforce representative (ERA, s 99, and Maternity and Parental Leave Regulations 1999);

(b) a health and safety case (ERA, s 100);

(c) a shop or betting worker who refuses to work on Sundays (ERA, s 101) or additional hours on Sundays (ERA s 101ZA);

(d) the exercise of a right under the Working Time Regulations (ERA, s 101A);

(e) performing a function as trustee of an occupational pension fund (ERA, s 102);

(f) performing a function of an employee representative (ERA, s 103);

(g) the making of a protected disclosure (ERA, s 103A);

(h) the assertion of a statutory right (ERA, s 104);

(i) the exercise of a right under the National Minimum Wage Act (ERA, s 104A);

(j) taking action with regard to a tax credit (ERA, s 104B);

(k) making or proposing an application for flexible working (ERA s 104C);

(l) refusing to accept employee shareholder status (ERA s 104G);

(m) membership or non-membership of a trade union (TULR(C)A, s 154);

(n) the taking of protected industrial action (TULR(C)A, s 238A);

(o) doing a wide range of actions in connection with the statutory procedure for recognition or derecognition (TULR(C)A, Sch A1, see para 21.61);

(p) doing acts in connection with rights under the Transnational Information and Consultation of Employees Regulations 1999, Companies (Cross Border Mergers) Regulations 2007, European Cooperative Society (Involvement of Employees) Regulations 2006, European Public Limited Liability (Employee Involvement) (Great Britain) Regulations 2009;

(q) doing acts in connection with an employee's rights under the Part-time Workers (Prevention of Less Favourable Treatment) Regulations 2000 (see para 2.85);

(r) the exercise of rights in connection with an application for flexible working (ERA, s 104C) (see para 6.128);

(s) taken action under the Fixed-Term Employees (Prevention of Less Favourable Treatment) Regulations 2002: see reg 6);

---

[114] [1999] ICR 511, EAT.

(t) undertaking jury service (see para 6.128);

(u) acted as a companion;

(v) selection for redundancy for any of these reasons (ERA, s 105);

(w) breach of the Employment Relations Act 1999 (Blacklist) Regulations 2010 (ERA s 104F);

(x) breach of the Time off Work for Study and Training provisions (ERA, s 63D) (ERA s 104E);

(y) pension enrolment (ERA s 104D).

17.78 In June 2013 s 13 of the Enterprise and Regulatory Reform Act added a new sub-s (4) to the ERA 1996 s 108. This removed the qualifying period for unfair dismissal where the principal reason for dismissal is an employee's political opinions or affiliation, although this is not an automatically unfair dismissal.

B. Reasons for the Dismissal

17.79 Although the Act lays down potentially fair reasons for dismissal, it will be convenient to make further sub-divisions, so that in practice a number of potential reasons for fair dismissal appear. This enables a more practical analysis to be made. Bearing this in mind, we can examine the general approach of the courts and tribunals to the problems of dismissals.

Inherent Inability

17.80 To dismiss an employee who is not capable of performing his job properly will be fair provided the employer acts reasonably in the circumstances. Thus, faced with the problem of an incompetent worker, what does the reasonable employer do? He enquires into the matter, to find out why the employee cannot do the job adequately. Has he been trained properly, so that he knows how the job should be done? Has he been properly supervised, been given an adequate job description? Does he have proper equipment, sufficient support staff and facilities? In other words, the employer's first task is to find out the reason for the alleged incompetence, and, so far as it is possible, do something about it from the employer's point of view.

17.81 For example, in *Davison v Kent Meters Ltd*[115] the claimant was dismissed for assembling nearly 500 components in the wrong sequence. She claimed that she had followed the pattern of work in accordance with the instructions received from her chargehand, but the latter denied having shown her how to assemble the parts, and maintained that she was entirely to blame for the errors. The employment tribunal thought that if the chargehand had not shown her what to do, he should have done so, and the mistakes were therefore hardly her fault. Further, he should have checked on her performance, and supervised her properly. Not surprisingly, the dismissal was held to be unfair.

17.82 A warning should not be given merely for the sake of conforming with a laid-down procedure, for this is to treat it as a mechanical system with no real significance. A warning is designed to do a job of work; it should have as its purpose the object of bringing an employee away from the brink of dismissal. It follows, therefore, that if the employee is suffering from an irredeemable incompetence, no amount of warnings will make any difference, and therefore there cannot be a need to issue them (*Sutton and Gates*

[115] [1975] IRLR 145.

Ltd v Boxall[116]). In *Littlewoods Organisation Ltd v Egenti*[117] the EAT pointed out that there is a distinction between disciplinary procedures and capability procedures. The former should be applied strictly, whereas this does not need to be so with regard to the latter. To give a warning in capability cases is not a matter of procedure; it is a matter of substance (*AJ Dunning & Sons (Shopfitters) Ltd v Jacomb*, para 12.84). In other words, the question is, would a warning have done any good? Would it have rendered this dismissal unnecessary? If the answer is yes, then the warning should have been given. If the answer is no, then, since no amount of warnings would make any difference, there is no need to give them. Thus in *Lowndes v Specialist Heavy Engineering Ltd* (see para 10.64) the claimant was dismissed after five serious and costly errors. No written warnings were given, and he was not allowed an opportunity to state his case. The dismissal was held to be fair; it would have made no difference had a different procedure been adopted. Nowadays, however, procedural fairness is essential (see para 12.22).

17.83 Finally, the reasonable employer will consider alternatives before he dismisses the employee. Is there some other work which can be offered within the level of competence of the employee? Would he accept it if it was offered? Would he make a success of it? Clearly, much will depend on the circumstances of the case. In *Bevan Harris Ltd v Gair* (para 12.85), the claimant, who had been employed as a foreman, was dismissed after 11 years' service for poor performance, about which he had been warned on four occasions. The employment tribunal held the dismissal to be unfair, because a reasonable employer would have demoted him rather than resort to dismissal. The decision was reversed by the EAT. The employer had given serious consideration to offering the claimant another job, but had decided against it. The small scale of the business, and the loss of confidence in the employee's abilities, meant that the decision to dismiss fell within the band of reasonableness and, in the circumstances, the dismissal was fair.

Neglectful Incompetence

17.84 Here we must consider the employee who could do the job, but is not achieving his potential. The object of the exercise is to bring him up to the standards which he is capable of reaching, and for this purpose the disciplinary procedure should be invoked, in accordance with the gravity of the matter.

17.85 If an employee is not working as well as he could, then a warning is appropriate; if he is refusing to obey instructions or is being generally uncooperative, then he should be told, firmly and by someone in authority, of the consequences which are likely to ensue. If the tribunal considers that had a clear warning been given a dismissal would not have been necessary (*Winterhalter Gastronom Ltd v Webb*[118]), then it will conclude that a dismissal without such warning having been given will be unfair (*Jones v GEC Elliott Automation Ltd*, para 12.84). An employee with long service is entitled to more consideration, if only because the employers can hardly be heard to say that it took them many years to discover his incompetence, but the fact that the employer has tolerated poor performance in the past is not conclusive, if the employee fails to respond to proper warnings (*Gozdzik v Chlidema Carpet Co*[119]). A newly appointed employee should be given a chance to prove himself, and not be judged on short-term results. Senior staff should have a greater appreciation of what is expected from them, whereas employees not in the managerial range should have greater attention paid to their requirements. If possible, the employer may consider giving the employee further training, should suitable facilities be available, assuming, that is, that the employee would be likely to benefit from such training. If the employee refuses to take

---

[116] [1979] ICR 67, [1978] IRLR 486, EAT.   [117] [1976] ICR 516, [1976] IRLR 334, EAT.
[118] [1973] ICR 245, [1973] IRLR 120, NIRC.   [119] IDS Brief 163.

advantage of this offer, at least the employer has acted in a reasonable manner, and a consequent dismissal may well be fair (*Coward v John Menzies (Holdings) Ltd*[120]).

17.86 If there is a minor act of neglect, a warning is appropriate, to be followed, as necessary, with a further or final warning. A serious act of neglect might lead to an immediate final warning. But there are some acts of neglect which dare not be repeated, and hence dismissal is not inappropriate. In *Taylor v Alidair Ltd*,[121] an airline pilot landed his aeroplane in a manner which caused some concern among the passengers and crew. After a proper investigation, it was decided that he had been negligent, and he was dismissed. This was held to be fair: there are some activities where the degree of skill required is so high, or where the potential consequences of a departure from the highest standards are so serious, that one failure is sufficient to justify dismissal. A warning in such cases is totally inappropriate.

17.87 The law which prevents unfair dismissal must not be used to impede the efficient management of business by compelling employers to retain incompetent employees (*Cook v Thomas Linnell & Sons Ltd*[122]), and once an employer has lost confidence in the employee's ability to do the job, then it is reasonable to dismiss and offer other employment should this be available. The employer is not bound to create a vacancy if none exists; but he should at least consider the possibility, and consider if the employee would make a success of it (*Brush Electrical Machines v Guest*[123]).

17.88 If an employee is dismissed because of his incapability, the correct test to apply is whether the employer honestly and reasonably held the belief that the employee was not competent, and whether there are reasonable grounds for that belief. It is not necessary for the employer to *prove* that the employee was incompetent (*Alidair Ltd v Taylor*[124]). In other words, the test under s 98(4) is a subjective one. The employment tribunal must consider the employer's state of mind as well as his reasons. But it is sufficient if the employer honestly believes on reasonable grounds that the employee is incompetent.

Long-term Sickness

17.89 An employee who is absent from work for a long time because of sickness or ill health is entitled to sympathetic consideration by the employer, but the employer can only be expected to act within sensible limits. The questions to be asked are (a) how long has the employment lasted, (b) how long had it been expected the employment would continue, (c) what is the nature of the job, (d) what was the nature, effect, and length of the illness, (e) what is the need of the employer for the work to be done, and to engage a replacement to do it, (f) are wages continuing to be paid, (g) why had the employer dismissed (or failed to do so), and (h) in all the circumstances, could a reasonable employer have been expected to wait any longer (*Egg Stores (Stamford-Hill) Ltd v Leibovici*, para 17.59, *BS v Dundee City Council*[125])? In other words, the employer is entitled to consider his business needs, as well as the employee's situation. An important question to consider is: 'has the time arrived when the employer can no longer reasonably be expected to keep the absent employee's post open for him?' (*Hart v AR Marshall & Sons (Bulwell) Ltd*, para 17.60). Thus if an employee is away for a long time, the employer should not dismiss as an automatic matter, but consider whether it is necessary to dismiss. The employer should make all necessary enquiries, from the employee and from his doctor, and if possible obtain an opinion from the firm's medical advisers (*East Lindsey District Council v Daubney*[126]).

---

[120] [1977] IRLR 428, EAT.   [121] [1978] ICR 445, [1978] IRLR 82.
[122] [1977] ICR 770, [1977] IRLR 132, EAT.   [123] EAT/382/76.
[124] [1977] ICR 446, [1976] IRLR 420, EAT; aff'd [1978] ICR 445, sub nom *Taylor v Alidair Ltd* [1978] IRLR 82, CA.   [125] [2013] CSIH 91.
[126] [1977] ICR 566, [1977] IRLR 181, EAT.

17.90 In all cases where dismissal on the grounds of ill health is being considered, there is a need for enquiry, consultation, warnings, a search for alternatives, etc, before the decision is taken (*A Links & Co Ltd v Rose*[127]). The purpose of consulting with the employee about his health is to weigh up the situation, balancing the need of the employer to get the work done against the employee's need for time in order to recover his health. Without such consultation, the employer may act precipitously, with unfair consequences. But consultation is not demanded by law; if it is clear that the consultation would not have made any difference to the result, a failure to consult does not make a dismissal unfair (*Taylorplan Catering (Scotland) Ltd v McInally*[128]).

17.91 Earlier cases had stated that an employer should warn an employee that unless he returns to work he will be dismissed, but this view is erroneous, for an employee cannot be warned that he has got to be in good health. However, the employer should make all proper and necessary enquiries from the employee, and not act in a precipitous manner. Perhaps the best way to express the employer's obligation is to say that he should treat the employee with sympathetic consideration, and that he should hold the job open for as long as is possible. In *Coulson v Felixstowe Dock & Rly Co Ltd*[129] the claimant was away from work due to ill health for considerable periods of time. He could no longer perform his duties, and was put on light clerical work. He was told that if he could not return to his old job, he would be dismissed, and was given six months in which to prove his fitness. However, he fell ill again and was dismissed. It was held that the employer had treated the employee with every consideration, but there must come a time when the employer cannot be expected to keep someone on who is not doing his work. The tribunal had to consider fairness to the business as well as to the employee.

17.92 On the other hand, in *Converform (Darwen) Ltd v Bell*,[130] the claimant was a works director who was off work because of a heart attack. He recovered, but the employers refused to permit him to return to work, as they thought there was the risk of another attack. His subsequent dismissal was held to be unfair. A risk of future illness cannot be used as a ground for fair dismissal unless the nature of the employment is such that the risk made it unsafe for the employee to continue in the job.

17.93 A good employer will try to fix a date by which time he must know when the employee expects to be able to give information about the likely date of return to work (*Marder v ITT Distributors Ltd*[131]), but once having explained and discussed the situation with the employee, the employer is entitled to make a decision in the light of the information available (*Spencer v Paragon Wallpapers Ltd*[132]).

17.94 In *Merseyside and North Wales Electricity Board v Taylor*[133] the Divisional Court held that there is no rule of law which requires the employer to create a special job for an employee who is off sick. Nor is there a rule that an employer is obliged to find alternative employment for an employee plagued by ill health. Each case must be judged on its own facts in the light of the employer's circumstances. It may be that the employer has some light work available of the kind which is within the employee's capacity to do, and the employee should be encouraged to take such a post, even at reduced rates of pay, before dismissal is considered.

17.95 In larger firms it may be possible for the company to place a sick employee in some form of holding department, so that he can recommence employment when fit, but there are certain legal problems about such a course which require further consideration. In

---

[127] [1991] IRLR 353, Ct of Sess.   [128] [1980] IRLR 53, EAT.   [129] [1975] IRLR 11.

[130] [1981] IRLR 195, EAT.   [131] [1976] IRLR 105.   [132] [1977] ICR 301, [1976] IRLR 373, EAT.

[133] [1975] ICR 185, [1975] IRLR 60, 10 ITR 52.

Burton v Boneham & Turner Ltd,[134] the management placed an employee in such a holding department after several spells of absence through illness. It was held that such conduct amounted in law to a dismissal, although in the circumstances, it was held to be fair. On the other hand, in *Parker v Westland Helicopters Ltd*[135] a sick employee was transferred from the department concerned with sick employees to a holding department, where she had to wait for a suitable vacancy before being employed again. As this was done with her agreement, on the facts it was held that no dismissal had taken place.

17.96 The legal significance of placing employees in a holding department has yet to be fully explored. In *Marshall v Harland & Wolff Ltd* (para 17.56) the NIRC held that such a transfer meant that the employee ceased to be employed in a legal sense, but the employers merely undertook some obligation to provide work if and when possible. If this is so, then the act of placing in the holding department could well be as the result of a frustrating event, and should not amount to a dismissal (*G F Sharp Ltd v McMillan*, para 15.26). On the other hand, it has been suggested (*O'Reilly v Hotpoint Ltd*[136]) that such transfer suspends the contract of employment. If this view is correct, then continuity will doubtless be preserved for redundancy and other purposes for 26 weeks (ERA, s 212(3)(a)), and presumably there is a legal (as opposed to moral) obligation to find an employee work when he recovers. It is clear that the matter should be subject to a defined policy which can be stated in the works/staff rules, so that the legal situation will be determined by the contractual obligations which can be laid down by the parties in accordance with the objective which they seek.

17.97 If an employee is retired (or dismissed) on ill-health grounds, the employment tribunal should not be concerned with whether or not the illness was caused or contributed to by the employer, but should consider whether the employer acted reasonably in dismissing the employee for that illness. The fact that the employer has caused the incapacity that led to the dismissal does not preclude a finding that the dismissal was fair, but in such circumstances the employer can be expected to go the extra mile in finding alternative employment for the employee, or put up with a longer period of sickness absence than would otherwise be reasonable (*McAdie v Royal Bank of Scotland*[137]).

17.98 Employers cannot be expected to go to unreasonable lengths in seeking to accommodate a sick employee, and what is reasonable is largely a question of fact and degree in each case (*Garricks (Caterers) Ltd v Nolan*[138]). There is no absolute rule that an employer must consult with the employee's general practitioner (and indeed, since this could result in a breach of professional confidence, it may not be a profitable exercise), although it may be desirable to do so if the employee gives his consent (see *Tower Hamlets London Borough v Bull*[139]). In the last analysis, the employer must act within the range of reasonable responses, depending on the circumstances (*Rolls-Royce Ltd v Walpole*[140]).

17.99 It is also the duty of the employee to keep the employer informed of the nature of the illness, and, where possible, the prognosis for a recovery. In *McGivney v Portman Mansions Management Ltd* the employee went off sick for six months, claiming to be suffering with 'stress'. However, he failed to produce any medical evidence of his condition, despite a number of requests from his employer for access to his medical records. He also refused to attend an appointment with an occupational therapist. His subsequent dismissal was held to be fair. He had failed to cooperate with his employer, and the dismissal was within the range of reasonable responses.

---

[134] IDS Supp 15.   [135] IDS Supp 15.   [136] (1969) 5 ITR 68, 113 Sol Jo 979, DC.
[137] [2007] EWCA Civ 806, [2007] IRLR 895.   [138] [1980] IRLR 259, EAT.
[139] [2001] All ER (D) 209 (May), EAT.   [140] [1980] IRLR 343, EAT.

17.100 The Equality Act 2010 (see para 4.1) makes significant changes to the law relating to the dismissal of long-term sick employees, for many sickness/ill-health absences may well come within the definition of a disability within the Act, although sickness, per se, is not a disability, and a person who is dismissed solely on account of sickness is not protected by the prohibition against discrimination on grounds of disability (*Chacon Navas v Eurest Colectividades SA*[141]). Thus dismissals on health-related grounds will be affected by the requirements for employers to make reasonable adjustments to cater for employees who are disabled within the meaning of the Act, and dismissal on the ground of long-term sickness will only be justified if no such adjustments are possible, or if the employee rejects them. A failure to consult a disabled employee about what reasonable adjustments can be made to his working conditions is not, by itself, a failure to make a reasonable adjustment. It is a matter to be taken into account, but it is not conclusive (*Spence v Intype Libra Ltd*[142]).

17.101 An employee who is away from work through illness etc is still within the pool of selection for redundancy, but the usual criteria of consultation etc must be applied (*Hill v General Accident Fire and Life Insurance Co*[143]).

Persistent Absenteeism

17.102 The employee who is persistently away from work (whether because of illness or other reasons) for short periods at a time presents a different problem. This employee can be cautioned about his absences; he can be confronted with his record, told that it must improve, and be given a period of time in which an improvement can be monitored. Indeed, the employer should not ignore the powerful medicinal effect of a final warning, and a failure to give one may mean that the employee is unaware that the situation is causing the employer great concern. The effect of such a warning might be to stimulate the employee into seeking proper medical advice in case there is an underlying cause of the continuous minor ailments, it may deter the employee from taking time off when not truly warranted, and it may even lead the employee to look for other work where such absences could be tolerated (*Smith v Royal Alfred Merchant Seamen's Society*[144]).

17.103 The employer should approach the situation with 'sympathy, understanding and compassion'. Factors to be taken into account include: (a) the nature of the illness, (b) the likelihood of it recurring, (c) the length of the various absences and the spells of good health in between, (d) the need of the employer to have that work done by that employee, (e) the impact of the absences on other employees, (f) the adoption and carrying out of the policy, (g) a personal assessment of the ultimate decision, and (h) the fact that the employee is fully aware that his employment will be terminated unless there is an improvement (*Lynock v Cereal Packaging Ltd*[145]).

17.104 At the same time, the employer can hold out a helping hand; he can enquire from the employee the nature of all these minor ailments, offer such medical help as the firm can provide, provide counselling, etc, in those cases where the employment is itself a major contributing factor to the illness, and so on.

17.105 In practice, it is essential to establish the reason for the absences, as this may well determine the appropriate procedural steps to be taken. For example, the employer may have issued a policy statement on alcohol or drug abuse, which may override standard procedures. In most cases, it will be necessary to interview the employee on his return to work, which will assist in establishing the reasons for the absence, assess the likelihood of recurrence, and determine whether the appropriate 'trigger' has been reached under

---

[141] [2007] All ER (EC) 59, [2007] ICR 1, [2006] IRLR 706.   [142] EAT/0617/06.
[143] [1998] IRLR 641, OH.   [144] HSIB 9.   [145] [1988] ICR 670, [1988] IRLR 510, EAT.

any attendance procedure. If an underlying medical condition is suspected, advice may be given on the need to seek further treatment. Alternative employment may be considered, or flexibility introduced into attendance improvement schemes. In other words, a great deal can be done to resolve the problem, rather than merely consider dismissal as a solution (*Kerrigan v Rover Group Ltd*[146]).

17.106 In *International Sports Ltd v Thomson*[147] the claimant was away from work for about 25% of the time, with a variety of complaints (all of which were covered by medical certificates) including dizzy spells, anxiety and nerves, bronchitis, virus infection, cystitis, arthralgia of the left knee, dyspepsia and flatulence. She was given a series of warnings, including a final warning, and before deciding to dismiss her, the company consulted their medical adviser. He saw no useful purpose in examining her, as none of the previous illnesses could be verified, there was no common link between them, and she was not suffering from any chronic illness. She was then dismissed, and the EAT held that the dismissal was fair. The company had undertaken a fair review of her attendance record, she had been duly warned and given the opportunity to make representations. A further medical investigation would have produced no worthwhile results. There must come a point in time when a reasonable employer is entitled to say, 'Enough is enough'.

17.107 It is normal for many firms to have contractual entitlement to a certain amount of sick leave, some of which may be regarded as 'certified' or covered by fit notes (formerly known as sick notes). Certainly, an employee should keep his employer informed by the proper means, and a failure to do so may mean that the employee contributes to his own dismissal and receives reduced compensation. But fit/sick notes, by themselves, can never be conclusive, for there are serious doubts about their factual validity. Thus, if an employer believes that a sick note is phoney, or may not be accurate, then he is entitled to disregard it (*Hutchinson v Enfield Rolling Mills Ltd*[148]). Otherwise a doctor's medical certificate should be taken at its face value unless there is some evidence to the contrary (*Taylor v Merseyside Electrics 2002 Ltd*[149]). In *Mainwaring v Corus UK Ltd*[150] the claimant had been signed off work by his doctor because of back problems. Following an anonymous tip-off from a colleague that the claimant might be malingering, the employers carried out an investigation, and a video was produced showing him to be walking normally, carrying shopping bags, etc. When shown the video, the doctor agreed that he would not have certified the claimant as being unfit for work had he known the truth. After a proper procedure the claimant was dismissed. It was held that the dismissal was fair. The reaction of the doctor to the video evidence overrode the initial medical certificate.

17.108 In *Wilkes v Fortes (Sussex) Ltd*[151] the EAT placed particular emphasis on a consideration of the size of the firm in determining whether or not it would be fair to dismiss an employee who is off work intermittently for sickness reasons. In a large firm, the disruption caused by such illnesses may be minimal; it is easy to have a float of overmanning to cover for absent employees. But in a small business, such absences may be extremely serious or even disastrous.

17.109 If a person's health is such that continued employment may well constitute a hazard, either to himself or to other employees, or is likely to cause damage to property, then provided the employer undertakes full consultation with the employee, and obtains expert medical opinion, this is capable of being a fair dismissal (*Spalding v Port of London Authority*[152]), and it is not necessary for the employer to wait until an accident occurs before

---

[146] Unreported.   [147] [1980] IRLR 340, EAT.   [148] [1981] IRLR 318, EAT.   [149] EAT/0162/07.
[150] EAT/53/07.   [151] IRRR, EAT.   [152] [1977] HSIB.

taking steps to dismiss (*Parsons v Fisons Ltd*[153]). In *Finch v Betabake (Anglia) Ltd*[154] the claimant was an apprentice motor mechanic. The employers received a report from an ophthalmic surgeon that the boy could not continue to work without undue danger to himself and to others. He was therefore dismissed. It was held that the circumstances in which an apprentice could be dismissed were limited, but in the circumstances, the dismissal was fair.

17.110 If the persistent absenteeism is due to factors other than ill health, then warnings, as appropriate, should be given. It has been suggested that a dismissal because of an unacceptable level of short-term persistent absenteeism should properly be considered under the heading of 'some other substantial reason' rather than capability or conduct (*Post Office v Wilson*[155]).

17.111 The ACAS Advisory Handbook gave some guidance to employers on how to handle persistent short-term absenteeism. It was stated that:

(a) absences should be investigated promptly, and the employee asked for an explanation;

(b) if there is no medical evidence to support frequent self-certified absences, the employee should be asked to consult with a doctor to establish whether medical treatment is advisable, and/or whether the underlying reason for the absence is work-related;

(c) if, following a full and careful investigation, there appears to be no valid reason (medical or otherwise) for the absences, the matter should be dealt with under the appropriate disciplinary procedure;

(d) if the absences are due to domestic problems, the employer should consider whether an improvement in attendance is likely;

(e) the employee should be told what improvement in attendance is expected, and warned of the likely consequences if this does not happen;

(f) if there is no improvement, the employee's age, length of service, and performance should be considered, as well as the availability of alternative work. These factors must be balanced against the effect of past and future absences on the business.

17.112 Finally, an employer would need to consider whether persistent absenteeism is due to a long-term illness of the kind covered by the Equality Act 2010 (see para 4.82), and hence appropriate consideration should be given to the need to make reasonable adjustments, where possible.

Lack of Qualifications

17.113 There have been very few cases concerning a lack of qualifications for the job as a reason for dismissal. In *Blackman v Post Office*[156] a telegraph officer was required to pass an aptitude test, but he failed after a maximum number of attempts. It was held that his dismissal was fair on the ground of lack of qualifications. But there must be a contractual obligation (express or implied) to hold the relevant qualification. In *Litster v M Thom & Sons Ltd*[157] the applicant was employed as a foreman fitter/driver. Government regulations required that special driving licences had to be obtained for drivers of heavy goods vehicles, and the claimant failed the necessary test. Nonetheless he was continued in employment as a fitter. His contract of employment contained no reference to the necessity of having an HGV licence. Following a dispute, he was told that unless he obtained such a licence, he would be dismissed. It was held that since his contract did not require him to hold that particular licence, a dismissal based on his lack of qualifications would be unfair.

---

[153] Unreported.   [154] [1977] IRLR 470.   [155] [2000] IRLR 834, CA.
[156] [1974] ICR 151, [1974] IRLR 46, NIRC.   [157] [1975] IRLR 47.

17.114 However, it may be permissible to go outside the formal requirements of the contract. In *Tayside Regional Council v McIntosh* (see para 3.28), the employers advertised for a vehicle mechanic, an essential requirement being that the successful applicant should have a driving licence. The claimant was appointed to the job, but his contract of employment made no mention of the need to hold a driving licence. He was subsequently disqualified from driving, and as there was no other suitable employment for him, he was dismissed. The EAT held that he had been fairly dismissed. The nature of the job clearly required the holding of a valid driving licence.

17.115 But even though it can be shown that the employee lacks the necessary qualification for the job, the employer must still act reasonably in treating that reason as a sufficient ground for dismissal. Thus in *Sutcliffe & Eaton Ltd v Pinney*[158] the claimant was dismissed from his job as a trainee hearing aid dispenser after he failed to pass the necessary examinations. It was held that the employers should have applied for an extension of his training period so that he could take the examination again. In other words, as always, the reasonable employer will look around for alternatives to dismissal.

Conduct Inside the Employment

17.116 Under this heading we can consider all those acts of the employee which occur during the performance of the contract, and which are alleged to have an adverse effect on that contract. Such acts may be sub-divided in accordance with their gravity, ie acts of a trivial nature (minor misconduct), serious matters (major misconduct), and extremely serious matters (gross misconduct). The importance of such a classification lies in the methods which are required to be adopted to solve the problem in question. For acts of minor misconduct, these can usually be dealt with by a warning (informal, then perhaps formal), but it would be wrong to utilise the full weight of a disciplinary sanction in order to deal with a trivial matter. Thus to give an employee a final warning 'if you come in late again you will be dismissed' is bound to lead to trouble at some later stage, for the sanction is out of all proportion to the offence. Such a person could be dealt with, for example, by a short period of suspension. Further, for some acts a single repetition would suffice to warrant dismissal (eg theft) and hence the warning would spell this out. But other acts may have to be monitored over a period of time (eg lateness, absenteeism), and hence the warning will indicate the period, spell out the improvement required, and state the ultimate sanction. An act of major misconduct could be handled by an immediate final warning, without the need to go through stages in a procedure (ie informal warning, first written warning, etc), for the seriousness of the matter is sufficient to leap over other stages. And an act of gross misconduct, once proven, can lead to instant dismissal without notice, for this amounts to a breach by the employee which in effect repudiates the contract.

17.117 For all acts of misconduct, the employer must show that he gave the matter a prompt and thorough investigation, that he gave the employee an opportunity to state his case, interviewed witnesses and collected evidence so far as it was possible to do so. Allegations of dishonesty involving breach of trust should be investigated with care. In *Stuart v London City Airport*[159] it was unreasonable for the employer not to look into evidence which might have shown that the employee was not dishonest. There are, however, limits to the power of an employer to investigate, and indeed, it may well be improper for him to do so on occasions. This is particularly true when the matter is to the subject of criminal charges or investigation by the police. Thus in *Carr v Alexander Russell Ltd*,[160] the claimant was dismissed when it was learned that the police had found some company

---

[158] [1977] IRLR 349, EAT.   [159] UKEAT/0273/12.
[160] [1979] ICR 469n, [1976] IRLR 220, Ct of Sess.

property in his possession, and that he was to be charged with theft. It was held that the employers had no duty to carry out any detailed form of enquiry, for it would have been improper of them to do so, and a subsequent trial might have been seriously prejudiced. This is dealt with further in Chapter 12.

17.118 There is no absolute prescription that an employee must be given an opportunity to explain his conduct before he is dismissed, though this course is clearly desirable. In *Parker v Clifford Dunn Ltd*[161] the employers received information from the police that the claimant had admitted stealing from the company. He was therefore dismissed in accordance with the works rules. He did not appeal through the procedure, and made no protestation of innocence. His dismissal was held to be fair; it was reasonable for the employers to rely on the police investigations rather than carry out their own. But the mere fact that the police intend to charge an employee with theft is not conclusive, as they may decide not to proceed with the charge, or the evidence may be too weak to secure a conviction, and so on. Some enquiry may therefore be necessary (*Scottish Special Housing Association v Cooke*[162]).

17.119 The acts which can constitute misconduct inside the employment are too numerous to categorise. Fighting, swearing, trading, drunkenness, betting, horseplay, incompetence, theft, neglect, dangerous or obstructive conduct, clocking offences, breach of safety rules, immorality, refusal to obey orders, breach of hygiene rules, insubordination, unauthorised absenteeism, disloyalty, breach of confidence, taking unlawful drugs, sleeping while on duty, computer hacking or seeking unauthorised access to a computer program, telling lies, unsuitable clothing, dishonesty, taking property without authorisation and lateness, have all, in their turn, been the subject of employment tribunal proceedings. To deal with such conduct, the employer must consider the gravity of the offence, its effect on the employment generally, and the previous history of the employee. In other words, the employer, it is submitted, must take into account the offence, and the offender.

17.120 Although misconduct may be grounds for a dismissal, it must not be used as an excuse for dismissal. The onus is on the employer to show what was the real reason for the dismissal. Thus if he uses the misconduct as a way of getting rid of the employee, this can be evidence of unfairness. On the other hand, if the employer welcomes the opportunity of dismissing the employee for reason of misconduct, his enthusiasm does not make the dismissal unfair. It is the true reason for the dismissal, and the manner in which it is carried out, which will determine the fairness or otherwise of the dismissal (*Associated Society of Locomotive Engineers and Firemen v Brady*[163]). Also, gross misconduct does not mean that dismissal will automatically be within the band of reasonable responses, as it depends on the individual circumstances of the case (*Brito-Babapulle v Ealing Hospital NHS Trust*[164]).

17.121 A tribunal should look at the actual reasons the employer had for dismissal, and not the reasons that he could have had. The tribunal should also assess overall fairness of a process which results in dismissal (*Robinson v Combat Stress*[165]).

17.122 It is not the function of the employment tribunal to substitute its views and opinions for those of management, but merely to decide if management has acted reasonably. For example, if an employee has committed an act of theft, it is for management to decide what should be done in the circumstances of the case, and provided a fair procedure is adopted, the eventual decision is that of management(*Trusthouse Forte Hotels Ltd v Murphy*[166]). Nor need the employers prove that an offence has been committed beyond reasonable doubt,

[161] [1979] ICR 463, [1979] IRLR 56, EAT.   [162] [1979] IRLR 264, EAT.
[163] [2006] IRLR 576, EAT.   [164] UKEAT/0358/12; on appeal [2014] EWCA Civ 1626.
[165] UKEAT/0310/14.   [166] [1977] IRLR 186, EAT.

for this would impose on them a higher commitment than would ever be possible to fulfil, and impose a duty which rightfully belongs to a court of trial. The employers must genuinely believe that the employee has been guilty of the misconduct in question, they must have reasonable grounds for that belief, and they must have carried out such investigation into the matter as is reasonable in the circumstances (*British Home Stores v Burchell*, see paras 12.5 and 17.74). In *Laurie v Fairburn*[167] the claimant was dismissed because the employers believed that she was stealing from them. The employment tribunal was not convinced that this was so, and held the dismissal to be unfair. This was reversed on appeal; the question is not whether or not the employee was guilty, or would have been found guilty if tried, but whether it was reasonable for the employers to dismiss her, taking into account all the circumstances and facts known to the employers at the time of the dismissal.

17.123 If an employee makes a confession, this is a fact which the employer is entitled to take into consideration when forming his views, and the rules about the non-admissibility of confessions made involuntarily (the Judge's Rules) have no application in such circumstances (*Morley's of Brixton Ltd v Minott*, see para 12.17).

17.124 Where an employee has pleaded guilty to a criminal offence, or been found guilty by the decision of a court or the verdict of a jury, it is reasonable for an employer to believe that the employee committed the offence. Any other conclusion 'would be ridiculous' (*P v Nottinghamshire County Council*, see para 12.18). This is so even if the employee alleges that he pleaded guilty on the advice of his lawyers, in order to avoid a prison sentence (*British Gas plc v McCarrick*[168]).

17.125 The fact that an employee faces criminal charges subsequently, and is acquitted on those charges, is also irrelevant to the issue of the fairness of the dismissal. In *Da Costa v Optolis*[169] the claimant was dismissed from his job as a book-keeper for not keeping proper accounts, and he subsequently faced criminal charges, though these ended in his favour. It was held that the fact the Crown Court had acquitted him did not preclude a finding by the employment tribunal that the dismissal was fair. The issues involved were different. In the Crown Court, it had to be decided whether he was guilty of the charge beyond reasonable doubt, whereas in the employment tribunal, it had to be shown whether the employer had reasonable grounds for dismissing him.

17.126 It must surely be sound policy for the employer to be consistent in his procedure, flexible in his decisions. Thus an employer may take into account the fact that the employee has had a long record of exemplary conduct (*City of Edinburgh District Council v Stephen*[170]), but the importance of such mitigating factors is a matter for the employer's discretion (*AEI Cables Ltd v McLay*[171]). In *Taylor v Parsons Peebles Ltd*[172] the claimant, who had been employed for 20 years without complaint, was dismissed for fighting. The EAT held the dismissal to be unfair. The company's policy had to be considered in the light of a reasonable employer's reaction to the incident. Given that the applicant had 20 years' good conduct, a reasonable employer would not have applied a rigid sanction of automatic dismissal. In failing to take account of mitigating circumstances, the employers had acted unreasonably. In *Hadjioannou v Coral Casinos Ltd* (see para 12.48) it will be recalled that the EAT stressed the need for flexibility in dealing with industrial misconduct, saying that a tariff approach was not correct.

17.127 An employee who admits that his conduct is unacceptable, and accepts advice and help to avoid any repetition, may be treated differently from an employee who refuses to

---

[167] IDS Brief 109.   [168] [1991] IRLR 305, CA.   [169] [1977] IRLR 178, EAT.
[170] [1977] IRLR 135, EAT.   [171] [1980] IRLR 84, Ct of Sess.   [172] [1981] IRLR 119, EAT.

accept responsibility for his actions, argues with management, or makes unfounded allegations that his colleagues have conspired to make false accusations against him (*Paul v East Surrey District Health Authority*, see para 12.48).

17.128 If the conduct in question amounts to gross misconduct, then this should be acted upon immediately by management, for a delay may lead the employment tribunal to conclude that the conduct was not so wrongful as to warrant the drastic punishment of instant dismissal, although in rare cases it is proper to dismiss summarily a long time after the event (*Refund Rentals Ltd v McDermott*[173]). Normally, it would be reasonable to suspend pending an investigation, but again, this counsel of perfection cannot always be followed (*Conway v Matthew, Wright & Nephew Ltd*, see para 12.68).

17.129 If the conduct falls under the heading of breach of works rules (eg smoking in prohibited areas, fighting, failing to observe safety precautions, etc) then provided the rule is a reasonable one, has been duly promulgated and brought to the attention of the employees, the tribunals will usually uphold management action (*Richards v Bulpitt & Sons Ltd*[174]), particularly if there has been an act of dishonesty (*British Railways Board v Jackson*, para 17.75). But a minor breach should not be treated as an excuse for dismissal, no matter how strongly worded the rule may be (*Ladbroke Racing Ltd v Arnott*, see para 12.47).

17.130 Before dismissing for gross misconduct, the employer should consider any alternative course of action, for it is not inconsistent with a finding of gross misconduct to offer the employee alternative employment in a different capacity (*Hamilton v Argyll and Clyde Health Board*[175]). Each case must be considered on its merits, taking into account the special facts and mitigating circumstances. If, in the past, an employee has not been dismissed for a similar offence, management should enquire into those circumstances. The dangers of a tariff or consistent approach in cases where there is no true comparability should be avoided (*Procter v British Gypsum Ltd*[176]).

17.131 Equally difficult is conduct by the employee which is strictly within his contractual rights, but which is obstructive in nature. In *Pengilly v North Devon Farmers Ltd* (see para 10.61) it was held that a refusal to work overtime, even though not compulsory within the terms of the employee's contract, warranted a dismissal, as the refusal was contrary to the normal practice, and the employee was trying to put improper pressure on the employer. But in *Burns v Ideal Timber Products*[177] it was held that a refusal to work overtime in order to get the employer to improve working conditions did not amount to improper pressure.

17.132 The conduct of the employee must in some way reflect on the employment relationship. In *Thomson v Alloa Motor Co Ltd*,[178] the applicant was employed as a petrol pump attendant. One day she finished work and drove off in her car, but collided with a petrol pump, causing substantial damage. She was summarily dismissed, because of the seriousness of the damage and the fact that her employers would have to sue her for compensation. The dismissal was held to be unfair. The accident had no bearing on her ability to do her work, it was an incident unlikely to be repeated, and her employers were undoubtedly covered by insurance.

17.133 While it may not generally be possible to dismiss an employee who is acting within the terms of the contract, it should be possible to call for a variation of that contract, or to terminate it and offer a new one (see Chapter 3). Provided the proper procedure is adopted, a subsequent dismissal may well be for 'some other substantial reason' (see para 17.144).

---

[173] [1977] IRLR 59, EAT.   [174] [1975] IRLR 134.   [175] [1993] IRLR 99, EAT.
[176] [1964] 3 All ER 731.   [177] [1975] IRLR 19.   [178] [1983] IRLR 403, EAT.

17.134 Other types of conduct which have been held to warrant dismissal include a refusal to wear the appropriate clothing required for the job (*Atkin v Enfield Hospital Management Committee*[179]), wearing provocative badges contrary to instructions and warnings (*Boychuk v Symons Holdings Ltd*[180]), carrying on sexual relations during business hours (*Newman v Alarmco*[181]), passing on information to a former employee of the firm who is working for a competitor (*Smith v Du Pont (UK) Ltd*[182]), breach of works rules (*Palmer v Vauxhall Motors Ltd*, see para 12.57), suspected dishonesty (*Parkers Bakeries Ltd v Palmer*, see para 12.16), breach of safety instructions (*Wilcox v HGS*[183]), fighting (*Parsons & Co Ltd v McLoughlin*[184]), being a drug addict (*Walton v TAC Construction Materials Ltd*[185]), taking drugs contrary to a zero-tolerance drugs policy (*O'Flynn v Airlinks the Airport Coach Co Ltd*[186]), refusal to go on a training course (*Minter v Wellingborough Foundries Ltd*[187]), unauthorised access to a computer (*Denco Ltd v Joinson*[188]), misusing the office computer to access hardcore pornography (*Hillingdon London Borough Council v Thomas*[189]), and so on.

17.135 Every employer is strongly urged to observe the provisions of the ACAS Code of Practice on Disciplinary and Grievance Procedures, and although a breach of the Code will not automatically make a dismissal unfair (*Lewis Shops Group v Wiggins*, see para 12.12), in practice it can be said that the provisions of the Code matter most when the decision to dismiss is at its weakest. Thus it is still possible to dismiss summarily for gross misconduct (*Retarded Children's Aid Society v Day*[190]), but procedural fairness should always be observed, and a failure to follow the Code's recommendations may lead to a finding that the dismissal was unfair, even though the compensation may be reduced because of the employee's contributory conduct.

Conduct Outside the Employment

17.136 The question which arises here is, what has it got to do with the employer what an employee does outside his working hours? The answer will depend on a number of factors, including the nature of the employment, the position held by the employee, the nature of the incident and its effect on the employer, on customers, on fellow employees, and so on. If it can be said that the conduct in question has an adverse effect on the employer's business, then a dismissal may be fair. For example, the conduct may be a conviction by a court of law for a criminal offence unconnected with the employment. In *Richardson v City of Bradford Metropolitan Council*[191] the claimant was a senior meat inspector, who was convicted of theft of money from his local rugby club on several occasions. When his employers were informed, he was suspended, but as there were no other suitable vacancies which could be offered to him, he was dismissed. This was held to be fair. The integrity of a public servant who was in a position of trust was of prime importance. In *Bradshaw v Rugby Portland Cement Co Ltd*[192] the claimant was dismissed following a conviction for incest with his own daughter, for which he was placed on probation by the Crown Court. The dismissal was held to be unfair. The offence had no bearing on his work as a quarryman, the firm's customers would not have objected to his continued employment, and his relationship with his fellow employees had not deteriorated to the extent that they objected to working with him. There must have been strong mitigating circumstances for the court to deal with the matter so leniently, and the tribunal did not see any reason to impose a

---

[179] [1975] IRLR 217, CA.   [180] [1977] IRLR 395, EAT.   [181] [1976] IRLR 45.
[182] [1976] IRLR 107.
[183] [1975] ICR 333, sub nom *Wilcox v Humphreys and Glasgow Ltd* [1975] IRLR 211; aff'd sub nom *Wilcox v HGS* [1976] ICR 306, [1976] IRLR 222, CA.   [184] [1978] IRLR 65, EAT.
[185] [1981] IRLR 357, EAT.   [186] [2002] All ER (D) 05 (Jul), EAT.   [187] [1981] IDS Brief 202.
[188] [1992] 1 All ER 463, [1991] ICR 172, [1991] IRLR 63, EAT.   [189] [2002] All ER (D) 202 (Sep), EAT.
[190] [1978] ICR 437, [1978] IRLR 128, CA.   [191] [1975] IRLR 296.   [192] [1972] IRLR 46.

further punishment. Clearly, different considerations would have applied had the applicant been (say) a schoolmaster. In *Gardiner v Newport County Borough Council* (see para 12.54) the claimant was a lecturer at an art college, in charge of a foundation course on which were pupils who were between the ages of 16–18. He was convicted of gross indecency, and his dismissal by the college was held to be fair. The tribunal held that *Bradshaw*'s case was no authority for saying that a person who receives a moderate punishment from the court is immune from dismissal, for the courts are frequently being reminded in mitigation that whatever punishment they impose is only part of the misfortune which will befall the accused. The employers could not be expected to waive the consequences which the courts had anticipated and possibly allowed for in fixing the penalty. Nor is it relevant that the employer never told the employee of the kind of conduct outside his employment which would warrant dismissal, for an employer cannot possibly specify or anticipate all the possible circumstances which may lead to a dismissal. To hold otherwise would mean that an employee would be safest from dismissal if he committed some act which was more outrageous than anyone ever envisaged.

17.137 If the employee is charged with a criminal offence, then clearly the employer will need to make a decision about whether the employment can continue, in advance of a hearing in the criminal courts. The employee should be interviewed (strictly, this is not part of the disciplinary procedure, because no breach of internal discipline has occurred), and invited to explain the position. If he intends to plead guilty, the employer can then make a decision, depending on the circumstances, nature of employment, position held, etc. If the employer considers that valuable customers would be lost if the employment continued, he should first attempt to ascertain the views of those customers, and not just make bland assumptions. If the employee states that he intends to plead not guilty, then ideally he should be suspended until the outcome of the criminal proceedings. Whether this suspension should be with pay or without pay is a matter of style and agreement, taking into account the length of time it will be before the hearing takes place, the circumstances of the employer's business, the seriousness or otherwise of the offence, and so on. If there is a collective agreement or a disciplinary procedure which provides that suspension on full pay will be appropriate where investigations cannot be completed, then that agreement or procedure must be followed (*Securicor Guarding Ltd v R*[193]).

17.138 Thus an employer is entitled to make a judgment based on the criminal conduct of the employee, as to whether or not the conviction has impaired the employee's ability to do the job and whether there has been a loss of confidence in the employee (*Robson v Brian Mills*[194]). In *Moore v C & A Modes*[195] the claimant was a section leader in a store, where she had been employed for 20 years. It was alleged that she had been caught shoplifting at another store. Her consequent dismissal was held to be fair. No one should be more alert to the damage caused by shoplifters than such an employee, and it was unreal to expect an employer in the retail trade not to dismiss an employee whom he believed to be stealing from another store. In *Mathewson v R B Wilson Dental Laboratory Ltd*,[196] the claimant was arrested during his lunch break for purchasing a small amount of cannabis. His subsequent dismissal was held to be within the range of reasonable responses which a reasonable employer might take.

17.139 'Moonlighting', ie the taking of additional employment outside normal working hours, may be grounds for dismissal if this has an adverse effect on the employer's business. It will be recalled (para 10.98) that in *Hivac Ltd v Park Royal Scientific Instruments Ltd* the

---

[193] [1994] IRLR 633, EAT.   [194] [1977] IRLIB.   [195] [1981] IRLR 71, EAT.
[196] [1988] IRLR 512, EAT.

employees were in breach of their contracts for which they could have been dismissed, although this was prevented at the time by the operation of the Essential Works Order. The court stated that it would be reluctant to impose on the employees a restriction which would hamper their ability to increase their earnings in their spare time, but on the facts they were inflicting great harm on the employer's business. In *Gray v C & P Pembroke Ltd* (see para 10.96) the claimant agreed to not engage in any other business without the written consent of the employer. Contrary to this agreement he took a part-time job with a rival company, and this was held to be a breach of faith for which he could be fairly dismissed. However, in *Nova Plastics Ltd v Froggatt*[197] the claimant was employed as an odd-job man. He was dismissed when it was discovered that he was working for a rival firm. The dismissal was held to be unfair. Having regard to the nature of his work as an odd-job man, he could hardly be contributing very seriously to the competition from the rival firm, and in the circumstances there was no breach of duty towards his own employer merely because he worked for a competitor in his spare time.

17.140 In some circumstances, it may be relevant to consider whether or not the outside activity is compatible with the dignity of the employee holding a particular post; in other circumstances an employer may be entitled to forbid an employee engaging in certain leisure pursuits or additional employment if the result is that the employee is too exhausted to follow his normal occupation. If an employee wishes to stand at a parliamentary or local election, this is of concern to the employer only if the activity spills over into the employment scene. For example, supposing a supervisor, who controls a labour force made up largely of immigrant workers, announces his intention of standing for election as a BNP candidate. It could be argued that the potential disruption likely to be caused to a contented workforce may well justify an employer dismissing the employee concerned, although the possible implications of the religion or belief provisions in the Equality Act 2010 would have to be considered (see para 4.157). In *Pay v Lancashire Probation Service*,[198] the claimant was dismissed from his job as a probation officer when it was discovered that in his spare time he was performing shows at various hedonist and fetish clubs, and also acted as a director of a company which sold bondage and sado-masochistic products. It was held that his dismissal was fair, because his activities were incompatible with his position, and there would be potential damage to the reputation of the employer if those activities became public knowledge. An argument that his rights under the Human Rights Act 1998, Art 8 (right to privacy) and Art 10 (freedom of expression) had been violated was not upheld, because of the justification defences provided by the Convention (see para 1.90).

17.141 The conduct in question must be such as to cause a loss of confidence in the employee. Thus in *Whitlow v Alkanet Construction Ltd*[199] the claimant was asked by the company's executive to do some work on the latter's house. There he met the executive's wife, and they went elsewhere and had sexual intercourse. His dismissal was held to be fair.

Redundancy

17.142 The commonest ground for a dismissal is for reason of redundancy. This will be considered in Chapter 18.

Statutory Restriction

17.143 An employer cannot be expected to continue to employ an employee if such employment would be contrary to the law. For example, if an employee is employed as a driver, and it is a term (express or implied) of his contract that he should hold a valid driving licence, then clearly, if he loses that licence, the employee is barred from pursuing that

---

[197] [1982] IRLR 146, EAT.   [198] [2004] ICR 187, [2004] IRLR 129, EAT.   [199] [1975] IRLR 321.

occupation by statute (Road Traffic Act 1974, s 84). Additionally, the employer may be guilty of an offence if he permits a disqualified driver to drive. But this does not mean that a dismissal will always be fair in such circumstances. The test is, as always, the reasonableness of the employer's action (*Sutcliffe and Eaton Ltd v Pinney*, para 17.115). He must consider the length of the disqualification, the needs of the business, whether the employee can do his job without driving a motor vehicle, whether alternative arrangements can be made, whether the employee could be given some other work to do until his licence is restored, and so on. In *Mathieson v WJ Noble*[200] the claimant was a salesman who was disqualified from driving. He made arrangements to engage a chauffeuse at his own expense to drive him around during the period of disqualification, but his employers decided to dismiss him. It was held that the employers had acted unreasonably in not giving him a chance to see if the new arrangements were satisfactory. This may be contrasted with *Appleyard v FM Smith (Hull) Ltd*,[201] where it was an essential requirement for the mechanics that they should hold valid driving licences so that they could test vehicles which they had repaired. When the claimant lost his licence, the company had given some thought to placing him elsewhere in the business, but this was not practicable in such a small firm, and his dismissal was held to be fair.

Some other Substantial Reason

17.144 It was never intended that these reasons for fair dismissal could constitute an exhaustive catalogue of the circumstances in which the employer would be justified in terminating the services of an employee, and there have been a number of cases where 'some other substantial reason' for the dismissal has been held to be fair. In *Wilson v Underhill House School Ltd*[202] the claimant was a schoolteacher in a school which was in financial difficulties, and which could not pay in full a pay award. All the other teachers agreed to take less, but she refused and was dismissed. Her dismissal was held to be fair for some other substantial reason. In *Farr v Hoveringham Gravels Ltd*[203] the company had a rule that employees must live within reasonable travelling distance of the firm, and they dismissed a manager who had moved to live 44 miles away. A person in his position may have to be called out in an emergency, and this would prove to be difficult in view of the distance involved. Hence the dismissal was fair.

17.145 It has to be recognised that frequently the legitimate interests of the employer in making a change in employment terms are irreconcilable with the equally legitimate interests of the employee. Thus a sound good business reason for a particular reorganisation has to be looked at in that context (*St John of God (Care Services) Ltd v Brooks*[204]).

17.146 Although an employee is not legally obliged to accept a variation in the terms of his contract, a refusal to do so may amount to a substantial reason for dismissal if it is in the commercial interests of the firm that a variation should be made, and it is a reasonable request to make in the circumstances. In *Muggridge and Slade v East Anglia Plastics Ltd*[205] the employers found it necessary to change the working hours, and fairly dismissed two women who refused to accept the change, and in *RS Components v Irwin* (see paras 3.89 and 19.25) the company fairly dismissed a salesman who refused to sign a restrictive covenant. But if an employee refuses to sign a restrictive covenant which is unreasonably wide, this will not be a potentially fair reason for dismissal. Nor is it necessary for the employee to make a counter-proposal; if the employer wants the benefit of a restraint clause, he must make sure that the proposal is a reasonable one (*Forshaw v Archcraft Ltd*[206]). However, a dismissal for refusing new contractual terms may be unfair if there is no immediate need for the variation (*Evans v Elemeta Holdings Ltd*[207]).

---

[200] [1972] IRLR 76.   [201] [1972] IRLR 19.   [202] [1977] IRLR 475, EAT.
[203] [1972] IRLR 104.   [204] [1992] ICR 715, [1992] IRLR 546, EAT.   [205] [1973] IRLR 163.
[206] [2006] ICR 70, [2005] IRLR 600, EAT.   [207] [1982] ICR 323, [1982] IRLR 143, EAT.

17.147 A change in employment terms may well be necessary even though these are to the detriment of the employee, if commercial necessity so dictates, for a contract of employment cannot remain static throughout the whole of its existence. In *Sycamore v H Myer & Co Ltd*[208] the claimant refused to accept a new payment system which would have resulted in his wages being reduced from £130 per week to about £90 per week. The new system was negotiated with the trade union because the old method of payment was clearly defective. All the other employees accepted the change, and it was held that the claimant's dismissal was for some other substantial reason, and fair in the circumstances. The new terms were not ungenerous, and had been negotiated with the trade union concerned.

17.148 A change in working hours does not give rise to a redundancy, but a dismissal due to a refusal to accept such a change consequent on a reorganisation may be for some other substantial reason (*Barnes v Gilmartin Associates*[209]). In *Martland v Co-operative Insurance Ltd*[210] the employer dismissed employees and offered to re-engage them on new contracts with changes to their terms and conditions of employment. It was held that the employees were dismissed for some other substantial reason and were not entitled to a redundancy payment.

17.149 The test in these cases is whether the offer of new terms is within the range of offers which a reasonable employer would make in the circumstances. The task of weighing the advantages to the employer against the disadvantages to the employee is merely one factor to be taken into account (*Richmond Precision Engineering Ltd v Pearce*, see para 3.103). Whether or not other employees have accepted the proposed changes, and whether a trade union has recommended acceptance of the changes, are relevant factors to be taken into account. The imposition of the new terms and conditions does not have to be solely on the ground that the changes are vital for the survival of the business, and other valid reasons may be equally acceptable (*Catamaran Cruisers Ltd v Williams*, see para 3.103).

17.150 If an employee is dismissed because he refuses to carry out an order which is not within his contractual obligations, this may be a factor in deciding whether or not he has been unfairly dismissed, but it is not determinative of the issue. There may be sound organisational reasons for the employer seeking to change working conditions or altering the terms of the contract. If the employee has been given ample warnings of the changes and ample time to discuss his concerns a dismissal for refusing to accept the changes could well be fair (*Farrant v Woodroffe School*, and see *Bateman v Asda Stores Ltd*, para 3.83).

17.151 A difficult situation arises when an employer knows that a disciplinary offence (eg theft) has been committed, but is unable to identify the actual person responsible. Can he then dismiss all the suspects? In *Parr v Whitbread & Co plc*[211] the claimant was a branch manager of an off-licence. There were three other employees working in the shop. It was discovered that the sum of £4,600 was missing, but the circumstances were such that each of the four employees had an equal opportunity of committing the theft. After carrying out a thorough investigation, all four were dismissed. It was found that the dismissal was for some other substantial reason, and fair in the circumstances. The following guidance was offered: (1) the act must be one which would justify dismissal if committed by an individual; (2) the employer must carry out a reasonable and thorough investigation; (3) as a result of the investigation, the employer must reasonably believe that one of the employees committed the act; (4) the employers must have acted reasonably in identifying the group of employees one of whom could have committed the act; and (5) as between the members of that group, the employer could not reasonably have identified the actual perpetrator.

---

[208] [1976] IRLR 84.   [209] EAT/825/97.   [210] EAT/0220/07.
[211] [1990] ICR 427, [1990] IRLR 39, EAT.

17.152 The employer does not have to dismiss all of the group, however, if he can show solid and sensible grounds for differentiating between members of the group. In *Frames Snooker Centre v Boyce*,[212] three managers had access to a safe in the employers' premises. After several burglaries had occurred, the police formed the view that each burglary was an inside job. There was no evidence against any of the managers, but the employer decided to dismiss two of them. He did not dismiss the third, because she was his daughter, and he had faith in her honesty and integrity. An employment tribunal held that the dismissal of the two managers was unfair because of the failure to dismiss all the suspects, but the decision was reversed on appeal. There is no 'all or none' principle in dismissing a group when it is not possible to identify the culprit. Equally, an inconsistency between sanctions given to two employees does not make a dismissal unfair, if there are differences between the two cases (*MBNA Limited v Jones*[213]).

17.153 A breakdown in confidence between an employer and a senior executive, for which the latter was responsible because of an inappropriate style of management, is capable of being some other substantial reason for the dismissal. But if a dismissal is procedurally unfair, it is still open to an employment tribunal to find that there was a 100% chance that a fair procedure would have reached the same result, and compensation may be reduced by that percentage (*Perkin v St George's Healthcare NHS Trust*[214]).

17.154 To dismiss one of two incompatible employees in order to restore harmony among the workforce (*Gorfin v Distressed Gentlefolk's Aid Association*[215]) may be fair provided that steps are taken to investigate the conflict and attempts are made to see whether or not an improvement in the relationship can be effected (*Turner v Vesteric Ltd*[216]). If an appointment is expressed to be of a temporary nature, pending the return to work of an absent employee, this could also constitute grounds which a tribunal may feel justified a dismissal. In particular, the Employment Rights Act 1996, s 106 provides that in two specific instances the dismissal of a temporary employee will be regarded as a substantial reason. These are where a temporary replacement is taken in because there has been a suspension on medical grounds, or a temporary appointment has been made to replace a woman who is absent on the grounds of pregnancy, childbirth, maternity or adoption. In these cases the replacement must be informed in writing of the temporary nature of the appointment, and that he/she may be dismissed when the absent employee returns to work. However, although such dismissal amounts to a substantial reason, it will be without prejudice to the application of the rule that the tribunal must find that the employer has acted reasonably in treating the reason as sufficient ground for dismissal.

17.155 If an employee indicates that he intends to resign his employment, with the result that the employer engages a replacement in anticipation, the employer is entitled to refuse to accept a late notification that the employee has changed his mind, and his dismissal may be fair for some other substantial reason (*Ely v YKK Fasteners Ltd*, see para 17.49).

17.156 An employment tribunal will not accept just any reason advanced by the employer as coming within the definition of another substantial reason. In *Wadley v Eager Electrical Ltd*[217] the claimant was a valued worker who had been employed for 17 years. His wife, who worked at the same firm, was summarily dismissed for theft, and the employers felt that they had lost confidence and trust in the applicant. They also felt that his continued employment would have an adverse effect on customers. His dismissal was held not to be for some other substantial reason. It was unfair to dismiss an employee because some other person in the household was fairly dismissed. But a dismissal because of third party

---

[212] [1992] IRLR 472, EAT.   [213] UKEAT/0120/15.   [214] [2005] IRLR 934.
[215] [1973] IRLR 290.   [216] [1980] ICR 528, [1981] IRLR 23, EAT.   [217] [1986] IRLR 93, EAT.

pressure may amount to some other substantial reason (*Davenport v Taptonholme for the Elderly*[218]). Where a client refuses to have a particular employee working for it, then provided the employer has done everything that he reasonably can to avoid or mitigate the injustice brought about by the stance of the client, but has failed to achieve a satisfactory result, then a subsequent dismissal of the employee will be fair (*Henderson v Connect (South Tyneside) Ltd*[219]).

17.157 It must be remembered that even though a reason is capable of being another substantial reason for the dismissal, the employer must still act reasonably in treating that reason as a sufficient reason for dismissal. To do this, he should have a full investigation of the problem, and explore any alternatives which may be available (*Scott Packing and Warehousing Co v Paterson*[220]). There is no absolute requirement that consultation with the employee should take place, but this is one of the factors to be taken into account in determining if the employer has acted reasonably (*Hollister v National Farmers' Union*, see para 3.103). In *Johnson v Tesco Stores Ltd*[221] the claimant made a false statement on his job application form. He was subsequently employed for 18 months before the falsity came to light, during which time he was perfectly satisfactory. Nonetheless he was dismissed, and this was held to be unfair. In *Debaughn v Star Cinemas (London) Ltd*[222] it was contrary to the company's policy to employ people who had had previous criminal convictions, particularly for violence, and they dismissed a doorman who had been employed satisfactorily for 12 months when it was discovered that he had failed to disclose a previous conviction for assault. This was held to be fair. The distinction between these cases lies in the fact that in the former case, there was no real need to act on the information which had come to light, whereas in the latter case the firm's policy could not admit of exceptions for very sound reasons.

17.158 It is frequently useful for an employer to plead or argue 'some other substantial reason' in addition to another reason advanced, for this enables him to have 'two bites at the cherry'. Thus, to dismiss an employee who has been sent to prison may be regarded as conduct or frustration or some other substantial reason. But whatever the 'label', the employer must always be prepared to show that he had acted reasonably in treating the reason as a sufficient reason for dismissing the employee (*Bouchaala v Trusthouse Forte Hotels Ltd*[223]). However SOSR is not a catch-all reason for employers who cannot find a more conventional reason for a dismissal. The reason has to be 'substantial' and also a fair process must be followed in all circumstances: *Leach v The Office of Communications (OFCOM)*.[224]

C. Dismissal for Asserting a Statutory Right (ERA, s 104)

17.159 It will be unfair to dismiss an employee because:

(a) he has brought proceedings against an employer to enforce a relevant statutory right; or

(b) he has alleged that the employer has infringed a right of his which is a relevant statutory right.

17.160 The relevant statutory rights for the purposes of s 104 are as follows:

(a) all the rights contained in ERA for which the remedy for infringement is to make a complaint or reference to an employment tribunal;

[218] EAT/559/98.   [219] [2010] IRLR 466.   [220] [1978] IRLR 166, EAT.   [221] [1976] IRLR 103.
[222] Unreported.   [223] [1980] ICR 721, [1980] IRLR 382, EAT.   [224] [2012] EWCA Civ 959.

(b) the following rights made under TULR(C)A—the right not to have the deduction of unauthorised or excessive trade union subscriptions or unauthorised payment to the union's political fund, right not to have action taken short of dismissal on the ground of union membership or non-membership, right to have time off work for trade union duties or activities, or to act as a learning representative;

(c) rights conferred by the Working Time Regulations and the Transfer of Undertakings (Protection of Employment) Regulations 2006.

17.161 It will also be unfair to select a person for redundancy on any of the grounds described (s 105(7)).

17.162 The right will apply irrespective of the employee's length of service, because no qualifying period of continuous employment is required.

17.163 It is immaterial whether or not the employee in fact has the right, or whether or not it has been infringed, as long as the employee makes the claim in good faith. Nor need the employee specify the right, as long as it is made reasonably clear to the employer what the right claimed to have been infringed was. Thus, for example, if an employee were to bring a claim before an employment tribunal alleging that he is entitled to a right contained in the Working Time Regulations, and he is dismissed in consequence, the dismissal would be in breach of s 104, irrespective of whether his claim was justified. Thus if an employee genuinely but mistakenly believes that he has the statutory right in question, or genuinely believes that an infringement of his statutory rights has occurred, a consequent dismissal would be unfair (*Philip Hodges & Co v Crush*[225]). The employee cannot be expected to know the precise legal terminology of the right, or the section number of the statutory provision alleged to have been infringed, and it is sufficient if the employee makes it reasonably clear to the employer what right he is relying on (*Jiminez v Nelabrook Ltd*[226]). It would appear that a mere proposal by the employer that a statutory right may be infringed (eg a proposal to reduce wages in circumstances which would amount to an unlawful deduction contrary to ERA, s 13) is not sufficient (*Mennell v Newell & Wright (Transport Contractors) Ltd*,[227] para 17.164).

17.164 But the employee must be able to identify the right alleged to have been infringed by the employer, and if he cannot show that he ever made an allegation that the employer had been in breach of a statutory duty, then the allegation could not be the cause of his dismissal (*Mennell v Newell & Wright (Transport Contractors) Ltd*).

17.165 The interesting thing about this right is that the 'dismissal' referred to in s 104 must inevitably include a constructive dismissal. Hence, if an employee feels that he is being deprived of his statutory rights, he can resign and make a claim accordingly.

D. **Other Dismissals**

17.166 For dismissals on grounds of trade union membership or non-membership, in closed shop situations, lockouts, strikes, and industrial pressure, see Chapter 21. Dismissal on grounds of sex, race, disability, or age are dealt with in Chapter 4, maternity dismissals in Chapter 6, and dismissals in health and safety cases in Chapter 11.

---

[225] EAT/1061/95.   [226] EAT 614/97.
[227] [1996] ICR 607, [1996] IRLR 384, EAT; revsd [1997] ICR 1039, [1997] IRLR 519, CA.

E. **National Security**

17.167 As already noted, there is a special procedure to be adopted by employment tribunals when dealing with complaints made by members of the security service which involve issues of national security.

Written Reasons for Dismissal (ERA, s 92)

17.168 When an employee is dismissed, either with or without notice, or where a limited-term contract terminates without being renewed, he is entitled to receive, on request, and within 14 days, a written statement of the reasons for his dismissal. This statement is admissible in any proceedings before a tribunal or a court. He will not be so entitled unless he has been continuously employed for two years (except for maternity or adoption reasons, see para 17.176).

A. **Adequacy of the Statement**

17.169 The employment tribunal must consider three issues, namely (a) was there a failure to provide written reasons, (b) was the failure unreasonable, and (c) are the particulars of reasons given inadequate or untrue?

17.170 The first issue will be largely a question of fact. The reasons must be contained in a document sent for the purpose of complying with the request. Filling in Form ET3 (respondent's reply to an application to an employment tribunal) is not sufficient compliance (*Rowan v Machinery Installations (South Wales) Ltd*, see para 13.42). Nor is it sufficient compliance to refer to other documents, although the sending of documents which contain those reasons is sufficient compliance with s 92 (*Kent County Council v Gilham*, see para 17.75).

17.171 On the second issue, the test of reasonableness is an objective one, ie the standard of behaviour to be expected from a reasonable employer. Thus in *Daynecourt Insurance Brokers Ltd v Iles*[228] the employers ignored a request for written reasons for dismissal following an instruction from the police not to answer any correspondence or deal with the matter which was the subject of an investigation, and it was held that the failure to comply was reasonable in the circumstances. Equally, if the employer genuinely and reasonably believes that no dismissal had taken place then a failure to provide written reasons would be reasonable (*Broomsgrove v Eagle Alexander Ltd*[229]). The fact that the employee knows of the reason does not render the failure to comply with the request reasonable.

17.172 But s 92 has to be strictly construed. In *Keen v Dymo Ltd*[230] the employers sent the written reasons by second class post, so that these arrived a day outside the 14-day period. This was held to be an unreasonable refusal to supply written reasons.

17.173 Finally, the reason given by the employer must be the true reason for the dismissal, but it does not have to be a reason adequate enough to justify the dismissal. That is a matter for subsequent investigation should the employee pursue his claim for unfair dismissal (*Harvard Securities plc v Younghusband*[231]). To be adequate under s 92, the written statement must be such that anyone reading it can know the essential reasons for the dismissal.

---

[228] [1978] IRLR 335, EAT.   [229] [1981] IRLR 127, EAT.   [230] [1977] IRLR 118.
[231] [1990] IRLR 17, EAT.

No particular technicalities are involved, and no particular form required (*Horsley Smith and Sherry Ltd v Dutton*[232]).

17.174 If the employee does not make a request for written reasons, he cannot complain that the reasons which were given were untrue, and an employment tribunal has no power to make an award under s 92 in the absence of any such request (*Catherine Haigh Harlequin Hair Design v Seed*[233]).

17.175 A complaint may be presented to an employment tribunal that the employer has unreasonably failed to provide a written statement, or that the statement which has been given is inadequate or untrue. If the tribunal finds the complaint well founded, it may make a declaration as to what it finds to be the employer's reasons for the dismissal, and must make an award of two weeks' pay (ERA, s 93). This award is not subject to the statutory maximum of (currently) £538 per week. The complaint can only be considered by an employment tribunal if it is presented together with a claim for unfair dismissal (ERA, s 93(3)).

B. Written Reasons for Dismissal on Grounds of Maternity or Adoption (ERA, s 92(4), (4A))

17.176 A woman is entitled to written reasons for her dismissal if she is dismissed at any time while she is pregnant, or after her childbirth in circumstances in which her ordinary or additional maternity leave period ends by reason of her dismissal. She does not need to have the requisite period of continuous employment, and she must be given the written reasons irrespective of whether or not she makes a request for them. The same rule applies if an employee is dismissed while absent from work during an ordinary or additional adoption leave period.

Interim Relief (ERA, ss 128–132)

17.177 If an employee complains that the reason for his dismissal was because he was exercising his rights under s 100(1)(a)–(b) (health and safety), s 101A(1)(d) (representative of the workforce for the purpose of the Working Time Regulations), s 102(1) (trustee of occupational pension schemes), s 103 (employee representative under TULR(C)A or Transfer of Undertakings Regulations), or s 103A (protected disclosure), he may make an application for interim relief. A similar application may be made under the provisions of TULR(C)A, ss 161–166 (dismissal for trade union membership and activities, etc) and TULR(C)A, Sch A1, para 161 (playing a role in proposing or opposing trade union recognition). The procedure and remedies are similar to those outlined at para 21.122.

Remedies for Unfair Dismissal

A. Reinstatement and Re-engagement Orders (ERA, s 113)

17.178 If an employment tribunal finds that the employee has been unfairly dismissed, it shall explain to him that it has the power to make an order that he be reinstated or re-engaged, and shall ask him if he wishes the tribunal to make such an order. If he expresses such a wish, the tribunal may make the necessary order.

17.179 The requirement for the employment tribunal to explain its powers to award reinstatement or re-engagement is mandatory. However, if there is a failure to do so (and

---

[232] [1977] ICR 594, [1977] IRLR 172, EAT.   [233] [1990] IRLR 175, EAT.

in practice many tribunals do so fail) this will not render any other award made a nullity. The order made without compliance with s 113 will only be set aside if the employee has been prejudiced, or if he has suffered an injustice, in consequence of the failure (*Cowley v Manson Timber Ltd*[234]).

17.180 If the order is for reinstatement, the employer shall treat the employee in all respects as if he had not been dismissed, and the tribunal may specify the amount of arrears in pay which are payable to the employee, and rights and privileges, including seniority and pension rights, which must be restored to him, and the date by which the order must be complied with. If the employee would have benefited from an improvement in his terms and conditions of employment had he not been dismissed, the order shall require him to have those improvements. If the tribunal orders re-engagement, this is an order that the employee be re-engaged by the employer or by his successor, or an associated employer, in employment comparable to that from which he was dismissed, or other suitable employment. The tribunal will specify the terms on which the re-engagement will take place, stating the identity of the employer, the nature of the employment (*Khan v Home Office*[235]), the remuneration, any arrears of pay, any rights or privileges which must be restored to him (including seniority and pension rights), and the date by which the order must be complied with. If in either case the tribunal makes an order in respect of arrears of pay it will take into account (for the purpose of reducing the employer's liability) any sums received by the applicant between the date of dismissal and the date of reinstatement or re-engagement, by way of wages in lieu of notice, *ex gratia* payments, remuneration received from another employer, social security benefits, and any other benefits as the tribunal thinks appropriate.

17.181 It must be stressed that the tribunal has a discretion in making either of these orders. It must first consider whether to make an order for reinstatement, and in doing so, it must take into account three considerations:

(a) whether the claimant wishes to be reinstated (but in *McBride v Scottish Police Authority (Scotland)*[236] a fingerprint officer who was acquitted of perjury in a criminal case was ordered by the tribunal to be reinstated, but it was impliedly accepted that her role would be a non-court going one, as prosecutors would not want to use her. She appealed as she did not want to accept such a restriction on her job. It was found by the Supreme Court that there was no evidence that such a restriction would be in breach of contract, and so the actual reinstatement did not have to be acceptable to both parties);

(b) whether it is practicable for the employer to comply with an order for reinstatement. If there is a loss of mutual trust and confidence between the employer and employee, reinstatement is not practicable (*Central and North West London NHS Foundation Trust v Abimbola*[237]);

(c) where the claimant caused or contributed to some extent to the dismissal, whether it would be just to order his reinstatement.

If the tribunal decides not to make an order, it shall then consider whether to make an order for re-engagement, and if so, on what terms. Again, there are three considerations to take into account:

(a) any wish expressed by the claimant as to the nature of the order;

(b) whether it is practicable for the employer or his successor or an associated employer to comply with the order;

[234] [1994] ICR 252, EAT; aff'd [1995] ICR 367, [1995] IRLR 153, CA.	[235] [2008] EWCA Civ 578.
[236] [2016] UKSC 27.	[237] EAT/0542/08.

(c) where the claimant has caused or contributed to some extent to the dismissal, whether it would be just to order his re-engagement, and if so, on what terms (see *Boots Co plc v Lees-Collier*[238]).

If a re-engagement order is made, it shall, so far as is reasonably practicable, be on terms which are as favourable as an order for reinstatement, unless the tribunal takes into account the contributory fault of the claimant.

17.182 The main restriction on making reinstatement or re-engagement orders appears to be the practicability of doing so. If a permanent replacement has been engaged in place of the dismissed employee, the tribunal shall not take this into account for the purpose of deciding whether it was practicable for the employer to comply with the order unless the employer shows:

(a) that it was not practicable for him to arrange for the dismissed employee's work to be done without engaging a permanent replacement; or

(b) that he engaged the replacement after the lapse of a reasonable time without having heard from the dismissed employee that he wished to be reinstated or re-engaged, and that when the employer engaged the replacement, it was no longer reasonable for him to arrange for the dismissed employee's work to be done except by a permanent replacement.

17.183 It is also submitted that earlier tribunal decisions on the impracticability of making reinstatement or re-engagement recommendations are still valid, for it should be noted that 'practicable' does not mean 'possible'. Thus the orders are unlikely to be made:

(a) if the dismissal was in a redundancy situation, or if reinstatement would result in redundancies (*Cold Drawn Tubes Ltd v Middleton*[239]);

(b) if the claimant is unfit for work (see *Rao v Civil Aviation Authority*[240]); or

(c) if there is some friction or personal animosity either with the employer or with fellow employees (*Coleman v Magnet Joinery Ltd*[241]); or

(d) if the employer is a small firm, with few staff, reinstatement or re-engagement should only be ordered in exceptional circumstances, as there is a close personal relationship between the parties which may make such an order impracticable (*Enessy Co SA v Minoprio*[242]); or

(e) if there is mistrust between the parties (*Nothman v London Borough of Barnet*[243]); or

(f) if the order is likely to be ineffective (*ILEA v Gravett*[244]); or

(g) if there has been a breakdown in trust or confidence between the employer and employee, eg if the dismissal was for alleged misconduct (*Wood Group Heavy Industrial Turbines Ltd v Crossan*[245]). The existence or absence of mutual trust and confidence are relevant factors to be taken into account when determining the question of the practicability of complying with an order for reinstatement or re-engagement (*Central & NW London NHS Trust v Abimbola*[246]). However, a simple assertion that re-engagement was not practicable because there had been a breakdown of trust and confidence between the employee and his managers as a result of the events that

---

[238] [1986] ICR 728, [1986] IRLR 485, EAT.   [239] [1992] ICR 318, [1992] IRLR 160, EAT.

[240] [1992] ICR 503, [1992] IRLR 203, EAT; on appeal [1994] ICR 495, [1994] IRLR 240, CA.

[241] [1974] ICR 25, [1973] IRLR 361; aff'd [1975] ICR 46, [1974] IRLR 343, CA.

[242] [1978] IRLR 489, EAT.

[243] [1978] ICR 336, [1977] IRLR 398, EAT; revsd [1978] 1 All ER 1243, [1978] ICR 336, [1978] IRLR 489, CA; aff'd [1979] 1 All ER 142, [1979] ICR 111, [1979] IRLR 35, HL.   [244] [1988] IRLR 497, EAT.

[245] [1998] IRLR 680, EAT.   [246] See n 235.

gave rise to the dismissal does not, by itself, prevent an order for re-engagement to be made. It may well be that the employee's contact with the managers responsible for his dismissal would be minimal (*Johnson Matthey plc v Watters*[247]); or

(h) if the employee's job has disappeared following a reorganisation (*Thamesdown Borough Council v Turrell*[248]).

17.184 In other words, the practicability of ordering reinstatement or re-engagement must be looked at in a subjective and pragmatic sense, bearing in mind the particular circumstances of the case. The employer is entitled to give a logical and reasonable explanation why there are no vacancies, and to make a commercial judgment about the best interests of the business. An employment tribunal is not entitled to substitute its own views for those of management, provided the decision not to re-engage is in the bracket of reasonableness, for the test is whether it is practicable, not whether it is possible (*Port of London v Payne*[249]). In practice, very few reinstatement or re-engagement orders are made, as very few applicants request this remedy. If an order is made for re-engagement, or reinstatement, and the former employer refuses to comply with it, there is no power to force the employer to do so. (*Mackenzie v University of Cambridge*[250]).

17.185 If an employee is reinstated or re-engaged following an order to that effect from the employment tribunal, his continuity of employment is preserved, and the period between his dismissal and reinstatement or re-engagement counts towards his continuity (Employment Protection (Continuity of Employment) Regulations 1996). This also applies if reinstatement or re-engagement follows a compromise agreement, or action taken by a conciliation officer, or a claim based on a designated dismissal procedure or following an ACAS sponsored arbitration award.

B. **Compensation (ss 117–127A)**

17.186 If the order for reinstatement or re-engagement is made, but its terms are not fully complied with, the tribunal may make an award of compensation of such amount as it thinks fit, having regard to the loss sustained by the claimant in consequence of the employer's failure to comply with those terms.

17.187 If an order is made, but the claimant is not reinstated or re-engaged at all, then the tribunal will make an award of compensation. This will be under three headings:

(a) basic award

(b) compensatory award

(c) additional award.

17.188 If no order for reinstatement or re-engagement is made, the tribunal will make an award which will consist of a:

(a) basic award

(b) compensatory award.

17.189 *Basic award (i).* In two instances this will amount to two weeks' pay, with a maximum of £538 per week in 2020–21 (these figures change in April each year). The two instances are:

(a) Where an employee's contract is renewed, or he is re-engaged under a new contract, he is not regarded as having been dismissed under his old contract (s 138). If the terms and conditions of the new contract (including capacity and place in which

---

[247] EAT/0236/0237/0238/06.   [248] Unreported.
[249] [1993] ICR 30, [1992] IRLR 447, EAT; aff'd [1994] ICR 555, [1994] IRLR 9, CA.
[250] [2019] EWCA Civ 1060.

he is employed) differ from the previous contract, and during the trial period the employer or employee terminates the contract for a reason connected with the difference, the employee will be treated as having been dismissed on the date on which his previous contract ended. If the reason for that dismissal was redundancy, he will be entitled to a minimum basic award of two weeks' pay (s 121(a)).

(b) Where there is an offer to renew the contract, or an offer of re-engagement under a new contract, and the provisions of the contract as to capacity and place of employment and other terms and conditions would not differ from the old contract, or if they do differ, but the offer constitutes an offer of suitable alternative employment, the employee is not entitled to a redundancy payment if he unreasonably refuses that offer (see para 18.28). This also applies if the employee unreasonably terminates the contract during the trial period. Nonetheless, he is entitled to a basic award of two weeks' pay (s 121(b)).

17.190 *Basic award (ii)*. Where a dismissal has been held to be unfair because the employee was selected for dismissal because of trade union membership or activities (TULR(C)A, s 152), or because he was designated to carry out health and safety activities or was a health and safety representative (ERA, s 100(1)(a)–(b)), or because he was a workforce representative under the Working Time Regulations (ERA, s 101A(d)), or was a trustee of an occupational pension scheme (ERA, s 102(1)), or an employee representative for consultation purposes (ERA, s 103), or was selected for redundancy for any of these reasons, the minimum basic award shall be £6,562 (2020–21).

17.191 *Basic award (iii)*. The basic award will depend on the number of years the employee has been employed (with a maximum of 20 years' service to count) and his normal week's pay (capped). There is no lower or upper age limit, and the tapering provision which used to apply to employees over the age of 64 was abolished by the Employment Equality (Age) Regulations 2006. There will be a multiplier of one half of a week's pay for each year's service below the age of 21, one week's pay for each year's service between the ages of 22 and 40, and one and a half week's pay for each year's service over the age of 41.

17.192 The amount of the basic award can be reduced in three circumstances (ERA, s 122).

(a) If the employer has made an offer to reinstate the employee, so that in all respects he would be treated as if he had not been dismissed, and the employee unreasonably refuses that offer, the employment tribunal may reduce the basic award by an amount it thinks to be just and equitable. (Note that if the offer is made with different terms and conditions, an unreasonable refusal will not justify reducing the basic award, although it may be relevant to reduce the compensation award, because the employee has failed to mitigate his loss.)

(b) If the employee's conduct prior to the dismissal (or, where notice was given, before notice of dismissal) was such that it would be just and equitable to reduce (or further reduce) the basic award, the employment tribunal may do so. Normally, the conduct in question would have caused or contributed towards the dismissal, but this is not essential so far as the employment tribunal's powers under this section are concerned. Indeed, conduct which only comes to light after the dismissal (which occurred before the dismissal) may be grounds for reducing the basic award, eg if it is subsequently discovered that the employee had set up a rival business during his employment, or had been stealing from his employer. But misconduct during the notice period is not a ground for reducing the basic award, even though it would not be just and equitable to make that award, although it may be grounds for reducing the compensation award.

It is not permissible to make a reduction of the basic award on grounds of contributory conduct if the reason for the dismissal was redundancy, except in those cases where the dismissal was for an inadmissible reason (trade union membership or activities (TULR(C)A, s 157), designated safety representatives (s 100), occupational pension scheme trustee (s 102), and employee representative (ss 101A and 103)), when the minimum basic award of (currently) £6,562 applies (s 120). In such cases, if the employee caused or contributed to the dismissal, there may be a reduction in the amount by which the minimum basic award exceeds the normal basic award (s 122(3)).

(c) If an employee was dismissed for reason of redundancy, and was given a redundancy payment, the amount paid by the employer or awarded by a tribunal is to be deducted from the basic award. Normally, this would extinguish the basic award altogether. But the fact that a redundancy payment was made will not extinguish the basic award if the real reason for the dismissal was not in fact redundancy (*Boorman v Allmakes Ltd*[251]).

17.193 The entitlement to a basic award is automatic once a dismissal is held to be unfair, and cannot be reduced on the ground that there has been no financial loss to the claimant (*Cadbury Ltd v Doddington*[252]). It is payable even if no compensation award is made (*British United Shoe Machinery Co Ltd v Clarke*[253]). It cannot be reduced on the ground that the claimant has failed to mitigate against his loss, because there is no provision to this effect (*Lock v Connell Estate Agents*[254]). And it cannot be reduced when an *ex gratia* payment or a severance payment is made, unless it is made clear that the payment is in respect of all compensation an employee is entitled to should the employee subsequently bring a claim in an employment tribunal (*Chelsea Football Club and Athletic Co Ltd v Heath*[255]). There is no requirement to make the same reduction in the basic and compensatory awards on the grounds of contributory conduct (*Optikinetics Ltd v Whooley*[256]).

17.194 When assessing a week's pay for the purpose of the basic and compensation awards, the employment tribunal must not disregard the employer's obligation to pay the national minimum wage, and must base the award on what the employee should have received under the National Minimum Wage Act (see Chapter 8), rather than on what he actually received (*Paggetti v Cobb*, see para 14.5).

C. Compensatory Award (ERA, s 123)

17.195 This award will be such amount as the employment tribunal considers just and equitable in all the circumstances, having regard to the loss sustained by the claimant in consequence of the dismissal, in so far as that loss is attributable to action taken by the employer, including any expenses reasonably incurred by him, and the loss of any benefits which he might reasonably have expected to have had (ERA, s 123(1)). Once an employment tribunal finds blameworthy conduct on the part of the employee which brought about his dismissal, it must reduce the compensation award by some proportion, under the just and equitable rule (*Optikinetics Ltd v Whooley*[257]).

17.196 Under the 'just and equitable rule' the employment tribunal has a wide discretion, even so far as awarding nil compensation in appropriate cases (*W Devis & Sons*

---

[251] [1995] ICR 842, [1995] IRLR 553, CA.   [252] [1977] ICR 982, EAT.
[253] [1978] ICR 70, [1977] IRLR 297, EAT.   [254] [1994] ICR 983, [1994] IRLR 444, EAT.
[255] [1981] ICR 323, [1981] IRLR 73, EAT.   [256] [1999] ICR 984, EAT.   [257] [1999] ICR 984.

Ltd v Atkins[258]). For example, in *Courage Take Home Trade Ltd v Keys*,[259] the claimant accepted a sum in settlement of his claim, but then continued with proceedings for unfair dismissal, because, as the settlement did not involve ACAS, it was not binding. The employment tribunal did not think it was just and equitable to make a compensatory award, and declined to do so. If, after the dismissal, it is discovered that the employee had been guilty of conduct before the dismissal which would have merited dismissal, then it may not be just and equitable to award full or any compensation (*W Devis & Sons Ltd v Atkins*, para 20.85), but post-termination conduct should not be taken into account (*Soros v Davison*[260]). If a redundancy dismissal is unfair because of the lack of consultation, the employment tribunal should assess the likelihood of there being a fair dismissal had there been proper consultation, and make an appropriate award on that basis (*Mining Supplies (Longwall) Ltd v Baker*[261]).

17.197 There is no limit on the amount of a week's pay for the purpose of calculating the financial loss, although there is a statutory maximum limit on the compensatory award. This is (currently) £88,519 or 52 weeks' pay, whichever is less (the latter element was introduced in July 2013). This can be exceeded if an additional award is made: see para 17.235. If the reason for the dismissal was because the employee acted as a health and safety representative (ERA, s 100) or because he made a protected disclosure (ERA, s 103A), or if he was selected for redundancy for either of those reasons, there is no limit on the amount of the compensatory award (s 124(1A)). The employment tribunal must assess the compensatory award judicially, and specify how it is made up, but they can, and do, use a 'broad brush' approach (*Norton Tool Co Ltd v Tewson*[262]). Only financial loss may be taken into account, for the object is to compensate the claimant, not to punish the employer for his wrong behaviour. The manner of dismissal cannot be the subject of a compensatory award, unless there is evidence that this has caused financial loss, eg if it affected the claimant's reputation, making him less attractive to future employers. Thus, unlike awards made in discrimination cases, no award can be made for injured feelings. It follows that if the claimant has lost nothing, eg if he has obtained other employment immediately, no award under this head can be made. The assessment of past losses should not be too difficult, but, when assessing future losses, the employment tribunal must inevitably indulge in a form of speculation. The burden of proof is on the employee to show the past and/or future loss, but this should not prove to be an onerous task in practice (*Adda International Ltd v Curcio*[263]).

17.198 Generally speaking, there are five headings to consider.

Immediate Loss of Earnings

17.199 The immediate loss is the loss incurred between the date the employment was terminated and the date when the employment tribunal assesses the loss. In some cases, a considerable time may have elapsed between these two dates, whilst issues of procedure and/or liability are being argued. Nonetheless, if the employment tribunal feels that the claimant has taken reasonable steps to mitigate his loss, the length of time which may have elapsed is irrelevant (*Gilham v Kent County Council (No 3)*[264]). The claimant's loss is assessed by reference to the net pay he would have received, although bonuses, overtime pay, and pay increases can be taken into account, had these been likely (*Mullet v Brush Electrical*

---

[258] [1976] 2 All ER 822, [1976] ICR 196, [1976] IRLR 16; on appeal [1977] AC 931, [1977] 2 All ER 321, [1977] ICR 377, [1976] IRLR 428, CA; aff'd [1977] AC 931, [1977] 3 All ER 40, [1977] ICR 662, [1977] IRLR 314, HL.   [259] [1986] ICR 874, [1986] IRLR 427, EAT.

[260] [1994] ICR 590, [1994] IRLR 264, EAT.   [261] [1988] ICR 676, [1988] IRLR 417, EAT.

[262] [1973] 1 All ER 183, [1972] ICR 501, [1972] IRLR 86, NIRC.

[263] [1976] 3 All ER 620, [1976] ICR 407, [1976] IRLR 425, EAT.

[264] [1986] ICR 52, [1986] IRLR 56, EAT.

Machines Ltd[265]). Tips which form part of normal remuneration (*Palmanor Ltd v Cedron*, see paras 14.4 and 17.26), expenses, to the extent they represent a profit in the hands of the employee (*S & U Stores v Wilkes*, see para 14.4), and the loss of the opportunity to obtain an enhanced redundancy payment (*Lee v IPC Business Press Ltd*[266]) are all part of the loss suffered. The loss of private use of a company car can be valued either by using the annual tables produced by the AA or RAC, or using the Revenue calculations. Free or subsidised accommodation, private medical insurance, subsidised mortgage schemes (*UBAF Bank Ltd v Davis*[267]), and luncheon vouchers are all benefits, the value of which can be calculated.

17.200 If, at the time when the employment tribunal assesses the loss, the employee has obtained fresh employment with the same or lower earnings, those earnings can be offset when assessing the net loss, but compensation does not end merely because an employee has found fresh employment (*Dench v Flynn & Partners*[268]). If, following a dismissal, an employee takes a new job that is temporary, or on probation, and he loses that job within a short time, this can result in further compensation being awarded. Losses do not automatically cease to be attributable to the first employer upon fresh employment being obtained (*Cowen v Rentokil Initial Facility Service (UK) Ltd*[269]).

17.201 A problem may arise if the employee obtains employment which is better paid, because then compensation will be based on his loss during the period of unemployment, but the excess between his old and new salary also falls to be deducted (*Ging v Ellward Lancs Ltd*[270]). However, because this can lead to an unfair result on occasions, the employment tribunal may fall back on the 'just and equitable' principle and ignore this rule, particularly when there has been a long period of time between the dismissal and the date when compensation is assessed (*Fentiman v Fluid Engineering Products Ltd*[271]). The principles to be adopted in these circumstances were set out by the EAT in *Whelan v Richardson* (para 17.205), where it was held that loss of earnings should be calculated from the date of dismissal up to the date when the applicant obtains higher paid permanent employment. Similarly, credit must be given in respect of earnings from self-employment (*Justfern Ltd v D'Ingerthorpe*[272]).

17.202 Income support and/or jobseeker's allowance is not deducted at this stage, but is subject to the recoupment provisions (see para 17.238). Any incapacity benefit received is also deducted from the compensation award (*Chan v London Borough of Hackney*;[273] *Morgans v Alpha Plus Security Ltd*[274]). The fact that a claimant was in receipt of incapacity benefit did not preclude the employment tribunal from awarding compensation for loss of earnings during the same period. Eligibility for incapacity benefit is based on 'deemed' incapacity for work, which does not mean that the claimant is in fact incapable of earning during that period (*Sheffield Forgemasters International Ltd v Fox*[275]). Housing benefit should not be deducted (*Savage v Saxena*[276]). Money received under an early retirement scheme or ill-health retirement scheme is not to be deducted (*Smoker v London Fire and Civil Defence Authority*[277]).

17.203 If an employee is dismissed without notice and without pay in lieu of notice, but nonetheless finds work within what would have been the statutory notice period, he is still entitled to receive compensation for that period, because that is a legal entitlement, not

[265] [1977] ICR 829, EAT.   [266] [1984] ICR 306, EAT.   [267] [1978] IRLR 442, EAT.
[268] [1998] IRLR 653, CA.   [269] EAT/0473/07, [2008] All ER (D) 70 (Apr).   [270] [1991] ICR 222n.
[271] [1991] ICR 570, [1991] IRLR 150, EAT.   [272] [1994] ICR 286, [1994] IRLR 164, EAT.
[273] [1997] ICR 1014, EAT.   [274] [2005] ICR 525, EAT.   [275] [2009] ICR 333, [2009] IRLR 192.
[276] [1998] ICR 357, [1998] IRLR 182, EAT.
[277] [1991] 2 AC 502, [1990] IRLR 271; revsd [1991] IRLR 22, CA; aff'd [1991] 2 AC 502, [1991] 2 All ER 449, [1991] ICR 449, [1991] IRLR 271, HL.

to be deducted from the compensatory award (*TBA Industrial Products Ltd v Locke*[278]). In *FATA Ltd v Addison*[279] it was held that full wages should be paid for what would otherwise have been the notice period, without regard to the principle of mitigation, as this was in accordance with good industrial relations practice. A tribunal cannot make an award greater than the loss suffered by the employee as a consequence of the dismissal so as to result in a bonus payment. Thus if an employee would only be entitled to statutory sick pay during what would have been the notice period, compensation can only be based on sick pay entitlement (*Langley and Carter v Burlo*[280]). But if the employee's notice period would have been particularly long (eg on the premature termination of a fixed-term contract), the additional notice period will not be added to the compensatory award, on the ground that the employee should have mitigated against his loss (*Vaughan v Weighpack Ltd*[281]). If the employee is dismissed without notice but given his proper entitlement in lieu of notice, credit for this sum must be given (*Addison v Babcock FATA Ltd*[282]), although the EAT in Scotland appear to have come to a different conclusion on this point (*Finnie v Top Hat Frozen Foods*[283]).

17.204 *Ex gratia* payments should always be offset, to the extent that these exceed the basic award (*Horizon Holidays Ltd v Grassi*[284]), as should severance payments (*Darr v LRC Products Ltd*[285]). Income tax rebates received by the employee during his period of unemployment should be ignored unless there are substantial sums involved (*MBS Ltd v Calo*[286]).

Future Loss

17.205 The employment tribunal must estimate the likely future loss, inevitably by indulging in speculation. They can take into account all the relevant circumstances, eg the age of the applicant and his general employability, his personal circumstances, his health (*Fougère v Phoenix Motors*[287]), local employment conditions, the scarcity of jobs in a particular trade, industry, the current economic climate (*MacNeilgae v Arthur Roye Ltd*[288]), and so on. They must form a judgment as to how long it will be before the claimant obtains comparable employment (*Courtaulds Northern Spinning Ltd v Moosa*, see para 17.207). There is no objection, in theory, to consider making an award for the rest of the claimant's working life (see *Morganite Electrical Carbon Ltd v Donne*[289]) although the existence of a maximum award of £88,519 or 52 weeks' pay will inevitably come into play at some point. If a claimant has become self-employed, future loss can be estimated to a point when he establishes an income comparable with that he has lost. As a general rule, the more senior the employee, the longer it may take him to obtain fresh employment, but the whole exercise is speculative. Of course, when assessing future loss, the employment tribunal will already have at its disposal much of the information needed on past losses, and will merely be projecting those losses forward for a period of time. Thus if the employee obtained new employment after the date of dismissal at a higher rate of pay, the employment tribunal should calculate the compensatory award from the date of the dismissal up to the date when the new employment commenced, and not up to the date when the tribunal makes the award (*Whelan v Richardson*, para 17.201,

---

[278] [1984] ICR 228, [1984] IRLR 48, EAT.

[279] [1988] QB 280, [1987] 2 All ER 784, [1987] ICR 805, [1987] IRLR 173.

[280] [2006] 2 All ER 1104, [2006] ICR 850, [2006] IRLR 460, EAT; aff'd [2006] EWCA Civ 1778, [2007] 2 All ER 462, [1007] ICR 390, [2007] IRLR 145, CA.   [281] [1974] ICR 261, [1974] IRLR 105, NIRC.

[282] [1987] ICR 45, [1986] IRLR 388, EAT; revsd [1988] QB 280, [1987] 2 All ER 784, [1987] ICR 805, sub nom *Babcock FATA Ltd v Addison* [1987] IRLR 173, CA.   [283] [1985] ICR 433, [1985] IRLR 365, EAT.

[284] [1987] ICR 851, [1987] IRLR 371, EAT.   [285] [1993] IRLR 257, EAT.

[286] [1983] ICR 459, [1983] IRLR 189, EAT.

[287] [1977] 1 All ER 237, [1976] ICR 495, [1976] IRLR 259, EAT.   [288] [1976] IRLR 88.

[289] [1988] ICR 18, [1987] IRLR 363, EAT.

but see *Dench v Flynn & Partners*, para 17.207). In *Wardle v Credit Agricole Corporate and Investment Bank (Calyon)*[290] the Court of Appeal gave guidance as to the correct approach to the duration of loss. It would be rare to award career-long loss. This should be done only in those cases where there was no real prospect of the employee obtaining another job. In most other cases, damages should only be awarded to the time when the employee was likely to obtain an equivalent job, ie where there was a more than 50% chance of obtaining an equivalent salary.

17.206 If the employment tribunal has evidence which would lead to the conclusion that the claimant would have lost his job anyway at some point in time, eg because of the redundancy situation, then that is a factor which should be taken into account when assessing the past and future loss of earnings (*Young's of Gosport Ltd v Kendell*[291]). Equally, a supervening event, eg illness, which arises after the dismissal, and which causes the claimant to be out of work for a long time, is not a loss which is attributable to the action taken by the employer. But if the illness was brought on to some extent by the employer's action, that is a matter which an employment tribunal can take into account, for a certain period of time at least (*Devine v Designer Flowers Wholesale Florist Sundries Ltd*[292]).

17.207 Since the employment tribunal is projecting the claimant's loss into the future, there is authority for the proposition that the employer should receive a discount of around 2–5% for accelerated payment, although there may be a premium of a similar amount in respect of a delayed payment (*Melia v Magna Kansei Ltd*[293]). It has been suggested that this brings into the calculations a complication which should not be introduced (*Les Ambassadeurs Club v Bainda*[294]). Losses which are too remote from the employer's actions should also be excluded. For example, if the claimant obtained permanent employment, that is a fact which will normally break the chain of causation, so that if he has lost that employment at the time when the employment tribunal is assessing compensation, the subsequent period of unemployment is not a future loss which could have been contemplated (*Courtaulds Northern Spinning Ltd v Moosa*, para 17.205). But this rule is not one of universal application, for the ultimate duty of the employment tribunal is to make an award which is just and equitable (see *Dench v Flynn & Partners*, para 17.228). There is also an overlap between the question of remoteness and the claimant's duty to mitigate against his loss, which can usually be resolved by the application of the 'just and equitable' principle (*Simrad Ltd v Scott*[295]).

In *Norton Tools Co Ltd v Tewson*, decided in 1972, it was held that only quantifiable pecuniary loss could be compensated for, and non-economic loss was not recoverable. In *Dunnachie v Kingston upon Hull City Council* (see paras 11.913 and 16.5), the Court of Appeal threw doubt on the correctness of that decision, holding that the provision in the Act which provided for compensation to be 'just and equitable in all the circumstances' could include a sum in respect of injury to feelings, pride, and self-respect. However, on appeal, the decision in the *Dunnachie* case was reversed by the House of Lords, who held that no award for non-economic loss of that nature may be made under the statutory provisions.

Expenses

17.208 The employment tribunal may award to the claimant any expenses reasonably incurred by him in consequence of the unfair dismissal. This could include money spent seeking fresh employment, eg on travelling to interviews, on buying or selling a home in order to

[290] [2011] IRLR 604, [2011] EWCA Civ 545.   [291] [1977] ICR 907, [1977] IRLR 433, EAT.
[292] [1993] IRLR 517, EAT.   [293] [2006] ICR 410, [2005] EWCA Civ 1547, CA.
[294] [1982] IRLR 5, EAT.   [295] [1997] IRLR 147, EAT.

obtain employment in a different area, or on setting up a new business (*Gardiner-Hill v Roland Berger Technics Ltd*[296]). However, legal expenses incurred in the bringing of the employment tribunal proceedings cannot be awarded under this heading, although there is a residue power for the employment tribunal to make an award of costs in appropriate cases (see para 20.109).

Loss of Statutory Rights

17.209 Since it will take some time before a claimant is employed in a new job long enough to obtain the benefit of a number of statutory rights (in particular, he will have to wait for a further year before he is protected against a future unfair dismissal), the employment tribunals will usually award a modest sum of between about £300 to £500 by way of compensation for this loss (*S H Muffett Ltd v Head*[297]). Also, in the case of a claimant who had a long period of service with his former employer, it is possible to make an award in respect of the loss of the right to have a long period of statutory notice (*Arthur Guinness Son & Co (Great Britain) Ltd v Green*[298]).

Loss of Pension Rights

17.210 The loss suffered by a claimant under this heading will sometimes depend on the type of pension scheme, ie final salary scheme or money purchase scheme. The former scheme does not depend on contributions to the fund by the employer and/or employee, whereas the latter schemes are so dependent. So far as the compensatory award is concerned, a claimant may have lost (a) pension rights accruing to him since the dismissal, (b) future pension rights, and (c) the loss of enhancement of accrued pension rights. To assist in resolving and quantifying the loss, reference may be made to the Government's Actuary's Guidelines 'Compensation for loss of pension rights—Employment Tribunals' (see *Greenhoff v Barnsley Metropolitan Borough Council*[299]). If, following a dismissal, an employee chooses to take his pension early, the value of his pension benefits should not be deducted from any compensation award (*Knapton v EEC Card Clothing Ltd*[300]).

17.211 When calculating the compensation awarded in respect of an unfair dismissal it is proper to take into account the fact that in any new employment it is almost impossible nowadays in the private sector to find a job that provides membership of a final salary pension scheme as opposed to a money purchase scheme (*Roberts v Aegon UK Corporate Services Ltd*[301]).

D. Reducing the Compensatory Award (ERA, s 123(4), (6))

The Reduction

17.212 In *British Labour Pump Co Ltd v Byrne*[302] it was held that where there was a procedural irregularity in an otherwise fair dismissal, eg a failure to consult in a redundancy situation, but it was shown that carrying out the proper procedure would have made no difference, then a consequent dismissal was nonetheless fair. This 'it makes no difference rule' was overturned in *Polkey v A E Dayton Services Ltd* (see para 12.14), except in those circumstances where the employer can show that carrying out a proper procedure would have been utterly useless or futile. Thus if an employee is caught literally or metaphorically with his hands in the till, it is perfectly possible for a dismissal to be unfair (eg, because the correct procedure has not been followed) but for nil compensation to be awarded on the ground that the employee contributed totally towards his dismissal (*Kristapaitis v Thistle Seafood Ltd*[303]).

---

[296] [1982] IRLR 498, EAT.   [297] [1987] ICR 1, [1986] IRLR 488, EAT.
[298] [1989] ICR 241, [1989] IRLR 288, EAT.   [299] [2006] ICR 1514.
[300] [2006] ICR 1084, [2006] IRLR 756, EAT.
[301] [2009] EWCA Civ 932, [2010] ICR 596, [2009] IRLR 1042, (2009) 106(31) LSG 18.
[302] [1979] ICR 347, [1979] IRLR 94, EAT.   [303] UKEATS/0033/09.

17.213 However, following from another decision of the House of Lords in *Devis v Atkins*[304] that 'it cannot be just and equitable that a sum should be awarded in compensation where in fact the employee has suffered no injustice by being dismissed', *Polkey* decided that where there has been a failure to follow a fair procedure, the compensation award (but not the basic award) may be reduced, potentially to nil if necessary.

Adjustment of Compensatory Awards (TULR(C)A, s 207A)

17.214 If it appears to the employment tribunal that an employer has unreasonably failed to comply with the ACAS Code on Disciplinary and Grievance Procedures (eg by failing to adopt the appropriate dismissal procedure), the tribunal may, if it considers it is just and equitable to do so, increase any award it makes to the employee by up to 25%.

17.215 Similarly, if the employee has unreasonably failed to comply with the ACAS Code (eg by failing to go through a grievance procedure) the tribunal may, if it considers it is just and equitable to do so, reduce any award it makes in favour of the employee by up to 25%.

17.216 The ACAS Code does not apply to redundancy dismissals or to the non-renewal of fixed-term contracts on their expiry.

17.217 The adjustments for breach of the ACAS Code only apply to cases brought under the 25 jurisdictions listed in Sch 2A of TULR(C)A.

Mitigation of Loss

17.218 A dismissed employee is under a duty to mitigate against his loss so far as possible (*Scottish and Newcastle Breweries plc v Halliday*[305]). This means that he should take reasonable steps to obtain other employment, taking into account his skills, personal circumstances, health, etc (*Fourgère v Phoenix Motor Co Ltd*[306]). Whether a claimant has taken such reasonable steps is a question of fact in each case (*Gardiner-Hill v Roland Berger Technics Ltd*, para 17.230). Thus, if an employer changes his mind about a dismissal, or recognises that it is unfair, and offers reinstatement or re-engagement on suitable terms which the employee unreasonably refuses, this may indicate that he has not taken reasonable steps to mitigate against his loss, and compensation may be reduced accordingly (*Hepworths Ltd v Comerford*[307]). A failure by an employee to invoke an internal appeals machinery is not a failure to mitigate against the loss (*William Muir (Bond 9) Ltd v Lamb*, see para 12.22), for the rules relating to mitigation apply to conduct after the dismissal (*McAndrew v Prestwick Circuits Ltd*[308]).

17.219 If, after being dismissed, the claimant decides to have a complete change of career, which involves retraining, the employment tribunal may find that such action was reasonable, and the loss of income during the training period may be the subject of compensation. A failure to seek alternative employment in such circumstances is not a failure to mitigate against the loss (*Orthet Ltd v Vince-Cain*[309]).

17.220 The burden of proof lies on the employer to show that the claimant has failed to mitigate against his loss (*Fyfe v Scientific Furnishing Ltd*[310]). An employment tribunal is not bound to consider this heading unless it is raised by the employer, along with some supporting evidence. The employment tribunal should identify the steps taken to mitigate the loss, find the date by which such steps would have produced an alternative income, and then reduce the amount of compensation by the amount of income which would have been earned (*Savage v Saxena*, para 17.202, and see *Hardy v Polk (Leeds) Ltd*, para 15.39).

---

[304] [1977] AC 931, [1977] 3 All ER 40, 8 BLR 57, [1977] ICR 662, [1977] IRLR 314.
[305] [1986] ICR 577, [1986] IRLR 291, EAT.　　　[306] [1976] IRLR 259.　　　[307] Unreported.
[308] [1988] IRLR 514, EAT; on appeal sub nom *Prestwick Circuits Ltd v McAndrew* [1990] IRLR 191, Ct of Sess.　　　[309] [2005] ICR 374, EAT.
[310] [1989] ICR 648, [1989] IRLR 331, EAT.

17.221 So far as mitigation is concerned, the following principles were laid down by the Court of Appeal in *Wilding v British Telecommunications plc*:[311]

(a) it is the duty of the employee to act as a reasonable person unaffected by the prospect of compensation from his former employer;

(b) the onus is on the former employer as the wrongdoer to show that the employee has failed in his duty to mitigate his loss by unreasonably refusing an offer of re-employment;

(c) the test of reasonableness is an objective one based on the totality of the evidence;

(d) in applying that test, the circumstances in which the offer was made or refused, the attitude of the former employer, and all the surrounding circumstances, including the employee's state of mind, should be taken into account;

(e) the court or tribunal should not be too stringent in its expectations of the injured party.

This was followed by the EAT in *Cooper Contracting Ltd v Lindsey*,[312] which summarised it that it is for the wrongdoer to show that the Claimant acted unreasonably in failing to mitigate. The tribunal emphasised that what has to be proved is that the Claimant acted unreasonably; he does not have to show that what he did was reasonable, and that the tribunal should not apply too demanding a standard to the Claimant; after all, he is the victim of a wrong and should not be put on trial as if the losses were his fault.

Contributory Conduct

17.222 Where an employment tribunal finds that the dismissal was to any extent caused or contributed to by any action of the claimant, it shall reduce the amount of the compensatory award by such proportion as it thinks just and equitable, having regard to that finding (ERA, s 123(6)). In *Nelson v BBC (No 2)*,[313] the Court of Appeal stated that there are three matters which must be taken into account under this heading. First, the action of the employee must be culpable or blameworthy; second, that action must have caused or contributed towards the dismissal; and third, it must be just and equitable to reduce the compensatory award by the specified proportion. For example, in *Scottish Co-operative Wholesale Society Ltd v Lloyd*[314] a dismissal was held to be unfair because no specific warnings had been given to the claimant. But he had failed to reply to complaints which had been made against him, failed to obey certain instructions, and failed to achieve a modest sales target. All these factors were held to be conduct which contributed towards the dismissal and were therefore grounds for reducing the compensatory award. A failure to follow works rules, using company property for private purposes, uncooperative conduct, failure to apologise for wrongful acts (eg swearing at a manager), failure to explain unauthorised absences, a refusal to give an explanation for certain conduct, failing to return to work on time after holidays, and so on, have all been held to be grounds for reducing the compensatory award.

17.223 Since the conduct must in some way be blameworthy or culpable, matters which are beyond the employee's control, eg ill health (*Slaughter v C Brewer & Sons Ltd*[315]), ought not to be taken into account. Similarly, an employee who is incompetent or incapable does not contribute to his dismissal, provided he is trying his best (*Kraft Food Ltd v Fox*), although if an employee is lazy, indolent, or does not make an effort to improve or avoid errors, he does so contribute. Further, the conduct in question does not have to be the main

---

[311] [2001] All ER (D) 03 (Apr), EAT; aff'd [2002] EWCA Civ 349, [2002] ICR 1079, [2002] IRLR 524.
[312] UKEAT/0184/15.   [313] [1980] ICR 110, [1979] IRLR 346, CA.
[314] [1973] ICR 137, [1973] IRLR 93, NIRC.   [315] [1990] ICR 730, [1990] IRLR 426, EAT.

reason for the dismissal; it is sufficient (for the purpose of reducing the compensatory award) for it to have played a material part in the dismissal (*Robert Whiting Designs Ltd v Lamb*[316]). A senior employee who is dismissed for serious misconduct must expect to have his compensatory award reduced substantially, for a higher standard of conduct is expected from him (*McPhail v Gibson*[317]).

17.224 It is unlikely that the employment tribunal would reduce the compensatory award in cases of constructive dismissal, but there is no reason in principle why this cannot be done, because the employee's conduct may have played a material part in the events which led to his resignation (*Morrison v Amalgamated Transport and General Workers' Union*[318]). For example, in *Polentarutti v Autokraft Ltd*,[319] the employee machined a number of defective hubcaps. Subsequently, the employer refused to pay him for working overtime, and he resigned, claiming constructive dismissal. Although his dismissal was held to be unfair, the employment tribunal reduced the compensatory award by two-thirds on the ground that his poor workmanship contributed to the dismissal. The EAT dismissed an appeal by the employee, holding that there was a sufficient link between the events in question which justified a reduction in the award. An employee who has been constructively dismissed must give credit for sums earned from other employment during what would otherwise have been the notice period. The Court of Appeal has held that the *Norton Tool* principle does not extend to cases of constructive dismissal (*Stuart Peters Ltd v Bell*[320]).

17.225 If a claimant was dismissed on the ground of his non-membership of a trade union, no reduction can be made in the compensatory award because he refused to join a trade union (see *Transport and General Workers' Union v Howard*[321]). Nor can a reduction be made if the dismissal was because of his trade union membership or activities (TULR(C) A, s 155). If an employee is dismissed because he took part in a strike, and it is subsequently held that that dismissal was unfair on ground of selective re-engagement (see para 21.101), a reduction for contributory conduct should not be made merely because he took part in the strike. It is only where there was some individual blameworthy conduct additional to or separate from the participation in industrial action that the employment tribunal should consider reducing the compensatory award (*Crosville Wales Ltd v Tracey*[322]).

17.226 Contributory conduct has resulted in some cases in a reduction as high as 80–90%, and for some time there was doubt as to whether it was a proper reduction to make, because there appears to be a logical inconsistency in saying that an employee was treated unfairly and yet contributed to that extent towards his dismissal. However, in *Maris v Rotherham Corpn*[323] the House of Lords thought that there was no particular problem in finding a dismissal unfair, yet reducing the compensatory award by 100%. Compensation should only be awarded when it is just and equitable to do so, and it cannot be just to award compensation when the employee was totally responsible for his dismissal. Nor is there an inconsistency in finding a dismissal unfair yet not awarding compensation.

17.227 The assessment of the percentage reduction to be taken into account because of contributory conduct is essentially a question of fact, to be determined by the employment tribunal (*Hollier v Plysu Ltd*[324]).

---

[316] [1978] ICR 89, EAT.   [317] [1977] ICR 42, [1976] IRLR 254, EAT.   [318] [1989] IRLR 361, NICA.
[319] [1991] ICR 757, [1991] IRLR 457, EAT.   [320] [2009] EWCA Civ 938.
[321] [1992] ICR 106, [1992] IRLR 170, EAT.
[322] [1993] IRLR 60, EAT; revsd sub nom *Tracey v Crosville Wales Ltd* [1996] ICR 237, sub nom *Crosville Wales Ltd v Tracey (No 2)* [1996] IRLR 91, CA; aff'd sub nom *Tracey v Crosville Wales Ltd* [1998] AC 167, [1997] 4 All ER 449, [1997] ICR 862, sub nom *Crosville Wales Ltd v Tracey (No 2)* [1997] IRLR 691, HL.
[323] [1974] 2 All ER 776, [1974] ICR 435, [1974] IRLR 147, NIRC.   [324] [1983] IRLR 260, CA.

Remoteness of Loss

17.228 The tribunal must compensate the employee for the loss caused by the employer's wrongful conduct. That loss does not cease when the employee finds new alternative employment, because it is quite possible for the loss to continue. Thus, if the new employment is at a lower rate of pay, or is of a temporary nature, or entails additional expense by way of travel, relocation etc, these factors can be taken into account when assessing the compensation. In *Dench v Flynn & Partners* (paras 17.203, 17.208, and 17.210), the claimant was unfairly dismissed. She obtained employment with another firm but this only lasted for two months. The Court of Appeal held that the tribunal was wrong to limit the compensation award up to the time when she had obtained the new employment. The question was whether her losses were attributable to her unfair dismissal.

17.229 If an employee decides not to seek other employment, but to make a career change by going on a training course, a tribunal may take the view that this is a reasonable course to take, having regard to the employee's age, the state of the employment market, the level of remuneration, the viability of the course, etc. However, there may well come a point in time when the loss suffered by the employee is too remote from the employer's wrongful action. Thus in *Simrad Ltd v Scott* (para 17.207) an electronics technician was unfairly dismissed. She decided to change career and took a course in nursing. Although the tribunal thought that she had acted reasonably in taking up a new career, the EAT held that compensation was not payable from the time she commenced the nursing course, because this was too remote to be attributed to the actions of the employer. However, a contrary conclusion appears to have been reached in *Orthet Ltd v Vince-Cain* (see para 17.218).

17.230 In some cases, it may well be reasonable for the employee to become self-employed, and this should not be held against him, when weighed against his employment prospects generally. In *Gardiner-Hill v Roland Berger Technics* (see paras 17.208 and 17.218) a 55-year-old managing director acted reasonably in setting up his own specialised business. Clearly, his initial loss was greater than if he had attempted to obtain immediate employment, but the loss was not too remote, although it could not be expected to go on indefinitely. Expenses reasonably incurred in setting up a new business are not too remote, but again, a sensible limit should be imposed.

E. Order of Adjustments to Compensation Awards

17.231 The tribunal must first ascertain the employee's loss in consequence of the dismissal, insofar as that loss is attributable to the action of the employer. The following adjustments to that amount may be made in the following order, where applicable:

(a) a deduction of any payment made to the employee as compensation for the dismissal (eg a payment in lieu of notice, or an *ex gratia* payment, but not an enhanced redundancy payment) (*Digital Equipment Co Ltd v Clements*[325]);

(b) a deduction of any sum earned by the employee by way of mitigation of the loss, or to reflect the failure by the employee to mitigate against the loss (ERA, s 123(4));

(c) a percentage reduction under the *Polkey* principle, reflecting the fact that the employer would have a fair reason for the dismissal had the relevant contractual disciplinary procedure been followed (*Rao v Civil Aviation Authority*, see para 17.184);

(d) an increase in the compensation because the employer has failed to follow the ACAS Code or a decrease in compensation because the employee has failed to comply with the ACAS Code;

[325] [1996] ICR 829, [1996] IRLR 513, EAT.

(e) an increase because the employer has failed to provide written particulars of employment (Employment Act 2002, s 38);

(f) a percentage reduction because the employee has contributed to the dismissal (ERA, s 123(6));

(g) the deduction of any enhanced redundancy payment to the extent that it exceeds the basic award (ERA, s 123(7));

(h) a deduction under the recoupment provisions.

17.232 After all these adjustments have been made, the statutory cap of (currently) £83,682 is applied.

F. **Additional Award (ERA, s 117)**

17.233 It will be recalled that if an employer totally ignores a tribunal order to reinstate or re-engage the employee, an additional award can be made. This order should not be made if the employer satisfied the tribunal that it was not practicable to comply with the order, but since the tribunal will have already considered this point when making the order (see para 17.178) it will presumably be open to the employer to adduce new evidence as to why it is not practicable to do so. Otherwise, if re-engagement or reinstatement is ordered and not complied with, and the reason for the dismissal was because of race, sex, or disability discrimination, or victimisation for trade union membership, employee representation, pension scheme trustee, breach of working time provisions, or health and safety reasons, there will be an additional award of between 26 and 52 weeks' pay. A week's pay for the purpose of the additional award shall not exceed £538 (2020).

17.234 However, in the case of a highly paid employee, or where proceedings have been considerably delayed, the total of the maximum of the basic, compensatory, and additional awards may not be adequate to meet the loss actually suffered and it may be cheaper not to comply with the reinstatement order. In such cases, ERA, s 124(3) enables an employment tribunal to make a compensation award which is at least equal to the amount of pay lost between the date of dismissal and what should have been the date of reinstatement or re-engagement, to show their disapproval of the employer's decision (see *Selfridges Ltd v Malik*[326]), at the same time taking into account the employee's conduct and failure to mitigate against his loss (*Mabirizi v National Hospital for Nervous Diseases*[327]).

17.235 Severance payments made may be deducted from the additional award to the extent that the basic and compensatory awards are exceeded (*Darr v LRC Products Ltd*, para 17.204).

G. **Interest on Awards**

17.236 By the Employment Tribunals (Interest) Order 1990, interest is payable on all tribunal awards (but not the recoupment element) after 42 days from the date the decision is recorded and sent to the parties. Interest is also payable on awards made by the EAT. Any award by way of costs or expenses is excluded. If on a review or appeal the award is varied, interest accrues on the amount as varied. However, by the Employment Tribunals (Interest on Awards in Discrimination Cases) Regulations 1996, interest on awards made in respect of injury to feelings may be made from the date of the act of discrimination to which the complaint relates.

---

[326] [1998] ICR 268, [1997] IRLR 577, EAT.   [327] [1990] ICR 281, [1990] IRLR 133, EAT.

17.237 The rate of interest is the rate currently prescribed under the Court Funds Rules 1987 and the Act of Sederunt (Interest in Sheriff Court Decrees or Extracts) 1975.

H. Recoupment of Jobseekers' Allowance

17.238 Under the heading of the compensation award, a sum of money is ascertained as the loss suffered, and the tribunal will then deduct from that sum the amount of jobseeker's allowance which the claimant has received. In fact, this amounts to the government providing a subsidy to the employers, and thus regulations have been passed enabling the government to recoup this money from the employer (see Employment Protection (Recoupment of Jobseeker's Allowance and Income Support) Regulations 1996). The consequence is that the tribunal must ascertain the prescribed element (which is the gross loss of earnings from the date of dismissal until the date of the hearing), and this may be withheld from the claimant until the Secretary of State has served a notice on the respondent to pay the whole or part of the prescribed element to the Department. When this has been received, the Secretary of State will pay to the claimant the sum due less the jobseeker's allowance he has received. Recoupment only applies in respect of the period for which compensation is assessed (*Hosnan v Al Baca Ltd*[328]).

17.239 Recoupment does not apply when a settlement is reached without a tribunal hearing, because private settlements (with or without the assistance of the conciliation officer) are not within the scope of the regulations.

Summary

- Unfair dismissal set out in the ERA, and can occur in several ways, eg non renewal of fixed term contract.
- The test for constructive dismissal is whether the employer's conduct amounted to a fundamental breach of contract entitling the employee to resign. The employee must resign as a result of the breach, and act reasonably expeditiously.
- Constructive dismissal can be fair dismissal depending on the facts.
- S98 ERA sets out grounds on which dismissal can be fair.
- Some dismissals, eg for asserting a statutory right, do not require a qualifying period, otherwise it is two years.
- The purpose of a warning is to bring the employee away from the brink of dismissal.
- Some other substantial reason not a catch-all—has to be substantial.
- An employment tribunal must not substitute its own views for those of employer.
- A dismissal can be fair if it was within the employer's range of reasonable responses.
- Written reasons for dismissal can be requested if the employee has two years' continuous employment.
- Remedies for unfair dismissal can be reinstatement, re-engagement or, most likely, compensation.
- Compensation is divided into basic award and compensatory award.

---

[328] Unreported.

18

Redundancy

Background

18.1 The basic purpose of the Redundancy Payments Act 1965 was to compensate a long-serving employee for the loss of a right which he has in a job. There may be other benefits or advantages, such as the need to encourage mobility of labour, redistribute economic skills, and assist in the process of rationalisation of resources, but whether such objects are being achieved must be a matter for the economist rather than the lawyer. The compensation paid is in respect of the loss suffered, and is not intended as a benefit to tide the redundant employee over a period of difficulty. Thus if a person is made redundant, he is entitled to his payment even if he obtains employment elsewhere immediately; similarly, he is entitled to claim jobseekers' allowance in addition to his redundancy money.

18.2 The Act has been repealed and replaced by corresponding provisions in the Employment Rights Act 1996, and in this chapter appropriate references will be made to the latter Act. The provisions relating to collective redundancies are to be found in the Trade Union and Labour Relations (Consolidation) Act 1992 as amended.

Provisions of the Employment Rights Act 1996

A. Persons Covered by the Act

18.3 The Act applies to 'employees', ie persons who have entered into a contract of service or apprenticeship. In order to qualify generally, the employee must have at least two years' continuous employment with that employer or with another employer where continuity is preserved (see ERA s 218, para 13.39).

18.4 The usual problem arises with the definition of the term 'employee', illustrated, perhaps, by *Challinor v Taylor* (see para 2.30), which shows one of the disadvantages of being self-employed. A partner is not an employee for redundancy purposes (*Burgess v O'Brien*[1]), nor is a clergyman working at a Mission (*Parker v Orr*[2]). A managing director or director of a company who has executive responsibilities may be an employee, in accordance with the principles set out by the Court of Appeal in *Secretary of State for the Department of Business, Enterprise and Regulatory Reform v Neufeld* (see para 2.14). Nor does the appointment of a receiver alter the position, for if he was an employee before that appointment, he can still be one following the appointment. A person may pay self-employed national insurance and yet be regarded as an employee, for, as we have already seen, this fact is not conclusive evidence as to the true status. The matter is one to be decided in each case on its own special facts.

---

[1] (1966) 1 KIR 99, 1 ITR 164. [2] (1966) 1 KIR 513.

B. **What is Dismissal? (s 136)**

18.5 A dismissal takes place if:

(a) the employer terminates the contract (with or without notice);

(b) a fixed-term contract expires without being renewed;

(c) the employee is employed under a limited-term contract and the contract terminated automatically on the completion of a particular task or upon the occurrence
or non-occurrence of a specific event, without the employment being renewed
(whether under the same contract or otherwise);

(d) the employee terminates the contract with or without notice in circumstances which
are such that he is entitled to do so by reason of the employer's conduct (*Millbrook
Furnishing Industries Ltd v McIntosh*[3]); and

(e) the employment is terminated by the death, dissolution, or liquidation of the employer, or the appointment of a receiver.

18.6 We saw in Chapter 3 that a variation of a contract may amount to a new agreement.
If the variation is accepted by both sides, then there is no dismissal, and continuity of employment is preserved. But a variation unilaterally imposed by the employer may amount
to a dismissal. In *Marriott v Oxford and District Co-operative Society (No 2)* (see para 3.96),
a foreman was told that he would be employed at a lower status and at a reduced rate of pay.
This was held to be a dismissal. If the employee accepts the changed situation for a short
time under protest there will still be a dismissal, though clearly there will come a point
when he will be deemed to have accepted the change if he continues in employment. If the
express or implied terms of the contract permit a variation, then no dismissal takes place
if the employer exercises his rights thereunder. If the contract of employment contains
a mobility clause, an employer can choose to exercise it rather than make the employee
redundant. As long as the decision is not made arbitrarily or capriciously, an employee cannot insist on being made redundant as an alternative (*Home Office v Evans*[4]). In *McCaffrey v
EE Jeavons & Co Ltd*[5] an express term of the contract stated that the employee should work
anywhere in the United Kingdom. He was asked to move from Bristol to Reading, but he
refused. His subsequent resignation was held not to amount to a dismissal.

18.7 If the employer and employee mutually agree to 'part company' this will not be a dismissal, unless there is a clear intention to this effect. But the fact that a contract specifically
states that it can only be determined by mutual consent or with appropriate notice does not
mean that if appropriate notice has not been given it must have been determined by mutual
consent (*Hellyer Bros v Atkinson*[6]). For example, some employers may call for 'volunteers'
to be made redundant, and they will qualify for redundancy payments despite their willingness to be dismissed (*Burton, Allton and Johnson Ltd v Peck*, see para 17.64), but a mutual
agreement whereby the employee accepts terms for early retirement does not constitute a
dismissal (*Birch and Humber v University of Liverpool*, para 17.64). If an employee is given
the option of being transferred to part-time working or being made redundant, and he
chooses the latter option, there is a dismissal for reason of redundancy, and it is not a consensual termination (*Lassman v De Vere University Arms Hotel*, para 17.64).

18.8 If an employee is told that there may be possible redundancies in the future,
he may be penalised if he acts precipitously. In *Morton Sundour Fabrics Ltd v Shaw*
(para 15.1) a foreman was warned of impending redundancies, and he left the firm to take

---

[3] [1981] IRLR 309, EAT.   [4] [2007] EWCA Civ 1089, [2008] ICR 302, [2008] IRLR 59.
[5] (1967) 2 ITR 636, DC.   [6] [1992] IRLR 540, EAT; revsd [1994] IRLR 88, CA.

other employment. His initiative went unrewarded, for it was held that as he had not been dismissed, he was not entitled to a redundancy payment (see also *International Computers v Kennedy*[7]).

18.9 As long as the employee is on the books of the firm, he is still employed, even though he is not working or not being paid. In *Marshall v Harland & Wolff Ltd* (paras 17.58 and 17.97) the employee was absent from work for 18 months because of illness. The company then decided to close down the works, and gave him four weeks' notice of dismissal. It was held that he was nonetheless entitled to a redundancy payment, for the employers had not discharged the burden of showing that the contract had come to an end by virtue of frustration through illness.

18.10 An employer may dismiss an employee with appropriate notice. If, during the period of that notice, the employee gives a written counter-notice, stating that he intends to leave before the notice expires, the employee is still regarded as having been dismissed. However, the employer is not bound to accept the counter-notice, and may (again in writing) inform the employee before the end of the counter-notice that he does not accept it, and require him to work until the expiry of the original period of notice. The sanction is that the employer may contest the redundancy payment, and the tribunal has power to reduce it either in whole or in part, as it thinks just and equitable. On the other hand, if there is a mutual agreement that the employee may leave early, this constitutes a variation of the employer's notice, not a consensual termination of the contract (see para 17.64). The employee, therefore, will still be regarded as having been dismissed (*McAlwane v Boughton Estates Ltd*, see para 15.10).

C. Dismissal for Reason of Redundancy (s 139)

18.11 For a claim to be made, the employee must be dismissed for reason of redundancy. In *Sanders v Ernest A Neale Ltd*[8] employees went on a work-to-rule campaign in protest against management actions. The employers sacked them, and eventually the factory closed down. It was held that they were not entitled to redundancy payments. They were dismissed because they would not give an undertaking to work normally, and the dismissals caused the redundancy, rather than the redundancy bringing about the dismissals (see *Baxter v Limb Group of Companies*,[9] para 21.103). There is a statutory presumption (s 163(2)) that if an employee is dismissed, it is presumed to have been for the reason of redundancy unless the contrary is proved. The burden of proof is on the employer to show the reason, and if none is forthcoming, or if the tribunal does not accept the reason as a genuine one, the statutory presumption will arise. However, if the employer does show a reason other than redundancy, the question may arise as to whether the dismissal was fair or unfair, but there will be no liability to redundancy payments.

18.12 A dismissal shall be for reason of redundancy if it is wholly or mainly attributable to:

(a) the fact that the employer has ceased, or intends to cease, to carry on that business for the purposes for which the employee was employed; or

(b) the employer has ceased or intends to cease to carry on that business in the place where the employee was employed; or

(c) the fact that the requirements of that business for employees to carry out work of a particular kind, or for them to carry out that work in the place where they were so employed, have ceased or diminished or are expected to cease or diminish.

---

[7] [1981] IRLR 28, EAT.   [8] [1974] 3 All ER 327, [1974] ICR 565, [1974] IRLR 236, NIRC.
[9] [1994] IRLR 572, CA.

Cessation of Business

18.13 This is a recognisable situation which produces a few legal problems. In *Gemmell v Darngavil Brickworks Ltd*[10] the firm closed down temporarily for a period of 13 weeks so that repairs could be carried out, and the dismissed employees were held to be redundant, as a temporary cessation is within the meaning of the Act. If the part of the business where the employee works is closed down, but the rest of the business (in its corporate sense) carries on, there is still a cessation of the business.

The Employer Moving his Place of Business

18.14 Section 139(1)(a)(ii) provides that a dismissal shall be for reason of redundancy if it is due to the fact that the employer has ceased to carry on business in the place where the employee was employed. According to the EAT, this is a factual matter, not a contractual one. In other words, the test to be applied is where, in fact, the employee worked, not where, under his contract, he was required to work. Thus in *Bass Leisure Ltd v Thomas*,[11] the employee worked from the company's depot in Coventry. It was then decided to close the depot and transfer it to a suburb of Birmingham, some 20 miles away. Her contract stated that the employer reserved the right to transfer her to any other alternative place of work in order to meet the needs of the business. After working from the new depot for a short while, she found that it involved too much travelling, and she resigned, claiming a redundancy payment. The EAT held that the place where she was employed was at Coventry, and that her contractual terms were evidential in defining the place of her employment. However, it was not permissible to take into account those terms which permitted a variation of the place of employment. The EAT also held that earlier decisions, which take into account mobility clauses (eg *United Kingdom Atomic Energy Authority v Claydon*, see para 10.58), were not to be followed. This view has been given the approval of the Court of Appeal in *High Table Ltd v Horst*,[12] where it was stated that the true test is a factual one, to be determined by the circumstances, and the mere fact that there was a mobility clause in the contract did not mean that 'the place where the employee was employed' extended to every place where he could be employed. If an employee only worked at one location for the purpose of his employer's business, the place where he was employed cannot be extended simply because there was a mobility clause (a contrary view appears to have been taken in *Home Office v Evans*,[13] see para 18.6). If an employee worked in different places, the contract would be helpful in determining the extent of the place where he was employed. However, the test of the suitability of alternative work (see para 18.28) would still need to be met.

18.15 If the employer moves his place of work, whether the move is sufficient to constitute a redundancy situation will be a question of fact, depending on the distance between the old and the new premises, and the resultant inconvenience caused to the employees affected. In *Managers (Holborn) Ltd v Hohne*,[14] the claimant was the manageress of premises in Holborn. The company decided to move its premises to Regent Street, a short distance away. It was held that it could not be said that there was an implied term in her contract that she would only work in Holborn. Both premises were in Central London, and easily accessible. To hold that the employers had broken the contract would mean that it would have been a breach had the employers moved just around the corner, even though the claimant's work or her travel had been completely unaffected.

---

[10] (1967) 2 ITR 20.   [11] [1994] IRLR 104, EAT.

[12] [1998] ICR 409, [1997] IRLR 513, sub nom *Hosdt v High Table Ltd* [1997] 28 LS Gaz R 25, CA.

[13] [2007] EWCA Civ 1089, [2008] IRLR 59, [2008] ICR 302.   [14] [1977] IRLR 230, EAT.

Surplus Labour

18.16 In this situation the employer requires fewer employees for existing work (*Carry All Motors Ltd v Pennington*[15]), or there is less work for existing employees (*Chapman v Goonvean and Rostowrack China Clay Co*[16]), and consequently some are redundant. The redundancy can arise because the work has been reorganised, thus requiring fewer employees to do the same work, or because of the introduction of labour-saving devices, or a change in the work pattern which requires the same number of employees but a different kind of skill, or one to whom different terms and conditions of employment will apply. But the time of day in which the work is to be performed does not make it 'work of a particular kind' so that if there is a reduction in the need for night workers, who are thus transferred to day working, this does not amount to a redundancy. In *Johnson v Nottinghamshire Combined Police Authority*,[17] clerks were employed from 9.30am to 5.30pm. It was decided to introduce a shift system whereby they would work from 8.00am to 3.00pm and from 1.00pm to 8.00pm in alternate weeks. The clerks refused to do the shift work, and were dismissed. It was held that the change in the hours was to promote greater efficiency, and they were not entitled to redundancy payments (see also *Barnes v Gilmartin Associates*, para 17.148).

18.17 This reasoning was confirmed by the Court of Appeal in *Lesney Products & Co Ltd v Nolan*,[18] where the company reorganised its working hours so that instead of the employees working one long day shift plus overtime, they were required to work two-day shifts. Employees were offered work on the double-day shift, and those who refused were dismissed. It was held that they were not entitled to redundancy payments. A redundancy only arises if there is a change in the terms and conditions of employment due to the fact that the employer's need for work of a particular kind is ceasing or diminishing. A reorganisation of work which results in reduced earning does not produce a redundancy situation if there is still the need for the same number of employees doing the same overall work, and the only change is that they earn less wages. The law should not inhibit the ability of the employer to reorganise the workforce so as to improve efficiency. The fact that overtime is reduced does not create a redundancy if the employer's requirements for the work to be done, and the employees to do the work, are the same as before. But if an employee is on a temporary contract, which is not renewed, this can be a redundancy, even though it is known at the time of his appointment that there would be no work for him at the end of the period. ERA, s 136(1)(b) clearly provides that a failure to renew a fixed-term contract is a dismissal for redundancy purposes, and this would be unnecessary if there was no entitlement to a redundancy payment on the expiry of such a contract (*Lee v Nottinghamshire County Council*[19]).

18.18 In *Hindle v Percival Boats Ltd*[20] the claimant was engaged in repairing wooden boats. The amount of work was declining because of the introduction of fibreglass, and it was uneconomical to retain his services, so he was dismissed because 'he was too good and too slow'. Although he was not replaced (a fact which is sometimes used to determine whether or not a redundancy exists) his work was carried out by other employees working overtime. A majority of the Court of Appeal thought that the employers had rebutted the presumption of redundancy. In another leading case (*North Riding Garages Ltd v Butterwick*[21]) the employee was the manager of a repair workshop. New employers took over the business, and introduced new working methods to which the employee could not

---

[15] [1980] ICR 806, [1980] IRLR 455, EAT.
[16] [1973] 1 All ER 218, [1973] ICR 50, 8 ITR 77, NIRC; aff'd [1973] 2 All ER 1063, [1973] ICR 310, CA.
[17] [1974] 1 All ER 1082, [1974] ICR 170, [1974] IRLR 20, CA.
[18] [1977] ICR 235, [1977] IRLR 77, CA.
[19] [1979] ICR 818, [1979] IRLR 294, EAT; revsd [1980] ICR 635, [1980] IRLR 284, CA.
[20] [1969] 1 All ER 836, CA.   [21] [1967] 2 QB 56, [1967] 1 All ER 644.

adapt. He was dismissed for incompetence and inefficiency, and applied for a redundancy payment. It was held that if the new methods had so altered the nature of the work that there was a lessening of the work of a kind he was formerly employed to do, this would amount to redundancy. On the facts, however, the overall requirements of the firm had not changed. It was the inability of the employee to change and adapt to new methods which brought about his dismissal.

18.19 In considering the definition of redundancy, earlier cases appear to have concentrated on the work which the employee actually did (the function test) and the work which the employee was obliged to do under his contract (the contract test); but in *Safeway Stores plc v Burrell*[22] it was stated that both these approaches were wrong, and that it is the statutory definition which must be considered. The true test requires employment tribunals to consider whether there was a diminution or cessation in the employer's requirement for *employees* to carry out work of a particular kind, and not to focus on the work of the individual employee.

18.20 The issue was finally resolved by the House of Lords in *Murray v Foyle Meats Ltd*[23] where it was held that the key word on which tribunals should concentrate is 'attributable'. Thus if a dismissal of an employee was 'attributable' to a diminution of the employer's need for employees, then it is irrelevant to consider either the contractual obligations or the functions which the employee performed. It can therefore still be a redundancy if the employee is dismissed when his own job remains, but the needs of the business for different kinds of employee reduce. In *Contract Bottling v Cave*[24] a group of staff with different roles were put into a pool, with the lowest scoring staff dismissed. Those who remained were retrained. There was a diminution in the needs of the employer to carry out work of several kinds, and the dismissals were attributable to this state of affairs, and so a 'bumping' or transferred redundancy situation existed.

D. Transferred Redundancy

18.21 If an employee is redundant, but, in accordance with a redundancy procedure, he is retained in another post because he has seniority, and the holder of that other post is consequently dismissed, can the latter claim that he was redundant? Such transferred or 'bumping redundancy' has been considered in a number of cases, the prevalent view being that such a claim is valid and statutorily correct. Thus, in *Elliott Turbomachinery v Bates*,[25] a redundant employee was transferred to the claimant's department, 'bumping' the applicant out of a job. It was held that he was redundant. This line of cases was supported by the EAT in *Safeway Stores Ltd v Burrell*, but another division of the EAT expressed disagreement (*Church v West Lancashire NHS Trust*[26]), where it was stated that a bumped employee was not dismissed for reason of redundancy, but rather because of the application of a procedure which required the dismissal of that employee to complete a reorganisation.

18.22 However, in *Murray v Foyle Meats Ltd* (para 18.20) the House of Lords approved *Safeway Stores Ltd v Burrell*, and thus a transferred redundancy is still a redundancy under the Act.

E. Presumption of Redundancy

18.23 Section 163(2) of ERA provides that if there is a dismissal, it is presumed to be by reason of redundancy, unless the contrary is proved. Thus if two employees are dismissed,

---

[22] [1997] ICR 523, [1997] IRLR 200, 567 IRLB 8, EAT.
[23] [1997] NI 429, NICA; aff'd [2000] 1 AC 51, [1999] 3 All ER 769, [1999] ICR 827, [1999] IRLR 562, HL.
[24] UKEAT/0525/12/DM.   [25] [1981] ICR 218, EAT.   [26] [1998] ICR 423, [1998] IRLR 4, EAT.

although only one is redundant, they are both entitled to rely on the statutory presumption (*Willcox v Hastings*[27]) in the absence of evidence to the contrary.

F. Renewal or Re-engagement (ERA, s 138)

18.24 If the employee's contract of employment is actually renewed, or he is re-engaged under a new contract made before the end of his previous contract, and the renewal or re-engagement takes place immediately on the end of that employment or within four weeks thereof, he will not be regarded as having been dismissed under the old contract. This does not apply if the new contract differs as to capacity, place of employment, or other terms and conditions of employment.

18.25 The employee is entitled to have a trial period of four weeks, or such longer period as may be agreed between the parties for the purpose of retraining the employee under that new contract. In the latter case the new agreement must be made before the employee starts to work under the new contract. It must be in writing, specifying the length of the trial period, and the terms and conditions of employment which will apply after the trial period. If before or during the trial period the employee terminates the contract, or the employer does so for a reason connected with the new contract, the employee shall be treated as being dismissed on the date on which his previous contract ended, and for the reason he was dismissed under that contract (*McKindley v William Hill (Scotland) Ltd*[28]). However, in *Hempell v W H Smith & Sons Ltd*[29] the EAT stated that this did not preclude an enquiry under s 98(4) to ascertain whether the dismissal during the trial period was fair or unfair. In other words, even if the employee accepts the job after a trial period, s 138(3) only provides that he has not been dismissed for reason of redundancy; he may (or may not) have been unfairly dismissed from his old job, and he is entitled to have that issue resolved by an employment tribunal (*Jones v Burdett Coutts School*[30]). If before or during the trial period the employee unreasonably terminates the contract, he shall not be entitled to a redundancy payment by reason of his dismissal from the previous contract.

18.26 The statutory right to a trial period of four weeks applies to employees who are dismissed by the employer, or whose fixed-term contracts have expired, and who have been offered renewal or re-engagement under the provisions of s 138. There is no additional common law trial period running alongside s 138 (*Optical Express Ltd v Williams*[31]).

18.27 Since an employee has a statutory right to a trial period, a refusal to offer him one may lead to a finding that his dismissal was unfair (*Elliot v Richard Stump Ltd*[32]). The statutory trial period of four weeks is four calendar weeks, not four working weeks (*Benton v Sanderson Kayser Ltd*[33]).

G. Offer of Suitable Alternative Employment (s 141)

18.28 If the employer makes an offer (whether in writing or not) to the employee to renew the contract of employment, or to re-engage him under a new contract, which is to take effect on the expiry of the old contract or within four weeks thereafter, then:

(a) if the provisions of that new contract as to capacity, place at which employed, and other terms and conditions of employment would not differ from the corresponding terms of the previous contract; or

[27] [1987] IRLR 298, CA.   [28] [1985] IRLR 492, EAT.   [29] [1986] ICR 365, [1986] IRLR 95, EAT.
[30] [1997] ICR 390, 571 IRLB 9, EAT; revsd [1999] ICR 38, [1998] IRLR 521, CA.
[31] [2007] IRLR 928, [2008] ICR 1, EAT.   [32] [1987] ICR 579, [1987] IRLR 215, EAT.
[33] [1988] ICR 313, [1988] IRLR 235, EAT; revsd [1989] ICR 136, [1989] IRLR 19, CA.

(b) these terms and conditions do differ, but the offer constitutes an offer of suitable employment,

and in either case the employee unreasonably refuses that offer, he will not be entitled to a redundancy payment.

18.29 When making an offer of alternative employment to an employee who is potentially redundant, the employer should provide the employee with as much information as is necessary to enable the employee to make an informed choice. In particular, the employee is entitled to know about the financial prospects in the alternative position (*Fisher v Hoopoe Finance Ltd*[34]). It is a question of fact and degree in each case. In *Sheppard v National Coal Board*[35] a redundant carpenter was offered a similar job which would have involved more travelling, less overtime, and the loss of certain fringe benefits. It was held that the additional travel was not excessive, and the loss of overtime did not, by itself, render the employment less suitable. The loss of the fringe benefits was more important, and it was held that the offer was not of suitable employment.

18.30 The suitability of the offer of alternative work must be assessed objectively, whereas to assess whether or not the employee's refusal is unreasonable (whether in relation to the offer to renew the old contract on the same terms or the offer of suitable alternative employment) it is permissible to take into account subjective considerations (*Cambridge & District Co-operative Society Ltd v Ruse*,[36] *Devon PCT v Readman*[37]). Thus the employee's own personal problems which may arise through taking up the offer are relevant factors. Domestic difficulties, inadequate or inconvenient travel facilities, lack of suitable educational facilities for children, loss of friends, have all been matters which have been held to constitute reasonable grounds for refusal of the offer (*Paton Calvert & Co Ltd v Westerside*[38]). The test is whether this employee made a reasonable decision on the basis of the facts that appeared before him, or ought reasonably to have appeared at the time. There is no room for the test of the range of reasonable responses of a reasonable employee (*Hudson v George Harrison Ltd*,[39] *Devon Primary Care Trust v Readman*[40]). An employee does not act unreasonably in refusing to accept alternative employment if he feels he cannot achieve a satisfactory standard in the new post (*Spencer v Gloucestershire County Council*[41]).

18.31 If an offer of alternative employment made to a redundant employee is only marginally suitable, this could impact on the reasonableness of the refusal to accept that offer. However, if the new job offer was overwhelmingly suitable, it would be easier for the employer to show that a refusal was unreasonable (*Commission for Healthcare Audit and Inspection v Ward*[42]).

18.32 But a personal whim or fad cannot constitute a reasonable refusal. In *Fuller v Stephanie Bowman (Sales) Ltd*[43] the claimant was a secretary working in Mayfair. The employers decided to move the office to Soho. The claimant rejected the offer of employment at the new premises, for these were above a sex shop, and as she was opposed to 'money for sex' activities, she found the move too distasteful. Her application for a redundancy payment failed. The tribunal pointed out that the commercial exploitation of sex was no less in Mayfair than in Soho (except, perhaps, a little more discreet), and if this was the basis of her reasoning, she should move away from London altogether. Her dislike of working near a sex shop was based on a personal fad, and thus it was held that she had unreasonably refused alternative employment.

---

[34] Unreported.   [35] (1966) 1 KIR 101, 1 ITR 177.   [36] [1993] IRLR 156, EAT.
[37] [2013] EWCA Civ 1110.   [38] [1979] IRLR 108, EAT.   [39] [2003] All ER (D) 381 (Mar), EAT.
[40] [2013] EWCA Civ 1110.   [41] [1985] ICR 223, EAT; rev [1985] IRLR 393, CA.
[42] UKEAT/0579/07/JOJ.   [43] [1977] IRLR 87.

H. Laying Off and Short-time Working (s 147)

18.33 An employer may find himself in a difficult economic situation which may be envisaged to be of a temporary nature, and he may decide, instead of dismissing his employees, to lay them off temporarily, or to put them on short-time. A lay-off is where there is no work for the employees and no remuneration provided; short-time working is defined as being where less than half the normal week's pay is earned. If the lay-off or short-time has lasted for more than four consecutive weeks, or more than six weeks in any 13, then the employee may give written notice (not more than four weeks after the lay-off or short-time has finished) that he intends to claim a redundancy payment. He must then give the requisite notice to terminate his contract, and will be entitled to be considered redundant. The employer may agree to meet the claim, or refuse to do so and serve a counter-notice within seven days on the ground that he reasonably expects to be able to provide at least 13 weeks' continuous employment without further resort to lay-offs or short-time working. If the claim or counter-notice is not withdrawn, the matter will be determined by the employment tribunal, which will consider whether or not there is a reasonable prospect of full employment for 13 weeks. If the counter-notice is withdrawn by the employer, or the 13 weeks' continuous employment fails to materialise, the employee is entitled to be paid redundancy money.

18.34 If the employer offers work, but the employee refuses the offer because the rate of pay is too low, the employer has still offered to provide the work, and if, had he accepted the work, the employee would have earned more than half a week's pay, there is no short-time working (*Spinpress Ltd v Turner*[44]).

18.35 But an employer has no inherent right to lay off workers as he chooses. In the absence of an express right to do so in the contract, such unilateral action can be regarded as a repudiation of the contract, and hence a dismissal. Thus (in theory) at least one week's notice should be given of such intended lay-off (*Johnson v Cross*[45]). But if the employer reserves the right to resort to a lay-off in the contract, the employee cannot treat this as a termination.

18.36 If the employer has a contractual right to lay off for an indefinite period (eg in the building industry) the employee's remedy is under s 148, and he cannot claim that the lay-off was for such an unreasonable length of time as to constitute a constructive dismissal (*Kenneth MacRae & Co Ltd v Dawson*[46]).

18.37 It should be noted that the introduction of short-time working, without any contractual authority to do so, could result in a claim being made for unauthorised deductions from wages under ERA, s 13 (*International Packaging Corpn (UK) Ltd v Balfour*, see para 8.19).

I. Time Off to Look for Work (ERA, s 52)

18.38 An employee who is dismissed for reason of redundancy shall be entitled, before the expiration of his notice, to be given reasonable time off during his working hours to look for new employment or to make arrangements for retraining. This right, however, only applies to employees who have been continuously employed for more than two years. The redundant employee is entitled to be paid at his appropriate hourly rate, and if the employer unreasonably refuses to allow him to have the time off, or fails to pay him for it, a complaint may be presented to an employment tribunal within three months. An award of up to two-fifths of a week's pay may then be made.

---

[44] [1986] ICR 433, EAT.   [45] [1977] ICR 872, EAT.   [46] [1984] IRLR 5, EAT.

18.39 It is not a prerequisite for time off that the employee should provide the employer with details of interviews or appointments he has made, as he is entitled to go to look for a job without having made any such arrangements. But if an employer thinks that the request for time off is not bona fide, it may be that he does not unreasonably refuse to permit it. The right to time off work and the right to a redundancy payment are independent of each other, so that an employee can claim time off work under s 52 irrespective of his entitlement to a redundancy payment, for example, if the employee has unreasonably refused alternative employment (*Dutton v Hawker Siddeley Aviation Ltd*[47]). The employee must have been given notice of dismissal by reason of redundancy, and had the requisite two years' continuous employment.

Fair/Unfair Redundancy Dismissals

A. Guidelines for Good Industrial Relations Practice

18.40 Although a redundancy situation may be grounds for dismissal, in respect of which the employee may be able to obtain a redundancy payment (see para 18.65), it does not follow that such a dismissal will automatically be fair, or that the employer acts reasonably in treating that reason as a sufficient ground for dismissal. In *Williams v Compair Maxam Ltd*[48] the EAT laid down five principles for good current industrial relations practice which should be adopted in appropriate circumstances:

(a) the employer will give as much warning as possible of impending redundancies so as to enable trade unions and employees to consider alternative solutions and seek alternative employment;

(b) the employer will consult with the unions as to the best means by which the desired object can be achieved with as little hardship as possible. In particular, the criterion for selection should be agreed, and the actual selection should be made in accordance with that criterion;

(c) the criterion for selection should not depend solely on the opinion of the person making the selection, but should be one which can be objectively checked;

(d) the employer must ensure that the selection is made in accordance with that criterion, and will consider any representations made;

(e) the employer will ascertain whether there is any alternative employment which can be offered.

18.41 However, the principles laid down in *Williams v Compair Maxam Ltd* are guidelines, not rules of law. They refer primarily to the situation found in large companies when a significant number of redundancies are being contemplated. They should be applied with caution in small firms (*Meikle v McPhail*, see para 9.58) or where there is no trade union involved. The principles should not be regarded as a shopping list with a finding of unfairness if one or more points have not been followed (*A Simpson & Son (Motors) v Reid*[49]).

B. Handling Redundancies

18.42 The fact that the employer has a redundancy policy is not, by itself, conclusive of anything. The employer must be prepared to justify that policy, and show, in particular, that

---

[47] [1978] ICR 1057, [1978] IRLR 390.   [48] [1982] ICR 156, [1982] IRLR 83, EAT.
[49] [1983] IRLR 401, EAT.

it is fair and non-discriminatory (*Whiffen v Milham Ford Girls' School*[50]). Whatever method of selection is used for redundancy purposes, it must be fair in general terms and reasonably applied in relation to the employee(s) concerned (*British Aerospace plc v Green*[51]). Bearing this in mind, there are three ways in which redundancies should be handled.

Consideration of Alternatives

18.43 Faced with a redundancy situation, the reasonable employer considers whether it is necessary to act on it, or whether there is some other way of dealing with the problem. For example, it may be possible to restrict recruitment, cut down on overtime, introduce work-sharing, introduce short-time working. In *Allwood v William Hill Ltd*[52] the employers closed down 12 betting shops and declared the managers redundant. No warning was given and no alternative employment within the company was offered. It was held that merely because a redundancy situation existed, it did not follow that the employees had to be made redundant. There was high wastage in the industry, and more effort should have been made to transfer them to other establishments, even on a temporary basis. The employers should also have considered retraining the employees until vacancies arose through wastage or expansion. It may be possible to offer a redundant employee another job which amounts to a demotion, and leave it to him to decide whether or not to accept (*Avonmouth Construction Co Ltd v Shipway*[53]).

18.44 The reasonable employer also takes steps to see if the employee can be absorbed elsewhere in the concern, or with associated companies (*Vokes Ltd v Bear*[54]), but the employer need only take such reasonable steps as are available for this purpose, and though an employment tribunal must scrutinise critically a complaint of unfair redundancy, it should also guard against adopting a standard which is unrealistic, and it should not find a dismissal unfair merely as a means of topping up an inadequate redundancy payment (*British United Shoe Machinery Co Ltd v Clarke*, see para 17.193). If an employer merely states that he decided not to offer a redundant employee alternative work, without advancing any reasons for the decision, he does not discharge the burden of showing that he has acted reasonably (*Thomas and Betts Manufacturing Ltd v Harding*[55]). If the employer has failed to act reasonably in searching a round for alternative employment, the employment tribunal must consider whether in fact any loss has accrued to the employee as a result of that failure, or whether in fact it made no difference. In the latter case, there could be a finding that the dismissal was consequently not unfair, or that even if it was unfair, no loss was suffered by the employee, and therefore he is not entitled to any compensation.

Lack of Consultation

18.45 To dismiss without warning or proper consultations, or without considering the recommendations of the Code of Practice relating to redundancies, may also result in a finding that a dismissal is unfair. But a failure to consult with the unions as provided by TULR(C)A, s 188 (see paras 18.69–18.71) does not by itself mean that a dismissal is unfair (*Forman Construction Ltd v Kelly*[56]). At the same time, consultation with trade unions does not preclude consultation with individuals (*Walls Meat Co Ltd v Selby*[57]). If the employer fails to consult with the affected individuals, he must supply a cogent reason why it was not possible to do so (*Holden v Bradville Ltd*[58]).

---

[50] [2001] EWCA Civ 385, [2001] ICR 1023, [2001] IRLR 468, [2001] All ER (D) 256 (Mar).
[51] [1995] ICR 1006, [1995] IRLR 433, CA.   [52] [1974] IRLR 258.   [53] [1979] IRLR 14, EAT.
[54] [1974] ICR 1, [1973] IRLR 363, NIRC.   [55] [1978] IRLR 213, EAT; aff'd [1980] IRLR 255, CA.
[56] [1977] IRLR 468, EAT.   [57] [1989] ICR 601, CA.   [58] [1985] IRLR 483, EAT.

18.46 The fact that the employer has established a policy not to consult in the event of redundancies being imminent, based on previous experience and the wishes of the work-force in the past, is not, per se, sufficient reason not to consult (*Ferguson v Prestwick Circuits Ltd*[59]), particularly when the criteria for selection are vague and subjective (*Graham v ABF Ltd*[60]). Even a small company is expected to act reasonably. Thus, if redundancy is being proposed, the size of the undertaking may affect the nature or formality of the consultation process, but it does not excuse the lack of consultation (*De Grasse v Stockwell Tools Ltd*[61]).

18.47 In *Mugford v Midland Bank plc*[62] the EAT suggested three propositions for the guidance of employment tribunals: (1) If there is no consultation with trade unions or individuals when redundancies are contemplated, a dismissal will normally be unfair, unless a reasonable employer would have concluded that consultation would be an utterly futile exercise; (2) consultation with a trade union does not of itself release the employer from an obligation to consult with individuals concerned; (3) it will be a question of fact and degree for the employment tribunal to consider whether such consultations as had taken place were so inadequate as to render a dismissal unfair. The lack of consultation by itself does not automatically lead to a finding of unfairness.

18.48 A mere warning that redundancies are being contemplated, coupled with an indication of the selection procedure, does not satisfy the requirements of a fair procedure. Consultation must be fair and genuine. An opportunity must be given to the affected employees to express their views (*Rowell v Hubbard Group Services*[63]). Thus in *Heron v Citilink-Nottingham*[64] the employers found it necessary to make significant economies, and dismissed the claimant without any warning. The EAT held that his dismissal was unfair. For there to be exceptional circumstances which obviate the need for consultation, it had to be shown that it was necessary to dismiss the applicant when they did, and at no later date. It may well be that had he been consulted, he may have been able to make suggestions as to how the situation could be ameliorated. He may have agreed to accept a more junior post, or work for a lower salary. Unless the employer consults the employee in such circumstances, the latter will have no opportunity to put forward any suggestions.

18.49 It had been suggested that a redundancy dismissal without consultation can only be fair if the employer took a deliberate decision not to consult (see *Robertson v Magnet Ltd (Retail Division)*[65]) but this view was rejected by the Court of Appeal in *Duffy v Yeomans and Partners Ltd.*[66] What matters is whether consultation would have been useless, taking into account the circumstances known to the employer at the time.

18.50 If a dismissal is unfair because of a failure to consult, the employment tribunal must consider whether consultation would have made any difference, or whether the employee would have had a chance of being retained in his employment. If the answer is uncertain, then a percentage assessment should be made to reflect the probability that he would have been retained (*Dunlop Ltd v Farrell*[67]), because the claimant must still show that a loss has resulted from the unfairness, and the employment tribunal must not speculate, guess, or indulge in conjecture. The claimant must show a sensible and coherent suggestion as to what was the result of the failure to consult or warn, and what would have happened had there been no such failure. The employer must then refute such suggestions (*Barley v Amey Roadstone Corpn Ltd*[68]). The employment tribunal may then decide that the failure

---

[59] [1992] IRLR 266, EAT.   [60] [1986] IRLR 90, EAT.   [61] [1992] IRLR 269, EAT.
[62] [1997] ICR 399, [1997] IRLR 208, EAT.   [63] [1995] IRLR 195, EAT.
[64] [1993] IRLR 372, EAT.   [65] [1993] IRLR 512, EAT.
[66] [1993] ICR 862, [1993] IRLR 368, EAT; aff'd [1995] ICR 1, [1994] IRLR 642, CA.
[67] [1993] ICR 885, EAT.   [68] [1977] ICR 546, [1977] IRLR 299, EAT.

made little or no difference, and reduce compensation to an amount they deem appropriate, to reflect the additional period of time by which the employee's employment would have been extended had consultations taken place (*Mining Supplies (Longwall) Ltd v Baker*, see para 17.199).

Proper Selection Procedures

18.51 It is the duty of the employment tribunal to examine the employer's procedures for selecting redundancies to ensure that these are fair. Even a selection system which is based on custom and practice in the industry can be challenged if it is unreasonable (*Watling & Co v Richardson*[69]). The tribunal is entitled to know (a) who made the decision to select, (b) what information was taken into account, and (c) upon what criteria the information was assessed (*Bristol Channel Ship Repairers Ltd v O'Keefe*[70]). Otherwise unfair selection for redundancy may also amount to an unfair dismissal. Faced with the decision of choosing which employee(s) shall be made redundant, the employer must engage in a genuine exercise in reaching his choice. The first decision that he should make is who should go in the pool for redundancy. There is no reason why there cannot be a pool of one, as long as choosing to do so is within the range of reasonable responses (*Wrexham GC v Ingham*;[71] *Capita Hartshead Ltd v Byard*[72]).

If there is an established procedure in existence, the employer should follow it; in the absence of such pre-arranged procedure, the general rule in industry for redundancy selection used to be based on the principle of 'last in first out' (LIFO), although this appears to be falling out of favour in recent times, being replaced by a more sophisticated system based on skills, flexibility, etc. Length of service as a criterion for redundancy selection is prima facie discriminatory against younger workers, although there is an exception in respect of service-related benefits where the service to be taken into account is five years or less. However, the use by an employer of a length of service criterion within a selection matrix for redundancy is a proportionate means of achieving a legitimate aim of advancing an employment policy that achieved a peaceable process of redundancy selection agreed with the recognised trade unions. Giving credit for length of service in a redundancy selection policy could be considered to be a benefit under reg 32 of the Employment Equality (Age) Regulations (*Rolls-Royce plc v Unite*[73]).

18.52 If there is no agreed procedure or customary arrangement, the employer may take into account long service, superior abilities, and experience, and the respective hardship caused. In *Selby and Tesse v Plessey Co Ltd*,[74] it was held that a selection based on an effective evaluation system, which was customary in the company, was fair. While having objective criteria is important, it is possible to go too far in the quest for objectivity. In *Mental Health Care (UK) Ltd v Biluan & Anor*,[75] employee capability was assessed entirely on the basis of competency tests, with no account taken of past performance. The employer chose an elaborate and HR-driven method which deprived it of the benefit of input from managers and others who actually knew the staff in question, and which by its very elaborateness could be difficult to apply consistently.

18.53 Adherence to a redundancy agreement made with a trade union is generally sufficient evidence to rebut unfairness (*Taylor v Conveyancer Ltd*[76]), though a failure to consult that union as provided by the agreement may be unfair. However, if the decision has

---

[69] [1978] ICR 1049, [1978] IRLR 255 333.
[70] [1977] 2 All ER 258, [1978] ICR 691, [1977] IRLR 13, EAT.
[71] UKEAT/0190/12/RN.   [72] UKEAT/0445/11/RN.
[73] [2009] EWCA Civ 387, [2010] ICR 1, [2009] IRLR 576.
[74] [1972] IRLR 36.   [75] UKEAT/0248/12/SM.   [76] [1972] IRLR 37.

to be made in a hurry for sound reasons, and consultations with the union or employees would result in serious delay, the employer does not act unfairly in failing to consult (*Guy v Delanair (Car Heater) Ltd*[77]). Selection for redundancy will also be unfair if it is discriminatory on grounds of sex, sexual orientation, race, disability, part-time worker, fixed-term employee, religion or belief, age, etc (see Chapter 4).

18.54 Although the actual selection criteria is for management to determine, it is sound practice to agree this in advance with trade unions. The more vague and subjective the criteria, the greater is the need to consult with affected employees (*Graham v ABF Ltd*[78]). It is the employer's responsibility to set up a fair system of selection, and to administer it fairly. If selection for redundancy is based on proper assessments, it is not for the employment tribunal to engage in a re-assessment exercise (*Eaton Ltd v King*[79]).

18.55 In *Clyde Pipeworks v Foster*,[80] selection for redundancy was based on a points system, which took into account bad time-keeping, workmanship, absenteeism, and merit on conduct. This procedure had been agreed with the unions, but they were not consulted about its implementation. It was held that there was no need to involve the unions in the detailed arrangements for selection for redundancy, provided the method was fair in general terms.

18.56 If a dismissal for redundancy is generally fair in terms of the procedure adopted and the selection criteria, it does not become unfair because of a failure by the employer to give the affected employees a right of appeal against their dismissal, even though an employee dismissed for gross misconduct would have that right. There is no suggestion in the Code of Practice that there should be a right of appeal against a dismissal for redundancy (*Robinson v Ulster Carpet Mills Ltd*[81]). The advantage of having an appeal machinery is that an original decision to dismiss for redundancy which is unfair can be cured if there is a complete rehearing on appeal (*Lloyd v Taylor Woodrow plc*[82]).

18.57 But if there is an appeal procedure, it must be operated fairly, and not be a mere sham. Thus, if selection for redundancy is based on a points system which had been agreed with union representatives, an employee is still entitled to know how his own marks had been calculated, otherwise he will have no material with which to present his case on appeal (*John Brown Engineering Ltd v Brown*[83]).

18.58 To select a woman for dismissal because she is pregnant, or on maternity leave of absence, would be unfair under s 99 (see para 6.56), but if a woman is made redundant because of the operation of a fair selection procedure then the fact that she is or was pregnant is coincidental, and has nothing to do with her selection. Her dismissal would be fair in accordance with the usual criteria (*Brown v Stockton-on-Tees Borough Council*[84]). Equally, a long-term sick employee may still be selected for redundancy, even though this terminates his entitlement to sickness pay under the employer's scheme (*Hill v General Accident Fire and Life Assurance Corpn plc*, see para 17.102). An employer must therefore not assess those who have been off work on parental leave (or sickness leave) on different criteria to those who have not been on leave (*Riezniece v Zemkopības Ministrija*[85]). (It is expected that that protection against redundancy for mothers returning to work will be extended by six months, and that this will also apply to parents returning from adoption and shared parental leave, but it is not yet known when this will come in.)

---

[77] [1975] IRLR 73.   [78] [1986] IRLR 90, EAT.
[79] [1995] IRLR 75, EAT; revsd sub nom *King v Eaton Ltd* [1996] IRLR 199, Ct of Sess.
[80] [1978] IRLR 313, EAT.   [81] [1991] IRLR 348, NICA.   [82] [1999] IRLR 782, EAT.
[83] [1997] IRLR 90, EAT.
[84] [1986] ICR 842, [1986] IRLR 432, EAT; aff'd [1987] ICR 897, [1987] IRLR 230, CA; rev [1989] AC 20, [1988] 2 All ER 129, [1988] ICR 410, [1988] IRLR 263, HL.   [85] Case C-7/12, [2013] IRLR 828.

18.59 The test is essentially not whether the employment tribunal agrees with the actual selection made by the employer, but whether the employer acted reasonably. Thus it is not the duty of the employment tribunal to decide who they would have made redundant had they had to make the choice, but to ensure that management acts from genuine motives. In *Grundy (Teddington) Ltd v Willis* (see para 17.73), the choice for making an employee redundant lay between two persons. Management chose one, but the employment tribunal held that this was unfair, in that the other should have been chosen. The EAT reversed this finding; the ultimate decision must remain with management, provided it acts fairly.

18.60 If an employee is given notice of dismissal, for reason of redundancy, and during that notice period new work becomes available, it may be unfair not to rescind the notice and offer further employment to him (*Stacey v Babcock Power Ltd*, see para 17.76). However, if the alternative employment becomes available after the employee's contract of employment has ended, an employer does not act unreasonably in failing to offer that employment to him (*Octavius Atkinson & Sons Ltd v Morris*, see para 16.15).

C. Unfair Selection for Redundancy (ERA, s 105)

18.61 It is unfair to dismiss a person for redundancy if the reason for his/her selection for dismissal was (a) health and safety reasons (s 100), (b) protected or opted-out shop worker (s 101), (c) refusal to comply with a requirement in contravention of the Working Time Regulations (s 101A), (d) acting as a trustee of an occupational pension fund (s 102), (e) acting as an employee representative (s 103), (f) making a protected disclosure (s 103A), (g) asserting a statutory right (s 104), (h) asserting a right under the National Minimum Wage Act (s 104A), (i) taking action to obtain a tax credit (s 104B), (j) taking action under the Transnational Information and Consultation of Employees Regulations 1999, (k) taking action under the Part-time Workers (Prevention of Less Favourable Treatment) Regulation 2000, or the Fixed-term Employees (Prevention of Less Favourable Treatment) Regulations 2002, or the Employment Equality (Age) Regulations 2006. Unfair selection for trade union membership and activities etc is covered by TULR(C)A, s 153. Unfair selection for redundancy by reason of pregnancy, maternity leave, parental leave, time off to care for dependants, and workforce agreement cases is dealt with in the Maternity and Parental Leave etc Regulations 1999 (see Chapter 6) and there is similar protection for persons who take paternity and adoption leave. Such dismissals will be automatically unfair, and no period of continuous employment is required.

D. Dismissal During the Period of Notice (s 140)

18.62 If an employee has been given due notice that he will be dismissed for reason of redundancy, and whilst he is working out that notice he commits an act of misconduct which is sufficiently serious to warrant his instant dismissal without notice, and he is summarily dismissed, the question will arise as to whether or not he is entitled to his redundancy payment. On the assumption that the dismissal was justified (eg because the employee refused to obey a lawful order (*Cairns v Burnside Shoe Repairs Ltd*[86]), or because the employee stole from the employer (*Jarmain v E Pollard & Co Ltd*)[87]), then the employment tribunal shall determine whether it is just and equitable that the employee should receive the whole or part of the redundancy payment, as it thinks fit. In *Lignacite Products Ltd v Krollman*[88] the claimant was given notice of redundancy. He was then found stealing from his employers and summarily dismissed. The employment tribunal reduced his redundancy pay by 40%, and the EAT upheld the decision. It is difficult to reconcile this decision with *Bonner v H Gilbert Ltd*.[89]

---

[86] (1966) 2 KIR 23, 2 ITR 75.   [87] (1967) 2 ITR 406.
[88] [1979] IRLR 22, EAT.   [89] [1989] IRLR 475, EAT.

18.63 If an employee is given notice of dismissal by reason of redundancy, and during his notice period he takes part in a strike, then although this is conduct which entitles the employer to terminate the contract without notice, the employee is not barred from getting the whole of his redundancy payment (s 143). However, if an employee is on strike, and then is dismissed for reasons of redundancy, his claim will fail. The reason is that s 140 of the Act provides that the employee will not be entitled to a redundancy payment if the employer, being entitled to terminate the contract of employment, terminates it, with or without notice. Since an employee who is on strike is in breach of his contract, the employer is entitled to terminate it. In other words, s 143 deals with the situation when an employee is dismissed for reason of redundancy, and then goes on strike. In *Simmons v Hoover Ltd*[90] employees who were actually on strike were dismissed for reason of redundancy, and it was held that s 140 operated and s 143 did not operate to save their claim.

Excluded Classes of Employees

18.64 The following employees are not eligible for, or will not be entitled to, a redundancy payment:

(a) a person employed under a fixed-term contract for two years or more, if before that term expires, he agrees in writing to exclude his rights to make a claim (s 197(3)). This is one of the very few circumstances when an employee can forgo his legal rights. However, this exclusion only applies to agreements which were made before 10 July 2002;

(b) a miscellaneous class of employees, ie share fishermen, holders of certain public offices (see s 159), those in employment by a government of an overseas territory (see s 160). Domestic servants employed in a private household *are* within the scope of the Act, unless the servant is a close relative of the employer (s 161);

(c) an agreement made between an employers' organisation and a trade union may provide exemption from the Act by a ministerial order on an application by both parties thereto, provided the conditions in s 157 are satisfied.

Claims for Redundancy Payments

18.65 A claim must be made to the employment tribunal within six months from the relevant date, which is the date of the expiry of the notice to terminate the employment, or the date when the contract expires, or the date on which a fixed-term contract comes to an end. The tribunal has a discretion to admit a claim which is outside the time limit if it thinks it would be just and equitable to do so, but no claim can be entertained after 12 months have elapsed. The claim, if admitted or successful, must be met by the employer. The amount of the claim will be determined by the length of time the employee has been employed, his normal week's pay, and his age.

18.66 The calculation of the amount of the redundancy payment will be determined in accordance with the rules on continuous employment (see Chapter 13), normal working hours, and a week's pay (see Chapter 14) and age. For each year's continuous employment below the age of 22 (with no lower age limit) an employee is entitled to one half of a week's pay; for each year's employment between the ages of 22 and 40, he will be entitled to one

[90] [1975] IRLR 263; aff'd [1977] QB 284, [1977] 1 All ER 775, [1977] ICR 61, [1976] IRLR 266, EAT.

week's pay; for each year's employment over (and including) the age of 41, he will be entitled to one and a half weeks' pay. There is no longer an upper or lower age limit, and the tapering provision which used to apply to employees over the age of 64 has been abolished. However, an employee will still have to have been employed for two years or more, and no more than 20 years' employment may be counted when calculating the payment. The maximum week's pay to count is (currently) £508. When making the payment, the employer shall give to the employee a written statement showing how the amount of the payment is calculated, and it is an offence, punishable on summary conviction by a fine not exceeding level 1 on the standard scale, not to do so (s 165). If an employer gives a lump sum to a redundant employee without indicating how it is made up, this may be regarded as an *ex gratia* payment, not intended to be by way of a redundancy payment (*Galloway v Export Packing Services Ltd*[91]).

Payments by the Secretary of State (ERA, ss 166–170)

18.67 If an employee claims that, despite taking all reasonable steps, the employer has failed or refused to make him a redundancy payment, or claims that the employer is insolvent, he may apply to the Secretary of State for a redundancy payment, to be paid out by the Insolvency Service (an executive agency of the Department for Business, Innovation and Skills). An employer will be insolvent if:

(a) he is an individual, and he has been adjudged bankrupt or made a composition or arrangement with creditors, or he has died and his estate falls to be administered under the Insolvency Act 1986 (there are comparable provisions for Scotland); or

(b) if a company, there has been a winding-up order or an administration order made, or a resolution for a voluntary winding up has been passed or a receiver or manager appointed.

18.68 Once the Secretary of State has made the payment due to an employer's insolvency, this will break continuity of employment for those employees who are re-engaged by virtue of the Transfer of Undertakings (Protection of Employment) Regulations 2006 (*Lassman v Secretary of State for Trade and Industry*,[92] and see Chapter 9).

Consultation on Redundancies (TULR(C)A, ss 188–192)

A. EC Directive on Collective Redundancies

18.69 Article 2 of the EC Directive on Collective Redundancies (75/129/EEC) lays down the principle that when an employer is contemplating collective redundancies, he shall consult with employee representatives. Although a Directive is generally enforceable against a state body (see *Foster v British Gas*, para 1.80) this Directive is not so unconditional or sufficiently precise as to be capable of direct enforcement (*Griffin v South West Water Services Ltd*[93]). Requirements for such consultations were provided for in the Employment Protection Act 1975, s 99, and repeated in the Trade Union and Labour Relations (Consolidation) Act 1992, s 188 (as amended by the Trade Union Reform and Employment Rights Act 1993).

---

[91] [1975] IRLR 306.
[92] [1999] ICR 416, [1999] IRLR 413, EAT; revsd sub nom *Secretary of State for Trade and Industry v Lassman (Pan Graphics Industries Ltd, in receivership)* [2000] ICR 1109, [2000] IRLR 411, CA.
[93] [1995] IRLR 15.

However, in *EC Commission v United Kingdom* (see para 1.84) infringement proceedings were brought alleging that neither the Transfer of Undertakings Regulations 1981 (see Chapter 9) nor the provisions of TULR(C)A correctly transposed the Directive, because there were no provisions which would require an employer to consult with employee representatives when the employer did not recognise a trade union. The UK Government argued that employee representation was traditionally based on the voluntary recognition by employers of trade unions, and therefore if an employer did not recognise a trade union, there were no 'employee representatives' with whom to consult. Nonetheless, the European Court held that the UK Government was in breach of the Directive. Legislation had to ensure that there was a mechanism whereby employee representatives were designated so as to enable employers to consult with them.

18.70 Section 188 of TULR(C)A was thus amended by the Collective Redundancies and Transfer of Undertakings (Protection of Employment) (Amendment) Regulations 1995, although it was not certain whether these regulations fully implemented the Directive, because although there arose a duty to consult with either trade unions or employee representatives, there was no mechanism by which those representatives could be elected. Thus the Collective Redundancies and Transfer of Undertakings (Protection of Employment) (Amendment) Regulations 1999 were passed to regularise the position. These latter Regulations make provision for the election of employee representatives (by inserting s 188A into TULR(C)A), and other changes).

18.71 However, there is still some doubt as to whether UK law adequately transposes the EC Directive. Section 188 requires consultation to take place when an employer is 'proposing' redundancies, whereas the Directive requires consultation when the employer is 'contemplating' redundancies (see *MSF v Refuge Assurance plc*[94]).

B. **Who and When to Consult**

18.72 Where an employer is proposing to dismiss as redundant 20 or more employees at one establishment within a period of 90 days or less, he shall consult with the appropriate representatives of any of the employees affected by the proposed dismissals (and not just those whom the employer proposes to make redundant), or may be affected by the measures taken in connection with those dismissals. The appropriate representatives are:

(a) if the employees are of a description in respect of which an independent trade union is recognised (whether or not the affected employees are members of the trade union concerned, see *Northern Ireland Hotel and Catering College v National Association of Teachers in Further and Higher Education*[95]), representatives of that union. Whether a trade union is recognised for the purpose of the consultation provisions is a question of fact (see Chapter 23). In any other case,

(b) either employee representatives who have been appointed or elected by the affected employees for some other purpose, who have authority to receive information or be consulted about proposed dismissals, or employee representatives who have been elected by the affected employees for consultation purposes, in an election which satisfies the requirements set out in s 188A.

If there is no recognised trade union, the employer must consult with either existing representatives or representatives elected for TUPE consultation purposes. If there are no trade union or elected representatives, the employer must invite the employees to elect

---

[94] [2002] ICR 1365, [2002] IRLR 324, [2002] All ER (D) 209 (Feb), EAT.   [95] [1995] IRLR 83, NICA.

representatives. If they fail to do so within a reasonable time, the employer must give each affected employee the information he would otherwise have given to the representatives (*Howard v Millrise Ltd*[96]). (Where in a proposed election for employee representatives, the number of candidates precisely matched the number of available places for elected employee representatives, the employer was entitled to treat them as 'elected' without proceeding to a formal ballot (*Phillips v Xtera Communications Ltd*[97]).)

18.73 The employer shall allow the appropriate representatives access to the employees affected, and shall afford those representatives such accommodation and facilities as may be appropriate, and time off work for training (ERA, s 61). An employee who is an employee representative, or a candidate for election as such, has the right not to suffer a detriment on the ground that he has performed any function or activity as such, the right to have time off with pay to perform his functions, and the right not to be unfairly dismissed because he performed any function or activity as such.

18.74 The consultation shall begin in good time, and, in any event, if the employer is proposing to dismiss 100 or more within 90 days or less, consultation shall begin at least 45 days before the dismissals take effect. (This was changed from 90 days in 2013.) If less than 100 but at least 20 are to be dismissed within the 90-day period, consultation must begin at least 30 days before the dismissals take effect. Employees who volunteer for redundancy are nonetheless dismissed for the purpose of including them in the head count of 20 or 100 respectively which triggers the collective consultation provisions (*Optare Group Ltd v TGWU*[98]).

18.75 Where there is a proposed transfer of undertakings (Chapter 9), s 198A of TULRCA 1992 allows a transferee who is proposing to make 20 or more employees redundant to start consulting about this before the date of the transfer, if the transferor consents.

What is an Establishment?

18.76 The term 'establishment' is not defined in the Act, and has thus been the subject of interpretation by the tribunals. In *Clarks of Hove Ltd v Bakers' Union*[99] it was held that separate premises can amount to one establishment, if there is no separate accounting, management, or trading. In *Barratt Developments (Bradford) Ltd v UCATT*[100] the company, which had its headquarters in Bradford, operated 14 building sites in Lancashire. On each site there was a temporary shed, with a telephone link to the headquarters. It was decided to reduce the labour force, and 24 employees were made redundant, being selected from eight different sites. It was held that all 14 sites were part of one establishment, and as there had been a failure to consult with the trade union, a protective award would be made.

18.77 However, in *Athinaiki Chartopoiia AE v Panagiotidis*[101] the European Court of Justice held that an establishment may consist of a single entity, having a certain degree of permanence and stability, which is assigned to perform one or more given tasks and which has a workforce, technical means, and a certain organisational structure allowing for the accomplishment of those tasks. The entity in question need not have any legal, economic, financial, administrative, or technical autonomy in order to be regarded as an 'establishment'. In *Rockfon A/S v Specialarbejderforbundet i Danmark* it was held that the

---

[96] [2005] ICR 435, EAT.   [97] [2011] IRLR 724.   [98] [2007] IRLR 931, EAT.
[99] [1978] 2 All ER 15, [1977] ICR 838, [1977] IRLR 264, EAT; revsd [1979] 1 All ER 152, [1978] ICR 1076, sub nom *Bakers' Union v Clarks of Hove Ltd* [1978] IRLR 366, CA.
[100] [1978] ICR 319, [1977] IRLR 403, EAT.   [101] Case C-270/05, [2007] IRLR 284, ECJ.

term 'establishment' must be understood as meaning the unit to which the workers who are made redundant are assigned to carry out their duties (see para 9.13). It is not necessary for the unit in question to have its own management structure which can carry out a redundancy programme independently.

In *USDAW & Anor v WW Realisation1 Ltd & Ors*,[102] where a chain of stores went into administration, the question arose as to the meaning of the word 'establishment' in the EC Directive, and so which employees should be consulted. Should the employer look at each store, or should it look at the whole undertaking when counting the number of employees being made redundant? The ECJ said that an establishment is the unit to which workers are assigned to carry out their duties, and not the undertaking as a whole. The employer was entitled to count each store as an establishment., even if this should result in uneven protection between an employer's different establishments. Where an employer has several establishments, consultation therefore only has to take place at establishments where it is proposed to dismiss at least 20 employees. There is no requirement to aggregate the number of dismissals across the whole undertaking. The court followed this in *Lyttle v Bluebird*,[103] finding that a single retail store is capable of being an 'establishment' for the purposes of Art 1(1)(a).

The Consultation Provisions

18.78 An employer is 'proposing to dismiss' employees as redundant (thus triggering the consultation provisions of the Act) when, 'following a diagnosis of the problem, specific proposals are formulated, with redundancies as one of the available options' (*Hough v Leyland DAF Ltd*[104]). 'Proposing to dismiss' means 'proposing to give notice of dismissal'. A proposal means something less than an actual decision that dismissals are to be made, and something more than a possibility that they may occur (*Leicestershire County Council v Unison*[105]). Thus where directors of a company were considering the options of either selling the business as a going concern or selling it as a development site, this amounted to a proposal to dismiss the workforce, even though no final decision had been reached on which option they would adopt (*Scotch Premier Meat Ltd v Burns*[106]).

18.79 The actual notice of dismissals can be issued during the consultation period, provided that the dismissals do not take effect until after the consultation period has elapsed. But if an employer issues dismissal notices the day after consultations begin, it may be thought that he does not intend meaningful consultations to take place (*National Union of Teachers v Avon County Council*[107]). Similarly, if the employer does not give the appropriate representatives sufficient time to consider the proposals before they are implemented, meaningful consultation is being denied (*Transport and General Workers' Union v Ledbury Preserves (1928) Ltd*[108]).

18.80 The purpose of consultation is to consult about ways of:

(a) avoiding the dismissals;

(b) reducing the numbers of employees to be dismissed; and

(c) mitigating the consequences of the redundancies (TULR(C)A, s 188(2)).

18.81 Consultation with employee representatives does not mean reaching an agreement, but should be undertaken by the employer with a view to reaching agreement. Thus, the

---

[102] Case C-80/14. [103] Case C-182/13. [104] [1991] ICR 696, [1991] IRLR 194, EAT.
[105] [2005] IRLR 920, EAT. [106] [2000] IRLR 639, EAT.
[107] [1978] ICR 626, [1978] IRLR 55, EAT. [108] [1986] ICR 855, [1986] IRLR 492, EAT.

consultation process must be genuine. If a redundancy situation is presented as a fait accompli, subsequent consultations may not be a genuine and open-minded review of the decision (*GMB and AEEU v Campbell's UK Ltd*[109]). In *Middlesbrough Borough Council v TGWU*[110] it was held that the consultations on avoiding redundancies had been a sham, because the decision on numbers had already been taken.

18.82 If a workplace is closing down, with the result that employees are made redundant, the employer is obliged to consult with the recognised trade union over the reasons for the closure, because the dismissals and the closure are inextricably linked. Further, the Information and Consultation of Employees Regulations 2004 (see para 23.144) require consultation over economic decisions, and it would be strange if this did not apply at a time when job losses were being considered (*UK Coal Mining Ltd v National Union of Mineworkers*[111]).

18.83 True consultation involves:

(a) consulting with employee representatives when the proposals are still at a formulative stage;

(b) giving adequate information to which those representatives can respond;

(c) giving adequate time for the response;

(d) a conscientious consideration by the employer of the response (*Rowell v Hubbard Group Services Ltd*, para 18.48);

(e) providing information about the reasons for the dismissals.

18.84 An employer does not warrant the accuracy of the information provided, and if he consults on the basis of a mistaken understanding of the effect of TUPE on the affected employees, this does not mean that there is a breach of the consultation provisions (*Royal Mail Group Ltd v Communication Workers Union*[112]).

18.85 But consultation does not imply agreement with those representatives, nor the adoption of any proposals made by them (*R v British Coal Corpn, ex p Price*[113]).

18.86 From 2013, the Trade Union and Labour Relations (Consolidation) Act 1992 (Amendment) Order 2013 provides that an employer does not have to consult during a collective redundancy exercise where fixed-term contracts come to an end, although he will have to if the redundancy is due to take place before the end of the fixed term or before the completion of the specified task.

A. Disclosures Required by the Employer

18.87 When consulting, the employer must disclose (in writing to the appropriate representative):

(a) the reasons for his proposals;

(b) the numbers and descriptions of employees whom it is proposed to dismiss as being redundant;

(c) the total number of employees of that description employed by the employer at that establishment;

(d) the proposed method of selecting the employees who are to be dismissed;

---

[109] Unreported.   [110] [2002] IRLR 332, [2001] All ER (D) 79 (May), EAT.
[111] [2008] ICR 163, [2008] IRLR 4.   [112] [2009] EWCA Civ 1045, [2010] ICR 83, [2009] IRLR 1046.
[113] [1993] ICR 720, [1993] IRLR 104.

(e) the proposed method of carrying out the dismissals, with due regard to agreed procedure, including the period over which dismissals are to take effect; and

(f) the proposed method for calculating any redundancy payments to be made, other than statutory redundancy pay (s 188(4)).

18.88 Having provided this information, the employer must consider any representations made by the appropriate representatives and reply to them. If he rejects any of those representations, he must state his reasons. It must be stressed that the employer's duty is to consult with the representatives. He does not have to reach any agreement, and the final decision is his. In *Perez v Mercury Display Ltd*[114] the employer consulted with a trade union about a redundancy. The employer wanted selection to take place on the basis of LIFO (in the days before age discrimination legislation), but the union wanted volunteers to be selected. The employer gave to the union his reasons for rejecting the representations, and dismissed the employees on the basis of LIFO. It was held that the employer had complied with his statutory obligations.

B. **Special Circumstances**

18.89 If there are special circumstances which render it not reasonably practicable for the employer to comply with any of the provisions relating to consultation or considering representations, he shall take all such steps as are reasonably practicable in the circumstances. Special circumstances may exist if a company becomes insolvent but insolvency per se is not a special circumstance, for reasonable and prudent management may well foresee such a possibility (*Clarks of Hove Ltd v Bakers' Union*, para 18.76). The sudden appointment of a receiver would be a special circumstance (*FTATU v Lawrence Cabinet*[115]). The loss of a key order (*AUEW v Cooper Plastics*[116]) and the unexpected failure to obtain a renewal of an important contract (*National Union of Public Employees v General Cleaning Contractors*[117]) have also come within this defence. But the fact that the employer genuinely believes that he has not recognised a trade union for the purpose of collective bargaining does not constitute a special circumstance which would render it not reasonably practicable to comply with the obligation to consult (*Joshua Wilson & Bros Ltd v Union of Shop, Distributive and Allied Workers*[118]). Special circumstances may also be said to exist if delicate negotiations are taking place which may be prejudiced if consultations are carried on with the union (*Association of Pattern Makers and Allied Craftsmen v Kirvin Ltd*[119]). A circumstance is likely to be special if it is sudden, as opposed to being gradual or foreseeable with reasonable prudence (*Union of Shop, Distributive and Allied Workers v Leancut Bacon Ltd*[120]). However, even though special circumstances exist, the employer must nonetheless take all such steps as are reasonably practicable to consult. If he fails to take such steps, there is still a breach of s 188(1A), although the special circumstances can operate to mitigate the amount of the protective award (*Shanahan Engineering Ltd v UNITE*[121]).

18.90 The dismissal of employees in order to make the sale of a business more attractive to buyers, or the absence of orders, are not special circumstances within the meaning of the Act (*GMB v Rankin and Harrison*[122]). A failure on the part of a person who controls the employer (eg a multinational corporation in control of a subsidiary) to provide information to the employer also does not constitute a special circumstance (s 193(7)).

---

[114] [1977] IRLIB. [115] IDS Brief 96. [116] IDS Brief 90. [117] [1976] IRLR 362.
[118] [1978] 3 All ER 4, [1978] ICR 614, [1978] IRLR 120, EAT. [119] [1978] IRLR 318.
[120] [1981] IRLR 295, EAT. [121] EAT/0411/09. [122] [1992] IRLR 514, EAT.

18.91 An employer does not fail to consult if he deals only with an accredited shop steward, for there is no requirement that the information should be conveyed to a full-time union official (*General and Municipal Workers' Union v Wailes Dove Bitumastic*[123]). The information shall be given to appropriate representatives, or sent by post to a notified address, or sent by post to the union's head office (s 188(5)).

C. Protective Award (TULR(C)A, s 189)

18.92 If the employer fails to consult as required by s 186, a trade union or an employee representative or an employee who has been or may be dismissed as redundant may present a complaint to an industrial tribunal (s 189). It further appears that an employee who has been dismissed for reason of redundancy may be able to bring a complaint that the employer has failed to invite potentially redundant employees to elect appropriate employee representatives as required by s 188. If the employer wishes to plead that it was not reasonably practicable for him to comply with these provisions, he must show that this was so, and that he took all reasonably practicable steps in the circumstances. Otherwise, if the tribunal finds the complaint to be well founded, it will make a declaration to that effect, and may also make a protective award, which is remuneration for a protected period for those employees who were dismissed (or whose dismissal was being proposed) and in respect of whom the employer has failed to comply with the legal requirements. The protected period is such time as the tribunal considers to be just and equitable, having regard to the seriousness of the employer's default, but shall not exceed 90 days.

18.93 A protective award can only be made in favour of those employees in respect of whom the trade union is recognised by the employer (*TGWU v Brauer Coley*[124]). Employees who are not of that description would have to bring their own claims under s 189 of TULR(C)A (failure to consult with appropriate representatives). Also, an individual complainant may only claim a protective award on behalf of himself, and not on behalf of all affected employees (*Independent Insurance Co Ltd v Aspinall*[125]).

18.94 If a protective award is made, every employee to whom it relates shall be entitled to one week's pay for each week of the protected period, with proportionate reductions in respect of a period which is less than one week. There is no maximum week's pay for the purpose of the protective award, because the statutory cap in ERA, s 227 does not include a protective award. If the employer has already made any payment to the employee in respect of any period falling within the protected period, or by way of damages for breach of contract, this will not reduce the employer's liability to pay remuneration under the protective award, and conversely, any payment made under a protective award will not reduce any liability to pay any sum due in respect of a breach of contract by the employer for that period.

18.95 If an employment tribunal finds that the employer is in default of the consultation provisions, then the making of a declaration to that effect is mandatory, but the amount of the protective award is discretionary. The purpose of the protective award is to provide for a sanction against an employer for being in breach of the statutory consultation provisions, rather than to compensate employees for the loss which they have suffered in consequence of the breach. The maximum period of 90 days' protective award should only be reduced if there were mitigating circumstances justifying a reduction to the extent which the tribunal considers appropriate (*Susie Radin Ltd v GMB*[126]). The presumption in favour of a 90-day

---

[123] [1977] IRLR 45.   [124] [2007] ICR 226, [2007] IRLR 207.   [125] [2011] IRLR 716.
[126] [2003] All ER (D) 192 (Sep), EAT; aff'd [2004] EWCA Civ 180, [2004] 2 All ER 279, [2004] All ER (D) 353 (Feb).

protective award applies whether the minimum consultation period is 30 days, because there are 20–99 employees being made redundant or 90 days (previously 45) where 100 or more employees are being made redundant (*Evans v Permacell*[127]).

18.96 An award for a failure to consult on redundancies is determined by the seriousness of the employer's default, not his ability to pay. Thus if the employer fails to consult and has become insolvent, a maximum award may still be made, the point being that it will be the Secretary of State who will have to pay (*Smith v Cherry Lewis Ltd*[128]). The protective award is essentially punitive in nature, and the employment tribunal should use the 90-day award as a starting point. However, mitigating factors can be taken into account so as to reduce the award, such as if the employer had taken some genuine steps to provide information or has attempted some form of consultation (*Amicus v GBS Tooling Ltd*[129]).

18.97 As a result of consultations with the appropriate employee representatives, there may well be an agreement that employees will leave the firm before the appropriate period of 90 or 30 days has expired. Whether the agreement has been reached with the employee representatives or employees on an individual basis, it is probably void by virtue of TULR(C)A, s 288, which prevents the contracting out of the various statutory rights. It is clear therefore that the dismissals will take effect before the end of the consultation period, and there will be a breach of the Act. However, on a complaint that the employer has failed to consult within the statutory period, the employment tribunal will make the mandatory declaration, but not a protective award (*Association of Scientific, Technical and Managerial Staffs v Hawker Siddeley Aviation*[130]).

18.98 If, during the protected period, the employee is fairly dismissed for some reason other than redundancy, or if he unreasonably resigns, then his entitlement to the protective award shall cease from the time his contract is terminated. If the employer makes an offer to renew the contract, or to re-engage under a new contract, so that the renewal or re-engagement would take effect before or during the protected period, or the offer constitutes an offer of suitable employment and the employee unreasonably refuses that offer, then he shall not be entitled to any payment under the protective award in respect of any period during which but for the refusal he would have been employed.

18.99 Once a protective award has been granted, then any individual employee may present a complaint to a tribunal that the employer has failed, in whole or in part, to pay him the remuneration under that award. If the complaint is well founded, the tribunal shall order the employer to make that payment (*Howlett Marine Services Ltd v Bowlam*[131]).

18.100 The fact that the employer has failed to consult in accordance with these provisions is irrelevant to the issue as to whether a particular employee's redundancy is fair or unfair (*Forman Construction Ltd v Kelly*, para 18.45).

18.101 It should be noted that, for the purpose of the consultation provisions only, the definition of redundancy is not the same as the one laid down in ERA, s 139. Under TULR(C)A, s 195, when considering the consultation provisions, references to dismissals for reason of redundancy are references to a dismissal not related to the individual concerned (or for a number of reasons not so related). This wider definition throws out some interesting possibilities. For example, suppose an employer decides to give lawful notice to all his employees, coupled with an offer to re-engage them all on changed terms of

[127] EAT/0350/07.   [128] [2005] IRLR 86, EAT.   [129] [2005] IRLR 683, EAT.
[130] [1977] IRLR 418.   [131] [2001] ICR 595, [2001] IRLR 201, [2000] All ER (D) 2494, EAT.

employment. Since this 'dismissal' is not related to an individual, it is submitted that prior consultations with employee representatives are required under TULR(C)A, s 195 (*GMB v Man Truck and Bus UK Ltd*[132]).

Notification of Mass Redundancies to the Minister (TULR(C)A, s 193)

18.102 If an employer is proposing to make redundant 100 or more employees at one establishment within 90 days, or 20 or more employees within 30 days, he must notify the Secretary of State of his proposals within 90 or 30 days respectively before any notice of redundancy has been issued. He must also give a copy of this notification to the representatives of any recognised independent trade union and/or to any elected representatives. If there are special circumstances which make compliance not reasonably practicable, he shall take all such steps as are reasonably practicable. But a failure on the part of a person who controls the employer to provide information to the employer does not constitute a special circumstance (s 193(7)).

18.103 An employer who fails to give the required notification to the Secretary of State may be prosecuted in the magistrates' court, and is liable on conviction to a fine not exceeding level 5 on the standard scale (TULR(C)A, s 194(1)).

Summary

- Redundancy legislation applies only to employees.
- Redundancy can be a fair reason for dismissal, but unfair selection can amount to an unfair dismissal.
- Section 136 ERA sets out what is a dismissal.
- A transferred redundancy is still a redundancy.
- The suitability of an offer of alternative work must be assessed objectively.
- An employee who has two years' service should be given reasonable paid time off work to look for new employment.
- An employer should have proper selection procedures and criteria to decide whom to make redundant.
- There is a formula for calculating statutory redundancy payments (and see Appendix B).
- There are provisions relating to consultation before redundancies are made.
- Payments can be made by the Secretary of State in the case of insolvent employers.

---

[132] [2000] ICR 1101, [2000] IRLR 636, EAT.

19

Duties of Ex-employees

Background

19.1 We saw in Chapter 10 that during the subsistence of a contract of employment, the relationship between an employer and employee is one of trust, confidence, and faith, and any course of conduct which is inconsistent with those obligations may well amount to a breach of contract. In this chapter we shall consider the more limited obligations which apply to an employee who is about to leave his employment (whether voluntarily or otherwise), or who has actually left that employment. The law must strike a delicate balance. On the one hand, an employee has a right to earn his living, and knowledge and skills obtained in his former employment will doubtless enable him to continue to do so; on the other hand, an employer is entitled to limited protection against an employee who may well be seeking to compete. An employer is not entitled to have protection from competition per se but he is entitled to have some limited protection in respect of confidential information, trade secrets, existing customers, etc.

Employees who are about to Leave their Employment

19.2 The mere fact that the employee is seeking employment with a competitor is not, by itself, a breach of the duty of fidelity, in the absence of any evidence that the employee is wrongfully seeking to disclose confidential information or trade secrets (*Harris & Russell Ltd v Slingsby*, see paras 15.9 and 17.18). In *Ranson v Customer Systems PLC*[1] Mr Ranson was an employee who was recruited in 2001 straight from university. His contract contained a confidentiality clause, but no post-termination restrictions. He gave notice and during the notice period had discussions with a number of his employer's clients (who were not people he usually dealt with) in relation to obtaining future work for himself. His employer brought an action alleging that he was in breach of his duties as an employee. The Court of Appeal held that his duty did not extend that far, although it would have done had he been a director, as a director owes a wider-ranging duty (see also *Shepherds Investments*, para 19.5).

If an employee steals information from his former employer, however, this gives rise to an equitable duty of confidentiality in respect of trade secrets and confidential information, particularly if the information would give competitors a commercial advantage and the employer from whom it was stolen suffers a detriment in terms of lost orders, etc (*JN Dairies Ltd v Johal Dairies Ltd*[2]). But an employee who is about to leave his employment might attempt to make preparatory steps, either during his working hours, or in his own time, to prepare himself for future employment. He may attempt to solicit customers or suppliers, poach staff, or use information which has been imparted to him in confidence. His status and position as an employee, the nature of the work he is seeking to do, the custom and practice of the industry, etc, may well be relevant factors to be taken into account when determining the rights of his employer.

[1] [2012] EWCA Civ 841.   [2] [2010] EWCA Civ 348.

19.3 If the employee engages in such activities during his working hours, or uses his employer's premises or equipment to do so, then doubtless he will be in breach of his duty of fidelity. Thus in *Roger Bullivant Ltd v Ellis*[3] a managing director left his employment in order to set up a rival business. He took with him copies of a card index, which listed the names and addresses of all the company's customers. This was held to be a breach of the implied duty of fidelity, and an injunction was granted to restrain him from entering into or fulfilling any contract made with or through any person whose name appeared on the card index. However, this does not necessarily apply if the employee pursues such activities in his own time and uses his own premises or equipment (*Balston Ltd v Headline Filters Ltd*[4]).

19.4 There appears to be a subtle distinction between a definite intention to compete with the employer and mere preparatory activities. Thus to tender for work already being undertaken by the employer (*Adamson v B & L Cleaning Services Ltd*, see para 10.53) or to rent and equip premises for his own business (*Lancashire Fires Ltd v SA Lyons & Co Ltd*, see para 10.70) or to approach customers with a view to doing business with them (*Wessex Dairies v Smith*, see para 10.98) or to copy out a list of the employer's clients with a view to approaching them after the employment has ceased (*Robb v Green*[5]) are clearly competing activities which will amount to a breach of the duty of faithful service. But an employee who merely indicates, whether by word or deeds, that he intends to compete with his employer at some future point in time is not acting in breach of his implied duty of fidelity (see *Laughton and Hawley v Bapp Industrial Supplies Ltd*, para 16.12).

19.5 As a general principle, an employee's duty of fidelity does not prevent him from competing with a former employer once he has left his employment, and the freedom to do so carries with it the freedom to prepare for future activities that the employee intends to pursue once he has left his employment (*Helmet Integrated Systems Ltd v Tunnard*, see para 10.56). But preparatory activities undertaken by directors or senior employees are more likely to constitute breaches of fidelity and fiduciary duties (*Shepherds Investments Ltd v Walters*;[6] see also *Caterpillar Logistics Services (UK) Ltd v de Crean*[7] and *Ranson v Customer Systems*, para 19.2). In any particular case, it will be necessary to identify the particular duties undertaken by the employee and to ask whether, in all the circumstances, he has placed himself in a position where he must act solely in the interests of his employer (*Nottingham University v Fishel*, see para 10.56).

19.6 If, while still employed, an employee seeks to entice away existing fellow employees, this can amount to a breach of the duty of fidelity, especially if the activities of the employee have gone beyond the mere preparatory stages. But the law on this point is not absolutely clear, and the position of the employee is very relevant. A managing director who seeks to entice away senior staff (*Marshall v Industrial Systems and Control Ltd*, see para 16.12) is more likely to be in breach of his duty of fidelity than a more junior member of staff (*Tithebarn Ltd v Hubbard*[8]).

19.7 An employer must not unreasonably withhold the provision of work where there is work available to be done. But this is subject to the qualification that the employees have not demonstrated in a serious way that they are not ready or willing to work, nor rendered it impossible or reasonably impracticable for the employers to provide work. Thus if an employee is in breach of his contract or other duties, then even though the contract is

---

[3] [1987] ICR 464, [1987] IRLR 491, EAT.   [4] [1987] FSR 330, [1990] FSR 385.
[5] [1895] 2 QB 1, 59 JP 695, 39 Sol Jo 921, 72 LT 686, 11 TLR 330; aff'd [1895] 2 QB 315, 59 JP 695, 64, 44 WR 25, [1895–99] All ER Rep 1053, 39 Sol Jo 653, 73 LT 15, 11 TLR 517, CA.
[6] [2006] EWHC 836 (Ch), [2007] IRLR 110.   [7] [2012] EWCA Civ 156.   [8] EAT/532/89.

ongoing the employer is not obliged to provide work. In *SG & R Valuation Services Co v Boudrais*[9] the employee, who possessed confidential information about the employer's business, but had acted in breach of his contractual obligations, resigned his employment. The employer sought to enforce the three-month notice period, which had the effect of creating a garden leave situation, even though there was no provision to this effect. It was held that the employee remained in employment during the notice period, and interim relief was granted to prevent him from working for a competitor during that period.

Garden Leave

19.8 Because of legal uncertainties which surround the enforcement of post-termination restrictive covenants, some employers seek to obtain some protection from their employees' future competition by inserting a 'garden leave' clause into their contracts. This clause operates when lawful notice of termination is given, either by the employee or employer. During the notice period, the employee is not required to work, but is entitled to his full contractual terms and conditions. For his part, the employee remains bound by the implied duty of fidelity, and cannot work for a competitor, nor disclose trade secrets or confidential information, etc.

19.9 There should be an express contractual term which permits the employer to put the employee on garden leave, and this should set out the rights and obligations of both parties. However, in an unusual case, it was decided that an employer can put an employee on 'garden leave' even where there is no express garden leave clause in their employment contract unless the employee has a 'right to work', or he would become 'de-skilled' by not working (*Christie v Johnston Carmichael*[10]). The garden leave requirement can only be enforced if it is reasonable in terms of the length of time it operates, and if it is intended to protect the employer's genuine interests. During the garden leave period the employer is entitled to have a limited protection against the employee going to work for a competitor, or disclosing confidential information (*Provident Financial Group plc v Hayward*, see para 10.16), and if the employee acts in a manner contrary to the agreement the employer's remedy is for an injunction and/or damages. These remedies, however, are discretionary. And if, contrary to the terms of the garden leave, the employee works for a non-competitor, or discloses information which is not confidential, this will not amount to a breach of the garden leave clause, but he may be in breach of his contract of employment, and the employer may terminate the contract and/or sue for damages.

19.10 Garden leave clauses though, like restrictive covenants, are inherently contracts in restraint of trade, and so will only be enforced by the courts if they are reasonable, ie justified by reference to the legitimate business interests of the employer. Whether or not a court will uphold such a clause is a matter of discretion, to be determined on the facts of each case. On the one hand, there may be little damage to the employee if he is held to the agreement, for he will still be receiving his pay and other contractual entitlements; on the other hand there could well be considerable potential damage to the employer if the employee goes to work immediately for a rival firm (*Euro Brokers Ltd v Rabey*[11]). The employer's legitimate interests have to be balanced against the employee's right to work, especially when it is necessary to practise and exercise his skills and talents (*William Hill Organisation Ltd v Tucker*, see para 10.16). After all, it is to be expected that senior employees will seek employment in the same line of business, and will not take kindly to enforced

[9] [2008] EWHC 1340 (QB), [2008] IRLR 770.   [10] [2010] IRLR 1016.   [11] [1995] IRLR 206.

idleness, even if they are being paid. And employers will sometimes have exaggerated fears as to the damage likely to be caused to their business if the employee takes employment with another firm (*JA Mont (UK) Ltd v Mills*[12]).

19.11 A garden leave clause does have one advantage over a post-termination restrictive covenant. If the latter is drafted too widely, it will be void and unenforceable. The covenant must stand or fall on its own terms (but see para 19.52), unless the court can use the 'blue pencil' rule to give it limited validity (see para 19.52). However, when considering a garden leave clause which is too wide in its operation, the courts appear to be quite willing to interpret it and, if necessary, modify it, so as to give effect to its intentions. Thus in *Symbian Ltd v Christensen*[13] the employee's contract, which was terminable on six months' notice, contained a clause which prohibited him from working for anyone during the notice period. The employers learned that he was about to work for a competitor, and applied for an injunction to restrain him from doing so. Clearly, this clause was too wide, for it would have prohibited the employee from working for non-competing employers in non-competing businesses, but the court modified the clause so as to prohibit him from working for the named competitor any time during the six-month notice period.

19.12 Similarly, the court can modify the length of the period of garden leave, and, if necessary, reduce it to a period of time which reflects the realities of the situation (*Provident Financial Group plc v Hayward*). Thus in *GFI Group Inc v Eaglestone*[14] a garden leave period was cut down from 20 weeks to 13 weeks, although in *Euro Brokers Ltd v Rabey* a six-month garden leave period was upheld.

19.13 There is no reason in principle why a garden leave clause cannot be followed by a post-employment restrictive covenant, in effect lengthening the period of time when the employee is prevented from entering into competing employment. The one period cannot be set off against the other. But the existence of a garden leave clause may be a factor to take into account when determining the validity of the restrictive covenant and, if the garden leave clause is exceptionally long, the courts may, on grounds of public policy, refuse to enforce any further protection based on a restrictive covenant (*Credit Suisse Asset Management Ltd v Armstrong*[15]).

Employees who have Left their Employment

19.14 During his employment, an employee will doubtless come across a considerable amount of information, some of which is likely to be of a confidential nature. Names and addresses of customers and suppliers, prices, production methods, secret processes, etc, are all likely to come his way. Thus when he leaves his employment, he does not leave with an empty mind, yet the disclosure of such information is capable of causing considerable harm to his former employer. The higher the status of the employee, the more likely it is that he will have in his possession confidential information, and therefore the wider the restraint will have to be if it is to afford adequate protection to his former employer. This is particularly true in certain areas of employment where specialised knowledge and connections are involved (*Thomas v Farr plc*[16]). To determine whether particular information falls into the

---

[12] [1993] IRLR 172, CA.   [13] [2001] IRLR 77, CA.   [14] [1994] IRLR 119.
[15] [1996] ICR 882, [1996] IRLR 450, CA.
[16] [2007] EWCA Civ 118, [2007] ICR 932, [2007] IRLR 419.

category of information which ought not to be disclosed after the employment has ceased, regard must be had to all the circumstances, and, in particular, to:

(a) the nature of the employment;

(b) the nature of the information;

(c) whether the employer regarded the information as being confidential, and whether the employee was informed of this;

(d) whether the information could easily be isolated from other information which the employee is free to use (*Faccenda Chicken Ltd v Fowler*[17]).

19.15 It appears that there are three classes of information which an employee may acquire during his employment. First, there is information which is trivial or easily available to the public at large. This clearly does not give rise to any implied term of confidentiality. Second, there is information which has been imparted to the employee, or which he learns during the course of his employment for the purpose of his employer's business. During the course of his employment this should not be the subject of unauthorised disclosure, but once the employment has ceased, it remains part of the employee's skill and knowledge, and can be used by him for his own benefit—if necessary, in competition with his former employer. The law does not seek to prevent an employee from using his skill and know-how, even though these were obtained during his employment (*Stenhouse Australia Ltd v Phillips*[18]), for to do so would amount to a restraint on competition per se. Thus in *Faccenda Chicken Ltd v Fowler* the employer sought an injunction to restrain two former employees from using their knowledge of sales and price information when they set up a competing business. It was held that this was not confidential information, and the application for an injunction was refused. Finally, there is information which has been imparted in confidence, or which clearly amounts to being a trade secret, such as secret processes, etc. This cannot be disclosed after the employment has ceased, unless there is a public interest in disclosure. A trade secret, as well as being specialised or technical information (such as chemical formulae or specialised processes), must be such that its disclosure would be liable to cause real or significant harm to the employer (*Lansing Linde Ltd v Kerr*[19]). Whether information is to be treated as being confidential, or whether something is a trade secret, will clearly depend on the facts of each case (*SBJ Stephenson Ltd v Mandy*[20]), and the mere fact that the employer seeks to regard it as such is by no means conclusive (*Jack Allen (Sales and Service) Ltd v Smith*[21]).

19.16 It will be obvious that the rule against disclosure is easier to state in theory than to enforce in practice, for it is not possible to wipe out from an employee's mind information which he has gained in the course of the employment and which he may properly place at the disposal of his new employer. A distinction must be drawn between trade secrets and confidential information on the one hand, and an employee's skill, knowledge, and general familiarity with his former employer's business on the other hand (*Lock International plc v Beswick*[22]). In *Printers and Finishers Ltd v Holloway* (see para 10.70) the claimants sought an injunction against their former works manager restraining him from disclosing certain confidential information which he had obtained during his employment. Some of this information was contained in documents which the defendant had taken with him, and an injunction was granted in respect of these and an enquiry

---

[17] [1985] 1 All ER 724, [1984] ICR 589, [1984] IRLR 61; aff'd [1987] Ch 117, [1986] 1 All ER 617, [1986] ICR 297, [1986] IRLR 69, CA.   [18] [1974] AC 391, [1974] 1 All ER 117, PC.
[19] [1991] 1 All ER 418, [1991] ICR 428, [1991] IRLR 80, CA.   [20] [2000] IRLR 233.
[21] [1999] IRLR 19, OH.   [22] [1989] 3 All ER 373, [1989] IRLR 481.

ordered to ascertain what damage, if any, had flowed from the defendant's breach of duty. So far as confidential matters which were in his memory were concerned, which related to the know-how and general processes of the claimant's business, these were not readily separable from his general knowledge of the whole trade, and it would not be unreasonable for him to recall particular skills of his former employer's business and use his skills for the benefit of his new employer. Consequently, an injunction relating to these matters was refused.

19.17 It is not necessary that the employer points out to the employee the precise nature or aspects of the production process for which protection as a trade secret is sought (*Lancashire Fires Ltd v SA Lyons & Co Ltd*, see paras 10.70 and 19.4).

19.18 However, if the information obtained, though confidential, relates to a breach of the law or wrongful act by the employer, then there is an entirely different situation, for 'there is no confidence as to the disclosure of an iniquity'. In *Initial Services Ltd v Putterill*[23] the defendant was employed as a manager by the claimants. After leaving his employment he gave information to a newspaper concerning the conduct of the claimants' business, in particular alleging that they had violated the Restrictive Trade Practices Act 1956 by entering into agreements with other laundries which ought to have been registered under that Act, and that they had issued circulars which were misleading to the public. The newspaper proposed to publish an article which would have made detrimental allegations about the claimants' business, and an injunction was sought. It was held that the disclosure would be justified as being in the public interest, and there was no confidence attached thereto.

19.19 If an employee does disclose information relating to the commission of a fraud, crime, or act of corruption by his former employer, he can rely on the defence of 'just cause' if the disclosure is made in the public interest. Thus in *Lion Laboratories Ltd v Evans*[24] two ex-employees gave information to a newspaper which showed that there were doubts about the reliability of a breathalyser approved by the Home Office. It was held that the information disclosed was of grave public concern, and would not be restrained (see now para 10.75 for protected disclosures).

19.20 An ex-employee is not in breach of the implied term of confidentiality in disclosing information relating to his former employer's insolvency, because the duty of confidentiality is much more restricted in scope after the employment has ceased than that which is imposed by the general duty of good faith during the employment (*Brookes v Olyslager OMS (UK) Ltd*[25]). Nor can an ex-employee be restrained from disclosing information to regulatory bodies (such as the then Financial Services Authority) which have a duty to investigate matters within their remit (*Re a Company's Application*[26]).

19.21 In the absence of an express covenant restricting post-employment activities, there can be no general restriction on an ex-employee canvassing or doing business with customers of his former employer, or competing with him in any way, and there is no implied term prohibiting this (*Wallace Bogan & Co v Cove*[27]). An ex-employee is entitled to make use of the skill and knowledge he has acquired in his previous employment (*United Sterling Corpn v Felton*[28]) and, although he can be restrained by a restrictive covenant not to disclose trade

[23] [1968] 1 QB 396, [1967] 3 All ER 145, CA.   [24] [1985] QB 526, [1984] 2 All ER 417, CA.
[25] [1988] IRLR 590, 601 IRLB 6, CA.
[26] [1989] Ch 477, [1989] 2 All ER 248, [1989] ICR 449, [1989] IRLR 477.
[27] [1997] IRLR 453, CA.   [28] [1974] IRLR 314.

secrets or confidential information, or not to compete with his former employer, such a covenant can only give reasonable protection in limited circumstances (*Herbert Morris Ltd v Saxelby*[29]).

A. Springboard Injunctions

19.22 Employees are generally entitled to enter into competition with their former employer in the absence of a valid restrictive covenant, and they are entitled to use the knowledge and expertise that they have acquired during their employment. It is not possible to isolate their accumulated skill and knowledge. However, if an employee deliberately copies information acquired during his employment (eg lists of customers) or other confidential information, he can be restrained from using it to his former employer's disadvantage. Further, there is a distinction between a duty of fidelity and the fiduciary duty. A duty of fidelity is implied into every contract of employment, which requires the employee not to do anything contrary to the employer's interests. Additionally, however, directors and others in senior positions have a separate and potentially more onerous fiduciary duty of acting solely and exclusively in the employer's interests. Thus in *Kynixa Ltd v Hynes*[30] a director and senior manager failed to disclose that for a period of two months they had been discussing possible employment prospects with a competitor, and in *Crowson Fabrics Ltd v Rider*[31] two senior employees set up their own company in competition with their former employer. In both cases it was held that the employees were in breach of their fiduciary duty.

19.23 Additionally, the aggrieved employer may apply for a springboard injunction to prevent the former employee from gaining a head start in the new business at the expense of the former employer if there is a serious breach of contract by the latter that could cause serious economic damage to the former employer (*UBS Wealth Management (UK) Ltd v Vestra Wealth LLP*[32]). Indeed, even though there may be the absence of a garden leave clause in their contracts, there may be an implied right to impose one in cases where the employees have so breached their contracts of employment (eg by seeking to take away confidential information and/or fellow employees with them) that they have indicated that they are unwilling to perform their contractual duties (*SG & R Valuation Services Co LLC v Boudrais*, para 19.7).

19.24 Springboard injunctions were originally used to stop an ex-employee from using confidential information, despite the fact that that information was in the public domain and others could be free to use it. However, in *UBS Wealth Management (UK) Ltd v Vestra Wealth LLP* a springboard injunction was used to prevent five former employees and their new employer (Vestra Wealth) from approaching UBS's clients and encouraging more UBS staff to leave in order to work for the defendants, in breach of their own duty of loyalty and fidelity. On the other hand, a springboard injunction was refused in *Utopia (UK) Ltd v Wright*,[33] there being little evidence that the defendants had gained any unfair competitive advantage.

Post-employment Restraints

19.25 We have seen that an employer cannot prevent an ex-employee from competing with him, nor from using the knowledge, skill, and experience gained during the employment.

---

[29] [1915] 2 Ch 57, 59 Sol Jo 412, 112 LT 354, 31 TLR 370, CA; on appeal [1916] 1 AC 688, 85 LJ Ch 210, [1916–17] All ER Rep 305, 60 Sol Jo 305, 32 TLR 297, HL.
[30] [2008] EWHC 1495 (QB).   [31] [2007] EWHC 2942 (Ch), [2008] IRLR 288.
[32] [2008] EWHC 1974 (QB), [2008] IRLR 965.   [33] [2007] EWHC 321 (QB).

The employer can, however, extract a promise that the ex-employee will not, for a limited period of time, use that knowledge etc to the disadvantage of the employer (*Spafax Ltd v Harrison*, see paras 17.34 and 17.37), provided the restriction is reasonably necessary for the protection of the employer's business. Thus if an employer has a genuine interest to protect, he can require the employee to sign a covenant, restricting the employee's future activities after the employment comes to an end. Normally, this covenant would be agreed at the commencement of the employment, but this is not essential. In *R S Components Ltd v Irwin*[34] the employer asked a salesman, who was already in employment, to sign a covenant which would have prevented him from soliciting business from the firm's customers for a period of 12 months after leaving the employment. The employee refused to do so, and in consequence was dismissed. It was held that the dismissal was fair for 'some other substantial reason' (see para 17.144).

19.26 There are several limitations on the right of the employer to impose such restraints, for the courts may disapprove of any agreement which has the effect of restraining a person from earning his livelihood in the future. The employer cannot take away the employee's skill, experience, and fund of knowledge which he has obtained during the employment, and, in particular, the employer cannot protect himself against competition per se. For example, in *SW Strange Ltd v Mann*[35] the defendant was employed by a firm of bookmakers as a manager. Most of the betting was done by telephone, and hence the defendant had little contact with customers. He agreed that after leaving his employment he would not engage in a similar business within a radius of 12 miles. After leaving his job, he set up as a bookmaker within the prohibited area. It was held that the restriction was void. The purpose of the covenant was not to give legitimate protection to the business interest of the employer, but was a naked attempt to prevent future competition. In *Re-Use Collections Ltd v Sendall & Anor*,[36] however, Mr Sendall had been employed for some years by a family-run company before it was taken over by the claimant in 2000. He had no written contract, and no post-termination restriction until 2013, when he signed a contract. It was common ground that consideration was required as this was a variation to Mr Sendall's contract. He then left and set up a rival business. The High Court held that his continued employment did not amount to consideration, and it was not clear on the facts that refusal to sign the draft contract would amount to dismissal or any other sanction. In the absence of consideration, therefore, the post-termination covenant was unenforceable.

19.27 The protection required by the employer must be contained in a restrictive covenant, agreed to by the employee prior to the end of the employment, and is subject to two general limitations. These are (a) the restraint must be designed to protect the legitimate interests of the employer, and (b) it must be reasonable, in terms of the activities prohibited, and in terms of time and area covered by the restraint. The fact that the employee is given a payment to enter into a restrictive covenant is a relevant factor to be taken into account, but it is not conclusive, and the restraint is still required to be justified (*Turner v Commonwealth and British Minerals Ltd*[37]). In addition, a restrictive covenant is not enforceable if the previous employer is no longer carrying on the particular type of work as a result of the departure of the claimant (*Phoenix Partners Group LLP v Asoyag*[38]).

19.28 There are four legitimate interests in respect of which the employer is entitled to limited protection, namely (a) trade secrets and confidential information, (b) existing customers and connections, (c) working for competitors, and (d) enticing existing employees.

---

[34] [1974] 1 All ER 41, [1973] ICR 535, [1973] IRLR 239, NIRC.   [35] [1965] 1 All ER 1069.
[36] [2014] EWHC 3852 (QB).   [37] [2000] IRLR 114, [1999] All ER (D) 1097, CA.
[38] [2010] EWHC 846 (QB), [2010] IRLR 594.

A. **Trade Secrets and Confidential Information**

19.29 The common law surrounding trade secrets has been built up over many years. On 9 June 2018 the Trade Secrets (Enforcement, etc) Regulations 2018 came into force, providing a parallel cause of action in this area. Regulation 3 confirms that the common law is still valid, and so an action can be brought in both common law and under the Regulations.

The common law

19.30 If an employer could not ensure that his employees would not pass on information concerning his secret processes, it might restrict the employment relationship to an extent where commercial initiative became impossible. The employer would not be able to trust the employee, furtive attempts would have to be made to disclose some information without disclosing all, industrial espionage would flourish, and employees would attempt to sell secrets by offering themselves on the labour market to the highest bidder. Research and development would be hampered and become unprofitable. So, at least, ran the economic theories of former ages, though with the advent of patent law the modern scene might be somewhat different. Nonetheless, the legal principles remain substantially the same. Thus if a trade secret, or a secret process, exists, the employer is entitled to have his employee's promise not to divulge that information to a future employer, at least, subject to possible limitations on time and area. In *Forster & Sons Ltd v Suggett*[39] the defendant was a works engineer concerned with a secret process in the glass-making industry. He covenanted that he would not divulge any trade secret or manufacturing process, and would not be employed by a competitor anywhere in the United Kingdom for five years after leaving his employment with the plaintiffs. It was held that the covenant was reasonable and enforceable.

19.31 It is not possible to restrain an employee from disclosing to a future employer a special method of organisation, as opposed to a secret process, for one must draw a distinction between objective knowledge, such as trade secrets and lists of customers, which are part of the employer's property, and subjective knowledge which has been acquired by the employee, such as his general knowledge of the trade or industry, or his organisational ability. In *Herbert Morris Ltd v Saxelby* (para 19.21) an engineer covenanted not to be engaged by a competitor for seven years after leaving his employment. This was held to be void, for it was a restraint on his technical skill and knowledge which he had acquired by his own industry, observation, and intelligence, and this could not be taken away from him. On the other hand, in *SBJ Stephenson Ltd v Mandy* (para 19.15), a covenant against the disclosure of any information relating to the company's business affairs which had come into the employee's possession whilst employed by the company was held to be valid. The identity of customers, prices charged, renewal dates, market information, and contractual arrangements were objective knowledge capable of being protected. But if an employer wishes to enforce a covenant against the disclosure of confidential information, he must be able to identify a perceived or actual harm from the disclosure which would justify the restraint (*Jack Allen Ltd v Smith*, para 19.15).

19.32 Another example is *Thomas Marshall Ltd v Guinle* (see para 15.26), where the defendant was appointed managing director of the claimant company under a ten-year service contract, which contained clauses against disclosing confidential information relating to the affairs, customers or trade secrets of the company, during his employment or after it ceased. He resigned after five years and set up his own competing business. The court granted an injunction against him from acting in breach of the agreement.

---

[39] [1918] 35 TLR 87.

Statutory regulation

19.33 The Trade Secrets EU Directive 2016/943 was intended to harmonise the law across the EU in relation to Trade Secrets. The law in the UK was already fairly developed, and so the Trade Secrets (Enforcement, etc) Regulations 2018 are intended to 'fill in the gaps'. Regulation 2 defines 'trade secret' (for the purposes of the regulations only) as one which is:

(a) secret in the sense that it is not generally known or readily accessible to people who normally deal with that kind of information,

(b) has commercial value because it is secret, and

(c) has been subject to reasonable steps to keep it secret.

19.34 The Regulations provide for a limitation period of six years and set out how this is calculated. Regulation 10 deals with the preservation of confidentiality during court proceedings. Regulation 11 sets out interim measures the court can order, such as the cessation or prohibition of use or disclosure of the trade secret and the seizure of suspected infringing goods to prevent them entering the market. The court can specify a reasonable period for the trade secret holder to bring a case before the court, otherwise there is a time limit of 20 working days after the interim order is made.

19.35 There are also a number of final remedies. Regulation 14 provides for an injunction, or Regulation 16 for compensation as an alternative to this if the person did not know or ought to have known that the trade secret was obtained from someone who was using or disclosing it unlawfully. Regulation 17 deals with assessment of damages if an action is successful.

B. **Existing Customers and Connections**

19.36 An employer is entitled to have a limited protection against an ex-employee dealing with existing customers, for this is part of the goodwill which has been built up over the years. A covenant can restrict the right to solicit or endeavour to entice away former customers, or to have post-employment dealings with such customers, but it is likely that such clauses should be limited to those customers with whom the ex-employee had some dealings, for otherwise the restraint is likely to be regarded as one designed to prevent competition (*Marley Tile Co Ltd v Johnson*[40]). A clause prohibiting the ex-employee from approaching the employer's customers, or persons with whom the employer had been negotiating or who were in the habit of dealing with the employer, may be reasonable, particularly if there is a relationship with potential customers which could be built up over a number of years, and the employee was in a position where he could form a bond with those customers (*International Consulting Services (UK) Ltd v Hart*[41]). In *GW Plowman & Sons Ltd v Ash*,[42] the defendant was employed as a sales representative. He covenanted not to canvass or solicit orders from any person who was a customer of the firm for a period of two years after leaving his employment. It was held that the restraint was valid, even though it extended to customers whom the employee did not know or with whom he had no contact during his period of employment. It was argued that the restraint was bad because it could apply to those customers who had ceased to do business with the firm, but the Court of Appeal thought that an employer was entitled not to abandon hope that such customers would return to do business once more. This was reiterated in *Coppage & Anor v Safety Net Security Ltd*.[43]

---

[40] [1982] IRLR 75, CA.   [41] [2000] IRLR 227.
[42] [1964] 2 All ER 10, [1964] 1 WLR 568, 108 Sol Jo 216, CA.   [43] [2013] EWCA Civ 972.

19.37 On the other hand, if an employee does not come into contact with such customers, then it cannot be argued that he has built up a special relationship with them so as to entitle the employer to extract a covenant restraining the employee from approaching them with a view to taking business away from the employer. A restrictive covenant that prevents an employee from soliciting or accepting business from his former employer's customers will be unenforceable if it extends to customers with whom the employee personally had no dealings (*WRN Ltd v Ayris*[44]). For example, if a firm is engaged mainly in trading in the south of England, and has few customers outside that area, a covenant restraining an employee from working in that type of business anywhere in the UK must of necessity be void, as being wider than legitimately required for the protection of the employer's business (*Dowden and Pook Ltd v Pook*[45]).

19.38 The position held by the employee may be relevant, too. An employer can scarcely claim that he fears competition from an ex-employee if, during the period of employment, he pays him a low wage, for this reflects the regard he has for his services (*M and S Drapers v Reynolds*[46]). Nor is an employer entitled to restrain competition by preventing the ex-employee from approaching persons who are not his customers. In *Gledhow Autoparts v Delaney*[47] the claimants employed the defendant as a commercial traveller. It was agreed that after leaving his employment, the defendant would not seek orders from any firm within the area in which he had previously operated. The restraint was held to be void, for as worded, it would have prevented him from calling on firms who were not then customers of the claimants, and was therefore a covenant designed to restrain competition. Nor can a covenant restrain an ex-employee from dealing with businesses which were not in competition with the employer (*Scully UK Ltd v Lee*[48]).

19.39 Moreover, the personality, temperament, and general make-up of an employee is his own possession, and there is thus no proprietary right in an employee's own personality which the employer can keep to himself as part of his own business (*Cantor Fitzgerald (UK) Ltd v Wallace*[49]).

19.40 The employer's 'connections' are also a legitimate object for protection. Thus an employment agency which supplied temporary staff to business clients was held to be entitled to extract and enforce a restrictive covenant from its own staff who dealt with the temporary staff (the connection) and the clients (*Office Angels Ltd v Rainer-Thomas*[50]).

C. **Working for Competitors**

19.41 We have seen (para 10.3) that the courts will not grant an injunction to compel a person to work for a particular employer, for this would amount to compulsory labour. Thus if an employee agrees that after leaving his employment he will not work for anyone, the courts will rarely enforce such an agreement because the employee will be faced with the alternative of being forced to work for his former employer or starve! But if the latter alternative does not exist, the courts may be more willing to enforce the agreement.

19.42 In *Littlewoods Organisation Ltd v Harris*,[51] the claimants ran a mail order business, their chief rivals being Great Universal Stores (GUS). The defendant worked for the

[44] [2008] EWHC 1080 (QB), [2008] IRLR 889.
[45] [1904] 1 KB 45, 48 Sol Jo 50, 89 LT 688, 20 TLR 39, CA.
[46] [1956] 3 All ER 814, [1957] 1 WLR 9, 101 Sol Jo 44, CA.
[47] [1965] 3 All ER 288, [1965] 1 WLR 1366, 109 Sol Jo 571, CA.   [48] [1998] IRLR 259, CA.
[49] [1992] IRLR 215.   [50] [1991] IRLR 214, CA.
[51] [1978] 1 All ER 1026, [1977] 1 WLR 1472, 121 Sol Jo 727, CA.

claimants in a senior position, and had access to confidential information about how the business was operated. He agreed that on leaving his employment, he would not work for GUS for a period of 12 months. He then resigned his position in order to take employment with GUS, and the claimants sought an injunction to restrain him. For the defendant it was argued that the covenant was too wide, and therefore void, for, as worded, it would have prevented him from being employed by GUS anywhere in the world, or by one of their companies which was not concerned with mail order. Nonetheless, the restriction was held to be valid by a majority of the Court of Appeal. It was held that where a covenant in restraint of trade was drafted in general terms, which without alteration could be construed in a sense which was not unreasonably wide in relation to the relevant confidential information or trade secrets for which the covenantee was seeking protection, the court could construe the covenant in that sense, thereby rendering it valid and enforceable. Accordingly, the covenant should not be construed as applying to the whole range of business carried on by GUS throughout the world, but only to the mail order business carried on in the United Kingdom. So construed, it was no wider than was reasonably necessary to protect the confidential information about the mail order side of the claimants' business, and it was thus enforceable. There is little doubt that this case represented a major shift in the judicial approach to the interpretation of restrictive covenants, though it is arguable that the conclusion is warranted on the special facts.

19.43 But the protection taken out by the employer must be in respect of his specific interests, and if it is too wide for this purpose, it will be void. In *Commercial Plastics Ltd v Vincent*,[52] the claimants employed the defendant to work on the production of PVC calendering sheeting for adhesive tape. The defendant agreed not to be employed by a competitor in the PVC calendering field for one year after leaving his employment. This restriction was held to be void. The protection legitimately required by the claimants could only be in respect of their own business, which was the production of adhesive tape. In fact, the covenant covered the whole field of calendering sheeting, and hence was too wide.

19.44 The covenant should only restrict what is necessary to protect the employer. In *Associated Foreign Exchange Ltd v International Foreign Exchange (UK) Ltd*[53] a 12-month non-solicitation restrictive covenant restraining a currency trader was not enforced. The employee did not hold a senior position, and in the market in which the employer operated, 12 months was longer than was reasonably necessary to protect its interests.

D. Enticing Existing Employees

19.45 A covenant which purports to restrict the right of an employee to solicit or entice other employees to leave the employer's employment and to work for another employer is generally void. Thus in *Hanover Insurance Brokers Ltd v Schapiro*[54] the defendant entered into a restrictive covenant with his employers which provided, inter alia, that for a period of 12 months after leaving his employment he would not 'solicit or entice any employees of the company to the intent or effect that such employee terminates that employment'. When the defendant left his employment, the employers sought an injunction to restrain him from acting in breach of the clause quoted. It was held that an employee has the right to work for any employer who is willing to employ him. Thus employees are not part of the assets of an employer—like stock-in-trade or goodwill and customers. A restriction which sought to prevent a person from poaching employees, irrespective of their expertise, technical knowledge, and/or juniority, and which could also apply to employees who were not in the

[52] [1965] 1 QB 623, [1964] 3 All ER 546, [1964] 3 WLR 820, 108 Sol Jo 599, CA.
[53] [2010] IRLR 964, [2010] EWHC (Ch) 1178.   [54] [1994] IRLR 82, CA.

particular employment when the defendant left, was clearly a restriction against competition, and therefore void (*TSC Europe UK Ltd v Massey*[55]).

19.46 In *Hanover Insurance Brokers Ltd v Schapiro* (para 19.45) a non-solicitation clause was held to be unenforceable because it applied to all employees, irrespective of their position or experience, but different considerations may apply if the covenant purports to restrain the poaching of 'an executive' or a person 'in a senior capacity', and, if necessary, the court will identify those who fall within such categories (*Alliance Paper Group plc v Prestwich*[56]). Further, the Court of Appeal has held that an employer has a legitimate interest in maintaining a stable, trained workforce in a highly competitive business (*Ingham v ABC Contract Services Ltd*[57]) which can be protected within the limits of reasonableness by means of a non-solicitation clause (*Dawnay Day Ltd v de Braconier d'Alphen*[58]).

19.47 Employers cannot agree to a restraint among themselves which would not be enforced if it was entered into by their employees. In *Kores Manufacturing Co Ltd v Kolok Manufacturing Co Ltd*[59] two companies, both engaged in the selling of carbon paper, agreed that they would not employ any person who had been employed by the other party for a period of five years after that person had left the other's employment. Had the restraint been imposed by a company on the employees, it would have been void. It was equally void having been made by the employers themselves.

E. Reasonableness of the Covenant

19.48 To assess whether or not a covenant in restraint of trade is reasonable, the courts will consider not only the subject matter of the restraint, but also the time and area within which it will operate. If the employer's business is worldwide, a worldwide restraint may be valid (*Nordenfelt v Maxim Nordenfelt Ltd*[60]), but if the employer's business operates in a limited geographical area, a restraint which purports to operate outside that area will not be valid (*Office Angels Ltd v Rainer-Thomas*, para 19.40). A covenant with no geographical limitation will normally be unenforceable (*Commercial Plastics Ltd v Vincent*), as will a covenant which purports to operate in a densely populated area, which is not reasonably necessary for the protection of the employer's connections (*Office Angels Ltd v Rainer-Thomas*, para 19.406). In *Hollis & Co v Stocks*[61] a covenant which restricted a solicitor from working within a ten-mile radius of Sutton-in-Ashfield in Nottinghamshire was upheld, but in *Mason v Provident Clothing and Supply Co Ltd*[62] a covenant restraining a canvasser from competing with his former employer anywhere within 25 miles from the centre of London was held to be void.

19.49 Where an unreasonable covenant had been imposed some years ago on what was then a junior employee, if it was unenforceable at the time it was agreed, it remained unenforceable regardless of the employee's promotion to a role where such a covenant might have been regarded as reasonable (*Bartholomews Agri Food Limited v Michael Thornton*,[63] following *Pat Systems v Neilly*[64]).

The time element of a restrictive covenant must also be reasonable. In *Herbert Morris Ltd v Saxelby* (paras 19.21 and 19.31) a seven-year restraint on an engineer was not upheld,

---

[55] [1999] IRLR 22.   [56] [1996] IRLR 25.   [57] Unreported.
[58] [1997] IRLR 285; aff'd [1998] ICR 1068, [1997] IRLR 442, CA.
[59] [1957] 3 All ER 158, [1957] 1 WLR 1012, 101 Sol Jo 799; aff'd [1959] Ch 108, [1958] 2 All ER 65, [1968] 2 WLR 858, 102 Sol Jo 362, CA.   [60] [1895] 1 QB 151, 64 LJQB 182, 71 LT 565, 11 TLR 26, CA.
[61] [2000] IRLR 712, CA.
[62] [1913] AC 724, [1911–13] All ER Rep 400, 57 Sol Jo 739, 109 LT 449, 29 TLR 727, HL.
[63] [2016] EWHC 648 (QB).   [64] [2012] IRLR 979.

although in *Nordenfelt's* case (above) a 25-year restraint was held to be valid. In the latter case, the worldwide nature of the business and the price paid for the employee's promise were significant factors in upholding the covenant. Time and area may be looked at together to assess the validity of the covenant. In *Fitch v Dewes*[65] a solicitor's clerk was prohibited from entering into the employment of another solicitor within a radius of seven miles of Tamworth Town Hall. Although this was a lifetime restraint, the modest area enabled him to work quite openly outside the geographical limit, and it was held to be valid. On this point see also *Associated Foreign Exchange Ltd v International Foreign Exchange (UK) Ltd.*[66]

19.50 The restriction cannot be worded in a manner which prevents the employee from obtaining non-competing employment (*Commercial Plastics Ltd v Vincent* (para 19.48)). For example, in *Fellowes & Son v Fisher*[67] the defendant was a conveyancing clerk employed by a firm of solicitors in Walthamstow. He agreed that for five years after leaving his employment, he would not (a) be employed or concerned in the legal profession anywhere within the postal districts of Walthamstow and Chingford, or (b) solicit any person who had been a client of the firm while he had been with them. After leaving his employment, he commenced work with another firm of solicitors who had offices in Walthamstow. The Court of Appeal refused to grant an injunction to restrain him. A restraint of five years which covered such a thickly populated area was undoubtedly too wide in the circumstances. Further, clause (a), as worded, would have prevented him from being employed as an assistant to a justices' clerk, or in the legal department of the local authority. In *Greer v Sketchley Ltd*,[68] the activities of the company were confined to the Midlands and London areas. The employee agreed that after leaving his employment he would not work for any similar business anywhere in the United Kingdom. This was held to be void; the fact that there was a problematical and possible expansion by the company into other areas of the country was too vague to justify such a wide restraint.

19.51 An area restriction will always be considered critically by the courts, since it will frequently amount to a covenant against competition, which would generally be unenforceable. Thus if such a restriction will do little to protect the employer (eg, because most of the orders are placed on the telephone), or if there is no functional connection with the area covered by the restriction and the areas associated with the employee's work, the restraint is likely to be void (*Office Angels Ltd v Rainer-Thomas*, paras 19.40 and 19.48). A covenant that has a time restriction is more likely to be enforceable (*Allen Janes LLP v Johal*[69]).

F. Interpreting a Covenant in Restraint of Trade

19.52 If a covenant is too restrictive, it will be totally void, and the courts will not enforce it or any part of it. They will not normally validate the agreement by altering it, for the test is whether the parties have in fact made a valid agreement, not whether they could have done so, and it must stand or fall on its own merits. Thus in *Wincanton Ltd v Cranny*[70] a non-competition clause prohibiting post-termination involvement 'in any capacity' with a competing firm was held to be void. The court refused to read into the covenant a reasonable coverage (see also *J A Mont Ltd v Mills*, para 19.10). Exceptionally, however, the courts may relax this strict interpretation by use of a device known as the 'blue pencil' rule.

[65] [1921] 2 AC 158, 90 LJ Ch 436, [1921] All ER Rep 13, 65 Sol Jo 626, 125 LT 744, 37 TLR 784, HL.
[66] [2010] EWHC 1178 (Ch), [2010] IRLR 964.   [67] [1976] QB 122, [1975] 2 All ER 829, CA.
[68] [1979] IRLR 445, CA.   [69] [2006] EWHC 286 (Ch), [2006] ICR 742, [2006] IRLR 599, Ch.
[70] [2000] IRLR 716, CA.

19.53 The court must be satisfied that (a) the unenforceable provision is capable of being removed without the necessity of adding to or modifying the wording of what remains, (b) the remaining terms continue to be supported by adequate consideration, (c) the removal of the unenforceable provision does not so change the character of the contract that it becomes different from that which the parties entered into, and (d) the severance must be consistent with public policy underlying the avoidance of the offending term (*Marshall v NM Financial Management Ltd*;[71] see also *Beckett Investment Management Group Ltd v Hall*[72]). This approach was confirmed by the Supreme Court in *Tillman v Egon Zehnder Limited*.[73]

19.54 If there are terms which are too wide, and others which are valid and reasonable, then the former may be struck out of the agreement altogether. If those terms which thus remain are valid, then they may be enforced. In *T Lucas & Co Ltd v Mitchell*[74] the defendant was employed by the claimants as a sales representative. He agreed that after leaving his employment he would not (a) deal in any goods similar to those which he had previously sold, or (b) solicit orders from or supply any such goods to any customer of the firm within the Manchester area. The first part of the covenant was clearly void, for this was a restraint on competition. The second part was clearly reasonable. Because there were two separate restraints, capable of being enforced separately, the excision of the first was possible without affecting the second.

19.55 Severance is possible if there is no grammatical difficulty in removing the offending words (*Business Seating (Renovations) Ltd v Broad*[75]). If that which remains is reasonable, the covenant will be enforced (*Rex Stewart Jeffries Parker Ginsberg Ltd v Parker*[76]). The courts will prefer an interpretation which gives effect to the parties' intentions, rather than invalidate it by using a literal interpretation (*Turner v Commonwealth and British Minerals Ltd*, see para 19.27).

19.56 If, in the particular circumstances of the case, there is 'a want of accuracy of expression' the court may be prepared to permit an interpretation which would give some sensible meaning to a covenant. Thus in *Business Seating (Renovations) Ltd v Broad*, a clause forbade a sales representative from canvassing, soliciting, or endeavouring to take away from the company the business of any client or customers. The nature of 'the business' was not defined, but its meaning could be inferred from the nature of the defendant's employment, and, as a matter of construction, it meant the business carried out by the company.

19.57 When construing a restrictive covenant, the courts would seek objectively to ascertain the intentions of the parties. Thus in *Hollis & Co v Stocks* (para 19.48) a restrictive covenant contained a clause prohibiting an assistant solicitor from working for a period of 12 months within a ten-mile radius. This clause was clearly too wide, because it would have prevented him from doing any sort of work, but the Court of Appeal upheld an injunction, arguing that it was clear that the clause was designed to prevent him working as a solicitor. The balance of convenience was in favour of granting the injunction, because damages were not an appropriate remedy, and it was not possible for his former employers to quantify the loss.

19.58 Where a restrictive covenant is ambiguous, a court can interpret a sensible meaning. Where, however, the clause is not ambiguous, but just badly drafted without thinking of the consequences, the employer has 'made its bed . . . and must now lie upon it'. The

---

[71] [1995] 4 All ER 785, [1995] ICR 1042, [1996] IRLR 20; on appeal [1997] ICR 1065, [1997] IRLR 449, CA.

[72] [2007] EWHC 241 (QB), revsd [2007] EWCA Civ 613, [2007] IRLR 793, [2007] ICR 1539.

[73] [2019] UKSC 32.   [74] [1972] 2 All ER 1035; revsd [1974] Ch 129, [1972] 3 All ER 689, CA.

[75] [1989] ICR 729.   [76] [1988] IRLR 483, CA.

Court cannot rewrite it (*Prophet PLC v Huggett*[77]). There is a tendency in some cases for the courts to attempt to ascertain the true intentions of the parties and give effect to them, even though some redrafting of the covenant is involved (*GFI Group Inc v Eaglestone*, para 19.12), but the principle remains that the court will not rewrite the covenant so that it has a meaning which is different from that which it has when properly construed.

19.59 A restrictive covenant that has been entered into between an employee and a holding company can be enforced, even though it is the subsidiaries that have the interests to protect. The law must take account of the realities of modern business organisation (*Beckett Investment Management Group Ltd v Hall*, para 19.53).

G. **Breach of Contract by the Employer**

19.60 There is a general rule that a party in breach of contract cannot rely on any of its terms in order to gain an advantage. Thus if an employer wrongfully dismisses an employee, he cannot enforce a restrictive covenant, for the whole of the contract will have been repudiated by him (*General Billposting Co Ltd v Atkinson*, see para 16.6). (Be aware, however, that if the dismissal is an unfair one, as opposed to a wrongful one, it has been held that it does not negate a restraint clause: *Lonmar Global Risks Ltd v West*.[78])

19.61 But in *Campbell v Frisbee* (a case which concerned a contract for services rather than a contract of employment) the High Court held that 'an employee's acceptance of an employer's repudiatory breach cannot displace the employer's established property rights, and these include his right in respect of confidential information'.[79] There is no justification for granting as a windfall to a wrongfully dismissed employee a present of his employer's trade secrets or other secrets or confidences. The wrongful dismissal may arise because of a dismissal without notice, or with insufficient notice, or contrary to a contractual disciplinary procedure (*Dietman v Brent London Borough Council*, see paras 16.19, 16.21, and 16.31), or breach of a fixed-term contract consequence on the dissolution of a partnership (*Briggs v Oates*[80]). It may even arise out of a constructive dismissal (*Cantor Fitzgerald International v Callaghan*, see para 3.33). But if a contract provides that it may be terminated by an employer on giving six months' notice or six months' pay in lieu of notice, an employer who adopts the latter option is not acting in breach of contract (*Rex Stewart Jeffries Parker Ginsberg Ltd v Parker*, para 19.55).

19.62 To avoid this rule, some employers resorted to inserting into the covenant a clause which stated that it was to apply 'howsoever the employment is terminated' or if the contract was terminated 'for whatever reason', etc. Such phrases do not, by themselves, render the covenant unenforceable by virtue of being unreasonable. Not every stipulation in a contract falls when there has been a fundamental breach by one side which has been accepted by the innocent party. Thus if an employee is dismissed for reason of misconduct, or he resigns his employment, the restrictive covenant may still be enforced, despite the presence of the above phrases. The fact that the offending term may apply to some circumstances, but not to others, will not invalidate the covenant (*Rock Refrigeration Ltd v Jones*[81]).

19.63 If an employee is dismissed for refusing to sign a restrictive covenant that is too wide, this is still capable of being 'some other substantial reason' for the dismissal (unless

---

[77] [2014] EWCA Civ 1013.   [78] [2011] IRLR 138, QBD.
[79] [2002] EWHC 328 (Ch), [2002] All ER (D) 211 (Mar); revsd [2002] EWCA Civ 1374, [2003] ICR 141, [2002] All ER (D) 178 (Oct).
[80] [1991] 1 All ER 407, [1990] ICR 473, [1990] IRLR 472.
[81] [1997] 1 All ER 1, [1997] ICR 938, [1996] IRLR 675, CA.

the dismissal is in fact a mere ruse to get rid of the employee), but the unreasonableness of the covenant becomes very relevant when determining the fairness of the dismissal. Thus, if it is plainly unreasonable, and not severable, it will be easier for the employment tribunal to conclude that the dismissal was unfair. On the other hand, if the covenant was arguably unreasonable or marginally capable of being severable, the tribunal should consider the employer's approach to the whole issue, including the time given to the employee to consider the proposal and the opportunity for him to obtain legal advice. Even if the covenant is plainly reasonable, the employer must still satisfy the requirements of a reasonable procedure (*Willow Oak Developments Ltd v Silverwood*[82]).

H. **Restrictive Covenants and Transfers**

19.64 It will be recalled (see Chapter 9) that if there is a transfer of an undertaking, the contracts of employment of the affected employees will pass automatically from the transferor to the transferee. It therefore follows that if the employee's terms and conditions include a restrictive covenant, then this will bind the employee if he subsequently leaves the transferee's employment. But the covenant needs to be considered in the light of the new situation, otherwise it may be unenforceable (see *Morris Angel & Son Ltd v Hollande*, para 9.32). Equally it is not possible to impose a restrictive covenant on an employee following a transfer, even though the employee agreed to it, if it was introduced by reason of the transfer (*Credit Suisse First Boston (Europe) Ltd v Padiachy*, para 9.40), because the employee is entitled to the terms and conditions which he enjoyed prior to the transfer, and it is irrelevant that he is better off as a result of the variation (*Credit Suisse First Boston (Europe) Ltd v Lister*, para 9.40). However, it does appear that any variation in a contract of employment which takes place unconnected with the transfer may well be valid.

I. **Remedies for Breach of Contract**

Injunctive relief

19.65 The prime remedy for the employer if the ex-employee acts in breach of the restrictive covenant is to seek an injunction restraining the breach.

19.66 In considering whether or not to grant an injunction, the court will take account of the 'balance of convenience' in accordance with the principles laid down in *American Cyanamid v Ethicon Ltd* (see paras 10.6 and 16.30). Three questions need to be asked: (a) is there a serious issue to be tried, (b) would damages be an appropriate remedy if the injunction is not granted, and (c) what is the likelihood of the plaintiff succeeding at a full trial? In *Lansing Linde Ltd v Kerr* (para 19.15) it was alleged that the defendant was in breach of a covenant which was designed to prevent him from working for a competitor for a period of 12 months after leaving his employment. The Court of Appeal held that an application for an injunction was rightly refused. The trial of the action would not have taken place until most of the period for which the injunction was sought would have expired. Thus the question was not only whether there was a serious issue to be tried, but also an assessment of the plaintiff's prospect of succeeding at that hearing. The injunction, if granted, would have effectively determined the case in the claimant's favour, and therefore the judge had been correct in considering as an additional factor the strength of the plaintiff's claim. In *ESL Fuels Ltd v Fletcher & Anor*[83] the first limb of the American Cyanamid test, namely

---

[82] [2006] ICR 55, [2006] IRLR 28, EAT; aff'd [2006] EWCA Civ 660, [2006] ICR 1552, [2006] IRLR 607, CA.
[83] [2013] EWHC 3726 (Ch).

'was there a serious issue to be tried?' was considered, but this did not preclude considering any clear conclusion on the merits that could be reached at the interim stage. In this
case, however, there was no clear preliminary conclusion. The case concerned trade secrets,
where an application for an interim injunction sought to prevent the defendants from selling a particular product which the claimant said was a trade secret that a former employee
had taken. The application was refused. Despite the status quo favouring the claimant,
the balance of convenience favoured the defendants. The effect of an interim injunction
would be catastrophic for the rival, a start-up company which would then be 'strangled at
birth', whereas the claimant could be adequately compensated if the claim was subsequently
found in its favour.

19.67 Even though an employee is in breach of his covenant, the granting of an injunction to restrain him from working for a competitor is a discretionary remedy, and will only
be granted if, on the balance of convenience, it is necessary to do so. In *GFI Group Inc v
Eaglestone* (paras 19.12 and 19.58) the defendant was required by his employment contract
to give 20 weeks' notice of termination. He, and two other highly paid employees, decided
to resign and work for a competitor. The other two employees were only required to give
four weeks' notice. The claimant sought an order to restrain the defendant from working in
breach of his contract until the end of the 20-week notice period, but the court decided to
uphold the restraint only for 13 weeks. The fact that two other employees had already commenced work for the competitor meant that the reality of the situation was that the damage
had already been done. It was not necessary for the protection of the claimant's interests to
hold the defendant to the full period of 20 weeks.

19.68 If there is a prima facie breach of a covenant not to deal with the employer's former
customers, the employer is entitled to an injunction even though the customer has inti-
mated that he will not do further business with the employer (*John Michael Design plc v
Cooke*[84]).

Search Orders

19.69 In addition (or as an alternative) to obtaining an injunction, the aggrieved employer
may seek a search order. This permits the employer to search the employee's premises or
home etc, and to remove documents, drawings, records, prototypes, or other specified
matter. The purpose is to prevent a defendant from destroying, hiding, or removing vital
evidence, and to enable the claimant to obtain inspection of any relevant matter in the
defendant's possession. A refusal to permit the search, and/or the removal, destruction, etc
of the evidence not only enables the courts to draw an adverse conclusion, but may also
amount to a contempt of court (*Anton Piller KG v Manufacturing Processes Ltd*[85]). Before
granting the order, the court must be satisfied (a) that there is a strong prima facie case,
(b) that the actual or potential damage to the plaintiff would be very serious, and (c) that
there is clear evidence that the defendant has in his possession incriminating matter, and
that there is a real possibility that he would destroy, hide, remove, or otherwise dispose of
it (*Lock International plc v Beswick*, para 19.16).

19.70 Search orders are not available in Scotland, although there is a separate procedure
by way of letters of request, under which a court may grant a commission and a diligence
for the recovery of documents relevant to pending litigation.

---

[84] [1987] 2 All ER 332, [1987] ICR 445, CA.
[85] [1976] Ch 55, [1976] 1 All ER 779, CA.

Damages

19.71 If the employer can show that he has suffered damage as a result of the breach, he may bring an action accordingly. The amount of damages to be awarded will be such as to put the claimant in the position he would have been in had the contract been performed. Thus in *SBJ Stephenson Ltd v Mandy* (paras 19.15 and 19.31) the defendant signed a restrictive covenant preventing him from disclosing confidential information, engaging in competing activities and soliciting staff of the employer, for a period of 12 months from the end of the termination of his employment. He resigned his position, and subsequently acted in breach of the covenant. The employers were successful in obtaining an injunction, and were subsequently awarded substantial damages in respect of loss of income from former clients and for future loss.

Account of Profits

19.72 An action for an account of profits is essentially based on the equitable principle of unjust enrichment, and is normally available only in those cases where there has been a breach of fiduciary duty or breach of the duty of confidence. Damages are assessed on the profits made by the defendant rather than on any proven loss by the claimant. Thus in *Nottingham University v Fishel* (paras 10.56 and 19.5) the defendant, a world-renowned fertility expert, was employed by the university. He carried out outside work for overseas clinics, from which he earned money. He also benefited financially from work performed by junior colleagues under his supervision. It was held that the university was entitled to an account of profits for this breach of fiduciary duty.

Actions Against Third Parties

19.73 An action for inducing a breach of contract may be brought against someone who induces an employee to breach his contract of employment (*Bents Brewery Co Ltd v Hogan*, para 10.69) or to break the terms of a restrictive covenant. As well as obtaining an injunction (*Hivac v Park Royal Scientific Instruments Ltd*, paras 10.93 and 17.141), the injured party may seek damages in tort (*British Industrial Plastics Ltd v Ferguson*[86]).

Training Agreements

19.74 An employer may permit an employee to go on a training course (possibly with paid leave of absence) under an agreement whereby the employee agrees to serve the employer for a specified period after completing the course. Clearly, such an agreement can be for the mutual benefit of both parties. The problem arises when the employee fails to serve the employer for the specified period. In *Strathclyde Regional Council v Neil*,[87] the defendant was employed by the claimants as a trainee social worker. She was given paid leave of absence to go on a training course, and signed an agreement to serve the council for two years after completing the course. The agreement also specified that if she left her employment before completing two years' service she would refund to the council a sum of money proportionate to the unexpired period of the contractual two years. After completing the course, she worked for the council for 15 months, and resigned her employment. It was held that the council could recover a proportion of their expenditure in respect of her salary, course fees, examination fees, and book allowance. The terms of the contract were not extravagant or unconscionable.

---

[86] [1938] 4 All ER 504, CA; aff'd [1940] 1 All ER 479, HL.
[87] [1984] IRLR 11, Sh Ct; aff'd sub nom *Neil v Strathclyde Regional Council* [1984] IRLR 14.

Summary

- There is a duty of fidelity between employer and employee.
- An employer is not entitled to have protection from competition per se, but is entitled to have limited protection re confidential information, existing customers, etc.
- Seeking employment with a competitor is not by itself a breach of the duty of fidelity.
- A distinction must be drawn between trade secrets and an employee's skill and familiarity with the employer's business.
- An employer cannot put an employee on garden leave if he has a right to work or would become de-skilled by not working.
- Garden leave must be of reasonable length and only to protect employer's genuine interests.
- An employer may apply for an injunction to prevent misuse of confidential information, etc.
- An employer cannot prevent an ex-employee from competing with him nor from using the knowledge, skill and experience gained during the employment, but can agree a restrictive covenant that employee will not use knowledge for a period of time.
- A covenant in restraint of trade must be reasonable not only re subject matter, but also in the time and area it will operate.
- A covenant which is too restrictive will be void.

20

Practice and Procedure

Background

20.1 We looked at employment tribunals and the employment appeal tribunal on Chapter 1. In this chapter we consider the practicalities of bringing a case to a tribunal or appeal, and will deal with the Employment Tribunals (Constitution and Rules of Procedure) Regulations 2013 ('the rules').

20.2 In the original scheme of things, employment tribunals (formerly known as industrial tribunals) were intended to be a cheap, speedy, and informal method of resolving employment disputes. The parties frequently represented themselves, and the employment judge would assist them in presenting their respective cases. However, the growth of employment rights over the years and the tremendous increase in the number of claims made resulted in more complex legal rules, frequently requiring the use of legal or other skilled representatives. In consequence, tribunal procedures became more formal and less flexible. The rules, which have been through several variations and amendments over the years, contain a number of provisions designed to speed up hearings, concentrate on relevant facts and information, and discourage weak claims.

20.3 The overriding objective of the rules is to enable tribunals to deal with a case justly, including, so far as is practicable, ensuring that the parties are on an equal footing, saving expense, dealing with the case in ways which are proportionate to the complexity of the issues, ensuring that the case is dealt with expeditiously and fairly while avoiding unnecessary formality and seeking flexibility in the proceedings. Proceedings at the actual hearing are therefore reasonably informal. The parties may represent themselves, or be represented by a solicitor or barrister, or a representative of a trade union or employers' association, or any other person whom they desire to represent them.

Making a Claim to an Employment Tribunal

20.4 An employee who wishes to seek the enforcement of a statutory right or to obtain a remedy for a breach of that right must present his claim to an employment tribunal within the appropriate time limit. An application for interim relief must be made within seven days of the dismissal, and a claim for a redundancy payment must be made within six months from the relevant date, although the employment tribunal has a discretion to extend the period for a further six months in certain circumstances if it is just and equitable to do so (ERA, s 164). Claims for equal pay must also be presented within six months from the termination of employment, as must a claim based on a dismissal connected with official industrial action (see para 21.101), and a claim against a trade union in respect of unlawful exclusion or expulsion.

20.5 The general rule is that all other claims must be presented within three months of the act complained of. Apart from two exceptions (and the extension afforded by early conciliation, below), this rule is mandatory (see paras 20.6 and 20.10). An employment tribunal has no jurisdiction to hear a claim that has been presented out of time. Thus, in *Rogers v Bodfari (Transport) Ltd*[1] a claim for unfair dismissal was made out of time, but the employer did not raise an objection. The employment tribunal decided that the dismissal was unfair. At an adjourned hearing to assess compensation, the employers raised the fact that the limitation period had elapsed, and the employment tribunal (reluctantly) dismissed the application on the ground that it had no jurisdiction to hear the claim in the first place. The decision was upheld on appeal. Neither the tribunal nor the parties can waive a jurisdictional provision.

Note that the clock stops when a prospective claimant contacts ACAS for early conciliation to take place, and only starts again when the ACAS 'Early Conciliation certificate' is issued (para 1.41). Early conciliation can last up to one calendar month, and can be extended by up to 14 days if ACAS feel there is a reasonable prospect of settling the case within that time.

There are two exceptions to the general three-month rule.

20.6 (a) *Not reasonably practicable.* If it was not reasonably practicable to present the claim within the three months, the claim may be presented within such period as the employment tribunal considers reasonable. If it was reasonably practicable to do so, that will generally be the end of the matter. Otherwise, it is for the employment tribunal to consider whether to exercise its discretion and permit the claim to be admitted within such period as it considers to be reasonable. In *Cambridge & Peterborough Foundation NHS Trust v Crouchman*[2] a claim was admitted outside the three-month limit where the claimant discovered new and crucial information that led him to believe that he had a viable claim.

20.7 In deciding whether or not to allow a claim out of time, the employment tribunal must enquire into the circumstances as to why it was not reasonably practicable to present the claim before the end of the relevant period. 'Practicable' in this connection means 'feasible' and it is a question of fact for the employment tribunal to determine (*Palmer v Southend-on-Sea Borough Council*[3]). The mere fact that there is a pending internal appeal will not by itself allow a claimant to say that it was not reasonably practicable to present a claim in time, but the question of the claimant's state of knowledge of the time limit is still relevant. In *John Lewis Partnership v Charman*,[4] the claimant pursued an internal appeal, not realising the time limit for an unfair dismissal claim. The question was whether he should have made proper inquiries, but the EAT, following *Marks & Spencer v Williams-Ryan*,[5] held that it was not reasonable to have expected him to do so until he knew the outcome of the appeal. *Palmer* was distinguished on the basis that in that case the claimant had been represented by a trade union which should have known of the time limit.

20.8 If the time limit expires on a non-working day (eg a Sunday) an application will be out of time if it is presented on the following day (*Swainston v Hetton Victory Club Ltd*[6]).

20.9 If an employee is dismissed on the 14th day of the month, the claim must be presented on or before the 13th day of the third month following. If the effective date of termination is the end of a month, and the month three months afterwards has no corresponding date (ie because it is a shorter month), the three-month period will expire on the last day of the relevant month. Thus if an employee is dismissed on 30th November, the claim must

---

[1] [1973] ICR 325, [1973] IRLR 172.   [2] [2009] ICR 1306.
[3] [1984] 1 All ER 945, [1984] ICR 372, [1984] IRLR 119.   [4] UKEAT/0079/11/ZT.
[5] [2005] ICR 1293.   [6] [1983] 1 All ER 1179, [1983] ICR 341, [1983] IRLR 164.

be presented on the 28th of the following February (or 29th, if it is a leap year: see *Pruden v Cunard Ellerman Ltd*[7]).

20.10 If an employee or his representative (eg trade union official or solicitor) are at fault in not presenting the claim in time, it is likely that the employment tribunal will refuse jurisdiction (*Times Newspapers v O'Reagan*[8]) but if an employee is blameless, it may be easier to infer that it was not reasonably practicable to present the claim in time (*Union Cartage Co Ltd v Blunden*[9]). Where the claimant's 'skilled adviser' has got the date wrong because of misleading information from the employer, an extension can be allowed (*Northamptonshire County Council v Entwhistle*[10]). If the employer expressly requests that the claim be delayed so that negotiations can take place with a view to reaching an amicable settlement, then it may not be reasonably practicable to present the claim within the time limits (*Owen v Crown House Engineering Ltd*[11]). Ignorance of one's rights is no excuse for not presenting a claim within the three-month period (*Avon County Council v Haywood-Hicks*[12]) but mistaken advice given by the staff of the employment tribunal may be a ground for extending the time limits (*London International College v Sen*[13]). If a claimant knows of the time limits, or has been advised of them, or if he is capable of looking after his own affairs, it is for the employment tribunal to decide how much weight to place on all the factors that have led to the claim being presented out of time (*Robinson v Post Office*[14]).

20.11 Having submitted that it was not reasonably practicable to comply with the time limits, the claimant must then go on to show that the claim was submitted within such period as the employment tribunal considers reasonable. Thus a claimant must rectify any delay as soon as he becomes aware of it, and there is no particular timescale involved. It is a matter for the employment tribunal to determine as a question of fact. Thus, in *James W Cook & Co Ltd v Tipper*[15] a claim was allowed to proceed that was presented two weeks after the time limit had expired, because the employment tribunal was satisfied that the claimant had been misled as to the true situation. At the same time, the employment tribunal is entitled to take into account the prejudice that may be caused to the employer by allowing a claim to proceed out of time and balance this against the disadvantage to the claimant (*Baynton v South West Trains Ltd*[16]). If the employer is aware of the facts and the reason for the delay (eg a claimant's ill health) a delay of months might not be unreasonable (*Whitbread plc v Rees*[17]).

20.12 (b) *Just and equitable.* So far as claims that are based on allegations of discrimination are concerned, the employment tribunal can extend the time limit if it is just and equitable to do so (*British Coal Corpn v Keeble*,[18] and see Equality Act 2010, para 4.222). This test is less stringent than the 'not reasonably practicable' test. Thus, in *Department of Constitutional Affairs v Jones*[19] an out-of-time disability discrimination claim was accepted when it was shown that the claimant's delay was in part due to the fact that he was reluctant to admit that his depression was severe enough to amount to a disability.

20.13 If the claimant was not aware of the facts that gave rise to a potential complaint until after the three-month time limit has expired (eg the alleged acts of race or sex discrimination: see *Berry v Ravensbourne National Health Service Trust*[20]) it will be just and equitable to allow the late submission of the claim, provided the claimant acts expeditiously once he is aware of the true state of affairs (*Machine Tool Industry Research Association v Simpson*[21]).

[7] [1993] IRLR 317.   [8] [1977] IRLR 101.   [9] [1977] ICR 420, [1977] IRLR 139.
[10] [2010] IRLR 740, EAT.   [11] [1973] 3 All ER 618, [1973] ICR 511, [1973] IRLR 233.
[12] [1978] ICR 646, [1978] IRLR 118.   [13] [1992] IRLR 292.   [14] [2000] IRLR 804.
[15] [1990] ICR 716, [1990] IRLR 386.   [16] [2005] ICR 1730.   [17] EAT/1292–1293/97.
[18] [1997] IRLR 336.   [19] [2007] EWCA Civ 894, [2008] IRLR 128.
[20] [1993] ICR 871.   [21] [1988] ICR 558, [1988] IRLR 212.

20.14 If the act complained of is a continuing one (eg race or sex or disability discrimina-tion, etc), which extends over a period, time will run from the end of the period (*Barclays Bank plc v Kapur*²²). The date on which the cause of action crystallised will depend on the facts of each case (*Clarke v Hampshire Electro-Plating Co*²³). If the claimant is ill during the three-month period, attention should be focused on whether the illness falls in the earlier part of the period or in the far more critical weeks leading up to the expiration of the period if the employment tribunal is considering whether to permit the claim outside the three months (*Schutz v Esso Petroleum*²⁴).

20.15 In a discrimination case, wrong advice by a legal adviser may be a valid excuse for not complying with the time limits, making it just and equitable to allow the claim to proceed (*Chohan v Derby Law Centre*²⁵), and a delay caused by the fact that the claim-ant was awaiting the outcome of a disciplinary hearing can also be taken into considera-tion (*Apelogun-Gabriels v London Borough of Lambeth*²⁶). When deciding how to exercise its discretion, the employment tribunal may refer to a checklist of factors set out in the Limitation Act 1980, s 33, which is used in personal injury cases, and use them as a guide, although these should not be elevated to the status of a legal requirement. These include (a) the length of and reason for the delay, (b) the extent to which the cogency of the evi-dence would be affected by the delay, (c) the extent to which the parties co-operated with requests for information, (d) the promptness with which the plaintiff acted once he knew of the facts which gave rise to the cause of action, and (e) the steps which the plaintiff took to obtain prompt advice once he realised that he had a possible cause of action.

20.16 All complaints must actually be received (*Secretary of State for Employment v Banks*²⁷) by the Employment Tribunal Central Office within the appropriate time limits (before midnight: see *Post Office v Moore*²⁸), although an application received by a regional office will be valid if presented in time (*Bengey v North Devon District Council*²⁹). Most ap-plications are now submitted electronically, but if the application does not arrive in time because of an abnormal delay in the post, the claimant will have to rely on the escape clause (*Beanstalk Shelving Ltd v Horn*³⁰). A claim which was presented 88 seconds late was held to be out of time in *Beasley v National Grid*.³¹ There is no grey area for complaints that are 'only a bit out of time'. It would be for the claimant to show that it was not reasonably practicable to bring the claim within the appropriate time limit.

20.17 Documents or letters dispatched by first class post are expected to arrive in the ordinary course of events on the second working day after posting; documents and letters sent by second class post are expected to arrive on the fourth working day after posting (*St Basil's Centre Ltd v McCrossan*³²). If there is a postal strike, appropriate allowances should be made (*Beanstalk Shelving Ltd v Horn*), although alternative means of delivery should be arranged. Working days are Monday to Friday but, technically, bank or public holidays are *dies non* (non-days), and time limits are accordingly extended (*Ford v Stakis Hotels and Inns Ltd*³³).

20.18 Thus if an application is posted, but arrives one day after the time limits have ex-pired, it is open to the employment tribunal to decide if the claimant could have reason-ably expected the application to be delivered in the ordinary course of the post. This is a

²² [1991] 2 AC 355, [1991] 1 All ER 646, [1991] ICR 208, [1991] IRLR 136.
²³ [1992] ICR 312, [1991] IRLR 490.   ²⁴ [1999] ICR 1202.
²⁵ [2004] IRLR 685.   ²⁶ [2001] EWCA Civ 1853, [2002] ICR 713, [2002] IRLR 116.
²⁷ [1983] ICR 48, EAT.   ²⁸ [1981] ICR 623, EAT.   ²⁹ [1977] ICR 15, EAT.
³⁰ [1980] ICR 273, EAT.   ³¹ [1980] ICR 273, EAT.
³² [1992] ICR 140, [1991] IRLR 455, EAT.   ³³ [1987] ICR 943, [1988] IRLR 46, EAT.

question of fact for the employment tribunal to determine on the evidence (*St Basil's Centre v McCrossan*[34]). On the post rules generally, see *Consignia plc v Sealy*.[35]

20.19 But if, though posted in time, an application does not appear to have been received by COET, prudence requires that the claimant (or his representative) should make further enquiries, because it should be obvious from the failure to receive an acknowledgment that something is amiss, and therefore confirmation should be sought as to its arrival. It follows that if nothing is done to check the receipt of an application which has in fact never arrived, a fresh application may well be out of time (*Capital Foods Retail Ltd v Corrigan*[36]). Indeed, a solicitor who submits an application on behalf of a client is expected to have a proper system operating which enables him to find out, contemporaneously, whether the conduct of business is taking a normal course, and to check, at or near the time, that replies which should have been received at a given date have in fact been received. Thus in *Camden and Islington Community Services NHS Trust v Kennedy*,[37] the claimant's claim for unfair dismissal had to be presented by 27 December. Her solicitor posted her application on 19 December, but although he expected to receive an acknowledgment by 5 January, he delayed checking with the tribunal office until 30 January, when he was told that it had not been received. He posted another application the following day. It was held that the claim was out of time. Solicitors practising in the field of employment law must be aware of the need to comply strictly with the appropriate time limits, and ensure that they have in place systems which ensure that time limits are complied with.

20.20 If, in error, a claimant names the wrong employer in his application, an employment tribunal may, at the request of the claimant or on its own motion, add any other person to be joined in the proceedings, even though this is done outside the normal time limit for presenting a claim. The employment tribunal may exercise its discretion to join the other party not only when the claimant has misnamed or misdescribed the respondent, but also when he has failed to identify the 'correct' employer (eg where his contract has been transferred by virtue of the Transfer of Undertakings (Protection of Employment) Regulations: see *Drinkwater Sabey Ltd v Burnett*[38]).

20.21 The general power to extend time limits on the ground that it is just and equitable to do so is to be used sparingly. The onus is on the applicant to show good reason, and the initial assumption is that an extension is to be the exception, not the rule (*Robertson v Bexley Community Centre*[39]).

20.22 The statutory time limits go to the employment tribunal's jurisdiction, and if a claim is presented out of time, the tribunal will be unable to hear the claim even though the employer fails to take the point (*Rogers v Bodfari (Transport) Ltd*,[40] para 20.5). But there is no time limit as such when it is proposed to add a new respondent, or substitute another one, to an application which has been lodged in time (*Drinkwater Sabey Ltd v Burnett*, para 20.20). If the claimant's claim is for breach of contract under the Employment Tribunals Extension of Jurisdiction Order, which is out of time, the employer's counterclaim, presented in time, can be proceeded with (*Patel v RCMS Ltd*, see para 1.23).

[34] [1992] ICR 140, [1991] IRLR 455, EAT.
[35] [2002] EWCA Civ 878, [2002] 3 All ER 801, [2002] ICR 1193, [2002] IRLR 624.
[36] [1993] IRLR 430, EAT.   [37] [1996] IRLR 381, EAT.   [38] [1995] ICR 328, [1995] IRLR 238, EAT.
[39] [2002] All ER (D) 78 (Jul), EAT; revsd [2003] EWCA Civ 576, [2003] IRLR 434, [2003] All ER (D) 151 (Mar).
[40] [1973] ICR 325, [1973] IRLR 172, NIRC.

A. Time Limits for Enforcing Community Rights

20.23 European law (ie the Treaty of Rome or EC Directives) does not specify any particular time limits for bringing proceedings when an employee is seeking to enforce a Community right. The general principle to be adopted was laid down in *Fisscher v Voorhuis Hengelo BV*, where the European Court held that national rules relating to time limits for bringing such actions were to be applied, providing that they are no less favourable than similar actions of a domestic nature, and do not render the exercise of rights conferred by Community law impossible in practice.

20.24 Thus, in principle, domestic time limits will apply, but the question arises: what are the time limits when it is discovered that UK law does not meet the requirements of EC law? Does time start to run from when the cause of action arose, or from when it is discovered that UK law is defective, or from when UK law is brought into line with EC law?

20.25 Part of the answer is to be found by considering the EC law which is being sought to enforce, bearing in mind that employment tribunals are creatures of statute, and may only exercise jurisdiction over matters specified in respective UK legislation. There have been a number of cases where the UK has failed to implement an EC requirement altogether, or failed to implement it fully or properly, and claimants have tried to re-open matters at a later date, arguing that time runs from when the UK should have implemented the article of the Treaty of Rome or Directive, as appropriate, or from when it was discovered that such a right existed. Generally speaking, these arguments will fail. Thus in *Biggs v Somerset County Council* (see paras 1.104 and 20.27) the claimant worked for 14 hours per week as a teacher. She was dismissed in 1976, after having been employed for less than two years. As the law then stood, she had no right to bring a claim for unfair dismissal, but following the decision in *R v Secretary of State for Employment, ex p Equal Opportunities Commission* (decided in 1994, see para 1.105), she immediately brought a claim for unfair dismissal, arguing that the qualifying threshold condition should be disapplied as being contrary to EC law. The Court of Appeal held that her claim was not brought within the requisite time limit of three months from the date of her dismissal. Although in 1976, when she was dismissed, she would have been unaware of the impact of s 2 of the European Communities Act 1972 or the effect of the decision of the European Court of Justice in *Defrenne v Sabena* (see para 1.72), her mistake was one of law, not of fact. There was no legal impediment to her bringing a claim and arguing that the restriction on part-time workers was indirectly discriminatory. The fact that she (and her advisers) did not fully understand the law at the time was not a ground for re-opening past transactions. The complaint was not presented within the time limit of three months, nor within a reasonable time after the expiry of that limit.

20.26 Similarly, in *Barber v Staffordshire County Council*,[41] the Court of Appeal refused to permit a claimant to bring a new claim based on EU law when an earlier claim had already been dismissed by an employment tribunal. The doctrine of issue estoppel applies.

20.27 However, the decision in *Biggs v Somerset County Council* (para 20.25) does not preclude all retrospective claims which are instituted as a result of a new interpretation of EC law. In *British Coal Corpn v Keeble* (see para 20.10) the EAT expressed the view that the decision in *Biggs* was only applicable to those cases where the claimant had failed to show that it was not reasonably practicable to bring the claim within the appropriate time limits. But, said the EAT, this did not apply to those cases where an extension of time is possible because it is 'just and equitable' to do so. Thus if a person is under a misapprehension of the law (eg due to some earlier legal ruling) a tribunal would still have a discretion

---

[41] [1996] 2 All ER 748, [1996] IRLR 209, sub nom *Staffordshire County Council v Barber* [1996] ICR 379, CA.

to grant an extension of time. This discretion is only available in the areas of sex, race, and disability discrimination, etc. Thus in *DPP v Marshall*[42] a transsexual person made a claim for unlawful discrimination three years after the date when the cause of action arose, but within three months from the date of a decision of the European Court which had decided that gender re-assignment came within the scope of the EC Equal Treatment Directive. The EAT upheld a tribunal's finding that it was just and equitable to permit the claim to be heard on its merits.

B. **Effective Date of Termination (s 97)**

20.28 So far as unfair dismissals are concerned, the claim must be presented within three months from the effective date of termination (EDT) of employment. This date can be:

(a) if the employment is terminated with notice, the date on which that notice expires; or

(b) if the employment is terminated without notice, the date on which the termination takes effect; or

(c) in the case of a limited-term contract (ie a fixed-term or a task contract: see para 17.20) which terminated by virtue of the limiting event without being renewed under the same contract, the date on which the termination takes effect.

In other words, the effective date of termination is the actual date when the employment comes to an end (*Alboni v Ind Coope Retail*[43]) and that date cannot be varied by any subsequent agreement between the parties. However, the notice that determines the effective date of termination can be varied, so that there can be a subsequent agreement that the effective date of termination can be brought forward or pushed backward, and time will start to run from the new date (*Palfrey v Transco plc*, see para 15.30).

20.29 Certain problems have arisen out of this. In *Dixon v Stenor Ltd*[44] Sir John Donaldson pointed out that there were four common situations. The first is where the employee is given notice, and works to the end of that notice. The second is where there is a summary dismissal, and the third is where the employee is given money in lieu of notice. These cases are fairly straightforward, but the fourth situation presented a problem. This was where the employee is dismissed with notice, but is not required to work the period of that notice. In effect, he is on paid garden leave, and his employment does not effectively terminate until the notice expires, even though he may not be working during that time. If he were to submit an application during this period, in effect it would be premature. However, ERA, s 111(3) provides that if a dismissal is with notice, a tribunal may consider a complaint notwithstanding that it is presented before the effective date of termination of the employment. In other words, an employee may bring a complaint as soon as he receives his notice, or within three months from the effective date of termination of his employment.

20.30 If an employee is dismissed, and pursues an appeal through the domestic procedures, there are two possibilities. If the procedure provides for an immediate dismissal, with the possibility of reinstatement should the appeal be successful, the EDT is the date of dismissal (*J Sainsbury Ltd v Savage*, see paras 4.200 and 12.39). If the procedure provides for a suspension of the dismissal with the possibility of it being lifted following a successful appeal, the EDT is the date when the appeal was dismissed should the dismissal be confirmed (*Drage v Governors of Greenford High School*[45]).

---

[42] [1998] ICR 518, EAT.   [43] [1998] IRLR 131, CA.   [44] [1973] ICR 157, [1973] IRLR 28, NIRC.
[45] [2000] ICR 899, [2000] IRLR 314, CA.

20.31 The fact that the employer retains the employee's P45 is irrelevant to the effective date of termination (*Newham London Borough v Ward*[46]).

20.32 If an employer dismisses an employee without notice, but gives him a payment in lieu of notice, the effective date of termination is the date of dismissal (ERA, s 97(1)). Consequently, if on that date the employee does not have the requisite length of continuous employment, he cannot pursue his claim for unfair dismissal, unless, of course, he can add on his statutory notice 'to pull him past the post' (s 97(2), see para 17.4). If notice of termination is given orally, the period of notice commences the day after it has been given, and the effective date of termination is calculated accordingly (*West v Kneels Ltd*, see paras 15.7 and 17.4).

20.33 If an employee is dismissed with notice, he may bring his claim before the notice period expires, ie before the effective date of termination (ERA, s 111(3)), but a warning of a possible dismissal in the future is not a dismissal, and hence the presentation of a claim may be premature (*Rai v Somerfield Stores Ltd*, para 17.13 and see para 18.8).

20.34 The effective date of termination cannot be earlier than the date on which the employee receives notice of the dismissal. Where an employer notifies an employee of his summary dismissal by letter sent in the post, the date of dismissal is the date the employee actually reads the letter, not the date when it is written, posted, or delivered (*Gisda Cyf v Barratt*[47]). In other words, it is the date that she is informed of the dismissal, even if this is before she reads the letter (*Robinson v Fairhill Medical Practice*[48]). There is no room for a doctrine of 'presumed or constructive knowledge' of a dismissal (*McMaster v Manchester Airport plc*, para 17.5). Although the parties may agree a prospective date of termination, they cannot agree a retrospective date, because the EDT is dependent on what actually happened, and not what they may have agreed to treat as having happened. In any case, a consensual arrangement to antedate the date of termination would be a provision which purports to limit the operation of the Act, which would be void under s 203(1) (*Fitzgerald v University of Kent at Canterbury*[49]).

20.35 It should be noted that s 97(2) ('pulling him past the post', see para 17.4) will extend the effective date of termination by the requisite statutory notice for the purposes of s 92 (right to have written reasons for dismissal), s 94 (unfair dismissal), s 119(1) (calculation of the basic award), and s 227(3) (increases the maximum allowable week's pay), but not for the purpose of computing the time limit within which a claim must be brought under s 111(2).

20.36 If an employee's claim is based on constructive dismissal, time will run from when the resignation is actually communicated to the employer, whether by written or oral communication or by conduct (*Edwards v Surrey Police*[50]). In so far as the employer's conduct may have resulted in the employee suffering a detriment, the three-month time limit runs from the date of that conduct, not from when the employee decides to treat the repudiatory breach as putting an end to the contract of employment (*Metropolitan Police Comr v Harley*).

20.37 If the employee resigns with notice, he may present his claim before that notice has expired (*Presley v Llanelli Borough Council*[51]), but if he resigns without notice, he can rely

---

[46] [1985] IRLR 509, CA.

[47] [2009] EWCA Civ 648, [2009] ICR 1408, [2009] IRLR 934, Supreme Court [2010] UKSC 41.

[48] UKEAT/0313/12/JOJ.

[49] [2003] All ER (D) 152 (May), EAT; revsd [2004] EWCA Civ 143, [2004] All ER (D) 262 (Feb).

[50] [1999] IRLR 456, EAT.　　[51] [1979] ICR 419, [1979] IRLR 381, EAT.

on the provisions of s 97(4) to 'pull him past the post' if he lacks the necessary period of continuous employment (see para 15.29).

C. **Restrictions on Contracting Out (ERA, s 203)**

20.38 Subject to the exceptions noted at para 20.50, an employee cannot voluntarily surrender or contract out of his statutory rights, and any statement or agreement to that effect is void. A private settlement between the parties, even one purporting to be in full and final settlement of all or any outstanding claims, cannot prevent an employee from pursuing the matter further in the employment tribunal, for an employee cannot opt out of his statutory rights.

20.39 Thus in *Council of Engineering Institutions v Maddison*[52] the employee accepted £1,600 in consideration that he would forgo any claim against his former employers. This was held to be unenforceable. The object of the legislation is to prevent hasty and imprudent agreements being entered into by the employee. On the other hand, such an agreement, whilst unenforceable, can be taken account of by the employment tribunal, and if it provides for compensation at a level not less than that which would have been awarded by the tribunal, then the employee will not have suffered any loss, and no further award will be made. Further, it will be recalled that an agreement for a financial settlement as a price for a resignation is not void under the Act (*Sheffield v Oxford Controls Co Ltd*, see paras 17.47 and 17.69). In practice, if an agreed settlement is reached, it is sound policy to call in the conciliation officer, thus turning the agreement into a binding one.

20.40 The exceptions to the rule are as follows:

(a) Any settlement made under the auspices of the conciliation officer from ACAS acting under his statutory powers, whether the settlement is made orally or in writing, will be binding on the parties (*Gilbert v Kembridge Fibres Ltd*, see para 1.43), and can be enforced. But the settlement will only apply to the matters contained therein. Thus if a settlement is made to an unfair dismissal claim made under ERA, this will not bar a subsequent claim under other legislation, eg Equality Act 2010 etc, unless such claims have been specifically excluded (*Livingstone v Hepworth Refractories Ltd*[53]). In the absence of precise language, signing a conciliation form does not necessarily bar a further claim by an employee based on facts of which the employee was ignorant at the time the agreement was signed (*Bank of Credit and Commerce International SA v Ali*, see paras 3.44 and 10.12).

Where a counsel, solicitor, CAB adviser, or member of a law centre, who has been named as a representative, holds himself out as having authority to negotiate and reach a settlement on behalf of a claimant, then, in the absence of any notice to the contrary, the other party is entitled to assume that the adviser has such authority. Thus an agreement reached between the adviser and the conciliation officer will be binding on the claimant whether or not the adviser has actual authority to enter into it. Thus the ostensible authority of the adviser extends beyond the pleadings and presentation of the case, but includes all the actual and potential issues which are known to the parties (*Freeman v Sovereign Chicken Ltd*[54]).

---

[52] [1977] ICR 30, [1976] IRLR 389, EAT.
[53] [1992] 3 CMLR 601, [1992] ICR 287, [1992] IRLR 63, EAT.
[54] [1991] ICR 853, [1991] IRLR 408, EAT.

(b) A collective agreement which provides for guaranteed remuneration where all parties have applied to the minister for an order excluding the right to receive guarantee pay under s 35. About 30 such orders have been made.

(c) A dismissal procedure agreement which provides for remedies at least as effective as ERA, which has been designated by the minister by order on an application by all the parties. However, such exclusion from statutory rights does not apply to failure to permit a woman to return to work after childbirth, dismissal for reason of pregnancy or childbirth, dismissal of protected shop or betting workers, dismissal for asserting a statutory right, and an inadmissible reason for redundancy.

(d) A collective agreement which provides for redundancy payments where all the parties have applied to the minister for an exemption order. A few such orders have been made under this provision.

(e) A settlement agreement under s 111A of the ERA (known as a compromise agreement until April 2014), which satisfied the following conditions:

(i)   the agreement must be in writing;

(ii) it must relate to particular proceedings;

(iii) the employee must have received advice from a relevant independent adviser as to the terms of the proposed agreement and its effect. An independent legal adviser is a qualified lawyer (barrister, solicitor, Fellow of the Institute of Legal Executives, or advocate), official, employee, or member of an independent trade union who has been certified in writing as being competent and authorised to give advice on behalf of the trade union, a worker at an advice centre who has been certified in writing as being competent to give advice on behalf of the centre, or a person of a description specified in an order made by the Secretary of State;

(iv) the adviser must have a professional indemnity insurance policy or be covered by a contract of insurance;

(v)   the agreement must identify the adviser; and

(vi) the agreement must state that the conditions regulating the compromise agreement under the Act are satisfied.

Settlement agreements may be made in respect of all those claims for which the employment tribunal has jurisdiction under the Employment Tribunals Act 1996, s 18(1), which covers most, though not all, of the rights contained in ERA, TULR(C)A (except a failure to consult with a trade union on redundancies), Equality Act, Part-time Workers (Prevention of Less Favourable Treatment) Regulations 2000, and Fixed-term Employees (Prevention of Less Favourable Treatment) Regulations 2002. Settlement agreements are binding in respect of the particular complaints mentioned therein. A further claim may be made (within the appropriate time limits) in respect of matters not within the terms of the agreement (*Lunt v Merseyside TEC Ltd*[55]). Thus the agreement should be drawn up in such a way that all matters which could be the subject of a complaint are effectively covered.

(f) An agreement to submit the dispute to arbitration under a scheme prepared by ACAS, which has been approved by the Secretary of State, under the provisions of TULR(C)A, s 212A (see para 1.46).

20.41 Strictly speaking, a settlement agreement can only settle those disputes which have actually been raised (as a concern, not necessarily as a tribunal claim) at the

---

[55] [1999] ICR 17, [1999] IRLR 458, EAT.

date of the agreement (*Lunt v Merseyside TEC Ltd*,[56] also see *McWilliam v Glasgow City Council*[57]). Thus very clear language must be used to ensure that a claimant releases claims or rights of which he is unaware or could not have been aware (*Hinton v University of London*[58]).

20.42 One distinction between an ACAS conciliation and a settlement agreement is that the conciliation agreement can be made in full and final settlement of all claims, whether actual or potential, whereas a settlement agreement 'must relate to the particular proceedings'. However, if the applicant (or his adviser) was aware of the possibility of further claims, the signing of a settlement agreement will be binding, because such additional claims would have been in contemplation when the agreement was signed (*Byrnell v British Telecommunications plc*[59]).

20.43 A settlement agreement is subject to the general principles of contract law and would, for example, be unenforceable if it was affected by a mistake or misrepresentation (*Industrious Ltd v Horizon Recruitment Ltd*[60]). In *Crystal Palace v Dowie*[61] a football manager stated that he wanted to leave his job in order to move closer to his family, and a settlement agreement was signed that released him from the liability to make payment of contractual compensation. In fact, he intended to join a neighbouring club. It was held that the club was entitled to damages for misrepresentation.

20.44 A settlement agreement may be the subject of a condition precedent which will nullify the agreement if the condition is not fulfilled prior to the date for payment. In *Collidge v Freeport plc*[62] the chief executive of a company warranted that there were no circumstances of which he was aware that would constitute a repudiatory breach on his part of his contract of employment. Before the employers paid a substantial sum under the agreement, it was discovered that the chief executive had been guilty of serious financial impropriety, and the financial payment was not made. The chief executive sued for the money, but his claim failed. The employers had protected themselves in the event that subsequent investigations showed that the promise was untrue.

20.45 A settlement agreement is a contract connected with employment, and as such it may be enforced in an employment tribunal under the provisions of the Employment Tribunals Extension of Jurisdiction Order 1994 (*Rock-It Cargo Ltd v Green*,[63] and see para 1.22) provided that the claim arises out of or is outstanding on the termination of the employee's employment. An agreement reached after the employee has left the employment may be enforced in the civil courts in the usual way (*Miller Bros & F P Butler Ltd v Johnston*[64]). A settlement agreement can only be made to settle a valid legal claim, and cannot be used for other types of agreements. In *Gibb v Maidstone & Tunbridge Wells NHS Trust*[65] a severance payment of £250,000 was made the subject of a settlement agreement between the chief executive and the trust in order to remove her from office in anticipation of a damaging report which was known to be critical of her leadership. Although the amount agreed upon, which was intended to take into account the public interest, was made with Treasury guidance, the Trust only paid £50,000, and the claimant sued for the balance. The Court of Appeal upheld her claim, holding that, in the circumstances, the payment was not irrational and was not ultra vires. There is an ACAS Code on Settlement Agreements (para 1.41).

[56] [1999] IRLR 458.　　[57] [2011] IRLR 568.　　[58] [2005] ICR 1260, [2005] EWCA Civ 532, CA.
[59] [2004] All ER (D) 78 (Nov) EAT.　[60] [2010] ICR 491, [2010] IRLR 204.
[61] [2007] EWHC 1392 (QB); [2007] IRLR 682.　[62] [2008] EWCA Civ 485, [2008] IRLR 697.
[63] [1997] IRLR 581, EAT.　　[64] [2002] ICR 744, [2002] IRLR 386.　　[65] [2010] EWCA Civ 678.

20.46 From the available figures, it would appear that more than half of the complaints are settled without a tribunal hearing, though the confidential nature of the work of the conciliation officer is such that we have little knowledge of the terms or circumstances. About 70% of the cases referred to conciliation officers are settled on the basis of some form of monetary payment by the employer. The bulk of the remaining cases are settled because the claimant withdraws the claim, and in a few cases, there will be an agreement for reinstatement or re-engagement. Any communication to the conciliation officer is not admissible in evidence without the consent of the party who communicated it. In *M and W Grazebrook Ltd v Wallens*[66] certain documents, which had been prepared by the personnel manager after the claimant had been dismissed, were shown to the conciliation officer. It was held that the documents were not covered by the privilege, for to find otherwise would enable a party to prevent disclosure of evidence by deliberately communicating it to the conciliation officer. On the other hand, if the documents had been specially prepared for the purpose of showing them to the conciliation officer then no disclosure can be ordered.

20.47 A claim under ERA, s 94 (unfair dismissal) has two objects. First, the claimant will be seeking a finding that he has a statutory remedy and, second, he will be seeking compensation. Both those matters are justiciable before the employment tribunal. Thus, if the employers offer to pay the maximum compensation which would be payable, this does not prevent the claimant from proceeding with his claim in order to obtain a finding that the dismissal is unfair, where the employers are unwilling to concede this (*Telephone Information Services Ltd v Wilkinson*,[67] but see *Nicolson Highlandwear Ltd v Nicolson*, where the EAT came to a different conclusion[68]).

20.48 It has been seen (para 20.38) that an agreement reached whereby an employee agrees to waive his statutory rights is generally void, subject to certain exceptions, and hence the fact that the employee has accepted a sum in settlement (even though this may be in excess of the statutory compensation limits) does not preclude an employment tribunal from hearing the claim (*NRG Victory Reinsurance Ltd v Alexander*[69]), and it is not vexatious or frivolous to pursue such a claim.

Employment Tribunal Procedure

20.49 The Employment Tribunals (Constitution and Rules of Procedure) Regulations 2013 lay down the procedural rules for claims brought before an employment tribunal. Schedule 1 lays down the general procedural rules, Sch 2 deals with national security issues and Sch 3 deals with equal value claims. The overriding objective of these Rules (set out in Sch 1 rule 2) is to enable employment tribunals to deal with cases fairly and justly, which includes:

(a) ensuring that the parties are on an equal footing;

(b) dealing with cases in ways which are proportionate to the complexity and importance of the issues;

(c) avoiding unnecessary formality and seeking flexibility in the proceedings;

(d) avoiding delay, so far as is compatible with proper consideration of the issues; and

(e) saving expense.

---

[66] [1973] 2 All ER 868, [1973] ICR 256, [1973] IRLR 139, NIRC.
[67] [1991] IRLR 148, EAT.   [68] [2010] IRLR 859.   [69] [1992] ICR 675, EAT.

To take account of the overriding objective, therefore, it is permissible to take account of the apparent skills and experience of a party or representative and any apparent inequality in such skills and experience, and adjust procedures accordingly. An example of avoiding delay and informality is that hearings can be conducted by electronic communication, including by telephone, so long as the parties and any members of the public can hear what the judge is hearing (Sch 1 rule 46). Tribunals should also encourage parties to use other means of settling their disputes, such as ACAS or mediation.

20.50 Although the procedural rules are detailed and precise, and are, in some respects, strictly construed, they should not be interpreted in such a way as to avoid injustice, or to drive away a possibly meritorious claimant or respondent (*Richardson v U Mole Ltd*[70]). Regard must always be had to the interests of justice. The rules must not be interpreted so as to prevent an employment tribunal from entertaining jurisdiction to hear a claim for which primary legislation has provided an employment right, and a mandatory requirement in the rules must not be taken to the point of denying a claimant access to the tribunal system.

A. Submitting a Claim

20.51 All claims must be presented to an employment tribunal office on the prescribed form (ET1), the only exceptions being certain claims brought under the National Minimum Wage Act, ss 19, 20, 22; proceedings brought by an employer under ERA, s 11, appeals against the industrial training levy, and appeals against an unlawful notice. A claim must contain the prescribed information, which basically will be the name and address of the claimant and respondent, and details of the claim. It must also include the Early Conciliation certificate number issued by ACAS (paras 1.41, 20.5). An incorrect number will lead to the claim being invalid (*E.ON Control Solutions Ltd v Caspall*[71]). If it is out of time because of an incorrect number it can be rejected (*Sterling v United Learning Trust*[72]). The Secretary of Tribunals must reject the claim if it does not provide the relevant names and addresses, or if it is not on the prescribed form, or if the tribunal does not have power to consider the claim (eg, because the claimant lacks the necessary qualifying conditions, or because the tribunal has no jurisdiction in the matter). The claimant can apply for reconsideration of this rejection within 14 days, on the basis that the rejection was wrong, or the defect has been rectified. If rectified, the claim shall be treated as having been presented the day it was rectified.

20.52 If the Secretary does refuse to accept the claim, he may refer the matter to an employment judge who will decide whether the claim should be accepted. The judge may invite the claimant to a pre-acceptance hearing, before he decides the matter.

20.53 It is the duty of the claimant to state (with as much precision as possible) the nature of the claim, but the employment tribunal will not investigate on its own motion every allegation made but not pursued by a party (*Mensah v East Hertfordshire NHS Trust*[73]). Generally a claimant will be precluded from bringing fresh proceedings in respect of a matter which could and should have been litigated in earlier proceedings (*Divine-Bortey v Brent London Borough Council*[74]).

B. Tribunal Fees

20.54 Between 2013 and 2017 there was a system of fees in the employment tribunal, but this was rejected in *UNISON, R (on the application of) v Lord Chancellor* [2017] UKSC 51,

---

[70] [2005] IRLR 668.   [71] [2019] UKEAT 0003/19.   [72] UKEAT/0439/14.
[73] [1998] IRLR 531, [1998] All ER (D) 260, CA.   [74] [1998] ICR 886, [1998] IRLR 525, CA.

the Supreme Court finding it unlawful as the level of fees prevented the common law right of access to justice and was discriminatory against women. It is possible, however, that there may be a different system of fees introduced in the future.

C. **Employer's Response**

20.55 A copy of the claim will be sent to the respondent employer, who must reply on the prescribed response form (ET3) within 28 days of it being sent to him, although an application may be made before the 28 days have elapsed for an extension of time. The response form must also contain the prescribed information, and be presented on time, or it will be rejected. An application can be made for a reconsideration of the rejection on the basis that it was wrong, or that the failure has been rectified. If rectified, the response shall be treated as having been presented the day it was rectified, and the judge has the power to extend time. If a response has been rejected, and there is no application for reconsideration, or if a respondent has an indication he will not contest the claim, an employment judge will decide if he can decide the case on the material before him. If not, a hearing will be fixed before a judge sitting alone.

   If a respondent does not receive a copy of the claim form due to errors in the name or address on the ET1, it cannot be said that he has been notified of the claim, and thus he cannot be penalised for failing to respond within the 28-day time limit (*Chowles t/a Granary Pine v West*[75]).

20.56 The 'label' which is attached to the response by the employer is generally irrelevant, as long as the response contains all the relevant information, for the actual legal position is a matter for the tribunal to determine on consideration of the factual evidence. Thus, if an employer submits that the reason for a dismissal was 'redundancy', and the facts are fully investigated by the tribunal, it is open to them to find that the reason was for 'some other substantial reason' (*Hannan v TNT-IPEC (UK) Ltd*[76]). All relevant defences should be pleaded, if necessary in the alternative (*Church v West Lancashire NHS Trust*, see para 18.21).

D. **Initial Consideration of Claim and Response**

20.57 The 2013 regulations added a 'sift' stage to the Employment Tribunal process (Sch 1 regs 27 and 28). This should be done as soon as possible after the receipt of the response. The employment judge has to look at the papers in the case, and if he considers either that the tribunal has no jurisdiction to consider the claim or response or that it has no reasonable prospect of success, he will dismiss it (or part of it, if the problem is with just part of it), and send a notice asking for written representations within a certain date. If representations are received, he shall either permit the claim or response, or fix a hearing to decide whether to permit it. The employment judge can also make any case management orders at this stage that he sees fit.

E. **Preliminary Hearings**

20.58 There are two types of hearing in the employment tribunal—preliminary hearings (an amalgamation of the pre-2013 pre-hearing reviews and case management hearings) and final hearings. At a preliminary hearing the judge can make case management orders, or deal with any other kind of issue. Preliminary hearings, which are generally heard by a

---

[75] UKEAT/0473/08.   [76] [1986] IRLR 165, EAT.

judge alone, replaced case management hearings and pre-hearing reviews from 2013. At a preliminary hearing the judge can consider the claim and response, issue case management orders (para 20.57), deal with any preliminary issue, consider whether a claim or response (or part of one) should be struck out, make a deposit order if he considers it necessary, and explore the possibility of settlement. There may be more than one preliminary hearing in a case, and a preliminary hearing can be treated as a final hearing if neither party would be prejudiced by this.

At a preliminary hearing the employment judge may determine interim or preliminary matters, issue directions, or, if he considers that the contentions put forward in relation to a matter to be determined by the tribunal have little prospect of success but are nevertheless arguable, order that party to pay a deposit not exceeding £1,000 as a condition of being permitted to continue to take part in the proceedings. When considering making a deposit order, the employment judge must first ascertain the ability of the party to comply with the order (*Hemdan v Ishmail & Anor*[77]). Note that a deposit order cannot be made just because a claimant's case is not clear as other case management orders are more appropriate (*Tree v South East Coastal Services Ambulance NHS Trust*[78]). If the deposit is not paid within the time limit, the claim or response (or the allegation to which the deposit order is made) may be struck out. If the deposit is paid it shall be refunded in full unless the tribunal makes a costs or preparation time order (see paras 20.109 and 20.113) on the ground that the party has conducted the proceedings unreasonably in persisting in having the matter determined.

20.59 An employment judge may strike out the claim (or defence) if it is considered that the case is so weak that it has no reasonable prospect of success, and ought not to be permitted to proceed to a hearing. Since no evidence is called for at a preliminary hearing, the striking out option will be applicable in those cases where there is no conflict of evidence, or where the evidence presented is self-explanatory, or where the matter has already been litigated. The employment judge may also strike out or amend any claim or response on the ground that it is scandalous or vexatious, or on the ground that the manner in which the proceedings have been conducted by or on behalf of the claimant or respondent has been scandalous, unreasonable, or vexatious. A claim may be struck out where there is intentional and contumelious fault by the claimant, or where there has been inordinate and inexcusable delay such as to give rise to a substantial risk that a fair trial is not possible or where there would be serious prejudice to the respondent (*Rolls Royce plc v Riddle*[79]). A claim or response may also be struck out if there is threatening or abusive conduct or intimidation against a party or witness. However, such action will only be taken if a fair trial is no longer possible (*Force One Utilities v Hatfield*[80]). It is only in exceptional cases that such a course of action should be taken (*Ezsias v N Glamorgan NHS Trust*[81]).

20.60 A restricted reporting order may be made in any case which involves an allegation of sexual misconduct or a disability case in which evidence of a personal nature is likely to be heard. The order will prohibit the publication of any identifying material, ie the names of the parties, until a decision on liability has been reached and entered into the register (*X v Metropolitan Police Comr*[82]). Such order cannot be made to protect the identity of a corporate employer who may be vicariously liable for the acts of its employees, even though its commercial reputation may suffer (*Leicester University v A*[83]). An employment tribunal can also make a 'permanent anonymity order', and anonymise its judgment if the loss of a claimant's anonymity would breach his right to privacy under the Human Rights

---

[77] [2016] UKEAT 0021.   [78] UKEAT/0043/17/LA.
[79] [2008] IRLR 873.   [80] [2009] IRLR 45.
[81] EAT/0705/05, EAT/0612/05; aff'd [2007] EWCA Civ 330, [2007] 4 All ER 940, [2007] ICR 1126, [2007] IRLR 603.   [82] [2003] ICR 1031, [2003] IRLR 411.
[83] [1999] ICR 701, [1999] IRLR 352, EAT.

Act (*A v B*).[84] There is no power, however, to exclude the press or members of the public (*R v Southampton Industrial Tribunal, ex p INS News Group Ltd*[85]). (For restricted reporting orders, see *Tradition Securities SA v Fariad*,[86] 'closed material procedure' where the claimant and his representatives can be excluded, see para 20.75.)

20.61 It is an offence punishable by a fine not exceeding level 5 on the standard scale to act in contravention of any restricted reporting order.

F. **Case Management**

20.62 An employment judge has a general power to manage proceedings in order to achieve the objectives of the Employment Tribunals (Constitution and Rules of Procedure) Regulations 2013 (para 20.4), and wide powers to issue directions on any matter he considers to be appropriate, whether on his own volition or on an application by either party. Directions may be given as to the manner in which proceedings are to be conducted (witness statements prepared and exchanged, agreed bundles of relevant documents, statement of agreed facts, skeleton arguments etc), and with regard to requiring additional information, extending time limits, provision of written answers to questions put, disclosure and/or production of documents, staying part of the proceedings, joining other respondents, postponing or adjourning proceedings, conducting a preliminary hearing, permitting an amendment to the claim or response, etc. If a direction is not complied with an employment judge may make an order in respect of costs or preparation time, and may, at a preliminary hearing or final hearing, make an order to strike out the whole or part of the claim or response, as appropriate, but this punitive power should only be exercised if a fair trial is not possible due to the failure to comply. If there is a last-minute compliance, with an acceptable explanation, it is not appropriate to strike out the claim or defence (*National Grid Co plc v Virdee*[87]). However, either party may apply for a review of directions given.

20.63 If a claimant is so unwell as to be able to proceed with the claim, and there is no prospect of being able to do so in the foreseeable future, it is open to an employment tribunal to strike out the claim altogether (*Peixoto v British Telecommunications plc*[88]).

20.64 Either party may apply to a tribunal for an order for further particulars or disclosure of documents, but such orders are not made as a matter of routine, but only if the party requiring the information can show that he will be prejudiced without such information (*White v University of Manchester*[89]). In particular, disclosure of documents will not be ordered to enable a party to indulge in a 'fishing expedition', ie to search for material in order to establish a case (*British Aerospace plc v Green*, see para 18.42; *Aon Ltd v JLT Reinsurance Brokers Ltd*[90]). An employment tribunal cannot order a party to produce 'evidence' or to create documentary evidence which was not in existence, because an order for discovery is limited to those documents which are in being (*Carrington v Helix Lighting Ltd*[91]). The party against whom an order for discovery of documents is made is under a continuing duty to disclose all relevant documents, right up to the conclusion of the hearing (*Scott v Commissioners of Inland Revenue*, para 20.98).

20.65 Documents which are produced in order to comply with an order for discovery may only be used for the purpose of the hearing, and not for any other cause of action. In *Riddick v Thames Water Board Mills Ltd*[92] an employee of the defendants wrote a

---

[84] [2010] IRLR 844, EAT.   [85] [1995] IRLR 247.   [86] [2009] IRLR 354.
[87] [1992] IRLR 555, EAT.   [88] [2008] All ER (D) 240 (May).
[89] [1976] ICR 419, [1976] IRLR 218, EAT.   [90] [2010] IRLR 600, [2009] EWHC 3448 (QB).
[91] [1990] IRLR 6, EAT.   [92] [1977] QB 881, [1977] 3 All ER 677, CA.

confidential memorandum about the manner of the claimant's dismissal, which was allegedly defamatory. The claimant got to know about the document as a result of an order for discovery, made during the course of a legal action brought against the employer. The action was settled, but the claimant brought a further action for defamation. It was held that the public interest required that documents which were compulsorily disclosed on discovery should only be used for the purpose of the action in which they were disclosed, and that each party impliedly undertook not to use them for any other ulterior or improper motive.

20.66 In complex cases, such as those alleging race discrimination (*Martins v Marks & Spencer plc*) or disability discrimination (*Goodwin v Patents Office*), or protected disclosure claims (*ALM Medical Services Ltd v Bladon*[93]), or where there are likely to be a large number of witnesses or a large number of documents, or many claimants (eg equal value claims), it is usual to have a hearing for preliminary directions, so as to ensure as far as possible that the parties and tribunal can identify the relevant issues to be determined.

20.67 If one party is seeking the disclosure of documents which the other side regards as being of a confidential nature, such as references, confidential assessments on the applicant or other employees, and so forth, the employment judge should himself inspect the document to satisfy himself that discovery is essential in order to dispose fairly of the proceedings. If he does decide that they should be disclosed, the interests of third parties can be protected by 'covering up', substituting names, and, in rare cases, hearing the proceedings in camera (*Science Research Council v Nassé*[94]). A tribunal should inspect confidential documents and decide what is not only relevant to issues actually in dispute but also necessary for the fair disposal of the proceedings (*Dhanda v TSB Bank plc*[95]).

20.68 If privilege is claimed from disclosure, a balance must be held between the public interest in non-disclosure and that of justice in the production of the documents (*Halford v Sharples*[96]). Communications between parties headed 'without prejudice' should be excluded from the evidence submitted, unless the material was such that without them a dishonest case was being presented (*Independent Research Services Ltd v Catterall*[97]).

20.69 Privilege from the disclosure of documents only applies to communications between clients and professional legal advisers, such as solicitors and barristers (*New Victoria Hospital v Ryan*[98]).

20.70 There is no general duty on a party to disclose any documents in his possession or power, in the absence of any formal order to that effect. However, if he voluntarily discloses documents, there is a duty not to be selective in that disclosure, and he must not withhold other documents if there is a risk that the non-disclosure might convey a false or misleading impression as to the nature of any document disclosed (*Birds Eye Walls Ltd v Harrison*[99]).

20.71 Attendance orders, compelling a person to attend as a witness, may also be made in appropriate circumstances. But a tribunal cannot direct that a representative chosen by a party to the proceedings shall not act as such (*Bache v Essex County Council*[100]).

---

[93] EAT/709/00, EAT/967/00, EAT, [2001] EWCA Civ 1183, CA, [2002] EWCA Civ 1085, [2002] ICR 1444, [2002] IRLR 807, CA.

[94] [1978] ICR 777, [1978] IRLR 201; on appeal [1979] QB 144, [1978] 3 All ER 1196, [1978] ICR 1124, [1978] IRLR 352, CA; aff'd [1980] AC 1028, [1979] 3 All ER 673, [1979] ICR 921, [1979] IRLR 465, HL.

[95] [2017] UKEAT/0294/17.   [96] [1992] ICR 146, EAT; aff'd [1992] 3 All ER 624, [1992] ICR 583, CA.

[97] [1993] ICR 1, EAT.   [98] [1993] ICR 201, [1993] IRLR 202, EAT.

[99] [1985] ICR 278, [1985] IRLR 47, EAT.   [100] [2000] 2 All ER 847, [2000] IRLR 251, CA.

20.72 If there are High Court proceedings between the employer and employee in which there are issues in common with an application for unfair dismissal, the employment judge has a discretion to order that the latter claim be postponed, pending the outcome of the High Court proceedings (*Carter v Credit Change Ltd*, para 16.28). He should take into account the convenience, expedition, and cost when exercising his discretion (*First Castle Electronics Ltd v West*[101]). The test to be applied is 'In which court is this action most conveniently and appropriate to be tried, bearing in mind all the surrounding circumstances, including the complexity of the issue, the amount involved, the technicality of the evidence and appropriateness of the procedure?' Thus, where a managing director was alleging a repudiatory breach of contract by the employers which was claimed to be a wrongful and unfair dismissal, the Employment Appeal Tribunal ordered that employment tribunal proceedings should be adjourned until after the hearing of the High Court action (*Bowater plc v Charlwood*[102] and see *GFI Holdings Ltd v Camm*[103]).

G. **Postponements**

20.73 A hearing can, in certain circumstances, be adjourned, but rule 30A of Employment Tribunal Rules 2013 sets out limitations to

- limit the number of postponements that can be granted to a party, in a single case, other than in exceptional circumstances;
- introduce a deadline after which applications for the postponement of a hearing would only be allowed in exceptional circumstances;
- place an obligation on tribunals to consider granting costs orders where late notice postponements are granted.

H. **The Final Hearing**

20.74 Hearings before an employment tribunal are reasonably informal, but must be held in public (*Storer v British Gas plc*[104]). An employment tribunal may only sit in private if:

(a) it would be against the interests of national security to allow evidence to be given in public;

(b) a person is giving evidence which he could not disclose without contravening a prohibition imposed by an enactment;

(c) the evidence has been communicated to a person in confidence; or

(d) the evidence is information which if disclosed in public, could cause substantial injury to an undertaking of the witness or in which he works for reasons other than its effect on collective bargaining (see rule 29, 1st Schedule).

20.75 However, it is permissible for a tribunal to hear certain evidence in private in order to protect the right to respect for private or family life, as required by Art 8 of the European Convention on Human Rights (*XXX v YYY*[105]). If a private hearing is ordered, this does not preclude the presence of a party's representative (*Fry v Foreign and Commonwealth Office*[106]). In addition, rule 94 provides for the adoption of a closed procedure whereby a person may be excluded from part of employment tribunal proceedings on grounds of national security, a witness may have his identity concealed, or proceeding can be held in

---

[101] [1989] ICR 72, EAT.   [102] [1991] ICR 798, [1991] IRLR 340, EAT.   [103] [2008] All ER (D) 74.
[104] [2000] 2 All ER 440, [2000] ICR 603, [2000] IRLR 495, CA.
[105] [2004] EWCA Civ 231, [2004] IRLR 137, [2004] All ER (D) 144 (Feb).   [106] [1997] ICR 512, EAT.

private. The Supreme Court found in *Home Office v Tariq*,[107] a case under the 2004 rules, that excluding a claimant and his representatives was not incompatible with EU law or the European Convention on Human Rights.

20.76 When dealing with a litigant in person, an additional responsibility falls on the employment judge to clarify exactly what is being alleged, and to ensure from the start of the proceedings that the parties know precisely what the issues are, and what ground is to be covered (*Akintola v Capita Symonds Ltd*[108]). A litigant in person is entitled to generous treatment and some leeway (*Shea v Marcos Fidelio*[109]).

20.77 If there is no prior settlement or withdrawal, the employment tribunal will hear the case. A date, time, and place for the hearing will be notified to the parties, although applications for adjournments will be considered on appropriate grounds. At the hearing, as a general rule, the burden of proof is on the claimant, and he should therefore give evidence first in order to support his allegations. In discrimination cases, the burden of proof is reversed: see Equality Act 2010, s 135.

20.78 If an employment tribunal is unable to come to a conclusion on a question of fact, they may apply the burden of proof. Thus in *Morris v London Iron and Steel Co Ltd*[110] the tribunal could not decide whether an employee had been dismissed had or resigned, and they held that he had not discharged the burden of proof which was on him to show that he was dismissed.

20.79 In unfair dismissal cases, if the dismissal is admitted, the employer will be required to give evidence first, and he must establish:

(a) the reason for the dismissal (or, if there is more than one reason, the principal reason, see *Smith v Glasgow City District Council*[111]), and

(b) that it was a statutory reason.

He should then seek to show that he acted reasonably in the circumstances.

20.80 From a practical point of view, the employer should recognise that there are a number of matters within his knowledge about which the tribunal may wish to learn, and therefore should be prepared to give evidence on these matters. Thus it is not sufficient to show a reason for dismissal; the reasonableness of acting on that reason must also be shown. If an employee is dismissed because of redundancy, an employer should normally lead evidence to show that there was a fair selection system and full consultation with the individual concerned and their trade union (if appropriate) and that efforts were made to find alternative employment, even if the applicant does not raise all these matters (*Langston v Cranfield University*[112]). If the dismissal is for incompetence, the employer would need to show all those matters which a reasonable employer should have considered before taking the decision to dismiss (see Chapter 17).

20.81 If one party is taken by surprise by the evidence of the other side, it will normally be possible to apply to introduce rebutting evidence, even if it is necessary to apply for an adjournment in order to produce the necessary evidence and/or witnesses. However, unreasonable applications for adjournments may be visited by an award of costs against the offending party, although costs cannot be awarded as a pre-condition for resuming a hearing (*Cooper v Weatherwise (Roofing and Walling) Ltd*[113]). An employment tribunal

---

[107] [2011] UKSC 34.   [108] [2010] EWCA Civ 405.   [109] UKEAT/0159/11/JOJ.
[110] [1986] ICR 629, EAT; revsd [1988] QB 493, [1987] 2 All ER 496, [1987] ICR 855, [1987] IRLR 182, CA.
[111] [1985] IRLR 79; aff'd [1987] ICR 796, [1987] IRLR 326, 1987 SC, HL 175.   [112] [1998] IRLR 172, EAT.
[113] [1993] ICR 81, EAT.

may permit a witness to be recalled for further examination, but should then give the other party an opportunity to make a further rebuttal (*Aberdeen Steak House Group v Ibrahim*[114]).

20.82 If an employment tribunal, on its own volition, takes a point which was not taken by the parties, natural justice requires that the parties should be alerted to the fact, so that they can be given an opportunity to present further evidence on the matter, and/or make further submissions (*Laurie v Holloway*[115]).

20.83 The standard of proof, ie the quantum of evidence which must be given in support of any particular allegation, must be sufficient to establish the balance of probabilities in that party's favour. The informality of tribunal procedure can sometimes mislead the parties into thinking that they can escape with a standard of proof which is in fact unacceptable. If the employer, for example, fails to prove the reason or the principal reason for the dismissal (*Smith v Glasgow City District Council*, para 20.79) or fails to show any reason, or gives a reason which the tribunal does not believe, then he will have failed to discharge the burden of proof which is placed on him, and the dismissal will be unfair. Although the tribunals will admit hearsay evidence in the proceedings, the weight which is given to such evidence is a matter for them to decide (*Coral Squash Clubs Ltd v Matthews*[116]) and they will seldom base a decision in favour of an employer on such evidence, particularly if it is controverted by the direct evidence (or denials) of the claimant (*Mawson v Leadgate Engineering Ltd*[117]). The tribunals will give such assistance as they can to a person who is not legally qualified or represented, but it is the duty of the parties to present all the relevant evidence before the tribunals, and applications of adjournments may be made if a party considers it necessary to call someone whose attendance was not thought necessary.

20.84 The evidential requirements in the employment tribunals are not the same as other courts. For example, in *Docherty v Reddy* (para 12.16), the claimant was dismissed for suspected theft. The tribunal permitted the employer to introduce evidence that the claimant had stolen on previous occasions. Such evidence would scarcely have been admissible in the criminal courts, as its probative value would have been exceeded by its prejudicial value, but the EAT held that the evidence was rightly admitted. The issues in the employment tribunals and the criminal courts are different; in this case, the tribunal had to decide if the employer had reasonable grounds for dismissing, and the claimant's previous conduct was a relevant factor to be taken into account.

20.85 Equally, whether a dismissal was fair or unfair can only be determined on the basis of the facts which were known to the employer at the time he dismissed the employee, and subsequent information which comes to light is only relevant if it confirms that reason. Such information cannot be admissible to show a separate and additional reason for dismissal, because when the employer dismissed the employee, he did not know of those facts. This can be illustrated by *W Devis & Sons Ltd v Atkins* (paras 17.199 and 17.216), where the company dismissed a manager for failing to follow company directives. After he had left, it was alleged that facts were discovered which indicated that he had been guilty of gross misconduct, and that he had been taking secret commissions from customers, for which he could have been dismissed summarily. The employment tribunal refused to allow such evidence to be called on the issue of the fairness of the dismissal, and this was upheld on appeal to the House of Lords. It was permissible to adduce evidence which was discovered after the dismissal to prove the fairness of that reason, but not for the purpose of showing that the employers had discovered subsequently another reason which would have enabled them to dismiss fairly. However, if the dismissal is found to be unfair, the subsequent

---

[114] [1988] ICR 550, [1988] IRLR 420, EAT.   [115] [1994] ICR 32, EAT.
[116] [1979] ICR 607, [1979] IRLR 390, EAT.   [117] [1972] IRLR 105.

evidence can then be admitted for the purpose of determining the remedies which would be considered by the tribunal.

20.86 If a claimant fails to attend the tribunal hearing, without good cause, the tribunal can dismiss the claim without having to be satisfied that the respondent could establish a good defence (*Roberts v Skelmersdale College*[118]), or adjourn to another date (with or without an order for costs), but if the failure to attend was due to a medical reason, the decision whether to postpone is one within the discretion of the tribunal. Adequate reasons for taking this course of action must be given (*Teinaz v London Borough of Wandsworth*[119]). If, having heard the claimant's case, the respondent makes a submission of no case to answer, on the ground that the claim is weak or misconceived, the tribunal should still continue to hear the respondent's evidence, for it is very rare that a submission of no case to answer can succeed (*Logan v Customs and Excise Comrs*[120]). The tribunal should always be prepared to hear evidence from the other side, except perhaps in the most hopeless or frivolous cases (*Hackney London Borough Council v Usher*[121]).

20.87 Otherwise, after considering all the facts, hearing the witnesses, and studying any evidence tendered, the employment tribunal must determine the issue on the basis of the relevant legal requirement. Thus if the issue is whether or not the employer has acted reasonably, this does not mean that the tribunal must agree with the employer's decision, for in many cases more than one course of action is possible, and an employer is not to be criticised because he adopts one in preference to another. It is not the duty of the tribunal to decide if they would have come to the same conclusion as the employer based on the facts which were within the employer's knowledge (*Ferodo v Barnes*, para 12.16), nor should the tribunal substitute their own judgment for that of the employer (*Donn v Greater London Council*, para 2.101), and any temptation to interfere with management prerogatives should be resisted. In *St Anne's Board Mills Co Ltd v Brien*[122] four employees refused to work with another employee, who they considered had been responsible for an accident. The employers investigated the matter, came to the conclusion that that employee was not to blame, and required the four to continue to work with him. They continued to refuse, and were dismissed. After considering the facts, the tribunal decided that the other employee had been responsible for the accident, and hence the four employees had not acted unreasonably in refusing to work with him. The dismissals were therefore unfair. On appeal, it was held that the question before the tribunal was not who was responsible for the accident, but whether the employers had acted reasonably in the circumstances. They had investigated the matter thoroughly and carefully, and come to certain conclusions. They had had the choice of dismissing an employee whom they considered to be blameless, or the four employees who were (in their view, wrongfully) refusing to work with him. In the circumstances, they had not acted unreasonably in dismissing the latter.

20.88 It is the practice of some employment tribunals to give an oral decision immediately the hearing finishes, and then promulgate the decision in writing at a later date. In rare cases it is possible for the employment judge, before such written promulgation, to announce his intention to recall the tribunal in order to reconsider some point of law which he has omitted to notice, or which was not drawn to his attention. While such practice is

---

[118] [2002] All ER (D) 145 (Nov), EAT; revsd [2003] EWCA Civ 954, [2003] ICR 1127, [2004] IRLR 69, [2003] All ER (D) 272 (Jun).

[119] [2001] All ER (D) 497 (Nov), EAT; aff'd [2002] EWCA Civ 1040, [2002] ICR 1471, [2002] IRLR 721, [2002] All ER (D) 238 (Jul).

[120] [2002] All ER (D) 360 (May), EAT; aff'd [2003] EWCA Civ 1968, [2004] ICR 1, [2004] IRLR 63, [2003] All ER (D) 388 (Jul).

[121] [1997] ICR 705, EAT.   [122] [1973] ICR 444, [1973] IRLR 309, NIRC.

unusual, there is no legal objection to it (*Hanks v Ace High Productions Ltd*[123]). However, it is not possible for an employment tribunal to depart from their oral decision when it is reduced to writing (*Arthur Guinness Son & Co (Great Britain) Ltd v Green*, para 17.209).

20.89 If, at the end of the oral hearing, both sides agree to put their submissions in writing, the employment tribunal must send a copy of each party's submission to the other party, and give a specified time in which any response is to be made. Such comments should be limited to the correction of factual errors and legal submissions on any new points of law raised (*Barking and Dagenham London Borough Council v Oguoko*[124]).

20.90 After all the evidence has been heard, and representations made, the tribunal will either give an oral judgment or reserve its decision to be given in writing at a later date. If an oral decision has been given, written reasons will only be provided if requested by one of the parties either at the hearing or within 14 days of the judgment.

20.91 The written reasons should include the following information:

(a) the issues which the tribunal has determined;

(b) details of issues not determined, and the reason why;

(c) any findings of fact relevant to those issues;

(d) a concise statement of the relevant law;

(e) how the relevant findings of fact and applicable law have been applied in order to determine the issues; and

(f) where the judgment includes an award of compensation, a table of how the amount has been calculated.

I. Allegations of Bias

20.92 Generally speaking, the tribunal will regulate its own procedure. However, within that parameter, a tribunal must not only act fairly but be seen to act fairly. Thus, an employment judge or member should not adjudicate on a case if s/he has some personal connection with either of the parties or some knowledge of the facts (over and above those facts which are presented in evidence), or has an interest in the outcome of the case. If a wing member has had contentious dealings with either party to the proceedings, this must be disclosed to the parties, as this would give rise to apparent bias, even though the actual identity of the parties is unknown to the member (*City and County of Swansea v Honey*[125]). In particular they must be careful not to show any animosity against a party or any form of bias, whether against a party to the proceedings or a representative. If there is any possibility of a conflict of interest arising, the employment judge should first seek to ascertain whether there is another employment judge (or tribunal member, as appropriate) who can hear the case. If not, he should give a full explanation (recorded or carefully noted, so as to avoid controversy about what was said), and, if there is a serious objection, as opposed to a fanciful one, give the party affected the option of having the hearing continued, or having it heard by a differently constituted tribunal (*Jones v DAS Legal Expenses Insurance Co Ltd*[126]).

20.93 So far as allegations of bias are concerned, there are two aspects to consider. The first is actual bias, where an employment judge or member may have some pecuniary or proprietary interest in the outcome of the case (see *Locabail Ltd v Bayfield*

---

[123] [1978] ICR 1155, [1979] IRLR 32, EAT.   [124] [2000] IRLR 179, EAT.   [125] EAT/0030/08.
[126] [2003] EWCA Civ 1071, [2004] IRLR 218, [2003] All ER (D) 425 (Jul).

Properties Ltd[127]). The second is apparent bias, where a fair-minded and informed observer, having considered all the facts, would conclude that there is a real possibility that the tribunal was biased. A comprehensive series of principles to be adopted in all cases where allegations of bias are made was set out by the EAT in *Hamilton v GMB (Northern Region)*.[128]

20.94 There is a difference between a tribunal member being rude and being biased, and the fact that the tribunal member is making facial gestures or his body language indicates a disapproval of the claimant's evidence does not, by itself, indicate that the member's mind has been made up (*Ross v Micro Focus Ltd*[129]).

20.95 There is a legal adage that justice must not only be done but must be seen to be done. This is also enshrined in Art 6 of the European Convention on Human Rights, which requires that an individual has the right to a fair and public hearing within a reasonable time by an independent and impartial tribunal established by law. Thus if there is a doubt about the impartiality of a member of the employment tribunal, the doubt should be resolved in favour of recusal. Apparent bias, as well as actual bias, is sufficient to disqualify a person from acting in a judicial capacity (*City and County of Swansea v Honey*[130]).

20.96 It can sometimes happen that during the course of the hearing, the tribunal may express a forcefully held opinion as to the merits of the case. This, by itself, does not indicate bias, as such views may well assist the parties in the manner in which they continue to conduct the proceedings. But the tribunal must indicate that the views expressed were only provisional, and that they remain open to persuasion to the opposite view (*Jiminez v Southwark London Borough Council*[131]).

J. Financial Remedies

20.97 Monetary awards in respect of proceedings brought before an employment tribunal are subject to the special rules applicable in each case (see Appendix A). In particular, it should be noted that in discrimination claims, there is currently no limit to the amount which may be awarded, and an award may also be made in respect of injury to feelings. Nor is there a limit to compensation awards in cases of health and safety and protected disclosure dismissals. Special rules are also applicable in claims brought under EU law (eg the Equal Treatment Directive) because 'full compensation' is required, and hence there is a difference in the stages at which percentage reductions are to be made for mitigation, contributory conduct, *ex gratia* payments, etc (see *Ministry of Defence v Hunt*[132]).

20.98 Aggravated damages may be awarded where the injury to the claimant was inflicted by conduct that was high-handed, malicious, insulting, or oppressive (*Alexander v Home Office*[133]). This head of damages is separate from any other awarded for injury to feelings (*Scott v Commissioners of Inland Revenue*, para 20.64).

Interest on Awards

20.99 An award made by an employment tribunal will attract interest, on a day-to-day basis, at the stipulated rate of interest, from the day after the date of judgment. If the award is paid within 14 days of the order, then no interest is payable. Interest is also not payable on costs awarded, nor on any part of the award which is subject to the recoupment provisions.

[127] (2000) 7 BHRC 583, [2000] 2 WLR 870.   [128] [2007] IRLR 391.
[129] EAT/0304/09.   [130] See n 124.   [131] [2003] EWCA Civ 502, [2003] ICR 1176, [2003] IRLR 477.
[132] [1996] ICR 554, [1996] IRLR 139, EAT.   [133] [1988] IRLR 190, CA.

20.100 Interest is still payable if the tribunal's decision is subject to appeal or review, but if the amount of the award is subsequently varied, interest is payable on the amount as varied (Employment Tribunals (Interest) Order 1990, as amended).

20.101 In cases of sex, race, and disability discrimination, and in equal pay claims, interest on awards will accrue from the date of the act of discrimination complained of (Employment Tribunals (Interest on Awards in Discrimination Cases) Regulations 1996, as amended).

Failure to Pay

20.102 There are penalties for employers who fail to pay awards or settlements set out in Sections 37A-37Q of the Employment Tribunals Act 1996. These include other financial liabilities such as awards of costs, employment tribunal fees, and settlements reached through the ACAS Early Conciliation Service.

20.103 From 18 December 2018, a naming scheme was introduced whereby employees can register employers with BEIS who have failed to pay at least £200 of a tribunal award (note that this does not extend to ACAS conciliated settlements). The employer has 14 days from the date of the naming notification letter to make written representations to BEIS outlining whether they fall under any of the exceptional circumstances for not being named under the scheme. Representations may be accepted if they meet the following criteria:

- Naming carries a risk of personal harm to an individual, their family or other employees;
- There are national security risks associated with naming in this instance;
- Other factors which suggest it would not be in the public interest to name the employer (employer to provide details);
- Where the employment tribunal has been paid in full and proof is submitted and verified.

K. **Reconsideration of Judgment**

20.104 An application may be made to an employment tribunal within 14 days from the time the decision was sent to the parties, asking for it to reconsider its decision (rules 70–73) if it is in the interests of justice to do so. This is not an appeal, and there are limited circumstances in which the tribunal will accede to such a request. The main reason stated by the legislation is where the interests of justice require a review. This general power can be illustrated by the case of *Berkeley Garage Ltd v Edmunds*[134] where the employers were told by officers from the Department of Employment that the claimant was bringing his case out of time. Consequently, they did not bother to attend the hearing. The tribunal found that it was not practicable for the claimant to have presented the case earlier, and proceeded to hear the case on its merits. When the employers discovered this, they applied for a review and a rehearing, which the tribunal refused. On appeal this was reversed, for the interests of justice clearly required that the employers be given an opportunity to present their side of the story. Similarly, in *Help the Aged Housing Association (Scotland) Ltd v Vidler*[135] the claimant was awarded £4,700 compensation for unfair dismissal, mainly on the basis that he was 60 years of age, and the tribunal thought that it would be a considerable length of time before he obtained further employment. Within two weeks of the tribunal's decision, he obtained employment. It was held on appeal that the tribunal should have exercised its

[134] [1975] ICR 228, [1975] IRLR 124, DC.   [135] [1977] IRLR 104, EAT.

powers of review and reviewed the compensation in the light of the new situation, for the original assessment was totally wrong. Because the claimant had obtained alternative employment so quickly, this altered the substratum of the tribunal's reasoning in computing the loss likely to be suffered, and hence it was in the interests of justice that there should be a review.

There are other reasons why a judge may reconsider a decision, such as:

(a) if the decision was wrongly made as a result of an error on the part of the tribunal's staff;

(b) if a party did not receive notice of the proceedings (*Hancock v Middleton*);[136]

(c) if the decision was made in the absence of a party entitled to be heard. If an employer fails to reply to a complaint by not returning the appropriate defence within the stated time he may be denied the right to be heard unless he can show some valid reason for this. But if a party is prevented from attending a hearing through illness, then the tribunal should consider whether the absence was for a genuine reason, and if his story is believed, a review should be granted (*Morris v Griffiths*[137]). In addition to seeking a review, the person applying should state in writing his reasons not only for the application, but also for contending that the decision of the employment tribunal was wrong. In *Drakard & Sons Ltd v Wilton*,[138] the employers did not attend a tribunal hearing as they believed that, once having made an offer of settlement to the conciliation officer, they would be contacted if any further steps were required. The EAT held that the tribunal should have granted a review. They should have enquired into the circumstances surrounding the failure to attend the hearing;

(d) new evidence comes to light, which could not have been discovered before. For example, if, after the claimant has been awarded compensation for unfair dismissal, new evidence comes to light that he had been defrauding the employer during the period of employment, so that it would have been possible to have dismissed him summarily, then this will be taken into account by the tribunal when it reviews the decision, and any previous award of compensation may be altered accordingly (*McGregor v Gibbings Amusements Ltd*[139]). It must be shown that the new evidence which has now become available could not have been presented at the original hearing, and the application should be accompanied by the substance of that new evidence, including, if possible, proofs of witnesses (*Simmons v Medway Welding Ltd*[140]).

20.105 Before refusing an application for reconsideration, the employment tribunal should give the claimant an opportunity to elaborate in writing the grounds which he intends to put forward (*Drakard & Sons Ltd v Wilton*[141]).

20.106 The power to reconsider only applies when the employment tribunal has made a decision. There is no power to review an actual settlement reached during or at the end of proceedings, where the tribunal has not made a finding on liability (*Larkfield of Chepstow Ltd v Milne*[142]).

20.107 An application for reconsideration may be made on the ground that there was an error in the proceedings, but not on the ground that the decision of the employment tribunal discloses an error of law, for that is a matter which must be dealt with on appeal to the EAT (*Trimble v Supertravel Ltd*[143]).

---

[136] [1982] ICR 416, EAT.   [137] [1977] ICR 153, EAT.   [138] [1977] ICR 642, EAT.
[139] [1975] ITR 64.   [140] [1973] ITR 373, NIRC.   [141] [1977] ICR 642.
[142] [1988] ICR 1, EAT.   [143] [1982] ICR 440, [1982] IRLR 451, EAT.

20.108 An employment tribunal may also reconsider its decision on its own motion. On reconsideration, the original decision may be confirmed, varied, or revoked. If it is revoked it may be taken again.

L. Costs

20.109 In some circumstances, the tribunal may make an order that one party makes a payment to the other party in respect of costs incurred. Notice must be sent to the party against whom the order may be made to give him an opportunity of arguing why the order should not be made. A costs order may only be made if the other party was represented at the hearing, ie either by a solicitor or barrister or a lay representative who charged for the service. The amount of costs is in the discretion of the tribunal. For a costs order to be made, a party or their representative must have acted 'vexatiously, abusively, disruptively or otherwise unreasonably', or their claim had 'no reasonable prospect of success'. A representative does not behave thus simply by acting for a client whose case is doomed to fail, or failing to advise the claimant that the case has little chance of success (*Mitchells Solicitors v Funkwerk Informations Technologies York Ltd*[144]). The fact that the party has legal expenses insurance is irrelevant when considering the question of costs (*Mardner v Gardner*[145]).

20.110 A costs order must be made in an unfair dismissal case where the claimant has expressed a wish to be reinstated or re-engaged not less than seven days before the hearing, and the hearing has been adjourned or postponed because the respondent has failed, without a special reason, to adduce reasonable evidence as to the availability of a suitable job. A costs order may be made if a preliminary hearing is postponed, or if a party has, in bringing the proceedings, or he or his representative has, in conducting the proceedings, acted vexatiously, abusively, disruptively, or otherwise unreasonably, or the bringing or conducting of the proceedings has been misconceived (ie has no reasonable prospect of success). If a claimant has brought proceedings based on evidence which is a lie, it is appropriate for an award of costs to be made against him (*Daleside Nursing Home Ltd v Mathew*[146]). Costs may also be awarded against a party who has not complied with a practice direction.

20.111 If the employer makes an offer to settle the claim prior to the tribunal hearing, which is unreasonably rejected by the claimant, the tribunal is within its rights to exercise a discretion and make an award of costs (*Kopel v Safeway Stores plc*[147]).

20.112 Costs, however, remain the exception rather than the rule in employment tribunals.

M. Preparation Time Order

20.113 A preparation time order may be made in favour of a party who was not legally represented at a hearing in order to compensate for the time spent on preparatory work directly relating to the proceedings, including time spent by legal or other advisers, but not in respect of time spent at the hearing. An application for a preparation time order must be made within 28 days from the issuing of the judgment. The amount of the order will be determined by the tribunal's assessment of the number of hours spent on preparation time by the party in whose favour the order is to be made, based on the information provided by that party, and the tribunal's own assessment of what it considers to be a reasonable and proportionate amount of time spent on such preparatory work with reference to the

---

[144] [2008] PNLR 29.   [145] EAT/0483/13.   [146] EAT/0519/08.
[147] [2003] IRLR 753, [2003] All ER (D) 05 (Sep), EAT.

complexity of the proceedings and the number of witnesses and documentation required. The ability of the party who is to pay must be taken into consideration.

20.114 A preparation time order must be made in unfair dismissal proceedings which have been postponed or adjourned and the claimant has expressed a wish to be reinstated or re-engaged but the respondent has failed, without a special reason, to adduce reasonable evidence as to the availability of a suitable job. An order may be made where a party has, in bringing the proceedings, or he or his representative has in conducting the proceedings, acted vexatiously, abusively, disruptively, or otherwise unreasonably, or the bringing or conducting of the proceedings has been misconceived, in that it has no reasonable prospect of success.

20.115 A tribunal cannot make a preparation time order and a costs order in favour of the same party in the same proceedings. If a deposit has been taken from a party as a condition of the claim going forward, that may be paid in part or full settlement of the costs or preparation time order. A costs order and a preparation time order may not both be made for the same party in the same proceedings.

N. **Wasted Costs Order**

20.116 A tribunal may make a wasted costs order against a party's representative to disallow or pay (or refund) to his client any wasted costs, which will cover any costs incurred by a party as a result of any improper, unreasonable, or negligent act or omission by that representative. However, such an order cannot be made against a representative who is not acting in pursuit of profit with regard to the proceedings. Before making such an order the tribunal must give the representative a reasonable opportunity to make oral or written representations, and take into account his ability to pay.

O. **Appeals**

20.117 It has already been noted (see Chapter 1) that the Employment Appeal Tribunal will hear appeals on points of law from employment tribunals, and on points of law from the decisions of the certification officer. An appeal on a point of law from the employment tribunals must be made within 42 days from the date when the document recording the full reasons for the decision was sent to the appellant (*Hammersmith London Borough Council v Ladejobi*),[148] not from the date on which under the normal postal rules they might be deemed to have been received (*Mock v IRC*),[149] although it is possible in exceptional circumstances to apply for an extension of time, but a good reason for the delay must be shown (*Duke v Prospect Training Services Ltd*[150]).

20.118 It will only be in the most exceptional cases that the EAT will relax the 42-day time limit for bringing an appeal. The principles set out in *United Arab Emirates v Abdelghafar*[151] remain good law, and only in exceptional circumstances will an extension be granted (*Jurkowska v Hlmad Ltd*[152]). Legal aid is available in the EAT, but it should be noted that a delay in obtaining legal aid, or the fact that the assistance of the Equality and Human Rights Commission is being sought for the purpose of pursuing an appeal, are not reasons for not adhering to the 42-day time limit. In particular, a Practice Direction issued by the EAT makes it clear that if an application for a review is made to an employment tribunal, this does not prevent the time for appealing from running (although this obviously does

---

[148] [1999] ICR 673, EAT.   [149] [1999] IRLR 785, EAT.   [150] [1988] ICR 521, [1989] IRLR 196, EAT.
[151] [1995] ICR 65, [1995] IRLR 243.   [152] [2008] EWCA Civ 231, [2008] ICR 841, [2008] IRLR 430.

not prevent an appeal against the refusal of the tribunal to grant the review), and further, if an employment tribunal makes a finding of liability, but adjourns the question of compensation, the time for appealing runs from the date of the decision, and is not suspended until the final matter of compensation has been dealt with. The EAT will also consider the motives of the appellant, the tactics used, whether the delay was intentional, the length of the delay, the merits of the appeal, and whether there would be any injustice or prejudice to the party who was successful before the employment tribunal (see *Aziz v Bethnal Green City Challenge Co Ltd*[153]).

20.119 Once an appeal to the EAT has been lodged, a preliminary hearing will take place. The appellant will be required to satisfy the EAT that it is reasonably arguable that the employment tribunal made an error of law. If so satisfied, the appeal will be allowed to proceed, and the EAT will make any appropriate directions to ensure that the appeal may be determined efficiently and effectively. A special form must be completed, enabling amendment to be made to the notice of appeal, giving time estimates for argument, and, if needed, requesting the employment judge's notes of evidence. If the appeal does not raise an arguable point of law, it will be dismissed at that stage. Only in very limited circumstances will an appellant be permitted to raise a point of law on appeal which was not canvassed before the employment tribunal (*Church v West Lancashire NHS Trust*, paras 18.21 and 20.56).

20.120 In *Secretary of State for Health v Rance*[154] the EAT gave guidance on the circumstances in which new points may be taken on appeal. Thus, a new point may be taken for the first time if it would be unjust to allow the other party to get away with a deception or unfair conduct, or if there is a glaring injustice in not permitting an unrepresented party to rely on evidence that could have been given to the employment tribunal, or if it is of particular public importance for a legal point to be decided, and so on. No further factual investigation must be required, and all the relevant material must be before the EAT (see also *Lipscombe v Forestry Commission*,[155] *Bennett v Governing Body of Pennoweth School*[156]).

20.121 An appeal from a decision of an employment tribunal can only hope to succeed if the employment tribunal have misdirected themselves in law, or entertained the wrong issue, or proceeded on a misapprehension or misconstruction of the evidence, or taken matters into account which were irrelevant to the decision, or reached a decision which no reasonable employment tribunal, properly directing themselves in law, could have arrived at. In *Neale v Hereford and Worcester County Council*,[157] May LJ propounded the so-called 'Biggles' test. He stated that the EAT should not interfere with the decision of the employment tribunal (except when they erred on a point of law) unless it was possible to say, 'My goodness, that was certainly wrong!' Thus, if there is evidence to support their decision, the EAT will not normally interfere, particularly where the questions of fact and degree are at issue. The task of the EAT is to hear appeals only on points of law (*Spook Erection Ltd v Thackray*[158]). It is not an error of law that the employment tribunal has misunderstood the facts (*British Telecommunications plc v Sheridan*[159]).

20.122 In *Piggott Bros & Co Ltd v Jackson*[160] the Court of Appeal stated that a decision of the employment tribunal can only be characterised as being perverse if it was not a permissible option. The EAT would have to identify a finding of fact which was unsupported by any

---

[153] [2000] IRLR 111, CA. [154] [2007] IRLR 665, EAT. [155] [2007] EWCA Civ 428.
[156] Employment Appeal Tribunal. 22 July 2008.
[157] [1985] IRLR 281, EAT; revsd [1986] ICR 471, sub nom *Hereford and Worcester County Council v Neale* [1986] IRLR 168, CA.
[158] [1984] IRLR 116, Ct of Sess. [159] [1990] IRLR 27, CA.
[160] [1992] ICR 85, [1991] IRLR 309, CA.

evidence or a clear self-misdirection of law. However, in *East Berkshire Health Authority v Matadeen* (para 12.72) the EAT held that in addition, 'perversity' was a free-standing basis for interfering with an employment tribunal's decision, if that decision 'was not a permissible option' or was 'a conclusion which offends reason' or 'so outrageous in its defiance of logic or of acceptable standards of industrial relations'. In particular, the EAT thought that the lay members were there to bring their experience and industrial judgment to the application of the law and to the decision to be reached on appeal. They were entitled to use that experience to ensure that employment tribunal decisions did not ignore generally acceptable standards. In *Yeboah v Crofton*[161] the Court of Appeal gave some guidance on whether an appeal based on perversity should be brought.

20.123 The weight to be attached to the evidence is a matter for the employment tribunal, and it is not permissible for the EAT to substitute their own views on this (*Eclipse Blinds Ltd v Wright*[162]). But an employment tribunal must consider whether a dismissal falls within the range of reasonable responses open to a reasonable employer, and not substitute their own judgment. A failure to adopt this approach may result in the decision not being a permissible option (*United Distillers v Conlin*[163]).

20.124 The notice of appeal should state quite precisely what point of law is to be argued. It is not sufficient to make a bald statement that the employment tribunal misdirected itself on a point of law without specifying the error or misdirection to be appealed against. As Phillips J has pointed out, to say that something is an error of law does not, without further explanation, make it so. Indeed, if it turns out that there is in fact no arguable point of law involved in the appeal, the EAT is quite likely to make an award of costs against the unsuccessful party. Further, if no arguable point is disclosed in the notice of appeal, the notice itself can be rejected by the EAT, so that the appeal will never be heard.

20.125 In the Practice Direction issued in 2008 the EAT made clear that copies of the notes taken by the employment judge will only be made available if they are necessary for the purpose of arguing a point of law on appeal. More latitude will be allowed to applicants who were not legally represented at the tribunal hearing (*Webb v Anglian Water Authority*[164]). The facts of the case will be found in the tribunal's decision, and any appeal must be based on the law as applied to those facts. However, it is permissible in argument to refer to the employment judge's notes for the purpose of clarifying any ambiguity in the case. If an appeal is based on the actual conduct of the case by the employment judge, or an allegation of bias by the employment judge or members (*Facey v Midas Retail Security*[165]), or some evidence contrary to that found by the tribunal, the claimant must first inform the Registrar of the EAT, so that this can be communicated to the respondent, and the views of the employment judge sought. The EAT will not interfere with an award of compensation unless it is more than a trifling matter. If the question of the amount of compensation is alleged to be an error of law, it must be of a substantial nature for the EAT to interfere (*Fougère v Phoenix Motor Co Ltd*, para 17.218).

20.126 The EAT does have power to hear new evidence on appeal, but only if a reasonable explanation is produced as to why the evidence was not put before the employment tribunal (see *Hygia Professional Training v Cutter*[166]). It must be shown that the existence of the new evidence could not have been known or foreseen, and that had it been available at the employment tribunal hearing, it would have had an important influence on either

---

[161] [2002] EWCA Civ 794, [2002] IRLR 634.   [162] [1992] IRLR 133, Ct of Sess.
[163] [1992] IRLR 503, EAT; *Conlin v United Distillers* [1994] IRLR 169, Ct of Sess.
[164] [1981] ICR 811, [1981] IRLR 494, EAT.   [165] [2001] ICR 287, [2000] All ER (D) 1306, EAT.
[166] (2007) 151 SJLB 1297.

the outcome of the case or the award of compensation (*Photostatic Copiers (Southern) Ltd v Okuda*[167]). The evidence must be credible, and of such a nature that it would have had a decisive effect on the tribunal's decision had they heard it (*Hussein v Mite Security Ltd*[168]). It is also possible to argue a new point of law, not canvassed before the employment tribunal, if the balance of justice so requires (*Russell v Elmdon Freight Terminal Ltd*, para 2.8).

20.127 If the decision of the employment tribunal is defective, because no reference or insufficient reference had been made to a particular aspect of the case, the EAT must not remit the case back to the employment tribunal for further amplification or clarification. The proper course is to allow the appeal and remit the case back for a further hearing (*Reuben v Brent London Borough Council*[169]). However, there is no objection to remitting a matter back to the employment tribunal for fuller reasons or an amplification of the reasons (*Barke v SEETEC Business Technology Centre*[170]) where the ground of appeal is the inadequate reasoning of the original decision (*Burns v Consignia plc (No 2)*[171]). The EAT is obliged to remit a case to an employment tribunal where there is an issue of fact to be decided, unless the parties agree otherwise (*Jafri v Lincoln College*[172]). Where the EAT remits a case back to the employment tribunal to consider certain specific issues, the tribunal has no jurisdiction to hear or determine matters outside the scope of those issues. In particular, there is no power to permit one party to amend its case so as to raise issues which were not previously before the employment tribunal (*Aparau v Iceland Frozen Foods Ltd (No 2)*[173]).

20.128 If there is a complaint about the actual conduct of the employment tribunal proceedings (eg that a member is falling asleep) this should be raised with the employment judge at the time, and not after the tribunal has reached its conclusions (*Red Bank Manufacturing Co Ltd v Meadows*[174]), although more serious matters, such as allegations of bias, can be raised at any time (*Peter Simper & Co Ltd v Cooke*[175]). The procedure to be followed in such cases was outlined by the EAT in *Facey v Midas Security* (para 20.125).

20.129 An appeal may be brought on the ground that the promulgation of the decision of the employment tribunal has been delayed for an unconscionable length of time. In *Kwamin v Abbey National plc*[176] it was suggested by the EAT that three and a half months should be the maximum time after the end of a case for the preparation and promulgation of all but the most complicated and lengthy judgments. If there is a delay beyond that time, the delay will be regarded as being culpable in the absence of a proper explanation. However, even though there is a delay, there is no automatic presumption that the decision will be set aside. It is for the party impugning the decision to show a material error or omission due to faulty recollection, so as to establish that the decision is unsafe by virtue of the delay.

P. Reviews by the Employment Appeal Tribunal

20.130 The EAT has power to reconsider its own decision on the grounds that (a) the order was wrongly made as a result of an error on the part of the tribunal or its staff, (b) a party did not receive proper notice of the proceedings, and (c) the interests of justice require such review. However, the purpose of a reconsideration is not to allow appeals to

[167] [1995] IRLR 11, EAT.   [168] UKEAT/0342/08.
[169] [2000] ICR 102, [2000] IRLR 176, EAT.   [170] [2005] EWCA Civ 578, CA.
[171] [2004] IRLR 425, [2004] ICR 1103.   [172] [2014] EWCA Civ 449.
[173] [1996] IRLR 119, EAT; revsd [2000] 1 All ER 228, [2000] IRLR 196, CA.
[174] [1992] ICR 204, [1992] IRLR 209, EAT.   [175] [1986] IRLR 19, EAT.   [176] [2004] IRLR 516, EAT.

be reheard and, in particular, a reconsideration will not be granted if an appeal has been lodged to the Court of Appeal (*Blockleys plc v Miller*[177]).

Q. **Vexatious Litigants (Employment Tribunals Act 1996, s 33)**

20.131 If the EAT is satisfied that any person has habitually and persistently and without reasonable grounds instituted vexatious proceedings or made vexatious applications before an employment tribunal or the EAT, then, on an application by the Attorney-General or the Lord Advocate, the EAT may make a restriction of proceedings order, the effect of which will be to debar that person from instituting proceedings or making applications without leave from the EAT. The hallmark of vexatious proceedings is that they have little or discernible basis in law, with the effect of subjecting the defendant to inconvenience, harassment, and expense out of all proportion to any gain likely to accrue to the claimant (*A-G v Wheen*[178]).

R. **Further Appeals**

20.132 An appeal will lie from the EAT to the Court of Appeal (in Scotland the Court of Session). Leave to appeal must be given by the EAT, but if this is refused an application for leave to appeal must be made to the Court of Appeal or the Court of Session. It must be shown that there is a genuine point of law of practical consequence involved (*Campbell v Dunoon and Cowal Housing Association Ltd*[179]).

The jurisdiction of the Court of Appeal is to hear appeals from the Employment Appeal Tribunal, not from the employment tribunal. The question before the Court of Appeal is whether the EAT erred in law in the judgment under appeal (*Balfour Beatty Power Networks Ltd v Wilcox*[180]) and it has emphasised many times that a decision at first instance will not be overturned merely because one of several reasons for that decision turns out to be wrong, as long as the overriding reason for the decision can be identified and upheld (*McLoughlin v Jones*[181]).

A further appeal will lie to the Supreme Court.

S. **National Security (ERA, s 193)**

20.133 There is a special regime to deal with cases involving issues of national security. The provisions of ERA dealing with protected disclosures do not apply in relation to employment for the purposes of the security service, the secret intelligence service, or the Government Communication Headquarters. Otherwise Crown employees (including the security services) may present claims to an employment tribunal, but claims for unfair dismissal and for victimisation on grounds of trade union membership based on ss 145A, 145B and 146 of TULR(C)A must be dismissed if it is shown that the action taken was for the purpose of safeguarding national security (Employment Tribunals Act, s 10). But it is still necessary to prove that the action was taken for the purpose of safeguarding national security, and although the action may be analogous with 'some other substantial reason' the employment tribunal is still entitled to consider the fairness or otherwise of a decision to dismiss in unfair dismissal cases (*B v BBA*[182]).

---

[177] [1992] ICR 749, EAT.
[178] [2000] IRLR 461, [2000] All ER (D) 767, EAT; aff'd [2001] IRLR 91, [2000] All ER (D) 2186, CA.
[179] [1992] IRLR 528, Ct of Sess.
[180] [2006] IRLR 258, EAT; aff'd [2006] EWCA Civ 1240, [2007] IRLR 63, CA.
[181] [2001] EWCA Civ 1743, [2002] QB 1312.   [182] [2005] ICR 1530.

2.134 In such cases, a specially convened employment tribunal will be convened, with special powers and procedures to ensure that secrecy and confidentiality are maintained. Proceedings (in whole or in part) will be held in private, the claimant/his representative may be excluded, and the disclosure of documents may be prohibited. If the claimant or his representatives are excluded, a special advocate may be appointed (Employment Tribunals (Constitution and Rules of Procedure) Regulations 2013, Sch 2 and r 94).

2.135 An argument that these provisions were incompatible with Art 6 of the Human Rights Act was rejected in *Home Office v Tariq*,[183] where the 'closed material procedure' was upheld, but it was also ruled that the claimant must be provided with the allegations against him in sufficient detail to enable him to give effective instructions to the special advocate, so as to enable the latter to challenge the allegations effectively.

2.136 It should be noted that these procedures apply in respect of all of the statutory jurisdiction of employment tribunals, including discrimination cases. Guidance on the approach to be adopted by employment tribunals when considering national security cases was given in *AB v Ministry of Defence*.[184] There must be cogent justification, and a judicial assessment on whether the interests of national security are at stake. The risks to the security services or the armed forces must be weighed against the principle of open justice. It is for the employment tribunals to make a necessary assessment when national security is involved.

Summary

- Most employment cases are brought in the employment tribunal, although some types of claim can be brought in the civil courts.
- Employment tribunals are much less formal than civil courts.
- There is no legal aid in employment tribunals.
- There is a three month time limit for most types of claim in the tribunal.
- A claimant has to obtain a certificate of early conciliation from ACAS before bringing a claim.
- Preliminary hearings are held for case management orders, in preparation for the final hearing.
- Costs are rarely awarded in the employment tribunal.
- Appeals can be made on points of law to the Employment Appeal Tribunal.

---

[183] [2011] UKSC 35.   [184] [2010] ICR 54.

21

Individual Trade Union Rights

Background

21.1 In this chapter we shall consider the rights of an individual in respect of his trade union membership and/or non-membership. These rights exist vis-à-vis a trade union or against an actual or potential employer. The relevant statutory provisions are contained in the Trade Union and Labour Relations (Consolidation) Act 1992 (TULR(C)A), which has been amended by subsequent legislation, and reference will also be made to a number of legal decisions.

Rights vis-à-vis a Trade Union

A. **Right not to be Excluded from any Trade Union (TULR(C)A, s 174)**

21.2 An individual cannot be excluded or expelled from any trade union unless:

(a) he does not satisfy an enforceable membership requirement contained in the rules of the union. Enforceable means the restriction of membership solely by reference to employment in a specified trade, industry, or profession, or occupational description, or the possession of a specified trade, industrial, or professional qualification or work experience;

(b) he does not qualify for membership by reason of the union operating only in a particular part of Great Britain;

(c) the union negotiates with one particular employer (or a number of particular employers who are associated) and the applicant is no longer employed by that employer;

(d) the exclusion or expulsion is entirely attributable to the applicant's conduct, and the conduct is neither 'excluded conduct' nor 'protected conduct'. Conduct is excluded if the individual ceases to be a member of a trade union, or to be employed by a particular employer or at a particular place, or is conduct for which an individual may not be disciplined by a union by virtue of s 65 of the Act (see para 21.9). Conduct is protected (see s 174(4A)) if the individual is a member of a political party, or ceased to be a member, but conduct which consists of activities undertaken by an individual as a member of a political party is not protected. This means that although a trade union cannot expel or exclude a person from membership because he is a member of a political party, he can be excluded or expelled because of his activities as a member of that political party.

21.3 In *ASLEF v United Kingdom*[1] a trade union expelled a member because of his membership of the British National Party. A court held that the expulsion was unlawful because of the provisions of s 174(1). However, the union appealed to the European

---

[1] [2007] IRLR 361.

Court of Human Rights, which held that to give associations that promote particular values no control over their membership was contrary to their freedom of association under Art 11 of the Convention. Thus s 174 was amended by the Employment Act 2008, which added s 174(4C) to TULR(C)A. This provides that conduct which consists of an individual being or having been a member of a political party is not protected conduct falling within s 174(4A) if the membership of that political party is contrary to (a) the rule of the trade union, or (b) an objective of the trade union. However, an exclusion or expulsion from the trade union is not permitted if the decision to exclude or expel is taken unfairly, or is contrary to the rules of the trade union, or if the individual would lose his livelihood or suffer exceptional hardship by reason of his not being a member of the trade union.

21.4 If a person's application for membership of a trade union is neither granted nor rejected within a reasonable period, he shall be treated as having been excluded from the union (s 177).

21.5 The significance of s 174 is two-fold. First, at common law a trade union was entitled to lay down the description of persons who were eligible to join, and could specify any qualification for membership it desired (see *Boulting v Association of Cinematograph, Television and Allied Technicians*[2]), and exclude a person on any ground (see *Faramus v Film Artistes' Association*[3]). The courts did take the view that a rule which operated arbitrarily and unreasonably was void as being against public policy (see *Nagle v Feilden*, para 10.16), but such cases were rare and, generally speaking, a trade union could control its own admissions, and the court had no power to order it to grant membership to any particular individual. Section 174 now overrides the common law in this respect. A trade union may lay down certain requirements for membership, as above, but otherwise must admit any person seeking to join.

21.6 The second significance of the law is that the principles of the Bridlington Agreement, which used to govern inter-union disputes arising from competition for members, and applied to TUC affiliated unions, can no longer be relied upon. Previously, if a trade union commenced recruitment in an area in which another union already had a substantial membership, the TUC could order the interloper to surrender the members gained in the recruitment drive (see *Rothwell v Association of Professional, Executive and Computer Staff and the Trade Union Congress*[4]). This is no longer possible, because the individual has an indefeasible right to join whichever union he pleases, and cannot be expelled as a result of any award made by the TUC Disputes Committee.

21.7 A union may still specify who is entitled to join as a member within the limits specified above, but it is submitted that even these requirements cannot be exercised in an arbitrary and unreasonable manner (see *Nagle v Feilden*[5]).

21.8 The remedy for a failure to admit or to expel an applicant to or from membership is dealt with at para 21.18.

B. Right not to be Unjustifiably Disciplined (TULR(C)A, ss 64–65)

21.9 The power of a trade union to take disciplinary action against a member, and the procedural rules which should be followed, are noted in Chapter 22. In addition, a member has the right not to be unjustifiably disciplined by the trade union. A member

---

[2] [1963] 2 QB 606, [1963] 1 All ER 716, CA.
[3] [1963] 2 QB 527, [1963] 1 All ER 636, CA; on appeal [1964] AC 925, [1964] 1 All ER 25, HL.
[4] [1976] ICR 211, [1975] IRLR 375.   [5] [1966] 2 QB 633, [1966] 1 All ER 689.

is unjustifiably disciplined if the reason for the disciplinary action was conduct by him which was:

(a) a failure to participate in or support a strike or other industrial action (whether by members of that union or by others) or indicate his opposition to or lack of support for any such strike or other industrial action; or

(b) something required from him by virtue of an obligation imposed by his contract of employment or other agreement made with his employer; or

(c) the making of an assertion that the union, or an official or representative or trustee of the union's property, has contravened or is proposing to contravene a requirement of the union's rules or any other agreement or legal provision, or attempts to vindicate any such assertion; or

(d) the encouraging of any person to perform an obligation imposed by virtue of a contract of employment or any other agreement; or

(e) the contravention by him of any requirement imposed by a determination which itself constitutes an infringement of his rights or of the right of any other individual; or

(f) failing to agree to, or withdrawing from, a check-off agreement; or

(g) resigning from a union, becoming a member of another union, or refusing to join any other union; or

(h) working with individuals who are not members of the union or any other union; or

(i) working for an employer who employs individuals who are not members of the union, or who are or are not members of any other union; or

(j) requiring the union to do something which the union is required to do on the requisition of any member; or

(k) an approach to the certification officer for advice or assistance on any matter whatsoever, or which involves any other person being asked for advice or assistance with respect to any assertion made under (c) above; or

(l) a proposal to engage in conduct outlined in paras (a) to (k) above, or preparatory conduct (s 65).

But a refusal to accept union policy that members should not take on additional work is not protected, because the policy is not 'other industrial action' (*Knowles v Fire Brigade Union*[6]).

21.10 Discipline, for the purpose of this section, is a determination made under the union's rules by an official of the union, or by a number of persons including an official:

(a) that an individual shall be expelled from the union (or branch or section). In *Transport and General Workers' Union v Webber*,[7] it was held that a recommendation that the claimant be expelled was not a determination for the purpose of s 174. Until an appeal against the recommendation had been heard, he was still a member of the union;

(b) that an individual shall pay any sum to the union (or branch or section) or to any other person whatsoever;

(c) that sums tendered by that individual in respect of any obligation to pay a subscription or other sums to the union (or branch or section) should be treated as unpaid or as paid for a different purpose;

---

[6] [1996] 4 All ER 653, [1997] ICR 595, [1996] IRLR 617, CA.
[7] [1990] ICR 711, [1990] IRLR 462, EAT.

(d) that that individual should be deprived of, or refused access to, benefits, services, or facilities which would otherwise be available to him as a member of the union. Suspending a member involves depriving him of benefits which accrue from union membership (*National and Local Government Officers' Association v Killorn*[8]);

(e) that another trade union (or branch or section) should be encouraged or advised not to accept that individual as a member; or

(f) that that individual should be subjected to any other detriment. Naming a person as a 'strike breaker' in a union circular, with the intention of causing him embarrassment is to subject that person to a detriment (*National and Local Government Officers' Association v Killorn*).

21.11 However, a member will not be unjustifiably disciplined if the reason for the disciplinary action was that he made an allegation that the union, an official, a representative, or a trustee had contravened the union's rules or an agreement or an enactment or rule of law, and the assertion was false, and the member knew it was false or otherwise acted in bad faith.

21.12 If a complaint relating to an expulsion is brought under s 174, and is declared to be well founded, no further complaint relating to that matter can be brought under s 64 (unjustifiable discipline).

C. Complaints of Unjustifiable Discipline (TULR(C)A, ss 66–67)

21.13 An individual who believes that he has been unjustifiably disciplined by a trade union may present a complaint to an employment tribunal, alleging that his rights have been infringed. The complaint must be presented within three months of the alleged infringement, unless the employment tribunal is satisfied that it was not reasonably practicable to present the complaint earlier, and that any delay in making the complaint was wholly or partially attributable to any reasonable attempts to appeal against the decision or to have it reconsidered or reviewed.

21.14 If the employment tribunal finds that the claimant has been unjustifiably disciplined contrary to s 64, they will make a declaration that the complaint is well founded. An application may then be made to an employment tribunal for an award of compensation, and an order that the union repay him any sum he has paid by way of a fine. The application must be made after four weeks but within six months of the declaration.

21.15 The amount of the award shall be such as the employment tribunal considers to be just and equitable in all the circumstances. The applicant is under a duty to mitigate against his loss, and the compensation award may be reduced if the infringement complained of was to any extent caused or contributed to by him. The amount of the award shall not exceed 30 times a week's pay (capped at £538 per week) plus £88,519. If on the date the application for compensation was made, the determination infringing the applicant's right not to be unjustifiably disciplined has not been revoked, or the union has failed to take steps to reverse anything done for the purpose of giving effect to the determination, the amount of compensation shall not be less than £10,022. An award of compensation for injury to feelings may be made (*Massey v UNIFI*[9]).

D. Right to Resign from a Trade Union (TULR(C)A, s 69)

21.16 In every contract of membership of a trade union, whether made before or after the passing of the Act, there shall be an implied term conferring a right on the member, on giving reasonable notice and complying with any reasonable conditions, to terminate his

[8] [1991] ICR 1, [1990] IRLR 464, EAT.		[9] [2007] EWCA Civ 800, [2007] IRLR 902, [2008] ICR 62.

membership of the union. In *Ashford v Association of Scientific, Technical and Management Staffs*[10] (decided under the provisions of the Industrial Relations Act 1971) the claimant wrote a letter of resignation to the union, which was to take immediate effect. This was not in accordance with the union rules, and subsequently expulsion proceedings were commenced. It was held by the NIRC that as the member had failed to give reasonable notice, he was bound by the union's rules. It was suggested that although it might be reasonable to invite members to state their reasons for resignation, it would not be reasonable to make such a statement a condition of resignation.

E. Right not to be Expelled from the Union (TULR(C)A, s 174)

21.17 The grounds upon which a person cannot be excluded from trade union membership (see para 21.2) apply equally to the right not to be expelled from a union. However, a person who resigns from the union because of dissatisfaction with the way the union is conducting its affairs cannot bring proceedings under s 174, for there is no such doctrine as 'constructive expulsion' (*McGhee v Transport and General Workers' Union*[11]). If a member ceases to be a member of the union on the happening of an event specified in the rules of the union, he shall be treated as having been expelled from the union (s 177).

F. Remedies for Wrongful Exclusion or Expulsion (TULR(C)A, ss 175–176)

21.18 A person who claims that he has been wrongly excluded or expelled from a trade union may present a complaint to an employment tribunal within six months from the date of the exclusion or expulsion, or, where it was not reasonably practicable to do so, within such further period as the tribunal considers reasonable. The fact that the internal appeal procedure has not been exhausted does not, by itself, render it not reasonably practicable to present the claim earlier (*GMB v Hamm*[12]). If the tribunal find the complaint to be well founded, it shall make a declaration to that effect. If the tribunal finds that the exclusion or expulsion was mainly attributable to 'protected conduct' (ie being or ceasing to be a member of a political party), it shall make a second declaration to that effect. A third declaration shall be made if the exclusion or expulsion was attributable to conduct which would have been contrary to the rules of the union.

21.19 If the application is declared to be well founded, and the applicant has been admitted or re-admitted to the union, an award of compensation shall be made which is just and equitable in the circumstances, and which may be reduced if the applicant caused or contributed to the exclusion or expulsion. If on the date when the application was made the applicant has not been admitted or re-admitted to the union, the tribunal shall award compensation (see para 21.15), but this minimum award does not apply where either of the above second or third declarations have been made, when the just and equitable rule will apply.

G. Right of Access to the Courts (TULR(C)A, s 63)

21.20 A member who is seeking a determination or conciliation of a dispute under the union's rules should first pursue his case through the union's internal disputes procedure before seeking recourse to the courts (*White v Kuzych*[13]). But irrespective of any provision in the union's rules, the member has an indefeasible right to apply to the courts any time after six months from when the union first receives his application to have the matter

---

[10] [1973] ICR 296, NIRC.   [11] [1985] ICR 503, [1985] IRLR 198, EAT.   [12] IDS Brief 682.
[13] [1951] AC 585, [1951] 2 All ER 435, PC.

determined or conciliated. However, if the delay is attributable to the unreasonable conduct of the union member, the court can extend the six-month period (ie to give the union more time to deal with the complaint).

21.21 The right to apply to the court after six months is of course without prejudice to a member's right to apply to the court at any time when, for example, an appeal cannot cure a defect because the action complained against is ultra vires or otherwise contrary to law.

H. Right to a Ballot before Industrial Action (TULR(C)A, s 62)

21.22 If a trade union calls on members to engage in a strike or other industrial action without the affirmative support of a ballot conducted in accordance with the stringent requirements of the Act, any member may apply to the court for an order seeking to have the authorisation or endorsement of the action withdrawn by the union. If the strike is not called by the specified person, or the Act's requirements relating to the functions of the independent scrutineer are not satisfied, or members have not been given an equal opportunity to vote, or a ballot has been held but a majority have not voted in favour, then the court will make such order as it considers appropriate for requiring the union to take steps for ensuring that there is no further inducement to take part in the action, and that no member engages in conduct after the making of the order by virtue of having been induced before the order to take part or continue to take part in the action.

21.23 The right to apply to the court for an order is thus available to an individual member of the union, whether or not the strike is actionable by anyone else (eg an employer, see para 23.46), and is additional to any right a member may have in respect of any breach which may have occurred of the trade union's rules. The right exists in respect of calls for any strike or other industrial action, whether or not the member is in breach of his contract of employment. Thus secondary action (see para 23.74) is covered.

21.24 A court may grant interlocutory or interim relief by ordering that the authorisation or endorsement of the industrial action is withdrawn, but it cannot order the union to hold a ballot. The right to bring an action under s 62 applies to self-employed persons, as well as to employees (s 62(8)).

21.25 Crown employees (who may not be employed under a contract of employment) are within the provisions of s 62 (see s 62(7)).

I. Other Individual Rights

21.26 A member of a trade union has the right to restrain the union from indemnifying unlawful conduct (see para 22.63), to bring an action against the union's trustees in respect of unlawful application of the union's property (see para 22.65), and to bring a complaint about the conduct of the ballot in respect of a political fund (see para 22.67). He has the right to inspect the register of members (see para 22.18) and examine the union's accounts, and can apply to the court if the union has failed to comply with the requirements relating to union elections, election addresses, appointment of a scrutineer, etc. These matters will be considered in Chapter 22.

Rights vis-à-vis an Employer

21.27 An individual worker has a number of legal rights against an actual or potential employer, as follows.

A. **Access to Employment (TULR(C)A, s 137)**

21.28 It is unlawful to refuse a person employment:

(a) because he is, or is not, a member of a trade union; or

(b) because he is unwilling to accept a requirement:

   (i) to take steps to become or cease to be, or to remain or not to become, a member of a trade union; or

   (ii) to make payments or suffer deductions in the event of his not being a member of a trade union.

21.29 A person shall be taken to have been refused employment if the person to whom he is applying:

(a) refuses or deliberately omits to entertain and process his application or enquiry; or

(b) causes him to withdraw or cease to pursue his application or enquiry; or

(c) refuses or deliberately omits to offer him employment of that description; or

(d) makes him an offer of such employment the terms of which are such that no reasonable employer who wished to fill the post would offer, and which is not accepted; or

(e) makes him an offer of such employment but withdraws it or causes him not to accept it.

21.30 The law is aimed at preventing any form of discrimination against a worker on the ground of his trade union membership. The employer is quite entitled to refuse to employ someone because of that person's previous trade union activities (eg a well-known militant, see *Birmingham City District Council v Beyer*[14]), because the refusal is not based on trade union membership, but disruptive conduct in his previous employment. Whether the employer thus refuses employment because of past trade union membership or past trade union activities is a question of fact for the employment tribunal to determine in accordance with the evidence. However, once the worker has entered employment slightly different considerations may apply (see *Fitzpatrick v British Railways Board*,[15] para 21.85).

21.31 The precise scope of s 137 is not clear. In *Harrison v Kent County Council*[16] the claimant had previously been employed for some 14 years, during which time he was known to be the leader of a long and bitter industrial dispute. He then left the employment, and subsequently applied for an advertised vacancy. He was refused employment. He argued that the refusal was because of his trade union membership, and hence contrary to s 137. The employers argued that he was refused employment because of his uncooperative attitude and anti-management style. His claim failed before the employment tribunal, but this was reversed by the EAT, who held that there was an overlap between trade union membership and activities. If a person was refused employment because of his trade union activities, it was open to an employment tribunal to find that he was refused employment because of his trade union membership. However, it should be noted that the decision in this case was made prior to the House of Lords' decisions in *Associated Newspapers Ltd v Wilson*[17] and *Associated British Ports v Palmer*,[18] where it was pointed out that there is a distinction

---

[14] [1978] 1 All ER 910, [1977] IRLR 211, EAT.

[15] [1990] ICR 674, EAT; revsd [1992] ICR 221, [1991] IRLR 376, CA.   [16] [1995] ICR 434, EAT.

[17] [1992] ICR 681, [1992] IRLR 440, EAT; [1994] ICR 97, sub nom *Wilson v Associated Newspapers Ltd* [1993] IRLR 336, CA; revsd sub nom *Associated Newspapers Ltd v Wilson* [1995] 2 AC 454, [1995] 2 All ER 100, [1995] ICR 406, [1995] IRLR 258, HL.

[18] [1993] ICR 101, [1993] IRLR 63, EAT; revsd [1994] ICR 97, [1993] IRLR 336, CA; revsd [1995] 2 AC 454, [1995] 2 All ER 100, [1995] ICR 406, [1995] IRLR 258, HL.

between 'the purpose' and 'the effect' of an act, and thus the decision in *Harrison* must be regarded as being of doubtful authority.

Job Advertisements (TULR(C)A, s 137(3))

21.32 Where a job advertisement (including every form of advertisement or notice, whether to the public or not), is published, which indicates (or might reasonably be understood as indicating) that the employment is only open to a person who is, or who is not, a member of a trade union, or make payments or suffer deductions (see para 21.28), then if a person applies for a job, and he is refused employment, it will be conclusively presumed that he was refused employment for that reason. Thus it is clear that all references to trade union membership or non-membership should be eliminated from job advertisements. However, the job advertisement per se is not unlawful (unlike advertisements which seek to discriminate on grounds set out in the Equality Act 2010, see para 4.211), and the only remedy is for an individual who has been refused employment to bring a personal complaint.

Unfair Practices (TULR(C)A, s 137(4))

21.33 Where there is an arrangement or practice under which employment is only offered to persons put forward or approved by a trade union, a person who is not a member of the trade union, and who is refused employment because of that arrangement or practice, shall be taken to have been refused employment because he is not a member of the trade union.

Employment Agencies (TULR(C)A, s 138)

21.34 The Act covers employment agencies, defined as any person who provides services for the purpose of finding employment for workers or for supplying employers with workers. In so far as the employment agency acts as an agent for an employer, the provisions of s 137 (see para 21.28) apply. In so far as the agency is acting in its own right, the identical provisions apply, and a person who has been refused the services of an employment agency (on grounds of his membership or non-membership of a trade union) will have a right to complain against the agency to an employment tribunal. Advertisements by employment agencies are also covered by identical provisions (s 138(3)).

Exceptions to the Act

21.35 The Act only deals with employment under a contract of service or apprenticeship. Thus it cannot apply to self-employed persons. Further, if a person is being considered for appointment or election to an office in a trade union, then s 137 does not prevent anything done for the purpose of securing the compliance with a condition that he be or become a member of the trade union, even though this would constitute employment. Thus it is not unlawful to insist that a trade union official becomes a member of the union concerned.

21.36 The unfair recruitment provisions do not apply to members of the armed forces, police, share fishermen, employees who work outside Great Britain, seamen registered on ships registered at ports outside Great Britain or who are not ordinarily resident in Great Britain, and when the minister issues an exemption certificate on the ground of national security.

Remedies under the Act (ss 139–142)

21.37 A person who considers that his rights have been violated under the Act may make a complaint to an employment tribunal within three months from the date of the act complained of, with the usual extension of time if it was not reasonably practicable to present it earlier. If the tribunal upholds the complaint, it must make a declaration to that effect, may award compensation, and may make a recommendation that the respondent takes action to obviate or reduce the effect on the complainant of the conduct which is the subject of the complaint. If the complaint is made against an employment agency and a prospective employer, there are provisions which permit the joinder of both parties, and any award of compensation may be apportioned between them, as the tribunal thinks just and equitable. It is also possible to join a third party (eg a trade union or shop steward) if the act complained of came about by virtue of industrial pressure.

21.38 The practical effect of legislation is that the pre-entry and post-entry closed shop is no longer lawful in Great Britain.

Trade Union Blacklists

21.39 Following an investigation by the Information Commissioner into the activities of an organisation called the Consulting Association, the Employment Relations Act 1999 (Blacklists) Regulations 2010 were passed. It was found that the Consulting Association was providing a number of companies with a list purporting to appraise the suitability of applicants for employment, with a strong emphasis on the names of trade unionists who were actual or potential 'troublemakers'. The Consulting Association has now ceased to exist, but the Blacklist Regulations are designed to prevent any resurgence of such activities.

21.40 Regulation 3 defines a prohibited list as a list that contains details of members of trade unions or persons who have taken part in the activities of trade unions, and is compiled with a view to being used by employers or employment agencies for the purpose of discrimination in relation to the recruitment or in relation to the treatment of workers.

21.41 Regulation 3 states that no person shall compile, use, sell, or supply a prohibited list (there are specific exceptions where it is permissible to draw up or use such lists). If a person is refused employment because a potential employer has relied on information supplied by a person who has contravened reg 3, a right of complaint exists to an employment tribunal. The refusal may come about because the employer has refused or deliberately omitted to entertain or process a job application or enquiry, or caused the job applicant to withdraw the application, or has refused to offer employment, or has made an offer of employment in terms that no reasonable employer would make, or withdraws an offer of employment, etc. It is also unlawful for an employment agency to refuse its services to a person for a reason relating to a blacklist.

21.42 If, in the absence of any other explanation, the employment tribunal finds that the employer or employment agency has contravened reg 3, or relied on information supplied in contravention of reg 3, the burden of proof will shift to the employer or employment agency to prove that there was no such contravention.

21.43 A complaint may be made to an employment tribunal before the end of three months beginning with the date of the conduct to which the complaint relates, or such further time as the employment tribunal considers reasonable, having regard, in particular, to when the facts to which the complaint relates came to the attention of the complainant. If the employment tribunal finds the complaint well founded, it shall make a declaration to that effect, and may make an order of compensation, and a recommendation that the respondent takes action for the purpose of obviating or reducing the adverse effect on the complainant.

21.44 A complaint may also be made if a person suffers a detriment for a reason that relates to a prohibited list, and it will be an automatically unfair dismissal if a person is dismissed (or selected for redundancy) because his employer has contravened reg 3 or relied on information supplied by a person in contravention of reg 3. There will be a minimum award of £5,000 (subject to a reduction in the event of contributory conduct) and a maximum of £65,300. Unlike other compensation limits, these are not subject to an annual review.

21.45 A person who has suffered because of an actual or apprehended contravention of reg 3 may, in the alternative, bring a claim for damages in a civil court for breach of statutory duty. Interim relief (an interim order in Scotland) is also available.

B. Inducements Relating to Union Membership or Activities (TULR(C)A, s 145A)

21.46 A worker has the right not to have an offer made to him by his employer for the sole or main purpose of inducing the worker:

(a) not to be or seek to become a member of an independent trade union;

(b) not to take part in the activities of an independent trade union at an appropriate time;

(c) to be or become a member of any trade union or of a particular trade union.

Inducements Relating to Collective Bargaining (TULR(C)A, s 145B)

21.47 A worker who is a member of an independent trade union which is recognised by his employer has the right not to have an offer made to him by his employer if:

(a) acceptance of the offer (together with the other workers' acceptance of similar offers) would have the result that the workers' terms of employment will no longer be determined by collective agreement negotiated by or on behalf of the union; and

(b) the employer's sole or main purpose in making the offer is to achieve this result.

21.48 A worker has the right to make a complaint to an employment tribunal on the ground that his employer has made him an offer in contravention of s 145A or 145B. It will be for the employer to show what his sole or main purpose was in making the offer. If the tribunal upholds the complaint, it shall make a declaration to that effect, and also award compensation to the worker of £4,294

21.49 The purpose of ss 145A and 145B (which were inserted into TULR(C)A by the Employment Relations Act 2004) is to prohibit 'sweetener payments' as an inducement to workers not to belong to trade unions, such payments being held by the European Court of Human Rights to contravene Art 11 of the European Convention (see *Wilson v United Kingdom*, para 1.109). Note that in *Kostal UK Ltd v Dunkley & Ors*[19] an employer made a one-off offer to the employees over the heads of the union, but crucially intended to continue to negotiate with the union. The Court of Appeal found, on the specific facts of this case, that this was not an unlawful inducement under s 145B. The wording of the offer was simply to break the impasse. If the employer had in fact made a direct offer which the employee could accept directly then that would have been contrary to the legislation. It is expected that this decision will be appealed.

---

[19] [2019] EWCA Civ 1009.

C. **Action Short of Dismissal (TULR(C)A, s 146, as amended)**

21.50 Every worker has the right not to be subjected to any detriment as an individual by any act, or any deliberate failure to act, by his employer, if the act or failure takes place for the purpose of:

(a) preventing or deterring him from being a member of an independent trade union, or penalising him for being so; or

(b) preventing or deterring him from taking part in the activities of an independent trade union at an appropriate time, or penalising him for doing so; or

(c) preventing or deterring him making use of trade union services at an appropriate time, or penalising him for doing so; or

(d) compelling him to become a member of a trade union.

Detriment, for the purpose of this section, is detriment short of dismissal.

21.51 The first matter to be determined is whether the action was taken against the worker 'as an individual'. If action is taken against a trade union this may affect an individual worker, but the action was not necessarily taken against him as an individual. In *F W Farnsworth Ltd v McCoid*,[20] a collective agreement provided that the employer had the right to derecognise a shop steward if his conduct was called into question. The employer notified the union that it intended to derecognise the claimant because his conduct was such that he was not suited to hold the office of shop steward. The claimant claimed that this derecognition constituted a breach of s 146(1). For the employer, it was argued that the action had not been taken against him as an individual, because it only affected his status as a shop steward, not as an employee. The argument was rejected. The Court of Appeal held that the purpose of s 146(1) was to allow an individual (in whatever capacity) to bring a complaint before an employment tribunal. However, it was thought that the employer could still successfully defend the action if it could show that the action taken was not for the purpose of preventing or deterring him from taking part in the activities of an independent trade union, but for the purpose of removing someone from the office of shop steward who was not fit for that role.

21.52 There is no breach of s 146 if the action taken (or omission) had the effect of so doing, if it was not done for that purpose. Thus in *Gallacher v Department of Transport*,[21] the claimant was a civil servant, who spent most of his working time carrying out trade union duties. He put his name forward for promotion to a higher grade, but was turned down because of his lack of management skills. He was told that the only way he could acquire those skills was by taking a line job, thus reducing the amount of time spent on trade union duties. He complained to an employment tribunal, who found that the advice given to him that he should spend more time gaining management experience was intended to deter him from spending time on trade union duties and activities. However, the EAT allowed the employer's appeal and that decision was upheld by the Court of Appeal. The employer's purpose was to ensure that only employees with sufficient line management experience were promoted. Thus any action taken was not for the purpose of deterring the applicant from exercising his statutory rights.

21.53 The 'appropriate time' for carrying out trade union activities or making use of trade union services means time which is outside his working hours, or at a time within his working hours at which, in accordance with arrangements agreed with or consent given by

---

[20] [1998] IRLR 362, EAT; aff'd [1999] ICR 1047, [1999] IRLR 626, CA.
[21] [1993] ICR 654, EAT; aff'd [1994] ICR 967, [1994] IRLR 231, CA.

his employer, it is permissible for him to take part in those activities. Such consent may be express, and will frequently be implied from the conduct of the parties. However, it would be rare that consent can be implied in the case of a shop steward who is not accredited (*Marley Tile Co Ltd v Shaw*[22]). A worker cannot just engage in trade union activities in working hours when he feels like it. Thus in *Brennan and Ging v Ellward (Lancs) Ltd*[23] the claimants left a site on which they were working to consult their trade union official, despite a warning that if they did so they would be dismissed. Although this may have amounted to trade union activities, it was not within the appropriate time for such activities.

21.54 In *Robb v Leon Motor Services*[24] the claimant was a long-distance coach driver. He was appointed shop steward. He was then told that he would have to drive other vehicles because of all the trouble he was causing, and he claimed that by taking him off better paid and more important work, he was being deterred from carrying out his trade union activities at an appropriate time. It was held that even though this was action taken against him short of dismissal, and even though it was done for the purpose of deterring him from taking part in trade union activities, he could not succeed. There was no attempt to stop him from taking part in union activities outside his working hours, and the activities he was engaged in within working hours were not done with any arrangement or with the consent of the employers. Consequently, he was not being deterred from taking part in trade union activity at the appropriate time.

21.55 Whether the activities in question are the activities of an independent trade union is an issue of fact for the employment tribunal to determine (*Marley Tile Co Ltd v Shaw*). There must be some institutional link, with the union or an accredited shop steward being involved. Individual requests or complaints, or group meetings which have no union connection, are outside the statutory protections (*Dixon and Shaw v West Ella Developments Ltd*[25]).

21.56 If there is a requirement (whether contractual or not) that in the event of a failure by the worker to become or remain a member of a trade union, he must make a payment (usually to charity), and a deduction is made from the worker's wages in consequence, this shall be treated as a detriment. Further, where a worker notifies the employer that he has ceased or will cease to be a member of a trade union as from a certain date, the employer will ensure that no amount representing his trade union subscription shall be deducted from the worker's pay (TULR(C)A, s 68, see para 21.79). If the employer fails to comply, the worker may seek a declaration in the county court. The court may make an order to ensure that the employer's actions are not repeated, but for any unlawful past deductions, the worker must seek a remedy in the employment tribunal under the provisions of s 23 of the Employment Rights Act 1996.

21.57 A complaint may be presented to a tribunal that an employer has taken action against a worker in violation of the above rights. The burden of proof is placed on the employer to show the purpose for which the action was taken, although it does not operate in the same way as in a discrimination claim. if the employer fails to establish the reason, it does not necessarily mean that it was for the reason put forward by the employee. It is open to the tribunal to find that the real reason was one that was put forward by neither side (*Dahou v Serco*[26]). This is similar to the approach in unfair dismissal, as shown in *Kuzel v Roche Products Ltd.*[27]

---

[22] [1978] ICR 828, [1978] IRLR 238, EAT; revsd [1980] ICR 72, [1980] IRLR 25, CA.
[23] [1974] IRLR 153, NIRC.   [24] [1977] IRLR 245; revsd [1978] ICR 506, [1978] IRLR 26, EAT.
[25] [1978] ICR 856, [1978] IRLR 151, EAT.   [26] [2016] EWCA Civ 832.   [27] [2008] EWCA Civ 380.

21.58 The employment tribunal may then make an award of compensation to the claimant either against the employer or the party who exercised the pressure, or partly against each of them as it thinks just and equitable in the circumstances (TULR(C)A, s 150).

21.59 The complaint must be presented within three months from the date of the last action complained of (see *Adlam v Salisbury and Wells Theological College*[28]), with the usual extension of time in cases where it was not reasonably practicable to present it earlier. If the tribunal upholds the complaint, it may make a compensation award as it considers just and equitable having regard to the claimant's loss, and the infringement of his rights, including any expenses incurred and any benefits he might have received but for that action. There is no limit (in theory) on the amount of compensation which can be awarded. The claimant must mitigate against his loss, and compensation is subject to a reduction on the ground of contributory conduct.

21.60 The basis of the award is to compensate the worker for any loss suffered, not for the purpose of imposing a fine on the employer. In *Brassington v Cauldon Wholesale Ltd*[29] an employer threatened to close his business down if he was forced to recognise a trade union. The claimant claimed this was action short of dismissal taken against him for the purpose of preventing or deterring him from joining an independent trade union, and with some hesitation, the EAT agreed that this was so and remitted the appeal back to an employment tribunal to assess compensation under TULR(C)A, s 149(2). Thus the infringement of a person's trade union rights will lead to an employment tribunal making a mandatory declaration, and compensation if the employee can show that he has suffered a loss. This could be, for example, stress causing ill health (*Cheall v Vauxhall Motors Ltd*[30]), injury to feelings as a result of being overlooked for promotion (*Cleveland Ambulance NHS Trust v Blane*[31]), the loss of the benefit of trade union advice or assistance, and so on.

D. Detriment and Dismissal in Statutory Recognition Cases (TULR(C)A, Sch A1)

21.61 We shall see (Chapter 23) that Sch A1 inserted into TULR(C)A sets out a statutory procedure whereby a trade union may obtain recognition or suffer derecognition. The Schedule also (in Pt VIII) provides protection for any worker (see para 23.6) against suffering a detriment because he did or did not do any of a wide range of actions in connection with the statutory procedure for recognition or derecognition, including supporting or opposing the application, influencing others to support or oppose the application, voting in a ballot, and so on (see para 156 of the Schedule). However, there will be no protection if what the worker did was unreasonable (is a breach of contract by the worker, eg a strike, unreasonable conduct on his part?). A worker may make a complaint to an employment tribunal, which may make a declaration, and may also award compensation to be paid by the employer in respect of the act or omission complained of; the amount shall be such as the tribunal considers to be just and equitable.

21.62 If the detriment amounts to the termination of the worker's contract, but that contract is not a contract of employment, the amount awarded by the tribunal may be the equivalent of the normal basic and compensatory awards which can be made in unfair dismissal cases under ERA, ss 119 and 124(1).

21.63 So far as workers who are employees are concerned, if the detriment amounts to a dismissal, that dismissal shall be regarded as being automatically unfair under ERA, Pt X.

---

[28] [1985] ICR 786, EAT.   [29] [1978] ICR 405, [1977] IRLR 479, EAT.   [30] [1979] IRLR 253.
[31] [1997] ICR 851, [1997] IRLR 332, EAT.

It will also be unfair to select an employee for redundancy if the reason was any of the above specified reasons.

21.64 Similar protections are given to employees who are employed under a fixed-term contract, and the normal qualifying periods of employment and the age limit provisions do not apply to any of the rights referred to earlier. Interim relief will also be available, as appropriate.

21.65 Workers who act or omit to act in circumstances which are outside the statutory procedure of Sch A1 must rely on those provisions which protect against detriment or dismissal in respect of trade union activities contained in TULR(C)A, ss 146 and 152 (see paras 21.50 and 21.85). Thus recruiting members, distributing literature, etc, with a view to obtaining recognition outside the statutory procedures will constitute trade union activities under the existing TULR(C)A provisions, and is thus protected (*Lyon v St James Press Ltd*[32]).

E. Time Off Work for Trade Union Duties (TULR(C)A, s 168)

21.66 An employer shall permit an employee of his who is an official of a recognized independent trade union to take time off work during his working hours, for the purpose of carrying out any duties as such officially concerned with:

(a) negotiations with the employer related to or connected with collective bargaining; or

(b) the performance on behalf of the employees of functions in relation to or in connection with matters falling within collective bargaining which the employer has agreed may be performed by the union; or

(c) the receipt of information from the employer and consultations by the employer concerned with redundancies (see para 18.69) and the transfer of an undertaking (see para 9.76).

21.67 The employer will also permit the employee to have time off work during working hours to undergo training in aspects of industrial relations which is relevant to the carrying out of those duties, and which has been approved by the TUC or by his union.

21.68 Time off work for this purpose is not confined to face-to-face meetings with the employers, but can also include preparatory or co-ordinating meetings in order to discuss forthcoming negotiations, as long as these are in connection with the collective bargaining purposes outlined in s 178 (*London Ambulance Service v Charlton*[33]).

21.69 A trade union official wishing to take time off work for training should show a copy of the syllabus to the employer. In *Menzies v Smith and McLaurin Ltd*[34] the claimant wished to go on a course relating to job security. The union sent a copy of the syllabus to the employers, showing that topics to be covered included import controls, North Sea Oil, EEC policies, and so on. The company decided that all this was not relevant to his trade union duties, but agreed to give him time off work (without pay) for trade union activities. He went on the course and then claimed his pay. It was held that he was not entitled to be paid. The syllabus clearly indicated that the course was not relevant to his duties as a trade union official.

21.70 The amount of time off, the purposes for which, the occasions on which, and any conditions subject to which time off may be taken are those that are reasonable in all the

---

[32] [1976] ICR 413, [1976] IRLR 215, EAT.   [33] [1992] ICR 773, [1992] IRLR 510, EAT.
[34] [1980] IRLR 180, EAT.

circumstances having regard to the relevant provisions of the code of practice issued by ACAS. The employer shall pay an employee who has taken time off for these purposes in accordance with his usual rate of remuneration. A failure to permit an employee to have time off under this section, or a failure to pay him for time off, may be the subject of a complaint to an employment tribunal by the aggrieved employee. In *Blower v CEGB*[35] the claimant, who was a night shift worker, was a member of a works committee which met during the day. His day shift colleagues were paid for attending, whereas he was not. It was held that he was not entitled to be paid. It was part of his union work that his leisure time would be eaten into; the law only requires time off to be paid for if it is during his normal working hours, not for time spent on trade union duties outside his working hours (see *Hairsine v Kingston-upon-Hull City Council*[36]).

21.71 Whether it is reasonable to have time off under s 168 is a question of fact for the employment tribunal, and its findings cannot be challenged in the EAT unless it took into account matters which ought not to be taken into account (*Thomas Scott & Sons (Bakers) Ltd v Allen*[37]).

F. Time Off Work for Trade Union Activities (TULR(C)A, s 170)

21.72 An employer shall permit an employee who is a member of a recognised independent trade union to take time off during the employee's working hours for the purpose of taking part in:

(a) any activities of that trade union; and

(b) any activities in relation to which the employee is acting as a representative of that union.

This might include, for example, attendance at a conference as a union delegate, etc, but the activities for which permission is to be granted do not include anything which involved the taking of industrial action, whether or not in contemplation or furtherance of a trade dispute. Nor does the lobbying of Parliament to protest against proposed legislation come within the definition of 'trade union activities', even if the lobby is organised by a trade union, because it is intended to convey political and ideological objections to the proposed legislation, and is not as such a trade union activity (*Luce v London Borough of Bexley*[38]).

21.73 Again, the amount of time off, the purposes, the occasions, and the conditions are those that are reasonable in all the circumstances having regard to the relevant provisions in the Code of Practice issued (see *Depledge v Pye Telecommunications Ltd*[39]). When determining the reasonableness of time off to be taken for a particular purpose, the nature, extent, and purpose of time off already taken by the employee may be taken into consideration (*Wignall v British Gas Corpn*[40]). It will be noted that the employer does not have to pay an employee for time taken off for trade union activities. A failure to permit time off for these purposes may be the subject of a complaint to an employment tribunal by the aggrieved employee.

G. Time Off Work for Trade Union Learning Representatives (TULR(C)A, s 168A)

21.74 An employer shall permit an employee of his who is a member of an independent trade union recognised by the employer, and a learning representative of the trade union, to take time off work during his working hours, with pay, for the purpose of carrying on

---

[35] Unreported.   [36] [1992] ICR 212, [1992] IRLR 211, EAT.   [37] [1983] IRLR 329, CA.
[38] [1990] ICR 591, [1990] IRLR 422, EAT.   [39] [1981] ICR 82, [1980] IRLR 390, EAT.
[40] [1984] ICR 716, [1984] IRLR 493, EAT.

552 INDIVIDUAL TRADE UNION RIGHTS

the following activities in relation to qualifying members of the trade union, ie members of the trade union who are employees of the employer of a description in respect of whom the union is recognised, and in relation to whom it is the function of the union learning representative to act as such.

21.75 The purposes in question are:

    (a) any of the following activities:

        (i)   analysing learning or training needs,

        (ii) providing information and advice about learning or training matters,

        (iii) arranging learning or training, and

        (iv) promoting the value of learning or training;

    (b) consulting with the employer about carrying on such activities; and

    (c) preparing for any of the above.

21.76 The trade union must give notice in writing to the employer that the employee is a learning representative of the trade union, and that he has undergone (or will be undergoing) sufficient training to enable him to carry on such activities. The training must be sufficient for the above purpose, having regard to any Code of Practice issued by ACAS or the Secretary of State. The amount of time off, the occasions on which, and any conditions subject to which time off may be taken are those that are reasonable having regard to any relevant provision of the Code of Practice.

21.77 An employee may present a complaint to an employment tribunal that his employer has failed to permit him to take time off as required by s 168A which, if the complaint is well founded, shall make a declaration, and may make an award of compensation.

21.78 A trade union member is entitled to reasonable time off work (without pay) for the purpose of having access to the services of his union learning representative. It will be unfair if an employee is dismissed because he brought proceedings to enforce his rights under s 168A.

H. **Check-off Arrangements (TULR(C)A, s 68)**

21.79 If a trade union and an employer have an agreement whereby the employer will deduct the union subscriptions from the worker's wages and pay this direct to the union (ie a check-off agreement) the employer shall ensure that the worker has authorised the deduction in a document which is signed and dated, that the amount of the deduction does not exceed the permitted amount, and that the authorisation is current on the day of the deduction. An authorisation once made will be operative until the worker withdraws it in writing. The permitted amount to be deducted is the amount of the union subscription. It is no longer necessary for the employer to give one month's notice in writing before deducting an increase in the union subscription, but the amount of the deduction will still have to be shown on the regular itemized pay statement, and the worker is free to withdraw from the check-off arrangement at any time (Deregulation (Deduction from Pay of Union Subscriptions) Order 1998).

21.80 The fact that the worker has given his authorisation to the deductions does not give rise to any obligation on the part of the employer to continue to make the deductions (s 68(9)). That is clearly a matter between the employer and the trade union.

21.81 A worker may bring a complaint before an employment tribunal that his employer has made a deduction in contravention of s 68. The complaint must be presented within three months from the date of the last deduction, with the usual extension of time if it was not reasonably practicable to present the claim earlier.

21.82 If the tribunal finds the complaint to be well founded, it shall make a declaration to that effect, and also order the employer to pay to the worker the unauthorized deduction (or unauthorised increase in subscription).

I. Deductions for the Political Fund of the Union (s 86)

21.83 If a member of a trade union informs the employer in writing that he is not a contributor to the political fund of the union, the employer shall ensure that no amount representing the contribution to the political fund is deducted from the employee's wages.

21.84 If a person alleges that his employer has wrongly deducted a political fund contribution, or has refused to deduct union dues, he may make a complaint to an employment tribunal within three months, and the tribunal may make a declaration, order the employer to pay the applicant the amount deducted in contravention of s 87, or make an order requiring the employer to take steps specified in relation to emoluments payable. In the latter case, if there is still a failure to comply, there is an ultimate sanction of two weeks' pay (TULR(C)A, s 87).

J. Dismissal on the Ground of Trade Union Membership or Non-membership, or Trade Union Activities (TULR(C)A, s 152)

21.85 The dismissal of an employee will be unfair if the reason (or principal reason) was because the employee:

(a) was, or proposed to become, a member of an independent trade union; or

(b) had taken part, or proposed to take part, in the activities of an independent trade union at an appropriate time, or made use of trade union services at an appropriate time, or had failed to accept an offer made in contravention of ss 145A–145B (inducement relating to union membership or collective bargaining, see para 21.46). 'Appropriate time' means time which is outside his working hours, or time within his working hours at which, in accordance with arrangements agreed with or consent given by his employer, it is permissible to take part in those activities. 'Working hours' means any time when the employee is required to work. A person is not taking part in trade union activities merely because he is a trade union activist, for one must distinguish between individual and trade union activities (*Chant v Aquaboats Ltd*[41]). Nor do the activities of an unofficial strike committee constitute trade union activities. But enlisting the help of a trade union official to assist in negotiations of terms and conditions of employment may constitute trade union activities (*Discount Tobacco and Confectionery Ltd v Armitage*[42]), (but see *Speciality Care plc v Pachela*[43]). Going on strike does not constitute trade union activities, but leading an official strike will (*Britool Ltd v Roberts*[44]).

If the employee is dismissed because the employer learns of his trade union activities in a previous employment (eg as a trade union activist), it would be inevitable that the employer was dismissing him because of the belief that he would be involved in trade union activities in his current employment, and thus the principal reason for the dismissal would be that the employee proposed to take part in trade union activities, and

---

[41] [1978] 3 All ER 102, [1978] ICR 643, EAT.   [42] [1990] IRLR 15, [1995] ICR 431, EAT.
[43] [1996] ICR 633, [1996] IRLR 248, EAT.   [44] [1993] IRLR 481, EAT.

hence the dismissal is unfair (*Fitzpatrick v British Railways Board*, para 21.30). But if the trade union activist has obtained employment by deceit (eg by changing his name) then a dismissal for that deceit may be fair, and the reason is not because of past or proposed trade union activities (*Birmingham City District Council v Beyer*, para 21.30);

(c) was not a member of any trade union, or a particular trade union, or had refused or proposed to refuse to become or remain a member (*Crosville Motor Services Ltd v Ashfield*[45]). This provision gives general rights to non-unionists not to be dismissed because of their non-membership of a trade union.

A distinction may be drawn between the fact of involvement in trade union activities and the manner of such involvement. Thus if, in the course of such activities, the trade unionist makes statements which are malicious, untruthful, or irrelevant to the matter in hand, his manner of conducting those activities may take him outside the protection of s 152 (*Bass Taverns Ltd v Burgess*[46]);

(d) had made use of trade union services at an appropriate time, or had failed to accept an offer which was made in contravention of ss 145A and 145B.

21.86 If a person is dismissed for any of the above reasons, it will be an unfair dismissal, and thus it is not necessary for him to have the normal qualifying period of employment of one year before he can bring his claim (TULR(C)A, s 154, and see *Carrington v Therm-A-Stor Ltd*[47]). Nor does the upper age limit exclusion apply. Taking part in a strike may be trade union activity, but it is not at an appropriate time (see para 21.66).

21.87 It is also an unfair dismissal to select a person for redundancy because of his trade union membership/non-membership, or his trade union activities, or making use of trade union services (TULR(C)A, ss 152(1)–153).

21.88 To select an employee for redundancy because of his trade union membership or non-membership or trade union activities would, of course, be manifestly unfair, but it must be shown that the circumstances constituting the redundancy applied equally to other employees who held positions similar to that employee, and that they were not dismissed. Thus in *O'Dea v ISC Chemical Ltd*,[48] the claimant, who was a senior shop steward, was paid as a technical services operator, although in fact he spent half of his working time working as a packaging operator and the other half on trade union activities. He was dismissed for reason of redundancy, although two other technical service operators were retained. It was held that his dismissal was not unfair. When considering his 'position' account had to be taken of his status as an employee, the nature of his work, and his terms and conditions of employment. The claimant could not compare himself with technical service operators because he did not do that job.

21.89 It does not need to be shown that the employer acted maliciously or with a deliberate desire to get rid of a trade union activist. Thus if an employee spends a major part of his working hours on trade union duties, with the result that he is given a poor assessment when redundancy selection procedures are being implemented, 'the reason' for his selection is his trade union activities, carried out at an appropriate time with the consent (albeit reluctantly given) of the employer, and hence his dismissal falls within s 152(1) (*Dundon v GPT Ltd*[49]).

---

[45] [1986] IRLR 475, EAT.   [46] [1995] IRLR 596, CA.
[47] [1982] ICR 8, EAT; revsd [1983] 1 All ER 796, [1983] ICR 208, sub nom *Therm A Stor Ltd v Atkins* [1983] IRLR 78, CA.   [48] [1996] ICR 222, [1995] IRLR 599, CA.
[49] [1995] IRLR 403, EAT.

K. Dismissal in Connection with Industrial Action (TULR(C)A, ss 237–239)

21.90 The law on dismissal for taking part in industrial action is somewhat complicated, and needs careful consideration. There are five different situations to consider.

21.91 The first situation arises when the employer conducts a lock-out. Here, the provisions of s 238(1)(a) apply, and if there is a dismissal, the 'no picking and choosing' rule applies.

21.92 The second situation arises when employees, who may be all union members, or some of whom may be union members (and some not), go on strike and the strike has not been authorised or endorsed by the trade union to which they belong. This is an unofficial strike, and the provisions of s 237 apply.

21.93 The third situation arises when none of those who go on strike or take industrial action are members of a trade union. This is not unofficial industrial action, and clearly it is not official industrial action. Here, a dismissed employee can only complain of unfair dismissal if the 'no picking and choosing' rule has been violated (s 238(2)).

21.94 The fourth situation arises when a union authorises or endorses industrial action, but the action is not protected by virtue of s 219 because the balloting provisions have not been complied with, or secondary action, etc is being taken. This is official unprotected industrial action, and the 'no picking and choosing' rules in s 238(2) apply.

21.95 The fifth situation arises when a union calls a protected strike, ie one that is protected by TULR(C)A, s 219 (immunity from actions in tort, see para 23.41), and the union has not lost its immunity through a failure to comply with the legal rules which would lead to such loss, eg it has complied fully with the balloting provisions (see ss 222–235). Here, the provisions of s 238A apply, and dismissed employees enjoy much greater protection.

21.96 There is a further subtle distinction between ss 237–238 and 238A. Sections 237 and 238 are both concerned with a dismissal which takes place *while* an employee was taking part in industrial action, whereas 238A deals with a dismissal *for* taking part in industrial action. In other words, ss 237 and 238 apply whenever an employee is dismissed during the industrial action, whereas s 238A will apply if the participation in the industrial action was the reason for the dismissal.

These situations can now be examined in more detail.

Dismissal in Connection with a Lock-out (TULR(C)A, s 238(I)(a))

21.97 A lock-out is the closing of a place of employment, or a suspension of the work, or the refusal by the employer to continue to employ his employees, done with a view to compelling those employees to accept terms and conditions of or affecting employment (ERA, s 235(4)). A lock-out by an employer is not necessarily a breach of contract by him (*Express and Star Ltd v Bunday*[50]). If an employee claims that he has been dismissed by virtue of the lock-out, an employment tribunal is precluded from determining whether or not such dismissal is fair or unfair unless it can be shown that (a) one or more of the relevant employees were not dismissed, or (b) if they were dismissed, they were re-engaged within three months from the date of dismissal, but the applicant was not offered re-engagement. The relevant employees are those who were directly interested in the dispute on the day of the lock-out (*H Campey & Sons Ltd v Bellwood*[51]).

---

[50] [1987] ICR 58, [1986] IRLR 477, EAT; revsd [1988] ICR 379, [1987] IRLR 422, CA.
[51] [1987] ICR 311, EAT.

Dismissal of Unofficial Strikers (TULR(C)A, s 237)

21.98 An employee who is dismissed after taking part in unofficial industrial action has no right to claim unfair dismissal. Further, if there is mass industrial action that causes enormous disruption to an employer's business, and which requires an immediate and firm response, the employer's policy of dismissing all employees who were absent without leave or explanation, but then trying to sort out the exceptional cases of genuine non-participation by way of an appeal process, amounts to a reasonable response (*Sehmi v Gate Gourmet London Ltd*[52]).

21.99 A strike or other industrial action will be unofficial unless:

(a) the employee is a member of the trade union, and the strike or other industrial action was authorised or endorsed by his trade union; or

(b) the employee is not a member of the trade union, but there are others who are taking part in the strike who are members of the trade union by which the strike or other industrial action has been authorised or endorsed.

21.100 In other words, if some or all of the employees who are taking industrial action are members of a trade union, and the union has not authorised or endorsed the industrial action, any employee who is consequently dismissed will have no claim for unfair dismissal, even if others who took part in the industrial action were not dismissed (s 237). If the trade union authorised or endorses the action, but then repudiates it, the action will become unofficial the next working day after the repudiation takes place. What amounts to a repudiation is set out in s 21 (see para 23.84). Thus an employer could dismiss the ringleaders of an unofficial strike without having to worry about the prospect of defending an unfair dismissal claim, subject to the exception in respect of protected reasons (see para 21.112).

Dismissal in Connection with Industrial Action (s 238(1)(b), (2)(b))

21.101 The third situation applies when none of those who are taking industrial action are members of a trade union. This is not official industrial action, because they are not members of a trade union, nor is it unofficial industrial action, presumably because there is no one to make it official. It is just industrial action. In these circumstances, if an employee is dismissed while taking part in industrial action, the tribunal shall not determine whether the dismissal was fair or unfair, unless it is shown that:

(a) one or more of the relevant employees (ie, those taking part in the industrial action) were not dismissed, or

(b) any such employee who was dismissed was offered re-engagement within three months of the claimant's dismissal, but the claimant was not so offered.

There is no requirement that the offer to re-engage must be in writing (*Marsden v Fairey Stainless Ltd*[53]).

21.102 Whether or not an employee is taking part in a strike or other industrial action must be determined as an objective fact. In other words, the test is 'what is the employee doing or omitting to do?' The subjective knowledge of the employer is not relevant (*Manifold Industries v Sims*, para 13.36).

21.103 An employee who is dismissed for taking part in a strike is not entitled to a redundancy payment, even if it can be shown that a subsequent redundancy situation is revealed.

---

[52] [2009] IRLR 807.   [53] [1979] IRLR 103, EAT.

In *Baxter v Limb Group of Companies* (para 18.11), dock workers refused to work overtime following a dispute with the employers over bonus payments. They were dismissed, and subsequently the employers discontinued using direct labour and contracted the work out. The dismissed employees argued that the employers had decided to dispense with direct labour, and had manoeuvred the employees into a position where it appeared that they were dismissed for taking part in a strike or other industrial action, whereas the real reason for the dismissal was redundancy. The Court of Appeal dismissed their claim. The industrial action was the reason for the dismissal and for the decision to use contract labour. TULR(C)A, s 238 prohibits an employment tribunal from considering whether a dismissal is fair or unfair if, at the date of dismissal, the employee *was taking part* in a strike or other industrial action. It does not say that the employee was dismissed *because* he was taking part in such action. In other words, if the dismissals caused the redundancy, a redundancy payment cannot be made (*Sanders v Ernest A Neale Ltd*, para 18.11).

21.104 It will be recalled that a strike is a breach of contract by the employee which entitles the employer to dismiss him. Provided the employer dismisses all the strikers, or offers all of them re-engagement after the strike is over within three months, the employment tribunal has no jurisdiction to hear any complaint. This is the 'no picking and choosing' rule (see *McCormick v Horsepower Ltd*[54]). But if an employer is selective in his dismissals or offers of re-engagement, those employees who have been excluded may bring claims in the employment tribunals. To avoid a finding of unfair dismissal, the employer must show that he has acted reasonably in not taking back those strikers who were not offered re-engagement. The question will be determined by the circumstances, having regard to the equity and substantial merits of the case (*Edwards v Cardiff City Council*[55]).

21.105 Further, the employer can re-engage an employee who has been dismissed for striking any time after three months from the time another striker was dismissed without exposing himself to a claim for unfair dismissal from the latter.

21.106 But if the employer (or an associated employer) re-engages a striker by mistake (eg in ignorance of the fact that he had been on strike) this gives the employment tribunal jurisdiction to consider a claim from a striker who has not been offered re-engagement (*Bigham v GKN Kwikform Ltd*[56]).

21.107 The three-month period is in the nature of a 'cooling-off' period, designed to enable industrial disputes to be settled on honourable terms. As long as the offer of re-engagement is made within that period, the employment tribunal has no jurisdiction to hear a claim by a person who does not wish to accept that offer (*Highland Fabricators Ltd v McLaughlin*[57]).

21.108 But the employer will lose the protection of s 238 if he seeks to dismiss before the strike has begun or after the strike is over. In *Heath v Longman (Meat Salesmen) Ltd*[58] employees went out on strike, but subsequently decided to return to work. One of them informed the employer that the strike was over, but when they returned to work they were dismissed. The NIRC held that since they had returned to work, they were no longer on strike, and hence the dismissals were unfair. In *Midland Plastics Ltd v Till*,[59] a letter was sent to the company management stating that unless certain demands were met, industrial action would commence at 11am. At 9.30am, the managing director spoke to four

---

[54] [1980] ICR 278, [1980] IRLR 182, EAT; aff'd [1981] 2 All ER 746, [1981] ICR 535, [1981] IRLR 217, CA.
[55] [1979] IRLR 303, EAT.   [56] [1992] ICR 113, [1992] IRLR 4, EAT.
[57] [1985] ICR 183, [1984] IRLR 482, EAT.
[58] [1973] 2 All ER 1228, [1973] ICR 407, [1973] IRLR 214, NIRC.   [59] [1983] ICR 118, [1983] IRLR 9, EAT.

employees, who confirmed that they would abide by the decision, and they were immediately dismissed. It was held that the employment tribunal were not precluded by s 238 from entertaining a complaint of unfair dismissal. The threat to take part in a strike was a mere display of power by one side to a dispute which is a substantial feature of industrial relations negotiations. As the dismissals took place before the strike, s 238 did not apply.

21.109 The offer of re-engagement must be made to the striking employee. A general advertising campaign offering employment to those who apply does not amount to an offer of employment to any particular individual. Such a campaign merely makes available the opportunity to be offered employment (*Crosville Wales Ltd v Tracey*, para 17.225).

21.110 If a dismissal is unfair because the employer has re-engaged some of the strikers contrary to TULR(C)A, s 238, compensation is not to be reduced on the ground of contributory conduct merely because the employees who were not re-engaged took part in the strike. There must have been some other sufficiently blameworthy conduct which makes it just and equitable to reduce their compensation, for example if the strikers' leaders were over-hasty or indulged in inflammatory language. The circumstances of each claimant must be examined to see whether *his* compensation should be reduced because of *his* conduct other than the mere fact that he was on strike (*Tracey v Crosville Wales Ltd*).

Official Unprotected Industrial Action

21.111 The fourth situation arises where a trade union calls a strike, but loses the protection of s 219 because:

(a) the strike was to enforce trade union membership (s 222); or

(b) unofficial strikers were dismissed (s 223); or

(c) secondary action was taken (s 224); or

(d) the strike was to impose union recognition requirement (s 225); or

(e) the balloting provisions of ss 226–234 were not complied with; or

(f) notice was not given to the employer (s 234A).

In these circumstances the strike is no longer protected under s 238A (see para 21.112), and hence the dismissal of employees on strike falls to be considered under the 'no picking and choosing' rule in s 238(2) (see para 21.101). The action may be official, but it is not protected industrial action.

Protected Industrial Action (s 238A)

21.112 Finally, protected industrial action is industrial action in respect of which the trade union will be immune from liability in tort by virtue of TULR(C)A, s 219, and has not lost that immunity by virtue of the above matters. Those who take part in such industrial action have the protections conferred by s 238A, which will arise if the date of dismissal is:

(a) within the protected period, which is the basic period of 12 weeks beginning with the first day of protected industrial action, plus any extension period brought about by an employer lock-out; or

(b) after the end of the protected period, but the employee had ceased to take part in the industrial action before the end of that period; or

(c) after the end of the protected period, but the employer had not taken such procedural steps as would have been reasonable for the purposes of ending the dispute. The procedural steps include complying with agreed procedures, resuming negotiations, unreasonably refusing the use of conciliation or mediation services, etc (s 238A(6)).

21.113 Any such dismissal is automatically unfair, and there is no qualifying period of employment or upper age limit which would otherwise defeat a claim. A claim may be presented before the end of six months from the date of dismissal, with the usual extension of time provisions. It will be equally unfair to select an employee for redundancy if the selection was because the employee took part in protected industrial action as defined in the above three categories (ERA, s 105(7C)). The action taken must be an official strike called by a trade union which itself would be protected under TULR(C)A, s 219 (see Chapter 23). If the union repudiates the official action, and thus the strike changes from being official to unofficial, employees are given a day's grace in which to cease their action, ie if they continue to be on strike beyond the next working day after the day on which the repudiation took place, they will lose their protection of s 238A.

21.114 To determine whether the employer has taken reasonable steps to resolve the dispute, regard shall be had to:

(a) whether the employer or the union have complied with procedures established by any collective agreement or other agreement;

(b) whether the employer or the union offered or agreed to commence or resume negotiations after the start of the protected industrial action;

(c) whether the employer or the union unreasonably refused, after the start of the protected industrial action, a request for conciliation services to be used;

(d) whether the employer or the union unreasonably refused, after the start of the protected industrial action, a request that mediation services be used.

21.115 In determining whether the employer has taken those steps, no regard shall be had to the merits of the dispute. If there is a dismissal contrary to s 238A, an employment tribunal cannot make an order for reinstatement or re-engagement until after the conclusion of the protected industrial action. Additional powers are given to tribunals to carry out pre-hearing reviews and to adjourn proceedings if they become aware that legal actions are being brought challenging the legitimacy of the industrial action in question.

Exceptions in Certain Cases (ss 237–238)

21.116 The general principle is that an employee has no right to claim unfair dismissal if at the time of the dismissal he was taking part in an unofficial strike or other unofficial industrial action (s 237). However, this does not apply if the reason for the dismissal (or selection for redundancy) was a protected reason, ie a reason which violates an employee's rights with respect to pregnancy, maternity or parental leave, health and safety, working time, employee representative matters, jury service, dependants, protected disclosure, or flexible working (s 237(1A)).

21.117 Similarly, if an employee believes that he was unable to claim that he was unfairly dismissed because at the date of the dismissal the employer did not act in violation of the 'picking and choosing' rule, then again, the employee's rights will revive if the reason for the dismissal was for one of the above reasons.

L. Dismissal due to Industrial Pressure (ERA, s 107)

21.118 If an employer is forced to dismiss an employee because of actual, or the threat of, industrial pressure by other employees, this may amount to an unfair dismissal. The reason is that ERA, s 107 provides that for the purpose of determining whether the employer has a statutory reason for dismissing, or whether the employer acted reasonably in dismissing, no account shall be taken of any industrial pressure (ie strike or other industrial action) which was put on the employer, and the question must be determined as if no such pressure had been exercised. In *Hazell Offsets v Luckett*,[60] the claimant was dismissed from his managerial post after trade union representatives had indicated that they would not co-operate with him. Clearly, the principal reason for the dismissal was the industrial pressure, but this could not be advanced as a reason. Since there was no other reason, the dismissal was unfair. The tribunal thought that this did not seem right, nor fair, but it was clearly what Parliament had decided. But if the employee was partly responsible for the threat of industrial action, this could amount to contributory conduct so as to warrant a reduction in the compensation awarded. Thus if the industrial pressure is exercised because of some personal animosity, and the employee is uncooperative in a difficult situation and, for example, refuses to move to another job, he may well have contributed to his dismissal (*Ford Motor Co Ltd v Hudson*[61]).

21.119 However, if on a claim for unfair dismissal the employer or the claimant claims that the employer was induced to dismiss the claimant because of pressure which a trade union or other person exercised on him by way of calling, organizing, procuring, or financing a strike, or threatening to do so, and the pressure was exercised because the claimant was not a member of any trade union or a particular trade union, then the employer or the claimant may, before the hearing of the complaint, join that person as a party to the proceedings before the employment tribunal. If the latter decides to make an award of compensation in favour of the claimant, but also finds that the employer was induced to dismiss him because of the pressure, the tribunal may make an award against that person instead of the employer, or partly against that person and partly against the employer. The amount shall be such as the tribunal considers to be just and equitable in all the circumstances (TULR(C)A, s 160).

M. **Selection for Dismissal on Grounds of Redundancy (TULR(C)A, s 153)**

21.120 We have seen that to select a person for dismissal on grounds of redundancy will be unfair if the reason for the selection was his membership or non-membership of a trade union. No qualifying period of continuous employment is required.

N. **Compensations for Dismissals (TULR(C)A, ss 155–158)**

21.121 In respect of compensation for dismissals for trade union membership or non-membership, there are rules relating to a minimum basic award, an additional award, as well as the usual compensation award (see Chapter 17).

O. **Interim Relief for Dismissed Trade Unionists or Non-unionists (TULR(C)A, ss 161–166)**

21.122 If an employee considers that he was unfairly dismissed because he was, or proposed to become, a member of an independent trade union, or had taken or proposed to take part in the activities of that union, or he was not a member of a trade union, he may present a complaint to an employment tribunal asking for an order that he be reinstated or re-engaged by the employer or, if this cannot be agreed upon, that he be suspended on full pay pending a settlement or a determination of the complaint. The employee must present the complaint before the end of seven days from the effective date of the termination of his employment, and must, if he is claiming he was dismissed because of his trade union

---

[60] [1977] IRLR 430, EAT.   [61] [1978] 3 All ER 23, [1978] ICR 482, [1978] IRLR 66, EAT.

membership or activities, accompany his complaint with a certificate signed by an author-ised official of the trade union concerned, stating that the employee was or had proposed to become a member, and that there were reasonable grounds for believing that the reason for the dismissal was the one alleged in the complaint. The signature of a trade union official is prima facie evidence that he is duly authorized to sign the certificate, but if this is chal-lenged, the onus is on the employee to show that the official had actual or implied authority to sign it (*Sulemany v Habib Bank Ltd*[62]).

21.123 The tribunal will give the employer seven days' notice before the hearing, but shall thereupon hear the complaint as soon as is practicable. If the tribunal comes to the conclusion that it is likely that it would uphold a complaint of unfair dismissal on one of the above grounds, it shall announce this preliminary finding and explain to the par-ties its powers. It will then ask the employer if he is willing to reinstate the employee, or re-engage him on terms and conditions which are no less favourable than he formerly enjoyed, pending the determination or settlement of the complaint. If the employer is willing to re-engage the employee in another job, and specifies the terms and conditions, the tribunal will ask the employee if he is willing to accept, and if so, an order to that effect will be made. If the employee is unwilling to accept the job on those terms and conditions, then, if his refusal is reasonable, the tribunal will make an order for the continuation of his contract of employment, but if his refusal is regarded as being unreasonable, no order will be made. If the employer fails to attend the hearing, or states that he is unwilling to reinstate or re-engage the employee, the tribunal will make an order for the continuation of the employee's contract of employment.

21.124 The effect of an order for continuation of the contract of employment is that if the employment has ceased, it will continue in force, or if it has not yet ceased, it will con-tinue when it does so cease, until, in either case, the determination or settlement of the complaint for the purposes of pay, seniority, pension rights, and other similar rights, and for determining for any purpose the period for which the employee has been continuously employed. The tribunal will also specify the pay due to the employee from the time of dismissal until the complaint is finally settled, but it will take into account any lump sum received in lieu of wages. At any time after making the order and before the determination by the tribunal, the employer or the employee may apply for a revocation or variation of the order on the ground that there has been a relevant change in circumstances. Also, the employee may apply to the tribunal on the ground that the employer has not complied with the terms of the order. If his complaint is that the employer has not paid the amount speci-fied, the tribunal will determine the amount due, and make it as a separate award for any other sum it gives by way of compensation. If the complaint relates to any other breach by the employer, then it shall make an award of compensation as it thinks just and equitable having regard to the loss suffered by the complainant.

21.125 An order for continuation of employment merely preserves the employee's rights; the employer does not have to permit him to come back to work, or to allow him on the premises.

21.126 On an application for interim relief, the employment tribunal must decide if the claimant can establish that he has a good chance of succeeding at a full hearing. This is a higher degree of certainty than a mere reasonable chance of success. 'Likely' means more than 'probable', and probable itself suggests more than an even chance (*Taplin v C Shippam Ltd*[63]).

---

[62] [1983] ICR 60, EAT.   [63] [1978] ICR 1068, EAT.

21.127 It will be extremely rare that an employer will admit that a person was dismissed because he engaged in trade union activity, and doubtless some other reason will be advanced. In *Forsyth v Fry's Metals Ltd*[64] the tribunal considered the evidence under four headings: (a) the extent of the alleged behaviour, (b) the extent of the employer's dissatisfaction with the employee, (c) the coincidence in time between the alleged behaviour and the initial steps taken towards dismissal, and (d) the coincidence in time between the behaviour and the actual dismissal. In this case, the claimant was dismissed for alleged poor work performance. There was little direct evidence of this; on the other hand, he had been instrumental in persuading most of the employees to join a trade union, and had been elected shop steward. On the facts, there was a likelihood that he would succeed in establishing his claim, and interim relief was granted.

21.128 On an application for interim relief, it is possible to join a person who is exercising pressure to bring about the dismissal (see TULR(C)A, s 160), and such a person shall be given notice of the time, date, and place of the hearing as soon as is reasonably practicable (s 162(3)).

Summary

- The law in relation to trade unions is mostly set out in the Trade Union and Labour Relations (Consolidation) Act 1992 (TULR(C)A).
- An individual has rights both in respect of union membership both against his union and against his employer.
- S/he cannot be excluded from a union except in certain circumstances, nor unjustifiably disciplined.
- An employer cannot refuse someone employment because they are or are not a member of a union.
- Blacklisting is prohibited.
- A worker has the right not to be offered inducements in relation to union membership or activities, such as collective bargaining.
- Officials of recognised unions have the right to time off work to carry out union duties and activities.
- An employee cannot be dismissed for taking part in official industrial action. Other rules apply for other types of strikes.

---

[64] [1977] IRLR 243.

22

The Law Relating to Trade Unions

Background

22.1 In this chapter we shall concentrate on the law as it affects the running of a trade union. All the relevant law is consolidated by the Trade Union and Labour Relations (Consolidation) Act 1992, as amended. In so far as earlier reported decisions were based on provisions in earlier (now replaced) legislation, references to the relevant statutory provisions have, for the sake of convenience, been transposed to the corresponding provisions of the 1992 Act.

What Constitutes a Trade Union?

A. **Definition of a Trade Union (TULR(C)A, s 1)**

22.2 A trade union is an organisation (whether permanent or temporary) which either:

(a) consists wholly or mainly of workers of one or more descriptions and whose principal purposes include the regulation of relations between workers and employers or employers' associations; or

(b) consists wholly or mainly of:

  (i) constituent or affiliated organisations which have those purposes; or

  (ii) representatives of such constituent or affiliated organisations, and in either case whose principal purposes include the regulation of relations between workers and employers or workers' and employers' associations, or include the regulation of relations between the constituent or affiliated organisations.

This definition discloses two functional bodies:

(a) a single trade union; and

(b) confederated organisations, such as the Trades Union Congress.

22.3 Whether or not a trade union has a 'legal personality' of its own was always a matter of some controversy. Section 10 provides that a trade union shall not be a body corporate, but shall nonetheless be capable of making contracts, suing and being sued in its own name, and being prosecuted for any offences committed in its name. As, however, it has no 'legal' existence, property must be held by its trustees, and any judgment, order, or award shall be enforced against the property held by the trustees. This does not apply to those organisations which were on the special register created by the Industrial Relations Act 1971 (see TULR(C)A, s 117) for these were professional organisations which engaged in collective bargaining on behalf of their members, and their legal personality stemmed from their charter of incorporation, or by virtue of incorporation under the Companies Acts. Such legal personality is to continue (about 12 such professional bodies are on the special register), but other than these, any registration by a trade union under the Companies Acts, or as a friendly society or an industrial and provident society, is void.

B. Listing of Trade Unions (TULR(C)A, s 2)

22.4 The certification officer (a post created in 1975 by the Employment Protection Act—see Chapter 1) has taken over and maintains a list of trade union organisations which were formerly held by the Registrar of Friendly Societies (s 257). On this list there will be organisations which were registered under the pre-1971 law (or formed as a result of an amalgamation of two or more bodies which were registered), all organisations registered under the Industrial Relations Act 1971, and all TUC affiliated trade unions. Any organisation (including employers' associations) which is not listed may apply for inclusion, submitting the appropriate fee, a copy of its rules, a list of officers, the address of its head office, and details of its name. The certification officer will refuse to enter on the list any organisation the name of which is the same as a previously registered or listed organisation, or a name which so closely resembles any such organisation as to be likely to deceive the public. If it appears to the certification officer that an organisation whose name is on the list is not a trade union he may remove it from the list, but not without giving notice of his intention to do so and considering any representations which may be made. An organisation which is aggrieved by the decision of the certification officer to refuse to enter it on the list, or a decision to remove it from the list, may appeal, either on a question of law or of fact, to the Employment Appeal Tribunal. Copies of the list shall be available for public inspection.

22.5 There are certain advantages of being a 'listed' trade union. First, it is evidence (but not conclusive evidence) that the body concerned satisfied the statutory definition. Second, there are procedural advantages in connection with the passing of property consequent on the change of trustees. Third, and perhaps the most significant of all, only a listed trade union can apply for a certificate of independence.

C. Certification of Trade Unions (TULR(C)A, s 6)

22.6 Any trade union which is on the list may apply to the certification officer for a certificate that it is an independent trade union. A union is independent if:

(a) it is not under the domination or control of an employer or groups of employers or an employers' association; and

(b) it is not liable to interference by an employer or any such group or association arising out of the provision of financial or material support or by any other means whatsoever tending towards such control (s 5).

If, after making enquiries, the certification officer decides that the union is independent he will issue a certificate accordingly; otherwise he will refuse to do so, but must give reasons for his refusal. Even if he grants the certificate, he may withdraw it if he is of the opinion that the union is no longer independent, but he must notify the trade union concerned of his intention, and may take into account any relevant information supplied by any person. An appeal by the trade union aggrieved will lie on a point of law or fact to the Employment Appeal Tribunal against the decision of the certification officer to refuse to grant, or to withdraw, a certificate.

22.7 Once granted, the certificate is conclusive evidence of the independence of the trade union, and in any proceedings before any court, the Employment Appeal Tribunal, the Central Arbitration Committee, or an employment tribunal, where the independence of the trade union is in issue and there is no certificate in force and no refusal, withdrawal, or cancellation recorded, the proceedings shall be stayed until a certificate has been issued or refused by the certification officer.

22.8 The certificate of independence has retrospective effect for a reasonable period before the date of the certificate and the issue of a certificate of independence on a particular date does not mean that the union was not independent before that date. If a union is certified to be independent on a particular date, it is inevitable that the union was independent for at the very least a modest period before that date and tribunals must adopt a reasonable and common-sense approach to this issue (*Bone v North Essex Partnership NHS Foundation Trust*[1]).

22.9 To understand the arguments about certification, it is necessary to make a short excursus into industrial relations. Some years ago there was an expansion of unionisation, particularly among so-called 'white-collar' workers and management. A considerable number of staff associations sprang up in order to exercise the sort of industrial pressure hitherto reserved for blue-collar workers. These staff associations are looked upon as not being 'proper' trade unions, and are sometimes referred to in a derogatory tone as being 'sweetheart unions' or 'house unions'. The test of independence for certification purposes is to permit through the net those unions which can demonstrate that they are truly independent, and not just the tame adjuncts of management. A considerable number of such staff associations have applied for and obtained certificates of independence; many have not bothered, on the ground that they can obtain by negotiation all the advantages which certification confers. Those that have succeeded in obtaining a certificate are criticised for bringing about a proliferation of trade unions (at a time when a reduction in the number of unions is thought to be desirable) and for not joining in with the existing established (ie TUC) trade unions.

22.10 The first case to be challenged under this branch of the law was *Blue Circle Staff Association v Certification Officer*.[2] In 1971 the staff association was formed for salaried staff at the instigation of higher management. Subsequently, changes were made to the association's constitution and an application was made for certification. It was held by the EAT that the certification officer was right in his refusal to grant a certificate. The association had not yet attained the freedom from domination by the employer under which it had lived since its formation. There is a heavy burden to show that it had shaken off such paternal control.

22.11 A different view of the realities of the scene was taken in *Association of HSD (Hatfield) Employees v Certification Officer*,[3] where the association was formed with the active encouragement of the employers, who shared the opposition of the association to proposals for nationalisation. After the decision to nationalise was taken, the new head of the industry visited the factory, and was met by a hostile demonstration organised by the association. A subsequent application for a certificate of independence was refused by the certification officer, and the association appealed to the EAT. It was held that the certificate should be granted. Under s 5(a) the organisation must show that it is not under the domination or control of the employer. This involves an examination of the factual situation, including finance, the extent (if any) of employer assistance or interference, history, rules, organisation, membership base, and general attitude. Under s 5(b) there is inevitably a degree of speculation, but the certification officer ought not to be unduly anxious about future possibilities as he always has the power to revoke the certificate if he thinks he should do so. On the facts of the case, the EAT was clearly impressed by the hostile demonstration, and held that as the association had demonstrated that it was 'fiercely independent of management' a certificate should be granted.

22.12 The fact that an association is company-based is not fatal to the association's independence, for there are many trade unions in industry which negotiate with a single

---

[1] [2014] EWCA Civ 652.   [2] [1977] 2 All ER 145, [1977] ICR 224, [1977] IRLR 20, EAT.
[3] [1978] ICR 21, [1977] IRLR 261, EAT.

employer (eg the Post Office, or civil service unions). Nor is the fact that the employer makes facilities available to a trade union destructive of its independence, for this may be seen as good industrial relations practice, and is in accordance with the Code of Practice on Time Off for Trade Union Duties and Activities. In *Squibb UK Staff Association v Certification Officer*,[4] a certificate of independence was refused because of fears of vulnerability to employer interference. This was based largely on the extensive facilities which were provided by the employer, which included time off with pay for the officials of the association when performing their duties, free use of office accommodation and rooms for meetings, the provision of free stationery, free use of the employer's telephone, photocopying, and internal mailing system, and a free check-off system. In view of the obvious limited resources of the association, and its narrow membership base, the certification officer thought that it would be very difficult to function effectively if these were withdrawn by the employer. The EAT held that nonetheless the certificate should be granted, but this decision was reversed by the Court of Appeal, and the original ruling of the certification officer was confirmed. The test of 'liability to interference' by the employer, which would be fatal to the association's independence, meant vulnerable to, or at risk of, interference. The degree of the likelihood of the risk was irrelevant as long as it was not insignificant.

22.13 If the continued existence of the staff association is dependent on the approval of the employer, then it is 'liable to interference' and hence cannot be an independent trade union (*Government Communications Staff Federation v Certification Officer*[5]).

22.14 The purpose of the organisation is important too—if its primary aim is merely to help provide representation at disciplinary and grievance hearings then it is not a trade union, as it does not have as its principal purpose the regulation of relations between workers and employers (*Akinosun (on behalf of General & Health Workers Union) v The Certification Officer*[6]).

Advantages of Certification

22.15 There are a number of advantages in having a certificate of independence, which benefit the union, its officials (including shop stewards), and members as follows:

(a) a member is entitled not to suffer a detriment (TULR(C)A, s 146(1)) or to be dismissed (s 152(1)) on grounds of trade union membership or activities, or making use of trade union services (s 152(1)). Interim relief is also available (s 161);

(b) an independent trade union may negotiate a dismissal procedure agreement which will replace individual statutory rights (ERA, s 110);

(c) an independent trade union may negotiate away the right of employees to strike (TULR(C)A, s 180);

(d) an independent trade union may negotiate a collective agreement modifying or derogating from rights contained in the Working Time Regulations and the Fixed-term Employees (Prevention of Less Favourable Treatment) Regulations 2002, and replace the statutory default scheme on parental leave under the Maternity and Parental Leave etc Regulations 1999;

(e) an official or member of an independent trade union can act as an independent adviser for the purpose of compromise agreements (ERA, s 203(3A));

(f) an independent trade union will be able to receive money from the Secretary of State under the trade union modernisation scheme.

---

[4] [1978] ICR 115, [1977] IRLR 355, EAT; revsd [1979] 2 All ER 452, [1979] ICR 235, [1979] IRLR 75, CA.
[5] [1993] ICR 163, [1993] IRLR 260, EAT.   [6] UKEAT/0180/13/RN.

22.16 If the independent trade union is recognised by the employer for collective bargaining purposes, then:

(a) it has the right to receive information for collective bargaining purposes (TULR(C)A, s 181);

(b) it has the right to be consulted on redundancies (TULR(C)A, s 188) and proposed transfers (Transfer of Undertakings (Protection of Employment) Regulations 2006);

(c) an official of the union is entitled to paid time off work for trade union duties, and unpaid time off work for trade union activities and to act as a union learning representative (TULR(C)A, ss 168–170);

(d) the union can appoint safety representatives under the Health and Safety at Work Act 1974, s 2;

(e) representatives of an independent trade union can act as employee representatives for the purpose of the Transnational Information and Consultation of Employees Regulations 1999, European Public Limited Liability (Employee Involvement) (Great Britain) Regulations 2009, Companies (Cross-Border Mergers) Regulations 2007;

(f) the union is entitled to receive information from an employer concerning occupational pension schemes (Pension Schemes Act 1993);

(g) the union will be entitled to receive information on recent and probable development of the undertaking's activities under the Information and Consultation Regulations (see para 23.144).

D. **Register of Members (s 24)**

22.17 A trade union shall maintain a register of the names and addresses of its members. The register shall be accurate and up to date, and may be kept by means of a computer.

22.18 A member is entitled to know whether there is an entry in the register relating to him, and be supplied with a copy of that entry. The person who has been appointed as an independent scrutineer for election purposes must also be permitted to inspect the register and be provided with an up-to-date copy of it (see para 22.47).

Confidentiality of the Register of Members (s 24A)

22.19 A trade union shall impose a duty of confidentiality on the independent scrutineer who has been appointed to oversee any ballot held on an election for office, political resolution, or resolution to approve an instrument of amalgamation or transfer. The scrutineer or independent person must not disclose any name or address on the register (except in permitted circumstances), and must take all reasonable steps to ensure that no such disclosure takes place. Disclosure will be permitted (a) when the member consents, (b) where required for the purposes of the discharge of functions by the certification officer or of the scrutineer under the terms of his appointment, or (c) where required for the purpose of investigating crime or of criminal proceedings.

Remedies (ss 25–26)

22.20 A member of a trade union who claims that the union has failed to comply with ss 24 or 24A may apply to the certification officer for a declaration to that effect (s 25), or, in the alternative, to the court (s 26). The certification officer can make an enforcement order requiring the union to remedy the breach and/or abstain from acts which might lead to a future recurrence of the same breach. Any member of the union (who was a member at the time of the declared failure) may apply to the court to force the union to comply with the order. An appeal against the decision of the certification officer may be made to the EAT.

Membership of a Trade Union

22.21 In principle, it is for the trade union to lay down the description of persons who are eligible to join, and this will usually be laid down in the union's rules (*Boulting v Association of Cinematograph, Television and Allied Technicians*, para 21.5). It follows that it cannot accept for membership someone who is not within the prescribed class, and cannot create a category of membership not provided for in the rules (*Martin v Scottish Transport and General Workers' Union*[7]). The rules may also specify a class of person who is not eligible to join (*Faramus v Film Artistes' Association*, para 21.5). However, a trade union cannot exclude a person from membership on arbitrary and unreasonable grounds (*Nagle v Feilden*, paras 21.5 and 21.7), nor can it discriminate against someone on the grounds set out in the Equality Act 2010 (although positive action is permitted in certain respects in section 158 of that Act).

22.22 However, notwithstanding anything contained in the union's rules, a person cannot be excluded (or expelled) from a trade union unless this is permitted by the provisions of TULR(C)A, s 174 (see para 21.2), and a person who is so excluded or expelled has the right to bring a complaint before an industrial tribunal or the EAT as appropriate.

22.23 There is no statutory definition of who is a 'member' of a trade union, and the term has to be looked at in its context. Thus, if a trade union has a class of 'limited members', who have restricted rights precisely defined in the union's rules, then they may not be 'members' for the purpose of voting in certain elections (eg on a proposal for the transfer of engagements, see *National Union of Mineworkers (Yorkshire Area) v Millward*[8]).

Rules of a Trade Union

22.24 At common law, a trade union was tainted with illegality because its rules and/or objects were in 'restraint of trade'. In the nineteenth century this led to certain problems; the trade unionists were prosecuted for criminal conspiracy, and the rules of the unions were generally unenforceable. The effect of the doctrine against restraint of trade on trade unions was nullified by the 1871 Trade Union Act (see now TULR(C)A, s 11), which provides that the purposes of a trade union or an employers' association shall not, by reason of being in restraint of trade, make any member liable for criminal conspiracy or make any agreement or trust void or voidable, nor shall the rules be unlawful or unenforceable by virtue of their being in restraint of trade (see *Goring v British Actors Equity Association*[9]). This also applies to incorporated employers' associations and special register bodies in so far as the purposes or rules relate to the regulation of relations between employers or employers' organisations and workers. It should be noted that Art 11 of the European Convention on Human Rights guarantees the right to freedom of association. Since the Convention now applies in the United Kingdom by virtue of the Human Rights Act 1998 (see para 1.105) it is arguable that the common law doctrine that trade unions are unlawful organisations (by virtue of having objects which are in restraint of trade) is no longer good law.

22.25 As long as a trade union complies with the various statutory requirements, there are no general restrictions on the rules which it may adopt. But the rules constitute a contract between the union and its members, and must be strictly observed.

A. **Disciplinary Action**

22.26 If the trade union wishes to take disciplinary action, by way of fines or forfeitures, or wishes to expel a member, such powers must be contained in the rules, otherwise they

---

[7] [1952] 1 All ER 691, HL.   [8] [1995] ICR 482, [1995] IRLR 411, EAT.   [9] [1987] IRLR 122.

cannot be exercised. In *Spring v National Amalgamated Stevedores and Dockers' Society*[10] the plaintiff was enrolled as a member of the defendant union contrary to the Bridlington Agreement, which was designed to prevent poaching of members among TUC affiliated unions. The TUC ordered the union to expel the members, which it did, but the expulsion was held to be void when it was discovered that the union rules contained no power of expulsion.

22.27 However, it is possible for the court to imply into the union's rules a power to discipline a member, although since such a power is penal and could involve serious consequences which would affect the reputation and livelihood of the member, an implied disciplinary power would only arise when there are compelling circumstances to justify it. In *McVitae v UNISON*[11] the claimant was a member of the National and Local Government Officers' Association (NALGO). Various complaints of intimidating, oppressive, and sexist conduct were made against him and disciplinary proceedings were arranged. However, before they could take place, NALGO amalgamated with two other unions to form Unison, and, following an investigation into the original complaints, Unison decided to re-institute the disciplinary proceedings. The claimant sought an injunction to prevent Unison from taking disciplinary action against him in respect of conduct which occurred prior to the union coming into existence.

There was no power in the instrument of amalgamation or the rules of the new union to discipline members in respect of conduct which occurred before its inception, but in the circumstances of the case, the court was prepared to imply such a power. The conduct in question was contrary to the rules of NALGO and Unison, and it could not have been intended that there should be a complete amnesty for conduct which occurred before the new union was created out of the amalgamation of the three unions.

22.28 If the rules specify the grounds on which disciplinary action may be taken, then the union must adhere to these grounds, and not proceed on others. Moreover, the courts have in the past exercised the power to interpret the rules of the union in accordance with the courts' understanding of the rules, not the union's. The interpretative power is particularly important in those cases where the rules are somewhat vague (eg 'conduct detrimental to the union' in *Kelly v National Society of Operative Printers' Assistants*[12]), although the legitimate interests of the union will be upheld. In *Evans v National Union of Printing, Bookbinding and Paperworkers*,[13] the rules provided that a member who acted contrary to the interests of the union might be expelled. The claimant absented himself from work on several occasions, contrary to an agreement between the union and the employers. As a result of such conduct, he was expelled. It was held that the expulsion was valid, for it was designed to uphold the success of the collective bargaining arrangements.

22.29 If the union rules provide for a procedure to be adopted in disciplinary cases, then that procedure must be strictly adhered to, and the smallest irregularity will be as fatal as the greatest. The rules cannot be so framed as to oust the jurisdiction of the courts by declaring that the decision of the union shall be final and binding (*Chapple v Electrical Trades Union*[14]), and if there is an appeal procedure which is denied to the aggrieved member, the expulsion will be invalid (*Braithwaite v Electrical Electronics and Telecommunications Union*[15]).

22.30 Although the statutory requirements that a trade union must act in accordance with the rules of natural justice have been repealed, it is submitted that the common law position remains unchanged. This means that a trade union, in the exercise of what is essentially a

---

[10] [1956] 2 All ER 221.   [11] [1996] IRLR 33.

[12] (1915) 84 LJKB 2236, 59 Sol Jo 716, 113 LT 1055, 31 TLR 632, CA.   [13] [1938] 4 All ER 51.

[14] [1961] 3 All ER 612.   [15] [1969] 2 All ER 859, CA.

quasi-judicial function, cannot expel a member without giving him a hearing, notifying him of the charges against him, and giving him an opportunity to rebut them (*Lawlor v Union of Post Office Workers*[16]). It also means that the officials of the union should avoid being placed in the position of being prosecutor, judge, and jury. In *Taylor v National Union of Seamen*,[17] the general secretary of the union dismissed the claimant for insubordination. When the claimant appealed to the executive council, the general secretary was the chairman of the meeting, and after the claimant had withdrawn, the meeting was treated to a long statement of matters which were not the subject of the charge, but which were prejudicial to him, and he had no opportunity of rebutting. It was held that the hearing of the appeal offended against the rules of natural justice.

22.31 A member who has been wrongfully expelled may apply for a declaration that he is still a member, an injunction restraining the union and its officials from acting on the purported expulsion, and damages for wrongful expulsion. In *Bonsor v Musicians' Union*,[18] the appellant was expelled by the branch secretary, when this power could only be exercised by the branch committee. In consequence, he could not get work, and was reduced to earning a living by scraping rust off Brighton Pier. It was held that as the expulsion was void, he could recover damages for wrongful expulsion.

22.32 In addition (as already indicated), whatever the rules may or may not state, a member of a trade union has a statutory right not to be unjustifiably disciplined (see para 21.9) or expelled from a trade union (see para 21.2) unless the discipline or expulsion is not prohibited by the statute, and may seek an appropriate remedy before an employment tribunal.

B. Conduct of Union Affairs

22.33 Membership of a trade union confers certain rights and privileges on the members, and they are entitled to damages if these are not forthcoming. If the rules provide that members shall be entitled to legal advice, then a union which fails to provide that advice, or negligently provides incorrect advice, may be sued for the loss which flows from that breach. The tremendous increase in the statutory rights of employees is bound to throw an additional burden on trade union officials, who now need to be as familiar with those rights as management. Thus it is submitted that if a trade union fails to apply for a protective award in appropriate circumstances, or negligently delays the presentation of a claim to an employment tribunal so that it becomes out of time, the aggrieved member will have a right of action against that union for damages. No breach of contract arises if the member fails to show that his action had a reasonable prospect of success (*Buckley v National Union of General and Municipal Workers*[19]), and in any case the union can fulfil the duty to use ordinary care and skill by handing over a potential claim to a firm of competent solicitors (*Friend v Institution of Professional Managers and Specialists*[20]).

22.34 In the conduct of union affairs, the officials can only act within the confines of the rules. Thus in *Weakley v Amalgamated Union of Engineering Workers*[21] the president of the union exercised a casting vote on a motion when the committee was equally divided. An injunction was granted restraining the union from acting on the motion, for, on a true construction of the rules, the president was not entitled to exercise a casting vote. But the officials may have implied power to do certain things which are in the interests of the union.

---

[16] [1965] Ch 712, [1965] 1 All ER 353.   [17] [1967] 1 All ER 767.
[18] [1954] Ch 479, [1954] 1 All ER 822, CA; revsd [1956] AC 104, [1955] 3 All ER 518, HL.
[19] [1967] 3 All ER 767.   [20] [1999] IRLR 173.   [21] (1975) 125 NLJ 621.

In *Hill v Archbold*,[22] two union officials brought an action in respect of matters which arose out of their employment. The actions were dismissed, but the union sought to pay the legal costs on behalf of the officials, though there was no provision in the rules for such expenditure. It was held that the union had implied power to do so, for the matter was incidental to their work as officials of the union.

22.35 A problem arises when a trade union takes action that benefits a majority of its members, but the end result is a detriment to a minority. In *GMB v Allen*[23] the union encouraged its members to agree to the settlement of an equal pay claim against a local authority, based on its policy to promote single status pay, preservation of jobs, and pay protection for those losing out. However, the end result was to seriously undervalue the claims of a number of women. The latter brought claims against the union alleging sex discrimination, which were upheld by the Court of Appeal. It was held that the striking of a deal by a trade union with a local authority, which established a single status common pay and grading structure, was indirectly discriminatory of women, since it applied a provision, criterion or practice that applied equally to men but was detrimental to a large number of women. Although the deal attempted to achieve compensation for some union members for past inequality as well as providing ongoing pay and employment protection for all members, which were legitimate aims, the means adopted by the union included mis-selling and manipulation, and were not therefore proportionate to the union's legitimate aim of achieving single status with a minimum of losers.

C. **Copy of the Rules (s 27)**

22.36 A trade union shall supply, at the request of any person, a copy of its rules, either free or on payment of a reasonable charge.

Executive Committee (TULR(C)A, s 46)

22.37 Every member of the principal executive committee of a trade union (including those members who are members by virtue of holding an office) shall be elected by a ballot at least every five years. A person who holds his membership of the principal executive committee as a result of an election may continue as a member or official for such period as may be necessary (not exceeding six months) to give effect to an election result. In such a ballot, every member of the union shall be entitled to vote, except:

(a) those members who as a class are excluded by the rules from voting;

(b) members not in employment;

(c) members in arrears; and

(d) members who are students, trainees, apprentices, or new members.

If the rules permit, it is possible to have voting restricted to special classes of membership, determined by reference to:

(a) trade or occupation;

(b) geographical area;

(c) separate sections of the union; or

(d) any combination of these.

---

[22] [1967] 2 QB 418, [1967] 1 All ER 1038; aff'd [1968] 1 QB 686, [1967] 3 All ER 110, CA.
[23] [2007] IRLR 752, EAT.

Voting at an election must be made by the marking of a ballot paper by the person voting, and every person entitled to vote (a) must be allowed to do so without interference or constraint imposed by the union or any of its members, officials, or employees, and (b) so far as is reasonably practicable, must be able to do so without incurring any direct cost. So far as is reasonably practicable, voting papers must be sent to voters by post, containing or accompanied by a list of candidates, and the voter must be given a convenient opportunity to vote by post. So far as is reasonably practicable, voting shall be in secret, and the result shall be determined by the counting of the number of votes cast for each candidate (with or without the transferable vote) and votes shall be fairly and accurately counted.

22.38 These provisions do not apply to trade unions which consist of representatives of constituent or affiliated organisations, merchant seamen who are ordinarily resident outside the United Kingdom, newly formed trade unions, or members of the principal executive committee who are near retirement. In a claim for detriment under this section the question whether a trade union is independent does not affect the jurisdiction of the employment tribunal (*Bone v North Essex Partnership NHS Foundation Trust* (para 22.8)).

22.39 The president and general secretary (or persons who hold equivalent positions) shall be deemed to be members of the principal executive committee (and hence subject to the balloting provisions) as will be any other persons, notwithstanding anything in the rules of the union, if they are permitted to attend and speak at the meeting of that committee, other than for the purpose of providing the committee with factual information or technical or professional advice.

22.40 However, a person who is the president or general secretary of the union, and who is neither a voting member of the principal executive committee, nor an employee of the union, is not required to be elected in the above manner if he holds his office for a period of less than 13 months. Nor does the president need to be re-elected if he has been elected within the previous five years to the post of general secretary or member of the executive.

22.41 Elections for the members of the principal executive committee shall be by means of postal ballot, but there is no need to hold a ballot if the election is uncontested. If voting is done by means of a transferable vote system, and the same number of votes are cast for the final candidates, there is an implied term in the union's rules that the candidate with the most first-choice votes shall be declared the winner, especially if this method has been used as a tie-breaker in the past (*AB v CD*[24]).

A. Election of Candidates (TULR(C)A, s 47)

22.42 No member of a trade union may be unreasonably excluded from standing as a candidate for election to any position unless he belongs to a class of which all members are excluded by the rules of the union. The rules of the union may give the executive committee of the union a discretion to decide certain prescribed qualifications for a union post, but not having the confidence of the executive committee is not a qualification (*Ecclestone v National Union of Journalists*[25]). No candidate shall be required to be a member of any political party.

If there is a tie between two candidates in a union election, and there is no express mechanism for resolving the tie, a tie-breaker must be implied into the union's rules (*AB v CD*).

---

[24] [2001] IRLR 808, [2001] All ER (D) 354 (May).   [25] [1999] IRLR 166.

B. Election Addresses (TULR(C)A, s 48)

22.43 Every candidate in an election for the principal executive committee must be provided with an opportunity of preparing an election address, in his own words, and submitting it to the union to be distributed to those who are entitled to vote. Such election addresses are to be sent out with the voting paper, and the candidates are not required to bear any expense for the production of these copies. The election address shall be sent out without any modification except at the request of or with the consent of the candidate, or where the modification is necessarily incidental to the method adopted for the production of the copy. The same method of production is to be used for the election addresses of all candidates. A trade union may determine that election addresses may not exceed a certain length (but must permit a minimum of 100 words), and may incorporate only such photographs or other matter as the union may determine. So far as is reasonably practicable, the union must ensure that the same facilities and restrictions with respect to the preparation, submission, length and modifications, and incorporation of photographs or other matter not in words are provided or applied equally to each of the candidates.

22.44 No person other than the candidate himself shall be subject to any criminal or civil liability in respect of the publication of a candidate's election address made under s 48.

C. Independent Scrutineer (ss 49, 75, 100A, 226B)

22.45 Before an election is held for positions in the principal executive committee, or a ballot is held on the approval of a political fund, or approving an instrument of amalgamation or transfer, or on the holding of industrial action, the trade union must appoint a qualified independent person as a scrutineer, who will carry out his functions without interference. A person will be eligible for such appointment if he satisfies the conditions laid down in the Trade Union Ballots and Elections (Independent Scrutineers' Qualifications) Order 1988–2010.

22.46 However, a scrutineer need not be appointed if there is a ballot on the holding of industrial action and the number of members entitled to vote does not exceed 50 (s 226C).

22.47 The union will supply the scrutineer with a copy of the register of members, which he will inspect as appropriate, and in particular if requested to do so by a member or candidate who suspects that it was not accurate or up to date. The name of the independent scrutineer must be sent to every member of the union by notice, or communicated to members in the same manner as when matters of general interest are brought to their attention. His name must also appear on any ballot paper.

22.48 The storage, distribution, and counting of ballot papers must be undertaken by an independent person, who may be the scrutineer or other person whose competence and independence are not in doubt (s 51A). The scrutineer must supervise the production and distribution of all voting papers, which are to be returned to him by those voting. He will retain them for one year after the announcement of the result of the election or ballot or, if the result is challenged before the certification officer or a court, until disposal is authorised.

22.49 As soon as is reasonably practicable after the last date for the return of the voting papers, the scrutineer shall make a report to the union, stating:

(a) the number of voting papers distributed;

(b) the number of voting papers returned to him;

(c) the number of valid votes cast in the election for each candidate, or, in a ballot, for each proposition;

(d) the number of invalid or spoiled votes returned; and

(e) the name of the person (if any) appointed as an independent person to count the votes.

22.50 The report will also state if he is satisfied that there was no contravention of any requirement imposed by law, that the arrangements for the ballot or election (including any security arrangements) minimised the risk of any unfairness or malpractice, and that he was able to carry out his functions without interference or anyone calling his independence into question. He will also state if he has inspected the register of members, and whether any such inspection has revealed any matter which should be brought to the attention of the union in order to ensure that it is accurate and up to date (s 52).

22.51 Within three months of receiving the scrutineer's report on an election (s 52(4)), on a political fund resolution (s 78(4)), or on an amalgamation or transfer resolution (s 100E(6)), the trade union shall send a copy to every member to whom it is reasonably practicable to send such a copy, or take all such steps for notifying the contents of the report to members of the union as it is the practice for the union to take when matters of general interest need to be brought to the members' attention. So far as ballots on industrial action are concerned, any person entitled to vote in the ballot, and the employer of any such person, is entitled to be supplied with a copy of the scrutineer's report on request. This may be supplied free of charge or on the payment of a reasonable fee.

D. **Remedies (s 54)**

22.52 Any member may apply to the High Court (or Court of Session) or the certification officer (but not both) for a declaration that the trade union has failed to comply with any requirement of the Act relating to secret ballots for trade union elections or relating to election addresses or to scrutineers. The court may make an enforcement order specifying the action which the trade union shall take in consequence of its failure to comply with the Act (s 56). The certification officer may grant the declaration, and, if necessary, make an enforcement order requiring the union to hold a fresh election (s 55). An appeal from the order of the Certification Officer may be made to the EAT.

Accounts, Records, etc (TULR(C)A, s 28)

22.53 Every trade union and employers' association shall keep proper records, and establish a satisfactory system of control over its cash holdings, receipts, and remittances. An annual return must be sent to the certification officer, with accounts duly audited. There are provisions in ss 32–42 detailing the matters which must be contained in the annual return including the salaries paid to, and the benefits provided for, the president, general secretary, and members of the executive committee, together with the qualifications, appointment, functions, and removal of auditors, and for the control over members' superannuation schemes. The annual return should also contain details of any industrial action taken, and details of political expenditure over £2,000 (s32ZA). Any person who refuses or wilfully neglects to perform a duty imposed by these provisions, or who alters a document required for those purposes, shall be guilty of an offence, punishable by a fine of up to levels 3 and 5 on the standard scale respectively.

22.54 An annual statement must be sent to all members of the union (or otherwise communicated to them) giving details of the union's income and expenditure, salaries paid to the president, general secretary, and executive members, and the income and expenditure of the political fund. The statement will also include prescribed information on the remedies to members who are concerned about any irregularities in the conduct of the union's affairs (s 32A).

A. **Right to Inspect Accounts (ss 29–31)**

22.55 A trade union shall keep its accounting records available for inspection for six years from 1 January following the end of the period to which those records relate.

22.56 Any member of a trade union may request to be permitted access to those records in respect of any period when he was a member. Such access shall be permitted within 28 days of the request and, unless otherwise agreed, at a reasonable hour and at the place where the records are normally kept. The member is entitled to take an accountant with him, and to take, or be supplied with, such copies or extracts from those records as he may require. The trade union may make a charge in respect of reasonable administrative expenses incurred (s 30).

22.57 If the trade union fails to comply with the member's request for access to the accounting records, the member may apply to the court or the certification officer (but not both), who may make such order as is considered appropriate for ensuring that that person:

(a) is allowed to inspect the records;

(b) is allowed to be accompanied by an accountant; and

(c) is allowed to take, or is supplied with, such copies of or extracts from those records as he may require (s 31).

22.58 The certification officer has the power to require the production of documents, take copies etc, and appoint an inspector to investigate the financial affairs of the union, if he suspects that the financial affairs of the union have been conducted in a fraudulent manner, or a person managing its affairs has been guilty of fraud, or the union has failed to comply with a provision of the Act or its own rules with relation to the conduct of its financial affairs (TULR(C)A, s 37B). The inspector has wide powers of investigation, and will report back to the certification officer.

Offences (ss 45–45C)

22.59 If a trade union refuses to supply a copy of its rules (s 27), fails to keep accounting records (s 28), fails to keep records available for inspection (s 29), fails to give members access to the accounts (s 30), fails to make an annual return (s 32) or make an annual statement to members (s 32A), breaches the auditing requirements (ss 33–37), or breaches the requirements relating to members' superannuation schemes (ss 38–42), it commits an offence. The offence will also be committed by every officer who is bound by the rules to discharge any of those duties, or, if there is no such officer, every member of the management committee. It will be a defence for the officer or member of the management committee to prove that he had reasonable cause to believe that some other competent person was authorised to discharge that duty. It is also an offence to wilfully alter a document, fail to produce a document, destroy, mutilate, or falsify a document relating to the financial affairs of the union, or fraudulently alter or delete anything in such document, or to make a false statement. The offences may be punishable by a fine or, in some circumstances, up to six months' imprisonment. A person who has been convicted under these provisions shall not hold office as a member of the executive, president, or general secretary for a period of five or ten years, depending on the offence.

A. Indemnifying Unlawful Conduct (s 15)

22.60 It is unlawful for any property of a trade union to be applied towards the payment for any individual, or towards the provision of anything for indemnifying an individual, in respect of any penalty which has been imposed on him for a relevant offence, or for contempt of court. A 'relevant offence' is any offence other than one which has been designated as an offence by the Secretary of State in relation to which s 15 does not apply.

22.61 If property has been so applied in contravention of this section, the equal amount of any payment is recoverable from the individual concerned by the trade union, and in the case of property, the individual shall be liable to account for its value. If the trade union unreasonably fails to make a claim against the individual, any member may apply to the court for authorisation to bring or continue proceedings on the union's behalf and at the union's expense.

B. Remedies Against Trustees (s 16)

22.62 If a member of a trade union considers that the trustees of the union's property are carrying out their functions so as to permit an unlawful application of the union's property, or are complying with an unlawful direction which has been given to them under the union's rules, he may apply to the court for an order. If the court is satisfied that the application is well founded, it may make such orders as it deems appropriate, including:

(a) requiring the trustees of the union to take all such steps as may be specified for the purpose of protecting or recovering the union's property;

(b) appointing a receiver (or judicial factor) of/on the union's property;

(c) the removal of one or more trustees.

22.63 Should the trustees act in contravention of the court's order, the court may remove all the trustees except those who can satisfy the court that there is good reason to allow them to remain a trustee.

Political Fund and Political Objects (TULR(C)A, ss 71–74)

22.64 The Act lays down the necessary requirements before a trade union can have a political fund and pursue political objects. A resolution to establish a political fund must be passed at least every ten years by a ballot of all the union's members, and if approved, a separate political fund may be created. The ballot must be by the use of a voting paper, and every person entitled to vote must be allowed to do so without interference from or constraint imposed by the trade union or any of its members, officials, or employees. The member must be able to vote without incurring any direct cost.

22.65 So far as is reasonably practicable, every person who is entitled to vote on a ballot concerning the establishment of a political fund must have the voting papers sent to him at his home or postal address, and be given a convenient opportunity to vote by post. The voting must be in secret, and the votes fairly and accurately counted (s 77).

22.66 If the political fund is established, no property of the trade union shall be added to that fund other than sums representing contributions made to the fund by the members or any other person and property accruing to the fund in the course of administering its assets. No liability of the political fund shall be met out of any other fund of the trade union. If there is no resolution in force establishing the political fund, no property shall be added to an existing fund (other than that which accrues in the course of administering the fund) and no union rule shall require any member to contribute towards the fund. The union may transfer the whole or part of the assets of an existing fund to such other fund of the trade union as it thinks fit. Where a resolution is passed rescinding an existing fund, the trade union may use the fund for a period of six months, but not so as to put the fund in deficit.

22.67 If a resolution to have a political fund ceases to have effect, the union shall take such steps to ensure that the collection of contributions to the fund is discontinued as soon as is reasonably practicable, and any contribution collected after the resolution ceases to have effect may be paid to any other fund of the trade union. If the trade union continues to collect contributions these are refundable at the members' request.

22.68 A member of a trade union who wishes to can opt into paying into the political fund, and can withdraw from paying by giving one month's notice. Within eight weeks of sending the annual return to the Certification Officer, a union must take all reasonable steps to notify members of their right to withdraw and that a member who does shall not in consequence be excluded from any benefit or disqualified from holding any office other than a position connected with the management of the political fund. Contributing towards the fund must not be a condition of membership. The Trade Union Bill 2015–16, if enacted, would change the opting-out provision to one of expressly opting in. The union would then have to ask the member again every five years.

22.69 The TUC has issued a 'Statement of Guidance' on political funds. It advises trade unions to draw up 'information sheets' about their political funds, and to inform members why there is a fund, make clear members' legal rights to opt out, state the current amount of the levy, and provide information on how members may contract out.

22.70 The political fund may be used for the following purposes:

(a) any contribution to the funds of, or the payment of any expense incurred by, a political party;

(b) the provision of any services or property for the use by or on behalf of a political party;

(c) the registration of electors, the candidature of any person, the selection of any candidate, or the holding of a ballot by the union in connection with any election to a political office;

(d) the maintenance of any holder of a political office;

(e) the holding of any conference or meetings by or on behalf of a political party, or any other meetings the main purpose of which is the transaction of business in connection with a political party;

(f) the production, publication, or distribution of any literature, document, film, sound recording, or advertisement the main purpose of which is to persuade people to vote for a political party or candidate or not to vote for it or him.

22.71 An allegation that a trade union has broken a rule as to the use to which the political fund may be put may be the subject of an investigation by the certification officer. In *Richards v National Union of Mineworkers*[26] a complaint was made that the union had spent money from the general fund sending members on a lobby of Parliament organised by the Labour Party, and had also paid money to a trade union consortium which was developing

---

[26] [1981] IRLR 247.

Labour Party headquarters. It was held by the certification officer that such expenditure was in furtherance of political objects, and he ordered that the money should come from the political funds of the union, not the general funds.

22.72 A member who claims that the union has applied its funds in breach of s 71 may apply to the certification officer for a declaration. After making the necessary enquiries, the certification officer may grant the declaration, specifying the amount of funds applied in breach of s 71 and any remedial action to be taken, and may specify any steps to be taken to ensure that the same or similar breach does not take place in the future (s 72A).

A. Complaints Over Political Fund Ballots (TULR(C)A, ss 79–81)

22.73 A member of a trade union who complains that a ballot on the political fund was taken otherwise than in accordance with the rules approved by the certification officer, or that there has been a failure to comply with those rules, may apply to the certification officer or to the court (but not both) for a declaration. The application must be made within one year from the date when the result of the ballot was announced.

22.74 The court may make an enforcement order, specifying the action which the trade union shall take in consequence of its failure to comply with the Act.

Breach of Union Rules (ss 108A–108B)

22.75 A member of the union who claims that there has been a breach of other rules of the union may apply to the certification officer for a declaration. The rules in question are:

(a) the appointment or election of a person to, or the removal of a person from, any office;

(b) disciplinary proceedings by the union (including expulsion);

(c) the balloting of members on any issue other than industrial action;

(d) the constitution or proceedings of any executive committee or of any decision-making meeting;

(e) such other matters as may be specified in an order made by the Secretary of State.

22.76 The application must be made within six months from the day when the breach occurred, or, if an internal complaints procedure was invoked, six months from when it was concluded. The certification officer is not entitled to consider a complaint about the discipline or dismissal of an employee of the union, as these are matters capable of being dealt with under the general law on individual employment rights.

22.77 The certification officer may refuse to consider the complaint unless reasonable steps were taken to resolve the issue by use of the internal complaints procedure, but if he hears the complaint he may make a declaration, and, if appropriate, an enforcement order, requiring the union to remedy the breach, or abstain from specified acts. An appeal from any proceedings under this section will lie to the EAT on a point of law.

Amalgamation and Transfers (ss 97–105)

22.78 Two or more trade unions may decide to amalgamate into one union, or a union may wish to transfer its engagements to another union. In both cases, the instrument of amalgamation or transfer must first be submitted to the certification officer for approval, and then voted upon by the members of the amalgamating unions or transferor union, as the case may be. The union must give the members a notice in writing, which either sets out the instrument of amalgamation or transfer, or gives an account of it so as to enable the member to form a reasonable judgment of its main effects. Section 100 of the Act provides that the instrument may be approved by a simple majority of votes recorded, unless the rules of the union specifically exclude this provision, in which case some other specified proportion of members will be required to approve.

22.79 An independent scrutineer must be appointed, who will supervise the production and distribution of the voting papers, inspect the register of members, and generally report to the union after the ballot has been concluded. Voting in the ballot shall be accorded equally to all members of the union, and the ballot papers will be numbered consecutively and sent to members' homes or postal address. The notice sent to members shall not contain any statement making a recommendation or expressing an opinion about the proposed transfer or amalgamation. A copy of the scrutineer's report must be sent to every member or otherwise suitably published.

22.80 A complaint about the procedure relating to an amalgamation or transfer may be made to the certification officer, who may make a declaration and an order specifying the steps to be taken before he will entertain the application (s 103).

Employers' Associations

A. Definition of Employers' Association (TULR(C)A, s 122)

22.81 An employers' association is defined as an organisation which either:

(a) consists wholly or mainly of employers or individual proprietors, and whose principal purposes include the regulation of relations between employers and workers or trade unions; or

(b) consists wholly or mainly of constituent or affiliated organisations with those purposes or representatives of such constituents or affiliated organisations, whose principal objects include the regulation of relations between employers and workers or between the constituent or affiliated organisations.

22.82 An employers' association may be incorporated under the Companies Acts, or may be an unincorporated association. In the latter case it shall nonetheless be capable of making contracts, or suing and being sued in its own name, and of being prosecuted in its own name. Its property, however, will have to be held by trustees, and any judgment, award, or order would have to be enforced against that property. A trade association, which is largely concerned with the business interests of employers, is not an employers' association within the statutory definition, but if it did have as one of its purposes collective bargaining objectives, or if it regulated the relations between organisations which have such objectives, it could be an employers' association. This is because the Act requires the principal objects of an employers' association to 'include' the statutory objects, not that the principal objects 'shall be' the statutory objects.

B. Listing of Employers' Associations (TULR(C)A, s 123)

22.83 The Act permits the employers' associations to be entered on the appropriate list, but there are few advantages of doing so. Many employers' associations are incorporated under the Companies Act, and therefore do not require trustees to hold property. They do not have provident funds, and do not require certificates of independence. Not surprisingly, fewer than half of employers' associations have bothered to become listed.

Summary

- The Certification Officer can certify that a trade union is an independent trade union.
- There are a number of advantages with being so certified, one of which is that it can negotiate collective agreements with the employers.
- The union must conduct its affairs in ways which are specified in the legislation and in its rules.
- Members of the executive committee must be elected by ballot every five years.
- Trade unions and employer associations must keep proper records and accounts.
- If the union fails to follow the rules set out in TULR(C)A it will commit an offence, which will also be committed by every officer who was bound to discharge those duties.
- There are specific rules about establishing a political fund and having political objectives.

23

Law Relating to Industrial Relations

Background

23.1 Since 1871, when trade unions were legalised by the Trade Union Act of that year, the history of industrial relations in the United Kingdom has been somewhat turbulent. This is partly due to conflicting ideologies, sometimes of a political nature, but mainly due to a conflict between those who favour individual as opposed to collective bargaining arrangements. A consideration of the extent to which the law should play a role in the control of industrial relations, and the precise nature of that law, has always been a subject for political controversy. Various governments of differing political persuasions have made their impact throughout the years, but, mainly due to the reforms pushed through in the Thatcher era, trade unions have now achieved a respectability and a role recognised by employers and confirmed by law. The whole story, though interesting from a legal and philosophical point of view, need not detain us in this book, but history has left its mark, and it is not possible to understand the present legal position without some reference to the previous law on this topic, though it is intended to keep such excursus to a minimum. In particular, it will be necessary to examine certain common law rules which, though they may now be only of historical importance, have shaped the legislative provisions.

23.2 Freedom of association, ie the right of an individual to join a trade union, is guaranteed by the European Convention on Human Rights and is now accepted in the United Kingdom as axiomatic. However, the right of a trade union to bargain and/or negotiate on behalf of its members is initially dependent on the willing co-operation of employers. Thus an employer may refuse to recognise a trade union, may recognise it for some purposes only (eg representation) or for all purposes (eg negotiations). Whether an employer recognises a trade union, and the extent of that recognition, are questions of fact; there need not be a formal agreement to confirm this (see para 23.4). Once recognition has been granted, various legal consequences will flow, including the right to receive information for collective bargaining purposes (para 23.15), the right to be consulted on redundancies (Chapter 18) and on transfers of the undertaking (Chapter 9) etc. Members of independent trade unions which are recognised by the employer are entitled to certain benefits, including time off work for union duties and activities, and have various protections from dismissal and detriment (Chapter 21).

23.3 One of the reasons for industrial unrest in the past was the reluctance of some employers to recognise a trade union for any purpose, for whatever reason. An attempt to force employers to recognise a trade union was made in the Employment Protection Act 1975, but this was not a success, and the provisions were subsequently repealed.

Trade Union Recognition

A. **Voluntary Recognition**

23.4 Employment tribunals appear to operate under the general rule that it is for the trade union to show that there is some formal agreement (not necessarily in writing) that it is recognised for collective bargaining purposes (*T&GWU v Dyer*[1]). The mere fact that there are employees who are trade union members, and that one of them negotiates, but without specific trade union authority, will not constitute recognition (*AUEW v Sefton Engineering*[2]). A history of consultation between an employer and a trade union was not sufficient to show that the trade union had been recognised for the purposes of collective bargaining. There must be clear evidence that a trade union has been recognised by an employer for collective bargaining purposes within the meaning of s 178 of TULR(C)A (*Working Links v Public and Commercial Services Union*[3]). Negotiations which may lead to recognition do not themselves constitute recognition (*T&GWU v Stanhope Engineering*[4]). Nor can recognition be inferred for the purpose of collective bargaining if a full-time union official represents an individual in a disciplinary proceeding (*T&GWU v Courtenham Products*[5]). The fact that an employer is a member of an association which negotiates with a trade union does not mean that the particular employer recognises the union (*NUGSAT v Albury Bros Ltd*[6]). Nor does recognition by a former employer by itself constitute recognition by a successor (*UCATT v Burrage*[7]). In *NUTGW v Charles Ingram & Co Ltd*[8] five propositions were established: (1) recognition is a mixed question of law and fact; (2) recognition requires mutuality; (3) there must be an express or implied agreement for recognition; (4) if the agreement was implied, there must be clear and unequivocal acts or conduct, usually over a period of time; (5) there may be partial recognition for some but not all purposes. Recognition for representation purposes only is not the same thing as recognition for negotiating purposes (*USDAW v Sketchley Ltd*[9]).

B. Statutory Recognition (TULR(C)A, Sch A1)

23.5 The Employment Relations Act 1999 lays down a new complex statutory procedure for recognition and derecognition of trade unions, which can be found in TULR(C)A, Sch A1. The detailed provisions, including time limits and balloting procedures, can be found in some 172 paragraphs of the Schedule (as amended), which additionally deal with semi-voluntary recognition, derecognition procedures, and protection of workers from detriments or dismissal on grounds relating to trade union membership or non-membership. However, the provisions do not apply where an employer employs fewer than 21 workers.

23.6 Schedule A1 is divided into nine parts, as follows:

Part I: statutory recognition;

Part II: voluntary recognition following a request for statutory recognition;

Part III: changes affecting the bargaining unit;

Part IV: derecognition, general;

Part V: automatic derecognition;

Part VI: derecognition of non-independent trade union;

Part VII: derecognition when a trade union loses its certificate of independence;

Part VIII: detriment and dismissal;

Part IX: general matters.

---

[1] [1977] IRLR 93, EAT.   [2] [1976] IRLR 318.   [3] UKEAT/0305/12/RN.
[4] IRLR (LIB (121)).   [5] [1977] IRLR 8.
[6] [1978] ICR 62, [1977] IRLR 173, EAT; aff'd [1979] ICR 84, [1978] IRLR 504, CA.
[7] [1978] ICR 314, EAT.   [8] [1978] 1 All ER 1271, [1977] ICR 530, [1977] IRLR 147, EAT.
[9] [1981] ICR 644, [1981] IRLR 291, EAT.

23.7 An independent trade union can apply to the Central Arbitration Committee (CAC) for a declaration requiring the employer to recognise it for collective bargaining purposes in respect of workers in a particular bargaining unit. CAC will grant the declaration if a majority of workers in the bargaining unit already belong to the trade union, or where the union obtains the support of a majority of those voting in a secret ballot, which consists of at least 40% of those entitled to vote. The employer and the union should then agree to a method of collective bargaining, although if they fail to do so, an application may be made by either party to CAC, who will impose one. Recognition, thus obtained, will last for a minimum of three years, and cannot be ended unilaterally by the employer even after the end of that time, unless the derecognition procedure has been followed (Pt I, paras 1–51). The manner in which collective bargaining is to be conducted is set out in the Trade Union Recognition (Method of Collective Bargaining) Order 2000, which is legally binding, and can be enforced by an order for specific performance.

23.8 An alternative method is an agreement for recognition, which will arise when the union makes an application to CAC for recognition, but then abandons it because the employer agrees voluntarily to recognise the union. Nonetheless, either side may still request CAC to impose a method of collective bargaining. An agreement for recognition will last for three years, but does not require the derecognition procedure to be followed to terminate it (Pt II, paras 52–63).

23.9 It should be noted that neither of the two procedures in paras 23.7 and 23.8 in any way affects existing voluntary collective bargaining arrangements, which will no doubt continue without the necessity of being underpinned by a statutory procedure. Indeed, if there is a collective agreement in force a statutory claim for recognition cannot succeed (TULR(C)A, Sch A1, para 35, see *R(NUJ) v CAC*[10]).

23.10 It is the task of CAC to determine the appropriateness of the bargaining unit. The employer has the right to make representations on such matters and, indeed, frame objections to the union's proposals. But as long as CAC takes such arguments into account, their function is to determine the appropriateness of the union's original proposals, and not to shop around seeking an alternative (*R (Kwik-Fit (GB) Ltd) v Central Arbitration Committee*[11]).

23.11 If, for whatever reason, the original bargaining unit is no longer considered to be appropriate, either side may apply to CAC to select a new bargaining unit. There are provisions which are designed to ensure that the new unit does not overlap with an existing bargaining unit (including balloting if necessary), and CAC can make arrangements for workers who consequently fall outside the original unit into a residual unit (Pt III, paras 64–95).

23.12 An employer may derecognise the union if the number of workers falls below 21, or if an application is made to CAC (by the employer or by the workers) for a secret ballot to be held, at any time after three years from a CAC declaration. There is a further procedure for the workforce to apply for the derecognition of a non-independent trade union (which had achieved voluntary recognition), and for dealing with the situation which arises if a trade union loses its independent status (Pts 4, 5, 6, 7, paras 96–155).

[10] [2005] IRLR 28.
[11] [2002] EWHC 277 (Admin), [2002] All ER (D) 111 (Feb); revsd [2002] EWCA Civ 512, [2002] ICR 1212, [2002] IRLR 395, [2002] All ER (D) 272 (Mar).

C. Employers' Training Policies (TULR(C)A, s 70B)

23.13 If a trade union has obtained recognition for collective bargaining purposes under Sch A1, and CAC has imposed a method of collective bargaining (and the parties have not agreed that the imposed method should not be legally binding), a trade union will be entitled to be consulted about the employer's policy on training for workers within the bargaining unit and the plans for training those workers during the following six months, and to receive information about training provided since the previous meeting. Two weeks before a meeting is held for this purpose, the employer must provide the union with whatever information is required to ensure that the union's representative can participate meaningfully in the meeting, and which it would be in accordance with good industrial relations practice for the employer to disclose. The employer shall take account of any written representations made by the union within four weeks from the date of the meeting. If the employer fails to comply with s 70B, the trade union may present a complaint to an employment tribunal, which may make a declaration and award compensation of up to two weeks' pay to each person who was a member of the bargaining unit.

Collective Bargaining (TULR(C)A, Sch A1, para 94)

23.14 The existing definition of collective bargaining refers to negotiations between a trade union and an employer on a wide variety of matters, including terms and conditions of employment, termination and suspension of employment, allocation of work, discipline, and physical conditions of work (TULR(C)A, s 178). However, for the purposes of Sch A1, the definition is more restrictive, with the following result:

(a) So far as existing voluntary arrangements are concerned, collective bargaining refers to those matters listed in TULR(C)A, s 178.

(b) Where statutory recognition is awarded under Pt I of Sch A1, collective bargaining refers to the three core issues of pay, hours, and holidays. There is no obligation to negotiate about matters falling outside these core areas (*British Airline Pilots' Association v Jet2.com Ltd*[12]).

(c) If the parties agree matters as the subject of collective bargaining (eg if there is an agreement for recognition under Pt II, or an agreement to change the agenda in relation to a new unit under Pt III), the matters are referred to in the agreement.

(d) If there is a new unit, or a residual unit under Pt III (with certain exceptions, see para 94(2)), collective bargaining means negotiations on the matters which were the subject of collective bargaining in the corresponding or parent unit.

A. Disclosure of Information (TULR(C)A, s 181)

23.15 For the purpose of all stages of collective bargaining it shall be the duty of the employer, on request, to disclose to representatives of a recognised independent trade union all such information relating to his undertaking as is in his possession, and is information without which the representatives would to a material extent be impeded in carrying on such bargaining, and is information which it would be in accordance with good industrial relations practice that he should disclose. In one of its earliest findings, the CAC held that the test of 'materially impeded' meant that the information should be

---

[12] [2015] EWHC 1110.

both relevant and important (*Institute of Journalists v Daily Telegraph*[13]). The employer need only make the disclosure to unions which are recognised by him. In determining what is good industrial relations practice, regard will be had to any Code of Practice issued by ACAS. If the trade union representatives so request the employer will disclose or confirm the information in writing, but he need not disclose:

(a) information the disclosure of which would be contrary to the national interest;

(b) any information which he could not disclose without breaking the law;

(c) information which he received in confidence;

(d) information relating to an individual, unless he has consented to the disclosure;

(e) information the disclosure of which would cause substantial injury to the employer's business for reasons other than its effect on collective bargaining;

(f) information obtained by the employer for the purpose of bringing or defending any legal proceedings.

23.16 The employer is not bound to produce, or allow the inspection of, any document, or to compile information where this would involve an amount of work or expenditure out of all reasonable proportion to its value in the conduct of collective bargaining.

23.17 If an independent trade union wishes to make a complaint that an employer has failed to disclose information which he is required to produce, it may report the matter to the CAC. If that body thinks that the complaint can be settled by conciliation it will refer the matter to ACAS, which will try to promote a settlement. If this does not prove possible, or if the complaint is not so referred, the committee will hear and determine the complaint. If it finds the complaint is wholly or partly well founded, it will issue a declaration, stating:

(a) the information in respect of which the complaint is well founded;

(b) the date on which the employer refused or failed to disclose the information; and

(c) a period (being more than one week from the date of the declaration) within which the employer ought to disclose the information. If, at the end of that period, the employer still fails to disclose, a further complaint may be made by the trade union.

23.18 The complaint may be accompanied by a claim relating to the terms and conditions of the employees, and if the employer still persists in his refusal, the committee may make an award that, in respect of the employees of any description specified in the claim, the employer shall observe the terms and conditions demanded, or other terms and conditions which the committee considers to be appropriate. These will form part of the contracts of employment of those employees from a date specified in the award, until varied or superseded by a further award or a subsequent collective agreement, or an express or implied agreement made between the employer and the employees which is an improvement on the award. As a general rule, CAC would consider the likely loss which flows from the failure to give the union the relevant information, and make an award accordingly.

B. Legal Liabilities and Legal Proceedings

23.19 At common law it is impossible for a trade union to engage in any effective industrial relations activity without falling foul of some well-established legal rule. An understanding

---

[13] IDS Supp 22.

of those liabilities is necessary in order to understand and appreciate the statutory protections which have been developed over the years.

Inducing or Procuring a Breach of Contract

23.20 It is a tort (civil wrong) for a person to induce another to break a contract to which the other is a party, or to procure a breach of that contract. In *Lumley v Gye*,[14] an opera singer contracted to sing at a theatre owned by the claimant. The defendant induced her to break that contract and sing for him instead. Clearly, the singer was liable for her own breach of contract, but it was held that the claimant could successfully sue the defendant for inducing her to break the contract. In terms of industrial relations, the tort is peculiarly appropriate (see, for example, the county court decision in *Falconer v ASLEF and NUR*[15]). An employer has a contract (of employment) with an employee. If a trade union official calls upon that employee to strike, the employee is breaking the contract (for which he can be dismissed—but see Chapter 21) but the union official (and possibly the union also) could be held liable for inducing a breach of that contract. Equally, if a trade union was to call for a secondary boycott, it may be furthering strike action, but it is also inducing (or procuring) a breach of a commercial contract. In *Torquay Hotel Co Ltd v Cousins*,[16] a trade union was in dispute with a hotel. A union official informed a company which was supplying oil to the hotel of the existence of the dispute, and instructed its members not to deliver oil supplies. It was held that an injunction would lie restraining the union officials from causing any fuel supplier to breach its contract to supply oil.

23.21 If a shop steward has express or implied authority to act on behalf of a trade union, then the union may be responsible for his actions unless it can shelter behind some legal protection (*Heatons Transport (St Helens) Ltd v Transport and General Workers' Union*, see para 3.7). But a union cannot be responsible for activities of unofficial committees of shop stewards, particularly when they are pursuing policies which are contrary to those of the union, and where union officials are trying to solve problems through machinery for negotiation and conciliation, while the shop stewards are taking militant industrial action (*General Aviation Services (UK) Ltd v Transport and General Workers' Union*[17]). However, in such a situation, the union must repudiate the activities in question (see para 23.84) if it wishes to retain its immunities.

23.22 For the tort of inducing or procuring or otherwise wrongfully interfering with contractual rights to be made out, five conditions must be satisfied: (1) it must be shown that the defendant persuaded or procured or induced a third party to break its contract with the claimant; (2) it must be shown that when the defendant so acted he had knowledge of the existence of the contract, if not its precise terms; (3) it must be shown that the defendant intended to persuade, induce, or procure a breach of that contract, because it is an essential prerequisite for establishing the tort of inducing a breach of contract that the alleged wrongdoer deliberately and specifically intended to induce the breach. A mere careless or negligent inducement will not suffice (*Mainstream Properties Ltd v Young*[18]); (4) the claimant must show more than nominal damage; (5) if the defendant puts forward the defence of justification, the claimant has to rebut that defence (*Timeplan Education Group Ltd v National Union of Teachers*[19]).

---

[14] (1853) 2 E & B 216, 22 LJQB 463, 17 Jur 827, 1 WR 432, [1843–60] All ER Rep 208.

[15] [1986] IRLR 331.

[16] [1969] 2 Ch 106, [1968] 3 All ER 43; aff'd [1969] 2 Ch 106, [1969] 1 All ER 522, CA.

[17] [1974] ICR 35, [1973] IRLR 355, NIRC; revsd [1975] ICR 276, CA; on appeal [1985] ICR 615, [1976] IRLR 224, HL.

[18] [2005] EWCA Civ 861, [2005] IRLR 964.   [19] [1997] IRLR 457, CA.

Conspiracy

23.23 A conspiracy is a combination of two or more persons to do an unlawful act, or a lawful act by unlawful means. Such acts could lead to a prosecution for criminal conspiracy (ie where the conspirators combine in order to pursue criminal objects) or an action for civil conspiracy where the alleged act constitutes a tort. Since trade unions are by necessity combinations, it is not surprising that they are particularly vulnerable to this form of legal constraint. For example, in *Quinn v Leathem*,[20] Leathem was a butcher who employed non-union labour. The union called upon him to dismiss them, but he refused to do so. Instead, he offered to pay the men's arrears of subscriptions if they were admitted into the union. This offer was rejected by the union officials, who wanted to teach the non-unionists a lesson 'and make them walk the streets for 12 months'. Munce supplied meat to Leathem, and the union threatened to call a strike of Munce's men unless supplies of meat to Leathem were cut off, and Munce complied with this request. It was held that the union officials had conspired together to cause harm to Leathem without lawful jurisdiction. Their legitimate trade union objectives could have been achieved by accepting Leathem's offer and admitting the men to membership, but in fact their subsequent conduct had been motivated by vindictiveness.

23.24 But the mere fact that an act causes harm does not, by itself, amount to a conspiracy. Clearly, a strike causes harm to an employer, but if the object is a legitimate one, eg obtaining higher wages, no actionable conspiracy exists (*Crofter Hand Woven Harris Tweed Co v Veitch*[21]). In *Scala Ballroom (Wolverhampton) Ltd v Ratcliffe*,[22] the claimants operated a colour bar at their dance hall. Officials of the Musicians' Union placed a boycott on the premises in protest. It was held that this was not a conspiracy to injure, for the combination was a legitimate furtherance of the union's interests.

Intimidation

23.25 This 'obscure and unfamiliar' tort was resurrected from oblivion in the controversial case of *Rookes v Barnard* (see para 3.76), where a shop steward threatened to call a strike at Heathrow Airport unless the claimant, a non-unionist, was dismissed. This 'threat' constituted a breach of contract, which was held to be an unlawful act (ie in the same way that a threat to commit an act of violence would be unlawful) and the defendants were held liable for intimidation.

Other Tort Liabilities

23.26 There are a number of other possible headings of legal liabilities which trade unions may run up against, including such headings as unlawful interference with trade business or employment, interference with future contracts, and so forth. Such torts are to be found in judicial hints rather than actuality, and the fear was of their emergence rather than their existence. With the increased statutory control over the conduct of trade unions, it is unlikely that these obscure torts will be revived.

23.27 But if there are unlawful acts committed by a trade union, an injured party may apply for an injunction to restrain the commission of such acts, and sue for damages in respect of any loss suffered, including, if necessary, exemplary damages (*Messenger Newspapers Group Ltd v National Graphical Association*[23]). A trade union can only defend itself if it can rely on the statutory protections.

---

[20] [1901] AC 495, 65 JP 708, 50 WR 139, [1900–3] All ER Rep 1, 85 LT 289, 17 TLR 749, HL.
[21] [1942] AC 435, [1942] 1 All ER 142, 166 LT 172, 58 TLR 125, HL.
[22] [1958] 3 All ER 220, [1958] 1 WLR 1057, 102 Sol Jo 758, CA.
[23] [1984] IRLR 397; aff'd [1984] 1 All ER 293, [1984] ICR 345, CA.

Statutory Protections

23.28 It is clear from paras 23.19 to 23.27 that if trade unions are to carry out their legitimate functions in industrial relations, they require protection from these headings of common law liability, and arguably against judicial ingenuity in developing new case law which would restrict their activities. This has been the object of statute law since 1906; it was a process which was carried on by the Industrial Relations Act 1971, and has been continued in TULR(C)A. But the statutory immunities are not a licence to do anything; they only provide a protective cover for trade unions when legitimate objectives are being pursued. These objectives are limited to acts done in furtherance or contemplation of a trade dispute, known as the 'golden formula', and it is to the wide meaning of this phrase that we must now turn.

A. 'Trade dispute' (TULR(C)A, s 244)

23.29 A trade dispute means a dispute between workers and their employers which relates wholly or mainly to one or more of the following:

(a) terms and conditions of employment, or the physical conditions in which any workers are required to work;

(b) the engagement or non-engagement or termination or suspension of employment, or the duties of employment, of one or more workers;

(c) the allocation of work or the duties of employment between workers or groups of workers;

(d) matters of discipline;

(e) membership or non-membership of a trade union on the part of a worker;

(f) facilities for officials of trade unions;

(g) machinery for negotiations or consultation, and other matters relating to the foregoing (ie (a)–(f) above), including recognition by employers or employers' associations of the right of a trade union to represent workers in any such negotiations or consultations or in the carrying out of such procedures.

23.30 The important change made by the Employment Act 1982 is that the dispute must relate 'wholly or mainly' to these matters. In *Mercury Communications Ltd v Scott-Garner*,[24] the claimants were granted a licence by the government to run a telecommunications system (the 'liberalisation' agreement), which effectively broke the Post Office monopoly. The government also proposed to privatise British Telecommunications. The Post Office Engineering Union opposed both the liberalisation and privatisation of the work, and gave instructions to its members not to do work which would enable the plaintiffs to connect to the British Telecommunications network. The claimants applied for an injunction to restrain the union from inducing a breach of contractual relations between themselves and British Telecommunications. The Court of Appeal granted the injunction. It was unlikely that the union would be able to establish at the trial that there was a trade dispute within the statutory definition. There was little evidence to support the union's contention that there was a dispute about the risk of loss of jobs. The reality was that the union was waging a campaign against the political decisions to liberalise and privatise the industry. But in *UNISON v Westminster County Council*[25] a dispute between a local authority and employees about

[24] [1984] Ch 37, [1984] 1 All ER 179, [1984] ICR 74, [1983] IRLR 485; revsd [1984] Ch 37, [1984] 1 All ER 179, [1984] ICR 74, [1983] IRLR 494, CA.
[25] [2001] EWCA Civ 443, [2001] ICR 1046, [2001] IRLR 524.

the proposed privatisation and contracting out of certain advisory services was held to be a dispute about terms and conditions of employment, and not a dispute about public policy. Similarly, a dispute about the reasonableness of an instruction from an employer can be a dispute about terms and conditions of employment within the meaning of s 244(1)(a) (*P v National Association of Schoolmasters/Union of Women Teachers*[26]).

23.31 In addition, there are three other circumstances to consider. First, a trade dispute will exist between a Minister of the Crown and a group of workers notwithstanding that the minister is not the employer of those workers, if the dispute relates to matters which have been referred for consideration to a joint body on which that minister is bound by statute to be represented, and which cannot be settled without the minister exercising a power.

23.32 For example, in *Wandsworth London Borough Council v National Association of Schoolmasters Union of Women Teachers*,[27] the defendants wished to ballot their members to protest against the excessive workload caused by the assessment requirements of the national curriculum, which had been imposed by the government. A local authority sought an injunction against the unions, arguing that the dispute was not about terms and conditions of employment but about the very idea of the national assessment, and this was a matter which could only be resolved by the Secretary of State exercising a power conferred by statute. It was held that the dispute was wholly or mainly about the workload imposed on teachers and, therefore, since it was about the terms and conditions of employment, the statutory protection (see para 23.34) applied, and the application for an injunction was refused.

23.33 Second, there is a trade dispute even though it relates to matters occurring outside the United Kingdom as long as the persons who are taking action are likely to be affected in respect of one or more of the matters mentioned at para 23.29. The third situation is more curious. In *Cory Lighterage Ltd v Transport and General Workers' Union* (see para 3.16), a lighterman named Shute decided to leave the union, and the employers were informed that none of the crew would sail if he did not pay his union dues. The employers had no quarrel with the union, for they accepted the principle of 100% unionisation, but they could not dismiss Shute under the Dock Workers Employment Scheme, so they sent him home on full pay. It was held that as there was no dispute between the employers and the union, the statutory protections did not apply. The employers did not resist the demands of the union, but rather acceded to them by taking Shute off the lighter. In line with the policy of giving the widest possible protection to trade unions in all actual and potential conflict situations, TULR(C)A, s 244(4) provides that an act, threat, or demand done or made by one party or organisation against another which, if resisted, would have led to a trade dispute with that other, shall, notwithstanding that because that other submits to the act or threat or accedes to the demand no dispute arises, be treated as done or made in contemplation or furtherance of a trade dispute.

23.34 There is no trade dispute if a strike is called about the terms and conditions of employment of employees of a third party who have never been employed by the employer with whom the union is in dispute, nor is there a trade dispute if it concerns the employment of the employees with a future unidentified employer. In *University College London Hospitals NHS Trust v UNISON*[28] the claimant entered into a contract with a consortium for the latter to build and run a new hospital. The union was opposed to the scheme, and sought to persuade the claimant to enter into a contractual agreement with the consortium

---

[26] [2001] EWCA Civ 652, [2001] ICR 1241, [2001] IRLR 532; aff'd [2003] UKHL 8, [2003] 2 AC 663, [2003] 1 All ER 993, [2003] ICR 386, [2003] IRLR 307.

[27] [1994] ICR 81, [1993] IRLR 344, CA.　　[28] [1999] ICR 204, [1999] IRLR 31, CA.

whereby the terms and conditions of staff who were transferred to the new hospital would receive equivalent terms and conditions of employment to those who were not transferred. When the claimant refused to accede to the demand, the union called a strike, which was approved in a ballot of members. An injunction to restrain the strike was confirmed by the Court of Appeal. The dispute was about the terms and conditions which would apply to another employer, and in respect of employees who may at some future stage be employed by that other employer. The dispute was not between 'workers and their employer', because, at this stage, neither the future employer nor the workers employed by him could be identified.

23.35 But a strike called for political reasons is not a trade dispute. In *BBC v Hearn*,[29] the Association of Broadcasting Staff threatened to stop a transmission of the Cup Final by satellite to South Africa, in protest of the alleged racist policies of the Government of that country. This would also have affected a number of other countries throughout the world. The Court of Appeal held that there was no trade dispute, and granted an injunction restraining the union from telling its members to break their contracts of employment and from inducing the BBC to break its contracts with other countries. In *Express Newspapers v Keys*,[30] three trade unions instructed their members to strike in response to a call sent out by the TUC for a one-day national stoppage in protest against government policies. It was held that this was a political strike, not in connection with a trade dispute, and injunctions were granted restraining the unions from inducing or procuring breaches of contract between the claimants and their employees.

23.36 In *Examite Ltd v Whittaker*,[31] a trade union called a strike against a firm called Baldwins Industrial Services, with the result that the company's business came to a standstill. A new company called Examite was formed, with two shares being issued, and it took over the business of Baldwins and engaged some of its former employees. The union continued the strike against the new company, as it was considered to be a sham, and the company sought an injunction to restrain the union officials from intimidating the employees and to restrain them from procuring a breach of contract. It was held that a trade dispute existed between the union and Examite. There was sufficient evidence to show that the company had been formed to take over the business formerly carried on by Baldwins. The 'hat' worn by the employer was irrelevant. The truth was that the new company was carried on by the same people who ran the old one, and the legal form it took was irrelevant.

B. 'In contemplation of'

23.37 Having obtained the formula for a trade dispute, for an act to come within the statutory protection, it must be in contemplation of that dispute. The act may be so done if it is committed before the dispute arises, but is imminent. However, the dispute must be more than a mere possibility. In *Bents Brewery Co Ltd v Hogan* (see paras 10.69 and 19.69) managers of a brewery were asked by a trade union official to obtain information about the firm's salaries, sales, etc. In providing this, the managers were in breach of their contract not to disclose confidential information to unauthorised persons (see Chapter 10). The union official was clearly inducing a breach of that contract, and it was held that his action was not in contemplation of a trade dispute, even though one may well have arisen at some future date. His actions may have been preparatory to the dispute, but were not in contemplation of one.

---

[29] [1978] 1 All ER 111, [1977] ICR 685, [1977] IRLR 273, CA.   [30] [1980] IRLR 247.
[31] [1977] IRLR 312, CA.

C. 'In furtherance of'

23.38 The act committed must also be in furtherance of the trade dispute, and not in furtherance of some other issue. In *Conway v Wade*,[32] a union official informed employers that unless a worker was dismissed there would be a strike. This was untrue, and the union official's actions were prompted by his desire to get the worker to pay a fine which was due to the union. It was held that although a trade dispute existed, the act was not done in furtherance of that dispute, but for some other motive. A more difficult problem arises when there is more than one motive for the acts in question, and some of the pre-1971 cases, which were decided on a much narrower definition of the term 'trade dispute' must now be viewed with greater care. For example, in *Huntley v Thornton*[33] the claimant was recommended for expulsion by the branch committee of a trade union, but this was not upheld by the national executive. Nonetheless, the local officials regarded him as being expelled, and took steps to ensure that he did not obtain employment. The judge thought that there was no trade dispute, but such conduct would nowadays clearly be covered by the new, wider definition. More interesting was the finding that some of the officials were not acting in furtherance of a trade dispute, but in furtherance of a personal grudge, and their actions were in the nature of a vendetta. In other words, if protection is sought for acts done in furtherance of a trade dispute, the predominant motive must be the advancement of legitimate objects, and trade unionists cannot use the cover of the statutory protection to pursue improper aims.

23.39 But not every action which flows from a trade dispute is necessarily in furtherance of that dispute. In *Beaverbrook Newspapers Ltd v Keys*,[34] a trade dispute existed between the *Daily Mirror* newspaper and a trade union, which resulted in a complete stoppage of production. The *Daily Express* decided to print more copies to cater for the increase in demand, but the general secretary of the printing union told his members not to handle the additional copies. The claimants applied for an injunction to restrain the union from inducing their employees to break their contracts of employment. It was held that the injunction would be granted. There was no trade dispute between the members of the defendant's union and the claimants, and the action would not further the dispute between the *Daily Mirror* and its employees.

23.40 Armed with the 'golden formula', we can now consider those statutory protections, and consider when the immunities will be lost.

Statutory Protection and Loss of Immunities

A. The Provisions of TULR(C)A, s 219

23.41 Subsection (1) provides that an act done by a person in contemplation or furtherance of a trade dispute shall not be actionable in tort on the ground only (a) that it induces another person to break a contract or interferes or induces any other person to interfere with its performance; or (b) that it consists of his threatening that a contract (whether one to which he is party or not) will be broken or its performance interfered with, or that he will induce another person to break a contract or to interfere with its performance.

---

[32] (1908) 24 TLR 604; on appeal [1908] 2 KB 844, 52 Sol Jo 748, 99 LT 634, 24 TLR 874, CA; revsd [1909] AC 506, [1908–10] All ER Rep 344, 53 Sol Jo 754, 101 LT 248, 25 TLR 779, HL.
[33] [1957] 1 All ER 234, [1957] 1 WLR 321, 101 Sol Jo 171.   [34] [1978] ICR 582, [1978] IRLR 34, CA.

23.42 This subsection does three things. First, it gives immunity against legal action to anyone who calls a strike or other industrial action and thus induces a breach of contract (of employment) by the strikers, or a breach of a commercial contract by any other person. It also covers any inducement which interferes with the performance of a contract. A strike includes any refusal to work for specified periods when workers would normally work, provided it is concerted, ie mutually planned. It does not have to be a total stoppage (*Connex South Eastern Rly v National Union of Rail, Maritime and Transport Workers*[35]). Whether an overtime ban is 'other industrial action' is a question of fact for the employment tribunal to determine (*Naylor v Orton & Smith Ltd*[36]). Second, the subsection provides immunity where a threat of strike or other industrial action is made, whether this is done by the actual strikers or some other person, eg a trade union official. Thus, the threat to call a strike—the unlawful act in *Rookes v Barnard* (paras 3.76 and 23.25)—is no longer actionable. Third, it protects those who threaten to induce a breach of contract or to interfere with its performance.

23.43 Section 219(2) provides that an agreement or combination of two or more persons to do or procure the doing of an act in contemplation or furtherance of a trade dispute shall not be actionable in tort if the act is one which, if done without such agreement or combination, would not be so actionable. This subsection is designed to nullify the law of conspiracy as applied to trade disputes (see para 23.23). If an act in contemplation or furtherance of a trade dispute would be actionable if done by one person, then a civil conspiracy would be committed if a group of persons did it. For example, if strikes commit a trespass by engaging in a sit-in, or commit a nuisance, or libel someone by picketing with defamatory placards, such conduct would be actionable if done by one person, and therefore no statutory protection exists.

23.44 Thus, in *News Group Newspapers Ltd v Society of Graphical and Allied Trades 1982*[37] the defendants were responsible for organising mass picketing at the claimant's premises at Wapping. This was held to be a public nuisance, intimidation, and an interference with commercial contracts, and injunctive relief was granted. But if the act was lawful if done by one person, it does not become an actionable conspiracy merely because a group of persons do it. Thus it is not unlawful for one person to threaten to strike or to go on strike. It therefore cannot be a conspiracy if more than one person does so. It is unlawful for one person to use violence; it will be a conspiracy for a group of persons to agree to use violence or actually to use it in a strike situation, and civil as well as potential criminal liability may arise.

23.45 However, it was suggested in *Meade v Haringey London Borough Council*[38] that the immunity of a trade union from actions in tort based on conspiracy may not apply if there is an inducement to break a duty laid down by statute. Thus, if a local authority is forced to close a school (which it is under a statutory duty to keep open) because of trade union pressure, the union officials may be liable for inducing a breach of statutory duty and will not be protected by TULR(C)A. But if the statutory duty can be re-arranged so that it can still be carried out, injunctive relief will not be granted (*Barretts & Baird (Wholesale) Ltd v Institution of Professional Civil Servants*[39]). Also, if there is no statutory obligation to break, a trade union cannot be liable for inducing an alleged breach (*Associated British Ports v Transport and General Workers' Union*[40]).

---

[35] [1999] IRLR 249, CA.   [36] [1983] ICR 665, [1983] IRLR 233, EAT.
[37] [1986] ICR 716, [1986] IRLR 227, CA.
[38] [1979] 2 All ER 1016, [1979] ICR 494, CA.   [39] [1987] IRLR 3.
[40] [1989] IRLR 291; on appeal [1989] 3 All ER 796, [1989] ICR 557, [1989] IRLR 305, CA; revsd [1989] 3 All ER 822, [1989] ICR 557, [1989] IRLR 399, HL.

B. **Loss of Immunities**

23.46 In recent years, the tactics adopted by trade unions in industrial disputes have not always attracted universal approval, and Parliament has intervened to place restrictions on certain types of activities, by limiting the immunity conferred by TULR(C)A, s 219. The objects are twofold: first, to ensure greater democracy in trade unions by requiring secret ballots to be held before strikes or other industrial action are called, so as to negate decisions made at mass meetings by a show of hands, or calls for action which may be unsupported by the rank and file; second, to prevent unnecessary hardship caused by industrial action to third parties who are in no way involved with or connected with the dispute. The primary purpose is to regulate official trade union action; unofficial action, though covered by the law, is seldom the subject of court proceedings (but see para 23.73). Consequently, the immunity provided by TULR(C)A, s 219 will be lost unless the legal hurdles below can be surmounted. Note also that the Trade Union Act 2016 is now in force and it creates further hurdles in terms of balloting thresholds, etc.

Secret Ballots before Industrial Action (TULR(C)A, ss 226–234A)

23.47 There is no legal requirement which insists that a ballot be called by the union before industrial action can be taken. However, a failure to do so will have the following legal consequences:

(a) industrial action which is authorised or endorsed by the union will not have the statutory immunity under s 219 from actions in tort, and an employer affected by the strike will be able to obtain an injunction and sue for damages;

(b) members of the trade union will be able to apply to the court for an order restraining the union from calling for strike action (TULR(C)A, s 62, see Chapter 21);

(c) any member of the public who suffers a reduction or delay in the quality or supply of goods or services may apply to the court for an injunction to restrain the strike (s 235A);

(d) employees who go on strike will not have the protection afforded by s 238A (para 21.112) although they will have the protection contained in s 238(1)(b) (para 21.101).

23.48 The balloting provisions contained in TULR(C)A, ss 226–235 have been amended by the Employment Relations Act 2004, and a Code of Practice on Industrial Action Ballots and Notice to Employers has been issued. They have also been amended by the Trade Union Act 2016 (TUA) (para 23.62 in). The requirements apply only to official industrial action. It should be noted that for the purpose of the balloting provisions (as with secondary action, see para 23.74) any reference to a contract of employment also includes a contract under which a person personally does work or performs services for another. Thus self-employed workers who are union members are covered by the statutory provisions.

23.49 An act done by a trade union to induce a person to take part in industrial action will not be protected unless the industrial action has the support of a ballot, and the other detailed requirements of TULR(C)A are satisfied (s 226). These are that, not later than seven days before the opening day of the ballot, the union must take reasonable steps to notify the employer of persons who are entitled to vote:

(a) that a ballot is to be held;

(b) the date of the opening day of the ballot;

(c) a list of the categories of employee to which the employees concerned belong, a list of the workplaces of the employees concerned, the total number of employees, together with the figures of the total number of employees concerned, the number of employees in each category, and the number of employees concerned who work at each workplace. The list and figures supplied must be as accurate as is reasonably practicable in the light of the information which the union possesses (s 226A(3A)).

23.50 As an alternative, if there is a union subscription arrangement in force (see para 21.83) the union may send the list and figures containing the information (s 226A(2) (c)(ii)). In either case, there is no need to name the actual employees who are to be balloted.

23.51 A sample voting paper is to be sent to the employer at least three days before the opening day of the ballot. If the employees concerned are not all to be sent the same voting paper, a sample of each form of voting paper is sent to any of them. Before the ballot is held, the union must appoint a scrutineer (see para 22.48), unless the number of those to be balloted is fewer than 50.

23.52 All those members of the trade union whom it is reasonable to believe (at the time of the ballot; see *London Underground Ltd v National Union of Rail Maritime and Transport Workers*[41]) will be induced by the union to take part in the industrial action must be balloted, and no other person (s 227(1)). A union's policy of not balloting members who are in arrears of subscriptions does not satisfy s 227(1) because such persons might nonetheless be induced to take part in strike action as a gesture of solidarity, and therefore are entitled to vote on the matter (*National Union of Rail, Maritime and Transport Workers v Midland Mainline Ltd*[42]). It is for the union to ensure that it has up-to-date information on the addresses of its members and their current job classifications. But if the union acquires new members, or if existing members transfer from employments which are not in dispute into the area of a dispute, immunity will not be lost, because it would hardly be reasonable for the union to believe that they would be induced to take part in the industrial action (s 232A). Section 232B provides that if there is a failure to comply with s 227(1), and the failure is accidental and on a scale which is unlikely to affect the result of the ballot, the failure must be disregarded. In *British Airways plc v Unite (No. 1)*[43] the union included in its ballot employees who had accepted voluntary redundancy, and who would not be employed by the time the strike action was due to start. An injunction to restrain the union from acting on the ballot was granted because although the court accepted that the failure to comply with s 227(1) was unintentional, it was not accidental.

23.53 So far as is reasonably practicable, a voting paper must be sent to the home address of the member, and he must be given a reasonable opportunity to vote by post (s 230(2)), although there is a review of the provision for electronic voting in s4 TUA. If a member is denied the opportunity to vote, and is subsequently induced to take part in the industrial action, the trade union will lose its statutory immunity (s 232A), but the inadvertent failure to supply a ballot paper to union members will be disregarded for all purposes if the failure was accidental and not likely to affect the result of the ballot (s 232B). An inadvertent mistake which leads a member not to be accorded an opportunity to vote in a ballot does not mean that the union loses its immunity for failing to follow the correct balloting procedure. If the failure was accidental, and not likely to affect the result, it can be disregarded. Inadvertently failing to give a member the opportunity to vote is not the same thing as denying him an entitlement to vote (*P v National Association of Schoolmasters/Union of Women Teachers*, para 23.30).

---

[41] [1996] ICR 170, CA.   [42] [2001] EWCA Civ 1206, [2001] IRLR 813.
[43] [2010] IRLR 423, [2009] EWHC 3541 (QB).

Separate Workplace Ballots (TULR(C)A, ss 228–228A)

23.54 The general rule about balloting is that a separate ballot shall be held for each workplace (s 228(3)), and industrial action will not be protected unless a majority of workers at that workplace voted in favour (s 226(3)). A person's workplace is a single set of premises (if that is where he works) or premises with which the person's employment has the closest connection (s 228, and see *InterCity West Coast Ltd v National Union of Rail Maritime and Transport Workers*[44]). This requirement does not apply where the union reasonably believes that all the members who are entitled to vote have the same workplace (s 228(2)).

23.55 If the union wishes to call an aggregate ballot of a genuine bargaining unit (instead of separate ballots), certain conditions must be satisfied. The entitlement to vote must be limited to all members of the union who, according to the union's reasonable belief, have an occupation of a particular kind, and are employed by a particular employer or any number of employers with whom the union is in dispute. There must be at least one of its members at each of the workplaces directly affected by the dispute, or the union must be balloting members of a particular occupational category who are employed by a particular employer or by a group of employers, or balloting all of its members who are so employed (s 228A).

Ballots for Overseas Members (TULR(C)A, s 232)

23.56 Generally, a trade union can elect whether or not to ballot overseas members (ie a person who is not a merchant seaman or offshore worker), who is outside Great Britain during the period of the ballot (s 232(3)) (Great Britain means England, Scotland, and Wales). However, if the ballot relates to industrial action involving Great Britain and Northern Ireland, or if a member is temporarily seconded to Northern Ireland, members in both countries must be balloted. If a trade union reasonably believes that a merchant seaman will be at sea or in a place outside Great Britain at the time of the ballot, then, if it is reasonably practicable, he is entitled to have a voting paper made available while on the ship or at the place where the ship is.

Voting Requirements (TULR(C)A, ss 229–231A)

23.57 Voting must be by means of marking a voting paper (but see 23.53 re possible electronic voting). This must state the name of the independent scrutineer, specify the address to which and the date by which it is to be returned, and be given one of a series of consecutive numbers, and marked with that number. The voting paper must contain the question (however framed) which requires the member to answer 'Yes' or 'No' whether he is prepared to take part in (or continue to take part in) a strike. A similar question must be posed if the issue is industrial action short of a strike, and for this purpose an overtime ban and a call-out ban will constitute industrial action short of a strike (*Connex South Eastern Ltd v National Union of Rail Maritime and Transport Workers*, para 23.42, being thus overruled). The requisite majority must be on each of the relevant questions, not the combined voting figures on both ballots (if two questions are being posed) (*West Midlands Travel Ltd v Transport and General Workers' Union*[45]). After all, a member might be willing to take part in industrial action short of a strike, but not a strike, and vice versa (*Post Office v Union of Communication Workers*[46]).

23.58 The TUA amended s229 to require further information on the ballot paper, to include a summary of the matter in issue, the type of industrial action to be taken, and the period within which the industrial action is expected to take place.

---

[44] [1996] IRLR 583, CA.   [45] [1994] ICR 978, [1994] IRLR 578, CA.
[46] [1990] 3 All ER 199, [1990] ICR 258, [1990] IRLR 143, CA.

23.59 The voting paper must also specify who, in the event of the vote being in favour of industrial action, is authorised to call upon members to take the industrial action. It is not necessary to name the individual in question, but he must be a person duly authorised either by the rules of the union, or the principal executive committee, or president or general secretary, or any other committee or official of the union (including shop stewards) (s 229(3), s 230(2)).

23.60 The ballot paper must contain the following statement: 'If you take part in a strike or other industrial action, you may be in breach of your contract of employment. However, if you are dismissed for taking part in a strike or other industrial action which is called officially and is otherwise lawful, the dismissal will be unfair if it takes place fewer than 12 weeks after you started to take part in the action, and depending on the circumstances may be unfair if it takes place later.' There must be no further comment or qualification on this statement.

23.61 Every person who is entitled to vote must be allowed to do so without interference from or constraint imposed by the union, or any of its members, officials or employees, and without direct cost. So far as is reasonably practicable, he must have the voting paper sent to his home address or other address as may be requested, and be given a convenient opportunity to vote by post (s 230(2)). The ballot shall be so conducted as to ensure that, so far as is reasonably practicable, voting is done in secret. The votes must be fairly and accurately counted, but accidental inaccuracies, which could not affect the result of the ballot, may be disregarded.

23.62 Originally the law required only a simple majority, but the TUA inserted into s226 a requirement of a 50% turnout, so that at least half of those eligible to vote must actually have voted in order for the ballot to be valid. A further requirement is that, in key public services, at least 40% of those eligible will need to have voted in favour.

23.63 As soon as is reasonably practicable after the holding of the ballot, the trade union shall inform all persons entitled to vote of the number of:

(a) individuals entitled to vote;

(b) votes cast;

(c) individuals answering 'yes';

(d) individuals answering 'no';

(e) spoilt papers; and

(f) whether the number of votes cast were at least 50% of those entitled to vote;

(g) for a public body, whether at least 40% voted 'yes'.

23.64 In *British Airways plc v Unite (No. 2)*[47] the trade union posted the results of a strike ballot on its website, distributed hard copy leaflets to members in crew centres, left the result in news-stands, made an announcement at a press conference, issued a press release, and sent emails and text messages to members who had signed up for these services. Not all the information was in the statutory form (eg percentage results were given, as opposed to the actual numbers). The employers obtained an interim injunction restraining the strike, but this was discharged by the Court of Appeal. Section 231 did not require that every member should receive an individual report of the full results, but rather that it be put where members can access it if they want to.

---

[47] [2010] EWCA Civ 669.

23.65 The union will also ensure that every relevant employer receives this information (s 231A), ie every employer who it is reasonable for the union to believe was the employer of any persons entitled to vote. A failure to do so would make subsequent industrial action unlawful.

23.66 A scrutineer's report will also be prepared, stating whether there were grounds for believing that the statutory grounds for holding the ballot were contravened, that the arrangements with respect to the production, storage, distribution, return, or handling of the voting papers, and the arrangements for the counting of the votes, including all security arrangements, were such as to minimise the risk of unfairness or malpractice, and that he was able to carry out his functions without interference from the trade union, or any of its members, officials or employees.

Effectiveness of the Ballot (TULR(C)A, ss 233–234)

23.67 A ballot will not be effective in so far as it relates to a call for a strike or other industrial action before the date of the ballot, or any such call after the ballot ceases to be effective (s 233(3)). In other words, industrial action cannot be subsequently validated by a ballot. But this does not require a union to adopt a neutral stance on the matter, and urging members to vote in favour of strike action is not the same thing as calling them to strike (*Newham London Borough Council v National and Local Government Officers' Association*[48]).

23.68 A ballot will also cease to be effective after six months from the date of the ballot, or such longer period not exceeding nine months, as may be agreed between the employer and the trade union. Industrial action which takes place after that time will not be supported by a ballot (*RJB Mining (UK) Ltd v National Union of Mineworkers*[49]). If, during the six- or nine-month period, industrial action is prohibited by a court order (eg on an application for a temporary injunction), and the order is subsequently discharged, or it lapses, the trade union may request the court to order that the period during which the prohibition took effect shall not count towards the six- or nine-month period. Once industrial action has started, it may continue indefinitely if necessary, and if at any time it is suspended (eg to enable negotiations to take place), a new ballot will not be required if the resumption of industrial action was part of the original dispute (*Monsanto plc v Transport and General Workers' Union*[50]), although if there is a fresh dispute a new ballot will be required (*Post Office v Union of Communication Workers*, para 23.58). *Post Office v Union of Communication Workers* was followed by the case of *Westminster Kingsway College v University and College Union*.[51] A ballot relating to a pay dispute in November 2013 led to a strike in December 2013. A further ballot in September 2014 for a further strike did not comply with the requirements. The union sought to rely on the first ballot to hold the second strike. The High Court granted an injunction relating to this. The proposed strike action in October 2014 was not a continuation of the action from December 2013. There had been a substantial interruption between the two, and 'what was authorized by ballot can cease to be authorised if industrial action is effectively discontinued'. The test to be applied was whether an ordinary trade union member would say that the original industrial action had come to an end. If so, then the original ballot could not be relied on for a further strike.

Notice of Industrial Action (TULR(C)A, s 234A)

23.69 An act done by a trade union to induce a person to take part in industrial action shall not be prevented from being actionable in tort by s 219 unless the union takes such steps as are reasonably necessary to ensure that the employer receives a relevant notice of the

[48] [1993] ICR 189, [1993] IRLR 83, CA.   [49] [1997] IRLR 621.
[50] [1987] 1 All ER 358, [1987] ICR 269, [1986] IRLR 406, CA.   [51] [2014] EWHC 4409.

industrial action within the appropriate period, ie the period beginning with the day when the union informed the employer of the result of the ballot, and ending with the 14th day before the day specified in the notice for industrial action to commence. The notice must be in writing, and must contain a list of the categories of employee to which the affected employees belong, a list of the workplaces, the total number of affected employees, and the number of affected employees who work at each workplace or a list of employees in respect of whom a union subscription arrangement (see para 21.79) is in force (s 234A(3)(a)(ii)). The 'affected employees' are those employees of the employer whom the union reasonably believes will be induced by the union to take part in the industrial action, but there is no need for the union to identify by name the employees concerned. The notice must state whether the industrial action is to be continuous or discontinuous, and if continuous, the date when it will commence, and if discontinuous, the dates when the action will take place.

23.70 In *Metrobus Ltd v Unite*[52] an injunction was upheld on a trade union restraining industrial action. The union had failed to notify the employer of the numbers and categories of employee involved in the action (contrary to s 226A), had failed to notify the employer of the outcome of the ballot as soon as was reasonably practicable (contrary to s 231A) and had failed to provide the employer with figures that were as accurate as reasonably practicable (contrary to s 234A). Minor failures relating to the provision of information about the results to union members, however, should not undermine the entire ballot process (*British Airways plc v Unite the Union (No. 2)*[53]). In maintaining the records, a union is only obliged, as far as is reasonable, to ensure that the records are accurate, but it is not reasonable to expect them to be perfectly accurate. Statutory requirements imposed on trade unions regarding ballots of members and notices to employers before calling a strike should be given a reasonably relaxed, practical, interpretation (*National Union of Rail, Maritime & Transport Workers v Serco Ltd*[54]). (In the case of *RMT v UK*, formerly *EDF Energy Powerlink v UK*,[55] it was suggested that the balloting requirements are in contravention of Article 11 of the European Convention, but the case was dismissed by the European Court of Human Rights on the specific facts of the case.)

23.71 Technically, if the union suspended industrial action (to enable negotiations to take place) a further seven days' notice would be required before the action could be resumed. However, s 234A(7B) now provides that if the union agrees with the employer that it will cease to authorise industrial action from a specified date (the suspension date) but that it may be again authorised with effect from a date not earlier than a specified date (the resumption date), then if the action is suspended, it may be resumed without the necessary notice being required.

Industrial Action to Enforce a Closed Shop (TULR(C)A, s 222)

23.72 Section 219 shall not provide an immunity in tort for acts done in furtherance or contemplation of a trade dispute if the reason for the act is that the employer is employing or proposes to employ a person who is not a member of a trade union or of a particular trade union. Immunity is also removed if the action is designed to put pressure on an employer into treating persons less favourably on grounds of their non-membership of a trade union.

---

[52] [2009] EWCA Civ 829, [2010] ICR 173, [2009] IRLR 851.

[53] [2010] IRLR 809, [2010] EWCA Civ 669.

[54] The joined cases *National Union of Rail, Maritime & Transport Workers (RMT) v Serco Ltd t/a Serco Docklands* and *Associated Society of Locomotive Engineers & Firemen v London & Birmingham Railway Ltd t/a London Midland* [2011] IRLR 399, [2011] EWCA Civ 226.

[55] (Application 31045/10) [2010] IRLR 114.

Industrial Action in Support of Unofficial Strikers (TULR(C)A, s 223)

23.73 We have noted that if a person goes on unofficial strike, and is dismissed, he has no right to claim that he has been unfairly dismissed (see para 21.90). Section 223 provides that s 219 will not prevent an act from being actionable in tort, if the reason for the action was that an employer had lawfully dismissed unofficial strikers.

Secondary Action (TULR(C)A, s 224)

23.74 The immunities conferred by s 219 will only apply when a trade union takes industrial action (supported by the appropriate ballot) vis-à-vis an employer with whom there is a trade dispute. In recent years, it became an increasingly popular technique to strengthen the effectiveness of such action by extending it to employers who were not themselves parties to the dispute, in the hope that pressure (direct or indirect) would be thereby exerted on the employer with whom there was a dispute. This is known as secondary action (see, eg, *Duport Steels Ltd v Sirs*[56]).

23.75 Secondary action is defined as when a person:

(a) induces another to break a contract of employment; or

(b) interferes or induces another to interfere with its performance; or

(c) threatens that a contract of employment under which he or another is employed will be broken, or its performance interfered with; or

(d) threatens that he will induce another to break a contract of employment, or to interfere with its performance;

and the employer under the contract of employment is not the employer party to the dispute (s 224(2)).

23.76 In these circumstances, nothing in s 219 shall prevent an act from being actionable in tort where one of the facts relied upon for the purpose of establishing such liability amounts to secondary action which is not lawful picketing.

23.77 The current definition of secondary action is wider than the original definition contained in the Employment Act 1980, and thus there are greater pitfalls for those who engage in such action. Secondary action must result in a breach of a contract of employment, whether or not there is a breach of a commercial contract. Further, the present definition extends the meaning of contract of employment to include the contract of a self-employed person who contracts personally to do work or perform services for another, thus closing a loophole revealed in *Shipping Co Uniform Inc v International Transport Workers' Federation*[57] (see TULR(C)A, s 224(6)).

23.78 The only type of secondary action which now remains lawful is peaceful picketing, as laid down in TULR(C)A, s 220 (see para 23.107), ie by workers who are (or were) employed by the employer who is a party to the dispute, and by a trade union official whose attendance is lawful by virtue of s 220(4) of the Act. Secondary picketing (ie at the gate of an employer who is a customer or supplier to the employer who is a party to the dispute) is not lawful.

23.79 The UK ban on secondary strikes, even where the secondary employer is closely associated with the primary employer, is lawful under Article 11, given the wide margin of appreciation (*RMT v UK*[58]).

---

[56] [1980] IRLR 112, CA; revsd [1980] 1 All ER 529, [1980] ICR 161, [1980] IRLR 116, HL.
[57] [1985] ICR 245, [1985] IRLR 71. [58] [2014] ECHR 366.

Pressure to Impose Union Recognition Requirement (s 225)

23.80 An act will not be protected by s 219 if it constitutes an inducement of a person to incorporate into a contract a term requiring a party to a contract for goods or services to recognise a trade union for the purpose of negotiating on behalf of workers employed by him, or to negotiate or consult with an official of a trade union (such a contract term would be void by reason of s 186, see para 23.124). Nor will an act be protected if it interferes with the supply of goods or services by inducing another person to break a contract of employment, the reason being that the supplier does not recognise or negotiate or consult with a trade union (see para 23.119).

C. Immunity of Trade Unions (TULR(C)A, s 20)

23.81 Section 14 of TULRA 1974 (which re-enacted provisions dating from the Trade Disputes Act 1906) conferred total legal immunity on trade unions in respect of most actions in tort. This immunity was repealed by the Employment Act 1982, and nowadays a trade union will be liable in tort if the protection of TULR(C)A, s 219 is not available. However, a trade union cannot be responsible for everything which is done in its name by its members, shop stewards, or officers, but only for those actions which have been authorised or endorsed.

23.82 A trade union will only be liable for inducing breaches of contract, or threatening that a contract will be broken, or for actions for conspiracy, if the act in question is authorised or endorsed by the union. An act shall be taken to have been endorsed or authorised by the trade union if it was done or authorised or endorsed by:

(a) any person empowered by the rules to do, authorise, or endorse the act; or

(b) the principal executive committee or the president or general secretary of the union; or

(c) by any other committee of the union, or any other official of the union (whether employed by the union or not).

23.83 Thus, under the current law, a trade union may be held to be legally liable not only for the acts of its full-time officials, but also for its shop stewards if they are authorised to do an act. Further, the liability arises for the acts of any committee (set up in accordance with the union's rules) and also for the acts of any group of members of which a shop steward was a member, and the purpose of which included the organising or coordinating of industrial action (TULR(C)A, s 20(4)). This is so notwithstanding anything in the rules of the union, or any contract or rule of law subject to the repudiation provisions, see para 23.86.

23.84 However, the union will not be liable if the act was repudiated by the principal executive committee or president or general secretary as soon as was reasonably practicable. Written notice must be given to the committee or official in question, without delay, and the union must do its best to give written notice of the fact and date of repudiation, without delay, to every member whom the union believes is taking part in the industrial action, and to the employer of every such member (s 21).

23.85 The written notice must be in the following form: 'Your union has repudiated the call (or calls) for industrial action to which this notice relates and will give no support to unofficial industrial action taken in response to it (or them). If you are dismissed while taking industrial action, you will have no right to complain of unfair dismissal.'

23.86 The repudiation will not be effective if the principal executive, president, or general secretary behave in a manner inconsistent with the repudiation (see *Richard Read*

(Transport) Ltd v National Union of Mineworkers (South Wales Area)[59]). If, within three months of the purported repudiation, a person who is a party to a commercial contract which has been interfered with by the unofficial industrial action so requests, the union must confirm the repudiation in writing.

D. The Effect of the Act

23.87 If a trade union calls for a strike or other industrial action in violation of the balloting provisions of the Act, or for a reason which is not permitted by the Act, it can be sued, and will not have the immunity conferred by s 219. An application may be made by an aggrieved person to the court for an injunction (*Solihull Metropolitan Borough Council v National Union of Teachers*[60]) and a failure to comply constitutes contempt of court, which would lead to a fine or imprisonment being imposed (*Express and Star Ltd v National Graphical Association*[61]) or sequestration of property (*Kent Free Press v National Geographical Association*[62]). Additionally, an action for damages could be brought against the trade union, subject to the limits on the amount which can be awarded, depending on the size of the trade union.

Amount of Damages (TULR(C)A, s 22)

23.88 If a trade union is sued successfully in tort, there are limits to the amount of damages which may be awarded. These limits are dependent on the size of the union's membership and are as follows:

fewer than 5,000 members, the limit is £10,000;

5,000 or more, but less than 25,000, the limit is £50,000;

25,000 or more, but less than 100,000, the limit is £125,000;

100,000 or more, the limit is £250,000.

23.89 These limits are applicable in each claim brought against the union, and are not global limits on each incident. Thus, if a trade union calls a strike in circumstances where it lacks legal immunity under s 219, each employee who has suffered damage may sue the union for up to the maximum sum, depending on the number of members it has. In addition, interest may be added to the award (*Boxfoldia Ltd v National Graphical Association*[63]). For example, in *Willerby Holiday Homes Ltd v Union of Construction, Allied Trades and Technicians*,[64] a trade union called a strike despite the fact that the pre-ballot notice did not conform to s 226A, the actual ballot did not conform to s 227(1), and the notice of strike action did not conform to s 234A. An award of damages amounting to £130,000 was made.

23.90 The limits do not apply to any action in tort in respect of personal injury caused by negligence, nuisance, or breach of statutory duty, nor to any breach of duty in connection with the ownership, occupation, possession, control, or use of property.

23.91 If damages, costs, or expenses are awarded against a trade union, these cannot be enforced against the 'protected property', ie property which belongs to trustees other than in their capacity as trustees of the union, property owned by members in association with

---

[59] [1985] IRLR 67.   [60] [1985] IRLR 211.
[61] [1985] IRLR 455; aff'd [1986] ICR 589, [1986] IRLR 222 (CA).   [62] [1987] IRLR 267.
[63] [1988] ICR 752, [1988] IRLR 383.   [64] [2003] EWHC 2608 (QB).

other members (ie common property), the property of an official who is not a member or trustee, political funds, and provident benefit funds.

Injunctions and Interdicts (TULR(C)A, s 221)

23.92 An injunction without notice is an application for a temporary injunction to restrain the commission of some act. It is usually made in great haste, and thus only the party applying will have the time and opportunity to argue the case and be represented. Section 221 states that the court shall not grant such an application if the party against whom the injunction is sought claims, or the court thinks he might claim, that the act was done in contemplation or furtherance of a trade dispute, unless all reasonable steps have been taken to give that person notice of the hearing and an opportunity has been given for that party to be heard.

23.93 If an application is made for an interlocutory injunction (ie restraining an act until the matter comes to trial), and the party against whom the injunction is sought claims that he acted in contemplation or furtherance of a trade dispute, the court shall, in exercising its discretion whether or not to grant the injunction, assess the likelihood of success of any defence which may be raised that the act complained of will be protected by the statutory immunities (s 221(2)). For the procedure in Scotland, see *NWL Ltd v Nelson and Laughton*.[65])

A. Injunctive Relief (TULR(C)A, s 20(6))

23.94 If a trade union is responsible for official or unofficial strike action under the provisions of s 20, then in any court proceedings arising out of the act in question, the court may grant an injunction requiring the trade union to take such steps as the court thinks appropriate for ensuring:

(a) that there is no, or no further, inducement of persons to take part in industrial action; and

(b) that no person engage in any conduct after the granting of the injunction because he was induced to take part in industrial action before the injunction was granted.

23.95 This appears to give the court power to order a trade union to take disciplinary action against those who continue to induce or take part in industrial action after it has been repudiated by the union. However, no court shall make an order of specific performance or grant an injunction if the effect is to compel an employee to work or attend any place for the doing of any work (s 236).

23.96 A failure by a trade union (or any other person) to observe the terms of an injunction amounts to contempt of court, in respect of which a fine and/or imprisonment or sequestration of property may be ordered (*Kent Free Press v National Geographical Association*, para 23.87).

B. Industrial Action Affecting an Individual (s 235A)

23.97 Any individual who claims that industrial action has been called by a trade union which is actionable in tort or which has not been supported by a ballot under s 226, and

---

[65] [1979] ICR 755, [1979] IRLR 321, CA; aff'd [1979] 3 All ER 614, [1979] ICR 867, [1979] IRLR 478, HL.

the effect of which is to prevent or delay the supply of goods or services, or reduce their quality, may make an application to the High Court or Court of Session. It is immaterial that the individual in question is entitled to be supplied with the goods or services in question. If the court is satisfied that the claim is well founded, it shall make such order as it considers appropriate for requiring the union to take steps for ensuring that no further act is done by him to induce any person to take part in the industrial action, and that no person engages in any conduct before the making of the order because he has been induced before the making of the order to take part in industrial action. This section also applies to Crown employment even though no contract of employment may exist.

23.98 The situation may sometimes arise where a trade union calls for industrial action which would otherwise be actionable in tort because the various statutory provisions have not been complied with, but (for whatever reason) the employer (or union members) are unwilling to seek to restrain the industrial action. In such circumstances, any individual, whether affected by the industrial action or not, can bring an application to the court, seeking an appropriate order.

C. Industrial Action and European Law

23.99 There may be circumstances when the right to strike is restricted by EC law. Article 43 of the Treaty of Rome provides that there shall be no restriction on companies of one member state establishing undertakings in the territory of another member state. In *International Transport Workers' Federation v Viking Line*[66] the issue arose as to whether collective action taken by a trade union aimed at preventing a ferry operator from registering one of its vessels in a foreign country in order to reduce labour costs constituted a restriction on the company's right to freedom of establishment. The Treaty provides that any such restriction might be justified by an overriding reason of public interest, provided it does not go beyond what is necessary to achieve that objective. In this case, a Finnish ship that sailed around the Baltic was running at a loss because of competition from Estonian ships operating on the same route. The owners sought to reflag the ship by registering her in Estonia, with the aim of benefiting from lower labour costs. This move was opposed by the trade unions concerned, and strike action was threatened. The owners sought a declaration that the action violated their right to freedom of establishment under Art 43. The European Court held that the collective action constituted a restriction within the meaning of Art 43, which could be justified by an overriding reason of public interest, such as the protection of workers, provided that the restriction was suitable for the attainment of that legitimate objective and did not go beyond what was necessary to achieve that objective. The case was referred back to the Court of Appeal for it to find on complex questions of 'suitability', 'necessity', 'proportionality', and whether the union had other means at its disposal that were less restrictive of freedom of establishment than the industrial action.

23.100 It is thought that the decision of the European Court of Human Rights in *Demir v Turkey* (see Chapter 1) does not sit easily with the decision in the European Court of Justice in *International Transport Workers' Federation v Viking Line*,[67] which requires trade unions to justify the proportionality of their actions. The *Demir* case appears to reverse this burden of proof, by ruling that the right to strike may only be limited in strictly defined circumstances.

---

[66] Case C-438/05, [2008] All ER (EC) 127, [2008] IRLR 143, ECJ.
[67] [2008] All ER (EC) 127, [2008] ICR 741, [2008] IRLR 143.

Legal Effect of Collective Agreements (TULR(C)A, ss 178–179)

23.101 A collective agreement is any agreement or arrangement made by or on behalf of a trade union on the one part, and one or more employers or employers' associations on the other part, relating to one or more of the matters contained in the definition of a trade dispute (see para 23.29). In essence, a collective agreement performs two functions. First, it lays down the guiding procedures which will govern the relationship between the signatory parties, by providing, for example, for the constitution of any joint body, or the procedure to be adopted in the event of a dispute or disagreement. Second, it will lay down patterns of terms and conditions of employment which are to cover union members, and possibly others as well, and which are to be observed by all federated and some assenting non-federated firms. Such terms and conditions are usually the minimum, not the maximum rate, so if national bargaining results in a particular award, this may frequently be supplemented at a local level by a further bout of negotiations.

23.102 So far as legal enforceability of these agreements is concerned, s 179 provides that any agreement shall be conclusively presumed not to have been intended by the parties to be a legally enforceable contract, unless the agreement is in writing, and contains a provision stating that the parties do intend the agreement to be legally binding (*Universe Tankships Inc of Monrovia v International Transport Workers' Federation*, see para 3.16). It is possible for the parties to state expressly that only part of the agreement is intended to be legally binding, and part not, in which case the parties' intentions will be given effect to, though it is possible to look at a non-legally binding part for the purpose of interpreting a part which is legally binding.

23.103 There must be an express statement to the effect that the parties intend the collective agreement to be legally enforceable (*Prison Service v Bewley*, see para 7.98). If the agreement states that the parties intend to be bound by it, this may indicate that it is intended to be binding in honour only, which would not satisfy the provisions of TULR(C)A, s 179 (*National Coal Board v National Union of Mineworkers*, see para 3.56).

23.104 The extent to which, and the circumstances in which, the terms of a collective agreement can be incorporated into the contract of employment of an individual employee have already been examined in Chapter 3. Section 180 lays down one further important rule. If a collective agreement, whether legally binding or not, contains a clause prohibiting or restricting the right of workers to engage in a strike or other industrial action, this particular clause shall not be incorporated into the individual contract of employment of any worker, unless the collective agreement:

    (a) is in writing;

    (b) contains a provision expressly stating that such term shall be or may be incorporated into such contract;

    (c) is reasonably accessible at the place of work of such a worker, and is available for him to consult during working hours; and

    (d) is one made by an independent trade union.

It should have been noted that this rule applies notwithstanding any agreement to the contrary, whether contained in a collective agreement or an individual contract of employment.

23.105 Thus, if a collective agreement provides that 'the union will not call a strike until the disputes procedure is exhausted', a breach of this clause would be governed by the law relating to the legal effect of the agreement, as mentioned at para 23.102. If the collective agreement states: 'The employees will not go on strike until the disputes procedure is exhausted', then this clause will only form part of the individual contract of employment if the conditions are fulfilled. The matter, however, is not really important, for a strike is likely to be a breach of most individuals' contracts of employment (whether or not it is in breach of the terms of a collective agreement) as it is a breach of the duty of faithful service (see Chapter 10) and a breach of contract of such importance that a striker may be dismissed.

23.106 However, if CAC grants a declaration imposing a statutory collective bargaining framework (see para 23.7) the procedure to be followed is legally binding, and can be enforced by specific performance (Trade Union Recognition (Method of Collective Bargaining) Order 2000).

Peaceful Picketing (TULR(C)A, s 220)

23.107 It shall be lawful for a person in contemplation or furtherance of a trade dispute to attend:

(a) at or near his own place of work; or

(b) if he is an official of a trade union, at or near the place of work of a member of that union whom he is accompanying and whom he represents;

for the purpose only of peacefully obtaining or communicating information, or peacefully persuading any person to work or to abstain from working. If a person works at more than one place, or at a place where it is impracticable to picket because of its location, his place of work shall be any premises from which he works, or from which his work is administered. A person whose employment has been terminated because of a trade dispute is allowed to picket at his former place of work.

23.108 S220A (as inserted by the TUA) sets out a requirement for the union to appoint a readily identifiable picket supervisor, who has to be present and carry a letter stating that the picketing is approved by the union.

23.109 An employee's 'place of work' means his principal place of work or base. It does not refer to premises which, during his work, he may visit from time to time (*Union Traffic Ltd v Transport and General Workers' Union*[68]).

23.110 Whether the picketing has taken place at or near the place of work is a question of fact and degree. In *Rayware Ltd v Transport and General Workers' Union*,[69] pickets stood at the entrance of a private estate, about three-tenths of a mile from the employers' premises. An application by the employers for an injunction to restrain unlawful picketing failed. The pickets could not get any nearer to their place of work without trespassing, and thus they were picketing lawfully near their place of work.

23.111 Section 220 only makes lawful the acts in para 23.107. If something else is done, the section provides no protection. Thus in *Piddington v Bates*,[70] a policeman wished to restrict the number of pickets who were outside a factory. When a striker tried to join the picket line, he was arrested, and charged with obstructing the policeman in the course of his duty. A conviction was upheld, for the policeman had acted on reasonable grounds that a breach of the peace might have occurred. In *Tynan v Balmer*,[71] a group of pickets walked

---

[68] [1989] ICR 98, [1989] IRLR 127, CA.   [69] [1989] 3 All ER 583, [1989] ICR 457, [1989] IRLR 134, CA.
[70] [1960] 3 All ER 660, [1961] 1 WLR 162, 105 Sol Jo 110, DC.
[71] [1967] 1 QB 91, [1966] 2 All ER 133, DC.

in a circle at the entrance of a factory in order to prevent traffic from entering and this was held to be an obstruction of the highway and a nuisance.

23.112 Nor do pickets have the power to stop vehicles, for traffic control is a matter for the police. In *Broome v DPP*[72] a trade union official stood in front of a lorry and attempted to persuade the driver not to deliver goods to a factory where a dispute was on. The police told him to get out of the way, but he refused, and he was arrested and charged with obstructing the highway, an offence under the Highways Act 1959. It was held that he was guilty of the offence. Views were expressed in *Broome's* case that the law gave no right to pickets to stop persons or vehicles, for that would indicate that those persons were under a duty to stop and listen. The purpose of the statute was to make attendance at a picket line lawful, and then only for the statutory purposes of peacefully communicating information, etc.

23.113 Mass picketing can also amount to the tort of public nuisance (unreasonable obstruction of the highway), private nuisance (interference with access to the highway), and intimidation (see *News Group Newspapers Ltd v Society of Graphical and Allied Trades 1982*, para 23.44). Thus, 'flying pickets' and mass demonstrations are clearly unlawful, the former because they will not normally be picketing at their own place of work, the latter because it is unlikely that it is for the purpose of peacefully persuading. In *Thomas v National Union of Mineworkers (South Wales Area)*,[73] it was held that mass picketing constituted a common law nuisance (as well as an offence under TULR(C)A, s 241(1)), for all citizens had the right to use the highway without harassment or unreasonable interference. Accordingly, injunctions were granted against various trade union officials to prevent them from organising, encouraging, etc, members of the union congregating at coal mines, other than for the statutory purpose of peacefully communicating information, numbers in such cases being restricted to six.

23.114 Section 219(3) of TULR(C)A provides that if an act is done in the course of picketing which is not lawful, then s 219 will not provide a defence to any action which may be brought. Thus, if a picket induces workers to break their contracts of employment, and he is picketing at some place other than his own place of work, he can be sued in tort, and the statutory immunity of s 219 will not be available to him. Thus, unlawful picketing may attract civil as well as criminal liabilities. A Code of Practice on picketing has been approved by Parliament laying down the parameters for peaceful picketing.

23.115 If a tort is committed by picketing, s 220 will provide a trade union with legal protection provided the picketing is lawful within that section. But if no tort has been committed, the statutory rules are basically irrelevant. Thus, in *Middlebrook Mushrooms Ltd v Transport and General Workers' Union*,[74] the employers were mushroom producers, employing some 300 workers. They wished to introduce certain cost-saving measures, but these were not agreed to, and the union called a strike. The employer then dismissed all those employees who went on strike.

The union then urged its members to attend at supermarkets which were supplied with the mushrooms by the employers, and hand out leaflets to members of the public, asking them not to buy the employers' mushrooms. The employers brought an action for an interlocutory injunction restraining the union and its officials from organising the 'pickets' outside the supermarkets. The judge held that there was a direct interference with the contracts between the employers and the supermarkets, and granted the injunction.

However, the Court of Appeal reversed the decision. There was nothing in the leaflets which were handed out to members of the public which was aimed at the managers of the

---

[72] [1974] AC 587, [1974] 1 All ER 314, [1974] ICR 84, [1974] IRLR 26, [1974] Crim LR 311, HL.
[73] [1986] Ch 20, [1985] 2 All ER 1, [1985] ICR 886, [1985] IRLR 136.
[74] [1993] ICR 612, [1993] IRLR 232, CA.

supermarket who placed orders with the employers. Thus the union was not seeking to persuade a party to the contract (ie the employers and the supermarkets) but members of the public, who, of course, had no contractual relations with the employers. It may well be that the managers of the supermarket might react to the reaction of the public (not to the picketing), but this, at most, would amount to an indirect inducement not to enter into future contracts, and, as no unlawful means had been used, the application for an injunction was dismissed.

23.116 If the industrial action is unofficial, and a trade union representative is routinely present when picketing is taking place, it will be presumed that he had sufficient knowledge of the unlawful element of the picketing to have endorsed those actions, and possibly to have, in practice, organised the unlawful activity which the union has not repudiated (*Gate Gourmet London Ltd v TGWU*[75]).

A. **Sit-in**

23.117 Workers who engage in a sit-in or work-in are in breach of their contractual licence to remain on the employers' premises (*City and Hackney Health Authority v National Union of Public Employees*[76]), and as such, if they refuse to leave after being given reasonable notice to do so, are committing the tort of trespass and interfering with business by unlawful means (*Norbrook Laboratories Ltd v King*[77]). It is possible to obtain an injunction against those involved, and also an employer may use the special expedited procedure to obtain possession of the property (see Ord 113 of the Rules of the Supreme Court).

23.118 If a trade union called for or authorised the sit-in or work-in, it would not be protected by the immunity conferred by s 219, even if a ballot was held, because the immunity in respect of interference with business by unlawful means was removed with the repeal of earlier legislation.

Union Recognition

A. **Union or Non-union Members Only Contracts (TULR(C)A, s 144)**

23.119 Any term or condition in a contract for the supply of goods or services shall be void in so far as it purports to require that the whole or part of the work shall be done by persons who are not members of a trade union (or a particular trade union), or who are members of a trade union (or a particular trade union).

23.120 It will be a tort of breach of statutory duty if, on the grounds of union membership or non-membership, a person:

(a) fails to include a particular person's name on a list of approved suppliers of goods or services;

(b) terminates a contract for the supply of goods or services;

(c) excludes a person from tendering for the supply of goods or services;

(d) fails to permit a person to submit a tender; or

(e) otherwise determines not to enter into a contract for the supply of goods or services.

[75] [2005] EWHC 1889 (QB), [2005] IRLR 881.   [76] [1985] IRLR 252, CA.
[77] [1982] IRLR 456; aff'd [1984] IRLR 200, NIRC.

23.121 Thus any person who suffers damage through the failure or refusal of another to enter into a contract with him for the supply of goods or services on the grounds of union membership or non-membership may sue for breach of statutory duty, and will be able to recover damages (subject to any general defences which may exist to such an action). Further, if there is pressure from any person to induce another to incorporate into a contract to which that other is a party any term or condition which would be void by the provisions in para 23.120 then s 219 shall not be a defence. Nor will s 219 be a defence if a person induces or threatens to induce another person to break a duty imposed by s 144. Thus if trade unionists threaten to strike unless an employer enters into a union labour only contract, or unless he removes non-union sub-contractors from a site, such acts will be actionable despite the general immunity of s 219 (see s 222(3)).

B. Prohibition on Union Recognition Requirements (TULR(C)A, s 186)

23.122 Any term or condition of a contract for the supply of goods or services shall be void in so far as it purports to require any party to the contract:

(a) to recognise one or more trade unions; or

(b) to negotiate or consult with any official of a trade union.

C. Refusal to Deal on Union Exclusion Grounds (TULR(C)A, s 187)

23.123 If a person maintains a list of approved suppliers of goods or services, or list of persons from whom tenders may be invited, and fails to include on that list a person who does not recognise trade unions, or terminates a contract for the supply of goods or services on that ground, or does other acts which prevent a person from being able to enter into a contract for the supply of goods or services because he does not recognise trade unions, such action will amount to a breach of statutory duty, and is actionable accordingly (subject to any relevant defences) by the person against whom the action was taken or by any other person adversely affected.

23.124 An act will not be protected by s 219 if it consists of inducing a person to impose a union recognition requirement contrary to ss 186–187 (see s 225).

Criminal Liabilities

23.125 Members of the armed forces and policemen have no right to strike, and it is unlawful to induce a member of the prison service to strike or commit a breach of discipline, which effectively prevents them from taking part in an official strike (Criminal Justice and Public Order Act 1994, s 127). Merchant seamen may lawfully terminate their contracts and give 48 hours' notice of strike action provided their ship is in a safe berth in the United Kingdom.

23.126 Sections 240–241 of TULR(C)A enact two provisions which may be relevant in trade disputes generally. The first is contained in s 240 of the Act, which provides that where any person wilfully and maliciously breaks a contract of service of hiring, knowing or having reasonable cause to believe that the probable consequences of his doing so, either alone or in combination with others, will be to endanger human life, or cause serious bodily injury, or to expose valuable property whether real or personal to destruction or serious injury, he shall, on conviction, be liable to a fine or to imprisonment for a term not exceeding three months.

23.127 The second provision is contained in s 241 of the Act. This states that every person who, with a view to compelling any person to abstain from doing an act which he has a legal right to do:

(a) uses violence to or intimidates such other person or his wife or children, or injures his property; or

(b) persistently follows such other persons from place to place; or

(c) hides any tools, clothes, or other property owned or used by such other person, or deprives him of or hinders him in the use thereof; or

(d) watches or besets the house or other place where such person resides, or works, or carries on business, or happens to be, or the approach to such house or place; or

(e) follows such other person with two or more other persons in a disorderly manner along any street or road,

then he shall be liable to a fine not exceeding level 5 on the standard scale or a term of imprisonment not exceeding six months, or both.

23.128 Section 241 was considered in the case of *Galt v Philp*,[78] where workers engaged in a 'sit-in', during which they locked and barricaded laboratories, thus preventing other employees from entering the rooms. This was held to be 'besetting' within the meaning of s 241(1)(a) and the individuals concerned were found guilty of an offence under the Act.

23.129 It must be remembered that TULR(C)A, s 219 only protects a person from civil liability, and does not give any immunity in respect of criminal acts.

A. Public Order Act 1986

23.130 This Act abolished the common law offences of riot, rout, unlawful assembly, and affray, and repealed the provisions of the Public Order Act 1936, relating to threatening behaviour likely to provoke a breach of the peace. A number of statutory criminal offences have been introduced by the new Act, which may be invoked when the conduct of industrial disputes gets out of hand. These are:

(a) *Riot* (s 1). This is where 12 or more people use or threaten to use violence for a common purpose which would cause a person of reasonable firmness to fear for his personal safety.

(b) *Violent disorder* (s 2). This has the same elements as *riot*, except that it applies when three or more persons are taking part.

(c) *Affray* (s 3). This also has the same elements as *riot*, except that only one person need be involved, and threats, by themselves, would not be sufficient.

(d) *Fear or provocation of violence* (s 4). It is an offence to use threatening, abusive, or insulting words or behaviour or to distribute or display any visual representation which is threatening, abusive, or insulting, where the act is intended or likely to make a person fear immediate violence, or to provoke immediate violence.

(e) *Harassment, alarm or distress* (s 5). This has almost the same elements as *fear or provocation of violence*, but the accused may defend himself by arguing that he had no reason to believe that a person alarmed was within his hearing or sight, or that his conduct was reasonable.

23.131 The Act also lays down rules for marches, processions, demonstrations, and public assemblies.

[78] [1984] IRLR 156.

B. Intentional Harassment

23.132 The Criminal Justice and Public Order Act 1994, s 154 creates the criminal offence of intentional harassment. This is committed if a person, with intent to cause another person harassment, alarm, or distress:

(a) uses threatening, abusive, or insulting behaviour, or disorderly behaviour;

(b) displays any writing, sign, or visible representation which is threatening, abusive, or insulting

so that the other person feels harassment, alarm, or distress.

23.133 This offence could be committed in a number of employment situations, including verbal or written abuse etc to those who cross picket lines, and harassment on grounds of race, sex, sexual orientation, disabilities, religion, and so on.

European Works Councils

23.134 The Transnational Information and Consultation of Employees Regulations 1999 came into force in January 2000, and implemented the European Works Council Directive 94/45/EC. The regulations were amended as from June 2011 by the Transnational Information and Consultation of Employees (Amendment) Regulations 2010 (SI 2010/1088) which gave effect to Directive 2009/38/EC. There is also government guidance which, although not legally binding, can be taken into account by tribunals. The effect of Brexit on European Works Councils is not yet known.

23.135 The regulations apply to undertakings and groups of undertakings with at least 1,000 employees in the European Economic Area (ie, the 28 member states of the EU and Norway, Liechtenstein, and Iceland), and at least 150 employees in each of two or more states. Employee numbers are calculated by adding together the number of employees in each month in a two-year period, and dividing the total by 24 (reg 6). An employee (or employee representative) may request information from the management for the purpose of determining whether the establishment or undertaking is part of a European-scale un-dertaking, and if there is a failure to supply the information, a complaint may be made to the Central Arbitration Committee, which can order the disclosure of the relevant infor-mation (reg 8), or, if it considers the matter to be beyond doubt, declare that the undertak-ing is a Community-scale organisation, ie within the scope of the regulations.

23.136 If there is a valid request by employees or their representatives (see reg 9) manage-ment shall set up a special negotiating body, charged with the task of determining the scope, composition, functions, and term of office of a European Works Council, or, as an alternative, the arrangements for an information and consultation procedure (regs 11–17). The members of the special negotiating body must be elected by ballot and organised by management, and an employee or employee representative may complain to CAC if there is dissatisfaction with the balloting plans. CAC can require that the ballot arrangements be modified so as to reflect the interests of UK employees. However, if there is already in existence a consultative com-mittee which has been elected by ballot and represents all UK employees, that committee may nominate its own members to be members of the special negotiating body.

23.137 Negotiations between management and the special negotiating body must be carried out in a spirit of co-operation, with a view to reaching agreement, either by es-tablishing a European Works Council or an information and consultation procedure. If necessary, one or more experts may be engaged to assist. If a Works Council is established, the agreement will determine the undertakings covered, the composition of the Works Council, its functions, venue, frequency and duration of meetings, financial and material resources to be allocated, and the duration of the agreement and procedure for renegotiation. If an information and consultation procedure is adopted, the agreement will specify a method by which the representatives are to meet to discuss the information conveyed to them, which must in particular relate to transnational questions which significantly affect the interests of the employees (reg 17).

23.138 If management fails to establish a European Works Council or an information and consultation procedure, or if the terms of the agreement are not complied with by management, a complaint may be made to the EAT, which can make an order specifying the steps which central management shall take, with the ultimate sanction of a penalty notice (up to £100,000) if there is a failure to take the required steps.

23.139 A person who is or was a member of the European Works Council or information and consultation representative (or an expert who was assisting) shall not disclose any information or document which has been in his possession by virtue of his position as such, which central management has entrusted to him on terms requiring it to be held in confidence. A breach of this duty is actionable, although not in respect of a protected disclosure (see para 10.75). Disputes as to whether it was reasonable for management to impose a requirement of confidentiality, as well as complaints that management have improperly withheld information which ought to be disclosed, may be referred for settlement to CAC.

A. Time Off Work for Members of a European Works Council (regs 25–27)

23.140 An employee who is:

(a) a member of a special negotiating body;

(b) a member of a European Works Council;

(c) an information and consultation representative; or

(d) a candidate for election as a member or representative

is entitled to take reasonable time off work, with pay (at the appropriate hourly rate), during working hours, in order to perform his functions as a member, representative, or candidate, or for training which is necessary for the exercise of his duties. He may bring a claim to an employment tribunal, that:

(a) his employer has unreasonably refused to permit him to take time off work; or

(b) has failed to pay him for taking time off work.

The complaint must be made within the usual time limit of three months (with the usual extension if it was not reasonably practicable to present it earlier). If the complaint is well founded, the tribunal will make a declaration, and order the employer to pay the amount to which the employee was entitled, or would have been had he taken the time off work.

B. Protection from Detriment and Dismissal (regs 28–33)

23.141 An employee who is:

(a) a member of a special negotiating body;

(b) a member of a European Works Council;

(c) an information and consultation representative; or

(d) a candidate for election as a member or representative

has the right not to be subjected to any detriment by an act or deliberate failure to act, or to be dismissed, on the ground that the employee performed any functions or activities as a member, representative or candidate, or made a request for time off work or for pay for time off work to perform those functions or activities.

23.142 Any employee (whether or not he is one of the categories in para 23.141) has the right not to be subjected to any detriment, or to be dismissed because he:

(a) took proceedings before an employment tribunal to enforce a right or secure an entitlement under the regulations;

(b) exercised an entitlement to complain to an appeal tribunal or CAC;

(c) requested information from management to ascertain whether the establishment is part of a Community-scale undertaking (see reg 7);

(d) acted with a view to secure that a special negotiating body, or European Works Council or an information and consultation procedure, did or did not come into existence;

(e) indicated that he supported or did not support any of those institutions;

(f) stood as a candidate for membership of a special negotiating body, or European Works Council or as an information and consultation representative;

(g) influenced the way in which votes were to be cast by other employees in a ballot under the regulations;

(h) voted in such ballot;

(i) expressed doubts as to whether the ballot was properly conducted; or

(j) proposed to do or declined to do any of the things mentioned in paras (d)–(i) above.

23.143 A complaint may be made to an employment tribunal by a person who alleges that he has suffered a detriment or been dismissed on any of the above grounds. The complaint must be made within the usual time limits. If the complaint relates to a detriment, and is well founded, the tribunal will make a declaration, and may award compensation, as it thinks just and equitable. If the complaint relates to a dismissal, reinstatement or re-engagement can be ordered, or the usual basic and compensation awards will be made (see Chapter 20).

C. Information and Consultation of Employees Regulations 2004

23.144 These regulations give effect to EC Directive 2002/14/EC and are designed to create a framework for informing and consulting with employees. They apply to all undertakings with more than 50 employees. However, they only apply to undertakings which have a registered office or a principal place of business in Great Britain.

23.145 An 'undertaking' is a public or private undertaking which carries out an economic activity, whether or not operating for gain (see reg 2). This can be an incorporated legal entity, or an unincorporated body such as a partnership, co-operative, charity, mutual society, building society, etc. An undertaking does not include a group of companies, and therefore each company within a group must make its own arrangements. However, certain parts of the public sector will not come within the scope of the regulations, although a Cabinet Office Code of Practice will apply to such bodies, and local authorities will be encouraged to adopt similar arrangements.

23.146 To determine how many employees are employed in the undertaking, an average is taken in respect of the previous 12 months. The monthly total of number of employees employed in each calendar month is added together, and that total is divided by 12. Part-time employees can be counted provided they work for a certain number of hours (see reg 4(3)).

D. Pre-existing Agreements (regs 8–9)

23.147 Many undertakings will already have a pre-existing agreement, which has been voluntarily negotiated outside of, or prior to, the regulations. If so, there is no requirement to enter into a new arrangement unless at least 40% of existing employees make a request, and this request is endorsed by a majority of those voting and 40% of those eligible to vote in a ballot. To be a valid pre-existing agreement, certain conditions must be met:

(a) The pre-existing agreement must be in writing. Thus, existing informal or customary arrangements will have to be formalised.

(b) All employees in the undertaking must be covered. This requirement may cause difficulties in practice, either in respect of members of senior management who are outside formal arrangements, or parts of the workforce not covered by a formal collective agreement.

(c) It must set out the manner in which the employer will give information to the employees or their representatives. This is the 'what', 'where', and 'how' requirement, which must be satisfied.

(d) It must have been approved by the employees. There can be an express approval, or an approval given by representatives of an independent trade union or other appropriate representatives.

E. Negotiated Agreements (reg 7)

23.148 In the absence of any such pre-existing agreements, there is no obligation on an employer to do anything. However, the statutory procedure may be triggered by a request from 2% of the employees (this was amended from 10% by the The Employment Rights (Miscellaneous Amendments) Regulations 2019 from 6 April 2020) to commence negotiations about the establishment of an information and consultation procedure. (If 2% would amount to fewer than 15 employees, or more than 2,500 employees, a valid request occurs if there is a request by 15 or 2,500 employees respectively.) Employees (or their representatives) may request data from the employer to determine the number of employees employed so as to ascertain whether or not the regulations apply. There are certain formalities to be observed when making the request.

23.149 The employer may, at this stage, seek a declaration from CAC that the request is not valid (eg because it lacks the relevant support from the employees, or because there is an insufficient number of employees employed in the undertaking, etc). If this is upheld by CAC, that will be the end of the matter, although there is nothing to prevent a further request being made once any apparent defect in the earlier request has been remedied. A request will not be valid if it is made within three years of a previous agreement having been made, or the standard provisions (see para 23.153) are deemed to apply.

23.150 Otherwise, the employer must enter into negotiations to reach a negotiated agreement. The regulations provide for the election or appointment of negotiating representatives, ensuring that they represent all the employees. Both parties should 'work in a spirit of co-operation and with due regard for the reciprocal rights and obligations, taking into account the interests of both the undertaking and the employees' (reg 21). Negotiations for an agreement should not last more than six months, although there is a certain flexibility with regard to the timetable. There may be a single agreement covering all the employees, but there may be separate consultation arrangements for different parts of the undertaking, because parts of an undertaking may have little in common with other sectors and have different activities. The agreement will provide for the appointment or election of information and consultation representatives. It must be signed on behalf of the employer and by all the negotiating representatives, or signed by a majority of them and either approved in writing by 50% of the employees or approved in a ballot of all the affected employees.

23.151 The agreement may provide that consultation will take place through representatives or provide for information and consultation to be provided or undertaken directly with the employees. The employer and employee representatives can agree arrangements about the coverage of the agreement, the methods chosen for providing information and consultation arrangements, the frequency with which information is provided, the subject-matter to be covered, and the methods adopted for the exchange of views and opinions. Statutory consultation requirements such as handling redundancies, TUPE transfers, health and safety consultations, etc may be included or excluded in the agreement, although if they are excluded they must still be observed in the usual manner. The agreement should consider how confidential information is to be handled, the resolution of disputes, and the circumstances in which the agreement can be reviewed, revised, or terminated.

23.152 It must be stressed that consultation is not collective bargaining. It is about the exchange of views and the establishment of a dialogue with the workforce. However, where the Standard Information and Consultation Provisions apply (see para 23.153), consultation about changing work organisation or contractual relations must be conducted with a view to reaching agreement, although employers will still be free to make the final decisions if there is disagreement within the consultation arrangements.

F. Statutory Default Provisions (reg 18)

23.153 If the employer fails to initiate negotiations following a valid employee request, or if they fail to reach a negotiated agreement, the Standard Information and Consultation Provisions (SICP) will come into effect. The employer must hold a ballot, under the supervision of a ballot supervisor, to ensure the election of the relevant number of information and consultation representatives (one representative for each 50 employees, subject to a maximum of 50 representatives). Thereafter, there are specific issues in respect of which the employer is to provide information and on which to consult with the representatives so elected. These are:

(a) the recent and probable development of the undertaking's activities and economic situation;

(b) the situation, structure, and probable development of employment within the undertaking and any anticipatory measures envisaged, in particular where there is a threat to employment within the undertaking;

(c) decisions which are likely to lead to substantial changes in work organisation or in contractual relations, including business transfers and collective redundancies.

23.154 The information provided must be given at such time, in such fashion, and with such content as to enable the representatives to conduct an adequate study, and to prepare for consultation.

23.155 There is a general requirement that if the employer provides information or documents in confidence, the recipient must not breach that confidence, unless he reasonably believes that the disclosure would be protected by virtue of ERA, s 43A (see Chapter 10). Additionally, the employer may withhold information the disclosure of which would seriously harm the functioning of, or would be prejudicial to, the undertaking. A representative who disputes that the information is confidential, or that disclosure would be harmful or prejudicial, may apply to CAC for a ruling.

23.156 An employee who is a negotiating representative or a SICP representative has the usual right to have time off work (with pay) to perform his duties as such. He will have the statutory protection against dismissal or detriment because he performed his functions as such or exercised his right to have time off work to do so. However, a dismissal will not be automatically unfair if the reason was that he disclosed information or documents in breach of his duty of confidentiality, unless he reasonably believed that the disclosure was a protected disclosure (see Chapter 10). An individual employee also has protection against dismissal or detriment if he took action to enforce his rights under the regulations (eg, by acting to secure a negotiated agreement, etc).

23.157 There is no such statutory protection for employees or representatives who have a pre-existing agreement, as these fall outside the scope of the regulations. Such rights as they have will be determined within the existing legal provisions (see especially Chapter 17).

G. Enforcement (reg 22)

23.158 Most of the rights contained in the regulations may be enforced by way of a complaint to the Central Arbitration Committee (CAC) (rights in respect of time off work, detriment, and dismissal may be enforced in the employment tribunal). There are some 14 types of complaints which can be made, ranging from a breach of the employer's obligation to provide information on the numbers of employees employed, through to a declaration as to whether the disclosure of certain information is covered by the confidence provisions. In most cases, CAC will issue a declaration, which will have effect as if made by the High Court (or Court of Session). There is a right of appeal to the EAT.

23.159 If the employer fails to hold a ballot for the election of SICP representatives, or if he fails to comply with the terms of a negotiated agreement or the SICP, and CAC finds the complaint well founded, the applicant may apply to EAT for a penalty notice. Unless EAT is satisfied that the failure was beyond the employer's control, or there was some other reasonable excuse, EAT may set a penalty of up to £75,000, depending on its gravity or other factors, including the reason for the failure, etc (see *Amicus v Macmillan Publishers Ltd*[79]).

23.160 The Department for Business, Innovation and Skills has issued Guidance Notes to the regulations. ACAS has issued 'Good practice advice'. CAC has issued 'A Guide for Employers and Employees to the role of the Central Arbitration Committee (CAC)'.

Summary

- There is a statutory recognition procedure for trade unions in TULR(C)A 1992.
- The act also sets out requirements for collective bargaining, such as disclosure of information, etc.
- The 'golden formula' allows industrial action to be lawful if it is limited to acts done 'in furtherance or contemplation of a trade dispute'.

---

[79] [2007] IRLR 885, EAT.

- There are specific balloting requirements that must be followed for industrial action to have immunity.
- There has to be a 50% turnout, and for key public services, at least 40% of those eligible need to vote in favour, for a ballot to be valid.
- Collective agreements are those agreed between trade unions and employers. They lay down the procedures to govern the relationship and patterns of terms and conditions to cover the relevant employees.
- There must be an express statement that the parties intend the collective agreement to be lawfully enforceable.
- Peaceful picketing of a person's own place of work is lawful. Secondary picketing of other premises is not permitted.

Appendices

Appendix A
Monetary Awards (as at 6 April 2020)

Appendix B
Statutory Redundancy Pay Calculation Table

Appendix A
Monetary Awards (as at 6 April 2020)

Statutory reference	Statutory right	Maximum rate	Maximum award
1. ERA s 12(4)	Itemised pay statement	None	Un-notified deduction for 13 weeks prior to application to an employment tribunal
2. ERA s 31(1)	Guarantee pay	£30 per day	£150 in any period of three months
3. ERA, s 69(1)	Medical suspension pay	None	26 weeks' pay
4. TULR(C)A 1992 s 149(2)	Action short of dismissal	None	Just and equitable
5. TULR(C)A 1992 s 172(2)	Time off work	None	Just and equitable (refusal to allow) or normal pay or average hourly earnings (failure to pay)
6. ERA s 54(3)	Time off to look for work or arrange for retraining	None	Two-fifths of a week's pay
7. ERA s 93(2)	Written reasons for dismissal	None	Two weeks' pay
8. ERA ss 118–124	Unfair dismissal	£538 per week	Basic award £16,140 (30 weeks' pay) Compensatory award £88,519 Additional award £13,988–£27,976 (26 to 52 weeks' pay)
9. TULR(C)A 1992 s 158(1) and (2)	Unfair dismissal for trade union membership or non-membership		**(a)** Reinstatement/ re-engagement not sought
		£538 per week	**(i)** Basic award £16,140 (minimum £6,562)
			(ii) Compensatory award £88,519
		£538 per week	**(b)** Re-instatement/ re-engagement sought, but IT makes no order
			(i) Basic award £16,140 (minimum £6,562)
			(ii) Compensatory award £88,519
			(c) Reinstatement/ re-engagement ordered but not complied with

Statutory reference	Statutory right	Maximum rate	Maximum award
		£538 per week	**(i)** Basic award £16,140 (minimum £6,562)
			(ii) Compensatory award £88,519
		£538 per week	**(iii)** Additional award £13,988–£27,976 (26 to 52 weeks' pay)
			(d) Reinstatement/ re-engagement ordered and complied with Compensation award— loss made good
10. ERA s 162	Redundancy pay	£538 per week	£16,140
11. ERA s 184	Rights on employer's insolvency	£538 per week	Arrears of pay £4,304 (8 weeks' pay maximum)
		£538 per week	Statutory notice £6,456 (12 weeks' pay maximum)
		£538 per week	Holiday pay £3,288 (6 weeks' pay maximum)
		£538 per week	Basic award £16,140
12. Equality Act	Protected characteristic	None	Just and equitable
13. TULR(C)A 1992 s 67(8)	Right not to be unjustifiably disciplined	£538 per week	£104,659 (30 weeks' pay plus amount of compensatory award)
14. TULR(C)A 1992 s 176(6)	Unreasonable expulsion/ exclusion from trade union membership	£538 per week	£104,659 (30 weeks' pay plus amount of compensatory award)
15. TULR(C)A 1992 s 189(4)	Protective award	None	Up to 90 days' pay
16. ET Extension of Jurisdiction Order 1994	Breach of contract	None	£25,000
17. TULR(C)A s 140(4)	Refusal to employ on TU grounds		£88,519
18. TULR(C)A s 70C	Consultation with union on training	£538	£1,076 (2 weeks' pay)
19. ERelA s 11(2)	Right to be accompanied	£538	£1,076 (2 weeks' pay)

Appendix B
Statutory Redundancy Pay Calculation Table

The redundancy payment due to each employee under the statutory redundancy payment scheme depends on his or her age and length of service (up to 20 years). This determines the number of weeks' pay due. The maximum week's pay to count is currently £538.

Age	2	3	4	5	6	7	8	9	10	11	12	13	14	15	16	17	18	19	20
									Service (years)										
17	1																		
18	1	1½																	
19	1	1½	2																
20	1	1½	2	2½	-														
21	1	1½	2	2½	3	-													
22	1	1½	2	2½	3	3½	-												
23	1½	2	2½	3	3½	4	4½	-											
24	2	2½	3	3½	4	4½	5	5½	-										
25	2	3	3½	4	4½	5	5½	6	6½	-									
26	2	3	4	4½	5	5½	6	6½	7	7½	-								
27	2	3	4	5	5½	6	6½	7	7½	8	8½	-							
28	2	3	4	5	6	6½	7	7½	8	8½	9	9½	-						
29	2	3	4	5	6	7	7½	8	8½	9	9½	10	10½	-					
30	2	3	4	5	6	7	8	8½	9	9½	10	10½	11	11½	-				
31	2	3	4	5	6	7	8	9	9½	10	10½	11	11½	12	12½	-			
32	2	3	4	5	6	7	8	9	10	10½	11	11½	12	12½	13	13½	-		
33	2	3	4	5	6	7	8	9	10	11	11½	12	12½	13	13½	14	14½	-	
34	2	3	4	5	6	7	8	9	10	11	12	12½	13	13½	14	14½	15	15½	-
35	2	3	4	5	6	7	8	9	10	11	12	13	13½	14	14½	15	15½	16	16½
36	2	3	4	5	6	7	8	9	10	11	12	13	14	14½	15	15½	16	16½	17
37	2	3	4	5	6	7	8	9	10	11	12	13	14	15	15½	16	16½	17	17½
38	2			5	6	7	8	9	10	11	12	13	14	15	16	16½	17	17½	18
39	2	3	4	5	6	7	8	9	10	11	12	13	14	15	16	17	17½	18	18½
40	2	3	4	5	6	7	8	9	10	11	12	13	14	15	16	17	18	18½	19
41	2	3	4	5	6	7	8	9	10	11	12	13	14	15	16	17	18	19	19½
42	2½	3½	4½	5½	6½	7½	8½	9½	10½	11½	12½	13½	14½	15½	16½	17½	18½	19½	20½
43	3	4	5	6	7	8	9	10	11	12	13	14	15	16	17	18	19	20	21
44	3	4½	5½	6½	7½	8½	9½	10½	11½	12½	13½	14½	15½	16½	17½	18½	19½	20½	21½
45	3	4½	6	7	8	9	10	11	12	13	14	15	16	17	18	19	20	21	22

46	3	4½	6	7½	8½	9½	10½	11½	12½	13½	14½	15½	16½	17½	18½	19½	20½	21½	22½
47	3	4½	6	7½	9	10	11	12	13	14	15	16	17	18	19	20	21	22	23
48	3	4½	6	7½	9	10½	11½	12½	13½	14½	15½	16½	17½	18½	19½	20½	21½	22½	23½
49	3	4½	6	7½	9	10½	12	13	14	15	16	17	18	19	20	21	22	23	24
50	3	4½	6	7½	9	10½	12	13½	14½	15½	16½	17½	18½	19½	20½	21½	22½	23½	24½
51	3	4½	6	7½	9	10½	12	13½	15	16	17	18	19	20	21	22	23	24	25
52	3	4½	6	7½	9	10½	12	13½	15	16½	17½	18½	19½	20½	21½	22½	23½	24½	25½
53	3	4½	6	7½	9	10½	12	13½	15	16½	18	19	20	21	22	23	24	25	26
54	3	4½	6	7½	9	10½	12	13½	15	16½	18	19½	20½	21½	22½	23½	24½	25½	26½
55	3	4½	6	7½	9	10½	12	13½	15	16½	18	19½	21	22	23	24	25	26	27
56	3	4½	6	7½	9	10½	12	13½	15	16½	18	19½	21	22½	23½	24½	25½	26½	27½
57	3	4½	6	7½	9	10½	12	13½	15	16½	18	19½	21	22½	24	25	26	27	28
58	3	4½	6	7½	9	10½	12	13½	15	16½	18	19½	21	22½	24	25½	26½	27½	28½
59	3	4½	6	7½	9	10½	12	13½	15	16½	18	19½	21	22½	24	25½	27	28	29
60	3	4½	6	7½	9	10½	12	13½	15	16½	18	19½	21	22½	24	25½	27	28½	29½
61+	3	4½	6	7½	9	10½	12	13½	15	16½	18	19½	21	22½	24	25½	27	28½	30

Index